BEYOND ELITE LAW

Access to Civil Justice in America

Are Americans making under $50,000 a year compelled to navigate the legal system on their own, simply give up because they cannot afford lawyers? We know anecdotally that Americans of median or lower income generally do without legal representation or resort to a sector of the legal profession that – because of the sheer volume of claims, inadequate training, and other causes – provides deficient representation and advice. This book poses the question: Whether we can at the current level of resources, both public and private, better address the legal needs of all Americans?.

Samuel Estreicher is the Dwight D. Opperman Professor of Law at New York University School of Law, where he directs the Institute of Judicial Administration and the Center for Labor and Employment Law. He is the Chief Reporter of the Restatement of Employment Law and recipient of the Labor and Employment Research Association's Susan C. Eaton Award for Outstanding Scholar-Practitioner. In addition to the law of the workplace, his areas of expertise include alternative dispute resolution, civil procedure, federal courts, foreign relations law, and administrative law.

Joy Radice is an associate professor at the University of Tennessee College of Law. Her research focuses on the civil access to justice gap, and how civil and criminal laws intersect to impact people with criminal records. She teaches in the Advocacy Clinic, directs a new Expungement Clinic, and teaches criminal law and a seminar on poverty, race, gender, and the law.

Beyond Elite Law: Access to Civil Justice in America

Edited by

SAMUEL ESTREICHER AND JOY RADICE

CAMBRIDGE
UNIVERSITY PRESS

CAMBRIDGE
UNIVERSITY PRESS

One Liberty Plaza, 20th Floor, New York, NY 10006, USA

Cambridge University Press is part of the University of Cambridge.

It furthers the University's mission by disseminating knowledge in the pursuit of education, learning, and research at the highest international levels of excellence.

www.cambridge.org
Information on this title: www.cambridge.org/9781107070103

First published 2016
Reprinted 2017

Printed in the United States of America by Sheridan Books, Inc.

A catalog record for this publication is available from the British Library.

Library of Congress Cataloging in Publication Data
Estreicher, Samuel, editor. | Radice, Joy, editor.
Beyond elite law : access to civil justice in America / edited by Samuel Estreicher, Joy Radice.New York : Cambridge University Press, 2016.
LCCN 2015045192 | ISBN 9781107070103 (hardback)
LCSH: Legal assistance to the poor – United States. | Legal aid – United States. | BISAC: LAW / General.
LCC KF336 .B49 2016 | DDC 344.7303/258–dc23
LC record available at http://lccn.loc.gov/2015045192

ISBN 978-1-107-07010-3 Hardback

Contents

Beyond Elite Law

Editors' Preface

Samuel Estreicher & Joy Radice

We are justly proud of the American legal system and the lawyers and judges who make it work. Our system, to the envy of much of the world, takes law seriously, aspires to reduce the gap between the law on the books and the law as lived, and strives to subject all within its remit to the rule of law. And yet, it remains, at its core, a system of elite law largely for the elite.

We are all engaged in elite law, whether as lawyers or academics. Each year, the law schools produce eager, bright graduates ready to provide legal services to a thin layer of the population – either by working for the major law firms that serve corporate America or for NGOs that practice law with an "impact" on important social issues. Some fortunate graduates find such work; others work for overburdened legal services or public defender officers, or hang a shingle, or practice in small firms although they are usually poorly prepared for the clientele they will encounter. Still many others drop out of the legal system entirely – perhaps their legal education will prepare them for a political or business career, or will not be relevant at all.

We hope in this book to spark a conversation that helps move us beyond elite law, to better align existing legal resources with the people who need representation or simply assistance in navigating bureaucracies but are not wealthy enough to access our "Cadillac" legal system and not poor enough to qualify for the limited supply of publicly supported legal aid.

There is a vital debate in the literature, which we explore, as to whether there is indeed a gap between the demand for legal services and the available supply of providers of such services. Survey instruments do not always faithfully capture underlying facts. Even if people "lump" their problems together in an undifferentiated bundle of hopes and anxieties and do not always see those problems as requiring legal services, one must ask whether able lawyers are in fact available for people making, say, under $50,000 a year for:

- nonfatal claims of medical malpractice;
- employment disputes not amenable to class action treatment;

- housing disputes involving landlord failure to make timely repairs;
- transactions like wills and guardianship, closings on a small business, purchasing a medallion to drive a taxicab, transferring property or arranging child custody between spouses seeking a divorce;
- consumer claims for a defective washer-dryer or automobile not living up to warranty;
- individuals seeking bankruptcy protection or reversal of an initial agency decision to deny unemployment compensation or social security disability benefits;
- veterans seeking mental health or other medical assistance from the daunting Veterans Administration; or
- immigrants seeking asylum or lawful residence status to escape the risk of deportation.

We know, anecdotally, that Americans of median or lower income generally do without legal representation in these types of situations or seek help from a sector of the legal profession that, because of the sheer volume of claims, inadequate training, and perhaps other causes, is a deficient source of representation and advice.

This book, we hope, will encourage the development of more systematic information to assist policymakers. We also know that most calls for reform in this area seek an unrealistic solution: increased public funding for civil legal services programs — when decades of budget cuts have resulted in a system that falls far short of meeting the basic legal needs of those considerably below the official poverty line. Although we support the "civil *Gideon*" movement, changes that require significant further public funding are not politically feasible for the foreseeable future.

The question for this book, and the central question for realistic policy improvements in this area, is whether, at the current level of resources (both public and private), we can do a better job of meeting the legal needs of Americans of median or lower income.

Some improvements involve a change in lawyer culture and acculturation encouraging lawyers, young and old, to see service to non-elite populations as part of their professional identity. Law schools have a role to play in terms of the values they transmit and the skills they impart. Law firms are key players as well, and they must consider refashioning pro bono programs that will provide needed training while being better directed to the goal of service to everyday Americans. Bar associations and courts must also advance service as a condition of membership in the bar.

Not all legal problems will in any foreseeable world attract able lawyers. System redesign is needed to help people better represent themselves in court proceedings or prepare necessary documents for transactions. The internet offers vital new avenues for effective self-representation, if coupled with proper professional advice.

Intermediary institutions, like labor unions, worker centers, and ombudspersons, can also play a critical role supplementing representation and self-representation. Bar groups should not be able to inhibit the development of such alternatives through enforcement of vague rules against the unauthorized practice of law.

Forums other than traditional courts can help reduce the cost and formality of dispute resolution, enabling individuals to represent themselves or obtain limited-purpose representation from lawyers.

Law schools, too, need to embrace their role in developing a culture of service. They need to wake up to the reality that most of their graduates will not end up in the elite law firms, even assuming they can find a job requiring legal training at all. What the schools can do is train students to acquire the core competencies of a lawyer so that when they begin practice their skills are better matched to the needs of their likely clientele. They can also make sure they have internalized standards of professional service and understand the underlying economics of practice so that they can provide quality representation and advice in a high-volume setting. Such a development, in itself, would make an enormous contribution to access to civil justice in America.

This book is the product of leaders in the field who have contributed chapters that address each of these issues. They are outstanding judges, lawyers, and academics who care about the problem of access to justice and are actively working on making the system work better. We are proud to be associated with them in this endeavor.

During the work on this book, our good friend and mentor, Ted Eisenberg of Cornell Law School, died. His chapter on improving the database on claiming and dispute-resolution activity reflects his contributions as a leading voice for empirical study of the legal system and for tackling head-on the problem of access. This book is dedicated to his memory.

S.E.
J.R.
February 1, 2016

Foreword

Dean Martha Minow

The most advanced justice system in the world is a failure if it does not provide justice to the people it is meant to serve. Access to justice is therefore critical.[1]

– Rt. Hon. Beverley McLachlin, Chief Justice of Canada (2007)

Where justice is denied, where poverty is enforced, where ignorance prevails, and where any one class is made to feel that society is an organized conspiracy to oppress, rob and degrade them, neither persons nor property will be safe.[2]

– Frederick Douglass

Neglected in today's headlines, blogs, and talk radio is a silent shameful crisis inflicting suffering and costing the nation money, legitimacy, and decency. Our justice system has become inaccessible to millions of people who are poor, of modest or even average means. As a result, every day, we violate the "equal justice under law" promise engraved on the front of the grand United States Supreme Court. Americans who cannot afford legal help routinely forfeit basic rights because they cannot afford to enforce them. Inherently wrong and unfair, our practices are also short-sighted. Studies show that each dollar spent on civil legal assistance can save three to six dollars of public funds needed to deal with the consequences.[3]

The problem is not remote. It affects people in every neighborhood. The law does not enforce itself, and so we all suffer when people cannot enforce their legal rights. But of course the brunt of the failure falls on veterans seeking benefits the nation guaranteed, victims of domestic violence needing legal protection, tenants and homeowners asserting their legal rights, and others who cannot find legal help.

This book brings together a dream team of participants, organized by fine editors and introduced by the heroic leaders, retired Chief Justice Wallace Jefferson of the Supreme Court of Texas and Chief Judge Jonathan Lippman of the New York Court of Appeals. The chapters offer vigorous descriptions of the problem, vivid accounts

[1] Justice in our Courts and the Challenges We Face, Address to the Empire Club of Canada (Mar. 8, 2007), available at http://speeches.empireclub.org/62973/data.

[2] 1886 on the 24th anniversary of Emancipation, Washington, DC, available at www.americanswhotellthetruth.org/portraits/frederick-douglass/.

[3] Martha Minow & Sharon Browne, *Funding Civil Legal Aid: A Bipartisan Issue*, THE HILL, Apr. 13, 2015, available at http://thehill.com/blogs/congress-blog/judicial/238480-funding-civil-legal-aid-a-bipartisan-issue (citing studies in New York and Massachusetts).

of long-term efforts, and detailed analyses of the multiple elements needed for an effective reform agenda. If scored for degree of difficulty, each of these elements would achieve high numbers.

Describing the scope of the problem is challenging because by its very nature, the problem encompasses people who are not visible to law offices and courts because the individuals lack knowledge and resources to make their way there. Analyzing existing sources of legal assistance is also a challenge as the book rightly enlarges the field to include comparisons with other nations and consideration of meaningful services other than the provision of a lawyer. Currently, the United States rates as 65th out of 102 nations in terms of access to and affordability of justice.[4] A full reckoning requires inclusion of criminal law and the impact of America's extraordinary incarceration levels on the civil justice needs of affected individuals and their families.[5]

So many do not even know when they have a right or defense to claim or when it is worthwhile to do so. The chapter authors advance understandings of the actual demand for legal services, and the results for those who never obtain full or even partial legal assistance. They offer a comparison with practices in other countries and estimate the scope of "lumping it" behavior as people give up without asserting their lawful rights. They outline the research necessary to gain deeper, reliable information about the scope of unmet legal needs. The book also includes critical chapters on the disparate impact of the justice access crisis on people of color, immigrants, and individuals caught in exceedingly complex situations.

With chapters on the promise and limitations of federally funded civil legal services, clinical legal education, law firm pro bono efforts, employee benefit plans, and local attorney referral programs, the book highlights the misalignment of incentives that contributes to failures to supply legal assistance for "routine" or "ordinary" problems. Improving access to lawyers requires analysis of the shifting cost structure and supply chains for legal services. Identifying the full range of existing and potential devices for compensation of attorneys and educational loan repayment and forgiveness programs, the chapters make a good start on work that over time should also include attention to different ways to organize people and digital resources to increase both efficiency and quality as further avenues for expanding access to legal help. Provision of legal help must include, as this book

4 World Justice Project, Rule of Law Index 2015, available at http://data.worldjusticeproject.org/; James Lamont, United States Ranks 65th for the Accessibility and Affordability of its Civil Justice, June 18, 2015, available at http://law.passle.net/post/102ctvr/united-states-ranks-65th-for-the-accessibility-and-affordability-of-its-civil-jus?TW.

5 Consider the problems posed by internet records that include arrests even when no conviction resulted. "One recent study found that 49 percent of African American men are arrested by 23. Further, this criminal-record penalty is twice as likely to punish black job seekers as it is white ones. This penalty also has fiscal ramifications: by one account, criminal records as a hurdle to employment cost the U.S. economy up to $65 billion each year." Jason Tashea & Jon Tippens, *Helping Expunge an Inaccurate Criminal Record*, The Blog: Huffington Post, Apr. 2, 2015, available at www.huffingtonpost.com/jason-tashea/helping-expunge-inaccurate-criminal-record_b_6988750.html. As expungement of a criminal records is not "do-it-yourself-friendly," lawyers or other sources of expertise are needed. *Id.*

does, procedural and substantive rules affecting class actions and other opportunities to aggregate claims.

America's failures to ensure access to justice will not be solved easily. There is no silver bullet. A major contribution of this book is the array of detailed ideas for reforms across multiple sectors, institutions, and practices. Hence, the book explores potential changes in bar admission rules, law school "incubator" programs to support the development of sustainable "low bono" and small firm practices, judicial financial assistance, substantive law changes to reduce traps for those who are self-represented, and modifications of bar rules to permit limited representation and non-lawyer involvement. Setting up laws and justice systems that require lawyers to navigate, and then making lawyers inaccessible, are not just features of the dark imaginations of fiction writers like Franz Kafka and Lewis Carroll. If we cannot provide lawyers, shouldn't we change the rules and procedures that require them? Chapter authors are attentive to both the opportunities and risks arising with expansion of mediation, arbitration, and grievance systems in person and online, new technologies and models to support self-help programs at courts and administrative agencies, and document production companies. An underlying theme is the obligation of lawyers to open channels for collaboration with and independent work by non-lawyers. Lawyers have not been able to resolve the justice gap. Labor unions, worker centers, social services agencies, and other "intermediate institutions" can be helpful but not if bar rules hamstring them.

Most disheartening are the avoidable tragedies. Knowing of people who would have kept their homes, their children, their jobs, their lives if their legal rights were enforced is so frustrating. But in this very frustration lies hope. Unlike so many tragedies of human suffering, the access to justice crisis can be fixed. Especially encouraging, this book includes vivid accounts of successful efforts. We should take heart. We should follow the examples of statewide access to justice commissions that are putting in motion key reform elements and efforts needed to build political will. Law firm leaders build strong pro bono into the culture and commitments of young and old lawyers and other staff. Bar associations exemplify what it looks like to pursue justice. Law schools demonstrate how service and education can change the lives of clients and future lawyers. Like those who have worked on access to justice in the past, a new generation can join the struggle. This book points the way. A. Philip Randolph said so well what will light the path: "Justice is never given; it is exacted and the struggle must be continuous for freedom is never a final fact, but a continuing evolving process to higher and higher levels of human, social, economic, political and religious relationship."[6]

[6] Bayard Rustin, A. *Phillip Randolph: Dean of Civil Rights*, 76 THE CRISIS No. 4, Apr. 1969.

Contributors

Samuel Estreicher is the Dwight D. Opperman Professor of Law at New York University School of Law, where he directs the Institute of Judicial Administration and the Center for Labor and Employment Law. He most recently served as Chief Reporter of the American Law Institute's Restatement of Employment Law (2015).

Joy Radice is an associate professor at the University of Tennessee College of Law, where she co-teaches the Advocacy Clinic, directs the Expungement Clinic, teaches criminal law, and also serves on the Knoxville Bar Association's Access to Justice Committee, co-chairing the Expungement Subcommittee.

Martha Minow is the Morgan and Helen Chu Dean and Professor of Law at Harvard Law School. She serves on the Board of Directors of the Legal Services Corporation as vice-chair and co-chaired its Pro Bono Task Force.

Wallace B. Jefferson is the former Chief Justice of the Supreme Court of Texas. He is currently a partner in the appellate specialty firm of Alexander Dubose Jefferson and Townsend LLP.

Jonathan Lippman is the former Chief Judge of the New York Court of Appeals and is of counsel to Latham & Watkins in New York.

Ian Weinstein is Professor of Law at Fordham Law School where he teaches criminal law, evidence and the the Fedral Litigation Clinic.

Gillian K. Hadfield is the Richard L. and Antoinette Schamoi Kirtland Professor of Law and Professor of Economics at the University of Southern California, where she directs the Center for Law and Social Science. She is a member of the World Economic Forum's Global Agenda Council for Justice.

Jamie Heine is a 2013 graduate of the Gould School of Law at the University of Southern California and an associate with the law firm Covington and Burling LLP.

The late Theodore Eisenberg was the Henry Allen Mark Professor of Law and Adjunct Professor of Statistical Sciences at Cornell Law School.

Russell Engler is a Professor of Law and the Director of Clinical Programs at New England Law | Boston. He serves on the Massachusetts Access to Justice Commission, the Steering Committee of the National Coalition for a Civil Right to Counsel, and the Strategy and Outreach Committee for the Self-Represented Litigation Network.

Rafael I. Pardo is the Robert T. Thompson Professor of Law at Emory University School of Law.

Laura Beth Nielsen is a professor of sociology and directs the Legal Studies Program at Northwestern University. She also is a Research Professor at the American Bar Foundation.

Amy Myrick received a PhD and JD from Northwestern University and served as a Doctoral Fellow at the American Bar Foundation. She is currently a staff attorney at the Center for Reproductive Rights.

Robert L. Nelson is the MacCrate Research Chair in the Legal Profession, American Bar Foundation and Professor of Sociology and Law at Northwestern University.

David Yin was a litigation associate at WilmerHale LLP and is presently serving as a law clerk for Judge Timothy Dyk on the U.S. Court of Appeals for the Federal Circuit.

Robert A. Katzmann is Chief Judge of the U.S. Court of Appeals for the Second Circuit, and advanced the creation of the Study Group on Immigrant Representation and the Immigrant Justice Corps.

Alina Das is an associate professor of clinical law at New York University School of Law, where she co-directs the Immigrant Rights Clinic.

Jeanne Charn is a senior lecturer on law at Harvard Law School where she co-founded the clinical program and directs the Bellow Sacks Access to Civil Legal Services Project.

David L. Noll is an assistant professor of law at Rutgers School of Law. He teaches civil procedure, federal courts, evidence, and related courses.

William D. Henderson is a Professor of Law and Val Nolan Faculty Fellow at the Indiana University Bloomington Maurer School of Law.

Andrew P. Morriss is the Dean and Anthony G. Buzbee Dean's Endowed Chair in Law at Texas A&M School of Law.

Margaret Drew is an associate professor at University of Massachusetts (Dartmouth) Law School where she is Director of Clinics and Experiential Learning.

Emily S. Bremer is an Assistant Professor of Law at the University of Wyoming College of Law, where she teaches legislation & regulation, international business transactions, and corporations.

Allen Charne served as Executive Director of the Legal Referral Service sponsored by the Association of the Bar of the City of New York and the New York County Lawyers' Association from 1983 to 2013.

Steven A. Boutcher is an assistant professor of sociology and public policy at the University of Massachusetts, Amherst.

Jonathan Remy Nash is Professor of Law and was the David J. Bederman Research Professor (2014–15) at Emory University School of Law.

Steven C. Bennett is a partner at Park Jensen Bennett LLP in New York City and an Adjunct Professor of Law at Hofstra University and New York Law schools.

Michael Z. Green is a professor of law at Texas A&M University School of Law where he served as the inaugural Associate Dean for Faculty Research & Development for four years.

Maggie Gousman is an attorney at the law firm of Jackson Lewis PC, where she practices labor and employment law.

John P. Frantz is the senior vice-president and general counsel of product and new business innovation at Verizon. He has served as the chair of Verizon's pro bono committee since the start of Verizon's pro bono program in 2009.

Randal S. Milch is a Distinguished Fellow at New York University Law School's Center on Law and Security. He previously was the executive vice-president, public policy, and general counsel of Verizon.

Adam Klein is a partner of Outten & Golden LLP and is the chair of the firm's Class action practice group.

Olivia Quinto is an associate at Outten & Golden LLP representing employees in class action wage/hour and discrimination cases.

Nantiya Ruan is the Hartje and Reese Chair in Lawyering Process and Professor of Practice at the University of Denver Sturm College of Law, as well as of counsel to Outten & Golden LLP.

Helaine M. Barnett is Chair of the New York State Permanent Commission on Access to Justice (formely the Task Force to Expand Access to Civil Legal Services in New York) and Adjunct Professor at New York University School of Law. She previously served as President of the Legal Services Corporation and as head of the Civil Division of The Legal Aid Society of New York.

Hon. Victoria A. Graffeo is a partner at Harris Beach PLLC, where she is leader She previously served a 14-year term on the New York Court of Appeals, was a Judge of the Appellate Practice and ADR Practice groups. On the Appellate Division, Third Department, a Supreme Court Justice in the Third Judicial District, and Solicitor General for the State of New York.

Luz Herrera is Assistant Dean for clinical education, experiential learning and public service at UCLA School of Law.

Ann Juergens is a professor of law at Mitchell Hamline School of Law in Saint Paul, Minnesota, where she teaches ethics, advocacy, and small firm practice and is Co-Director of Clinics.

Reid Kress Weisbord is Vice-Dean, Professor of Law and Judge Norma L. Shapiro Scholar at Rutgers Law School.

Rachel Ekery served as staff counsel to Chief Justice Wallace B. Jefferson of the Texas Supreme Court. She is currently a partner in the appellate specialty firm, Alexander Dubose Jefferson & Townsend LLP.

Benjamin H. Barton is the Helen and Charles Lockett Distinguished Professor of Law at the University of Tennessee College of Law.

E. Patrick McDermott is a professor of management/legal studies at the Franklin P. Perdue School of Business and Director of Research and Evaluation at the Center for Conflict Resolution at Salisbury University.

Ruth Obar is a Senior Research Fellow at the Center for Conflict Resolution at Salisbury University.

Christopher R. Drahozal is the John M. Rounds Professor of Law at the University of Kansas School of Law. He is an Associate Reporter for the Restatement of the U.S. Law on International Commercial Arbitration and assisted the Consumer Financial Protection Bureau with its empirical study of consumer financial services arbitration.

Peter B. "Bo" Rutledge is Dean of the University of Georgia School of Law and the Herman E. Talmadge Chair of Law.

Michael Delikat is the global chair of the employment law practice group at Orrick, Herrington & Sutcliffe.

Lisa Lupion is an employment attorney in the New York office of Orrick, Herrington & Sutcliffe.

Ariel B. Woldar is tax and employee benefits associate at Hughes Hubbard & Reed LLP in the New York office.

David S. Sherwyn is the John and Melissa Ceriale Professor of Hospitality Human Resources at Cornell University, the Academic Director of the Cornell Institute for Hospitality Labor and Employment Relations, and a Stephen H. Weiss Presidential Fellow.

Zev J. Eigen is a consultant and expert on data analytics, labor law, and employment law.

Alexander J. S. Colvin is the Martin F. Scheinman Professor of Conflict Resolution at the ILR School, Cornell University, and serves as Associate Director of the Scheinman Institute on Conflict Resolution and Associate Editor of the *ILR Review*.

Kelly Pike is Assistant Professor of Work and Labour Studies at York University, Canada, where she is also a faculty affiliate of the Global Labour Research Centre.

Michael J. Wolf is the Settlement Judge and Director of Collaboration & ADR at the U.S. Federal Labor Relations Authority, where he helps federal government agencies and labor unions resolve complex workplace disputes.

Ann C. Hodges is Professor of Law at the University of Richmond where she teaches and labor and employment law and nonprofit organizations.

Aaron Halegua is a lawyer consultant and Research Fellow at both the U.S.-Asia Law Institute and the Center for Labor and Employment Law at the New York University School of Law.

Kate Levine is Acting Assistant Professor of Lawyering at New York University School of Law and will be joining the law faculty of St. John's University School of Law in the fall 2016.

Paul Salvatore is a member of Proskauer and Rose's executive committee and former co-chair of its global labor & employment law department.

Terry Meginniss is a partner in Gladstein, Reif & Meginniss, and is the general counsel of SEIU Local 32BJ.

Lisa Dewey serves as the U.S. Pro Bono Partner at DLA Piper LLP and Director of New Perimeter, the firm's global pro bono initiative.

Sara K. Andrews is senior international pro bono counsel at DLA Piper LLP and Assistant Director of New Perimeter, the firm's global pro bono initiative.

Richard Gruenberger is Counsel & Director of U.S. Pro Bono Programs at DLA Piper LLP and leads the firm's veterans, hunger, and client partnership initiatives.

Anne Geraghty Helms is Director & Counsel of U.S. Pro Bono Programs at DLA Piper LLP, focusing her practice on criminal and juvenile justice.

Roberta Ritvo served as senior pro bono counsel at DLA Piper for several years before leaving the firm in late 2014.

Daniel L. Greenberg is Special Counsel for Pro Bono Initiatives at Shulte, Roth & Zebel LLP in New York. He was formerly President and Attorney-in-Chief of The Legal Aid Society of New York.

Lynn M. Kelly is the Executive Director of the Association of the Bar of the City of New York's City Bar Justice Center. Her experience includes directing MFY Legal Services, clinical law teaching and litigating at The Legal Aid Society in New York City.

Randy Hertz is Vice-Dean, Professor of Clinical Law, and Director of Clinical and Advocacy Programs at New York University School of Law.

Natalie Gomez-Velez is a professor of law at the City University of New York (CUNY) School of Law, where she has served as Associate Dean for Academic Affairs and currently is director of the Center for Latino/a Rights and Equality.

Royal Furgeson is the founding Dean of the UNT Dallas College of Law and a retired United States District Judge.

Ellen Pryor is a professor of law and associate dean for academic affairs at the UNT Dallas College of Law.

Cheryl Wattley is a professor and Director of Experiential Education at the UNT Dallas College of Law, where she directs experiential programming and teaches criminal law, interviewing, and counseling.

Valerie James is Assistant Dean & Director of Admissions & Scholarships at UNT Dallas College of Law, where she oversees admissions and scholarship programming school.

Eric Porterfield is an assistant professor of law at UNT Dallas College of Law. He teaches in the areas of civil procedure, evidence, and legal writing.

Overview

Hon. Wallace B. Jefferson, former Chief Justice, Supreme Court of Texas

Thirty years ago, then-president of Harvard University Derek Bok delivered a stinging assessment of our justice system.[1] He observed that our country, which prides itself on efficiency and fairness, "has developed a legal system that is the most expensive in the world, yet cannot manage to protect the rights of most of its citizens."[2] He famously observed that "[t]here is far too much law for those who can afford it and far too little for those who cannot."[3]

How have Americans fared in the thirty years since then?

For those who can afford it, we have a top-notch legal system. Highly qualified lawyers, who know the art of cross-examination and who compose scholarly briefs, help courts dispense justice fairly and efficiently. But that kind of representation comes at a price. More often, litigants lack wealth, insurance is absent, and public funding is not available. Some of our most essential rights – those involving our families, our homes, and our livelihoods – are the least protected.

Veterans languish an average of eight months before the government processes their claims for disability, pension, and educational benefits.[4] Their poverty rate has increased.[5] They face physical and mental trauma, and they comprise 20% of the homeless population.[6] They experience significantly higher rates of unemployment than nonveterans.[7]

[1] See Derek C. Bok, *A Flawed System of Law Practice and Training*, 33 J. Legal Educ. 570 (1983).

[2] *Id.* at 574.

[3] *Id.* at 571.

[4] See James Dao, *Veterans Wait for Benefits as Claims Pile Up*, N.Y. Times, Sept. 28, 2012, at A1 (noting the average claims-processing rate in 2012).

[5] See Nat'l Ctr. for Veterans Analysis & Statistics, U.S. Dep't of Veterans Affairs, Health Insurance Coverage, Poverty, and Income of Veterans: 2000 to 2009, at 9 (2011), available at www.va.gov/vetdata/docs/SpecialReports/HealthIns_FINAL.pdf ("In 2000, about 5.0 percent of Veterans were living in poverty. By 2009, the poverty rate for Veterans was 6.3 percent").

[6] *United States: Leave No Veteran Behind*, Economist, June 4, 2011, at 38, available at www.economist.com/node/18775315 (noting that "[n]early a fifth of the homeless population in the United States are veterans" and that more face physical and mental challenges).

[7] Marta Hoes, Comment, *Invisible Wounds: What Texas Should Be Doing for the Mental Health of Its Veterans*, 13 Tex. Tech Admin. L.J. 369, 373 (2012) (comparing the unemployment rate of veterans with the national average and finding the former to be elevated in comparison to the latter).

The financial crisis has created ripple effects throughout society. Lower- and middle-income homeowners and tenants are grappling with legal issues as never before.[8] Facing foreclosure or eviction, they can little afford representation to protect their rights. Over the past several years, high numbers of consumers and small businesses have sought bankruptcy protection.[9]

American children are also at risk when interacting with the legal system. A family's lack of resources dramatically affects domestic matters, like custody and child support. Apart from that, families must grapple with issues involving juvenile justice. Texas has one of the largest school systems in the nation, with more than 4.4 million students.[10] Children who misbehave in school are often issued tickets and may be charged with Class C misdemeanors.[11] They must appear in court to contest the charges, but they have no right to counsel.[12]

Cash-strapped families forgo representation, often with devastating consequences, such as arrest warrants and criminal records.

In 2013, I delivered the annual William J. Brennan, Jr. Lecture on State Court and Social Justice at New York University School of Law. My speech, titled "Liberty and Justice for Some: How the Legal System Falls Short in Protecting Basic Rights,"[13] focused on the ways in which our system fails to protect not just the poor, but also the middle class. Statutory rights to counsel generally apply only to the indigent, as do most pro bono efforts.[14] Legal aid eligibility is generally capped at 125% of federal poverty guidelines.[15] Thus, a family of four with an income of

[8] See Aleatra P. Williams, *Real Estate Market Meltdown, Foreclosures and Tenants' Rights*, 43 IND. L. REV. 1185, 1187 (2010) ("The consequence of the current real estate market collapse and the resulting foreclosures and their effect on the tenant market is unparalleled in history").

[9] Although data suggest that consumer and small business bankruptcies may now be declining, their levels remain elevated, with 2010 levels more than three times what they were in 2006. See *Drop in Small Business Bankruptcies Outpaces Decline in Consumer Bankruptcies*, EQUIFAX, 1 (2011), www.equifax.com/ecm/pressroom/BankruptcyDataPrimerFinal.pdf (charting the rate of small business and consumer quarterly petitions for bankruptcy from the first quarter of 2006 through the last quarter of 2010).

[10] See TEX. APPLESEED, TEXAS'[S] SCHOOL-TO-PRISON PIPELINE: DROPOUT TO INCARCERATION 3 (2007), available at www.texasappleseed.net/pdf/Pipeline%20Report.pdf (finding that at least 4.4 million students attend public schools in the state's 1037 school districts).

[11] See Wallace B. Jefferson, *Recognizing and Combating the "School-to-Prison" Pipeline in Texas*, NAT'L CTR. FOR STATE COURTS, available at www.ncsc.org/sitecore/content/microsites/futuretrends2012/home/Otherpages/SchoolToPrisonPipelineInTexas.aspx (last visited Oct. 11, 2013).

[12] See TEX. APPLESEED, TEXAS'[S] SCHOOL-TO-PRISON PIPELINE: TICKETING, ARREST & USE OF FORCE IN SCHOOLS 71 (2010), available at www.texasappleseed.net/images/stories/reports/Ticketing_Booklet_web.pdf (noting that juveniles in Texas do not have a right to appointed counsel in Class C misdemeanor cases and observing that young people may plead guilty to such charges simply because they are unaware of viable defenses)

[13] Portions of this preface were derived from that speech, which was published as: Hon. Wallace B. Jefferson, *Brennan Lecture: Liberty and Justice for Some: How the Legal System Falls Short in Protecting Basic Rights*, 88 N.Y.U. L. REV. 1953 (2013). See also Chapter 28 by Rachel Ekery in this volume.

[14] See, e.g., TEX. FAM. CODE § 107.013(a)(1) (West Supp. 2012) ("In a suit filed by a governmental entity in which termination of the parent-child relationship is requested, the court shall appoint an attorney ad litem to represent the interests of . . . an indigent parent of the child who responds in opposition to the termination.").

[15] Financial Eligibility Policies, 45 C.F.R. § 1611.3(c)(1) (2012).

$30,000 generally will not qualify for services.[16] But after that family pays for shelter, sustenance, and the other necessities of daily life, it is unlikely that the family will be able to afford a lawyer for even the most basic legal necessities.[17]

With no real alternative, litigants are increasingly representing themselves. Although there are no comprehensive statistics on self-represented litigants in our nation's courts,[18] an American Bar Association (ABA) survey found that 60% of state judges recently noted an increase in the number of litigants representing themselves.[19]

Yet, we have more lawyers than at any time in our history. "In 1960, there was one lawyer for every 627 people in the United States";[20] today, there is one for every 252.[21] Certainly, it can be argued that more lawyers are necessary in an increasingly complex world. Nevertheless, it is ironic that, as litigants are increasingly forced to represent themselves, law school graduates cannot find jobs.[22] What accounts for this mismatch, and how can we ensure that our system is accessible to all segments of our society?[23]

Increased pro bono work by lawyers is always a good idea, and many lawyers do step in to help those who could not otherwise afford their services. New York now requires bar applicants to complete fifty hours of pro bono legal work.[24] Many law schools mandate pro bono service from their students[25] and have created legal clinics providing excellent representation for the indigent.

[16] But see 45 C.F.R. § 1611.5(a) (2012) (noting that in some instances, eligibility may be capped at 200% of the federal poverty guidelines by household size as determined by the Department of Health and Human Services); see also Notice, 78 Fed. Reg. 5182, 5183 (Jan. 24, 2013) (establishing a poverty guideline of $23,550 for a four-person household). Thus, in some instances, a household of four making less than $47,100 can qualify.

[17] See Susan D. Carle, *Re-Valuing Lawyering for Middle-Income Clients*, 70 FORDHAM L. REV. 719, 721 (2001) ("The fact is that the majority of Americans live on quite modest incomes and lack the discretionary spending power necessary to purchase expensive legal services in today's market").

[18] See Nathan Koppel, *More Strapped Litigants Skip Lawyers in Court*, WALL ST. J., July 22, 2010, at A4 (noting the lack of such statistics).

[19] *Id.*

[20] Robert C. Clark, *Why So Many Lawyers? Are They Good or Bad?*, 61 FORDHAM L. REV. 275, 275 (1992).

[21] Dividing the number of people in the United States by the number of attorney shows that there is one attorney for every 251.94 people. See PAUL MACKUN & STEVEN WILSON, U.S. CENSUS BUREAU, POPULATION DISTRIBUTION AND CHANGE: 2000 TO 2010, at 4 tbl.2 (2011), available at www.census.gov/prod/cen2010/briefs/c2010br-01.pdf (showing total U.S. population as 308,745,538).

[22] Catherine Rampell, *The Lawyer Surplus, State by State*, N.Y. TIMES (June 27, 2011, 11:35 AM), http://economix.blogs.nytimes.com/2011/06/27/the-lawyer-surplus-state-by-state/ (noting that "across the country, there were twice as many people who passed the bar in 2009 . . . as there were [job] openings").

[23] One explanation focuses on financial incentives. See John O. McGinnis & Russell D. Mangas, Op-Ed., *First Thing We Do, Let's Kill All the Law Schools*, WALL ST. J., Jan. 17, 2012, at A15 (observing that the steep cost of legal education results in higher legal fees, making legal services unaffordable to the middle class "at a time when increasing complexity demands more access to these services" and concluding that "the current system leaves citizens underserved and young lawyers indebted").

[24] N.Y. COMP. CODES R. & REGS. tit. 22, § 520.16 (2013) (imposing the pro bono requirement on graduates who will be admitted to the bar on or after January 1, 2015, and following an examination); see also Joel Stashenko & Christine Simmons, *Lippman Unveils Rule Detailing Bar Admission Pro Bono Mandate*, 248 N.Y. L.J., Sept. 20, 2012, at 1 (reporting on the new requirement). See Chapter 24 by Judge Graffeo in this volume.

[25] See Robert Granfield, *Institutionalizing Public Service in Law School: Results on the Impact of Mandatory Pro Bono Programs*, 54 BUFF. L. REV. 1355, 1364 (2007) ("While mandatory pro bono

But encouraging or even requiring pro bono representation cannot match the scale of the problem. In 2009, Texas attorneys provided as many as 2.5 million hours of free legal or indirect services to the poor.[26] While this is impressive, we are still meeting only about 20–25% of the civil legal needs of low-income Texans.[27] Even if we required every Texas lawyer to represent at least one client pro bono, we would serve less than 40% of indigent individuals in need of legal services,[28] to say nothing of the millions of middle-class individuals who need representation. In Southwest Texas alone, 2.6 million people qualify for legal aid.[29] That means there are 21,000 potential clients for every lawyer employed by the region's main legal aid office.[30] This situation is echoed across the country.[31] Increased funding would help provide more services. But in today's economic climate, even maintaining existing funding has proved challenging.[32]

Neither money nor additional pro bono work is enough.[33] And if neither money nor increased pro bono service will suffice to meet the challenge, what more can we do?

remains hotly contested within the organized bar, the majority of American law schools have already implemented some type of pro bono program and many have adopted mandatory requirements").

26 D'Arlene Verduin & Paul Ruggiere, *State Bar of Texas Survey of 2009 Pro Bono*, Tex. Access to Just. Comm'n, at i(Mar. 31, 2010), available at www.texasatj.org/files/file/Pro%20Bono%20Survey%202009.pdf.

27 *Facts and Figures*, Tex. Access to Just. Comm'n, available at www.texasatj.org/facts (last visited Oct. 11, 2013).

28 Tex. Access to Justice Comm'n, A Report to the Supreme Court Advisory Comm. from the Texas Access to Justice Comm'n on the Court's Uniform Forms Task Force 5 (2012).

29 *Who We Are*, Tex. Rio Grande Legal Aid, available at www.trla.org/about/whoweare (last visited Oct. 11, 2013).

30 *Id.*

31 See Gillian Hadfield, *Lawyers, Make Room for Nonlawyers*, CNN (Nov. 25, 2012, 12:25 PM), available at www.cnn.com/2012/11/23/opinion/hadfield-legal-profession (arguing that "the demand for ordinary legal help is simply too massive to meet with increased court funding, legal aid or pro bono work"); chapter by Professor Hadfield in this volume.

32 There has been a persistent campaign in Texas for legal aid funding. See Letter from Wallace B. Jefferson, Chief Justice, Supreme Court of Tex., and Nathan L. Hecht, Justice, Supreme Court of Tex., to Royce West, Tex. State Senator2 (June 1, 2011), available at www.supreme.courts.state.tx.us/advisories/Letter_West_060111.pdf (seeking funding for basic civil legal services for indigent Texans). In 2011, the Texas legislature authorized gap funding for legal aid. See Press Release, Tex. Access to Just. Comm'n, Texas Access to Justice Commission and Foundation Applaud the Texas Legislature for Providing Funding for the State's Legal Aid System (July 21, 2011), available at www.texasatj.org/commissionandfoundationapplaudlegislature (describing the Texas Legislature's appropriation of $17.5 million for civil legal aid and $7.6 million for county indigent defense programs to compensate for a decline in IOLTA funding); see also H. Con. Res. 22, 82d Leg., 1st Called Sess. (Tex. 2011) (commending members of the Texas Supreme Court for advocating for funding "to ensure that all citizens have equal access to the civil justice system").

33 Derek Bok, echoing a call for reform that still rings true, has argued:

> [M]oney alone will not suffice. In cases involving . . . disputes that touch the lives of ordinary folk, judges will have to develop less costly ways of resolving disputes . . . Likewise, lawyers will need to devise new institutions to supply legal services more cheaply. Such changes, in turn, will undoubtedly force the organized bar to reexamine traditional attitudes toward fee-for-service and the unauthorized practice of law.

Bok, supra note 1, at 580.

A great deal. Fortunately, Professors Estreicher and Radice, along with the judges, scholars, and lawyers involved in *Beyond Elite Law: Access to Civil Justice in America*, have comprehensively studied the barriers to justice faced by many Americans. The book begins by examining the current state of access to, and sources of assistance for, legal services by working Americans. It provides an overview of the many challenges to accessing our system, with a particular emphasis on the issues faced by self-represented litigants.

But this volume does not only examine the problems, it outlines a reform agenda to mitigate them. Every aspect of the legal system, from legal education through delivery of services, is covered. Innovative approaches, involving both the private and public sectors, are presented to help us ensure that ordinary Americans can get the legal services they need.

The book's final section, "Creating a Culture of Service," is a must-read for anyone involved in the delivery of legal services. The section examines ways in which law firms, bar associations, and law schools can help deliver equal justice to all Americans. The creative solutions to some of our system's woes are nothing short of inspiring.

The phrase "access to justice" is often thought of in terms of providing legal services to the poor. It is that, to be sure, but an accessible justice system requires that all segments of our society be able to utilize it. Viewed this way, our remedies must be more expansive as well.[34] Just as no single issue created the barriers, there is no unitary solution.

The legal profession must adapt to evolving procedures and times and must embrace change, even if that change sometimes comes at our own expense. Too often, when faced with issues that might adversely affect the bottom line, our profession acts less like a profession and more like a trade.[35] When vast segments of our society are unable to utilize the legal system, we must examine whether we should change the way legal services are delivered and how courts can create more accessible systems. A two-tiered justice system denies "liberty and justice for all." We can do much better. This book shows us how.

[34] See Lawrence M. Friedman, *Access to Justice: Some Historical Comments*, 37 FORDHAM URB. L.J. 3, 15 (2010) (noting that "access to justice is a complex issue" and that "[a] solution to the 'problem' depends on how the problem is defined and what policy goals one wishes to reach").

[35] See, e.g., George C. Harris & Derek F. Foran, The Ethics of Middle-Class Access to Legal Services and What We Can Learn from the Medical Profession's Shift to a Corporate Paradign, 70 Fordham L. Rev. 775, 804 (2001).

Overview

Hon. Jonathan Lippman, former Chief Judge, New York Court of Appeals

The United States has the best legal system in the world. Our adversarial system of justice requires opposing parties to present the best evidence for their respective arguments before an impartial judge or jury. It is critical, in making the system, that both sides are well-represented. Our system is imperiled, however, when the cost of legal assistance is so prohibitively expensive that litigants are forced to represent themselves pro se and to navigate the complicated legal system on their own. Today, more and more people are unable to afford the high cost of legal help in matters that impinge upon the basic essentials of life.

As Chief Judge of the State of New York, I see this scenario playing out all too often in our courtrooms each and every day. An unfair job termination, an unexpected illness or disability, or a wrongful foreclosure can deal a devastating financial blow to a working family. Many Americans do not understand how costly and out of reach legal services are until something calamitous happens in their lives. In New York and around the country, the current economic downturn, traumatic government spending cuts on the federal, state, and local level, and the impact of natural disasters like Superstorm Sandy only make access to justice more difficult for ordinary citizens. The number of Americans eligible for publicly funded legal assistance is at an all-time high, with 61.8 million people around the country living at or below 125% of the federal poverty line, but the funding levels are wholly inadequate to meet the need.[1] For Americans who do not meet the criteria to qualify for legal aid, paying hundreds of dollars an hour for a lawyer is simply not a financially feasible option.

One of the major issues that we grapple with in court administration is that precisely when state budgets are tightened and reined in as the economy declines, the need for legal services has ballooned. Our mission in the courts to mete out justice to litigants regardless of economic station is preeminent and must transcend these developments. Equal justice is one of the central tenets of our justice system. The safeguards and protections built into the law do us no good if the average person cannot access the courthouse doors. As U.S. Supreme Court Justice Lewis Powell once said, "Equal justice under law is not merely a caption on the facade of the

[1] Legal Services Corporation, LSC's Fiscal Year 2014 Budget Request, June 2013, available at www.lsc.gov/sites/default/files/LSC/lscgov4/LSC_FY2014_Budget_Request_FINAL_6-10-2013.pdf.

Supreme Court building, it is perhaps the most inspiring ideal of our society. It is one of the ends for which our entire legal system exists … it is fundamental that justice should be the same, in substance and availability, without regard to economic status."[2] The seriousness of this challenge cannot be understated. As a society, we cannot allow great swaths of our population to be shut out from the justice system. Access to justice is not a luxury, affordable only in good times, and it cannot be allowed to fluctuate with the ups and downs of economic booms and busts. It is a right for all, not an entitlement for the rich and powerful only.

Without a doubt, equal justice is curtailed when so many people cannot afford a lawyer to help them with life-altering legal problems. Each year, more than 2.3 million New Yorkers appear in civil courts without a lawyer, including more than 98% of tenants in eviction cases, 99% of borrowers in consumer credit cases, over 95% of parents in child support matters, and close to half of all homeowners facing foreclosure proceedings.[3] These unrepresented litigants often end up misdirecting their efforts by unnecessarily filing petitions or by filing the wrong documents as they go through the court system unassisted.[4]

In response to these difficulties, the New York court system has created a model to encourage earmarked public funding for civil legal services for the poor and people of limited means – $70 million in the 2014–15 fiscal year. This is by far the most state funding in the country for this purpose, and yet it is only the tip of the iceberg in terms of the tremendous need. We have also redoubled our efforts within the judiciary and in partnership with the bar to assist the unrepresented, by opening more Offices for the Self-Represented in our high-volume courthouses, expanding Volunteer Lawyer for the Day programs that provide lawyers for litigants who cannot afford one, and by expanding pro bono programs throughout New York. While these innovative efforts are beneficial in mitigating the shortfall in affordable legal services, by no means do they provide a comprehensive solution to this staggering problem.

Beyond Elite Law: Access to Civil Justice in America fills a gaping hole in the literature on how to assess and attack the problem of access to justice. Professors Samuel Estreicher and Joy Radice have carefully assembled contributions from the foremost legal thinkers and practitioners on how to analyze the problem of access to justice, the current state of available legal services for working Americans, and ways to improve our justice system and to increase the contributions from the bar.

The following chapters consider the issue of access to justice for working Americans from all angles of the problem. The book begins by looking at case studies on self-representation in bankruptcy, immigration, employment, and other matters and then examines how law schools, publicly funded legal services organizations, bar associations, law firms, and nongovernmental organizations provide legal assistance to those who cannot afford the high legal fees of a market-rate lawyer.

2 Lewis F. Powell, Jr., Address to the American Bar Association Legal Services Program, ABA Annual Meeting, Aug. 10, 1976.

3 2010 Report to the Chief Judge, Task Force to Expand Civil Legal Services in New York, at 1, 12; 2012 Report to the Chief Judge, Task Force to Expand Civil Legal Services in New York, at 15.

4 2012 Report to the Chief Judge, Task Force to Expand Civil Legal Services in New York, at 10.

These chapters are an invaluable and vital resource in helping to understand the impediments to affordable legal representation. The second half of the book considers what is being done around the country to address the justice gap. The status quo is simply an untenable posture, and the entire legal community must continue to test and implement innovative solutions to this immense crisis. As Justice Brandeis noted, the states may act as laboratories of democracy that try novel social experiments without risk to the rest of the country.[5] This book presents some of the most creative and successful ideas toward solving the problem of the public's limited access to legal services, including lowering the costs of attorney representation, increasing the pro bono contributions from the bar, utilizing alternative dispute resolution, facilitating non-lawyer legal assistance, and using intermediary organizations such as labor unions and immigrant centers.

The editors also include a section on creating a culture of service within the legal profession, a topic that is near and dear to my heart. While many individuals may be drawn to being a lawyer because of a desire to argue in court, to debate weighty constitutional issues, or simply to provide a stable income for their families, all members of the bar need to be reminded that the practice of law is a profession that is dedicated, first and foremost, to serving our clients and the communities around us. Lawyers must have an understanding that access to justice should be available to all people regardless of their station in life, and they must strive toward that ideal. The responsibilities of the profession must be a part of every lawyer's DNA – instilled from the very first day of law school and put into practice until retirement and beyond. It is not enough to say that this is the best we can do. The values of justice, equality, and the rule of law, must not buckle under the strain of financial pressure, budget constraints, or apathy toward our fellow men and women. In New York, I have made it a priority to encourage and spur increased pro bono involvement from the bar, by mandating that applicants to the bar contribute 50 hours of pro bono work[6] before they are admitted to practice and by urging mandatory reporting of pro bono hours. This book highlights the many ways that law firms, bar associations, and law schools can all contribute to cultivating a culture of service among lawyers.

As a nation, we have recently passed the 50th anniversary of the landmark U.S. Supreme Court decision in *Gideon v. Wainwright*, which established an indigent defendant's right to appointed counsel. The Supreme Court famously stated, "[I]n our adversary system of criminal justice, any person haled into court, who is too poor to hire a lawyer, cannot be assured a fair trial unless counsel is provided for him. This seems to us to be an obvious truth."[7] The Supreme Court recognized that the "noble ideal" of fair courts could not be realized if a poor man had to face his accusers without a lawyer to assist him. This principle holds true in criminal cases, but civil cases involving the basic essentials of life are every bit as critical to one's existence and well-being as the loss of liberty itself. The support for "civil *Gideon*" is growing, as a diverse coalition of bar associations, judicial leaders, academics, service providers, and others are collaborating to raise awareness about the dramatic

5 *New State Ice Co. v. Liebmann*, 285 U.S. 262, 311 (1932) (Brandeis, J., dissenting).

6 See Chapter 24 by my colleague Judge Graffeo in this volume.

7 *Gideon v. Wainwright*, 373 U.S. 335, 344 (1963).

need for civil legal services, to expand legal representation by finding permanent funding streams, and to encourage greater lawyer volunteerism.

To ensure access to justice for working Americans, we must continue to foster dialogue and encourage the development of imaginative and original solutions, two things that this volume does so well. This book is a clarion call to judges, lawyers, and political leaders to stand up and be counted when equal justice is so seriously at risk.

PART I

Current State of Access to Legal Services

1

Access to Civil Justice in America:

What Do We Know?

Ian Weinstein

Ian Weinstein reviews the body of research that describes what we know about access to civil justice for Americans of modest means. He looks at the problem from two perspectives: the demand side of those who present unmet civil legal needs and the supply side of providers that offer legal assistance to this population. Weinstein evaluates surveys that attempt to quantify the civil legal needs for this population and studies of how Americans fare when they represent themselves. The chapter closes with an inventory of the different civil legal service providers assisting Americans of limited means, from pro bono lawyers to government-funded legal aid organizations.

The crisis in access to justice for low- and moderate-income Americans has been the subject of renewed attention by the federal government,[1] states,[2] and private groups[3] in recent years. There is also a renaissance of access to justice

[1] In 2010, the United States Department of Justice created the Access to Justice Initiative "to address the access-to-justice crisis in the criminal and civil justice system." *The Access to Justice Initiative*, U.S. DEP'T OF JUSTICE, available at www.justice.gov/atj/ (last visited Aug. 5, 2014).

[2] More than thirty states have established Access to Justice Commissions or other groups focused on facilitating access to civil justice. See *State ATJ Directory*, AM. BAR ASS'N, available at www.americanbar.org/groups/legal_aid_indigent_defendants/initiatives/resource_center_for_access_to_justice/state_atj_commissions.html (last visited Aug. 7, 2014). For a discussion of access to justice issues across the nation, see ABA RESOURCE CTR. FOR ACCESS TO JUSTICE INITIATIVES, ACCESS TO CIVIL JUSTICE FOR LOW-INCOME PEOPLE: RECENT DEVELOPMENTS (2012), available at www.americanbar.org/content/dam/aba/administrative/legal_aid_indigent_defendants/ls_sclaid_atj_ccj_report_jan2012.authcheckdam.pdf. One of the most active state groups in recent years has been the New York Task Force. The Task Force's reports are available at *Task Force to Expand Access to Civil Legal Services in NY*, N.Y. STATE UNIFIED COURT SYSTEM, available at www.nycourts.gov/ip/access-civil-legal-services/index.shtml (last visited Aug. 5, 2014); for a fuller discussion of developments in New York, see Barnett, Chapter 23, and Graffeo, Chapter 24, in this volume.

[3] See, e.g., Peter L. Markowitz et al., Accessing Justice: The Availability and Adequacy of Counsel in Immigration Proceedings, New York Immigrant Representation Study (2011), available at www.cardozolawreview.com/content/denovo/NYIRS_Report.pdf (hereinafter N.Y. Immigrant Representation Study); Nabanita Pal, Facing Foreclosure Alone: The Continuing Crisis in Legal Representation (Brennan Center for Justice 2011), available at www.brennancenter.org/publication/facing-foreclosure-alone-continuing-crisis-legal-representation; Joy Moses, Ctr. for Am. Progress, Grounds for Objection: Causes and Consequences of America's Pro Se Crisis and How to Solve the Problem of Unrepresented Litigants

research,[4] a body of work that illuminates many dark corners of our system of civil justice. While people of means have ready access to lawyers, the courts, and the burgeoning system of private dispute resolution, most low- and moderate-income Americans with legal problems either do not use the civil justice system at all attempt to navigate it on their own without counsel.

Since the mid-1970s, surveys conducted by the American Bar Association (ABA) and the Legal Services Corporation (LSC) have shown that 80% of the legal needs of low-income Americans[5] and more than 50% of the legal needs of moderate-income Americans[6] remain unmet.[7] Data also confirm that underfunded civil legal aid providers must turn away many Americans who seek representation for their civil legal problems.[8]

But even as we learn more, there remain many gaps in our understanding of how the market, regulatory policy, legal rules, and social forces shape the supply of legal services. The first part of this chapter will present what we know about the need or demand for legal services among low- and moderate-income Americans, and the second part will describe the sectors of the legal profession that provide these services. Viewed from both demand and supply perspectives, the crisis in access to civil justice in America presents a clear challenge to our commitment to justice.

(2011), available at www.americanprogress.org/issues/open-government/report/2011/06/22/9721/grounds-for-objection/ (reporting on the pro se crisis); *Resource Center for Access to Justice Initiatives*, Am. Bar Ass'n, available at www.americanbar.org/groups/legal_aid_indigent_defendants/initiatives/resource_center_for_access_to_justice.html (last visited Aug. 5, 2014).

4 See Catherine R. Albiston & Rebecca L. Sandefur, *Expanding the Empirical Study of Access to Justice*, 2013 Wis. L. Rev. 101, 101 (2013).

5 The federal test for eligibility for representation by an LSC-funded program is a household income at or below 125% of the federal poverty level. In 2009, 56.8 million Americans lived in eligible households. Additionally, more than 55 million Americans who were over 60 years of age in 2009 also qualified for some LSC-funded programs. See Rebecca L. Sandefur & Aaron C. Smyth, Access Across America: First Report of the Civil Justice Infrastructure Mapping Project 10 (2011).

6 There were 122,459,000 households in America in 2012, and their median income was $51,017. Sixty percent of households had incomes of $64,582 or less. Eighty percent of households had incomes below $104,096, and only 5% of households had incomes of $191,157 or greater. Carmen DeNavas-Walt et al., U.S. Dep't of Commerce, U.S. Census Bureau, Income, Poverty, and Health Insurance Coverage in the United States: 2012 6, 9 (2013), available at www.census.gov/prod/2013pubs/p60–245.pdf.

7 Deborah L. Rhode, *Access to Justice: An Agenda for Legal Education and Research*, 62 J. Legal Educ. 531, 531 (2013) (noting that more than four-fifths of the legal needs of the poor remain unmet, and citing literature reviews on that data). See generally Rebecca L. Sandefur, *The Impact of Counsel: An Analysis of Empirical Evidence*, 9 Seattle J. for Soc. Just. 51 (2010) (hereinafter Sandefur *The Impact of Counsel*); Russell Engler, *Connecting Self-Representation to Civil Gideon: What Existing Data Reveal about When Counsel Is Most Needed*, 37 Fordham Urb. L.J. 37 (2010).

8 See Rhode, supra note 7, at 535–42; Legal Servs. Corp., Documenting the Justice Gap in America: The Current Unmet Civil Legal Needs (lsc) Low-income Americans 9–12 (2009) (hereinafter LSC 2009 Report).

THE DEMAND FOR CIVIL LEGAL SERVICES

Assessing Legal Needs

Barbara Curran's 1977 study, *The Legal Needs of the Public: The Final Report of a National Survey*,[9] launched the modern era[10] of empirical work on of access to civil justice in America. Published by the ABA, the study sought "to determine the circumstances under which the public seeks the advice or help of lawyers and to identify factors that appear to influence decisions to consult or not to consult lawyers."[11]

Curran asked two sets of questions – how often do Americans need legal services, and what do they do when they have that need. The study relied upon data collected from 2,064 survey respondents, each of whom was presented with twenty-nine different "problem situations." Each situation described a scenario in which consulting a lawyer would have been a reasonable response, such as an incident causing damage to one's home, a dispute with a landlord, or a car accident involving an injury.[12] Each time a respondent replied that he or she had encountered the situation presented, the respondent was counted as having experienced an incident of legal need, regardless of whether the respondent had understood that the situation raised a legal issue or sought legal assistance.

Curran found that Americans experience an average of 4.8 legal problems in their lifetimes for which consulting a lawyer would be reasonable.[13] The most common kinds of legal problems involved acquisition of real property, damage to property, wills, divorce, and disputes about major purchases. The incidence of legal problems was higher among white people, those with more discretionary income, and those with more education.[14]

What did people do when confronting situations calling for consultation with an attorney? Curran found that the use of legal services and the "nature, quality and effectiveness of legal services received, as perceived by the recipients, vary substantially . . . by type of legal problem."[15] For example, only 29% of people who reported job discrimination also reported that they had taken any action in response.[16] By contrast, more than 80% of those who faced a problem involving property damage took action, and more than 80% of those who took action did so, in part, by seeking

9 Barbara Curran, *The Legal Needs of the Public: The Final Report of a National Survey* (1977).
10 *Id.* at 1–9 (reviewing the legacy of prior research).
11 *Id.* at 9.
12 The problem situations covered a broad range of legal subject-matter including real property, employment, consumer, estate planning, marital and domestic, tort, criminal, and constitutional law.
13 Curran, supra note 9, at 100. As the study looked at cumulative experience, incidence predictably increased with the age of the respondent.
14 *Id.* at 100–102.
15 *Id.* at 260–61.
16 *Id.* at 137.

the assistance of a lawyer.[17] The study also found "small but important differences in opinions and perceptions about lawyers, the courts and the legal system among different demographic subgroups."[18] Relatively disadvantaged groups were more likely to have high regard for lawyers and at the same time, to feel more "pessimism about how well the system would serve them."[19]

More than fifteen years would pass before the next national survey of access to justice in America. *Legal Needs and Civil Justice: A Survey of Americans* was published by the ABA in 1994.[20] This study presented respondents with sixty-seven factual scenarios, raising a broader array of legal issues than the Curran study.[21] More than 3,000 households were contacted, and respondents were asked if anyone in the household had experienced any of the situations in the prior year.[22] As in the earlier study, each affirmative response was counted as an incident of legal need, and respondents were not required to conceive of their own situation as one entailing a legal issue or requiring legal representation. The larger sample size of the 1994 study, as compared to the 1977 study, permitted comparison between the legal needs of low-income people and those with moderate incomes.[23]

About half of all households surveyed – 47% of low-income households and 52% of moderate-income households – experienced at least one legal need as defined by the survey in the prior year.[24] Both the 1977 and the 1994 studies offer evidence that Americans regularly experience civil legal problems. Curran's shorter list of scenarios, omission of public benefits as a category, and decision to ask respondents to recollect a lifetime's worth of problems are all reasons to think that the 1977 study undercounted legal need. Subsequent

[17] *Id.* at 137–38.
[18] *Id.* at 264.
[19] *Id.*
[20] Comprehensive Legal Needs Study Advisory Grp., Am. Bar Ass'n, Legal Needs and Civil Justice: A Survey of Americans, Major Findings from the Comprehensive Legal Needs Study (1994), available at www.americanbar.org/content/dam/aba/migrated/legalservices/downloads/sclaid/legalneedstudy.authcheckdam.pdf (hereinafter ABA 1994 Study). For the data upon which the ABA 1994 Study relied, see Roy W. Reese & Carolyn A. Eldred, Inst. for Survey Research at Temple Univ., Legal Needs Among Low-Income Households: Findings from the Comprehensive Legal Needs Study 52 tbl.5–8, 56 tbl.5–12 (A B A. 1994); and Roy W. Reese & Carolyn A. Eldred, Inst. for Survey Research at Temple Univ., Legal Needs Among Moderate-Income Households: Findings from the Comprehensive Legal Needs Study (ABA 1994) (hereinafter Reese & Eldred).
[21] *Id.* at 7.
[22] While the 1977 study collected data on the respondents' experiences over the course of their entire lives, the 1994 study inquired about respondents' experiences limited to the previous year. See *id.* at 7–8.
[23] Over 40% of those surveyed in the 1994 study were from moderate-income households. See *id.* at 9. The study defined "low-income" households to include those whose occupants' combined annual incomes were below 125% of the poverty level, while "moderate-income" households included occupants whose combined annual incomes exceeded 125% of the poverty level but were less than $60,000. See *id.* at 7. That line demarcating low- from moderate-income marks the threshold for eligibility for most publicly financed legal aid services.
[24] *Id.* at 9. Of the households that experienced legal need, about half experienced multiple legal needs.

researchers have followed the ABA in seeking data on household experiences over a single year. Rebecca Sandefur used the ABA's data as a baseline to extrapolate the incidence of legal need from census data. She concluded that 100 million Americans, living in more than 44 million households, experience a non-trivial civil legal issue every year.[25]

The 1994 ABA study also found that the kinds of legal problems people experienced varies with income.[26] Although both low- and moderate-income people most frequently reported legal needs in the areas of personal finance and consumer issues, the two groups had little else in common.[27] Low-income households reported higher need than moderate-income households in the areas of housing and property, family and domestic issues, and public benefits. Moderate-income households were twice as likely to face legal issues related to estate planning, wills, and advanced directives, and they were also significantly more likely to deal with legal issues related to employment and economic or personal injury.[28]

Respondents in the 1994 study were also asked how they addressed their legal needs, if they sought and received legal help, and, if not, why not. About 40% of the respondents managed their legal affairs on their own, regardless of income.[29] Among the 60% who did not handle their legal matters on their own, respondents from low-income households were more likely to do nothing while those from moderate-income households were more likely to access the civil justice system. While 39% of the moderate-income households went to court, only 29% of the low-income households used the legal system. Moderate-income households were also more likely to address their legal needs by consulting a non-lawyer third party for help – 22% of the moderate-income households took that approach, in comparison to 13% of the low-income households.[30]

When the researcher compared the two groups to determine what the most "formal" action a certain household was likely to take to address its legal needs, they found that nearly 40% of low-income households took no action (the most common response for such households) while nearly the same number of moderate-income households accessed the legal system (the most common response for moderate-income households). Only 29% of low-income households used the civil legal system.[31] People in low-income households were less likely to perceive

[25] Sandefur, *The Impact of Counsel*, supra note 7, at 56.

[26] See ABA 1994 Study, supra note 20, at 10–12.

[27] *Id.* at 11.

[28] *Id.*

[29] *Id.* at 17 (reporting that 41% of low-income and 42% of moderate-income respondents handled any legal issues on their own).

[30] See *id.* See also, Reese & Eldred, supra note 20, at 22 (noting that accountants and insurance companies were the most frequently consulted non-legal professionals and that other third party assistance was provided by community groups, regulatory agencies, and union or professional groups).

[31] See *id.*

themselves as having a legal problem, less likely to address it themselves, less likely to seek legal assistance, and less likely to access the civil justice system than those in homes with greater financial resources.[32] Conversely, members of low-income households were more likely to think that legal assistance would not help address their problem than those in moderate-income homes.[33]

In 2005,[34] more than ten years after the second ABA study, and again in 2009,[35] the LSC published national data on the frequency with which low-income Americans sought legal assistance from its programs but were turned away without representation.[36] Researchers surveyed 137 LSC grantee programs to determine how many low-income individuals contacted LSC programs in person, by phone, or online, and how many people who would have otherwise qualified for legal assistance were turned away for lack of available services.[37]

The LSC found that its grantee programs in 2004 served 901,067 clients and turned away 1,085,838 potential clients.[38] In 2009, 889,155 clients were served, and 944,376 potential clients were turned away.[39] The LSC concluded that for every low-income American served by one of its legal aid programs, another low-income American was turned away because the program lacked funding to represent that person.[40] In total, nearly 1 million people who seek legal assistance from LSC go unserved each year.[41]

The 2009 LSC study also presented a compilation of state-level data showing that family law and housing problems are the most common legal issues for low-income people.[42] For example, a 2010 New York Task Force report noted that housing problems are common, along with issues presented by health insurance and employment law.[43] Illinois reports establish that the most common legal

[32] See *id.* at 21.

[33] People in moderate-income households were half as likely as those in low-income households to cite cost as an impediment to receiving legal services (8%), but they were almost twice as likely as those in low-income households to believe that the legal issue was not a problem that required legal services (18%). See *id.*

[34] See Legal Servs. Corp. (LSC), Documenting the Justice Gap in America (2005) (hereinafter LSC 2005 Report).

[35] See LSC 2009 REPORT, supra note 8.

[36] The LSC called this the "justice gap." See *id.* at 1.

[37] See *id.* at 2, 9–12; see also LSC 2005 REPORT, supra note 34, at 3, 5–8.

[38] See *id.* at 7.

[39] See LSC 2009 REPORT, supra note 8, at 11.

[40] See *id.* at 12; LSC 2005 REPORT, supra note 34, at 7.

[41] See LSC 2009 REPORT, supra note 8, at 9; LSC 2005 REPORT, supra note 34, at 5.

[42] See *id.*, at 11; LSC 2005 REPORT, supra note 34, at 7.

[43] See TASK FORCE TO EXPAND ACCESS TO CIVIL LEGAL SERVICES IN NEW YORK: REPORT TO THE CHIEF JUDGE OF THE STATE OF NEW YORK (2010), available at www.nycourts.gov/ip/access-civil-legal-services/PDF/CLS-TaskForceREPORT.pdf (hereinafter TASK FORCE 2010 REPORT TO THE CHIEF JUDGE). For details concerning issues presented by health insurance and employment law, see *id.* at app. 17, at 30, available at www.nycourts.gov/ip/access-civil-legal-services/PDF/CLS-Appendices.pdf.

problems are in consumer law followed by housing, family law, and public benefits.[44] New Jersey data also highlight the prevalence of housing issues among low-income residents.[45]

Limitations of the National Data

The overall picture is clear: Americans have many civil legal problems, few of which are resolved in court with the assistance of counsel, and poor people face more housing and family law problems than others. It is difficult, however, to say more with precision. The national legal-needs survey is dated, and methods used in the survey are widely acknowledged to undercount need.[46] The compilation of state data in the 2009 LSC study shows significant local variations[47] raising a question about the usefulness of generalizing at the national level.

Recent work also highlights the key insight that legal need is not static, and the decision to seek legal counsel, or engage with the civil legal system without counsel, is influenced by multiple factors. Albiston,[48] Hadfield,[49] Kritzer,[50] and Sandefur[51] each note that availability of counsel is not the only factor — perhaps not even the most significant factor — influencing whether or not a person presented with a legal problem recognizes it as such and seeks assistance. Instead, many Americans either ignore their legal problems or do not seek a lawyer.[52] While cost and availability play a role, many say that they ultimately decide not to seek a legal resolution because they do not think it will change the outcome; some express a preference for self-help. The literature emphasizes the importance of deepening our understanding of how and why Americans often ignore their legal problems, seek answers outside the legal system, or engage the civil legal system without representation.

44 Lawyers Trust Fund of Ill., The Legal Aid Safety Net: A Report on the Legal Needs of Low-Income Illinoisans 18 (2005), available at www.ltf.org/wp-content/uploads/2013/02/legalneeds.pdf (hereinafter The Legal Aid Safety Net).

45 Legal Servs. of N.J., Unequal Access to Justice: Many Legal Needs, Too Little Legal Assistance 28 (2009), available at www.lsnj.org/pdfs/povertyresearchinstitute/legalneeds2009.pdf.

46 *Id.* (citing Pascoe Pleasence et al., *Failure to Recall: Indications from the English and Welsh Civil and Social Justice Survey of the Relative Severity and Incidence of Civil Justice Problems, in* Access to Justice 43, 60 (Rebecca L. Sandefur ed., Emerald Group, 2009)); Rhode, supra note 7, at 534–36 (noting multiple reasons to think surveys undercount need); On the necessity of a new national survey of legal need, see Eisenberg, Chapter 3 in this volume.

47 See LSC 2009 Report, supra note 8.

48 See Albiston & Sandefur, supra note 4, at 104.

49 See Hadfield & Heine, Chapter 2 in this volume.

50 See Herbert M. Kritzer, *Examining the Real Demand for Legal Services,* 37 Fordham Urb. L.J. 255, 256–57 (2010).

51 See Rebecca Sandefur, *The Importance of Doing Nothing, in* Transforming Lives: Law and Social Process 112, 115–16 (Pascoe Pleasence et al. eds., 2007).

52 For a comparative perspective, see Hadfield & Heine, Chapter 2 in this volume.

Self-representation

While it is widely acknowledged that many Americans represent themselves in civil litigation, there is no national data on the frequency of self-representation.[53] There are, however, state[54] and local studies and reports[55] that note the large and growing numbers of self-represented litigants, particularly in landlord–tenant, family law, immigration, and other areas of law in which low- and moderate-income people often litigate.[56]

Compared to represented parties, pro se litigants tend to be poor, less educated, and, in recent years, more often women. In Maricopa County, Arizona, in 1997, 55% of pro se litigants in court actions had annual incomes below $25,000, and 83% had annual incomes below $40,000. In 1999, Florida found that 69% of the pro se litigants in family law cases earned less than $20,000 each year, and 56% of them were women. Data from Idaho, Minnesota, and Maryland paint a similar picture of the pro se litigant as disproportionately poor, young, less educated, and female.[57]

State-level reports offer details about the number of pro se litigants and the kinds of cases in which people represent themselves. In New York, for example, the Task Force on Access to Justice's 2010 report surveyed low-income New Yorkers on their legal needs, reviewed data generated by the New York Office of Court Administration (OCA), and queried judges across the state and legal service organizations.[58] Each year, more than 2.3 million people were unrepresented in civil legal proceedings in the New York State courts, not counting actions in town and village courts.[59] The crushing number of pro se litigants is particularly acute in the New York City housing and family courts. According to the 2010 report, 98% of tenants did not have representation in eviction cases in recent years. In New York City family courts in more than 611,000 proceedings, 74% of litigants were

[53] See generally John M. Greacen, *Self-Represented Litigants and Court and Legal Services Responses to Their Needs: What We Know*, Ctr. for Families, Children & the Courts Cal. Admin. Office of the Courts (2003), available at www.courts.ca.gov/partners/documents/SRLwhatweknow.pdf.

[54] See infra notes 57–65 and accompanying text.

[55] See generally *Self-Representation Resource Guide*, Nat'l Ctr. for State Courts, available at www.ncsc.org/Topics/Access-and-Fairness/Self-Representation/Resource-Guide.aspx (last visited Aug. 6, 2014) (linking to reports from several localities); Kira Krenichyn & Nicole Schaefer-McDaniel, Ctr. For Human Env't, Graduate Ctr. of City Univ. N.Y., Results From Three Surveys in New york City Housing Courts (2007), available at www.brennancenter.org/publications; Task Force on Unrepresented Litigants, Boston Bar Ass'n, Report on Pro Se Litigation (1998), available at www.bostonbar.org/prs/reports/unrepresented0898.pdf; see also Greacen, supra note 53 (discussing local data).

[56] Virtually every study highlights the very high percentage of pro se litigants in family law and housing court cases. By contrast, a survey of Washington State Courts showed that only 3% of litigants in cases involving torts and commercial law were pro se, as were 20% of those in cases involving property rights. See Greacen, supra note 53, at 5–6.

[57] See *id.* at 4–5.

[58] See Task Force 2010 Report to the Chief judge, supra note 43, at 3.

[59] See *id.* at 12.

unrepresented in 2009. [60] Ninety-three percent of the litigants in child support proceedings were pro se, with another 4–5% receiving only partial assistance of counsel.[61]

In 2004, the Judicial Council of California reported that 4.3 million Californians appeared pro se in the state's courts each year. In family law matters in the California courts, 67% of all petitioners were pro se and both parties were unrepresented in 75% of the child custody cases and in an additional 14% of those cases, only one party was represented.[62] In testimony to the California Commission on Access to Justice in 2011, James Brosnahan, a member of the Commission, stated, "[w]e know in California the six out of ten people in the middle class who go to civil court are unrepresented and that eight out of ten who are below the – at or below the poverty line go unrepresented."[63] Data from Illinois show that 66% of the low-income litigants were pro se,[64] while in New Hampshire, 85% of civil cases had at least one pro se litigant.[65]

Pro se litigants are also found in other courts and fora. The *New York Immigrant Representation Study* found higher rates of pro se representation among those detained during the pendency of their immigration case, a particular problem in these technical, high-stakes cases. Immigrants represented themselves in 55,999 cases involving at least one hearing in an immigration removal proceedings in New York City, Long Island, and the Lower Hudson Valley between October 1, 2005, and July 13, 2010. In those cases, 7,198 immigrants were detained. Of that group of detainees, 60% (4,818) were unrepresented throughout the immigration proceedings against them. In contrast, of the 48,801 who were not detained while the case was pending, only 27% (10,060)

[60] The more than 611,000 proceedings do not include parental neglect and abuse cases where parents are guaranteed counsel by law.

[61] See TASK FORCE 2010 REPORT TO THE CHIEF JUDGE, supra note 43, at 17 (citing testimony and written submissions of the Honorable Fern Fisher, Deputy Chief Administrative Judge for the New York City Courts).

[62] Task Force on Self-Represented Litigants, Judicial Council of Cal., Statewide Action Plan for Serving Self-Represented Litigants 50 (2004), available at www.courts.ca.gov/documents/selfreplitsrept.pdf.

[63] James Brosnahan, Chair of San Francisco Hearing, Reporter's Transcript of Hearings: November 30, 2011 at the Hearings on California's Civil Justice Crisis 122 (Nov. 30, 2011) (transcript available at http://californiahearings.files.wordpress.com/2012/01/transcript-from-11-30-11-hearing-in-san-francisco-full1.pdf).

[64] See THE LEGAL AID SAFETY NET, supra note 44.

[65] See N.H. TASK FORCE ON SELF-REPRESENTATION, CHALLENGE TO JUSTICE: A REPORT ON SELF-REPRESENTED LITIGANTS IN NEW HAMPSHIRE COURTS (2004), available at www.courts.state.nh.us/supreme/docs/prosereport.pdf. Every reporting state notes high rates of pro se litigants in at least some of its courts; however, the data are quite fragmented. Two large states, California and New York, report the overall count of pro se litigants in their courts in a given year and the rates of pro se litigants in particular subsets of cases. Other states report rates of low-income pro se litigants, but they do not report data on the overall number of pro se litigants. Categories of case types, measures of income level, and other reporting variables are not standardized, making direct comparisons impossible and greatly complicating meta-analysis.

were unrepresented.[66] Although federal courts show relatively low levels of overall pro se representation as compared to state courts, major exceptions are federal habeas and civil rights cases filed by prisoners,[67] bankruptcy cases,[68] and employment discrimination cases.[69] In the twelve months ending June 30, 2011, nearly 73,000 civil cases were filed pro se in the federal courts,[70] out of a total of 282,895 civil cases filed in that period.[71] About two-thirds of all pro se cases were filed by prisoners in fiscal year 2010. In that same period, 9% of the bankruptcy cases nationwide (more than 130,000 out of more than 1.5 million total case filings) were filed by pro se petitioners.[72] In the Central District of California, 27.1% of the bankruptcy filings were pro se in fiscal year 2010, and in the District of Arizona the figure was 20.8%. An analysis by the Administrative Office of the U.S Courts reveals persistent regional differences in rates of pro se representation with the South having historically lower rates. It also notes that rates of self-representation in bankruptcy appear higher in regions hardest hit by the mortgage foreclosure crisis.[73]

Pro se litigants face daunting hurdles, having to navigate multiple fora and procedures systems designed by and for educated, highly trained professionals. While recent research suggests there are circumstances where representation may not result in better outcomes,[74] and incompetent representation may be worse than no representation at all, pro se litigants generally achieve worse outcomes than their represented counterparts.[75]

John Greacen summarizes data about the length of time and cost of cases with at least one unrepresented litigant. While some pro se cases take longer to

66 N.Y. Immigrant Representation Study, supra note 3, at 8 tbl.1. For a fuller discussion of the immigration law context, see Katzmann, Chapter 8, and Das, Chapter 9 in this volume.

67 See Greacen, supra note 53, at 8.

68 *By the Numbers – Pro Se Filers in the Bankruptcy Court,* Third Branch News (Oct. 2011), available at www.uscourts.gov/news/TheThirdBranch/11-10-01/By_the_Numbers–Pro_Se_Filers_in_the_Bankruptcy_Courts.aspx (hereinafter *By the Numbers*).

69 See Myrick, et al., Chapter 6 in this volume; see also Laura Beth Nielsen, Robert Nelson & Ryon Lancaster, *Individual Justice or Collective Legal Mobilization? Employment Discrimination Litigation in the Post Civil Rights United States*, 7 J. Empirical Legal Stud. 175, 188 (2010).

70 *IN-DEPTH: Leveling the Playing Field: Help for Self-Filers,* Third Branch News (July 2011), available at www.uscourts.gov/news/TheThirdBranch/11-07-01/IN-DEPTH_Leveling_the_Playing_Field_Help_for_Self-Filers.aspx.

71 James C. Duff, Admin. Office of the U.S. Courts, Judicial Business of the United States Courts: 2010 Annual Report of the Director (2010), available at www.uscourts.gov/uscourts/Statistics/JudicialBusiness/2010/JudicialBusinespdfversion.pdf.

72 *Bankruptcy Filings Up 20 Percent in June,* Third Branch News (Aug. 17, 2010), available at www.uscourts.gov/news/NewsView/10-08-17/Bankruptcy_Filings_Up_20_Percent_in_June.aspx.

73 See *By the Numbers*, supra note 68. For a fuller discussion of the pro se representation in bankruptcy, see Pardo, Chapter 5 in this volume.

74 See Engler, Chapter 4 in this volume.

75 See generally Sandefur *The Impact of Counsel*, supra note 7 (marshaling studies and arguing that despite questions about the data and methodology, litigants have better legal outcomes when represented by a lawyer); Engler, supra *note* 7 (analyzing studies on lawyer effectiveness).

resolve, more of them appear to take less court time, apparently because pro se litigants file fewer motions and require fewer hearings or trials than represented litigants.[76] There are many pro se litigants in America's civil courts, but we know very little about why Americans represent themselves in legal matters. All agree that supply-side factors – such as client resources, limited availability of publicly-funded legal services, limited availability of lawyers practicing in the areas of greatest need, and limited availability of representation by non-lawyers – are significant factors, as is the American tendency to ignore legal problems or to deal with them outside the legal system or without the assistance of a lawyer.[77]

Although some data suggest that people who face litigation almost always choose representation when it is offered,[78] the studies mostly capture only those who sought representation and usually focus on defendants, litigants who do not choose to enter the legal system but are responding to a lawsuit brought by another. We know less about those who bring suits without counsel and those with transactional or planning needs.

THE SUPPLY OF CIVIL LEGAL SERVICES FOR LOW- AND MODERATE-INCOME AMERICANS

Another area of emerging research is empirical study of the supply side of the civil legal justice system. Most research on the supply of legal services, however, has focused on the wealthiest Americans and the lawyers who serve them.[79] While low-income people have received some attention through studies of those who provide free legal services, the legal representation of moderate-income Americans has been largely ignored.

Generally, there are four sources of civil legal services in the United States: the private bar, government-financed legal service providers, pro bono work of the private bar, and unbundled legal services or non-lawyer legal assistance. Most practicing American lawyers are in the private bar, which is the marketplace that provides most of the legal services used by low- and moderate-income Americans. Many, however, are priced out of the market for private legal services, and while legal aid and pro bono programs make a significant contribution, much legal need remains unmet.

[76] See Greacen, supra note 53, at 8–12.

[77] See Rebecca L. Sandefur, *The Fulcrum Point of Equal Access to Justice: Legal and Nonlegal Institutions of Remedy*, 42 LOY. L.A. L. REV. 949 (2009); Kritzer, supra note 50.

[78] For a discussion of the frequency with which offers of free legal representation are refused, see CURRAN, supra note 9. See also D. James Greiner & Cassandra Wolos Pattanayak, *Randomized Evaluation in Legal Assistance: What Difference Does Representation (Offer and Actual Use) Make*, 121 YALE L.J. 2118 (2012); LSC 2009 REPORT, supra note 8.

[79] See Hadfield & Heine, Chapter 2 in this volume.

Fee-Generating Civil Legal Services

The private bar constitutes about three-quarters of all lawyers practicing in America[80] and is the largest provider of civil legal services to low- and moderate-income Americans. Analyzing data collected for the 1994 ABA survey of Americans' legal needs, Rebecca Sandefur concludes that even among low-income Americans, about 75% of all contacts with lawyers are with members of the private bar and involve the payment of fees for legal services.[81] In about 25% of the situations in which low-income people turned to lawyers in the private bar, the type of legal problem they had was one in which a contingent fee is usually available, e.g., a tort action. The data do not reveal how often such a fee was recovered.[82] In more than half the cases in which a low-income person received the assistance of counsel, there was some payment of fees by the party seeking legal advice.[83] We know that the private market supplies almost all of the professional legal services used by middle-income people; most in this group are ineligible for publicly-financed legal aid and many pro bono programs.

The price of legal services is a barrier. Consider a poor person (household income at or below 125% of the federal poverty line or $29,437 for a family of four)[84] facing a common civil legal problem involving, say, housing, finances, or family. Most often, that person cannot afford a lawyer and will go unrepresented unless they receive one from resource-strapped government-funded legal aid. For moderate-income Americans (the median income in America was just over $51,000 in 2012 and

80 According to the Program on the Legal Profession (PLP) at Harvard Law School, in 2007 there were between 760,000 and 1.1 million lawyers in America. The lower bound of that range reflects surveys by the U.S. Bureau of Labor Statistics intended to reflect the number of people currently earning income from legal practice. The higher bound of that range is drawn from ABA data based on Martindale-Hubbell listings and intended to reflect all licensed lawyers whether or not they obtain income from their legal work. The PLP estimates s that about 75% of American lawyers are in private practice, 16% are in government, 8% are in business, and 2% are in education, while 0.4% work for interest groups and 0.3% work for public interest groups. *Analysis of the Legal Profession and Law Firms (as of 2007)*, Harvard Law School Program on the Legal Profession (2007), available at www.law.harvard.edu/programs/plp/pages/statistics.php (last visited Aug. 7, 2014) (hereinafter *Analysis of the Legal Profession and Law Firms*). Of the 600,000 to 700,000 lawyers in private practice, about 60% of their time is spent serving corporate or group clients, while fewer than 40% of the private bar's services go to individuals. See Hadfield & Heine, Chapter 2 in this volume.

81 Rebecca Sandefur, *Lawyers' Pro Bono Service and American-Style Civil Legal Assistance*, 41 Law & Soc'y Rev. 79, 82–83 (2007) (hereinafter Sandefur, *Lawyers' Pro Bono Service*). This discussion relies upon Reese & Eldred, supra note 20 at tbls. 5–8 and 5–12.

82 For a fuller discussion of the impact of contingency fee arrangements on access to justice, see Noll, Chapter 11 in this volume.

83 See Sandefur, *Lawyers' Pro Bono Service*, supra note 81

84 The Department of Health and Human Services posts the poverty guidelines online every year. See 2013 *Poverty Guidelines*, U.S. Dep't of Health & Human Servs., available at http://aspe.hhs.gov/poverty/13poverty.cfm (last visited Aug. 6, 2014). The guideline was 23,350 for a family of four. Using the LSC eligibility requirement of 125%, the best-off eligible family of four would have a yearly income of $29,437 or just under $2,500 a month in gross income. In 2009, almost 57 million Americans lived in households at or below the poverty guideline. See Sandefur & Smyth, supra note 5.

the top 60% of households had incomes up to almost $65,000 annually),[85] legal fees are often a large and usually unexpected expense. Half of all Americans lack an adequate emergency savings fund, and many have no savings at all.[86]

Poor- and moderate-income Americans who secure representation are more likely to hire a lawyer to meet their legal needs than to have one provided free of charge.[87] They are also likely to have a legal need but find themselves priced out of the market for legal services. Compared to legal-aid organizations and the pro bono work of the private bar, the private, fee-generating legal marketplace is by far the largest provider of legal services, and it has the greatest capacity to address Americans' unmet legal needs. Some of the barriers to increasing its role in access to civil justice for Americans of modest means are discussed elsewhere in this book.[88]

Civil Legal Aid

The second source of civil legal services are organizations that provide free legal services to eligible clients. These organizations include about 4,000 lawyers in LSC offices[89] and about the same number of lawyers in more than 650 civil legal aid offices funded by sources that are not affiliated with LSC.[90] The LSC is required by law to establish and publish eligibility requirements for all clients who receive legal services through LSC-funded programs.[91] Current regulations restrict eligibility to those in households with income at or below 125% of the federal poverty guideline,[92] with limited exceptions permitted for those with income at or below 200% of the guideline.[93] The non-LSC affiliated providers include a diverse array of privately funded groups, organizations funded by state and local agencies, and law school clinics.[94] These programs establish their own eligibility requirements with some following the LSC rules and others imposing other restrictions. In this sector, resource constraints and, to a lesser degree, legal constraints limit supply to levels well below the demonstrated need.

85 See DENAVAS-WALT et al., supra note 6.

86 See Ann Carrns, *Half of Americans Still Lack 3-Month Emergency Fund*, BUCKS BLOG (June 25, 2012, 10:57 AM), available at http://bucks.blogs.nytimes.com/2012/06/25/half-of-americans-still-lack-3-month-emergency-fund/?_r=0 (reporting on a survey showing that half of Americans do not have sufficient savings to cover three months of household expenses).

87 See Sandefur, *Lawyers' Pro Bono Service*, supra note 81.

88 See Hadfield & Heine, Chapter 2 in this volume, the marketplace for legal services and Bremer, Chapter 14, on the impact of educational debt on young lawyers.

89 Those 4,000 lawyers serve about 1 million Americans each year and turn away around 1 million others. See supra notes 46–49 and accompanying text.

90 See Sandefur, *Lawyers' Pro Bono Service*, supra note 81.

91 42 U.S.C. § 2996f(a)(2)(A). See Charn, Chapter 10 in this volume on the evolution of legal services.

92 45 C.F.R. § 1611.3(c).

93 45 C.F.R. § 1611.5.

94 On the limited services offered by law school clinics, see SANDEFUR & SMYTH, supra note 5, at 11.

In 2009, an LSC study reported that 7,931 attorneys provided legal aid to low-income Americans, either in LSC-funded programs or in non-LSC-funded programs, at a ratio of one lawyer for every 6,415 low-income individuals who would qualify for legal assistance.[95] Those lawyers work in about 850 different organizations.[96] By contrast, the ABA legal needs survey noted that 577,906 attorneys in private practice provided legal services to the general population during the same period. There was one lawyer in private practice for every 429 people – a ratio fifteen times greater than the ratio of legal aid lawyers to people in poverty.[97]

Of course lawyers in private practice perform a very wide range of legal work and represent many corporate and group clients.[98] The nearly 8,000 lawyers who provide free civil legal services primarily represent individuals in dispute-oriented matters of low to moderate complexity. Only 1% of all lawyers (no more than 8,000 of the grand total of 760,000 to 1.1 million lawyers in America)[99] devote themselves full-time to providing civil legal services to Americans unable to afford a lawyer.

Nationally, legal aid programs are supported by a mix of federal, state, and private money.[100] Federal funding has decreased as need has increased.[101] In 2009, spending on this sector of civil legal services was about $1.3 billion,[102] out of a total annual spending of about $250 billion on legal services in the United States.[103] In 2009, LSC funding accounted for about $355 million, states and localities gave about $195 million, and Interest on Lawyers' Trust Accounts (IOLTA)[104] contributed about $112 million.[105]

Funding for legal aid varies by region. In 2011 the Civil Justice Infrastructure Mapping Project, funded primarily by the American Bar Foundation, published the first report of efforts to paint a comprehensive, state-by-state picture of what civil justice services are available to Americans, how they are funded, and how they are

95 See LSC 2009 REPORT, supra note 8, at 20; LSC 2005 REPORT, supra note 34. See ALAN W. HOUSEMAN, CTR. FOR LAWAND SOC. POLICY, CIVIL LEGAL AID IN THE UNITED STATES (2009).

96 *Id.* at 2. (discussing estimate of 864 civil legal aid programs, exclusive of pro bono programs identified by the ABA, of which 137 were LSC grantees, leaving more than 700 other civil legal aid programs).

97 See LSC 2009 REPORT, supra note 8, at 20.

98 About 60% of the time of lawyers in private practice is spent serving corporate or group clients, while less than 40% of the private bar's services go to individuals. See Hadfield, Chapter 2 in this volume.

99 See *Analysis of the Legal Profession and Law Firms*, supra note 81.

100 See SANDEFUR & SMYTH, supra note 5.

101 See Rhode, supra note 7, at 532 n.2.

102 See HOUSEMAN, supra note 96, at 12.

103 See Hadfield & Heine, Chapter 2 in this volume.

104 IOLTA programs generate income from funds held by lawyers on behalf of clients. Frequently, client funds are held for too short of a time and are not large enough to generate net interest. When pooled, those funds generate net interest, which is then allocated to legal aid programs and client protection funds. When client funds are sufficiently large or held long enough to generate net interest, it goes to the client. On IOLTA generally, see *Commission on Interest on Lawyers Trust Accounts*, AM. BAR ASS'N, available at www.americanbar.org/groups/interest_lawyers_trust_accounts.html (last visited Aug. 6, 2014).

105 See HOUSEMAN, supra note 95, at 12.

regulated.[106] The report highlights the regional variations in availability of services. The 2011 report notes that "geography is destiny," in the sense that the availability of services across America turns not on the kind or magnitude of problem faced but rather where the person seeking services lives. This finding is consistent with Houseman's 2009 report, which notes that the highest-funded states – clustered in the Northeast, Mid-Atlantic, Midwest, and West – fund at rates ten times greater than those in South and Rocky Mountain West, the lowest funded.[107] The overall funding for legal aid in the United States has increased fairly steadily since 1980, but much of that growth has come from states, localities, and private sources. LSC funding has not kept pace with those sources; rather, it has declined in recent years.[108]

Eligibility restrictions also limit the supply of civil legal services to low-income Americans. Financial eligibility is the key criteria, and LSC programs are also restricted to serving citizens and specified categories of aliens,[109] and in undertaking certain classes of cases.[110] LSC programs may not engage in class action litigation.[111] And LSC grantees must spend 12.5% of their basic grant on the involvement of private attorneys in delivering services.[112] LSC-funded programs serve about 1 million Americans each year, but the funding and client-eligibility constraints force LSC-funded programs to turn away at least that number each year.[113]

The rest of the civil legal aid system is comprised of approximately 700 privately funded legal services offices across the nation that are not affiliated with LSC.[114] This is a diverse group of providers, including bar associations,[115] private not-for-profits, law school clinics,[116] and religiously affiliated organizations, many quite small and specialized. Some, such as the Legal Aid Society of the District of Columbia, provide a very significant portion of services in their communities.[117] While these groups do not face the legal restrictions imposed upon LSC, many have specialized missions that restrict representation to particular case types or populations. In theory, these groups could address gaps created by LSC restrictions or they could respond to

[106] See Sandefur & Smyth, supra note 5, at v.
[107] See Houseman, supra note 96, at 12; see also Sandefur & Smyth, supra note 5, at 17–20.
[108] See id. (noting an increase in non-LSC funding but a decline in real dollars for LSC programs).
[109] See 45 C.F.R. § 1611.
[110] See 28 U.S.C. § 2996(f)(b).
[111] 45 C.F.R. § 1617.3.
[112] See 45 C.F.R. § 1614.2; see also Houseman, supra note 96, at 21 (reporting that in 2007, pro bono private attorneys represented clients in almost 65,000 LSC cases).
[113] For fuller discussion of publicly funded legal services, see Radice, Chapter 15, in this volume
[114] See Sandefur, *Lawyers' Pro Bono Service*, supra note 83, at 83.
[115] For discussion of Bar Association programs, see Charne, Chapter 16 and Kelly, Chapter 45 in this volume.
[116] For discussion of law school clinics, see Drew & Morriss, Chapter 13, Charn, Chapter 10, Radice & Hertz, Chapter 47, and Gomez-Velez, Chapter 48 in this volume.
[117] See generally Legal Aid Soc'y of D.C., available at www.legalaiddc.org/ (last visited Jan. 9, 2014).

other particular local needs. There is, however, little national, regional, or local coordination beyond some basic efforts to coordinate delivery of existing services through statewide or regional phone hotlines, referral services, and some of the Access to Justice Commissions.[118]

Low and Pro Bono Legal Services

The third source of legal services for low-income and moderate-income Americans is pro bono[119] and "low bono"[120] (discounted) legal services provided by the private bar. This group is even more heterogeneous than the civil legal aid sector, as it is comprised of practitioners in every kind of private practice setting.

The ABA has conducted three national surveys of the pro bono work of American lawyers. Data were collected in 2004, 2008, and 2011.[121] The 2011 data formed the basis of the 2013 report,[122] which concluded that on average, American lawyers devoted 56.5 hours each year to providing free legal services to persons of limited means[123] and groups serving that population with a median of 30 hours annually.[124] Only 20% of all lawyers surveyed reported providing no free legal services to qualified clients, and 62% reported that they provide 20 or more hours each year.

118 See Sandefur & Smyth, supra note 5, at 22–24 (discussing coordination).

119 Rule 6.1 of the *ABA Model Rules of Professional Conduct* requires lawyers to "aspire to render at least 50 hours of pro bono public legal services per year" and says that a substantial majority of the hours should be provided to persons of limited means or non-profit organizations that assist persons of limited means without fee or expectation of a fee. Model Rules of Prof'l Conduct R.6.1 (1983), available at www.americanbar.org/groups/professional_responsibility/publications/model_rules_of_professional_conduct/rule_6_1_voluntary_pro_bono_publico_service.html (hereinafter Model Rule 6.1).

120 Lawyers have long discounted fees and written off uncollectible fees. In recent years, organized efforts to encourage discounted, or low bono, legal services for low- and moderate-income people have developed as part of the growing access to justice movement. One example is lowbono.org, a group for "solo and small firms committed to serving their communities," created by the Law School Consortium Project. See Lowbono.org, available at www.lowbono.org/ (last visited Aug. 6, 2014); see generally Herrera, Chapter 25 in this volume.

121 See *Research and Statistics in Pro Bono*, Am. Bar Ass'n, available at www.americanbar.org/groups/probono_public_service/research_pro_bono.html (last visited Aug. 6, 2014).

122 The 2011 data were gathered in 2,876 online surveys. Results were then weighted so the composition of the sample matched the national population of lawyers in respect to practice setting. The study's authors discuss the problems of selection bias, improper weighting, and the possibility that respondents will shade their responses toward socially desirable answers, and they describe the ways in which the study minimizes those risks. See Janet Buczek et al., ABA Standing Comm.on Pro Bono and Pub. Serv., Supporting Justice III: A Reportonthe Pro Bono Work of America's Lawyers A-1-A-4 (2013), available at www.americanbar.org/content/dam/aba/administrative/probono_public_service/ls_pb_Supporting_Justice_III_final.authcheckdam.pdf (hereinafter Supporting Justice III).

123 The phrase "persons of limited means" is drawn from Rule 6.1 of the *Model Rules of Professional Conduct*. See Model Rule 6.1, supra note 119. Income-eligibility standards for clients were not further defined by the study. Twenty-three percent of the respondents reported that a referring agency had reviewed the clients' eligibility and another 7% reviewed financial documents themselves. More than half relied upon their general knowledge of the client's situation or the client's representations. See Supporting Justice III, supra note 122, at 16.

124 See Supporting Justice III, supra note 122, at vi, 5–6.

Almost three-quarters of that service went to individuals, and the remainder was distributed to organizations that address the needs of persons of limited means.

Large law firms with institutionalized pro bono programs have become a significant source of civil legal services in recent years.[125] About half the pro bono hours are provided by firms of 250 lawyers or more.[126] A significant number of very large law firms have hired pro bono coordinators or other full-time employees whose major focus is coordinating pro bono activities at the firm.[127] While these programs do not face legal restrictions on the types of cases they may handle, business conflicts tend to discourage firms from taking on employment, mortgage foreclosure, estate planning, and bankruptcy matters.[128]

In addition to pro bono service, a significant group of lawyers provide reduced-fee, or low-bono, legal services. The data show that 74% of lawyers in private practice provided reduced-fee services or uncompensated public service activities other than the free services for qualified individuals or groups serving a qualified population that distinguish pro bono from low bono.[129] Of those, about 40% provided legal services for reduced fees in three or more legal matters.[130] Again, the data suggest that between 1.5 and as many as 3 million legal matters receive the attention of a lawyer who accepts reduced fees for the representation. Low and pro bono legal services provided by the private bar play a significant role in access to justice for low- and moderate-income Americans and also play an important expressive function for the legal profession.

Other Sources of Legal Services

The fourth sector of the supply of legal service providers are the emerging providers of new kinds of legal services, including educational and support programs for pro se litigants, and unbundled legal services, as well as legal services provided by non-

[125] See Scott L. Cummings & Deborah L. Rhode, *Managing Pro Bono: Doing Well By Doing Better*, 78 FORDHAM L. REV. 2357 (2010).

[126] See Boutcher, Chapter 17 in this volume. *After the JD*, a longitudinal study of newly certified lawyers by the American Bar Foundation and NALP Foundation for Law Career Research and Education, reported that about half of total pro bono hours by private practice lawyers came from lawyers in firms with more than 250 attorneys. See RONIT DINOVITZER ET AL., AM. BAR FOUND. & NALP FOUND. FOR LAW CAREER RESEARCH & EDUC., AFTER THE JD: FIRST RESULTS OF A NATIONAL STUDY OF LEGAL CAREERS 37 tbl.4.3 (2004); see also Rebecca L. Sandefur, *Lawyers' Pro Bono Service and Market-Reliant Legal Aid*, *in* PRIVATE LAWYERS AND THE PUBLIC INTEREST 95, 101 (Robert Granfield & Lynn Mather eds., 2009).

[127] See Dewey et al., Chapter 43 and Greenberg, Chapter 44 in this volume.

[128] See Lawrence M. Friedman, *Access to Justice: Some Historical Comments*, 37 FORDHAM URB. L.J. 3, 19 (2010).

[129] When reduced fees were charged, the average reduction was 48%. Examples of public service other than legal services for qualified people include training or teaching on legal issues, bar committee service, and grassroots community advocacy. See SUPPORTING JUSTICE III, supra note 122, at 8–9. For more discussion of low bono services, see Herrera, Chapter 25, and Juergens, Chapter 26 in this volume.

[130] See SUPPORTING JUSTICE III, supra note 122, at 8–9.

lawyers[131] and the growing use of new technologies, particularly in planning and transactional contexts,[132] rather than dispute resolution. This sector is both the most innovative and the most limited source of legal services, displaying creativity, fragmentation, and great geographic variation.[133] These sources are discussed elsewhere in this volume. [134]

CONCLUSION

To meet the demand for civil legal services, we rely on the market and on underfunded legal aid – a highly fragmented and uncoordinated approach. The barriers to legal assistance are so high that low- and middle-income individuals *often* ignore their legal problems, address them outside the courts, or represent themselves.

[131] For a discussion of non-lawyer representation, see Hodges, Chapter 39, Halegua, Chapter 40, and Levine, Chapter 41 in this volume.

[132] See Weisbord, Chapter 27, on transactions in this volume.

[133] See SANDEFUR & SMYTH, supra note 5, at v.

[134] See Ekery, Chapter 28 on court facilitation of pro se representation, Engler, Chapter 29 on limited representation, and Barton, Chapter 30 on online resources.

2

Life in the Law-Thick World:

Legal Resources for Ordinary Americans

Gillian K. Hadfield & Jamie Heine

Gillian Hadfield and Jamie Heine demonstrate that a very small percentage of the legal resources in the vast U.S. legal market is delivered on behalf of poor or middle-income people – indeed, overall the U.S. devotes fewer resources on a per case basis to courts, judges, legal aid, and even in some cases lawyers than Western European countries. Americans of modest means are more likely to "lump" their legal problems together and do nothing about them than their European counterparts. One important factor is the greater availability of non-lawyer assistance in Europe, which suggests an important avenue for U.S. reform.

Ours is a law-thick world.[1] Most advanced market democracies are pervaded by laws and rules that structure social and economic relationships. Ordinary people, businesses, and institutions alike interact with rules and legal principles both formally and informally on a daily basis: the "defining circumstances"[2] of everyday life – employment, consumer transactions, family dynamics, financial matters, and more – all have legal dimensions. The United States has a particularly complex and expansive civil legal system, partly because of America's uniquely adversarial approach to law and policy.[3] Navigating the web of complex rules that comprises our social and economic framework requires legal resources — legal information, advice, documents, representation; the rule of law presumes access to the civil legal system and legal resources. But what does the landscape of legal resources look like for ordinary Americans? Are we living in an environment that is thick with law but thin on legal resources?

Unfortunately, we know very little about the legal—resource landscape, especially when it comes to services for Americans of average means. We don't have a national federally funded research agency like the National Institutes of Health,

[1] This article was originally published in the *Fordham Urban Law Journal*, as Gillian K. Hadfield, *Higher Demand, Lower Supply*, 37 Fordham Urb. L. J. 129 (2010).

[2] Pascoe Pleasence, Alexy Buck, Nigel Balmer, Aoife O'Grady, Hazel Genn & Marisol Smith, Causes of Action: Civil Law and Social Welfare 13 (2004).

[3] Robert A. Kagan, *Adversarial Legalism: The American Way of Law* (2001).

which distributes over $30 billion in 50,000 grants annually to medical researchers who collect, analyze, and are often required to share, data on disease, medical procedures and the impact of interventions.[4] We don't have the legal equivalent of public health departments, tracking the legal health of communities. We don't have the legal analogs of specialists in epidemiology, studying the causes and patterns of legal problems in communities. While legal academia produces thousands of articles published in law reviews each year, such research typically focuses on law itself, not the public or markets the law serves. The major well-funded and regularly conducted studies on the legal system that do exist focus on the market for corporate legal services.[5] As a result, systematic efforts to collect data about the health of legal systems for ordinary individuals are few and far between.

Of the small number of studies analyzing the performance of the legal system for non-corporate clients almost all focus on the delivery of legal services to the poor as a form of charity or welfare assistance. While obviously of high significance, assessing only this segment of legal markets is a bit like assessing the performance of the U.S. health care system by asking only how well Medicaid and free clinics work. It treats the issues of access and cost for citizens as if they were entirely questions of the appropriate levels of charity (pro bono) and welfare spending. But the vitality of our legal systems is a matter of great importance throughout the income distribution. We all make decisions on a daily basis that rely on our understanding of the legal rules that structure our relationships with family, neighbors, schools, manufacturers, governments, and more.

Casually, most of us in the legal profession know that the bulk of civil legal services are ultimately provided not to ordinary people but to corporations. The 1995 Chicago Lawyers' Survey – one of the very few systematic efforts to assess the allocation of legal work across client sectors – estimated that only 29% of Chicago lawyers' efforts went to providing legal services to individuals or small businesses.[6] The "personal plight" category – comprised of civil rights, criminal defense, divorce, family, and personal injury plaintiff work – accounted for a mere 16% of total effort.[7] Both of these figures indicated drops relative to 1975 (from 40% and 21%, respectively);[8] the survey has not been updated but in all likelihood there have been comparable drops in the past twenty years as well.

In this chapter we pull together the small and disconnected bits of available data on the legal resources available to ordinary Americans – the best we can do to shed

4 *NIH Budget*, Nat'l Insts. of Health, available at www.nih.gov/about/budget.htm (last visited Sept. 9, 2013).

5 See, e.g., Citi Private Bank, Annual Survey of Law Firm Financial Performance (conducted annually for the past twenty-five years); Altman Weil, Law Firms in Transition Survey (conducted annually for the past five years); ALM Legal Intelligence, Survey of Law Firm Economics (conducted annually for the past forty years).

6 John P. Heinz, Edward O. Laumann, Robert L. Nelson & Ethan Michelson, *The Changing Character of Lawyers' Work: Chicago in 1975 and 1995*, 32 Law & Soc'y Rev. 752, 765 (1998).

7 *Id.*

8 *Id.*

some light on the performance of the U.S. legal markets serving non-corporate clients. We draw on some data from other countries to put our limited U.S. data into perspective. The goal is to try to get a handle on the health of the legal markets serving ordinary citizens as a whole. Our results suggest that, while the United States has a robust legal system with nearly twice as many lawyers per capita as most other countries, ordinary Americans have very little access to reasonably priced legal help in navigating that system.

We begin with a "macro" view, comparing the resources at an aggregate level that are devoted to the legal system in the United States as compared with other countries. Here we find evidence of a surprising fact: although public expenditure, legal aid, numbers of judges, and numbers of lawyers are comparable (or high) on a per capita basis, the much greater volume of cases in the United States implies that the United States devotes far fewer resources to supporting the legal system on a per case basis. That is, Americans choose or have no choice but to go through court-based processes at much higher rates, but compared to other countries, there are fewer public dollars, judges and even lawyers available to them when they do so. We then turn to a "micro" view, reviewing the available studies that track individual legal needs and the frequency with which individuals choose (or have no choice but) to represent themselves in court, comparing studies conducted at the national and state levels in the United States with studies carried out in comparably rich legal settings.

We identify here a troubling indication that Americans are led to "lump" their legal problems and do nothing about them at higher rates than is the case in these other countries. Looking closely at these studies suggests that one reason might be that Americans have fewer places to turn for legal help: environments in which people have more open regulatory systems that allow a wider variety of professionals to assist people with legal problems – not just lawyers, as is the case in the United States – appear to be ones in which people are significantly less likely to do nothing when troubles emerge. That is important: ignoring legal problems is likely to cause more problems. Moreover, both ignoring legal problems and muddling through without legal help undermines our confidence that the complex legal rules and entitlements we have put in place are, in fact, accomplishing the objectives they are designed to achieve.

THE MACRO VIEW: AGGREGATE LEGAL RESOURCES

The legal services industry in the United States is a multi-billion dollar industry and accounts for just under half of the revenue generated by the global legal services industry.[9] In 2010, legal services provided by private practitioners generated $204 billion[10] in gross domestic product in the United States; total receipts for law

[9] U.S. International Trade Commission, Recent Trends in U.S. Services Trade: 2011 Annual Report, at 7.2 (July 2011).

[10] U.S. Bureau of Economic Analysis, Gross Domestic Product by Industry 2010 (Value Added by Industry Table).

firms was $237 billion.[11] Neither figure counts legal services provided within corporations, government, legal aid providers, or other private associations, which account for 18% of all lawyers.[12] If we "gross up" these numbers to value the contributions of lawyers in these other settings, the total size of the legal services sector in the United States is thus roughly $249 billion in GDP terms and $289 billion in expenditures on legal services. By way of comparison, in 2010 GDP in educational services was $166 billion; health care services $1.1 trillion; agriculture $158 billion; food, beverage, and tobacco products $219 billion; securities, commodities contracts, and investments $181 billion; and computer system design and related services $183 billion.

While the U.S. legal services market is massive, ordinary citizens consume well under half of these resources. Of the roughly $289 billion spent on legal services, approximately 34% is consumed by individuals as part of personal consumption expenditures ($97.7 billion in 2010).[13] Another 1%[14] ($2.89 billion) can be attributed to services provided by legal aid lawyers and public defenders. Some share, but it is not possible to easily say how much, of the expenditure on government lawyers other than legal aid and public defenders may be attributable to providing services to individual Americans; in some sense, one could classify all of those expenditures (approximately $23 billion or 8%) as being on behalf of ordinary citizens. But clearly much of this expenditure is of little personal use to individuals. This suggests that at most 42% of legal services, and more reasonably a bit more than 35%, are serving the needs of individual citizens as opposed to corporations and businesses.

These figures comport with data from the only U.S. study of the allocation of legal effort across different types of matters and clients. As we noted earlier, the Chicago Lawyers' Survey estimated that in 1995 Chicago lawyers devoted 29% of total effort to services for individual or small business clients.[15] These figures probably understate the total share of all legal services statewide and nationwide because of the concentration of corporate law firms in this major financial center.[16] These numbers are in line with the census-based estimate presented earlier that approximately 35% of all legal services in the United States are available to individuals as opposed to corporations or governments.

[11] U.S. Census Bureau, Service Annual Survey 2010 Current Business Reports, t.6.3 (2012).

[12] American Bar Foundation, *The Lawyer Statistical Report* 2013(2005 data). Seventy-five percent of lawyers work in private practice, 4% are inactive or retired, 3% serve in the judiciary, and 1% in legal academia.

[13] U.S. Bureau of Economic Analysis, Personal Consumption Expenditure Underlying Detail Tables, t.2.4.5U (Personal Consumption Expenditures by Type of Product), 2010.

[14] ABA, Lawyer Demographics 2013.

[15] John P. Heinz et al., supra note 6.

[16] Correcting for this and looking province-wide in Ontario, one of us (Hadfield) together with Ronit Dinovitzer estimated that in 1998 Ontario lawyers devoted 42% of their effort in total to services for individual as opposed to corporate clients; in Toronto, a city of comparable size and financial significance as Chicago, the figure was 31%. We also estimated that an additional 10% worked in government. (Unpublished data on file with authors.)

In the abstract and in isolation, it is difficult to say whether this share of legal services devoted to ordinary citizens' interests is "enough." In theory, if ordinary citizens demanded more legal services, the legal services market could supply them; and, of course, the ordinary citizen benefits from the operation of a well-regulated and efficient market and thus from the availability of legal services to corporate entities as well. To add further perspective on these numbers, we have calculated what the personal share of the legal services market represents in terms of available legal effort and how this has changed over the last few decades.

In 1990, expenditures by households on legal services totaled $82.9 billion in 2012 dollars. At that time, the average hourly rate for lawyers in small firms (less than 20 lawyers, where we find most of the lawyers providing services to individuals) was roughly $209 in 2012 dollars.[17] Based on the total U.S. population for that year, this implies an average of 1.6 hours per person for the year or 4.3 hours per average household.[18] Conducting the same calculation for 2012 (total expenditures of $105.1 billion and an average hourly rate of $263 for small-firm lawyers, both in 2012 dollars[19]) yields an average of 1.3 hours per person or 3.3 hours per household, a decline of 30%.[20]

How does this compare with the availability of legal resources for those who live in comparably or even less law-thick environments around the globe? We do not have comparable data on personal expenditures on legal services and average hourly rates in other countries with which to do similar calculations. But we do have comparative data on expenditures in the legal system as a whole for a large set of European countries[21] and it is to these data that we turn for (again, rough) estimates of the availability of legal resources in the economy as a whole for ordinary citizens to address their relationships with and through the legal system.[22]

[17] This figure is based on Altman-Weil, Inc., The Survey of Law Firm Economics (2015), which is a self-selected proprietary survey and subject to substantial error. It is, however, the only quasi-systematic data we are aware of for hourly rates nationally in this year. We took a straight (unweighted) average of rates for those with 4–5 years' experience and those with 11–20 years' experience for firms with less than 9 and 9–20 lawyers and inflated based on the Consumer Price Index.

[18] Based on population estimate for 1990 of 248,790,925 and a household estimate of 93,347,000 (www.census.gov).

[19] This figure is based on Altman Weil data for 2012, taking a straight average of rates for equity and non-equity partners and associates in firms of less than 9 and 10–24 lawyers.

[20] Based on population estimate for 2012 of 313,873,685 and household estimate of 121,084,000, available at www.census.gov.

[21] European Commission for the Efficiency of Justice, *European Judicial Systems: Edition 2012 (data 2010): Efficiency and Quality of Justice*. In all data reported later, euros are converted to U.S. dollars at an exchange rate of $1 = €0.785.

[22] Justice Earl Johnson Jr. first drew attention to just how low the U.S. expenditure on civil legal aid was relative to other advanced market democracies. Earl Johnson Jr., Equal Access to Justice: Comparing Access to Justice in the United States and Other Industrial Democracies, 24 Fordham Intl. L. J. S83 (2000).

Table 2.1 provides data for the United States and a selection of European and Anglo-American countries showing total population, total public expenditure on courts, public prosecution and legal aid, total numbers of criminal and civil cases, and total numbers of judges and lawyers. These data should be read carefully, keeping in mind the potential for differences in the categories of what is counted and how data requests in the European survey were interpreted.[23] U.S. criminal cases include serious crimes and misdemeanors but exclude the 56.3 million traffic cases that also appear in state courts; the European data cover both serious crimes and misdemeanors but purport to exclude administrative offences and those processed by the police such as minor traffic offences. Civil cases include all non-criminal filings in the U.S. state and federal courts but exclude filings before administrative agencies that are not appealed to a court.

The count of judges for the United States includes all full-time federal and state judicial officers including magistrates, but does not include judicial officers sitting *pro tem* (temporary judges) or administrative law judges in state or federal governments; in the European data, we include full-time professional judges and exclude part-time professional judges and lay-judges. The count of lawyers includes both advocates and legal advisors who are members of a bar. This is a particularly difficult number to compare. While the count of lawyers who belong to a bar association in the United States is a very good measure of the availability of legal advice and representation – as only these people can provide these services – in most other countries bar membership is not co-extensive with an authorization to provide services. As we discuss in more detail, below, in both the United Kingdom and the Netherlands, for example, anyone may provide legal advice, although only bar members are counted here. In many European countries lawyers who are employed by a company, government, or organization need not – in some cases may not – be a member of the bar and thus are not counted. With these caveats in mind, Table 2.2 calculates the availability of legal resources per person and per case in the system.

Table 2.2 presents a stark picture. While U.S. public expenditure per capita on courts, judges, prosecutors, and legal aid is the highest among this set of both advanced and transitioning countries, when we take into account the vastly higher

[23] It is particularly important to note that the data reported here differ substantially from data reported in Christian Wollschlager, *Exploring Global Landscapes of Litigation Rates*, in SOZIOLOGIE DES RECHTS: FESTSCHRIFT FUR ERHARD BLANKENBURG (Jurgen Brand & Dieter Strempel eds., 1998). Wollschlager reports many more cases per capita for Germany than the data here; this is because he includes summary debt collections that are excluded here. Although Germany has by far the highest number of cases per capita in his data, and the United States ranks fifth just ahead of the United Kingdom and Hungary, he notes that if the summary debt cases are excluded, the United States is the highest per capita after Israel (p. 583). In addition Erhard Blankenburg, *The Infrastructure for Avoiding Civil Litigation: Comparing Cultures of Legal Behavior in The Netherlands and West Germany*, 28 LAW & SOC'Y REV. 789 (1994), suggests that the Netherlands has a much lower and Germany a much higher number of cases than is reported here. We were unable to determine from the published studies what might account for these differences; one possibility is change over time. Blankenburg appears to be drawing on data from the 1980s.

TABLE 2.1 *Total resources and cases.*

Country	Population	Public expenditure on courts, prosecutors & legal aid ($B)	Legal aid ($ M)	Criminal cases (M)	Civil cases (M)	Judges	Lawyers
United States	313,914,040	56	3,600*	20.8	28.6	31,930	1,268,011
France	65,026,885	5	460	1.1	2.3	6,945	51,758
Germany	81,751,602	11	487	1.2	5.8	19,831	155,679
Hungary	9,986,000	0.5	0.4	0.3	0.7	2,891	12,099
Netherlands	16,665,799	2.5	457	0.4	1.5	2,530	16,728
Poland	38,200,000	2.2	30	1.1	6.2	10,625	29,469
U.K. (England and Wales)	55,200,000	5.7	3,211	1.9	2	4,913	165,128

Sources: ABA Commission on Ethics 20/20 Working Group on Alternative Business Structures, Issue Paper Concerning Alternative Business Structures (2011); European Commission for the Efficiency of Justice, Report on European Judicial Systems (2012, 2010 data; includes contested and uncontested matters but excludes administrative matters and land registry); U.S. Census Bureau; Bureau of Justice Statistics, Justice Expenditure and Employment Extracts 2010 (July 1, 2013); Examining the Work of State Courts: An Analysis of 2010 State Court Caseloads (Court Statistics Project 2012); Federal Judicial Center Annual Report of the Director: Judicial Business of the United States Courts (2012); American Bar Foundation Lawyer Demographics (2013); Alan W. Houseman, Civil Legal Aid in the United States: An Update for 2013 (November 2013); Bureau of Justice Statistics, Indigent Defense Services in the United States, FY 2008-2012-Updated (April 21, 2015)(2012 data from Annual Survey of Government Finances)

* Estimate includes public and private charitable sources for civil legal aid and indigent criminal defense.

numbers of cases in the U.S. court system, public expenditure per case is significantly lower than in other advanced democracies; only relative to the amounts spent in emerging market democracies that are still seeking to build the rule of law in their countries does the U.S. expenditure level look high. Publicly financed legal aid per capita in the United States is lower than in the Netherlands and the United Kingdom[24] and higher than in other advanced and emerging democracies; but legal aid per case is well below that expended in other advanced democracies except Germany, exceeding only the low levels available in Hungary and Poland. Legally trained personnel also appear to be much less available in the United States when we take into account the number of cases in the United States. The number of judges per capita in the United States is significantly lower than in Germany, Poland, and Hungary, and comparable to the levels in France, the Netherlands, and the United Kingdom. But again the intensity of legal demand in the United States, as measured by the number of cases, reveals that per case there are far fewer judges available in the United States than in any of these European countries: roughly half as many as in the United Kingdom and the Netherlands, roughly a third of those available in France, and less than one-quarter of those in Germany and Hungary. Lawyers do not clearly make up all of the difference: while there are more lawyers, counted as bar members per capita in the United States than in this set of comparison countries, again the numbers per case reveal that the United Kingdom, with significantly more judges per case, also has more than one and a half times as many lawyers per case. The U.S. numbers per case look in Table 2.2 to be higher than in France, Hungary, the Netherlands, and Poland – but European bar members do not have the complete monopoly on provision of legal services that they do in the United States and so the European numbers are (perhaps significantly) understated. Moreover, given that we are ultimately interested in legal services available to individuals as opposed to businesses, the relatively large corporate sector in the United States and the fact that many in-house corporate lawyers in European countries are not counted as members of the bar also suggest that the U.S. figure of the availability of lawyer assistance to ordinary Americans is an overstatement.

Not all the lawyers in these counts, of course, are delivering litigation-related services such as those that would be demanded by individuals (and businesses – the data here do not separate out client types) in court cases. But we can interpret the number of cases in the courts as an indicator of the level of overall demand in the economy for legal inputs for the planning and management of social and economic relationships. There is no clear or singular interpretation of the substantially higher

[24] The United Kingdom recently announced significant cuts to its legal aid budget: £320 million per year by 2014–15 and an additional £220 million per year by 2018–19. Ministry of Justice, Transforming Legal Aid: Delivering a More Credible and Efficient System, Consultation Paper CP 14/2013, at 5. These numbers do not reflect any cuts. These cuts would be a 15% reduction in aid per case and per 100,000 people, though the number of cases could decline if less legal aid is available.

TABLE 2.2 *Comparative resources per person and per case.*

Country	Public spend per capita	Public spend per case	Legal aid per capita	Legal aid per case	Judges per 100,000 persons	Judges per 100,000 cases	Lawyers per 100,000 persons	Lawyers per 100,000 cases	Criminal cases per 100,000 persons	Civil cases per 100,000 persons	Total cases per 100,000 persons
United States	$178	$1,136	$12	$75	10	65	404	2,567	6,626	9,111	15,737
France	$77	$1,471	$7	$135	11	204	80	1,522	1,692	3,537	5,229
Germany	$135	$1,571	$6	$70	24	283	190	2,224	1,468	7,095	8,563
Hungary	$50	$500	$0	$0	29	289	121	1,210	3,004	7,010	10,014
Netherlands	$150	$1,316	$27	$241	15	133	100	880	2,400	9,000	11,401
Poland	$58	$301	$1	$4	28	146	77	404	2,880	16,230	19,110
U.K. (England and Wales)	$103	$1,462	$58	$823	9	126	299	4,234	3,442	3,623	7,065

number of cases per capita in the United States: this could be because of more law, greater willingness to use courts as opposed to alternative means for dispute resolution, and/or higher levels of unmet needs for ex ante legal advice, planning, and dispute resolution assistance. But this is precisely what makes the strikingly low levels of legal resources so salient: U.S. socioeconomic life is, as Robert Kagan[25] has emphasized, substantially more reliant on law and legal management of relationships and yet the United States devotes far fewer resources to providing the legal services needed to translate law on the books into law on the ground.

THE MICRO-VIEW: LEGAL NEEDS

We turn now to a view closer to that ground. Few studies have attempted to quantify the legal needs ordinary Americans face. Existing data suggest that at least half of all households face a legal problem each year and those households who face legal problems average several per year. These studies likely undercount the extent of legal needs faced by ordinary people because they focus on erupted legal problems, but exclude instances where legal information and advice could aid in planning conduct and avoiding or mitigating legal problems upfront. This section explores the legal needs of ordinary Americans and how Americans respond to those needs. What we find suggests that while Americans face legal needs at rates comparable to those faced by people in other countries, Americans are more likely to take no action to resolve these problems. When they do take action, they do so with fewer legal resources available to them: the expenditure data we reviewed in the last section imply that the average household secures an average of less than half an hour of legal assistance per year with legal problems and what studies we have of this phenomenon suggest that Americans represent themselves in court more often than do people in other countries.

U.S. Civil Legal Needs and the Availability of Legal Help

Civil legal needs surveys can help us get a better sense of people's demand for legal services and their experiences as participants in the legal system. In 1993 the American Bar Association (ABA) conducted a study assessing the legal needs of the poor (defined as those living at or below 125% of the poverty line), and those with moderate income (those with incomes falling in the middle 60% of the income distribution).[26] The study defined "legal needs" as problems or disputes households had encountered, such as substandard housing, job loss, or divorce, and that could potentially be addressed through the civil legal system. With few exceptions (review

[25] Robert A. Kagan, *Adversarial Legalism: The American Way of Law* (2001).

[26] ABA, Legal Needs and Civil Justice: A Survey of Americans, Major Findings from the Comprehensive Legal Needs Study *7 (1994). In 1993, the top household income in this group was $60,000, approximately $97,000 in 2013 dollars. *Id.*

of documents for a real estate transaction, for example) the focus of the study was on ex post dispute resolution and the nature of the legal assistance that might be offered.

The study found that approximately 51% of households (47% of poor households and 52% of moderate-income households) had experienced one or more legal needs in the previous year. The average number of problems experienced by those with legal needs was 2. Of those with legal needs, 38% of the poor sought assistance from a third party for resolution of the problem, 29% from a specifically legal third party such as a lawyer (21%) or other legal/judicial actor or entity (8%).[27] Thirty-eight percent did nothing to resolve their problem,[28] a course of action that has come to be called "lumping it" in the literature.[29] Among moderate-income households, assistance from a third party was sought for 51% of problems, 39% from a specifically legal source (lawyers 28%, other legal/judicial 12%), and 26% of moderate-income households lumped their problems.[30]

There has been no national study of legal needs in the United States in the two decades since this ABA study was published. State-level surveys have been conducted and they paint a largely similar picture. Table 2.3 summarizes the findings of 17 state legal needs surveys. Twelve[31] of the surveys report legal needs experienced by low-income individuals or households. Georgia, Montana, Nevada, and Oregon surveyed households of low- and moderate-income; Arizona included households of all incomes. The list of problems provided to respondents was relatively consistent across states.

The data in Table 2.3 paint an even grimmer picture of the legal environment facing ordinary Americans than the ABA study. It is clear from this collection of state studies that the incidence of legal problems occurred at least in 50% of households identified by the ABA study; the fact that numbers at least this high are consistently found in almost all state surveys supports the reliability of this estimate. A straight average across those states providing estimates at the household level suggests roughly 60% of American households are dealing with a legal problem at any one time.[32] Moreover, a rough calculation taking a straight average across the state studies suggests the average number of problems in households experiencing problems has increased from the 2 found by the ABA to 3. The rate at which poor

27 *Id.* at *17.

28 *Id.* at *17–18.

29 Marc Galanter may have been the first to use this phrase. See Marc Galanter, *Why the "Haves" Come Out Ahead: Speculations on the Limits of Legal Change*, 9 Law & Soc'y Rev. 95 (1974).

30 *Id.*

31 New Jersey conducted a small-sample survey of higher-income households as well but these results are not generalizable to the larger population. We report only the lower-income New Jersey results. In addition, our research identified studies done in Arkansas, Idaho, Minnesota, and Nebraska. The published reports from these studies, however, do not provide enough detail to develop statistics comparable to those shown for other states in Table 2.3.

32 Although most of the state surveys focus on the poor, the 1993 ABA study found little difference in the prevalence of problems between poor- and moderate-income households; if anything, moderate-income households reported more problems.

TABLE 2.3 *State legal needs surveys.*

State	Year	Prevalence of legal needs (% of households unless noted)	Average number of legal needs (respondents with at least one problem)	No steps taken to resolve problem	Contact with lawyer or legal institution (% of problems unless noted)
Alabama^{+}	2006	48%	3.6	20%	16%
Arizona$^{\wedge}$	2007	32% (individuals)	–	24%	16%
Connecticut^{+}	2002	65%	4.1	33%	10%
Georgia$^{\pm}$	2007–08	62%	4.6	28%	8%
Illinois^{+}	2004	49%	3.5	–	16%
Massachusetts^{+}	2002	67%	3.6	45%	< 19% (hhs, or head of households, at least one problem)
Montana$^{\pm}$	2004	–	>3.5	–	16%
Nevada$^{\pm}$	2007	68%	2.4	–	9% (hhs, all problems)
					20% (hhs, at least one problem)
New Jersey^{+}	2007	33% (individuals)	2.3	23%	14%
New York^{+}	2010	47%	> 2.0	>56%	17% (hhs, at least one problem)
Oregon$^{\pm}$	1999–2000	82%	3.9	–	18%
Tennessee^{+}	2003	70%	4.7	25% (biggest problems)	24–40% (biggest problems)
Utah^{+}	2005–06	68%	1.3	–	13% (hhs)
Vermont^{+}	2001	50% (est.)	2.2	30%	9%

Virginia[+]	2005–06	55%		3.4	42%	< 32% (HHs, at least one problem)
Washington[+]	2002–03	87%		3.3	–	12%
Wisconsin[+]	2006	45%		2.1	–	12% (HHs, all problems) 27% (HHs, at least one problem)

[+] Low-income

^ All-income

± Low- and moderate-income

Sources: State Legal Needs Studies, available at www.nlada.org/Civil/Civil_SPAN/SPAN_Library/document_list?topics=000055&list_title=State+Legal+Needs+Studies%3A+Reports&start=1.

Georgia: Report excludes from the "no action" category. those who took no action but reported satisfaction with result (48%); results in chart are estimated to adjust to include those for comparability with other studies.

Massachusetts: Percentage contacting lawyer is upper bound because not corrected for those who contacted more than one type of legal provider (private lawyers, legal aid).

Montana: Average number of legal needs is across all households, including those with no legal needs.

New Jersey: Measure is incidence, not prevalence – includes only new legal needs in a given year – does not include problems pending from prior years; no action includes problems not yet resolved; higher-income sample analyzed in full report but not generalizable to full population.

New York: Percent taking no action is upper bound because 56% reported taking no action on any problem.

Nevada: Average number of legal needs is reported as average number of categories in which problems occurred; actual number of legal problems may be higher.

Tennessee: Average number of legal needs is estimate based on average number of problems in categories reported.

Vermont: Excludes households without phones.

Virginia: Percentage contacting lawyer is upper bound because not corrected for those who contacted more than one type of legal provider (private lawyers, legal clinic, legal aid).

Wisconsin: Average number of legal needs is reported as average number of categories in which problems occurred; actual number of legal problems may be higher.

Americans lump their problems seems about as high in these studies as in the ABA study: averaging across the studies limited to low-income households, the rate is about 36%, compared with 38%; the two studies that included higher-income households and reported data on this show the same average rate (26%) as the ABA study. Finally, it appears that the 1993 ABA estimate of the likelihood that Americans receive help from a lawyer when dealing with legal problems is high relative to what the states are finding in these studies conducted a decade or so later. Again a rough calculation taking a straight average across the states that present a clear number on this (that is, excluding MA, NV, NY, TN, UT, VA, and WI), suggests that fewer than 13% of poor and 15% of moderate-income Americans have contact with a lawyer or other legal provider; this is substantially lower than the 29% (poor) and 39% (moderate income) rates found by the ABA.

A drop in legal help is consistent with the census data on expenditures on personal legal services that we reviewed earlier. Using the rough estimates of hourly rates for lawyers in small firms that we calculated there, the 1993 ABA estimate that the average household experienced one legal problem a year[33] for 1990 and a straight average of the number of problems (2) per household reported by the state surveys[34] for 2012, we estimate that in 1990 American households were able on average to draw on approximately four hours of legal time to address a legal problem and in 2012 they were able to draw on significantly less than half that amount: approximately an hour and a half.

An hour and a half of legal help per problem is a very low number, and yet it is still an overestimate. The legal needs surveys only ask about erupted civil problems – a dispute over employment or a foreclosure or a denial of health care or the risk of injury to or a diminished relationship with a child – and these are the only problems we included in our earlier estimate. Our count of problems excludes the demand for legal assistance with criminal matters where public defender help is unforthcoming or inadequate. It excludes the demand for legal assistance before problems arise, such as legal advice in assessing a complex mortgage offer or employment options or insurance coverage or the potential for conduct to influence custody of a child. If for every dispute-related need there is an ex ante advice-related need (as appears to be the case for large corporations[35]), this implies that today the average household is

33 This is based on the estimate that half of households experience problems and the average number of problems in these households is two; this averages to one per household across all households.

34 These surveys are of problems facing poor households but the ABA Legal Needs Survey suggests that the rate for poor households is not significantly different from that for moderate-income households. Table 2.1 reports average problems per household with a problem and the percentage of households with problems; we have calculated the average number across all households for each state and taken a straight average. We have excluded the data for New Jersey from this calculation because it is based on problems per individual, as well as the data for Montana because the survey does not report the percentage of households experiencing problems.

35 Mark Chandler, General Counsel of Cisco Systems Inc, reports that total legal expenditures in his company are 0.3% of company revenue with 0.16% coming from non-litigation expenses, available at www.law.com/jsp/ihc/PubArticleIHC.jsp?id=1188291741577.

able to draw on less than an hour's worth of legal advice or assistance in dealing with the points at which their everyday lives intersect with the legal system in such a way as to require them to assess legal rights or consequences.

The low rate at which Americans obtain legal assistance with their legal problems is also indicated by the information we have about publicly financed legal aid. According to the ABA, only 1% of American lawyers are either legal aid lawyers or public defenders;[36] the number of legal aid attorneys providing civil legal services was calculated by the Legal Services Corporation (LSC) to be 7,931, just over one-half of 1% of all U.S. lawyers.[37] Moreover, the availability of legal aid in practice is characterized by "fragmentation and inequality" and "geography as destiny."[38] Many who seek free legal assistance are turned away. LSC, the only federally funded legal aid agency, reported in 2009 that, as a result of resource limitations, LSC-funded programs were only able to serve half of the poor who sought assistance.[39]

What do Americans do when they do not obtain help from lawyers with their legal problems? The U.S. civil legal needs surveys indicate that a large fraction of them – roughly a third – do nothing at all; the state surveys indicate that in some settings the number among the poor is closer to one-half. There can be many reasons that people take no action: they may not think the effort is worth it, they may not know what to do, they may have nowhere affordable to turn to, they may be too overwhelmed by this and other problems to act. Even with the caveat that not all decisions to do nothing are evidence of a failure of the legal system to provide adequate assistance,[40] however, the rates at which Americans lump their problems is troubling. The legal-needs surveys consistently identify serious legal issues, where failure to obtain any legal advice generates significant risk that outcomes will not be the ones judged by the law to be fair and appropriate – people losing homes they are entitled to keep, being unpaid when they are entitled to payment, or losing jobs on wrongful grounds; children put at risk or deprived of parental contact, legislated benefits, or adequate health care. Moreover, failure to act on legal problems can also breed more problems. Several researchers have found that legal problems tend to occur in clusters, with initial problems triggering others.[41] The loss of a job or a failure to

[36] ABA, Lawyer Demographics (2013), available at www.americanbar.org/content/dam/aba/migrated/marketresearch/PublicDocuments/lawyer_demographics_2012_revised.authcheckdam.pdf.

[37] LSC, Documenting the Justice Gap in America: The Current Unmet Civil Legal Needs of Low-Income Americans 20–21 (2009), available at www.lsc.gov/JusticeGap.pdf.

[38] Rebecca L. Sandefur & Aaron C. Smyth, *Access Across America 2011: First Report of the Civil Justice Infrastructure Mapping Project* (October 7, 2011).

[39] See note 37 supra.

[40] See, e.g., Herbert M. Kritzer, *To Lawyer or Not to Lawyer: Is that the Question?*, 5 J. Leg. Stud. 875 (2008) (arguing based on empirical evidence that the decision to obtain a lawyer is explained by several variables and that not all those who can afford to hire a lawyer choose to do so).

[41] Currie analyzes the phenomenon of trigger problems, which lead to a cascade of other difficulties. He also emphasizes the momentum of legal difficulties, estimating in his Canadian study that vulnerability to additional problems increases with the number of problems: the probability of a second

collect on amounts owed under a contract can lead to failures to pay rent or meet mortgage or other debt payments; financial stress can lead to marital stress and relationship breakdown; relationship breakdown can lead to employment or financial problems. Failing to act on legal problems may only lead to more legal problems – perhaps partly as a consequence of the failure to discover what taking action can accomplish. The person who responds to not being paid by going to small claims court, for example, discovers how that process works; they learn a bit more about the law; and they learn a bit more about themselves. This can be of benefit to them personally and to their communities when they are the ones to whom others turn for advice. Failing to do anything about half or more of these problems is clearly evidence of a large gap between what we think are the legal rules in our communities and people's actual experiences in facing their legal needs. While Americans on average encounter as many as two legal problems each year, their actual experiences with the legal system are quite thin.

In some cases people choose, or have no choice but, to become involved with courts: the problem may be too serious to be ignored and may require judicial orders – for child custody or bankruptcy, for example – or a person may be sued (for collection, divorce, foreclosure, probate, etc.) and forced to deal with the legal system. The numbers above indicate that when Americans do interact with the court system, they do so with little legal help. The ABA data may mask this phenomenon – they count as legal help contact with judicial institutions but this includes those who do not seek out judicial help but rather are drawn into legal processes and may not find any of it to be legally helpful; moreover, court personnel in the United States cannot give litigants legal advice as they respond to summonses or participate in hearings and there is only so much judges can do without risking the loss of neutrality. Indeed, it is judges – under pressure to help the hapless – who are the most deeply aware of the crisis of unrepresented litigants in their courtrooms.

The annual Judicial Business report of the U.S. Courts provides information on the number of pro se[42] filings in U.S. federal district courts. In 2012 roughly 28% of all filings in U.S. district courts were by pro se litigants. Roughly 65% of these were filed by prisoners challenging prison conditions or civil rights. Of filings by non-prisoners, 12% were filed by pro se litigants.[43] To put this in perspective – recognizing that

problem for someone experiencing one is 32%; the probability of a third for someone facing two is 39%; the probability of a sixth for someone facing five (a phenomenon experienced by 8% of his sample) is 41%. Ab Currie, THE LEGAL PROBLEMS OF EVERYDAY LIFE: THE NATURE, EXTENT AND CONSEQUENCES OF JUSTICIABLE PROBLEMS EXPERIENCED BY CANADIANS at 43–44 (2007).

42 The literature on pro se litigants uses "pro se," "pro per" (California), "self-represented," "unrepresented," and "litigant in person" interchangeably. All are used to indicate a litigant who does not have an attorney appearing on his or her behalf in court or conducting his or her litigation.

43 U.S. Federal Courts, Judicial Business of the United States Courts 2012, Table C-13. Although the methodology is unclear, it appears that this only counts cases with pro se filing party and does not include pro se defendants.

much of the litigation in federal district courts involves businesses and other organizations enforcing contracts or responding to regulation – social security, civil rights, and labor cases make up about 7% of the caseload in federal district courts; torts account for less than 1%, are rarely filed without a (contingency fee) lawyer, and frequently are filed by corporate plaintiffs. This suggests a significant portion of ordinary individuals in federal district courts are pro se. A review of federal bankruptcy courts – which handle approximately 1.5 million cases a year, five times as many as federal district courts – indicates that in 2011 approximately 9% of bankruptcy petitions were pro se. The figure reaches as high as 27% in high-filing districts such as the central district of California.[44]

The vast majority of U.S. litigation, however, occurs in state courts – approximately 95%. Here the rates of self-representation are much higher, even in general civil filings, a category that includes a large share of corporate, government, and organizational litigants[45] who invariably have attorney representation.[46] A 2004 New Hampshire study (2001 data) found that one party is self-represented in 48% of general civil cases in the state.[47] A 2005 study of all types of cases in Woodbury County, Iowa, found that 58% of cases have a self-represented litigant.[48] A 2004 California study found that 16% of petitioners at filing are self-represented in general civil matters.[49] The California number underestimates, probably substantially, the level of self-representation in general civil litigation because it does not include defendants; nor does it reflect the rate of representation throughout the case or at disposition (many petitioners may choose to file a case while represented, but do not maintain representation throughout).

More dramatic evidence of the rate at which ordinary Americans deal with courts without legal help is provided by studies that focus on the types of cases that involve matters that individuals generally cannot ignore or where they are brought in as

44 Ninety-six percent of bankruptcy filings in 2011–12 were non-business. Judicial Business of the U.S. Courts, Table F-2 (2012). A review of pro se debtors in bankruptcy court in Massachusetts also found that 96% of cases filed in 1997 were non-business or consumer filings, of which roughly 6% were pro se. Boston Bar Association Task Force, supra note 44, at 31 (citing National Consumer Law Center, Self-Representation in the Bankruptcy Court: The Massachusetts Experience), available at www.bostonbar.org/prs/reports/unrepresented0898.pdf.

45 Recall, for example, the Chicago Lawyers Study which showed that in 1995 only 29% of legal work was done for personal rather than corporate, organizational or government clients, and only 16% in personal plight cases, which are the matters we expect to see in court.

46 *Roland v. California Men's Colony*, 506 U.S. 194, 201–202 (1993).

47 State of New Hampshire Judicial Branch, Challenge to Justice: A Report on Self-Represented Litigants in New Hampshire Courts (January 2004).

48 Report of the Joint Iowa Judges Association and Iowa State Bar Association Task Force on Pro Se Litigation (May 18, 2005). The study reports statistics for the Woodbury County district court (state trial level) from a random sampling of schedules from the week of June 7, 2004.

49 Judicial Council of California, Task Force on Self-Represented Litigants, Statewide Action Plan for Serving Self-Represented Litigants (2004). The California study is based on judicial officer and court staff estimates as well as data from the Judicial Branch Statistical Information System.

defendants. Studies of domestic relations and housing cases, for example, consistently reveal very high levels of self-representation. Nationwide, in a study of 16 large urban trial courts in 1991–92, the National Center on State Courts found that 72% of domestic relations cases had at least one self-represented party and in 18% of cases both parties were self-represented.[50] State-by-state studies confirm the national trend. In 1991, the ABA sponsored the first major study on self-represented litigants in domestic relations cases, conducted in Maricopa County, Arizona. The study found that the percentage of domestic relations cases involving a self-represented litigant rose from 24% in 1980 to 47% in 1985 to 88% in 1991.[51] Both parties were self-represented in 52% of these cases.[52] Subsequently, numerous state or local studies have been conducted. The Washington study found that from 1995 to 2001, pro se litigants were involved in 80% of paternity cases and 95% of domestic violence petitions.[53] A California study of child support cases found that neither parent was represented in 65% of cases in 2005, though this was a decrease from 2001.[54] The New Hampshire study reported that nearly 70% of domestic relations cases in state trial courts have one pro se party and 97% of domestic violence cases had one pro se party.[55] A Washington study found that from 1995 to 2001, pro se litigants were involved in 80% of paternity cases and 95% of domestic violence petitions.[56] A Utah study found that 83% of divorce cases and 87% of protective order cases had at least one self-represented litigant.[57] An eight-week study in Florida in 1999 revealed that 65% of domestic relations cases began with at least one self-represented party, which grew to 85% in Miami by the end of the case.[58] A 1997 Boston Bar Association study

[50] Stephan Landsman, *Pro Se Litigation*, 8 ANN. REV. L. & SOC. SCI. 231, 239 (2012) (citing John Goerdt, Divorce Courts: Case Management, Case Characteristics, and the Pace of Litigation in 16 Urban Jurisdictions (1992)).

[51] John M. Graecen, Self-Represented Litigants and Court and Legal Services Responses to Their Needs: What We Know, prepared for the Center for Families, Children & the Courts California Administrative Office of the Courts (undated) (citing Bruce Sales, Connie Beck & Richard Haan), Is Self-Representation a Reasonable Alternative to Attorney Representation in Divorce Cases? St. L. Univ. L. J. (1993). Available at www.courts.ca.gov/partners/documents/SRLwhatweknow.pdf.

[52] Boston Bar Association Task Force, supra note 44, at 1 (citing Sales, Beck & Haan, supra note 51).

[53] Judicial Services Division, Administrative Office of the Courts, An Analysis of Pro Se Litigants in Washington State 1995–2000 (2001), t.1.

[54] Judicial Council of California, Review of Statewide Uniform Child Support Guideline 2005, at 52 (2006).

[55] New Hampshire Supreme Court Task Force on Self-Representation, Challenge to Justice: A Report on Self-Represented Litigants in New Hampshire Courts, 2, 9 (Jan. 2004).

[56] Judicial Services Division Administrative Office of the Courts, An Analysis of Pro Se Litigants in Washington State 1995–2000 (2001), t.1.

[57] Committee on Resources for Self-Represented Parties, Strategic Planning Initiative Report to the Judicial Council (Utah, July 2006) at 5.

[58] John M. Graecen, Self-Represented Litigants and Court and Legal Services Responses to Their Needs: What We Know, prepared for the Center for Families, Children & the Courts California Administrative Office of the Courts, at 7 (citing Office of the Florida State Court Administrator, Report to the Florida Legislature on Family Court Self-Help Programs (1999)).

found that 69% of cases in Probate and Family Court in several counties in Massachusetts had at least one unrepresented party.[59] A 2010 New York study found that 97% of parents in New York City and 95% of parents outside New York City are unrepresented in child support cases.[60] Ninety-nine percent of tenants in New York City are unrepresented in eviction cases, 99% of borrowers in New York City are unrepresented in consumer credit cases, and 44% of homeowners are unrepresented in foreclosure cases throughout New York state.[61] The Utah study found that 98% of evictions cases have a self-represented litigant.[62] The New Hampshire study found that tenants were unrepresented in 90% of landlord–tenant cases. The Boston Bar Association report found that 79% of litigants in the Northeast Housing Court were unrepresented in 1997; with 50% of landlords and 92% of tenants in summary process actions being unrepresented.[63] The Boston Housing Court found that in 1996 90% of tenants were unrepresented in summary process eviction actions.[64]

These statistics indicate that in some of life's most important defining circumstances self-representation is by far the norm. Together with the U.S. legal needs surveys, the data on legal expenditures and the fraction of lawyers in the United States who provide legal aid services, a clear picture emerges: the great majority of ordinary Americans navigate the law-thick world without legal help. This is in stark contrast to complex commercial and tort litigation. For instance, the Washington study found that only 2–3% of tort and commercial cases involve self-represented litigants. Similarly, a 1995 Bureau of Justice Statistics report examining 45 trial courts found that only 3% of tort cases involve a self-represented litigant.[65]

Comparisons With Other Countries

In this section, we look at comparable data on civil legal needs and pro se representation in other advanced market democracies. Again the data are incomplete and difficult to evaluate but we see nonetheless evidence of significant differences, differences that we believe reflect the thin nature of the landscape of resources available to ordinary Americans dealing with the legal world.

[59] Boston Bar Association Task Force, supra note 44, at 8.

[60] The Task Force to Expand Access to Civil Legal Services in New York, Report to the Chief Judge of the State of New York (November 2010).

[61] Id.

[62] Committee on Resources for Self-Represented Parties, Strategic Planning Initiative Report to the Judicial Council (Utah, July 2006), at 5.

[63] Boston Bar Association, supra note 44, at 15.

[64] *Id.* at 16.

[65] Judicial Services Division Administrative Office of the Courts, An Analysis of Pro Se Litigants in Washington State 1995–2000 (2001); Steven K. Smith, Carol J. DeFrances, Patrick A. Langan & John Goerdt, Tort Cases in Large Counties, Civil Justice Survey of State Courts 1992 (1995).

Since the 1993 ABA study, legal needs surveys have been conducted in at least fifteen countries.[66] The gold standard for these surveys was developed by Hazel Genn in England in 1996.[67] Genn's methodology involved face-to-face interviews, presenting individuals with a series of cards listing types of problems – which were not identified as "legal" problems but which were "justiciable" in the sense that they were potentially resolvable using legal means. This methodology, with refinements, has since been used in several countries, and has been administered multiple times in England and Wales.

First a caution: surveys differ substantially across different jurisdictions and the results are not directly comparable. Most country studies survey all income levels; the ABA surveyed only the bottom 80% of the income distribution and most of the state studies focus only on poor households. Some studies ask whether anyone in the household has experienced a problem; others ask only the respondent about their problems. Some studies ask about problems in the last year – like most U.S. studies do – but some ask about problems in the last three or five years. This could increase the rate of problem reporting, although this does not follow as obviously as one might think: many problems are multi-year problems and, as at least one study has shown, people tend to remember and report the same number whether asked about one year or a longer period.[68] Studies differ in terms of whether they include a signal of the interest of the researchers in specifically "legal" problems: the original ABA study did not but some do. There is evidence that people do not always characterize their problems as "legal" even if a solution might at least in part be found through legal processes. The 2010 New York study, for example, first asked people if they had experienced "legal problems" in the past year; 94% said "no."[69] Researchers then asked if people had experienced any of a list of specifically identified problems which clearly have legal dimensions – such as problems with child support, foreclosure, eviction, denial of benefits, job discrimination and so on. Forty-seven percent reported having at least one such problem.[70]

Studies that include the reference to "legal" problems may therefore underreport them. Some studies expressly ask people about problems that were difficult to solve; others (like the ABA study) do not screen for triviality upfront, although they may (like the ABA study) frame some problem

[66] For a comprehensive review of these surveys, see Pascoe Pleasence, Nigel J. Balmer & Rebecca L. Sandefur, PATHS TO JUSTICE: A PAST, PRESENT AND FUTURE ROADMAP (2013).

[67] Hazel Genn, *Paths to Justice: What People Do and Think about Going to Law* (1999).

[68] Pascoe Pleasence, Nigel J. Balmer & Stian Reimers 2010, *Comparing Apples and Oranges: Methodological Issues Affecting the Comparative Analysis of the Public's Experience of Legal Problems* (undated presentation), University College of London, (on file with authors).

[69] The Task Force supra note 60, at Appendices 16.

[70] *Id.* at 17.

categories as asking about a "major," "serious," or "important" problem. This may not have as big an effect as one might think; people tend to forget[71] or leave out less important problems. Surveys can differ somewhat in the list of problems they ask about – some (e.g., ABA 1993) ask about small business difficulties, for example, but most do not. Different survey techniques – in person, on the phone, online – can also influence responses. People may be more willing to report some types of problems online than in person; they may be more inclined to censor out less important issues when face-to-face. Internet and (usually landline) phone methods too can influence the mix of respondents, making it harder to reach people without internet connections or who do not use landlines.[72]

With these caveats in mind, however, evaluating the U.S. studies in light of studies from other countries is nonetheless illuminating about the legal landscape facing Americans. Table 2.3 presents data from the 1993 ABA study and rough averages from the combined state studies conducted between 2000 and 2010 together with results from a set of other comparable countries. The data indicate that the rate at which Americans report experiencing justiciable problems is comparable to the rate in other countries. Certainly there is nothing to suggest here that the U.S. studies are out of line with experiences in comparable market democracies with high per capita income and highly developed legal systems. And there is no reason to think the U.S. number is inflated, relative to other studies, by trivial or inconsequential matters. The U.S. study asked about the broadest range of problems (although it lacked a catch-all "other" category that several other studies use to compensate for a more restricted list of specific examples) but it also frequently used language such as "difficult" or "important" to qualify the type of problem in which the surveyor was interested. There is, however, evidence that the rates at which Americans do nothing about their legal problems is high relative to these comparison countries. Certainly, none of these studies reports "no action" rates anywhere close to the 50% range we see in some of the state surveys. But nor do these countries seem to reach rates in the 30% range that we see at the lower end in the state surveys and in the 1993 ABA national study. It is striking that the rates of no action picked up in several of these surveys – specifically those from the United Kingdom and from the Netherlands – are on the order of 5–10%. This includes the 6% rate in the Dutch study – where the use of the internet to conduct the survey might have been predicted, if anything, to have swept in more problems that people just didn't think were worth doing

[71] Pascoe Pleasence, Nigel J. Balmer & Tania Tam, *Failure to Recall: Indications from the English and Welsh Civil and Social Justice Survey of the Relative Severity and Incidence of Civil Justice Problems*, 12 ACCESS TO JUSTICE: SOCIOLOGY OF CRIME, LAW AND DEVIANCE Vol. 12, 43–65 (Rebecca L. Sandefur ed., 2009).

[72] For an extended analysis of differences in survey methodology across national studies, see Paths to Justice, supra note 67.

TABLE 2.4 *Actions taken by those reporting legal problem.*

Country (year of data collection)	Prevalence (reference period, years) [reference group]	Took no action	Dealt with problem alone or informally	Contact with lawyer	Contact with other legal provider or judicial institution	Contact with provider not authorized to provide legal help
U.S. National Poor + Middle Income (1993)	51% (1)[hh]	29%	23%	26%	11%	11%
U.S. State Average (2000–10)	62%(1)[hh]	33%	–	14%	–	–
Australia (2008)	50% (1)[ind]	18%	31%	16%	13%	36%
Canada (2006)	45% (3)[ind/partner]	22%	44%	9%	–	22%
England & Wales (1997–98)	40% (5)[ind/partner]	5%	35%	27%	33%	n/a*
England and Wales (2010)	33% (1.5)[ind/partner]	10%	60%	7%	22%	n/a
Netherlands (2009)	61% (5)[ind]	6%	42%	10%	42%	n/a
N. Ireland (2005)	36% (3)[ind]	14%	26%	17%	43%	n/a
Scotland (1998)	26% (5)[ind/partner]	3%	31%	29%	36%	n/a

Sources: ABA, Legal Needs and Civil Justice: A Survey of Americans, Major Findings from the Comprehensive Legal Needs Study (1994); Ab Currie, The Legal Problems of Everyday Life: The Nature, Extent and Consequences of Justiciable Problems Experienced by Canadians (2007); Christie Coumarelos, Deborah Macourt, Julie People, Hugh M. McDonald, Zhigang Wei, Reiny Iriana & Stephanie Ramsey, 7 Legal Australia-Wide Survey: Legal Need in Australia (2012); Hazel Genn, Paths to Justice: What People Do and Think about Going to Law (1999); Pascoe Pleasence, Nigel Balmer, Ash Patel, Andrew Cleary, Tom Huskinson & Toby Cotton, Civil Justice in England and Wales: Report of Wave 1 of the English and Welsh Civil and Social Justice Panel Survey (2011); B.C.J. van Velthoven & C.M. Klein Haarhuis, Paths to Justice in the Netherlands (2009); Tony Dignan, Northern Ireland Legal Needs Survey, Report prepared for Northern Ireland Legal Services Commission (2006); Hazel Genn, Paths to Justice Scotland (1999).

n/a applies to countries that do not restrict the practice of law to bar-licensed lawyers, which the United Kingdom and the Netherlands do not.

U.S. National: Phone survey supplemented by in-person of non-phone households.

U.S. State Average: Straight averages when data available from state surveys in Table 2.3; prevalence excludes AZ, NJ; no action excludes TN; contact with lawyer is contact with lawyer or legal institution and excludes MA, NV, NY, TN, UT, VA, WI.

TABLE 2.4 (continued)

Australia: Phone; research purpose framed as "legal"; problem set included criminal, which was second-most prevalent problem; contact with lawyer includes court personnel and community law centers; contact with other legal is estimated minimum;[73] contact with non-legal provider is maximum, excluding estimated minimum of non-legal advisors who gave legal advice.

Canada: Phone survey; no action includes those who took no action due to perceived triviality of problem – excluding these, 17% took no action; non-legal includes informal; "alone or informally" is alone only.

England & Wales 1997–98, Scotland, Northern Ireland: In-person survey; actions taken excludes those who took no action due to perceived triviality of problem.

England & Wales 2010: In-person; other legal estimated by subtracting contacts with lawyers from total contacts with formal advisors.

Netherlands: Internet survey; allocation of contacts across lawyers, other legal and non-legal are estimates based on transition matrix.

anything about.[74] Even if we are cautions about the difficulties comparing across different surveys, this seems substantially lower than the rates found in American studies. The rates observed in Canada and Australia also appear significantly lower than the ABA study and the lower rates in the state surveys, although the difference is not as striking and may be attributable to methodological differences.

Interpreting the significance of the numbers in Table 2.4 in terms of access to legal help is a bit more complex. First, given the multiple caveats about comparing data from different surveys and the variance across studies, Table 2.4 probably should not be interpreted to support a finding that Americans are more or less likely to handle their legal problems on their own or with only informal help from friends and family. It's possible the United States is low on this number, but we would need a much closer look to decide that. Second, there is no suggestion here that Americans contact lawyers about their legal problems more or less frequently than elsewhere. The rate of contact with a lawyer from the 1993 ABA study is relatively high (27%) – but quite comparable to what we see in England and Wales in 1997 and Scotland in 1998. The average from the U.S. state studies is significantly lower – 14% – but so, too, are the rates in all the other country studies conducted in the 2000s. Collectively, the evidence suggests that use of lawyers may have fallen in many places from the 1990s to the 2000s. We may think that

73 Minimum estimated by considering advice received from non-legal advisors when these are main advisor and using largest rate reported from: advice on legal rights or procedures; help with legal documents; help with court or tribunal proceedings or preparation; help with formal dispute resolution. See Christie Coumarelos, Deborah Macourt, Julie People, Hugh M. McDonald, Zhigang Wei, Reiny Iriana & Stephanie Ramsey, 7 Legal Australia-Wide Survey: Legal Need in Australia, p. 130, Table 6.14 (2012).

74 One concern with internet surveys is that they can be biased because those who have internet access may be a wealthier group or one with more resources to bring to bear on problems. In the Netherlands in 2011, for example, 94% of households had internet access, the highest rate in Europe. Eurostat STAT/11/188, December 14 2011. In 2009, the year the Netherlands legal needs study was conducted, 90% of households had internet access. Eurostat, Broadband and connectivity – households (code isoc_bde15b_h).

14% – or even 27% – is low relative to an ideal, but we cannot glean from the comparison with other countries that the United States is in a significantly different predicament.

There does seem to be support, however, for the possibility that Americans have access to less legal help overall than individuals in these comparison countries. First, we see that rates of self-representation in settings where there is little choice about being in court are significantly lower in other countries than they are in the United States. A 2004 study of family law cases in the United Kingdom, for example, found that there was at least one self-represented litigant in 70% of adoption cases, 19% of cases involving financial matters such as child support and property orders, 61% of divorce cases, 33% of Children Act cases, and 28% of domestic cases involving restraining orders.[75] In the Australian Family Court[76] 17% of finalized cases and 27% of trials had at least one self-represented litigant.[77] A study in the Canadian province of British Columbia found that 11.5–24.6% of litigants were self-represented in family matters.[78] A New Zealand study from 2006 to 2007 found that at least one self-represented litigant was present in care of children cases roughly 35% of the time, domestic violence cases roughly 35% of the time, care and protection cases roughly 25% of the time, and dissolution, relationship property, and other family matters less than 5% of the time.[79] Although some of these numbers are high, they are still significantly below the percentages – some topping 95% – reported in comparable American family law cases.

Finally, that Americans navigate the legal world with less legal help than in comparable countries is suggested by the data in Table 2.4 about help from legal providers other than lawyers. Looking at the American, English/Welsh and Scottish studies from the 1990s – with relatively high and comparable lawyer rates – we see that people in the United States appear significantly less likely to get legal help from non-lawyer providers. The same is true if we compare the average from the U.S. state studies – where the "contact with lawyer" number includes other legal providers – and the other country studies

[75] Richard Moorhead & Mark Sefton, Litigants in Person: Unrepresented Litigants in First Instance Proceedings at 7, 31, Table 9 (2005). We categorize as "self-represented" those unrepresented litigants who were fully or partially active in the case. This excludes unrepresented parties who do not participate at all; this category in the United States is generally treated as a case of default and these litigants are generally excluded from counts of pro se litigants.

[76] The Family Court is a federal Australian court with jurisdiction over family and child support matters. This court does not have jurisdiction in the State of Western Australia.

[77] Family Court of Australia, Annual Report 2011–12. A 2002 study found that 31% of litigants in contested cases at first instance were self-represented and 18% in appeal cases had been self-represented at some stage. E. Richardson et al., Self-Represented Litigants: Literature Review, Australian Centre for Court and Justice System Innovation, at 25 (citing Rosemary Hunter et al., The Changing Face of Litigation: Unrepresented Litigants in the Family Court of Australia (Research Report) Law and Justice Foundation (August 2002)).

[78] British Columbia Justice Review Task Force, Exploring Fundamental Change: A Compendium of Potential Justice System Reforms 23, n.15 (2002).

[79] Melissa Smith, Esther Banbury & Su-Wuen Ong, Self-Represented Litigants: An Exploratory Study of Litigants in Person in the New Zealand Criminal Summary and Family Jurisdictions 34, fig.1 (2009).

conducted between 2000 and 2010. These other countries demonstrate significantly higher rates at which people seek out those who can provide legal help. To understand the numbers in Table 2.4, however, requires a better understanding of the scope of legal resources available to individuals in different countries. We turn to this now.

Regulation of Legal Resources

Legal resources available to ordinary persons include lawyers and other providers of legal advice, the court system, and legal aid. The scope of legal resources in the United States is relatively narrow; the World Justice Report ranks the United States below the Netherlands, Germany, Sweden, the United Kingdom, Australia, Canada, and France on access to civil justice.[80] Currently, all U.S. states permit only licensed lawyers to practice law.[81] The market for legal services is regulated by state bar associations, which impose qualitative restrictions on who may practice law and what the "practice of law" includes.[82] State definitions of the "practice of law" generally include the provision of almost any legal service or advice, with limited exceptions in some consumer-service areas.[83] An ABA task force defined the "practice of law" as "the application of legal principles and judgment to the circumstances or objectives of another person or entity."[84] This definition suggests that the provision of all legal services in the United States is limited to licensed attorneys. Moreover, ethical rules in all states except the District of Columbia (which has modest exceptions) prohibit lawyers from providing legal services in organizations that are to any extent owned, managed, or financed by non-lawyers; lawyers are also prohibited from entering into contractual arrangements with non-lawyers in any setting that can be interpreted to mean that the lawyer is splitting a fee with a non-lawyer. Lawyers must provide services directly to clients; they cannot be employed to do legal work for the

80 Mark David Agrast, Juan Carlos Botero, Joel Martinez, Alejandro Ponce & Christine S. Pratt, The World Justice Project: Rule of Law Index 2012–13, 27, fig.1 (2013).

81 This changed with Washington State's introduction in 2014 of a license for the (inartfully named) Limited License Legal Technician. See www.wsba.org/Licensing-and-Lawyer-Conduct/Admissions/Limited-Licenses-and-Special-Programs/Non-Lawyers-and-Students/Legal-Technicians. New York is also looking to develop pilot programs for non-lawyer assistance in housing, consumer debt and elder law fields. See www.nycourts.gov/press/PDFs/PR13_07.pdf. In other states, non-lawyers may only serve as a scrivener, filling in a blank form on behalf of another person and providing general legal information. California and Arizona license legal document preparers but this licensing does not expand their powers beyond those generally available in states without specific licensing requirements.

82 Gillian K. Hadfield, *Legal Barriers to Innovation: The Growing Economic Cost of Professional Control of Corporate Legal Markets*, 60 Stan. L. Rev. 1689, 1706–11.

83 *Id.* at 1706–708. See also ABA, State Definitions of the Practice of Law, available at www.americanbar.org/groups/professional_responsibility/task_force_model_definition_practice_law.html (compilation of state definitions of practice of law).

84 Hadfield, Legal Barriers to Innovation, supra note 82, at 1693, quoting ABA Task Force on the Model Definition of the Practice of Law, Report to the House of Delegates (Aug. 11, 2003), available at www.abanet.org/cpr/model-def/recomm.pdf.

public by organizations (such as consumer associations) or corporations.[85] These restrictions prohibit lawyers from contracting with document or question-and-answer web platforms or other service delivery mechanisms, such as retail stores or banks, for the provision of legal help.[86]

Canada, Australia, and France also have relatively restrictive systems. Like the United States, these countries prohibit anyone other than a bar-licensed lawyer from providing legal services, which include giving advice, drafting contracts, or assisting with the completion of documents. Anyone with a legal problem in these three countries is limited to the choice of finding and then paying for a private attorney, although Australia was the first jurisdiction in the world to permit non-lawyers to own legal practices.[87]

The legal systems in many other countries are much more open, providing a broader range of sources for legal assistance. Finland, which has been characterized as the most open legal system,[88] does not restrict who can provide legal advice or represent others in court.[89] Sweden maintains a comparably open system.[90] Slightly more restrictive, but still quite open legal systems include the United Kingdom and the Netherlands, both of which reserve little other than representation in courts to licensed lawyers; there are no restrictions on who may provide legal advice. The United Kingdom permits non-lawyers to provide legal advice and licenses a variety of competing professional groups (including barristers, solicitors, legal executives, and licensed conveyancers) to perform most legal tasks. The Netherlands also has multiple legal providers, including non-lawyer legal professionals, legal insurers who provide legal assistance through staff lawyers or paralegals, social workers who have additional training in legal matters and are employed by larger cities and towns to provide advice to constituents, government networks of legal advisors operating as a legal "help desk" through offices, websites, chat systems, telephone and email advice, providing legal information, referrals to lawyers and up to 30 minutes of individualized advice; and student-staffed legal clinics operated independently of law schools but supervised by lawyers. The United Kingdom also permits legal services to be provided through non-lawyer-owned

85 There are some narrow exceptions: lawyers working for non-profit organizations can assist people with immigration matters pro bono; unions and political associations such as the NAACP are protected by the First Amendment, and may provide staff attorneys to assist their members; in some states (e.g., Texas), insurers may use staff attorneys to defend an insured under a policy that promises to pay legal costs of defense when there is no conflict of interest with the insurer. For a discussion, see Gillian K. Hadfield, *The Cost of Law: Promoting Access to Justice through the (Un)Corporate Practice of Law*, 38 Int'l Rev. of Law and Econ. 43 (2014).

86 See id.

87 See Christine Parker, Tahlia Gordon & Steve Mark, *Regulating Law Firm Ethics Management: An Empirical Assessment of an Innovation in Regulation of the Profession in New South Wales*, 37 J. of L. & Soc'y 466 (2010).

88 SEO Economic Research, Regulation of the Legal Profession and Access to Law, at 61, t.3.8.

89 Frank H. Stephen, *The European Single Market and the Regulation of the Legal Profession: An Economic Analysis*, 23 Managerial Decis Econ 115, 116 (2002).

90 Id.

organizations, including both for-profit and non-profit corporate entities,[91] and does not place restrictions on what in the United States is called fee-sharing. One consequence of the more open regulatory regime is that there are increasingly robust online services available to provide one-on-one legal advice or assistance with legal matters such as filing for divorce or seeking a change in spousal or child support orders.[92] In Germany, lawyers do not have a monopoly on legal representation; numerous persons and entities can represent clients in civil cases.[93] In Hungary, lawyers do not have a monopoly on legal representation, even before a county court in civil matters, but only lawyers may represent clients in civil cases before appeals courts and the Supreme Court.[94] In Poland, lawyers only have a monopoly on representation of criminal defendants; in civil cases, family members, joint participants, associations, or trade unions may represent clients in court.[95]

There are also differences in the types of financial assistance available to ordinary individuals seeking legal services. Most countries have some form of legal aid, usually with income cutoffs to determine eligibility. Some countries provide loans or insurance for legal expenses. For instance, Germany provides loans to low-income individuals for legal aid services. While the loans are required to be repaid if the borrower is financially able to do so, in practice loans are repaid only 15% of the time.[96] Sweden's legal system offers legal expense insurance instead of legal aid and 97% of residents have add-on legal expense insurance. Seventy-five percent of Finns have a legal expense insurance policy;[97] Finland provides legal aid in addition. 40% of Dutch households have legal insurance, at a cost of approximately $250, which provides access to staff lawyers or paralegals (although often excludes family and criminal matters.)

This comparison adds to our understanding of the legal needs surveys discussed in the previous section. In reporting the data on contact with legal providers in Table 2.4, we distinguished between lawyers and others authorized to provide legal assistance. In the United States, there really are no other entities besides lawyers authorized to provide legal assistance; this category in the 1993 ABA study

[91] Cooperative Legal Services, operated as part of the Cooperative Group, a consumer cooperative, for example, began operation in 2006. It was one of the first three entities licensed to provide legal services as what the UK regulatory scheme calls an alternative business structure (an organization or corporation other than a traditional law firm partnership) in 2012. Prior to that licensing, it could not provide access to solicitors, but it could provide assistance with legal advice, completion of documents and do-it-yourself support for legal actions.

[92] See Hadfield, *The Cost of Law*, supra note 85; and Gillian K. Hadfield, *Innovating to Improve Access: Changing the Way Courts Regulate Legal Markets*, 143 DAEDALUS 83 (2014).

[93] European Commission for the Efficiency of Justice, Scheme for Evaluating Judicial Systems 2011, Germany, 75–76.

[94] Id., Hungary, 72–73.

[95] Id., Poland, 36.

[96] SEO Economic Research, Regulation of the Legal Profession and Access to Law, at 45.

[97] Id. at 45–46.

largely refers to contact with courts. But in countries with much less restrictive systems such as the Netherlands and the United Kingdom, any formal advisor is potentially a source of legal advice; we noted in Table 2.4 that there really is no category of formal advisors who are not authorized to provide legal help.[98] These non-lawyer sources of legal assistance play a substantial role in raising the rates at which citizens in these countries enjoy some legal help in dealing with legal problems above those we see in the United States despite the fact that rates of assistance from a lawyer do not appear to differ.

The apparently greater access to diverse sources of legal help in the United Kingdom and the Netherlands may also provide insight into the rates at which people lump their problems rather than try to deal with them. Table 2.4 indicates that the lowest rates of "no action" are found in the Netherlands and the countries of the United Kingdom. In these countries, people with legal problems are not faced with the stark choice between locating an affordable lawyer, doing nothing, or going it alone. They can also turn to the volunteer-staffed Community Advice Bureau, government networks of legal help desks, online services, insurers, banks, grocery stores, unions, consumer organizations, and more. It seems quite possible that this range of options makes a strategy for action both more visible and more accessible, woven more securely into everyday settings and forms of interaction.

Also on this line of reasoning, what is currently reported as self-help – acting on one's own or with help only from friends and family and not a formal advisor – may also be indicative of a more generous legal resource landscape. The high rate of self-help in the 2010 England and Wales survey is particularly intriguing here. On the one hand, it may indicate a failure of the legal environment relative to 1997 – and certainly access to legal aid during this period has been significantly cut back.[99] It may, as the researchers suggest, reflect only the fact that the 2010 survey asked about all problems, not only those that were difficult to solve – potentially sweeping in a larger number of problems that were in fact amenable to self-help (although this seems inadequate to explain the 25-point increase in self-help). But the increase in self-help may also reflect the changing landscape in the United Kingdom, with more resources available for self-helpers. Many of these services may not have been reported as consultation with an advisor; and the survey design does not appear to solicit information about whether people used, for example, an online or retail service for help answering questions about legal rights and procedures, filing for a "d-i-y" ("do-it-yourself") divorce, preparing a will, or navigating probate.

The question we want to raise then is this: are the apparently higher rates at which we see Americans lumping their problems in the ABA and state surveys a consequence of the more restrictive scope of legal help available to them? Or are they just evidence that although Americans may be facing on average two or

98 This does not mean that all contacts with formal advisors resulted in legal assistance.

99 See Roger Smith, After the Act: What Future for Legal Aid?, Justice Tom Sargant Memorial Annual Lecture 2012 (Oct. 16, 2012).

more justiciable problems in a year, they simply choose not to do anything about them, despite having reasonable options to respond?

We need to be cautious here because simple differences in rates alone are not enough to support an inference of something more fundamentally different in these legal settings given the differences in the survey and reporting methods. The surveys from England, Wales, and Scotland, which report the lowest rates of "no action," exclude from the denominator cases in which the respondent says he or she took no action because the problem wasn't important enough. The researchers take care to document in those reports,[100] the impact of what they call the "triviality threshold" is very small.[101] Nonetheless, given the absence of careful cross-national studies, it is impossible to say whether or not there is a causal relationship between the legal resource landscape and the rates at which people take no action on their problems or deal with them on their own is correct. Clearly, the data suggest that the rate at which Americans lump their problems cannot easily be written off to triviality or choice. Instead the data should be interpreted as a potentially important indicator of the paucity of options available for resolving legal issues.

CONCLUSION

American society is often seen as emblematic of the rule of law, and its adversarial legalism makes it a particularly dense legal environment. But the evidence presented above about Americans' experiences with the legal system and the availability of legal resources paints a different picture than that envisioned by a highly law-based society. The evidence is suggestive only. The data that we have reviewed do not control for the nature of legal problems, the opportunity for problems to be resolved in less litigious ways, and the resources necessary to achieve that goal. The thinness of the available data simply do not allow for such careful comparison, although they clearly suggest the need for such a study to be conducted.

The results, as rough and ready as they are, nonetheless do present a serious challenge to the American legal profession, which has, for the last 100 years, claimed exclusive authority to regulate the entire legal system in the United States.[102] The profession's assertion of regulatory authority has arguably blocked the capacity for federal or state regulatory or policy responses to the crises in U.S. legal systems.

[100] Genn, *Paths to Justice*, supra note 67, at 37; Hazel Genn & Alan Patersm, *Paths to Justice* Scotland 50 (2001).

[101] Notably, the survey methodology in England & Wales was changed with the 2010 survey, eliminating the triviality threshold. Moreover, the survey questions in 2010 only asked about "problems" and not, as in the original Genn approach used in 1997, problems that were "difficult to solve." Here we do see an increase in the no action rate in England & Wales – from 5% to 10% – between 1997 and 2010, but not a major leap upwards.

[102] See Thomas M. Alpert, *The Inherent Power of the Courts to Regulate the Practice of Law: An Historical Analysis*, 32 BUFF. L. REV. 525 (1983); Hadfield, supra note 82; Hadfield, *The Cost of Law*, supra note 85.

What accounts for the significantly lower level of legal resources – public expenditure, legal aid, judges, and (for Germany and the United Kingdom) lawyers – available at the macro level in the United States as compared to other advanced market democracies? For the more than 50% decline over the past fifteen years in the total effective number of hours of legal services per household per problem? For the more than 50% drop in the use of lawyers' services by the poor in addressing their problems in the decade since the 1993 ABA study? The lack of systematic data makes causal analysis difficult and speculative. Clearly we need substantially more attention to detailed study of the nature of legal systems and how they shape and meet the demand for legal services. In this concluding section we offer some preliminary thoughts on how those studies should be framed.

The access problems in the U.S. legal system are largely conceptualized by the profession as problems of the ethical commitments of individual lawyers to assist the poor and the failure of federal and state bodies to provide adequate levels of funding to legal aid agencies and the courts. The first conceptualization fails, we believe, to come to grips with the dimensions of the problem, which cannot be solved with an increase in pro bono efforts, as welcome as such an increase would be. Pro bono currently accounts for less than 2% of legal effort in the country. Even if every lawyer in the country did 100 more hours a year of pro bono work, this would amount to an extra twenty-five minutes per U.S. person a year, or about thirty minutes per dispute-related (potentially litigation-related) problem per household using the average number of legal problems reported in the state legal needs surveys.[103] This does not even begin to address the realistic demands that ordinary households have for ex ante assistance with navigating the law-thick world in which they live, some of which could reduce the need for ex post legal representation in litigation and crisis.

The problem is not a problem of the ethical commitment of lawyers to help the poor. Nor is an increase in public legal aid likely to make a substantial impact. The cost of just one extra hour of legal aid on each dispute-related problem per household would be on the order of $64 billion annually at a market rate of $263 per hour.[104] Even if we thought we could find enough lawyers willing to supply that help at $150 an hour, this level of assistance would entail a more than ten-fold increase in current U.S. levels of public and private (charitable) legal aid funding. Again, more legal aid funding would be welcome and is clearly called for, but it cannot make a serious dent in the nature of the problem.

So what is the problem? The bits of data we can see in the comparative analyses are suggestive of an important role for the regulatory and policymaking structure

[103] We are using here an estimate that there are approximately 1.3 million licensed lawyers in the United States (ABA, *Lawyer Demographics* (2012)). See note 104 for estimates of households and problems.

[104] Average calculated from Altman Weil data for lawyers working in solo or small firm (fewer than 24 lawyers) practice in 2012. See supra note 19. We are using here an estimate that there are approximately 121 million households in the United States and taking the average number of problems per household (2) reported in the state legal needs surveys.

governing legal markets in the United States. The United States stands largely alone in the world in terms of the extraordinary extent to which the bar and judiciary wield exclusive authority for shaping the cost and market structure of legal goods and services. Some of this difference can be seen to come from the structure of the courts and legal profession as elements of the civil service bureaucracy in countries such as Germany and France. This way of structuring courts and delivering legal services locates policy and funding decisions squarely within a government agency. In addition, civil law systems emphasize a much broader role for the judge, as opposed to parties and their lawyers, in the conduct of litigation. This arguably accounts for the substantially higher allocation of resources to the court systems in Germany, with many more judges per case. But the United Kingdom is a powerful counterexample to the hypothesis that we are seeing a difference between common law and civil code systems. The United Kingdom clearly devotes substantially more resources to the provision of legal services to ordinary citizens, measured in terms of public expenditure, legal aid, or judges per "case," even though the United Kingdom follows the common law practice of much greater reliance on the adversarial resources of parties to structure litigation. What explains this?

The importance of investigating with careful empirical studies the hypothesis that the regulatory system accounts for the failure of the U.S. legal system to provide an adequate level of legal inputs for ordinary people becomes even more apparent when the data from the Netherlands, which has a comparably open system allowing many non-lawyer service providers, is viewed alongside that of the United Kingdom. The striking difference in the rate at which people do nothing in response to legal difficulties between the United States (29% or higher[105]) and the United Kingdom (10%) and the Netherlands (6%) is highly suggestive of the role that a robust system of legal inputs plays in making a legal system a real, rather than apparent, basis on which everyday lives are structured. A careful study of how different regulatory regimes influence not only the use of legal resources in resolving problems once they have erupted but also the use of these resources ex ante to decide what transactions and relationships to enter into, leave, modify, and so on is clearly called for by these results.

Those concerned with access to justice have long emphasized how the extreme approach to unauthorized practice of law in the United States drastically curtails the potential for ordinary folks to obtain assistance with their law-related needs and problems. Key contributions have been made in this regard by Deborah Rhode,[106]

[105] Twenty-nine percent is the figure from the ABA study; the state legal needs surveys report rates ranging from 21% to 53%.

[106] Deborah L. Rhode's *Policing the Professional Monopoly: A Constitutional and Empirical Analysis of Unauthorized Practice Prohibitions*, 34 STAN. L. REV. 1 (1981); *Professionalism in Perspective: Alternative Approaches to Non-Lawyer Practice*, 1 J. INST. FOR STUDY LEGAL ETHICS 197 (1996); *In the Interests of Justice: Reforming the Legal Profession* (2003); Rhode, *Access to Justice* (2004).

David Luban,[107] and Barlow Christensen.[108] American lawyers often take for granted that it is natural that anyone who wishes to practice law must be an authorized member of a bar association and subject to the admissions, ethical, and disciplinary controls of the profession, including the judiciary. The regulatory problem, however, goes beyond a straightforward restriction on supply. The more fundamental problem with the existing regulatory structure is traceable to the fact that the American legal profession is a politically unaccountable regulator, which lacks the funding levers and policymaking apparatus needed for a sector that is a huge share of the American economy and one that plays an increasingly important role in a rapidly changing and decentralized economic system.

The problem is one of urgent need for structural reform in the regulatory and policy/funding system responsible for the critical infrastructure of market democracy, particularly one that draws as heavily as the American system does on law and legalism to structure economic, political, and social relationships. We hope this chapter helps paint a clearer picture of the legal needs of and legal resources available to ordinary people. With a better grasp on the dimensions of the problem, we hope it can be more readily tackled.

[107] David Luban, *Lawyers and Justice: An Ethical Study* (1988).

[108] Barlow F. Christensen, *The Unauthorized Practice of Law: Do Good Fences Really Make Good Neighbors – or Even Good Sense?*, 1980 AM. B. FOUND. RES. J. 159 (1980); See Levine, Chapter 41 in this volume.

3

The Need for a National Civil Justice Survey of Incidence and Claiming Behavior

Theodore Eisenberg

This chapter by the late distinguished Cornell Law professor proposes the development of a national civil justice survey to improve our base of knowledge of civil justice needs. Using a large data sample from households across the country, this survey would estimate the incidence of civil legal problems that people face, and document how they address them, if they do at all. It would gather demographic data about the respondents including where they live and their age, gender, race, and income level. The survey data would offer a comprehensive tool for understanding what civil legal needs exist and how they might be addressed.

Civil justice issues play a prominent role in society. Family law issues such as divorce[1] and child custody, consumer victimization issues raised by questionable trade practices,[2] and tort issues raised by surprisingly high estimated rates of medical malpractice,[3] questionable prescription drug practices,[4] and other behaviors are part

1 See, e.g., Betzaida Tejada-Vera & Paul D. Sutton, Nat'l Ctr. for Health Statistics, Ctrs. for Disease Control & Prevention, Births, Marriages, Divorces, and Deaths: Provisional Data for 2007 (2008) (hereinafter Nat'l Ctr. for Health Statistics), available at www.cdc.gov/nchs/data/nvsr/nvsr56/nvsr56_21.pdf. This article was originally published as Theodore Eisenberg, *The Need for a National Civil Justice Survey of Incidence and Claiming Behavior*, 37 Fordham Urb. L. J. 17 (2010). Reproduced with the permission of the journal and Theodore Eisenberg.

2 See, e.g., Fed. Trade Comm'n, Consumer Fraud and Identity Theft Complaint Data: January-December 2007 (2008), available at www.ftc.gov/opa/2008/02/fraud.pdf.

3 See, e.g., Chunliu Zhan & Marlene R. Miller, *Excess Length of Stay, Charges, and Mortality Attributable to Medical Injuries During Hospitalization*, 290 JAMA 1868 (2003).

4 See, e.g., Gregory D. Curfman et al., Expression of Concern: Bombardier et al., "Comparison of Upper Gastrointestinal Toxicity of Rofecoxib and Naproxen in Patients with Rheumatoid Arthritis," N Engl J Med 2000; 343:1520–528, 353 New. Engl. J. Med. 2813, 2813 (2005) ("It now appears . . . from a memorandum dated July 5, 2000, that was obtained by subpoena in the Vioxx litigation and made available to the New England Journal of Medicine, that at least two of the authors knew about the three additional myocardial infarctions at least two weeks before the authors submitted the first of two revisions and 42 months before publication of the article"); see also Theodore Eisenberg & Martin T. Wells, *Statins and Adverse Cardiovascular Events in Moderate Risk Females: A Statistical and Legal Analysis with Implications for FDA Preemption Claims*, 5 J. Empirical Legal Stud. 507 (2008) (questioning the marketing of the world's best-selling prescription drug); Editorial, Cholesterol Drug Bombs, N.Y. Times, Jan. 16, 2008, at A22 ("[I]t was . . . very disturbing to learn this week that a heavily promoted cholesterol-lowering drug had flunked a clinical trial of its effectiveness in reducing fatty deposits in arteries. The two companies that reap billions from the drug had been cynically sitting on the results for more than a year").

of the fabric of daily life. Policymakers and interest groups regularly debate and assess whether civil problems are best resolved by legislative action, agency action, litigation, alternative dispute resolution, other methods, or some combination of actions. Yet we lack systematic quantitative knowledge about the primary events in daily life that generate civil justice issues. This chapter explores the desirability of, and issues related to, creating what I refer to as a national civil justice survey (NCJS), analogous to the National Crime Victimization Survey (NCVS).

The NCVS is the primary source of information on criminal victimization.[5] The survey enables the Bureau of Justice Statistics (BJS) to estimate the likelihood of many crimes "for the population as a whole as well as for segments of the population such as women, the elderly, members of various racial groups, city dwellers, or other groups."[6] In 2005, U.S. residents age twelve or older experienced about twenty violent crimes per 1,000 people and about 150 property crimes per 1,000 people.[7] In comparison, decades-old national research on incidence of civil problems suggests that adults experience a long-term risk of serious personal injury at the rate of 120 per 1,000 and a risk of serious property damage of 400 per 1,000.[8] A more geographically limited early 1980s survey found that a three-year risk of having a civil justice grievance was 416 per 1,000.[9] The rate of civil justice incidents plainly is high enough to warrant systematic quantitative knowledge of their patterns.

SELECTED AVAILABLE CIVIL JUSTICE DATA AND THEIR LIMITATIONS

Important and useful civil justice data exist. BJS projects as well as those of other federal agencies supply much of that information. BJS data tend to focus on the end point of the civil disputing process – litigation – and not on the underlying pattern of grievances and claiming behavior that generate observable disputes.[10] Other data

5 Bureau of Justice Statistics (BJS), U.S. Dep't of Justice Criminal Victimization Data Collections, available at www.ojp.gov/bjs/cvict.htm#Programs.

6 *Id.*

7 Shannan M. Catalano, BJS National Crime Victimization Survey: Criminal Victimization, 2005 1 (2006) (hereinafter NCVS 2005), available at http://bjs.ojp.usdoj.gov/index.cfm?ty=pbdetail&iid=766 (follow "PDF" hyperlink).

8 See Barbara A. Curran, The Legal Needs of the Public: The Final Report of a National Survey 104 (1977).

9 See Richard E. Miller & Austin Sarat, *Grievances, Claims, and Disputes: Assessing Adversary Culture*, 15 LAW & SOC'Y REV. 525, 537 (1980–1981).

10 See Thomas H. Cohen & Steven K. Smith, BJS, Civil Trial Cases and Verdicts in Large Counties, 2001 (2004) (hereinafter BJS 2001), available at http://bjs.ojp.usdoj.gov/index.cfm?Fty=pbdetail&iid=559; Carol J. DeFrances & Marika F.X. Litras, BJS, Civil Trial Cases and Verdicts in Large Counties, 1996 (1999), available at http://bjs.ojp.usdoj.gov/index.cfm?ty=pbdetail&iid=560; Lynn Langton & Thomas H. Cohen, BJS, Civil Bench and Jury Trials in State Courts, 2005 (2008) (hereinafter BJS 2005), available at http://bjs.ojp.usdoj.gov/index.cfm?ty=pbdetail&iid=554; Steven K. Smith et al., BJS, Tort Cases in Large Counties (1995), available at http://bjs.ojp.usdoj.gov/index.cfm?ty=pbdetail&iid=864.

sets, for topics like divorce rates and patient safety data,[11] might already provide adequate information about particular topics.[12] In general, however, sources of civil justice data about other topics are sporadic and depend on reporting by intermediaries rather than by those experiencing the problems. Similar to data collection methods used for crime victimization, a household-level survey could provide the most reliable information to assess the true extent of civil-justice-related activity. For purposes of this chapter, I try to include a reasonably comprehensive list of civil justice topics that might be included in an NCJS. If it is determined that satisfactory information is already systematically gathered about one or more of the topics, the necessary scope of a national civil survey would be reduced accordingly. In order to illustrate the utility of an NCJS, I first focus on how it might enhance the utility of existing BJS data in relation to civil justice.

Reading Civil Justice Data Contain Surprises

Existing BJS civil justice initiatives have already established their value by providing significant insights into civil justice system performance. The BJS and the National Center for State Courts (NCSC) make available online and through print reports the best existing information about state courts, including trial outcomes and filings.[13] For example the BJS Report, Civil Trial Cases, and Verdicts in Large Counties, reports time trends from 1992 to 2001, in the number of civil trial cases and the amount of jury awards.[14] These data shed light on the operation of our civil justice system, in which the vast majority of cases and trials are adjudicated in state court.

Some core BJS-NCSC results are truly striking. In 1992, state courts in the nation's seventy-five largest counties are estimated to have concluded 22,451 trials. By 2001, state courts in these counties concluded only 11,908 trials, a reduction of 47.0%.[15]

[11] See Agency for Healthcare Research and Quality, U.S. Dep't of Health and Human Servs., National Healthcare Quality Report 101 (2008), available at www.ahrq.gov/qual/nhqr08/nhqr08.pdf; Nat'l Ctr. for Health Statistics, supra note 1.

[12] The National Health Interview Survey (NHIS) provides information about injuries. See Nat'l Ctr. for Health Statistics, Ctr. for Disease Control & Prevention, About the National Health Interview Survey (NHIS), available at www.cdc.gov/nchs/nhis/about_nhis.htm. The most inclusive category of external injury cause codes in the NHIS is code E9288 or E9289 ("other" or "unspecified" accident). See Wis. Dep't of Health Servs., Injury E-Codes, available at http://dhs.wisconsin.gov/wish/main/shared/4CodeInjuryHosp.htm. These constitute about 520,000 out of 3.6 million NHIS "other" accidents in the 2005, NHIS. Nat'l Ctr. for Health Statistics, U.S. Dep't of Health and Human Servs., ICPSR04606-v1, HHIS, 2005, available at www.icpsr.umich.edu/icpsrweb/ICPSR/studies/4606/sda. But these data do not readily allow one to assess if a civil grievance would be warranted.

[13] See Nat'l Ctr. For State Courts, Court Statistics Project, available at www.nscsonline.org/D_Research/csp/CSP_Main_Page.html (last visited Nov. 10, 2009); Bureau of Justice Statistics, Publications, available at www.ojp.usdoj.gov/bjs/pubalp2.htm (last visited Nov. 10, 2009).

[14] BJS 2001, supra note 10, at 8–9.

[15] *Id.* at 9 tbl.10.

By 2005, the estimated number had fallen to 10,813, a decline from 1992 of 51.8%.[16] The sharpest decreases came in product liability and real property cases, with reductions of 76.0% and 80.1%, respectively, from 1992 to 2001.[17] But by 2005, product liability trials had increased by 42.2% and real property trials had increased by 14.8% since 2001.[18] The BJS-NCSC data, through a methodology consistently applied over the course of fourteen years, thus conclusively established the reduction in trials in state courts. The vanishing trial and its implications for the justice system has been the topic of extended discussion.[19] With respect to amounts awarded at trial, the results are equally interesting. In 1992, the median jury award in all tort cases, adjusted for inflation to 2005 dollars, was $71,000.[20] In 2001, the median award was only $31,000, a statistically significant decline, followed by a 6.5% increase in 2005 to $33,000.[21] During that same period, awards were down in automobile cases, and up in product liability and medical malpractice cases.[22]

NCSC data on time trends in case filings, though limited to the subset of states that report information on a consistent basis, are noteworthy as well. For example, Figure 3.1 shows a long-term decline in tort filings, accompanied by a more modest decline in medical malpractice filings and little pattern in product liability filings.[23]

Limitations of Existing Civil Justice Data and the Benefits of a National Civil Justice Survey

So we have, as exemplified by tort statistics, a downward trend in filings, a downward trend in the number of trials, and a long-term downward trend in median awards. As telling as these data are, we cannot fully know what to make of them because we lack information about the possible number of grievances and disputes underlying them.

To show why, let's continue to pursue torts as an example. It is one thing if NCSC's declining tort filings are observed in light of a background of a stable rate of tort incidents over time. It is quite another if declining tort filings are observed and the rate of tort incidents per capita either has

[16] BJS 2005, supra note 10, at 9 tbl.10.

[17] BJS 2001, supra note 10, at 9 tbl.10.

[18] BJS 2005, supra note 10, at 9 tbl.10.

[19] See, e.g., Marc Galanter, *The Vanishing Trial: An Examination of Trials and Related Matters in Federal and State Courts*, 1 J. Empirical Legal Stud. 459, 459 (2004).

[20] BJS 2005, supra note 10, at 10 tbl.11.

[21] *Id.*; BJS 2001, supra note 10, at 9 tbl.11.

[22] BJS 2005, supra note 10, at 10 tbl.11.

[23] Empirical Nat'l Ctr. for State Courts, Examining the Work of State Courts, 2006: A National Perspective from the Court Statistics Project, available at www.ncsconline.org/D_Research/csp/2006_files/ewsc-2007wholedocument.pdf.

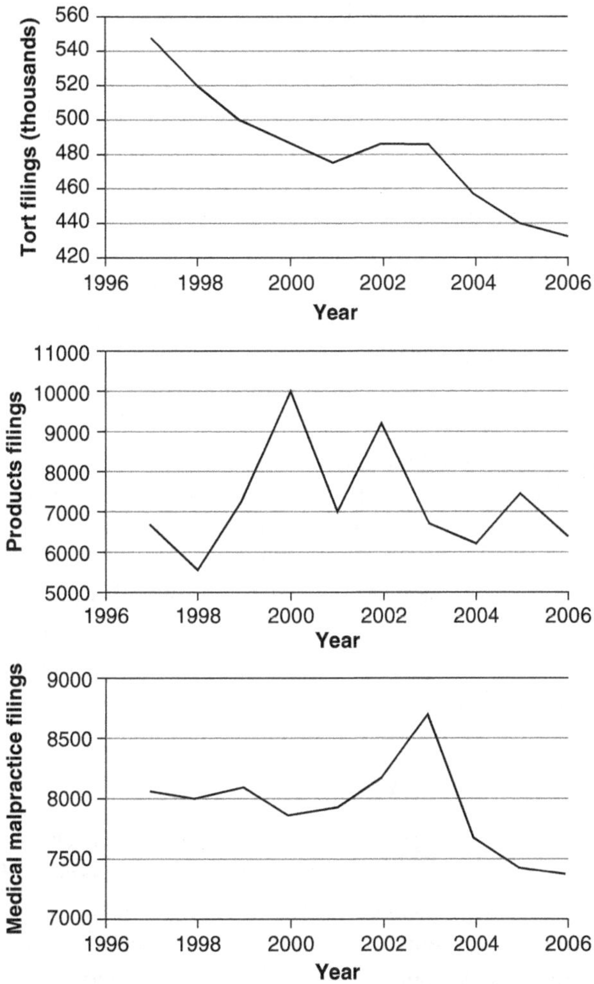

FIGURE 3.1. State court tort, products, medical filings, 1997–2006.

substantially increased or decreased. Unless we know about the number of underlying tort incidents, interpreting filings data are subject to unavoidable limitations.

Policy-makers cannot tell if legislative or other initiatives have had an effect in the expected direction or in an unintended one. It may be that tort reforms that reduce liability exposure increase the number of tort incidents. This would need to be balanced against the presumed litigation savings in order to fully understand outcome patterns. This uncertainty is, of course, equally true of other civil justice subject areas, including consumer problems such as credit card and mortgage disputes.

Gathering systematic data about the rate of underlying tort and other civil justice incidents over time has other important benefits, though not directly related to case filing and outcome patterns. Estimations of the rate of tort incidents, and the rate at which incidents are satisfactorily resolved, would yield important knowledge about the need for access to civil justice. Specifically, are civil legal services available to those who need them? Are they differentially available based on income, race, gender, or other factors? And how much access to civil justice is in fact needed? An NCJS could provide information beyond that used to note the difficulties in supplying legal services at reasonable costs. By regularly gathering information about types of injuries due to products or medical procedures we could have information relevant to important social issues such as whether rates of possibly tortious behavior change over time. This would help assess the impact of changes in state and federal law on underlying activity.

Thus, helping to understand the systematic civil justice data we do have, identifying the civil justice needs of citizens, and helping to assess the effects of changes in statutory and decisional law, are among the benefits that a systematic time series of data, based on valid national samples, could help supply. My proposal is that BJS, in cooperation with other agencies if necessary, formulate and implement an NCJS analogous to its current National Crime Victims Survey. Such an undertaking would be substantial and the rest of this chapter focuses on some of the issues that arise in developing such a survey.

WHAT TO TRACK?

Since the contemplated NCJS cannot be based on objectively observable court activity like filings or trials, the proposed survey generates questions of methodology about what a civil justice incident or need is. Designing a survey assessing civil-justice needs requires identifying events or occurrences that are considered to be needs. Such events and occurrences may not always be self-evident, even to respondents.

The Nature of the Activities Generating Civil Justice Needs

Fortunately, thoughtful work exists and can be built on by BJS in designing an NCJS. The earliest major modern study, regarded as a touchstone in the field of the incidence of civil justice problems, is the ABA/ABF project published in Barbara A. Curran's 1977 book, *The Legal Needs of the Public: The Final Report of a National Survey*.[24] One part of the survey used in Curran's study consisted of inquiring into "actual problem situations with which respondents might have been confronted at one or more times in their lives."[25] The other part of the Curran survey that is directly relevant for present

[24] Curran, supra note 8, at 103–104.
[25] *Id.* at 20.

purposes elicited information about the use of lawyers for the delivery of legal services.[26] This included information about what the lawyer did on behalf of the respondent, including appearing in court or at some other hearing.[27]

Richard Miller and Austin Sarat, writing in 1980 as part of the Wisconsin Civil Litigation Research Project (CLRP), provided a helpful and more formal discussion of the events that might lead to legal action.[28] The litigated dispute that ends up in court must be the result of an underlying grievance. Citing others, Miller and Sarat describe a grievance as "an individual's belief that he or she is … entitled to a resource which someone else may grant or deny …"[29] A grievance thus begins a litigated dispute, but not all grievances lead to litigated disputes. The aggrieved party might not even communicate his or her belief about entitlement to the "someone else"; that is, no claim in or out of court is made. That would end the matter at the grievance stage. The aggrieved party might communicate the belief to the "someone else"; that is, a claim is made, at least out of court. The response in some cases will be satisfactory. That would end the matter at what might be called the claim stage. A claim may be made and no satisfactory response received. One would then have something worthy of the name "dispute." At the end of this stylized process, one might observe a formal civil dispute. Miller and Sarat provide a useful chart (Table 3.1) to summarize this grievance to formal dispute process.[30]

If the aggrieved party decides to pursue the matter, a lawyer or other appropriate third party might be consulted. So an NCJS may want to ask not only about the grievance–claim–dispute–civil legal dispute stages. It may also want to ask what steps were taken to consult lawyers or others at each stage. Many lawsuits are filed without counsel, but one does not know which of the filed lawsuits were considered by counsel. Similar questions were included in the Curran study.[31]

The Subject Areas of Civil Justice Activities

In addition to tracking the activities beginning with a possible grievance that may lead to a civil dispute, a civil justice survey needs to disaggregate grievances by specific subject areas. The aggregated category "civil justice" problem is too general to provide the kind of information needed. Almost all legal phenomena vary by the

[26] *Id.* at 26–27.
[27] *Id.* at 349 (Question 16).
[28] Miller & Sarat, supra note 9, at 534.
[29] *Id.* at 527 (citing Jack Ladinsky & Charles Susmilch, Conceptual and Operational Issues in Measuring Consumer Disputing Behavior (Univ. of Wis. Law Sch. Disputes Processing Research Program, Working Paper No. 1981–3, 1981)).
[30] *Id.* at 528.
[31] Curran, supra note 8, at 341–53.

TABLE 3.1 *Definitions of disputing stages.*

	Belief that one is entitled to a resource controlled by another party	Voicing that belief to the other party	Rejection of claim	"Litigable" claims
Grievance	X			
Claim	X	X		
Dispute	X	X	X	
Civil legal dispute	X	X	X	X

subject matter of case categories[32] and so data on refined subsets of the civil justice supercategory are needed.

Different studies have taken different approaches to subdividing the possible range of civil justice areas. Table 3.2 reports the subject areas defined by Curran's 1977 study (I exclude crimes from the list as beyond the scope of a civil justice survey).[33]

Miller and Sarat provided a different but overlapping taxonomy of civil problem types. They provided a bit more detail about the makeup of their major categories. Table 3.3 reports their categorization of civil grievances.[34]

Important limitations attend using a fixed list to identify incident legal problems.[35] These include the survey instrument signaling to the respondent that a problem is a legal one without the respondent having regarded it as such. A predefined list also risks limiting responses to problems previously defined as being legal. The actual legal needs may be new ones, not previously known, such as systematic identity theft. A list also risks under-reporting problems that are not on the list. The lengthier the list, the more likely a respondent might not think he or she has a legal problem unless it appears on the list. And the survey methodology, of course, risks the reluctance of respondents unwilling to provide information to strangers about important personal matters that they may regard as private. Some steps may be taken to ameliorate these concerns,[36] but some are inherent in the contemplated venture.

32 See, e.g., Theodore Eisenberg et al., *Juries, Judges, and Punitive Damages: Empirical Analyses Using the Civil Justice Survey of State Courts* 1992, 1996, *and* 2001 *Data*, 3 J. EMPIRICAL LEGAL STUD. 263, 279 fig.5 (2006) (showing substantially different rates of punitive damages awards in motor vehicle cases and cases with and without bodily injury).

33 Curran, supra note 8, at 21.

34 Miller & Sarat, supra note 9, app. 1 at 566.

35 See *id.* at 534 n.5.

36 See *id.*

TABLE 3.2 *Curran ABF/ABA subject areas of civil subject matter areas.*

Ownership of real property
Rental of real property
Purchase of real property
Purchase of personal property
Credit transactions
Jobs and wages
Violation of civil or constitutional rights
Marital matters
Problems involving state, local, or federal governmental agencies
Torts
Problems involving children
Wills and estate planning
Estates

Information to be Gathered about Civil Justice Incidents and Related Matters

For each purported civil justice grievance, one must decide how much information to gather as part of an NCJS. One must of course gather information about the actual civil justice grievances themselves, but additional information is clearly desirable. For example, both the ABA/ABF study and the CLRP study included information about respondent demographics.[37] The pursuit and processing of the purported grievance is also important. Was a claim made with or without a lawyer? Was counsel consulted? Was a legal action or other formal proceeding commenced? What was the resolution of the grievance? This information allows assessing the rate at which respondents seek redress of grievances and the role of counsel and the courts. Both the ABA/ABF and CLRP studies included such information,[38] though the ABA/ABF study focused less on courts and more on the nature of lawyer use.[39]

Another major civil justice study focused exclusively on accidental injuries and gathered more detail about those injuries than the ABA/ABF or CLRP studies. Deborah Hensler et al., in a RAND Institute for Civil Justice project, interviewed about 26,000 households by telephone about all sources of compensation for injuries, and followed up with about 2,800 telephone interviews limited to liability-claiming behavior.[40] The scale of the project was limited to one form of claiming behavior. RAND stated, "[We] did not have the resources to explore how Americans view and

[37] See Curran, supra note 8, at 23, 122–30 (reporting incidence of legal problems by sex, race, education, income, and age); Miller & Sarat, supra note 9, at 552 (reporting associations between claim rates and income, race, sex, age, and education).

[38] See Curran, supra note 8, at 134–62 (describing use of lawyer services); Miller & Sarat, supra note 9, at 551–54 (describing claim rates per grievance, success rates, and more).

[39] See Curran, supra note 8, at 134–62.

[40] See Deborah H. Hensler et al., Compensation for Accidental Injuries in the United States 3 (1991).

TABLE 3.3 *Miller/Sarat aggregation of specific grievances into problem types.*

1. Tort	Auto accident; work injury; other injury to or damage to property of a household member.
2. Consumer	Problem with a major purchase, medical services or other services; problem with home builder,* or a home repair or improvement contractor.*
3. Debt	Problem collecting money from an employer, debtor or insurance company; disagreement with a creditor or other problems paying debts; problems with a mortgage.*
4. Discrimination	Employment problems (denied a job or promotion, lost a job, problems with working conditions, harassment, or being paid less because of discrimination); problems in schooling or education; buying or renting housing; or any other problems because of discrimination.
5. Property	Problems over what was permissible to build;* boundary lines;* someone else using the property;* or other problems with ownership or use,* excluding problems with business or rental property.
6. Government	Problems collecting social security, veterans, or welfare benefits or tax refunds; obtaining services from local government; obtaining any other government benefits or services; problems with any agency which claimed household owed money; other problems with a government office or agency.
7. Divorce*	Post-divorce problems: property division, alimony, and child support, visitation, or custody.
8. Landlord–tenant*	Problems over rent; eviction; condition of the property, or other problems with a landlord.
9. Other	Problems cited in response to a final, general probe for other problems; problems with the ownership or division of property jointly owned with someone outside of the household;* problems involving violation of civil rights, other than discrimination.

Note: * denotes grievances ascertained for households at risk.

interact with other systems, such as workers' compensation or their own insurance claims adjusters."[41] Nevertheless, the study gathered extensive information about claiming behavior with respect to accidental injuries, specifically: accident circumstances, nature and severity of the injury, health care and other direct expenditures and work loss associated with the injury, sources of compensation, amount of compensation from all sources, and liability-claiming behavior.[42]

The designers of an NCJS would have to decide whether such detail about each incident should be gathered, given that the scope of civil justice problems in an

[41] *Id.*
[42] *Id.*

NCJS would have to be broader than the narrower class of problems studied by RAND.

PRIOR RESEARCH METHODOLOGIES AND RESULTS ON CIVIL INCIDENTS

The Curran survey was intended to examine the legal needs of the public by interviewing a representative sample.[43] The target number of respondents was 2,000; 2,064 interviews were completed.[44] The complex survey design used a random sample of the continental United States Standard Metropolitan Statistical Areas (SMSAs) and counties outside SMSAs.[45] Within each selected SMSA or county, it drew a random sample of block groups and within these blocks, randomly selected a sample of about 100 households.[46] The results reported in the study cannot reasonably be summarized in a short chapter, but a key set of results for present purposes is reported in Table 3.4.[47]

The leading problem area reported by respondents relates to real property acquisition. Over 70% of respondents reported at least one real property acquisition problem and 40% reported at least two such problems.[48] Other areas with high rates of problems were major purchases, wills, divorce, serious personal injury, and serious damages to property.[49]

Observations were weighted by the population of each judicial district so that the five samples could be combined. Weights were calculated to preserve the actual number of observations. Numbers in parentheses are the total upon which the reported proportions are based.

Data for the CLRP were collected by a telephone survey.[50] The geographic scope was narrower than the Curran study, but the proportion of households surveyed within the selected geographic area was substantial. The survey was administered in January 1980 to approximately 1,000 randomly selected households in each of five federal judicial districts: South Carolina, Eastern Pennsylvania (which includes Philadelphia), Eastern Wisconsin, New Mexico, and Central California (which includes Los Angeles).[51] The time frame assessed was narrower than in Curran's study. The Miller-Sarat respondents were asked "whether anyone in their household had experienced one or more of a long list of problems within the past three years."[52]

43 Curran, supra note 8, at 32.
44 *Id.* at 33–34.
45 *Id.* at 33.
46 *Id.*
47 *Id.* at 103–104 tbl.4.8.
48 See *id.* at 104–105.
49 *Id.* at 104.
50 Miller & Sarat, supra note 9, at 534.
51 *Id.*
52 *Id.*

TABLE 3.4 *Results of ABA/ABF Curran study.*

		No. of adults who had problem per 1,000 adults in the population	
Question	Problem type	At least once	At least twice
	Real property		
7	Acquisition	710	400
8	Interference with ownership	50	10
10	Serious dispute with home builder	20	<10
12	Serious dispute on home repair contract	40	<10
14	Serious dispute with mortgagee	20	0
	Employment matters		
26	Serious difficulty collecting pay (excl. garnishment)	60	10
27	Job discrimination	90	30
	Consumer matters		
16	Eviction	40	<10
17	Serious dispute with landlord	90	10
18	Serious dispute on major purchase	140	30
20	Serious dispute with creditor	50	10
21	Repossession	30	<10
25	Garnishment	30	<10
	Estate planning		
57	Wills	270	–
61	Inter vivos trust	50	10
	Estate settlement		
52	Death of spouse	100	10

	Marital		
52	Divorce	150	20
55	Separation (custody/support)	10	–
56	Alimony/support	30	–
	Governmental		
34	Serious difficulty with municipal service	70	–
35	Serious difficulty with municipal/county agency	50	–
36	Serious difficulty with state agency	40	–
37	Serious difficulty with federal agency	50	–
	Torts		
38	Serious personal injury to respondent	120	20
39	Serious property damage to respondent	400	190
40	Serious personal injury or property damage by respondent	60	10
49	Serious injury to child of respondent	80	10
40F, 41	Crimes by Respondent	40	10
	Constitutional Rights		
28	Infringement of constitutional rights	80	40
	Juvenile Matters		
50	Child of respondent had serious problem with juvenile authorities	60	20

Naturally, one would expect problem rates to be lower, but for many problem types, substantial rates were reported. For present purposes, the key results are reported in Miller and Sarat's article, reproduced in Table 3.5.[53]

Almost 16% of households reported a tort grievance within a three-year period and almost 9% of consumers reported a grievance involving at least $1,000 in the same period.[54] The Miller-Sarat threshold for consumer grievances was $1,000.[55] Given the prominence of class-action policy discussions and activity, the $1,000 limitation might be ill-advised. In assessing aggregate litigation activity, it is important to know whether respondents believe they have a grievance about a matter, even if the matter is small. Many consumer and other class actions involve low stakes and recoveries per class member.[56]

Table 3.5 and the underlying study can make useful contributions to the design of a civil justice survey. First, note the range of topics covered. The table distinguishes among eight categories of civil justice grievances, of which torts is just one. The table could be expanded to include pre-divorce family related matters, including spousal or partner abuse.

Second, the data contain several important results. The "claims" rate is high, about 80% or more, for all categories other than discrimination, where it is only 29.4%.[57] In other grievance categories, the claims rate is so high that there is little room for statistically significant variation. In all categories other than torts, more than half of the claims resulted in disagreement or disputes. The torts dispute rate, 23.5%, is comparatively low.[58] It would be desirable to separate the torts results by automobile and non-automobile claims. The massive, routinized automobile insurance system likely leads to satisfactory claims resolution in a higher percentage of cases than in less routine torts. Evidence from the RAND study confirms the need to separately consider motor vehicle accidents. RAND found that 89% of motor vehicle incidents lead to someone taking action compared to 16% of on-the-job products-associated injuries and 7% of non-work products-associated injuries.[59]

Given a dispute, the rate of lawyer use varies. In two areas, post-divorce matters and torts, lawyer use was over 50%, with a notably higher rate in post-divorce grievances than in torts grievances. This is likely because attorneys often had already been consulted in connection with the divorce itself and only 24% of households were at risk for post-divorce problems. The high lawyer use rate in torts cases may be related to the low dispute rate in torts cases. Most torts grievances led to claims but not to disputes. The substantial filtering process likely results in high stakes or quite

53 *Id.* at 537 tbl.2.
54 *Id.*
55 *Id.* at 534, 566.
56 See, e.g., Theodore Eisenberg & Geoffrey P. Miller, *Incentive Awards to Class Action Plaintiffs: An Empirical Study*, 53 UCLA L. Rev. 1303, 1324 fig.1 (2006).
57 Miller & Sarat, supra note 9, at 537 tbl.2.
58 *Id.*
59 Hensler et al., supra note 40, at 121, 127.

TABLE 3.5 *Grievances, claims, and outcomes: rates by type of problem.*[a]

	All grievances	Torts	Consumer	Debt	Discrimination	Property	Government	Post-divorce	Landlord
Grievances[b] (percentage of households)	41.6 (5,147)	15.6 (5,147)	8.9 (5,147)	6.7 (5,147)	14.0 (5,147)	7.2 (3,798)[c]	9.1 (5,147)	10.9 (1,238)[c]	17.1 (2,293)[c]
Claims (percentage of terminated grievances)	71.8 (2,491)	85.7 (559)	87.3 (303)	94.6 (151)	29.4 (595)	79.9 (193)	84.9 (240)	87.9 (51)	87.2 (307)
Disputes: (percentage of claims)									
a. No agreement	32.0	206	37.1	23.9	58.0	32.1	40.7	37.7	55.0
b. Agreement after difficulty	30.6	20.9	37.6	60.6	15.5	21.8	41.4	49.3	26.7
	–	–	–	–	–	–	–	–	–
c. Dispute	62.6 (1,768)	23.5 (467)	75.0 (263)	84.5 (142)	73.5 (174)	53.9 (154)	82.1 (203)	87.0 (45)	81.7 (267)
Lawyer use[d] (percent of disputes)	23.0 (1,100)	57.9 (107)	20.3 (197)	19.2 (120)	13.3 (128)	19.0 (84)	12.3 (163)	76.9 (39)	14.7 (218)
Court filling[d] (percent of disputes)	11.2 (1,093)	18.7 (107)	3.0 (197)	7.6 (119)	3.9 (128)	13.4 (82)	11.9 (159)	59.0 (39)	7.3 (218)

TABLE 3.5 (*Cont'd*)

	All grievances	Torts	Consumer	Debt	Discrimination	Property	Government	Post-divorce	Landlord
Success of claims (percent of claims)									
a. No agreement (0)	32.0	2.6	37.1	23.9	58.0	32.1	40.7	37.7	55.0
b. Compromise (1)	34.2	85.4	15.2	23.5	11.3	9.7	18.3	35.5	10.3
c. Obtained whole claim (2)	33.8	11.9	47.7	52.6	30.7	58.3	41.0	26.8	34.6
	100.0	100.0	100.0	100.0	100.0	100.0	100.0	100.0	100.0
d. Success scale mean[e]	1.02 (1782)	1.09 (479)	1.11 (265)	1.29 (142)	0.73 (174)	1.26 (154)	1.00 (203)	0.89 (45)	0.80 (267)

[a] Observations were weighted by the population of each judicial district so that the five samples could be combined. Weights were calculated to preserve the actual number of observations. Numbers in parentheses are the total upon which the reported proportions are based.

[b] Proportions are of households reporting one or more grievances of each type.

[c] These are proportions and numbers of households at risk. Households at risk of property problems are those owning their own home, apartment, or land within the three-year period (73.8% of all households). Households at risk of post-divorce problems were the 24.0% of all households which had a divorced member. The 44.2% of households which rented within the three years were at risk of landlord problems.

[d] The number in these rows differ slightly due to missing data.

[e] The success of claims was scaled 0, 1, or 2: 0 if no agreement was reached, 1 if the agreement was a compromise, and 2 if the entire claim was met.

Source: Richard E. Miller & Austin Sarat, Grievances, Claims, and Disputes: Assessing Adversary Culture, supra note 9.

contested matters ripening into disputes. Such a process should be expected to lead to consultation with lawyers at unusually high rates, 57.9% in the case of torts disputes.

The process of consulting with lawyers tends to be associated with filtering disputes away from court filings. Across all categories of disputes, lawyers were used in 23% of disputes and court filings resulted in 11.2% of disputes. Working from grievances to court filings can be done by noting that 71.8% of grievances lead to claims, 62.6% of claims lead to disputes, and 11.2% of disputes lead to court filings. Multiplying through yields about 4% of grievances ending in court filings. In the CLRP data, only about one torts dispute in three led to a court filing and only about 4% of torts claims led to a court filing. RAND found that "about one injury in ten leads to an attempt to collect liability compensation."[60] Motor vehicle incidents tend to inflate the overall rate. "[I]n nonwork, non-motor-vehicle accidents, only three injuries out of 100 lead to liability claims."[61]

RAND's data on consulting attorneys is difficult to compare with CLRP data because the CLRP data do not separately report on motor vehicle cases. In motor vehicle cases, RAND reports that 18% of injured persons hire a lawyer.[62] In occupational injuries, 6% hire a lawyer and in other injury contexts, 1% hire a lawyer.[63]

As noted earlier, prior studies gathered information on customary demographic categories and all of the results reported here could be subdivided by income, race, sex, age, and education.

CONCLUSION: THE BENEFITS AND PLAUSIBILITY OF A NATIONAL CIVIL JUSTICE SURVEY

The need for information about civil justice issues and the results of previous studies suggest that a major civil justice survey is warranted. Problems are prevalent enough to warrant systematic assessment of their presence and pursuit. The uses to which systematic data about these areas could be put are great. For example, trends over time in serious personal injury or property damage could provide insight into the tort system's effect on primary behavior, and the effect of policy initiatives on the tort system. An NCJS would also have a synergistic effect with other datasets. Systematic knowledge about civil justice grievances over time would enhance the value of BJS-NCSC data about case filings and trials. And an NCJS would provide the best available information about claiming rates and disputing rates by U.S. residents.

Studies reviewed here also suggest that an NCJS is feasible. The sample sizes in the ABA/ABF, CLRP, and RAND studies suggest that a civil justice survey of

60 *Id.* at 120.
61 *Id.*
62 *Id.* at 123.
63 *Id.*

magnitude similar to the NCVS would yield highly meaningful results. Each year, the NCVS collects data from a nationally representative sample of 77,200 households comprised of nearly 134,000 persons on the frequency, characteristics, and consequences of criminal victimization in the United States.[64] A civil justice project of similar scope, building on BJS expertise, would dwarf prior efforts described here, which included a maximum of about 26,000 households. A sufficiently larger sample would allow a breakdown of results by state or locality, which would be helpful to assess whether interstate variation might reveal real property acquisition systems that are associated with a reduced incidence of problems.

64 See, e.g., NCVS 2005, supra note 7, at 11.

4

When Does Representation Matter?

Russell Engler

When does legal representation make a difference? Russell Engler reviews the existing research on the question and discusses the limitations of these studies. More work is needed, he concludes, to identify the factors that determine when lawyers make a difference; and greater receptivity should be shown for modes of assistance for the unrepresented that fall short of full representation by a licensed lawyer.

UNDERSTANDING THE QUESTION OF WHEN DOES REPRESENTATION MATTER

While a great deal of literature attempts to address the question of the importance of representation by lawyers in civil matters, the question framed that way masks the key Access to Justice concerns. Judges routinely report that they believe litigants are better off with lawyers, obtaining worse outcomes when they appear without counsel;[1] many judges have further identified the burdens on the legal system that flow from the pro se litigants.[2] As a result, guidance for judges often counsels judges to warn litigants of the perils of self-representation. Legal services lawyers staunchly believe that their clients are better off with representation. Opposing lawyers not only report that the absence of representation can have an adverse impact on the represented parties, but are generally prohibited by the ethical rules from giving advice to unrepresented parties, other than the advice to obtain counsel.

1 Report to the Chief Judge of the State of New York, 15–18 (November 2010) (hereinafter NY Report I), available at www.nycourts.gov/ip/access-civil-legal-services/PDF/CLS-TaskForceREPORT.pdf; Report to the Chief Judge of the State of New York, 19–21 (Nov. 2011) (hereinafter NY Report II), available at www.nycourts.gov/ip/access-civil-legal-services/PDF/CLS-2011TaskForceREPORT_web.pdf; Report to the Chief Judge of the State of New York, 15–16 (November 2012)(hereinafter NY Report III), available at www.nycourts.gov/ip/access-civil-legal-services/PDF/CLS-TaskForceREPORT_Nov-2012.pdf.

2 *Judges' Views of Pro Se Litigants' Effect on Courts*, 40 CLEARINGHOUSE REV. 228 (July–August 2006).

The most common reason that litigants appear without counsel in civil matters is that they cannot afford a lawyer.[3] While the concept of "unbundled" legal services offers the promise of providing choice to clients to retain lawyers for only those tasks for which they needed a lawyer's expertise, the evolution of unbundling is two stories: a story about clients with resources, for whom choice might be a reality, and a story about clients with few to no resources for whom the choice is to receive unbundled help or no help at all.[4]

In the Access to Justice context, therefore, the questions involving the importance of representation become more contextual than absolute. An inescapable reality embedded in the question is a scarcity of resources.[5] Given that there are insufficient resources to provide full representation to all litigants in a given context, when should resources be allocated to full representation and when might lesser forms of assistance suffice? The reality of scarcity is essential in understanding the empirical work regarding representation. Not surprisingly, it is perilous to attempt to draw too many conclusions from a few studies, as opposed to identifying trends that emerge from the body of work as a whole.

OVERVIEW OF EMPIRICAL WORK

The Methodologies Employed

The reports and more formal studies that inform our understanding of the importance of representation employ an array of methodologies. The most common form involves the review of case records, typically those in the court or administrative agencies.[6] In these studies, the researchers search the case files, sorting the cases between those involving represented litigants and unrepresented ones and comparing the results. Separately, or in combination with the review of case files, some

[3] *Handing Cases Involving Self-Represented Litigants,: A National Bench Guide for Judicial Officers*, 1–2 (2008), available online at www.selfhelpsupport.org/library/folder.42613-Communication_Protocol; John M. Greacen, Self-Represented Litigantsand Courtand Legal Services Responsesto Their Needs: What We Know 12 (2002), available at www.courts.ca.gov/partners/documents/SRLwhatweknow.pdf; Office of the Deputy Chief Admin. Judge for Justice Initiatives, Self-Represented Litigants: Characteristics, Needs, Services, The Results of Two Surveys 3–4 (2005), available at www.nycourts.gov/reports/AJJI_SelfRep06.pdf; Russell Engler, *And Justice for All—Including the Unrepresented Poor: Revisiting the Role of Judges, Mediators, and Clerks*, 67 Fordham L. Rev. 1987, 2046–47 (1999).

[4] Unbundled, or limited assistance or discrete task, lawyering involves the provision of a portion of the full service package provided in the traditional lawyer–client relationship. See Engler, Chapter 29 in this volume.

[5] See, e.g., Bonnie Rose Hough & Justice Laurie Zelon, *Self-Represented Litigants: Challenges and Opportunities for Access to Justice*, 47 Judges J. 30, 32 (Summer 2008).

[6] See generally Russell Engler, *Connecting Self-Representation to* Civil Gideon: *What Existing Data Reveal about When Counsel is Most Needed*, 37 Fordham Urb. L. J. 37 (2010) (hereinafter *Connecting Self-Representation to Civil* Gideon).

studies rely on observations of the proceedings[7], interviews,[8] surveys[9] of the various participants, and case studies in the form of narratives[10] to illustrate the trends identified through other methods.[11] Sandefur's research relies on meta-analysis: studying a series of reports that allows her to draw conclusions across substantive areas.[12]

While these studies consistently show that unrepresented parties achieve worse outcomes in many scenarios than represented ones, many are vulnerable to "selection bias": their results may be skewed because of the choices of lawyers, in selecting stronger cases, or of clients, in seeking out lawyers where their cases are stronger.[13] Kritzer and Sandefur, while acknowledging the possibility of selection bias, conclude that disparities in outcomes between represented and unrepresented parties are too stark for selection bias to provide a complete explanation.[14]

The methodology of randomized control trials addresses the problem of selection bias. However, in large part because of the practical difficulty of conducting randomized control trials that capture real-life circumstances, few published studies are based on such trials.[15] Moreover, the methodology raises a different

7 See, e.g., David L. Eldridge, The Making of a Courtroom: Landlord-Tenant Trials in Philadelphia's Municipal Court 65–69, 130–42 (2001) (unpublished Ph.D. dissertation, University of Pennsylvania) (studying 153 hearings in Philadelphia's Landlord-Tenant Court); Barbara Bezdek, *Silence in The Court: Participation and Subordination of Poor Tenants' Voices in Legal Process*, 20 HOFSTRA L. REV. 533 (1992).

8 See, e.g., NY Report III, supra note 1, at 16–18; NY Report II, supra note 1, at 21–23; NY Report I, supra note 1, at 29–31.

9 *Id.* See, also, KIRA KRENICHYN & NICOLE SCHAEFER-MCDANIEL, RESULTS FROM THREE SURVEYS IN NEW YORK CITY HOUSING COURTS (2007), available at www.policyarchive.org/bitstream/handle/10207/8683/threesurveys.pdf?sequence=1.

10 See, e.g., NY Report I, supra note 1, at 29–31; BOSTON BAR ASSOCIATION, *The Importance of Representation in Eviction Cases and Homelessness Prevention* 24–25 (2012) (hereinafter *The Importance of Representation in Eviction Cases and Homelessness Prevention*), available at www.bostonbar.org/docs/default-document-library/bba-crtc-final-3-1-12.pdf.

11 Kritzer's work illustrates one way in which the methodologies may be used in combination: "I employed a mixed research strategy that combined statistical assessment of outcomes with observation of processes." See, HERBERT M. KRITZER, LEGAL ADVOCACY: LAWYERSAND NONLAWYERS AT WORK 21 (1998) (studying data from Wisconsin from the mid-1970s to the mid-1990s).

12 See, e.g., Rebecca L. Sandefur, *The Impact of Counsel: An Analysis of Empirical Evidence*, 9 SEATTLE J. FOR SOC. JUST. 51, 51–52 (2011) (hereinafter *The Impact of Counsel*); Rebecca L. Sandefur, *Money Isn't Everything: Understanding Moderate Income Households' Use of Lawyers' Services, in* MIDDLE INCOME ACCESS TO JUSTICE 223, 223 (Michael J. Trebilcock, Anthony J. Duggan & Lorne Mitchell Sossin eds., 2012). Rebecca Sandefur, *Elements of Professional Expertise: Understanding Relational and Substantive Expertise through Lawyers' Impacts*, 80 AM. SOCIOL. REV. 909–933 (2015)(hereinafter The Elements of Professional Expertise).

13 *Id.* at 81–83.

14 KRITZER, supra note 11, at 33–37; Sandefur, "Elements of Expertise" supra note 12, at 912, 924.

15 Two of the published studies are in the housing area, one in the area of unemployment benefits and one that deals with of juvenile cases. Carroll Seron et al., *The Impact of Legal Counsel on Outcomes for Poor Tenants in New York City's Housing Court: Results of a Randomized Experiment*, 35 LAW & SOC'Y REV. 419, 423–26 (2001) (housing); D. James Greiner, Cassandra Wolos Pattanayak & Jonathan Phillip Hennessey, *The Limits of Unbundled Legal Assistance: A Randomized Study in a Massachusetts District Court and Prospects for the Future*, 126 HARV. L. REV. 901 (2013) (housing)

set of questions and concerns. First, the studies may not actually be able to report on the impact of representation. After potential clients are randomized into two groups, those offered representation and those not, some potential clients offered representation may decline to accept representation, while some of those not offered representation may obtain representation elsewhere. The Greiner studies therefore reported the impact of "an offer of representation" rather than "representation," a decision that led critics to question the utility of the studies. Second, the technique is criticized for placing undue burdens on those providing assistance.[16] Third, a randomized control study focused on individual outcomes will shed little light on systemic impacts such as benefits from representation that might accrue to others, including the legal system more generally. The studies involving randomized control trials, therefore, make an important contribution, but do not by themselves nullify the findings of other studies using different methodologies.

Courts (Housing, Consumer, and Domestic Relations Cases)

In eviction cases, tenants rarely are represented by counsel; the typical case pits a represented landlord against an unrepresented tenant. Regardless of whether tenants appear or default, settle or go to trial, raise defenses or do not, the result invariably is a judgment for the landlord. One variable that often can halt the swift judgment for the landlord is representation for the tenant, with the likelihood of eviction dropping precipitously. Represented tenants default less often, obtain better settlements, and win more often at trial.[17]

Two published housing studies, using the randomized control study methodology to eliminate selection bias, find significant differences in case outcomes for represented tenants, in comparison to those who did not receive full representation. Comparing case outcomes for those offered representation in Manhattan Housing Court, Seron found that where a tenant was represented, a final judgment was entered against him or her in 21.5% of the cases, compared with final judgments in

(hereinafter *The Limits of Unbundled Legal Assistance*); D. James Greiner & Cassandra Wolos Pattanayak, *Randomized Evaluation in Legal Assistance: What Difference Does Representation (Offer and Actual Use) Make*, 121 YALE L.J. 2118, 2171–196 (2012) (unemployment Compensation); W. Vaughn Stapleton & Lee E. Teitelbaum, IN DEFENSE OF YOUTH: A STUDY OF THE ROLE OF COUNSEL IN AMERICAN JUVENILE COURTS, Russell Sage Foundation (1972) (juvenile). Professor Greiner and his co-authors completed another study in the housing area that has been posted on SSRN, but not published. D. James Greiner, Cassandra Wolos Pattanayak & Jonathan Phillip Hennessey, *How Effective Are Limited Legal Assistance Programs? A Randomized Experiment in a Massachusetts Housing Court* (September 1, 2012), available at http://papers.ssrn.com/sol3/papers.cfm?abstract_id=1880078 (hereinafter How Effective Are Limited Legal Assistance Programs?).

16 See Clare Pastore, *California's Sargent Shriver Civil Counsel Act Tests Impact of More Assistance for Low-Income Litigants*, 47 CLEARINGHOUSE REV. 97, 106 (July–August 2013).

17 *Connecting Self-Representation to Civil* Gideon, supra note 6, at 46–51.

50.6% of the cases involving unrepresented tenants.[18] The favorable results for tenants were reflected in other measures of outcomes as well, with stipulations involving represented tenants more likely to include a rent abatement for the tenant (31.3% compared to 2.3%) and more likely to require repairs (63.8% to 25.4%);[19] warrants of eviction also issued far less often for represented tenants compared to unrepresented ones (10% compared to 44.1%).[20] The Seron study concludes that "low income tenants with legal representation experience significantly more beneficial outcomes than their counterparts who do not have legal representation, independent of the merits of the case."[21]

In the Greiner study, involving Quincy District Court near Boston, lawyers from Greater Boston Legal Services screened cases to identify a subset of eviction cases meeting articulated criteria. The lawyers then provided full representation to the tenants randomly assigned to the treated group and advice, combined with assistance in the preparation of pleadings and motions, to the tenants randomly assigned to the control group.[22] On the key question of whether tenants retained possession of the premises, two-thirds of the treated group did as compared to one-third of the control group.[23] Regarding financial benefits, including rent waived and damage payments from landlords to tenants, those in the treated group again fared far better than those in the control group. While tenants in the control group received financial benefits equivalent to an average of two months' rent, those in the treated group received almost five times as much – the equivalent of nine-and-a-half months of rent.[24] The benefits from full representation accrued without increasing the burden on the court.[25]

18 Seron, supra note 15, at 428. The tenants were recruited from among the tenants responding to nonpayment of rent petitions and waiting in line at the Clerk's office in Manhattan Housing Court; they were then sorted into control and treatment groups through a five-step process developed in collaboration with the Administrative Judge of the Civil Court. *Id.* at 423–24. Five variables were selected to test the effect of the program on substantive legal outcomes, and four additional variables were selected to measure the effect of the program on the efficiency of the Court. *Id.* at 426.

19 *Id.*

20 *Id.*

21 *Id.* at 421. The study also found that representation reduced the use of motions and increased the time to final disposition without increasing the number of court appearances.

22 The Limits of Unbundled Legal Assistance, supra note 15, at 917–19.

23 *Id.* at 908, 926–28. The Greater Boston Legal Services (GBLS) lawyers added that, for the one-third of the members of the treated group who were considered to have "lost possession," some did so of their own volition and most did so on their own terms, often finding more suitable housing. Boston Bar Association, *The Importance of Representation in Eviction Cases and Homelessness Prevention*, at 16 (2012) (hereinafter *The Importance of Representation in Eviction Cases and Homelessness Prevention*), available at www.bostonbar.org/docs/default-document-library/bba-crtc-final-3-1-12.pdf.

24 The Limits of Unbundled Legal Assistance, supra note 15, at 908, 928–31.

25 *Id.* at 932–36. An unpublished companion study found no difference between the control and study group although, as with the unemployment study, many tenants in the control group received extensive assistance from lawyers. How Effective Are Limited Legal Assistance Programs?, supra note 15. Not only did the lawyers assisting litigants in the "treated" group provide a level of assistance that more closely resembled unbundled assistance than full representation, but a substantial portion of

Steinberg's housing study is unique in that it compares the results achieved by three types of litigants: (1) unrepresented litigants, (2) those receiving partial representation by lawyers (sometimes referred to as "unbundled assistance"), and (3) those receiving full representation by lawyers.[26] The study, which did not involve a randomized control trial, compared the results for tenants who received no legal assistance at all and those who received full representation through Stanford's Community Law Clinic with those receiving two forms of partial assistance from a local legal services office: ghostwriting assistance through a half-day housing clinic and one-time negotiation assistance in a mandatory settlement conference.[27]

Steinberg's findings offer a grim account of the effectiveness of these forms of partial assistance in the setting she studied. Both in terms of retaining possession or, where tenants had to move, the length of time before which they had to move, the partial assistance rendered had no measurable impact for tenants; they fared as poorly as those who received no assistance at all, and worse than those who received full representation.[28] Represented tenants also paid less money to landlords when they were ordered to pay and were awarded damages from landlords more often; tenants receiving unbundled assistance again fared as poorly as those receiving no assistance, and far worse than those receiving full representation.[29] Neither form of partial assistance involved in this study resulted in a different success rate.[30] In terms of procedural outcomes, partially assisted tenants were less likely to default and more likely to raise cognizable defenses than wholly unrepresented tenants; there was, however, no improvement in outcomes.[31]

Empirical studies of courts in other areas also suggest that representation counts. Studies involving debt collection cases consistently show that represented debtors obtain far better results than unrepresented ones, who default at a high rate and, when they appear, typically succumb to pressure from the represented creditor and

the control group received a comparable level of assistance by the same lawyers. The Importance of Representation in Eviction Cases and Homelessness Prevention, supra note 10, at 18–20. As a result, the Boston Bar Association Task Force that partnered with Greiner and his co-authors concluded that "[b]oth pilot projects prevented evictions, protected the rights of tenants, and maintained shelter in a high rate of cases"; "[t]he findings of both pilot studies confirm that extensive assistance from lawyers is essential to helping tenants preserve their housing and avoid the potential for homelessness, including all of the far-reaching tangible and intangible costs to tenants and society generally that are associated with homelessness." *Id.*, at 2–3.

26 Jessica K. Steinberg, *In Pursuit of Justice? Case Outcomes and the Delivery of Unbundled Legal Services*, 18 Geo. J. Pov. Law & Pol'y 453, 463 (2011).

27 *Id.* at 457, 477–78. The legal aid office was the Legal Aid Society of San Mateo County. *Id.* The study, which was limited in scope and did not involve randomized controls, was designed with the assistance of Sandefur, and involved a review of files from court sorted by the type of assistance received. *Id.*, at 457, n.19, 480 and 496–97. With the negotiation assistance, the legal aid lawyers offered assistance to tenants who had previously received assistance at a legal aid housing clinic. *Id.* at 478.

28 *Id.* at 483–85.

29 *Id.* at 485–88.

30 *Id.* at 488–90.

31 *Id.* at 490–95.

the court to settle on terms less favorable than those obtained by represented debtors.[32] Studies in the family law area are more complicated to evaluate because it is not always clear what constitutes a favorable outcome.[33] Nevertheless, represented parties in these studies are more likely to obtain sole custody when the other side is without counsel, and shared custody when both are represented by counsel; represented parties also are more successful in obtaining protective orders than unrepresented ones.[34]

Agencies (Unemployment, Immigration, and Other Benefits Cases)

The methodological issues in the area of family law disappear with administrative agency decisions involving government benefits, where wins and losses present clearer instances of a favorable outcome. Kritzer's study includes extensive analysis of data involving Social Security disability appeals and unemployment appeals from Wisconsin.[35] With Social Security disability appeals, Kritzer found that represented claimants were successful in 60–70% of their appeals, while unrepresented claimants succeeded at rates as low as 30% and as high as 55%. Although the success rates varied from year to year, the gap based on representation status ranged consistently from 15–30% each year.[36] Kritzer also reported data regarding the success rates for claimants appearing with non-attorney representatives. For each year reported, claimants represented by non-attorneys fared far better than unrepresented ones, but slightly less well than those represented by attorneys.[37]

Kritzer's study of unemployment compensation appeals in Wisconsin demonstrated that represented claimants fared better regardless of the nature of the claim.[38] Represented claimants won 44.2% of the cases in which they appealed, compared to 29.7% for unrepresented claimants; when broken down by the nature of the claim, a comparable gap remained for appeals involving misconduct cases, with a smaller gap for cases in which the employee allegedly quit.[39] The same did not hold true for

[32] Connecting Self-Representation to Civil *Gideon*, supra note 6, at 55–58. The most common methodologies include reviews of court files, observations and interviews. *Id.*, at nn. 77–86.

[33] Greiner & Pattanayak, supra note 15, at 2165–66.

[34] Connecting Self-Representation to Civil *Gideon*, supra note 6, at 51–55.

[35] Kritzer, supra note 11, at 111–20. As noted previously, Kritzer used a mix of statistical analysis and observation of processes. *Id.*, at 21.

[36] *Id.* at 117 chart.

[37] *Id.*

[38] *Id.* at 23–77.

[39] *Id.* at 34–39. In misconduct cases, represented claimants prevailed in 50.8% of their appeals, compared to a 37.9% success rate for unrepresented claimants. *Id.* at 37. With "Quit" cases, the overall success of the claimants dropped, but the benefits of representation remained, as 26.3% of represented claimants prevailed in these cases, while only 17.4% of claimants won on appeal. *Id.* at 38. Considering all appeals, and not simply those in which the claimant appealed, represented claimants won 50.4% of the cases, compared to unrepresented claimants who prevailed in 41.5% of the cases. *Id.* at 34.

employers. While represented employers prevailed in 58.4% of the appeals, unrepresented employers prevailed almost as often (57.3%).[40]

Greiner and Pattanyak's initial article urging randomized controls concerned unemployment benefits cases and challenged the prior research.[41] They reported the results of a randomized control study of the impact of an offer of representation by the Harvard Legal Aid Bureau to claimants for unemployment benefits. The study not only reports no difference in outcomes between the control (no offer) and treated (offer) group, but suggests that claimants in the treated group might have been *harmed* by the offer of representation due to delays in the receipt of benefits without apparent countervailing gain. The Greiner–Pattanyak study created quite a stir, particularly in the legal services community. Critics questioned the decision to study the impact of an "offer of representation" rather than "representation," noting that "nearly half of the control group were represented by counsel," many of whom were legal services lawyers. These critics maintained that the Greiner–Pattanyak paper did not shed much light on the impact of representation itself. [42] Others questioned the applicability of findings involving the impact of law-student assistance to the larger question of the impact of lawyers.[43]

A pair of studies in the Immigration area, drawn from a review of government records, reveals a dramatic difference in outcomes for represented and unrepresented claimants. Kerwin reports that represented immigrants obtain relief in removal proceedings at significantly higher levels than those without representation, regardless of the nature of the proceedings.[44] Schoenholtz and Jacobs similarly

[40] *Id.* at 34. Earlier studies also reported a 15% gap between represented and unrepresented claimants, but no variation in success rates based on representation for employers. See, *Connecting Self-Representation to Civil* Gideon, supra note 6, at 61 n.100.

[41] Greiner & Pattanayak, supra note 15. For their critical analysis of the existing research, see *id.* at 2171–96.

[42] See Bob Sable, *What Difference Representation – A Response*, Concurring Opinions (Mar. 28, 2011), available at www.concurringopinions.com/archives/2011/03/what-difference-representation-a-response.html#more-42104. At the time, Sable was the Executive Director of Greater Boston Legal Services. For Professor Greiner's defense, see his *The Centrality of Abstracts? A Response to Bob Sable's and David Udell's Comments on "What Difference Representation? Offers, Actual Use, and the Need for Randomization"*, Concurring Opinions (Mar. 28, 2011), available at www.concurringopinions.com/archives/2011/03/the-centrality-of-abstracts-a-response-to-bob-sables-and-david-udells-comments-on-what-difference-representation-offers-actual-use-and-the-need-for-randomization.html#more-42420; Greiner & Pattanayak, supra note 15, at 2127–32.

[43] David Udell, *What Difference Presentation?*, Concurring Opinions (Mar. 28, 2011), available at www.concurringopinions.com/archives/2011/03/what-difference-presentation.html#more-42280 (referring to the "the experience gap that exists between the HLAB students and the 'other service providers' who represented members of the control group"; "[t]his experience gap may thus be expected to conceal the effectiveness of the HLAB students' performance while highlighting any delay caused by the HLAB students' performance").

[44] Donald Kerwin, *Charitable Legal Programs for Immigrants: What They Do, Why They Matter and How They Can Be Expanded*, IMMIGR. BRIEFINGS, No. 04–06, June 2004 (studying data from the Executive Office or of Immigration Review, U.S. Dept. of Justice, for Fiscal Year 2003). In asylum cases, success rates were 39% for represented, non-detained persons, compared to 14% for unrepresented, non-detained persons, dropping to 18% and 3%, respectively, where the persons were detained.

found a dramatic difference in the success rates for represented asylum seekers as opposed to unrepresented ones: represented asylum seekers referred through the affirmative process, in which the applicant applies for asylum prior to the initiation of removal proceedings, were six times more likely to be granted asylum than unrepresented ones.[45]

With the Greiner–Pattanayak study serving as an important exception, the unifying finding in studies involving administrative proceedings is that the success rate for represented claimants is usually 15–30% greater than for unrepresented claimants. [46] The level of success varies by type of benefit case involved, the grounds for appeal, the nature of the claim, and its procedural posture as well.[47]

Meta-Analysis

In contrast to the studies that focus on a particular type of case in a particular setting, Sandefur's body of work "takes the form of meta-analysis – a quantitative research synthesis that uses the findings of extant research to produce a summary of general knowledge about a given phenomenon."[48] Sandefur focuses "on a single empirical question: how much does lawyer representation affect who wins and loses in adjudication?"[49] Sandefur concludes that when "people are represented by attorneys, they are, on average, more likely to win in adjudication than people who are unrepresented. But how much more likely varies . . . widely across different kinds of civil justice problems and different studies of lawyers' impact."[50]

Sandefur's approach attempts to move beyond the question of where representation by lawyers affects outcomes, but also to shed light on *why* representation mattered."[51] Sandefur concludes that "[o]ne factor that seems to shape variation in the magnitude of the lawyers' impact is procedural complexity – the complexity of the documents and procedures necessary to pursue a justice problem as a court case

In suspension of deportation cases, 62% of represented, non-detained persons received relief, compared to only 17% of unrepresented, non-detained persons, with the figures dropping to 33% and 0%, respectively, where the persons were detained. The numbers are higher in each instance for non-detained immigrant persons than for detained ones. *Id.*

45 Andrew I. Schoenholtz & Jonathan Jacobs, *The State of Asylum Representation: Ideas for Change*, 16 Geo. Immigr. L.J. 739, 743 (2002) (analyzing data provided by the INS Asylum Office for fiscal years 1998 and 1999, and the first seven months of 2000). Those placed in the defensive posture, which occurs if the INS apprehends an individual before he files an affirmative application, were four times more likely to be granted asylum if they were represented. *Id.* at 743.

46 Connecting Self-Representation to Civil *Gideon*, supra note 6, at 51–55.

47 *Id.*

48 The Impact of Counsel, supra note 12, at 62. For Professor Sandefur's exploration of the challenges of this methodological approach and the restrictions on the studies that can be considered, see *id.*, at 62–64.

49 *Id.*

50 *Id.* at 51–52.

51 Catherine R. Albiston & Rebecca L. Sandefur, *Expanding the Empirical Study of Access to Justice*, 2013 Wisc. L. Rev. 101, 106, (discussing many of the limitations of randomized control trials).

appears to account for some of the lawyers' effect on case outcomes."[52] Sandefur describes this as "relational expertise" – skill at negotiating the interpersonal environments in which professional work takes place – may be a crucial component explaining the success representatives have in assisting vulnerable litigants who otherwise might be ignored by decision-makers.[53]

LESSONS FROM THE EMPIRICAL WORK

As Sandefur's analysis reflects, the lessons from the body of empirical work regarding the importance of representation reveal that the effectiveness of representation relates to a variety of factors beyond simply whether a party is represented.

The Representatives

One set of variables that affects outcomes of cases is the quality of the representatives and their tactics. Consistent with Sandefur's conclusion regarding the importance of "relational expertise" of the representatives, Greiner and his co-authors attribute dramatic results achieved on behalf of tenants by the legal services lawyers in Quincy District Court in part to their expertise, including their litigation approach.[54] Greiner et al. discuss at length the outreach, screening, and intake system devised, the litigation style adopted and the model of service delivery.[55]

Kritzer's studies of social security disability and unemployment appeals underscore the importance of expertise in a forum as a key ingredient of the advocates' success. Kritzer ultimately concludes that formal legal training is less crucial than day-to-day experience in the unemployment cases setting, and that it is the combination of general advocacy skills, knowledge of specific hearing practices and players, and substantive knowledge of the relevant law that characterizes the most effective advocates.[56] Kritzer identifies the following as part of the key role: preparing the party for the hearing room situation, helping to frame the issue, bringing the evidence to make the case, and asking the questions to make the case.[57]

In the social security setting, Kritzer describes the importance of a "knowledgeable, experienced" advocate and articulates the differences between the inexperienced, experienced, and "very best" advocates.[58] Kritzer identifies differences that potentially make lawyer representation effective: "the rigor with

52 The Impact of Counsel, supra note 12, at 52.
53 See The Elements of Professional Expertise, supra note 12, at 924–25.
54 The Limits of Unbundled Legal Assistance, supra note 15, at 936–48.
55 *Id.* at 936–42 and 945–47.
56 Kritzer, supra note 11, at 23–77.
57 *Id.* at 37–43.
58 *Id.* at 133–49. The difference is notable not simply because of the types of cases they accept, but the greater credibility afforded by judges to the best advocates and the strengths of these advocates in presenting their cases. *Id.*

which they screen and select cases, the thoroughness of their preparation, their credibility with the administrative law judges, and how strongly they feel about winning."[59] The "very best" or "specialist" lawyers clearly stood out in Kritzer's observations "in terms of their confidence, their thoroughness, and their detailed knowledge of the system (both in the legal sense and in the people sense)."[60] Monsma and Lempert, in their study of public housing hearings in Hawaii, suggest that the increase in the success rate over time for represented litigants was due in part to the growing expertise of the representatives.[61]

Where the representation is provided by lay advocates, including law students, the effectiveness of the representation will turn on whether the representatives have received specialized training for advocacy in the particular context. Kritzer's unemployment study found both that inexperienced law students and low-paid advocates for employers tended to be less effective than other representatives but also that skilled lay advocates can rival skilled lawyers in certain settings, since they can acquire advocacy skills and specialized knowledge of the forum, law and players without formal training in the law.[62] Authors of one study from England conclude that "specialization, rather than professional status, seems to be the best guarantee of such protection."[63]

The Forum – Judge or Hearing Officer, Court or Agency

A second set of variables that impacts case outcomes involves the individual decision-maker and features of the forum more generally. Kritzer's descriptions of the hearing processes for social security and unemployment cases reflect the heavy role played by the individual judges in shaping the flow of evidence, not to mention the conclusions drawn from the evidence.[64] Data from the U.S. Department of Homeland Security on immigration cases reveal dramatically the disparity in outcomes based on the identity of the judge.[65] A study of Philadelphia's housing court found that two of the four significant independent variables related to the judge.[66]

59 *Id.* at 139.

60 *Id.* at 146.

61 Karl Monsma & Richard Lempert, *The Value of Counsel: 20 Years of Representation before a Public Housing Eviction Board*, 26 Law & Soc'y Rev. 627, 663 (1992).

62 Kritzer, supra note 11, at 76.

63 Richard Moorhead, Avrom Sherr & Alan Paterson, *Contesting Professionalism: Legal Aid and Nonlawyers in England and Wales*, 37 Law & Soc'y Rev. 765, 799 (2003).

64 See Kritzer, supra note 11, at 26–32, 127–32.

65 See, Jaya Ramji-Nojales *et al.*, *Refugee Roulette: Disparities in Asylum Adjudication*, 60 Stan. L. Rev. 295 (2007).

66 Eldridge, supra note 7, at 130–42. Eldridge found that tenants were nineteen times more likely to win their cases when an attorney represented them. *Id.* at 135–37. He employed a multi-method design to test the significance of eight variables, four of which ultimately proved to be significant. *Id.* at 135. The strongest association was between tenant representation and hearing outcome. *Id.* at 135–37. Two other significant variables related to the judge: whether a case was heard by Judge "J" and whether a judge makes a pro-landlord argument throughout the course of the hearing. *Id.* at 135.

Where the decision-maker or forum tends to favor one category of litigants over another, the favored litigants would have less of a need for representation since much of the key work is being performed by the court. Thus, various studies of courts handling housing cases identify the courts' orientation favoring the claims of landlords,[67] while studies of debt collection cases observe a similar favoritism toward plaintiffs, acting as if their complaints were presumptively valid;[68] representation in these settings would be more important for tenants and debtors and less important for creditors and debtors.

The Applicable Law

The substantive[69] and procedural[70] law at issue in a particular proceeding constitute additional variables that will impact the outcome of cases. Tenants in jurisdictions or types of housing that recognize robust affirmative defenses and counterclaims would stand a better chance of retaining possession than those in private, unregulated housing in a jurisdiction that recognizes few defenses. While represented claimants in the immigration studies fared better than unrepresented ones regardless of the nature of the proceeding, the overall success rate for represented parties varied from a low of 18% to a high of 62%, depending on the claim.[71] The success rate for represented claimants in Social Security Disability Appeals drops between the initial administrative hearing and the reconsideration stage.[72] Where the substantive law affords few remedies for litigants, the results may be equally bleak whether the litigant is represented or not; where viable claims may be raised – or unknowingly waived – representation may be essential.

Regarding procedures, Sandefur's meta-analysis concludes that it is precisely where the procedures are most complex – "the complexity of the documents and procedures" – that the lawyer's craft seems to be most needed. Studies of representation for tenants in the New York City Housing Courts emphasize the complexity of housing laws – an "impenetrable thicket, confusing not only to laymen but to

67 For example, Eldridge refers to the "judges' orientation to eviction by virtue of [the landlords'] complaint." Eldridge, supra note 7, at 142. Spencer Rand describes the system as one that reflects "that it was created by landlords to work in a landlord's favor; . . . [i]t is rare that I have found a client proceed pro se and not end up with a possession order against her." Spencer Rand, *Teaching Law Students to Practice Social Justice: An Interdisciplinary Search for Help Through Social Work's Empowerment*, 13 Clinical L. Rev. 459, 496–97 (2006)

68 Barbara Yngvesson & Patricia Hennessey, *Small Claims, Complex Disputes: A Review of the Small Claims Literature*, 9 Law & Soc'y Rev. 219, 226 (1975) (observing a favoritism afforded to plaintiffs in small claims courts).

69 See, Connecting Self-Representation to Civil *Gideon*, supra note 6, at 74–75.

70 See, *id.* at 75–76.

71 See, Kerwin, supra note 44, at 6; Schoenholtz & Jacobs, supra note 45, at 743.

72 See William D. Popkin, *The Effect of Representation in Nonadversary Proceedings—A Study of Three Disability Programs*, 62 Corn. L. Rev. 989, 1024–27 (1977) (discussing data from the 1970s and showing a success rate of 71% for represented claimants and only 48% for unrepresented ones, but a success rate of 20% at the reconsideration stage).

lawyers."[73] Not surprisingly, simplification of court procedures and forms has become an important theme in Access to Justice initiatives. As barriers to access are lowered through reducing procedural complexity and other means, the need for representation may lessen.

Alternatives to Full Representation

The empirical work concerning the impact of representation tends to mask a further set of variables: for those not receiving full representation by a lawyer, what forms of assistance, if any, are they receiving in a particular context? As discussed above, not only does the operation of the courts vary from jurisdiction to jurisdiction and courtroom to courtroom, but self-help and limited assistance programs, using an array of public and private lawyers, lay advocates and court personnel, have emerged in a variety of configurations.[74] Even if the focus narrows to a comparison between the impact of full representation versus partial or "unbundled" assistance provided by lawyers, the comparison does not bring to light the full spectrum of different interventions. Partial assistance might involve the preparation of pleadings, telephone or in-person advice, assistance on a brief, or even a court appearance by a lawyer.

At a more basic level, it is often difficult to determine what forms of assistance various litigants have in fact received, particularly where evaluation efforts are focused on results reflected in case files; as a result, we may be classifying as "self-represented" someone who has received substantial assistance.[75] The Greiner–Pattanayak unemployment study provides a cautionary tale here: a substantial portion of the "control group" actually obtained representation, complicating the assessment of the impact of representation.[76]

[73] 89 *Christopher Inc. v. Joy*, 318 N.E.2d 776, 780 (N.Y. 1974).

[74] Greiner et al. describe the way in which each intervention can be evaluated through the use of a randomized control trial, as part of their description of a robust research agenda for the future. See The Limits of Unbundled Legal Assistance, supra note 15, at 954–59.

[75] A recent study of self-represented litigants (SRL's) in three Canadian provinces revealed that 53% of the SRL's sampled had been represented by an attorney earlier in the action. Dr. Julie MacFarlane, *The National Self-Represented Litigants' Project: Final Report: Identifying and Meeting the Needs of Self-Represented Litigants, Executive Summary*, 9 (May 2013), available at www.representing-yourself.com/index.php?option=com_content&view=article&id=99&Itemid=97.

[76] In Greiner's unpublished Housing Court study, Supra note 15, not only did the lawyers assisting litigants in the "treated" group provide a level of assistance that more closely resembled partial assistance than full representation, but a substantial portion of the control group received a comparable level of assistance by the same lawyers. The Importance of Representation in Eviction Cases and Homelessness Prevention, supra note 23, at 18–20. Greiner et al. discuss at length the levels of assistance provided to the control and treated groups in. How Effective Are Limited Legal Assistance Programs, supra, note 15, at 17–21. "[A]bout 57% of the cases that went to litigation took up this offer" and other forms of assistance were available as well. *Id.* at 20.

The Litigants

The characteristics of litigants also should be viewed as variables, impacting not only a prediction as to how a litigant may fare absent assistance, but also how much, and what type of, assistance a litigant may need. Unrepresented litigants typically are poor and disproportionately are minorities. A study of the effectiveness of hotlines in the United States found that clients who rated their outcomes most favorably "were significantly more likely to be white, English-speaking, [and] educated at least to the eighth grade."[77] Language or literacy, race/ethnicity, education and other "special barriers" that included a family member with a disability or serious health problem and transportation day care problems, were among the factors that rendered hotline callers less likely to be able to achieve favorable outcomes based on the advice.[78] Bedzek's study of Baltimore Rent Court cases confirms the feelings of powerlessness for those who appear in court with representation. [79]

The variables identified in the preceding sections combine to underscore the crucial role of power and power imbalances in the legal system. The substantive law, procedures, decision-maker and forum may provide power in certain ways for some types of litigants, at the expense of others. Business interests, larger landlords, and repeat players generally may wield more power than litigants who typically are poor, facing barriers such as those involving health, education and lack of child care. Unfamiliarity with the forum's process may further disadvantage some litigants, while representation itself provides a source of power.

IMPLICATIONS

The question of when representation matters is a nuanced one involving considerations that include analysis of the variables beyond representation. This reality has implications both for further empirical work and for policy decisions involving the need for counsel and the allocation of scarce resources designed to promote access to justice. For example, the importance of full representation by a lawyer in a particular forum or with a particular type of case may depend greatly on the alternatives to representation in that setting, and a study that fails to uncover that crucial information may cloud the analysis it intended to illuminate. At a more basic level, the implications underscore the need for precision in framing research questions, both to insure that the information new research yields sheds light on the questions to which we most urgently need answers and to allow meaningful comparative analysis with respect to prior works.

[77] Connecting Self-Representation to Civil *Gideon*, supra note 6, at 71.

[78] Jessica Pearson & Lanae Davis, The Hotline Outcomes Assessment Study, Final Report – Phase III: Full-Scale Telephone Survey 1, 46–51 (2002), available at www.nlada.org/DMS/Documents/1037903536.22/finalhlreport.pdf.

[79] Bezdek, supra note 7.

At the policy level, conclusions involving not only the impact of representation, but also the crucial role of the other variables identified in the previous section, should provide important clues in designing various forms of assistance that require choices about where we should presume full representation by a lawyer and where lesser forms of assistance stand a better chance of providing effective help. The greater the level of power imbalance between the parties, and the greater the barriers facing the unrepresented litigant, the greater the level of intervention that will be needed to provide meaningful assistance. For litigants with higher education and fewer barriers, navigating systems with less procedural complexity, substantive law that affords relief at least on paper, and more user-friendly and accommodating courts, more limited forms of assistance might suffice. The allocation of expert advocates, whether as direct representatives or supervisors in a particular setting, as opposed to inexperienced advocates, should be analyzed with these realities in mind as well.

These considerations should also inform conversations regarding the need for a civil right to counsel. I have articulated elsewhere a synthesis that recognizes a civil right to counsel as part of an overarching Access to Justice strategy, which includes three prongs:

(1) changes in the operation of the forum, including the expansion of the roles of the court system's or administrative agency's key players, such as judges, court-connected mediators and clerks, to require them to assist unrepresented litigants as necessary to prevent a forfeiture of important rights;
(2) the use of assistance programs, rigorously evaluated to identify which most effectively protect litigants from the forfeiture of rights; and
(3) the adoption of a civil right to counsel where the expansion of the roles of the key players and the assistance programs do not provide the necessary help to vulnerable litigants.[80]

The three-pronged analysis points the way to a targeted representation model, which serves as a middle ground between a categorical right to counsel and a case-by-case approach.

Full representation by skilled advocates with expertise in a particular setting remains an essential component to any strategy designed to provide meaningful access. The importance of representation extends beyond the outcomes of individual cases, impacting communities, legal systems, and government coffers as

[80] See, e.g., Russell Engler, *Towards a Context-Based Civil Gideon through Access to Justice Initiatives*, 40 Clearinghouse Rev. 196 (July–August 2006). For an explanation of the three prongs, see, *id.* at 42–43. I have also explored how the pieces of the comprehensive strategy are in place and the progress occurring, primarily at the state level, with activities at each of the three prongs. Russell Engler, Turner v. Rogers *and the Essential Role of the Courts in Delivering Access to Justice*, 7 Harv. L. & Pol'y Rev. 31, 45–50 (2013).

well. As we test new innovations and develop new research, we must accept as a starting point that, particularly where basic human needs are at stake, vulnerable litigants on the wrong end of power imbalances should be presumed to need full representation by a skilled representative. Our promise of the balanced scales of justice requires nothing less.

5

Self-Representation and the Dismissal of Chapter 7 Bankruptcy Cases

Rafael I. Pardo

It is difficult to demonstrate empirically that representation matters. But Rafael Pardo's discussion of his and other empirical work shows that represented debtors fare much better than self-represented debtors in individual Chapter 7 bankruptcy cases. Pardo suggests this is due in part to the complexity of the Bankruptcy Code.

The primary substantive relief that bankruptcy law provides to a financially distressed debtor is a discharge releasing him from personal liability for his pre-bankruptcy debts.[1] But filing for bankruptcy does not guarantee that a debtor will be afforded such relief. The path to discharge involves a process laden with myriad procedural requirements. Failure to comply with them can result in a death knell for the debtor's financial rehabilitation – specifically, dismissal of the debtor's case.

Bankruptcy law is highly specialized and technical, including the provisions that relate to bankruptcy cases filed by individuals.[2] Accordingly, to successfully navigate the complex path that ultimately culminates in a discharge, the assistance of an expert will be indispensable. Nonetheless, when individuals seek bankruptcy relief, they can either go it alone or seek the assistance of an attorney.[3] For self-represented debtors, the question arises whether that

[1] See, e.g., 11 U.S.C. §§ 524(a)(2), 727(b). This chapter draws on and excerpts (with some revisions) from my previously published work on the topic of self-representation in Chapter 7 cases involving individual debtors. See Rafael I. Pardo, *An Empirical Examination of Access to Chapter 7 Relief by Pro Se Debtors*, 26 Emory Bankr. Dev. J. 5 (2009).

[2] See, e.g., *Dignity Health v. Seare* (In re *Seare*), 493 B.R. 158, 221 (Bankr. D. Nev. 2013); *In re Malewicki*, 142 B.R. 353, 357 (Bankr. D. Neb. 1992); 1 Nat'l Bankr. Rev. Comm'n, Bankruptcy: The Next Twenty Years 79 (1997).

[3] Self-representation does not necessarily mean that the debtor will lack assistance. Some debtors may enlist the aid of others, which falls short of formal legal representation. One example of such assistance is that of a bankruptcy petition preparer (BPP), which the Bankruptcy Code defines as "a person, other than an attorney for the debtor or an employee of such attorney under the direct supervision of such attorney, who prepares for compensation a document for filing." 11 U.S.C. § 110(a)(1) (2012). The Code sets forth standards governing the activities of BPPs and provides for civil remedies in the event of noncompliance. See *id.* § 110.

decision makes them worse off than they otherwise would have been had they enlisted the assistance of an expert attorney.

This question has particular salience in the context of individuals who seek relief under Chapter 7 of the Bankruptcy Code. In a Chapter 7 case, an individual debtor must give up all non-exempt assets in exchange for a discharge. Year in and year out, Chapter 7 cases account for the majority of bankruptcy filings by individuals.[4] Prior empirical research has shown that self-represented debtors in Chapter 7 fare worse than their represented counterparts. This chapter offers new empirical evidence suggesting that the plight of self-represented debtors in Chapter 7 has not improved and that serious access to justice concerns persist.

THE NATURE OF LEGAL REPRESENTATION IN CHAPTER 7 CASES INVOLVING INDIVIDUAL DEBTORS

Although bankruptcy is formally a judicial process, much of the process historically has been and continues to be managerial and ministerial in nature.[5] For a debtor to voluntarily access the federal bankruptcy forum, he or she must file a case under the operative chapter of the Bankruptcy Code pursuant to which the debtor wishes the case to proceed (e.g., Chapter 7).[6] The case itself is an administrative proceeding within which disputes may, but need not, arise.[7]

A court must grant an individual Chapter 7 debtor a discharge unless the debtor falls within a particular class of individual, usually defined by reference to a limited set of circumstances that relate to debtor fraud or misconduct in connection with the bankruptcy case.[8] An objection to a Chapter 7 debtor's discharge must generally be filed no later than sixty days after the first date set for the meeting of creditors,[9] which must be set no earlier than twenty days and no later than forty days after the date that the Chapter 7 debtor filed for bankruptcy.[10] Accordingly, approximately three months after filing for bankruptcy, a Chapter 7 debtor will likely know whether a discharge will be forthcoming.[11] Most courts will enter a discharge order without requiring the debtor to appear in court on the rationale that doing so would impose

4 See Admin. Office of the U.S. Courts, *Bankruptcy Statistics*, www.uscourts.gov/Statistics/BankruptcyStatistics.aspx (last visited May 28, 2015).

5 See Richard B. Levin, *Towards a Model of Bankruptcy Administration*, 44 S.C. L. Rev. 963, 965–68 (1993).

6 See 11 U.S.C. § 301(a) (2012).

7 *Menk v. Lapaglia (In re Menk)*, 241 B.R. 896, 910 (B.A.P. 9th Cir. 1999).

8 11 U.S.C. § 727(a).

9 Fed. R. Bankr. P. 4004(a). A court, however, may extend for cause the time for filing an objection to discharge. *Id.* 4004(b).

10 *Id.* 2003(a).

11 Failure of a party in interest to file a complaint objecting to discharge within the time allotted by the Bankruptcy Rules precludes denial of a Chapter 7 discharge, unless procedural considerations – such as an extension of the time for filing a complaint objecting to discharge or a pending motion to dismiss the debtor's case – warrant otherwise. See *id.* 4004(c)(1).

unnecessary costs on the debtor.[12] At its essence, then, a Chapter 7 case involves properly filling out forms so as to ensure that the case is processed seamlessly and ultimately results in discharge.[13]

While the possibility of dismissal for a deficient filing has always existed, extensive amendments to the Bankruptcy Code in 2005 expanded the grounds for dismissal of a debtor's Chapter 7 case. These amendments – the Bankruptcy Abuse Prevention and Consumer Protection Act of 2005 (BAPCPA)[14] – made access to Chapter 7 relief more complex, especially by increasing the amount of disclosures required of individual debtors.[15] The increased complexity, in turn, has increased the importance of obtaining representation.[16]

The disclosure requirements are generally an integral component of bankruptcy as a collective proceeding that aims to distribute the debtor's assets for the benefit of creditors. The marshalling and distribution functions of a bankruptcy proceeding can only be carried out properly with adequate information regarding the debtor's financial circumstances (e.g., assets, liabilities, income, and expenses).[17] Accordingly, the Bankruptcy Code has structured a self-reporting system pursuant to which a debtor must make such disclosures.[18] Prior to BAPCPA's enactment, the Bankruptcy Code required a debtor's filing to include: (1) a list of creditors, (2) a schedule of assets and liabilities, (3) a schedule of current income and expenditures, and (4) a statement of the debtor's financial affairs.[19] Failure of a Chapter 7 debtor to file any of these documents within fifteen days after the

[12] Elizabeth Warren & Jay Lawrence Westbrook, The Law of Debtors and Creditors 229 (6th ed. 2009).

[13] See 1 Henry J. Sommer et al., Consumer Bankruptcy Law and Practice § 7.1.1, at 85 (John Rao ed., 9th ed. 2009).

[14] Bankruptcy Abuse Prevention and Consumer Protection Act of 2005 (BARCA), Pub. L. No. 109–8, 119 Stat. 23, 23–217.

[15] See, e.g., Ad Hoc Comm. on Bankr. Court Structure and Insolvency Processes, ABA Section of Bus. Law, *Working Paper: Best Practices for Debtors' Attorneys*, 64 Bus. Law. 79, 84, 85 (2008). It should be noted that the increased complexity has likely exacerbated the negative effects of poor-quality lawyering, thus making the need for an attorney who is highly skilled and competent more imperative than ever. See Lois R. Lupica, *The Consumer Bankruptcy Fee Study: Final Report*, 20 Am. Bankr. Inst. L. Rev. 17, 121–24 (2012). Accordingly, representation alone might not help individual debtors obtain successful outcomes. See *id.* at 104 (noting "perception [by attorneys, panel trustees, and bankruptcy judges] that there may be price undercutting, and sub-quality work being performed by lawyers less experienced in consumer bankruptcy practice").

[16] See Jean Braucher, *A Guide to Interpretation of the 2005 Bankruptcy Law*, 16 Am. Bankr. Inst. L. Rev. 349, 372 (2008); A. Mechele Dickerson, *Race Matters in Bankruptcy Reform*, 71 Mo. L. Rev. 919, 951 (2006); *cf.* Richard I. Aaron, *Access to Justice: Consumer Bankruptcy*, 2006 Utah L. Rev. 925, 936; Henry J. Sommer, *Trying to Make Sense Out of Nonsense: Representing Consumers Under the "Bankruptcy Abuse Prevention and Consumer Protection Act of 2005,"* 79 Am. Bankr. L.J. 191, 191 (2005).

[17] See *Siegel v. Weldon* (In re *Weldon*), 184 B.R. 710, 715 (Bankr. D.S.C. 1995); Sommer, supra note 13, § 7.1.1, at 85.

[18] See 11 U.S.C. § 521.

[19] *Id.* § 521(1) (2000) (amended 2005).

commencement of the case provided cause for the U.S. Trustee to move for dismissal of the case.[20]

With BAPCPA's enactment, an individual debtor must now also file: (1) copies of all payment advices received from an employer in the two months preceding the bankruptcy filing; (2) a statement of monthly net income, itemized to show how the amount is calculated; and (3) a statement disclosing any reasonably anticipated increase in income or expenditures for the year following the bankruptcy filing.[21] A Chapter 7 debtor who fails to file any of these documents not only faces possible dismissal upon a motion by the U.S. Trustee, but also faces *automatic* dismissal of the case for failure to file any of these documents within forty-five days after filing for bankruptcy.[22] A debtor must also file a certificate of pre-bankruptcy credit counseling and the debtor's federal income tax return from the tax year preceding the bankruptcy filing.[23] Failure to file the certificate presumably provides cause for any party in interest to move to dismiss the debtor's case,[24] whereas failure to file the tax return requires the court to dismiss the debtor's case, unless the debtor's noncompliance resulted from circumstances beyond the debtor's control.[25]

Individual debtors thus face a variety of procedural hurdles in gaining access to the federal bankruptcy forum. Chapter 7 debtors must also contend with the specter of an abuse dismissal based on the means test, a formulaic statutory directive that requires courts to presume abuse of the bankruptcy system by Chapter 7 debtors whose debts primarily consist of consumer debts (consumer debtors) and who seemingly have an ability to repay their debts from future income.[26] As part of the schedule of current income and expenditures that all debtors must file,[27] a Chapter 7 debtor must also include a statement of the debtor's current monthly income and calculations that determine whether the presumption of abuse arises under the means test.[28] The official forms for documenting these calculations consist of fifty-seven items,[29] the first fourteen of which must be completed by most debtors.[30]

[20] *Id.* § 707(a)(3). Subsequent to BAPCPA's enactment, a debtor's failure to file such documents still constitutes cause for the U.S. Trustee to move for dismissal of the case. *Id.* § 707(a)(3) (2012).

[21] *Id.* § 521(a)(1)(B)(iv)–(vi) (2012).

[22] *Id.* § 521(i)(1). There are some narrow exceptions to this rule. See *id.* § 521(i)(3) (allowing extension of time to file documents that does not exceed an additional forty-five days); *id.* § 521(i)(4) (granting the court discretion under a narrow set of circumstances not to dismiss the debtor's case, but only upon motion of the trustee before expiration of initial forty-five day period for filing mandated disclosures).

[23] *Id.* § 521(b)(1) (credit-counseling certificate); *id.* § 521(e)(2)(A) (tax return).

[24] *Id.* § 707(a)(3); *In re Dyer*, 381 B.R. 200, 206 (Bankr. W.D.N.C. 2007).

[25] 11 U.S.C. § 521(e)(2)(B).

[26] See *id.* § 707(b)(1), (b)(2)(A)(i).

[27] See *id.* § 521(a)(1)(B)(ii).

[28] See *id.* § 707(b)(2)(C).

[29] See Official Form B 22A1 (Chapter 7 Statement of Your Current Monthly Income); Official Form B 22A2 (Chapter 7 Means Test Calculation).

[30] Debtors whose debts are *not* primarily consumer debts are not subject to an abuse-dismissal motion, see 11 U.S.C. § 707(b)(1), and thus do not have to complete a statement of their current monthly income, see Official Form B 22A1 Supp (Statement of Exemption from Presumption of Abuse Under § 707(b)(2)).

Furthermore, for any debtor whose annual income is greater than the median family income for a family of comparable size to the debtor's household, that debtor must complete the remaining forty-three items relating to calculation of the means test.[31]

Evidence strongly indicates that Congress cast an overly broad net when it designed the abuse dismissal framework – that is, the vast number of debtors do not fall within the class of individual targeted by the complex statutory scheme. For example, during the six-year period spanning the 2006 and 2011 U.S. government fiscal years, less than 1% of consumer Chapter 7 cases involved an abuse dismissal motion (with the exception of the 2007 fiscal year during which 1.1% of the cases involved such a motion).[32] Thus, the overwhelming majority of individual debtors have been forced to grapple with the collateral effects of a statute never intended to reach them.

Predictably, these effects have had an adverse impact on a debtor's access to Chapter 7 relief. First, filing fees and expenses have increased for consumer debtors.[33] Second, the combination of new liability provisions for attorneys who represent consumer debtors[34] and the deluge of paperwork have exacerbated the due-diligence burden borne by attorneys who represent consumer debtors.[35] This, in turn, has likely increased the costs of legal representation. For example, in her national study of consumer bankruptcy fees, Professor Lois Lupica found that, when controlling for a variety of explanatory factors that could account for the costs of legal representation, attorney's fees in Chapter 7 consumer cases were, on average, $258 higher (in inflation-adjusted 2005 dollars) subsequent to BAPCPA's enactment.[36] The increase in legal costs has likely made representation unaffordable for some debtors, forcing them either to file without the assistance of counsel or not to file at all.[37] Self-represented debtors run the risk of being denied access to the bankruptcy forum if they fail to comply with the myriad filing requirements.[38]

Furthermore, some debtors are not required to complete a statement of current monthly income because of certain qualified military service. See 11 U.S.C. § 707(b)(2)(D); Official Form B 22A1 Supp.

31 See *id.* § 707(b)(7); Official Form B 22A2.

32 See Stephen J. Spurr & Kevin M. Ball, *The Effects of a Statute (BAPCPA) Designed to Make It More Difficult for People to File for Bankruptcy*, 87 AM. BANKR. L.J. 27, 41 & n.52, 42 tbl.3 (2013).

33 See, e.g., Robert J. Landry & Amy K. Yarbrough, *An Empirical Examination of the Direct Access Costs to Chapter 7 Consumer Bankruptcy: A Pilot Study in the Northern District of Alabama*, 82 AM. BANKR. L.J. 331, 335–38 (2008); Lupica, supra note 15, at 68 & n.123, 87–88.

34 See 11 U.S.C. §§ 526(c)(2), 707(b)(4) (2012).

35 See Aaron, supra note 16, at 945; Lupica, supra note 15, at 100–102, 121–22; Eugene R. Wedoff, *Means Testing in the New § 707(b)*, 79 AM. BANKR. L.J. 231, 278 (2005).

36 See Lupica, supra note 15, at 86.

37 See Aaron, supra note 16, at 947; Lupica, supra note 15, at 99; Keith M. Lundin, *Ten Principles of BAPCPA: Not What Was Advertised*, AM. BANKR. INST. J., Sept. 2005, at 1, 70; Sommer, supra note 16, at 230; *cf.* Jean Braucher, *Means Testing Consumer Bankruptcy: The Problem of Means*, 7 FORDHAM J. CORP. & FIN. L. 407, 408 (2002).

38 See Aaron, supra note 16, at 947 ("Pro se bankruptcy drops the cost of lawyering, but the new law is salted with little land mines making the savings foolish and deceptive"); Dickerson, supra note 16, at 951 n.181 ("[F]iling *pro se* is not a realistic option.... [G]iven the complexity of BAPCPA's filing and

Finally, if the complexity of the system has discouraged skilled and competent attorneys from continuing to represent consumer debtors,[39] then the quality of the supply of legal representation may have been adversely affected.[40] In sum, the radical overhaul of the system has created the conditions for disproportionately impacting access to Chapter 7 relief by self-represented debtors. The remainder of this chapter explores the disquieting signs of this disproportionate impact.

PRIOR EMPIRICAL RESEARCH

Prior empirical research has consistently documented worse outcomes for self-represented debtors in Chapter 7 cases filed by individual debtors. Two of these studies and some of their salient findings will be briefly discussed here: (1) my study that was published in 2009 (the "2009 Pardo Study"),[41] and (2) the Consumer Bankruptcy Fee Study by Professor Lois Lupica that was published in 2012 (the "Lupica Study").[42]

The 2009 Pardo Study

The 2009 Pardo Study explored whether BAPCPA had a disproportionate impact on the ability of self-represented individual debtors to access Chapter 7 relief. The study examined dismissal rates in cases that were originally commenced under Chapter 7 and filed by individual debtors in the U.S. Bankruptcy Court for the Western District of Washington from 2003 through 2007.[43] The study hypothesized (1) that dismissal rates for self-represented debtors would be statistically significantly higher than for represented debtors; and (2) that dismissal rates for post-BAPCPA, self-represented debtors would be statistically significantly higher than for pre-BAPCPA, self-represented debtors.[44] Analyses of the data supported both hypotheses.[45] Among other things, the study focused on the effect of BAPCPA on the dismissal of a case based on the debtor's failure to file the information required by the Bankruptcy

reporting requirements, it is even more likely that a *pro se* petition will be dismissed because of procedural defaults").

[39] See Alan D. Eisler, *The BAPCPA's Chilling Effect on Debtor's Counsel*, 55 Am. U. L. Rev. 1333, 1334 (2006) 1334; Lupica, supra note 16, at 122.

[40] See Lupica, supra note 15, at 104, 122–23.

[41] Pardo, supra note 1.

[42] Lupica, supra note 15. For additional research documenting worse outcomes for self-represented debtors in Chapter 7 cases, see, for example, Adam M. Langley et al., *The Case for a Constitutional Bankruptcy Court*, 88 Am. Bankr. L.J. 515, 542 n.131 (2014); Angela Littwin, *The Affordability Paradox: How Consumer Bankruptcy's Greatest Weakness May Account for Its Surprising Success*, 52 Wm. & Mary L. Rev. 1933, 1971–72, 1973 tbl.3a (2011).

[43] Pardo, supra note 1, at 21–22.

[44] *Id.* at 19.

[45] See *id.* at 23–25.

Code (as opposed to having been dismissed for some other reason).[46] The study found that the odds of dismissal on this basis for post-BAPCPA, self-represented debtors were 4.42 times greater than for pre-BAPCPCA, self-represented debtors; 4.14 times greater than for post-BAPCPA, represented debtors; and 11.68 times greater than for pre-BAPCPA, represented debtors.[47] These findings suggested that the combination of lack of representation and filing for bankruptcy post-BAPCPA had a negative effect on the probability of a debtor overcoming the procedural hurdles that impede access to Chapter 7 relief.[48]

The Lupica Study

The Lupica Study sought to address "issues related to the institutional framework of consumer bankruptcy by not only measuring and monetizing the cost of access, but by also examining the incentives and constraints imposed by the system."[49] At the heart of the study's investigation was "the hypothesis that following BAPCPA's enactment, the cost of accessing the consumer bankruptcy system increased."[50] The study's quantitative analysis focused on a national random sample of 11,221 Chapter 7 and Chapter 13 cases filed by consumer debtors ("consumer cases") between 2003 and 2009 in ninety federal judicial districts.[51] The study briefly devoted attention to comparing self-representation rates prior and subsequent to BAPCPA to explore the theory that the increased costs of access to the bankruptcy system may have made debtors "less likely to engage an attorney and more likely to file their case *pro se*."[52] The study found that, subsequent to BAPCPA, there was a statistically significant decrease in the proportion of all Chapter 7 cases (i.e., asset and no-asset cases[53]) filed by self-represented debtors – specifically, 7.4% for pre-BAPCPA cases compared to 5.8% for post-BAPCPA cases, a drop of 1.6 percentage points.[54] The study, however, did not compare case outcomes between represented

46 See *id.* at 27–31.
47 *Id.* at 30.
48 *Id.* at 32.
49 Lupica, supra note 15, at 28.
50 *Id.*
51 *Id.* at 29, 46.
52 *Id.* at 81.
53 In a no-asset case, the debtor does not have nonexempt assets for liquidation and distribution to creditors. Historically, more than 90% of Chapter 7 cases filed by individual debtors have been no-asset cases. See, e.g., Lois R. Lupica, Am. Bankr. Inst. & Nat'l Conference of Bankr. Judges, The Consumer Bankruptcy Creditor Distribution Study 6 (2013).
54 Lupica, supra note 15, at 82; *id.* app. III, at 139 tbl.A-7. The 2009 Pardo Study also found a statistically significant decrease along the same line. See Pardo, supra note 1, at 18 n.60 (reporting that the self-represented rate in the Western District of Washington dropped from 18.8% for pre-BAPCPA cases to 13.2% for post-BAPCPA cases and that the difference between the observed and expected values was statistically significant). The Lupica Study further found that, when disaggregating the data pursuant to various case characteristics (i.e., focusing on asset and no-asset cases as two subsets, and then further

and self-represented cases. Nonetheless, the study provides sufficient detail to estimate discharge rates in the two types of cases.

Among the study's sample of Chapter 7 consumer cases, there were 4,151 pre-BAPCPA cases and 3,149 post-BAPCPA cases, for a total of 7,300 cases.[55] Of the 4,151 pre-BAPCPA cases, there were 414 asset cases and 3,737 no-asset cases.[56] Of the 3,149 post-BAPCPA cases, there were 333 asset cases and 2,816 asset cases.[57] The study further reports discharge rates in the Chapter 7 cases. For pre-BAPCPA cases, the discharge rate was 92.5% in asset cases and 98.8% in no-asset cases.[58] For post-BAPCPA cases, the discharge rate was 95.8% in asset cases and 97.2% in no-asset cases.[59] Finally, the study reports the percentage of asset and no-asset cases filed by self-represented debtors, as well as the percentage of asset and no-asset cases involving self-represented debtors who received a discharge. For pre-BAPCPA cases, the percentage of cases filed by self-represented debtors was 5.8% for asset cases and 7.6% for no-asset cases.[60] For post-BAPCPA cases, the percentage of cases filed by self-represented debtors was 3.3% for asset cases and 6.1% for no-asset cases.[61] For pre-BAPCPA cases in which a discharge was granted, the percentage of cases filed by self-represented debtors was 6.0% for asset cases and 7.4% for no-asset cases.[62] Finally, for post-BAPCPA cases in which a discharge was granted, the percentage of cases filed by self-represented debtors was 2.8% for asset cases and 5.5% for no-asset cases.[63]

With these figures, one can estimate pre-BAPCPA and post-BAPCPA discharge rates in the Lupica Study's Chapter 7 consumer cases. First, the discharge rates for pre-BAPCPA cases were 98.3% for cases filed by represented debtors and 96.1% for cases filed by self-represented debtors. Second, the discharge rates for post-BAPCPA cases were 97.6% for cases filed by represented debtors and 87.4% for cases filed by self-represented debtors.

focusing on discharged cases and dismissed cases within those two subsets), the statistically significant decrease mostly persisted. See Lupica, supra note 15, app. III, at 139 tbl.A-7. Finally, while the national trend, according to AOUSC data, was an increase in the self-represented filing rate between 2007 and 2012, see Fig. 5.1, the median and mean filing rates over this period of time were 7.4% and 7.5%. When these figures are compared to the 7.4% nationwide, pre-BAPCPA, self-represented filing rate reported in the Lupica Study, the comparison suggests that the post-BAPCPA rate has finally returned to the pre-BAPCPA level (and will eventually surpass it if the rate continues to increase during the next several years).

55 Lupica, supra note 15, at 67 tbl.2.

56 See *id.*

57 See *id.* Accordingly, there were a total of 747 asset cases and 6,553 no-asset cases, for a grand total of 7,300 cases. These figures slightly differ from the figures reported elsewhere in the study due to a discrepancy in the number of no-asset cases. See *id.* at 53 (reporting a total of 7,350 Chapter 7 cases, which consisted of 6,603 no-asset cases and 747 asset cases).

58 *Id.* at 68.

59 *Id.*

60 *Id.* at 82; *id.* app. III, at 139 tbl.A-7.

61 *Id.*

62 *Id.*

63 *Id.*

Based on these estimates, one witnesses that the discharge rates were higher for represented debtors than self-represented debtors regardless of the time period – specifically, 2.2 percentage points higher for pre-BAPCPA cases and 10.2 percentage points higher for post-BAPCPA cases. Furthermore, while the post-BAPCPA discharge rate for represented debtors was slightly lower than their pre-BAPCPA discharge rate (97.6% compared to 98.3%, a mere drop of seven-tenths of a percentage point), the post-BAPCPA discharge rate for self-represented debtors was dramatically lower than their pre-BAPCPA discharge rate (87.4% compared to 96.1%, a drop of 8.7 percentage points). These findings are consistent with unreported findings from the 2009 Pardo Study.[64]

EMPIRICAL EXAMINATION OF THE CONSEQUENCES OF SELF-REPRESENTATION

This chapter now presents empirical evidence from a case study that examines the ability of self-represented debtors to access Chapter 7 relief (the "2014 Pardo Study"). Dismissal of a debtor's case is used as the metric for failure to access Chapter 7 relief. The rationale for selecting this metric is based on the fact that dismissal of a debtor's case will dispositively result in the failure of the debtor to obtain a discharge and thus bankruptcy's fresh start. Obviously, a debtor's case remaining within the bankruptcy system will not dispositively result in a discharge insofar as the debtor's circumstances may warrant denial of discharge.[65] That said, the reality is that, of the 79,649 non-dismissed Chapter 7 cases in this study, 99.3% resulted in a discharge for the debtor.[66] In other words, remaining within the system virtually guaranteed access to Chapter 7 relief.

Notably, in the non-dismissed cases, represented debtors fared somewhat better than self-represented debtors in obtaining discharges. While the overall share of non-dismissed cases involving a discharge was approximately 99.3%, represented debtors had a discharge rate that was approximately 2.8 percentage points higher than self-represented debtors (99.5% compared to 96.7%).[67] In terms of odds, a represented debtor's odds of obtaining a discharge were approximately 212 to 1,

64 In the 2009 Pardo Study, the discharge rates were higher for represented debtors than for self-represented debtors regardless of the time period – specifically, 4.6 percentage points higher for pre-BAPCPA cases (99.0% compared to 94.4%) and 16.0 percentage points higher for post-BAPCPA cases (98.0% compared to 82.0%). Furthermore, while the post-BAPCPA discharge rate for represented debtors was slightly lower than their pre-BAPCPA discharge rate (99.0% compared to 98.0%, a mere drop of one percentage point), the post-BAPCPA discharge rate for self-represented debtors was dramatically lower than their pre-BAPCPA discharge rate (94.4% compared to 82.0%, a drop of 12.4 percentage points).

65 See supra note 9 and accompanying text.

66 This finding is similar to the 2009 Pardo Study's finding that 99.7% of non-dismissed Chapter 7 cases resulted in a discharge for the debtor. See Pardo, supra note 1, at 19 n.65.

67 The difference between the observed and expected values is statistically significant ($p < 0.0001$) according to a chi-square test with one degree of freedom.

in contrast to 30 to 1 for self-represented debtors. Accordingly, in the non-dismissed cases, the odds of discharge for a represented debtor were seven times higher than those of self-represented debtors.

Importantly, however, the overwhelming majority of non-dismissed cases involving denial of discharge occurred as a result of the debtor's failure to file a certification indicating that he or she completed an instructional course concerning personal financial management (the "financial management course"). This ground for denial of discharge was a product of BAPCPA.[68] The official form for the certification consists solely of one page,[69] and the certification must be filed in a Chapter 7 case within 60 days after the first date set for the meeting of creditors, unless the court extends the deadline.[70] Failure to do so will result in a denial of discharge.[71] Of the 531 non-dismissed cases involving denial of discharge, approximately 81.2% (i.e., 431 cases) involved denial of discharge based on the debtor's failure to file proof of completion of the financial management course, but there was no statistically significant association between the represented status of the debtor and denial of discharge on this basis.[72]

While denial of discharge in a non-dismissed case is undoubtedly part of the story regarding Chapter 7 relief, those cases constitute only slightly more than a quarter (approximately 26.5%) of the cases involving negative outcomes.[73] Moreover, the vast majority of those cases involve denial on a ground that is not statistically significantly associated with the represented status of the debtor. Accordingly, a focus on dismissal rates presents a more refined approach to examining the failure of debtors to access Chapter 7 relief. Consistent with the findings of the 2009 Pardo Study, it is hypothesized that dismissal rates for self-represented debtors will be statistically significantly higher than for represented debtors. Analyses of the data provide support for this hypothesis.

Study Design

Before presenting the findings from the 2014 Pardo Study, a description is warranted of some of the salient characteristics of the study's location, the Western District of

[68] See BAPCA, supra note 14, § 106(b)(3), 119 Stat. 23, 38 (codified at 11 U.S.C. § 727(a)(11) (2012)).

[69] See Official Form 23 (Debtor's Certification of Completion of Postpetition Instructional Course Concerning Personal Financial Management).

[70] Fed. R. Bankr. P. 1007(c).

[71] 11 U.S.C. § 727(a)(11); Fed. R. Bankr. P. 4004(c)(1)(H).

[72] Of the debtors who were denied a discharge, failure to file proof of completion of the financial management course was the basis for the denial for approximately 83.4% of the represented debtors and 76.9% of the self-represented debtors. The difference between the observed and expected values is not statistically significant at the 5% level ($p = 0.071$) according to a chi-square test with one degree of freedom.

[73] There were 2,005 cases that resulted either in dismissal (1,474 cases) or denial of discharge (531 cases).

Washington (the "Western District"), which consists of nineteen counties,[74] both rural and metropolitan. It is estimated that the District's population of persons age eighteen and over in 2012 was 4,172,607.[75] Nearly three-quarters (73.9%) of that population resided in four counties – Clark, King, Pierce, and Snohomish Counties – with the remainder scattered over fifteen counties.[76]

Consumer debtors in the adult population (eighteen years and older) of the Western District file for Chapter 7 relief at a slightly higher rate than the national average, as evidenced by (1) data from the U.S. Census Bureau on the adult population[77] and (2) data from the Administrative Office of the U.S. Courts (AOUSC) on bankruptcy filings.[78] For example, in 2012, the average number of Chapter 7 consumer cases filed nationwide for every 1,000 adults was 3.4 cases. During the same year, the average number of Chapter 7 consumer cases filed in the Western District for every 1,000 adults was 4.1 cases.[79]

Also, the estimated proportion of self-represented Chapter 7 cases filed by individuals in the Western District slightly differs from the national proportion during the six-year period from 2007 through 2012. Estimating this proportion presents some difficulty. While the AOUSC tracks the number of cases filed by self-represented debtors by the chapter of the Bankruptcy Code under which the case was filed, the AOUSC does not disaggregate the number according to whether the case involved predominantly business or nonbusiness debt.[80] On the other hand, the AOUSC does track the total number of cases filed (whether by self-represented or represented debtors) both by chapter and by the predominant nature of the debt (i.e., business or nonbusiness).[81]

To estimate the proportion of Chapter 7 cases filed by self-represented debtors using AOUSC data, only one option exists for the numerator – the total number of Chapter 7 cases filed by self-represented debtors. While this number will consist only

[74] Those counties are Clallam, Clark, Cowlitz, Grays Harbor, Island, Jefferson, King, Kitsap, Lewis, Mason, Pacific, Pierce, San Juan, Skagit, Skamania, Snohomish, Thurston, Wahkiakum, and Whatcom Counties. See 28 U.S.C. § 128(b) (2012).

[75] See U.S. Census Bureau, Annual Estimates of the Resident Population for Selected Age Groups by Sex for the United States, States, Counties, and Puerto Rico Commonwealth and Municipios: April 1, 2010 to July 1, 2012 (2013).

[76] See *id.*

[77] See *id.*; U.S. Census Bureau, 2012 American Community Survey 1-Year Estimates (2012).

[78] See Admin. Office of the U.S. Courts, supra note 5.

[79] In 2012, there were 816,271 nonbusiness Chapter 7 filings in the nation, and the adult population nationally was 240,203,630. By comparison, there were 17,310 nonbusiness bankruptcy filings in the Western District of Washington, and the adult population in the District was 4,172,607.

[80] See Administrative Office of the U.S. Courts, Table F-28 (U.S. Bankruptcy Courts - Bankruptcy Cases Filed by Pro Se Debtors, by Chapter).

[81] See Administrative Office of the U.S. Courts, Table F-2 (U.S. Bankruptcy Courts - Business and Nonbusiness Cases Commenced, by Chapter of the Bankruptcy Code"). For further discussion regarding the manner in which the AOUSC classifies business and nonbusiness filings, see U.S. Gov't Accountability Office, Report No. GAO-09–28, Judiciary Should Take Further Steps to Make Bankruptcy Data More Accessible 14 (2008).

of cases filed by individual debtors (given that legal entities must be represented by counsel), some of those cases will involve debtors whose debts primarily consist of business debts. Importantly, however, among individual cases, the proportion involving primarily business debts has historically been very small.[82] On the other hand two options exist for the denominator – either the total number of Chapter 7 cases filed or the total number of Chapter 7 nonbusiness cases filed. The former will involve cases filed by individuals (whose debts are predominantly either business or nonbusiness debts) and legal entities, whereas the latter will only involve cases filed by individuals whose debts are predominantly nonbusiness debts (thus excluding cases filed by individuals whose debts are predominantly business debts). Accordingly, using the total number of Chapter 7 cases filed as the denominator will underestimate the self-represented proportion; and using the total number of Chapter 7 nonbusiness cases filed as the denominator will overestimate the self-represented proportion – but probably only slightly so given that there are very few cases filed by individuals whose debts involve predominantly business debts. The better estimate is likely produced by using the total number of Chapter 7 nonbusiness cases filed.

Estimating the self-represented proportion in this manner, AOUSC data indicate that the proportion of Chapter 7 cases filed by self-represented debtors in the Western District slightly differs from the national proportion during the six-year period from 2007 through 2012. As illustrated in Figure 5.1 below, the percentage of self-represented debtors in the Western District was greater than the national percentage during the 2007, 2008, and 2009 calendar years.

On the other hand, the national percentage exceeded the percentage in the Western District during the 2010, 2011, and 2012 calendar years. The median and mean percentages in the Western District during this six-year period were, respectively, 8.1% and 8.5% of the Chapter 7 nonbusiness cases. In contrast, the median and mean percentages nationwide during the same period were, respectively 7.4% and 7.5% of the Chapter 7 nonbusiness cases.

Descriptive Statistics and Bivariate Analyses

The data for this study, obtained from the Office of the Clerk of Court (the "Clerk's Office") for the U.S. Bankruptcy Court for the Western District of Washington, consist of some of the information that the Clerk's Office internally tracks for individual cases. These case-level data are derived from the self-reported information provided by the debtor to the court in the debtor's petition and accompanying schedules,[83] and they are generally available to the public through the Public Access to Court Electronic Records system.

[82] See, e.g., Robert M. Lawless & Elizabeth Warren, *The Myth of the Disappearing Business Bankruptcy*, 93 CAL. L. REV. 743, 773 tbl.2 (2005).

[83] The Clerk's Office provided the same types of data for the 2014 Pardo Study as it did for the 2009 Pardo Study. For a specific listing of these types of data, see Pardo, supra note 1, at 21 n.77.

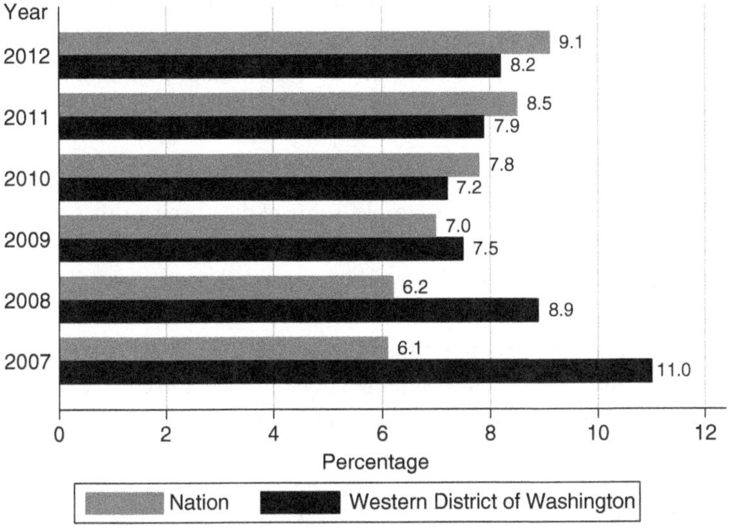

FIGURE 5.1. Estimated percentage of self-represented Chapter 7 cases by calendar year.

Source: Author's calculations based on Administrative Office of the U.S. Courts, Tables F-2 (U.S. Bankruptcy Courts – Business and Nonbusiness Cases Commenced, by Chapter of the Bankruptcy Code) and F-28 (U.S. Bankruptcy Courts – Bankruptcy Cases Filed by Pro Se Debtors, by Chapter).

The Clerk's Office provided information on all voluntary Chapter 7 cases of individual debtors that were filed in the Western District during the five-year period beginning on January 1, 2008, and ending on December 31, 2012. Excluded from the study are cases that were originally commenced under a chapter other than Chapter 7 (e.g., Chapter 13) but subsequently converted to Chapter 7, as well as cases that were originally commenced under Chapter 7 but subsequently transferred to another federal judicial district. In total, the dataset from which this study's findings are derived consists of 81,127 cases (the "study population").

According to these data, self-represented debtors filed approximately 7.7% (i.e., 6,252 of 81,127) of all voluntary cases in the study population. Before exploring the ability of self-represented debtors to access Chapter 7 relief, this section presents some of the financial characteristics of these self-represented debtors. In addition to the financial data provided by the Clerk's Office, the following financial characteristics have been calculated using the data from the Clerk's Office: (1) the debtor's monthly disposable household income, measured as the difference between the debtor's monthly household income and expenses on a debtor-by-debtor basis; (2) the ratio of the debtor's annual household income to the amounts set forth in the poverty guidelines established by the U.S. Department of Health and Human

Services (poverty ratio);[84] and (3) the number of years' worth of household income that the debtor would have had to devote to fully repay his or her total debt, measured by the ratio of total debt to the debtor's annual household income (the debt-to-income ratio). Table 5.1 sets forth these characteristics with all figures adjusted to 2013 dollars.

The financial characteristics indicate the magnitude of hardship faced by self-represented debtors. Consider, for example, some of the characteristics of the median self-represented debtor. With an annual household income of approximately $26,298, the median debtor would be hard-pressed to make daily ends meet. The disposable income data further reinforce this point. The household of the median self-represented debtor operated at a razor-thin monthly surplus of $43. Given the low monthly expense figure of $2,270, the median self-represented debtor was not likely to be a spendthrift, but instead was likely to devote monthly income to meet basic needs such as housing, food, and transportation. The proximity of the household of the median self-represented debtor to the poverty line further suggests that, more likely than not, the median debtor had little flexibility, if any at all, to reduce monthly expenses. The household of the median debtor generated income that placed it barely twice over the poverty line, thus conjuring the image of a household eking out a minimal existence.[85] Under these conditions, the median self-represented debtor was expected to cope with the crushing total debt load (i.e., the combined amount of secured debt, priority unsecured debt, and nonpriority unsecured debt) of $62,845. The median debtor would have had to devote nearly five years' worth of household income to fully repay this debt (assuming, of course, that the amount of debt would not increase by virtue of interest or other charges and that the debtor's household would live expense free). Simply put, the median self-represented debtor was in horrible financial shape.

Moreover, as set forth in Table 5.2, according to a series of two-sided, nonparametric Wilcoxon rank-sum tests, a statistically significantly association existed between the represented status of debtors and select financial characteristics, with

[84] The poverty guidelines constitute a simplified version of the federal poverty threshold and are administratively used to determine financial eligibility for certain federal assistance programs. See Annual Update of the HHS Poverty Guidelines, 78 Fed. Reg. 5182, 5183 (Jan. 24, 2013). Because HHS poverty guidelines for any given calendar year approximate the U.S. Census Bureau poverty thresholds from the previous calendar year, see *id.*, the poverty guidelines from a given calendar year (e.g., 2013) were used to calculate the poverty ratio in cases filed in the prior calendar year (e.g., 2012).

[85] For example, the 2013 HHS poverty guidelines define the poverty line for the contiguous United States as a household with income of $11,490 for the first member and $4,020 for each additional member. See *id.* Importantly, the reported poverty ratios in all likelihood *overestimate* the amount by which the debtor's income exceeded the poverty line. The data provided by the Clerk's Office did not include the debtor's number of dependents, the debtor's marital status, or the household size of the debtor. For a singly filed case, the poverty ratio was calculated assuming that the debtor's household consisted of one individual. For a jointly filed case (i.e., a case filed by spouses, see 11 U.S.C. § 302(a) (2012)), the poverty ratio was calculated assuming that the debtor's household consisted of two individuals. In other words, the poverty ratio was calculated using the most conservative estimates of family size. If the family size were larger, the poverty guideline figure (i.e., the denominator in the ratio) would be larger, thus reducing the ratio of the debtor's annual income to the poverty line.

TABLE 5.1 *Financial characteristics of Chapter 7 individual cases filed in the U.S. Bankruptcy Court for the Western District of Washington, 2008–12.*

	Represented cases				Self-represented cases			
Financial characteristics	Mean	Median	Observed	Missing	Mean	Median	Observed	Missing
Real property	$140,225	$6,733	74,111	764	$60,775	$0	5,376	876
Personal property	$32,675	$18,433	74,291	584	$18,699	$6,731	5,560	692
Secured debt	$173,855	$43,028	74,179	696	$77,563	$2,268	5,412	840
Priority unsecured debt	$3,449	$0	73,971	904	$6,171	$0	5,362	890
Nonpriority unsecured debt	$88,383	$51,044	74,284	591	$80,892	$39,227	5,514	738
Monthly income	$3,642	$3,413	73,629	1,246	$2,911	$2,244	5,148	1,104
Monthly expenses	$3,793	$3,374	74,188	687	$2,618	$2,270	5,461	791
Monthly disposable income	−$151	$158	73,553	1,322	$296	$43	5,089	1,163
Debt-to-income ratio	7.3	1.7	73,206	1,669	49.7	4.9	4,734	1,518
Poverty ratio	3.3	3.2	73,629	1,246	2.8	2.2	5,148	1,104

Source: 2014 Pardo Study.
Note: N = 81,127. All dollar amounts have been rounded to the nearest dollar and have been adjusted to 2013 dollars.

TABLE 5.2 *Correlation between represented status and select financial characteristics.*

Represented status	Median	Mean	N	Missing values
	Amount of monthly income			
Represented	\$3,413	\$3,642	73,629	1,246
Self-represented	\$2,244	\$2,911	5,148	1,104
Wilcoxon rank-sum test: $z = 39.225$ ($p < 0.0001$)				
	Amount of monthly disposable income			
Represented	\$158	–\$151	73,553	1,322
Self-represented	\$43	\$296	5,089	1,163
Wilcoxon rank-sum test: $z = 4.672$ ($p < 0.0001$)				
	Debt-to-income ratio			
Represented	1.7	7.3	73,206	1,669
Self-represented	4.9	49.7	4,734	1,518
Wilcoxon rank-sum test: $z = -40.397$ ($p < 0.0001$)				
	Poverty ratio			
Represented	3.2	3.3	73,629	1,246
Self-represented	2.2	2.8	5,148	1,104
Wilcoxon rank-sum test: $z = 37.390$ ($p < 0.0001$)				

the financial situation of self-represented debtors consistently worse than that of their represented counterparts. Specifically, represented debtors had statistically significant (1) lower amounts of monthly income and disposable income, (2) higher debt-to-income ratios, and (3) lower poverty ratios (i.e., closer to the poverty line).

One of the reasons that a debtor may choose to self-represent is that the cost of legal counsel is prohibitively expensive. Professor Angela Littwin has previously documented a statistically significant association between a debtor's income and his or her represented status, with self-represented debtors having lower incomes than represented debtors.[86] She has interpreted this finding to "suggest[] that cost played a major role in

[86] See Littwin, supra note 43, at 1965–67, 1967 tbl.2.

the decision of whether to hire a bankruptcy lawyer."[87] Standing alone, the data from the 2014 Pardo Study cannot support the inference that the debtors with relatively lower income chose to self-represent because they could not afford to pay legal counsel. That said, data from the Lupica Study evidence a marked increase in the Western District of Washington in the average amount of attorney's fees charged in no-asset Chapter 7 cases that resulted in a discharge – specifically, the average amount charged post-BAPCPA was approximately 52% higher than the amount charged pre-BAPCPA.[88] Adjusting the post-BAPCPA average fee amount to 2013 dollars, the average self-represented debtor in the 2014 Pardo Study would have had to save slightly more than three months' worth of disposable income to pay the average $920 fee for Chapter 7 representation. For debtors facing crushing debt burdens, this would be a daunting proposition to say the least.

As for case outcomes, in the absence of a relationship between the self-represented status of a Chapter 7 debtor and dismissal of the debtor's case, one would expect to see approximately 1.8% of all Chapter 7 cases dismissed (i.e., the proportion of dismissed Chapter 7 cases observed in the study population). The data reveal, however, that approximately 13.0% of the Chapter 7 cases involving self-represented debtors were dismissed, in stark contrast to approximately 0.9% of cases involving represented debtors.[89] Table 5.3 sets forth these findings.[90]

A comparison to the dismissal rates for post-BAPCPA debtors from the 2009 Pardo Study reveals that the debtors from the 2014 Pardo Study fared slightly better.

[87] See *id.* at 1965.

[88] Lupica, supra note 16, app. V, at 165 tbl.A-23. The average amount charged (in 2005 dollars) for such cases in the Western District of Washington was $508.98 pre-BAPCPA (compared to $654 for the national pre-BAPCPA average) and was $771.53 post-BAPCPA (compared to $968 for the post-BAPCPA average). *Id.* at 69, app. V, at 165 tbl.A-23. Although these amounts were nominally less than the national averages, the percentage increase in the Western District of Washington (52%) was greater than the national percentage increase (48%). See *id.*

[89] Analysis pursuant to a chi-square test with one degree of freedom indicates that there is less than a 0.0001 probability that random chance alone would have yielded a difference as large as that witnessed between the observed and expected values.

[90] One might ask whether the statistically significant difference in the dismissal rates of represented and self-represented debtors can be attributed to a selection-effect problem – specifically, that attorneys will be discouraged from representing debtors who have "weaker" cases. If the "weaker" cases are more likely to be dismissed, then the higher dismissal rates for self-represented cases might not be attributable to lack of representation but rather to the merits of the debtor's case. This concern is minimal, however, given the context of this study. As detailed above, individual debtors who seek Chapter 7 relief must overwhelmingly contend with procedural hurdles rather than substantive ones. See supra notes 6–32 and accompanying text. Additionally, prior research has estimated that approximately 85% of Chapter 7 individual cases are dismissed for procedural reasons (e.g., failure to file required information, failure to attend the meeting of creditors, failure to pay the bankruptcy filing fee) that are unrelated to what would be deemed to be the merits of the debtor's case. See Pardo, supra note 1, at 27 tbl.3. Finally, to the extent that there may be other selection effects in this context, research has shown that those effects do not impact outcomes. See, e.g., Angela Littwin, *The Do-It-Yourself Mirage: Complexity in the Bankruptcy System*, *in* BROKE: HOW DEBT BANKRUPTS THE MIDDLE CLASS 167 (Katherine Porter ed., 2012) (providing empirical evidence that "[w]ell-educated debtors may be more apt to attempt bankruptcy without legal assistance, but they are no more likely to succeed").

TABLE 5.3 *Dismissal disposition by represented status of debtor.*

	Dismissal		
Represented status	No	Yes	Total
Represented	74,207	664	74,871
	(99.11)	(0.89)	(100.00)
Self-represented	5,442	810	6,252
	(87.04)	(12.96)	(100.00)
Total	79,649	1,474	81,123
	(98.18)	(1.82)	(100.00)

Note: Row percentages are reported in parentheses. The *p*-value from a chi-square test with one degree of freedom is less than 0.0001.

The 2009 Pardo Study covered, in part, slightly more than the two-year period immediately following BAPCPA's effective date (i.e., the 806 days spanning October 17, 2005 through December 31, 2007). During this time, there were a total of 12,021 Chapter 7 individual cases. Represented cases totaled 10,439, of which 109 were dismissed (approximately 1.0%); and self-represented cases totaled 1,582, of which 237 were dismissed (approximately 15.0%).[91] The odds of dismissal for post-BAPCPA cases from the 2009 Pardo Study were 0.0106 to 1 for represented cases and 0.1762 to 1 for self-represented cases.[92] In contrast, during the five-year period following the post-BAPCPA period from the 2009 Pardo Study (i.e., January 1, 2008, through December 31, 2012), the odds of dismissal for represented cases were 0.0089 to 1 for represented cases and 0.1488 to 1 for self-represented cases. When dividing the odds of dismissal for post-BAPCPA represented cases from the 2009 Pardo Study by the odds of dismissal for represented cases from the 2014 Pardo Study, one witnesses that the odds of dismissal were 1.2 times higher for the 2009 Pardo Study debtors. Likewise, when dividing the odds of dismissal for post-BAPCPA self-represented cases from the 2009 Pardo Study by the odds of dismissal for self-represented cases from the 2014 Pardo Study, one witnesses that the odds of dismissal were 1.2 times higher for the 2009 Pardo Study debtors.

But even though the self-represented debtors from the 2014 Pardo Study faced a lower dismissal rate than their counterparts from the 2009 Pardo Study, the odds of dismissal for self-represented debtors relative to the odds of dismissal for represented debtors were equally terrible for the self-represented debtors from both studies. The odds of dismissal for the post-BAPCPA self-represented cases from the 2009 Pardo Study were approximately 16.6 times greater than the post-BAPCPA represented cases from that study.[93] Similarly, the odds of dismissal for the self-

[91] See Pardo, supra note 1, at 24 tbl.2.

[92] *Id.* at 25 tbl.3.

[93] *Id.* at 25.

represented cases from the 2014 Pardo Study were approximately 16.7 times greater than the represented cases from that study. In other words, self-represented debtors have not been able to close the dismissal gap.

The dismissal rate, of course, does not shed light on the *reasons* for dismissal. If the dismissal of cases involving self-represented debtors has occurred for reasons unrelated to the increased burdens imposed by BAPCPA, then the theorized account of the adverse effect of BAPCPA on self-represented debtors would have weak empirical support and thus would not be a compelling theory. This concern warrants an exploration of the grounds for dismissal of the cases in the study population.

Approximately 34.9% of the dismissed cases (i.e., 515 of 1,474) in the 2014 Pardo Study population were classified by the Clerk's Office as having been dismissed on the ground that has been theorized as likely having the most disparate impact on self-represented debtors due to the increased procedural hurdles imposed by BAPCPA – namely, failure of the debtor to file the information required by statute or rule. Accordingly, one might say that procedural requirements have created a barrier for a considerable number of Chapter 7 debtors. In order to ascertain whether this barrier has disproportionately blocked self-represented debtors in their attempts to access Chapter 7 relief, one can examine the percentage of dismissed cases that were dismissed as a result of the debtor's failure to file information while controlling for the self-represented status of the debtor.

In the absence of a relationship between the self-represented status of a Chapter 7 debtor and dismissal of the debtor's case on the ground of failure to file information, one would expect to see approximately 34.9% of all dismissed Chapter 7 cases to be dismissed on this basis (i.e., the proportion of Chapter 7 cases dismissed for failure to file information that were observed in the study population). The data reveal, however, that approximately 46.1% of the dismissed Chapter 7 cases involving self-represented debtors were dismissed for failure to file information, in stark contrast to approximately 21.4% of cases involving represented debtors. The difference between the observed and expected values is statistically significant. Table 5.4 sets forth these findings.

Among the dismissed cases, then, the odds of dismissal as a result of failure to file information were 0.8535 to 1 for self-represented cases and 0.2720 to 1 for represented cases. Put another way, a self-represented dismissed case was approximately 3.1 times more likely to have been dismissed on this basis than a represented dismissed case. The data thus suggest that the lack of representation had a negative effect on the probability of a debtor overcoming the procedural hurdles that impede access to Chapter 7 relief. If nothing else, consider that, among the 810 dismissed cases involving self-represented debtors, approximately 46.1% (i.e., 373 of 810) were dismissed on the basis of failure to file information. The plight of the would-be

TABLE 5.4 *Ground for dismissal by represented status of debtor.*

	Dismissal for failure to file information		
Represented status	No	Yes	Total
Represented	522 (78.61)	142 (21.39)	664 (100.00)
Self-represented	437 (53.95)	373 (46.05)	810 (100.00)
Total	959 (65.06)	515 (34.94)	1,474 (100.00)

Note: Row percentages are reported in parentheses. The *p*-value from a chi-square test with one degree of freedom is less than 0.0001.

Chapter 7 debtor in the Western District of Washington who is self-represented has continued to be dire.[94]

CONCLUSION

During the five-year period of the 2014 Pardo Study, there were 81,123 Chapter 7 cases commenced by individual debtors in the Western District of Washington, of which 1,474 were dismissed. Of those dismissed cases, only 40 were dismissed on the basis of abuse – that is, only 2.71% of the dismissed cases and a mere 0.05% of all cases. In other words, nearly every debtor who filed for bankruptcy relief in the Western District during this period of time was a non-abusive debtor. And yet, every one of these debtors was forced to contend with the onerous requirements of a law that screens for abuse.

Evidence from this study suggests that, by virtue of not being able to obtain attorney representation to assist in deciphering BAPCPA's convoluted system, some self-represented debtors fail to access the benefit of bankruptcy's fresh start. Instead, they experience a false start. If forgiveness of debt is going to be a cornerstone of our society (as it has been for more than a century), then policy-makers must confront the issue of access to justice for self-represented debtors.

94 Post-BAPCPA self-represented debtors from the 2009 Pardo Study also fared worse than represented debtors in terms of dismissals based on failure to file information. See *id.* at 28–30.

6

Racial Disparities in Legal Representation for Employment Discrimination Plaintiffs

Amy Myrick, Robert L. Nelson & Laura Beth Nielsen

Myrick, Nelson and Nielson evaluate the role of race in the decision to file pro se in employment discrimination litigation. The authors show that black plaintiffs are 2.5 times more likely to file pro se than white plaintiffs, a disparity that is larger than any other plaintiff characteristics tested, including sex and occupation. Data from employment discrimination cases further indicate that pro se plaintiffs have significantly worse litigation outcomes than those with representation.

This chapter uses statistical analysis to show that minority plaintiffs in employment discrimination lawsuits – in particular African Americans – are much more likely than white plaintiffs to file without a lawyer. This difference is salient because pro se plaintiffs have significantly worse litigation outcomes than those with representation. Furthermore, we show that pro se plaintiffs tend to misunderstand their legal issues and feel that the courts have failed them. While past access to justice initiatives have addressed these negative consequences of lacking a lawyer, they have not systematically examined racial differences in representation rates, or tried to explain why these differences exist. Remarkably, access to justice approaches have largely overlooked race, instead focusing primarily on poverty as a barrier to finding a lawyer. This chapter shows that race matters in representation rates. It then examines possible reasons for this ignored but troubling disparity. We show that race operates in complex ways, both for minority plaintiffs seeking lawyers, and for the lawyers who decide whether to accept them as clients.

PRO SE LITIGATION: DATA AND PAST FINDINGS

Compared to represented plaintiffs, pro se plaintiffs were significantly more likely to have their cases dismissed or lose on summary judgment, and were less likely to reach early settlement. This empirical evidence proving the serious disadvantage that pro se status entails is consistent with other access to justice research on various types of legal action.[1] Although we know of no other studies that look specifically at the outcomes for pro se employment discrimination plaintiffs, a growing body of work shows that employment discrimination litigation in general disfavors plaintiffs.[2] In addition, research on pro se plaintiffs suggests that they suffer most when they file claims involving complex or document-intensive areas of law, and that such issues may compel plaintiffs to seek an attorney instead of attempting to self-represent.[3] Because employment discrimination law meets these criteria, we would expect pro se rates to be low. However, 20% of employment discrimination plaintiffs in our sample filed their claims unrepresented, and other studies have shown pro se rates to be similarly high.[4] Employment discrimination is thus an area of law in which plaintiffs face serious hurdles to success, especially if unrepresented. And yet they often lack lawyers.

Apart from socioeconomic class, little research has systematically analyzed group characteristics such as sex or race as they relate to representation rates, nor have scholars asked how such characteristics might operate.

WHO HAS A LAWYER? RACIAL DISPARITIES IN REPRESENTATION

The data used throughout this chapter come from our large-scale, multi-method study of employment discrimination litigation in U.S. federal courts. We test

1 An expanded version of this chapter was originally published as Amy Myrick, Robert L. Nelson & Laura Beth Nielsen, *Race and Representation: Racial Disparities in Legal Representation for Employment Civil Rights Plaintiffs*, 15 N.Y.U. J. Legis. & Pub. Pol'y 705 (2012). See Rebecca L. Sandefur, *The Impact of Counsel: An Analysis of Empirical Evidence*, 9 Seattle J. Soc. Just. 51, 51–52 (2010) (combining the results of multiple studies to conclude that "when people are represented by attorneys, they are, on average, more likely to win in adjudication than are people who are unrepresented"). Carroll Seron, Gregg Van Ryzin & Martin Frankel, *The Impact of Legal Counsel on Procedural Outcomes for Poor Tenants in New York City's Housing Court: Results of a Randomized Experiment*, 35 Law & Soc'y Rev. 419 (2001) (showing benefit of counsel through unique experimental design). But see studies by James Greiner et al., *Randomized Evaluation in Legal Assistance: What Difference Does Representation (Offer and Actual Use) Make?*, 121 Yale L.J. 2118 (2012); *The Limits of Unbundled Legal Assistance: A Randomized Study in a Massachusetts District Court and Prospects for the Future*, 126 Harv. L. Rev. 901 (2013); How Effective Are Limited Legal Assistance Programs? A Randomized Experiment in a Massachusetts Housing Court (Sept. 1, 2012).

2 Compared to other kinds of cases in district courts, employment discrimination plaintiffs fare poorly in many ways. See generally Charles A. Brown, *Employment Discrimination Plaintiffs in the District of Maryland*, 96 Cornell L. Rev. 1247 (2011); see also Pat K. Chew & Robert E. Kelley, *Unwrapping Racial Harassment Law*, 27 Berkeley J. Emp. & Lab. L. 49, 54–55 (2006); Kevin M. Clermont & Stewart J. Schwab, *Employment Discrimination Plaintiffs in Federal Court: From Bad to Worse?*, 3 Harv. L. & Pol'y Rev. 103, 104–105 (2009) (recent decline in employment discrimination claims may reflect plaintiffs' consistently poor outcomes over time).

3 See Sandefur, supra note 1, at 52 (combining the results of multiple studies to conclude that "[o]ne factor that seems to shape variation in the magnitude of lawyers' impact is procedural complexity – the complexity of the documents and procedures necessary to pursue a justice problem as a court case appears to account for some of lawyers' effect on case outcomes").

4 Kevin M. Clermont & Stewart J. Schwab, *How Employment Discrimination Plaintiffs Fare in Federal Court*, 1 J. Empirical Legal Stud. 429, 434 (2004); John Doyle et al., *Report of the Working Committees to the Second Circuit Task Force on Gender, Racial and Ethnic Fairness in the Courts*, 1997 Ann. Surv. Am. L. 117, 343 (1997) (reporting that "plaintiffs in [employment discrimination cases] often appear pro se, and do not understand the law or the court's procedures").

TABLE 6.1 *Select plaintiff characteristics by legal representation.*

	Pro se throughout	Filed pro se, gained counsel	Lawyer throughout	Total
Race***				
African American	20.79%	12.13%	67.09%	100% (635)
White	8.37%	3.35%	88.28%	100% (478)
Hispanic	21.38%	6.38%	72.34%	100% (94)
Asian American	25.58%	19.95%	60.47%	100% (43)
Other	6.52%	5.98%	87.50%	100% (184)
Missing	13.35%	5.46%	81.09%	100% (238)
Total	14.77%	7.72%	77.51%	100% (1,672)
Sex**				
Male	18.24%	8.08%	73.68%	100% (817)
Female	11.47%	7.45%	81.09%	100% (846)
Missing	11.11%	0	88.89%	100% (9)
Total	14.77%	7.72%	77.51%	100%(1,672)
Occupation***				
Management, business, or professional	8.64%	5.50%	85.85%	100% (509)
Service, sales, and office or administrative support	16.20%	9.37%	74.43%	100% (747)
Natural resources, maintenance, construction, production, transportation	16.39%	8.03%	75.59%	100% (299)
Other	15.38%	15.38%	69.23%	100% (13)
Missing	29.81%	4.81%	65.38%	100% (104)
Total	14.77%	7.72%	77.51%	100%(1,672)

*** Chi-square probability = 0.0001; ** chi-square probability = 0.01.

whether a wide range of plaintiff characteristics and legal features affect whether employment discrimination plaintiffs have lawyers. We find that racial and ethnic minorities, in particular African Americans, are much less likely to have lawyers than white plaintiffs.

Plaintiffs in our dataset fell into three categories: (1) those who had a lawyer for the duration of their case; (2) those who filed alone but later obtained a lawyer (sometimes through court appointment); (3) and those who never had a lawyer. Table 6.1 shows that African Americans, Asian Americans, and Hispanics; men; and those employed in non-managerial or professional positions were more likely than their counterparts in the respective categories of race, sex, and occupation to lack a lawyer throughout their cases. Conversely, white plaintiffs and those identified as "other" were more likely to be represented throughout, as were women, and people

TABLE 6.2 *Logistic regression models predicting pro se filing and gaining counsel.*

	(1) Filed pro se	(2) Filed pro se but gained counsel
Plaintiff's race		
African American	2.540^{***} (3.86)	1.332 (0.64)
White	Reference group	
All other	1.948^{***} (3.29)	1.359 (0.70)
Plaintiff's sex		
Male	1.327 (1.70)	0.718 (−1.28)
	Female Reference group	
Plaintiff's occupation		
Managerial or professional	0.474^{***} (−3.50)	2.059 (1.89)
Service, sales, office administrative	1.005 (0.03)	2.037^{*} (2.24)
	Blue collar and other Reference group	
Other plaintiff Characteristics		
Age	1.012 (0.77)	0.997 (−0.11)
Job tenure	0.969^{**} (−2.68)	1.040^{*} (2.20)
Union member	1.905^{**} (2.58)	0.956 (−0.12)
Legal claim		
Title VII – race	1.833^{**} (2.87)	0.926 (−0.25)
Title VII – sex	1.080 (0.40)	1.089 (0.26)
Title VII – retaliation	0.933 (−0.38)	0.571 (−1.78)
Title VII – other	0.865 (−0.40)	0.381 (−1.04)
ADEA – age	0.992 (−0.03)	0.742 (−0.57)
ADEA – retaliation	1.324 (0.82)	1.471 (0.56)
ADA – disability	1.434 (1.47)	0.664 (−0.91)
ADA – retaliation	0.825 (−0.50)	0.919 (−0.11)
42 U.S.C. 1981	0.425^{***} (−4.12)	3.381^{***} (3.30)
42 U.S.C. 1983	0.633 (−1.27)	1.145 (0.17)
Constitutional claim	0.853 (−0.32)	1.128 (0.12)
Other statutory claim	0.325^{***} (−6.04)	0.774 (−0.70)
Type of discrimination		
Hiring	1.282 (0.93)	0.385 (−1.66)
Firing	0.891 (−0.71)	0.872 (−0.50)
Sexual harassment	0.457^{**} (−2.66)	0.655 (−0.81)
Conditions of employment	1.057 (0.32)	1.957^{*} (2.29)
Pay	0.851 (−0.66)	1.204 (0.48)
Other legal features		
Discrimination by a specific perpetrator	1.352 (1.86)	0.677 (−1.47)
Disparate impact	0.734 (−0.81)	1.307 (0.40)
EEOC		
Negative finding on the merits	6.624^{***} (10.57)	0.661 (−1.54)
No finding returned	Reference group	

TABLE 6.2 (continued)

	(1) Filed pro se	(2) Filed pro se but gained counsel
Positive finding on the merits	0.647 (−0.98)	1.024 (0.03)
Constant	0.0863*** (−3.47)	0.388 (−0.79)
N	1,672	376
pseudo-R^2	0.244	0.110

Exponentiated coefficients; *t*-statistics in parentheses.
* $p < 0.05$, ** $p < 0.01$, *** $p < 0.001$.

with high-level jobs. In the intermediate category, African Americans, Hispanics, and especially Asian Americans appear more likely than whites to file pro se but gain a lawyer, as do men relative to women, and people who are not managers or professionals.

These patterns are intriguing. While we might expect plaintiffs with higher occupational status to be more likely than others to obtain lawyers given their greater resources and potential for greater damages as higher-paid employees, it is surprising to find significant differences by race and sex. It is necessary to determine whether the effects of some characteristics are explained by other variables. For example, it could be the case that managers are more likely to have lawyers, regardless of race, but that whites are more likely to be managers. Such a pattern would imply a different kind of access problem than one showing that all whites, regardless of occupation, are advantaged.

Table 6.2 presents logistic regression models for two categories of representation status: whether a plaintiff filed their case pro se and whether a plaintiff who filed pro se gained counsel later in the litigation process. The first model (Column 1) analyzes our full sample of 1,672 cases to show which plaintiff and case characteristics are linked to pro se status at filing. The second model (Column 2) only analyzes the 376 cases that were filed pro se, showing which characteristics are related to gaining a lawyer after filing. The first model is our main focus, given that conventional process theories assume plaintiffs will have a lawyer from the beginning to assist with case preparation and the filing itself. The second model tests whether plaintiffs who lack a lawyer at filing may fix the problem by getting one later. In both models, we look for systematic patterns that might show disadvantage to particular groups.

The results in Column 1 of Table 6.2 demonstrate the strong influence of race in the employment discrimination litigation system. Compared to white plaintiffs (the reference group), African Americans are 2.5 times as likely to file pro se. This gap is greater than the difference between our "Other" category (which includes Hispanic and Asian American minorities) and whites. Still disadvantaged, the "Other" group is 1.9 times more likely than whites to lack counsel at filing. Moreover, in addition to the race of the plaintiff, race claims filed under Title VII are about 1.8 times more likely to be filed without the benefit of counsel. This effect controls for the race of plaintiffs – in other words, it is not explained by the fact that more minorities than whites file Title VII race claims. Instead, these filers of Title VII race claims are disadvantaged apart from the plaintiff's race, perhaps suggesting other reasons that these cases do not find lawyers.

As for occupation, plaintiffs in managerial jobs are less than half as likely to file pro se as the "blue collar" group (odds ratio = .47), and the effect is statistically significant. Plaintiffs with longer job tenure are also less likely to file pro se. On average, each year on the job reduces the odds of pro se filing by about 10% (odds ratio = 0.9). Complicating the pattern in Table 6.1, the sex variable shows that men are more likely than women to file pro se, but the effect is not statistically significant, meaning that it might be explained by random variation. Finally, union members were almost twice as likely as non-union members to lack a lawyer (odds ratio = 1.9), and this difference is statistically significant. This unexpected pattern may suggest that union members believed they had other resources to draw upon, making formal representation (perhaps at cost) unnecessary. This could also reflect a concentration of union members in low-income jobs. While our controls for occupation partly address this, we do not have an income measure to fully test the possibility.

Moving on to legal attributes, the particular statute under which a claim is filed is significantly related to the presence of a lawyer at filing. Race bias claims under Title VII of the Civil Rights Act of 1964[5] race claims are more likely to be filed pro se, net of other factors, and at the EEOC level are the most frequent type of filing in this system. The individuals filing race claims under Title VII may be more willing to file a claim on their own, or lawyers may dislike these cases. We will consider these possibilities in more detail later. In contrast, claims filed under 42 U.S.C. § 1981 are less than half as likely to be filed pro se (odds ratio = 0.43), and all "other statutory" claims are only a third as likely (odds ratio = 0.33). This may suggest that only lawyers have the legal knowledge to select these statutes over something more common like Title VII. Or, it could mean that plaintiffs who have fact patterns that fit the elements for these statutes are more likely to attract lawyers. Our model cannot differentiate between these causal mechanisms. Among the types of alleged discrimination, sexual harassment claimants are less likely to file pro se, and this effect does not appear because these claimants are more likely to be women. Sexual harassment may thus be a type of grievance that attracts lawyers, or people who experience sexual harassment may be unwilling to self-represent.

5 42 U.S.C. §2000e et seq.

Finally, there is a very strong association between filing pro se and an adverse finding by the EEOC when determining whether the charge has merit.[6] Plaintiffs who have received adverse findings are 6.6 times more likely to file pro se compared to plaintiffs who receive no finding. Interestingly, a supportive EEOC finding does not significantly increase the chances of getting a lawyer relative to no finding. Again, this is an instance in which the direction of the effect is ambiguous. It may be that when the EEOC finds against a charging party, it discourages lawyers from taking that case. It may also be that complainants represented by counsel are more likely to shape the EEOC outcome to avoid such a negative finding.

Our second analysis (Column 2) tests whether some of these disparities are mitigated by pro se plaintiffs who add lawyers after initial filing, possibly through a court appointment. With a few exceptions, we do not see this pattern in the model for the probability of gaining counsel after filing pro se. Employees in service, sales, and administrative positions are significantly more likely to gain counsel, as are employees with longer tenure. But while African Americans and "Other" minorities are slightly more likely than whites to add counsel, these effects are neither large nor significant. For legal features, Title VII race claims are not more likely to gain lawyers; the only significant legal predictors are claims under Section 1981, which attract lawyers at more than three times the rate of other statutes, and claims of discrimination in employment conditions, which are about twice as likely to gain lawyers. Thus, the lack of representation for African Americans, other minorities, and persons making Title VII race claims is not redressed after a pro se filing.

Table 6.2 demonstrates that both the social characteristics of plaintiffs and the nature of their legal claims are associated with whether they have a lawyer at filing and over the course of litigation. Most striking is the continuing significance of race – as a plaintiff characteristic and as a characteristic of the legal claim – to patterns of legal representation. These analyses compare all groups to whites, showing that whites are by far the most represented group. Between African Americans and other minorities, African Americans remain at a disadvantage; they are 2.5 times more likely to file pro se than whites, while other minorities are 1.9 times more likely. This disparity is larger than any other plaintiff characteristics we tested, including sex and occupation. This pattern holds even controlling for the effects of occupation, other plaintiff characteristics such as age and union membership, and for a variety of legal factors including the basis for the claim and the nature of alleged discrimination. But what explains this racial disparity?

THE PRO SE PLAINTIFFS IN THE SAMPLE

We interviewed a total of 100 individuals who were parties or lawyers in a systematically selected subsample of cases, which was drawn from the larger set

6 *Id.* § 2000e-5(b).

TABLE 6.3 *Race, gender, and representation status of interviewed plaintiffs.*

	Pro se entirely	Represented for at least part of case	Total
African American men	5 (50%)	5 (50%)	10 (100%)
African American women	1 (14%)	6 (86%)	7 (100%)
White men	1 (8%)	12 (92%)	13 (100%)
White women	1 (8%)	10 (91%)	11 (100%)
Total	N = 8	N = 33	N = 41

of 2,100 federal employment civil rights case filings in our statistical dataset. These included 41 plaintiffs, of whom 8 filed pro se. Six of the 8 were African American: 5 men and 1 woman. The qualitative data thus broadly mirror the large dataset used in the model presented earlier: about 20% of respondents were pro se, and of these 75% were black and 25% were white. The pro se African American plaintiffs that were interviewed spoke at length about their reasons for not having a lawyer.

The Problem of Finding a Lawyer: the Plaintiffs' View

Prominently, lack of information about the legal process creates a barrier to representation. Billy Dee among our interviewees, for example, did not see his claim as a legal issue, and then mistakenly believed that the EEOC would represent him. Because plaintiffs must first file with the EEOC, which typically produces a right to sue letter but no discrimination finding, uninformed plaintiffs may decide to simply file their federal claims as the next step in the process. Absent information and knowledge, they may not understand the importance of finding a lawyer for their claim to survive in federal court. Other pro se African American plaintiffs clearly lacked information about aspects of the legal process.

While existing research shows that the question of whether plaintiffs perceive legal complexity predicts whether they obtain a lawyer, there are no recent surveys of how legal knowledge differs across demographic groups. However, social science research shows definitively that African Americans receive less education than whites at every level from high school graduation to graduate degrees. In addition, African Americans tend to be segregated in low-status jobs, without access to training or advancement opportunities, and do not receive equivalent positive socialization or opportunities to build "human capital" even in better jobs. If, on average, African American plaintiffs have lower levels of knowledge and information about the law because of these systemic disparities in education and personal development opportunities, they may be more likely to file cases on their own. Our interviews do not allow us to generalize at this level, but do support the mechanism.

Trust in lawyers and their motives also emerged as an issue in the interviews. Chris Burns, for example, felt that lawyers were rejecting his case because they did not want to take on the government, not because his claim lacked merit. Marjorie Turner had mixed feelings about lawyers, although she reported believing them when they said her case was frivolous, and said she withdrew it as a result. Philip Jacobson was not convinced when a lawyer told him that filing while he was still employed would accomplish little, so he proceeded on his own. Studies have shown racial differences in trust of counseling professionals and criminal defense lawyers. At the group level, if African American plaintiffs are less trusting of civil lawyers and their advice, they may be more likely to forgo representation.

Searching for a lawyer is a complicated and time-consuming process. Plaintiffs who have jobs and family obligation, may lack the material and emotional resources to invest in calling multiple lawyers and organizations while fulfilling their other obligations. This is especially true for plaintiffs who do not have lawyers, or ties to them, in their personal networks, and thus must turn to directories or legal aid providers. Because African Americans generally have smaller professional networks, they may be less likely to find a lawyer. Additionally, racial differences in care obligations and household organization, all well documented in the social science literature, may impede the search at the group level. Even transportation is less accessible to urban minority populations because of suburbanization and its effects on public transit policy. Given the resource-intensive nature of the search, which we will demonstrate in more detail later when interviewing represented plaintiffs, racial disparities in access to social and material resources could contribute to the disparity.

Several plaintiffs mentioned the cost of a lawyer as a problem, although not always in a straightforward way. Franklin Williams recalled that at the time of his case, he preferred to self-represent rather than pay an attorney. Mortgaging his house had been an option that he dismissed based on confidence in his and his wife's abilities. Chris Burns and Philip Jacobson felt they could not afford lawyers' fees of $2,700 and $500, respectively. They made cost–benefit assessments based on their knowledge of the legal process and the perceived value of representation. Our interviews suggest that cost is not a straightforward barrier to obtaining a lawyer. Instead, plaintiffs' decisions about how to spend their resources depend on how plaintiffs view the law, the legal profession, and their chances of success. A low-income plaintiff might decide to pay for a lawyer, at serious hardship, if she thought it crucial. Our findings are in line with other access to justice research that complicates the role finances play in use of legal services – plaintiffs' views of those services are part of the equation. Racial differences in such perceptions might then interact with income disparities to explain why African American plaintiffs are less likely to have lawyers.

What about the merits? Is it possible that, as a group, African American plaintiffs have weaker cases that lawyers reject, forcing them to file pro se? We acknowledge that our data do not allow an objective assessment of case merits, either statistically or through interviews. Yet, unmeritorious cases do not seem to be the main reason that African American plaintiffs are less likely to have lawyers. Instead, the resources required to find and retain a lawyer are unequally distributed. Resources include forms of human and social capital, among them legal knowledge, trust in lawyers, and personal connections to lawyers. Resources also include time and money to invest in searching for a lawyer. Social science research shows clearly that inequitable social structures in the United States offer minorities less education, wealth, and income, and limit their professional networks in ways that exacerbate disparities. Because the lawyer search process draws on all these resources, minorities are likely disadvantaged relative to whites.

What Worked? Insight from Represented Plaintiffs

Although this chapter focuses mainly on the experiences of pro se African American plaintiffs, some additional insights can be gained by considering the accounts of represented plaintiffs. This dataset includes thirty-three interviews with members of this group, including eleven African Americans. A few salient themes emerged to show what the process of securing a lawyer entails.

First, many represented plaintiffs talked about the time-consuming process of seeking a lawyer. Many plaintiffs who successfully secured attorneys reported consulting with several before finding the right one. Some said they were initially rejected by lawyers who told them to seek second opinions, forcing them to decide whether to persist. These plaintiffs shrugged off rejection and used additional resources to pursue different paths to representation.

Plaintiffs who secured lawyers generally seemed to have access to more resources of the kind that the pro se plaintiffs in our sample lacked. Several knew lawyers personally, or had them in their social networks.

Some represented plaintiffs found their lawyers through directories or publicly available sources instead of personal connections, but they often had additional resources with which to approach the search. Robert Lester, a forty-nine-year-old white professional claiming age discrimination, obtained a list from the ABA and "just went down the list."

As a group, the represented plaintiffs were not very specific about how they paid for the lawyers they retained. Several talked about shopping around for an option that they could afford, but knew that they had a budget to work with. The more flexible tone with which represented plaintiffs talked about money is itself a difference from some of our pro se plaintiffs, who felt immediately that they could not afford a lawyer and did not seriously consider shopping around.

At least two plaintiffs said they used their ability to acquire and demonstrate legal knowledge to compensate for a lack of financial resources. Matthew Brown persisted because "every time I met with one of these lawyers, I'd try to squeeze a question in," thereby learning more about his case. Ultimately, Brown learned that if he filed pro se he could request a court-appointed lawyer, which he did successfully.

THE LAWYERS' PERSPECTIVE

What can we learn from the lawyers' perspectives, and are their thoughts consistent with plaintiffs' beliefs? Twenty plaintiffs' attorneys representing a range of practice specialties, sizes, and prestige levels – from solo practice generalists to lawyers engaged in pro bono work through large firms to an elite national class action specialist – explained how they select clients.

Screening

Every plaintiffs' attorney interviewed stressed that he or she accepted a very small fraction of potential discrimination clients, with several estimating a 10% or smaller acceptance rate. This high selectivity drove their client selection process. Many lawyers also said they were intentionally pessimistic in their assessment, aiming to weed out clients who were not serious. Most described screening that took place before they would agree to meet a potential client or discuss their case details.

While lawyers claimed to have an ability to assess the merits of a case almost instantly, their initial screening methods seem to favor some clients for reasons unrelated to case merits. They favor clients who know how to quickly and compellingly "sell" their case, or who have a personal vouching connection that takes them past the first call. They also select for clients who know to read discouraging assessments for what they are: a test of commitment, and a professional disclaimer, instead of a clear rejection. Because many lawyers charged fees for these early assessments, poor clients are disadvantaged at screening. These patterns would likely work against some African American plaintiffs, who statistically are poorer and – as a correlate of educational disparities and segregation in low-level jobs – might be less experienced at making compelling phone presentations to strangers expressing disbelief.

Demeanor

After the initial phone call, most plaintiffs' attorneys said a large part of their decision whether to accept a client was based on her mannerisms or demeanor at the initial meeting. Some assessed clients specifically for how they were likely to interact with their attorney. Harry Morgan, a prominent African American civil rights lawyer, said he had a "sixth sense" for "difficult" clients. Attorneys also said that demeanor related to client credibility, or simply whether their claims of discrimination were true. Some attorneys assessed demeanor in terms of whether a client would interact favorably with a judge or jury.

These observations might help explain the underlying pattern of underrepresented African American plaintiffs in Title VII race discrimination plaintiffs if lawyers tend to unfavorably assess the demeanor of minority plaintiffs, viewing them either as "difficult" to work with, not credible, or unlikely to present well to a judge or jury.

Plaintiffs' Preparation

Apart from demeanor, several attorneys said they were more likely to accept clients who came to their initial meetings with documents or background work, or who seemed likely to be willing and able to assist with their case preparation going forward. A few lawyers recalled cases that they would have rejected had it not been for background work a client had already done to develop his claim.

These lawyers responded positively to clients' foresight in requesting and assembling documentary evidence. The preference some lawyers showed for prepared clients might disadvantage African American plaintiffs who, statistically, are likely to have less education, more likely to work in jobs with less access to documents or opportunities to request them, and perhaps more likely to have less general legal knowledge about the litigation process as a consequence.

Attroney Corpentation

There was wide variation in the sample as to how lawyers negotiated payment.

Contingency

Attorneys who worked on contingency based client-acceptance decisions on projected recovery. For these lawyers, liability was separate from, and less relevant than, potential damages. Factors that lawyers considered in assessing recovery included the plaintiff's salary, which would serve to calculate back pay, so higher salaries were favored, and whether the plaintiff found a new job immediately after being fired, which could mitigate lost wages, and thus limit damages. Given that recovery depended largely on a clients' salary, one lawyer said that regardless of merits, "if they were like low wage earners, like $3,000 a month, I would not be interested in filing a lawsuit or anything like that."

This cutoff, equivalent to $36,000 per year, would exclude many African American workers, given that the average income for an African American full-time worker in 2010 was $28,964. White, non-Hispanic full-time workers, by contrast, averaged $41,656 in annual salary in 2010. Our data suggest that lawyers ask about salary as part of the client screening process, sometimes in an initial phone call. The contingency fee structure disadvantages low- and middle-income clients.

Hourly

Lawyers who followed hourly billing schemes were less directly concerned with how much a claim might recover. Because they were guaranteed payment regardless of outcome, damages were less significant to their decision-making. Hourly fee payment plans with up-front retainers would be out of reach for plaintiffs lacking substantial financial assets, which would include many African American plaintiffs. Most lawyers described hourly-fee arrangements as an option for plaintiffs who could not convince contingency lawyers to accept their cases. In other words, they expanded the representation prospects for only those plaintiffs who could afford it.

Pro Bono or Informal

Lawyers who claimed to have personal or ideological commitments to the plaintiffs' side sometimes described indifference to financial gain. Lawyers who reported taking cases without regard for payment generally said they selected them based on legal interest or sympathy for a client.

IMPLICATIONS

Systemic Implications: A Problem with the Individual Litigant Model

Lawyers are almost certainly necessary to improving outcomes against experienced employers, even if they are not sufficient to do so. Since minority plaintiffs do not obtain lawyers as readily as whites, their ability to influence the system may be further curtailed. Racial disparities in representation mean that the groups most affected by discrimination lack the resources to mount effective challenges through the courts. This is an additional strike against the individual litigant model. Beyond that, it poses a paradox in which the Civil Rights Act of 1964 – enacted largely to help minorities – ends up better serving non-minority groups who have more legal help to effectively enforce it.

Implications for Litigants: Legal Confusion and Disillusionment

Disparities in representation suggest that minorities, more than whites, may have a negative litigation experience that leaves them disillusioned with the courts. Several of the pro se plaintiffs interviewed sensed that the legal system was operating over their heads, and viewed them as irrelevant or incompetent while denying them respect. For them, the experience of going to court was confusing and degrading, on top of the unhappy workplace situations that led them to sue.

Afterwards, their accounts show major, persistent misunderstandings about their cases. This pattern is problematic regardless of whether plaintiffs have "good cases" that might prevail on the merits with the help of a lawyer. Even if plaintiffs are in court pro se because they misunderstand the law, the appropriate redress is for them to learn more about the legal system and its limitations, not for them to be disparaged and made to feel that their subjective experiences of discrimination are not valid. Because minorities are more likely than whites to be unrepresented, these negative experiences have troubling implications for equality in the courtroom.

Policy Suggestions

EEOC Reforms

Employment discrimination litigation is complicated by the requirement that plaintiffs exhaust their remedies through the EEOC, the federal agency charged with enforcing Title VII, the Age Discrimination in Employment Act, the Americans with Disabilities Act, and select other antidiscrimination statutes. Only after the EEOC has issued a finding (which may include "reasonable cause," "no reasonable cause," or administrative closure), and a right to sue letter, can a federal suit be filed. The interviewed plaintiffs, both pro se and represented, tended to misunderstand this process, or otherwise felt that it was a waste of time. Some reported confusion when visiting the EEOC office to file the claim. Others thought that the right to sue letter they received at the end of the EEOC review was a positive finding of discrimination, or meant that the EEOC would act as their lawyer.

Adding to the confusion, most states maintain separate offices or commissions to deal with workplace rights under state law. There is wide variation across states in how these bodies function. Some offices have their own review processes that are similar to the EEOC. Some have dedicated attorneys that may agree to represent clients.

Both the EEOC and state equivalents could take steps to assist pro se claimants. An obvious option is to increase levels of direct representation, where agency attorneys accept clients. Budget constraints at the federal level and in many states seem to preclude this at present. Some have argued that transforming the EEOC into a direct services agency would detract from systemic change activities. Alternatively, the EEOC could enhance its collective regulatory role, bringing suit against employers when there is evidence of widespread discrimination practices or policies instead of focusing on specific incidents. This would entail a shift away from the individual litigant model in favor of a government oversight and enforcement approach.

Short of individual or collective representation, EEOC policy could focus on better education of clients. This could happen both in person, when claims are filed, and through the mail over the course of the review processes. Based on our interviews, the terminal "permission to sue" letter seems especially important in directing claimants' next steps. It should convey information clearly in accessible language, explain that the claimant is not represented, and outline options for finding a lawyer prior to filing.

Inform Plaintiffs about the Law and Legal Process

Because legal beliefs have complex social determinants, there is no easy way to change how people view lawyers and the legal system. For example, trust in attorneys cannot easily be encouraged. Education efforts that try to explain the complexity of the legal system (and related benefits of counsel) seem dubious, and might deter people from pursuing claims; this is true even though perceived case complexity seems to promote lawyer use. Instead, the process itself seems to best educate plaintiffs about how lawyers operate. Thus, assuming that some pro se plaintiffs file unrepresented because they do not feel the benefits of counsel justify the cost, the court should provide subsequent opportunities to add a lawyer when litigation realities emerge. Ideally, courts could facilitate that process through an appointment model.

Because minority plaintiffs may be likely to know fewer lawyers personally, outreach through specialized directories and clinics could also have benefits. For general education purposes, clinics that run information sessions describing the legal process might be useful; currently, phone calls to lawyers who also serve as high-volume screeners seem to be a primary source of plaintiff information, and these calls do not serve to educate as much as evaluate.

Court Appointments

Federal law authorizes courts to appoint lawyers in civil cases. There is wide variation across federal courts in how appointments function; local court rules usually outline the steps. Example criteria include case merits as set forth in the pleadings, issue complexity, the presence of conflicting evidence, the litigant's capability to self-represent, and the litigant's access to other lawyers. The availability of panel lawyers is a constraint that varies widely by district. A task force assessing courts in the Second Circuit concluded that compensating lawyers for litigation costs would allow for greater participation. Better recruitment and possible compensation of a reserve panel might improve these programs.

Because the appointment process requires judges to evaluate plaintiffs, cultural and social awareness is crucial to avoiding racial disparities. For example, denying a plaintiff counsel because her pleadings were not compelling might disadvantage plaintiffs who lacked educational attainment, or who were unfamiliar with the legal system. Our interviews included three plaintiffs who successfully requested court-appointed lawyers; all were well-educated, legally knowledgeable people who felt comfortable in the courtroom. Judges should self-examine the basis of their decisions, and courts should keep statistics with racial breakdowns to guard against disparities.

Solutions within the Bar

Our interviews suggest that lawyer screening practices may be vulnerable to racial bias. Legal practitioners should be attentive to this possibility. In addition, the fee structures that disadvantage groups with low recovery prospects likely also disadvantage minorities. Interviewed pro bono lawyers did not use the same profit-driven criteria. Thus, more pro bono services might ease the racial disparity. Currently, employment discrimination does not seem to have been identified as an area of pro bono need.

Help for Plaintiffs Who Proceed Pro Se

While more available and affordable legal services might shift the cost–benefit calculus, some plaintiffs will still file pro se. Judges should make efforts to explain requirements, invite questions, and give plaintiffs leeway where appropriate, especially when setting and enforcing deadlines. Courthouse resources including help desks might assist pro se plaintiffs with standard tasks such as filing motions. Help desk staffers could also help translate legal jargon and offer a neutral perspective to plaintiffs. Some federal districts have extensive help desk programs while others lack them. Future research might evaluate whether help desks actually benefit plaintiffs and in what ways.

CONCLUSION

Access to justice research has not looked systematically at racial patterns of lawyer use. Our mixed-methods study of employment discrimination litigation revealed a troubling disparity. Minority plaintiffs, especially African Americans, are much less likely than white plaintiffs to have lawyers. Since employment discrimination law is intended to assist marginalized groups in the workplace, including minorities, this finding suggests a flaw in the redress system.

Because social inequities are entrenched and slow to change, the onus for improvement may lie with the legal community. Legal reformers have taken steps to equalize access. Adding race to the picture makes such efforts even more imperative. Otherwise, legal services function to reinforce system-wide disparities aligned with race.

7

The Unemployment Action Center:

A Student-Driven Response to a Legal Need

David Yin

In New York unemployment insurance hearings, the vast majority of claimants represent themselves when they appeal the denial of their claim. There are virtually no lawyers for these claimants. In New York City, students from several law schools, with nominal support from their institutions, have maintained since 1981 a legal aid office, the Unemployment Action Center, to address the need for representation. This chapter by NYU graduate David Yin offers an example of how law students can make a difference in administrative forums, like public housing hearings, welfare hearings, licensing hearings, and truancy hearings, where most litigants represent themselves and a license to practice law is not required to provide trained assistance.

America's system of unemployment insurance (UI) was created in the midst of the Great Depression as a primary component of the Social Security Act of 1935.[1] The unemployment benefit, a cash payment disbursed to unemployed individuals, fulfills a dual role of providing individuals with temporary support when they lose their jobs, and sustaining consumer spending to stimulate local economies. The UI system is a prophylaxis against and a treatment for economic recessions.[2] The system is funded by a federal payroll tax on employers,[3] against which a partial credit may be claimed if the employer paid into a state-administered unemployment insurance fund.[4] This mode of funding has encouraged all states to enact and administer their own UI programs. Today, all 50 states, the District of Columbia, Puerto Rico, and the Virgin Islands have UI regimes for their workers, administered under state-set eligibility criteria and benefit levels.[5] Federal law, however, prescribes the

1 42 U.S.C. §§ 503–505 (2012).

2 See generally Wayne Vroman, *The Role of Unemployment Insurance as an Automatic Stabilizer during a Recession*, IMPAQ International (July 2010), available at http://wdr.doleta.gov/research/FullText_Documents/ETAOP2010-10.pdf.

3 Federal Unemployment Tax Act, 26 U.S.C. § 3301 (2012).

4 *Id.* § 3302.

5 See *Comparison of State Unemployment Laws*, U.S. Dept. of Lab. (2009), available at www.ows.doleta.gov/unemploy/uilawcompar/2009/comparison2009.asp.

minimum standards that states must meet to have their programs certified for federal funding.[6]

In New York, UI benefits are available to a worker who is "totally unemployed": receiving no income for services for a given workweek and unable to engage in the usual employment for which the worker is reasonably fitted by training or education.[7] The worker must have achieved certain monetary eligibility by receiving income during a "base period" prior to becoming unemployed.[8] The worker must also be able to work, be available to work, and be actively seeking work.[9] Additionally, a UI claimant may be disqualified from receiving benefits if the claimant left the prior position voluntarily without good cause, or if the involuntary unemployment was caused by the worker's misconduct in the prior position or criminal activity.[10] The unemployment benefit does not fully replace a worker's former income. Generally, the benefit payment will be about half of the worker's previous income, and capped at a maximum amount – in New York, the weekly cap is currently $405.[11] The nationwide average unemployment benefit was about $300 per week in 2012.[12] Most states, including New York, allow workers to collect unemployment benefits for up to 26 weeks. In practice, most claimants find new jobs before the maximum number of weeks have run.[13] In some states, workers may be eligible

6 See 26 U.S.C. §§ 3303–304; see generally Samuel Estreicher & Gillian Lester, Employment Law 133–34 (2008). Under federal law, a state UI program is certified only if the state creates a public employment agency to administer the benefit; the agency must have procedures in place for merit-based selection of personnel, and for claimants to receive a fair hearing before an impartial tribunal. 42 U.S.C. § 503(a). States must deposit employer tax revenue in an interest-bearing account that can be accessed only for the payment of benefits. 26 U.S.C. § 3304(a). The tax may be experience-rated, whereby employers who lay off fewer workers are subject to a reduced rate of contributions, *id.* § 3303 (a)(1), although states use different methods to incorporate experience rating in the calculation of the employer's UI tax. See Estreicher & Lester, supra, at 134–35. Finally, federal law imposes certain coverage and eligibility criteria. See *id.* §§ 3304–306.

7 N.Y. Lab. L. § 591(1) (McKinney 2013). See also, e.g., Fla. Stat. § 443.036(44)(a) ("[A]n individual is 'totally unemployed' in any week during which he or she does not perform any services and for which earned income is not payable to him or her").

8 See N.Y. Lab. L. § 520 (defining "base period"); *id.* § 527 (describing the income the claimant must have received during the base period in order to file a valid claim).

9 *Id.* § 591(2).

10 See *id.* § 593 (describing disqualification from benefits, and stating that voluntary separation is not a disqualification if there is "good cause" including, but not limited to, compelling family reasons).

11 For example, in New York, the benefit is currently calculated at about 46–48% of the worker's previous weekly income. See N.Y. Lab. L. § 560.5. The maximum weekly benefit in New York is currently $405. *Before You Apply For Unemployment: Frequently Asked Questions*, N.Y. Dept. of Lab., available at https://labor.ny.gov/ui/claimantinfo/beforeyouapplyfaq.shtm.

12 Chad Stone & William Chen, *Introduction to Unemployment Insurance*, Center on Budget and Policy Priorities (Feb. 6, 2013), available at www.cbpp.org/cms/index.cfm?fa=view&id=1466.

13 In 2012, claimants collected unemployment benefits for an average of about 17 weeks. Average Duration of Persons Collecting UI Benefits, *Unemployment Insurance Chartbook*, U.S. Dept. of Lab., available at http://workforcesecurity.doleta.gov/unemploy/chartbook.asp.

for an added 13–20 weeks of benefits under an extended benefits program if their state is experiencing high unemployment. Additionally, Congress has, from time to time, provided for the temporary extension of unemployment benefits for individuals who have exhausted their state benefits.[14]

The UI Administrative Process

While unemployment benefits are a long-established statutory right, the process of obtaining benefits is not always easy. In New York, a claimant first files a claim for benefits with a Labor Services Representative at a UI office, and describes the circumstances surrounding his loss of employment.[15] A claimant is generally eligible for benefits, for example, if the employer laid off workers due to lack of business, or if the worker was not able to meet performance and production requirements. But because, as discussed, a claimant is not eligible for benefits if the claimant was discharged for misconduct, or if the claimant left employment voluntarily without good cause, the factual circumstances of the separation may become contested by claimants or employers.[16] In some cases, the Labor Services Representative may contact the employer to verify the claimant's story. The official will then make an initial determination on whether the claim is approved, and send a Notice of Determination to the claimant and employer describing the reasons for the determination.[17] Either the claimant or employer may contest an initial determination as erroneous and request a redetermination by the Labor Services Representative on the basis of new or corrected information.[18]

[14] Most recently the federal Emergency Unemployment Compensation (EUC) program was established by the Supplemental Appropriations Act, Pub. L. No. 110–252 (2008) and last extended by the American Taxpayer Relief Act of 2012, Pub. L. No. 112–240 (2012). This program provided for the availability of UI to up to 99 weeks in many U.S. states between 2009 and 2012. However, the EUC program ended in December 2013, and there is presently no federal extension program as of June 15, 2014.

[15] N.Y. LAB. L. §§ 596–97.

[16] See, e.g., id. § 593(1) & (3) ("No days of total unemployment shall be deemed to occur after a claimant's voluntary separation without good cause" and "[n]o days of total unemployment shall be deemed to occur [if] a claimant lost employment through misconduct in connection with his or her employment ..."); FLA. STAT. § 443.101(1)(a) (disqualifying an individual who has "voluntarily left work without good cause," and defining "good cause" as: "that cause attributable to the employing unit which would compel a reasonable employee to cease working or attributable to the individual's illness or disability requiring separation from his or her work"; further disqualifying individuals "discharged for misconduct connected with his or her work"); CAL. UNEMP. INS. CODE § 1256 ("An individual is disqualified for unemployment compensation benefits if the director finds that he or she left his or her most recent work voluntarily without good cause or that he or she has been discharged for misconduct connected with his or her most recent work"); Boynton Cab v. Neubeck, 296 N.W. 636, 640 (Wis. 1941) (defining "misconduct").

[17] N.Y. LAB. L. § 597.

[18] *Id.* § 597(3). See also Matter of Council, 523 N.Y.S.2d 212 (N.Y. App. Div. 1987).

Subsequently, either the claimant or employer may appeal the Labor Services Representative's initial determination at "a fair hearing before an impartial tribunal."[19] In New York, this hearing is conducted by an Administrative Law Judge (ALJ) employed by the state Department of Labor. The ALJ hearing provides an opportunity for each side to present evidence and call witnesses. It is this first-level appeal of the initial determination that is the common subject of study in the scholarship on unemployment compensation appeals. The ALJ's decision may, in turn, be reviewed in a second-level appeal to the Unemployment Insurance Appeal Board, an independent body appointed by the governor of New York.[20] Final decisions of the Appeal Board may be further appealed in state court.[21]

An employer has an economic incentive to challenge unemployment benefit awards because the employer's UI tax may be increased if there are successful benefits claims made by its former workers. In New York, an employer may qualify for a "stable employment benefit" that will reduce the employer's tax rate.[22] Since each successful claim by a former employee can result in thousands of dollars in increased UI tax payments for the employer,[23] the employer has a real financial interest in contesting initial benefits determinations by appealing to an ALJ. For example, a hypothetical company in New York with ten employees in 2012 would have paid $3,670 more at the highest UI tax rate imposed on the employers who lay off the most workers, compared to the average UI tax rate.[24] According to Herbert

[19] 42 U.S.C. § 503(a)(3). Each state's unemployment compensation laws must provide "[o]pportunity for a fair hearing, before an impartial tribunal, for all individuals whose claims for unemployment compensation are denied."

[20] N.Y. Lab. L. § 621.

[21] *Id.* § 624. See also *Requesting a Hearing*, N.Y. Dept. of Lab., available at http://labor.ny.gov/ui/aso/hearing2.shtm.

[22] Every employer has an account within the UI fund reflecting UI payments by the employer; an "experience rating" charge is a debit to the employer's account reflecting the payment of UI benefits. N.Y. Lab. L. §§ 581(1)(a)–(e). When benefits paid exceed the account balance, the balance is negative, and the DOL assigns a higher contribution rate than if the balance were positive. *Id* § 581(2) (prescribing employer contribution rates based on negative or positive account percentage, and the account's size relative to the size of the UI fund); see also *UI Rates and Employer Account Percentages*, N.Y. Dept. of Lab., available at www.labor.ny.gov/ui/bpta/empacct.shtm (last visited Nov. 30, 2013); Jay Goltz, 20,000 *Reasons Not to Hire Someone*, N.Y. Times Small Bus. Blog (Feb. 3, 2010), available at http://boss.blogs.nytimes.com/2010/02/03/20000-reasons-not-to-hire-someone/ ("The important point for business owners to know is that when the state pays out claims to a company's former employees, that company's unemployment tax rate goes up").

[23] See Ian Mount, *As Jobless Claims Rise, Businesses Try to Manage the Burden of Benefits*, N.Y. Times (Oct. 19, 2011), available at www.nytimes.com/2011/10/20/business/smallbusiness/managing-unemployment-premiums-in-a-time-of-joblessness.html ("A typical unemployment claim against a business increases the amount that business pays in state premiums in a range of $4,000 to $7,000 over a three-year period . . .").

[24] For example, in 2012, a New York employer could have paid as little as $77 per employee at the lowest UI rate assigned to employers with the best experience rate – those laying off the fewest employees. The average UI rate was $390 per employee, while the maximum rate per employee was $757. See *Significant Measures of State Unemployment Insurance Tax Systems*, U.S. Dept. of Lab. (2012), available at http://ows.doleta.gov/unemploy/finance.asp.

Kritzer, author of a study on unemployment compensation appeals in Wisconsin, "[s]ophisticated employers go to significant lengths to minimize the unemployment compensation taxes that they pay."[25]

Of course, workers also have an incentive to challenge unfavorable initial claim determinations in a hearing before an ALJ. But they may often be less able to represent themselves than employers, who are often repeat and sophisticated players in the unemployment benefits system. While the New York Department of Labor does not report data on representation at ALJ hearings, it is estimated by one experienced New York employment lawyer that around 70% of hearings involve represented employers, while only around 5% of claimants are represented.[26] Employers may be represented at hearings by attorneys, unemployment cost control companies, or by representatives from their internal personnel departments.[27] Workers, however, are less able to obtain representation to advocate on their behalf. In New York, only attorneys and agents registered with the Unemployment Insurance Appeal Board may represent any party in exchange for compensation in any proceeding, limiting the supply of representation (however, anyone may represent a claimant if no compensation is involved).[28] Compensation for services rendered to claimants – but not employers – must be approved by the appeals board, which will consider (i) the total benefit allowed; (ii) the time spent in representation; (iii) the factual complexity involved; and (iv) other factors the board deems relevant.[29] Importantly, a claimant's attorney or agent can only be paid for successful hearing representations; no equivalent paternalism shields employers from paying unsuccessful lawyers, so representing claimants is a riskier proposition than representing employers. Additionally, no attorney will be appointed to represent a claimant in ALJ hearings or proceedings before the appeal board; appointment of an attorney for a claimant is possible only if the employer

[25] See HERBERT M. KRITZER, LEGAL ADVOCACY: LAWYERS AND NONLAWYERS AT WORK 24 (1998); see generally ESTREICHER & LESTER, supra note 6, at 134–36 (discussing experience rating and its effect on employer decisions to engage in layoffs).

[26] Interview with David A. Raff, Partner, Raff & Becker, in New York, NY (Dec. 27, 2013) on file with author (discussing the history of the Unemployment Action Center and the operations of the unemployment insurance system in New York state); see also KRITZER, supra note 25, at 25 (reporting that in Wisconsin, about 9.2% of claimants had an advocate, about two-thirds of whom were lawyers).

[27] *Id.*

[28] See N.Y. LAB. L. § 538(1)(b) (McKinney 2013) ("In any proceeding under this article a party may be represented by an agent, but no fees for services rendered by such agent shall be allowable unless such agent is registered with the or is an attorney"); N.Y. COMP. CODES R. & REGS. tit. 12, § 465(c) (setting requirements for registration as a non-attorney agent authorized to represent claimants, including attainment of a high school diploma and at least sixteen hours of experience in legal or administrative proceedings). The practice of requiring registration for non-lawyer agents to represent claimants for a fee varies from state to state. Compare N.J. Rev. Stat. § 43:21–6.2 (requiring registration of authorized non-lawyer agents in New Jersey), with WIS. STAT. § 108.105 (requiring no qualifications for non-attorney agents to represent claimants for a fee, but providing grounds for suspension of the privilege to represent claimants in Wisconsin).

[29] N.Y. Lab. L. § 538(1)(c).

appeals an administrative determination in court. All of these factors reduce the supply of experienced representation available to claimants, and increase their need for pro bono representation.

Unemployment Action Center

Students at New York University School of Law (NYU) founded the Unemployment Action Center (UAC) in 1981; it was incorporated as a nonprofit in 1985. The UAC was created after the cessation of an employment law clinic[30] at NYU upon the departure of its long-time faculty director, David Raff, in 1980.[31] Students still wanted to assist workers on employment law matters, and searched New York state statutes for provisions allowing non-attorneys to help workers. With Mr. Raff's assistance, they discovered that UI claimants could be represented by anyone, non-attorneys and non-registered agents alike, as long as no fee was collected.[32] A church near the law school donated the organization's first office and phone line, and the UAC began taking cases in 1981. Today, through the UAC, NYU students are joined by law students at Cardozo, Columbia, Fordham, Hofstra, and New York Law School in providing free legal services to UI claimants in their first-level appeals before an ALJ.

The UAC is a nonprofit corporation managed by a board of directors comprised solely of law students. Individual chapter leadership councils at each of the six participating law schools in New York State provide support and training to new volunteers. Chapters typically offer multiple training sessions at the beginning of each semester, each run by student leaders from that chapter. The training sessions are three to four hours long, and take prospective volunteers through the history of the UAC, a synopsis of unemployment insurance law in New York, and the timeline of a UAC case. Volunteers are shown in mock interviews how to discuss cases with claimants prior to a hearing before the ALJ, and taught how to gather evidence in support of the claimant's theory. Finally, the trainers stage a mock hearing with an "appropriately stern/irritable" mock-ALJ. The UAC allows new volunteers to take UAC cases immediately after the training, but new volunteers are often paired with experienced volunteers on their first cases, and the relatively experienced chapter leaders make themselves available to discuss cases and legal strategies with volunteers.

Chapter dues, currently set at $5,000 per school, are paid annually by the member law schools, and comprise the primary source of funding for the UAC. The UAC's

30 The employment law clinic has since been revived at NYU Law, primarily focusing on federal litigation in the fields of employment discrimination, Family and Medical Leave Act violations, and violations of minimum wage laws. See *Civil Litigation-Employment Law Clinic*, NYU LAW, available at www.law.nyu.edu/academics/clinics/semester/civil-litigation-employment-law (last accessed June 15, 2014).

31 Interview with David Raff, supra note 26.

32 *Id.*

modest, one-person office is presently provided by NYU and is located in the basement of one of the law school's residence halls. The nonprofit has a single full-time employee, an office administrator, who screens claimants, assigns cases, and oversees day-to-day operations for every chapter.

After an initial determination of unemployment benefits by the Labor Services Representative, either the employee or the employer may appeal the determination in a hearing before an ALJ. If such a hearing is requested, a notice of hearing is sent to both parties, seven to ten days before the hearing date. The notice of hearing contains contact information for organizations that offer free legal advice to employee claimants, such as the Workers Defense League, Legal Aid, and the UAC.[33] Claimants call the UAC office and leave voicemails with some basic information – the claimant's name, phone number, hearing date, and hearing location. The voicemail greeting also instructs the claimant to gather the notice of hearing and the notice of determination, so the UAC office administrator can perform a full intake. The UAC fields as many as 60 calls a day – typically, claimants will call and leave messages with every pro bono organization listed in the notice of hearing.[34] The UAC office administrator listens to each voicemail, and attempts to call back each claimant, trying at least three times, if necessary, to perform a full intake interview.

The office administrator performs around 10–15 full intakes each day, and ultimately selects two to three cases to present to student volunteers. The primary barrier to the UAC accepting a case is if the hearing date is too soon for a student volunteer to be found. There is no income requirement to be represented by the UAC. The screening process is a coarse filter as far as legal claims go. While some claimants are screened out because they do not fulfill the basic legal criteria for receiving unemployment benefits (e.g., unavailability to work), the office administrator does not turn away claimants with merely difficult legal cases, such as contested quit cases or firings where the employer alleges malfeasance. In this manner, the UAC may take cases that other pro bono legal services organizations staffed by attorneys may have screened out. Because one of the UAC's primary motivations is to provide students with legal experience, they can be less selective in the merits of the case.[35] Instead, the full intake provides an opportunity for the office administrator to perform a basic assessment of the claimant's credibility – an *obviously* dishonest or clearly unstable claimant will not be referred to a volunteer. Language also presents a significant barrier, as the UAC does not have the resources to provide an interpreter for non-English-speaking claimants at the intake level.

33 For many years, the UI Appeal Board refused requests by the UAC to appear on the notices of hearing mailed to claimants, even though the UAC had assisted claimants in thousands of cases. The UAC was finally listed in 2007, when Leonard Polletta became Chairman. *Id.*

34 Interview with Marisa Voila, Office Administrator, Unemployment Action Center (Aug. 22, 2013) (discussing the operations and intake process of the UAC).

35 Interview with David Raff, supra note 26.

Thus, the office administrator may not be able to return voicemails left in a foreign language.

This screening method is far from perfect. It favors, for example, claimants who decide to call the UAC and leave a voicemail, claimants with a working understanding of English, and claimants in good mental health. Claimants without these attributes are not necessarily less entitled to UI benefits. The unfortunate irony is that the UAC is unable to assist those who are the least able to assist themselves, without any representation, in hearings before an ALJ. A claimant who cannot leave a voicemail in English is even less likely to be able to research the relevant English-language case law and UI Appeal Board precedents. A claimant who cannot coherently narrate a factual background to the UAC stands little chance of persuading an ALJ. This measure of selection bias is not lost on the UAC, but absent a substantial change in its finances, there are no immediate prospects for providing representation in these difficult cases.

At the end of each day, the UAC office administrator sends an email to volunteers with that day's claimant referrals. Volunteers typically request cases very quickly, but the office administrator makes the final assignment, attempting to balance the number of cases per school and per volunteer, and forming teams if there are first-time volunteers. Since the UAC relies on student participation, the pool of advocates fluctuates along with the academic year. Each semester's final exam season brings a drought of volunteers, and the UAC often must turn away many claimants when their hearing dates overlap with the most hectic periods of law school. During the summer months, however, the UAC recruits law student interns who each take two new cases a week.[36]

Once a UAC student advocate is assigned to a case, the first step is to schedule a meeting with the claimant to hear the claimant's story and review documents relating to the employment and the UI claim (which the student will request the claimant bring to their first meeting). This first meeting typically takes place at the state Department of Labor (DOL), where the advocate can also request to view the claimant's file kept by the Department. Reviewing the DOL file allows the student advocate and claimant to discuss strategies for rebutting adverse documentation, and identify defenses to evidence likely to be submitted by the employer or the Labor Services Representative who made the initial determination.

Getting a claimant to present their whole story to the student advocate is not always easy, yet it is a vital ingredient of successful representation. A claimant contacts the UAC at a tremendously unsettling period of his life, having recently lost a job, being shuttled around the UI system, and having benefits denied or challenged. Voicemails left for the UAC often sound frustrated and defensive; some claimants view the UAC as part of an unfriendly and impersonal system.

[36] Interns are eligible to receive funding for completing public interest internships during the summer, e.g., NYU students can receive the School's Public Interest Law Center funding.

The claimant interviews require advocates to practice a lawyering skill that is rarely taught and even less frequently exercised in law school: earning the trust and cooperation of a client. Advocates first remind the claimant that they are law students, and the scope of representation is limited to helping the claimant secure unemployment benefits. While there is no attorney–client privilege, advocates do promise to maintain confidentiality to their fullest ability. From there, advocates, who are disproportionately first-year law students, must project confidence and competence in interviewing the claimant and explaining to them the legal principles and obstacles involved.

After the first meeting, the advocate develops a case theory for why the claimant is entitled to UI benefits. UAC student leaders encourage advocates, during training, to research statutory sources and case law. A particularly helpful resource, published by the DOL, is the Interpretation Service Index, a curated digest of binding precedents from the UI Appeal Board and courts.[37] With the claimant's assistance, the advocate gathers evidence needed to support the legal theory, e.g., correspondence with the employer, time cards, pay stubs, medical records, letters from healthcare providers, employee handbooks, telephone records. An advocate can also find witnesses who can corroborate parts of the claimant's story. At the second meeting with the claimant, the advocate prepares the client for direct examination, the admission of evidence, and cross-examination. The advocate also coaches the client on proper protocol, attire, and demeanor during the hearing before the ALJ.

At the hearing itself, the student advocate conducts a direct examination of the claimant and the claimant's witnesses. Advocates are expected to cross-examine the employer or the employer's witnesses, make objections where necessary, and preserve objections to process failures for appeal. An important role for the advocate is to be vigilant for violations of the claimant's procedural rights in ALJ hearings: e.g., a party must have a translator if one is needed; the judge must grant greater weight to sworn testimony as opposed to hearsay; the claimant is entitled to a default judgment in appeals from initial benefit determinations by the employer if the employer fails to appear.[38] Finally, the advocate will present a brief closing argument emphasizing important testimony and legal precedent.

Claimants receive a decision from the ALJ in two to four weeks. If the claimant does not obtain benefits, the claimant may appeal the ALJ decision to the Appeal Board, but it is the individual advocate's decision whether to continue with the appeal. Since the Appeal Board rarely overturns the ALJ,[39] the UAC concentrates its resources at the hearing level. On a pragmatic level, the limitations of the

37 *Electronic Interpretation Service*, N.Y. Dept. of Lab., available at https://labor.ny.gov/ui/aso/interpservice.shtm. While many unemployment insurance documents and forms are available in other languages, the Interpretation Service appears to be available only in English.

38 See Barcia v. Sitkin, 865 F. Supp. 1015 (S.D.N.Y. 1994).

39 See also Andrew Stettner & Rebecca Smith, *Down But Not Out: Reviving the Promise of Unemployment Insurance in New York*, National Employment Law Project (Dec. 2006), available at http://nelp.3cdn.net/c1a6cda56ce5013529_rkm6b5gig.pdf (showing U.S. Department of Labor data

academic calendar and the lack of professional and institutional supervision make appeals to the Appeal Board, a longer process than the ALJ hearing, less suitable for a student organization. However, if the claimant receives benefits, and the employer appeals, then the UAC advocate will continue with the appeal and will submit briefs on behalf of the claimant.

Unemployment Action Center's Record

The office administrator collects data on every case taken by a student advocate. The UAC reports that claimants "have been awarded benefits in approximately 60% of the cases in which they were represented by a UAC advocate … [T]he estimated city-wide average success rate [is] less than 30% for unrepresented claimants."[40] This corroborates other studies of representation in UI cases, which find that represented claimants prevail at a significantly higher rate than unrepresented claimants.[41] The UAC's success rate is particularly impressive given their screening process. Unlike paid attorneys or registered agents, the UAC does not select cases based on the prospect of future remuneration – it receives none. The financial incentive may skew the data on the success rates of represented claimants, because there is typically a selection bias in determining which claimants receive representation. While the UAC does screen out some claimants based on language or credibility concerns, the UAC can afford, as a nonprofit, not to be as discriminating in trying to choose probable legal winners.

that from 1994 to 2004, claimant appeals to the UI Appeal Board were only successful between 5–10% of the time); Interview with David Raff, supra note 26.

40 *About the UAC*, Unemployment Action Center, available at http://uac-ny.org/?page_id=18 (last visited Dec. 12, 2013); The most recent measure of UAC data was based on cases taken from Summer 2010 through the end of the 2013–2014 academic year. Across all member schools, the UAC completed cases for 1,128 claimants during this period, and was informed by claimants of the hearing result in 672 cases. Of the cases with known results, the claimant prevailed in obtaining benefits 71% of the time. This matched the success rate of the New York City pro bono legal assistance organization Volunteers of Legal Service (VOLS), which also provides legal services to claimants in UI appeals through its Unemployment Insurance Advocacy Project. In 2013, VOLS received calls to its UI hotline from 2,274 claimants. 539 claimants received brief advice and counseling, and 122 received full legal representation. Eighty-six of the 122 prevailed and won benefits, and 18 lost; 9 claimants withdrew, 4 claimants had their attorneys withdraw, and 5 cases remain pending. E-mail from Bill Lienhard, Executive Director, Volunteers of Legal Service, to author (July 1, 2014).

41 See *Unemployment Insurance Advocacy Project*, Volunteers of Legal Service, available at www.volsprobono.org/projects/unemployment-insurance-advocacy-project (reporting that in New York, "more than 90% of claimants are unrepresented. Only about 28% of unrepresented claimants win their hearings. When claimants are represented by a lawyer, their odds of securing these crucial benefits nearly triple. In 2013, for example, 83% of claimants represented through [Volunteers for Legal Services] won unemployment benefits"); Herbert M. Kritzer, Legal Advocacy: Lawyers and Nonlawyers at Work 34 (1998) (finding that, overall, claimants won 41.5% of appeals when unrepresented, and 50.4% of appeals when represented); see generally Russell Engler, *Connecting Self-Representation to Civil* Gideon: *What Existing Data Reveal About When Counsel is Most Needed*, 37 Fordham Urb. L.J. 37, 60–61 (2010).

In an attempt to measure the efficacy of free student-driven legal representation, Jim Grenier and Cassandra Pattanayak published a controversial study of UI services offered by the Harvard Legal Aid Bureau (HLAB).[42] In their study, UI claimants with first-level appeals from initial determinations of claimant benefits or denial of benefits – hearings before an ALJ – were randomized into a "treatment" and a "control" group. Harvard students offered the "treatment" group assistance from HLAB, but this offer was not extended to the "control" group, which was referred to other legal aid organizations that might take up their case. Interestingly, not everyone in the "treatment" group who received offers of representation accepted those offers; and many members of the "control" group who did not receive representation from Harvard students did obtain representation from other legal services organizations. The authors found that members of the "treatment" group were no more likely to prevail on their benefits claim than members of the "control" group, who did not receive offers.[43] But, the authors found that cases in the "treatment" group took an average of 42% longer (from an average 37.3 days from HLAB intake to ALJ decision, to 53.1 days) for the claimant to receive an ALJ decision.[44] The authors concluded that the "treatment" group thus experienced unnecessary delay while having the same likelihood of prevailing as members of the "control" group. And for those who did prevail, that delay was costly. Delays in the receipt of benefits are particularly harmful because unemployed claimants rely on benefit income, and the policy objectives of the UI system is only achieved if the benefits are rapidly disbursed.[45]

It is not clear whether the supposed harm of delayed resolution from the offer of representation also occurs for claimants receiving assistance from the UAC. Massachusetts law requires its agency tasked with administering the UI benefit – the Department of Unemployment Assistance – to make "every reasonable effort to complete" first-level appeals of initial determinations within forty-five days of the request for an ALJ hearing;[46] and claimants can expect an ALJ decision one to two weeks after the hearing. Similarly, in New York, a notice of hearing is typically sent seven to ten days before a hearing date, and claimants are instructed to expect a decision from the ALJ within two to three weeks.[47] One explanation for the

42 D. James Grenier & Cassandra W. Pattanayak, *Randomized Evaluation in Legal Assistance: What Difference Does Representation (Offer and Actual Use) Make*, 121 YALE L.J. 2118 (2012).

43 *Id.* at 2149. On average, 76% of claimants in the "treatment" group and 72% of claimants in the "control" group prevailed in the ALJ hearing.

44 *Id.* at 2153–55.

45 See *id.* at 2137.

46 MASS. GEN. LAWS ANN. ch. 151A, §39(b)(5) (2011).

47 *Hearing Process*, NY DEPT. OF LAB., available at http://labor.ny.gov/ui/claimantinfo/HearingProcess.shtm; see also *Lower Authority Appeals Time Lapse*, UNITED STATES DEPARTMENT OF LABOR EMPLOYMENT & TRAINING ADMINISTRATION, available at http://ows.doleta.gov/unemploy/btq.asp (last accessed June 10, 2014) (showing that in New York, in 2013, a decision was rendered in a first-level appeal before an ALJ within 30 days in 63% of cases, and within 45 days in 83% of cases).

delay found by Grenier and his coauthor is that student representatives request hearing postponements in order to investigate a case.[48] However, this practice is uncommon among UAC advocates, and the screening process is designed to not accept cases that have imminent hearing dates.[49] More importantly, if the harm of offers of free legal services representation is that it results in a delayed judgment, the best solution may be simply for the state to better enforce its timeliness guidelines.

Aside from helping successful claimants, the UAC also provides a service to unsuccessful claimants. It helps claimants understand why they were denied benefits, often because the legal question can turn on the events of a single critical day, and the ALJ does not consider the laundry list of grievances either party may have. By providing representation, the UAC promotes acceptance of the legitimacy of the UI system, which to many claimants may seem to be a bureaucratic maze.

Despite its success, the UAC faces challenges in growing and improving its services. The improvements in screening and intake that Grenier and Pattanayak recommend are costly, and the UAC only has one employee to handle intake. The current chapter dues are $5,000 per school, but not every school is able or willing to pay the full amount. The UAC also faces competition for student attention from other volunteer organizations and clinics. An innovative new rule governing the admission of attorneys to the New York State bar that requires new applicants to have completed fifty hours of pro bono service promises to increase the number of law students interested in pro bono opportunities, but currently does not benefit the UAC because the organization's independent model lacks the requisite faculty or attorney supervision to be a qualifying source of pro bono work.[50]

The UAC has demonstrated consistent success in helping claimants obtain unemployment benefits. By exposing law students to the quasi-adversarial mini-trial of an ALJ hearing, the UAC also educates students in practical legal skills. And even without pro bono credit, the UAC helps inculcate a spirit of volunteerism that encourages future lawyers to continue to invest in their community by helping those who cannot otherwise afford representation.

48 Grenier, supra note 42, at 2172.

49 E-mails from Rebecca Riddell, Chair of Regional Board of Directors 2014–15, Unemployment Action Center, to author (June 16, 2014).

50 N.Y. Comp. Codes R. & Regs. tit. 22, § 520.16 (2014).

8

Immigrant Representation:

Meeting an Urgent Need

Hon. Robert A. Katzmann

State and federal judges across the country have led innovative initiatives to address civil access to justice problems that they see in their courtrooms every day. In this chapter, Chief Judge Katzmann of the U.S. Court of Appeals for the Second Circuit describes how over 50 lawyers in New York formed a study group to identify and promote ways to improve the level of legal assistance for immigrants. Among the group's successes has been the creation of the Immigrant Justice Corps, which engage senior lawyers working together with recent graduates to provide counsel and representation for immigrants facing deportation or otherwise needing to navigate the American courts and administrative agencies.

Until recently, immigration cases were a very small part of the work of the Second Circuit. In 1999, when I started as a court of appeals judge, the immigration docket was a minuscule percentage of our workload. But within a few years, the immigration docket approached 40% of the case load – and, as a result, our Court developed procedures to manage such cases, devised largely by Jon Newman under the chief judgeship of John Walker. This system continues to this day. Since 2006, We have adjudicated more than seventeen thousand immigration cases. In all too many cases, I could not but notice a substantial impediment to the fair and effective administration of justice: the too-often deficient counsel of represented noncitizens. For immigrants, the stakes could not be greater – whether they can stay in the United States, whether they will be separated from their loved ones, often their children. In all too many cases, I had the sense that if only the immigrant had competent counsel at the very outset of immigration proceedings where the record is made with lasting effect – long before the case reached the court of appeals where review is limited – the outcome might have been different, the noncitizen might have prevailed.

Wanting to do something, I took the opportunity of the Marden Lecture of the New York City Bar[1] in 2007, to challenge the New York legal establishment and others interacting with that establishment – law firms, bar associations, nonprofits,

[1] Robert A. Katzmann, The Legal Profession and the Unmet Needs of the Immigrant Poor, Orison of the Bar of the city of S. Marden Lecture (Feb. 28, 2007), *in* 62 Record of. Ass'n of the Bar N.Y.C. 287 (2007). A slightly revised, footnoted version can be found in Robert A. Katzmann, *The Marden Lecture:*

corporate counsel, foundations, law schools, state and local government, the media, the immigration bar, senior lawyers and retirees, providers of continuing education and training, and think tanks – to step up activity to help address the large – and largely unmet – need in noncitizen communities. Justice, I said, should not depend upon the income level of immigrants.[2]

STUDY GROUP ON IMMIGRANT REPRESENTATION

I did not know what the reaction would be, but the response was, and has been, very gratifying. With the guidance of several outstanding lawyers, beginning with Peter Eikenberry and Robert Juceam, I started a working group in 2008, the Study Group on Immigrant Representation, consisting of some fifty lawyers from a range of firms; nonprofits; bar organizations – the Federal Bar Council, the New York City Bar, the New York State Bar Association, the New York Lawyers County Association, the American Immigration Lawyers Association; immigrant legal service providers; immigrant organizations; law schools; federal, state and local governments; as well as my excellent colleague, Judge Denny Chin. Our method is to bring together key participants from the federal, state, and city governments, the private bar, bar associations, nonprofits, legal service providers, immigrant organizations, philanthropies, and law schools, as part of a collaborative effort to promote the fair and effective administration of justice.

Over the past several years, Study Group activities have included these initiatives:

(1) I proposed the creation an Immigrant Justice Corps (IJC) to represent noncitizens, consisting of young lawyers, senior lawyers, and college graduates, who would serve for two or three years – a program launched in January 2014 with substantial planning support and initial funding from the Robin Hood Foundation, and with additional generous support from the JPB Foundation and other foundations.[3] The IJC is the country's first national fellowship program, piloted initially in New York City, wholly dedicated to meeting the need for legal assistance for immigrants seeking

The Legal Profession and the Unmet Needs of the Immigrant Poor, 21 GEO. J. LEGAL ETHICS 3 (2008) [hereinafter Katzmann, *The Marden Lecture*]. Copyright © 2014–2016 by Robert A. Katzmann, Chief Judge, United States Court of Appeals for the Second Circuit. Excerpts of remarks delivered by Judge Katzmann upon receiving the Learned Hand Medal from the Federal Bar Council on May 1, 2012, in New York City. The full version can be found in Robert A. Katzmann, *Bench, Bar, and Immigrant Representation: Meeting an Urgent Need*, 15 J. LEGIS. & PUB. POL'Y. 586 (2012).

2 Katzmann, *The Marden Lecture*, supra note 1, at 5.

3 Kirk Semple, *Seeking Better Legal Help for Immigrants*, N.Y. TIMES, Jan. 28, 2014, available at www.nytimes.com/2014/01/29/nyregion/service-program-will-recruit-law-school-graduates-to-help-represent-immigrants.html?_r=0.

citizenship and fighting deportation.[4] The IJC will substantially add to the capacity of nonprofit providers to offer counsel for noncitizens, and will create a new generation of lawyers committed to serving noncitizens.

(2) In 2010, the Study Group spearheaded an assessment of the representational needs of indigent noncitizens facing removal in New York – the New York Immigrant Representation Study. A product of the study is the New York Immigrant Family Unity Project (NYIFUP), the nation's first system of institutionally provided deportation defense using an assigned counsel model. In a major breakthrough, with funding provided by the New York City Council, every person in detention in New York City will have legal representation.

(3) We have undertaken two major conferences, one at Fordham Law School and Cardozo Law School, the latter with retired Justice John Paul Stevens participating, out of which we have produced a series of studies and reports published in the Fordham[5] and Cardozo[6] law reviews.

(4) We met with Attorney General Holder, Senator Schumer, and others, after which, in 2010 – the Attorney General announced the creation of a Legal Orientation Program in New York, enabling nonprofit providers to counsel immigrants in group settings and individually.

(5) We devised a pilot project to stimulate greater law firm pro bono activity with the support of the Leon Levy Foundation, the Federal Bar Council, Human Rights First, and law firms of Cleary Gottlieb, Sullivan & Cromwell, Fried Frank, Morrison & Foerster, and WilmerHale. In this program, potential asylum clients are first screened at the New York Immigration Court, and the law firms then take the asylum cases pro bono.

(6) We have joined with bar organizations to recruit, successfully, more pro bono lawyers.

(7) We have developed, in collaboration with other organizations, training sessions for deferred law firm associates so that they could devote their deferral years to immigrant representation.

(8) We have spurred the creation of law school clinics – the prime exemplar being the Kathryn O. Greenberg Immigration Justice Clinic at Cardozo Law, under the leadership of two wholly dedicated, vigorous deans, David Rudenstine and Matthew Diller.

4 The Immigrant Justice Corps website is at www.justicecorps.org.

5 Symposium, *The Robert L. Levine Distinguished Lecture: Overcoming Barriers to Immigrant Representation: Exploring Solutions*, 78 Fordham L. Rev. 453 (2009) (including articles, reports, and commentaries of the Study Group on Immigrant Representation); see also Mark Hamblett, *Lawyers Target "Assembly Line" Practice, Abuse of Poor Immigrants*, N.Y. L.J., Jan. 4, 2010, at 1 (discussing the symposium).

6 Symposium, *Innovative Approaches to Immigrant Representation: Exploring New Partnerships*, 33 Cardozo L. Rev. 331, 331–619 (2011).

(9) Study Group members have worked with state, local, and federal governments to explore ways that consumer law could be used to root out fraudulent legal service providers.

(10) Responding to federal initiatives to combat immigration fraud, the Study Group, in concert with the American Immigration Lawyers Association and other organizations, in 2011 sponsored two days of intensive training in immigration law for non-immigration lawyers.

A lot more could be said about each of these initiatives. With your indulgence, I'd like to say more about a foundational cornerstone of our activities – the securing of data that allowed us with confidence to develop a coherent approach to address the problems at hand.

NEW YORK IMMIGRANT REPRESENTATION STUDY

Senator Daniel Patrick Moynihan often said that you're entitled to your own opinion, but not to your own facts. I couldn't agree more. Thus, I thought it important that the Study Group move from anecdote to comprehensive data, so that the problem could be better defined and addressed. To that end, Study Group members have undertaken the New York Immigrant Representation Study (NYIRS),[7] chaired by Professor Peter Markowitz of Cardozo Law School, Professor Stacy Caplow of Brooklyn Law School, and Claudia Slovinsky. That study, with the support of the Leon Levy Foundation and the Governance Institute, is a two-year project in collaboration with the Vera Institute of Justice. The study provides, for the first time ever, comprehensive data about the scope of the immigrant representation challenge in New York (part one, year one) and a plan for addressing it (part two, year two, be issued at the end of 2012). [8]

I present to you now a few of those findings because they powerfully show the depth of the problem:

First. "A striking percentage of detained and non-detained immigrants appearing before the New York Immigration Courts do not have representation."[9] In New York City:

- "Sixty percent of detained immigrants do not have counsel by the time their cases are completed."

[7] See generally Peter L. Markowitz et al., *Accessing Justice: The Availability and Adequacy of Counsel in Removal Proceedings*, 33 CARDOZO L. REV. 357 (2011) (reporting the results of Part 1 of the New York Immigrant Representation Study Report) (hereinafter *Accessing Justice I*). For part II, which proposed the model for the New York Family Unity Project, see NYIRS Steering Committee, Accessing Justice II: A Model for Providing Counsel to New York Immigrants in Removal Proceedings (2012), available at www.cardozolawreview.com/content/denovo/NYIRS_ReportII.pdf.

[8] *Accessing Justice I*.

[9] *Id.* at 363.

- "Twenty-seven percent of non-detained immigrants do not have counsel by the time their cases are completed."

Second. The study found that the Department of Homeland Security's detention and transfer policies create significant obstacles for immigrants facing removal to obtain counsel.

- At the time of the study, Immigration and Customs Enforcement transferred "almost two-thirds (64%) of those detained in New York to far-off detention centers (most frequently to Louisiana, Pennsylvania, and Texas) where they face the greatest obstacles to obtaining counsel" (a practice that has essentially ended, in part, due to the study's findings).
- "Individuals who are transferred elsewhere and who remain detained outside of New York are unrepresented 79% of the time."

Third. "The two most important variables affecting the ability to secure a successful outcome in a case (defined as relief or termination) are having representation and being free from detention. The absence of either factor in a case – being detained but represented or being unrepresented but not detained – drops the success rate dramatically. When neither factor is present the rate of successful outcomes drops even more substantially."

- "Represented and released or never detained: 74% have successful outcomes."
- "Unrepresented but released or never detained: 13% have successful outcomes."[10]
- "Represented but detained: 18% have successful outcomes."
- "Unrepresented and detained: 3% have successful outcomes."

I think we can all agree that having a lawyer, preferably a good one, makes a substantial difference.

Fourth. "Grave problems persist in regard to deficient performance by lawyers providing removal-defense services."

- "New York immigration judges rated nearly half of all legal representatives as less than adequate in terms of overall performance . . ."

Fifth. "According to the providers surveyed, detained cases are least served by existing removal-defense providers."

Sixth. "[T]he two greatest impediments to increasing the capacity of existing providers are a lack of funding and a lack of resources to build a qualified core of experienced removal-defense providers."[11]

These dramatic findings give us a sense of the immensity of the task before us.

[10] *Id.* at 364.
[11] *Id.* at 364–65.

WHAT YOU CAN DO?

You might be wondering what can you – the assembled lawyers here – do? I see so much talent in this room. I encourage and welcome the involvement of all of you here: firm leaders who set the tone, partners who serve as mentors for young lawyers, senior lawyers and associates alike. Any lawyer who has successfully represented a noncitizen can tell you of the deep satisfaction of helping a person in need, of helping to keep a family intact, of frankly becoming a hero to that immigrant and immigrant family, with the not insubstantial additional benefit to the attorney and firm of honing legal skills through that representation. Such honing of skills can enhance lawyering in other areas of practice.

We are all shaped by our personal histories. As I reflect on my subject tonight, immigrant representation, my own family's past no doubt plays a part. My father is a refugee from Nazi persecution, my mother the child of Russian immigrants. I can still hear the accents and voices of my own relatives, who escaped persecution, who wanted to become part of this great country, and who, through their toil and belief in the American dream, made this great nation even greater. When we work to secure adequate representation for immigrants, not only are we faithful to our own professional responsibilities, not only do we further the fair and effective administration of justice, but we also honor this nation's immigrant experience.

9

Self-Representation, Civil *Gideon*, and Community Mobilization in Immigration Cases

Alina Das

Alina Das describes the severe lack of legal representation for immigrants facing deportation and reviews research showing that representation would make a difference in the outcome of these removal proceedings. She also evaluates the potential for reforming the system from various perspectives, including pro se initiatives, right-to-counsel litigation, and community mobilization.

Immigration issues are American issues. One out of every eight people living in America is an immigrant, whose status or lack thereof may place them at risk of deportation.[1] One out of every five children is the child of an immigrant, and over 16 million people in America live in families with at least one undocumented immigrant. And the threat of deportation is significant. Immigration law is complex and lawful immigrant status – whether as a visa holder, refugee/asylee, lawful permanent resident, or individual with some other form of authorization to remain in the country – is difficult to obtain and keep. Authorization may expire and even forms of "permanent" status are subject to revocation because of past criminal conduct and other civil immigration violations. Under the various grounds of "removal" (the legal term for deportation), nearly 400,000 individuals are deported each year.[2]

The immigration system is largely a system of self-representation. Forty-one percent of noncitizens end up representing themselves in removal proceedings.[3]

1 Data from Randy Capps & Karina Fortuny, *Immigration and Child and Family Policy*, URB. INST. & CHILD TRENDS ROUNDTABLE ON CHILDREN IN LOW-INCOME FAMILIES 3 (2006), available at www.taxpolicycenter.org/UploadedPDF/311362_lowincome_children3.pdf; Joanna Dreby, *How Today's Immigration Enforcement Policies Impact Children, Families, and Communities*, CTR. AM. PROGRESS (Aug. 20 2012), available at www.americanprogress.org/issues/immigration/report/2012/08/20/27082/how-todays-immigration-enforcement-policies-impact-children-families-and-communities/

2 U.S. Dep't of Homeland Security, U.S. Immigration and Customs Enforcement (ICE), ERO Annual Report, FY 2013 ICE Immigration Removals, at 1, available at www.ice.gov/doclib/about/offices/ero/pdf/2013-ice-immigration-removals.pdf.

3 U.S. Dep't of Homeland Security, 2013 YEARBOOK OF IMMIGRATION STATISTICS, at G1, available at www.justice.gov/eoir/statspub/fy13syb.pdf (hereinafter YEARBOOK).

The number is much higher for the detained immigrant population, where over 80% are pro se.[4] Categorized as a "civil" legal process, removal proceedings do not provide a right to counsel. Instead, individuals in removal proceedings must rely on the limited resources of nonprofit legal service providers or pay for private representation. Although causation is unclear, those without legal representation are ten times more likely to be deported than those with counsel. Moreover, those with counsel may not receive effective representation, given the wide variation in quality among those who represent immigrants in removal proceedings.[5]

MEASURING OUTCOMES FOR PRO SE LITIGANTS IN IMMIGRATION CASES

Nationwide statistics from the U.S. Department of Justice's Executive Office for Immigration Review demonstrate that, in fiscal year 2011, 52.9% of represented noncitizens in removal proceedings received a successful outcome (defined as case termination, relief from removal, or other basis for case closure) as compared to only 5.2% of unrepresented noncitizens.[6] Of course, these numbers alone do not necessarily account for the effect that other factors may have on the outcomes. For example, the detention of a noncitizen during her removal proceedings presumably has a significant effect both on her ability to find an attorney and her ability to defend her case. Similarly, the nature of one's charges and the availability of relief on the merits may also affect one's ability to find an attorney.[7]

Some more targeted studies have attempted to measure these factors with more precision, and lend support to the conclusion that representation itself plays a significant role in case outcomes. For example, a New York study[8] compared outcomes for represented and unrepresented individuals who were not in detention, finding that 74% of represented, non-detained individuals achieved a successful outcome in their removal case, as compared to only 13% of unrepresented, non-detained immigrants.[9] Detention was a significant factor in and of itself, lowering

[4] Nina Siulc et al., Vera Institute for Justice, Improving Efficiency and Promoting Justice in the Immigration System: Lessons from the Legal Orientation Program 1 (2008), available at www.vera.org/download?file=1780/LOP%2BEvaluation.

[5] The quality of lawyering in the immigration field is notoriously low, see Robert A. Katzmann, *The Legal Profession and the Unmet Needs of the Immigrant Poor*, 21 Geo. J. Legal Ethics 3, 6–10 (2008). The system is ripe for abuse by "notarios" and other immigration "consultants" who take advantage of the complexities of the system, see Mary Dolores Guerra, *Lost in Translation: Notario Fraud – Immigration Fraud*, 26 J. Civ. Rts. & Econ. Dev 23 (2011).

[6] Data provided to author from the U.S. Department of Justice, Executive Office of Immigration Review.

[7] Mark Noferi, *Cascading Constitutional Deprivation: The Right to Appointed Counsel for Mandatorily Detained Immigrants Pending Removal Proceedings*, 18 Mich. J. Race & L. 63, 78 (2012) (noting the possibility of a "selection effect" due to the complexity of immigration cases in the detention context).

[8] New York Immigrant Representation Study Report, *Accessing Justice: The Availability and Adequacy of Counsel in Immigration Proceedings*, 33 Cardozo L. Rev. 357, 362 (2011).

[9] *Id.* at 363–64.

successful outcome rates in both categories, but it did not negate the difference attributed to representation.[10]

An earlier study based on 2003 data found similar results nationwide – significant gaps in outcome between represented and unrepresented respondents among both the detained and non-detained population.[11] Gaps were found with various subsets of relief sought, including adjustment of status, asylum, and cancellation of removal for lawful permanent residents.

Some studies have applied more rigorous regression analysis to control for other factors that might influence grant rates. In a study of asylum cases, scholars applied multivariate regression analysis to control for several factors that might otherwise influence the decision of the judge to grant or deny asylum, including the judge's gender and professional background, and the asylum applicant's family ties in the United States.[12] They ultimately concluded that representation alone increased the rate of the success in the case substantially, other measurable factors held constant.[13]

These studies all suffer from a significant selection bias issue. Representation rates may be influenced by clients' resources and their likelihood for relief from removal – two factors which may have an independent impact on the outcome in a case. These studies would have to randomly assign lawyers to the clients whose case outcomes are being measured to be certain that representation fully accounts for the higher success rate.

CAUSES OF THE FAILED SELF-REPRESENTATION SYSTEM

Several features of the immigration system may account for the poor outcomes for the self-represented in immigration cases.

Complexity

The complexity of immigration law makes it difficult for pro se noncitizens to navigate alone. The grounds for removability alone are confusing. Removability is

10 See *id.*

11 Donald Kerwin, *Charitable Legal Programs for Immigrants: What They Do, Why They Matter, and How They Can Be Expanded*, 04–06 IMMIGR. BRIEFING 1 (2004) (finding that, in FY 2003, 87% of represented, non-detained persons were granted adjustment of status, compared to 70% of unrepresented, non-detained persons; that 29% of represented, non-detained persons were granted asylum, compared to 14% of unrepresented, non-detained persons; that 68% of represented, non-detained persons received cancellation of removal for lawful permanent residents, compared to 60% of unrepresented, non-detained immigrants; and that similar gaps were found in comparison among represented and unrepresented detainees).

12 Jaya Ramji-Nogales, Andrew I. Schoenholtz & Philip G. Schrag, *Refugee Roulette: Disparities in Asylum Adjudication*, 60 STAN. L. REV. 295, 339–40 (2007).

13 *Id.* at 340. The study found that represented asylum seekers were three times as likely to receive a grant in immigration court as unrepresented asylum seekers. Previous studies have confirmed similar gaps. See Andrew I. Schoenholtz & Jonathan Jacobs, *The State of Asylum Representation: Ideas for Change*, 16 GEO. IMMIGR. L.J. 739, 743 (2002).

divided into two categories, inadmissibility and deportability.[14] The grounds of inadmissibility apply to individuals seeking admission to the United States, immigrants in the United States who have never been admitted or who are seeking to adjust their status, and immigrants with lawful status who are returning to the United States after a trip abroad.[15] And grounds of deportability apply to immigrants who have been lawfully admitted to the United States. Both categories include seemingly overlapping grounds, which may be misleading.

For example, while both deportability and inadmissibility are triggered by certain criminal offenses, the types of criminal offenses, the existence of exceptions, the nature of the adjudication – for example, whether a conviction is required – vary between grounds of inadmissibility and deportability.[16] An admission of, or conviction for, one "crime involving moral turpitude" (a term defined by case law, not the statute) will make a noncitizen inadmissible unless it falls into the "petty offense" exception: where the term of imprisonment was no more than six months and the maximum penalty for the offense did not exceed one year.[17] By contrast, only one conviction will suffice for most grounds of deportability, but a conviction for one "crime involving moral turpitude" alone will not make a person deportable, unless it was committed within five years of admission to the United States and punishable by at least a year in jail – with no "petty offense" exception available.[18] The Immigration and Nationality Act (INA) is filled with terms that are repeated with important differences in application or meaning within different parts of the immigration statute.

Removal proceedings themselves are a multi-stage process, adjudicated within a division of the U.S. Department of Justice (DOJ) Executive Office for Immigration Review.[19] An Immigration Judge, an employee of the DOJ, presides over an adversarial hearing, with the government represented by a trial attorney from Immigration and Customs Enforcement (ICE).[20] If the Immigration Judge finds the respondent removable as charged, then the Immigration Judge must decide whether the respondent is eligible for any forms of relief from removal. Each of these forms of relief has its own set of eligibility requirements, which may including criminal-offense bars – which may or may not match the ground of removal that triggered the hearing in the first place – as well as other requirements relating to hardship to one's

[14] See 8 U.S.C. § 1229a (describing removal proceedings for deciding the inadmissibility or deportability of noncitizens).

[15] See *id.* § 1182 (specifying grounds of inadmissibility).

[16] *Compare id.* § 1182 (generally applying to a person "convicted of, or who admits having committed, or who admits committing acts" specified in the statute) *with* id. § 1227 (generally applies to a person "convicted of" an offense specified in the statute).

[17] *Id.* § 1182(a)(2)(A).

[18] *Id.* § 1227(a)(2)(A)(i).

[19] U.S. Dep't of Justice, Exec. Office for Immigration Review, Factsheet: Immigration Court Process in the United States (May 2005), available at www.justice.gov/eoir/press/05/ImmigrationCourtProcess2005.pdf.

[20] See 8 U.S.C. § 1101(b)(4) (defining "immigration judge" to mean "an attorney whom the Attorney General appoints as an administrative judge within the Executive Office for Immigration Review").

relatives, the status of those relatives, the timing of one's application, and other factors that differ based on the type of relief sought.

Once an Immigration Judge determines that the respondent is eligible for relief, the judge will hold a hearing to consider evidence, including testimony, relevant to whether the relief should be granted. Throughout the proceedings, both ICE and the noncitizen have the right to submit relevant documents bearing on removability, eligibility for relief, and discretionary factors in support of or adverse to the granting of such relief.

The complexity of the grounds of removability and the bars to relief seem quite formidable for any self-represented individual to master. Even seasoned attorneys have difficulty fully understanding the various bars and triggers for removability.[21] The criminal bars in particular are problematic, as the federal statute often does not define the relevant categories in a clear way. For example, a lawful permanent resident faces deportation and bars to most forms of relief from removal if she is convicted of an "aggravated felony."[22] The immigration statute defines an "aggravated felony" by a list of twenty-one sub-definitions, which may cross-reference other statutes or provide a generic definition of a type of offense.[23] Despite the terminology, aggravated felonies include offenses that are neither aggravated nor felonies. The issue of whether a state or federal offense trigger is an "aggravated felony" has sparked considerable litigation, with the Supreme Court having to weigh in to clarify the scope of the sub-definitions seven times in the last decade.

Given the complexity of the law, a pro se noncitizen's ability to identify and present legal arguments in defense to removal or in support of eligibility for status or relief is limited.

Detention

Each year, over 400,000 noncitizens are detained in immigration detention facilities pending their removal or removal proceedings.[24] Under federal law, ICE has broad discretion to detain individuals with pending removal charges or a final removal order, and in many cases must detain those individuals under "mandatory detention" laws. Some noncitizens are held under laws that do not permit a bond hearing;

21 Careen Shannon, *To License or Not to License? A Look at Differing Approaches to Policing the Activities of Nonlawyer Immigration Service Providers*, 33 CARDOZO L. REV. 437, 446 (2011) (noting that the complexity of immigration law "discourages many lawyers from specializing in this area"); Jill Family, *Beyond Decisional Independence: Uncovering Contributors to the Immigration Adjudication Crisis*, 59 U. KAN. L. REV. 541, 551 (2011) (describing the "harshness, complexity, and opacity of substantive immigration law" as a reason for the lack of legal representation).

22 See 8 U.S.C. § 1101(a)(43)(A)-(U) (defining the term "aggravated felony" by list of subcategories of offenses).

23 See *id.*

24 U.S. Dep't of Justice, Office of Immigration Statistics, Annual Report, Immigration Enforcement Actions 2012 (Dec. 2012), at 5, available at www.dhs.gov/sites/default/files/publications/ois_enforcement_ar_2012_1.pdf (stating that ICE detained 477,523 people in 2012).

while others who are entitled to a bond hearing and receive bond determinations remain detained because they cannot afford to pay for their release.[25] The combined effects of mandatory detention laws and high bond rates have resulted in a large detained population in the immigration system.

Several aspects of the immigration detention system hamper effective self-representation. The federal government relies heavily on county jails and private prisons to hold immigrant detainees.[26] These facilities, scattered across the country, each have their own rules regarding visitation, telephone access, law libraries, and other services that may facilitate or hinder self-representation. While the federal government has issued Performance-Based National Detention Standards (PBNDS) in an attempt to provide minimum standards for acceptable detention conditions in these facilities, the PBNDS are unenforceable.[27] Over the years, a number of studies and reports have decried the conditions in these facilities.[28] While the PBNDS require facilities to maintain electronic and hard-copy legal resources, many facilities do not comply with these standards.[29] Moreover, legal resources are available in English, and county jails and private prisons are not unequipped to provide necessary language assistance to detainees.

Another factor is the role of geography and detainee transfers. Under federal law, ICE may detain a noncitizen in any facility in the country. Many of the detention facilities that ICE uses are in Southern United States, including remote rural areas with no local counsel or nonprofit organizations.[30] For example, 64% of New York City detainees are transferred to far-away detention facilities, mostly in Pennsylvania, Louisiana, and Texas.[31]

[25] See 8 U.S.C. § 1226(a) (authorizing the Attorney General to detain and release noncitizens pending removal proceedings); see also New York Immigrant Representation Study, supra note 8, at 376 (indicating prohibitively high bond amounts may result in high detention rates for individuals who are not subject to mandatory detention).

[26] Detention Watch Network, About The U.S. Deportation and Detention System, available at www.detentionwatchnetwork.org/resources (last visited Sept. 23, 2014).

[27] Dora Schriro, *Improving Conditions of Confinement for Criminal Inmates and Immigrant Detainees*, 47 Am. Crim. L. Rev. 1441, 1451 (2010).

[28] See, e.g., Amnesty International, Jailed without Justice: Immigration Detention in the U.S.A. (2009), available at www.amnestyusa.org/pdfs/JailedWithoutJustice.pdf (hereinafter Jailed Without Justice) (documenting human rights violations in ICE detention facilities); National Immigrant Justice Center, Isolated in Detention: Limited Access to Legal Counsel in Immigration Detention Facilities Jeopardizes a Fair Day in Court 7–8 (2010), available at www.immigrantjustice.org/isolatedindetention (hereinafter Isolated in Detention) (emphasizing the lack of access to legal counsel in detention facilities).

[29] See Noferi, supra note 7, at 78–79; Jailed Without Justice, supra note 28, at 32; Broken System, supra note 28, at 33.

[30] See, e.g., Human Rights Watch, A Costly Move: Far and Frequent Transfers Impede Hearings for Immigrant Detainees in the United States (2011), available at www.hrw.org/node/99660 (hereinafter A Costly Move); Office of Inspector General, Dep't of Homeland Security, OIG 10–13, Immigration and Customs Enforcement Policies and Procedures Related to Detainee Transfers, (2009), available at www.dhs.gov/xoig/assets/mgmtrpts/OIG_10–13_Nov09.pdf.

[31] New York Immigrant Representation Study, supra note 8 at 363.

Governmental and nongovernmental groups have collaborated to attempt to address these issues through the "Legal Orientation Program" (LOP) with some success. LOPs, which aim to provide noncitizens with advice about the removal system and available forms of relief so that they may better represent themselves and make decisions about their cases, exist in 25 facilities.[32] Studies demonstrate that LOPs improve case processing times and case outcomes for participants.[33] In some cases, outcomes may even approximate those for represented immigrants.[34] Nonetheless, the same studies also conclude that representation is more effective at producing higher grant rates among detainees overall.[35] LOP is also available only in a small percentage of the approximately 250 facilities that hold immigrant detainees nationwide.[36]

Traditional pro se assistance models, emphasizing written materials and presentations and the simplification of court processes, are difficult to implement successfully in the removal context. Given the complexity of immigration law and the prevalence of language, mental health, and educational limitations among immigrant respondents, the development of effective pro se written materials is particularly challenging. In addition, traditional pro se assistance programs are generally unable to provide the type of fact-specific analysis of the law or the ongoing support that a pro se litigant would need throughout the stages of a removal case.[37] A significant commitment of financial resources would also be required to bring such programs to every detention facility and immigration court in the country.

Access to Evidence

The rules of evidence are lax in the immigration context and do little to help pro se immigrants access the necessary evidence to litigate their cases. The Federal Rules of Evidence are not binding in immigration court. For example, immigration courts typically permit hearsay evidence and apply lower standards for the authentication of documents.[38] Federal courts have repeatedly held that the "sole test for admission of evidence is whether the evidence is probative and its

32 See Vera Inst. for Justice, Legal Orientation Program, available at www.vera.org/project/legal-orientation-program (describing the Legal Orientation Program).

33 See Vera Inst. for Justice, Legal Orientation Program: Evaluation and Performance and Outcome Measurement Report, Phase II 65–66 (May 2008), available at www.vera.org/sites/default/files/resources/downloads/LOP_evalution_updated_5-20-08.pdf.

34 *Id.* at 65.

35 *Id.*

36 Detention Watch Network, supra note 26.

37 *Id.*; see also Richard Zorza, The Self-Help Friendly Court: Designed from the Ground up to Work for People without Lawyers 17 (2002), available at www.zorza.net/Res_ProSe_SelfHelpCtPub.pdf.

38 See, e.g., *Solis v. Mukasey*, 515 F.3d 832, 835–36 (8th Cir. 2008); *Vatyan v. Mukasey*, 508 F.3d 1179, 1185 (9th Cir. 2007); *Yongo v. INS*, 355 F.3d 27, 30–31 (1st Cir. 2004).

admission is fundamentally fair."[39] While respondents have the right to a "reasonable opportunity" to cross-examine witnesses, immigration courts recognize "practical limitations on this right."[40] Immigration Judges do not generally allow discovery, remitting the noncitizens to seek out their own evidence.[41] Immigrants may move to suppress evidence against them, but the standard for suppression is significantly higher in immigration court than in criminal court proceedings.[42]

Government attorneys have access to both immigration and criminal records, and may choose which documents to disclose to the immigration court in support of its case. Pro se immigrants routinely see these documents for the first time in immigration court when they are presented to the judge, and immigration courts generally do not require the government to supply the immigrant with the full record or other potentially exculpatory information. Instead, pro se immigrants must go through onerous, and at times, costly channels to obtain these records.

The most troubling example is access to one's own "Alien File" or "A-File." The A-File is a compilation of all records held by federal agencies related to an individual's immigration case, including evidence of prior applications filed along with attachments and outcomes, entry and exit records, and references to criminal records identified as part of the immigration process.[43] The government may access the A-File and supply documents from the file as it processes application forms or prosecutes a removal case. A noncitizen's ability to access his or her own A-File is limited, however. While some individual ICE offices will share portions of an A-File with a noncitizen in removal proceedings at his or her request, the vast majority of offices require the noncitizen to file a Freedom of Information Act (FOIA) request. Such requests typically take months to process, and immigrants must therefore come to their removal hearings unprepared with the evidence necessary to support their claims. One federal court has recognized that noncitizens have a statutory right to their A-File during their removal proceedings,[44] but the government has not meaningfully altered its practice of requiring noncitizens to file an FOIA request outside that jurisdiction to access their full file.[45]

39 *Nyana v. Ashcroft*, 357 F.3d 812, 816 (8th Cir. 2004) (quoting *Espinoza v. INS*, 45 F.3d 308, 310 (9th Cir. 1995).
40 *Matter of Devera*, 16 I. & N. Dec. at 269; see also Garry Malphrus, *Expert Witness in Immigration Proceedings*, 4 Immigr. L. Advisor 2 (2010) (collecting cases that limited the scope of inadmissible hearsay evidence).
41 See C. Gordon et al., *Immigration Law & Procedure* § 3.07 (2008).
42 See *INS v. Lopez-Mendoza*, 468 U.S. 1032, 1050–51 (1984) (exclusionary rule not applicable unless egregious or widespread violations).
43 See Special FOIA Processing Track for Individuals Appearing before an Immigration Judge, 72 Fed. Reg. 9017, 9018 (February 28, 2007) (describing the components of an A-File).
44 See *Dent v. Holder*, 627 F.3d 365, 374 (9th Cir. 2010).
45 Attorneys continue to push the issue in jurisdictions beyond the Ninth Circuit. See Legal Action Center, Practice Advisory: Dent v. Holder and Strategies for Obtaining Documents from the Government during Removal Proceedings (June 12, 2012), available at www.legalactioncenter.org/sites/default/files/dent_practice_advisory_6-8-12.pdf.

As a result of the lax evidentiary rules, pro se immigrants have few tools at their disposal to access the documents or subpoena the witnesses necessary to present their cases.

Administrative Resources and the Role of the Immigration Judge

The current self-representation system relies heavily on the role of the Immigration Judge to help individuals who are pro se. Under federal regulations, Immigration Judges are required to advise noncitizens of the availability of free legal services in their district.[46] When noncitizens are unable to find counsel, Immigration Judges are also required to inform noncitizens about the availability of various applications for relief.[47]

Immigration Judges are, of course, limited in their role and cannot substitute for adversarial representation. Before a noncitizen may proceed to relief, he or she must first raise any challenges to the grounds of removal and establish relief eligibility. Immigration Judges are not required to identify or preserve arguments on behalf of a noncitizen with respect to grounds of removal. Even with respect to eligibility for relief, judges generally rely only on the record before them in identifying the relief for which a noncitizen might be eligible.[48] Thus unrepresented immigrants begin at a disadvantage, as they may not be able to develop a record that establishes their eligibility for relief. Nor may Immigration Judges help noncitizens prepare their cases, other than agreeing to provide noncitizens with additional time to gather evidence or contact potential witnesses.

Even within the limited role they do play, however, there are constraints. Immigration Judges have massive caseloads and few resources. For example, in fiscal year 2010, approximately 268 immigration judges received 325,326 proceedings – which averages to 1,214 proceedings per judge.[49] Immigration judges experience pressure to complete cases and clear backlogs, at the price of giving each case the attention it may deserve. Without sufficient law clerks and trainings to help Immigration Judges identify potential legal issues in their cases, they must rely on the arguments and briefing supplied by the parties. In pro se cases, this may mean that the only legal arguments being considered are those supplied by the government attorney.

46 See 8 C.F.R. § 1240.10(a)(2) ("[T]the Immigration Judge shall ... [a]dvise the respondent of the availability of free legal services").

47 See *id.* § 1240.11(a)(2) ("The Immigration Judge shall inform the alien of his or her apparent eligibility to apply for any of the benefits enumerated in this chapter and shall afford the alien an opportunity to make application during the hearing").

48 See *Moran-Enriquez v. INS*, 884 F.2d 420, 422 (9th Cir. 1989) ("IJs are not expected to be clairvoyant; the record before them must fairly raise the issue")

49 Juan Osuna, Acting Director, Executive Office for Immigration Review, Statement before the Committee of the Judiciary, United States Senate Hearings on Improving Efficiency and Ensuring Justice in the Immigration Court System 1 (May 18, 2011), available at www.judiciary.senate.gov/pdf/5–18–11%20Osuna%20Testimony.pdf.

The immigration system is filled with institutional barriers to fair adjudication of pro se cases. Reform of any one of these aspects of the immigration system – simplifying the eligibility process for relief hearings, reducing reliance on detention, strengthening evidentiary rules, or providing administrative resources and support to Immigration Judges – would enhance the role of self-representation.

BRIDGING THE GAP IN REPRESENTATION

Pro Bono Representation

Scholars and commentators have identified several groups in the legal community that can play a more significant role in representing immigrants. As described in detail in the previous chapter, Judge Katzmann of the U.S. Court of Appeals for the Second Circuit has helped organize legal service providers, law firms, and nonprofit groups to address this issue in New York, and has identified several ways in which legal professionals may fill current gaps in representation.[50]

Federal law already takes a relatively expansive view on representation in immigration cases. Attorneys may represent noncitizens in immigration cases, whether or not the immigration court or administrative body is in the state in which the lawyer is admitted to practice.[51] Law students and law graduates not yet admitted to the bar may represent noncitizens in immigration cases if supervised and permitted by the court or administrative body.[52] Non-lawyers can also represent immigrants facing removal proceedings. For example, "reputable individuals" related personally or professionally to a noncitizen in removal proceedings can serve as his or her representative if they have "good moral character" and the permission of the immigration court or administrative body.[53] It is unclear how often "reputable individuals" appear in immigration cases. A far more common category of representatives are "accredited representatives."[54] These representatives are non-attorneys from organizations that agree to undergo an accreditation process with the U.S. Department of Justice in order to represent noncitizens in immigration cases. "Accredited representatives" are often affiliated with organizations that also employ immigration lawyers, although this is not always the case.

Given the expansive class of individuals and organizations who may represent noncitizens in removal proceedings, why are the rates of representation so low? The answers are similar to the institutional factors that hinder effective self-representation. The complexity of the law, particularly in removal proceedings, often discourages legal representatives who may otherwise be familiar with aspects

50 See Katzmann, Chapter 7 in this volume.
51 8 C.F.R. § 1292.1(a)(1).
52 Id. § 1292.1(a)(2).
53 Id. § 1292.1(a)(3).
54 Id. § 1292.1(a)(4).

of immigration law. In cases involving detained clients, there may be few free legal services available near their detention center.

Greater outreach among bar groups has achieved some success in encouraging lawyers to take on more cases, particularly involving detained clients.[55] In New York, immigrants whose cases remain in one of the two New York City immigration courts have much higher rates of representation than those who are transferred to courts in other areas.[56] This is due in part to nonprofit organizations that play a key role in facilitating representation recruiting lawyers and law school clinics, as well as universal representation efforts in the detained court, described in further detail later.

Unbundled legal services or limited representation could permit attorneys to represent immigrants for discrete parts of their case. For example, lawyers could represent mandatorily detained immigrants for the limited purpose of challenging the legality of their detention without bond.[57]

Non-lawyers could also play a key role in representation in removal proceeding as they do in other types of administrative hearings.[58] Some have argued that accredited representatives and other non-lawyers may do more harm than good because of the inability of the immigration agency to monitor and sanction ineffective representation.[59] Others contend that accredited representatives are able to fill important needs and that, with some tailored reforms, the accredited representative program could play a critical role in providing quality representation while reducing litigants' vulnerability to notario fraud.

In the context of both lawyers and non-lawyers, greater attention is being paid to the issue of *quality* representation. Courts and advocacy organizations alike have bemoaned the poor quality of legal representation in many cases, noting that in

55 Adams & Lasker, Lori Adams & Alida Y. Lasker, *The Asylum Representation Project and the Leon Levy Fellowship at Human Rights First: An Innovative Partnership to Increase Pro Bono Representation for Indigent Asylum-Seekers*, 33 CARDOZO L. REV. 417 (2011) (discussing ways the success of a pilot Asylum Representation Project and how it can be expanded to other nonprofit providers offering representation for relief other than asylum); Jojo Annobil, *The Immigration Representation Project: Meeting the Critical Needs of Low-Wage and Indigent New Yorkers Facing Removal*, 78 FORDHAM L. REV. 517, 521 (2009) (describing New York City-based programs offering representation and providing suggestions for expansion).

56 New York Immigrant Representation Study, supra note 8, at 367–70.

57 See Noferi, supra note 7, at 122–24 (arguing that, if full representation is not possible, attorneys could provide representation at "*Joseph* hearings," which provide immigrants the opportunity to challenge whether they are properly included in the mandatory detention statute); Matter of Joseph, 22 I&N Dec. 799 (BIA 1999).

58 Benjamin H. Barton & Stephanos Bibas, *Triaging Appointed-Counsel Funding and Pro Se Access to Justice*, 160 U. PA. L. REV. 967, 972 (2012); Barbara Allison Clayton, Comment, *Are We Our Brother's Keeper's?: A Discussion of Nonlawyer Representation before Texas Administrative Agencies and Recommendations for the Future*, 8 TEX. TECH. ADMIN. L.J. 115, 130 (2007).

59 M. Isabel Medina, *The Challenges of Facilitating Effective Legal Defense in Deportation Proceedings: Allowing Nonlawyer Practice of Law Through Accredited Representatives in Removals*, 53 S. TEX. L. REV. 459 (2012) (arguing that the representation crisis in immigration law should not be solved through accredited, non-lawyer representation).

some cases immigrants would have been better off pro se.[60] Lawyers and accredited organizations serving immigrants, like Immigration Judges, are overburdened by massive caseloads. Even where legal representatives are able to identify potential arguments against removal, "[c]arrying too many cases results in filing barely competent, boilerplate submissions that omit the detailed facts vital to distinguishing meritorious cases from non-meritorious challenges to removal."[61]

Some advocacy groups have responded by promulgating minimum standards to help guide legal representatives on the best practices for effective representation in immigration cases.[62] Government and nongovernment agencies have also sought greater enforcement, to weed out incompetent counsel and to prevent the unauthorized practice of law.[63] In addition, an effort is underway to reform the accredited representative system, both to increase the quality of those organizations authorized to represent noncitizens, and to reduce barriers to entry among well-meaning organizations who have found it too difficult to provide quality representation to seek such authorization.[64]

Despite these efforts, low rates of quality representation still remain.

Civil *Gideon*

Litigating Civil Gideon

Scholars have been arguing that due process requires the right to counsel in immigration cases for decades.[65] In *Gideon v. Wainwright*,[66] the Supreme Court held that the Sixth Amendment requires states to provide counsel for indigent

60 LaJuana Davis, *Reconsidering Remedies for Ensuring Competent Representation in Removal Proceedings*, 58 Drake L. Rev. 123, 141–42 (2009) (noting remarks by courts and government officials bemoaning the poor quality of immigration representation); Felinda Mottino, Vera Inst. of Justice, Moving Forward: The Role of Legal Counsel in Immigration Court 39 (2000), available at www.vera.org/sites/default/files/resources/downloads/353.409747_MF.pdf.

61 *Id.* at 143.

62 New York State Bar Ass'n, Report of the Special Committee on Immigration Representation, available at: www.nysba.org/Content/NavigationMenu90/SpecialCommitteeonImmigrationRepresentationHome/SCIRFinalReportApproved.pdf (approving standards to guide the effective practice of immigration law).

63 See Emily A. Unger, *Solving Immigration Consultant Fraud Through Expanded Federal Accreditation*, 29 Law & Ineq. 425, 429 (2011) (examining the problem of fraud by immigration consultants); Andrew F. Moore, *Fraud, the Unauthorized Practice of Law and Unmet Needs: A Look at State Laws Regulating Immigration Assistants*, 19 Geo. Immigr. L.J. 1, 3 (2004) (analyzing state laws attempting to regulate the provision of immigration services by non-attorneys).

64 Shannon, supra note 21, at 454–56 (2011) (discussing the need for reforming the accredited representative program).

65 See, e.g. Beth J. Werlin, *Renewing the Call: Immigrants' Right to Appointed Counsel in Deportation Proceedings*, 20 B.C. Third World L.J. 393, 423 (2000); David A. Robertson, *An Opportunity to Be Heard: The Right to Counsel in a Deportation Hearing*, 63 Wash. L. Rev. 1019, 1040 (1988).

66 Courts have uniformly rejected a Sixth Amendment right to counsel in removal cases. See *Michelson* v. INS, 897 F. 2d 465, 467–68 (10th Cir. 1990); *United States v. Campos-Ascencio*, 822 F. 2d 506, 509 (5th Cir. 1987); *Lozada v. INS*, 857 F.2d 10, 13 (1st Cir. 1988); *Rios-Berrios v. INS*, 776 F. 2d 859, 862 (9th Cir. 1985).

defendants in felony cases.[67] While the Sixth Amendment does not apply in civil cases, the Fourteenth Amendment provides all persons with the right to due process of law, including notice and an opportunity to be heard.[68] Due process requires an opportunity to be heard in removal proceedings, in part due to the serious consequences at stake.[69]

The Supreme Court has not, however, recognized a per se constitutional right to counsel in every case that may involve impingement of a liberty interest. Rather, it has applied a balancing test,[70] identifying three factors that should guide courts in determining what due process requires: (1) the private interest at stake; (2) the "risk of an erroneous deprivation of such interest through the procedures used, and the probative value, if any of additional or substitute procedural safeguards"; and (3) the government's interest, including "the fiscal and administrative burdens that the additional or substitute procedural requirement would entail."[71] If the factors weigh in favor of the right to counsel, either as a per se right or on a case-to-case basis, then the government must provide counsel.

The Supreme Court has already recognized that the private interest at stake in removal proceedings is significant, making it possible to meet the first prong of the test. The Court has long described deportation as "the equivalent of banishment or exile"[72] and the "loss . . . of all that makes life worth living."[73] More recently, the Court has described deportation as a "penalty" more severe in some cases than criminal punishment.[74]

The second *Matthews* factor test similarly leans in favor of the right to counsel because the consequences of an erroneous deprivation are severe: separation from one's family and community; economic loss; harm to one's family, particularly to children who may have to rely on foster care; and the possibility of persecution and

[67] 372 U.S. 335, 344 (1963).

[68] *Yamataya v. Fisher*, 189 U.S. 86, 100–101 (1903) (stating that due process of law generally implies an "opportunity to answer").

[69] *Id.* (recognizing that due process requires that noncitizens be given notice and an opportunity to be heard regarding their right to remain in the United States).

[70] See *Matthews v. Eldridge* 424 U.S.319 (1976) (determining the constitutionality of an impingement of liberty by weighing the private interest affected and the government interest served); see also *Turner v. Rogers*, 564 U.S. 431 (2011) (applying the *Matthews* framework to the question of whether the right to counsel is required in civil contempt proceedings); *Lassiter v. Dep't of Social Services*, 452 U.S. 18, 27–31 (1981) (applying the *Mathews* framework to the question of whether the right to counsel is required in parental rights termination proceedings). Notably, some have argued that a stricter test should apply in the context of removal proceedings in light of the Supreme Court's decision in *Padilla v. Kentucky*, 130 S. Ct. 1473 (2010), recognizing a Sixth Amendment duty for defense counsel to advise noncitizens of the immigration consequences of their pleas. See Noferi, supra note 7, at 70 n. 24 (citing Daniel Kanstroom, *The Right to Deportation Counsel in Padilla v. Kentucky: The Challenging Construction of the Fifth-and-a-Half Amendment*, 58 UCLA L. Rev. 1461 (2011) and Peter L. Markowitz, *Deportation is Different*, 13 U. Pa. J. Const. L. 1299 (2011)).

[71] *Matthews*, 424 U.S. at 335.

[72] *Delgadillo* v. *Carmichael*, 332 U.S. 388, 391 (1947).

[73] *Ng Fung Ho v. White*, 259 U.S. 276, 284 (1922).

[74] *Padilla*, 130 S. Ct. at 1481.

even death.[75] Plus the issues that must be resolved are quite complex, Immigration Judges are not sufficiently trained, and the opposing counsel – the U.S. Department of Homeland Security – specialize in removal proceedings.

The third factor involves an assessment of the government's interest, including fiscal and administrative burdens. The provision of counsel to every noncitizen placed in removal proceedings is no doubt expensive in the aggregate.[76] However, unlike contexts where the appointment process itself may cause delay in an otherwise quick administrative process, the average case processing time for a removal proceeding is 553 days.[77] The provision of counsel would presumably result in some cost savings in terms of increased efficiency in court processing.[78] In addition, counsel would help root out unnecessary detention and cases that may merit termination or administrative closure early in the process.[79] On the whole, as many commentators have argued, the balance leans in favor of the appointment of counsel.

The federal courts of appeals, however, have rejected these arguments and no court has recognized a per se right to counsel in removal proceedings.

Because of this failure, arguments have turned to applying the right to counsel only to certain classes of immigrants facing removal – children, including unaccompanied minors; asylum seekers; detainees; the mentally ill; lawful permanent residents; and noncitizens facing removal for criminal convictions.[80] This piecemeal approach may prove more successful in litigation. In *Franco-Gonzales v. Holder*, a federal district court held that mentally ill noncitizens could proceed in their class action litigation for the appointment of counsel in their cases.[81] A similar

[75] Werlin, supra note 65, at 405–408.

[76] Noferi, supra note 7, at 118 (estimating that it would cost $40 million to provide counsel to indigent immigrant detainees nationwide, although this represents only a small fraction of overall costs in the system); The New York Immigrant Family Unity Project: Good for Families, Good for Employers, Good for All new Yorkers (2013), available at http://populardemocracy.org/sites/default/files/immgrant_family_unity_project_print_layout.pdf (hereinafter Family Unity Report) (estimating an annual cost of $7.4 million to provide universal representation for detained immigrant New Yorkers).

[77] Transactional Records Access Clearinghouse, Immigration Court Backlog Reaches an All Time High (Mar. 13, 2013), available at http://trac.syr.edu/whatsnew/email.130313.html.

[78] Noferi, supra note 7, at 118–19 (arguing that case processing efficiencies and other cost savings would outweigh the cost of providing the right to counsel); Davis, supra note 60, at 162; see also Family Unity Report, supra note 76, at 10–15 (estimating cost savings for government and private entities if universal representation is provided to detained immigrant New Yorkers).

[79] Davis, supra note 60, at 161 ("The early appointment of counsel would also help immediately identify and resolve erroneous charges and detentions in days – rather than in weeks, months, or even years").

[80] Anne R. Traum, *Constitutionalizing Immigration Law on Its Own Path*, 33 Cardozo L. Rev. 491, 543 (2011).

[81] *Franco v. Holder*, 767 F. Supp. 2d 1034, 1061 (C.D. Cal. 2010); see also Amelia Wilson & Natalie H. Prokop, *Applying Method to the Madness: The Right to Court Appointed Guardians Ad Litem and Counsel for the Mentally Ill in Immigration Proceedings*, 16 U. Pa. J. L. & Soc. Change 1, 26–28 (2013).

class action lawsuit seeking the appointment of counsel for unaccompanied minors in removal proceedings is pending.[82]

Policy Efforts to Achieve Civil Gideon

Given the piecemeal nature of this approach and the limited success that litigation has had so far, civil *Gideon* efforts have also focused on legislative approaches. In New York, a group of judges, lawyers, and professors have proposed a state-funded program to meet the needs of detained noncitizens facing removal in New York immigration court.[83] Estimating the yearly cost at $7.4 million, the proposal would provide every indigent detained immigrant facing removal proceedings within New York State with a lawyer.[84] The model contemplates contracts for representation within a small group of institutional providers, overseen by one centralized coordinating agency.[85] The institutional providers would also be funded to provide the necessary language services, social work and mental health services, expert services, and investigative services.

These efforts have already resulted in local funding for a universal representation program for detained individuals in the New York City area. In 2013, the New York City Council allocated $500,000 in funding for the representation of detained, indigent New Yorkers whose cases are heard in the Varick Immigration Court.[86] The pilot project was the first in the country to provide public funding for an indigent defender system in immigration court. In 2014, the New York City Council extended the funding to create a full representation program, allocating $4.9 million for all detained, indigent New Yorkers in removal proceedings in New York City and nearby courts in New Jersey.[87] This may spark other states or localities to adopt similar mechanisms.[88]

[82] *J.E.F.M. v. Holder*, No. 2:14-cv-01026 (W.D.Wa., filed Jul. 9, 2014), available at http://legalactioncenter.org/sites/default/files/Counsel%20Complaint.pdf.

[83] Accessing Justice II: A Model for Providing Counsel to New York Immigrants in Removal Proceedings (2012), available at www.cardozolawreview.com/content/denovo/NYIRS_ReportII.pdf (hereinafter Accessing Justice II).

[84] Family Unity Report, supra note 76, at 5 (estimating an annual cost of $7.4 million to provide universal representation for detained immigrant New Yorkers).

[85] Accessing Justice II, supra note 83.

[86] See New York City Council Press Release, *Speaker Quinn, Council Members & Immigrant Rights Groups Announce Pilot Program Providing Legal Counsel For Immigrants Facing Deportation*, available at http://council.nyc.gov/html/pr/071913nyifup.shtml; Kirk Semple, *New Help for Poor Immigrants Who Are in Custody and Facing Deportation*, N.Y. Times (Nov. 6, 2013), available at www.nytimes.com/2013/11/07/nyregion/new-help-for-poor-immigrants-who-are-in-custody-and-facing-deportation.html?ref=nyregion&_r=1& (describing new pilot program).

[87] See Vera Institute, New York Family Unity Project, available at www.vera.org/project/new-york-immigrant-family-unity-project.

[88] Similar efforts have led to the allocation of funding for representation for unaccompanied minors and families in San Francisco. See CBS-San Francisco, *San Francisco Allocates $2.1M to Legal Aid for Unaccompanied Minors, Families Facing Deportation* (Sept. 16, 2014), available at http://sanfrancisco.cbslocal.com/2014/09/16/san-francisco-allocates-2–1m-to-legal-aid-for-unaccompanied-minors-

Unfortunately, the full expense of a universal representation program – even accounting for potential savings to taxpayers – may be a difficult commitment for some states or localities to make.[89] There is some precedent for the expansion of mandated representation in other civil contexts. For example, in the family court context, states have created mechanism to provide parents with the right to counsel in certain proceedings. However, these efforts are often in response to state court decisions recognizing a due process concern. It is unclear whether states or localities would have the political will to fund universal representation in the absence of a mandate.

FROM SELF-REPRESENTATION TO COMMUNITY MOBILIZATION

What other options may pro se litigants seek to access justice in immigration proceedings? One possibility is the role of community education before the removal process begins – programs aimed at educating immigrants about the triggers that lead to deportation; the eligibility requirements and proper avenues for seeking asylum, adjustment of status, and citizenship; and the problems that arise from hiring notaries or unscrupulous lawyers to complete immigration paperwork and applications.[90]

A second possibility is the role of community mobilization in immigration cases. There is a growing movement to bring community members into the courtroom, to observe the proceedings, speak out for the pro se litigant, marshal community resources to meet the individual's specific needs, and serve as a check on injustice from the judge and opposing counsel. In the immigration context, two New York City-based organizations, Families for Freedom and the New Sanctuary Coalition, have developed models for community-involved defense committees and accompaniment programs for immigrants facing removal.[91] Defense committees, composed of family members, church leaders, and even lawyers, help the immigrant facing removal to consider his or her strategic choices in immigration court, gather information and evidence in support of the case, marshal legal resources, and attend hearings.

Similar models exist in other legal services contexts. Another New York City-based organization, Common Law, brings community members into foreclosure auctions and creates "court support" teams to accompany pro se homeowners in

families-facing-deportation-david-campos-central-america-el-salvador-guatemala-honduras-mexico-undocumented/.

89 See Family Unity Report, supra note 76, at 10–15 (estimating $1.9 million in health insurance and foster care savings to New York State, with an additional $4 million in savings to New York employers).

90 See Unger, supra note 63, at 440 (noting the role that community organizations play in combating notario fraud through information about reporting fraud, hotlines, clinics, and other forms of direct assistance).

91 See Families for Freedom website, available at www.familiesforfreedom.org; New Sanctuary Coalition of New York website, available at www.newsanctuarynyc.org/.

foreclosure proceedings for individuals facing eviction.[92] While attorneys with the organization prepare clinics to orient homeowners to the legal process, participating homeowners appear pro se in court along with other community members. The San Jose, California-based Albert Cobarrubias Justice Project encourages "the active engagement of families and communities" to help defendants in criminal court feel supported.[93]

These types of projects go one step beyond the traditional community education programs by incorporating a community organizing model and bringing community support into the courtroom. There are no studies that have examined whether such programs are effective in closing the gap in outcomes between pro se and represented litigants, or what other effects they may have on the behavior of the judge or counsel in the courtroom. However, anecdotal evidence indicates that people who participate in the programs feel more satisfaction with the justice system. Moreover, in the immigration context, such programs may improve the likelihood that an individual may receive some form of prosecutorial discretion.[94]

On a larger scale, undocumented youth organizing and activism led directly to the Obama Administration's creation of the "deferred action for childhood arrivals" program, which grants two-year renewable reprieves to qualifying immigrants.[95] The role of community mobilization in immigration cases warrants more attention given the crisis in representation.

CONCLUSION

Evidence has repeatedly shown that the lack of legal representation increases an immigrant's chance of deportation. The best possible long-term solution may be a combination of government-funded counsel for indigent immigrants in removal proceedings, with greater transparency and community involvement in the court process. In the meantime, efforts to close the gap through increased pro bono attorney representation, the exploration of carefully regulated non-lawyer representation, the expansion of assisted self-representation programs and community education and mobilization are critical to helping immigrants defend themselves in removal proceedings.

92 Jay Kim & Karen Gargamelli, *Courtrooms as Spaces for Activism*, MOBILIZING IDEAS (Feb. 24, 2013, at 7:01 AM), available at http://mobilizingideas.wordpress.com/2013/02/04/courtrooms-as-spaces-for-activism/.

93 *Id.*

94 See AMERICAN IMMIGRATION COUNCIL, UNDERSTANDING PROSECUTORIAL DISCRETION IN IMMIGRATION LAW (Sept. 9, 2011), available at www.immigrationpolicy.org/just-facts/understanding-prosecutorial-discretion-immigration-law.

95 Miriam Jordan, *Anatomy of a Deferred-Act Dream*, WALL STREET JOURNAL (Oct. 14, 2012), available at http://online.wsj.com/news/articles/SB10000872396390443982904578046951916986168 (describing the process by which undocumented youth moved the Obama Administration to create a deferred action program).

PART II

Sources of Legal Services Assistance for Working Americans

10

Evolution of Legal Services in the United States:

From the War on Poverty to Civil *Gideon* and Beyond

Jeanne Charn

Jeanne Charn, a pioneer in the field of clinical legal services for poor people, describes how the U.S. anti-poverty-thrust of the legal services movement in the 1960s led to a divergence of U.S. policy from government policy in England and other countries where the goal was to assure legal assistance for all. Charn calls for a broader definition of legal assistance that offers meaningful legal assistance without necessarily guaranteeing an attorney.

Since the 1990s the main policy agenda of access to justice activists in the United States has been an effort to obtain a civil *Gideon* – a guarantee of attorneys for everyone the market cannot serve.[1] The civil *Gideon* movement rests on two, lawyer-centric assumptions. The first is that access requires the assistance of an attorney.[2] The second is that, but for cost barriers, people would flood lawyers' offices seeking representation. These assumptions are belied by the experience of government-funded legal services in the United States and peer nations, and by empirical research on the public's responses to law-embedded problems.

While the civil *Gideon* movement has had little success, new ways of providing legal assistance have emerged. Innovation in service delivery is producing a diverse supply side that increasingly incorporates technology, encourages self-help, supports institutional reforms that enable self-help, and is keenly attuned to consumer preferences.[3] In what follows, I argue that a diverse, consumer-centered delivery system with many types of providers is the best policy – better than a Civil *Gideon* – if our goal is to substantially reduce access disparities not just for the poor but for moderate- and middle-income people as well.

1 National Coalition for a Civil Right to Counsel, available at www.civilrighttocounsel.org; National Center for Access to Justice, available at http://ncforaj.org.

2 The American Bar Association (ABA) policy includes a "strong presumption" that an attorney is required to meet the "basic human needs" identified in ABA House of Delegates Resolution 112A (Aug. 7, 2006). Available at www.abanet.org/advocacy/legal_professional_involvement.

3 See Harvard Program on the Legal Profession Conference, *Disruptive Innovations in the Market for Legal Services*, Mar. 6, 2014. Available at www.law.harvard.edu/programs/plp/pages/kenny_event.php.

ANTI-POVERTY WARRIORS IN THE OEO YEARS

In the United States we have never had a right to lawyer assistance in civil matters.[4] Government-funded legal services began in 1965 as a component of the Johnson administration's War on Poverty. The Office of Economic Opportunity (OEO) Legal Services focused exclusively on the very poor and rejected universal access as a goal. OEO leadership prioritized law reform and systemic change over service to individuals and evaluated its grantees accordingly.

Many OEO lawyers embraced legislative and test case reforms[5] and had remarkable success litigating poor people's issues in the Supreme Court.[6] Others pursued systemic change at the local level in alliance with mobilized community groups. Lawyers who took this approach encouraged self-help, employed lay advocates, and preferred a community-led strategy to a lawyer-led strategy.[7]

A COMPARATIVE PERSPECTIVE: THE ENGLISH JUDICARE MODEL

The founders of OEO Legal Services were aware that in 1949 England had adopted a Legal Aid and Advice Act with the quite different goal of guaranteeing legal assistance to all, regardless of means.[8] The English system was built upon the following core principles:

- Assistance should be available not only to the poor but to the middle class as well. At the outset in 1949, approximately 80% of the population was eligible for free or partially subsidized legal assistance.
- Assistance for poor people should be free but those with higher incomes should contribute to costs of service.[9]

4 A right to counsel exists in some states in a narrow range of cases – intervention in the parent–child relationship or appointment of substitute decision-makers for adults lacking competence to manage their own affairs due to mental illness or other serious disabilities. Jeanne Charn, *Foreword*, 7 Harv Law & Policy L. Rev. 1 (2012); Laura K. Abel & Max Rettig, *State Statutes Providing for a Right to Counsel in Civil Cases*, 40 Clearinghouse Rev. 245, 252–70 (2006).

5 Jack Katz, Poor People's Lawyers in Transition (1982)

6 Susan Lawrence, The Poor in Court: The Legal Services Program and Supreme Court Decision Making (1990).

7 See, Stephen Wexler, *Practicing Law for Poor People*, 79 Yale L. J. 1049 (1970). Wexler makes an uncompromising case for prioritizing community mobilization and community-led efforts over lawyer-led approaches. See also Gary Bellow, *Steady Work: A Practitioner's Reflections on Political Lawyering*, 31 Harv. Civ.Rts.-Civ.Libs L. Rev. 298 (1996).

8 The Alliance for Legal Aid, *The History of Legal Aid*, Save Legal Aid, available at www.savelgalaid.co.uk/history.html.

9 The English loser-pays system complicates the contribution and merits reevaluation.

- Requests for assistance should be assessed for merit.
- The government should bear the costs of the program.
- To assure independence of counsel, bar organizations, not the government, should administer the program.
- Services should be provided by the private bar and reimbursed by the government.
- Barristers and solicitors should receive adequate remuneration from the government for their services.
- Eligible consumers should have choice of provider from among members of the bar who participate in the legal aid scheme.

Subsequently, many nations, including Canada, Australia, New Zealand, Belgium, the Netherlands, and the Scandinavian countries, enacted legal aid programs that guarantee attorney assistance at government expense in civil as well as criminal matters.[10] These entitlements reach people of modest means while the English and Dutch guarantee some services to the middle class. Legal aid enjoys broad public support even though the price tag is high. All these countries spend more than the United States – as much as ten times more per capita – on their legal aid programs.[11] Debate has focused on how to control escalating costs but the existence of government-funded legal aid has never been threatened. Cost concerns have led to lowered eligibility and narrowing types of matters covered, but within these constraints everyone who is eligible and seeks service gets it.

The OEO legal aid program not only rested on different principles, it relied on a different mode of service delivery. Most nations follow the English model of private bar pay-per-case that has come to be known as "judicare."[12] In contrast, the OEO program delivered services through not-for-profit offices that hired full-time lawyers.

The law reform/systemic change approach of OEO lawyers generated fierce opposition. Conservatives opposed to the OEO activist agenda were willing to support what they viewed as the apolitical goal of helping people on an individual basis. They advocated a judicare delivery system to rein in the law-reform agenda of the staffed offices. The solo and small-firm private bar, then and now the main source of legal assistance for people of modest means, sided with conservatives. A highly politicized debate ensued that derailed judicare as a service option in the

10 Richard Moorhead & Pascoe Pleasence, *Access to Justice after Universalism*, 30 J. Law Soc. 1 (March 2003).

11 Richard Zorza, *Making an International Case*, LSC Equal Justice Magazine, Summer 2003. In Britain the Cameron government has cut funding for civil legal aid by 30% to about 1.5 billion pounds, the equivalent of over $2.3 billion. U.S. Annual funding for the Legal Services Corp. (LSC) is less than $400 million and funding from all sources in the United States is about $1.2 billion, much less than what the British government provides. Britain has nearly twice the funding for a population of less than 60 million while the United States makes do with half that for a population that exceeds 300 million.

12 See A Reader on Resourcing Civil Justice (Alan A. Paterson & Tamara Goriely eds., 1997).

United States. The staffed model prevailed and the private bar's role was relegated to pro bono service, that is, to charity.[13]

With the election of Richard Nixon to the presidency in 1968, the OEO program faced cutbacks, even termination. Eventually its functions were transferred to the Legal Services Corporation (LSC). This was a compromise that included restrictions on the types of substantive cases that poverty lawyers could undertake and on the remedies they could pursue on behalf of their clients. [14] However, the new structure offered some assurance of independence from outside political interference. Despite these hopes, with the election of Ronald Reagan in 1980 and the "contract with America" coalition that led to Republican majorities in both houses of Congress in 1995, existential threats to the federal legal services program continued.

THE TURN TO "CIVIL GIDEON"

The survival of government-funded legal services required a change in rationale that would, incidentally, align it more closely with the access goals of the English model. LSC's first president, Thomas Ehrlich, stated in congressional testimony in 1976: "Legal assistance is no longer part of a war against poverty. Rather that assistance is established as a basic right of citizenship."[15]

Decades after the birth of OEO legal services, the "civil *Gideon*" movement has emerged as a strategy to increase resources by securing a broad right to counsel in civil matters.[16] In 2006 the ABA voted to place its prestige and resources behind a categorical right to counsel in areas of "basic human need" defined as shelter, sustenance, safety, health, and child custody. The ABA policy asserts that these "categories are considered to involve interests so fundamental and important as to require governments to supply low-income persons with effective access to justice as a matter of right . . ." Further, the ABA states that "[t]here is a strong presumption this mandates provision of lawyers in all such cases."[17]

Dozens of state bar organizations have formally endorsed the ABA civil *Gideon* resolution, but the movement has had little success.[18] State court judges routinely preside over courtrooms with mostly unrepresented parties, legal aid organizations continue to turn away many more people than they serve, and the needs of

[13] See generally Scott L. Cummings & Rebecca Sandefur, *Beyond the Numbers: What We Know – and Should Know – About American Pro Bono*, 7 HARV. L & POL REV. 83 (2012); Rebecca L. Sandefur, *Lawyers 'Pro Bono Service and American-Style Legal Assistance*, 41 LAW & SOC. REV. 79 (2007).

[14] See Earl Johnson, Jr.'s authoritative and detailed three-volume account of the history of legal services in the United States from its charitable origins in the nineteenth century to the Obama administration, TO ESTABLISH JUSTICE FOR ALL: THE PAST AND FUTURE OF CIVIL LEGAL AID IN THE UNITED STATES (2014).

[15] Id. at 451.

[16] National Coalition for A Civil Right to Counsel; supra note 1.

[17] See note 2.

[18] *See Turner v. Rogers*, 564 U.S. 431 (2011).

moderate- and middle-income people have never been a policy focus of the academy or the access to justice community.

I have argued elsewhere that a lawyer-centric civil *Gideon* of the type supported by the ABA has both conceptual and practical problems and will not, standing alone, meet the access needs of millions of Americans. [19] First, an open-ended, categorical entitlement to lawyer services is inconceivable in the present economic climate.[20] Second, costs will escalate when poor people with lawyers face moderate-income people who cannot afford legal help and so must have appointed lawyers. Third, assuring lawyers for everyone may heighten formality, proceduralism, and delays that undermine substantive justice. Fourth, people in crises are likely to get priority for appointed counsel, depleting resources for advice services that might have averted the crisis in the first instance. Fifth, quality will be at risk when inexperienced or poorly prepared lawyers become the norm as is so often the case for criminal defendants. Finally and perhaps most importantly, the focus on lawyers diverts attention from the potential for access gains through new service approaches and reform of "institutions of remedy"[21] – the courts, agencies, and penumbra of less formal processes and arrangements that the public turns to for resolution of law problems.

Ironically, the stalled civil *Gideon* movement has created a space for service innovations in which lawyers play a more limited role. Innovations that began as stopgap measures while waiting for *Gideon* have proved effective – even superior – to conventional adversarial lawyer assistance.[22] For example, court-based self-help services are now firmly established in most states. Plain language, easy-to-use forms, informational materials, and advisors of the day (lawyers, law students, and in some instances lay people) allow many claimants to effectively self-represent.

State court judges and administrators as well as innovators in legal aid and private law offices continue to invent new ways of providing services – important reforms that are covered elsewhere in this volume.

PEER NATIONS AND THE CONSUMER PERSPECTIVE

While continuing civil *Gideon*–like guarantees of universal access to lawyers, legal aid policy-makers in peer nations are funding advice services, assistance from lay advocates, and support for "self-helpers." [23] Some countries have deregulated the bar

[19] Jeanne Charn, *Celebrating the Null Finding: Evidence-Based Strategies for Improving Access to Legal Services*, 122 YALE L. J. 2016, 2217–32 (2013).

[20] See Hadfield & Heine, Chapter 2 in this volume; see Gilian K. Hadfield, Higher Demand, Lower Supply? A Comparative Assessment of the Legal Resource Landscape for Ordinary Americans, 37 FORDHAM URB. L. J. 129 (2009).

[21] Rebecca L. Sandefur, *Fulcrum Point of Equal Access to Justice*, 42 *Loyola of L. A. L. Rev.* 949 (2009).

[22] See, e.g., Rebecca Aviel, *Why Civil* Gideon *Won't Fix Family Law*, 122 *Yale L.J.* 2106 (2013).

[23] Civil Justice Council, *Access to Justice for Litigants in Person (or self-represented litigants): A Report and Series of Recommendations to the Lord Chancellor and the Lord Chief Justice*, November 2011, available at www.judiciary.gov.uk/JCO%2FDocuments%2FCJC%2FPublications%2FCJC+papers%2FCivil

in order to incentivize the market to produce new, lower cost services designed to attract moderate- and middle-income consumers.[24] No doubt cost concerns play a role in the expansion of advice services, particularly if further research shows that early interventions are effective as well as less costly. However, though cost per case may go down, overall system costs may not decrease and may even increase when services that consumers prefer increase usage.

A large body of survey research documents that, contrary to the widely held assumptions of the bar, the public is not eager to access conventional lawyer services. The research examines consumer perspectives on "justiciable problems" meaning problems that have "legal aspects, legal consequences, and (potentially) legal solutions" but "may never be understood or treated as a legal problem" by consumers.[25] Legal-aid researchers in Scotland and in Britain refined earlier methods and began surveys via in-person interviews of a representative sample of the entire population. Many other countries have undertaken similar studies.[26]

This research provides detailed information about the incidence of justiciable problems and the "claiming behavior" of poor, middle-income, and wealthy strata of the population. It suggests that people with justiciable problems often do not see legal dimensions or legal remedies and that when such problems are ignored or tolerated, they cluster and compound. Moreover, people with justiciable problems often turn to non-lawyer advisors more often than lawyers and cost may not be the most important of the many reasons people do not seek lawyer assistance.

The UK researchers who pioneered "justiciable problem" research offered educational programs to help the public find and use lawyer services but these efforts had little effect. Policymakers shifted gears and began to offer advice services in ways that research showed the public preferred. The United Kingdom has a national system of Citizens Advice Bureaus (CABs)[27] dating from the aftermath of World War II when Britain was rebuilding its economy and laying the foundations of its modern welfare state. CABs are a trusted brand, well known and well regarded by the public. By offering advice services through the CABs, local councils, and civic organizations, legal aid policymakers hoped to increase claiming behavior by the public.

+Justice+Council+-+Report+on+Access+to+Justice+for+Litigants+in+Person+(or+self-represented +lit; Cite to International Legal Aid Group (ILAG) websites.

24 Vanessa Rakel, Paul Anderson & Jonathan Edwards, "Tesco Law: The Big Bang in the UK Legal Industry," on file with the author; Harvard Law School Program on the Legal Profession, "remarks of Chris Kenny, Chief Executive of Legal Services Board of UK, Harvard Law School (March 5, 2014), available at www.law.harvard.edu/programs/plp/pages/kenny_event.php; Patrick Lamb and Paul Lippe, New Normal blog (march 19, 2014), available at www.abajournal.com/legalrebels/new_normal/.

25 Sandefur, Fulcrum of Equal Justice, supra note 21.

26 See Hadfield & Heine, Chapter 2 in this volume.

27 www.citizensadvice.org.uk/index/getadvice.htm.

Sociologist Rebecca Sandefur compared the findings of an English and Welsh Civil Justice Survey[28] fielded when informal advice services had increased,[29] with the findings of the 1994 ABA survey of legal needs in the United States.[30] She focused on money and housing problems. The experience of justiciable problems was common across the United States, England, and Wales in that most problems never reached lawyers or the legal system, and cost was seldom cited as the main barrier to access.[31] However, in other respects the public's response was markedly different in England and Wales than in the United States. Sandefur attributes the differences to the helping resources available to people with civil justice problems. "In the United States, people respond to their money and housing problems by choosing between what is broadly available: law or nothing. In the United Kingdom, where a wider variety of assistance with civil justice problems is available, people respond to justiciable money and housing problems in a wider variety of ways."[32]

The UK data show a dramatic drop between 2001 and 2007 in the number of people who took no action (from 20% to 8.8%),[33] and a strong preference for non-legal third-party advisors even though the United Kingdom *guarantees* low- and moderate-income people access to free or low-cost lawyers. Notwithstanding this categorical guarantee, nearly *four times* as many people opted for informal advice service over lawyers. As Sandefur points out: "Institutions of remedy not only receive clients, they also create their clienteles."[34]

Although the United Kingdom continues to guarantee access to lawyers, policy-makers have made a major commitment to advice services because when "a delivery system offers consumers many choices in addition to... lawyer services, consumers are both more likely to seek help ... and less likely to seek lawyer services."[35] That is, when people have a choice between lawyers and readily available, informal advice givers, we have a lot of evidence that they prefer the informal advisors, at least in the first instance. Advice services reach people who would not go to a law office and may

28 Pascoe Pleasence, Causes of Action: Civil Law and Social Justice (2006) comparing results of 2001 and 2004 surveys.

29 See e.g., Legal Services Research Centre, Outreach Advice Fact Sheet (2010), available at http://webarchive.nationalarchives.gov.uk/20130128112038/http://www.justice.gov.uk/downloads/publications/research-and-analysis/lsrc/2010/FactSheetDebtOutreach August2010.pdf.

30 ABA Consortium on Legal Needs and the Public, Legal Needs and Civil Justice: A Survey of Americans (1994), available at www.americanbar.org/content/dam/aba/migrated/legalservices/downloads/sclaid/legalneedstudy.authcheckdam.pdf.

31 Sandefur, supra note 21, at 968.

32 Id. at 968.

33 Pascoe Pleasence, Nigel Balmer, Tania Tam, Alexy Buck, Marisol Smith & Ashish Patel, Civil Justice in England and Wales: Report of the 2007 English and Welsh Civil and Social Justice Survey, pp. 46, 53–54 (2008). Available at http://webarchive.nationalarchives.gov.uk/20130128112038/http://www.justice.gov.uk/downloads/publications/research-and-analysis/lsrc/2008/2007CSJS.pdf.

34 Sandefur, supra note 22, at 971. See also Laura Abel, *Designing Access: Using Institutional Design to Improve Decision Making about the Distribution of Free Civil Legal Aid*, 7 Harv. L. Pol'y L. Rev. 61 (2012).

35 Jeanne Charn, *Legal Services for All: Is the Profession Ready?* 42 Loy. L.A. L. Rev. 1021, 1054 (2009).

reach them when limited assistance could avert the need for more intensive, expert, and costly intervention.[36] In these crucial respects a mixed model, consumer-driven delivery system is superior to a civil *Gideon*.

A GUARANTEE OF ACCESS TO LEGAL ADVICE AND ASSISTANCE AND, SOMETIMES, TO LAWYERS

The lessons are clear from the experience of legal aid in the United States and abroad and from justiciable problem research. If we want to increase access to legal services, we cannot think only about more lawyers. We must focus on the preferences of consumers, and we must diversify the sources of assistance we offer. The early years of the OEO legal services program fostered many examples of this client-centered approach. Reexamining that history and reengaging the basic commitment to understanding and respecting the preferences of those we seek to help is solid ground on which to mount efforts to reduce access disparity.

I propose a guarantee of access to legal advice and assistance that might, but would not necessarily, mean access to a lawyer.[37] It is time for a chain of legal aid walk-in advice clinics. Court budgets should support state-of-the-art information services, particularly since the Supreme Court has recently held that court-based self-help may be required in certain circumstances to assure due process for unrepresented parties.[38]

Fortunately, the bench and bar in many states are already far down the path of a mixed model, consumer-centered delivery system. Vibrant sectors of innovation exist not only within legal aid offices but also in the private bar, which is the only recourse for the middle class and people of moderate means. For years the lower trial courts have been engaged in reforms that support self-representation, which in turn enables discrete task (unbundled) legal services from the private bar and from legal services lawyers.

The challenges going forward are related to a radically changed legal services landscape and not to any failure of imagination or unwillingness to innovate. This changed landscape[39] has at least three dimensions. First, funding for civil legal services, adjusted for inflation, is about 50% greater than in 1980 – the high point of

[36] Charn, Null Finding, supra note 19, at 2224.

[37] Jeanne Charn & Richard Zorza, Civil Legal Assistance for All Americans, 2005, available at www.law.harvard.edu/academics/clinical/bellow-sacks/Templates/index.htm.

[38] See *Turner v. Rogers*, supra note 18 (holding due process does not require provision of a lawyer at public expense for an indigent defendant in a civil contempt hearing for non-payment of child support but does require facilitation of self-help with respect to access to information and forms). See Null Finding, supra note 19; Russell Engler, *Turner v. Rogers* and the Essential Role of the Courts in Delivering Access to Justice, 7 Harv. L. & Pol. Rev. 31 (2012).

[39] See generally Access Across America: The First Report of the Civil Justice Infrastructure Mapping Project (October 2011). The study, which was completed under the auspices of the American Bar Foundation, systematically collected data and compared civil legal resources available in all fifty states. Available in all fifty states.

federal funding. However, funding comes from a great many sources. Although LSC continues to be the single largest funder, it is a minority funder, providing about a third of total dollars. Two-thirds of funding for civil legal services comes from state and local sources.

Second, as a result of the devolution of funding to state and local sources, disparities among states are large and growing. Some states have no resources beyond LSC funds – under $15 per eligible person – while the best-funded states may have as much as ten times more per capita, not counting pro bono and similar in-kind resources. The problem of disparities of this magnitude among states will be difficult to solve and, at present, is not on the agenda of any policymakers.

Third, the fragmentation of funding leaves civil legal aid with no policy center, adds complexity, weakens coordination, and creates inefficiencies that result in less service for dollar spent. Critical decisions about what type of cases programs accept for service and the types of services they provide are made at the program or law office level except when funders specify a particular purpose, or prohibit types of services. Although many states have Access to Justice Commissions that have the power to convene and recommend, they have no authority over funds, do not make policy, and usually have no staff and no capacity for research or data gathering.

This is the daunting terrain on which we must find ways to expand access to legal assistance for everyone the market cannot serve.

11

The Effect of Contingent Fees and Statutory Fee-Shifting

David L. Noll

Contingent-fee and statutory fee-shifting provisions shift costs away from the client and to the back end of the litigation. David Noll's analysis suggests that even with these arrangements, only a limited number of attorneys are willing and able to finance plaintiff-side litigation. The result is that the demand for legal assistance in cases with fee-shifting devices exceeds the supply of lawyers who handle these cases. Noll concludes that alternative payment arrangements that place the burden of costs on the lawyer will not solve the affordability problem.

Litigation is time-consuming, and the complexity of American law and importance of understanding court procedure place pro se litigants at a demonstrable disadvantage to counseled parties. But, for the victim of a legal injury, the cost of representation may be so high that the only viable way to assert a claim is to proceed pro se. The high cost of legal services therefore can lead to a denial of justice in a very practical sense. Though an individual is formally entitled to a remedy, the cost of claiming makes obtaining one impossible.

Such access-preclusive costs result in part from two norms governing attorney fees in the United States: the "American" rule of attorney fees, whereby litigants are responsible for their own attorney fees,[1] and the practice of charging for legal services on an hourly basis. It is therefore unsurprising that legal policymakers have attempted to expand court access by authorizing departures from those norms. "No win no fee" contingent-fee agreements and statutory fee-shifting provisions both modify the timing of payment for legal services; instead of being paid as services are rendered, an attorney is paid upon obtaining a recovery. In the case of fee-shifting provisions, ultimate responsibility for the cost of legal services is also transferred to the losing defendant.

But what effect do these ameliorative mechanisms have on the basic problem of access-preclusive costs? Do they ensure that individuals with meritorious claims are able to make use of the civil justice system?

[1] See *Alyeska Pipeline Serv. Co. v. Wilderness Soc'y*, 421 U.S. 240, 247 (1975) ("In the United States, the prevailing litigant is ordinarily not entitled to collect a reasonable attorneys' fee from the loser").

In one sense the answer is easy. Domestic relations disputes, for instance, make up a significant proportion of Americans' legal problems, but the coverage of fee-shifting statutes in this context is sporadic, and ethical rules generally prohibit contingency fees paid to outcomes such as a divorce.[2] In this discrete context, alternative payment devices do not expand access to justice because they are not legally available. One can go further and ask the same questions about areas that are the bread and butter of the civil justice system – torts, contracts, property, and claims under regulatory statutes. Do alternative payment devices overcome the problem of access-preclusive costs in these other areas?

The answer may be "not much." Alternative payment devices undoubtedly enable some forms of litigation that Americans of ordinary means could not afford on an hourly-fee basis; few persons are willing or able to finance a complex products liability or medical malpractice suit out of pocket. But to determine the effect on the overall availability of civil justice, one must consider the characteristics of the broader market for legal services. In this market, the limited supply of attorneys that are willing and able to finance plaintiff-side litigation, combined with competition for their services, suggest that changes to the way attorneys are paid will have a modest effect on overall access to justice. Contingency fees and statutory fee-shifting, on this account, are primarily *determinants* of which clients and claims receive representation rather than a *general solution* to the problem of access-preclusive costs.

To appreciate the point, it is useful to contrast two models of alternative payment devices. Proponents of such devices have suggested that the devices are capable of overcoming the problem of access-preclusive costs, if only they were generally available. Taken to its logical limits, this "enabling" model posits that alternative payment devices are capable of ensuring access to justice for the majority of Americans' legal needs.

A second, "determinant" model is more skeptical. While this model shares most of the enabling models' assumptions, it emphasizes that a variety of factors constrain the overall supply of legal services, and that cases financed through alternative payment devices compete for representation with other uses of attorneys' time and money. Thus, instead of viewing alternative payment devices as a *general* solution to the problem of access-preclusive costs, the determinant model sees the devices as a means of influencing *which* of a larger universe of clients and claims receive legal representation.

The models are not necessarily exclusive; alternative payment devices probably enable some forms of claiming *and* influence attorneys' selection of cases for representation. Nonetheless, it is useful to consider which is more consistent with what we know about the civil justice system to get a sense of the justice-enabling potential of alternative payment devices.

2 E.g., American Bar Assn, Model Rules of Prof'l Conduct R. 1.5(d) (1983).

FINANCING LITIGATION THROUGH CONTINGENT FEES AND STATUTORY FEE-SHIFTING

The contingent-fee agreement and statutory fee-shifting provisions share an intuitive logic: when the cost of legal services prevents individuals from making use of the courts, modify the client's ordinary obligation to pay for services as they are performed. Under a contingent-fee agreement, services are financed by a law firm until the client obtains a recovery out of which the firm's fee can be paid. A law firm likewise finances the costs of litigation when a statutory fee-shift is available, but financial responsibility for the firm's services is shifted to the losing party if the lawsuit succeeds.

Contingent-Fee Agreements

The first of the devices to emerge was the contingent-fee agreement. From the founding of the republic through the 1830s or 1840s, attorney fees generally were paid out of the "costs" of litigation, which courts awarded in amounts specified in statutory tables. The statutory tables failed to keep up with inflation, however, and elite lawyers seeking to charge higher fees lobbied for authority to charge privately negotiated rates. The lawyers' lobbying succeeded and the use of negotiated fees became widespread, subject only to a check for patently "unreasonable" fees.

Once the price of legal services is determined by contract, the problem of access-preclusive costs arises. In a market where the price of a service is determined by supply and demand, it is inevitable that some potential purchasers will be unable or unwilling to pay the market price. The "no win no fee" contingent-fee agreement attempts to ameliorate the unaffordability of legal services by making the client's obligation to pay contingent on a monetary recovery. If the client obtains a recovery, the lawyer's fees are paid from it. If no recovery is obtained, the client is under no obligation to pay for the lawyer's services.

The legality of the contingent-fee agreement is now well-established, but this was not always the case. At common law, the doctrines of champerty and maintenance prohibited splitting the proceeds of a claim and financial support of litigation by someone lacking a "bona fide" interest in the claim. Well into the nineteenth century, prominent state courts held that contingent-fee agreements violated these doctrines because an attorney with no relation to the underlying dispute effectively acquired an interest in the client's recovery in consideration for providing services on spec. The restrictions began to erode in the mid-nineteenth century, however, and by the turn of the twentieth century it was widely accepted that a client could make payment of the attorney's fee contingent on a recovery. Today, contingent-fee agreements can lawfully be used in most types of litigation, though they continue to be prohibited in certain criminal and domestic relations matters.[3]

[3] Id. R. 1.5(d) (2012).

In popular imagination an attorney paid via a contingent fee retains one-third of the recovery plus out-of-pocket expenses, and this contract structure is indeed used in the majority of contingent-fee representations.[4] Nonetheless, research by Herbert M. Kritzker has found significant variation in the structure of contingent-fee agreements. In a survey of Wisconsin lawyers, 31% of respondents reported using agreements in which the fee varied based on contingencies such as trial or appeal, and 5% reported relying on other kinds of contracts, such as those providing for an hourly fee until the first settlement offer and a percentage fee of any recovery above that amount.[5]

Most cases in which lawyers are compensated by a contingent fee are personal injury cases.[6] However, such arrangements are found in many other areas, including workers' compensation, non-personal injury torts, civil rights, property, and tax disputes.[7] Although the client in most contingent-fee representations is an individual, corporate purchasers of legal services have made increased use of contingent-fee agreements in recent years.[8]

Statutory Fee-Shifting

Around the time that the lawfulness of contingent-fee agreements became accepted, statutory fee-shifting provisions began to appear. "Three federal statutes, the voting rights legislation of 1870, the Interstate Commerce Act of 1887, and the Sherman Act of 1890, allowed successful plaintiffs to recover their legal expenses in addition to liquidated damages, ordinary damages, or a treble damage award."[9] The structure of the Sherman Act (as later amended by the Clayton Act) is typical. The act creates a private right of action to "encourag[e] private challenges to antitrust violations."[10] As an incentive to private enforcement, it permits courts to award prevailing plaintiffs "the cost of suit, including a reasonable attorney's fee."[11]

Today, the combination of a private cause of action and fee-shifting provision is a standard feature of state and federal regulatory statutes. A 1984 survey of state legislation identified 1,974 state statutes that provide some form of

[4] See Herbert M. Kritzker, Risks, Reputations, and Rewards: Contingency Fee Legal Practice in the United States 39 tbl 2.4 (2004).

[5] Id. at 39–40 & tbl. 2.4

[6] See Kritzker, supra note 4, at 36 & tbl. 2.2.

[7] See Peter Karsten, *Enabling the Poor to Have Their Day in Court: The Sanctioning of Contingency Fee Contracts, A History to 1940*, 447 DePaul L. Rev. 231, 248 (1998).

[8] See, e.g., Robert E. Litan & Steven C. Salop, *Reforming the Lawyer-Client Relationship through Alternative Billing Methods*, 77 Judicature 191 (1994); Darlene Ricker, *The Vanishing Hourly Fee*, 80 A.B.A. J. 66 (1994).

[9] See John Leubsdorf, *Toward a History of the American Rule on Attorney Fee Recovery*, 47 Law & Contemporary Probs. 9, 25 (Winter 1984).

[10] *Reiter v. Sonotone Corp.*, 442 U.S. 330, 344 (1979).

[11] 15 U.S.C. § 15(a) (2012).

fee-shifting.[12] A 2008 report identified 293 fee-shifting provisions in the U.S. Code. Since then, Congress has continued to make use of the device.[13]

The exact language used to authorize fee-shifting varies across statutes. In functional terms, however, nearly all statutes prioritize the *assertion* as opposed to defense of claims. While a prevailing plaintiff often is entitled to fees as a matter of course,[14] the successful defendant must typically show that litigation was frivolous, unreasonable, or without foundation to recover attorneys' fees.[15] The reason for this differential treatment is Congress's decision to make use of private litigation to enforce public regulatory policy. A plaintiff bringing suit under a regulatory statute creates a positive external effect insofar as the plaintiff functions as "a 'private attorney general,' vindicating a policy that Congress considered of the highest priority."[16] Such law suits are, in effect, subsidized through the fee-shifting provision.

The Contingent Fee and Statutory Fee-Shift as a Financing Device

Both the contingent-fee and statutory fee-shifting provisions are intended to enable litigation that could not be brought if an individual paid for legal services out-of-pocket on an hourly-fee basis. They do so via the omnipresent "buy now, pay later" device familiar from credit cards, big-screen TVs, and used cars. In view of this similarity, it may be helpful to note some of the characteristics of the contingent fee and statutory fee-shifting as a financing device before considering their effect on access to justice. Seen from this perspective, the first and most important characteristic of both the contingent fee and statutory fee-shifting is that the law firm, or the lawyer alone if self-employed, finances the litigation.[17] Until a recovery is obtained, the law firm pays for the services of its attorneys (and often the costs of litigation). A client can therefore bring a claim with virtually no risk of incurring liability for attorney fees and costs.

This has a number of implications for the processing and valuation of claims. First, the fact of law-firm financing means that firms that rely on contingent fees and statutory fee-shifting are likely to maintain an inventory of claims. The decision to represent a case without upfront payment is a kind of investment – ex ante, the firm does not know whether it will recover the time and money it dedicates to the case – and as with other investments, risk can be reduced through diversification. Firms

[12] Note, *State Attorney Fee Shifting Statutes: Are We Quietly Repealing the American Rule?*, 47 Law & Contemp. Probs. 321 (Winter 1984).

[13] Henry Cohen, CRS Report for Congress, Awards of Attorneys' Fees by Federal Courts and Federal Agencies 64–114 (Jun. 20, 2008).

[14] See *Newman v. Piggie Park Enters., Inc.*, 390 U.S. 400, 401–402 (1968).

[15] See *Christiansburg Garment Co. v. Equal Employment Opportunity Comm'n*, 434 U.S. 412, 421 (1978).

[16] *Newman*, 390 U.S. at 402.

[17] Jonathan T. Molot, *Litigation Finance: A Market Solution to a Procedural Problem*, 99 Geo. L.J. 65, 90 (2010).

that make use of alternative payment devices therefore can be expected to maintain a portfolio of cases, to diversify the risk the firm is exposed to from any single case.

One consequence of this is cross-subsidization among the firm's clients. The proceeds from one group of cases fund the next generation of cases, the proceeds of which fund the next, and so on. Thus, the resources a firm can dedicate to prosecuting a claim depend importantly on the financial strength of the prosecuting firm. Not only the individual case's expected recovery but also the success of prior generations of litigation affect a firm's capacity to invest resources in prosecuting a claim.[18]

Although not a financing characteristic as such, contingent-fee agreements and statutory fee-shifting also introduce a unique conflict of interest into the attorney–client relationship. In a variety of circumstances, such as where there is a small chance of obtaining an outsized recovery, it may be in the client's interest to continue litigating but the attorney's interest to settle (or vice versa).[19] Despite ethical rules that mandate the client exercise unfettered control over settlement decisions, there are well-known examples in which the decision to settle seemingly served the lawyer's interests rather than the client's.[20]

TWO MODELS OF ALTERNATIVE PAYMENT DEVICES

Both of the dominant alternative payment devices used in the United States are thus attorney-funded forms of litigation financing. Where the cost of legal services prevents an individual from making use of the courts, a law firm represents her with the expectation of recovering payment from the client's recovery or the losing party. Return, then, to the central problem animating this chapter: To what extent do these devices address the barrier to justice created by the high cost of legal services?

In a system that follows the American rule, there are at least two ways to understand alternative payment devices. First, such devices can be understood as a general solution to the problem of access-preclusive costs, an understanding I term the *enabling* model. According to this model, attorney-funded financing devices ensure access to justice for Americans of ordinary means, or at least are capable of doing so if they were generally available. Alternatively, attorney-funded financing devices can be seen as a means of determining which of many possible cases are litigated, an

[18] This fact potentially explains the dominance of a handful of firms in high-cost areas such as securities litigation. See Institutional Shareholder Services Inc., The Securities Class Action Services (SCAS) 50 (for 2011), available at www.issgovernance.com/files/private/SCAS502011.pdf (last accessed May 3, 2013).

[19] For a classic treatment, see John C. Coffee, Jr., *Understanding the Plaintiff's Attorney: The Implications of Economic Theory for Private Enforcement of Law through Class and Derivative Actions*, 86 COLUM. L. REV. 669, 687–90 (1986).

[20] See *Kamilewicz v. Bank of Boston*, 92 F.3d 506 (7th Cir. 1996) (class action settlement in which many class members suffered a loss after deductions for attorney's fees and costs). Further examples are available at S. Rep. No. 109–14, at 14–20 (2005), reprinted in 2005 U.S.C.C.A.N. 3, 44.

understanding I term the *determinant* model. This model posits that the level of legal services available to potential litigants primarily reflects factors other than the norms governing attorney payment. Because they do not affect the overall level of available services, alternative payment devices are capable of changing the makeup of litigated cases, but cannot overcome the problem of access-preclusive costs.

The Enabling Model

The basic premise of the enabling model is that there is a universe of claims existing in the world that would be asserted if only the cost of legal services did not prevent aggrieved individuals from securing legal representation. By modifying attorney-payment practices, policymakers facilitate assertion of these claims. When recognizing alternative devices, policymakers unfailingly invoke the model. For example, the stated purpose of the Civil Rights Act Attorney's Fees Act of 1976 is "to ensure 'effective access to the judicial process' for person with civil rights grievances."[21]

The Determinant Model

A second way to understand alternative payment devices emphasizes the devices' role in shaping which cases are litigated over their capacity to enable claiming that would otherwise be too expensive to maintain. The model posits that other constraints limit the overall availability of legal services, and that cases financed via alternative payment devices compete for attorney representation with one another as well as with cases financed on a traditional fee-for-services basis. The key feature of alternative payment devices, accordingly, is to modify *which* cases are litigated. By modifying the payoff from representing particular claims and clients, alternative payment devices encourage some forms of litigation over others.

The determinant model shares many of the basic assumptions of the enabling model. Thus, the determinant model assumes that a significant factor in attorneys' choice of clients and claims to represent is the fee available from the representation. Attorneys see representations as an investment whose expected value is a function of the probability of success on the merits and the available fee. All other things being equal, attorneys will choose representation with a higher expected fee.

The determinant model further assumes that through modification of attorney-payment devices, legal policymakers can encourage representation of certain claims and clients. When the coverage of alternative payment devices is less than universal, authorizing a new device or expanding the payoff of existing devices increases the expected payoff from covered representations by establishing a new source of money

21 *Blanchard v. Bergeron*, 489 U.S. 87 (1989) (quoting *Hensley v. Eckerhart*, 461 U.S. 424, 429 (1983)).

from which attorney fees can be paid (the client's recovery or defendant's pockets) and permitting an attorney to take from it.[22]

Where the determinant model differs from the enabling model is its broader assumptions about the market for legal services. In contrast to the enabling model, the determinant model does not assume that attorneys will materialize to represent clients and claims whenever the potential for collecting a fee from a judgment or the defendant is present. Instead, it assumes a supply of lawyers constrained by, among other things, the requirement that a law firm finance litigation and the fact that attorneys seek to maximize their own profits in selecting claims and clients for representation.

The first constraint is the limited supply of lawyers for cases requiring upfront attorney financing. To represent a case on an alternative payment basis, it is not enough that a law firm be willing to represent the client and have the competence to do so. Instead, the firm must also be able to finance the costs of litigation – i.e., the out-of-pocket costs and the opportunity cost of attorneys' time. Indeed, since no particular case is guaranteed to succeed, a firm must as a practical matter be able to finance a portfolio of cases to be assured of recovering her investment. This constrains the supply of lawyers able to undertake litigation financed via an alternative payment device, because lawyers who are willing and able to finance a portfolio of cases only make up a fraction of the total population of attorneys. A freshly minted attorney cannot finance a major securities fraud case.

The second constraint is competition among clients or claims for the limited number of competent lawyers willing to finance plaintiff-side litigation. When claims and clients compete for representation in a world of constrained supply, the effect of recognizing or expanding alternative payment devices is as much *allocational* as justice-enabling. The recognition or expansion of an alternative payment device will cause attorneys to compare the expected payoff in the area the device covers with the payoff from other areas of practice, including those covered by other payment devices and areas in which clients pay by the hour. If the payoff in the newly covered area is high enough, attorneys will select representations in that area over alternatives. That choice, in turn, will have a negative effect on the availability of representation in less lucrative areas. As a result, authorizing an alternative payment device is not guaranteed to have a positive or negative effect on the overall availability of legal services.

In short, the determinant model sees fee-allocation devices as a means of influencing attorneys' selection of cases for representation rather than a way of broadly ensuring access to justice. In extreme form, it implies that alternative payment devices have no effect, on net, on the overall availability of legal services.

[22] See Sean Farhang, The Litigation State: Public Regulation and Private Lawsuits in the U.S. 30–31 (2010); see also Judith Resnik, *Money Matters: Judicial Market Interventions Creating Subsidies and Awarding Fees and Costs in Individual and Aggregate Litigation*, 148 U. PA. L. REV. 2119, 2130–40 (2000).

The model therefore implies that modifications to the baseline rules governing attorney payment are more likely to generate changes in the universe of litigated cases than to create a "new proud profession of 'little lawyers' serving the little man."[23]

Evaluating the Models

The two models of alternative payment devices sketched earlier both assume that attorneys respond to financial incentives in selecting cases for representation but differ in their real-world implications. The logic of the enabling model is that alternative payment devices are capable of overcoming the problem of access-preclusive costs. By contrast, the determinant model predicts that alternative payment devices will primarily reallocate scarce legal services.

The models are not necessarily exclusive. Nevertheless, it is useful to compare the models because doing so sheds light on the capacity for changes in attorney-payment norms to address the problem of access-preclusive costs. To the extent the enabling model is accurate, there is a simple solution to the problem of access-preclusion costs: authorize more alternative payment devices. To the extent the determinant model is accurate, it suggests other devices are needed to address access-preclusive costs. Which, then, better captures the actual effect of alternative payment devices?

One way of approaching that question is to consider the supply of lawyers. Is it consistent with the determinant model's assumption of constrained supply? Or does the supply of lawyers vary with changes in the availability of alternative payment devices?

In the twentieth century, there are two significant time periods to account for. Until the 1970s, the number of lawyers as a proportion of the total employed population in the United States remained relatively constant, at approximately 0.3%.[24] During this period, the determinant model's assumption of a constrained supply of lawyers holds. All else being equal, if an alternative payment provided access to justice during this time period, it was because lawyers were reallocating services from less lucrative clients and claims to those covered by an alternative payment device.

The story is more ambiguous with respect to the second period. From 1970 until 2000, the number of lawyers as a proportion of the employed population roughly doubled, with lawyers making up approximately 0.7% of the workforce by the turn of the millennium.[25] As noted earlier, the availability of statutory fee-shifting greatly increased beginning in the late 1960s. One obvious explanation for the

[23] Albert A. Ehrenzweig, *Reimbursement of Counsel Fees and the Great Society*, 54 CAL. L. REV. 792, 796 (1966).

[24] Ian D. Wyatt & Daniel E. Hecker, *Occupational Changes During the 20th Century*, MONTHLY LABOR REV., Mar. 2006, at 41.

[25] Id.

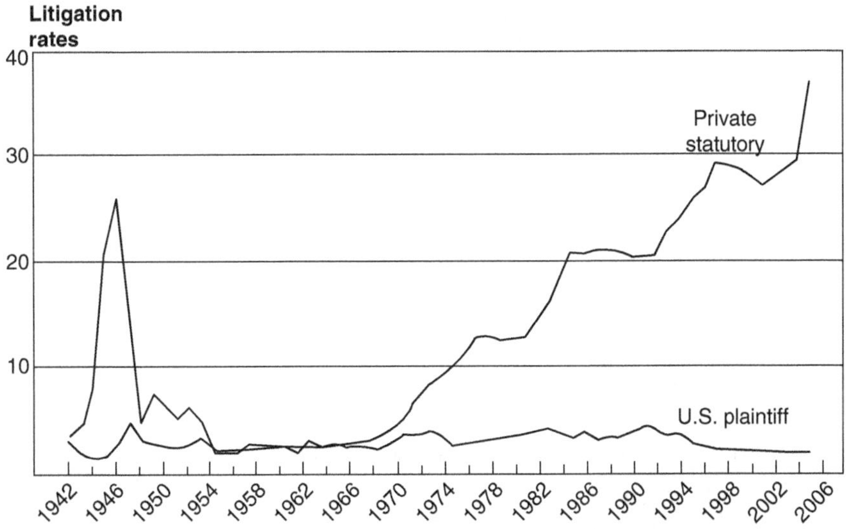

FIGURE 11.1. Rates of private statutory and U.S. plaintiff litigation, 1942–2005. (*Source:* Sean Farhang, The Litigation State: Public Regulation and Private Lawsuits in the United States. 12 (2010))

increase in the supply of lawyers during the same time period is that the availability of statutory attorney fees increased the attractiveness of employment as an attorney, leading to the gradual creation of a bar primarily engaged in fee-shifting work. A comparison of the number of lawyers and the incidence of private litigation under federal regulatory statutes seems to provide support for this interpretation. Figure 11.1 summarizes rates of private litigation from 1942 through 2005. Figure 11.2 shows the percentage of the U.S. workforce made up of lawyers and judges from 1900 to 2000. Increases in both litigation rates and percentage of population employed as attorneys beginning around the 1960s suggest that the enactment of fee-shifting devices at the beginning did, in fact, expand the pool of lawyers willing and able to represent clients who could not pay for legal services on an hourly-fee basis.

But there is a competing explanation. The same time period of 1970–2000 saw similar growth in *other* professions, including computer specialists, accountants and auditors, educators, engineers, and healthcare providers.[26] If the increase in the number of lawyers was caused by the same underlying forces that caused the general increase in the number of professionals – the decreasing competitiveness of American manufacturing, the information technology revolution, the growth of international trade, and the increasing complexity of business activities – it is not clear that the availability of attorney fees is responsible for the growth in the number

[26] Id. at 38–40.

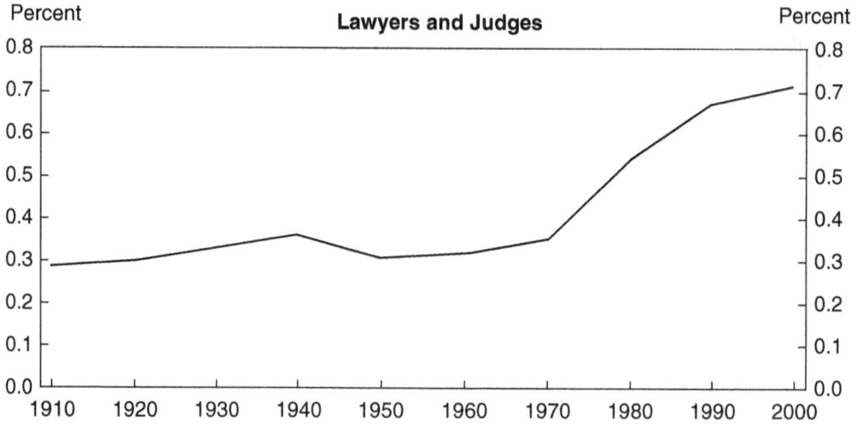

FIGURE 11.2. Lawyers and judges as a proportion of total employment, 1900–2000. (*Source:* Ian D. Wyatt & Daniel E. Hecker, Occupational Changes During the 20th Century, Monthly Lab. Rev., Mar. 2006, at 41.)

of lawyers. Indeed, if those same forces increased the demand for legal services paid for on a fee-for-service basis, it is not clear that the greater number of lawyers increased access to justice for Americans of ordinary means.

In short, the supply story is ambiguous. Without a statistical analysis, it is difficult to say whether it is characterized by constrained supply, as the determinant model predicts.

Another way of evaluating the models is to consider the allocation of legal services. Given that it views alternative payment devices as a general solution to the problem of access-preclusive costs, the enabling model predicts at least a rough correspondence between reports of legal needs and observed litigation patterns, with exceptions for areas such as domestic relations where the use of alternative payment devices is unlawful. The determinant model predicts a mismatch.

Here the data seem to favor the determinant model. The most recent comprehensive survey of Americans' legal needs was conducted by the American Bar Association (ABA) in 1994.[27] Based on interviews of 3,000 low- and moderate-income households, researchers identified the areas in which individuals were likely to encounter legal problems. The nine most common were: (1) personal finance and consumer (disputes reported by approximately 18% of households); (2) housing and property (11–15%, depending on household income); (3) "community and regional" problems such as inadequate

[27] ABA Consortium on Legal Services and the Public, Legal Needs and Civil Justice: A Survey of Americans: Major Findings from the Comprehensive Legal Needs Study (1994), available at www.americanbar.org/content/dam/aba/migrated/legalservices/downloads/sclaid/legalneedstudy.authcheckdam.pdf.

police services (12%); (4) family and domestic (12%); (5) employment (7–12%); (6) personal/economic injury (6–10%); (7) estates and directives (5–10%); (8) health (4–5%); and (9) public benefits (2–4%).[28]

That distribution of problems is not reflected in statistics of litigated cases. Rather, cases that are litigated align more closely with the coverage of alternative payment devices that support a competitive fee. For example, a 2005 survey of state court trials conducted by the U.S. Department of Justice's Bureau of Justice Statistics found that most trials involved high-value tort claims.[29] Trials most frequently involved motor vehicle accidents (35%), medical malpractice (9%), and premises liability (7%).[30] Contract claims by a seller-plaintiff – an area in which claimants do not typically require an alternative payment device to finance litigation – accounted for 10.7% of trials. 9.6% of trials involved claims by a buyer plaintiff, and 4.1% involved claims of fraud.[31]

In federal court, litigation also is concentrated in areas covered by an alternative payment device and capable of supporting a competitive attorney's fee. In the twelve-month period ending March 31, 2012, the five most common types of cases commenced in federal district court (excluding prisoner cases) were personal injury, civil rights, labor law, intellectual property, and real estate. In four of those areas – personal injury, civil rights, labor, and intellectual property – fee-shifting is available or litigation is lucrative enough to support competitive contingent fees.[32] Only one area, real estate, is neither covered by a fee-shifting regime nor likely to generate damages awards from which a contingent attorney's fee can be recovered. Table 11.1 summarizes the findings from the ABA legal needs survey, the BJS study of state court litigation, and the 2012 report. There is not a clear relationship between reported legal needs and litigated cases.

Of course, differences between reported legal needs and the makeup of litigated cases do not definitively prove that alternative payment devices allocate representation toward favored areas. Litigants' failure to recognize legal injury, informal dispute resolution, selection effects, and other factors could explain why certain disputes that are common in the real world are not regular

28 Id. at 3. The results of the 1994 study differ from the last major national study of legal needs, conducted in 1974. See Barbara A. Curran, The Legal Needs of the Public: The Final Report of a National Survey (1977). In the 1974 survey, "more respondents had been involved in the acquisition of real property (710 per 1,000 adults) than in any other single problem situation presented. Serious property damage (400 per 1,000) and wills (270 per 1,000) were the second and third most experienced [problem]. In only three other situations did more than 10% of respondents report at least one occurrence: divorce (150 per 1,000), serious dispute on major purchase (140 per 1,000), and serious personal injury (120 per 1,000)." Id. at 104.

29 See Bureau of Justice Statistics, Special Report, Civil Bench and Jury Trials in State Courts, 2005 (Oct. 2008).

30 Id. at 2.

31 Id.

32 See, e.g., Civil Rights Act of 1964, 42 U.S.C. § 2000e-5(k); Fair Labor Standards Act, 29 U.S.C. § 216(b); Copyright Act, 17 U.S.C. § 505.

TABLE 11.1 *Legal needs versus litigated cases.*

Most frequently reported legal problems (1994 ABA Survey)	Most-litigated cases (2005 BJS Survey of State Court Litigation)	Most-litigated cases (2012 FJC report)
Personal finance	Motor vehicle accidents	Personal injury
Housing and property	Medical malpractice	Civil rights
Community and regional	Premises liability	Labor
Family and domestic	Contract claims – buyer plaintiff	Intellectual property
Employment	Fraud	Real estate
Personal/economic injury		
Estates and directives		
Health		
Public benefits		

subjects of litigation. Even so, the prevalence of disputes covered by alternative payment device and paucity of non-covered disputes within the universe of litigated cases is striking.

Lastly, the enabling and determinant models can be compared by considering how attorneys actually select which cases to represent. Are attorneys' descriptions of case-selection practices consistent with the suggestion that alternative payment devices provide a general solution to the problem of access-preclusive costs? Or do those practices suggest that alternative payment devices are driving the cases selected for representation?

Here the well-known existence of case-screening casts doubt on the accuracy of the enabling model. There is significant evidence that, in considering whether to undertake representation of a new client, attorneys routinely take into account factors unrelated to the merits. In his study of Wisconsin lawyers, Kritzker found that attorneys declined to represent clients both because liability would be difficult to establish *and* because the damages were too low to support an attractive contingent fee.[33] The same phenomenon occurs in areas of litigation where statutory fee-shifting is available. Despite the availability of court-ordered attorney fees, attorneys report declining to represent clients whose injuries would not support a substantial contingent fee.[34]

[33] Kritzker, supra note 4, at 84–88. For a recent survey confirming the point, see Joanna Shepherd, *Uncovering the Silent Victims of the American Medical Liability System*, 67 VAND. L. REV. 151 (2013) (in survey of medical malpractice practitioners, "over half of the respondents indicated that cost factors – either insufficient damages or the expense of bringing the claim – were the primary reasons for rejecting cases").

[34] See Julie Davies, *Federal Civil Rights Practice in the 1990's: The Dichotomy between Reality and Theory*, 48 HASTINGS L.J. 197, 232, 234 (1997) ("[E]mployment practitioners interviewed unequivocally asserted that the amount of damages is a primary consideration in deciding whether to take a case").

Such screening is entirely consistent with the determinant model, which posits a limited supply of lawyers choosing cases on the basis of their expected payoff. But it poses a problem for the enabling model, which sees contingent fees and fee-shifting as a general solution to the problem of access-preclusive costs. If non-trivial numbers of clients are denied representation for reasons unrelated to the merits of a claim, it is difficult to see how alternative payment devices are guaranteeing access to justice.

A comprehensive empirical analysis of the enabling and determinant models is beyond the scope of this chapter. However, statistics on the supply of lawyers, the concentration of litigation in areas covered by fee-allocation devices, and the existence of attorney case screening suggest that the determinant model better captures the role of fee-allocations devices in the U.S. legal system. Alternative payment devices, it would seem, are a seriously incomplete solution to the problem of access-preclusive costs.

IMPLICATIONS

If the determinant model better captures the effect of contingent fees and statutory fee-shifting provisions, what difference does that make?

As an initial matter, the model highlights a disconnect between rhetoric used to justify alternative payment devices and their real-world effect. Traditionally, alternative payment devices have been justified on the ground that they enable litigants who cannot otherwise afford legal services to vindicate rights. But if the devices serve primarily to reallocate legal representation, their effect is somewhat different. Enabling some kinds of claiming means disabling others, as attorneys redirect representation to areas covered by an alternative payment device.

The more immediate point is that many marginal decisions about alternative payment devices do not necessarily affect the overall availability of legal services to Americans of ordinary means. This point is important for legislatures, who must ensure that regulatory statutes contain sufficiently robust enforcement mechanisms. It also is important for courts, whose decisions determine the availability and scope of alternative payment devices.

Ultimately, then, the determinant model underscores the persistence of the problem of access-preclusive costs. If fee-allocation devices are justice-allocating rather than justice-creating, the problem of access-preclusive costs is larger than the American rule, and tools other than alternative payment devices are needed to ensure that meritorious claims are litigated. The promise and perils of those tools are the subject of the remainder of this volume.

12

The Market for Recent Law Graduates

William D. Henderson

William Henderson's chapter highlights changes in the market for recent law graduates that reveal a substantial divergence between the growing supply of recent law graduates and the reality of fewer jobs in the private sector. Declining opportunities for young lawyers are offset only in part by the emergence of "JD Advantage" jobs where a law degree is helpful though not required.

Drawing upon publicly available sources of information, there are at least three significant patterns that affect the economics of legal education: (1) a steady increase in the number of law schools and graduating law students; (2) a three-decade-long decline in the percentage of entry-level jobs in private practice that predates the more recent decline in large law firm employment; and (3) in the gradual rise of a new category of post-law school employment, now called "JD Advantage" jobs, where the law degree is not required but potentially advantageous.

This third category signals a fundamental change in the entry-level market for law graduates. Data from multiple sources, including salary information, suggest that the rise of the JD Advantage category is less a product of non-legal employers seeking to hire entry-level JDs than the inability of the traditional legal services economy to fully absorb the number of graduates exiting law school each year. That might change in the years to come, however, as law schools reengage with the market and cultivate professional opportunities for their students along the vast boundaries between law and business, government, and the nonprofit sectors.

SURGE IN SUPPLY OF GRADUATING LAWYERS

Figure 12.1 shows for 40 years the number of law school graduates that is steady and upward sloping. Since 1973, the number of law graduates has increased from 27,800 to 46,500 (+67.5%); the number of ABA-accredited law schools has increased from 151 to 201 (33.1%); the average size of the typical graduating class has increased from 184 to 231 (28.8%).

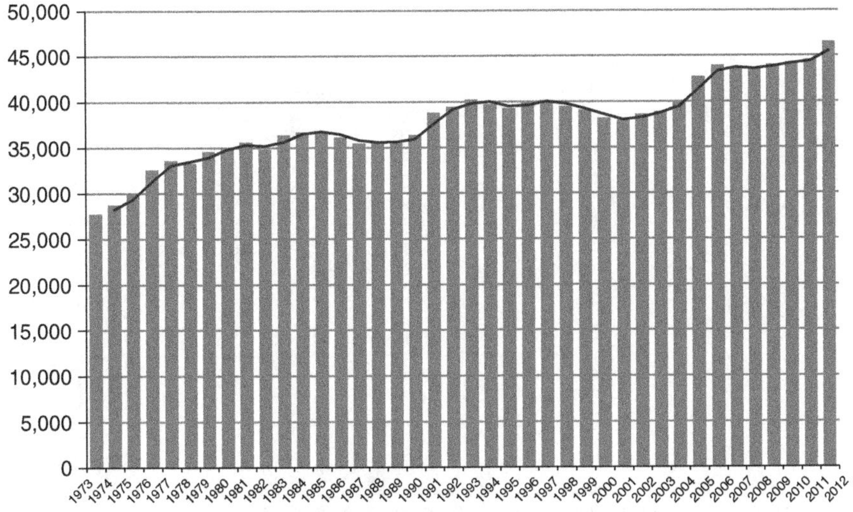

FIGURE 12.1. Number of JD/LLB graduates from ABA-accredited law schools.
Source: ABA.

Is this increase in lawyer production driven by a true market need for more lawyers? This is a difficult question to answer authoritatively because legal demand is so difficult to measure. The best evidence on demand for legal services, albeit indirect, probably comes from the Chicago Lawyer I and II studies,[1] which were based on a representative sample of roughly 800 Chicago lawyers drawn in 1975 and 1995. Comparing the two samples that are separated by two decades, the researchers observed that lawyers who served organizational clients (i.e., corporations) grew much faster than lawyers who served primarily individuals. Likewise, lawyers serving organizations enjoyed large gains in real income whereas lawyers serving individuals experienced a decline.

The Chicago Lawyer studies suggest demand moving in two different directions – higher demand for lawyers who serve corporations, lower demand for lawyers servicing people. More recent data show that demand for organizational lawyers, at least at the entry level, has dramatically softened. As shown in Figure 12.2, between 2002 and 2012, the number of summer associates at law firms who participate in the on-campus interview process (more than 500 law firms nationally) declined from 11,800 to 5,400.[2] This drop spans a full decade and predates the 2008–09 economic crisis.

In short, the supply of law graduates has been growing significantly faster than demand. When this dynamic sets in, basic economic principles tell us that law graduates will experience growing unemployment and underemployment.

[1] See John P. Heinz & Edward Laumann, The Social Structure of the Bar (rev. ed. 1994) (Chicago Lawyer I); John P. Heinz et al., Urban Lawyers: The New Structure of the Bar 99 (2005) (Chicago Lawyer II).

[2] William D. Henderson, *Sea Change in the Legal Market*, NALP Bulletin (Aug. 2013).

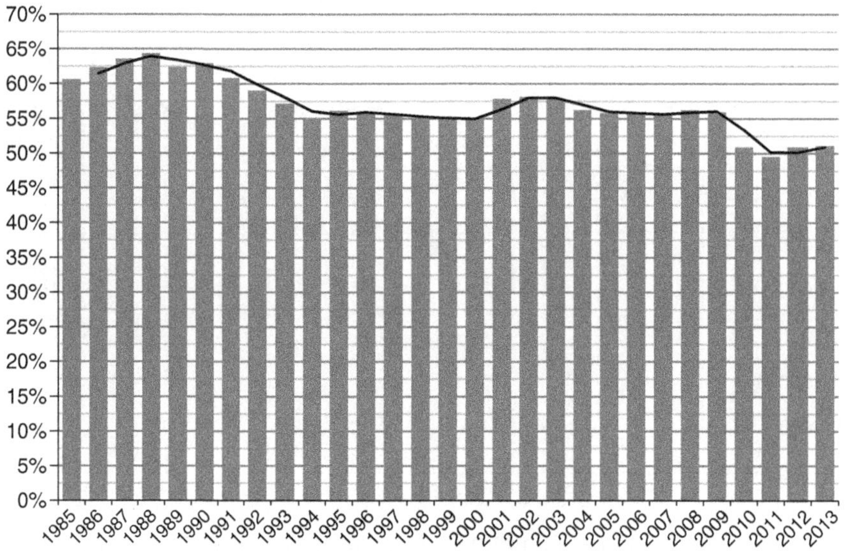

FIGURE 12.2. Percentage of employed law grads starting careers in private practice. *Source: NALP.*

DECLINE IN PRIVATE PRACTICE ENTRY-LEVEL JOBS

"Big firm" hiring is clearly down. But as shown in Figure 12.2, a more troubling trend is a three-decade-long decline in the percentage of law graduates who begin their careers in private practice of any kind. Metrics related to private practice are important to legal educations because these entry-level jobs are the most remunerative. For the class of 2013, the median starting salary for all law school graduates was \$62,500 compared to a median of \$95,000 for lawyers working in law firms. The reduction in entry-level private practice jobs (at least in percentage terms, if not absolute numbers) is problematic for law schools because these jobs are often used to justify higher law school tuition and debt levels.

It is worth noting that the data on private practice shown in Figure 12.2 include law school graduates who begin their careers as solo practitioners. As a historical matter, there is a very strong negative correlation between the number of law graduates taking jobs in large firms of 25 lawyers or more, which are generally viewed as more stable and remunerative, versus the number starting their careers as solo practitioners.[3] Yet according to data published by the National Association for Law Placement (NALP), there appears to be a relative low ceiling for the number of law graduates who are willing to start their own law practice within their first year out of law school. As summarized in Figure 12.3, the proportion of new graduates who become solos has never been higher than 7.6% (in 1982) and in general it has been trending downward.

[3] Based on NALP data from 1982 to 2013, the correlation is stunning: –0.93.

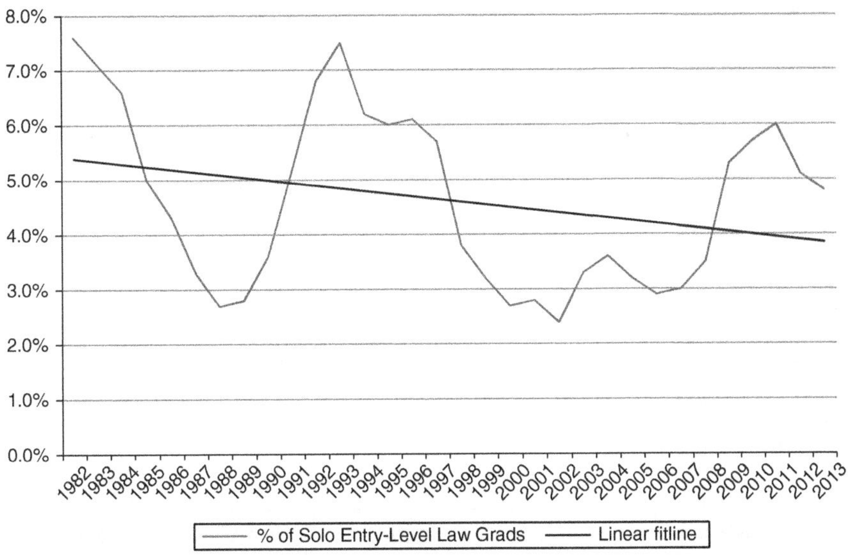

FIGURE 12.3. Percentage of entry-level law grads employed as solo practitioners.
Source: Calculated from NALP data.

Rather than hanging their own shingle, it is likely that most junior lawyers would prefer the safety net of working with one or more experienced lawyers during the first few years out of law schools, as most law graduates realize they lack the skills successfully to open an office of their own. This logic becomes more compelling as the law become more complex, voluminous, and specialized. Yet, in an over-saturated legal market that is not growing, entry-level legal jobs become harder to obtain because it is uneconomical for senior lawyers to hire and train new law graduates beyond a very low replacement rate.

This downward trend has been occurring for nearly 30 years, yet we are only acknowledging it now because we have to deal with its fallout.

INCOMPLETE ABSORPTION OF LAW SCHOOL GRADUATES

When the production of lawyers is higher than the number of lawyers needed to serve the needs of paying clients, the basic principles of supply and demand suggest that lawyer incomes will, as a result, trend downward over time. Yet, declining lawyer incomes is not the only predictable effect that flows from an oversupply of law school graduates. Faced with a traditional legal economy that cannot absorb the full number of law graduates, some sizeable portion are going to seek and obtain entry-level employment outside the legal field.

I refer to this possibility as "incomplete absorption." The incomplete absorption of law graduates is likely the primary driver behind the growth of "JD-Advantage"

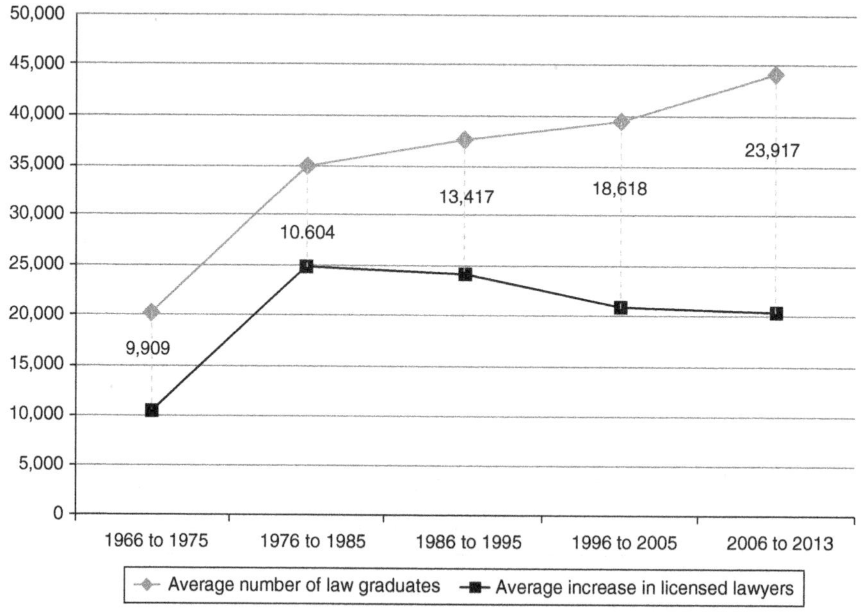

FIGURE 12.4. Law school graduates versus change in the number of licensed lawyers, 10-year averages.

Source: Calculated from data obtained from ABA.

jobs, a category of employment that is now formally tracked by the American Bar Association (ABA) and NALP and given full weight as an employment outcome in *U.S. News & World Report* law school rankings methodology. If the incomplete absorption theory is accurate, it will likely be reflected in two trend lines on lawyer demographics. First, the increase in the number of licensed lawyers in the United States will, over time, increasingly lag behind the number of newly minted law school graduates. Second, the licensed bar will become older over time. As shown later, there is clear evidence that both of these trends have been unfolding for several decades.

Figure 12.4 shows the relationship between the increase in total lawyer population and the number of the newly minted law school graduates. After the mid-1980s, the increase in the number of lawyers begins to diverge from the number of law school graduates. This is surprising because the size of the graduating classes in the 1950s and 1960s is the same as the cohort that is, by dint of a 40-year career, most likely to be exiting the legal profession in the 1990s and 2000s. Yet, numerically, graduates of that era represent a relatively small group of lawyers. In the fall of 1952, 1L enrollment at the 124 ABA-accredited law schools was only 13,111. In contrast, by 1992, this figure had increased to 42,793. Ten years later, the figure was 48,433. With so few lawyers exiting the profession and so many students graduating from law school, the

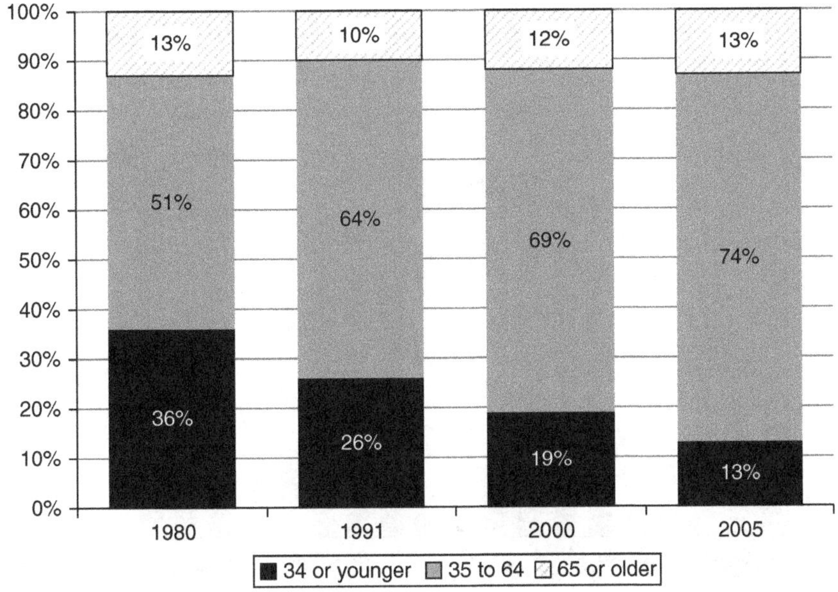

FIGURE 12.5. Breakdown of licensed bar by age.

Source: American Bar Foundation (ABF), Lawyer Statistical Reports.

two trend lines should not be diverging. A simple explanation for this divergence, however, is that fewer and fewer law school graduates are getting absorbed into the licensed legal profession.

The incomplete absorption of younger graduates is further corroborated by Figure 12.5, which breaks down the demographics of licensed bar by age and year. Between 1980 and 2005, the median age of a lawyer in the United States climbed from 39 to 49.[4] This demographic shift is so stark that it is hard to fathom that we legal educators failed to recognize the trend and understand and anticipate the consequences it would have for our students.[5]

4 See ABA, Legal Profession Statistics, Lawyer demographics table – current, online at www.americanbar.org/content/dam/aba/administrative/market_research/lawyer-demographics-tables-2014.authcheckdam.pdf.

5 Indeed, the shifting age demographic is so stark that my first impulse was to question the reliability of the data. In the case of longitudinal data, it is only reliable if the conditions for data collection are stable over time. For many years, Martindale–Hubbell was the definitive legal directory for the legal profession. Its value was its completeness. With the advent of the internet, the utility of Martindale–Hubbell has declined, particularly for younger lawyers. Martindale–Hubbell attempts to track lawyers who did not subscribe to the directory because the universal listing is perceived as key to the Directory's value. To illustrate this point, consider that in 2005, the *Lawyer Statistical Report* (which relies on Martindale–Hubbell data) counted 995,000 lawyers. According to the ABA, the total number of lawyers licensed in the United States (compiled from state bar roles) was 1,105,000, and that almost certainly includes some double counting of lawyers licensed in more than one state. This rough 10% gap between ABA and ABF figure is relatively stable for the sample years that overlap (1980, 1991, 2000, and 2005). While I have no doubt that younger lawyers are becoming harder to hunt down

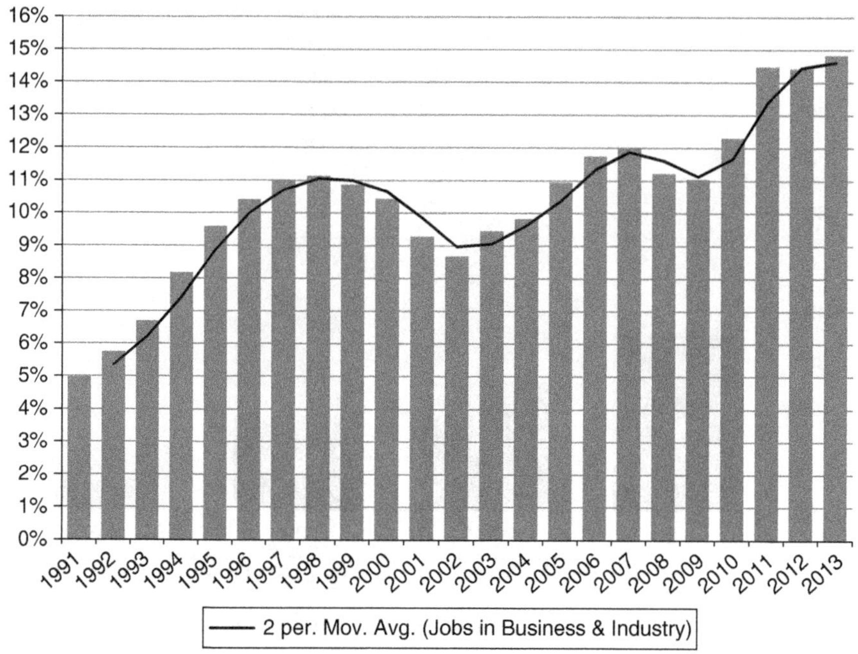

FIGURE 12.6. Percentage of jobs in business and industry, 1991–2013.

Source: NALP.

As the proportion of entry-level jobs in private practice has declined, law graduates have in fact been obtaining employment in other job settings, including those settings outside the legal industry. As shown in Figure 12.6, between 1991 and 2013, the proportion of graduates taking entry-level jobs in business and industry increased from 5.0% to 14.8%. In absolute numbers, the total number of entry-level jobs in this sector more than tripled (from 1,926 to 6,935).

Although jobs in business and industry are growing, a breakdown by industry reveals no clear pattern by business or industry sector. According to data published by NALP, the business and industry category for 2012 includes jobs in accounting (5% of all business and industry employment), banking (13%), insurance (5%), technology / e-commerce (9%), and temporary staffing as contract attorneys (8%). Sixty-one percent of the remaining jobs are distributed in other sectors. Further, only 30% of all business and industry jobs require bar-passage, a proportion that has been stable since NALP began reporting these statistics in 2001 (a low of 26.9% in 2003, a high of 34.2% in 2006 and 2007). The implication is that most of these entry-level jobs are not in-house legal positions where the graduates are working as lawyers.

because of cell phones and home-based offices, it is doubtful that the trend lines reported here are being driven by difficulties in data collection that vary by demographics.

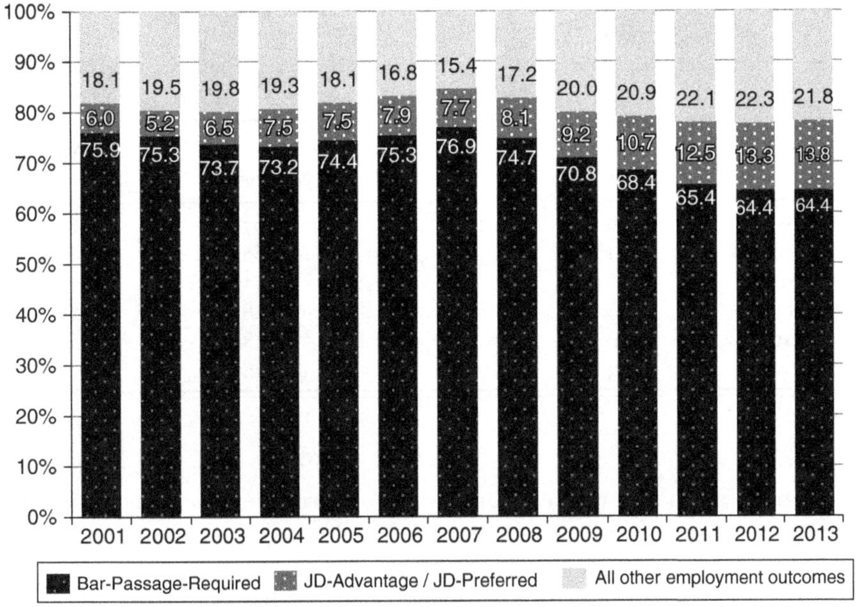

FIGURE 12.7. Breakdown of JD-Advantage versus Bar-Passage-Required jobs, 2001–13.

Sources: Calculated from NALP and ABA data.

The fragmentation of the traditional entry-level legal market can also be evaluated by trend lines on the proportion of law graduates with entry-level jobs that do not require bar-passage. If the broader legal market is softening, the law degree may provide an advantage in obtaining other professional employment; in other cases, limited employment opportunities may cause more law graduates to take jobs with no connection to their legal training. Fortunately, NALP has been tracking these categories since 2001. The trend lines are presented in Figure 12.7. Consistent with an overall softening of the entry-level legal market, the proportion of Bar-Passage-Required jobs has dropped from 75.9% (class of 2001) to 64.4% (class of 2013).[6] During this same period, the proportion of JD-Advantaged jobs has increased from 6.0% to 13.8%.

JD-Advantage jobs are clearly becoming more important as a source of entry-level jobs, yet these jobs are also important for gaining or maintaining institutional prestige. As noted earlier, *U.S. News & World Report* changed its methodology for employment at 9 months to weight equally in its rankings formula Bar-Passage-Required and JD-Advantage jobs.[7] Despite this change, we know very little (a) about

[6] These figures include part-time and short-term employment outcomes, which are higher than the official ABA figures commonly published in the legal press. However, these subcategories are a relatively recent innovation for which there is limited historical data. So trend analysis is limited to part-time and full-time jobs combined.

[7] To receive full weight, both types of jobs must also be full time and long term (at least 1 year in duration). Recently, the measurement period was extended to 10 months to accommodate jurisdictions where summer bar results are reported until the winter of the following year.

TABLE 12.1 *Salary comparisons of JD-Advantage and Bar-Passage-Required jobs, class of 2013.*

	JD-Advantage			Bar-Passage-Required		
Sector	Number	%	Median salary	Number	%	Median salary
Business	2,936	48	$65,200	1,967	8	$65,000
Law firms	1,211	20	$40,000	17,968	71	$100,000
Government	936	15	$51,264	3,117	12	$52,000
Academic	540	9	$49,000	188	1	$48,000
Public Interest	510	8	$46,000	2,088	8	$45,000
Total	6,133	100		25,328	100	

Source: NALP.

the content and range of these career paths, (b) whether law school training is relevant to these careers, and (c) whether JD-Advantage careers are, on balance, a prudent investment of time and money for law school graduates.

Table 12.1 compares JD-Advantage and Bar-Passage-Required jobs for the Class of 2013. Although Business is the largest source of JD-Advantage jobs (48%), the jobs are spread across numerous sectors. Also, it is worth noting that the median entry-level salaries for JD-Advantage and Bar-Passage-Required jobs are nearly identical within each sector. The one very large exception is law firms, where JD-Advantage pays a median of $40,000 versus $100,000 for a Bar-Passage-Required job. Law firms still provide the largest and best-paying jobs for law school graduates. Yet, the economic problem confronting legal education is that there are too few of these jobs for the number of students graduating from law schools. Students from a relatively small number of elite law schools enjoy excellent access to these opportunities. The rest of the law school hierarchy, however, is much more alike than they are different.[8]

CONCLUSION

The trend lines presented in this essay are not complicated but they do convey a hard message. Legal education is producing too many graduates for the traditional legal economy to absorb. The economic consequences are borne by law school graduates who struggle to find a paid position upon graduation that justifies the time and expense of three years of legal education. As a group, law school graduates are highly educated and motivated. So when faced with poor prospects

[8] See, e.g., Chris Zorn, *Similarities in Employment Status: What Do the Data Say?* LAWYER METRICS BLOG, Feb. 24, 2015, online at http://lawyermetrics.com/2015/02/24/similarities-in-employment-status-what-do-the-data-say/.

in the entry-level legal economy, it is not surprising that a large number eventually find paid professional employment at the boundaries of law and other sectors. As this trend continues, the common narrative on what it means to be a law school graduate is bound to change, as many JD-Advantage graduates will blaze new trails. If law schools want to take credit for this eventual reinvention of the law degree, we legal educators need to study the career paths of our graduates and use those findings to retool our curricula in a way that maps onto a national economy and a changing legal industry.

13

Clinical Legal Education and Access to Justice:

Conflicts, Interests, and Evolution

Margaret Drew & Dean Andrew P. Morriss

Margaret Drew and Andrew Morriss argue that the internal politics of legal education has impeded clinical programs from fully meeting their two primary goals: serving unmet legal needs and preparing law students to be lawyers. As clinics evolved and clinicians fought for equal tenure status, clinical programs experienced a shift from service clinics that provided direct legal representation to issue-based and impact litigation clinics. The authors propose greater integration of clinical legal education and the more traditional law school curriculum to achieve the two original purposes of clinics: to teach students the law and skills in a live-client legal practice, and reverse the trend away from service clinics that fill unmet legal needs.

Virtually everyone agrees that there are large unmet needs for legal services among people and organizations that cannot afford them. Similarly, there is widespread agreement that law schools do a substantially less than perfect job of preparing students to practice law, a role that could be enhanced by expanding the curriculum beyond traditional doctrinal courses to focus on more practical training for the practice of law.[1] Even though opinions differ on exactly how much more practical training law schools ought to provide and how they ought to provide it, blending the doctrinal and clinical perspectives offers a potential solution to both problems: establish law clinics that would enable students to gain live client experience solving real legal problems in courts, government agencies, and organizations, while simultaneously providing additional legal services for the poor and enhancing the practical training of new lawyers. Both these goals were part of the initial impetus for

[1] See Rebecca Sandefur & Jeffrey Selbin, *The Clinic Effect*, 16 CLINICAL L. REV. 57 (2009); Rachel J. Littman, *Training Lawyers for the Real World Part One*, N.Y. ST. B.J., September 2010; Rachel J. Littman, *Training Lawyers for the Real World Part Two*, N.Y. ST. B.J., October 2010; Lauren Carasik, *Renaissance or Retrenchment: Legal Education at A Crossroads*, 44 IND. L. REV. 735 (2011); Mitchell D. Hiatt, *Why the American Bar Association Should Require Law Schools to Increase and Improve Law Students' Practical Skills Training*, 45 CREIGHTON L. REV. 869 (2012).

establishing law school clinics in the late 1960s, when clinical education became the reform *du jour.*[2]

While law school clinics have become an almost universal part of law school course offerings, they have not fulfilled their initial promise to change the face of legal education by making it noticeably more practice-oriented, a result of law schools' separation of clinical training from the rest of the law school curriculum. Rather than incorporating clinical training into a coherent overall curriculum, law schools have largely minimized the effect of clinical education on non-clinical training. As a result, the impact of clinical legal education on legal education generally has been muted. And although clinics have provided many American law students with an opportunity for some practical training while in school, they are unable to serve more than a relatively small portion of the poor's unmet legal needs.[3] In part, this is because there are relatively few clinics relative to the size of the unmet need – even if every law student enrolled in a clinic focused on individual client needs, significant needs would remain unmet. It is also due to the balance clinics must strike between the demands of their educational mission and their ability to serve clients. Since their first priority is to teach legal skills, clinics must serve fewer clients than they might if they were focused on the efficient delivery of services. But clinics are not meeting their full potential in this regard because the limited capacity to serve unmet legal needs is exacerbated by the internal politics of legal education.

Our thesis is that there are three primary tensions within the law schools that affected how clinics and experiential legal education more generally evolved. First, clinics have been burdened with serving two masters: they are educational institutions, with a responsibility to focus on students' development as lawyers; at the same time they are expected to help meet unmet legal needs for lower income and vulnerable populations. These roles often conflict, and we argue, the conflicts have grown more frequent as clinical legal education evolved, both with respect to the volume of cases and the type of cases accepted into clinics. Second, the "fit" of clinics within legal education creates its own tensions between clinical and non-clinical faculty. Differences in compensation, status, scholarship demands, and teaching responsibilities as well as the often-physical separation between clinics and the rest of a law school create additional tensions that can interfere with both missions. Third, the current crisis in legal education exacerbates these tensions

[2] Peter A. Joy, *The Ethics of Law School Clinic Students as Student-Lawyers*, 45 S. TEX. L. REV. 815, 821 (2004).

[3] Jane H. Aiken & Stephen Wizner, *Teaching and Doing: The Role of Law School Clinics in Enhancing Access to Justice*, 73 FORDHAM L. Rev 997–101 (2004) ("the educational focus of clinical courses, and the many other claims on the time of clinical teachers and clinic students, make it unrealistic to expect law schools to play a significant role in addressing the access to justice problem"). See also, www.lsc.gov/sites/default/files/LSC/pdfs/documenting_the_justice_gap_in_america_2009.pdf at 11, (documenting the number of individuals whom legal service organizations could not serve due to the organizations' limited resources).

because clinics are – despite the generally lower pay for clinical faculty relative to doctrinal faculty – more expensive on a per student-credit-hour basis than doctrinal courses. At the same time, student and employer demand for "practical" training has increased.

EVOLUTION OF CLINICAL LEGAL EDUCATION

As Brian Tamanaha notes, "law schools are run *for* law professors."[4] As a result, the evolution of clinical legal education within law schools must be explained by examining the interests and behavior of law school faculties. In this section we focus on faculty (both clinical and doctrinal) interests to examine this evolution with the goal of predicting how clinics' roles may evolve in the future and the implications of that future evolution for meeting the legal needs of the poor.

The Emergence of Clinics

Efforts to provide practical training through clinical education have a long history. The earliest clinics were typically volunteer law offices or opportunities for students to earn academic credit while working in legal aid offices.[5] At least as early as the Carnegie Foundation for the Advancement of Teaching's 1921 report on legal education, there have been calls for expanding clinical legal education to enhance skills training.[6] The initial efforts to add practical elements through supervised practice were modest, with the first full-fledged in-house clinical program established at Duke in 1931.[7] Efforts to make more substantial changes were largely rejected. Only a handful of other law schools developed clinics over the next few decades.

In general, from the early twentieth century, using the American Bar Association (ABA) and the American Association of Law Schools (AALS) to enforce the rules, legal elites pushed law schools toward an academic model focused on scholarship and theory and away from "practical" training.[8] This evolution suited bar elites (concerned that the "wrong" sort of people, e.g., immigrants and blacks, were becoming lawyers) and helped keep lawyers' incomes high by restricting competition.[9] It also suited law faculty who were able to distinguish themselves as

4 Brian Z. Tamanaha, FAILING LAW SCHOOLS 8 (2012) (emphasis in original).

5 Joy, supra note 2, at 818.

6 Alfred Zantzinger Reed, Training for the Public Profession of the Law (1921).

7 Joy, supra note 2, at 820.

8 See Olufunmilayo Arewa, Andrew P. Morriss & William Henderson, *Enduring Hierarchies in American Legal Education*, 89 INDIANA L. J., 946–56 (2014).

9 Harry First, *Competition in the Legal Education Industry (I)*, 53 N.Y.U. L. REV. 311, 332 (1978) ("Predicted anticompetitive conduct, organized by the AALS, has been rampant for more than seventy years. Finally, restrictions on output, lack of innovation, and uniformity – again predicted by applying our economic model to legal education – have successfully been sought"); Harry First, *Competition in*

"elite" by separating from practical study and teaching.[10] This also meant that legal education did not focus on the immediate legal needs of the poor but rather on what were perceived as more high-status areas of legal thought.[11] Thus the structure of legal education exacerbated the problem of access to the legal system for the poor by restricting competition in education that might have led to lower-cost education and by restricting the number of lawyers and so increasing the costs of legal services.

Despite periodic calls for greater practical training over the next few decades, little changed in legal education until the late 1960s. Only just over a quarter of ABA-accredited law schools (35 of 126) had clinics in the late 1950s, for example.[12] As late as 1967, "clinical legal education barely existed."[13]

Clinics expanded into the mainstream of American legal education only after "Ford Foundation funding fueled the widespread expansion of in-house clinical programs" in law schools nationwide[14] and, in particular, began "to pour cash into proposals to establish clinical programs submitted by elite law schools filled with bored students demanding greater relevance."[15] In addition, student demands for more practice-oriented and more "relevant" courses grew in the late 1960s, pushing

the Legal Education Industry (II), 53 N.Y.U. L. REV. 1049, 1072–73 (1979) (hereinafter First, Competition II); Robert Stevens, LAW SCHOOL: LEGAL EDUCATION IN AMERICA FROM THE 1850S TO THE 1980S, (The Lawbook Exchange, Ltd. reprint 2001, original pub. 1983) at 175 (quoting Dean Edward Lee of the then-unaccredited John Marshall Law School in Chicago in 1924 that the cooperative relationship between the ABA and AALS was the product of a "group of educational racketeers"); George B. Shepherd, *No African-American Lawyers Allowed: The Inefficient Racism of the ABA's Accreditation of Law Schools*, 53 J. LEGAL EDUC. 103, 134 (2003) ("By imposing high costs, the system has closed the legal profession to most people with lower incomes. Because black families have lower incomes and less wealth than most other groups, the high entry price that the ABA imposes is a filter, like the academic accreditation requirements, for eliminating blacks from the legal profession"); Robert Stevens, *The Nature of a Learned Profession*, 34 J. LEGAL EDUC. 577, 583 (1984) ("The organized bar fell down in the past because some members of the ABA and many State bars used an extended period of education not to produce a broadly based, technically competent, ethical, socially responsible bar, but rather as an opportunity to ensure the maintenance of the Anglo-Saxon male hierarchy").

10 Arewa et al., supra note 8, at 957–62.

11 Of course, the poor sometimes have need for constitutional lawyers. See, e.g., *Brown v. Bd. of Educ.*, 347 U.S. 483, 495 (1954); *Gideon v. Wainwright*, 372 U.S. 335, 342 (1963); *Goldberg v. Kelly*, 397 U.S. 254 (1970). But they also have vast needs for lawyers to handle more prosaic matters dealing with landlord–tenant issues, criminal law, marital law, bankruptcy, etc. At least some of the time, turning these needs into constitutional issues is less productive than focusing on the immediate problem (although some of the time the reverse is also true). Consider *State v. Shack*, 277 A.2d 369 (N.J. 1971), in which a legal services program litigated a case to the New Jersey Supreme Court against opponents who did not even bother to appear. The resulting precedent, although appearing in casebooks, has had almost no impact on the development of the law. (It is rarely cited and seems not have been followed by any court.) See Andrew P. Morriss, *Review of Jesse Dukeminier & James E. Krier, Property (4th Ed. 1998)*, 22 SEATTLE U. L. REV. 997, 1003–1005 (1999) (describing *State v. Shack's* irrelevance to law).

12 Peter A. Joy & Robert R. Kuehn, *The Evolution of ABA Standards for Clinical Faculty*, 75 TENN. L. REV. 183, 187 (2008).

13 Laura Kalman, Yale Law School and the Sixties: Revolt and Reverberations 28 (2005).

14 Joy, supra note 2, at 821.

15 Kalman, supra note 13, at 28.

schools to seek to find ways to satisfy that demand.[16] By 1978 there were over 100 clinics at the 167 ABA-accredited law schools.[17] The ABA's development of a Model Student Practice Rule in 1969 also helped prompt states to adopt such rules,[18] making clinics easier to establish within law schools. By end of 1970s, thirty states had adopted student practice rules.[19] U.S. Department of Education (DOE) funding replaced Ford Foundation money and continued to fuel expansion of clinics until 1997.[20]

Clinical education's success in the legal academy was thus primarily the result of the combination of student demand for greater practice relevance and the appearance of outside funding. It was not the result of doctrinal faculties' desires to change what they did in the classroom or administrative response to ABA and other criticism and recommendations. Indeed, the primary trends in legal education outside of clinics have been a shift toward more theoretical scholarship and teaching, through "law and ..." courses and writing.[21] As a result, clinical education represented something added on to the existing curriculum, not a reshaping of how law is taught. (Whether it should be or not is, of course, a separate question.)

The Conflict Over Status

Although law schools generally welcomed the infusion of Ford Foundation and DOE funds, and the clinics purchased with them, clinics' place in law schools and even the methodology of clinical teaching was "unsettled" at first.[22] Skills training – "the most commonly-cited educational purpose" of clinics— [23] was (and remains) associated with low prestige in the legal academy.[24] This is not surprising in light of the larger evolution of the legal academy, which had an increasing focus on legal

[16] *Id.*, at 80, 152, & 360.

[17] Joy & Kuehn, supra note 12, at 187; James P. White, *Law School Enrollment Continues to Level*, 66 A.B.A. J. 724, 724 (1980) (In the fall of 1978, 121,606 students were registered at the 167 ABA-approved law schools).

[18] Joy, supra note 2, at 821–22.

[19] Suzanne Valdez Carey, *An Essay on the Evolution of Clinical Legal Education and Its Impact on Student Trial Practice*, 51 U. Kan. L. Rev. 509, 516 (2003).

[20] Joy & Kuehn, supra note 12, at 188.

[21] See Law Schools and Professional Education: Report and Recommendation of the Special Committee for a Study of Legal Education of the American Bar Association 78, n. 191 (1980) (noting that as early as the mid-1960s, "professors at high resource schools tended to support a theoretical orientation to law ..."). See also Richard A. Posner, *The Decline of Law as an Autonomous Discipline: 1962–1987*, 100 Harv. L. Rev. 761 (1987); George L. Priest, *The Growth of Interdisciplinary Research and the Industrial Structure of the Production of Legal Ideas: A Reply to Judge Edwards*, 91 Mich. L. Rev. 1929 (1993); Graham C. Lilly, *Law Schools Without Lawyers? Winds of Change in Legal Education*, 81 Va. L. Rev. 1421 (1995); Stephen M. Feldman, *The Transformation of an Academic Discipline: Law Professors in the Past and Future (or Toy Story Too)*, 54 J. Legal Educ. 471 (2004).

[22] Carey, supra note 19, at 517.

[23] *Id.*, at 517–18.

[24] Rose Voyvodic & Mary Medcalf, *Advancing Social Justice through an Interdisciplinary Approach to Clinical Legal Education: The Case of Legal Assistance of Windsor*, 14 Wash. U. J. L. & Pol'y 101, 106

scholarship of a more theoretical and interdisciplinary nature at the expense of doctrinal work.[25] Within the established hierarchy of legal education, the schools at the top were those whose non-clinical faculty had begun to focus more on theoretical scholarship and less on doctrinal writing.[26] The parallel expansion of "case" books into "cases and materials" books meant classrooms were also shifting away from doctrinal focus and into broader analyses of the law.[27] Thus, the expansion of clinics came at the time when law schools were increasingly turning away from a doctrinal focus. Indeed, the rising student demand for "practical" skills that helped expand clinics may have been partially a result of this same shift, as students who wanted to learn to be lawyers – rather than professors – were getting less of what they sought in "regular" classrooms.

Clinical faculty were quick to identify the need for "security . . . and prestige" to commensurate with their doctrinal colleagues as an important concern, with the issue raised in some of the early clinical faculty meetings.[28] The ABA addressed the status issue for the first time in 1979 in its Crampton Report, in which it pushed for expanding clinical education.[29] Similar reports from other ABA groups and joint ABA–AALS reviews soon followed.[30] The ABA briefly adopted an interpretation of its standard on tenure that included clinical faculty in 1980, but reversed course quickly after "a negative reaction from some law schools."[31] Clinical faculty in turn reacted negatively to the ABA's reversal. For example, the director of American University's clinical program argued that

(2004) ("within legal education, there is a sense of 'academic illegitimacy' associated with clinical legal education when it is perceived as 'skills training,' and therefore lacking in academic rigor").

25 See Tom Ginsburg & Thomas J. Miles, *Empiricism and the Rising Incidence of Coauthorship in Law*, 2011 U. Ill. L. Rev. 1785, 1795 (2011) (noting that "[m]ore and more entry-level [legal teaching] candidates have PhDs in social sciences like economics or political science"); Stephen M. Feldman, *The Transformation of an Academic Discipline: Law Professors in the Past and Future (or Toy Story Too)*, 54 J. Legal Educ. 471 (2004); Richard A. Posner, *The Decline of Law as an Autonomous Discipline: 1962–1987*, 100 Harv. L. Rev. 761(1987); Richard A. Posner, *The Present Situation in Legal Scholarship*, 90 Yale L.J. 1113 (1981); Graham C. Lilly, *Law Schools Without Lawyers? Winds of Change in Legal Education*, 81 Va. L. Rev. 1421 (1995); George L. Priest, *The Growth of Interdisciplinary Research and the Industrial Structure of the Production of Legal Ideas: A Reply to Judge Edwards*, 91 Mich. L. Rev. 1929 (1993); William M. Landes & Richard A. Posner, *Influence of Economics on Law: A Quantitative Study*, 36 J.L. & Econ. 385 (1993); Charles W. Collier, *Interdisciplinary Legal Scholarship in Search of a Paradigm*, 42 Duke L.J. 840 (1993).

26 Arewa et al., supra note 8, at 969.

27 Margaret Martin Barry, Jon C. Dubin & Peter Joy, *Clinical Education for The Millennium: The Third Wave*, 7 Clinical L. Rev. 1, 40 (2000).

28 Joy & Kuehn, supra note 12, at 189.

29 Section of Legal Educ. and Admissions to the Bar, Am. Bar Ass'n, Report and Recommendations of the Task Force on Lawyer Competency: The Role of the Law Schools (1979).

30 Joy & Kuehn, supra note 12, at 191

31 *Id.*, supra note 12, at 195 (quoting Roy Stuckey, A Short History of Standard 405(e), at 1 (Apr. 1994) (unpublished manuscript)).

> law schools treat clinicians with something approaching disdain ... [T]he law schools withhold the symbols and perquisites of the profession from us. They deny us promotions and titles. They deny us voting rights and salaries of other faculty members.[32]

The controversy dragged on through the 1980s, with the ABA eventually abandoning a proposed requirement that law schools "shall" provide status equivalent to tenure to clinical faculty, weakening the standard to merely state that they "should" do so.[33]

Despite the ongoing conflict over clinical faculty status, clinics got a further boost with the "MacCrate Report"[34] in 1992, in which the bar (once again) criticized law schools for failing to sufficiently train new graduates, giving schools a reason to place a renewed emphasis on clinical opportunities,[35] as well as the addition of simulation and other courses designed to provide practical skills. Responding to the concerns identified in the MacCrate Report, the ABA amended its accreditation standards to require "live-client or other real life practice experiences" in 1996[36] and, at the same time, clinicians succeeded in changing the standard to require tenure or its equivalent and equal status for clinical faculty,[37] giving clinics additional legitimacy within law schools. Opposition to equivalent status for clinical faculty has continued, however, spearheaded by the Association of Law Deans of America.[38] One divide in the debate was over the purpose of tenure rights granted to doctrinal faculty and how clinicians' roles did or did not fit within a similar model. The failure of many doctrinal faculty to treat clinicians' concerns as valid exacerbated the tension between the two groups. The problem has continued to fester, with the 2007 Carnegie Foundation for the Advancement of Teaching report on legal education emphasizing both the need for clinical education and the problem that having such courses taught by faculty "that has lower academic status" made such courses appear to be "of secondary intellectual value and importance."[39]

This short history of clinical education's position in the academy reveals as a consistent theme the clinical faculty's struggle for status, prestige, and job security within the legal academy. Whether one views this struggle as one by a marginalized group for equality or as rent-seeking, or some of both, the struggle is a central conflict that has consumed considerable time and effort over the last forty years. We argue that one response to this conflict was a shift by clinicians away from lower-status

32 Beverly T. Watkins, *Teachers of Clinical Law Seek Recognition, Better Treatment*, CHRON. HIGHER EDUC., Jan. 19, 1983, at 14.

33 This is described in great detail in Joy & Kuehn, supra note 12, at 197–206.

34 The "MacCrate Report" is formally the American Bar Association, Section of Legal Education and Admissions to the Bar, *Report of the Task Force on Law Schools and the Profession: Narrowing the Gap* (July 1992).

35 Carey, supra note 19, at 529 ("The contemporary call to provide clinical opportunities for students is primarily linked to the 1992 McCrate Report").

36 ABA Standard 302(c)(2).

37 Id. 405(c). See also Joy & Kuehn, supra note 12, at 210–13.

38 See Joy & Kuehn, supra note 12, at 213–23 (detailed description of dispute).

39 William M. Sullivan et al., Educating Lawyers: Preparation for the Profession of Law 88 (2007).

service clinics and toward broader law reform and impact clinics that advance more theoretical training. This shift advanced the search for status in two ways. First, "[s]ervice-modeled clinics ... usually involve the litigation of routine cases in areas such as family law, landlord-tenant law, public benefits law, and consumer law."[40] These are less prestigious areas of legal scholarship and legal practice (at least in the view of most law faculty). Shifting into law reform work allows clinicians to focus on higher-prestige areas of the law.[41] The shift also relieves clinicians of the emotional stress that continuous exposure to the neediest clients can bring. Second, some social critics argued for "political lawyering" in the form of impact litigation as a more appropriate role for clinics.[42] For example, one clinician described environmental law clinics' legal reform efforts as "lawsuits filed to protect the sanctity of the environment or to protect people and animals from the adverse effects of environmental abuse."[43] Others argue that global initiatives are an important avenue of expanding access to justice regimes. Regardless of the merits of such an educational mission – and it certainly seems like a different one from that embodied in the

[40] Carey, supra note 19, at 530.

[41] For example, see Harvard's Health Law and Policy Clinic where students "will participate in a broad range of national and state law and policy initiatives aimed at increasing access to quality, comprehensive health care for poor and low-income individuals and families – especially those living with chronic medical conditions"; or one-time New York University's Constitutional Transitions Clinic and Colloquium where the "mission is to support sustainable democratic change by providing comparative knowledge, and assisting in democratic reform, and influencing policies and politics" in the Middle East; and the many policy and legislative advocacy clinics at schools such University of California, Berkeley, NYU, University of Pennsylvania, Loyola, and the University of Kansas.

[42] Peter Margulies, 3 MICH J. GENDER & L. 493 (1996); Voyvodic & Medcalf, supra note 24, at 108–109 ("[C]linical legal education, so history reveals, neither necessarily nor naturally facilitates transformative practice. In practice, clinical legal education has often been (and continues to be) permeated by the same vision of law and lawyering that informs classroom instruction. Indeed, many authors have critiqued law school clinics for their failure to reflect critically about justice or about practice norms, and for the control and manipulation to which they routinely subject clients."); id. at 106, 108 ("While the goal of integrating social values into legal education has long been central to the clinical legal education movement, this aspect of legal education has also been critically examined (and found wanting) in respect of legal education's ability to effectively advance a social justice agenda.") Proponents of impact clinics argued that service work was insufficiently "transformative," helped to perpetuate idealized notions of fairness that fail to accord with the realities of poverty and discrimination," and failed to adequately politicize the law. If students were to learn "to appreciate the context in which the [client's] problems arise; this requires an understanding of the social realities in which clients live." Voyvodic & Medcalf, supra note 24, at 128. One individual's "understanding of social realities" is another's ideological indoctrination, of course, and the introduction of such efforts into clinics created at least a perception that clinics had a definite political view. As a result of this criticism, "a faction of clinics has gone from representing individual clients in conventional types of cases to engaging in mass litigation efforts where legal and societal reform are the primary goals". Carey, supra note 19, at 531. Clinicians can then use clinics as a vehicle for "numerous possibilities for advancing a social justice agenda in both professional education and practice." *Id.*., at 101. In these clinics, students would receive "exposure to a social justice mission within a guided practice setting" which will provide them "not only with a key linkage between their legal education and their practice competence, but also with the intellectual foundation for a long-term engagement with the advancement of social justice." Id., at 114.

[43] Carey, supra note 19, at 536.

periodic calls for greater skills training evidenced in the MacCrate Report and the Carnegie Foundation report – such a mission is different in type from the focus of service clinics on "help[ing] ordinary people with their common legal problems such as divorces and other family law disputes, consumer and immigration issues, landlord/tenant matters, and bankruptcies."[44] It is also a mission with higher status within the academy than assisting individuals in sorting out a child support problem, addressing a misdemeanor charge, or solving a dispute with a landlord.

Students learn from both these types of experiences, although they may be learning different lessons. Students who practice in controversial areas of law are introduced to broader forces that might oppose legal actions. Students can explore what positions might be legally weak and assess which clients are likely to follow through with protracted litigation. The student then is provided a vehicle for assessing what may be theoretically ideal but impractical remedies while encouraging the client to consider at what point the client wishes to settle. Further, these cases can be useful for teaching students negotiating strategy in a context where the client may be merely symbolic.

More recently, clinics have added a new focus beyond traditional social change-oriented activities. A recent development in clinical education is the creation of transactional clinics. For example, a business clinic at George Washington University serves "clients that are best described as 'microbusinesses' employing from one to five persons with less than $5,000 in start-up capital."[45] Similarly, the University of Pennsylvania's Small Business Clinic's mission is to both "educate students through practice so that they may acquire the skills and ethical consciousness necessary to become highly competent transactional law practitioners, and ... to provide legal services to small businesses and nonprofit organizations that cannot afford to purchase these services in the commercial market."[46] Such work fits readily into the service model while offering a chance to deliver services in higher prestige areas of the law and without the same political overtones that disturb some critics of issue clinics. Transactional clinics also acknowledge the needs and interests of students who are not drawn to more traditional litigation clinics and provide an avenue of skills training in a broader range of areas.

Clinics of all sorts provide necessary opportunities to teach students to sort through ethical issues and strategic planning. Many clinicians we know view themselves as teachers first and practitioners second,[47] and so view doctrinal faculties as their peers rather than the members of the broader legal community (even if the doctrinal faculty do not always acknowledge this). For people primarily

[44] Carey, supra note 19, at 530–32.

[45] Eric J. Gouvin, *Learning Business Law by Doing It*, Bus. L. Today (Sept./Oct. 2004), at 53, 55.

[46] Dina Schlossberg, *An Examination of Transactional Law Clinics and Interdisciplinary Education*, 11 Wash. U. J. L. & Pol'y 195, 195 (2003).

[47] This is a potential distinction between clinical faculty and externship supervisors, although externship supervisors may also see themselves as having a broader role.

identifying themselves as teachers, the goals of clinical education development centers on defining teaching goals.

If the clinicians or the law schools incorporate service to the poor as part of clinical education,[48] the school may benefit from providing a needed community service. For example, the University of Alabama clinic played an important role in post-tornado relief by quickly responding to the legal needs created by the disaster that struck Tuscaloosa and other parts of Alabama in April 2011.[49] Incorporation of the law school into the local community becomes secondary, if not lost entirely with many non-service clinics. For example, in 2001 students from the International Human Rights Law Clinic at American University advised the Framework Convention Alliance (FCA), a coalition of non-governmental organizations involved in negotiations on the Framework Convention on Tobacco Control (FCTC), on appropriate enforcement mechanisms for the treaty. Clinic students conducted extensive research and drafted detailed recommendations and proposed language regarding reporting obligations, monitoring requirements, and dispute settlement procedures under the FCTC. In November 2001 the students traveled to Geneva to brief the FCA during the third round of FCTC negotiations.[50]

While this no doubt was a worthwhile and exciting endeavor for the students, there was little benefit to the local DC community in which the clinics are located.[51] Whether or not the law school desires to benefit the local community, and engender the goodwill that typically follows, is something faculty should consider when approving new clinics. Schools of means may pay less attention to this factor since they have sufficient resources to fund both service and interest clinics. Of course, this is not to say that alliance with doctrinal faculty concepts of intellectually valid work is the only motivation for interest clinics. After years of supervising students in service clinics, clinicians may become weary of doing the same types of cases over and over or decide that their political preferences require a more systemic assault on existing legal rules.

Our conclusion from this brief review of the development of clinical legal education is that clinicians' search for equivalent status and/or rents within the academy played an important role in the shift to diversify away from the service clinic model. Particularly as legal scholarship has grown more interdisciplinary and theoretical, doctrinal scholarship has declined in value, and JD/PhDs (and just plain

48 State student practice rules require that students represent those who could not otherwise afford legal services. See, for example, Massachusetts Supreme Court Rule 3:03 Legal Assistance to the Commonwealth and to Indigent Criminal Defendants, and to Indigent Parties in Civil Proceedings.

49 See Alabama Law Wins 2012 CLEA Award for Excellence in a Public Interest Project (May 1, 2012) available at www.law.ua.edu/blog/news/alabama-law-wins-2012-clea-award-for-excellence-in-a-public-interest-project/ (describing clinic's response).

50 Richard J. Wilson et al., *The Work of the International Human Rights Law Clinic at American University: 12 Years of Operation*, (May 2002), available at www.wcl.american.edu/clinical/annual_2002.pdf?rd=1.

51 American University has sustained its service clinics while expanding into interest clinics. Service clinics include domestic violence, tax, and civil litigation. Available a www.wcl.american.edu/registrar/clinics.cfm.

PhDs) have grown in number in the legal academy, the status gap between practitioners within law schools and "regular" faculty has grown, intensifying pressure to close the gap by awarding tenure and elevating clinical faculty's role in governance. Resolving those issues is well beyond the scope of this chapter; the crucial point is that these forces are likely to continue to push clinics away from what is perceived as "low-status" service work even if clinicians achieve formal equality in tenure and governance. The appearance of transactional clinics in higher-prestige areas may offer a partial means of alleviating such pressures while still providing service opportunities, but will not be sufficient to resolve the underlying tension.

Stress in the Market for Legal Education

One way to understand legal education is as a business that must generate sufficient revenue to cover its costs.[52] Indeed, law schools must often do more than cover their costs – for many universities, law schools have been major sources of revenue a long time. The adoption of the case method made law schools "the university cash cow[s]"[53] by allowing schools to teach large numbers of students with minimal capital investment in classrooms and relatively few faculty. Compared to sciences that required expensive laboratories or humanities or social sciences, where large classes were hard to sustain in the face of student preferences for smaller classes, law schools were able to limit competition by restricting the number of schools and so play the role of an oligopolist[54] and extract economic rents from their students both in the form of tuition and improved faculty working conditions derived from pedagogically unsound teaching methods (e.g., large classes, virtually no feedback during the semester, grades based on single examinations). This played a major role in shaping U.S. legal education.[55]

For the most part, American law schools are staffed by doctrinal subject, full-time faculty with relatively light teaching loads (compared to other sectors of higher education) who place great emphasis on faculty scholarship for a professional school.[56] Full-time study by students dominates the field. All this redounds to the

[52] See Richard A. Matasar, *The Two Professionalisms of Legal Education*, 15 Notre Dame J. L. Ethics & Pub. Pol'y 99, 103 (2001) (business and legal education "are inextricably linked. Simply put: [the dean's] job is running a business").

[53] Kalman, supra note 13, at 24.

[54] Evidence of the oligopoly status of American law schools is the remarkable lack of diversity of approaches among law schools. See, e.g., Lawrence C. Foster, *The Impact of the Close Relationship between American Law Schools and the Practicing Bar*, 51 J. Legal Edu. 346, 347 (2001) ("The first-year curriculum is nearly identical at all American law schools: legal writing and research, contract law, property law, criminal law, torts, and civil procedure, with some law schools also introducing aspects of constitutional law. In the second and third year, most courses are elective"). On the oligopolistic nature of law schools, see First, Competition (I) and Competition (II), supra note 9.

[55] Tamanaha, supra note 4, at 39–53; Arewa et al., supra note 8, at 946–68.

[56] Marin Roger Scordato, *The Dualist Model of Legal Teaching and Scholarship*, 40 Am. U. L. Rev. 367, 373 (1990) ("It is currently the common wisdom that tenure and promotion are attainable at most law

benefit of the faculty. As Deborah Rhode noted, "In a *New York Times Magazine* profile, one faculty member put the point bluntly: whatever its other faults, 'law school works pretty well for us.'"

Law school administrations and law faculties thus share considerable economic rents derived from the potent combination of a stranglehold on admission to the bar through the requirement of graduation from an ABA-accredited law school as a condition of taking the bar in many states;[57] inexpensive and non-capital-intensive methods of instruction; and control of the ABA-accreditation process by legal education insiders.[58]

The faculty and administration's enjoyment of these rents are challenged by clinicians and clinical programs in two ways. On a per student basis, clinics are costly to operate, much costlier than large section courses.[59] Supervising students practicing law takes more attention per student than asking questions in a classroom: even a "small" section in a doctrinal course at most law schools exceeds the size of a clinic. Expanding clinics thus threatens to introduce a thirsty new competitor for the stream of milk from the "cash cow."

Second, as the mainstream of the legal academy becomes more theoretical and interdisciplinary, many clinics remained largely practical (which was, after all, an important original point of clinical education) and focused in many cases on non-prestigious areas of the law such as consumer protection, landlord–tenant, and family law. Clinicians' efforts to gain a larger share of the economic rents generated by the larger enterprise are thus resisted by doctrinal faculty, who may hold the same disdain for direct service clinical practice areas as they have for many practicing lawyers.[60]

By conforming to the expectations of the "regular" faculty and meeting promotion standards that reflect the desires of doctrinal faculty rather than reflect the realities of clinical teaching, they hope to gain a greater share of the benefits of the enterprise. In other words, the key to acceptance by doctrinal faculty is (rightly or wrongly) perceived as the need to "look" more like doctrinal faculty.[61] How much long-term

schools by faculty who have compiled a record of solid published scholarship coupled with classroom teaching that does not provoke active complaints from students").

57 Herb D. Vest, *Felling the Giant: Breaking the ABA's Stranglehold on Legal Education in America*, 50 J. Legal Edu. 494, 496 (2000) ("In response to the swelling ranks of lawyers and the perceived competition from new schools, the ABA teamed up with the Association of American Law Schools to lobby state legislatures and supreme courts to begin requiring graduation from an ABA-approved law school in order to gain admission to the state bars").

58 Tamanaha, supra note 4, at 12–19.

59 *Id.*, at 59–60; see also, Peter A. Joy, *The Cost of Clinical Legal Education*, 32 *B.C.J.L. & Soc. Just.* 309, 327 (2012) (section on "Comparing Costs before Cutting Them").

60 Amy B. Cohen, *The Dangers of the Ivory Tower: The Obligation of Law Professors to Engage in the Practice of Law*, 50 Loy. L. Rev. 623, 632 (2004) ("One of the most unfortunate collateral effects of the tendency for law professors to identify first and foremost as scholars and academicians and to distance themselves from practicing lawyers is the apparent disdain many professors feel and perhaps even express towards practice and practitioners").

61 This has also led to the development of legal fellowship programs that train relatively inexperienced lawyers to be clinical teachers. Fellows are exposed to clinical pedagogy as well as scholarship.

benefit to students will be sacrificed with this shift remains to be seen. For example, making time for increased scholarship production may require a school to offer fewer clinic slots per clinician, reducing student and client access.[62] While there may be sound business reasons for developing or expanding interest clinics to teach particular skills, to prepare students for large and mid-size firm practice, or to meet student demands as part of a student retention strategy, the economics of which types of clinics will attract students to the law school may ultimately determine the type of clinic offerings.

The demand for greater status, evolving teaching preferences, and job security are colliding with the current economic crisis in legal education, caused by the dramatic drop in applications over the past few years, together with the shrinking job market for law graduates. This puts additional strain on the relationship between clinics and doctrinal education. On the one hand, there is a greater demand for skills-based education to prepare students for a job market in which small firms and solo practice are more likely outcomes. Without the additional training previously provided to some students by large law firms, new graduates are often unable to accomplish even simple legal tasks despite three years of post-graduate education. On the other hand, when the pie is shrinking (or even static), it is harder to resolve conflicts between faculty groups by giving something to both. With some schools facing 20–30% drops in applications or more, and class sizes shrinking in an effort to hold on to existing LSAT and UGPA medians for entering classes, tuition-dependent schools face the prospect of making cuts in programs. From the doctrinal side, clinics may appear an expensive luxury. From the clinical side, subsidizing doctrinal faculty scholarship with low teaching loads that require more hires to cover basic courses also appears like a luxury. The partial integration of clinics into law schools since the 1970s – made possible with few sacrifices by other interest groups within legal education by the rising revenues during the fat years – has not prepared legal education for a thoughtful resolution of this conflict.

The tension that then develops in clinical faculty hiring is whether to favor relatively inexperienced clinicians who may have limited subject matter experience but who are more likely to write articles versus the more experienced practitioner who may bring a greater depth of knowledge and skill to a particular clinic but who may have little interest in scholarship.

62 Tamanaha, supra note 4, at 34 (noting that extending tenure to clinicians "has an effect that is counter to their function: it prompts clinicians to engage in scholarship, traditionally the sine qua non of tenure. This is odd in several ways. The nature of the position is to train lawyers in a practice context-and clinicians are hired based on criteria tied to this function, primarily including substantial practice experience. Clinicians can be scholars, of course, but that is not what they are mainly selected for, in contrast to doctrinal faculty, for whom scholarly potential is the all-determining criterion for obtaining a position. Clinicians relentlessly criticize the emphasis on scholarship in law schools, yet now they hanker to do it themselves in order to qualify for tenure. To produce enough high-quality scholarship to earn tenure, furthermore, clinicians must be given time away from the clinics they have been hired to teach, thereby increasing the cost of the clinic-someone else must supervise the cases in their absence").

We suggest that the changes to legal education demanded by the shifting marketplace will be delayed, if not hindered, if decision-making is left to traditional faculty processes. Since preservation of status and/or attainment of status often drive faculty discussions, many law schools will experience ongoing resistance to change, risking further decline in enrollment and student satisfaction. With the demand for experiential learning increasing, law school existence for all but a handful of schools may rest on the ability to change to satisfy market demand. Faculty of all sorts must adjust their agendas to support the best interests of the law school and the needs of students rather than focus on furthering what may be economically unrealistic individual interests.

For access to justice, these pressures are likely to lead to further subordination of what was already a secondary goal of providing underserved communities with legal services. Faced with the extraordinary revenue pressures on many schools, clinics' clients are far behind internal constituencies in law schools in access to law school resources. Even within clinical budgets, serving clients with low-status needs is likely to rank lower than meeting clinicians' desire for greater status and job security. Indeed, the economic pressures heighten the demand for job security (although even traditional tenure cannot protect faculty against cuts for economic reasons). Economics might drive resource sharing, status, and job security in an effort to shift law school culture to one that supports student needs.

Legal education is at a crossroads. As William Henderson, Brian Tamanaha, and others have described, the industry is facing a dramatic decline in revenues that threatens the existing model.[63] Change is coming and addressing it will require addressing, and perhaps resolving, the tensions described earlier. Law schools must do a much better job of explaining how they deliver skills that produce employment opportunities whose value exceeds the cost of attending law school. Whatever the explanation turns out to be at particular schools, it surely will involve a greater skills component than legal education has historically included. Standing alone, the current clinic model is an insufficient answer in part because of these tensions. We now turn to an exploration of the current status and role of clinics.

CLINICAL LEGAL EDUCATION TODAY

Peter Joy, associate dean and former director of clinics at the Washington University (St. Louis) School of Law and a thoughtful commentator on clinical legal education, calculates that more than a third of law school graduates take an in-house clinical course during law school, a percentage that has been growing in recent

63 William D. Henderson, A *Blueprint for Change*, 40 PEPPERDINE L. REV. 461 (2013); Tamanaha, supra note 4, at 160–66.

years.[64] While calculations based on the data from recent ABA statistics suggest that this number is likely a bit smaller than one-third, it is still substantial. In addition, clinical slots are unevenly distributed among law schools, giving some students greater opportunities to participate in a clinic than others while providing nearby residents larger clinical programs offering greater access to much-needed legal services. Consequently, residents of some areas are provided greater opportunities to have their legal needs met by a clinical program than residents of areas with relatively fewer clinics.

Moreover, clinics vary considerably from school to school in the type of legal needs they serve. Some clinics concentrate on providing low-income clients with access to basic legal assistance for immigration, taxes, divorces, landlord–tenant disputes, and other individual needs, while other clinics focus on broader litigation designed to produce systemic changes in policy through class action or other representative action suits, legal challenges to policies focused on producing policy changes, or assisting with lobbying or other non-courtroom measures designed to achieve policy changes. In a relatively recent development, a growing number of clinics focus their efforts outside the United States. As noted, students from the International Human Rights Law Clinic at American University advised the Framework Convention Alliance on appropriate enforcement procedures under the Framework Convention on Tobacco Control. In a project that combined individual representation with international advocacy, students at Columbia's Human Rights Clinic drafted briefs and framed oral arguments for presentation of a U.S. domestic violence case heard by the Inter-American Human Rights Commission.[65]

These internationally focused clinics illustrate an important tradeoff between clinical work that focuses on providing legal services to the poor, who might not otherwise have access to representation, and clinic work that does not. To some degree, American clinical legal education has shifted away from clinics doing work for individuals who cannot afford legal services and toward clinics doing work that might be described as long-term social impact work. For the sake of convenience, we will refer to individually oriented clinics providing legal services in traditional civil and criminal cases or transactions as "service clinics" and social impact clinics as "impact clinics." Whatever the merits of this shift, it also limits the ability of clinics to meet unmet legal individual needs of the poor in the United States, although it may increase access internationally.[66]

[64] Peter A. Joy, *The Ethics of Law School Clinic Students as Student-Lawyers*, 45 S. Tex. L. Rev. 815, 817 (2004). Joy's calculations are detailed in note 7 of his article. On the growth in clinic enrollments, see Id at 823–24.

[65] See decision of the Inter-American Council on Human Rights' in *Lenahan (Gonzales) v. United States of America*, Case 12.626, Inter-Am. Comm'n, H.R., Report No. 80/11 (2011).

[66] Defining the parameters of the relevant population is an issue to which relatively little attention has been paid. One of us has argued that a broader conception than national borders is needed in other areas. See Andrew P. Morriss & Roger E. Meiners, *Borders and the Environment*, 39 Envt'l L. 141 (2009).

Let us first consider the extent and distribution of clinic resources nationally – law schools are not distributed in a way to deliver resources to the areas in greatest need. To the extent that the needs of the poor for access to legal services are larger than can be met by clinical programs (as they are), this may not matter to a clinic's design. Any given law clinic is likely to have a sufficient population of low-income individuals to absorb the full capacity of the clinic to provide services. To the extent that clinics are considered an important part of an overall plan to provide access to legal services, however, these disparities may be worth considering in allocating resources to increase clinical resources in underserved jurisdictions. Funding sources concerned primarily with unmet legal needs generally direct funds to areas of the greatest need making rural areas or others with particular underserved populations, such as immigrants, more likely to benefit from government grants. Private grants might be more focused on substantive area of service, such as entrepreneurial or tax clinics. Moreover, justifications for grant-funded clinical programs in terms of unmet legal needs are typically benchmarked with quantitative measures of the services provided, a demand that can work against clinical teaching as will be discussed later. Further, the geographic mismatch between law clinic slots and poverty populations is likely exacerbated by law schools' distribution *within* states. This may place a greater burden on some law schools to support clinics without any outside funding. This is common where the schools are located in areas where legal service organizations may be the primary beneficiaries of government grants. This lack of clinic funding may be relieved where legal service organizations are willing to partner in grant applications but substantial sharing of grant resources in those circumstances may be unrealistic.

In addition to the geographic distribution of clinical slots, the distribution of clinic slots among law schools of different ranks is also relevant. Although the *U.S. News & World Report* rankings of law schools have many imperfections,[67] these rankings nonetheless provide a sorting of law schools into categories that roughly approximate some significant differences. The top 16 ranked schools have remained quite stable (albeit with minor movements) since *U.S. News* began serious efforts at ranking and these schools are clearly distinguished from their competitors in the remainder of the publication's "first tier."[68] Similarly, while there may be quibbles on the margin, there is little doubt that the employment outcomes from a third- or fourth-tier school are generally quite different from those of a first-tier school.

These differences express themselves in clinics in three ways. First, schools with greater numbers of graduates entering directly into solo practice or joining small to medium-sized firms may emphasize skills training at the expense of impact work and

67 See Andrew P. Morriss & William D. Henderson, *Measuring Outcomes: Post-Graduation Measures of Success in the U.S. News & World Report Law School Rankings*, 83 IND. L. J. 791 (2008); William D. Henderson & Andrew P. Morriss, *Student Quality as Measured by LSAT Scores: Migration Patterns in the U.S. News Rankings Era*, 81 IND. L. J. 163 (2006).

68 Henderson & Morriss, supra note 67, at 178.

TABLE 13.1 *Law clinics* 1998/99–2008/09.

	Median clinical slots/ total students (%)		Total clinical slots		Total clinic slots/total students	
U.S. News rank	1998/99	2008/09	1998/99	2008/09	1998/99	2008/09
1–15	15.5	18.3	2,609	3,392	0.19	0.23
16–29	16.3	14.9	2,269	2,345	0.18	0.18
30–50	15.5	21.0	2,040	3,540	0.18	0.23
51–100	10.9	13.9	3,673	6,234	0.12	0.15
Tier 3	9.7	14.7	3,376	3,367	0.13	0.16
Tier 4	8.0	10.6	2,659	3,671	0.11	0.12
All (including unranked schools)	12.6	14.3	17,325	23,108	0.13	0.16

so focus on service clinics. Second, schools with greater prestige may find service work less worthwhile because it is perceived to not carry with it the intellectual pedigree that impact work does. Third, student demand for clinical experiences is likely to be different at top-tier and lower-tier law schools. At the top of the hierarchy, where students are generally more secure that they will end up in the high end of the bimodal distribution of new legal jobs,[69] students may look for experiences that they may be unable to replicate in their post-law school experiences. While relief from the tedium of three years of coursework is a common motivation in seeking a clinical experience, the final units of which they perceive as adding little marginal value, students at the lower end of the law school hierarchy may be more motivated by the need to acquire skills that will enable them to earn a living upon graduation.

Table 13.1 shows the ratio of offered clinic slots to total JD student enrollments for two points in the evolution of clinical education. We chose 1998/99 as a benchmark year for the *U.S. News* era. The 2008/09 figures depict schools before the current admissions crisis appeared. A ratio of 0.33 would indicate that there were sufficient clinic slots for each student to take a clinic. Not all clinic slots offered are filled (the median percentage filled using ABA-reported data is 87%), which summarizes these data for different segments of the law school market. Clinical opportunities are unevenly distributed across the market, with much higher ratios of slots to students at the top and in the lower half of the first tier than elsewhere. Growth has also been uneven, with increases at the top 15 and schools ranked 30–50 dwarfing the modest increments at schools ranked between 16 and 29.

[69] William D. Henderson, *Are We Selling Results or Resumes?: The Underexplored Linkage between Human Resource Strategies and Firm-Specific Capital*, Indiana Legal Studies Research Paper No. 105, available at http://papers.ssrn.com/sol3/papers.cfm?abstract_id=1121238 (2008).

TABLE 13.2 *Change in clinic positions* 1998/99–2008/09.

	Δ Total clinical positions 1998/99–2008/09	Δ Total students 1998/99–2008/09	Median Δ clinical positions/students 1998/99–2008/09 (%)
U.S. News rank 1–15	759	796	3.3
U.S. News rank 16–27	222	256	4.4
U.S. News rank 30–50	992	798	5.3
U.S. News rank 51–100	970	1,952	1.4
U.S. News Tier 3	750	1,199	1.5
U.S. News Tier 4	1,781	7,216	4.8
All (including unranked schools)	5,820	12,217	4.6

Growth has also been substantial in seats in law schools. The substantial growth in fourth-tier schools through 2008 reflects both the increased number of such schools (13 since 1998/99), including Florida Coastal with a total student body of almost 1,400 students in 2008/09, and the expansion of Thomas Cooley in Michigan, which grew by 2,000 total students in the ABA statistics.

The interesting pattern in clinical program growth is in the top tier, where clinics expanded on virtually a one-to-one basis compared to student bodies, increasing the clinic/student ratios, with increases at lower-tier schools not keeping pace with expansions in the student body but still outpacing the 1:3 growth rate necessary to offer each new student a chance at a clinic in the second and third tiers.

The types of clinics offered at schools are quite different. Table 13.3 lists the number of different types of clinics at some schools from each of the top three tiers. The categorization is based on the clinic descriptions on schools' websites; unfortunately these descriptions do not generally include the number of slots in individual clinics, making it impossible to tell whether some clinics are substantially larger than others.

Two features of clinics from this small sample are of interest. First, while issue clinics exist outside the top tier, they are a smaller proportion of clinics in the lower-ranked schools. It thus appears that a greater proportion of clinical legal education resources are being devoted to the provision of access to the legal system at lower ranked schools compared to higher ranked schools. Second, there are a considerable number of issue clinics doing everything from providing "assistance to environmental groups interested in policy reforms" (Yale) to "work[ing] to prevent gentrification on low income neighborhoods" (Harvard) to "travel to Africa to document human rights abuses and strategize human rights initiatives" (Stanford). While the data are insufficient to say exactly how many clinical resources are being devoted to such projects rather than individual service cases, it would appear reasonable to assume

TABLE 13.3 *Sample clinic distribution (2008).*

			Number of clinics			
School	2008 *U.S. News* rank	Clinic slots/ students (%)	Service clinics	Prosecution, small business, government agency clinics	Clients + issue clinics	Issue clinics
Yale	1	88.1	8	3	4	6
Harvard	2	31.4	18	6	2	7
Stanford	2	38.8	3	2	2	3
Geo. Wash.	20	10.1	7	2	1	5
Boston U	21	27.8	2	1	2	1
Emory	22	10.9	1		1	3
Geo. Mason	38	28.7	3	2		1
U Arizona	38	15.0	2	1	1	1
UC Hastings	38	15.9	5	4	2	2
Pepperdine U	59	19.0	3		1	1
Temple U	59	6.8	2	1		
U Kentucky	59	6.3	1			
U Missouri	59	9.7	3	1		
GA State	77	16.5	2			
Penn. St. U	77	42.7	7		2	
Rutgers	77	16.2	2			
Rutgers	77	24.4	4	1	1	3
Santa Clara	77	27.1	1	1	1	1
Stetson U	100	16.1	2	3		
Syracuse U	100	15.8	6	1		
Drake U	T3	27.1	5			1
Franklin Pierce	T3	32.8	5	2		3
Gonzaga	T3	23.9	4	2		1

that one student traveling to Africa to work on human rights issues would likely cost more to support than a considerable number of students handling landlord–tenant disputes in New Haven. Moreover, while preventing "gentrification on" neighborhoods might involve some aspect of service work, it likely results in resources being devoted to issues outside the scope of individual client goals.[70] Of course, resource-rich schools like Yale and Harvard may offer both types of clinics, but presumably

[70] Some of these measures may be valuable in their own right as well. It may be, for example, that New Haven benefits considerably from prevention of gentrification. (More likely, it seems that some residents of New Haven benefit and others do not.) One of the prime motivating forces for New Haven's gentrification is Yale's presence in the community and so using university resources to slow the process might be considered by those opposed to gentrification as an appropriate means of mitigating

TABLE 13.4 *Clinical offerings, all law schools (2013).*

	Service	Issue	Service + issue	Prosecutorial, small business, or gov't agency
Top 16	8.53 (7)	3.65 (3)	0.88 (0)	1.82 (1)
17–50	6.78 (6)	1.52 (1)	0.37 (0)	1.30 (1)
51–100	5.84 (5)	1.29 (1)	1.14 (1)	1.43 (1)
101–143	5.38 (5)	1.58 (1)	1.00 (1)	1.48 (1)
Unranked	4.33 (3)	1.07 (1)	1.00 (1)	1.67 (1)

even they could offer more service-oriented clinics if they funded fewer issue clinics on the margin. Nonetheless, clinical resources are being devoted to programs that, at the least, deemphasize individual client representation in favor of a broader approach to social issues.

More broadly, we examined clinics at all schools by counting those listed on schools' websites in July 2013.[71] Table 13.4 gives the average and median (in parentheses) number of clinics for the various tiers of schools by type.

Not surprisingly, the top tier law schools have both more clinics and more issue clinics. However, issue clinics have expanded into the rest of the law school hierarchy, if in smaller numbers.

We think it is clear that law schools cannot provide enough clinics to solve the problem of access to justice on their own. Nonetheless, at least some commentators believe that law schools do make a meaningful contribution to addressing the legal needs of the poor through clinics, if only because there are so few other resources for the poor. For example, Peter Joy concludes that

> The impact of clinical legal education in providing access to the courts for those unable to afford lawyers has been significant . . . Many in-house clinic student-lawyers, as well as those students certified as student-lawyers in some externship programs, join the mere 5,000 to 6,000 lawyers representing the forty-five million Americans who are so poor that they qualify for civil legal aid.[72]

Even if they are not sufficient, law school clinics seem to be a necessary part of the provision of access to justice for the poor given the overwhelming amount of unmet needs.

This survey suggests several important facts about clinical legal education and its place in the academy.

Yale's impact. See Rhiannonn Bronstein et al., *In Expanding Yale Should Avoid Gentrification*, Yale Daily News (Jan. 28, 2008) available at www.yaledailynews.com/articles/view/23182.

71 Clinics were classified by having a research assistant examine the name and description from the website. While not perfect, we think the broad trends accurately reflect the current state of clinical education.

72 Joy, supra note 2, at 824.

- As law schools expanded, clinics expanded with them. There are more accredited law schools and more law school clinics in those law schools today than there have been at any time since the beginning of ABA accreditation. What remains to be seen is whether the current decline in admissions will lead to fewer slots in the future.
- During the boom, higher-ranked law schools added clinics and clinic slots more rapidly than lower-ranked law schools, with the greatest per-student growth in the top 50.
- The term "clinic" encompasses a wide range of course offerings. There are service-oriented programs aimed at providing direct legal services to individuals unable to afford lawyers, with a goal of generating a caseload on which law students might gain practical training. There are also impact clinics that focus on litigation, treaty negotiation, and other activities designed to address broader social problems while providing law students with opportunities to participate in those forms of lawyering directly or indirectly.
- Service clinics are an important part of the overall solution to access to justice for the poor.
- The reduction in law school applications and class sizes is likely to limit the ability to expand the resources devoted to clinical legal education.

In the next section, we turn to examining the implications of these trends.

CLINICS, LEGAL EDUCATION, AND LEGAL NEEDS

We have sketched a fairly dire picture of the state of legal education. Law school economics, however, might propel the change toward integrating clinical and doctrinal teaching with a force that professional reports have failed to accomplish in large measure. Let us conclude by offering predictions and recommendation for modest reforms that might ameliorate the problems we have identified.

We identified three tensions in clinics' relationship to the rest of legal education: the status conflict between doctrinal and clinical faculty; the resource conflict between teaching and providing legal services; and the economic tension within law schools. The future is uncertain, but these are our predictions for how the resolution of these tensions will affect the ability of law school clinics to provide legal services for underserved sectors of the population while improving respect for the work of both clinicians and other faculty within the law school community.

We predict that for those schools where faculty are willing to place self-interest aside and respond to market demand, clinical faculty will ultimately prevail in their efforts to gain equal status in law schools, obtaining tenure (or its equivalent), higher pay, sabbaticals, a stronger role in governance, and the other perquisites of full-time tenured faculty status. We believe that they will prevail not because their arguments are necessarily strong on the merits but because their arguments are based on an appeal to fairness.[73] As clinical faculty become more valuable to the law school's marketing and student retention, the fairness argument becomes more palatable to the rest of the faculty. In addition, as clinicians become more influential in faculty decision-making, they will become more persuasive in changing tenure criteria to support enhancement of teaching skills as well as writings on clinical pedagogy in addition to more traditional academic writing.[74]

We predict that the trend toward impact clinics will continue and that service clinics will decline in relative and perhaps absolute number, at least in the upper reaches of the law school hierarchy. So long as schools seek the infusion of outside money, clinical opportunities will be limited by those who believe that clinics cannot be supported or justified due to high faculty–student ratios. With enhanced status for clinicians at those schools that favor more interest clinics will come the need to reduce teaching loads to allow more traditional scholarship during the pursuit of tenure, sabbaticals, research leaves, and the like. The cuts will likely come from service clinics that can accept fewer students due to the need for more intensive supervision, rather than the more prestigious impact clinics. As a result, access to justice will be reduced from a combination of three factors. First, the price of status will be greater involvement of doctrinal faculty in selecting and reviewing clinical faculty; this will exert pressure to select clinical faculty with more elite credentials. The elite model of clinics, which is more focused on issue clinics, will thus be transmitted downward in the hierarchy. Second, the pressure for equivalent scholarly production will create an incentive for clinical faculty to find ways to teach in areas that reinforce their scholarly interests, just as doctrinal faculty now frequently teach a seminar in their areas of interest. This will push clinical faculty's teaching in more "big picture" directions, as they strive to write articles that will succeed in the marketplace for prestigious placements. Third, the pressure for placement will push clinicians to write (and so teach) more constitutional law and other subjects that dominate in elite journals rather than focusing on family law, landlord–tenant law, and other fields that have largely vanished from the pages of top law reviews.[75]

73 In our experience, law faculties are collectively astonishingly unable to make absolute judgments and instead often rely heavily on fairness arguments in making decisions on everything from hiring to tenure. Even individuals within the legal academy are often unwilling to make absolute judgments of quality. For example, tenured outside reviewers sometimes decline to review a promotion and tenure candidate's work rather than write a negative evaluation letter.

74 At present, while "clinical tenure" promotion criteria may include service and teaching skills, faculty often overemphasize any criterion for scholarship contribution.

75 One of us discusses this in Olufunmilayo Arewa, William D. Henderson, Peter A. Hook & Andrew P. Morriss, *Subject Matter Trends in Legal Scholarship* (Working paper on file with authors). See also Carissa Alden et al., Trends in Federal Judicial Citations and Law Review Articles, 1 (2007), available at http://graphics8.nytimes.com/packages/pdf/national/20070319_federal_citations.pdf. In a 2007 study, editors of the Cardozo Law Review examined articles published in five of the most cited law reviews (California Law Review, Columbia Law Review, Harvard Law Review, New York University Law Review, and The Yale Law Journal) in 1960, 1980, and 2000. The editors classified the

There is some hope that law schools can play a role in improving access to legal services, should they embrace the changes occurring outside the academy in the market for legal services. As Richard Susskind and William Henderson have both shown, clients' access to the legal system is being dramatically changed by non-traditional legal services providers.[76] Briefly, an entire new industry has sprung up aimed at providing low-cost legal services outside the "bespoke tailor" model of legal services. In one such business model, a small number of lawyers create the raw materials for a business process that automates construction of legal documents through structured interviews.[77] Many of these firms are targeting previously underserved segments of the market for legal services, beginning with the problems of middle-class and poor clients.[78] This model implemented by some law school incubators, as well.[79]

This model offers law school clinics a possible reconciliation of the high-status work they need to maintain clinicians' status within the academy and the demand for high-volume legal work among clients. Students working in traditional service clinics might move on to a project constructing the forms, interviews, and other materials necessary to produce a legal process outsourcing solution to particular community problems. The documentation of the process and scholarly analysis of the issues that inform the solution could provide the clinicians with the raw material for substantive scholarship (admittedly not likely constitutional law) while bolstering a clinic's ability to bring large-scale services to a broader population. Particularly if overall enrollments in law schools continue to decline, we think this may be one approach for expanding access to legal services through clinics. The model fails to provide traditionally valued skills such as client-centered interviewing but does provide some service experience at low cost to the institution. And if paired with a local court to provide more effective assistance to pro bono litigants, this or similar models could provide student service to the poor while exposing the students to both legal substance and procedure as well as an introduction to court personnel who may be positive resources for students who enter into practice.

Another route to resolving these tensions is to blur the distinction between "clinical" and "doctrinal" courses by expanding the range of courses law schools offer. It has been observed more than once that there is little justification for the third year of law school beyond the extraction of tuition.[80] Law professors have

articles as "practical," "theoretical," or "both practical and theoretical." *Id.* at 1–2. Their study found that, in 1960, the five law reviews published a total of 48 "practical" articles, 36 "both practical and theoretical" articles, and 21 "theoretical" articles. *Id.* at app. D. By 2000, the journals published 6 "practical" articles, 45 "both practical and theoretical" articles, and 68 "theoretical" articles. *Id.*

76 Richard Susskind, THE END OF LAWYERS? (2008); William D. Henderson, *A Blueprint for Change*, 40 PEPPERDINE L. REV. 461, 470–78 (2013).

77 Susskind, supra note 76, at 100–104, which discusses several examples of innovative automated document assembly.

78 Id.

79 www.umassd.edu/justicebridge/.

80 See Samuel Estreicher, *The Roosevelt-Cardozo Way: The Case for Bar Eligibility After Two Years of Law School*, 15 NYU J. LEG. & PUB. POL'Y 599 (2012). See Estreicher & Milch, Chapter 50 in this volume.

wonderful jobs and not all of the reasons our work life is so satisfying are related to the receipt of rents. We have the opportunity to interact on a daily basis with students who, for the most part, are smart, engaging, and eager. We are able to work on subjects that interest us, to freely disseminate even the most crackpot ideas, and to teach at prestigious universities with fewer years of graduate study than almost any other discipline while being paid better than most of our university colleagues outside the law schools. Even if we gave up some of the rents we now enjoy, by redoubling our efforts to add value to our students' careers, we would still enjoy these attributes of our jobs. Adding value is unlikely to be accomplished by offering one more large section class with a three-hour exam. We must find ways to teach our students how to be better lawyers with sharp practical skills and an appreciation of how the ongoing study of the theoretical is essential to best practice lawyering.[81]

One suggestion is to blend the clinical and academic experience. The possibilities are endless. One example would be to combine a clinical experience of representing individuals in appeals of denials of social security claims, while concurrently engaging in a study of both historical development of the current social security scheme and the law surrounding it together with study of how other countries approach the needs of the disabled (or not). Such a course might examine the modern expansion of the disability insurance roles,[82] the problem of review of decisions of administrative law judges,[83] and the administrative challenges of mass programs that require individualized assessments.[84] Simultaneously delving into how the social security system fits into the larger administrative law framework would enrich the educational experience. Creating a capstone course that combined all of these would provide a broader context for the student's understanding of the legal system generally as well as the problems of the poor. Cooperative teaching in such a context would at least partially eliminate the difference between doctrinal and clinical faculty. In light of the history of clinical legal education, resolving existing tensions between clinical and doctrinal faculty is necessary before any significant change in law schools' ability to help resolve the larger problem of access to justice can occur.

[81] This is not a plea for more "practical" courses alone. We are convinced that even extremely theoretical subjects like Law & Economics have the potential to add value if they contribute to a student's ability to analyze and understand a client's legal problems.

[82] See David H. Autor & Mark G. Duggan, *The Growth in Social Security Disability Rolls: A Fiscal Crisis Unfolding*, 20 J. Econ. Persp. 71 (2006) (attributing growth to 1984 changes in statute increasing share of recipients with comparatively low-mortality conditions, increasing average duration of disability spells, rise in after-tax DI income replacement rate, and increased coverage due to higher female labor force participation); John Merline, 5.4 *Million Join Disability Rolls Under Obama*, Investor's Business Daily (April 20, 2012) (describing fiscal impact of added recipients and attributing some of the increase to the recession).

[83] See Paul R. Verkuil & Jeffrey S. Lubbers, *Alternative Approaches to Judicial Review of Social Security Disability Cases*, 55 Admin. L. Rev. 731 (2003) (describing problems with efforts to institute review process for ALJ decisions).

[84] See Jerry L. Mashaw, Bureaucratic Justice: Managing Social Security Disability Claims (1985).

14

Loan Repayment Assistance and Access to Justice

Emily S. Bremer

Emily Bremer questions the widely-held notion that loan forgiveness programs are a viable approach to increasing access to affordable lawyers. The chapter presents data showing that reducing law graduates' debt through these programs does not significantly increase their chances of becoming lawyers for the middle class or the poor.

Loan repayment assistance programs have long been viewed as an effective way for law schools to neutralize the effect of debt on job choice and encourage law school graduates to take relatively low-paying jobs serving the public interest.[1] Whatever the virtues of law school loan repayment assistance programs, however, expanding access to justice does not appear to be chief among them. Although counterintuitive and seemingly at odds with the anecdotal evidence, empirical studies have consistently shown that educational debt is a weak determinant of job choice. Educational debt matters. But not as much as other factors such as wage differentials and career aspirations. The available data suggest that loan repayment assistance programs are generally ineffective in encouraging students to take positions that would not otherwise interest them. Nor does it appear likely that such programs meaningfully increase the aggregate number of public interest or other low-paying but socially beneficial jobs available to law school graduates. Rather, these programs seem primarily to subsidize graduate employment in jobs that would likely exist without the programs. In addition, the programs often support graduates working in government or nonprofit advocacy organizations, which generally do not provide direct legal services to underserved populations.

This chapter urges that law schools should resist pressure to overinvest in loan repayment assistance programs and would be wiser to provide career-contingent scholarships if access to justice is their objective.

[1] See, e.g., Emily A. Benfer, *Bending the Arc*, 16 Geo. J. on Poverty L. & Pol'y 283, 283–84 (2009); Robert E. Hirshon, *Graduating Under Pressure*, 87 A.B.A. J. 6 (Nov. 2001), at 6. As used in this chapter, the term "public interest" refers to positions in legal aid organizations, public defenders offices, not-for-profit organizations, and government.

LAW SCHOOL LOAN REPAYMENT ASSISTANCE PROGRAMS

The first law schools to create loan repayment assistance programs did so in the late 1970s and early 1980s,[2] in response to concerns that increasingly heavy student debt loads were driving an observed decline in the share of law school graduates taking public interest positions.[3] The cost of legal education was expanding at a seemingly unsustainable rate, resulting in increased educational debt burdens for law school graduates.[4] The number of new lawyers annually entering the profession had also increased steadily in the 1980s – 46,528 lawyers joined the profession in 1989, a 52% increase over the 30,707 who had joined in 1975.[5] During the same time period, however, the percentage of recent graduates taking public interest positions declined from nearly 26% to just over 16%.[6] Although rising student debt was not the only factor that might have explained this apparent shift in recent law graduates' job choices,[7] the belief that loan repayment assistance programs could reverse the trend gained widespread professional acceptance quickly.[8] In 1988, the American Bar Association (ABA) House of Delegates adopted a resolution urging law schools to create programs to provide debt relief to graduates who accepted low-paying public interest jobs.[9] At the time, the federal government provided little such assistance, and law school programs were widely viewed as the best viable option for reversing the perceived effect of debt on graduate job choice.[10] Many law schools heeded the ABA's advice, resulting in a flurry of new loan repayment assistance programs in the early nineties, before a recession intervened, slowing the pace at which new programs emerged.[11]

The start of the twenty-first century brought with it a renewed effort – given force by two high-profile reports on the still-growing debt problem – to expand the

[2] See Equal Justice Works, Financing the Future: Responses to the Rising Debt of Law Students 6–7 (2d ed. 2006), available at www.equaljusticeworks.org/sites/default/files/financing-the-future2006.pdf (hereinafter Financing the Future). Harvard Law School appears to have created the first loan forgiveness program, in 1978. See *id.*

[3] See, e.g., Luize E. Zubrow, Is Loan Forgiveness Divine? Another View, 59 Geo. Wash. L. Rev. 451, 496 (1991).

[4] See, e.g., James P. White, *The Impact of Law Student Debt Upon the Legal Profession*, 39 J. Legal Educ. 725, 727 (1989); see also John R. Kramer, *Who Will Pay the Piper or Leave the Check on the Table for the Other Guy*, 39 J. Legal Educ. 655, 657 (1989) (hereinafter Kramer, *Pay the Piper*).

[5] Zubrow, supra note 3, at 496 & n.134.

[6] See *id.* at 496 n.133. These figures exclude judicial clerkships. See *id.* The data identify "public interest" and "government" positions as distinct categories, but I use the former term to refer to both categories together. See supra note 1.

[7] See *id.* at 496–97.

[8] See Oscar G. Chase, *Financing Legal Education: Loan Forgiveness Programs*, 39 J. Legal. Educ. 623, 625 (1989).

[9] White, supra note 4, at 733.

[10] The emergence of federal educational debt relief is discussed infra.

[11] See Hirshon, supra note 1, at 6. The problem of low levels of entry into public service persisted, however, with just 3.3% of law school graduates accepting government and public interest positions in 1998. See *id.*

availability of loan repayment assistance.[12] Delivered in 2002, the first report was a joint effort of Equal Justice Works, the National Association for Law Placement (NALP), and the Partnership for Public Service and was entitled *From Paper Chase to Money Chase: Law School Debt Diverts Road to Public Service*.[13] This report, the *Paper Chase* report, provided the first empirical support for the conventional wisdom that law school debt is a principal obstacle to recruiting and retaining public interest lawyers. The report's most influential finding was that 66% of third-year law students responding to a survey said that law school debt prevented them from considering a career in the public sector.[14] The report further heralded loan repayment assistance programs as "possibly the most viable solution" to the problem.[15] A year later, in 2003, the ABA Commission on Loan Repayment and Forgiveness, a special group convened in 2001, delivered its final report, *Lifting the Burden: Law Student Debt as a Barrier to Public Service*.[16] The report revealed that law school tuition had continued to skyrocket, that nearly 87% of law school graduates had borrowed to pay for their legal education, and that "the amount borrowed by many law students exceeded $80,000."[17] Relying heavily on the *Paper Chase* report's statistics, the *Lifting the Burden* report further concluded that "[h]igh student debt bars many law graduates from pursuing public service careers" and forces many graduates to leave such positions after just a few years.[18] The group's core recommendation was for law schools and the federal government to create new loan repayment assistance and forgiveness programs and to expand the programs that were already in place.[19]

Law schools responded favorably to this recommendation, resulting in a proliferation of loan repayment assistance programs designed to support law school graduates faced with heavy debt and low salaries.[20] In 2003, the ABA reported that approximately fifty-six law schools offered such a program to their graduates.[21] Within just a few years, eighty-one law schools reported having operational loan

[12] See Financing the Future, supra note 2, at 6.

[13] See Equal Justice Works, NALP, and the Partnership for Public Service, From Paper Chase to Money Chase: Law School Debt Diverts Road to Public Service (2002), available at www.americanbar.org/content/dam/aba/migrated/marketresearch/PublicDocuments/lrapsurvey.authcheckdam.pdf (hereinafter Paper Chase).

[14] *Id.* at 19

[15] Although Georgetown's support was conditioned on Ms. Long's staying in public interest work for five years, it appears that she left Utah Legal Services after less than two years, see www.linkedin.com/pub/rebecca-long-okura/7/720/368, and, in 2004, opened her own law firm in Salt Lake City, see http://longokura.com/about/attorney-bios/. *Id.* at 35.

[16] ABA Comm'n on Loan Repayment and Forgiveness, Lifting the Burden: Law Student Debt as a Barrier to Public Service (2003), available at www.americanbar.org/content/dam/aba/migrated/legalservices/downloads/lrap/lrapfinalreport.authcheckdam.pdf (hereinafter Lifting the Burden).

[17] *Id.* at 10; see *id.* at 16–27 (examining the economics of law school attendance).

[18] *Id.* at 10; see *Id.* at 27–28 (discussing empirical support for conventional wisdom regarding debt and public interest work); see also *id.* at 38–46 (recommendations to the federal government); 48–51 (recommendations to law schools).

[19] *Id.* at 11–13.

[20] See Financing the Future, supra note 2, at 6–7.

[21] Lifting the Burden, supra note 16, at 47.

repayment assistance programs.[22] As of 2006, that number exceeded one hundred.[23] These programs have been further buttressed by the federal government's expansion of federal educational debt relief, which is discussed in the next section.[24]

Most law school programs provide support only to graduates working full time in qualifying, "public interest" positions.[25] Only two schools – Harvard Law School and Yale Law School – offer low-income protection plans that provide support based exclusively on financial need.[26] Although programs vary in their details,[27] almost all use some combination of the following requirements to define eligibility and available support levels:

- *Qualifying Employment.* At most schools, assistance is available only for those working full time in the "public interest," which is typically defined to include public defenders and legal aid attorneys, as well as graduates working for nonprofit organizations and in government. Private, for-profit law practice, whether in a firm or solo practice, is rarely eligible, regardless of the type of services being provided.[28] Almost all programs require that a graduate's work be "law-related."[29]
- *Income Caps or Ceilings.* Law schools typically impose relatively strict income ceilings that further limit participant eligibility. Of fifty-three schools reporting data for 2004–05, nine set the ceiling at $35,001–$40,000, twenty set the ceiling at $40,001–$45,000, twelve set the ceiling at $45,001–$50,000, seven set the ceiling at $50,001–$55,000; and five set the ceiling at $55,001–$60,000.[30]
- *Income Calculation Methods.* Different programs calculate qualifying income in slightly different ways, but usually with the same goal of determining the extent of each graduate's genuine financial need. Schools may or may not consider factors other than salary, such as available assets and spousal income, in determining eligibility and award levels.

[22] Financing the Future, supra note 2, at 6; *but* see Philip G. Schrag & Charles W. Pruett, *Coordinating Loan Repayment Assistance Programs with New Federal Legislation*, 60 J. Legal Educ. 583, 588 (2011) (stating that 76 law schools had loan repayment assistance programs as of 2008).

[23] *Id.* at 6.

[24] See generally Schrag & Pruett, supra note 22.

[25] See supra note 1.

[26] Harvard's program covers only "law-related" employment, while Yale's does not impose even that modest limitation. See Harvard Law School, Student Financial Services, Low Income Protection Plan (LIPP), available at http://hls.harvard.edu/dept/sfs/lipp/; Yale Law School, Career Options Assistance Program (COAP), available at www.law.yale.edu/admissions/cost-financial-aid/post-graduate-loan-repayment/about-coap. Loan forgiveness programs at the University of Michigan Law School and New York University School of Law began as low-income protection plans, but have subsequently been restricted to support only those graduates who take public interest positions. See Zubrow, supra note 3, at 456 n.5.

[27] See Schrag & Pruett, supra note 22, at 588.

[28] See David H. Vernon, *Educational Debt Burden: Law School Assistance Programs – A Review of Existing Programs and a Proposed New Approach*, 39 J. Legal Educ. 743, 766 & n.30 (1989).

[29] See note 26.

[30] Financing the Future, supra note 2, at 13.

- *Qualifying Debt*. There is also a fair degree of variation in terms of which loans are included in the financial need calculation. In 2004–05, of the seventy-three reporting schools, thirty-four included some or all undergraduate loans in the qualifying debt calculation, twenty-nine schools included some or all postgraduate loans, thirty-two schools included bar study loans, and five schools included non-educational loans.[31]
- *Time Limits on Participation*. Most schools limit participation to a certain number of years following graduation. Of forty-five schools reporting data for 2004–05, twenty-four limited participation to five years or less, two schools limited participation to six to eight years, seventeen schools limited participation to ten years, and two schools limited participation to fifteen years.[32]

Graduates must ordinarily apply annually to participate in their school's program and provide documentation demonstrating eligibility and financial need. To take advantage of more favorable tax treatment, most law school programs are structured to provide assistance in the form of short-term loans and not grants.[33] At the end of the program year, provided the graduate remains in eligible employment, the loan is forgiven.[34]

Law school loan repayment assistance programs have been consistently criticized for being underfunded and imposing too-rigid eligibility requirements.[35] As the data presented earlier suggest, income ceilings are often set quite low. As a consequence, relatively few graduates qualify to receive assistance.[36] Law schools at the top of the rankings (which I will term "elite law schools") offer the most generous programs and typically have sufficient funding to support all eligible graduates who apply for assistance.[37] For most schools, however, available funding is insufficient to meet the

[31] *Id.* at 15.

[32] *Id.* at 13.

[33] See *id.* at 16. Section 108(f) of the Internal Revenue Code excludes from gross income student loan amounts discharged "pursuant to a provision of such loan under which all or part of the indebtedness of the individual would be discharged if the individual worked for a certain period of time in certain professions for any of a broad class of employers." 26 U.S.C. § 108(f)(1); see Rev. Rul. 2008–34, 2008–2 C.B. 76. This rule does not apply, however, if loan repayment assistance is provided in the form of a grant. See, e.g., *Moloney v. Comm'r*, T.C. Summary Op. 2006–53, available at www.ustaxcourt.gov/InOpHistoric/moloney.sum.WPD.pdf. Some law schools nonetheless provide loan repayment assistance in the form of grants. See Schrag & Pruett, supra note 22, at 589.

[34] In some programs, a graduate must remain in eligible employment for several years before his or her law school will begin to forgive these loans. For example, participants in NYU's program must remain in eligible employment for 36 months before loan forgiveness begins. At the end of the year during which the participant reaches 36 months, all outstanding loans are forgiven, and further loans are then forgiven annually for as long as the participant remains in the program. See New York Univ. School of Law, Loan Repayment Assistance Program (LRAP), LRAP FAQs, available at www.law.nyu.edu/financialaid/lrap/lrapfaq.

[35] See, e.g., Paper Chase, supra note 13, at 35.

[36] E.g., Vernon, supra note 28, at 745, 757.

[37] Telephone Interview with Charles DeRubeis, Director of Financial Aid, Columbia Law School (Feb. 21, 2013) (hereinafter DeRubeis Interview); Telephone Interview with Joel Schoenecker, Director, NYU Law Office of Student Financial Services (Feb. 12, 2013) (hereinafter Schoenecker Interview).

needs of all graduates, and awards are too small to make much of a dent in graduates' large debt loads. In 2004–05, the median annual award was $3,500, and "[o]ut of 62 reporting schools, 37 schools or 60 percent, disbursed average annual awards of less than $4,000."[38] Meanwhile, "[t]he average annual law school debt payment for a graduate is about $7,500 for an in-state resident public school graduate and $12,000 for a private school graduate."[39] Average award amounts vary widely by school. In 2008, the average award nationwide was $7,021, but per-school averages varied from $600 to $26,978.[40] Strict eligibility requirements allow schools to give effect to funding priorities in the face of limited resources.[41] Schools may also provide only modest support to individual graduates in order to spread limited funding across a greater number of graduates.[42] If available funding turns out to be insufficient to provide support for all eligible graduates in a particular year, schools may either adjust award amounts to accommodate everyone or distribute available funds in order of demonstrated financial need or on a first-come, first-served basis.[43]

Despite the increasing number of law school loan repayment assistance programs, the number of graduates participating in such programs has remained relatively small, and the vast majority of assistance is provided to graduates of elite law schools. As of 2004–05, seventy law schools reported providing loan repayment assistance to a total of 1,778 law school graduates.[44] That figure represents just a tiny fraction of all law school graduates – if all 1,778 had been members of the class of 2004 (and they assuredly were not), they would represent just over 4% of the 40,018 students who graduated from 186 ABA-accredited law schools that year.[45] This should not be surprising: most law school loan repayment assistance programs are very small. Of sixty-three schools reporting relevant data for 2004–05, eighteen funded more

38 Financing the Future, supra note 2, at 10.

39 *Id.* at 10.

40 See Schrag & Pruett, supra note 22, at 589.

41 See Vernon, supra note 28, at 758, 761.

42 See, e.g., L. Kinvin Wroth, *Access to Justice: The Problem of Law Student Debt*, 30 Vt. B. J. & L. Dig. 28, 29 (2004) ("Because the [Vermont Law School loan repayment assistance] program seeks to make as many awards as possible each year, individual annual awards rarely exceed 50 percent of the annual payment amount and are often less than that").

43 See, e.g., The George Washington Univ. Law School, Career Development Office, Loan Reimbursement Assistance Program (LRAP) FAQs 2 (2010), available at www.law.gwu.edu/Careers/currentstudents/Documents/Informational%20Handouts/2010%20Updated%20Handouts/2010%20LRAP%20FAQs.pdf ("If funds are insufficient to provide the formula amount for all selected applicants at the time awards are being made, the amount of the loan awards may be adjusted. Eligible applications received after the first application deadline may be funded to the extent funds remain available"); Univ. of California Davis School of Law, Loan Repayment Assistance program, plan 3 (June 2009), available at https://law.ucdavis.edu/financial-aid/files/LRAP-ByLaws-November-2014.pdf ("In event of insufficient funding, applicants with greatest need and lowest income will be funded first").

44 Financing the Future, supra note 2, at 7.

45 See *NALP, Jobs & J.D.'s: Employment and Salaries of New Law Graduates – Class of* 2004, *Class of* 2004 *Selected Findings* (2005), at 2, available at www.nalp.org/uploads/160_selectedfindings04.pdf.

than twenty graduates, while twenty-seven reported funding fewer than ten graduates.[46]

Although law schools run most of the available loan repayment assistance programs, some state governments, federal agencies, bar associations, and public interest employers have their own programs. As of 2003, a handful of states were operating or had authorized loan repayment assistance programs[47] and other state legislatures and bar associations were in various stages of considering or establishing such programs.[48] In seven other states, privately run statewide loan repayment assistance programs were available,[49] and bar associations were in the process of creating or advocating for the creation of additional programs.[50] At last count, there were at least twenty-five statewide programs.[51] In 1990, Congress authorized federal agencies to provide loan repayment assistance to employees, although it was not until 2000 that the Office of Personnel Management promulgated the regulations necessary for agencies to exercise that authority.[52] In 2011–12, four agencies provided financial support to a total of eight employees.[53]

FEDERAL LOAN REPAYMENT ASSISTANCE AND FORGIVENESS PROGRAMS

In recent years, the federal government has significantly changed the financial landscape for law school graduates, by effectively creating a federal loan repayment assistance program.[54] This program includes loan repayment assistance in the form of an income-based repayment option for federally guaranteed and federal direct loans,[55] coupled with two types of loan forgiveness that eliminate remaining debt

[46] FINANCING THE FUTURE, supra note 2, at 7.

[47] See LIFTING THE BURDEN, supra note 16, at 52; COMMITTEE ON LEGAL EDUCATION AND THE ADMISSION TO THE BAR, ASSOCIATION OF THE BAR OF THE CITY OF NEW YORK, LAW SCHOOL DEBT AND THE PRACTICE OF LAW 14 (2003), available at www.abcny.org/pdf/report/lawSchoolDebt.pdf (hereinafter DEBT AND THE PRACTICE OF LAW).

[48] See DEBT AND THE PRACTICE OF LAW, supra note 47, at 14, 15; *but* see PAPER CHASE, supra note 13, at 33 (reporting, in 2002, that "currently six states and more than 40 legal employers also offer some form of LRAP").

[49] See DEBT AND THE PRACTICE OF LAW, supra note 47, at 17.

[50] See *id.* at 17–18.

[51] List available at www.equaljusticeworks.org/ed-debt/students/loan-repayment-assistance-programs/state-LRAPs/state-contacts (last visited Nov. 7, 2015). Some public-interest employers even provide debt relief for the law school graduates they employ. See DEBT AND THE PRACTICE OF LAW, supra note 47, at 18–19.

[52] See PAPER CHASE, supra note 13, at 37.

[53] *Id.* at 37.

[54] See Schrag & Pruett, supra note 22, at 590. As this section explains, the federal government has structured educational debt relief differently than have the law schools, but the result is much the same and is commonly referred to as a federal "loan repayment assistance program."

[55] Income-based repayment will ultimately replace its failed predecessor, income-contingent repayment. See Higher Education Amendments of 1992, Pub. L. 102–325; 34 C.F.R. pt. 685; see generally

after ten years (for those in public-service positions)[56] or twenty-five years (for all others). The key to this long-sought[57] federal approach to student debt relief was the College Cost Reduction and Access Act of 2007 (CCRAA),[58] which paved the way for the two core features of the program: income-based repayment and the federal Public Service Loan Forgiveness (PSLF) Program.[59]

Income-based repayment allows graduates with high debt levels and low incomes to reduce the monthly payments on their federally guaranteed and federal direct educational loans.[60] The plan uses a formula that limits monthly payments based on income. If a borrower would pay less using this formula than he would on a "standard" ten-year repayment plan,[61] then he is deemed to have a "partial financial hardship" and may choose to repay his loans using the income-based repayment plan.[62] The formula limits a borrower's annual payment obligation to 15% of "discretionary income," defined as the difference between the borrower's adjusted gross income and 150% of the federal poverty level for a family the size of the borrower's family. The borrower's monthly payment is established at one-twelfth of this annual payment obligation.[63] For example, take an unmarried law school graduate with a total debt at graduation of $125,000 at 6.8% interest and an annual income of $62,467.[64] Using income-based repayment, this graduate would owe $570 per month, which is $868.50 less than the $1,438.50 that would be due under a

Philip G. Schrag, *The Federal Income-Contingent Repayment Option for Law Student Loans*, 29 HOFSTRA L. REV. 733 (2001) (hereinafter Schrag, Income-Contingent Repayment).

56 The Department of Education defines employment in "public-service organizations" expansively, such that it includes what we refer to here as "public interest" positions, see supra note 1, plus a wide variety of other types of work in private organizations, see 34 C.F.R. § 685.219 (b).

57 See, e.g., Vernon, supra note 28, at 28; see also White, supra note 4, at 732.

58 See generally Schrag, Federal Student Loan Repayment Assistance, infra note 104 (thoroughly analyzing relief provided by the 2007 Act).

59 See 34 C.F.R. § 685.219; Schrag & Pruett, supra note 22, at 590; see generally Schrag, Federal Student Loan Repayment Assistance, infra note 104. In 2008, Congress also created additional loan forgiveness programs specifically for prosecutors, public defenders, and civil legal aid lawyers. See 20 U.S.C. § 1078–12 (Civil Legal Assistance Attorney Student Loan Repayment Program); 42 U.S.C. § 3797cc-21 (John R. Justice Prosecutors and Defenders Incentive Act of 2008); Schrag & Pruett, supra note 22, at 595.

60 See, e.g., 34 C.F.R. §§ 682.215 (income-based repayment plan for the Federal Family Education Loan (FFEL) Program), 685.221 (income-based repayment plan for the William D Ford Federal Direct Loan Program).

61 The statutory term "standard repayment plan" refers to a repayment schedule "with a fixed annual repayment amount paid over a fixed period of time, not to exceed 10 years." 20 U.S.C. § 1078(b)(9)(A). Some have objected that a ten-year payment plan should no longer be considered "standard" because graduates today have a wider array of repayment options available to them and often select income-sensitive, graduated, or extended repayment plans to accommodate higher federal debt loads. See Philip G. Schrag, *Failing Law Schools – Brian Tamanaha's Misguided Missile*, 26 GEO. J. LEGAL ETHICS 387, 398–99 (2013) (hereinafter Schrag, Misguided Missile).

62 See 34 C.F.R. § 685.221(a)(4).

63 See 3 IA. § 685.221(b).

64 This would be the 2012 salary for a GS-11 attorney employed in Washington, DC. See OFFICE OF PERSONNEL MANAGEMENT, SALARY TABLE 2012-DCB, available at www.opm.gov/policy-data-oversight/pay-leave/salaries-wages/2012/general-schedule/dcb.pdf.

standard ten-year repayment plan.[65] Borrowers must reapply for income-based repayment annually, and payment amounts increase as income rises. After twenty-five years, provided certain conditions are met, any remaining loan balance is forgiven.[66]

Under PSLF, graduates working full time in public service may have the remainder of their educational debts forgiven after just ten years.[67] The law defines "public service" broadly, to include employment in any level of government (local, state, tribal, or federal), in any nonprofit 501(c)(3) organization, and with many other types of private organizations.[68] The law requires eligible borrowers to make 120 months of loan payments while engaged in eligible employment, but does not require this employment be continuous.[69] Loan forgiveness under PSLF is tax-free.[70]

PSLF is available only for loans taken out directly from the federal government, although such loans represent an increasing share of all educational borrowing.[71] Congress set down this path in 2006, when it raised the ceiling for Stafford borrowing for graduate and professional education[72] and created a new federally guaranteed loan program, Grad Plus, that allows graduate and professional students to borrow the difference between the Stafford borrowing limit and the cost of attendance at a fixed interest rate of 7.9%.[73] More recently, the government has taken steps to replace all federally guaranteed loans with direct loans from the federal government. This shift began administratively in 2008, after Congress, concerned that the troubled credit market would be unable to meet demand for educational financing, authorized the Department of Education to buy up federally guaranteed loans.[74] In 2010, as part of healthcare reform legislation, Congress

65 See IBR Calculator, available at www.ibrinfo.org/calculator.php.

66 See, e.g., 34 C.F.R. § 685.221(f).

67 See 35 C.F.R. § 685.219.

68 See supra note 56; Schrag & Pruett, supra note 22, at 592.

69 See 34 C.F.R. § 685.219(c); Dep't of Educ., Federal Student Aid, Public Service Loan Forgiveness Program, Questions and Answers for Federal Student Loan Borrowers 4, available at http://studentaid.ed.gov/sites/default/files/public-service-loan-forgiveness-common-questions.pdf.

70 See Schrag & Pruett, supra note 22, at 593 & n.33.

71 See Heather Jarvis & Kelly Carmody, An Employer and Employee Guide to Public Service Loan Forgiveness (Aug. 2012), available at http://askheatherjarvis.com/uploads/images/PSLF%20Guide%20for%20Public%20Interest%20Employers%20and%20Employees%20August%202012.pdf. Students that have other federally-guaranteed loans, such as FFEL loans, must consolidate their debt in federal direct loans before those loans become eligible for forgiveness under PSFL. See 34 C.F.R. § 685.219(b); U.S. Department of Education, Office of Federal Student Aid, Income-Based Plan, available at http://studentaid.ed.gov/repay-loans/understand/plans/income-based (last visited Nov. 7, 2015).

72 See Higher Education Reconciliation ACT (HERA) of 2005, Pub. L. No. 109–171. HERA raised the annual borrowing limit from $18,500 to $20,500.

73 See Schrag & Pruett, supra note 22, at 590.

74 See Michael C. Macchiarola & Arun Abraham, *Options for Student Borrowers: A Derivatives-Based Proposal to Protect Students and Control Debt-Fueled Inflation in the Higher Education Market*, 20 Cornell J. L. & Pub. Pol'y 67, 98–100 (2010).

terminated all private, federally guaranteed student loans and replaced them with federal direct loans under the Student Aid and Fiscal Responsibility Act (SAFRA).[75]

Federal loan repayment assistance has created new opportunities for law schools and their graduates. Law schools now have the opportunity to coordinate their own loan repayment assistance programs with the federal program.[76] Because income-based repayment significantly reduces a graduate's monthly loan payment, law schools are able to cover a greater percentage of that payment at significantly reduced cost.[77] This allows schools to spread the same level of funding across a greater number of graduates. As of January 2011, seven law schools had modified their programs to take advantage of this opportunity.[78] In addition, law schools that have not previously been able to secure sufficient funding to start a program may now be able to do so by taking a similar approach. For graduates, the new federal program makes it possible to reduce monthly debt service obligations regardless of the type of employment they secure. Graduates working in public service may reap even greater benefits through PSLF, particularly if their law school does not provide adequate (or any) loan repayment assistance.

Federal loan repayment assistance also presents new challenges. While the federal programs may alleviate financial hardship for some borrowers, they do not solve the problem of increasing tuition and heavy debt loads. To the contrary, the further liberalization in federal lending rules that has accompanied the new programs[79] may further fuel the now decades-long rise in tuition.[80] It is generally recognized that the widespread availability of federally guaranteed educational loans has helped drive up law school tuition.[81] Income-based repayment also creates a new problem for heavily indebted law school graduates: negative amortization. Although the plan alleviates financial hardship in the short term, opting to use it may cause graduates' debt burden to *grow*, sometimes significantly, as unpaid interest compounds. Affected graduates must hope to remain in qualifying employment long enough to eradicate the increased debt.

75 See Health Care and Education Reconciliation Act of 2010, Pub. L. 111–152, §§ 2001–213, 124 Stat. 1071–1081 (codified in scattered sections of 20 U.S.C.). "[B]y converting the loan guarantees into an income-producing asset, the federal budget was reduced by $61 billion over 10 years." William D. Henderson & Rachel M. Zahorsky, The Law School Bubble: How Long Will It Last if Law Grads Can't Pay Bills?, A. B.A. J. (Jan. 1, 2012).

76 See generally Schrag & Pruett, supra note 22.

77 See supra at note 65 and accompanying text.

78 Schrag & Pruett, supra note 22, at 583–84.

79 See supra notes 72–73 and accompanying text.

80 See generally Macchiarola & Abraham, supra note 74 supra.

81 See, e.g., John A. Sebert, *The Cost and Financing of Legal Education*, 52 J. Legal Educ. 516, 525 (2002); White, supra note 4, at 729.

THE LAW SCHOOL CRISIS

There is widespread agreement that legal education in the United States is in crisis – a reality that will undoubtedly complicate any effort to reevaluate loan repayment assistance from a pure access to justice perspective.[82] The challenges of steadily rising tuition and educational debt, which first spurred the development of these programs, have only intensified. As Figure 14.1 shows, average tuition and expenses at the nation's law schools have continued the steady upward climb that first triggered concern nearly three decades ago.

Similarly, the debt levels that initially spurred the loan repayment assistance movement dwarf those now routinely taken on by law school graduates.[83] In the early 1990s, the concern was that it was becoming common for students to take out cumulative undergraduate law school debts of $40,000–$60,000.[84] Today, the problem is both broader and deeper: approximately 90% of law students take out loans to pay for their legal education, and the average law school debt exceeds $100,000.[85] As shown in Figure 14.2, in the single decade between 2002 and 2011, the average law school debt for graduates of private law schools has grown from $70,147 to $124,950, an astounding 78% increase.[86]

These figures, which are merely averages and do not include undergraduate debt, likely underestimate many graduates' actual debt levels.[87]

The problem of increasing debt is compounded by the dismal employment outcomes that many, perhaps even most, law school graduates face. The most recent employment data reveal that, nine months out of graduation, only 56% of the class of 2012 had secured full-time positions in law practice.[88] Even graduates from top tier law schools are reportedly having difficulty finding full employment.[89] Whether these difficulties are merely a product of the recent recession or reflect permanent structural changes in the legal services market is a matter of some debate.[90] That is a

[82] See generally BRIAN Z. TAMANAHA, FAILING LAW SCHOOLS (2012); see also, e.g., Richard W. Bourne, *The Coming Crash in Legal Education: How We Got Here, and Where We Go Now*, 45 CREIGHTON L. REV. 651 (2012).

[83] See, e.g., Sebert, supra note 81, at 521–22.

[84] David L. Chambers, *The Burdens of Educational Loans: The Impacts of Debt on Choice and Standards of Living for Students at Nine Law Schools*, 42 J. LEGAL EDUC. 187, 187 (1992) (hereinafter Chambers, *Burdens of Educational Loans*).

[85] Letter from The Coalition of Concerned Colleagues, to The A.B.A. Task Force on Legal Education (Mar. 2013), available at www.americanbar.org/content/dam/aba/administrative/professional_responsibility/taskforcecomments/032013_coalition_revcomment.authcheckdam.pdf.

[86] Data from the ABA, available at www.americanbar.org/content/dam/aba/administrative/legal_education_and_admissions_to_the_bar/statistics/avg_amnt_brwd.authcheckdam.pdf.

[87] See, e.g., Tamanaha, supra note 82, at 109–10.

[88] Jordan Weissmann, *The Job Crisis at Our Best Law Schools Is Much, Much Worse Than You Think*, THE ATLANTIC, Apr. 9, 2013, available at www.theatlantic.com/business/archive/2013/04/the-jobs-crisis-at-our-best-law-schools-is-much-much-worse-than-you-think/274795/.

[89] Weissmann, supra note 88.

[90] Compare STEVEN J. HARPER, THE LAWYER BUBBLE: A PROFESSION IN CRISIS (2013), with Richard A Epstein, *The Rule of Lawyers*, WALL ST. J., May 5, 2013.

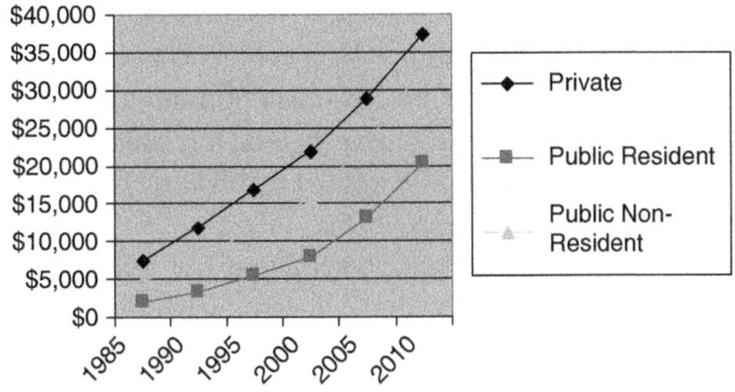

FIGURE 14.1. Average law school tuition and expenses, 1985–2010.

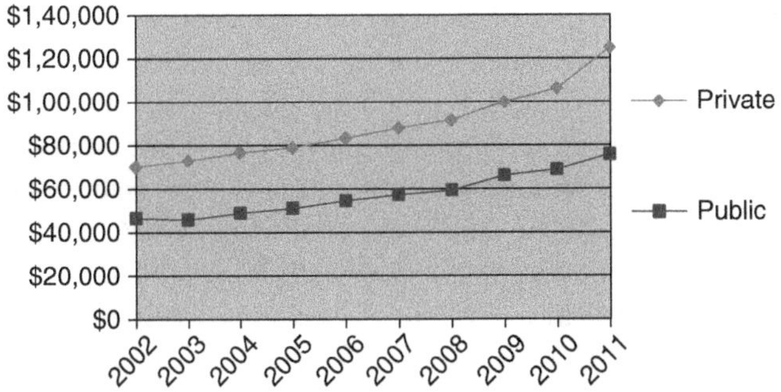

FIGURE 14.2. Average law school debt 2002–11.

question that only time will answer definitively. For now, however, many are quite reasonably questioning whether attending law school is worth the cost.[91] The number of students applying and enrolling in law schools has declined considerably in recent years and appears likely to continue declining.[92] Even if this phenomenon is arrested in the short term, lower enrollment figures may be the new normal for law schools.

Although these problems are not new ones, they have now reached levels that threaten the viability of some law schools and perhaps even the overall health of the justice system.[93] As in past market downturns, some have urged that additional debt

[91] See, e.g., Tamanaha, supra note 82; see also ABA COMM'N ON THE IMPACT OF THE ECONOMIC CRISES ON THE PROFESSION AND LEGAL NEEDS, THE VALUE PROPOSITION OF ATTENDING LAW SCHOOL (Nov. 2009), available at www.americanbar.org/content/dam/aba/migrated/lsd/legaled/value.authcheck dam.pdf; but see Michael Simkovic & Frank McIntyre, *The Economic Value of a Law Degree* 49, available at http://papers.ssrn.com/sol3/papers.cfm?abstract_id=2250585 (Apr. 13, 2013) ("Applying reasonable discount rates, we estimate the mean lifetime value of a law degree in 2012 dollars as of the start of law school to be approximately $1,000,000 before taxes, and $700,000 net of taxes").

[92] See, e.g., Catherine Ho, *Law School Applications Continue to Slide*, WASH. POST, June 2, 2013, available at http://articles.washingtonpost.com/2013-06-02/business/39697850_1_american-bar-association-accredited-law-school-legal-job-market.

[93] E.g., FINANCING THE FUTURE, supra note 2, at iii ("The mortgage-sized debt burdens of law school graduates have far-reaching effects that harm the legal profession and our justice system").

relief, including through expanded loan repayment assistance, is the answer (or at least part of it).[94] Some law schools are taking action accordingly. For example, in March 2013, Northwestern University Law School announced that it would be reducing incoming class sizes by 10%, maintaining a relatively modest 3% tuition increase, and increasing the availability of financial aid funds – including for loan repayment assistance – by 25% over two years.[95]

In this climate, it is particularly important for law schools to carefully and candidly assess what they can reasonably expect to achieve through a loan repayment assistance program. A persistent difficulty in evaluating the performance of existing programs is that they have been created, maintained, and expanded based on a variety of intermingled and sometimes conflicting reasons.[96] Some have argued that excessive educational debt burdens are problematic because they might "affect adversely decisions law graduates make on behalf of their clients"[97] and deter graduates in practice from fulfilling pro bono obligations.[98] Others have argued debt prevents graduates from accepting low-paying public interest positions and that loan forgiveness programs are necessary to enable law school graduates to accept and remain in such positions.[99] At other times, the issue is not that public interest positions go unfilled, but that they are filled with less qualified candidates.[100] Still others have argued that loan repayment assistance is necessary to promote socio-economic and racial diversity in law school classes and, more broadly, the legal profession.[101] Finally, as a practical matter, law schools often advertise their loan repayment assistance programs, using them as one of many ways to compete with each other for students.[102]

This chapter takes a simpler approach by evaluating loan repayment assistance programs according to a single, straightforward metric: do the programs expand access to justice?

[94] In 2011, the ABA House of Delegates adopted a resolution urging Congress to further expand loan forgiveness to indebted graduates who were not covered by the previous overhaul. See ABA Young Lawyers Division, Report to the House of Delegates, Resolution 111A (adopted Aug. 8–9, 2011), available at www.abajournal.com/files/111a.pdf.

[95] Samantha Bonkamp, *NU Law to Cut Class Sizes, Hold Tuition in Check*, Chic. Trib., Mar. 11, 2013, available at http://articles.chicagotribune.com/2013–03–11/business/chi-nu-law-to-cut-class-sizes-hold-tuition-in-check-20130311_1_class-sizes-nu-law-law-school.

[96] E.g., Paper Chase, supra note 13, at 35 (noting that law schools provide loan repayment assistance programs "for many reasons").

[97] Vernon, supra note 28, at 759; see also Debt and the Practice of Law, supra note 47, at 2, 26; Zubrow, supra note 3, at 518.

[98] See, e.g., Vernon, supra note 28, at 759.

[99] See, e.g., Paper Chase, supra note 13, at 7.

[100] See, e.g., Lifting the Burden, supra note 16, at 28.

[101] See, e.g., Schrag, *Misguided Missile*, supra note 61, at 388.

[102] See Chase, supra note 8, at 625 (noting that uniform support for loan forgiveness "probably is due to competition between major law schools for desirable students and to the understandable wish on the part of law faculties to aid in the public interest endeavor").

LOAN REPAYMENT ASSISTANCE AND ACCESS TO JUSTICE: THE EMPIRICAL EVIDENCE

The question of whether law school loan repayment assistance programs expand access to justice is an empirical one, although it can be evaluated from several different perspectives. First, how do debt and the availability of loan repayment assistance affect graduates' job choices? Widespread support for such programs has long been rooted in the conventional wisdom that high debt loads prevent students from pursuing low-paying positions in the public interest. But do they? And if so, can a school reverse that effect and encourage more students to pursue lower-paying careers by providing generous loan repayment assistance? Second, in the aggregate, can law school loan repayment assistance programs increase the number of jobs available in the legal services market to graduates who want to provide direct legal services to underserved populations? Finally, do existing loan repayment assistance programs support law school graduates in such jobs or do they more often support graduates working for government offices or nonprofit organizations that do not provide such direct legal services?

The Supply of Lawyers: Influencing Graduate Job Choice

Intuition and Anecdotal Evidence

The most compelling evidence of the need for law school loan repayment assistance programs has long been intuitive and anecdotal. Intuitively, high monthly loan payments seem likely to deter or prevent law school graduates from accepting low-paying public interest jobs. This intuition is frequently confirmed by the experiences of individual law graduates,[103] highlighted by the press, who carry heavy debt loads into entry-level public interest positions.[104] Some of these anecdotes suggest that loan repayment assistance programs are a necessary precondition for graduates to accept public interest positions right out of law school. For example, in 2001, the *A.B.A. Journal* told the story of Rebecca Long, a Georgetown University Law Center graduate who was able to accept an entry-level position with Utah Legal Services that paid just $31,000 per year because Georgetown covered 100% of the monthly payments on Ms. Long's total of $116,000 in educational debt.[105] Other anecdotes suggest that if loan repayment assistance is not available, graduates who take

[103] Some anecdotes focus on the experiences of public interest employers. See, e.g., DEBT AND THE PRACTICE OF LAW, supra note 47, at 22–23.

[104] DEBT AND THE PRACTICE OF LAW, supra note 47, at 3; see also Philip G. Schrag, *Federal Student Loan Repayment Assistance for Public Interest Lawyers and Other Employees of Governments and Nonprofit Organizations*, 36 HOFSTRA L. REV. 27, 29 (2007) (hereinafter Schrag, *Federal Student Loan Repayment Assistance*).

[105] See Margaret Graham Tebo, *The Debt Conundrum*, 87 A.B.A. J. 42 (Mar. 2001).

entry-level public interest positions will be unable to stay in them for very long.[106] One such story appeared in a *New York Times* profile of Paula J. Clifford, a law school graduate earning just $26,000 per year as a prosecutor in Bristol, MA, and forced to continue bartending in order to service her $70,000 educational debt.[107]

Student Surveys

The conventional wisdom that debt prevents law school graduates from taking low-paying public interest positions finds further support in survey data – when asked, students and public interest employers report that educational debt affects job choice.[108] The most well-known survey data were provided by the 2002 "Paper Chase" study, which reported that 66% of student respondents said that law school debt prevented them from considering public interest positions.[109] In the same study, 83% of student respondents said that $6,000 per year in loan repayment assistance would increase their interest in a federal government job.[110] Similarly, public interest and non-federal government employers that reported difficulties recruiting and retaining attorneys overwhelmingly cited low salaries (89% and 92%, respectively) and educational debt (92% and 82%, respectively) as the biggest contributing factors.[111] Like their student counterparts, the majority of employer respondents said that loan repayment assistance provided by third parties such as law schools can improve attorney recruitment (56%) and retention (50%).[112]

Over the years, other surveys of students and public interest employers have yielded statistics similar to those contained in the "Paper Chase" report. In 1988, when debt levels were relatively low by today's standards, 45% of graduating law students responding to a survey by the George Washington University National Law Center cited debt as "determinative" or a "very important factor" in job choice.[113] A survey administered by mail in 2002 by a Committee of the New York State Bar

[106] See, e.g., Curtis Caton, *Legal Community Works Toward Forgiveness of Student Debt*, 28 B. LEADER 8, Jan./Feb. 2004, at 21.

[107] Janothan D. Glater, *High Tuition and Low Pay Drain Public Interest Law*, N.Y. TIMES, Sept. 12, 2003, at A1. Ms. Clifford is now a partner in a Boston law firm. See www.bonnerkiernan.com/news-31.html.

[108] See, e.g., Survey of New Admittees Regarding Law student Debt and Post-Law School Employment: *(Survey Conducted February 24, 2011)*, 72 ALA. LAW. 193 (2011).

[109] See PAPER CHASE, supra note 13, at 19. The percentages were higher for students who ultimately accepted jobs in business (75%), large private law firms (78%), and small private law firms (83%). See *id.* at 19, 20.

[110] See *id.* at 6. Forty-six percent said that $6,000 per year in loan repayment assistance would make them "much more interested" in federal government employment, while 37% said it would make them "somewhat more interested." *Id.*

[111] See *id.* at 30. Sixty-eight percent of respondent employers reported difficulty recruiting attorneys, while 62% reported difficulty retaining attorneys. See *id.*

[112] See *id.* at 37. The small number of employers who reported directly offering students some form of loan repayment assistance (13% of the respondents) were more likely to view their own programs as an effective tool for both recruitment (approximately 83%) and retention (76%).

[113] Chase, supra note 8, at 625 n.1 (citing ABA, 1 Faculty Briefing No. 4, at 1 (Chicago, Ill., 1988)).

Association yielded similar results. Of twenty-nine responding public service employers, 64% reported that debt impeded efforts to recruit and retain attorneys.[114] Most recently, the first results of the "After the JD" study, released in 2004, showed that "[s]eventy percent of the 'After the JD' respondents said that when they looked for their first legal job, the goal of paying off debt was one of their top concerns."[115] The second results from this longitudinal study, released in 2009, revealed that, even years out of law school, 42% of respondents "said that having educational debt had a fairly strong influence on their job choice."[116] The "AJD" study similarly showed that indebted students whose first job was a public interest position viewed loan repayment assistance as very important to their job choice.[117] Oddly enough, these sentiments shifted just a few years into their careers.[118]

As debt levels have risen, then, students have increasingly viewed educational debt as a barrier to public service and loan repayment assistance as a substantial benefit. So too have public service employers. But are these mere sentiments? Or do students' observed conduct also support the conventional wisdom that debt affects job choice and that loan repayment assistance programs can successfully mitigate that effect?

School-Specific Studies of Students' Observed Job Choices

In a 1992 study, Professor David L. Chambers evaluated whether students' observed job choices reveal a strong relationship between debt and job choice. The Chambers study was based on a questionnaire that nine law schools distributed right before graduation to students in the class of 1989.[119] The nine schools were divided into two groups. Group A schools had lower tuition rates, many students without jobs lined up at graduation, and many graduates working in government, small firms, or non-practice settings. In contrast, Group B schools had higher tuition rates, were located

114 See Lifting the Burden, supra note 16, at 28. "Those that did not report such difficulties tended to be the federal and state government agencies that paid higher salaries."

115 Ronit Dinovitzer et al., After the JD: First Results from a National Study of Legal Careers 72 (The NALP Foundation for Law Career Research and Education and the American Bar Foundation 2004), available at www.americanbarfoundation.org/uploads/cms/documents/ajd.pdf (hereinafter AJD I).

116 Ronit Dinovitzer et al., After the JD II: Second Results from a National Study of Legal Careers 80 (The NALP Foundation for Law Career Research and Education and the American Bar Foundation 2009), available at www.law.du.edu/documents/directory/publications/sterling/AJD2.pdf (hereinafter AJD II).

117 See AJD I, supra note 115, at 72.

118 See AJD II, supra note 116, at 81 ("Curiously, loan repayment assistance programs (LRAPs) are not identified by ... respondents [in public interest jobs or nonprofits] as particularly important factors in their ability to repay their student loans, though LRAPs were more important for them than for respondents in any other setting").

119 See Chambers, *Burdens of Educational Loans*, supra note 84, at 187, 190. The nine law schools that participated in the study included three public and six private schools. *Id.* at 188 n.2. "The rate of response ranged from about 40 percent of the class at one school to over 95 percent at another, with a median of 65 percent." *Id.* at 190.

in areas with a higher cost of living, and had a "large majority of students" with jobs lined up at graduation, mostly in large law firms.[120] The survey asked students whether they had secured post-graduation employment and what type of work they expected to be doing upon graduation or (if applicable) after a clerkship. The survey also inquired about the student's expected salary, marital status and spousal income, total educational debt, cumulative law school grade point average, gender, and race/ethnicity.[121] In addition to measuring actual student conduct and controlling for the students' background, the study included several measures of individual school context that gave the study greater depth. The number of employers interviewing at each school during the 1988–89 school year provided a rough measure of the students' employment opportunities. Median LSAT scores and undergraduate GPAs of the entering class were used as a proxy for employers' perceptions of the quality of the schools' graduates. Finally, a ratio of the mean salaries for respondents at each school who took jobs in the public sector and small firms and those who took jobs in large firms was used to measure how wide the salary gap appeared to the schools' students.[122]

This more nuanced empirical evaluation of students' actual job choices tells a different story than the surveys, suggesting that educational debt is at most "mildly and weakly" related to job choice and that other factors have a much greater influence.[123] The data suggested that "for each $10,000 increase in a student's debt, there is a roughly 3-percent decrease in the probability that the student will take a job in government, legal services, or a small firm and a 3-percent increase in the probability of taking a job in a larger firm."[124] When the analysis was conducted for each school individually, the results were "murkier."[125] For while the relationship between debt and job choice ran in the same direction for each school, the relationship was statistically significant for only three of eight schools.[126] Furthermore, both law school grades and the number of interviewers at a school had a greater influence on students' job choices than did debt levels.[127]

A larger and similarly nuanced study of the job choices of students at NYU School of Law and the University of Michigan Law School confirmed that, in choosing what type of job to accept upon graduation, other considerations matter much more

[120] See *id.* at 189.
[121] See *id.* at 228.
[122] See *id.* at 194–95.
[123] *Id.*
[124] *Id.*
[125] *Id.*
[126] See *id.* One school had to be omitted from this analysis because it did not provide information about the students' grades, a factor that proved to have a greater effect on job choice than debt. See *id.* at 199 n.26.
[127] Chambers, *Burdens of Educational Loans*, supra note 84, at 200–201; see also Christa McGill, *Educational Debt and Law Student Failure to Enter Public Service Careers: Bringing Empirical Data to Bear*, 31 Law & Soc. Inquiry 677, 683 (2006).

than debt. Professors Lewis A. Kornhauser and Richard L. Revesz constructed two data sets – one consisting of student data culled from NYU's records for 1,370 of 1,601 graduates from the classes of 1987–90,[128] and one consisting of student data obtained through surveys filled out by 1,445 of 2,627 graduates from Michigan's classes of 1982–88.[129] The dependent variable was job choice, with employment outcomes broken down into three categories: non-elite for-profit jobs, elite for-profit jobs, and not-for-profit jobs.[130] The independent variables included race and gender, career plans, law school performance, debt, and wages.[131] The analysis revealed that law school performance, career plans, and wages affected job choice more than debt. At NYU, law school debt had a statistically significant effect only for African American and Latino women, and only on the choice between elite for-profit and not-for-profit jobs.[132] At Michigan, debt level had a statistically significant effect only for women, for whom higher debts increased the relative probability of taking a non-elite for-profit job over a not-for-profit job or an elite for-profit job over a not-for-profit job.[133]

The empirical analysis of student job choice further suggests that even the most generous loan repayment assistance program is unlikely to have much influence on the number of students who choose to take public interest positions.[134] At NYU, Kornhauser and Revesz estimated that, in the aggregate, "[o]nly about 3% of the individuals who took for-profit jobs (either elite or non-elite) absent loan forgiveness would have, instead, taken a not-for-profit job as a result of a full loan forgiveness program."[135] The projected aggregate effect was even smaller – about 1% – for the Michigan sample.[136] Interestingly, for most demographic groups at the two schools, the projected influence of loan repayment assistance "may simply have resulted by chance."[137]

[128] See Lewis A. Kornhauser & Richard L. Revesz, *Legal Education and Entry into the Legal Profession: The Role of Race, Gender, and Educational Debt*, 70 N.Y.U. L. Rev. 829, 892 (1995). The researchers omitted from the study all students for whom complete information was not available through the school's records, external sources (e.g., Martindale–Hubbell directories), or some combination of the two. See *id.* at 892 & nn. 213–14.

[129] See *id.* at 901–902. The total response rate was thus 55%, *id.* at 902, and the researchers carefully considered the demographic variation and its implications, see *id.* at 902–903.

[130] See *id.* at 893–95, 903–904. The categories were defined slightly differently for each school, to account for differences in the market realities in New York and Chicago. See *id.* at 903–904.

[131] See *id.* at 895–901, 903–907. There was slight variation in how the dependent variables were defined for each school, primarily as a result of the different ways in which the information was collected at each school (i.e., school records versus student surveys). See *id.* at 903–907.

[132] See *id.* at 915, 919.

[133] See *id.* at 918, 919.

[134] See *id.* at 927–30.

[135] *Id.* at 928. A "full loan forgiveness program" is one under which graduates accepting a not-for-profit job "would not have needed to make *any* debt-service payments." *Id.* at 927 (emphasis added). Interestingly, for African American and Latino women at NYU, the projected effect of such a program was much greater – more than one-third might have taken a not-for-profit job if offered full loan forgiveness. *Id.* at 929.

[136] See *id.* at 929, 930. Here, too, however, the projected effect was greater (approximately 10%) for certain demographic groups, specifically African Americans and Latinos. See *id.* at 930.

[137] *Id.* at 929; see also *id.* at 930.

Longitudinal studies of students' observed job choices

The findings of the school-specific empirical studies of student job choice are corroborated by an empirical evaluation of data obtained in two longitudinal studies of student job choice. One of these studies was conducted in the early 1990s, while the other was initiated in the early 2000s and is ongoing.

The first longitudinal study was the "Bar Passage Study," an examination of legal education and entry into the legal profession conducted by the Law School Admissions Council (LSAC). This study followed 2,290 students at 172 law schools from the time they entered law school in 1991 until they passed the bar and entered the legal profession. The study included student data, supplemented by information provided in follow-up questionnaires administered annually for three years.[138] Although the data had some limitations,[139] they also had some advantages over data used in earlier studies. One important advantage is that the data were substantively rich, including measures of students' career aspirations, summer employment experiences, and actual job choices.[140] Another advantage is that the study produced data from the full range of law schools nationwide.

An empirical analysis of the LSAC data confirmed that there is "no significant relationship between debt and whether a graduate entered the [public interest] job sector."[141] As in previous studies, the data strongly suggest that job choice is a nuanced calculus involving a variety of considerations. Debt is only one of these considerations – and it is not the most important. In this study, the students who were most likely to take entry-level positions in public interest and government were those who: (1) entered law school with the desire to pursue a public interest career; and (2) worked in a public interest job during the summer following their second year of law school.[142] At the same time, 76% of the students who came to law school with public interest aspirations did *not* ultimately take public interest positions.[143] Although there could be many explanations, these graduates were underrepresented in the most lucrative practice settings, and so were probably not lured away from public interest work by significantly higher wages.[144] This suggests that the supply of public interest jobs "may have been an important factor" leading otherwise interested graduates to accept positions outside of the public interest sector.[145]

Data from a second longitudinal study, the "After the JD" study, corroborate the conclusions drawn from the LSAC data. The "After the JD" study is a joint enterprise of the NALP Foundation for Law Career Research and Education and the ABA,

[138] See McGill, supra note 127, at 692.
[139] See *id.* at 694.
[140] See *id.* at 693.
[141] *Id.* at 700.
[142] See *id.* at 702.
[143] See *id.* at 703.
[144] See *id.* at 704.
[145] *Id.* at 703.

which began in the early 2000s and is ongoing.[146] The study is a ten-year project tracking the professional experiences of more than 5,000 lawyers, a sample that is representative of the lawyers first admitted to the bar in 2000.[147] To date, the project has generated two reports. The first report, released in 2004, focused on the first few years of the study participants' legal careers, while the second report, released in 2009, analyzed data collected when the participants were about seven years out of law school.[148] The first report found that the data do "not support th[e] assertion" that "debt accrued while attending law school prevents law school graduates from taking public service positions in the legal profession when they leave law school."[149] This finding held constant in the study's second report.[150] Indeed, the results suggested that, although graduates "feel the weight their debt in a more global way," there is not "a strong correlation between levels of debt and job choice."[151]

The "After the JD" study confirms something implicit in the body of empirical research on the relationship between debt and job choice: with respect to the questions of whether and to what extent debt affects job choice, there is considerable tension between students' expressed sentiments and observed conduct. Students worry about their debt and how it will affect their lives. If you ask them whether loan repayment obligations and assistance programs are important considerations, they will overwhelmingly reply in the affirmative. But students' observed conduct tells a different and more complex story. Debt and loan repayment assistance certainly matter, but study after study has shown that, at least when it comes to job choice, other factors matter more. The lesson is that, although loan repayment assistance programs may attract prospective students and signal that a law school is taking action to address student debt and further the public interest, law schools should look elsewhere if they are serious about achieving access to justice results.

The Demand for Lawyers: Influencing the Legal Services Market

To successfully expand access to civil justice, law school initiatives like loan repayment programs must not merely influence students to take socially beneficial jobs – they must result in an overall increase in the number of such jobs available in the legal services market.[152] Loan repayment assistance programs do not directly create

[146] Gita Z. Wilder, *Law School Debt and Urban Law Schools*, 36 Sw. U. L. Rev. 509, 509 (2007); see AJD I, supra note 115.

[147] See AJD I, supra note 115, at 13–14.

[148] See AJD II, supra note 116, at 12.

[149] Wilder, supra note 146, at 509; see AJD I, supra note 115; AJD II, supra note 116.

[150] AJD II, supra note 116, at 80.

[151] *Id.* at 80.

[152] See, e.g., Zubrow, supra note 3, at 533 ("The central issue is whether the money spent by law schools on loan forgiveness will increase the legal services produced in the public interest sector"). It is possible that loan repayment assistance programs may improve the qualifications of the graduates who accept public interest jobs. See, e.g., Lifting the Burden, supra note 16, at 28. But this is a matter of

jobs.[153] Instead, they provide support to graduates who have secured qualifying employment with third-party employers.[154] And "even without the issue of student and attorney debt, public interest and government organizations face a variety of challenges in recruiting and retaining legal talent."[155] Many other factors, which are beyond the control of law schools, are likely to have a greater effect on the number of public interest positions available in the legal services market. These factors include the availability of core funding and public interest employers' resource allocation decisions.[156] This is probably also true for positions providing middle-income legal services. When there is a shortage of jobs in a particular sector – whether public interest or middle-income services – it seems unlikely that generous loan repayment support will be sufficient to overcome market reality.[157] As previously noted, an analysis of data collected by LSAC suggested that the restricted supply of public interest positions was a significant factor leading students who were otherwise interested in such positions to accept employment in other sectors.[158] Market realities may also partially explain why the number of participants in law school loan repayment assistance programs has remained relatively small.[159]

Through what mechanism would law school loan repayment assistance programs effectuate an increase in the aggregate number of public interest (or middle-class service) jobs available in the legal services market?[160] Presumably, it would be by subsidizing qualifying employment, thereby enabling the affected employers to stretch limited core funding to hire a greater number of graduates. Note, however, that this result is only possible if the employers are paying each graduate less than they might have paid in the absence of law school loan repayment assistance.[161]

Viewed from this perspective, it seems possible that law school loan repayment assistance programs may be somewhat counterproductive. The original motivation for establishing these programs was to address the wage gap between the private and public sectors of the legal services market. And, as we have seen, empirical studies have consistently shown that the wage gap is a more powerful influence on student job choice than are debt levels. To increase the number of positions available in a particular sector of the economy, however, loan repayment assistance programs

substitution. The potential access to justice effects of loan repayment assistance require not substitution, but expansion.

[153] A recent increase in the number of law school graduates employed in legal services has been attributed to law schools funding fixed-duration job opportunities for their own graduates. See NALP, *Legal Services Jobs – Are They Up or Down?*, Oct. 2012, available at www.nalp.org/oct12research_lscjobs.

[154] See Vernon, supra note 28, at 744.

[155] PAPER CHASE, supra note 13, at 11.

[156] See, e.g., Zubrow, supra note 3, at 496–97.

[157] See, e.g., FINANCING THE FUTURE, supra note 2, at iii.

[158] See supra at notes 142–145 and accompanying text.

[159] See FINANCING THE FUTURE, supra note 2, at 7; see also supra at notes 44–46 and accompanying text (discussing the small participation rate in law school loan repayment assistance programs over time).

[160] See generally Zubrow, supra note 3.

[161] See generally *id.*

would need to exert sufficient downward pressure on market salaries in the targeted sector (whether public interest or middle-income services) to enable employers to hire more attorneys using the same level of available funds.[162] One scholar has accordingly suggested that, if loan repayment assistance programs have their desired aggregate effect, it may come at the cost of exacerbating the wage differential between the public and private sectors.[163] One possible consequence is that "graduates with no educational debt may be driven out of the market because of a decrease in wage rates," while eligible employment becomes marginally more attractive to those with debt.[164] This suggests a possible substitution effect.[165] If commitment to public interest work is, as some studies have suggested, a stronger predictor of student job choice than financial considerations, there may be a more pernicious consequence of the "success" of loan repayment assistance programs: lawyers willing to sacrifice financial security to do socially beneficial or personally rewarding work might be punished for their choices with artificially depressed wage rates.[166]

Supporting What Kinds of Jobs?

A final way to evaluate the extent to which loan repayment assistance programs expand access to justice is to consider the kind of the jobs supported by existing programs. Do existing programs actually support graduates serving underrepresented populations? If so, which populations?

A close look at NYU's loan repayment assistance program is illuminating. NYU's Office of Student Financial Services provided a list of the names of employers of NYU graduates who participated in the school's loan repayment assistance program during each program year from 2005 through 2012.[167] Using publicly available information, I examined the 544 employers in program year 2012[168] and sorted each employer into one of nine categories: (1) federal government; (2) state or local government;[169] (3) nonprofit organization; (4) nonprofit organization that

[162] See Vernon, supra note 28, at 759.
[163] See generally Zubrow, supra note 3.
[164] See *id.* at 533.
[165] See *id.* at 573.
[166] *Cf.* Vernon, supra note 28, at 760 ("The assistance programs, thus, tend to relieve pressure on employers to increase salaries to more reasonable levels").
[167] Some program participants had more than one employer during the program year. All such employers were included in the list. Participants who graduated in 1998–2001 were not subject to the requirement that their employment be in the "public interest." As a result, some of the employers included in the list would not be considered to provide qualifying employment under the program's current requirements.
[168] A comparison of the employer lists for program years 2005–11 provides some assurance that the 2012 list fairly represents the types of employers that are typically the indirect beneficiaries of NYU's loan repayment assistance program.
[169] NYU's program provides assistance to graduates who accept judicial clerkships with the intention of taking public-interest positions at the end of the clerkship. These jobs are therefore reflected in the count of federal, state, and local government employers.

provides substantial direct legal services;[170] (5) legal aid and public defender; (6) sole practitioner or law firm; (7) international organization; (8) academic institution; and (9) other. The distribution of employer types is provided in Table 14.1.

These data suggest that most of jobs supported by NYU's loan repayment assistance program do not entail the provision of direct legal services to underserved populations.[171] Indeed, 54% of employers were governments, nonprofit organizations that primarily engage in research and advocacy, international organizations, and academic institutions. On the other hand, approximately 44% of the employers provide direct legal services: about 13% were nonprofit organizations that provide substantial direct legal services to underrepresented or vulnerable populations, about a quarter were legal aid and public defender organizations, and roughly 6% were sole practitioners or law firms. For the most part, however, these nonprofit, legal aid, and public defender employers appeared to provide services primarily to indigent and poor clients. It thus appears likely that NYU's program supports few (if any) graduates who represent clients who are underrepresented but of average means.

The extent to which law school loan repayment programs support graduates engaged in traditional law practice (i.e., client representation) varies. For example, of the graduates receiving support from Columbia's loan repayment assistance program in 2012–13, 6% worked for public interest law firms, 40% were employed in nonprofit organizations, 31% worked in government, 16% were in clerkships, and 4% were employed in legal academia.[172] Some schools' programs specifically exclude from eligibility certain types of traditional law practice. Thus, in 2008, thirteen of seventy-six law school programs did not cover prosecutors.[173] A program's other eligibility requirements may affect the distribution of supported employment, including for particular classes of graduates over time. For example, "[b]ecause salaries are higher, government attorneys are likely to earn their way out of eligibility more quickly th[a]n lawyers in nonprofit organization positions."[174]

Further examination of program eligibility requirements across law schools suggests that NYU's experience may be typical. If the primary goal is to expand access to justice, most law school loan repayment assistance programs appear poorly designed to achieve it. Although a graduate's work must usually be "law-related," the requirement is defined broadly, capturing many positions that do not involve representing clients. For example, at NYU, to be eligible, a position must "involve law," which

170 This differentiation between different types of nonprofits was made in an effort to provide a more accurate assessment of the extent to which NYU's loan repayment assistance program supports graduates who provide direct legal services to underrepresented populations.

171 The data do not reveal jobs, but rather employers. Nonetheless, the type of employer provides a rough indication of the type of work performed by participating graduates.

172 DeRubeis Interview, supra note 37.

173 See Schrag & Pruett, supra note 22, at 588.

174 FINANCING THE FUTURE, supra note 2, at 13.

TABLE 14.1 *Jobs supported by NYU's loan repayment assistance program in 2012.*

Federal gov't	State or local gov't	Nonprofit	Nonprofit providing direct legal services	Legal aid and public defender	Sole practitioner or law firm	Int'l	Academic	Other
80 (14.7%)	68 (12.5%)	103 (18.9%)	73 (13.4%)	132 (24.3%)	33 (6.1%)	10 (1.8%)	33 (6.1%)	12 (2.2%)
All gov't: 148 (27.3%)		All nonprofit: 176 (32.3%)				Int'l and academic: 43 (7.9%)		
Total gov't and nonprofit: 324 (59.6%)			Total providing direct legal services: 238 (43.8%)			All other: 55 (10.1%)		

Total number of graduates participating in the program: 544

Total providing direct legal services: 238 (43.8%)

Total not providing direct legal services: 294 (56.2%)

Other: 12 (2.2%)

may mean that the position requires a JD as a minimum educational requirement, is "often held by members of the legal profession," or generally requires the graduate "to use his or her legal training to a significant degree."[175] Eligible employment is thus not limited to positions that require bar admission and entail representing clients. As at NYU, many graduates who receive loan repayment assistance do not provide legal services, but rather are employed for nonprofit organizations that focus on advocacy or other policy work that is one (or more) step removed from client representation.[176] This approach recognizes that there may be many socially beneficial but low-paying ways for graduates to use their law degrees. But if a law school's goal is to expand access to justice for underrepresented populations, then such a permissive eligibility requirement may result in a misallocation of resources.

Similarly, most programs define "public interest" in a way that is both under- and over-inclusive from an access to justice perspective. "Public interest" typically includes jobs in organizations that provide poverty legal services,[177] employment with tax-exempt nonprofit organizations, and work for local, state, and federal governments.[178] At some schools, positions with international nongovernmental organizations, judicial clerkships, and academic positions may also qualify.[179] This approach has benefits. It recognizes there are many different kinds of socially beneficial but low-paying jobs available to law school graduates. And by using an employing organization's tax-exempt status as a proxy for "socially beneficial," schools are able to avoid making more nuanced eligibility determinations that might be controversial or politically charged.[180] On the other hand, a broad definition of "public interest" renders this core eligibility requirement over-inclusive to the extent that it funds a variety of non-practice positions in nonprofit and nongovernmental organizations, judicial clerkships, and academia. At the same time, it is often under-inclusive, rendering ineligible those graduates who work in solo practices, small law firms, or other settings in which the work primarily involves providing legal representation to low-income, middle-income, or other traditionally

[175] NYU Law, Financial Aid, Loan Repayment Assistance Program (LRAP), Eligible Employment, available at www.law.nyu.edu/financialaid/lrap/EligibleEmployment/index.htm.

[176] Schoenecker Interview, supra note 37; see also Zubrow, supra note 3, at 502.

[177] Poverty lawyers include those working in legal aid, as public defenders, or in other organizations that provide civil or criminal legal services to low-income and indigent populations that could not otherwise afford such services. See Zubrow, supra note 3, at 501–502.

[178] See Financing the Future, supra note 2, at 12.

[179] See, e.g., Schrag & Pruett, supra note 22, at 588 (reporting that only twenty-four of seventy-six law school programs operational in 2008 supported judicial clerks); Zubrow, supra note 3, at 501–502.

[180] *Cf.* Zubrow, supra note 3, at 527 ("Programs that require students and their families to subsidize, through tuition payments, the activities of public interest organizations that are contrary to their belief may impinge upon students' associational rights"); Vernon, supra note 28, at 759–60 (noting the lurking danger that donors may put pressure on schools to incorporate political considerations into the eligibility determinations).

underserved populations.[181] The mismatch between eligibility requirements and legal services provision should not be surprising – it is a natural consequence of the mixed motives for law school loan repayment assistance programs.

Finally, it may bear noting that most law school loan repayment assistance is provided by elite law schools.[182] As of 2000, although approximately fifty schools offered loan repayment assistance programs, nearly 70% of the total funds available were distributed to graduates of just six law schools.[183] That figure has held constant – in 2008, the same six law schools also provided 70% of the funds.[184] Nonetheless, an empirical study of aggregate law school data pulled from several different sources revealed that "[i]rrespective of the salary gap, elite law schools were significantly less likely to send graduates into" public interest jobs.[185] This further supports the proposition that loan repayment assistance programs, no matter how generous, have little effect on job choice.

THE CASE AGAINST EXPANDED LOAN FORGIVENESS

Resisting Pressure to Expand Loan Repayment Assistance

The empirical evidence is substantial and persuasive: law school loan repayment assistance programs are an ineffective tool for expanding access to justice. Support for these programs, however, seems impervious to these empirical findings. The conventional wisdom remains that debt is determinative of job choice and that debt relief, in the form of loan repayment assistance and forgiveness, is essential to ensure that enough law graduates pursue careers in the public interest.[186] And some contend that, even if the conventional wisdom is wrong in the public-interest context, it might hold in other, less profitable practices, including those serving the legal needs of middle class Americans.[187] Others have likewise assumed that debt inhibits lawyers in private practice from doing pro bono work.[188] Several decades of

[181] Graduates in these kinds of positions are now able to use income-based repayment. But schools faced with limited funding for loan repayment assistance may need to continue relying on strict eligibility requirements to effectuate funding priorities.

[182] See, e.g., Lisa Stansky, *About Those Loans . . . Secure your financial future by arming yourself with debt management strategies and repayment options*, 29 STUDENT LAW. 24 Mar. 2001, at 29 ("Loan repayment assistance programs are most common at well-endowed elite schools").

[183] See LIFTING THE BURDEN, supra note 16, at 47.

[184] See Schrag & Pruett, supra note 22, at 588.

[185] See McGill, supra note 127, at 691. The data, all from 2004, were drawn from the *U.S. News and World Report* law school rankings, the ABA and LSAC's *Official Guide to Law ABA-Approved Schools*, and NALP's *Jobs and JDs* Placement Statistics. See *id.* at 685.

[186] See, e.g., Jeanine L. DeBor, *From the ACBA: Loan Repayment Assistance Programs Ease Debt for Public Interest Attorneys*, 12 LAWYERS J. 3 (2010) ("Whether a law student's journey leads him/her to a job in public service or the private sector will, unfortunately, depend upon the amount of debt he/she incurs as a result of his/her law school education").

[187] DEBT AND THE PRACTICE OF LAW, supra note 47, at 1–2; see also *Survey of New Admittees*, supra note 108.

[188] See Wroth, supra note 42, at 28.

experience with existing law school loan repayment programs provides ample reason to question these intuitive appeals. In seeking ways to encourage public interest work and expand access to justice to Americans of average means, law schools should focus on finding more targeted, transparent approaches to fill the legal services gap.

The current crisis in legal education may, however, make it difficult for schools to neatly separate access to justice goals from the pervasive challenges of astronomical educational debt, uncertain employment opportunities, and declining law school enrollments. In this climate, limiting loan repayment assistance to graduates pursuing public interest careers as traditionally defined seems inadequate.[189] Indeed, there can be little justification for exclusively providing benefits to graduates working in the public interest when the "law school subsidies do not in fact increase representation of the poor or other underserved groups."[190] At the same time, many still subscribe to the conventional wisdom regarding the relationship between debt and job choice and have plausibly suggested that the current debt crisis is not just worse in degree, but also different in kind, from previous crises. If would-be lawyers seek employment in other fields to avoid high debt and uncertain employment outcomes out of law school, the entire justice system may suffer.[191] And as enrollments decline, loan repayment assistance programs may become more appealing to law schools for competitive reasons. In short, law schools may face significant pressure to expand or create new programs regardless of the empirical evidence that such programs are not an effective way to expand access to justice.

From this perspective, the emergence of federal loan repayment assistance and forgiveness programs may be a double-edged sword. On the one hand, it may amplify pressure for schools to create or expand their own loan repayment assistance programs. After all, coordinating with the federal program will substantially bring down the cost to law schools of providing full support to a greater number of graduates.[192] In this sense, the federal program undermines the long-prevailing truth that "loan forgiveness programs are very expensive, and there is substantial doubt that school-sponsored programs will ever assist a large number of students at more than a very few schools."[193] On the other hand, there are reasons for schools to be cautious in going down this path. Income-based repayment and PSLF may prove

[189] *Cf.* Debt and the Practice of Law, supra note 47, at 29 ("[L]aw schools have an obligation to be responsive to the needs of all of their students, and not just those interested in public interest law").

[190] Zubrow, supra note 3, at 547.

[191] See White, supra note 4, at 734.

[192] See generally Schrag & Pruett, supra note 22. This opportunity may not last – some have raised concerns that the federal loan repayment assistance program will not be financially sustainable and that its costs may exceed its benefits. See, e.g., Beth Akers & Matthew M. Chingos, Student Loan Safety Nets: Estimating the Costs and Benefits of Income-Based Repayment 2 (Brown Center on Education Policy at Brookings, Apr. 2014), available at www.brookings.edu/research/papers/2014/04/14-income-based-repayment-akers-chingos ("[W]e recommend that policy makers revise the existing income-based repayment programs to eliminate forgiveness, or at least significantly reduce its generosity").

[193] Sebert, supra note 81, at 525.

to be just the newest "mechanisms that will make the debt burden feel lighter than it actually is."[194] Law schools must educate their students about the responsibilities and potential consequences of heavy educational debt, including by honestly addressing the negative amortization that may result from reliance on income-based repayment. This is not a new need,[195] but it has taken on greater importance in the current crisis. Finally, law schools must take seriously the opportunity costs of investing in loan repayment assistance programs. Although law schools may be able to create these programs with fewer resources, the time, energy, and money that schools devote to such programs will still be significant. And if those resources are dedicated to loan repayment assistance, they will not be available to support other initiatives, including those that may hold greater promise for addressing "the excessively high cost of legal services to [the middle class and] prospective lower-income clients, to which the cost of education may make only a small contribution."[196]

Finding Effective Ways to Achieve School-Specific Goals

Law schools may seek to achieve other goals – aside from expanding access to justice – by operating loan repayment assistance programs. These goals may include making law school more affordable for poor or middle-income students, successfully competing with other law schools for students, and cultivating a reputation for producing well-trained attorneys both capable of and dedicated to providing top-notch legal services to underserved populations.

The results of a controlled "Innovative Financial Aid Study" strongly suggest that well-designed scholarship programs may be a more effective way for law schools to achieve these goals. The "Innovative Financial Aid Study" was initially proposed by Professors Kornhauser and Revesz[197] and was conducted at NYU School of Law for a subset of students in the classes of 1998–2001.[198] The study used a lottery to randomly allocate income-contingent tuition subsidies, in the form of public service scholarships, among the 270 students who elected to participate in the study.[199] The 141 student participants who won the lottery received a career-contingent scholarship that "provided a grant for two-thirds tuition that converted to a loan in the event a recipient did not pursue a public interest law career."[200] The remaining 129 student participants who lost the lottery "had to take out interest-free loans at the beginning of each year, but were eligible for loan repayment from NYU after graduation to

194 Kramer, *Pay the Piper*, supra note 4, at 656.
195 See, e.g., Stansky, supra note 182, at 26.
196 Schrag, *Misguided Missile*, supra note 61, at 387; *but* see TAMANAHA, supra note 82, at 27.
197 See Kornhauser & Revesz, supra note 128.
198 Erica Field, *Educational Debt Burden and Career Choice: Evidence from a Financial Aid Experiment at NYU Law School*, 1 AM. ECON. J. APPLIED ECON. 1, 3 (2009).
199 *Id.* at 3–4.
200 *Id.* at 3.

cover tuition debt accrued during law school."[201] The study was designed to eliminate any direct or indirect difference in the monetary value of the two aid packages.[202] In addition, neither aid package was merit-based or entailed "any extra curricular activities, organized meetings, or special coursework."[203] Finally, lottery outcomes were announced at different times for different class years involved in the study, allowing researchers to evaluate the effect of the two aid packages on both application and enrollment decisions.[204] Entrance and exit surveys were used to track changes in the students' personal ranking of the importance of fifteen job characteristics.[205] Other data included information about the students' background, career goals, personal debt, academic performance, clinical course work, participation in extracurricular activities, summer job placement, and biennial employment information for six years following graduation.[206]

If a law school seeks to increase the percentage of its own graduates who accept positions providing legal services to underrepresented populations, the results of the "Innovative Financial Aid Study" suggest that career-contingent scholarships will be more effective than income-contingent loan repayment assistance.[207] Indeed, students who received a career-contingent scholarship in the study were 36% more likely to choose careers in the public interest.[208] The results also suggest that a law school may be able to compete more effectively with other law schools for students by offering career-contingent scholarships.[209]

Finally, this study may provide an explanation for the apparent tension, previously discussed, between what students say about debt and loan repayment assistance and what their observed job choices reveal. Recall that the "Innovative Financial Aid

[201] *Id.* at 4. Lottery losers were permitted to reapply for a PSS in their second and third years of law school, a complicating factor for which the study was designed to account. See *Id.* at 10–11.

[202] See *id.* at 4–8. "The only difference in the financial value of the two aid packages is the potential risk associated with the nonbinding nature of the LRAP agreement. In particular, neither the existence of LRAP nor its benefits formula was guaranteed to remain constant for ten years after law school applicants entered the job market." *Id.* at 9.

[203] *Id.* at 9. These aspects of the IFAS were designed to equalize employment opportunities and eliminate non-financial explanations for any differences in the students' job choices.

[204] See *id.* at 11. Data were drawn from six sources, including "law school applications; financial aid applications; law school academic records; first-year entry surveys on work experience, personal debt, career goals, and job preferences; third-year exit surveys identical to the entry survey but including school and summer activities; and work experience surveys mailed biennially for six years after graduation." *Id.* at 4.

[205] *Id.* at 18.

[206] *Id.* at 4.

[207] As previously discussed, it is likely that an individual school's success in this regard reflects a substitution of its graduates for the graduates of other law schools and not an increase in the aggregate number of graduates accepting these positions.

[208] Field, supra note 198, at 15.

[209] *Id.* at 12. "In 1999, lottery winners were 30 percent more likely to attend NYU, while in 2000 lottery winners enrolled at NYU at twice the rate of lottery losers. The numbers suggest that 18.5 percent of lottery winners in the classes of 1999 and 2000 would not have attended NYU had they lost the lottery." *Id.* at 13.

Study" was designed to ensure that the scholarships given to students in the treatment group were financially equivalent to the loan repayment assistance offered to students in the control group. The students' preferences and experiences during law school remained remarkably consistent across both treatment and control groups,[210] so the effectiveness of career-contingent scholarships cannot be attributed to increased social consciousness resulting from participation in the program.[211] A careful analysis of the data thus reveal that "choosing a well-paid private sector job appears to be a tradeoff students make in response to the psychological stress associated with securing a livable wage in public interest law."[212] This suggests that debt has psychological costs that cannot be compensated by retrospective financial assistance.[213] Regardless, "[t]he policy implication for a school interested in increasing its supply of graduates to the public interest sector is straightforward. By distributing career contingent scholarship funds before rather than after graduation a law school can increase its rate of public interest placement."[214]

CONCLUSION

Law schools are foundational institutions bound by the legal profession's obligation to protect the integrity of the justice system and ensure that the legal needs of all members of society are met. This obligation has taken on new urgency and complexity as law schools grapple with the current crisis. Loan repayment assistance programs have long been heralded as the best hope for addressing simultaneously the needs of law students, law schools, and the public. But these goals and interests are distinct, and law schools should not merely assume that providing loan repayment assistance is an effective way to achieve them all. As in the early days of loan repayment assistance movement, intuition and anecdotal evidence strongly suggest that education debt is determinative of job choice and that loan repayment assistance can encourage more graduates to accept low-paying positions, including those in solo practices and small firms that serve the legal needs of middle-class and working Americans.[215] Several decades of experience with public interest loan repayment assistance programs, however, provide solid empirical evidence that contradicts this enduring conventional wisdom.

[210] See Field, supra note 198, at 18–19. Interestingly, the only significant shift in the pattern of preferences was that students who received career-contingent scholarships ranked salary and benefits as more important at the end of law school than they did at the beginning of law school. *Id.* at 18. These students also performed significantly better in their third year, perhaps in part due to the "greater competition for the limited supply of prestigious and reasonably paid public interest jobs." *Id.*

[211] See *id.* at 18–19.

[212] *Id.* at 19.

[213] *Cf.* Zubrow, supra note 3, at 491–92 ("The loan forgiveness standard of social justice appears to be from each, according to his unwillingness to borrow, and to each, according to his proclivity to borrow and inability to earn").

[214] Field, supra note 198, at 19.

[215] See Vernon, supra note 28, at 745.

In developing ways to expand access to justice, law schools should not ignore the empirical evidence that loan repayment assistance programs are ineffective as a tool for expanding access to justice. Instead, they should redirect their limited resources to new and more promising approaches. These approaches may include improving practical training and equipping students with the business and financial knowledge they will need to operate solo practices or start small law firms. Changes to state bar rules may be needed to facilitate academic experimentation, including the reintroduction of an optional two-year legal education. Law schools might also support the deliberative, ethical development of new technologies that hold the promise of expanding the availability of basic legal services in a cost-effective way. In these and other endeavors, collaboration among members of the bar, bench, and academy will be necessary to ensure that the legal needs of all Americans are met.

15

Federally Funded Civil Legal Services

Joy Radice

Legal services organizations funded in part by federal grants have provided a national safety net of civil legal assistance for the poor since the 1970s. In this chapter, Joy Radice explains how legal service offices are structured and funded, who is eligible for their free legal assistance, and how local legal services organizations triage their resources and stretch their shrinking federal dollars to reach as many eligible people as possible.

The Legal Services Corporation (LSC) is the largest source of funding for civil legal services in the country. Its grantees include 799 field offices and over 4,000 attorneys nationwide.[1] In 2013, LSC, which is funded by Congressional appropriations, provided its grantees $342,778,665. The LSC offices in turn closed over 758,689 cases involving three basic types of legal assistance defined by the LSC's regulations: legal advice and counsel (60% of closed cases in 2013), brief services (16% of closed cases), and extended legal services (25% of closed cases).[2]

This chapter examines how this network of programs is structured, who qualifies for LSC-supported legal services, and what type of assistance is provided. Over the past two decades, Congressional funding has declined dramatically, while the number of Americans who financially qualify for LSC assistance has increased to about 65 million according to U.S. Census Bureau estimates.

LSC CLIENT DEMOGRAPHICS

LSC grantees serve clients in all 50 states and every U.S. territory – from dense metropolitan areas to rural counties where lawyers might have to travel for hours to visit clients. LSC clients are farmers, tenants, parents, students, and veterans. The majority of clients, 70%, are women, while 15% are seniors over 60, and only 2% are children. LSC clients are also diverse racially and ethnically (see Table 15.1).

1 Legal Services *Corporation* (LSC), *Annual Report* (2013) at 1, 5.
2 LSC, *By the Numbers: The Data Underlying Legal Aid Programs* (2014), available at www.lsc.gov/about/lsc-numbers-2013 (last visited June 2015) (hereinafter LSC Data Underlying Legal Aid Programs).

TABLE 15.1 2013 *client race and ethnicity.*

Ethnic group	Total individual clients	Percent served	Percent in poverty
White	348,570	46.0	44.2
African American	211,964	28.0	20.7
Hispanic	131,521	17.3	27.2
Native American	20,087	2.6	1.4
Asian or Pacific Islander	18,686	2.5	4.1
Other	27,506	3.6	2.4
Total	758,334	100.0	100

Source: LSC Data Underlying Legal Aid Programs, supra note 2.

TABLE 15.2 2015 *Legal Services Corporation income guidelines: 125% of the federal poverty guidelines.*

Household size	Gross income level caps
1	$14,713
2	$19,913
3	$25,113
4	$30,313
5	$35,513
6	$40,713
7	$45,913
8	$51,113
For each additional household member, add:	$5,200

Source: Appendix to 1611, LSC 2015 Income Guidelines, 45 C.F.R. § 1611.5(a).

ELIGIBILITY FOR LSC-FUNDED SERVICES

To be eligible for LSC-funded civil legal services, an applicant's pre-tax income must fall at or below 125% of the federal poverty guidelines and, as Table 15.2 shows, that number is keyed to the size of a person's household.[3] Federal regulations require LSC to establish maximum income levels for eligible households based on the federal poverty guidelines published by the Department of Health

[3] See Section 1007(a)(2) of the Legal Services Corporation Act, 42 U.S.C. § 2996f(a)(2). Since 1982, HHS has been responsible for updating and issuing the Federal Poverty Guidelines. DHS's Federal Poverty Guidelines are, by law, based on the Census Bureau's Federal Poverty Thresholds, which are calculated using gross income before taxes. 42 U.S.C. § 9902(2).

and Human Resources (DHS).[4] Then local LSC grantees are responsible for developing financial eligibility charts to reflect local differences including factors like the "cost of living in the service area" or "availability and cost of legal services provided by the private bar and other free or low cost legal services providers."[5]

Table 15.2 presents how low household income limits were set in 2015, capping eligibility for a single person at $14,713 a year and a family of five at $35,513.[6] Each LSC grantee organization must also set undefined "reasonable" asset ceilings as well, but can exclude assets like "a principal residence, vehicles used for transportation . . . and other assets which are exempt from attachment under state or federal law."[7] For an applicant to be eligible for LSC assistance, income and assets should fall below both ceiling levels.

The income guidelines merely define eligibility; they do not guarantee representation. The LSC regulations also give grantees discretion to exceed those ceilings up to 200% of the poverty line.[8] Also, asset ceilings can be waived for "unusual circumstances"[9] and income determinations can take into account "medical or nursing home expenses," "seasonal variations in income," "dependent care," transportation, educational activities, or fixed debts that make it otherwise impossible to afford a lawyer.[10]

CONGRESSIONAL PROHIBITIONS

LSC grantees operate under certain Congressional restrictions. For example, LSC cannot provide legal assistance to defendants in criminal cases,[11] individuals in prison,[12] and individuals seeking to file collateral habeas attacks on convictions.[13] LSC is also prohibited from representing anyone living in public housing if the potential client has been charged or convicted with illegal drug activity.[14] Undocumented immigrants[15] and individuals involved in assisted suicide, abortion, and desertion[16] are all categorically excluded as well.

[4] Annual Update of the HHS Poverty Guidelines, 80 Fed. Reg. 3236 (Jan. 22, 2015).

[5] LSC 2015 Income Guidelines, 45 C.F.R. § 1611.3(g)(Sept. 7, 2015).

[6] *Id.* § 1611.3 Appendix to 1611 (hereinafter Appendix to 1611).

[7] *Id.* § 1611.3(d)(1).

[8] LSC 2015 Income Guidelines, 45 C.F.R. § 1611.5(a). By way of comparison with Table 15.2 the 200% income guideline grants eligibility to a single person earning up to $23,540 a year and a family of five earning $56,820 annually.

[9] 45 C.F.R. § 1611.3(d)(2)(2015).

[10] *Id.* § 1611.5.

[11] 42 U.S.C. § 2996(b)(2); 45 C.F.R. §§ 1613, 1610.2(a)(4), (unless a court appoints an LSC grantee organization).

[12] 45 C.F.R. § 1637.

[13] 42 U.S.C.§ 2996(f)(b)(3); 45 C.F.R. § 1615.

[14] *Id.* § 2996(b)(2); 45 C.F.R. §1634.1.

[15] 45 C.F.R. § 1626.

[16] 42 U.S.C. § 2996(f)(b)(10).

Congress precludes funding for services that go beyond individual legal representation. In 1996, Congress restricted legal services organizations from representing clients in class action litigation (at trial or on appeal), or serving as amicus curiae for a class action.[17] LSC organizations also cannot lobby or take positions on referenda.[18]

FEDERAL FUNDING

The bulk of Congressional appropriations for LSC is distributed as basic field grants[19] that fund the direct legal representation of clients, covering everything from administrative overhead to lawyer and staff salaries. In addition to direct legal services to clients, LSC programs are required to spend 12.5% of their LSC grant to increase the private bar's pro bono involvement in representation that serves low-income individuals. Grantees organize ways to engage the private bar in representing eligible clients, including setting up "Saturday bar" legal clinics, creating hotlines or interactive online websites, and partnering with the local bar in recruiting and training private lawyers. In 2013, private lawyers closed 79,189 pro bono cases, 10% of the total number of cases closed by LSC grantee organizations.

Congressional appropriations have declined from $479 million ($117 million in 1974 adjusted for 2013 dollars) to $341 million in 2013. Three significant reductions have occurred: in 1982, appropriations declined by 25%; in 1996, appropriations declined by 30.5%; and in 2012, appropriations declined by 14%. These reductions have had a real impact. In 2012, when funding was cut by almost 14%, the number of closed cases shrunk by 10% – which translates into almost 100,000 fewer cases. Regardless of whether this loss measures cases involving advice only or full representation, the number is stark.

Non-LSC funding sources have increased as LSC funding shrinks. In 2013, 61% (or $542 million) of the overall money raised by grantees was from non-LSC money, which included state and local grants, interest on lawyer trust accounts, and private donations.

One problem with turning to non-LSC funds is that not all LSC organizations can or have successfully tapped other sources, making LSC grant reductions significantly more severe for some organizations than others who have made up for the shortfall. For example, Colorado Legal Services receives 71% of its $3.67 million revenue from non-LSC funding. In contrast, Legal Services of Alabama relies on LSC grants for 78% of its funding, in a state where 25% of the population is poor. For organizations like Legal Services of Alabama, LSC

17 42 U.S.C. § 2996(e)(d)(5).

18 *Id.* § 2996(f)(b)(7); 45 C.F.R. § 1612.

19 There are three types of field grants: basic field general, basic field Native American, and basic field immigrant.

reductions are severe and translate into immediate staff reductions and fewer closed cases.

STRUCTURE OF LSC-FUNDED ORGANIZATIONS

LSC funds statewide, regional, and local organizations, and grantees have discretion as to how to deliver legal services to the poor. Some LSC grantees use their grants to fund only legal advice or help hotlines; most offer a broader spectrum of services, including legal representation.

Statewide LSC programs

In twenty-eight states, LSC funds centrally administered, statewide legal-services programs that disseminate their LSC grant to local field offices.[20] Statewide programs differ dramatically and reflect the legal needs and density of their residents living below the poverty line. LSC statewide grants range from just over $500,000 in Delaware to $9 million in North Carolina.

Some statewide programs focus heavily on providing pro se legal advice and online forms. In Vermont, where only 0.15% of the total U.S. poverty population lives, the second lowest in the country, LSC provides $562,867 to the Law Line of Vermont, a statewide hotline that provides free consultation and advice. This funding is 90% of the hotline's revenue. Four staff attorneys and a paralegal help callers strategize about cases, understand their rights, and prepare documents to file.[21]

In another low-poverty state, Delaware, LSC funds a statewide organization, the Legal Services Corporation of Delaware, with a little over $500,000, similar to Vermont's grant. But unlike Vermont, the Delaware organization also raises over $800,000 from non-LSC sources. This funding level supports two local offices in Wilmington and Dover providing more traditional legal assistance, and a website offering a range of self-help information and forms from "bankruptcy basics" to filing for divorce.[22] With virtually the same LSC grant and the same size poverty population as Vermont, the Legal Services Corporation of Delaware offers more legal assistance geography matters. When it comes to the type and degree of legal help available for low-income clients.

Legal Aid of North Carolina, the largest statewide LSC grantee, draws $9 million in LSC funding, and raises $14 million or 62% of its budget through non-LSC

[20] *Id.* In 2013, these states were: Alabama, Alaska, Colorado, Connecticut, Delaware, Hawaii, Idaho, Indiana, Iowa, Kansas, Maine, Maryland, Montana, Nevada, New Hampshire, New Mexico, North Carolina, North Dakota, Oregon, Oklahoma, Rhode Island, South Carolina, Utah, Vermont, Washington, West Virginia, and Wyoming.

[21] Vermont Legal Aid, which does not receive LSC money, is the major legal services provider in Vermont.

[22] www.lscd.com.

revenue. This funding supports 24 field offices and 8 special projects across the state. The special projects include the Senior Law Project in Asheville, which provides a statewide helpline for seniors, and the Farmworker Unit in Raleigh, which represents migrant and seasonal workers for violations of workers' rights including compensation claims and claims for substandard housing conditions.

Regional LSC grantees

Similar to statewide grantees, regional LSC grantees divide funding between local field offices. Each regional program operates independently with separate budgets, staff, reporting requirements, website resources, and boards of directors.

As an example, in Texas, the second largest state, with over 26 million people and about 9% of the U.S. poverty population, there are three regional LSC grantees (in the east, northwest, and Rio Grande regions). Each regional office receives over $7 million in an annual LSC grant and almost doubles that amount in its non-LSC funding. Texas Rio Grande Legal Aid serves 68 counties, both rural and urban, in southwest Texas. It is the third largest legal services provider in the country with over three dozen practice areas, and serves about 25,000 clients a year with over 2.6 million southwest Texans who are eligible for its services.

Because the regional programs are independent nonprofits and have different budgets, donors, and poverty rates in their regions, some regional programs could have a greater capacity to offer legal help than others. Eligible LSC clients would then have better odds of receiving legal assistance if they live in a particular part of the state. Without an overseeing entity attempting to fairly allocate resources throughout the state, there could be great disparities.

Urban LSC offices

Legal service providers in large cities with high concentrations of poverty receive some of the highest LSC grants. This third level of service delivery allows these individual nonprofits to act independently from their regional or statewide counterparts. For example, in Georgia, which has 3.5% of the U.S. poverty population, the Atlanta Legal Aid Society receives a $2.7 million grant to support its work, while the Georgia Legal Services Program receives a $6.7 million LSC grant. Their service areas are vastly different. Georgia Legal Services focuses its attention on the needs of rural Georgians including farmworkers, homeowners, and seniors. Six counties in Georgia have no lawyers and 56 others have fewer than 15. The legal needs of low-income Georgians in these counties differ dramatically from the urban poor in Atlanta. Atlanta Legal Aid Society offers a broader focus, representing seniors, the disabled, families, and people living with HIV in family law, predatory lending, unemployment, and housing cases.[23]

[23] www.atlantalegalaid.org/ar.pdf.

Concentrations of poverty in cities result in larger LSC grants, and most cities have significant non-LSC funders. The largest LSC grant to a single legal services provider is $12 million dollars for Legal Services NYC, which raises over $40 million in non-LSC revenue. LSC grantees in Chicago and Los Angeles receive LSC grants of $6 million and $6.8 million, respectively.

LSC'S CASELOADS

Types of Services

LSC organizations offer three different types of legal assistance as defined under LSC regulations: "advice and counsel," "brief services," and "extended services."[24] The LSC Case Service Report Handbook explains how grantees should determine in which category to include closed cases, and each grantee is responsible for collecting its own data annually in an automated management system as a part of the LSC grant's reporting requirements.[25]

In "advice and counsel" cases, legal assistance is "limited to the review of information relevant to the client's legal problem(s) and counseling the client on the relevant law and/or suggested course of action."[26] The LSC regulations further explain that advice and counsel "does not encompass drafting of documents or making third-party contacts on behalf of the client."[27] LSC's guidance to grantees explains that an example of a case closed and categorized as legal advice is "the advocate ascertained and reviewed relevant facts, exercised judgment in interpreting the particular facts presented by the client and in applying the relevant law to the facts presented, and counseled the client concerning his or her legal problem."[28]

There are different reasons that might contribute to not offering full legal representation for clients receiving advice from LSC lawyers.[29] Some legal problems may not fall into the types of cases the LSC grantee covers. For example, some grantee organizations do not work on healthcare issues, so even if a person is eligible the grantee would not be able to offer assistance. At other times, specialized units, like a grantee's housing unit, may close intake temporarily when the number of cases exceeds the capacity of that grantee's attorneys. Some eligible clients may not have good prospects for prevailing and the lawyer evaluating the case may determine that it would not be worth spending limited resources on their case.

"Brief services" cases, which make up 16% of the closed cases, are defined as "legal assistance in which the recipient undertakes to provide a discrete and time-limited

24 45 C.F.R. §1611.2(a), (e), and (f).

25 LSC, Case Service Report Handbook (2008, amended 2011) at 3 (hereinafter Case Service Report Handbook).

26 45 C.F.R. §1611.2(a).

27 *Id.*

28 Case Service Report Handbook, supra note 29 at 20.

29 Telephone interview with former LSC Chair Helaine Barnett, June 5, 2015.

service to a client beyond advice and consultation, including but not limited to activities, such as the drafting of documents or making limited third party contacts on behalf of the client."[30] The LSC Handbook for grantees explains that a case closed under this category includes "communications by letter, preparation of a simple legal document such as a routine power of attorney, or legal assistance to a *pro se* client that involves assistance with preparation of court or other legal documents."[31]

"Extended services" are defined as "legal assistance characterized by the performance of multiple tasks incident to continuous representation." The LSC regulations' examples of extended services are: "representation of a client in litigation, an administrative adjudicative proceeding, alternative dispute resolution proceeding, extended negotiations with a third party, or other legal representation in which the recipient undertakes responsibility for protecting or advancing the client's interests beyond advice and counsel or brief services."[32]

The LSC handbook requires grantees to record the exact type of extended service provided through six distinct categories.[33] For example, the category of administrative agency decision includes cases where the grantee "represented a client in an administrative agency action that resulted in a case-dispositive decision by the administrative agency or body, after a hearing or other formal administrative process."[34] "[N]egotiated with settlement" cases can only include "cases in which an appearance has been entered before a court or administrative agency as counsel of record; or cases in which the settlement was reached prior to the program's entry as counsel of record, provided that the program was actually representing the client in the negotiations (not assisting a *pro se* client) and provided that there is documentation of the settlement in the case file."[35] The handbook offers more direction to grantees about the specific types of extended services.

Table 15.3 breaks down the 758,689 closed cases reported in 2013 by LSC organizations into these three categories to show that the vast majority of closed cases, 457,874 cases or 60%, were advice only. Table 15.4 shows how that percentage is consistent for all case types. Both Tables 15.3 and 15.4 show that when advice cases and brief services cases are combined, they account for 75% of the closed LSC caseloads, making these types of limited or unbundled legal services the predominant type of assistance that legal aid offers eligible clients.

30 45 C.F.R. §1611.2(e).
31 Case Service Report Handbook, supra note 29 at 21.
32 45 C.F.R. §1611.2(f).
33 Case Service Report Handbook, supra note 29 at 21–23.
34 *Id.* at 21.
35 *Id.* at 21–22.

TABLE 15.3 2013 *LSC – closed cases by type of service.*

Reason for closure	Total cases closed	Percentage
Advice and counsel	457,874	60.4
Brief services	122,330	16.1
Extended services	176,734	23.3
Other	1,751	0.2
Total	758,689	100

Source: LSC Data Underlying Legal Aid Programs, supra note 2.

TABLE 15.4 2013 *total closed cases by type.*

	Total closed	Percentage of total closed cases	Advice and counsel (as % of total)	Brief services (as % of total)	Extended services (as % of total)
Family	249,843	32.9	61	11	28
Housing	207,614	27.4	66	14	20
Income maintenance	91,961	12.1	54	18	28
Consumer	83,463	11.0	71	12	17
Health	27,571	3.6	51	30	19
Employment	22,447	3.0	59	22	19
Individual rights	15,289	2.0	50	22	28
Juvenile	13,415	1.8	36	13	51
Education	5,947	0.8	38	33	29
Miscellaneous	41,139	5.4	43	45	12
Total	758,689				

Source: LSC Data Underlying Legal Aid Programs, supra note 2.

LSC organizations also offer legal assistance that cannot be easily quantified, through pro bono clinics, online self-help tools, community education workshops, referral services, and hotlines. Each service helps people understand their legal rights, when legal assistance is needed, and where to find help. Thousands of people use these services, but the impact is more difficult to see. For example, in one year, 305,429 people attended LSC community–education presentations, 49,672 attended pro se workshops, and 13 million people used LSC websites downloading 1.5 million self-help forms.[36] Over 10% of all cases closed are ones where private attorneys handled the case pro bono, and this number has been steadily increasing over the past decade.[37]

[36] LSC Data Underlying Legal Aid Programs, supra note 2.
[37] Id.

TABLE 15.5 *Family – cases closed.*

Type	Number	Percentage of family cases	Percentage of total LSC cases closed
Adoption	2,277	0.9	0.3
Custody/visitation	71,196	28.5	9.4
Divorce/separation	92,127	36.9	12.1
Guardianship	5,055	2.0	0.7
Name change	3,065	1.2	0.4
Parental rights termination	1,594	0.6	0.2
Paternity	5,593	2.2	0.7
Domestic abuse	43,619	17.5	5.7
Support	18,754	7.5	2.5
Other family	6,563	2.6	0.9
Total	249,843	100.00	32.9

Source: LSC Data Underlying Legal Aid Programs, supra note 2.

Types of cases

The majority of legal aid cases center around only half a dozen key subject areas of concern to low-income Americans. Table 15.4 presents the breakdown of LSC cases in 2013 by general cases type.

Family law cases

Historically, a third of all legal services cases involve family law issues, where legal assistance helps stabilize families in crisis. Although clients are represented in a range of cases in family court, three areas make up about 80% of the family law caseload: divorce or separation, custody or visitation, and domestic abuse. These lawyers help parents who need to keep or seek custody of children, and assist predominantly women and their children with securing legal protection from an abusive relationship. Other cases include helping family members adopt or seek custody of abandoned children, filing for child support to improve the financial deficits of single-parent households, and representing a married person in a divorce or separation. Table 15.5 sets out the types of cases involved in the family category.

Housing cases

The second largest category, which represents 27% of all cases, protects an immediate basic need: housing. As Table 15.6 indicates, the majority of these cases, 116,453, involve private landlord–tenant disputes where tenants are facing eviction proceedings or fighting for improved living conditions. The 2007 mortgage crisis also sparked the establishment of foreclosure units in LSC organizations. Lawyers specialize in helping homeowners in foreclosure raise important legal defenses, renegotiate mortgages, or challenge unlawful predatory lending practices. For some LSC

TABLE 15.6 *Housing – cases closed.*

Type	Number	Percentage of housing cases	Percentage of total cases closed
Federally subsidized housing	36,335	17.5	4.8
Homeownership/real property (not foreclosure)	8,476	4.1	1.1
Private landlord/tenant	116,453	56.1	15.3
Public housing	11,068	5.3	1.5
Mobile homes	3,505	1.7	0.5
Housing discrimination	1,006	0.5	0.1
Mortgage foreclosures (not predatory lending/practices)	19,550	9.4	2.6
Mortgage predatory lending/practices	807	0.4	0.1
Other housing	10,414	5.0	1.4
Total	207,614	100	27.4

Source: LSC Data Underlying Legal Aid Programs, supra note 2.

grantees, housing may exceed family law cases, especially in urban areas, where large percentages of the low-income population live in rent-stabilized units or public housing, or receive federal Section 8 vouchers.

Employment issues

Over 20,000 cases help people challenge unlawful employment practices and withheld wages. The migrant farmworker projects described earlier account for many of these cases, where workers are fighting for safe working conditions and fair wages.

Consumer issues

Eleven percent of cases protect vulnerable consumers from deceptive lending and sales practices, aggressive debt collection practices, repossession and garnishment of wages, and fraudulent contracts. Cases also include representation in bankruptcy filings and negotiating debt relief.

Government benefits

Almost a quarter of all LSC cases offer legal assistance to obtaining or restoring government benefits that were allegedly unlawfully denied or terminated. Public assistance, food stamps, disability benefits, veterans' benefits, and healthcare benefits create a critical safety net keeping many low-income families afloat. Yet application procedures and administrative hearings can be daunting without lawyers who can navigate these systems.

LSC organizations also represent categories of vulnerable people who include children, seniors, domestic violence survivors, and veterans.

CONCLUSION

In July of 1974, the Legal Services Corporation Act passed both houses with bipartisan support. Through this legislation, Congress recognized that our system of justice requires equal access to the courts and defined a "need to provide high quality legal assistance to those who would be otherwise unable to afford adequate legal counsel." To date, Congress has failed to allocate sufficient funding to achieve that goal.

Still, the LSC structure – the dissemination of block grants to over one hundred LSC organizations throughout the country – provides one model for building a legal services infrastructure that can serve thousands of people using different service delivery approaches. But LSC's history shows that declining federal funds are insufficient to meet this vulnerable population's growing legal needs, which has required legal services organizations to do more than rely on federal government appropriations. Many organizations have doubled their budgets with other funding sources, engaged pro bono attorneys to take cases and staff advice clinics, and they use technology and education to help people represent themselves.

16

New York's Lawyer Referral Services

Allen Charne

For well over 75 years, local bar associations have connected Americans of average means to reputable, affordable legal services through lawyer referral programs. This chapter describes the experience of one of the oldest programs in the country, New York City's Legal Referral Service (LRS). Looking at data collected over a ten-year period, from 2003 to 2013, Allen Charne, the former long-time executive director of LRS, examines the legal needs of clients who called in for help and the actual legal fees they paid. He also describes the competitive selection process for the LRS attorney panel.

ABA-approved lawyer referral services provide basic legal information, explain what lawyers do, help the client understand whether a problem is actually a legal problem, and help identify the right legal resource to respond to legal problems through a telephone hotline and internet communications. These clients include people who do not qualify for free legal services, or who have legal needs that are not served by free legal aid. Many callers have no previous experience with lawyers. Others had disappointing experiences with lawyers and seek a recommendation from a reliable source. The referrals can be to attorneys in private practice who specialize in addressing a particular legal issue, government and private agencies, or various pro bono programs depending on a person's ability to pay.

This chapter focuses on the work of New York City's Legal Referral Service (LRS) program, one of the oldest programs in the country. To accomplish this, the referral service develops selective attorney qualification standards and procedures that help provide the public with competent, ethical, and responsive legal service. This chapter describes the types of legal needs that LRS responds to, the legal fees collected by these cases over a period of 10 years, and the process for selecting attorneys for its approved attorney panel.

A BRIEF HISTORY OF LRS

In 1946 two leaders of the New York legal profession, Harrison Tweed, president of The Association of the Bar of the City of New York (the City Bar), and Joseph

Proskauer, president of the New York County Lawyers' Association, joined forces to create the Legal Referral Bureau (now the Legal Referral Service) in New York City. *The New York Law Journal*, on October 21, 1946, announced: "The Association of the Bar of the City of New York and the New York County Lawyers Association are in the process of establishing a legal referral service whereby a person having some means to pay and seeking legal advice for a moderate fee may be referred to a competent and reliable lawyer willing to render such service." More than 100 lawyers had already applied when the article was published.

Lawyers who applied to be panel members agreed to charge $5.00 for an initial consultation of up to 30 minutes. If further advice or representation was required, the fee arrangement was subject to agreement between the client and the lawyer. The public was informed about the service through brochures that were distributed in libraries and articles that appeared in New York newspapers.

Finding the right lawyer, especially in metropolitan areas where many law offices were removed from residential neighborhoods, became more difficult. The old method of relying on recommendations of friends and family was less useful than the recommendation of a source that knew more about the lawyer's background and experience and could understand the client's issues. From its beginnings, the Legal Referral Service employed lawyers on staff to help evaluate legal issues and guide clients.

The LRS has been not only a source for direct referrals, but it has also marshaled lawyers to work on pressing legal issues. During the early 1950s, the LRS recruited lawyers to oppose the excesses of McCarthyism, particularly in civil service, private employment, and the entertainment industry. The 1960s brought increased needs for civil rights lawyers. The LRS recruited lawyers to represent the inmates at Attica. LRS panel members handled conscientious objector, draft, discharge upgrades, and military issues during the wars in Korea and Vietnam.

Beginning in 1975, many thought that the arrival of lawyer advertising would sound the death knell for lawyer referral services. To the contrary, calls increased almost in relation to the increased lawyer advertising. The proliferation of advertising on television, radio, billboards, and print media led people to seek out an independent, reliable resource to connect people with competent legal representation.

Beginning in 1985, taking into account staffing and equipment requirements to improve the service, the LRS oversight committee approved a plan to begin collecting from participating lawyers a percentage of the fees generated by LRS Referrals. This was consistent with suggestions from the American Bar Association's Standing Committee on Lawyer Referral and Information Services.

In 1989, following a long review process by state and local bar association and lawyer referral experts from both the public and private sector, the American Bar Association adopted Model Rules for the operation of public service lawyer referral programs. The overriding concern of the Model Rules was and continues to be

TABLE 16.1 *Number of referrals in most active areas (2003–13).*

Torts and negligence including defense	41,129
Family law	39,079
Labor and employment law	27,765
Landlord–tenant	27,749
Wills, trusts, and estates	20,787
Real property	14,570
Immigration	12,571
Business and corporations	10,367
Bankruptcy	861
Consumer law	8,344

Source: N.Y.C.B.A. data

consumer protection. Lawyer referral services that comply with the Model Rules are entitled to use the logo "ABA Approved" on websites, pamphlets, and promotional materials. The New York City Bar Association endorsed the Model Rules and became the first lawyer referral service in New York State to be ABA approved.

Lawyer referral requests reflect needs related to economic and social conditions, a wide range of tort matters, divorce filings, employment discrimination, and wage-and-hour employment issues, the housing market, and immigration. Mass disasters in New York from 9/11 to Hurricane Sandy also create new legal needs that LRS responds to. The ten most active areas of legal referrals are listed in Table 16.1.

FEES COLLECTED FROM LRS REFERRALS

When LRS refers individuals to lawyers, lawyers report whether they take the case and how much revenue the case generates. LRS receives a percentage of the attorney's fees, which keeps LRS funded and properly staffed. Fee agreements with panel members were set up to have the least impact on lawyers who handle lower-fee matters. If the attorney's fee is below \$600, there is no additional fee paid to LRS. If the attorney's fee is between \$600 and \$10,000, LRS receives 6% of the fee collected by the lawyer. A higher percentage is collected for the large-fee matters, many of which are handled by the lawyer on a contingency fee basis. The lawyer is not permitted to increase the fee to the client to compensate for the amount paid to the bar association. For matters generally handled on a contingency fee basis, such as personal injury, workers compensation and social security, there is no consultation fee. For matters normally handled on an hourly or flat fee basis, the consultation fee is \$35 (raised from \$25 in 2008).

Among the thousands of clients referred to panel members, the vast majority of those who hire lawyers for additional services pay fees in a low to moderate fee range.

Table 16.2 presents fee range data over an 11-year period of cases referred by the LRS. Over this period, 75.6% of the clients referred by LRS paid fees below \$2,000,

TABLE 16.2 *NYC legal referral service fees in different fee ranges (January 1, 2003, to December 31, 2013, as of September 4, 2013).*

Number of cases	Fee range	Attorney fees	Case fees	Consult $	Percentage of matters
452	$50,000+	$588,858,176	$6,042,747	$7,800	1.0
2,368	$10,000–$49,999	46,236,263	2,482,012	53,768	5.4
7,822	$2,000–$9,999	34,486,621	1,388,046	204,476	18
5,179	$600–$1,999	6,231,673	255,451	150,738	11.9
27,732	Less than $600	2,001,406	8,565	$872,672	63.7
43,553	Total	$147,814,140	$11,526,960	$1,350,140	100.0
				# $25–$35 consults	45,005

Source: N.Y.C.B.A. data

and 93.5% paid fees of less than $10,000. This table also shows that LRS refers a range of fee-generating cases. This is important to LRS because many lawyers with successful practices choose not to join a lawyer referral service fearing that such services refer only pro bono and very low fees matters. LRS balances lower-end referrals with more typical-fee matters to attract highly qualified panel members in all areas of law and to generate the income necessary to fund the service.

LRC OPERATIONS AND STAFF

The LRS staff includes ten lawyers responsible for handling tens of thousands of calls and thousands of emails and written correspondence received each year. The staff screens hundreds of calls daily, and on average, about one-third of the callers are referred to private lawyers. The lawyers on staff handling the initial calls are able to explain to the caller whether referral to a private lawyer would be helpful and to make practical suggestions. The two-thirds that are not referred to private lawyers are provided with basic legal information, referrals to bar association clinics, the City Bar Justice Center Hotline (see kelly, Chapter 45 in this volume), appropriate agencies, available on the website www.nylawhelp.org. To make sure that language is not a barrier, five of the lawyers on the LRS staff, including the Managing Attorney, are fluent in Spanish. And calls can be handled in all other languages through the Language Line interpreter service to which the LRS subscribes.

Any caller referred to a panel member may consult with an experienced attorney for only $35 for the first half an hour. No consultation fee is charged for matters such as personal injury, medical malpractice, social security, and workers compensation where attorneys receive contingency fees based on the amount recovered for the client.

COMMITTEE OVERSIGHT

The sponsoring bar associations appoint a committee of lawyers and judges to provide guidance and direction and to oversee various functions of the LRS. The committee plays an active role in the review of panel applicants, assessment of complaints, and adoption and revision of standards for panel members.

If a question is raised as to the suitability of a lawyer to continue receiving referrals, whether because of fee disputes, client communication problems, competence, refusal to meet with referred clients, or violation of the Rules of Professional Conduct, the lawyer may be suspended from receiving further referrals and an investigative subcommittee appointed to assess and recommend further action.

The LRS Committee has established rules governing panel members. For example, panel members must have professional liability insurance. They must agree not to charge any fee for the first half an hour's consultation beyond the initial $35 consultation fee. For any services beyond this first consult, panel members must provide clients with written retainer agreements. And if a fee dispute arises between a panel member and a referred client despite a written retainer, the attorney also agrees to mandatory fee arbitration at the client's request. The fee arbitration rules are more extensive than those required of lawyers in New York.

LRS SPECIALTY PANELS AND QUALIFICATION STANDARDS

Currently there are twenty-six major panel categories and within those, there are over 100 subcategories of specialty areas. Depending on the specialty area, some subcategories are further subdivided based on the complexity of the matter and the level of experience an attorney requires to receive referrals. For example, Matrimonial and Family Law, Negligence, Tax, and Trusts and Estates include three levels of experience ranging from Level 1 for basic, uncomplicated matters to Level 3 for the most complex, unusual, or substantial matters. This allows for the most appropriate referral for a client's specific needs as determined by the referral counselor.

DEVELOPMENT OF PANELS AND QUALIFICATIONS CRITERIA

The staff and the committee undertook beginning in 1985 a complete review of panel categories and the establishment of objective experience requirements. Major panel categories were expanded from 13 to 26.

PANEL APPLICATION PROCESS

To become panel members, lawyers must first complete a comprehensive written application form. For each area of law that they want to be considered for, applicants must send summaries of three matters they handled and writing samples. The importance of this part of the application is emphasized in the cover letter, which accompanies the application and advises the applicant to: "Pay particular attention to question 20, which requires descriptions of specific matters and issues in your area of expertise. Your descriptions must include a summary of particular matters ... the discovery, investigation, or other preparation, the final results and how your client benefited from your representation."

LRS staff review the initial applications by lawyers hoping to be panel members, and confirm the lawyers are in good standing to practice law and have professional liability insurance. Disciplinary and grievance committees are checked for pending complaints and past findings of misconduct.

At every stage of the application, referral, and quality control process, LRS staff are involved. The Managing Attorney and the Executive Director review the application, participate in the interview, and review client responses to satisfaction questionnaires. This enables the staff to know much more about the lawyers they recommend than would be possible from just reviewing a simple application.

The number of years the lawyer has been admitted to practice does not guarantee that the lawyer will be accepted as a panel member. The LRS applicant evaluation process requires a personal interview by a qualifications subcommittee, which includes the Managing Attorney or the Executive Director of the LRS, one or more attorney(s) chosen from a pool of highly experienced lawyers in the relevant legal area(s), and a member of the LRS Committee.

Any member of the interview panel may request additional information from the applicant.

The interview provides an opportunity to assess the candidate's substantive legal knowledge, and consider important subjective criteria such as the attorney's ability to communicate effectively, deal with ethical issues, understand the practicalities involved in a particular type of practice, and explain billing practices. Panel applicants are also required to produce copies of their retainer agreements and describe how they explain their fees and communicate with the client at all stages of a case. The interview reveals information that cannot be gleaned from a written application alone.

The role of experienced lawyers in the interview and evaluation process is invaluable. Applicants have occasionally stated on paper that they had handled certain matters, but more in-depth questioning revealed that an applicant handled only a small part of the work or was under another attorney's direction. It is only by having highly experienced practitioners as a part of the review that deficiencies are spotted. By the end of the interview, the interviewers have a good sense whether the candidate should be recommended for panel membership.

An unsuccessful candidate is told the reason for the denial. This is helpful particularly when the candidate may want to reapply. Even if these candidates do not reapply, providing constructive criticism can help propel them to improve their practice or encourage them to develop further professionally.

COMPLAINTS AND QUALITY CONTROL

LRS also reviews the competence, ethical practices, and client relations of panel members. Such information may be revealed as a result of the client follow-up forms, newspaper or law journal articles, lawyer grievance proceedings, and fee dispute committee reports. When positive information is received, it is generally shared with the panel member, placed in the panel member's file to be accessible to the LRS staff and Committee, and may also be shared as models for other panel members. Negative information, especially referred clients, is taken seriously. Sometimes the complaint is a simple misunderstanding, but at other times LRS staff may attempt to resolve the issue by calling the panel member.

Public interest and upholding the integrity and reputation of the LRS are the touchstones that inform the decisions made by the LRS Committee. As issues arise and are dealt with, the Committee often tries to prevent future similar incidents through protective measures for clients and educating panel members. Much discretion is built into the LRS Committee's quality control procedures; this discretion is set forth in the agreement signed by panel members.

CONCLUSION

The Legal Referral Service makes a continuing effort to provide callers with competent, responsive legal counsel, and basic legal information. Yet, the service is continually responding to new challenges. As lawyers' fees continue to rise, new ways of providing legal services through electronic means, unbundled legal services, bar association and law school clinics are evolving. The LRS is committed to making referrals in a way that is responsive to the new demands as well as the new supply of legal resources.

Some of the greatest benefits that LRS provides include the ability of any person to speak to an LRS staff attorney for free. The attorneys on staff are not there just to quickly screen out non-paying callers, or those with problems that lawyers do not handle. If no referral is made, the LRS staff explains why. Anyone with a legal problem who is referred to a panel member knows that the panel member will never charge more than $35 for an initial half-an-hour consultation regardless of the lawyer's regular hourly rate. If a pro bono resource is appropriate, the LRS staff lawyer will make that suggestion. And in the rare instance where there is a dispute between the panel member and the client, LRS will try to help resolve the dispute.

APPENDIX I SUMMARY OF MODEL RULES FOR LAWYER REFERRAL SERVICES

Adopted by the American Bar Association House of Delegates 8/93

1. A qualified service shall be operated in the public interest and shall provide information regarding government and consumer agencies, which may assist the client, and provide referrals to lawyers, pro bono programs and other legal service providers. The service may be privately owned so long as the primary purpose is public service.
2. Membership in the service should be open to all licensed attorneys in the geographical area served who meet the requirements of the service. Charges for membership in the service must be reasonable. Membership may not be restricted by the particular geographical areas or subject areas.
3. The service must require its members to maintain malpractice insurance or to provide proof of financial responsibility.
4. The combined fees and expenses charged to a client by a service and the lawyer to whom the client is referred shall not exceed the combined fees and expenses the client would have incurred if no referral service were employed.
5. No fee generating referral may be made to any lawyer who has an ownership in, who operates, or who is employed by the service, or to their law firm. Referrals may be made to lawyers who are members of the board or governing committee of the service so long as they do not receive any preferential treatment.
6. The service must periodically survey client satisfaction with its operations and shall investigate and take appropriate action regarding any complaints against panelists, the service or its employees. The survey may be by mail or by phone and need not involve every client.
7. The service must establish procedures for the admission, suspension or removal of a lawyer from any panel. The procedures must be clearly articulated in the service's materials. The procedure may include peer review, but other procedures are permissible. The procedure must include an appeal process.
8. Subject to the rules of the service's jurisdiction, the service may, in addition to a referral fee, receive a percentage of the fee earned by the lawyer to whom a referral is made. Any such fees received may be used only for the reasonable operating expenses of the service or to fund public service activities of the service or its sponsoring organization.
9. The service must establish subject matter panels and establish minimum requirements for eligibility. The number of subject panels necessary will

vary from service to service depending upon the needs of the community served. Requirements for eligibility should include sufficient experience to ensure that the lawyer is qualified in the field of practice. The service should require proof of compliance with the requirements so established, which may include certification in affidavit or affirmation form.

APPENDIX II MAJOR PANEL CATEGORIES

Major Specialty Panels:

- Administrative Law
- Bankruptcy
- Business & Corporations
- Civil Appeals
- Consumer Law
- Contracts
- Criminal Law
- Education Law
- Employment/Labor Law
- Entertainment Law
- Family Law
- Immigration Law
- Insurance Law
- International Law
- Intellectual Property
- Other
- Landlord/Tenant
- Mediation
- Moderate Means/Clinic Reduced Fee Client
- Real Property
- Securities
- Tax
- Torts/Negligence
- Wills, Trusts & Estates
- Workers Compensation

17

Growth of Large Law Firm Pro Bono Programs

Steven A. Boutcher

"Big law" pro bono programs are a growing source of legal assistance for poor and working Americans. Steven Boutcher discusses the evolution of these pro bono programs since the 1960s and presents data on the number of hours lawyers have spent on pro bono over the past two decades and the types of cases involved.

A quiet revolution has taken hold across the American legal profession, which has had profound implications for the delivery of legal services to individuals of limited means. Although this revolution has not gone unnoticed, its presence has transformed traditional notions of legal professionalism, law firm practice, and contemporary public interest advocacy. The revolution is the institutionalization of pro bono programs, which has swept contemporary law firm practice.

THE RISE OF A PROFESSIONAL PRO BONO MOVEMENT

Over the last few decades, pro bono has experienced a growing resurgence across the legal profession.[1] This is, in part, reflected in the sheer growth of empirical research on the topic, but is also indicated by the increasing importance that pro bono has come to play as an important component of the contemporary access to justice movement.[2] These developments mark the advent of a contemporary pro bono movement, which has swept the legal profession in response to long-standing

[1] See, e.g., Scott L. Cummings, *The Politics of Pro Bono*, 52 UCLA LAW REV. 1 (2004); Deborah L. Rhode, *Pro Bono in Principle and in Practice: Public Service and the Profession* (Stanford: Stanford University Press, 2005); Rebecca L. Sandefur, *Lawyers' Pro Bono Service and American-Style Civil Legal Assistance*, 41 LAW SOC. REV. 79 (2007); Steven A. Boutcher, The Institutionalization of Pro Bono in Large Law & Firms: Trends and Variation Across the AmLaw 200; Robert Granfield & Lynn Mather, Pro Bono, the Public Good & The Legal Profession, in Private Lawyers and the Public Interest: The Emerging Role of Pro Bono in the Legal Profession (Robert Granfield & Lynn Mather eds., 2009)

[2] Scott L. Cummings & Rebecca L. Sandefur, *Beyond the Numbers: What We Know – & Should Know – About American Pro Bono*, 7 Harv L. & POL. REV. 83 (2013).

criticisms that American lawyers were stinting on their professional responsibilities to serve the poor.[3]

Although the contemporary pro bono movement appears to have taken root across the profession, this was not always the case. Historically, pro bono was conceived and dispensed largely as charity from individual lawyers. Until as recently as the middle of the twentieth century, pro bono was delivered through the ad hoc, idiosyncratic interests of individual attorneys. Consequently, the services that were picked up were extremely limited and directed toward local charitable organizations or elite cultural institutions, such as the symphony or opera. This changed during the 1960s with the advent of President Johnson's "War on Poverty," which shifted the meaning of pro bono from one rooted in *noblesse oblige* to a focus on "access to justice" – targeting direct legal services for the poor through the mobilization of government and legal services lawyers. The 1980s marked an era of retrenchment in providing legal services to the poor and the beginning of the shift toward the privatization of public interest law.[4] At the same time, the profession slowly began to institutionalize pro bono in an effort to "fill the gap" in legal services. Paradoxically, this began at the same time that the profession was undergoing increasing commercialization and stratification across the bar.

Early attempts to organize pro bono had limited success across large firms, and was largely tied to direct competition for elite law students. During the 1960s and 1970s, the emergence of the public interest field, competition with the legal services movement, and increased social movement activism drew elite law school graduates away from the big firm in search of jobs where they could pursue social change.[5] In response to this competition for talent, some large firms began to formalize pro bono programs in order to recruit these students.[6] However, as the lure of social activism began to recede in the late 1970s and 1980s, large firms no longer felt pressured to pursue organized pro bono programs, and commitment to pro bono waned.[7]

It wasn't until the turn of the twenty-first century that a new wave of formal pro bono departments took off as large firms saw their profits soar and the number of large firms increased. However, the new pro bono wave was markedly different from its predecessor of the 1960s. For example, Joel Handler and his colleagues identified only 24 formalized programs in large firms in 1973,[8] but now pro bono departments can be found in many of the top

[3] See, e.g., Anthony T. Kronman, *The Lost Lawyer: Failing Ideas of the Legal Profession* (1993); Sol M. Linowitz, *The Betrayed Profession: Lawyering at the End of the Twentieth Century* (1994).

[4] Cummings, supra note 1, at 26–27.

[5] Jerold Auerbach, *Unequal Justice: Lawyers and Social Change in Modern America*, 278–79 (1976); Michael J. Powell, *From Patrician to Professional Elite: The Transformation of the New York City Bar Association*, 161–65 (1988).

[6] Joel F. Handler, Ellen Jane Hollingsworth, & Howard S. Erlanger, *Lawyers and the Pursuit of Legal Rights*, 123, (1978).

[7] *Id.* at 123.

[8] Handler et al., supra note 6, at 123.

firms across the country, centralizing the administration of a firm's pro bono practice.[9] These programs, often staffed by a pro bono manager, implement and structure the firm's pro bono practices as well as provide rotating opportunities that connect associates with a network of nonprofit organizations seeking assistance.[10]

FACTORS PRECIPITATING THE INSTITUTIONALIZATION OF PRO BONO

The emergence of the large law firm over the course of the second half of the twentieth century created the infrastructure that institutionalized pro bono rests upon. Over this period, there was an explosion in the number, size, and geographic diffusion of large firms.[11] Initially centered in New York City, large firms sprang up across the country in other metropolitan areas, including Chicago, San Francisco, Los Angeles, Dallas, and Atlanta.[12] The big firm is such a pervasive organizational form within the American legal profession that it has now expanded into secondary markets, and has increasingly gone global.[13]

The contemporary field of large law firms has dramatically expanded compared to the field just fifty years ago. Galanter and Palay report that by the late 1950s, only 38 firms had over fifty lawyers, but by 1985, that number had increased to 508 firms.[14] Today, the large firm is much larger than its predecessor. In 2008, for example, the average number of lawyers across the *AmLaw* 200 law firms was 557 lawyers. The largest firm in 2008 had 3,626 lawyers, which stands in stark contrast to the largest firm in the past – in 1968 the largest firm had 169 lawyers and by 1988 the largest firm had 962 lawyers.[15]

The growth of the large firm has led them to increasingly bureaucratize their organizational structures.[16] Pro bono became another avenue of this process, due, in

[9] Steven A. Boutcher, *From Policy to Practice: Assessing the Effect of Large Law Firm Pro Bono Structure on Pro Bono Commitment*, 52 Stud. Law, Politics & Soc. 145 (2010).

[10] Scott L. Cummings & Deborah L. Rhode, *Managing Pro Bono: Doing Well by Doing Better*, 78 Fordham L. Rev. 2357 (2010).

[11] Marc Galanter & Thomas M. Palay, *Tournament of Lawyers: The Transformation of the Big Law Firm* (1991).

[12] Erwin Smigel, *The Wall Street Lawyer: Professional Organization Man?* (1969); Wayne K. Hobson, *The American Legal Profession and the Organizational Society*, 1890-1930 (1986).

[13] Carole Silver, *Globalization and the U.S. Market for Legal Services – Shifting Identities*, 31 Georgetown J. Int. Law 1093 (2000).

[14] Galanter and Palay, supra note 11, at 46.

[15] *Id.*

[16] Robert L. Nelson, *Partners with Power: The Social Transformation of the Large Firm* (1988); see also, John P. Heinz, Robert L. Nelson, Rebecca L. Sandefur, & Edward O. Laumann, *Urban Lawyers: The New Social Structure of the Bar*, 107 (2005).

part, to the increasing necessity of tracking the growing volume of pro bono activities.[17]

This growth also provided the organizational slack that spurred the resources to increase the amount of pro bono work undertaken within the firm. As firms grew, the equilibrium between client demand for legal services and the supply of lawyers was knocked off balance. There were now more lawyers housed in the firm than were sometimes necessary for the number of ongoing case matters. Thus, the extraneous supply of lawyers could be easily shifted into pro bono work during a lull in fee-generating work. Furthermore, the increasing profitability of large firms provided the economic means to take on nonpaying pro bono work without it being a large resource cost to the firm.

Pro Bono as a Recruitment Tool

The exponential growth of large firms over the last few decades has led to increased competition for top recruits from elite law schools, which expanded the market for pro bono programs within law firms.[18]

Organizing a formal program became an effective way to demonstrate to top recruits that the firm was doing interesting pro bono work. During recruitment, many firms will include the pro bono coordinator in their interview process, linking top recruits with an interest in pro bono work with the firm's pro bono program. As pro bono programs continue to diffuse across many large firms, it has become difficult for firms to differentiate their pro bono programs from their peers. Prior to institutionalization, firms that moved first with organizing their pro bono programs had an edge over their peers in using pro bono as an effective recruitment tool. However, this has become increasingly difficult to demonstrate in the contemporary period; firms now simply have to demonstrate that they have a program in order to signal their compliance to institutionalized pro bono norms.

Although pro bono appears to continue to play an important recruitment tool for firms, it is unclear how the recent recession has affected student interest in pro bono during the recruitment process. As students continue to face an uncertain legal profession that is still recovering from the recession and firms continue to lay off associates, defer recent hires, and reduce their recruitment classes, pro bono might be less important to the student than simply getting a job offer, especially when facing increasing debt loads. Thus, although advocates continue to argue that pro bono is an important recruitment tool to attract elite students, there is no strong evidence that it actually affects the recruitment outcomes of law firms. However,

[17] Cummings & Rhode, supra note 10, at 10 (arguing that "as firms grew bigger and more bureaucratic, it became harder to maintain decentralized systems with lawyer-initiated volunteer work ... such systems were ill-suited to prevent potential conflicts of interest").

[18] Stephen Daniels & Joanne Martin, *Legal Services for the Poor: Access, Self-Interest, and Pro Bono*, 12 Sociology of Crime, Law & Deviance 145, at 154 (2009).

there is some recent evidence that does support the idea that elite students are motivated, in part, by the pro bono opportunities when looking for their ideal jobs and pro bono managers regularly regard potential recruits as a central constituency to reach through their programs.[19]

A Decline in Federally Funded Legal Services

As part of the general trend toward decentralizing governmental support for social services, federal funding for legal services has decreased sharply since the early 1980s.

The current system of civil legal assistance in the United States is no longer primarily centralized through the federal government, but funded in a piecemeal fashion through a host of alternative sources. The private bar has become one vital source of civil legal assistance funding – so much, in fact, that by the late 1990s, the increasing recruitment of private lawyers to assist the poor meant that pro bono legal work had become the "largest component of civil legal assistance in the United States."[20]

The Professional Bar

Responding to the restructuring of federal legal services and the long-standing critiques of increasing commercialization of the legal profession, the professional bar has been a major contributor in building the current pro bono movement.

Organizations such as the American Bar Association (ABA) Standing Committee on Pro Bono and Public Service, the Pro Bono Institute, and Pro Bono Net have focused on facilitating lawyers' commitment to pro bono. These professional organizations, in addition to the numerous non profits that receive support from organized pro bono programs, regularly give awards to firms and individual lawyers for their pro bono achievements, further publicizing the pro bono cause across the profession. Most important in this professional network is the Association of Pro Bono Counsel (APBCo), which is dedicated to the development of pro bono counsel within large firms. This specialized association was formed in 2006 and now includes over 120 members across 85 large firms.[21]

The Rise of Law Firm Rankings

The rise of *American Lawyer* rankings, and in particular the "A-List," has created conditions that have facilitated institutionalized pro bono in ways both internal and external to the firm. *American Lawyer* is a national law magazine founded in 1978

[19] Robert Granfield, *The Meaning of Pro Bono: Institutional Variations in Professional Obligations among Lawyers*, 41 LAW SOCIETY REV. 113 (2007); see also Steven A. Boutcher, *Rethinking Culture: Organized Pro Bono and the External Sources of Law Firm Culture*, 8 U. ST. THOM L.J. 108 (2011).

[20] Sandefur, supra note 1, at 85.

[21] Available at www.probonocounsel.org.

that tracks large law firm trends through a variety of surveys, including the AmLaw 100 and AmLaw 200 surveys on the economics of the largest 100 and 200 firms, respectively.

Internally, the rankings provide an opportunity for committed individuals inside of the firm to press for increased commitment by firm managers, who espouse the rhetoric of pro bono as a component of their firm's historic culture.[22] Additionally, the rankings have led some firms to specifically structure their pro bono policies and practices in ways to extract higher ratings. For example, some firms have mandated that attorneys commit at least 20 hours toward pro bono in order to facilitate a higher score on American Lawyer's "A-List" rankings, which includes the percentage of the firm working at least 20 hours a year as one component in its larger composite score. Externally, the rankings allow firms to compare themselves relative to their peers, which spurs increased competition to outperform each other in the rankings.

CONTEMPORARY TRENDS IN PRO BONO PARTICIPATION AND GOVERNANCE

The institutionalization of pro bono across the field of large law firms has a direct effect on how firms organize their pro bono programs, which in turn affects the level of law firm participation within the pro bono system. Here, I discuss some contemporary trends in pro bono participation, focusing on how much time is devoted to pro bono, how they organize their pro bono programs, and the issues they target.

Field-Level Participation

Since 1998, *American Lawyer* has been surveying the top 200 firms about their pro bono programs, including information on the firm's total pro bono hours, the average participation rates per lawyer, and the percent distribution of the firm's lawyers engaging in pro bono work.[23] The trend in overall participation has been one marked by a gradual increase in total hours across the field of large firms. Figure 17.1 shows the increasing trend in participation between 1998 and 2011. In 1998, just over two million hours of pro bono were contributed among the top 200 firms, which increased to a high of 5.7 million hours in 2009. However, due, in part, to the recent economic recession, total pro bono output decreased to 4.9 million hours in 2011, dropping by about 14% from the high point of 2009.

[22] Boutcher, supra note 19, at 120–21.

[23] In 1994, *American Lawyer* began surveying large firms on their pro bono participation rates. Between 1994 and 1998, *American Lawyer* included only the top 100 firms, which was then expanded to include the top 200 firms in subsequent years. Here, I focus on the full field of 200 firms, commonly referred to as the AmLaw 200.

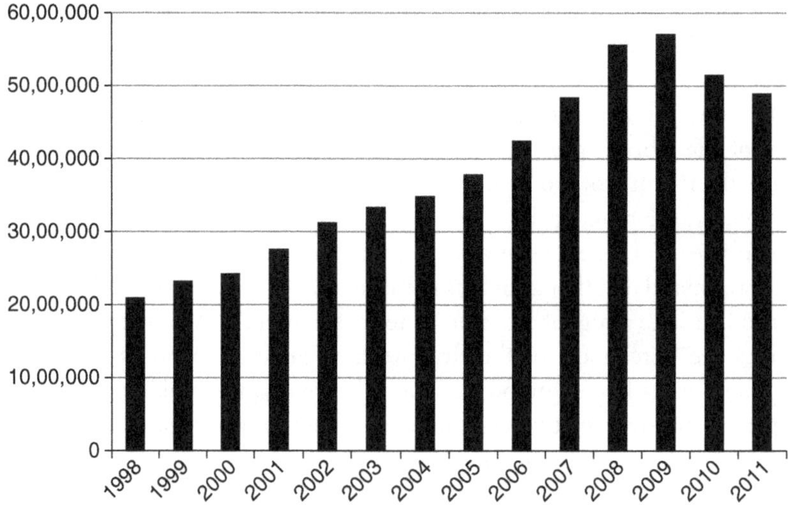

FIGURE 17.1. Total hours of pro bono, 1998–2011.
Source: Calculated from *America Lawyer.*

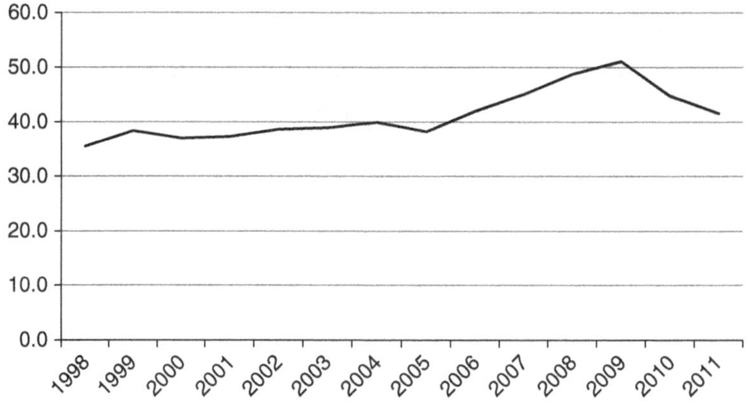

FIGURE 17.2. Average hours of pro bono per lawyer, 1998–2011.
Source: Calculated from *America Lawyer.*

A measure of total hours provides one indicator of how much pro bono work is provided, but it is, in part, a function of how many firms report their data to *American Lawyer* each year along with the overall growth in the number of lawyers entering these firms from one year to the next. To control for this, another measure of pro bono participation is the average hourly output per lawyer. Figure 17.2 shows the trend in terms of the average hours of pro bono work per lawyer over time. In 1998, lawyers donated 35.5 hours of pro bono work on average across the field. This gradually increased through the decade to a high of 51.1 hours per lawyer on average in 2009. Like total hours, the average decreased due to the recession, dropping by almost 19% to 41.6 hours per lawyer on average in 2011. An important point to note here is that only in

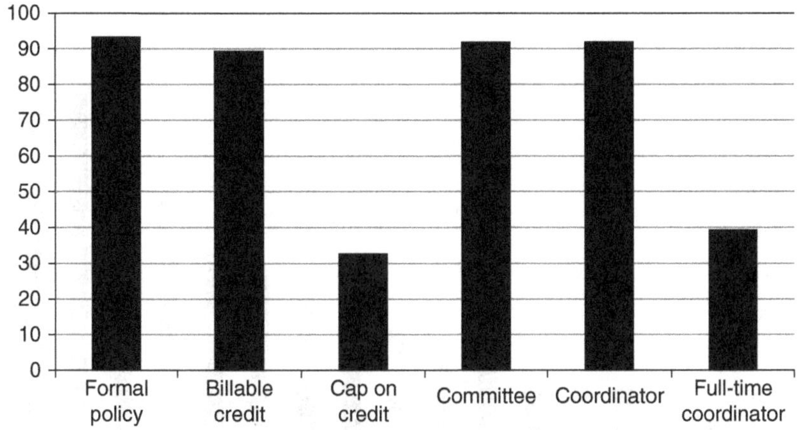

FIGURE 17.3. Distribution of various pro bono governance structures, 2005–06 (percentage of firms reporting various pro bono structures).
Source: Calculated from vault Guide, supra note 25.

2009 did the field reach the 50-hour voluntary guideline outlined in ABA Model Rule 6.1.

Both measures of pro bono participation suggest that from the late 1990s to 2009, the trend was toward increasing pro bono output among the field of large firms. Although I cannot say for certain, it appears that this trend would have continued to gradually tick upward if the recession had not happened in late 2008, resulting in a decline in overall pro bono services from large firms.

Incentivizing Pro Bono

Although firms have integrated pro bono into their organizational structure, they are still primarily oriented toward generating billable hours, which are in direct competition with pro bono hours. In an effort to incentivize associates to take on pro bono cases without risk of adding additional time to their already demanding workloads, many firms now give credit for pro bono time to count as a portion of their billable hours.[24] As Figure 17.3 indicates, just over 89% of large firms surveyed reported having this in their policy.[25] Although most firms included this type of policy, there was wider divergence around the question of whether to cap the number of hours credited. About one-third of the firms surveyed indicated that they did include a cap on the amount of pro bono that counts toward billable hours. Of these firms that included a cap, close to 40% included up to 50 hours, 18.4% had a cap of 100 hours, and 10.5% allowed up to 150 hours.

[24] Boutcher, supra note 9, at 154–56.

[25] Data presented in Figure 17.3 was collected from the *Vault Guide to Law Firm Pro Bono Programs* (2007), which includes data on 140 *American Lawyer* firms. For a description of this data source, see, Boutcher, supra note 9 at 156.

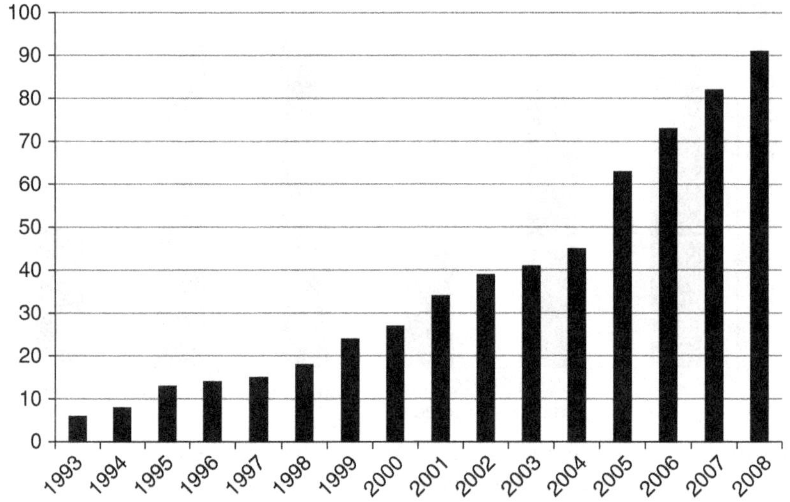

FIGURE 17.4. Cumulative growth of the pro bono coordinator, 1993–2008. Source: Cumming & Rhode, supra note 10, see note 26.

In terms of how the firms manage their pro bono programs, an overwhelming majority (92%) of firms reported having a committee that oversaw the firm's staffing and handling of pro bono cases. These committees often combine partners with associates within each office as well as across offices. Moreover, most firms (92%) had a designated individual (or a team in some cases) of coordinators managing the firm's pro bono practice. Some coordinators are responsible for administering the pro bono program in addition to their billable practice, while other firms staff the coordinator as a full-time manager, completely organizing all facets of the firm's pro bono program. Firms varied more in terms of whether they hired a full-time or part-time coordinator. Among the firms reporting they had a coordinator, 39.4% had someone full time compared to 60.6% that had a part-time coordinator.

Limited data exist to illustrate the diffusion of the coordinator position across large firms. Figure 17.4 shows the cumulative rise of the pro bono coordinator position across large firms.[26] Scott Cummings and Deborah Rhode found that there has been a dramatic growth in the pro bono coordinator position over the last decade. There were a total of 91 pro bono positions in 2008 across a total of 78 firms, demonstrating a remarkable expansion from a decade earlier where only 18 positions existed in 1998 and only 6 in 1993.[27]

[26] Data for Figure 17.4 was generously shared by Scott Cummings.

[27] Cummings & Rhode, supra note 10, at fn. 77 (reporting that "Of the 127 firms that responded, 49 stated that they had no pro bono counsel positions, leaving 78 firms with such positions during the period covered by the rankings. The number of positions reported (91) is greater than the number of firms (78) because some firms had more than one pro bono counsel position")

In prior research, I found that differences in how a firm structures its pro bono program have important consequences for firm participation.[28] For instance, firms that had a formal policy, provided billable hour credit for pro bono work, and had a pro bono coordinator all tended to have higher levels of pro bono participation compared to firms that lacked those governance structures. Moreover, the content of those policy differences also mattered; firms that had a full-time coordinator did more pro bono on average compared to firms that had a part-time coordinator, and firms that had no cap on the amount of pro bono hours that could count toward billable hours also had higher levels of participation per lawyer. Thus, how a firm structures its pro bono program has important consequences for pro bono outcomes.

THE TARGETS OF PRO BONO

Much of the literature on pro bono focuses on the supply side of the pro bono system, analyzing the various inputs into the pro bono system. There is a relative absence of scholarship focused on where pro bono is actually directed. What types of issues and organizations does large firm pro bono serve, and where are there glaring gaps in coverage? ABA Model Rule 6.1, which outlines the profession's voluntary pro bono responsibility, lists the variety of types of organizations where pro bono services should be directed. However, ABA Model Rule 6.1 also gives priority to organizations that focus on "persons of limited means." This would include the many legal services organizations that channel legal assistance to low-income individuals. Given the guidelines listed by the ABA, we could expect that much of large firm pro bono should be directed at these types of organizations. However, very little is known whether this is actually true in practice.

Drawing from two different data sources, this section provides a snapshot of the issues that contemporary large firm pro bono programs assist. Table 17.1 reports survey data from a sample of pro bono managers in large firms, illustrating the popularity of different issues sorted by the percentage of firms reporting working in that area.[29, 30] Two areas received universal coverage: every firm reported working on children/youth and immigration issues. Many issues received widespread coverage, including civil liberties, civil rights, human rights, LGBT rights, and homelessness. Issues such as animal rights, consumer protection, and environmental protection received much lower support among firms, though more than half of those surveyed reported

[28] Boutcher, supra note 9, at 155–56 (showing that different types of pro bono policy can affect pro bono participation in the firm).

[29] Data for Table 17.1 were collected and generously shared by Scott Cummings.

[30] Scott L. Cummings, *The Pursuit of Legal Rights – and Beyond*, 59 UCLA L. Rev. 506, 536 (2012), (noting that his survey "was sent to eighty APBCO firm counsel, forty-two (53 percent) of whom responded to a question asking whether the U.S. offices of their firm have handled pro bono cases in designated issues areas over the past five years").

TABLE 17.1 *Pro bono issue areas.*

Issue	Percentage of firms reporting working in area
Children/youth	100
Immigration	100
Arts/cultural	98
Civil liberties	98
Community/economic development	98
Family	98
Civil rights	95
Housing	95
Human rights	95
LGBT	95
Criminal	93
Elder law	93
Homelessness	93
Public benefits	93
Employment	88
Disability rights	86
Education	86
Women's rights	86
Voting	83
Health	81
Election law	76
Animals	69
Consumer protection	69
Media/technology	69
Environmental protection	62
Labor	52
Reproductive rights	36
Indian law	26
Other	26

Source: Cummings, supra note 30; see note 29.

working in those areas. Labor issues received coverage by just over half of the firms and the areas of reproductive rights and Indian law garnered sparse coverage.

Table 17.2 shows the distribution of pro bono issues from organizational data I compiled for a recent study about the issues to which pro bono is directed.[31]

[31] Steven A. Boutcher, *Lawyering for Social Change: Pro Bono Publico, Cause Lawyering, and the Social Movement Society*, 18 Mobiliz. Int J 179 (2013). Data from Table 17.2 was collected from the *Vault Guide to Large Firm Pro Bono Programs, 3rd Edition* (2007). The *Vault Guide* included pro bono information for a total of 146 law firms. The organizational data were coded from the following question: "List up to 10 organizations for which your firm performed pro bono legal services in 2004 and 2005."

TABLE 17.2 *Distribution of pro bono issues.*

Issue	Percentage of firms listing at least one organization in issue area
Civil rights/civil liberties	67.39
Children	57.25
Women's rights	46.38
Health/disability	43.48
Human rights/international	39.13
Housing/homelessness	35.51
Prisoner's rights	29.71
Immigration	29.71
Nonprofits	24.64
Economic development	23.19
Other	16.67
LGBT	15.94
Education	10.14
Environment	13.04
Elder	10.87
Veteran	6.52
Religion	6.52
Labor	5.07
Animals	4.35
Government	2.90
Poverty	2.90

Source: Calculated from Vault Guide, supra note 25.

The distribution of issues largely maps on to the previous distribution, but with important differences. First, none of the issue areas received universal coverage. For instance, although the issue areas of civil rights and civil liberties, and children, received the largest amounts of coverage from firms, the amount of coverage was much lower than in the previous dataset (67.4% vs. 98%). Second, whereas the majority of firms in Table 17.1 reported taking pro bono cases across most issues, Table 17.2 suggests that most substantive areas receive coverage by fewer than half of the firms. For instance, 69% of firms reported taking on animal rights cases in Table 17.1, but only 4.35% of firms reported working in that area in Table 17.2. Thus, the data in Table 17.2 present a more differentiated field of pro bono representation, suggesting that firms make varied strategic decisions about where to devote their pro bono resources.[32]

[32] The differences in coverage between Tables 17.1 and 17.2 are important to note. The differences between datasets may be due to the different sources of data and how the issues areas were gathered. Table 17.1 reports survey data collected from pro bono coordinators across a small sample of large firms that asked them to simply list if they worked in each particular issue area. Table 17.2 reports data

What factors direct firms to represent some issue areas over others? Although the data presented in this chapter cannot answer this question, I offer some speculation of factors that may be driving the connections between firms and pro bono organizations. Like other areas of legal practice, pro bono lawyering is driven by relationships.[33] These relationships can be structured in a variety of ways. For instance, firm partners, or associates, may serve on the boards of different organizations, playing a brokering role between the two. This brokerage role may make it easier for the organization to tap into the pro bono resources of the firm. Additionally, some organizations may have structured their operations to more easily capture firm resources, relying heavily on volunteer labor while others draw from multiple resource streams.

Another mechanism for channeling pro bono toward some issues over others may have to do with the idiosyncratic, personal tastes of associates who do the bulk of pro bono work in law firms, suggesting a bottom-up process of issue selection. Issues that are personally rewarding to the individual attorney or perceived as more interesting could receive more support than issues that are perceived as uninteresting or outdated. However, considering the extent to which personal tastes are randomly distributed across attorneys in a firm, we should see less differentiation across issues than illustrated in Table 17.2 and more variation than Table 17.1 suggests.

Finally, firms may select issues that are "safe" in order to avoid irritating current, and potential, clients. Direct positional conflicts will necessitate avoidance. However, most pro bono cases do not pose a direct ethical conflict with clients, but may contain broad, issue-based conflicts that influence decisions about what issues to take on.[34] For instance, positional conflicts may shape the likelihood that a firm is willing to take on labor or environmental issue when their clients are engaged in related legal matters. Thus, how broad or narrow a firm to defines their issue-based conflicts will shape the decisions about where to channel pro bono resources.

In reality, firms probably decide where to direct their pro bono resources not as a function of personal networks or individual taste, but most likely, a combination of factors all operating at the same time, and at odds with each other. The issues that predominate across large firms are most likely not motivated by the functional needs of American society in any given year, but is largely driven by social factors internal, and external, to the individual firm. Thus, as Granfield and Mather argue, "The type of pro bono work undertaken within a law firm . . . reflects the social, economic, and even political context of the firm."[35]

collected from a survey of large firms about the organizations they assist, which were then coded according to primary issue area, and includes a larger sample of firms.

[33] See, e.g., Phillip R. Lochner, *The No Fee and Low Fee Legal Practice of Private Attorneys*, 9 Law & Society Rev. 431 (1975).

[34] See, e.g., Norman W. Spaulding, *The Prophet and the Bureaucrat: Positional Conflicts in Service Pro Bono Publico*, 50 Stan. L. Rev. 1395 (1998).

[35] Granfield & Mather, supra note 1, at 11.

CONCLUSION

This chapter has outlined the expansion of pro bono work being done in large law firms across the United States. The expansion of these programs has led to the institutionalization of pro bono across this segment of the elite bar, leading pro bono to become largely taken for granted within contemporary firm governance. This is not to suggest that it is not contentious in its implementation, especially with respect to decisions about where resources should be directed. Nonetheless, the amount of pro bono work has increased substantially across the field of *American Lawyer* law firms. The expansion in time devoted to pro bono work is coupled with governance structures supporting its growth and providing a strong foundation to sustain itself. However, decisions about how much time to devote to pro bono work are intimately connected to firm-level and field-level factors, as the trends outlined earlier show regarding the relationship between the recession and aggregate hours across the firms.

The growth of pro bono across large firms should mean an increase in access to civil justice for Americans. As more lawyers are mobilized to provide pro bono work inside of law firms, more individuals and organizations should be able to access legal assistance. However, growth in supply does not necessarily mean more equitable access to increasing pro bono resources. Indeed, as shown earlier, the expansion of pro bono in large firms has resulted in a channeling of some issues over others, and some organizations are better able to leverage those resources than others.

What role can large firm pro bono programs play in providing legal assistance to working Americans? The growth of pro bono in large firms might suggest that there are increasing resources to help working Americans gain legal assistance. However, because Model Rule 6.1 privileges "no fee or expectation of fee" in defining what qualifies as pro bono, most large firm pro bono may ignore working and middle-class individuals that do not fit the traditional criteria of "persons of limited means."[36] Thus, under current ethical rules, large firm pro bono programs may not be a viable source of legal assistance for working Americans. Expanding what counts as legitimate pro bono services to include reduced-fee services would be a first step to including more Americans under these programs.[37] Another potential mechanism for expanding who fits within traditional pro bono representation would be for the creation of intermediary organizations to structure their missions to serve working and middle-class Americans. This would be especially important given that most

[36] ABA Model Rule 6.1: Voluntary Pro Bono Service, available at www.americanbar.org/groups/professional_responsibility/publications/model_rules_of_professional_conduct/rule_6_1_voluntary_pro_bono_publico_service.html.

[37] Leslie C. Levin, *Pro Bono and Low Bono in the Solo and Small Firm Context*, in Private Lawyers and the Public Interest (Robert Granfield and Lynn Mather, eds., 2009).

large firms work with organizations and not individuals.[38] Creating new organizations that can generate strong relationships with large firms could broaden the traditional targets of contemporary pro bono to include Americans of average means that are currently underserved by existing organizations.

Institutionalized pro bono appears to be a prominent feature of large firm governance for the foreseeable future. Although contemporary programs privilege organizations working with "persons of limited means," the expansion of pro bono resources presents a mix of new opportunities and constraints for expanding access to civil justice to a broader set of Americans that find themselves increasingly unable to access legal services through traditional markets.

[38] Heinz et al., supra note 16.

18

Institutionalizing Pro Bono

Samuel Estreicher & Jonathan Remy Nash

U.S. law firms expend considerable resources supporting the pro bono activities of their lawyers. This chapter by Estreicher and Nash explores the reasons for law firm pro bono practices and suggests that more attention be paid to the training opportunities for junior lawyers that can be provided by a pro bono program that emphasizes assistance to individuals and groups on "retail" matters where legal assistance of any kind is typically unavailable. A questionnaire is offered to help law firms assess what they do in their pro bono programs.

Why do large law firms engage in pro bono matters? One answer is that legal services on pro bono matters provide a benefit to society. Often pro bono projects involve provision of critical services to individuals and groups who may otherwise lack access to competent legal representation. Where this is the case, lawyers are making an important societal contribution, and fulfilling an ethical obligation of their profession.

Pro bono matters also provide an opportunity for young lawyers to deal with clients and issues they would be unlikely to encounter, and hence to develop skills not ordinarily called upon in the course of at least their junior years of billable work. Such engagements thus offer an attractive training opportunity for young lawyers that, from the firm's standpoint, poses no risk to its paying clients. Law firms also use the prospect of pro bono work as a means to recruit and retain young associates. Pro bono matters also may improve the public image of law firms that underwrite them. From the firm's vantage, the benefits to society in helping to address social needs are important but may be secondary to the instrumental benefits.

If there is a positive relationship between commitment to pro bono activities and measures of firm performance, such a finding may encourage firms to expand their underwriting of pro bono work by their associates. On the other hand, if a positive relationship is lacking or has become attenuated over time, firms may reassess their commitment to pro bono activities or implement controls to better further instrumental objectives.

We offer an overview of large law firm pro bono[1] practices. Our discussion consists of four parts. First, we consider the demand for pro bono services.

Second, we discuss the supply of pro bono services by large law firms. We include a brief overview of collaboration with public interest organizations – which tends to be the way that large law firms currently deliver pro bono services.

Third, we explore two explanations for *why* large law firms might devote nontrivial resources to the provision of pro bono services. One account sees pro bono service provision as driven by lawyers' – and in particular individual partners' – political or ideological commitments and their understanding of professional obligations. Another approach views pro bono as driven by economic considerations. From the latter perspective, for example, it is important that pro bono matters provide valuable opportunities for junior lawyers to gain experience or for the firm to attract legal talent.

Fourth, recognizing that there is a dearth of empirical data from which one might discern which of these theories has greater explanatory power, we present a simple survey instrument for law firm pro bono administrators to complete that might help fill the informational gap. The data such a survey could produce would be valuable to law firms, those seeking pro bono help, and bar organizations and court systems seeking to improve the delivery of pro bono services.

DEMAND FOR LAW FIRM PRO BONO PRACTICES

We begin with the demand for pro bono services. Legal services tend to be expensive. While the market will tend to ration legal services to those who value it most,[2] not all those who would value or need legal services have the resources to purchase them.[3] It is foreseeable, then, that the market may not deliver legal services to some who value or need them.

The 1960s witnessed expansion and development of government programs designed to provide some modicum of legal services to the poor.[4] The advent of

[1] We leave to the side the question of what exactly constitutes pro bono. See Deborah L. Rhode, *Where is the Public in Lawyers' Public Service? Pro Bono and the Bottom Line* 3–12, *in* PRIVATE LAWYERS AND THE PUBLIC INTEREST: THE EVOLVING ROLE OF PRO BONO IN THE LEGAL PROFESSION 251, 252–53 (Robert Granfield & Lynn Mather eds. 2009) (hereinafter PRIVATE LAWYERS AND THE PUBLIC INTEREST); Cynthia Feathers, *The New York State's Experience: How Should Pro Bono Be Defined to Emphasize Service to the Poor While Encouraging Broad Public Service*, in *id.*, at 267.

[2] See, e.g., Jonathan Remy Nash, *Framing Effects and Regulatory Choice*, 82 NOTRE DAME L. REV. 313 323 (2006).

[3] See, e.g., Saul Levmore, *Voting with Intensity*, 53 STAN. L. REV. 111, 117–18 (2000).

[4] See Robert L. Abel, *State, Market, Philanthropy and Self-Help as Legal Services Delivery Mechanisms*, *in* PRIVATE LAWYERS AND THE PUBLIC INTEREST, supra note 1, at 295, 296.

these programs also gave rise to new demands for legal services, such as challenges to the denial of government benefits.[5]

Demand for legal services is not limited to litigation.[6] As charitable and public-interest organizations have proliferated, so has the demand for transactional services by these groups. These organizations have resource issues and often need to incorporate, rent, and purchase office space, as well-qualified lawyers and other staff.

ROLE OF LARGER LAW FIRMS IN THE DELIVERY OF PRO BONO SERVICES

On the supply side, during the initial rise in demand for pro bono services during the 1960s, the government was the principal provider of any legal services to the poor, whether directly or through legal services paid for with government funds. But this funding source has been significantly diminished in recent decades as political resistance developed to having the government fund legal challenges to systemic practices of government and private companies.[7]

The rise in demand in the 1960s and thereafter for pro bono services coincided with the growth in the number and size of of large law firms.[8] Today, private lawyers who perform pro bono services are principally employed by large law firms.[9] For complex litigation and transactions, a large law firm may be the only practical option: Large law firms have the necessary resources to do such work, including a significant number of associates who might be interested in spending part of their time doing pro bono work. As Professor Boucher relates in his chapter in this volume, virtually every law firm of any significant size maintains a pro bono legal services program; few small firms do so.

WHY DO LARGE LAW FIRM SUPPLY PRO BONO SERVICES?: TWO EXPLANATIONS

Why have large law firms become involved in supplying pro bono services? After all, just because large law firms have the resources to conduct a lot of pro bono work does not mean that they will agree to do so. Large law firms are creatures of the market. They grew because of economic demand, and they thrive on representing institutional and wealthy clients. Why, then, would they undertake to provide pro bono

5 See Charles A. Reich, *The New Property*, 73 YALE L.J. 733 (1964).

6 See Garth C. Grissom, *Pro Bono and the Transaction Lawyer*, 9 GEO. J. LEGAL ETHICS 929 (1996).

7 See *Abel*, supra note 4, at 3–4; Scott L. Cummings, *The Politics of Pro Bono*, 52 UCLA L. REV. 1, 19 (2004).

8 See Cummings, supra note 7, at 33; see generally Marc Galanter & Thomas Palay, *The Transformation of the Big Law Firm*, *in* LAWYERS' IDEALS/LAWYERS' PRACTICES 31 (Robert L. Nelson, David M. Trubek & Rayman L. Solomon eds. 1992).

9 See Galanter & Palay, supra note 8, at 52; Cummings, supra note 7, at 33–41.

services? We see two categories of explanations: explanations exogenous to the market and explanations endogenous to it.

Most commentators offer explanations external to the market. They often view pro bono work as undertaken primarily to serve the professional or ideological commitments of their lawyers or clients.[10]

Those holding this view point to state bars that require licensed lawyers to engage in pro bono work. New York, for example, mandates that all new lawyers devote 50 hours a year of pro bono service.[11] Sometimes, the law schools impose a pro bono service requirement before students can receive a JD degree.[12] Many large law firms have accepted the "pro bono challenge" of local bar associations under which firms are called upon to contribute some percentage of their billable hours to pro bono.[13] In some firms, a pro bono commitment is part of the "office culture."[14]

Some lawyers may also see pro bono work as a means of vindicating their political and ideological commitments.[15]

In part because of the emphasis on non-market motivations, few commentators have recognized that market-based factors also create an incentive for large law firms to engage in pro bono activities. For the firm, economic incentives will be important drivers in influencing the benefits of pro bono involvement outweigh, or at least are perceived to outweigh, their costs.

We begin by observing that pro bono activities can be time-consuming. The time spent on pro bono is time that one cannot devote to billable matters (i.e., those matters engaged in with a profit motive).[16] An attorney's billable hours generally

[10] See, e.g., Deborah A. Schmedermann, *Pro Bono Publico as a Conscience Good*, 35 Wm. Mitchell L. Rev. 977 (2009); Deborah L. Rhode, *Pro Bono in Principle and in Practice*, 53 J. Leg. Educ. 113 (2003) (arguing that pro bono emanates from, and can be designed better to further, altruistic goals); cf. Robert Granfield, *The Meaning of Pro Bono: Institutional Variations in Professional Obligations among Lawyers*, 41 Law & Soc'y Rev. 113 (2007) (arguing that individuals' views of pro bono are influenced and ultimately molded by the professional setting in which they find themselves working); but see Jim Hales, *Why I Selfishly Accept Pro Bono Cases*, 22 Nev. Law. 21 (2014).

[11] For discussion, see Graffeo, Chapter 24 in this volume.

[12] E.g., Ronit Dinovitzer & Bryant G. Garth, *Pro Bono as an Elite Strategy in Early Lawyer Careers*, *in* Private Lawyers and the Public Interest, supra note 1, at 115.

[13] For discussion, see Cummings, supra note 7, at 40; Esther F. Lardent, *Structuring Law Firm Pro Bono Programs: A Community Service Typology*, *in* The Law Firm and the Public Good 59, 78–82 (Robert A. Katzmann ed. 1995); Barrington D. Parker, Jr., *Monitoring Compliance with the ABA Law Firm Pro Bono Challenge*, *in* Lawyers' Ideals/Lawyers' Practices, supra note 8, at 158.

[14] See Cynthia Fuchs Epstein, *"Issues Entrepreneurs": Charisma, Charisma-Producing Events, and the Shaping of Pro Bono Practices in Large Law Firms*, *in* Private Lawyers and the Public Interest, supra note 1, at 211.

[15] See Galanter & Palay, supra note 8, at 52. On the evolution of conceptions of lawyers' obligation to serve the public, see Russell G. Pearce, *The Lawyer and Public Service*, Am. U. J. Gender Soc. Pol'y & L. 171 (2001); Susan P. Shapiro, Tangled Loyalties: Conflict of Interest in Legal Practice 242 (2002).

[16] Some claim that pro bono service correlates with high billable hours and other measures of productivity. See James L. Baillie, *It Helps the Bottom Line – Really*, Bus. Law Today, Jan./Feb. 1997, at 50; Jack W. Londen, *The Impact of Pro Bono Work on Law Firm Economics*, 9 Geo. J. Legal Ethics 925, 925 (1996).

have a major effect on compensation and even job security. Pro bono matters are generally not billable, and the extent to which they "count" toward an attorney's minimal billable-hours requirement for a bonus or for retention is often capped (if they really count at all).

Effective economic incentives to engage in pro bono must more than offset this cost to the lawyer's salary and promotional opportunity.[17] As we examine economic factors that contribute to law firms undertaking pro bono activities, we first identify reasons why lawyers consider it in their interest to engage in such work; and then consider why firms support these efforts.

First, pro bono activities offer lawyers – especially junior lawyers – the opportunity for networking. They likely will interact with other lawyers at their firms. They also may meet lawyers from other large firms, the government or nonprofit sector who are engaging in similar activities.

Second, pro bono work may help build a lawyer's reputation. Indeed, it may enhance a lawyer's reputation among communities with which the lawyer is likely be especially concerned: other lawyers, judges, clients,[18] and the public at large.[19] Members of these communities may view the lawyer more favorably, as more able, and perhaps be more likely to send the lawyer work in the future.

Third, pro bono practice can be a source of training for lawyers.[20] Junior lawyers working on billable matters often do not get front-line responsibility, and sometimes garner only relatively mundane assignments. Pro bono offers the possibility of more responsibility and more substantive assignments.

We have just offered three reasons why attorneys might perceive a benefit to engaging in pro bono activities, but none of these provides a robust motivation for a firm's pro bono program. The incentives for pro bono we have identified – networking, reputation, and training – may apply to attorneys of all levels of experience but, as we have indicated, we expect them to be especially enticing for junior attorneys. Moreover, the benefits that networking and training offer will tend to accrue in the future, while the time taken away from billable worker is experienced in the present. The question thus arises whether, even if junior associates would choose to engage in pro bono work if left to their own devices, should we expect law firm management to expend concrete resources in promoting pro bono activity?

[17] Pro bono engagements may also lead to conflicts with paying clients' representation – whether because of a technical conflict of interest, or simply because a position that should be advanced on behalf of the pro bono client conflicts with one that may be advanced for paying clients; the latter's interest will generally prevail. See Shapiro, supra note 15, at 166–67.

[18] See Ronald J. Tabak, *Integration of Pro Bono into Law Firm Practice*, 9 Geo. J. Legal Ethics 931, 931 (1996).

[19] See Londen, supra note 16, at 926; Debra Burke, Reagan McLaurin & James W. Pearce, *Pro Bono Publico: Issues and Implications*, 26 Loy. U. Chi. L.J. 61, 78 (1994).

[20] See, e.g., Londen, supra note 16, at 926; Tabak, supra note 18, at 931; Strossen, supra note 1, at 2143–44; Burke, McLaurin & Pearce, supra note 19, at 78.

One answer is that, for some firms, the interests of management and junior lawyers will be aligned (or at least will be perceived to be so). We anticipate that this will especially be the case for firms that have better retention rates for their junior associates, or that anticipate a long-term involvement with exiting associates who are placed in positions that will help maintain client relationships.

Aside from training opportunities, pro bono activities are an important recruitment and retention tool. In order to attract and retain the best associates, a law firm must have a significant pro bono program. In the end, it may not be that the best associates actually engage in pro bono activities, and indeed that may not matter on this account. The fact the firm has a significant pro bono program enhances the firm's general reputation in the market. As a general matter, young lawyers are likely to factor in firms' pro bono activities in assessing firms' reputations and ultimately in deciding which firm to work for. A mathematical example may be helpful to understand the underlying dynamic. Our assumption is that firms that eschew pro bono activity will be less able to attract and retain the best associates. Consider that a firm will earn profit B_1 from "Associate #1" if she does not engage in pro bono, and profit B_2 if she does (with $B_1 > B_2$, by assumption). If faced with this choice, the firm would prefer for Associate #1 not to engage in pro bono matters.

Let us say, however, that the firm will not be able to hire Associate #1 if it does not allow her to engage in at least some pro bono work.[21] Instead of Associate #1, the firm will hire "Associate #2," who is not as qualified or hardworking. And let us further say that the firm's profit from Associate #2 (even doing no pro bono work) will be B_3, with $B_2 > B_3$ by virtue of Associate #1's edge in ability or diligence over Associate #2.[22] We can easily assemble the firm's preference ranking thus:

Preference rank	Condition	Profit to firm
1	Associate #1 works and does no pro bono work.	B_1
2	Associate #1 works and does pro bono work.	B_2
3	Associate #2 works and does no pro bono work.	B_3

While the firm might prefer, hypothetically, to hire Associate #1 and have her do no pro bono work, once the firm adopts a "no pro bono work" policy, it cannot hire Associate #1. Given that result, the firm will prefer to allow pro bono work so that it can hire (and retain) Associate #1.

21 The stylized example could work as well if the result of not allowing Associate #1 to engage in pro bono work was not that the firm could not hire her in the first instance, but rather that the firm could retain her only as it provided pro bono opportunities.

22 The increase in profit might result from Associate #1's superior competence or efficiency, for example.

One troubling question is why would potential junior associate applicants have sufficient leverage to achieve this outcome? First, realize that large law firms prefer to hire so-called "elite" junior lawyers from the best law schools with the best grades, and that there is a limited supply of such lawyers. They may seek such lawyers because they are likely to become talented, profitable partners, because the firm acquires reputational benefits in the marketplace from being able to hire young stars, or some combination of both. A firm's pro bono program enhances the firm's ability to attract and hire junior talent.

Second, consider why junior lawyers might demand the chance to work on pro bono matters. We offered earlier three reasons – networking, reputation, and training – why junior associates might see it in their self-interest (even if it is not in the firm's interest) to do so. In addition, there is a pro bono scenario that mixes market-based reasons and reasons exogenous to the market. "Elite" junior lawyers[23] may be the category of attorneys who, confident they can readily obtain a big firm position, are more likely to have political or ideological commitments or to profess to have them.[24] These junior lawyers may trade on their strong desire to do pro bono work (a factor exogenous to market concerns) to convince firms (who are interested in hiring them for market-based reasons) to allow them to do pro bono work.[25] Moreover, even for junior associates who do not themselves necessarily want to engage in pro bono activities, the presence of such a program is seen as a factor that positively influences firms' reputations and attractiveness to young talent. Indeed, publicity may provide an information base that allows would-be associates, and the public generally, to compare large firms on the metric of pro bono. The *American Lawyer*'s survey of firm pro bono activities is a prime example,[26] as is law firm participation in the "pro bono challenge."[27] While junior associates left to their own devices might have trouble assessing firms' pro bono commitments, these rankings allow prospective employees to consider this factor at a very low cost.

[23] See Dinovitzer & Garth, supra note 11, at 126 (survey of lawyers admitted to the bar in 2000; finding that "elite law graduates rate pro bono opportunities more highly than do graduates of lower tier law schools"); Cummings, supra note 7, at 33 (among "elite law school graduates, many ... care deeply about pro bono opportunities").

[24] See Dinovitzer & Garth, supra note 11, at 122; Robert Granfield & Philip Veliz, *Good Lawyering and Lawyering or the Good: Lawyers' Reflections on Mandatory Pro Bono in Law School*, *in* PRIVATE LAWYERS AND THE PUBLIC INTEREST, supra note 1, at 53; Deborah A. Schmedermann, *Priming for Pro Bono: The Impact of Law School on Pro Bono Participation in Practice*, *in* PRIVATE LAWYERS AND THE PUBLIC INTEREST, supra note 1, at 73.

[25] Dinovitzer and Garth find, however, that junior associates value the opportunity to do pro bono, but do not uniformly value having more pro bono hours over fewer hours. Dinovitzer & Garth, supra note 11, at 130 ("[E]ngaging in any amount of pro bono compared to none increases satisfaction with the power track, while the number of pro bono hours does not have a significant relationship with this form of satisfaction").

[26] See Feathers, supra note 1, at 274.

[27] See sources cited in note 12.

THE NEED FOR EMPIRICAL STUDY OF LAW FIRM PRO BONO SERVICE DELIVERY

We set out earlier two explanations for why large law firms would opt to deliver pro bono services. One focuses on lawyers' motivations to "do the right thing" or to live up to professional obligations. A second approach instead turns to market considerations. Each of these theories independently explains why large law firms might decide to provide pro bono services. But which theory is a more accurate description of the real world? We call here for future empirical research to shed light on this question. As an opening suggestion, we describe a survey instrument that could learn more about what firms do and why they do it in the pro bono space.

There is considerable empirical information on the question of how many hours of pro bono service large law firms provide. However, the question of which theory better explains law firm participation turns not on how many hours of service are provided. Rather, it turns on the motivations of the partners at these firms who engage in or authorize pro bono work. A better understanding of what firms are trying to accomplish and whether those programs, as presently constituted, promote those objectives will help firms assess whether they need to change what they are doing to better promote those objectives.

There are substantial obstacles to gathering such information. For one thing, it is likely that many partners would be unwilling to divulge their motivations. Moreover, even if they were willing, it may be that they would be tempted to make their motivations seem more altruistic than they really are. Indeed, in some cases, it might be that an individual has convinced himself or herself of a motivation that is not really at work (or at least not doing as much work as he or she would like to admit).

Another research strategy looks not to uncover lawyer motivations directly, but rather uses the type of matters handled in large law firm pro bono practices as a proxy for motivation. If law firms seek in large measure to use pro bono as a means to train junior attorneys, one would expect to see law firm pro bono dominated by relatively small matters that need not, and generally do not, raise novel issues requiring more hours than routine issues. Moreover, pro bono matters would extend beyond litigation to corporate, real estate, and tax matters capable of being addressed without significant associate time. On the other hand, if pro bono matters serve principally to vindicate partners' professional obligations or ideological commitments, one would expect to see more high-profile matters, more work promising an impact on the law and social policy, and more collaboration with advocacy organizations, rather than to serve the retail legal needs of individuals or groups. Finally, to the extent that court cases tend to attract media coverage, one would expect to see litigation dominate law firm pro bono practices.

We have designed a modest survey instrument that might, were it administered by law firm pro bono leadership, shed light on these questions. The survey, attached here as an appendix, asks about partners' motivations for instituting and maintaining pro bono practices. In addition, recognizing that such inquiries might be futile or simply provide less than reliable information, the survey also seeks information about the actual substance of law firms' pro bono practices. It does this in terms of time, types of clients, and whether pro bono practices are centered on litigation matters.

Gathering information of this sort would be valuable for academic purposes. It would also be helpful to law firm leaders who may unknowingly have pro bono programs that are not well designed to achieve the firm's articulated objectives. It would, in short, help law firms better design their pro bono programs to fulfill their goals. It would also help bar organizations and court systems to improve the delivery of pro bono services. Finally, it might help many who are currently unable to obtain pro bono services to obtain the representation that they need.

APPENDIX: DRAFT SURVEY INSTRUMENT

A. ADMINISTRATION OF PRO BONO PROGRAM

How many lawyers do you have in your firm?
Where is the headquarter office of the firm located?
Does your firm have an office- or firm-wide pro bono administrator?
  Yes/No
  Office-wide___
  Firm-wide____
  Both____
If so, is that person an attorney?
  Yes/No
If so, is that attorney engaged full time in pro bono work, including oversight of various programs?
  Yes/No
Does the firm have a policy of setting a maximum number of hours associates may devote to pro bono matters?
  Yes/No
If so, what is the maximum number of hours associates may devote to pro bono work?
  Number of hours per year____
Does the firm have a policy of setting a minimum number of hours lawyers must devote to pro bono matters?
  Yes/No
If so, what is the minimum number of hours lawyers must devote to pro bono work?
  Number of hours per year____
Does the firm count any or all pro bono hours performed by associates in determining whether associates receive a bonus?
  No more than ____ hours per year
  All hours count___

Does the firm count any or all pro bono hours performed by associates in determining whether associates are to be promoted to partner?

No more than ____ hours per year

All hours count___

B. NATURE OF PRO BONO MATTERS

Does your firm undertake any litigation-based pro bono work?

Yes/No

Does your firm undertake any transaction-based pro bono work (including corporate and tax advice)?

Yes/No

Approximately what percentage of the pro bono work at your firm is litigation-based (as opposed to transaction-based)?

_____

Approximately what percentage of the pro bono work at your firm involves the direct provision of legal services to individuals as opposed to rendering assistance to lawyers in organizations?

_____

Approximately how many of your lawyers are involved in handling cases referred to the firm or identified as needing representation by a court?

_____

Approximately how many attorney hours are involved in handling cases referred to the firm or identified as needing representation by a court?

_____

C. PRO BONO HOURS

What is the total number of attorney hours per year involved in pro bono work?

Approximately what percentage of the total number of attorney hours (billable and non-billable) do pro bono hours constitute?

How many lawyers were engaged in pro bono work in the past year?

_____

How many lawyers are engaged in 5 or more hours of pro bono work per month?

_____

How many lawyers are engaged in 10 or more hours of pro bono work per month?

_____

How many lawyers are engaged in 15 or more hours of pro bono work per month?

_____

D. SELECTION AND SCREENING OF PRO BONO MATTERS

Does the firm centrally select or screen pro bono matters?

Yes/No

Does the firm work with organizations that provide pro bono opportunities for your lawyers?

Yes/No

If so, what is the nature of the referral agency and what percentage of pro bono matters come from these sources?

Government____

Private nongovernmental organization (including bar association)____

Private law firm (including public interest organization)

Law School Clinic_____

Are decisions about which pro bono matters to take on made according to a standard set of criteria (whether written explicitly or otherwise)?

If the answer to the previous question is "Yes," please select from the following the criterion/criteria according to which pro bono matters are selected or screened. Please select all that apply.

__ The source of the referral (e.g., from the local bar association)
__ Whether the matter is litigation-based or transaction-based
__ The types of legal issues raised by the matter
__ The type or characteristics of client to be represented
__ The type of experience attorneys working on the matter are likely to receive
__ The likelihood of favorable media coverage of the matter

Please use numbers 1, 2, 3, 4 to rank the firm's principal objectives in running a pro bono program for its lawyers, with 1 being most central and 4 least central:

___ Training of lawyers
___ Publicizing the firm's accomplishments
___ Recruitment of lawyers
___ Other

Are there pro bono matters engaged in by the firm's lawyers that result in a fee to the firm?

Yes/No

If so, approximately how many hours of lawyer time were devoted to such matters in the previous year?

_____ hours per year

19

Pro Bono as a Second Career

Steven C. Bennett

Retried attorneys are an untapped source of legal assistance. Steven Bennett discusses how nonprofits, legal services organizations, and law schools could engage a generation of lawyers and navigate them to a second legal career to help meet the civil legal needs of the poor and middle-income Americans.

Long viewed as an "untapped resource,"[1] employment of senior and otherwise retired lawyers, on a pro bono or "low bono" basis[2] to fill the "justice gap" in America has become especially important in light of recent economic developments and government funding limitations. The "baby boomer" generation, now entering traditional retirement years, has increasingly adopted an "active" approach to retirement,[3] with the expectation that "second (or even third) acts," often including public service, will become the norm for retirees. Any predictions that this huge force of retired attorneys can single-handedly alleviate the nation's legal assistance crisis, however, would be exaggerated.[4] While such lawyers may help reduce the

1 See John Fulmer, *Attorneys Emeritus Filling the Gaps*, THE DAILY RECORD, available at www.nydailyrecord.com (June 29, 2010) (noting "untapped resource" of lawyers, including 40% of lawyers in New York who are close to retirement age); Stephanie Edelstein & Jan May, *Senior Attorney Volunteers: A Resource for Legal Services Programs*, CLEARINGHOUSE REV. 619, 621 (Oct. 1993); American Bar Association, Commission on Second Season of Service, Informational Report to the Board of Governors, available at www.abanet.org (Feb. 2007).

2 See Luz E. Herrera, *Encouraging the Development of "Low Bono" Law Practices*, 14 U. MD. L.J. OF RACE, RELIGION, GENDER & CLASS 1, 2 (2014) ("In order to address the unmet legal needs of individuals in our country, the legal profession must advance an affordable legal services agenda that includes lawyers who provide competent legal services at reduced or 'low bono' rates").

3 See An Interview with H. Guy Collier, The Senior Lawyer Public Interest Project, Wash. Lawyer, available at www.dcbar.org (Dec. 2006) (noting "current phenomenon among this group [senior lawyers] to reinvent the idea of retiring, to reinvent what to do once one is ready to transition out of one's career"); ABA Commission on Law and Aging, Report to ABA House of Delegates, www.americanbar.org (May 2006) (goal to "promote the concept of 'active retirement' while expanding the pool of volunteers available" to meet needs).

4 See Marc Galanter, *"Old and in the Way": The Coming Demographic Transformation of the Legal Profession and Its Implications for the Provision of Legal Services*, 1999 WIS. L. REV. 1081, 1105 ("The juxtaposition of a desperate need for public service work and the presence of skilled lawyers with an inclination to take up that work is not in itself sufficient to bring about an enlargement of the

problem, they cannot alone solve it. Instead, policies aimed at efficiently harnessing as much of this potential resource as possible must be the central focus for policymakers, social service professionals, and bar leaders. This chapter addresses some fundamental realities that will determine the shape of such efforts.

RECRUITMENT

Despite decades of efforts, the reality remains that most lawyers (active or retired) do not focus on serving low-income populations. Those who take on pro bono obligations, moreover, often are recruited into the process (versus finding opportunities on their own).[5] The best predictor of future pro bono activity is prior experience with pro bono activity.[6] Successful transition of retired lawyers into pro bono participation thus may turn on the ability of programs to identify appropriate target populations, and recruit them, before retirement, into the world of volunteer work. Programs that recruit volunteers at law firms, for example, may also aim at helping lawyers, as they retire, transition into more pro bono activities. Effective recruitment, moreover, may turn on finding "champions" for pro bono activity, who can help influence their peers through direct communications.[7] Senior lawyers may be particularly adept at such peer recruitment.[8]

public services sector . . . We need to think about facilitating this transition"); see also Marty Martinson & Meredith Minkler, Civic Engagement and Older Adults: A Critical Perspective, 46 The Gerontologist 318 (June 2006) (baby boomers "have the potential to become a social resource of unprecedented proportions") (quotation omitted, emphasis added).

5 See ABA Standing Committee on Pro Bono and Public Service, Supporting Justice III: A Report on the Pro Bono Work of America's Lawyers, available at www.americanbar.org at vii (Mar. 2013) (3/4 of attorneys reporting pro bono work indicated "they do not seek out pro bono opportunities; the opportunities find them"; when contacted, 7 in 10 "took advantage of the opportunity"); see also Stephanie Edelstein & Jan May, Senior Attorney Volunteers: A Resource for Legal Services Programs, Clearinghouse Rev. 619, 619 (Oct. 1993) ("While there are senior attorneys who are knowledgeable about legal services and offer their assistance, most have to be recruited. The experiences of early senior attorney programs teach us that relying exclusively on mass mailings or notices in the bar newsletter for recruitment does not work ... The most effective projects have approached potential volunteers through their peers").

6 Deborah L. Rhode, Senior Lawyers Serving Public Interests: Pro Bono and Second Stage Careers, 22 The Professional Lawyer 1, 27 (2011) (noting that "the best predictor of volunteer work after retirement is work prior to that stage," such that "programs should target experienced attorneys before they take inactive status"); ABA Standing Committee on Pro Bono and Public Service, Supporting Justice III: A Report on the Pro Bono Work of America's Lawyers, available at www.americanbar.org at 34 (Mar. 2013) (in survey, 50% of lawyers who did no pro bono in prior year had "never done any at all in their careers").

7 See Legal Services Corporation, Report of the Pro Bono Task Force, available at www.lsc.gov at iv (Oct. 2012) (suggesting that judges and bar leaders help recruit new pro bono lawyers, especially in rural areas, and draw attention to the "crisis" in legal services).

8 See Deborah L. Rhode, supra note 6, at 26 (through "personal solicitation," senior lawyers can serve as "pied pipers," securing commitments to pro bono programs from law firms and lawyers). Another effective method of recruitment may be through religious institutions. See James L. Perry & Jeffrey L. Brudney, *What Drives Morally Committed Citizens? A Study of the Antecedents of Public Service Motivation*, 68 Public Admin. Rev. 445, 452–53 (May/June 2008).

Lawyers differ in their background and experiences, and in their inclinations toward public service.[9] Levels of commitment to pro bono work, in particular, may vary greatly.[10] Many senior lawyers may hesitate to make a substantial commitment of their time, especially where the activities fall outside the range of their prior professional experience. Thus, another key to effective recruitment may lie in finding projects of limited scope,[11] within the areas of senior lawyer expertise and schedule limitations.[12] Developing systems of matching needs with interests, especially via low-cost alternatives such as the internet, certainly should be a priority.

A creative approach to the definition of "pro bono" work seems in order. Pro bono work need not be confined to the traditional role of a lawyer representing an indigent client in court. Senior lawyers may be particularly useful in administrative rather than "front line" roles with legal service organizations.[13] Options for non-legal forms of service also abound,[14] as do forms of "limited" legal service.[15]

[9] See Scott L. Cummings & Rebecca L. Sandefur, *Beyond the Numbers: What We Know – And Should Know – About American Pro Bono*, 7 Harv. L. & Policy Rev. 83, 92 (2013) ("Existing research reveals that lawyers do pro bono for a variety of different reasons, some consistent with an ethic of public service or social transformation, others more consistent with a 'business case,' such as developing skills or cultivating clients"); Deborah L. Rhode, *Senior Lawyers Serving Public Interests: Pro Bono And Second Stage Careers*, 22 The Professional Lawyer 1, 26 (2011) (senior lawyers "vary considerably" in background and priorities).

[10] See Deborah L. Rhode, *Rethinking The Public In Lawyers' Public Service: Pro Bono, Strategic Philanthropy, and the Bottom Line*, 77 Fordham L. Rev. 1435, 1443 (2009) (noting phenomenon of lawyers who want to do pro bono work in theory, but in practice, "don't want to make the commitment") (quotation omitted).

[11] For some senior lawyers, home or other "remote" forms of work, with populations of particular interest to seniors, may be preferable. See Legal Services Corporation, Retired and Inactive Lawyers and Volunteer Involvement, available at www.lsc.gov (Dec. 1, 2007) (noting example of volunteers who assist legal services staff to provide estate planning; volunteers work both remotely and at legal services offices, and make home visits to clients); Holly Robinson, No Longer on Their Own: Using Emeritus Attorney Pro Bono Programs to Meet Unmet Civil Legal Needs, available at www.abanet.org (2008) at 1 (senior lawyers may be "more readily used to reach out to provide legal services to homebound residents, residents of hospitals" and "others who are unable to come to an office or clinic").

[12] See ABA Standing Committee on Pro Bono and Public Service, Supporting Justice III: A Report on the Pro Bono Work of America's Lawyers, available at www.americanbar.org at vii (Mar. 2013) (majority of lawyers surveyed agreed that "being offered opportunities to provide limited scope representation would encourage lawyers to do more pro bono"); Mary Pat Toups, Senior Lawyers Organizing & Volunteering: A National Profile, available at www.americanbar.org (June 1996) ("senior lawyers, many of whom are retired or semi-retired, want flexibility incorporated into their pro bono activities").

[13] See Deborah L. Rhode, supra note 6, at 26 (experience suggests that "some of the best uses of seniors are in project development, management and fundraising"); see also Stephanie M. Wildman, *Democracy and Social Justice: Founding Centers for Social Justice in Law Schools*, 55 J. Legal Educ. 252, 267 (2005) (calling for systems to identify alumni, friends, and foundations interested in funding social justice work, and establishment of alumni/community advisory boards, with faculty and student involvement, to foster interlocking networks).

[14] See Holly Robinson, No Longer on Their Own, supra note 11, at 4 (noting array of potential non-legal applications of senior lawyer talent, including community legal education programs, mentoring less experienced attorneys, outreach activities, service on boards of social service agencies, assistance with fundraising, and legislative research and advocacy).

[15] See Legal Services Corporation, Pro Bono Programs: Best & Promising Practices, available at www.lsc.gov (2014) (noting examples of "limited service" opportunities, including provision of legal advice to

TRAINING AND SUPPORT

Even where the time provided by volunteers is entirely unpaid, significant costs may attend to the operation of a senior lawyer volunteer program. Most legal aid programs do not focus their efforts on the use of senior volunteers.[16] Many senior lawyers, moreover, lack experience in the areas where low-income clients most need assistance.[17] For certain areas of public service practice (such as death penalty representation), training requirements may be quite extensive. For other areas, existing training resources may suffice.[18] Further, solo and small-firm lawyers (the majority of lawyers in this country)[19] on retirement may lose access to office space and administrative support.[20] Free CLE offerings may serve as an inducement to senior volunteers who wish to maintain their bar membership.[21] Other senior lawyers prefer to withdraw from bar membership (or take "inactive" status) and

pre-screened clients, through telephone interviews; single-day monthly advice and referral clinics; and monthly clinics via Skype connections).

16 See An Interview with H. Guy Collier, The Senior Lawyer Public Interest Project, Wash. Lawyer, available at www.dcbar.org (Dec. 2006) ("We don't see organizations creating a special role for senior lawyers, as most of them have roles for lawyers of any age"); F. William McCalpin, *Where Are the Senior Lawyers?*, 3 EXPERIENCE 5 (1992–93) (survey finds "no programs using only senior lawyers" but many "general pro bono programs attracting senior lawyers").

17 See New York State Unified Court System, Attorney Emeritus Program: Volunteer Recognition, available at www.nycourts.gov (2011) (noting that "many" emeritus attorneys "have no prior experience in the areas in which they are now volunteering"); Marc Galanter, "Old and in the Way": The Coming Demographic Transformation of the Legal Profession and Its Implications for the Provision of Legal Services, 1999 WIS. L. REV. 1081, 1105 ("There is some basis for concern about the mismatch between legal services work and skills of lawyers from private practice").

18 Less expensive (and more generally available) forms of training may exist. See Legal Services Corporation, Pro Bono Programs: Best & Promising Practices, available at www.lsc.gov (2014) (noting examples of training and support, including: manual with overview of civil pro bono work, library of support materials; interactive forms; instructional videos; and free continuing legal education).

19 See ABA Serves Solo and Small-Firm Lawyers with New Online Resource Center, available at www.abanow.org (2010) ("It is estimated that the United States has about 435,000 solo law practitioners (comprising about 48% of private-practice lawyers)"); Clara N. Carson, The Lawyer Statistical Report: The U.S. Legal Profession in 2000, at 28 (2004) (as of 2000, 74% of lawyers were in private practice; of those, 48% were in solo practice, and an additional 15% were in firms of two to five lawyers).

20 See ABA Commission on Law and Aging, Report to ABA House of Delegates, available at www.americanbar.org (May 2006) ("[The traditional pro bono] system is not well-suited to lawyers who do not maintain an office or administrative support, who no longer carry professional liability insurance, who may be unfamiliar with the issues about which low and moderate income individuals most commonly seek advice, and who may be living in a state in which they are not licensed"); F. William McCalpin, *Where Are The Senior Lawyers?*, 3 EXPERIENCE 5 (1992–93) (survey indicates that "only a small number of the nearly 70,000 senior lawyers over age 60 in the United States are doing pro bono work"; those "least likely to engage in pro bono are fully retired").

21 See ABA Standing Committee on Pro Bono and Public Service, Supporting Justice III: A Report on the Pro Bono Work of America's Lawyers, available at www.americanbar.org at 33 (Mar. 2013) (suggesting offers of free or reduced-fee CLE as an incentive to volunteer); David Godfrey & Erica Wood, Emeritus Attorney Programs: Best Practices and Lessons Learned, available at www.americanbar.org (Sept. 2010) at 12 (senior lawyers frequently seek ways to "sharpen their skills"; offer of CLE and training is an "excellent tool for recruiting" and "encourages attorneys to accept referrals").

forgo the expense of malpractice insurance.[22] Thus, for many legal service programs, the cost of training and supporting senior volunteers may deter development of effective usage programs.

One potential solution to this problem is use of senior attorneys in non-legal functions at legal service institutions. Senior lawyers may provide useful assistance as (unpaid) board members and fund-raisers, and in other administrative roles supporting the organization. Senior lawyers, moreover, might aid an institution by providing mentoring and training assistance to the institution's staff and lawyers. Senior lawyers may also work with full-time lawyers at an institution, serving solely as advisors, where full-time lawyers retain primary responsibility for representation of clients. Other forms of service may operate largely independent of legal aid organizations (other than for referral purposes), and focus on community legal education efforts, rather than direct representation of clients.

A further model for support of senior lawyer pro bono assistance operates on the premise that law firms may provide some of the essential ingredients (office space, support staff, malpractice insurance) that might otherwise tax the resources of legal service organizations. Although the economic downturn may have inhibited law firm interest in pro bono work, legitimate business reasons still exist for law firms to keep senior lawyers in "consulting" roles, providing transition services for clients and training for junior lawyers, and in the process supporting pro bono activities.[23] Some senior lawyers may require an income source, in addition to administrative support; law firm (or legal aid) temporary consulting work may offer (at least partial) solutions there as well. Forms of (subsidized) fellowships may also encourage senior participation.

LAW SCHOOL COLLABORATION

Although the primary mission of law schools, generally speaking, does not consist of service to low-income clients, inculcation of the values of public service should be an essential element of law school training. Further, the development

[22] See Sharon Katz, Making Pro Bono Work: A Pro Bono Practice in Retirement, NYSBAJ (Jan. 2014) at 31 (retired attorneys working on pro bono matters require work space, professional support, administrative and technological support, and malpractice insurance coverage; work arrangements also should not adversely affect retirement benefits); ABA Standing Committee on Pro Bono & Public Service, Senior Lawyers, available at www.apps.americanbar.org (2013) (noting licensing, malpractice insurance, office space and other issues that may serve as "barriers" to senior lawyer pro bono project work); Legal Services Corporation, Report of the Pro Bono Task Force, available at www.lsc.gov at 5 (Oct. 2012) (lawyers involved in pro bono have needs, including training, advice, and malpractice insurance coverage).

[23] See Esther Lardent, Reena Glazer & Kellen Ressmeyer, *"Old and Making Hay:" The Results of the Pro Bono Institute Firm Survey on the Viability of a "Second Acts" Program to Transition Attorneys to Retirement through Pro Bono Work*, 7 CARDOZO PUB. LAW, POLICY & ETHICS J. 321, 326–27 (2009) ("second acts" programs could be of use to law firms in "transitioning attorneys to retirement, providing continuity for clients, providing training and mentoring opportunities for young attorneys, and meeting the firm's professional obligation to provide pro bono services").

of practice-ready new lawyers may offer one method of helping to meet the demand for lower-cost legal services, while absorbing some of the "glut" of new lawyers in the profession.[24] The cost of law school clinics and other experiential training, coupled with the frequent lack of practical experience in conventional law school faculty,[25] suggests the possibility of use of outside lawyers (including pro bono senior lawyers) as one method to augment law student experiences.

Such assistance may take the form of outside lawyers serving as adjunct faculty. Outside lawyers, moreover, might team-teach, or guest-teach, along with established faculty, to provide "real-world" input into conventional coursework. In addition, although not necessarily a primary focus for law schools, and not necessarily the most efficient form of service,[26] outside lawyers also can assist law school clinics as they provide assistance to low-income clients, while helping to train students in the norms of legal practice.[27] Experienced outside lawyers, moreover, can assist law students in developing new forms of legal aid to under-served populations,[28] including research assistance to pro bono practitioners, "cyber" clinics, and support for small businesses in affected communities.[29]

[24] See Andrea Remynse, *Preventing Self-Regulation from Becoming Self-Strangulation: The Application of Deregulation and Independent Oversight to Allow the U.S. Legal System to Adapt to Market Forces Currently Threatening Lawyers, Law Schools and Access to Justice*, 22 MICH. ST. INT'L L. REV. 1149, 1180 (2014) (suggesting that "new forms of legal education would be the most efficient way to create new legal service providers").

[25] See Debra Moss Curtis, *Teaching Law Office Management: Why Law Students Need to Know the Business of Being a Lawyer*, 71 ALB. L. REV. 201, 210–11 (2008) (law schools tend to employ full-time faculty with little or no experience providing personal legal services).

[26] See Jane H. Aiken & Stephen Wizner, *Teaching and Doing: The Role of Law School Clinics in Enhancing Access to Justice*, 73 FORDHAM L. REV. 997, 1005 (2004) (noting "many inefficiencies built into the design of most law school clinics that result in limiting the numbers of clients represented and cases handled").

[27] See Alicia E. Perhoples & Amanda M. Spratley, *Engaging Outside Counsel in Transactional Law Clinics*, 20 CLINICAL L. REV. 1, 3, 9 (2014) (suggesting possibility of law school clinics collaborating with a "range" of outside attorneys, and suggesting that outside attorneys may be more willing to take on pro bono clients "if they know that a clinic is willing to assist"); Thomas A. Gilligan, The Beginning and the End of Pro Bono Professionalism, for the Defense 86, 87 (May 2013) ("Perhaps the ideal program . . . would match up law students at the dawn of their careers in need of pro bono qualifying hours with emeritus lawyers in search of service in the twilight of theirs").

[28] See Marsha M. Mansfield & Louise G. Trubek, *New Roles to Solve Old Problems: Lawyering for Ordinary People in Today's Context*, 56 N.Y. SCH. L. REV. 367, 368–69 (2011–12) (new technology and new forms of collaboration create opportunities for "new roles and tools" to serve low-income clients; law schools can serve as "incubators" for experimentation, while providing training for students to assume new roles after school). For one example of such a system of collaboration, see About Law without Walls, available at www.lawwithoutwalls.org (2014) (program to team academic, lawyer, and entrepreneur mentors to develop business plans to tackle main problems facing legal education and legal practice, with the goal of "innovation in the legal services market" and "enhanced job prospects" for students).

[29] See Stephen Falla Riff, *Using Business Law to Build Social and Economic Infrastructure in Low-Income Communities*, 20 J. AFFORDABLE HOUSING & COMMUNITY DEV. L. 5 (2010–11) (noting that public interest law organizations and law school clinics can help support economic and social development in low-income communities through provision of aid to small businesses); see also Dina Schlossberg, *An Examination of Transactional Law Clinics and Interdisciplinary Education*, 11 WASH. U. J. L. &

EVALUATION AND IMPROVEMENT

Despite the creation of a Senior Lawyer Division at the ABA some 30 years ago,[30] organized thinking about methods to overcome the unique obstacles involved in the use of senior lawyers for public service is relatively new. A significant challenge for legal service organizations, for example, may lie in dealing with declining skills in an aging population of practitioners. Similarly significant (though unrelated) challenges may arise with stay-at-home lawyers, who may offer a great resource, but with unique limitations on their availability.

Systems for evaluation and improvement of programs thus appear essential. It is not simply a matter of "throwing bodies at the problem" of legal service inadequacies.[31] That way lies confusion of mission, and dissatisfaction for all concerned.[32] Instead, the goal should be creation of relatively specific plans for use of senior lawyers,[33] coupled with a system of supervision, and evaluation of the results of any organized program.[34] By these means, successful programs can be identified, and offered as models for others to follow.[35]

POLICY 195, 199–200 (2003) (describing clinic offering transaction-related legal services to nonprofit organizations and small businesses).

30 See Stephen N. Maskaleris & Corinne P. Maskaleris, *The First 25 Years of the Senior Lawyers Division*, 21 EXPERIENCE 16 (2011) (noting creation of ABA Senior Lawyers Division in 1984).

31 See generally David Eisner, Robert T. Grimm, Jr., Shannon Maynard & Susannah Washburn, The New Volunteer Workforce, Stanford Social Innovation Rev. 32, 34 (Winter 2009) (suggesting that good volunteer management practices include: matching skills with appropriate assignments; recognizing contributions of volunteers; measuring the impact of volunteers annually; providing volunteers with training and development; and training paid staff to work with volunteers).

32 See David Eisner, Robert T. Grimm, Jr., Shannon Maynard & Susannah Washburn, *The New Volunteer Workforce*, STANFORD SOCIAL INNOVATION REV. 32, 32 (Winter 2009) (although nonprofits "rely heavily" on volunteers, most do a "poor job" of managing them; as a result, "more than one-third of those who volunteer one year do not donate their time the next year – at any nonprofit").

33 See Legal Services Corporation, Pro Bono Programs: Best & Promising Practices, available at www.lsc.gov (2014) (plans should include: a description of the needs of the client community; specification of ways that attorneys are to be used; staffing structures; strategies to recruit, retain, and recognize volunteers; process to identify and route cases; and quality assurance procedures).

34 See Deborah L. Rhode, *Access to Justice: An Agenda for Legal Education and Research*, 62 J. LEGAL EDUC. 531, 535 (2013) (noting that, although various groups collect some information on services for low-income populations, "it is highly fragmentary and frequently leaves out certain providers, such as attorneys offering pro bono, 'low bono' (reduced rate) or 'unbundled' (partial) representation").

35 Thus, for example, "emeritus" attorney programs have grown in popularity, and specific suggestions for implementation of such programs have been developed. See Holly Robinson, No Longer on Their Own: Using Emeritus Attorney Pro Bono Programs to Meet Unmet Civil Legal Needs, available at www.abanet.org (2008) at 6 (offering checklist for creation of emeritus attorney program, including program administration, registration requirements, outreach and recruitment, training, malpractice coverage, evaluation and volunteer recognition); see also Holly Robinson, *Checklist for Creating an Emeritus Attorney Pro Bono Participation Program*, 29 BIFOCAL 5 (Nov. 2007).

A HOPEFUL NOTE

Development and implementation of effective new programs for use of senior attorneys will take time, but the efforts are certainly merited. "Emeritus attorney" programs, for example, began more than thirty years ago. Fostered by ABA calls to action, these programs have now spread to a majority of states. Such programs are far from perfect, but they show the potential for creative approaches to the problems of legal assistance to under-served communities, through the use of senior attorneys.[36]

[36] See Kelly S. Terry, *Do Not Go Gentle: Using Emeritus Pro Bono Attorneys to Achieve the Promise of Justice*, 19 Geo. J. on Poverty L. & Policy 75 (2012) (surveying value of senior lawyer emeritus programs in providing legal service to low-income clients); Report of the New Jersey State Bar Association's Pro Bono Task Force: Closing the Justice Gap (May 2012) at 42 (suggesting that emeritus programs may be "more resource-intensive than would be justified by potential new additions to the ranks of pro bono volunteers," and noting the need to "take other steps to educate attorneys" approaching or at retirement about pro bono options); Joel Stashenko, Courts Approve Increase in CLE Bonus for Lawyers Who Offer Pro Bono Service, available at www.newyorklawjournal.com (Mar. 9, 2012) (noting that, in New York State, only 242 out of 45,600 eligible lawyers have signed up for "emeritus" status).

20

Employer-Provided Legal-Services for Employment Claims

Michael Z. Green

Legal service insurance or employee benefits are an understudied subject in the access-to-justice literature. Michael Green discusses the different types of legal service plans, how they work, and the ways that these plans help companies avoid ethical problems that can arise from opposing unrepresented employees when mediating or arbitrating employment disputes. His chapter focuses on one company's successful experience with a legal service plan for its employees.

Many employment disputes involve legal claims brought by employees without legal representation.[1] Inability to obtain adequate legal representation can create a significant hurdle for employees in resolving a dispute with their employer.[2] The lack of legal representation for employees in discrimination suits has reached a crisis level as employees only find lawyers to help them about 5% of the time.[3] When they pursue their claims, employees tend to lose lawsuits more than 90% of the time.[4] Even if an employee obtains that rare court win, a strong chance of being reversed on appeal makes the overall prospects even worse.[5]

[1] See Michael Z. Green, *Finding Lawyers for Employees in Discrimination Disputes as a Critical Prescription for Unions to Embrace Racial Justice*, 7 U. PA. J. LAB. & EMP. L. 55, 64–66, 72–77 (2004); Ann C. Hodges, *Mediation and the Transformation of American Labor Unions*, 69 MISSOURI L. REV. 365, 372–73, 394–95 (2004). With the approval of the editors, this chapter is a shorter version of my prior publication which addressed this topic in more detail. See Michael Z. Green, *Ethical Incentives for Employers in Adopting Legal Service Plans to Handle Employment Disputes*, 44 BRANDEIS L. REV. 395 (2006).

[2] See Roberto L. Corrada, *Claiming Private Law for the Left: Exploring Gilmer's Impact and Legacy*, 73 DENV. U. L. REV. 1051, 1067 (1996); Samuel Estreicher, *Saturns for Rickshaws: The Stakes in the Debate over Predispute Employment Arbitration Agreements*, 16 OHIO ST. J. ON DISP. RESOL. 559, 563–64 (2001).

[3] Lewis L. Maltby, *Employment Arbitration and Workplace Justice*, 38 U.S.F. L. REV. 105, 106–107 nn.1–3 (2003).

[4] See Michael Selmi, *Why Are Employment Discrimination Cases So Hard to Win?*, 61 LA. L. REV. 555, 560–61 (2001) (describing how claimants lose discrimination cases more than 90% of the time).

[5] See Kevin M. Clermont & Stewart J. Schwab, *How Employment Discrimination Plaintiffs Fare in Federal Court*, 1 J. EMPIRICAL LEGAL STUD. 429, 451–52 (2004).

This chapter describes one way that employers can bridge this legal representation gap for their employees. Legal-service plans[6] can be a reasonable and affordable employee benefit that resembles a group health plan.[7] If employees can obtain legal counsel through legal service plans, they can fairly overcome the hurdle to employment dispute resolution that the lack of legal representation currently presents.[8] Lawyer participation in legal service plans offered to public groups or organizations continues to rise.[9]

LEGAL SERVICES PLANS: A PARTIAL SOLUTION TO THE NEED FOR LEGAL REPRESENTATION AND A VALUABLE HUMAN RESOURCES BENEFIT FOR EMPLOYEES AND EMPLOYERS

In 1975, the organized bar stopped opposing the use of legal service plans, and instead embraced the concept by including them in the Model Rules.[10] Legal service plans can bridge the significant legal representation gap for the working class who cannot normally afford legal services. A 2001 report stated that "[e]mployer- paid [legal service] programs cover 7.6 million Americans, with Hyatt Legal Plans and the United Auto Workers being the largest providers."[11]

6 "A legal service plan is a prepaid or group legal service plan or a similar delivery system that assists prospective clients to secure legal representation." American Bar Assn (ABA), MODEL RULES OF PROF'L CONDUCT R. 7.2 cmt. 6 (2002).

7 David Narkiewicz, *A 21st Century Blueprint for Providing Legal Services to the Middle Class*, 26 AUG. PA. LAW. 20, 28 (2004) "Legal services plans similar to health care HMOs exist now for the middle class" under the approach that "the middle-class consumer, perhaps in conjunction with an employer or membership organization, pays a monthly fee for the right to receive certain personal legal services from a participating attorney in a legal services plan").

8 See Brian Heid & Eitan Misulovin, Note, *The Group Legal Plan Revolution: Bright Horizon or Dark Future?*, 18 HOFSTRA LAB. & EMP. L.J. 335 (2000) (describing the benefits of legal service plans for employees); see also Julia Field Costich, Note, *Joint State-Federal Regulation of Lawyers: The Case of Group Legal Services under ERISA*, 82 KY. L.J. 627 (1993) (discussing legal service plans as an employment benefit and its regulation).

9 See Wayne Moore & Monica Kolasa, *AARP's Legal Services Network: Expanding Legal Services to the Middle Class*, 32 WAKE FOREST L. REV. 503 (1997) (describing the expansive legal service plan available to members of the American Association of Retired Persons (AARP)); Narkiewicz, supra note 7, at 29 (stating that "AARP currently has a legal services network with more than 1,000 participating attorneys"). some lawyers have made their services available through legal service plans via the internet or online auctions. See Jennifer Vaculik, Note, *Bidding by the Bar: Online Auction Sites for Legal Services, Inc.*, 82 TEX. L. REV. 445 (2003); Narkiewicz, supra note 7, at 29 (describing Fee Bid, Legal Match and Med Law Plus websites that pits lawyers against each other based on the lowest bidder).

10 See Judith L. Maute, *Pre-Paid and Group Legal Services: Thirty Years after the Storm*, 70 FORDHAM L. REV. 915, 916–17, 926–28 (2001) (describing historical opposition to legal service plans by the organized bar as attitudes around ABA's until change in 1975 leading to the acceptance of legal service plans under the Model Rules).

11 Maute, supra note 10, at 935 (footnote omitted).

There are typically two types of legal-service plans, either access plans or comprehensive plans.[12] Access plans exchange a prepayment for "advice and consultation" and charge additional fees for services beyond that.[13] Comprehensive plans are "designed to meet 80% to 90% of an average person's legal needs in a given year" by paying "[p]remiums or membership fees . . . to a third party," and "all legal services covered by the plan are available at no additional charge except for deductibles and co-payments."[14] The premium cost then varies based on services and relies on the use of a panel of lawyers in private practice who must meet certain qualifications.[15] A majority of legal service plans tend to focus on telephone services, while more comprehensive legal services usually warrant a higher premium.[16]

Also, a key distinction in legal service plans is whether they are open or closed.[17] A closed plan restricts and an open plan expands the choices of attorneys for the plan.[18] Some plans do not cover certain types of cases, e.g., criminal or preexisting cases.[19] Under most plans, an employee cannot use the group legal services to sue their employer.

PROFESSIONAL RESPONSIBILITY CONCERNS AS A MOTIVATION

A change to The American Bar Association (ABA)'s Model Rule 1.8(f) of the Rules of Professional Conduct opened the door for use of legal-service plans. Model Rule 1.8(f) provides:

> A lawyer shall not accept compensation for representing a client from one other than the client unless: (1) the client gives informed consent; (2) there is no interference with the lawyer's independence of professional judgment or with the client-lawyer relationship; and (3) information relating to representation of a client is protected as required by Rule 1.6 [confidentiality of information].[20]

Comment 11 to Rule 1.8(f) recognizes that third parties such as "a relative or friend, an indemnitor (such as a liability insurance company) or a co-client (such as a corporation sued along with one or more of its employees)" may pay for a lawyer's compensation as long as "there will be no interference with the lawyer's independent professional judgment and there is informed consent from the client."[21] Also, Model Rule 5.4(c) prohibits a lawyer from permitting "a person

[12] See Types of Legal Services Plans, 14 Emp. Coord. Personnel Manual § 12:119 (2005); see also Costich, supra note 8, at 635 n.63 (describing different types of legal service plans).

[13] See Types of Legal Services Plans, supra note 12.

[14] *Id.*

[15] *Id.*

[16] *Id.*

[17] *Id.*; see also Maute, supra note 10, at 925 (noting the battles within the organized bar about open versus closed legal plans).

[18] See Types of Legal Services Plans, supra note 12.

[19] *Id.*

[20] See Model Rules of Prof'l Conduct R. 1.8(f) (2002).

[21] *Id.* R. 1.8 cmt. 11.

who recommends, employs, or pays the lawyer to render legal services for another to direct or regulate the lawyer's professional judgment in rendering such legal services."[22] An attorney's participation in an employer-sponsored legal service plan does not present a concern as long as the attorney performs his duties without being controlled or influenced or dominated by the plan or the employer.

The continued growth of employment dispute resolution systems and persistent legal and ethical issues involving an unrepresented employee now warrant serious concern.[23] Some examples of ethical issues that arise for a lawyer of a corporation who has a pro se party on the other side of litigation:

1. The pro se party asks you to explain a test articulated in a case.
2. The pro se party asks for your legal advice in mediating a claim.
3. The pro se opposing party talks to employees of you client's company, and you want to challenge it.

With the ethical minefields involved in dealing with an unrepresented employee as demonstrated by these hypothetical examples, employer's counsel should recommend that their clients make legal assistance available through some form of legal service plan.

HALLIBURTON BROWN & ROOT'S LEGAL-SERVICES PLAN

Halliburton/Brown & Root is a global construction and engineering company. Its Dispute Resolution program offers four resolution options to employees that includes both inside and outside company processes along with "an employee benefit designed to ensure fairness ... [and] access to legal counsel of the employee's choosing."[24] The first level of the program is an Open Door Policy that "encourag[es] employees to first contact a supervisor or manager with their dispute."[25] The second level is a "conference" that could lead to a "loop back" to level one, an in-house mediation, or a move to levels three or four.[26] The third level is mediation conducted by an outside mediator involving legal rights.[27] Finally, the fourth level consists of arbitration involving legal rights.[28] In the first two years of operation, Brown & Root learned

22 See MODEL RULES OF PROF'L CONDUCT R. 5.4.

23 See Kenneth L. Jorgensen, *Counsel for the Organization: Employee Conflicts*, 61 AUG. BENCH & B. MINN. 12 (2004); Gregory V. Mersol, *Ethical Issues in Class Action Employment Litigation*, 20 LAB. LAW. 55 (2004); Nancy J. Moore, *Conflicts of Interest for In-House Counsel: Issues Emerging from the Expanding Role of the Attorney-Employee*, 39 S. TEX. L. REV. 497 (1998).

24 William L. Bedman, *The Future of ADR from Litigation to ADR: Brown & Root's Experience*, 50 DISP. RESOL. J., 8, 8.

25 See Andrea McGrath, *The Corporate Ombuds Office: An ADR Tool No Company Should Be Without*, 18 HAMLINE J. PUB. L. & POL'Y 452, 481 (1997) (footnotes omitted).

26 *Id.* at 482.

27 *Id.*

28 *Id.*

that "[e]ven with an employee benefit plan which compensates employees for their legal expenses, fewer than 80 employees have requested the assistance of counsel" and in "two-thirds of the arbitrations which have occurred, the employees have elected to proceed without the use of legal counsel."[29] Furthermore, after more than "10 years of the program, about 7,700 disputes were handled."[30] Of those disputes, "about 90% got resolved within the company, and the remaining 10% were resolved through mediation or arbitration."[31] These numbers suggest that the Brown & Root dispute resolution program allows quick and fair resolutions without them spiraling into a federal case. The employees must trust the program and the employer enough not to use lawyers very often, even though they are available to them through the legal service plan.[32]

The "Employment Legal Consultation Plan" of Brown & Root states that its "purpose is to provide certain specified legal services for all Employees of Brown & Root who have a Dispute with the Company which is subject to the Brown & Root Dispute Resolution Plan."[33] The legal consultations "are paid much like benefits under [Brown & Root's] medical plan, that is, you pay a deductible and a copayment" and "Brown & Root pays the balance."[34] The participant pays a plan deductible amount of $25 and then 10% of the balance, while Halliburton/Brown & Root pays the remaining 90% up to a maximum annual benefit of $2,500 per employee.[35] "For example, if the legal consultation was $1,000, you would pay a plan deductible amount of $25 and then 10% of $975 or $97.50" and Halliburton/Brown & Root "would pay $877.50."[36]

Under the legal plan, an attorney consults with an employee and is available to negotiate or mediate the dispute. If that fails, the attorney represents the employee in a proceeding by a referee, including any necessary discovery and preparation for the proceeding.

Some of the key limitations on the benefits under Halliburton/Brown & Root's Employment Legal Consultation Plan are that "no benefits are payable for services rendered after a decision by a Referee," and "no benefits will be paid in excess of $2,500 with respect to the representation of any one Participant per calendar year."[37] Further monetary requirements as mentioned earlier include payment of "a $25

[29] Bedman, *supra* note 24, at 13.

[30] See Sally Roberts, *Employer Concerns Slow Growth in Mandatory ADR*, 38 Bus. Ins. 22 (Feb. 16, 2004).

[31] *Id.*

[32] Of course, a contrary reason for the results could be that employees are lulled into thinking that they do not need lawyers or they just decide that they can handle their claims without lawyers. Even if that is true, the legal service plan allows those employees who really want legal representation but could not normally obtain it to now have it.

[33] E. Patrick McDermott & Arhtur Eliot Berkeley, Alternative Dispute Resolution in the Workplace: Concepts and Techniques for Human Executives and Their Counsel 129, 161 (1996).

[34] *Id.* at 129.

[35] *Id.*

[36] *Id.*

[37] *Id.*

deductible for each dispute" and then "the Plan shall pay 90% of the fees approved by the Director up to the pre-approved amount in relation to each dispute."[38]

With respect to selection of the attorney, the director of the Halliburton/Brown & Root Plan can set up panels of attorneys for employee to choose from.[39] The Plan does not require that a participant "consult an Attorney from a Panel as a condition of receiving benefits under this Plan."[40] Instead, participants "may consult with a lawyer or any other adviser of [their] choice."[41] A participant is "not required, however, to hire a lawyer to participate in arbitration," and if the participant chooses "not to bring a lawyer to arbitration, [Brown & Root] will also participate without a lawyer."[42] Attorneys are paid directly by the plan's director.[43] The payment of withholding and payroll tax related to the benefit "shall be made directly to the applicable taxing authority in satisfaction of the tax withholding requirements with respect to the benefits provided."[44]

The Halliburton/Brown & Root Legal Service Plan certainly does not represent the only legal service plan being offered as an employee benefit to resolve internal employment disputes in some fashion.[45] Nevertheless, it represents a very successful example that has now been in place for more than a decade. Other companies do have similar programs or variations. At a minimum, the Halliburton/Brown & Root experience demonstrates that employees may be able to find legal services.

Given the focus of so many employers on developing comprehensive conflict resolution programs for their employees, employers are starting to recognize that offering legal service plans as an employee benefit will also operate "as a means of increasing employee trust, and therefore usage, of the program, resulting in resolution of conflicts before they ripen into disputes."[46] Each employer can reap these same benefits by designing a legal service plan that fits its particular culture.[47]

38 *Id.* at 164.
39 *Id.*
40 *Id.*
41 *Id.* at 136.
42 *Id.*
43 *Id.*
44 *Id.* at 165.
45 See F. Peter Phillips, *Mediation Is Alternative to Adjudicating Disputes: Internal Employment Dispute Management Programs are New Trend*, 26 NAT'L L.J. No. 41, § 4, at 1 (June 14, 2004) (describing how "a division of General Electric 'will reimburse the employee up to $2,500 for attorney's fees incurred for mediation, provided that a complete settlement is reached at mediation'" and noting how many employer-sponsored dispute resolution programs call for the employer to pay all or almost all of the costs including legal costs). See Thomas J. Stipanowich, *ADR and the "Vanishing Trial": The Growth and Impact of "Alternative Dispute Resolution,"* 1 J. EMPIRICAL LEGAL STUD. 843, 875–912 (2004) (describing several thoughtfully designed conflict management systems and their use in various companies).
46 Phillips, supra note 45, at 1.
47 See F. Peter Phillips, *Ten Ways to Sabotage Dispute Management: Read Between the Lines to Learn What it Takes to Run a Successful Program*, 49 HR MAG., Sept. 1, 2004, at 164 (asserting that companies

CONCLUSION

With little hope of successfully navigating a hostile court system, employees can find better opportunities for resolution of employment discrimination claims through alternative dispute resolution (ADR). Likewise, employers fearing the potential of a hostile jury verdict in the court system may find ADR to be a viable mechanism to resolve employment discrimination claims. Whether in court or through ADR, a fundamental problem continues to plague any form of dispute resolution system for employment discrimination claims – the inability of employees to obtain legal counsel. In addition to concerns about the overall dispute resolution system integrity, the unrepresented or pro se employee presents a host of ethical challenges for all parties to the dispute, especially the employer and the employer's counsel. Accordingly, employers and their repeat player legal counsel should explore the benefit of providing legal services to employees through a legal service plan.

Following the model of Brown & Root, employees and employers can capitalize on the value of legal service plans as a component of a comprehensive and well-designed employee conflict resolution program. Employers who provide their employees with a legal service plan will escape a number of ethical challenges that may arise with the unrepresented or pro se employee. These employers will also see the marketing value of providing a unique employee benefit and reap the reward from having better relations with their employees. Employees will know that their employer has designed a dispute resolution system intended to provide employees with fairness and voice through a win-win approach. Once employers start to help their own employees obtain legal services for resolving their employment disputes, the ethical incentives to adopt these legal service plans may end up being merely a nice complement to the overall human resource and conflict resolution benefit for all those involved.

should not just copy "excellent, cutting-edge employment dispute resolution systems" of other companies like "Halliburton, UBS, Johnson & Johnson or any other foresighted companies" and should instead focus on the "distinct corporate ethos and different management style" of the company involved).

21

Company-Provided Legal Services

Maggie Gousman, John P. Frantz & Randal S. Milch

Over the past few decades, corporations have joined the ranks of pro bono pioneers, in significant numbers creating their own pro bono programs and leveraging their relatively small in-house counsel resources through partnerships with nonprofits, law firms, and bar associations. Although many corporations predictably help by providing advice on corporate law matters, other areas, like family law, contracts, veterans' assistance, are also common. This chapter authored by verizon's in-house counsel looks at Verizon's pro bono initiative, which has grown to engage more than 70% of its U.S. attorneys over the past five years in representing domestic violence survivors, veterans, immigrants, and nonprofit groups.

Fifteen years ago, only a small number of corporate legal departments had pro bono programs. Today, legal departments of all sizes across a wide range of industries are participating in pro bono.[1] The majority of Fortune 100 companies and many of the Fortune 500 have created, or are moving to create, formal pro bono programs. To help improve the effectiveness of these efforts, corporate legal departments are working with partners – law firms, legal service organizations, bar associations, and Association of Corporate Counsel (ACC) Chapters – to provide pro bono services.

There are a number of reasons for this growth. Companies are increasingly focused on social responsibility, and pro bono creates opportunities for the legal department to participate in skills-based volunteer efforts. Many in-house lawyers were introduced to strong pro bono programs in prior law firm jobs and wish to continue participating in similar meaningful work. Finally, the success of in-house programs has created a virtuous circle, as the accomplishments of pioneers in this area have challenged and encouraged other companies to get involved.

[1] See, e.g., List of Corporate Pro Bono Challenge Signatories, Corporate Pro Bono, available at www.cpbo.org/cpbo-challenge/list-of-challenge-signatories/ ("List of Challenge Signatories"); Corporate Pro Bono, 2012 *Benchmarking Report: An Overview of In-House Pro Bono*, Corporate Pro Bono, 3–4 (Mar. 2013) (describing the range of industries and sizes of in-house legal departments that have made a commitment to pro bono) ("Benchmarking Report").

OVERVIEW OF IN-HOUSE PRO BONO

Hundreds of companies have developed and implemented formal pro bono programs.[2] Despite a number of challenges facing in-house lawyers – constraints on time and resources, obtaining malpractice insurance, a perceived mismatch of legal experience and client needs, and ethics restrictions – many still participate in a wide range of pro bono efforts.

According to a recent Benchmarking Report published by Pro Bono Institute, legal departments are providing pro bono assistance to a wide range of communities in need. Overall, the study identified fifteen types of clients served by in-house pro bono programs, including victims of domestic violence, nonprofits, children and the organizations assisting them, veterans, emergency responders, the elderly and organizations assisting them, immigrants, schools, and criminal defendants.

Legal departments cover many areas of law for their corporations and therefore are able to provide advice on a broad range of legal subjects to their pro bono clients. Predictably, corporate law is the most common area covered by in-house pro bono work. Other popular areas of law include family law, contracts and commercial law, and immigration law. Corporate legal departments commonly undertake more than a dozen types of pro bono projects, including advice-only clinics, intake clinics, transactional work for nonprofits and small businesses, document drafting, educational and training projects, and litigation.

Two organizations in particular, the Pro Bono Institute and Corporate Pro Bono, have initiated and facilitated in-house pro bono projects. Established in 1996, the Pro Bono Institute (PBI) explores and identifies "new approaches to and resources for the provision of legal services to the poor, disadvantaged, and other individuals or groups unable to secure legal assistance." In 2000, PBI partnered with the ACC to create a joint project called Corporate Pro Bono (CPBO). CPBO works to increase the amount of pro bono work performed by in-house counsel and to enhance the pro bono culture of in-house legal departments by providing consulting services, targeted research and publications, online information and services, and outreach and educational programming.

Since its inception, CPBO has worked with over 500 legal departments and ACC Chapters to help them create or advance their pro bono programs. One initiative to measure the growth of in-house pro bono is the Corporate Pro Bono Challenge℠. To date, more than 120 legal departments have joined the Challenge, which is a simple, voluntary statement of commitment to pro bono service that allows legal departments to benchmark and communicate their support for pro bono. The Corporate Pro Bono Challenge℠ is now the standard for in-house pro bono, and sets a goal of 50% participation by legal department staff.

2 Benchmarking Report, supra note 1, at 2.

VERIZON'S PRO BONO PROGRAM

Verizon launched its pro bono program in November 2009. The central challenge was to create a single program that would provide meaningful opportunities for the roughly 400 attorneys, and hundreds of legal staff, that Verizon employs throughout the country. This was a complex undertaking, in part because most pro bono opportunities are based on local partnerships with nonprofits and legal aid providers, and establishing these relationships across a wide geography was not practical in the few months Verizon had allocated to designing the program. Verizon addressed this problem by partnering with a law firm, DLA Piper LLP (DLA), that already had a pro bono program matching the broad footprint of the company's legal department.

Verizon's pro bono program is given structure by the company's pro bono policy, which states that the purpose of the program "is to assist the Legal Department in providing important pro bono services to people and organizations that could not otherwise afford them." Participation in the program is voluntary, but "[e]very member of the Legal Department is encouraged to devote at least 25 hours per year to pro bono service." Volunteers can work on pro bono matters for up to 100 hours per year, during work time, without securing any additional approvals.

Verizon's pro bono program is focused on education, aiding victims of domestic violence, and providing support for returning veterans. Verizon's pro bono policy defines pro bono work broadly, to "include legal advice or representation provided to individuals or organizations that cannot afford to pay, as well as activities that aid legal service organizations or promote the administration of justice." The policy also states that the committee "may sponsor or encourage particular non-legal activities and may adopt particular causes in an effort to provide members of the Legal Department with meaningful opportunities to give back to the community."[3] The policy does not endorse representation of criminal defendants due to the time and resources needed to provide effective representation, unless the representation is required by court order. It also discourages volunteers from taking on matters that require "trials or hearings exceeding two consecutive days, or five days total, due to the strain such matters will place on the Legal Department's limited resources."

Verizon's pro bono committee oversees the program. To ensure all projects are covered by the company's malpractice insurance, the committee must approve all pro bono work in advance and in writing. The committee also assesses the program's effectiveness; ensures pro bono matters are adequately staffed and supervised, and

[3] Including community service options allows more non-attorneys to participate in the program. Volunteers join Habitat for Humanity build days; prepare holiday gifts for homeless shelters and domestic violence shelters; and work at local food banks. One of Verizon's most popular projects is the Street Law Corporate Diversity Pipeline Program. Through this program, volunteers visit local high schools and teach on various civil law topics including contracts, trademark, dispute resolution, advertising law, and employment law. Attorneys also regularly participate on panels that discuss legal careers for kids from disadvantaged backgrounds.

that training, materials, and assistance are available to volunteers; and addresses any other issues that may arise in connection with the program. The committee publishes a newsletter every three to four months as well as a yearbook detailing the various projects completed each year. The committee is headed by a pro bono chair and is comprised of representatives from the legal department of all Verizon business units. There are a number of regional coordinators on the committee who assist in the administration of the program across the United States.

In order to stay in touch and remain on track, Verizon's pro bono committee has monthly conference calls with DLA's full-time pro bono attorneys to plan upcoming events. Verizon and DLA have also used technology to keep the program focused and organized. The team uses electronic meeting rooms, online training programs, and webinars to train volunteers and coordinate case work. Project approval and tracking systems are used to ensure all work is properly documented. The committee also created a website where helpful documents and information, such as the pro bono policy, pro bono FAQs, and model engagement and termination letters are posted and can be accessed by volunteers. The website also has a link to a current list of upcoming events and committee member contact information.

Participation in Verizon's program has remained strong since its inception. In 2010, the program's first full year, more than 50% of Verizon's domestic attorneys participated. In 2011–13, participation was at or above 60%. In 2014, participation grew to over 72% of domestic attorneys, with 32% of attorney participants working on more than one project and more than 400 total volunteers working in the program. Volunteers have contributed thousands of hours to work in the pro bono program. A key to this success is the involvement of senior-level attorneys, who participate actively and encourage attorneys and staff in their groups to be part of the program.

VERIZON'S PRO BONO PROGRAM: CASE STUDIES

Domestic Violence Immigration Clinics

Domestic violence immigration clinics are a signature part of Verizon's pro bono program. When Verizon first began including immigration applications for domestic violence victims as part of its pro bono program, attorneys were taking cases one-by-one and only one attorney would work on each. After realizing how difficult it was to secure widespread volunteer participation using this model, Verizon and DLA worked together to create a new clinic model. One of the committee's primary objectives in managing Verizon's program is to lower barriers to participation and make it easier for volunteers to deliver impactful service to clients. These clinics provide the ideal balance – delivering vital services to clients while packaging the work in a way that volunteer attorneys can handle it quickly and efficiently.

At these clinics, Verizon and DLA volunteers in Washington, D.C. Northern Virginia, New York, and San Francisco helped clients complete and submit their

U Visa applications to the United States Citizenship and Immigration Services (USCIS). The U Visa "is designed for noncitizen crime victims who have suffered substantial physical or mental abuse flowing from criminal activity [in the United States] and who have mustered the courage to cooperate with government officials investigating or prosecuting such criminal activity."[4] U Visa status allows the recipient to obtain an employment authorization document and receive certain public assistance benefits.

The U Visa application requires the victim to submit a personal statement detailing the events of the crime and the victim's subsequent cooperation with officials, as well as any supporting documentation to prove the necessary elements.[5] These documents might include police reports, medical records, identification documents, counselor statements, and copies of protective orders. Further, law enforcement must sign an immigration form that is included as a supplement to the application.[6] Sometimes clients already have all of these supporting documents; more often, they need the volunteer attorneys to help them obtain these records. In the end, the attorneys help the clients put together the affidavits that outline their story, gather all the necessary documentation, and submit the application.

Legal services partners are critical to the success of these clinics. To date, Verizon and DLA have held clinics in conjunction with Ayuda (an immigration services organization) in Washington, DC, and Virginia, My Sisters' Place and City Bar Justice Center in New York, and Asian Pacific Islander Legal Outreach in San Francisco. These organizations provided training to volunteers, screened the clients, and mentored the volunteers throughout the clinic. As an example, the training for one clinic in New York was set up as a webinar so both Verizon and DLA could participate without traveling. Soon after the training, but prior to the clinic, My Sisters' Place sent the files of clients they had prescreened for the clinic to DLA. Verizon and DLA attorneys were then teamed up to put together the available supporting documents, with the idea of having almost the entire application, with the exception of the affidavit, put together before the clinic to ensure they could make the most of their time with the client.

In the typical set-up, on the morning of the clinic, the attorneys meet and discuss what needs to be done during the time they will have with the client that day. The clients then arrive and the attorney-teams work with the clients to draft the affidavit the application requires. The interview process typically takes four to five hours. The goal is to have the affidavit complete by the end of the day and the entire application filed as soon as possible. However, not all clients have complete files, so the attorneys have to help them obtain the proper supplemental documentation sometime after the clinic, which can delay submission of the application.

4 *U Visa Fact Sheet*, Immigrant Women Program, Legal Momentum, available at www.legalmomentum.org/assets/pdfs/wwwuvisafactsheet-2.pdf.

5 See USCIS Form I-918, Petition for U Nonimmigrant Status, at 2.

6 See USCIS Form I-918, Supplement B, U Nonimmigrant Status Certification (Form I-918B).

The clinic model has proven to be superior to handing out cases individually for several reasons. First, the clinic reduces barriers to volunteer participation by compressing the work into a manageable, scheduled event, thereby removing the logistical burdens of gathering files, scheduling client meetings, and coordinating with the partner organization from volunteers. Second, the clinic model prompts attorneys to get started and sets deadlines for them to finish. This is advantageous because it keeps cases from dragging along and provides volunteers with an assurance that the time commitment for the project is not open-ended and indefinite. Third, a lawyer from the partner organization is on-site for all the client meetings at the clinic. This expert attorney can help volunteers issue-spot and can answer questions, giving the volunteers more confidence in their ability to complete a project in an unfamiliar area of the law. Finally, additional support is widely available and easy to coordinate at the clinic, including from other volunteer attorneys, the law firm, and from non-attorney staff who can serve as translators, help to gather needed information, and draft documents.

The pronounced impact of these clinics is clear. Virtually all of the applications developed in the clinics that have been acted upon by the Department of Homeland Security have been approved, and many are still pending. The clinic model has allowed Verizon and DLA to increase the number of clients they are helping, decrease the time it takes to do so, and instill confidence in the volunteers who are helping these greatly appreciative individuals.

Combat-Related Special Compensation Cases for Veterans

Many servicemen and women incur long-term or permanent disabilities from injuries that are connected to their military service. These disabilities end military careers and reduce or eliminate veterans' earning potential in the civilian community. In 2002, Congress created the right to Combat-Related Special Compensation (CRSC) – enabling military retirees with more than 20 years of service and disabilities that were incurred in combat or other hazardous duty to receive both Veterans' Administration (VA) Disability Compensation and Department of Defense (DOD) Military Retirement. In 2008, Congress expanded CRSC – to allow veterans with qualifying disabilities and fewer than 20 years of service to receive a portion of their DOD Military Retirement while still getting the full amount of VA Disability Compensation.

The National Veterans Legal Services Program (NVLSP) is an independent nonprofit organization that works to ensure veterans, active duty personnel, and their families receive the benefits to which they are entitled. Verizon, DLA, and NVLSP worked together to create and pilot a new program, which is now part of the broader Lawyers Serving Warriors® program, in which attorneys can efficiently assist veterans with their CRSC claims.

Once the program was structured, NVLSP developed training for volunteers interested in helping with a CRSC claim. Verizon conducted two training sessions in its largest offices – one of which was webcast to all of the company's legal offices and to DLA – so that attorneys and legal staff interested in the project could learn how to handle the cases. The trainings were two hours long and provided volunteers with a comprehensive and detailed guide on how to help combat-disabled veterans secure CRSC. Now there is an option to watch that second webcast online. The recorded training includes PowerPoint slides, training handouts, and step-by-step instructions on how to assist a client with a claim. In addition to providing training, NVLSP recruits and screens veterans' and service members' benefit cases and then refers clients to Verizon and DLA. NVLSP also provides substantive mentoring to attorneys as needed, assists with client outreach if a client is non-responsive, and works with paralegal teams at DLA to obtain Claims Files (C-Files) from the VA so they can be passed to the attorney.

Verizon's role in the partnership is to provide volunteers to staff the CRSC matters. Following training, over 50 Verizon attorneys and legal staff began working on cases representing almost 30 disabled veterans. Once a Verizon attorney volunteers to represent a veteran, he or she must complete the training and then review the client's existing VA C-File, which contains identifying information, in-service and veteran medical files, military service history files, and VA adjudicatory files. After reviewing the file, the attorney contacts the client to discuss the nature of the case and the parameters of the representation. The client must then sign an engagement letter. After speaking with the client, if the attorney finds he or she does not have the most recent VA or personnel files for the client, they must be requested. After identifying all evidence that supports a CRSC finding for eligible conditions, the attorney fills out the CRSC Application, which involves assisting the client in drafting a declaration describing the events surrounding the disability and how it meets the CRSC criteria. The attorney also must submit a short legal brief describing how each claimed disability is combat-related using supporting medical, personnel, and witness evidence the attorney gathered. When the application and brief are completed, they are submitted to a review board at the relevant branch of the military. Decisions usually are sent to the client within a few months. If a claim is denied, the veteran can seek reconsideration by submitting clarifying or additional documentary evidence or appeal to a Board for Correction of Military Records.[7] Verizon tracks the status of each matter as well as records results and reports them to DLA and NVLSP.

DLA also provides attorneys who handle cases in the same manner, and has an internal mentor who assists attorneys at the firm and Verizon with any substantive questions that arise during the representation. In addition, DLA plays a large role in ensuring that the program runs smoothly and efficiently. The firm's paralegals assist NVLSP in obtaining records from the VA and provide volunteers instructions on

7 See, e.g., U.S. Air Force Fact Sheet, *CRSC Denial, Appeal Process*, available at www.afpc.af.mil/library/factsheets/factsheet_print.asp?fsID=9718&.

training and access to the eRoom and client records. Throughout a case, an attorney can contact a DLA paralegal if he or she needs help navigating the eRoom, has an administrative question about the assignment, or needs to transfer his or her case to another attorney. The paralegal also tracks the status of client cases every two to three months and compiles statistics to ensure that attorneys are staying on top of their work and achieving the desired results. Finally, she sends CRSC decision letters to NVLSP once she receives them from the attorneys.

DLA also provides the online infrastructure of the program through their eRoom. The eRoom contains everything an attorney needs to represent his or her client. It provides the attorneys not only with training and guidance materials to review before taking a case, but with sample engagement letters, briefs, and appeal requests that can be used throughout the representation.[8] The eRoom also holds all the client's records; when an attorney volunteers, DLA provides the attorney with instructions on how to access the eRoom so they can view the client's files.

Together, Verizon and DLA have taken over 150 CRSC cases and have received many positive results. Scores of applications have been approved in whole or in part. The clients are receiving an average of $274 per month,[9] and received an average retroactive payment of $13,207,[10] although some monetary awards have been substantially higher. The monthly payments will be adjusted automatically for inflation and for any changes in the veteran's disability ratings.

The clients are not the only ones that benefit from these cases. One Verizon attorney said: "My experience assisting my client with his CRSC application was incredibly rewarding. It felt great when he advised me that his application had been approved. I am grateful for the opportunity that was presented to me to give back something to someone who has sacrificed so much for our country."

Veterans' Clinics

Since Verizon's main office in New Jersey is near the VA Lyons campus, it made sense to consider this large VA facility as a base for a new partnership. After a brainstorming session during a planning call, one of DLA's pro bono counsels contacted the VA, which ultimately agreed that it would be beneficial for the veterans under its care to have direct and easy access to attorneys. DLA met with VA staff at the Lyons campus to outline an ambitious framework for a clinic that would assist veterans on a wide range of legal issues. They drafted a memorandum of understanding that defined the roles DLA Piper and the VA would play in organizing and maintaining the clinic. Soon thereafter, Verizon and DLA began recruiting volunteers for their inaugural veterans' clinic.

[8] The eRoom also contains copies of statues and guidance relevant to CRSC, reference materials, and materials on how to understand and work with clients with post-traumatic stress disorder.

[9] Based on reported results for 21 clients.

[10] Based on reported results for 13 clients.

Each partner plays a vital role in the program. The VA helps recruit veterans to sign up for the clinics and provides space in their facilities where the volunteers can meet the veterans. DLA is instrumental in organizing the overall program. The firm creates the training materials used by the volunteers, interfaces with the VA on all planning and logistical details for the clinic; hosts and runs the clinic at the VA; provides volunteer attorneys to meet with veterans; works with local nonprofits to assist veterans who have longer-term issues after the clinic; and performs all follow up, including representing some clients outside of the clinic.

Verizon's role is recruiting volunteers to staff the clinic. The Verizon attorneys who volunteer must review a binder of materials detailing the main legal issues veterans face before the clinic. The binder outlines New Jersey law on the most prevalent issues veterans face including family law; housing and landlord–tenant law; driver's license suspension; criminal record expungement; and disability.

DLA and Verizon volunteers staff the three-hour clinic every other month. Veterans are scheduled to meet a lawyer for fifteen to twenty minutes. Some questions are easily handled, for example, by a letter to a judge or family member. Other issues are more complex and are referred to one of many legal services organizations in the state. In addition to the most common issues, veterans have asked the volunteers about numerous other issues, and the volunteers have done whatever they can to help.

The clinic allows the volunteer attorneys to provide effective assistance quickly and easily. Hundreds of veterans have received assistance at the clinics. The VA has received positive feedback about the usefulness of the clinic to veterans across the state, and the clinic has served as a model for others in additional VA hospitals as well.

Nonprofit Organizations

Verizon provides representation and training on legal issues to a wide range of nonprofit organizations. Two groups that help Verizon connect with nonprofit clients are Pro Bono Partnership and Corporate Pro Bono.

Pro Bono Partnership (PBP) "provides business and transactional legal services to nonprofit organizations serving the disadvantaged or enhancing the quality of life in neighborhoods in Connecticut, New Jersey, and New York."[11] Each month, PBP provides its list of available nonprofit projects to the pro bono committee at Verizon. When a specific project fits into one of the focus areas of Verizon's pro bono program – domestic violence, education, and support for returning veterans – PBP flags those projects for Verizon. Once a lawyer from Verizon expresses interest in a project, PBP provides that lawyer with detailed information about the project and any documents to be reviewed. PBP then coordinates a call to introduce the

[11] About Pro Bono Partnership, Pro Bono Partnership, available at www.probonopartner.org/Pages/about-us/about-us.

volunteer to the client. A PBP staff attorney is assigned to oversee each matter undertaken by a Verizon volunteer to provide any support needed and act as a resource for any issues that require expertise in unfamiliar areas of law. Finally, PBP makes templates, toolkits, and other resource documents available for its volunteers so that they can educate themselves about new issues.

Since Verizon began working with PBP, 103 attorneys have worked on 165 different matters. Projects include direct client representations in many different areas, including labor, tax, intellectual property, real estate, corporate, and education law, as well as workshops for nonprofits addressing areas of common interest, such as contract drafting, compliance, and employment law.

These matters are an ideal fit for in-house counsel to handle on a project-by-project basis. Typically, these projects are in the attorney's field of expertise, and he or she is providing that expert assistance to a different client that needs help. This work is beneficial not only to the nonprofits, but also to the communities that these groups help to serve.

Verizon has also provided representation to nonprofits through CPBO's Clinic in a Box^{SM} Program. CPBO and Verizon began working together at the start of Verizon's pro bono program when CPBO provided consultation to Verizon. In 2010, CPBO, Verizon, and DLA worked together to host Verizon's first clinic program in Arlington, Virginia. The clinic is an off-the-shelf model designed to create pro bono opportunities for legal departments and ACC Chapters. Developed by CPBO, these half-day legal audit clinics provide in-house counsel the opportunity to advise nonprofit organizations or small businesses. Verizon has sponsored or participated in numerous such clinics since launching its pro bono program.

For the in-house volunteer, the clinic is a half-day commitment divided into two parts – training and advice. During the first 90 minutes of the clinic, volunteers receive the training necessary to assess the legal health of a local nonprofit organization or small business. Experts from a law firm instruct the in-house lawyers on identifying legal issues that affect nonprofits or small businesses, usually in the areas of corporate governance, employment, real estate, tax, intellectual property, and general corporate law. DLA has typically provided this training at Verizon's clinics, often in conjunction with volunteers from other pro bono providers such as PBP or the DC Bar Community Economic Development Project. For the remainder of the clinic, in-house attorneys meet with the leader of a local nonprofit or small business in pairs or small groups and lead the client through a legal audit checklist, spotting issues and providing legal advice when needed. To the extent legal issues arise that cannot be resolved at the Clinic, volunteers have the option to provide ongoing pro bono representation to the client or to ask the law firm or public interest partner to assist in the matter.

Clinics are organized at Verizon's request. When a request is made, CPBO begins to look for clients to participate in the clinic and provides Verizon with all its materials. Once identified, CPBO prepares invitations and confirmation letters to be sent to the clients. CPBO then pairs these clients with Verizon volunteers for the clinic. After the clinic, CPBO follows up with the clients and volunteers to obtain feedback and help coordinate any ongoing work.

Verizon is responsible for recruiting volunteers for the clinic and providing a location for the clients to meet the attorneys. If a volunteer decides to provide ongoing representation to a client, Verizon also manages the matter as part of the overall pro bono program.

The clinics deliver multiplying benefits because they help nonprofits to resolve legal issues and focus on their core missions, and thereby serve their communities more effectively. The clinic also affords legal departments a replicable model for delivering pro bono services and is a good fit for in-house attorneys because it allows them to leverage their existing legal skills and expertise on behalf of a broader base of clients. The clinics also foster closer ties among corporations and their communities.

SUGGESTIONS FOR IMPROVING CORPORATE PRO BONO PROGRAMS

Creating partnerships is vital to the success of a corporate pro bono program. Law firm partners can be particularly helpful because they often have extensive existing programs and relationships with nonprofit organizations that can help to ensure a ready supply of clients and provide the support needed to complete projects effectively. For their part, law firms are eager to partner with their clients to help deepen relationships and create opportunities to work with in-house attorneys on a new set of positive, collaborative projects. Once a partnership is created, a company's attorneys can benefit greatly from pairing with the firm's attorneys on pro bono matters. This helps with workload management and allows a company's attorneys comfortably to handle matters that may be outside their expertise. The firm can also assist with the many details of program administration. Creating a law firm partnership can help a company translate its commitment to pro bono into a dynamic, growing program.

Legal service partners are also necessary for a pro bono program to succeed. Pro bono opportunities are typically either local in nature or involve a specific group of potential clients who are bound together by a set of common issues. Either way, legal service organizations and nonprofits are on the front lines of serving these individuals every day, and partnering with these groups is essential to having efficient, productive interactions with clients. Legal service organizations can provide training to attorney volunteers, perform client intake, provide and communicate with clients, and mentor volunteers throughout projects. The in-house partner can provide volunteers to take cases, develop new projects, and help to ensure that clinics and cases run smoothly. The partnerships created within a program allow each participant to deliver more impactful service to clients than either could alone.

It is also critical for pro bono coordinators to package work in a way that facilitates volunteer involvement. The two most common hurdles to pro bono participation are concerns about an open-ended time commitment that could conflict with other work responsibilities, and a reluctance to take on matters in an unfamiliar area of the law. Turning matters that are commonly thought of as one-by-one client representations into clinics helps to create a structure for volunteers who otherwise might be reluctant to participate. Clinics also provide volunteers a ready opportunity to work with mentors from legal service organizations and partner with other attorneys. Centralizing logistical work is likewise an important function within a pro bono program that can lower barriers to participation. The eRoom, for example, allows Verizon and DLA to gather and distribute files in an organized and efficient manner, saving time for volunteers and allowing clients to revive benefits sooner.

Company commitment is also central to the success of a pro bono program. Programs flourish in companies that have a broader culture of volunteer engagement. A significant part of the process of building a pro bono program is creating a culture of participation and spreading that culture to smaller offices. Participation in the pro bono program by senior attorneys in the department, including the general counsel and his direct reports, is the best way to help create and spread this culture. Pro bono events can be structured as team-building exercises, allowing whole groups in a department to participate together. A strong pro bono committee is also important. Verizon's pro bono committee helps organize, plan, and conduct events; find volunteers for each event; match volunteers with clients; and publicize the program's work. Members of the committee also personally volunteer to take on cases and attend many events throughout the year.

Finally, it has been tremendously valuable at Verizon to bring in pro bono law clerks to assist with the administration of the program. Often, corporate pro bono programs are limited more by the capacity of the committee members to plan events than the willingness of volunteers to participate. There are many talented law students who are committed to public service and eager for an opportunity to work in a corporate legal department. This is an ideal match. Law clerks, whether volunteers or paid, can assist with developing new opportunities and partnerships, planning events, recruiting volunteers, tracking participation, writing newsletter and yearbook articles that help to publicize the good work of volunteers, and assist directly with pro bono representations. Their assistance can be instrumental in helping a program to grow.

ETHICS RULES LIMITING PARTICIPATION BY IN-HOUSE COUNSEL

One additional issue merits discussion in this chapter. Many in-house counsel interested in pro bono work are unnecessarily limited by state ethics rules on multi-jurisdictional practice. Often, corporate counsel do not have bar admission in the state where their office is located and are subject to registration requirements that authorize them to represent only their employer. Many states do not expressly permit these attorneys to do pro bono work, and those that do often impose unnecessary restrictions.[12]

For example, many states limit corporate counsel who are not barred in the jurisdiction to working with an approved list of legal services providers, usually under the supervision of another attorney who is a member of that state's bar.[13] The rule in South Carolina is typical, and provides that an in-house attorney not licensed in the state may only provide pro bono services if the attorney

> is associated with an approved legal services organization which receives, or is eligible to receive, funds from the Legal Services Corporation or is working on a case or project through the South Carolina Bar Pro Bono Program [and] ... performs all activities authorized by this rule under the supervision of an attorney (Supervising Attorney) who is a regular member of the South Carolina Bar employed by, or participating as a volunteer for, the legal services organization or the South Carolina Bar Pro Bono Program and who assumes professional responsibility for the conduct of the matter, litigation, or administrative proceeding in which the attorney participates.[14]

Other states allow pro bono practice but only for a limited time. California limits service to three years, Maryland to two years, and Georgia to eighteen months – all in conjunction with various other restrictions on service.[15]

It is widely understood that "more people than ever need free legal services – while at the same time, states are cutting their legal aid budgets."[16] "These unnecessary bans and restrictions limit the number of in-house counsel who provide pro bono services, reduce the number of clients served, and increase burdens on already overworked legal services organizations."[17]

CPBO has been at the forefront of urging changes to restrictive practice rules to empower non-locally licensed in-house counsel to provide pro bono services in the jurisdictions where they work. CPBO formed a task force on the subject, brought the topic to the attention of the Conference of Chief Justices, and drafted numerous resources, such as reports, articles, and model language. The Multijurisdictional Practice Task Force, comprised of in-house counsel from across the country, along

[12] A complete summary of this issue, and a state-by-state summary of the rules, can be found in: Corporate Pro Bono, Multijurisdictional Practice in the U.S.: In-House Counsel Pro Bono, available at www.cpbo.org/wp-content/uploads/2015/04/MJP-Guide-2015-April.pdf; Summary of Multijurisdictional Practice Rules by State, Corporate Pro Bono, Apr. 2015, at 4–6 (CPBO Ethics Summary).

[13] *Id.* at 3, 6–10.

[14] SC App. Ct. Rule 405(m).

[15] CPBO Ethics Summary, supra note 13, at 6–8.

[16] Randal S. Milch, *Letting In-House Counsel Serve Their Communities through Pro Bono Services*, Corporate Counsel (Oct. 29, 2012), available at www.law.com/corporatecounsel/PubArticleCC.jsp?id=1202576522258&26Letting_InHouse_Counsel_Serve_Their_Communities_Through_Pro_Bono_Services.

[17] *Id.*

with CPBO and ACC, develops strategies and resources to advocate for changes to state practice rules. CPBO has worked with the ACC, in-house leaders on the ground, and others in numerous jurisdictions including Connecticut, Florida, Illinois, Iowa, Massachusetts, Minnesota, New York, Ohio, and Virginia.

A number of states have been successful in their efforts to change ethics rules to allow unrestricted pro bono participation by in-house counsel. For example, Verizon and other commentators urged a change in Virginia's restrictive ethics rules in April 2010 during a forum sponsored by the Chief Justice of the Virginia Supreme Court. This led the Virginia State Bar and the Virginia Bar Association to also recommend a change. On April 15, 2011, the Supreme Court of Virginia approved a new rule that became effective immediately and allowed "Virginia corporate counsel admitted in States other than the Virginia to do pro bono work,"[18] and unleashed the "resources of 800 corporate attorneys to help with the pro bono crisis."[19] The Virginia rule is now a model rule. It states: "Notwithstanding the restrictions set out in Part I(f) above on the scope of practice, a lawyer certified pursuant to Part I of this rule may, and is encouraged to, provide voluntary pro bono public services in accordance with Rule 6.1 of the Virginia Rules of Professional Conduct."[20]

Other states have also succeeded in their reform efforts. In 2013, Minnesota approved a reform that allows in-house counsel who are barred outside the state to practice pro bono. Under Minnesota's "newly amended Rule for Admission to the Bar, a lawyer licensed as house counsel or temporary house counsel [can] provide pro bono legal representation to a pro bono client referred to the lawyer through an approved legal services provider."[21] The Illinois Supreme Court likewise changed its rule dealing with in-house pro bono participation.[22] The new rule no longer requires in-house counsel to be supervised by an attorney licensed in Illinois and does not limit in-house attorneys to working with pre-approved legal aid organizations. Massachusetts also loosened its past restrictions and now authorizes "in-house counsel [to] provide pro bono under the auspices of either (1) an approved legal services organization or (2) a lawyer admitted to practice and in good standing in the

[18] *The Virginia Supreme Court Approved Proposal by the Joint Virginia State Bar and Virginia Bar Association Corporate Counsel Pro Bono task Force to Amend Virginia Supreme Court Rule* (V.S.C.R.) 1A:5, Virginia State Bar Professional Guidelines (Apr. 15, 2011), available at www.vsb.org/pro-guidelines/index.php/rule_changes/item/the-joint-virginia-state-bar-and-virginia-bar-association-corporate-counsel.

[19] Milch, supra note 16.

[20] V.S.C.R. 1A:5 Part I(g).

[21] China Terrell, *Minnesota allows in-house counsel barred outside Minnesota to serve pro-bono*, Advocacy, Association of Corporate Counsel (Jan. 22, 2013), available at http://advocacy.acc.com/2013/01/minnesota-expands-pro-bono-to-authorized-in-house-counsel/; see also *Order Promulgating Amendments to the Rules for Admission to the Bar*, Supreme Court of Minnesota, ADM10–8008 (Jan. 17, 2013), available at www.mncourts.gov/Documents/0/Public/Clerks_Office/Rule%20Amendments/2013–01–17%20Bar%20Admission%20Amendments%20(2).pdf.

[22] Ill. Sup. Ct. R. 716(g) & 756(k).

Commonwealth of Massachusetts."[23] Iowa[24] and Connecticut[25] have also amended their practice rules to permit expanded pro bono participation by in-house counsel.

New York has likewise a sweeping and significant change to its rules. The prior rule stated that an in-house attorney not barred in New York can "provide legal services in this State only to the single employer entity or its organizational affiliates" and "only on matters directly related to the attorney's work for the employer entity."[26] Since the rule only authorized practice on behalf of the employer, in-house attorneys who were not barred in New York could not work on pro bono matters that involve issues of New York law. On December 2, 2013, New York Court of Appeals Chief Judge Jonathan Lippman, joined by Senior Associate Judge Victoria Graffeo and representatives from CPBO, Verizon, and other advocates of reform, announced the change. The new rule provides that an attorney registered as an in-house counsel "may provide pro bono legal services in this State in accordance with New York rules of Professional Conduct."[27] The new rule became effective on December 4, 2013.

These reform efforts must continue for corporate counsel to meet their full potential in pro bono. The rules adopted in Virginia and New York strike the right balance. Their widespread adoption would eliminate a significant hurdle to pro bono participation among in-house counsel.

Even with ethical and practical obstacles for in-house counsel, there has been a sea change of pro bono activity to respond to the crisis in legal services for individuals of average means. Several states have lifted bar admissions limitations on pro bono work, and more will likely follow their lead. Verizon's case studies offer one replicable road map for how to establish far-reaching pro bono programs that engage lawyers. One critical component to Verizon's success is the commitment to partner with a law firm or legal services organization to administer the programming and training of volunteer attorneys. Another is to make innovative efforts to package pro bono work in a manner that is attractive and efficient for volunteers and for clients. Finally, CPBO and PBI are there as a vital resource to support the creation of new pro bono programs and partnerships for companies interested in moving forward.

[23] MA S.J.C. Rule 4:02(9)(b); *Massachusetts Joins the Club!*, The PYEye, Pro Bono Institute (Feb. 6, 2013), available at http://thepbeye.probonoinst.org/2013/02/06/massachusetts-joins-the-club/.

[24] See Iowa Court R. 31.16(3)(b).

[25] See Connecticut Authorized House Counsel Sec. 2–15A(c)(5).

[26] 22 NYCRR Part 522.4(a).

[27] 22 NYCRR Part 522.8.

22

Individualized Justice in Class and Collective Actions

Adam Klein, Olivia Quinto & Nantiya Ruan

Class action lawsuits are procedural mechanisms that allow the aggregation of legal claims. They provide an important means by which Americans of modest means can obtain lawyers to take on a group of related legal claims in instances where individual recovery is often too small or risky to support litigation. In this chapter, the authors discuss how individual plaintiffs can actively participate and retain their voice in the class action mechanism.

Class actions are, for all practical purposes, the only means of relief where a single plaintiff's claim is too small to support individual litigation and "private attorney generals" are needed to diffuse the costs and risks among the affected members of the class.[1] But little is written about the individual, justice-seeking plaintiff within the class. Is her voice heard amid the clamor of the advocates, among the throngs in the class? Can individuals realize justice in today's class action? Our experience is yes – if certain precautions are taken to both ensure and incentivize active participation, as well as remedy individual harms within the parameters of class relief.

PROTECTING INDIVIDUAL VOICES

At first, the notion of prioritizing individual voices seems fundamentally antithetical to class actions. Class actions allow a court to treat a group of individuals as one unit based on their common nucleus of facts, being subjected to uniform policy of the defendant, and presuppose that a single judgment can provide relief for each member of the class.[2] Such uniform treatment into one action promotes judicial economy and avoids duplicative waste of resources, as well as the potential of unfair disparate outcomes. But "due to the efficiency-fairness dialectic in class

1 See, e.g., Nantiya Ruan, What's Left to Remedy Wage Theft?: How Arbitration Mandates That Bar Class Actions Impact Low-Wage Workers, 2012 Mich. St. L. Rev. 1103, 1118 (2012).

2 For an overview of Federal Rule 23 requirements and statutory collective actions (of wage and hour rights, as well as Equal Pay Act and Age Discrimination claims), see, generally, Scott Moss & Nantiya Ruan, *The Second-Class Class Action: How Courts Thwart Wage Rights by Misapplying Class Action Rules*, 61 Amer. Univ. L. Rev. 523 (2011) (hereinafter Second-Class Class Action).

actions,"[3] a natural tension results between the collective and the individual in the class action framework.[4]

This tension, however, is not insoluble: "Numerous instances will arise where authorizing a class action will actually serve as a catalyst to the attainment of individualist goals and the furtherance of individualist values.[5]" This is particularly true if one views class actions as an "an aggregation of individuals, a complex joinder device"[6] rather than a collection of individuals forming one entity. In the successful litigation of class actions, individual voices are critically important in the following ways.

HIGHLIGHTING INDIVIDUAL VOICES: THE CLASS REPRESENTATIVE

Modern class action procedures require at least some evidence of participation by class representatives, recognizing that individual voices do matter to the litigation. Class representatives (or "named plaintiffs") must participate by representing the interests of the absent class; third-party representation is no longer allowed. Their claims must be typical of the class and they must prove they will "fairly and adequately protect the interests of the class."[7]

Through the role of class representative, the individual's story is highlighted and stands in for the experience of other class members. This effect was most recently apparent in the country's largest class action lawsuit: *Wal-Mart Stores v. Dukes*.[8] Originally filed in 2001, the face of the lawsuit was a single African American woman named Betty Dukes, who started at Wal-Mart for $5.00 an hour and worked her way up the corporate ladder only to face gender discrimination in both pay and promotion. Ms. Dukes, at first, "found [herself] standing alone, but [she] wasn't standing alone."[9] By the time it reached the U.S. Supreme Court in 2011, the class numbered 1.5 million women.[10] Ms. Dukes – and other class representatives like her – have been able to use the class action both as an opportunity to unite and lead a group of individuals with common contentions to stand up in court *and* as a vehicle to be heard on the bully pulpit. Ms. Duke's use of the class action mechanism to garner

[3] Elijah Yip and Eric K. Yamamoto, *Justice Ruth Bader Ginsburg's Jurisprudence of Process and Procedure*, 20 U. Haw. L. Rev. 647, 691 (1998).

[4] See Martin H. Redish, Wholesale Justice: Constitutional Democracy and the Problem of the Class Action Lawsuit 135 (2009). See also *Culver v. City of Milwaukee*, 277 F.3d 908, 910 (7th Cir. 2002) (Posner, J.).

[5] *Id.* at 126.

[6] Alexandra D. Lahav, *Two Views of the Class Action*, 79 Fordham L. Rev. 1940 (2011).

[7] Fed. R. Civ. P. 23(a).

[8] 131 S. Ct. 2541 (2011).

[9] Monee Fields-White, *She's Taking on Walmart*, The Root, June 24, 2010, available at www.theroot.com/articles/culture/2010/06/interview_betty_dukes_on_the_walmart_genderbias_lawsuit.1.html.

[10] *Dukes*, 131 S.Ct. at 2547.

support for her plight ignited grassroots action[11] and a public policy response: on the ruling's first year anniversary, lawmakers introduced the Equal Employment Opportunity Restoration Act of 2012, a proposal to restore the effective use of group actions for claims arising under Title VII of the Civil Rights Act of 1964.[12]

However, *Walmart Stores v. Dukes* and its progeny also stands for a seismic shift in the way class actions are litigated and the burden of individualized proof shouldered by named plaintiffs in these type of cases.[13] Under Rule 23, to maintain a class action, a party must meet the following requirements: numerosity, commonality, typicality and an adequate representative of the putative class (i.e., the named plaintiffs and class counsel). The party must also provide evidentiary proof of at least one of the 23(b) elements, such as the predominance of common legal questions or facts and that the class action is the superior vehicle to resolve the dispute.

In *Walmart Stores v. Dukes*, the Supreme Court focused on Rule 23's commonality requirement – "the rule requiring a plaintiff to show that there are questions of law or fact common to the class"[14] – and denied class certification because plaintiffs lacked "significant proof" that Walmart engaged in a "general policy of discrimination."[15] Instead, the Court heightened the standard of proof of commonality to a "rigorous"[16] level, holding that satisfying the commonality element required plaintiffs to identify "answers to common questions."[17] As a result, for the individual named plaintiff, this heightened standard has meant that her class claims must flow from a "common contention ... capable of class-wide resolution" in the form of a common biased testing procedure or a common discrimination policy.[18]

Moreover, *Walmart v. Dukes* can be viewed as signaling judicial skepticism against all of Rule 23's class action requirements, making the adequacy of the named representative in maintaining her responsibility to represent the class paramount.[19] Class representatives must remain active throughout the litigation so as to buttress the impression that they have not ceded authority to their lawyers.[20]

[11] Jessica Sabah, *Dozens Rally on Anniversary of Wal-Mart Employee Discrimination Ruling*, Scripps-Howard Foundation, June 20, 2012, available at www.shfwire.com/dozens-rally-anniversary-wal-mart-employee-discrimination-ruling.

[12] H.R. Con. Res. 5978, 112th Cong, (2012) (unenacted).

[13] See also *Comcast Corp. v. Behrend*, 133 S. Ct. 1426 (2013); *Amgen Inc. v. Conn. Ret. Plans & Trust Funds*, 133 S. Ct. 1184 (2013).

[14] 131 S. Ct. at 2550–51 (internal citations omitted).

[15] *Id.* at 2553–54, 2555–56 ("Other than the bare existence of delegated discretion, respondents have identified no 'specific employment practice' – much less one that ties all their 1.5 million claims together. Merely showing that Wal-Mart's policy of discretion has produced an overall sex-based disparity does not suffice").

[16] *Id.* at 2551.

[17] *Id.* at 2554 (emphasis added).

[18] *Id.* at 2551.

[19] Michael R. McDonald & Damian V. Santomauro, *Cutting the Strings Pulling the Puppet Class Representative*, Commer. Lit. (Gibbons P.C., NJ), July 2013, available at www.gibbonslaw.com/UserFiles/Image/DRI%20-%20McDonald%20Santomauro.pdf.

[20] See *Middleton v. Arledge*, 2008 U.S. Dist. Lexis 77352, at *35 (S.D. Miss. Mar. 31, 2008).

This includes being knowledgeable about the litigation and the facts of their claims,[21] understanding their role as class representative,[22] and actively participating in the prosecution of the case.[23] The latter includes communicating with class counsel, responding to discovery, and taking part in the decision-making process of the litigation. In addition, class representatives have a fiduciary obligation to her fellow class members, ensuring that settlement allocations for the class are driven by fairness. All this highlights the pivotal role an individual – specifically the named plaintiff – can play in a class action.

KEEPING ONE'S VOICE: USE OF DECLARATIONS

Becoming a class representative is not the only role in class action suits that highlights individual claims. The use of declarations is also a powerful means for an individual to assert her voice. Before certifying a Rule 23 class action, a court must determine whether there are common questions of fact and law between the putative class members.[24] To do so, a court relies on evidence from putative class members other than the class representatives. This evidence largely takes the form of declarations – signed statements that convincingly tell the declarant's story.[25]

Declarations are a powerful tool: they can support or work to defeat class certification. They remain an important means by which individuals in the putative class reclaim their individual voice. In fact, submitting declarations have been deemed as an important exercise of free speech.[26] In *Ali v. USA Cab Limited,*[27] for example, the plaintiff alleged in a wage and hour suit that the defendant misclassified its drivers as independent contractors. The court denied class certification based on 20 declarations signed by putative class members who detailed their work experience with the company and asserted that they set their own schedules, provided their own supplies, chose which fares to accept, established their own rates, and chose when to use their cars for personal errands.[28] Such means of self-expression guarantees that an

[21] See *Rolex Employees Retirement Trust v. Mentor Graphics Corp.*, 136 F.R.D. 658, 666 (D. Or. 1991; *Jones v. CBE Group, Inc.* 215 F.R.D. 558, 568–69 (D. Minn. 2003); *Wein v. Master Collectors*, 1995 U.S. Dist. Lexis 21622, at *11–12 (N.D. Ga. Aug. 15, 1995).

[22] *Price v. United Servs. Auto. Ass'n*, 2012 U.S. Dist. Lexis 97179, at *21–22 (W.D. Ark. Mar. 16, 2012), *adopted by* 2012 U.S. Dist. Lexis 95659 (W.D. Ark. July 11, 2012); *Scott v. N.Y. City Dist. Council of Carpenters Pension Plan*, 224 F.R.D. 353, 356 (S.D.N.Y. 2004).

[23] *Bodner v. Oreck Direct*, LLC, 2007 U.S. Dist. Lexis 30408, at *3 (N.D. Cal. Apr. 25, 2007); *Strykers Bay Neighborhood Council, Inc. v. New York*, 695 F. Supp. 1531, 1537 (S.D.N.Y. 1988); *Ballan v. Upjohn Co.*, 159 F.R.D. 473, 486 (W.D. Mich. 1994).

[24] Fed. R. Civ. P. 23 (a)(2).

[25] See Marcy Hogan Greer, A Practitioner's Guide to Class Actions 33 (American Bar Association 2010).

[26] *Parris v. Superior Court*, 109 Cal. App. 4th 285 (2003).

[27] 176 Cal. App. 4th 1333 (2009).

[28] *Id.*

employee's subjective determination of his circumstance is not completely subsumed under and determined by the collective body.

LEAVING THE DECISION TO PARTICIPATE WITH THE INDIVIDUAL

An important, but often overlooked, aspect of class litigation is the ability of class members to decide for themselves whether to participate. In the most common types of class actions, plaintiffs who meet the class definition have the option whether, and to what extent, they wish to participate. Only under Rule 23(b)(1) classes are the parties "obliged by law to treat the members of the class alike" and therefore, all class members are automatically part of the class without an opportunity to bow out.[29] Under Rule 23(b)(2) classes, members seek mainly injunctive or declaratory relief against a party who acted "on grounds that apply generally to the class," and while not guaranteed opt-out rights, courts are well within their discretion to allow it.[30]

For workers with common claims of unlawful treatment, whether for discrimination in pay or promotion, failure to pay wages, or other similar workplace claims, plaintiffs typically bring claims under Rule 23(b)(3) for money damages (where all class members suffered a common harm and are part of the class unless they affirmatively opt-out),[31] or if bringing Fair Labor Standards Act (FLSA), Age Discrimination in Employment Act, or Equal Pay Act claims, under their statutory collective action mechanism under FLSA § 216(b). Both Rule 23(b)(3) and FLSA § 216(b)'s opting in/out mechanisms serve to guarantee an individual's due process rights, leaving the ultimate choice to participate up to the individual. [32] Rule 23(b)(3) requires minimal due process of class action, which requires notice, an opportunity to be heard, and a right to opt-out and adequate representation.[33]

Under §216(b), putative class members who are "similarly situated" must "opt-in" with a consent form if they choose to join the lawsuit.[34] Plaintiff's counsel then sends notice to the potential class members informing them of their opt-in rights.[35] Opting-in to a collective action under the FLSA means each opt-in is a claimant

[29] As the Supreme Court observed, Rule 23(b)(1) applies when separate actions risk multiple court orders inconsistent with each other or the rights of non-parties, such where the party "is obliged by law to treat the members of the class alike (a utility acting toward customers; a government imposing a tax) or where the party must treat all alike as a matter of practical necessity." *Amchem Prods., Inc. v. Windsor*, 521 U.S. 591, 614 (1997).

[30] *Martens v. Smith Barney, Inc.*, 181 F.R.D. 243, 260 (S.D.N.Y. 1998) (collecting appeals court decisions in limited fund and employment discrimination class actions in which the courts held that neither Rule 23 (b)(1) or (b)(2) required notice or the opportunity to opt out of the class action; rather "it is within judicial discretion to ... [grant] such rights").

[31] Fed. R. Civ. P. 23(b)(3).

[32] For a discussion, see Steven T. O. Cottreau, *The Due Process Right to Opt Out of Class Actions*, 73 N.Y.U. L. Rev. 480 (1998).

[33] Fed. R. Civ. P. 23(b)(3).

[34] 29 U.S.C. §216(b).

[35] See *Myers v. Hertz Corp.*, 624 F.3d 537, 554 – 555 (2d Cir. 2010).

with an individual stake in the litigation. Thus, each opt-in is a party plaintiff and has an opportunity to tell her own story via the discovery process, including deposition, document production, or representative testimony.[36]

Many FLSA wage and hour collective suits focus on two kinds of violations: (1) allegations of misclassification, where nonexempt employees are classified as exempt depriving them of overtime compensation; and (2) non-payment of off-the-clock compensable work, usually in the context of pre-shift and post-shift activities or work performed during meals or break periods. Such cases are driven by the active participation of individual class members because of the detailed evidence required to prove such claims.

Generally, in wage and hour suits, damages in class actions are calculated to reflect the individual's own hours worked. But this is particularly challenging in litigation involving "off the clock" or unpaid hours, where documentation of working hours is usually non-existent. Typically, the only way to discover employees' unpaid working hours is to interview the workers and reconstruct their typical work hours in order to calculate damages. Thus, the individual experience becomes paramount. Moreover, in many pre- and post-shift unpaid work cases, damages to each individual are often very small, but when added in aggregate with other claims, the overall damages become more meaningful. The adage that there is power in numbers may be trite, but – particularly in the context of off-the-clock class action wage and hour litigation – remains true.

Lastly, as is true for all civil litigations, class actions have a high settlement rate. Class representatives, and sometimes non-named plaintiffs who have an active role in the suit, become key participants in the settlement negotiations. Whether through structured mediation, settlement conferences overseen by the court, or more informal party negotiations, active class members often provide valuable insight into settlement offers and can counsel the plaintiffs' counsel about the reasonableness of the offer, especially regarding non-monetary relief, such as changes to corporate policy and other injunctive relief. Such "on the ground" intelligence is extremely valuable to negotiating a comprehensive and suitable class relief.

ENSURING AND REWARDING ACTIVE PARTICIPATION

For workers facing unlawful employer conduct, whether through wage theft, discrimination and hostile work environments, or other workplace violations, the first hurdle is their ability to "name and claim"[37] such conduct as "unlawful" and

[36] See A.G. King & C. C. Ozumba, *Strange Fiction: The "Class Certification" Decision in FLSA Collective Actions*, 24 Lab. Law. 267 (2009); James M. Finberg & Peder J. Thoreen, *The Use of Representative Testimony and Bifurcation of Liability and Damages in FLSA Collective Actions*, ABA Section of Labor and Employment Law, Nov. 8, 2007, available at http://apps.americanbar.org/labor/annualconference/2007/materials/data/papers/v1/032.pdf.

[37] See William L.F. Felstiner et al., *The Emergence and Transformation of Disputes: Naming, Blaming, and Claiming*, 15 Law & Soc. Rev. 631, 631–54 (1980–81).

recognize the need for lawful remedy. Next, the aggrieved workers must be sufficiently motivated to seek judicial redress, a daunting decision in the current culture of disenchantment with class actions, attorneys, and the U.S. legal system in general. Then, they must find their way to an experienced and receptive plaintiffs' attorney, willing and able to represent their interests.

Potential class representatives and representing attorneys engage in a lengthy and valuable process of fact investigation and claim recognition. As required by Fed. R. Civ. P. 11 and the heightened pleading standard of recent Supreme Court decisions,[38] this investigative process requires significant time and effort, including: interviewing witnesses and potential clients and class members; researching business practices; and researching causes of action and past litigations. It also requires significant resources from the attorneys, given that the worker of average means is unable to afford such legal services and the attorneys will have to work on a contingent basis in hopes of being ultimately successful and recovering their fees and expenses through fee shifting statutes. Only after that investigative and analytical process is complete and successful will a complaint be drawn and filed.

The workers' participation at this early stage is critical. But why would a worker of average means take any time out of her work and personal lives to attend to such a process? For hourly workers (the majority of low-income workers), any time not working is lost money. Moreover, the risks associated with suing one's employer, either current or former, are daunting.[39] In the employment context, where workers are often blacklisted if they are considered "trouble makers," plaintiffs who sue their employers are particularly vulnerable to retaliation.[40] Even former employees risk retaliation from their current employers and put their ability to secure future employment at risk as well.[41]

[38] To survive a motion to dismiss, a plaintiff must plead "enough facts to state a claim to relief that is plausible on its face." *Bell Atl. Corp. v. Twombly*, 550 U.S. 544, 570, 127 S.Ct. 1955, 167 L.Ed.2d 929 (2007); see also *Ashcroft v. Iqbal*, 556 U.S. 662, 129 S.Ct. 1937, 1950, 173 L.Ed.2d 868 (2009) ("[O]nly a complaint that states a plausible claim for relief survives a motion to dismiss").

[39] See *Frank v. Eastman Kodak Co.*, 228 F.R.D. 174, 187 (W.D.N.Y. 2005); *Parker v. Jekyll & Hyde Entm't Holdings, L.L.C.*, No. 08 Civ. 7670, 2010 WL 532960, at *1 (S.D.N.Y. Feb. 9, 2010) ("Enhancement awards for class representatives serve the dual functions of recognizing the risks incurred by named plaintiffs and compensating them for their additional efforts").

[40] See *Frank*, 228 F.R.D. at 187–88; see also *Velez v. Majik Cleaning Serv., Inc.*, No. 03 CIV 8698, 2007 WL 7232783, at *7 (S.D.N.Y. June 25, 2007) (observing that the plaintiffs "exposed themselves to the prospect of having adverse actions taken against them by their former employer and former co-workers").

[41] See *Parker*, 2010 WL 532960, at *1 ("[F]ormer employees put in jeopardy their ability to depend on the employer for references in connection with future employment"); *Silberblatt v. Morgan Stanley*, 524 F. Supp. 2d 425, 435 (S.D.N.Y. 2007) (recognizing that former employees face risks to their future employability when they serve as plaintiffs).

Representative plaintiffs play a crucial role in bringing justice to those who would otherwise be hidden from judicial scrutiny.[42] Service awards (sometimes called "incentive" or "enhancement" awards) "provide an incentive to seek enforcement of the law despite these dangers."[43] Service awards provide an additional recovery amount to acknowledge the additional burdens and risks that they face beyond those required by the rest of the class. Despite some judicial criticism,[44] they are common in class action cases and serve to compensate plaintiffs for the time and effort expended in assisting the prosecution of the litigation, the risks incurred by becoming and continuing as a litigant, and any other burdens sustained by such plaintiffs.[45] Accordingly, "[i]ncentive awards are not uncommon in class action cases and are within the discretion of the court."[46] Courts have also

[42] See, e.g., *Velez v. Majik Cleaning Serv.*, No. 03 Civ. 8698, 2007 WL 7232783, at *7 (S.D.N.Y. June 25, 2007) ("[I]n employment litigation, the plaintiff is often a former or current employee of the defendant, and thus, by lending his name to the litigation, he has, for the benefit of the class as a whole, undertaken the risk of adverse actions by the employer or co-workers") (internal quotation marks omitted); see also Nantiya Ruan, *Bringing Sense to Incentive Payments: An Examination of Incentive Payments to Named Plaintiffs in Employment Discrimination Class Actions*, 10 EMP. RTS. EMP. POL'Y J. 395 (2006).

[43] *Parker*, 2010 WL 532960, at *1.

[44] *Radcliffe v. Experian Info. Solutions Inc.*, 715 F.3d 1157, 1164–67 (9th Cir. 2013) (criticizing conditional incentive awards as corrupting the adequacy of class representatives); *Rodriguez v. W. Publ'g Corp.*, 563 F.3d 948, 960 (9th Cir. 2009) (criticizing incentive agreements entered into by class counsel and representatives); *Staton v. Boeing Co.*, 327 F.3d 938, 977–78 (9th Cir.2003) (settlement agreement denied because the awards request indicated that the class representatives "more concerned with maximizing [their own] incentives than with judging the adequacy of the settlement as it applies to class members at large"); *Partridge v. Shea Mortg. Inc.*, No. 07-4230, 2008 WL 5384542, *1 (N.D. Cal. Dec. 22, 2008) (denying $15,000 incentive award due to Court's concern that incentive payments induces class representatives to accept sweetheart settlements that favor the interests of class counsel over the interests of the class); *Weseley v. Spear, Leeds & Kellogg*, 711 F. Supp. 713, 720–21 (E.D.N.Y. 1989) (noting that "if class representatives expect routinely to receive special awards in addition to their share of the recovery, they may be tempted to accept suboptimal settlements at the expense of the class members whose interests they are appointed to guard"); *Women's Comm. for Equal Employment Opportunity v. Nat'l Broad. Co.*, 76 F.R.D. 173, 180 (S.D.N.Y. 1977) ("[W]hen representative plaintiffs make what amounts to a separate peace with defendants, grave problems of collusion are raised"). See also Theodore Eisenberg & Geoffrey Miller, *Incentive Awards to Class Action Plaintiffs: An Empirical Study*, 53 UCLA L. REV. 1303, 1311–13 (2006) (hereinafter Eisenberg, *Incentive Awards to Class Action Plaintiffs*).

[45] See, e.g., *McMahon v. Olivier Cheng Catering and Events, LLC*, No. 08 Civ. 8713, 2010 WL 2399328, at *9 (S.D.N.Y. Mar. 3, 2010). Service awards fulfill the important purpose of compensating plaintiffs for the time they spend and the risks they take. *Massiah v. MetroPlus Health Plan, Inc.*, No. 11 Civ. 5669, 2012 WL 5874655, at *8 (E.D.N.Y. Nov. 20, 2012).

[46] *Frank v. Eastman Kodak Co.*, 228 F.R.D. 174, 187 (W.D.N.Y. 2005); see *Toure v. Amerigroup Corp.*, No. 10 Civ. 5391, 2012 WL 3240461, at *6 (E.D.N.Y. Aug. 6, 2012) (approving awards of $10,000 for each class representative); *Palacio v. E*TRADE Fin. Corp.*, No. 10 Civ. 4030, 2012 WL 2384419, at *7 (S.D. N.Y. June 22, 2012) (approving awards of $6,500 to class representatives); *Sewell v. Bovis Lend Lease, Inc.*, No. 09 Civ. 6548, 2012 WL 1320124, at *14–15 (S.D.N.Y. Apr. 16, 2012) (approving payments of $10,000 and $15,000); *Willix v. Healthfirst, Inc.*, No. 07 Civ. 1143, 2011 WL 754862, at *7 (E.D.N.Y. Feb. 18, 2011) (approving awards of $30,000, $15,000, and $7,500 to class representatives and opt-ins); *Khait v. Whirlpool Corp.*, No. 06 Civ. 6381, 2010 WL 2025106, at *9 (E.D.N.Y. Jan. 20, 2010) (approving awards of $15,000 and $10,000). Courts routinely approve service awards in wage and hour class and

approved service awards for non-representative plaintiffs who have provided valuable services to the class.[47]

The amount of the award is discretionary but must be reasonable, and it typically ranges from a few thousand to several thousand dollars.[48] In examining the reasonableness of a requested service award, courts consider: (1) the personal risk incurred by the named plaintiffs and opt-in plaintiffs; (2) the time and effort expended by the named plaintiffs and opt-in plaintiffs in assisting the prosecution of the litigation; and (3) the ultimate recovery in vindicating statutory rights.[49]

Courts recognize the important factual knowledge that plaintiffs bring to employment and wage class and collective actions, including information about employer policies and practices that affect wages.[50] Both representative (named) plaintiffs as well as non-named plaintiffs often contribute significant time and effort to a class case after it has been investigated and filed. They provide detailed factual information regarding their hours worked, their job duties, defendants' policies, and other information relevant to their claims, and submit declarations in support of plaintiffs' motion for class or conditional certification pursuant to Rule 23 or Section 216(b).

collective actions. See, e.g., *Toure v. Amerigroup Corp.*, No. 10 Civ. 5391, 2012 WL 3240461, at *6 (E.D.N.Y. Aug. 6, 2012) (approving awards of $10,000 for each class representative); *Lovaglio v. W & E Hospitality, Inc.*, No. 10 Civ. 7351, 2012 WL 2775019, at *4 (S.D.N.Y. July 6, 2012) (approving service awards of $10,000 for each named plaintiff); *Sewell v. Bovis Lend Lease, Inc.*, No. 09 Civ. 6548, 2012 WL 1320124, at *14–15 (S.D.N.Y. Apr. 16, 2012) (approving service payments of $10,000 and $15,000); *Reyes v. Altamarea Grp., LLC*, No. 10 Civ. 6451, 2011 WL 4599822, at *9 (S.D.N.Y. Aug. 16, 2011) (approving service awards of $15,000 and $5,000); *Willix v. Healthfirst, Inc.*, No. 07 Civ. 1143, 2011 WL 754862, at *7 (E.D.N.Y. Feb. 18, 2011) (approving awards of $30,000, $15,000, and $7,500 to class representatives and opt-ins); *Khait v. Whirlpool Corp.*, No. 06 Civ. 6381, 2010 WL 2025106, at *9 (E.D.N.Y. Jan. 20, 2010) (approving awards of $15,000 and $10,000 to named plaintiffs).

47 See, e.g., *Toure*, 2012 WL 3240461, at *6 (approving awards of $5,000 for opt-ins who participated in discovery); *Palacio*, 2012 WL 2384419, at *7 (approving awards of $3,000 for opt-in plaintiffs); *In re Wells Fargo Loan Processor Overtime Pay Litig.*, MDL No. 07–1841, 2011 WL 3352460, at *11 (N.D. Cal. Aug. 2, 2011) (approving incentive awards of $1,000 each for six opt-in plaintiffs); *Wren v. RGIS Inventory Specialists*, No. 06 Civ. 5778, 2011 WL 1230826, at *38 (N.D. Cal. Apr. 1, 2011) *supplemented*, 2011 WL 1838562 (N.D. Cal. May 13, 2011) (approving incentive award of $2,500 for opt-in plaintiff).

48 See, e.g., *Toure v. Amerigroup Corp.*, No. 10 Civ. 5391, 2012 WL 3240461, at *6 (E.D.N.Y. Aug. 6, 2012) (approving awards of $10,000 for each class representative); *Lovaglio v. W & E Hospitality, Inc.*, No. 10 Civ. 7351, 2012 WL 2775019, at *4 (S.D.N.Y. July 6, 2012) (approving service awards of $10,000 for each named plaintiff); *Sewell v. Bovis Lend Lease, Inc.*, No. 09 Civ. 6548, 2012 WL 1320124, at *14–15 (S.D.N.Y. Apr. 16, 2012) (approving service payments of $10,000 and $15,000); *Reyes v. Altamarea Grp., LLC*, No. 10 Civ. 6451, 2011 WL 4599822, at *9 (S.D.N.Y. Aug. 16, 2011) (approving service awards of $15,000 and $5,000); *Willix v. Healthfirst, Inc.*, No. 07 Civ. 1143, 2011 WL 754862, at *7 (E.D.N.Y. Feb. 18, 2011) (approving awards of $30,000, $15,000, and $7,500 to class representatives and opt-ins); *Khait v. Whirlpool Corp.*, No. 06 Civ. 6381, 2010 WL 2025106, at *9 (E.D.N.Y. Jan. 20, 2010) (approving awards of $15,000 and $10,000 to named plaintiffs).

49 *Frank*, 228 F.R.D. at 187; *Roberts v. Texaco, Inc.*, 979 F. Supp. 185, 200 (S.D.N.Y. 1997).

50 See *Frank*, 228 F.R.D. at 187 (recognizing the important role that plaintiffs play as the "primary source of information concerning the claims [,]" including by responding to counsel's questions and reviewing documents); *Parker*, 2010 WL 532960, at *1 (recognizing efforts of plaintiffs including meeting with counsel, reviewing documents, formulating theory of case, identifying and locating other class members to expand settlement participants, and attending court proceedings).

Named plaintiffs also inform putative class members of the lawsuit and respond to document requests and interrogatories. Defendant employers faced with a class case often notice not only named plaintiffs for deposition, but also any witness or declarant that have provided information to the plaintiffs in support of the class claims.

Yet service awards typically represent only a very small percentage of the total recovery of the class.[51] In respect to the duty owed to absent class members and to avoid the appearance of collusion, courts are wary to approve service awards that represent a greater percentage of the recovery, avoiding any unfairness to the absent class. But continuing to provide even modest service awards helps to incentivize needed class participation.

SAFEGUARDING INDIVIDUALIZED RELIEF WITHIN CLASS TREATMENT

Class actions bring together an aggregate of individuals, whose "substantive rights ... remain individually held and are simply brought in one proceeding."[52] Courts utilize several class mechanisms to honor individual rights, including the use of sub-classes, final approval hearings, and separate damage hearings, when applicable. All function as a way for the individual to either register one's dissent or approval of the decisions made by the collective and safeguards individual interests by leaving each member with a core principle of autonomy: choice.

Sub-Classes to Preserve Differences

Individualized relief within the class is supported through Federal Rule 23(c) (4) (B), which permits a court to create subclasses "when appropriate."[53] Before they may be certified, subclasses must satisfy the same Rule 23 class action requirements.[54]

[51] See, e.g., *Palacio*, 2012 WL 2384419, at *7 (approving awards representing approximately 3.3% of the settlement); *Parker*, 2010 WL 532960, at *2 (finding that service awards totaling 11% of the total recovery were reasonable "given the value of the representatives' participation and the likelihood that class members who submit claims will still receive significant financial awards"); *Frank*, 228 F.R.D. at 187 (approving award of approximately 8.4% of the settlement). Meanwhile, in a decade-long study, researchers discovered that when given, incentive awards on average, only made up 0.02% of the class recovery. The averaged total award was $128,803 with a median of $18, 190. These awards were often split between several class representatives and on average each received approximately $4,357. "The size of total incentive awards was strongly associated with the size of the class recovery, the recovery per class member, the amount of attorney' fees awarded, and the award of costs and expenses." Eisenberg, *Incentive Awards to Class Action Plaintiffs*, supra note 44, at 1308.

[52] Redish, supra note 4, at 127.

[53] Fed. R. Civ. P. 23(c)(4)(B).

[54] *Retired Chicago Police Ass'n v. City of Chicago*, 7 F.3d 584, 599 (7th Cir. 1993); *Roby v. St. Louis Southwestern Ry. Co.*, 775 F.2d 959, 961 (8th Cir. 1985).

Through this mechanism, divergent interests among class members can be addressed, but in isolation from the rest of the class who do not share a particular claim, avoiding the adequacy requirement by allowing both the subclass and global class to be certified under Rule 23.[55] By creating a subclass of similarly situated plaintiffs, the common class claims continue while still preserving and addressing any singular claim affecting only particular members. As the Supreme Court explained in *Amchem Products, Inc. v. Windsor*, subclasses provide a means of preventing the "shortchanging absentee class members."[56]

Final Approval Hearings and the Right to Dissent

Under Rule 23 (e), the district court must approve a class action settlement to protect the interests of the class members.[57] To do so, the presiding court holds a final approval hearing, allowing the litigants and all class members, an opportunity to be heard on the merits of the settlement. Prior to the hearing, court-approved notice must be sent to the class detailing how individual class members can exclude themselves from the suit by submitting a written request for exclusion. By choosing this option, an individual class member opts to not receive any settlement payments in exchange for being free to pursue her own claims against the defendant.

Moreover, the notice must also instruct class members that they can a file a notice of intention to appear at the final approval hearing. This allows dissenting class members to speak to the presiding judge about the fairness of the settlement, the proposed plan of allocation, or the attorney fees and reimbursements. Such means "inhere to the individual, recognizing class members as rights holders who are entitled to pursue their own litigation and to have their say in the pending class action."[58]

Separate Damages Hearings and Bifurcating Liability and Damages

Upon a finding of liability, the class suit enters a damages phase, which can entail either an individualized approach or an aggregate approach to proof of damages.[59] Under the individualized approach, each class member answers written discovery

[55] See Susan Bisom-Rapp, *The Use of Subclasses in Class Action Suits Under Title VII*, 9 Indus.Rels. L. J. 116 (1987). Subclass designation tends to occur in three situations: (1) if there is a presence of divergent interests; (2) if there is a presence of conflicting interests; or (3) if there are management concerns of the court.

[56] 521 U.S. 591, 627 (1997).

[57] Fed. R. Civ. P. 23(e) (requiring fairness hearings before approval of settlements in class actions).

[58] Alexandra D. Lahav, *Two Views of the Class Action*, 79 Fordham L. Rev. 1940 (2011).

[59] James M. Finberg & Peder J. Thoreen, *The Use of Representative Testimony and Bifurcation of Liability and Damages in FLSA Collective Actions*, ABA Section of Labor and Employment Law, Nov. 8, 2007.

and then attends an individualized hearing to address the specific damages she suffered.[60] Under the aggregate approach, each class member is awarded a proportional amount of the total relief. Accordingly, if suitable, individualized relief can be addressed, and often times at defendants' urging is routinely used, in multidistrict litigation suits.[61]

Bifurcating liability and damages is another instance where a class action suit can serve individualized relief. The determination of class-wide liability informs the scope of damages in a wage and hour collective action. Issues to be decided in the liability phase include the applicable statute of limitations, the necessity of liquidated damages, entitlements to prejudgment interest, and whether overtime pay needs to be calculated under state or federal law (applicable to hybrid FLSA/Rule 23 class action suits).[62] In a situation where the case is bifurcated, these issues will be decided before the damages phase, "allowing for discovery and proof relating to damages that are properly targeted and bounded – e.g. limited to eligible individuals, eligible time periods, applicable pay rates, and relevant remedies."[63]

Lastly, bifurcating class disputes can provide a process for individualized resolution once class liability is found. Rule 23(c)(4) allows for isolating the common question of liability while leaving the issue of damages for later individual hearings. Pursuant to Rule 23(c)(4), which allows for class certification "with respect to particular issues," courts can bifurcate the issue of liability for class-wide resolution from damages determinations.[64] Such a process highlights the advantage of individualized damage assessment but still benefiting from findings based on class-wide evidence. Additionally, class settlements can "establish a new dispute resolution process ... as an exclusive forum ... [for] all alleged claims" by members of the class.[65] In some specific circumstances, where a large corporation is targeted for similar but highly individualized workplace violations, it makes sense to implement a dedicated process for resolving disputes through a knowledgeable panel of arbiters.

CONCLUSION

Critics of class action suits argue that the "vast majority of cases produced no benefits to most members of the putative class[,]" enriching only the lawyers who represent them.[66] However, such critique is intentionally deceptive. The reality is that

60 *Id.*
61 See *id.*
62 *Id.*
63 *Id.*
64 See, e.g., *In re Nassau Cnty. Strip Search Cases*, 461 F.3d 219 (2d Cir. 2006).
65 *Martens v. Smith Barney, Inc.*, 181 F.R.D. 243, 261 (S.D.N.Y. 1998).
66 See, e.g., Mayer Brown LLP, *Do Class Actions Benefit Class Members? An Empirical Analysis of the Class Actions*, available at http://blogs.reuters.com/alison-frankel/files/2013/12/mayerbrownclassaction study.pdf. This report looks only at consumer class actions.

employment class actions against large corporations can yield significant settlement figures, providing robust relief to individual class members: Novartis ($175 million)[67]; Coca-Cola ($192.5 million)[68]; Texaco ($176 million)[69]; Microsoft ($96.9 million)[70]; Smith Barney ($98 million)[71]; Home Depot ($65 million)[72]; Staples ($38 million)[73]; Morgan Stanley ($46 million)[74]; Sprint/Nextel ($57 million)[75]; IBM ($65 million)[76]; UPS ($87 million)[77]; and Albertsons ($53.5 million).[78] Class litigation is a necessary tool for plaintiffs, mitigating the tremendous risks against of litigation especially gigantic corporate entities. Even where claims have relatively low value[79], class members might still prefer to litigate collectively if it renders justice on principle and deters bad actors from continuing their harmful practices and affecting others like them.[80]

Finally, those critics who like to characterize class action lawyers as merely chasing settlement windfalls gloss over the reality that victims of any illegal activity – such as those individuals whose employer fails to compensate them for a full day's work – do in fact need legal representation, otherwise they "would be left to fend for themselves."[81]

[67] See *Velez v. Novartis*, No. 04–09194 (S.D.N.Y. final approval granted on Nov. 30, 2010).

[68] See *Abdallah v. Coca-Cola Co.*, No. 1:98–3679 (N.D. Ga. final approval granted on June 7, 2001).

[69] See *Roberts v. Texaco, Inc.*, No. 94–02015 (S.D.N.Y. final approval granted on Jan. 3, 1997).

[70] See *Vizcaino v. Microsoft*, No. 93–00178 (W.D. Wash. final approval granted on Mar. 26, 2001).

[71] See *Bahramipour v. Citigroup Global Mkts. Inc.*, No. 04–4440 (N.D. Cal. final approval granted on May 24, 2006).

[72] See *Butler v. Home Depot, No. 94–04335 (N.D. Cal.* final approval granted on Jan. 14, 1998).

[73] See *Williams v. Staples*, No. 816121 (Cal. Super. Ct. final approval granted on Nov. 2007).

[74] See *Augst-Johnson v. Morgan Stanley & Co.*, No. 06–1142 (D.D.C. final approval granted on Oct. 26, 2007).

[75] See *Williams v. Sprint/United Mgmt. Co.*, No. 03–02200 (D. Kan. final approval granted on Sep. 10, 2007).

[76] See *Rosenburg v. Int'l Bus. Machs. Corp.*, No. 06–0430 (N.D. Cal. final approval granted on July 11, 2007).

[77] See *Cornn v. United Parcel Serv. Inc.*, No. 03–02001 (N.D. Cal. final approval granted on Apr. 9, 2007).

[78] See *In re Albertsons Inc., Employment Litigation Practice*, No. 98–0215 (D. Idaho final approval granted on Mar. 22, 2007).

[79] In a study of class action settlements of several categories of employment law claims, researchers found that the mean individual potential recovery is about $8,419, while the median is $2,180. The largest individual potential recoveries involve discrimination plaintiffs, which has a mean individual potential recovery of $12,255 and a median of $7,652. Meanwhile, state wage-hour claims can garner individual plaintiffs $10,861 and ERISA and FLSA claims are both worth approximately $6,000 per individual plaintiff. see Samuel Estreicher & Kristina Yost, *Measuring the Value of Class and Collective Action Employment Settlements: A Preliminary Assessment*, 6 J. of Empirical Legal Studies 768, 778 (Dec. 2009).

[80] But see Mark Moller, *The Anti-Constitutional Culture of Class Action Law*, Regulation (Summer 2007) at 50.

[81] Katie Melnick, *In Defense of the Class Action Lawsuit: An Examination of the Implicit Advantages and a Response to Common Criticisms*, 22 St. John's J. Legal Comment. 755 (2008).

Low-income workers and historically marginalized groups benefit particularly from class action suits, which have used "collective litigation [to] serve [] loftier goals than just dispute resolution."[82]

The Supreme Court emphasized the power of this vehicle in *NAACP v. Button*[83]:

> In the context of [civil rights'] objectives, litigation is not a technique of resolving private differences; ... It is ... a form of political expression. Groups which find themselves unable to achieve their objectives through the ballot frequently turn to the courts ... For such a group, association for litigation may be the most effective form of political association.[84]

For instance, in one stunning example, the state of Mississippi reported an increase in income in 2013, primarily due to a $1.25 billion settlement paid out to black farmers in the state who had long suffered racial discrimination by the Agricultural Department. The settlement, divided among 18,000 farmers, allocated roughly $69,500 per class member.[85] To these Mississippi farmers, the class settlement is not small potatoes.

82 See George A. Martinez, *Race Discrimination and Human Rights Class Actions: The Virtual Exclusion of Racial Minorities from the Class Action Device*, 33 J. LEGIS. 181, 182 (2007).

83 371 U.S. 415 (1963).

84 *Id.* at 425.

85 Niraj Choksh, A *Discrimination Settlement Was So Big It Skewed Mississippi's Income Data*, The Washington Post, Dec. 19, 2013, available at www.washingtonpost.com/blogs/govbeat/wp/2013/12/19/a-discrimination-settlement-was-so-big-it-skewed-mississippis-income-data/.

PART III

Fashioning a Reform Agenda

23

New York State Task Force to Expand Access to Civil Legal Services

Helaine M. Barnett

Over the past decade, state courts have been at the forefront of seeking to increase access to legal assistance and facilitating self-representation in civil cases. In this chapter, Helaine Barnett, former president of the Legal Services Corporation, describes her work on the Task Force to Expand Access to Civil Legal Services in New York, which was set in motion by former New York State Chief Judge Jonathan Lippman. The statewide task force first set out to assess the needs of New Yorkers who did not have legal assistance and then framed solutions around those findings.

"Equal Justice under Law" is a founding principle of our nation dating back to the Preamble of the Constitution and a concept that is familiar to most Americans. We all believe that rich or poor, we should be treated equally in our courts. Although equal access to justice remains an ideal, the reality is very different for those unable to afford the assistance of counsel in civil cases. Unlike in criminal cases, there is no constitutionally established right to counsel in civil cases for those who cannot afford it, even in cases involving essential issues such as housing, healthcare, child custody, or protection from domestic violence. For people of limited means, the result is that in the vast majority of civil cases where crucial issues are at stake, they have to navigate a complex legal system alone.

There is a system of civil legal services available to those who cannot afford counsel that addresses a small percentage of the need, supported by funding from a variety of sources. The biggest source of funding is the Legal Services Corporation (LSC), a private, nonprofit corporation created by Congress in 1974 that distributes funding from annual federal appropriations to 134 independent legal services providers throughout the country, in every state and territory of the United States.[1] Current LSC funding is at about $375 million annually, to serve an eligible population of over 63 million Americans, the number of people who meet the

[1] Legal Services Corporation Act, 42 U.S.C. §2996 *et seq.* (2013); Legal Services Corporation, *Fact Sheet on the Legal Services Corporation*, available at www.lsc.gov/about/what-is-lsc. See Radice, Chapter 15 in this volume.

qualifying criteria of earning no more than 125% of the federal poverty level.[2] LSC funding supports programs to assist the 1 in 5 Americans at that income level or below, which is currently $30,313 for a family of four.[3]

Until the economic crisis of the last several years, another significant source of funding was Interest on Lawyer Trust Accounts (IOLTA), which currently provides under $100 million in funding nationally.[4] Every state has an IOLTA program, which distributes the interest earned in accounts containing short-term deposits of client funds held in trust by lawyers, to support civil legal services programs.[5] The remainder of funding supporting civil legal services comes from a combination of state, local, private, and charitable sources.[6] In addition, pro bono representation by the private bar and by law school clinical programs plays an important role in providing legal assistance to needy Americans.

All of these sources for assistance combined do not come close to meeting the need. In 2005 and 2009, LSC issued two reports on "Documenting the Justice Gap in America," which showed that for every person served by LSC-funded programs, at least one person is turned away due to lack of resources.[7] When I was president of LSC, we coined the term "justice gap" to describe the difference between what we have promised, the ideal of justice for all, and what we actually provide. Studies by the American Bar Association and numerous state studies in recent years all confirm that there is a serious "justice gap," as only a small percentage of those needing civil legal assistance are able to obtain it.[8]

The problem has been greatly exacerbated in the last several years due to the economic downturn and foreclosure crisis, and the resulting increases in poverty,

2 Consolidated and Further Appropriations Act, 2015, Pub. L. 113–235, 128 Stat. 2130, 2207 (2014); 45 C.F. R. §1611.3 (c)(1)(2015)(eligibility at 125% of the poverty level). LSC's budget request for Fiscal Year 2016, based on demonstrated need, is $487 million. Legal Services Corporation, *LSC's Fiscal Year 2016 Budget Request*, available at www.lsc.gov/fy2016-budget-request.

3 45 C.F.R. §1611 Appnx. A (2015); Legal Services Corp. (LSC), What Is LSC? Available at www.lsc.gov/about/what-is-lsc.

4 Email from Bev Groudine, Staff Counsel, Comm'n on IOLTA, Am. Bar Assoc., to author (Oct. 6, 2011)); Terry Carter, No Longer Flush, ABA Journal, March 2013, at 61.

5 IOLTA programs, now in all 50 states, originated in Florida. See In Re Interest on Trust Accounts, 356 So. 2d 799 (Fla. 1978); *In the Matter of Interest*, 402 So. 2d 389 (Fla. 1981).

6 In total, these resources currently amount to about $1.4 billion a year. Alan Houseman, *The Crisis in Civil Legal Aid*, available at www.acslaw.org/acsblog/the-crisis-in-civil-legal-aid. In comparison, the legal services market accounts for over $200 billion of gross domestic product in the United States. See U.S. Bureau of Economic Analysis, Table, Gross Output by Industry in Current Dollars, Quantity Indexes by Industry, Price Indexes by Industry, available at www.bea.gov/industry/iedguide.htm#gdpia_ad_it.

7 LSC, Documenting the Justice Gap in America 4 (2005); Legal Services Corporation, Documenting the Justice Gap in America, The Current Unmet Civil Legal Needs of Low-Income Americans 1 (2009).

8 See, e.g., D.C. Access to Justice Commn. & D.C. Consortium of Leg. Servs. Providers, Rationing Justice: The Effect of the Recession on Access to Justice in the District of Columbia 1 (2009), available at www.legalaiddc.org/documents/RationingJusticeReport..pdf); Pennsylvania IOLTA Board, Results of the Pennsylvania Access to Justice Act 2 (2009); Mississippi Access to Justice Commission, Report of the Public Hearings on the Unmet Civil Legal Needs of Low Income Mississippians 13 (2010).

unemployment, and homelessness. In the last decade, unprecedented natural disasters such as Hurricane Katrina and most recently Hurricane Sandy have created countless additional civil legal needs that persist for years. At the same time, the economic downturn and the pressures on government budgets have caused steep declines in the resources available for civil legal services. LSC funding has been greatly reduced in the last few years, from $420 million in fiscal year 2010 to about $375 million currently.[9] The decline in economic activity and the drop in interest rates have resulted in drastic reductions in IOLTA funding, with the national total falling below $100 million, from $371 million prior to the crisis.[10] The economic downturn has also meant severe cuts to state and local government budgets and a decline in private and charitable resources as well, causing legal services programs to close offices and lay off staff.

CREATION OF TASK FORCE TO EXPAND ACCESS TO CIVIL LEGAL SERVICES IN NEW YORK

Against this background, in a Law Day speech delivered on May 3, 2010, New York State Chief Judge Lippman outlined a major statewide effort to address civil legal services. In his remarks, he noted that while equal justice is central to our system, the reality is that New York, much like the rest of the nation, is falling short of that ideal.[11]

Chief Judge Lippman announced that what was needed was a comprehensive, systemic approach to providing counsel to the indigent in civil cases, not just an ad hoc approach, single initiative or pilot program.[12] As a centerpiece of this effort to establish a comprehensive approach to providing legal assistance to low-income New Yorkers in civil legal matters, the Chief Judge established a statewide Task Force to Expand Access to Civil Legal Services in New York ("Task Force"). He announced that he would preside over annual public hearings on the issue of unmet civil legal services needs in New York in order to make recommendations to the Legislative and Executive branches of the state government on how to expand access to justice.[13] The newly created Task Force was charged with assisting in organizing the first ever judiciary hearings in all four judicial departments of the state to evaluate the unmet need for civil legal assistance.[14]

9 Consolidated and Further Appropriations Act, 2015, Pub. L. 113–235, 128 Stat. 2130, 2207 (2014); LSC, Funding History at www.lsc.gov/congress/funding/funding-history.

10 See supra note 4.

11 Chief Judge Jonathan Lippman, Law in the 21st Century: Enduring Traditions, Emerging Challenges, available at www.nycourts.gov/ctapps/LD10Transcript.pdf.

12 *Id.* at 18.

13 *Id.*

14 *Id.* at 19. The hearings were to be held in each of New York's four Appellate Divisions, with the Chief Judge presiding along with the Presiding Justice of that division, the Chief Administrative Judge and the president of the New York State Bar Association.

The Task Force, which I have been honored to lead since its creation, plays a central role in implementing the actions needed to achieve the goal of the Chief Judge's initiative. The 30-member Task Force includes representatives of the judiciary, civil legal services providers, the private bar, state and local government, funders, law schools, as well as business, labor, and community leaders. The New York state legislature is also represented, as the Chairs of the Judiciary Committees of both the Assembly and the Senate are Ex Officio members of the Task Force.[15] The Chief Judge gave the Task Force a broad mission of setting the agenda and preparing for the hearings, documenting the unmet need in New York State, identifying priorities and required resources, making recommendations based on its independent research in an annual report, and advocating for expanded civil legal services as well as ways to improve the efficiency and effectiveness of the delivery of civil legal services.[16]

The creation of the Task Force was well received, with support from the other branches of government. In June 2010, the State Legislature passed a resolution commending the initiative.[17] Both houses requested that the Chief Judge report annually to the Governor and the Legislature on the findings of the hearings and the Task Force recommendations.[18]

WORK OF THE TASK FORCE

Documenting the Need

To establish the foundation of its work, the Task Force in its first year commissioned a legal needs study to obtain a valid estimate of how many New Yorkers are unable to obtain civil legal assistance. Although previous national studies established that most Americans who cannot afford counsel in civil cases are unable to get representation, it was important to have a well-documented, updated estimate of the need in New York. The study was conducted by a respected research firm; it was a telephone survey designed to target New Yorkers at or below 200% of the federal poverty level.[19] This level describes about six million New Yorkers.[20] The study, conducted in August of 2010, found that 47% of respondents (representing almost 3 million New Yorkers) reported having a civil legal problem in the past year involving critical needs such as housing, employment, healthcare, public benefits, and domestic and

[15] The Task Force to Expand Access to Civil Legal Services in New York, Report to the Chief Judge of the State of New York iii (2012)(hereinafter 2012 Report).

[16] *Id.* at 20.

[17] State of New York Legislative Resolution, Senate No. 6368, Assembly No. 1621 (July 1, 2010).

[18] The Task Force to Expand Access to Civil Legal Services in New York, Report to the Chief Judge of the State of New York 8 (2010) (hereinafter 2010 Report); State of New York Legislative Resolution, Senate No. 6368, Assembly No. 1621 (July 1, 2010).

[19] 2010 Report at 11. Lake Research Partners conducted the legal needs study.

[20] *Id.* at 27.

family law issues.[21] Many of the respondents reported not seeking legal help.[22] Based on the survey findings, an estimated 1.2 million New Yorkers had three or more civil legal problems in the preceding year.[23] Considering the 260,000 actual cases closed by New York legal services providers in 2009, the Task Force estimated that at best only about 20% of those with civil legal needs were being helped.[24]

The Task Force's other fact-finding efforts confirmed the results of the study. A review of data from the New York state court system, as well as a survey of frontline judges and civil legal services providers, indicated that most New Yorkers who cannot afford counsel go without assistance in civil cases.[25] The Task Force found that approximately 2.3 million New Yorkers appear annually in court and face the civil legal system without the assistance of counsel.[26] In many of the most common types of cases in New York, such as Family Court matters or landlord–tenant cases, the rates of unrepresented litigants are extremely high.[27]

The Task Force studies in subsequent years have confirmed the level of the need. The economic crisis continues, as federal data show increasing rates of poverty in the last several years.[28] New York civil legal services providers have reported that they are turning away the same or more potential clients.[29]

Hearing Testimony

Beyond the statistics, the Task Force has prepared the hearings presided by the Chief Judge each year in the four Appellate Divisions. The hearings have produced an important record of testimony about the impact of the lack of civil legal services throughout society. Testimony has been heard from: veterans with post-traumatic stress disorder who were wrongfully denied disability benefits;[30] victims of human trafficking;[31] seniors facing the loss of their homes after a lifetime of work;[32] cancer

[21] 2010 Report at 11. The study was based on a poll of a statistically valid sample of low-income New Yorkers. The survey asked questions about specific civil legal issues. *Id.*

[22] 2010 Report at 27.

[23] *Id.*

[24] 2010 Report at 28.

[25] 2010 Report at 12.

[26] *Id.*

[27] 2010 Report at 17. Family court statistics show that 74% of the litigants are unrepresented. In New York City, 99% of the tenants in landlord–tenant cases are unrepresented. *Id.*

[28] The Task Force to Expand Access to Civil Legal Services in New York, Report to the Chief Judge of the State of New York 15–16 (2011) (hereinafter 2011 Report). Census data indicate a significant increase in the poverty rate in the last few years. See Press Release, United States Census Bureau, Census Bureau Releases 2011 Income and Poverty Estimates for All Counties and School Districts (Dec. 12, 2012) available at www.census.gov/newsroom/releases/archives/income_wealth/cb12–242.html.

[29] 2011 Report at 17. The need has in all likelihood increased, as the reports from legal services providers predated the effects of Superstorm Sandy.

[30] 2013 Report at 22.

[31] 2010 Report at 30.

[32] *Id.*

patients who received life-sustaining medical care that had been improperly denied;[33] domestic violence survivors who received civil legal assistance to escape abuse;[34] and many victims of Hurricane Sandy who required assistance to help save their homes and obtain federal emergency benefits.[35] For these individuals, the representation they received from civil legal services providers has been life-altering, and in several cases possibly life-saving.

The hearings have also featured testimony from frontline judges who see the impact of the lack of civil legal assistance on a daily basis. Judges and court staff have to spend considerable time explaining the proceedings to unrepresented litigants, slowing down the court system and that in many cases, it is difficult for judges to get the facts or evidence that lead to fair outcomes.[36] High-profile witnesses from the business community have testified in the hearings, arguing for the importance of civil legal services. An efficient, effective civil justice system is important to the business community, and large numbers of unrepresented litigants slow down the courts.[37] In addition, officials at all levels of government testified on the impact of lack of civil legal assistance. District attorneys testified about the impact of crime resulting from a failure to resolve underlying civil legal issues such as homelessness and lack of mental health services.[38] Other witnesses described the detrimental effects throughout society. Physicians testified about the illnesses and injuries resulting from problems with housing, public benefits, domestic violence, and elder law issues that go unresolved.[39] Educators described the struggles of students who cannot keep up with their studies due to homelessness.[40] Religious leaders, including the Archbishop of New York, testified on the impact of foreclosures and unemployment on the deterioration of neighborhoods.[41]

Cost-Benefit Analysis

Beyond the benefits to vulnerable low-income New Yorkers, the Task Force decided to look at whether state funding for the provision of civil legal assistance brings additional economic benefits to New York and contributes to cost savings for the State and local governments. As a result, an important aspect of the annual reports of the Task Force has been a cost-benefit analysis. The Task Force has established that funding for civil legal assistance is a good investment, through studies showing that

33 2011 Report at 21.
34 2013 Report at 22.
35 *Id.*
36 2011 Report at 20–21.
37 *Id.* at 18, quoting testimony of Buckmaster de Wolf, General Counsel of GE Global Research.
38 2010 Report at 31.
39 *Id.* at 32.
40 *Id.* at 31.
41 2012 Report at 8.The full list of witnesses at the Task Force hearings can be found in the report appendices. See 2010 Report App. 4; 2011 Report App. 6; 2012 Report App. 5, 2013 Report App. 6.

$1 in spending for civil legal assistance results in more than $6 of positive economic return for the State, in addition to having a positive impact on the operations of the courts, on represented litigants and on businesses.[42]

Over the years, the Task Force retained independent consulting firms on a pro bono basis to analyze costs and benefits of increased civil legal assistance.[43] Using updated federal government data and drawing on additional research, the analysis showed that New York State could save $85 million in current annual costs associated with domestic violence. If the provision of civil legal services could prevent domestic violence, the State could avoid direct costs such as medical care, hospitalization, counseling, as well as indirect costs of the loss of the victim's work productivity.[44] A separate analysis revealed that at least $116 million in cost savings to State and local governments result from avoiding evictions and homelessness and keeping low-income New Yorkers in their homes rather than shelters.[45]

For the 2013 Report, the Task Force obtained an updated study to analyze the amount and impact of federal benefits obtained through civil legal assistance, a new analysis of the benefits of civil legal services for child and spousal support, and a new evaluation of the impact of advice and brief legal services.[46] The updated analysis showed that the value of federal funds brought into New York State in benefits such as Social Security, Medicaid, and Medicare rose to $457.7 million, an $80 million increase from the analysis of 2011 data.[47]

The analysis showed the benefit of obtaining child and spousal support benefits through civil legal services generated at least $5.1 million in additional benefits.[48] The analysis also considered, for the first time, the benefits of advice and brief services to low-income New Yorkers. Because New York does not currently record the results of advice and brief services, the study looked at analogous data from Pennsylvania.[49] By applying the success rates in Pennsylvania cases where advice and brief services were provided, the analysis indicated that the value of additional Supplemental Security Income, Social Security Disability, Medicaid and child and support payments in New York was $53.7 million.[50] In summary, the Task Force's

42 2012 Report at 18–19.

43 Navigant Consulting and Cornerstone conducted analysis for the 2011 report pro bono. 2011 Report at 23–25. NERA Consulting analyzed the 2012 report and provided an updated analysis for the 2013 report, provided extensive pro bono assistance, and we were also aided by lawyers from the Cheif Judge's office, the law firms of Task Force members, and the law firm of Sullivan & Cromwell LLP.

44 2011 Report at 23.

45 *Id.* at 25.

46 The Task Force to Expand Access to Civil Legal Services in New York, Report to the Chief Judge of the State of New York 22–24 (2013) (hereinafter 2013 Report).

47 *Id.* at 24.

48 *Id.* at 25.

49 *Id.*

50 *Id.* at 26.

cost/benefit analysis continues to demonstrate that funding civil legal services provides a sound return in economic benefits to New York State.[51]

TASK FORCE SUCCESSES AND RECOMMENDATIONS

Increased Funding

From the beginning of the Task Force's work, it has been clear that the most direct way to provide more civil legal services in New York is to establish a stable source of funding, specifically through the State Judiciary Budget. Since the Task Force determined that at best 20% of the need in New York is being met, to solve the problem simply through funding increases would require a five-fold increase in total funding, from about $200 million from all sources to $1 billion.[52] The Task Force realized that any requests for budget increases had to be realistic, in light of the unprecedented pressures on all state budgets in recent years, including New York's. Accordingly, the Task Force recommended a multi-year plan to increase by half the current overall $208 million funding for civil legal services. Therefore, the Task Force initially set a goal of increasing the total resources for civil legal services by half.[53]

The Task Force in its 2010 report recommended $25 million in funding for the 2011–12 budget, and that the allocation increase until it reached $100 million annually in permanent, stable civil legal services funding by the fourth year.[54] Despite the enormous projected deficits faced by the State and the request by the Governor and Legislature for a $170 million reduction in the Judiciary budget, the Chief Judge was able to allocate $12.5 million of the State Judiciary Budget to expand access to civil legal assistance pursuant to the Task Force's 2010 recommendations.[55] In addition, he addressed the drastic fall in IOLA resources, which had shrunk to $6.5 million by 2009,[56] by allocating $15 million in IOLA rescue funding.[57] In the second year, the Task Force recommended $25 million in civil legal services funding and $15 million for IOLA, which was obtained.[58] In the third year, the Task Force recommended an additional $15 million in funding for civil legal services, for a total of $55 million, $40 million for civil legal services funding and $15 million in IOLA rescue funding.[59] The Chief Judge included these amounts

[51] Analysis for the 2014 Report indicated that the total value of federal benefits to low-income New Yorkers in 2013 was $518.5 million, with a multiplier effect of $769 million of value to the State. The Task Force to Expand Access to Civil Legal Services in New York, Report to the Chief Judge of the State of New York 3 (2014) (hereinafter 2014 Report).

[52] 2010 Report at 38.

[53] *Id.* at 39.

[54] *Id.*

[55] 2011 Report at 5.

[56] 2010 Report at 34.

[57] 2011 Report at 5.

[58] 2012 Report at 5.

[59] *Id.* at 13.

in the Judiciary Budget, and the recommended amounts were obtained.[60] In its 2014 report, the Task Force recommended another increase of $15 million, reaching an unprecedented level of funding of $85 million for 2015.[61] With the appropriations obtained to date, the Task Force is well on its way toward its goal of $100 million. The increases in funding, which make New York the national leader in state funding for civil legal services, are exceptional achievements in light of the continuing pressure to reduce state spending in general.[62]

The Task Force set priorities for the use of the additional resources. It established that the funding should be used to assist New Yorkers with civil legal matters that involve the essentials of life: housing (including evictions and foreclosures and homelessness), family matters (including domestic violence), and access to healthcare, education, and subsistence income[63] (including wages, disability benefits and consumer debt).[64] The Task Force also found that the most vulnerable New Yorkers in need of civil legal aid include both those living below the federal poverty level ($24,250 for a family four) and those living below 200% of the federal poverty level ($48,500 for a family of four).[65] Therefore, priority for civil legal assistance should be given to those living in poverty as defined by the Federal Government and the "working poor" living at below 200% of that level.[66] In addition, the Task Force emphasized early intervention and expanded community education in these matters, to avoid having cases end up in court if possible.[67] It also recommended that the legal services made possible through the funding should be provided by organizations with staff that have the requisite knowledge and experience in civil legal services.[68]

The Task Force recommended the funds be allocated throughout the State in accordance with these guidelines.[69] Also, on the Task Force's recommendation, the Chief Judge established an Oversight Board consisting of the Chief Administrative Judge of the Courts, the Chair of the Task Force and the Chair or the IOLA Board to oversee the Request for Proposals and decision-making process for the allocation of these funds, with assistance from the Office of Court Administration (OCA).[70]

60 New York State Senate, Report on the Enacted State Fiscal Year 2013–2014 Executive Budget 60, available at www.nysenate.gov/files/pdfs/2013–2014%20Enacted%20Budget%20Fact%20Sheet.pdf.

61 2014 Report at 8.

62 The funding increases have made significant impact. Funding grantees handled 384,974 cases in 2013–14, a substantial increase from the 267,965 cases handled the previous year. The number of unrepresented litigants fell from 2.3 million to 1.8 million. 2014 Report at 7.

63 2010 Report at 40.

64 *Id.*

65 HHS Poverty Guidelines for 2015 at www.federalregister.gov/articles/2015/01/22/2015–01120/annual-update-of-the-hhs-poverty-guidelines.

66 2010 Report at 40.

67 *Id.*

68 *Id.* at 41.

69 *Id.*

70 2010 Report at 41. The current Oversight Board consists of Hon. A. Gail Prudenti, Chief Administrative Judge of the Courts, Helaine M. Barnett, Chair of the Task Force, and Benito Romano, Chair of the IOLA Board. 2012 Report at 5.

While the increases in funding for civil legal services are critically important, the Task Force realized that non-monetary recommendations were also important, as it would not be possible to address its goals purely through seeking increases in funding.

Pro Bono Recommendations

While attorneys in private practice in New York State are already providing a high level of pro bono legal assistance for low-income clients, the Task Force concluded that additional reporting and other initiatives will enhance the efforts. Accordingly, the Task Force made a number of recommendations on pro bono work.

The Task Force recommended that New York Rule of Professional Conduct 6.1 be amended to increase the number of aspirational pro bono hours from 20 to 50 annually.[71] The Task Force also examined the effect of mandatory reporting of pro bono hours and monetary contributions to organizations providing legal services to low-income clients. The Task Force found that the seven states that have mandatory pro bono reporting show a significant increase in pro bono as a result of that requirement.[72] It therefore recommended the biennial attorney registrations process be revised to include a requirement to report pro bono hours and monetary contributions. [73] The Administrative Board of the Courts approved both of these steps.[74] The pro bono reporting requirement was announced on May 1, 2013.[75] The state bar expressed opposition to the rule based on privacy and coercion grounds.[76] After a series of meetings with the leadership of the New York State Bar Association, the Administrative Board of the Courts approved modifications to the rule providing for

[71] 2012 Report at 32. The Task Force recommendation sets the number of aspirational pro bono hours at 50 hours. Independently from the Task Force, Chief Judge Lippman announced and implemented a new rule requiring new applicants to the New York bar to provide 50 hours of qualified pro bono service starting in January 2015. 22 NYCRR Part 520.16, available at www.nycourts.gov/attorneys/probono/Rule520_16.pdf. See Graffeo, Chapter 24 in this volume.

[72] 2012 Report at 35.

[73] *Id.* at 32. The Task Force recommended that the existing rule concerning public access to attorney registration information remain in effect. The Report states that "[t]he Task Force expects and intends that the public availability of reported pro bono hours and monetary contributions will serve to encourage greater giving and higher participation." *Id.* at 35.

[74] Chief Judge Jonathan Lippman, The State of the Judiciary 2013 at 13, available at www.nycourts.gov/ctapps/news/SOJ-2013.pdf.

[75] New York State Unified Court System, Press Release, Chief Judge Announces New Attorney Registration Pro Bono Reporting Requirement (May 1, 2013) at www.nycourts.gov/press/PDFs/PR13_06.pdf.

[76] The New York State Bar Association expressed opposition to the rule based on privacy grounds, potential coercive effect, and the lack of opportunity to comment on the proposed rule before it went into effect. New York State Bar Association Letter to Chief Judge Jonathan Lippman, June 26, 2013, available at www.nysba.org/AM/Template.cfm?Section=Home&Template=/CM/ContentDisplay.cfm&ContentID=244698. After a series of meetings, Chief Judge Lippman agreed that the data will be confidential until April of 2015. Pete Brush, Public Disclosure of Pro Bono for NY Attorneys Put on Hold, available at www.law360.com/articles/472565/public-disclosure-of-pro-bono-for-ny-attys-put-on-hold.

anonymous reporting, an expanded definition of pro bono, and publication of the data only in the aggregate.[77]

In addition, the Task Force recommended that Part 522 of the Rules of the Court of Appeals for the Registration of In House Counsel be amended to permit attorneys registered in New York as in-house counsel to provide pro bono services.[78] The Chief Judge appointed a committee to draft a new in-house counsel pro bono rule which was announced on December 2, 2013, so that such registered in-house counsel can now provide civil legal services.[79]

Greater Law School Involvement

In its 2011 report, the Task Force found that greater law school involvement could help reduce the justice gap and that New York's 15 law schools could work more closely together with each other, legal services providers, private practitioners, and the courts.[80] To encourage greater coordination between all these stakeholders, the Task Force convened a day-long event at the Benjamin N. Cardozo School of Law titled "A Conversation About the Role of Law Schools in Helping to Meet the Essential Civil Legal Needs of Low Income New Yorkers" on May 22, 2012.[81] The program brought together, for the first time, the deans and faculty of the State's 15 law schools as well as legal services providers, members of the Judiciary, Office of Court Administration, and leaders of the bar.[82] At the Conference, four work groups were formed to focus on pro bono efforts, postgraduate opportunities, clinical and other experiential learning, and curriculum development, all aimed at increasing the impact of law schools on civil legal services.[83] Six key recommendations were made as a result of the Conference. One was to convene the Conference on an annual basis.[84] This recommendation was implemented as the

77 New York State Bar Association, Message from the President: Changes to the Mandatory Pro Bono Reporting Requirement at www.nysba.org/probonorequirement/.

78 2012 Report at 35.

79 Press Release, New York State Unified Court System, New Rule Permits Thousands of Out-of-State Lawyers Employed as In-House Counsel in NY to Provide Legal Services on Behalf of New York's Needy, available at www.nycourts.gov/PRESS/2013_11_27_in_house.pdf, 22 NYCRR § 522.8. In other non-monetary recommendations, the Task Force recommended consideration should be given to revising continuing legal education requirements for newly admitted unemployed lawyers to encourage pro bono participation and that the Continuing Legal Education Board should examine the advisability of allowing newly admitted unemployed lawyers to fulfill some number of the skills, practice management and professional practice credit requirements, but not the ethics and professionalism credits, with pro bono service. 2012 Report at 36. These recommendations have not yet been implemented.

80 2011 Report at 34.

81 2012 Report at 25.

82 *Id.*

83 *Id.* at 26.

84 *Id.*

second annual Conference was convened on May 16, 2013, at the New York Law School and the third on May 12, 2014, at CUNY School of Law.[85] The fourth annual Conference was held at Fordham Law School on May 11, 2015. A second recommendation was the creation of a statewide Law School Access to Justice Council consisting of a representative from each of the 15 New York law schools.[86] This recommendation has been implemented and the initial meeting of the Council took place on May 16, 2013.[87]

The Law School Conference in 2013 focused on the best practices to implement the 50-hour pro bono rule for bar admission, postgraduate programs for graduates serving low-income communities, coordination efforts to mobilize law students and faculty following natural disasters and incorporating access to justice in the law school curriculum. The recommendations from the 2013 Conference are included in the Task Force's 2013 Task Force Report to the Chief Judge.[88]

In the 2014 Task Force Report, the Task Force recommended that the annual law school conferences continue.[89] The Task Force also recommended the development of best practices to supervise law students performing pro bono work, expanding access to justice activities in law school curricula, including access to justice concepts in the bar examination, consideration of the role of law schools in working with non-lawyer advocates, and encouraging law schools to develop pathways to promote participation in the Pro Bono Scholars Program.[90]

"Court-Navigators" Initiative

At the 2012 hearing in the First Department, there was testimony about the increased use of non-lawyers to provide certain types of legal assistance as part

[85] 2014 Report at 23.

[86] 2012 Report at 27.

[87] *Id.* at 26. The other recommendations are to support recent law school graduates who are building new practices that respond to the justice gap; provide law students with an understanding of the justice gap through changes in law school curricula; create an online system to match law students with legal services providers; and establish a uniform student practice order. *Id.* at 28–30.

[88] 2013 Report at 28–30.

[89] 2014 Report at 23.

[90] *Id.* at 23–26. The 2014 Report made three additional recommendations. First, the Task Force recommended that the Chief Judge convene a meeting of the managing partners of the major law firms in New York City to encourage adoption of a policy that partners reaching retirement age be strongly recommended to provide pro bono services to low-income clients in matters affecting the essentials of life. 2014 Report at 33. Second, the Task Force recommended that the Administrative Board of the Courts consider ways to offer additional guidance to judges on exercising judgment in the interest of the fair administration of justice, when dealing with pro se litigants. *Id.* at 34. Third, the Task Force encouraged the continued development of unified, simplified state forms. *Id.*

of the solution.[91] Non-lawyers already play an important role in many types of cases.[92] In 2012, Washington State made significant changes to its justice system, creating a scheme of Licensed Legal Technicians to formally establish a licensed, non-lawyer position in order to assist a greater number of litigants in civil courts.[93] Given these developments, the Task Force recommended the creation of an Advisory Committee on non-lawyer advocates, which Chief Judge Lippman appointed.[94] The Advisory Committee created pilot programs to allow non-lawyer advocates to provide out-of-court assistance in discrete substantive areas, such as in housing, family, consumer credit, and elder law.[95] The Advisory Committee evaluated critical issues such as scope of work and the regulatory scheme such as licensing and certification.[96] In February 2014, the Chief Administrative Judge of the Courts issued an order creating the Court Navigators program permitting qualified non-lawyers called "Navigators" to provide essential, non-legal services, without cost.[97] The pilot program provides assistance in consumer credit matters in Civil Court, Bronx County, and in the Housing Part of Civil Court, Kings County.[98] The order states that the Chief Administrator of the Courts will establish minimum qualifications, education, and training standards for Court Navigators.[99] The order also states the duties and limitations of Court Navigators, specifying the types of assistance that they can and cannot provide to unrepresented litigants in those courts.[100]

91 Professor Gillian K. Hadfield of the University of Southern California presented extensive testimony on the potential of using non-lawyer advocates. 2012 Report at 37–38.

92 The Task Force found that a variety of non-lawyer entities provide advocacy assistance to low-income New Yorkers. For example, many community-based organizations help low-income New Yorkers with housing problems and obtaining subsistence benefits. Other examples include non-lawyer courthouse-based services that provide useful information to litigants but not individualized assistance and non-lawyer organizations devoted to preventing domestic violence that help with obtaining orders of protection and safety plans. In addition, the Task Force found that non-lawyer advocates are providing assistance in administrative hearings and proceedings involving public benefits such as federal food stamps, Medicare, Medicaid, unemployment insurance, and workers' compensation. 2012 Report at 36–37.

93 Washington State Supreme Court, Admission to Practice Rule 28 (2012).

94 Roger Maldonado, an attorney in private practice and Chair of New York City Bar Association's Council on Judicial Administration and Fern Schair, Chair of the Feerick Center for Social Justice at Fordham Law School, were appointed to head the Advisory Committee. Press Release, New York State Unified Court System, Chief Judge Names Members of Committee Charged with Examining How Non-Lawyer Advocates Can Help Narrow New York's Justice Gap (May 28, 2013), available at www.nylj.com/nylawyer/adgifs/decisions/052913release.pdf; Chief Judge Jonathan Lippman, The State of the Judiciary 2013 at 13–14 (Feb. 5, 2013).

95 2012 Report at 39.

96 *Id.*

97 Administrative Order of the Chief Administrative Judge of the Courts, February 10, 2014.

98 *Id.*

99 *Id.*

100 *Id.* Navigators may accompany the unrepresented party to court appearances and may answer factual questions posed by the judge. *Id.*

Dealing with Unrepresented Litigants

The Task Force made a recommendation based on the testimony of front-line judges about how they have to walk a "fine line" in explaining the process and the law to unrepresented litigants while remaining fair to both sides.[101] The judges were concerned about a potential violation of Section 100.3 of the New York Code of Judicial Conduct, which requires judges to perform their duties impartially and diligently.[102] In response, the Task Force looked at the ABA Model Judicial Code Rule 2.2 on Impartiality and Fairness, which provides that it is not a violation of the rule for judges to "make reasonable accommodations to ensure unrepresented litigants the opportunity to have their matters fairly heard."[103] Twenty-five states have language to that effect in their rules on judicial conduct. The Task Force recommended that New York include similar language in the New York rules.[104]

The Office of Court Administration (OCA) issued a proposed amendment to Section 100.3 for public comment, to add a new provision stating that "[i]t is not a violation of this Rule for a judge to make reasonable efforts to facilitate the ability of unrepresented litigants to have their matters fairly heard."[105] Amending the rule is intended to help alleviate the concerns expressed by New York judges and allow them greater leeway in explaining procedures to the many unrepresented litigants who appear before them. The new provision, Section 100.3(b)(12), became effective on March 26, 2015.[106]

Given that there will continue to be a large number of unrepresented litigants, the Task Force also recommended improvements in other resources important to pro se litigants, such as the various websites of New York courts. The Task Force found that they were not uniform or user-friendly, and recommended changes to make them more consistent, add more logical and useful links to other resources, and to increase the amount of materials translated in languages other than English.[107] The Task Force recommendation contributed to an award-winning overhaul of the Office of Court Administration website.[108]

The Task Force has recognized that technology has the potential to increase access to justice and extend the impact of resources available for civil legal assistance. In its 2014 report, the Task Force made a number of technology recommendations, including the creation of a pilot program for online screening and intake, an initiative to seek

[101] 2011 Report at 20.
[102] New York Code of Judicial Conduct §100.3.
[103] ABA Model Judicial Code Rule 2.2
[104] Task Force Letter to Judge Lippman (May 31, 2012)(on file with author).
[105] John W. McConnell Memorandum (Jan. 24, 2013)(on file with author).
[106] New York Code of Judicial Conduct § 100.3(b)(12) at www.nycourts.gov/rules/chiefadmin/100.shtml#03.
[107] 2011 Report at 32.
[108] 2013 Report at note 21.

pro bono IT assistance from large law firms, a technology baseline for New York civil legal services providers, and the convening of a statewide technology conference.[109] The first Statewide Technology Conference was held at Columbia Law School on July 23, 2015.

In addition, the Task Force has emphasized efforts to prevent matters from reaching the courts if possible, in order to maximize the benefits from limited resources for civil legal services. The use of alternative conflict resolution would also be beneficial. The Task Force concluded that OCA could encourage alternative conflict resolution by identifying more individuals who are qualified to serve as mediators, publishing brochures explaining the benefits of alternative conflict resolution, and encouraging both parties and judges to consider it an option in cases where it is appropriate.[110] The recommendations in varying degrees are being implemented on an ongoing basis.[111]

CONCLUSION

In just a few years, New York State has become a leader in addressing the justice gap and has established a systemic approach to improving access to justice that has had significant impact. Above all is the fact that the Chief Judge has been able to create a permanent, stable, civil legal services funding stream within the State Judiciary Budget in a time of unprecedented cuts in state budgets nationwide. The millions in additional funding since the launch of the effort has translated into thousands of additional cases handled, affecting tens of thousands of needy New Yorkers in life-altering or life-saving ways.[112] The Task Force has built a factual record on the size of the unmet need for civil legal services, the impact on the lives of New Yorkers as well as its economy, The Task Force has established that funding for civil legal assistance is a good investment, through studies showing that $1 in spending for civil legal

[109] 2014 Report at 27.

[110] 2013 Report at 36. OCA would encourage alternative conflict resolution only in appropriate cases, and not, for example, in cases involving domestic violence. In the 2013 Report, the Task Force recommended that the New York State Unified Court System consider developing an online dispute resolution platform that could be used by unrepresented parties in appropriate types of cases, again not in domestic violence cases or other cases where the power imbalance between the parties is inextricably tied to the legal system. *Id.* 36.

[111] Several recommendations from the 2012 Task Force report have been implemented, such as the creation of new, simplified uniform state forms such as a landlord–tenant non-payment answer form, a consumer debt answer form, a foreclosure preliminary conference order form, and a child support modification form, as well as training for Town and Village Court Justices and Clerks. 2013 Report at 8–9. Another area of ongoing work by the Task Force is in the area of technology. In the 2013 Report, the Task Force recommended that providers use the range of free resources available to increase access, that providers address pressing needs for enhancements in technology systems, and that providers take advantage of pro bono technology assistance from law firms. 2013 Report at 32.

[112] *Id.* at 7.

assistance results in more than $6 of positive economic return for the state besides having a positive impact on the operations of the courts, on represented litigants, and on businesses. And as of June 2015, the Task Force became the Permanent Commission on Access to Justice. The Task Force has brought together every important group in the legal profession and beyond, from the bar, the judiciary, legal services providers, law schools, government officials, funders, business, labor, and community leaders to make them all participants in addressing the problem of lack of equal access to justice.

24

New York's 50-Hour Pro Bono Requirement

Hon. Victoria A. Graffeo

Engaging law students in pro bono work before graduation can instill in them a professional ethic of volunteer work that they carry throughout their careers. Victoria Graffeo, former New York State Court of Appeals judge, describes New York's mandatory 50-hour pro bono rule, the first of its kind, which requires all applicants to the New York bar who sit for the bar examination to complete 50 hours of qualifying pro bono work. Because the rule does not set any income requirements for pro bono clients, it has the potential to help middle-class as well as poor Americans meet their legal needs.

On Law Day in 2012, Chief Judge Lippman announced several new initiatives directed at easing the crisis in civil legal services.[1] One proposal – the first of its kind in the nation – was directed at law students. Judge Lippman explained:

> If pro bono is a core value of our profession, and it is – and if we aspire for all practicing attorneys to devote a meaningful portion of their time to public service, and they should – these ideals ought to be instilled from the start, when one first aspires to be a member of the profession. The hands-on experience of helping others by using our skills as lawyers could not be more of a pre-requisite to meaningful membership in the bar of our state.[2]

Chief Judge Lippman recognized that the pool of law students preparing for the legal profession represented a valuable and untapped resource. To be admitted to the New York bar, applicants will be required to perform 50 hours of pro bono work.[3] This chapter describes the evolution of the 50-hour pro bono requirement and how it will be administered in the hope that it can serve as a model for other states addressing similar gaps in access to civil justice.[4]

1 Chief Judge Jonathan Lippman, Law Day Remarks 2–4 (May 1, 2012), available at www.nycourts.gov/whatsnew/Transcript-of-LawDay-Speech-May1–2012.pdf.

2 *Id.* at 3–4.

3 Rules of the New York Court of Appeals 520.16.

4 A similar pro bono requirement for prospective attorneys is currently under consideration in California, Montana, and New Jersey (see www.americanbar.org/groups/probono.html; Daniel Wiessner, "NJ court officials consider pro bono rule for aspiring lawyers," Thomson Reuters News & Insight (Oct. 22, 2012), available at http://newsandinsight.thomsonreuters.com/Legal/News/2012/10_-_October/NJ_court_officials_consider_pro_bono_rule_for_aspiring_ lawyers/).

SETTING UP AN ADVISORY COMMITTEE[5]

Chief Judge Lippman appointed 15 members representative of the profession to serve on the Advisory Committee and develop the 50-hour requirement.[6] Members included law school faculty, current and former state and federal judges, legal services providers, current and former bar leaders, and practitioners from law firms with well-established pro bono programs. I co-chaired the committee with Alan Levine, former chair of the Board for New York's Legal Aid Society.

The Advisory Committee worked under a tight 5-month deadline to gather relevant data about bar admissions and other factors, such as existing law school pro bono programs. The committee also solicited comments about the new requirement from a range of constituent groups and responded to their feedback. The committee's ultimate goal was to make recommendations for what would qualify as pro bono work and how the hours would be documented.

NEW YORK BAR ADMISSION

The 50-hour pro bono requirement would impact the diverse pool of applicants who seek admission to the New York bar. In 2012, the New York State Board of Law Examiners processed 17,692 applications to take the New York bar exam and 15,745 candidates sat for the examination.[7] This pool of test-takers consisted of graduates from the 15 New York law schools, candidates from other states, and over 4,000 candidates from more than 100 countries. A serious consideration for the Advisory Committee was how to develop a rule that accounted for the fact that more than half of the candidates sitting for the bar examination will have obtained their legal educations outside of New York State.

Any change to the bar admission rules would impact the work of either the State Board of Law Examiners or the Character and Fitness Committees, which are the two groups responsible for bar admission. The State Board of Law Examiners, comprised of five practicing attorneys appointed by the New York Court of Appeals,[8] reviews the credentials of bar examination applicants, develops and grades

[5] Report to the Chief Judge of the State of New York and the Presiding Justices of the Four Appellate Division Departments, Advisory Committee on New York State Pro Bono Bar Admission Requirements (Sept. 2012), available at www.nycourts.gov/attorneys/probono/ProBonoBarAdmissionReport.pdf.

[6] A list of the members of the Advisory Committee on New York State Pro Bono Bar Admission Requirements can be found at

[7] Report to the Chief Judge, supra note 5 at 4–5. Although over 17,000 applications were received in 2012, not all applicants were found eligible and some applicants failed to appear on the test dates.

[8] The names of the chairperson and members of the New York State Board of Law Examiners can be found on the New York State Board of Law Examiners' website: www.nybarexam.org/AboutUS/AboutUs.htm.

the New York portion of the Bar Exam, and administers the two-day examination in February and July.[9] In addition, the Board recommends the adoption of rules governing admission credentials, determines appeals from administrative denials of requested accommodations in testing, conducts hearings on misconduct charges, and participates in national discussions of bar admission issues.[10]

Unlike most other states, the Board does not have responsibility for reviewing matters pertaining to the character and fitness of applicants applying for admission to practice law.[11] In New York, such issues are determined by Character and Fitness Committees appointed by each of the four intermediate appellate courts, the Appellate Divisions of the New York Supreme Court.

Given New York's large and diverse volume of applicants, a successful pro bono admissions model in New York would hopefully be replicable by other states.

LAW SCHOOLS AS COLLABORATORS

Law schools will play a tremendous part in the implementation of the 50-hour rule. The Advisory Committee solicited comments from the 200-plus American Bar Association-approved law schools in the United States, including the 15 New York Law Schools. Two of the New York law schools had a mandatory pro bono requirement for graduation,[12] and the others encouraged student participation in pro bono activities, some through special recognition or monetary awards.

New York law school deans, who were generally supportive of the proposal, met with the committee to air their concerns. They unanimously requested that clinical courses be deemed eligible, regardless of whether academic credit was earned, since these educational settings provide intensive training and supervision, and students have found their clinical placements to be beneficial and meaningful educational experiences. But all of the deans stressed that the number of available clinical slots would be insufficient to meet the anticipated demand for pro bono projects under the proposed requirement and the high cost associated with the low student-to-instructor ratio in clinical instruction would make it difficult to expand clinical offerings. The deans also requested that the pro bono requirement not apply to 2012 graduates so that law schools could (1) implement administrative and budgetary adjustments to carry out the pro bono initiative, and (2) make appropriate

9 New York Judiciary Law § 463; New York Court Rules § 6000.6(a).

10 Candidate eligibility for the New York bar examination is governed by Part 520 of the Rules of the Court of Appeals for the Admission of Attorneys and Counselors at Law (see 22 NYCRR 520.3–520.6).

11 National Conference of Bar Examiners and American Bar Association Section of Legal Education and Admissions to the Bar, Comprehensive Guide to Bar Admission Requirements 4 (2013), available at www.ncbex.org/assets/media_files/Comp-Guide/CompGuide.pdf.

12 Columbia Law School (www.law.columbia.edu/center_program/public_interest/pro_bono) and the Touro College Jacob D. Fuchsberg Law Center (www.tourolaw.edu/PublicServiceInitiatives/?pageid=51).

arrangements with legal services providers, bar associations, and law firms in their regions to ensure the availability of adequate pro bono options for students.

CRITICAL INPUT FROM LEGAL SERVICES AND BAR ASSOCIATIONS

Legal services providers throughout the state offered feedback to the committee. These organizations explained the problems encountered in the delivery system for legal services to the poor and discussed the various ways in which law students can help. Although enthusiastic to receive this help, they made clear that they did not have the staff or resources to track the hours students would spend on their assignments, nor did they want to be responsible for maintaining records related to compliance with the 50-hour rule.

Bar association leadership participated in roundtable discussions and submitted written comments about the rule. Given the national implications of a pro bono admission rule, the Pro Bono Institute in Washington, DC, and the Association of Pro Bono Counsel offered critical advice in defining what types of pro bono work would qualify under the proposal.

THE DEFINITION OF QUALIFYING PRO BONO WORK

Chief Judge Lippman's primary objective of the pro bono requirement is to dedicate more resources to the needs of the poor and low-income New Yorkers who are unable to afford legal representation. Another aim, however, is to expose law students and bar applicants to the wide range of problems confronting the poor, who have difficulty navigating the justice system, and to convey that practicing law comes with a responsibility to serve others. If aspiring lawyers experience the intangible personal satisfaction from pro bono work, future generations of attorneys should be more inclined to volunteer for pro bono assignments, thereby increasing the resources available for civil legal representation.

After receiving feedback from the constituencies that would be most affected by the new requirement, the committee summarized its findings and made recommendations to the Chief Judge about how to define the 50-hour pro bono rule in light of these objectives. Key recommendations include the following.

Law-Related Work in the Public Interest

The Advisory Committee identified two pillars of the definition of qualifying pro bono projects. First, the work must be law-related, that is, the work must involve the use of legal skills or involve law-related activities that are appropriate for performance by law students and other bar applicants. General charitable projects, however worthwhile and encouraged by law schools, will not qualify. Examples of qualifying activities include helping a person complete legal forms, assisting a litigant prepare for a court appearance, engaging in legal research and preparing memoranda of law, participating in a community legal education project, or drafting basic legal documents. There are no specific income or asset eligibility requirements set forth in the rule for defining what constitutes a pro bono client – the providers of legal services or law school clinics establish any income restrictions. Since the goal of the pro bono requirement is to enhance resources available to persons who would otherwise not have access to or afford legal representation, students are to be encouraged to work on assignments in furtherance of the objectives of the pro bono rule or that involve the provision of government services.

Mandatory Attorney-Supervision

The second mandatory feature of qualifying pro bono work is that the work must be supervised by an attorney admitted to practice and in good standing in the jurisdiction where the work is performed; or by a law school faculty member, an adjunct professor, or instructor; or, in the case of a judicial clerkship or an internship with a court, by a judge or an attorney employed by the court system. This requirement assures that law students and lawyers aspiring to join the New York bar receive adequate training, guidance, and evaluation and that the people they serve receive appropriate legal advice or service. It also protects against the risk that participants will unwittingly engage in the unauthorized practice of law, a criminal offense in New York.[13]

Pro Bono Project for Academic Credit and Paid Work Qualify

The Advisory Committee engaged in extensive deliberations on whether academic credit received for student participation in a law school clinic would qualify as pro bono work. This was a controversial topic. Under the traditional definition, pro bono, derived from the term "pro bono publico," was legal work for the underserved undertaken for the public good without charge.[14] Yet, the committee had to weigh the expected demand for pro bono assignments by thousands of law students each year against the availability of pro bono options suitable for law students, especially during the early years of the initiative.

The law school deans contended that law school clinical courses, whose missions comply with pro bono objectives, certainly offer students training, supervision, and profession-ready experiences consistent with the aspirations of the 50-hour rule. To exclude these clinical courses from pro bono eligibility because the students received academic credit could have struck a serious blow to the popularity of clinical programs – a result contrary to the organized bar's call for greater emphasis

[13] The unauthorized practice of law in New York is a crime under New York Judiciary Law sections 485 and 485-a. See generally Levine, Chapter 41 in this volume.

[14] Bryan A. Garner, *A Dictionary of Modern Legal Usage*, 711–13 (3rd ed., 2011).

on practical skills training in legal education.[15] The Advisory Committee concluded that clinical legal education serves a valuable purpose, not just in terms of skills training, but because students are exposed to the needs of clients who receive legal assistance without charge. Clinical experiences will count as qualifying work only if the services provided are of a pro bono nature and, preferably, to a low-income or indigent client. The hours that a student devotes to working on a pro bono project in a properly supervised law school clinic qualifies under the 50-hour rule, provided that the hours spent on instructional training do not exceed the time attributable to the actual pro bono work. Since only law-related work qualifies, travel time, clerical work, or organizational tasks do not count toward the 50-hour requirement.

The committee also had to decide whether pro bono work done while the student received a salary paid by a legal employer or a stipend from a law school could be eligible for fulfilling the pro bono requirement. The law schools pointed out that some students receive stipends from their schools to assist with living expenses during summer internships, particularly summer positions with legal services organizations, public interest groups, or government offices. Other students may be paid a salary by law firms for employment during the summer or academic year for work on pro bono projects. Again, the receipt of such compensation would ordinarily exclude these activities from the realm of pro bono service. But the value of student experiences while working on pro bono client matters and the need to create sufficient and varied options for law students led the Advisory Committee to conclude that work on a firm's or organization's pro bono cases should qualify, provided that the clients do not pay a fee for the services.

Similarly, it was decided that law school graduates who obtain salaried legal employment prior to bar admission may count the hours spent on a firm's qualifying pro bono cases, provided that no special compensation or bonus is received in recognition of the pro bono work. This allowance was necessary to accommodate the large number of persons who receive their legal educations outside of New York or the United States. Such candidates may not be aware of the 50-hour pro bono requirement during the course of their legal education, or they may decide to wait until they receive their bar examination results before undertaking compliance with the 50-hour rule. In these scenarios, work will qualify under the rule only if the clients receiving legal services are not charged a fee.

DEFERRED COMPLIANCE REJECTED

The Advisory Committee rejected a recommendation that applicants be allowed to defer compliance with the pro bono requirement until after bar admission, delaying pro bono work to the first or second year of practice. Given that many individuals

[15] New York State Bar Association, Report of the Task Force on the Future of the Legal Profession 38–50 (Apr. 2, 2011), available at www.nysba.org/AM/Template.cfm?Section=Task_Force_on_the_Future_of_the_Legal_Profession_Home&Template=/CM/ContentDisplay.cfm&ContentID=48108.

admitted to the New York bar, particularly applicants from other states or foreign countries, may not intend to practice in New York, a deferral option would be difficult to enforce in an equitable manner. It might be possible to track the compliance of newly admitted attorneys who remain in New York, but those who return to their home states or countries after securing a New York license would have a greater ability to avoid fulfilling the pro bono requirement without incurring any consequence.

Even for New York lawyers, enforcement of a deferral option raised difficult questions, such as whether noncompliance should be a subject of attorney discipline and, if so, the appropriate penalty. This could result in the imposition of significant administrative burdens on the Appellate Divisions, the entities that oversee attorney discipline. Moreover, implementing a pro bono requirement by threat of disciplinary action against fledgling attorneys hardly seemed consistent with the goals underlying the initiative. The Advisory Committee therefore proposed a bright-line rule requiring completion of the pro bono requirement by all applicants as a condition to bar admission.

DOCUMENTING PRO BONO HOURS

Applicants for admission – not their pro bono supervisors – are responsible for maintaining records that document the hours spent on qualifying pro bono work. The Advisory Committee recommended that applicants document their pro bono hours in Affidavits of Compliance for each law firm, agency, or clinic, and then file these affidavits with their bar admission packet. This process mirrors the other materials, like verification of employment, that applicants are required to provide during the bar admission process. The applicant is responsible for specifying when and where the pro bono work was performed and attesting to the truth of the information provided. The applicant's supervisor is also responsible for certifying the pro bono hours. The Advisory Committee drafted the pro bono affidavit and recommended that it be available electronically.[16]

THE FUTURE OF THE PRO BONO REQUIREMENT

To begin implementation of the 50-hour requirement, the Advisory Committee developed several resources including a weblink with frequently asked questions, and a telephone line and an email address for inquiries.[17] The committee will

[16] The Affidavit of Compliance can be found at www.nycourts.gov/attorneys/probono/AppforAdmission_Pro-BonoReq_Fillable.pdf.

[17] www.nycourts.gov/attorneys/probono/baradmissionreqs.shtml. The telephone number, 1–855–227–5482, and e-mail address, ProBonoRule@nycourts.gov, are available for inquiries not addressed by the other materials.

continue to address issues that arise as bar applicants, law schools, law firms, and other groups create pro bono work that satisfies the new rule.

Although the 50-hour pro bono requirement is in its early stages, it has gained national attention as an innovative way of tackling the demand for legal representation that, to date, has outstripped the availability of voluntary pro bono assistance from the practicing bar. Despite the fact that New York's bar has a long and honorable tradition of pro bono service,[18] more needs to be done. There is no better time than during the course of legal education to instill core values of the legal profession – the need for ethical conduct, service to others, and equal justice under the law.

[18] Henry M. Greenberg Looking Back on Pro Bono Service, presentation at the Historical Society of the New York Courts Program on Pro Bono: New York Lawyers and Public Service – Looking Back and Looking Forward (Feb. 19, 2013). Webcast available at www.courts.state.ny.us/history/programs-events/society-events-past.html.

25

Starting a "Low Bono" Law Practice

Luz Herrera

Given that Americans of average means cannot afford the average hourly rate that most attorneys charge, Luz Herrera discusses how lawyers can realistically offer "low bono" fee arrangements, charging clients of limited means significantly lower hourly rates. She discusses how law schools, bar associations, legal aid organizations, and courts can help promote low bono models.

In order to address the unmet legal needs of individuals in our country, the legal profession must advance an affordable legal services agenda that includes lawyers who provide competent legal services at reduced or "low bono" rates. Low bono fee arrangements are a system of billing that takes into account the financial constraints and the legal needs of average-means Americans. In a low bono fee arrangement, a lawyer agrees to charge her client a lower rate for her services.

UNDERSTANDING LOW BONO

Although the term "low bono" may be new, the practice of offering reduced legal fees is not. The concept of low bono is memorialized in ABA Model Rule of Professional Conduct 6.1(b)(2). This particular subsection states that in addition to aspiring to provide 50 hours of free legal services each year, lawyers should also "provide any additional services through . . . delivery of legal services at a substantially reduced fee to persons of limited means."[1] Comment 7 of ABA Model Rule 6.1 explains that lawyers who offer "a modest fee for furnishing legal services to persons of limited means" comply with the rule despite the stated preference for pro bono services.[2] Today, most states recognize reduced fees, or low bono, as an alternative expression of a lawyer's public service commitment.

[1] ABA Model Rule ("MR") 6.1(b)(2) (2002).

[2] For more on the preference of pro bono in ABA MR 6.1 and recommendations for changes, see Leslie C. Levin, *Pro Bono and Low Bono in the Solo and Small Firm*, in PRIVATE LAWYERS & THE PUBLIC INTEREST 155–79 (Robert Granfield & Lynn Mather ed., 2009).

The practice of lawyers offering "low bono" rates is not fully embraced by all who support offering more affordable legal services. Some object to describing the practice of reduced rates as low bono because the word "low" communicates an inferior priority that can discredit the practice. Others caution that the problem with low bono is that the economic benefit is on the backs of the lawyers who are usually not always in the strongest economic position to subsidize legal fees. Those who understand the plight of solo and small firm lawyers, therefore focus on advancing an agenda for affordable legal services primarily through limited scope representation at market hourly rates.

Many attorneys unbundle their services and offer them at low bono rates, but the practice of limiting the scope of representation is not synonymous to low bono. While the practices of low bono and unbundling are great tools in making lawyers more accessible to modest-means clients, limiting the scope of representation does not necessarily reduce a lawyer's hourly rate. However, lawyers who offer low bono rates often do so by unbundling their services and offering flat fee options for average-income Americans.

THE ECONOMIC CHALLENGE

Starting and maintaining a low bono law practice can be personally rewarding but it also poses a number of financial challenges for a lawyer. Starting a low bono law practice requires that an attorney identify a market niche for her services. Low bono practices must be informed by the needs of the community but defined by the personal attributes of the lawyer.

To properly articulate the financial portion of a business plan for a low bono law practice, a lawyer first needs to understand what he needs to earn to cover his living expenses. Table 25.1 offers examples of conservative but realistic budgets of approximately $3,200 per month or $38,400 per year for

TABLE 25.1 *Estimated personal expenses.*

	Lawyer only	Lawyer + 1 dependent
Housing	$1,500	$2,000
Automobile	$300	$300
Auto. insurance	$250	$250
Health insurance	$250	$500
Food	$400	$600
Utilities	$100	$150
Cell phone	$100	$100
Entertainment	$300	$300
Miscellaneous	$300	$300
TOTAL	$3,500	$4,500

a single attorney and $4,200 per month or $50,400 annually for a lawyer with two dependents.[3]

The specific needs and priorities of each lawyer will require an adjustment to these figures. This table does not take into account student or consumer debt; nor does it account for any savings. The basic idea is that lawyers need to quantify how much they need to earn to meet monthly expenses.

A business plan also requires a clear articulation of the cost of doing business. Today's lawyers can build viable practices by leveraging technology to reduce the cost of providing quality legal services. While a physical space to meet clients is important for establishing a presence in a community, most client communications are now done telephonically or through cloud-based case management programs. A growing number of attorneys now operate virtual law practices from their homes. The internet has revolutionized law practice so much that legal research, client billing and even court filing can all be done from an attorney's laptop.[4]

Aside from a stable office location, a good computer, a scanner, and a printer, attorneys starting low bono law practices need malpractice insurance, mentors, and access to legal research platforms. In exchange for an annual fee, most bar associations offer its members group discounts on law office management tools, malpractice insurance, marketing programs, continuing legal education, and networking events. Law school alumni associations and postgraduate programs can play a significant role in helping new attorneys forge relationships with good mentors. In addition, law schools and law libraries are usually available to members of the bar for free or for a nominal fee. A realistic law practice budget in Table 25.2 illustrates basic line items adding up to expenses of $1,875 per month, i.e., $22,500 per year:

TABLE 25.2 *Basic law office start-up expenses.*

Expense	Monthly cost	Annual cost
Office space	$500	$6,000
Malpractice insurance	$300	$3,600
Marketing/client development	$250	$3,000
Subscriptions & dues	$200	$2,400
Healthcare	$200	$2,400
Phone, internet, utilities	$200	$2,400
Office supplies	$150	$1,800
Case management software	$ 75	$ 900
	$1,875	$22,500

3 These estimated expenses exceed current Internal Revenue Service Collection Financial National Standards and anticipate living expenses in San Diego, California, which is in the top ten most expensive cities in the country.

4 Lawyers starting their law practices today need to establish secure servers and internet connections to maintain client confidentiality.

These expenses are approximate and will change based on the location of the low bono law practice. The estimate for office space is based on shared office suite arrangements or renting an empty office space in an existing law firm with extra space. The cost of malpractice insurance varies depending on the substantive area of practice and the number of years the attorney has been practicing. In California, a new lawyer can obtain malpractice insurance that includes unlimited hours of continuing legal education training for about $500.[5]

This budget does not account for the initial start-up funds needed to invest in professional attire, furniture, and equipment (computer, printer, and scanner). Lawyers starting their law practices can find reasonably maintained office furnishings and equipment with a budget of $2,000–$3,500. Many shared office arrangements already come with furnishing and access to copy machines. Many lawyers set up eFax accounts and internet-based phone systems that are less expensive than traditional phone lines. Online case management tools that facilitate client billing, record keeping, and client communication are also available for about $ 50–$75 per month. New technology is allowing lawyers to keep their costs down but they must ensure that their communications mechanisms are arranged in a way that does not run afoul of the professional obligation to keep client confidences. For guidance on how to incorporate technology into law practices, attorneys must consult their state bar associations for an articulation of the best ethical approaches.

Understanding how to price legal services for a targeted group of legal services consumers is key to developing the low bono practice. In the examples offered here, the lawyer has a monthly budget of $3,500 for living expenses and a $1,875 for business expenses. Based on these budgets, let us assume a total budget for monthly expenses of $5,000 for an attorney with no dependents.

Assuming the going rate for legal services in a particular market is $300, a low bono rate would range between $75 and $180. Lawyers who work in law offices with little or no administrative support should expect to spend 40–50% of their time on administrative tasks related to managing their caseload and their business. If a lawyer wanted to only work 40 hours per week, he would at most bill 20 hours per week. Assuming the attorney works and collects payment for each of those 20 hours, a sample income based on a low bono hourly rate would be as shown in Table 25.3.

These gross figures may sound great to lawyers with starting salaries of $45,000–$65,000 or who are doing contract work at rates of $50–$75. However, after deducting taxes, the costs of doing business, and personal expenses, lawyers' rates cannot go too low before they begin to affect the viability of the practice.

[5] Lawyer Mutual Insurance Company, Strong Start Program, www.lmic.com/policies_offered/strong_start_program (describing a new type of malpractice insurance for lawyers going into solo practice who have been licensed for three years or less at an affordable rate of $500 for the first year premium).

TABLE 25.3 *Low bono rate income projections.*

	Weekly	Monthly	Annual
$50 20 hours	$1,000	$ 4,000	$ 48,000
$75 20 hours	$1,500	$ 6,000	$ 75,000
$100 20 hours	$2,000	$ 8,000	$100,000
$125 20 hours	$2,500	$10,000	$125,000
$150 20 hours	$3,000	$12,000	$150,000

TABLE 25.4 *Cost of maintaining a low bono law firm.*

	Lawyer only		Lawyer + one dependent	
Gross income	$75,000	$100,000	$125,000	$150,000
Taxes (@35%)	–$26,250	–$35,000	–$43,750	$52,500
Personal expenses	–$42,00	–$42,00	–$54,00	–$54,00
Business expenses	–$22,500	–$22,500	–$22,500	–$22,500
Disposable income	–$16,150	$ 100	$4,350	$20,600

There are three areas that will impact the low bono rate an attorney can offer: tax liability, educational debt, and consumer debt. For the purpose of illustration, after deducting business expenses, the tax liability for a self-employed lawyer is estimated at about 35%.[6] Based on 20 billable hours per week on a 50-week year, Table 25.4 presents examples of what it would cost to maintain a low bono law firm.

The rough net figures given in Table 25.4 reveal that after considering tax liability and personal and business expenses, lawyers have little or no disposable income. Table 25.4 reveals that it is difficult for a lawyer to only offer rates of $75 and bill only 20 hours. An attorney with a client base that can only pay $75 an hour will have to bill more hours, reduce living or business expenses, or offer low bono services at a higher rate. Lawyers who have significant student or consumer debt will have to determine if there is a loan repayment plan that works.[7] For lawyers who are not able to cover their debt burden with disposable income, building a low bono law practice may be difficult, if not impossible.

Offering reduced rates requires lawyers to set forth a business plan for their law practices. A business plan helps define the law firm's mission, client base, and

6 Tax liability for a self-employed lawyer will depend on the amount of business expenses, personal exemptions, and other considerations, which requires that each attorney consult a tax professional.

7 The specifics of loan repayment programs are beyond the scope of this chapter. However, it is important to note that some income contingent repayment programs still require loan payments based on gross income, which may not necessarily account for expenses associated with self-employment.

marketing strategies as well as financial projections. Fees for low bono services may be collected through the traditional hourly rate model, as flat fees for unbundled services, or delivered through other flexible fee structures such as extended payment plans. Business plans for low bono law firms may also offer a mix of low bono and market rates.

DEVELOPING THE LOW BONO FRAMEWORK

As a profession, we are well aware of the economic reality of most legal services consumers but we have failed to develop the proper infrastructure to encourage lawyers to build affordable and sustainable legal services models. Encouraging the development of a low bono framework requires a paradigm shift that reimagines what law schools, bar associations, courts, and even legal services organizations, can do to encourage the development of low bono law practices. Such a framework requires that we place the needs of average legal services consumers at the center of our legal service delivery system but also acknowleges the economic needs of Main Street lawyers.

Legal and Business Education

Law schools are the most instrumental in forming new lawyers' preferences. Law schools can do more to promote low bono services by providing greater career counseling in this area, integrating more law practice management courses that incorporate delivery of legal services discussions, and developing postgraduate programs, including attorney incubators that encourage low bono rates.

If a law school has a significant number of its graduates in solo and small firm practice, it should have personnel available to help students and alumni think through the practical and financial considerations of providing low bono services. Law schools should communicate that starting their own offices is a common experience for many lawyers. Solo and small firm lawyers constitute the largest segment of lawyers in our country. In fact, almost two-thirds of private practitioners work in law offices of five attorneys or less, with 49% as solo practitioners.[8]

These attorney are more likely to offer personal legal services than lawyers who work for government or large corporate law firms. The American Bar Association (ABA) does not require law schools to offer courses on the business of law or on the

[8] Seventy-five percent of all lawyers work in private practice. Of those, 49% have been identified as solo practitioners and another 16% as working in offices of 2–5 lawyers. In contrast, only 1% of lawyers work in public defender or legal aid offices, 1% work private associations, 8% work as government lawyers, and 20% work in law firms of more than 50 lawyers. See Lawyer Demographics, ABA Market Research Dep't (2015).

delivery of legal services as part of a lawyer's training. However, instruction on how lawyers can make a living by serving a large underserved market can help dispel the notion that lawyers are only for the elite.

Most law students do not see themselves as entrepreneurs or anticipate becoming small business owners. When they become lawyers, they generally lack a roadmap on how to use their professional training to generate their own salaries. Law office management, access to legal services, and the business of law should be integrated into the law school curriculum. These courses help students understand how legal services are delivered and the cost of providing such services. It opens their eyes to a greater range of available roles for them in the profession. Such curriculum can be easily integrated into courses on professional responsibility and clinical education but may also have a role in other parts of the curriculum, particularly as a small component of lawyering skills courses. Classes that delve into the business of law inevitably lead to a discussion on who can pay for lawyers at market rates. These discussions can help students think more strategically about building networks, identifying a client base, and fulfilling their professional obligation to ensuring access to law for low- and average-income Americans. In addition to helping law students think about creating viable business plans, law schools can offer post-graduate programs to support new lawyers who launch their law practices and incentivize the offering of low bono rates.

Networking and Referral Services

For decades, law school alumni offices have offered continuing legal education programming and organized alumni networking events for their graduates. The first effort to support solo and small firm lawyers to provide low bono rates was launched in 1997 as the Law School Consortium Project (LSCP), formed by several law schools through a grant from the Open Society Institute. The most enduring projects to result from the LSCP program were Civil Justice, Inc. at University of Maryland Francis King Carey School of Law (Maryland School of Law) and the Community Legal Resource Network at City University of New York (CUNY) School of Law.[9]

Civil Justice, Inc. at Maryland, for example, is an independent nonprofit entity that operates a referral service for a network of solo and small firm lawyers who offer reduced-rate legal services. Civil Justice, Inc. has staff that facilitate mentoring and networking opportunities that include informal counseling by law school faculty and co-counseling arrangements with more experienced attorneys. It also offers its

9 See Gomez-Velez, Chapter 48 in this volume, which discusses the Community Legal Resources Network.

attorney members assistance in managing their law practices to help them comply with ethical obligations.

Postgraduate Residency and Incubator Programs

A number of law schools have started postgraduate programs to train new lawyers and provide more affordable legal services. Most of the postgraduate programs are attorney incubator programs that follow a similar model to CUNY's Incubator for Justice.[10] The attorney incubator models are borrowed from the business community's practice of providing support services for new businesses to increase the likelihood of success through startup support, including office space, law practice management training, and in-house mentoring.[11]

In exchange for supporting the training on the tools needed to becoming self-sustaining, incubator programs require that their participants offer free and reduced-fee legal services to the underserved population.

These programs make setting up a law office less daunting for lawyers without much experience in running their own businesses. At the same time, they help address the growing need for affordable legal services. A lawyer who is building a client base understands that a handful of clients at $100 an hour is better than no clients at $300. Getting paid a contract hourly wage of $ 25–$50 is helpful for new lawyers to get experience but many soon realize they can keep more money in their pockets by taking on their own clients at $75–$150 an hour. Low bono practices encourage lawyers to be mindful of a community's legal needs.

In addition to the solo and small firm incubators, Pace University School of Law, Arizona State University Sandra Day O'Connor College of Law, and Georgetown University Law Center created postgraduate residencies for graduates in low bono law firms. The difference between postgraduate residency programs and the attorney incubators is that residency programs pay their recent graduate "residents" a stipend or salary for engaging in low bono work. Residency programs have experienced attorneys supervise the work of residents and focus more on substantive training than client development. As a result, residency programs are more costly than incubators.

These postgraduate programs are relatively new and little data are available on their effectiveness. However, according to the ABA Standing Committee on

[10] See Gomez-Velez, Chapter 48 in this volume, which discusses CUNY's Incubator for Justice. The Incubator for Justice is no longer operating. In its place, CUNY is launching CUNY Law Works – a program that offers graduates shared space to operate law offices. Telephone interview with Liz Newman, Director of the Community Legal Resource Network at CUNY, Nov. 16, 2015.

[11] For more information on business incubators, see the National Business Incubator Association at www.nbia.org.

the Delivery of Legal Services, there are now approximately fifty of these post graduate programs. Most of them offer graduates the opportunities to pilot law firm models focused on developing sustainability through low bono practices.

Bar Association Support

Some bar associations promote low bono rates by offering modest means panels through their lawyer referral and information services. Individuals seeking assistance from modest means panels must usually demonstrate proof of income before the bar association's administrative team refers the matter to an attorney on the panel. These programs have established income guidelines that go up to 300% of the federal poverty guidelines. They educate legal services consumers about the limited scope representation that a lawyer provides for reduced rates, and make it easier for the lawyer to engage in this work by limiting the subject matter of the modest means panel. Attorneys are vetted to participate on the panel and must carry malpractice insurance. The requirements for attorneys to participate in these panels vary, but all require a level of minimum competency that is achieved through experience, training, or mentoring by more experienced lawyers.

A 2008 Survey of Modest Means Panels by the ABA LRIS Committee revealed that modest means panels' rates range from $40 to $125 per hour.[12] Some require clients to deposit retainer fees that can be as high as $1,000. While these modest means panels facilitate the provision of low bono work, many programs do not have enough attorneys who participate to address the need. Recruiting for modest means is easier when these programs offer lawyers training, mentors, and other resources to facilitate a reduced fee.

State bar-led access to justice entities are also engaged in promoting greater options for average-income Americans by encouraging lower-rate legal fees. The Colorado Access to Justice Commission developed a Modest Means Task Force in 2012. After months of research across the United States, the task force released a report that recommends that its bar association employ the following tools to encourage more attorneys to take on modest-means clients:

- offer a tool kit that helps lawyers establish modest-means practices;
- distribute business planning software to help lawyers determine how to bill and set up viable law firms serving modest-income clients;
- develop a mentoring program for lawyers who represent modest-means clients;

[12] American Bar Ass'n Standing Committee on Lawyer Referral and Information Service (LRIS), 2008 Modest Means Survey, at www.americanbar.org/content/dam/aba/migrated/legalservices/lris/clearinghouse/downloads/2008_modest_means_survey.authcheckdam.pdf.

- establish a program to train lawyers how to provide modest-means representation;
- develop a lawyer information database for coordinators of self-represented litigation programs; and
- build a listserv to connect attorneys offering reduced rates to modest-means clients.

A number of state bar associations already offer some of the resources Colorado's Access to Justice Commission recommends but few have proposed such a comprehensive blueprint to encourage the sustainability of attorneys who offer low bono fees.[13]

California is also in the process of exploring its involvement in programs to address the unmet needs of average-income individuals. In its final report of its first phase on admissions regulation reform, the Task Force on Admissions Regulation Reform stated its belief that an infrastructure to support modest-means legal service delivery required the bar's encouragement.[14] In its final Phase I report, the California Task Force on Admissions Regulations Reform acknowledges that modest-means legal services are "a vastly underdeveloped part of the legal economy,"[15] and as a result recommended 50 hours of pro bono or low bono services become a new requirement for admission to the California bar.[16] In addition, the California Access to Justice Commission's Modest Means/Incubator Task Force launched a statewide pilot program to support modest-means incubator programs to learn more about modest-means delivery systems.[17]

A number of bar associations are promoting new attorney incubator programs that incorporate reduced-fee services. The Kansas City Metropolitan Bar Association and the Missouri Bar Association were the first bar associations to develop relationships with a law school to launch an incubator program. In November 2010, the University of Missouri Kansas City School of Law (UMKC) announced the launch of its attorney incubator program.[18] The program was a natural development that was

[13] The Iowa State Bar Association supports its members by offering an affordable library of legal documents called IowaDocs. See www.iowadocs.net. The Iowa State Bar Association owns the copyright to the legal documents, which it automates using HotDocs. *Id.* The program helps attorneys customize hundreds of routine forms for low rates. See www.iowadocs.net/rates.cfm. Also, state bar organizations such as the Maryland State Bar Association (MSBA) already organize annual conferences for new lawyers and individuals starting their own practices. Available at www.msbasoloconerence.org/.

[14] Jon B. Streeter et al., Task Force on Admissions Regulation Reform: Phase I Final Report, June 24, 2013, pp. 8–10.

[15] *Id.* at 9.

[16] *Id.* at 16. The California State Bar Task Force on Admissions Regulation Reform is in the process of developing the rules and regulations to implement its regulations.

[17] Meeting Materials for December 10, 2013 California Commission on Access to Justice.

[18] Steve Vockrodt, UMKC Incubator Preps Lawyers for Small, Solo Practices, Kan. City Bus. J. (Nov. 12, 2010).

supported by the bar association's efforts to support solo and small firm lawyers through an annual conference and also UMKC's commitment to supporting the development of lawyer entrepreneurship amongst their graduates. The annual conference is a two-day gathering that is family friendly and includes a range of programs on law practice management, ethics, and substantive legal issues. The Missouri State Bar hosts a listserv that connects solo and small firm lawyers that was started at the first Solo and Small Firm Conference in 1996.[19] UMKC developed the Solo and Small Firm Institute in 2004 that offers workshops and classes to students and attorneys that focus on business planning, founding, and operating a law firm.[20] The Solo and Small Firm Institute curriculum is taught by faculty UMKC, the Missouri-Kansas City Henry W. Bloch School of Business and Public Administration. The curriculum helps prepare lawyers to understand the importance of marketing and business planning that permits the delivery of low bono services.[21] Applicants to the incubator are selected in part by their statement of a commitment to offer free and low bono services to the local community.[22] The Kansas City Metropolitan Bar Association and the Missouri Bar Association were also involved in facilitating in-kind donations and money to support the incubator.

The Columbus Bar Association developed Columbus Bar inc as a pilot incubator program in April 2011 as part of their professional development center.[23] Columbus Bar inc selected recent law graduates from local law schools to participate in a one-year program to help them launch solo practices.[24] The incubator offers office space in the same building as the Columbus Bar Association and through its attorney network offers participants mentoring on "client intake, billing practices, law office management, marketing, case management, discovery, and other practice-related topics."[25] Incubator participants pay rent for furnished and equipped office space. But the bar association helps subsidize their costs by sending participants referrals from the bar's lawyer referral service.[26] In exchange for support and mentoring,

[19] What you need to know about SFIG: Solo and Small Firm Committee Listserver, available at www.mobar.org/weblinks/sfig-new-subscribers.pdf.

[20] MKC School of Law Launches Solo and Small Firm Incubator, University of Missouri-kansas City (Oct. 29, 2010).

[21] The UMKC incubator also provides support in law office management and mentoring to start law practices. See *id.*

[22] To be admitted applicants must submit a business plan that includes the intended practice areas, a marketing plan, three years of financial projections, and a statement of commitment to offer free or low bono legal services to the local community.

[23] Columbus Bar Announces New Incubator Program, columbus bar association (Jan. 21, 2011), available at www.cbalaw.org/articles/news/recent-news/2011/1631.

[24] *Id.*

[25] *Id.*

[26] The Columbus Bar Association also offers sponsorship opportunities and accepts in-kind donations for individuals wishing to subsidize start-up costs for lawyers. They have sponsorship packages at $2,000, $5,000, and $10,000 levels. In exchange, sponsors receive recognition in bar publications and

participants agree to take on at least one pro bono case from the Columbus Bar Association's Lawyers for Justice program.[27]

The Chicago Bar Foundation provided seed funding to start the Justice Entrepreneurs Project (JEP) in June 2013. The Chicago Bar Foundation, through various resources including law school stipends, subsidizes the cost of office space for the first six months in exchange for participation in pro bono work. In the second six months of the program, the attorney participants pay $300 per month for their office space, and $500 per month in each of the last six months in the program. While JEP represents that its attorneys do not offer discounted or low bono rates, its program focuses on leveraging technology to unbundle services at below market rates. The Chicago Bar Foundation leverages its existing relationships to provide JEP participants with malpractice insurance, supervised training on pro bono cases, and mentoring that encourages their participants to think not just about their own viability but about reinventing the way legal services are delivered.

Role of Courts

The Unified Judicial System in South Dakota offers one example of how courts can fund legal services for people of average means. In March 2013, South Dakota passed a law to launch a pilot program that subsidizes lawyers to work and live in rural areas (with populations of 10,000 or less) for a minimum of five years.[28] Although a fifth of the U.S. population lives in rural communities, only 2% of small law firms are located in those communities.[29] The program accommodates up to 16 participants who receive an annual $12,000 stipend for each of the five years they maintain a law practice and live in the rural community.[30] While the stipend may not seem like a large amount for lawyers who graduate with large debt loads, each payment equals 90% of tuition and other fees at the University of South Dakota School of Law.[31] The program is financed through a partnership between the State Bar of South Dakota, which contributes 15% of the stipend, each county that hosts a lawyer, which pays 35% of the lawyer's stipend, and the Unified Judicial System, which is responsible for 50% of the stipend.[32]

promotional materials. See Columbus Bar Ass'n, Columbus Bar Professional Development Center, available at www.cbalaw.org/cba_prod/Main/Resources/Legal-Professionals/inc/Sponsor.aspx.

27 *Id.*

28 Debra Cassens Weiss, South Dakota Lures Lawyers to Rural Areas with Annual Subsidies, ABA J. Apr. 9, 2013, 6:43 AM CST. See Rural Attorney Incentive Program – South Dakota Senate Bill No. 218, House Bill 1096, 88th Session of Legislative Assembly, 2013. See also South Dakota Unified Judicial System, Rural Attorney Recruitment Program, ujs.sd.gov/Information/rarprogram.aspx.

29 Ethan Bronner, *No Lawyer for Miles, So One Rural State Offers to Pay*, N.Y. TIMES, April 18, 2013.

30 *Id.*

31 Recruitment Assistance Pilot Program Contract/Letter of Agreement for Contractual Services, p. 1.

32 *Id.*

The judicial branch has committed to allocating $96,000 per year to pilot this program.[33]

The New York Unified Court System, led by Judge Fern Fisher, has set up a court program that promotes the provision of unbundled legal services by recent law graduates to help modest-income Americans in housing court.[34] Efforts in the New York Courts, led by Justice Fern Fisher, include the development of a housing court apprenticeship program. The New York Housing court has an existing Volunteer Lawyer for a Day program where experienced attorneys volunteer to represent tenants in housing court on nonpayment proceeding.[35] Through collaboration with CUNY School of Law, these volunteer attorneys are now providing mentorship and supervision to recent law graduates waiting for bar results. The program, called the LaunchPad for Justice, teams up CUNY law graduates with a volunteer lawyer to provide representation in court to an otherwise self-represented litigant. While they wait for bar results, recent graduates are trained in the law and procedure necessary to represent individuals in housing court.[36] In order to implement this model, the Supreme Court amended the student practice rules to allow for recent graduates to practice while waiting for bar results. In addition, some seed funding was available through public sources to provide recent graduates with modest stipends for their work. The partnership requires development, training, and coordination by court personnel but through the LaunchPad for Justice, many average-income self-represented litigants obtain representation they would otherwise forgo.[37] The program also introduces future lawyers to the need for affordable legal services and the opportunity to offer discrete task representation.

The Civil Justice Infrastructure Mapping Project of the American Bar Foundation found that every state in the United States has information online to help self-represented litigants and 98% of states have a selection of legal forms on those websites.[38] Further, more than 70% of states have at least one court-based self-help center that offers members of the public information and assistance to help

[33] The court will contribute $6,000 per year for each lawyer after the county and the state bar make their contributions. *Id.* This program mirrors a federal medical program that offers medical professionals as much as $60,000 tax-free for two years of service in underserved communities. See the National Health Service Corps at nhsc.hrsa.gov.

[34] See generally N.Y. State Courts, Access to Justice (2010) (describing various Access to Justice initiatives established in the New York State Courts), available at www.courts.state.ny.us/ip/nya2j/.

[35] Hon. Fern Fisher, Best Practices for the Administration of Court-Sponsored Volunteer Lawyer for the Day Programs (Limited Scope/Unbundled Legal Service Programs) 2 (Jan. 2010), available at www.nycourts.gov/ip/nya2j/pdfs/NYSA2J_ BestPracticesVLFD.pdf.

[36] Natalie Gomez-Velez, *Structured Discrete Representation to Bridge the Justice Gap: CUNY Law School's LaunchPad for Justice in Partnership with Courts and Communities*, 16 CUNY L. Rev. 21, 38 (2012).

[37] *Id.* at 38–40.

[38] Rebecca L. Sandefur, Access Across America: First Report of the Civil Justice Infrastructure Mapping Project, 12, ABA Civil Infrastructure Mapping Project (Oct. 2011).

them represent themselves.[39] The growing resources for legal services consumers provide options that are less costly than lawyers to sophisticated legal services consumers. Yet, these self-help resources are not always sufficient for individuals who face language barriers, suffer through emotional trauma, or quite simply are not sophisticated enough to overcome confusing procedural issues. When they face these obstacles, courts should offer these individuals referrals to lawyers and others who offer reduced rate services.

Chapter 41, which covers the role of courts in defining who is authorized to practice law, presents examples of how courts are issuing limited licenses to practice law to a new class of legal practitioners as a way to respond to this crisis in legal representation.[40] The judiciary will ultimately determine which legal issues and procedures benefit most from assistance by limited license practitioners, attorneys, and self-represented litigants. Existing policy and budget priorities indicate support for the self-represented but not for lawyers who offer reduced rates. While not all legal problems require the assistance of lawyers, having low bono services offered by attorneys is an essential part of an affordable legal services agenda.

Legal Aid

A number of legal aid organizations support low bono work by private lawyers. These legal aid entities use a portion of their budget to pay the private bar to take on cases for legal-aid-eligible clients they cannot take on due to conflicts or capacity of their staff.[41] These programs, which exist primarily in rural communities, identify private lawyers who understand legal aid's client base and can provide competent representation for a fraction of the market rate. Legal aid usually contracts with attorneys to perform a range of services with a set low bono fee payment schedule. Legal aid screens the client, connects them with the attorney, and then pays for the services rendered after the lawyer submits proof of completion of the work.

Legal aid organizations are also supporting the development of low bono law practices by referring cases they cannot take on to local incubator programs. For example, the Memphis Area Legal Services (MALS) has partnered with Memphis Bar Association (MBA), the University of Memphis Cecil C. Humphreys School

[39] *Id.* Additionally, 59% of states have courthouses with computer terminals to assist self-represented litigants. These computers use software that explains how to respond to a claim. *Id.*

[40] See Levine, Chapter 41 in this volume.

[41] Legal aid organizations that receive funding from the Legal Services Corporation are required to spend 12.5% of their budgets on involving the private bar. See 45 C.F.R. § 1614.1 (2008). For a discussion of the genesis of the private attorney involvement requirement, see Luz E. Herrera, *Rethinking Private Attorney Involvement through a Low Bono Lens*, 43 Loy. L.A. Law Rev. 1, 25–8 (2009).

of Law, and the Service Corps of Retired Executives (SCORE) to create Esq. Build – The Memphis Bar Association Sole Practitioner Incubator.[42] Participants pay a $50–$100 monthly fee to MALS in exchange for office space. Participants provide their own office equipment and are required to perform ten hours of pro bono work per month for MALS.[43] Like most other incubator programs, participants must submit an application to participate in the Esq.Build.[44] Once in the program, lawyers attend training programs, develop a marketing strategy and obtain preference in securing court-appointed cases.[45] Since these lawyers are renting space in MALS's offices, legal aid lawyers can greatly influence their training. By engaging in the training of the private bar, legal aid organizations are able to vet future Main Street lawyers, leverage their resources, and gain new supporters.

The Legal Aid Society of Orange County (LASOC) has maximized its opportunities to collaborate with the private bar and encourage the development of low bono law practices. In addition to using some of its budget to pay private lawyers low bono rates, it runs a lawyer referral program and helps fund its legal aid program by collecting referral fees from private attorneys. LASOC also recently developed the Bar Waiter Program and the Lawyer Entrepreneur Assistance Program (LEAP) to engage recent law graduates in pro bono work. The Bar Waiter Program participants volunteer with LASOC by working pro bono on routine legal aid cases in the areas of domestic relations, tenant rights, and consumer issues. In exchange these recent law graduates obtain training, access to LASOC's brief bank, and relationships with the local bar. The Lawyer Entrepreneur Assistance Program (LEAP) connects new solo lawyers to LASOC's training, network, and lawyer referral service in exchange for pro bono work. Lawyers are trained to do intake by working LASOC's hotline, they are taught to put together a client file, and work alongside legal aid lawyers in LASOC's family, bankruptcy, and tenant law clinics. In a ten-month period, LASOC reported that 32 LEAP attorneys made 143 appearances for 103 low-income litigants. Participants in both programs were responsible for closing 298 LASOC cases in family law, housing, bankruptcy, wage claims, guardianships, civil harassments, and conservatorships. LASOC is working with the local bar association and law schools to provide law office management training for these lawyers. All of these efforts to engage the private bar in pro bono and low bono work helps LASOC obtain support and funding that would otherwise be absent.

[42] ESQ.Build – The Memphis Bar Association Sole Practitioner Incubator, available at www.memphis.edu/law/esq_build_app.pdf.

[43] *Id.*

[44] To participate in Esq.Build, lawyers or individuals waiting for bar results must have graduated from the University of Memphis Cecil C. Humphreys School of Law in the last three years, be a member of the MBA, and carry professional liability insurance. *Id.* See also The University of Memphis, Cecil C. Humphreys School of Law Career Services, available at www.memphis.edu/law/career/esq build.php.

[45] *Id.*

Legal aid organizations and their clients have much to gain from such collaborations.

CONCLUSION

Bar associations, law schools, courts, and legal aid organizations should embrace low bono as a solution for meeting the unmet legal needs of average-income Americans. The concept of a low bono practice must come to mean a business enterprise that allows lawyers to charge reasonable rates for the demographic they serve. Through lower-than-market legal fees, unbundled legal services at full rates, flat-fee pricing, and other flexible-fee structures, attorneys can attract clients who otherwise will forgo legal representation or resort to more affordable non-attorney options. Ultimately the availability of more legal services at lower fees has a positive impact on both lawyers and legal services consumers.

26

Toward a More Effective and Accessible Solo and Small Firm Practice Model

Ann Juergens

Juergens provides concrete strategies for solo and small firm practices including crafting transparent fee arrangements with clients, outsourcing or automating non-lawyer tasks, creating service hubs of legal and non-legal professional services, leveraging local community connections to complement bar ties, creating a web presence, and using law student externs.

The lawyers most in touch with the civil justice needs of average Americans are those in solo and small firms. They are a crucial yet undervalued resource for closing the access gap. To meet more need, solo and small practitioners must reimagine the ways that their services actually add value to the lives and transactions of average Americans. They must distill and enhance the value of their services even as they work to lower their cost to clients. Finally, lawyers must improve the ways that the value and risks of their services are communicated to average Americans.[1]

DISTILLING THE ESSENTIAL IN THE SOLO AND SMALL FIRM SERVICE MODEL

In the current climate, the benefit small firm lawyers may bring to peoples' lives and transactions is not apparent to most moderate-income Americans. While lawyers once controlled access to most legal information, that is no longer the case. Small firm lawyers have relied heavily on the skills of building relationships and trust in their service to middle-income clients, but now they must do more. They must focus their efforts, and become more sophisticated and certain about the ways they add value. This should lead them to remove, automate, or outsource the non-essential, then offer a more concentrated and individualized – and more valuable – set of services for middle-income clients.

[1] This essay is part of an ongoing work. See Ann Juergens, *Valuing Small Firm and Solo Law Practice: Models for Expanding Service to Middle-Income Clients*, 39 Wm. Mitchell L. Rev. 80 (2012).

As one common example, small-firm lawyers who learned to draft wills or file articles of incorporation can no longer go through a series of standard questions and charge clients by the hour for creating documents that the client can access for $100 or less on the internet. Rather, these lawyers must investigate when these forms are not sufficient or cannot be easily used by potential clients. They must explore new ways to serve by concentrating on families who need to plan for the long-term care of a disabled family member or on small enterprises that face more complex questions like those raised by regulatory agencies or licensing agreements.

The Force-Field of Fee Arrangements

Traditional fee arrangements are one force that have kept lawyers from becoming more client-centered in communicating the content and value of their work. For one thing, people can learn almost nothing about the costs, benefits, and risks of a lawyer's services until they spend some minutes with the lawyer in contemplation of hiring her. The profession has made it maddeningly difficult for average Americans to learn how the variety, cost, and quality of lawyer services compare to alternative services in the marketplace.

After they access basic fee information, potential clients generally must evaluate the costs of hiring a lawyer based on the lawyer's hourly rates or flat fees.[2] Hourly billing does little to inform clients how much money they risk if they hire the lawyer. An hourly rate measures value by the amount of lawyer's time but does not allow clients to monitor the lawyer's efficiency. Middle- and lower-income clients often find hourly rates too risky. Flat fees cap client costs but are not necessarily responsive to clients' difficulty in learning the benefits and non-monetary risk of lawyers' services. Clients are usually given the choice to simply take or leave the flat fee option, rather than being engaged in an interactive process where the client acquires the information she needs to decide whether the benefits will be worth the risk of the outlay. That may be changing in some areas of law, yet few industries operate with so little regard for the client-customers' perspective.

To escape this force that repels clients, lawyers must reimagine their services from the clients' point of view and adjust their fee arrangements accordingly.

Research Alternative Approaches from the Clients' Point of View

A lawyer who wants to distinguish her services and attract clients who would otherwise go without service, do for themselves, or buy help from non-lawyers, must research the alternatives open to middle-income clients in her areas of practice. What would many potential clients do when thinking about how to respond to

[2] Contingency fees, prevalent in personal-injury cases, are not discussed here because the problem of access to justice for injury cases is not as serious, because contingency fees in most cases do not depend upon the client's ability to pay.

a debt collector or to start a small business? Pose a question on the internet, of course. Ask "How do I answer a debt collection complaint?" or "Do I need to incorporate my small business?" or "Is my elderly parent eligible for a nursing home under Medicare?" and thousands of potential sources for solving those queries will appear.

The next step is to analyze the comments or reviews that follow the web articles, government brochures, business offers, or blog posts. What seems satisfactory and unsatisfactory to people about the answers and assistance they are finding? How do lawyers and the law fit into the picture, or are they in the picture at all?

Such an analysis should sensitize any lawyer to what people say is the problem with seeking lawyers' representation: many believe that a lawyer will be unaffordable, that a lawyer's help will not be worth the cost, that lawyers will only make things worse or stupidly complex. One will learn that many people facing challenges or contemplating changes have no idea that consulting a lawyer – for example, for planning before quitting a job or dealing with a bad contractor or trying to move an elder relative into assisted living – could help them at all.

Interviews with former clients and potential clients about their perceptions of value are another step for lawyers seeking to identify the value added by the work they do. One small firm sent a law student assistant to the local court self-help desk to interview people seeking advice there about perceptions of lawyer value, or lack of it, in family law matters. Volunteering at local pro se clinics is another way for lawyers to learn the views of the large segment of people attempting to resolve a legal matter without a lawyer.

Articulate How Your Legal Services are Different

Through these web searches, conversations, and analyses, small firm lawyers should begin to articulate the ways their service is distinct in quality or kind from that obtainable without a lawyer. If the lawyer cannot identify those differences, she must reframe her services so that she can do so.

For example, a small firm specializing in elder law might explain that their expert knowledge of the ever-changing rules governing Medicare translates into advice about moving a parent into a nursing home that will be accurate and tailored to the family's situation. They work closely with social workers and social service providers to ensure the elder is placed in a care situation within her means and eligibility. The lawyers work out their fees with the family in light of many factors that take the clients' views into account: the money that is at risk if Medicare eligibility is not preserved; the needs of the elder that are likely to escalate; and, perhaps most importantly, the value of the peace of mind that the family is seeking at a stressful transition time. Some of these concerns are consistent across clients, others are weighed very differently by families.

It is not so difficult to discern that the hallmark lawyer skills are wise counsel, advocacy before judicial tribunals, and competent analysis, i.e., knowledge of the law and how it applies in a person's individual situation. Another distinction is that the tort and lawyer licensing system allow clients to hold lawyers responsible for knowing the most up-to-date rules. This is not the case for most non-lawyer providers of law services. These skills and accountability are not readily available from sources other than lawyers; filling out forms with guided questions and basic information about legal requirements are readily available.

The value of a competent lawyer's advice, advocacy, analysis, and accountability to clients can be a challenge to measure in terms of money. It takes discussions with clients, good judgment, and trial and error to discern, for example, the dollar value of peace of mind. The value can be expressed in fee agreements that are based upon a combination of flat fees, contingency upon success (unless prohibited as in family law matters), gradually decreasing or escalating sums, and units of dollar measurement lifted from the client's situation, e.g., a fee that is the equivalent of three months' rent in a tenant matter, or of two months' wages in an employment matter.

Focus Lawyer Time on Advice, Advocacy, and Analysis

Proper use of non-lawyer help is critical to a successful small firm practice and to providing services at a reasonable cost.

For example, small immigration firms usually employ paralegals to fill out and manage the many documents required for citizenship and visa applications, saving the lawyers' time for knowing the latest law, advising, and, when needed, advocacy before a judge. Any lawyer who is filling out forms that do not require substantial advocacy judgment is not operating efficiently.

Some tasks may be outsourced to the client herself, as when a potential client is asked to fill out an intake questionnaire via the firm's website before a first meeting with a lawyer. That intake form can then be amplified during a face-to-face meeting. This allows the lawyer to read routine information quickly and concentrate her time with the client on matters that are essential to needed advice, advocacy, or analysis.

When client and lawyer decide to enter into a relationship, case management technology can take client information from the electronic intake form to automatically open a matter in the firm's system. Technology also may automatically generate an electronic case file with subfolders, a billing account, populate dates into an individual and master calendar, and so forth.

Routinize as many tasks as possible through electronic case and document management systems. In the last year or so, security has advanced so that many of these are now based in the cloud, allowing for further efficiency. For example, to avoid multiple duplications of key client documents, a system can post those documents to a closed room on the cloud. Then client, paralegal, even accountant and other interested parties may access them via a web portal. This is both far more efficient and less risky than sending the documents as attachments on emails to multiple addresses, to computers that may have varying levels of privacy and security. (Security of knowledge and case management systems and the cloud is crucial but beyond the scope of this chapter.)

A knowledge management system can assist a small firm to curate and leverage the knowledge that is created within the firm. While it is arguable that a solo practitioner is able to keep in her head most of the knowledge that she has gained in the course of work, this argument fails as soon as you add another person or two to the small practice. How do two heads gain access to the work that the other has done? They do so through frequent conversations, of course, but also by crafting a searchable knowledge base of their work. That requires tagging most documents that are produced for future retrieval and reference. It also means that small firms should recruit the most technology-friendly member to keep refreshing firm systems for retaining their knowledge. Tagging systems need review and updating. As each client matter is closed, it should be scrutinized for valuable information. Ways to reuse that knowledge must be developed and encouraged.

Telephones with internet capacity have become essential to practitioners and myriad apps are helping small firm lawyers become more accessible and effective. There is an app, for example, that allows the lawyer to scan a business card when she meets a potential client or referral source out in the community. The app sends the card to an electronic file with a note of the date and location that it was added to the database. If that person eventually calls the lawyer's "office," information about the point of first contact pops up on the phone. This jogs the lawyer's memory of the contact before answering the call. It is no surprise that the lawyer who uses this app is out of her office frequently, networking with her micro-enterprise clients or working on her laptop in a spot where she may be able to hand out her own card to a future potential client.

The idea is to use non-lawyers and technology to strip from the lawyer's time those tasks that need not be performed by her, and then to focus her efforts upon the other value she brings to the relationship with the client.

Embrace the Benefits of Being Small

Lawyers are more accessible to clients when they think small. Clients build relationships through contact with individual lawyers, not through the larger entity. Small firms are able to keep their overhead lower than larger firms, so their fees can be more affordable. Lower fixed costs allow small firms greater flexibility in adapting their systems to client needs, including the need for less lawyer work.

One solo learned through conversations that small enterprises often want to be able to tell another that they were "going to call their lawyer." This solo lawyer designed a service that fulfilled peoples' wish to say that. Clients paid him a modest fixed fee – about $150 – each month for the right to phone or email him three times for legal advice. The cost was transparent and fixed, and the value of verbalizing that they had a lawyer in their corner was gained. On top of that was the value of the advice that was given during the occasional calls.

Arrangements for such small pieces of work may be more feasible in settings with enterprises, including nonprofits and unincorporated community organizations, or with ongoing transactions when the lawyer has a relationship with the client that is continuing. Yet the concept could be useful in family law, elder law, and other consumer settings. Unbundling of legal services is discussed in Chapter 29, titled Limited representation and ethical challenges, by Russell Engler.

Develop a Transparent Fee Structure in Collaboration with the Client

Once a small firm lawyer has delved into understanding her services from the clients' points of view, and has framed her services distinctly in light of that study, she can put her insight to work on developing value-based client contracts.

In using this model for billing, lawyers must work collaboratively with each client to decide on the set of services and fees that suit her. Client perceptions of value must be taken into account alongside the lawyer's needs – for the lawyer has to pay the rent too.

Transparency is vital in this lawyer–client exchange of information about perceptions and needs. Value-based billing presumes that risks of the representation should belong not only to the client, but be shared by the lawyer. How does a lawyer facilitate such candor? This is where relationship and trust-building skills are invaluable.

Transparency as a goal compels the development of a new norm, that of posting some discussions of fees on lawyers' websites. To ensure that citizens are making fair comparisons, however, small firms should include website narratives about how the lawyer's services are different from those available elsewhere, in particular from non-lawyers.

The process of designing value-based fees can be assisted when fee examples are posted with explanations of the potential value of each. This may entail a website story about the value that a client gained when the lawyer succeeded with an unemployment appeal or nonprofit formation or compliance audit.

The goal is to migrate the law-related and lawyer services down to the least expensive levels possible, while maintaining quality and competence. A solo or small firm lawyer needs research-based information, and access to experience and judgment to discern when a person needs the highest or lowest level of service or, in fact, no lawyer service at all. Setting the appropriate level of service also requires frank exchanges about the consequences of each level and the risks in each. Only the client and lawyer can decide how much risk of time, reputation, and treasure each is willing and able to take. That calculus is rarely the same from one client to the next.

One of the most challenging aspects of these conversations is for the lawyer to make relatively reliable predictions of outcome for the client. When thin experience supplemented by good research fails to provide usable predictions, lawyers must be candid about that as well. Unpredictability is part of the risk that the client must weigh, as must the lawyer.

In sum, the transition to value billing and setting of services involves a more collaborative approach to decision-making between lawyer and client. These are not take-it-or-leave-it transactions. If an exceptional, unanticipated event merits further legal service, another fee structure can be agreed upon. And if the lawyer work is more complex or urgent, a higher payment may presumably be due to the lawyer because of the higher value to the client.

ANTICIPATING CLIENT NEEDS THROUGH CONNECTIONS WITH THE COMMUNITY

People generally understand that it would be wise to consult and, if feasible, hire a lawyer when they are served with a lawsuit or need a child support order.

But when they start an enterprise, contemplate the details of an employment contract, ponder planning for their elderly parent to move out of the family home, are trying to persuade the regional governing entity to approve a zoning change or facilitate the transition to solar energy or train police in dealing with disabled citizens, many people do not think of engaging a lawyer.

Lawyers can add value in any of these scenarios when they are knowledgeable, skilled advocates, with creative problem-solving abilities. Yet they must find means for communicating to Americans of average means that they can help in such settings, in ways that are affordable.

Create Community Ties that Complement Bar Association Ties

Engagement with the community where one works is a primary means by which lawyers build a practice in small firm settings. Solo and small firm practitioners have the advantage that small entities are able to integrate more readily into the community where they work. Their work worlds are not populated largely by lawyers, and their offices may be anywhere, not only in a large building in a commercial district but next door to people of modest means. The lawyer who knows her neighbors, who has coffee at the local shop, who buys bread and birthday cards and beer at local businesses, who participates in school-based meetings and community events in the same area where she works, is likely to have rich contact with modest-means people and micro-enterprises – potential clients – during that social intercourse.

Lawyers who find a community, embed themselves and learn its justice and social issues, generally will be able to see potential work all around. Small and solo firm lawyers have an advantage in knitting themselves into middle-income communities in that most are of that income group, even if the top part of it. The challenge is to make a living by addressing the community's justice issues.

Form Service Hubs

To facilitate community members' decisions to use lawyers who live among them, lawyers may find similarly oriented businesses and non-lawyer service providers and form a service hub together. The concept is to put useful and related services and goods nearby each other or in the same building and to cooperate in making a kind of one-stop shop. This happens traditionally when lawyers and banks and accountants, realtors and mortgage brokers and title examiners find offices in the same building or very near one another, then assist one another with business deals, real estate transactions, debt collection, and so forth.

New kinds of co-location and collaboration create opportunities for average Americans to come into contact with useful lawyers. Small law firms find synergies when they co-locate with health practitioners, social workers, designers, computer engineers, payroll specialists, social entrepreneurs, or, say, urban farmers, wedding cake bakers, and other businesses and service providers. Startups often need legal advice, permits, trademarks, variances.

The ABA Model Rules of Professional Conduct do not facilitate much sharing between lawyers and non-lawyers, but those boundaries are not so high that lawyers should avoid collaborations. The confidentiality of client files and communications must be protected, so internet walls, security, and training of personnel, if any, must be strong. Financial arrangements must comply with the strictures of Model Rule 5.4 – Professional Independence of a Lawyer. This means that lawyers cannot enter financial partnerships with non-lawyers, nor share fees with them.

Yet American lawyers need not wait for the professional rules to change as they did in England to allow non-lawyer investment in their firms. Lawyers and non-lawyers *may* pay rent to a common landlord, consult freely on client matters (with client permission) or on local issues, work in collaboration with one another on behalf of clients, share a website front page, or refer clients back and forth between themselves.[3]

For example, small firm estate and elder law specialists in rural Minnesota are pairing with hospitals and skilled nursing facility personnel to offer packages of life care coordination to families of the elderly. This kind of medical–legal partnership is

[3] Referral arrangements are best left uncompensated in order to avoid problems with rules governing lawyer advertising, as in ABA, Model Rule of Professional Conduct 7.2(b)(4). Many service providers and businesses recommend each other without expectation of payment, as the goodwill that is generated rewards them over the long term. Even without a payment arrangement, it is a wise gesture to let the client know "the existence and nature of the [non-exclusive] agreement," as Rule 7.2(b)(4) requires when a lawyer gives something of value to another for recommending the lawyer's services.

becoming more common, and is another take on service hubs that puts lawyers in close contact with non-lawyers who need their expertise to serve their constituents. Possible combinations are myriad.

Community Education Matters – on the Web and on the Ground

Hand in hand with the goal of gaining clients, lawyers who emphasize value for clients understand that learning about legal matters is a means of empowering any community. The long-term goal is for community members to be able to advocate their own interests with the institutions that affect them. At the end of the day, every good lawyer, like good teachers and good parents, seeks to increase the independence of her clients, not their dependence. In my own experience with community-based solo practice and in teaching collaborations with solo and small firm lawyers, that professional approach ensures that some clients will return for trusted counsel again and again for years.

A current essential method for practitioners to engage the legal and justice issues of people is, of course, the World Wide Web. Solo and small firm lawyers gain most of their new clients by word of mouth: in my study of Minnesota small firm lawyers, their sources of clients were almost all referrals from other people, satisfied clients and other attorneys, social workers and non-lawyer professionals.[4] They understood that their practices depended upon the quality of their relationships and on their ability to help clients with decisions that could not be managed by computers and non-lawyers.

Lawyer websites often are out of touch with the visual digital age. The sites lack faces, photographs, stories, color, and interactive features – they tend to be dreary and seem aimed at lawyers, not client communities. Any solo or small firm lawyer based in a community must seek to draw people of modest means to its website, then give them information they can use. If the visitor learns something, she may eventually contact the lawyer directly for more services.

Website design is critical in the twenty-first century. It conveys the identity and values of the firm visually, before a word is read. Though most lawyers report they gain clients through word of mouth, we also know that the first thing most consumers do when preparing to hire services is use a search engine to investigate the recommended service provider's website before making direct contact.

Web presences are good places (but not sufficient) to demonstrate that a lawyer knows how to collaborate. This is especially important for those seeking work as advisors and problem solvers, arenas that call for more collaboration skills than that of the traditional litigator-warrior. When establishing service hubs, as mentioned earlier, a collaborative website for the location and its services is one way to communicate those values. Regular guest blogging on a nonprofit service provider's

[4] Juergens, supra note 1, at 112.

website is another path to the synergies of cooperation and to educating the community over the web.

Lawyers have become mainstays in community education presentations and every law graduate should have some training in how to stand up in front of groups of nonlawyers and explain the workings of the law. Lawyers seeking to connect with modest-means clients will find them in all kinds of public spaces and meeting places, from gatherings of caregivers needing support to ex-felons seeking employment and housing to nonprofit administrators gathering for workshops.

Use of Law Student Interns/Externs

Law student externs or volunteers can offer critical assistance to practitioners who are seeking deeper understanding of their communities. As law schools expand real-life practice settings for student learning, opportunities are arising for small firm lawyers to work with students. Community-based practitioners should link up with the law school closest to them and find ways to work with one or two law students each semester.

Accreditation rules for law schools and federal and state wage-hour laws require that any student doing work for no wages – whether for credit or not – must be benefiting from a truly educational experience, guided by both a field supervisor and a faculty member.[5] And ethics rules require that no client be charged for any work that a student provides for free or for academic credit.

Law student extern projects must be chosen carefully to comply with the goals of the law school program that may allow the placement, and to fulfill the law students' learning goals. Yet they are often worth the trouble. Students have energy and the insight of new eyes on projects in the community that the lawyer wishes to advance. Again, if the endeavor is a fee-earning one, many law schools would not approve the placement. Similarly, law students cannot be paid for any work for which they receive credit. Appropriate tasks for students include straight-ahead legal research; gathering data on the efficacy of representation in certain settings, as discussed elsewhere in this chapter and book; the creation of consumer education content for a website or for presentation at a community meeting; fact investigation, especially that which takes the student out into the community itself; mapping of expenditures on education or crime control or municipal development for use in policy reform projects; framing an online video game aimed at teaching young people the ins and outs of how to expunge their criminal records – the list is voluminous.

[5] ABA Standard for Accreditation 305, available at: www.americanbar.org/content/dam/aba/publications/misc/legal_education/Standards/chapter_3_2012_2013_aba_standards_and_rules.authcheckdam.pdf. The Fair Labor Standards Act of 1938, as amended, 29 U.S.C. 201, *et seq.*, regulates wages and hours of work. For detail on the Labor Department's criteria for permissible unpaid internships, see Fact Sheet #71: Internship Programs Under The Fair Labor Standards Act, available at www.dol.gov/whd/regs/compliance/whdfs71.htm.

Small practitioners should get to know the person who directs externships at the salient law school and seek guidance on the most rewarding activities for students. The practitioner, in turn, may educate the director on the kinds of experiences students might have in their practice. Potential student externs themselves, when asked, often have wonderful ideas for how to execute a community project that aims to build neighborhood awareness, trust, and links between citizens of average means and the legal resources in the area. This is especially true when a law student has preexisting ties to the community involved.

Nonprofit organizations, government, and unpaid (traditional pro bono) work need not hold the monopoly on public service. Solo and small firms are surely competent to articulate justice projects that arise from their communities, then ask for law student help in accomplishing them. The price is supervision and feedback and lots of mutual learning. The payoff is better connections between local citizens of average means and the small practitioner. In the long run, the hope is for a payoff of healthier communities.

ONGOING COMPETENCE AND QUALITY CONTROL

As lawyers gather and then disseminate accurate information about the impact of their services to clients, as lawyers adjust their cost structures and create value-billing fee agreements individually in collaboration with clients, the lawyer discipline system needs to catch up. Value billing holds potential for new forms of abuse by lawyers. But it also promises new ways to hold lawyers accountable for delivering the value promised, more than simply for expending a certain amount of time.

In my study of lawyers whose clients were in the middle 60% of income, quality control and competence were identified as prime challenges.[6] They were named the most important skills for sustaining practice by 26% of the study sample, second in frequency only to the skill of building relationships and trust. Half of the study participants had fielded ethics complaints; one lawyer was disbarred after the study was completed for his serious errors in handling client trust funds and for failures in client communication. The primary means of maintaining quality were informal: personal vigilance and small networks of experienced mentors to whom they would turn for consultation.

In a culture that seeks transparency and accurate information about lawyer services, there are nonetheless few means for average Americans to learn facts that enable them to avoid lawyers who are not competent. The profession's methods for making members answer for incompetence and bad quality control simply are not effective. Lawyers tend to go easy on their peers within a disciplinary system that also governs their own actions.[7] When lawyers steal from clients or use money from their

6 Juergens, supra note 1, at 110–11.

7 David R. Barnhizer, *Abandoning an "Unethical" System of Legal Ethics*, 2012 Mich. State L. Rev. 347 (2012).

trust accounts improperly, they may be prosecuted or disciplined or both. But when lawyers hurt clients through incompetent case handling or by running up fees needlessly, the bar relies on the tort-malpractice system to administer corrective action. If the person damaged by a lawyer is a moderate-income American, it is less likely that she will have damages sufficient to secure a lawyer for a malpractice case against an incompetent lawyer. It is also less likely that she will seek out yet another lawyer to help when the first problem was caused by a bad lawyer.

The system needs stronger incentives for competent behavior. David Barnhizer argues for new legislation, i.e., a statutory consumer protection system, that among other things would require lawyers to give written upfront estimates of cost and establish stringent consumer warranties of service quality.

CONCLUSION

Solo and small law practices have an advantage when it comes to working with middle-income clients – many of them are in the middle-income group themselves. This is as it should be. It is also one of the most salient reasons why solo and small firm practitioners hold the most promise for bridging the justice gap for Americans of average means.

That bridge now needs new struts and a roadbed. The legal profession, one lawyer at a time, must lower fees and its own expectations for income. Lawyers must reimagine how to make a living with clients of average means by gathering data and focusing on being valuable to them, which means offering something distinct from what people now can find outside lawyers' offices. They must help at an appropriate level of service on their law-related conflicts and contracts and neighborhood improvement projects. They will need to collaborate competently with clients and with a multitude of other service providers, even as they nurture their distinct identity as wise counselors, knowledgeable advocates and, it is eventually to be hoped, as peacemakers and community builders.

27

Facilitating Homemade Wills

Reid Kress Weisbord

Can we simplify legal processes so that individuals and their families can structure their affairs, including planning for the distribution of their estate when they die, without recourse to lawyers? In this chapter, Reid Weisbord offers an approach for facilitating the writing of wills that avoids some of the legal pitfalls than can bedevil self-help in this area. He proposes the use of a simplified will form that would be attached to a state income tax return that removes barriers to drafting a will and creates a vehicle for states to promote testacy.

Decades of empirical studies reveal that although most Americans intend to make a will, surprisingly few execute one. Most individuals die without a will, allowing the default rules of intestacy to govern the disposition of property at death. This is problematic because most Americans cannot correctly identify their intestate heirs, so the absence of a will creates the possibility that default rules may fail to carry out the decedent's probable intent. Among many possible adverse consequences, unintended intestacy can cause financial hardship, uncertainty, and frustrated expectations for the decedent's intended beneficiaries. The default rules of intestacy are also structurally unsuitable for the large and growing population of nontraditional families because heirship is limited to individuals related to the decedent by marriage, blood, or legal adoption.

This chapter explores the possibility that complexities embedded in the will-making process itself are at least partly responsible for the high rate of unintended intestacy. Unlike other acts of legal significance, such as entering into a marriage or consumer contract, the will-making process is unfamiliar to most individuals and requires legal drafting and compliance with testamentary formalities. Negative public perceptions about the will-making process discourage lay testation, and many individuals are reluctant to deal with a lawyer for reasons of cost or privacy. Those perceptions most likely arise from the law's historic hostility toward homemade wills and self-representation in the estate-planning context. For more than

A longer version of this chapter was published as Reid K. Weisbord, *Wills for Everyone: Helping Individuals Opt out of Intestacy*, 53 B.C. L. Rev. 877 (2012).

a century, courts have required strict compliance with statutorily imposed formalities for executing a will; failure to comply, even in cases of harmless error, led to the will's rejection from probate. The ostensible purpose of the strict compliance doctrine, which is still applied in most American jurisdictions, is to prevent the probating of fraudulent wills, but some courts and scholars have gone so far as to exalt the complexity of the testamentary process as policy designed to deter self-representation. Those commentators, believing that homemade wills are unreliable and breed litigation, argue that testators should be channeled to competent estate-planning lawyers who are most capable of implementing the decedent's intent. But that method of deterring self-representation has backfired because most individuals are channeled to intestacy rather than estate-planning lawyers. This chapter argues that the complexity of the will-making process deters the exercise of testamentary freedom by imposing substantial transaction costs, including the cost of professional counsel or the investment of time necessary to draft a formal will without a lawyer, and those transaction costs are not offset by any benefit.

Over the last thirty years, two aspects of inheritance law reform have demonstrated movement away from the strict compliance regime, arguably a mark of progress toward universal access to the will-making process. First, increased recognition of curative doctrines, such as the harmless error rule and the doctrine of substantial compliance, has lessened but not eliminated the cost of innocent noncompliance with testamentary formalities in some jurisdictions. Second, the recognition of statutory form wills in a handful of states represents a positive step toward facilitating lay testation, but existing forms are not effectively channeled, are still somewhat complex, and require compliance with testamentary formalities (including witness attestation, for validity). Prior reform efforts, although well intended, have failed to reduce the high long-term rate of intestacy.

This chapter proposes further simplification to promote universal access to the will-making process through the use of more effectively channeled statutory form wills. The most notable proposal is the creation of a testamentary schedule, an optional form will attached to the state individual income tax return that could be filed and updated electronically. By integrating the income tax and estate-planning processes, the testamentary schedule would encourage the exercise of testamentary freedom by interacting with the testator annually at the optimal moment – when preparing legally significant tax documents that in many cases take into account considerations relevant to estate planning (e.g., potential beneficiaries and the nature and extent of property). The substantive design of the testamentary schedule would improve upon existing statutory form wills by simplifying language and providing testators with greater flexibility regarding distribution of their estates. To assist lay testators, the state should provide complimentary software akin to the commercial "TurboTax" program, enabling testators to generate a draft will based upon user responses collected during an electronic interview.

THE HIGH RATE OF INTESTACY AND ITS COST

Testamentary freedom must be exercised affirmatively during life by executing a will, and the law strongly favors will-making by granting special protections for testate estates. The Constitution protects testamentary freedom so long as the decedent executes a will, but the Constitution provides no protection if the decedent died intestate because she intentionally relied on the default rules of heirship.[1] Likewise, state inheritance law favors wills through rules of construction giving effect to a testamentary document if the alternative is partial or complete intestacy.[2] Courts also make every effort to adhere to the testator's expressed or construed intent when a will exists.

Over the last few decades, American law has dramatically expanded the power of testation by vesting the dead hand with unprecedented control over property once owned by the decedent. Congress scaled back estate tax rates dramatically and increased the amount of wealth transferable without any transfer tax liability. At the same time, many states enacted dynasty trust legislation authorizing trusts up to 1,000 years in duration, theoretically allowing the decedent to control property for many generations after death. For the wealthy, those reforms were powerfully complementary – dynasty trust legislation enabled enduring control over private property while federal transfer tax reform greatly expanded the quantum of property subject to that control. Americans now have more power to control the disposition of property at death than ever before. In stark contrast to the sweeping scope of testamentary freedom, scholars agree that a high rate of intestacy has persisted throughout most of American history. In the eighteenth and nineteenth centuries, wills were uncommon except among the wealthy. Most recently, a 2009 publication estimated that 65% of Americans do not have a will.[3] A 2006 nationwide survey found that 68% of respondents lacked a will.[4] Both estimates corroborate older studies reporting similar findings that most individuals who lack a will never obtain one.[5]

For most Americans, therefore, intestacy statutes govern the disposition of probate property at death. By design, intestacy statutes reflect a legislative presumption that most individuals prefer property to pass to surviving family members, generally

[1] *Hodel v. Irving* 481 U.S. 704, 715 (1987).

[2] Rules of construction, such as doctrines to resolve ambiguous language, are often used by courts to avert intestacy through interpretation of testamentary language. Importantly, however, courts have not applied presumptions favoring the exercise of testamentary freedom in the context of statutory rules governing the *validity* of wills.

[3] Mary L. Fellows et al., *Public Attitudes about Property Distribution at Death and Intestate Succession Laws in the United States*, AM. B. FOUND. RES. J. 321, 335 (1978). Wendy S. Goffe & Rochelle L. Haller, *From Zoom to Doom? Risks of Do-It-Yourself Estate Planning*, EST. PLAN. (Apr. 2011), at 27.

[4] Alyssa A. DiRusso, *Testacy and Intestacy: The Dynamics of Wills and Demographic Status*, 23 QUINNIPIAC PROB. L.J. 36, 41 (2009).

[5] See, e.g., Contemporary Studies Project, *A Comparison of Iowans' Dispositive Preferences with Selected Provisions of the Iowa and Uniform Probate Codes*, 63 IOWA L. REV. 1041, 1070 (1978).

defined as the surviving spouse and blood relatives, to the exclusion of friends, cohabitants, favorite charities, or anyone else. Scholars argue that principles of testamentary freedom mandate agreement between heirship rules and probable intent because to do otherwise would create a trap for the uninformed. Although there are notable exceptions, such as inheritance rights for same-sex couples in jurisdictions that do not recognize such relationships, intestacy statutes tend to reflect the probable intent of most individuals.

However, there are several adverse consequences associated with unintended intestacy. Most significantly, dying intestate is problematic in the significant number of cases where the decedent's intended beneficiaries are not heirs. Intestacy is also unsuitable for a large and growing population of nontraditional families, which includes relationships other than those defined by consanguinity, marriage, or legal adoption. Intestacy statutes fail to account for probable intent in nontraditional families because the legislature cannot (or will not) make presumptions about probable intent when the decedent's relationship to intended beneficiaries is not clearly defined by traditionally accepted indicia of familial status. Because most Americans are unsure of how their property would be distributed by intestacy, the absence of a will creates uncertainty regarding the succession of property at death and can lead to frustrated expectations for the surviving family at a time of grief and emotional turmoil. The unintended descent of property by intestacy can also lead to fractionated interests held as tenants in common by multiple heirs. This is problematic because tenants in common must coordinate and obtain consent from fractional owners before maintaining or selling the property.

Even when intestacy statutes correctly anticipate the decedent's intended beneficiaries, dying intestate can lead to undesirable, costly, and acrimonious guardianship and administration contests, which could otherwise be avoided by executing a will. Guardianship issues are an especially important consideration for individuals with minor children. Upon the death of a parent with a minor child, a court must appoint a responsible adult, known as a "guardian of the person," to care for the surviving child left without a legal guardian. During life, the parent may nominate a guardian of the person by will, but failure to nominate forces the court to select from a statutory hierarchy of possible guardians to care for the child without direction from the decedent parent. Further, if an unmarried single parent dies intestate, all or most of the estate passes to the decedent's children, but a court proceeding may be necessary to appoint a "guardian of the estate" or conservator of the child's property.[6] During life, it is advantageous for the minor child's parent to nominate the guardian of the estate or conservator; such nominations are typically made by will. Guardianship concerns are most prescient for the large and growing population of unmarried parents in the United States; the 2010 Census reported

[6] The same concerns are present if both parents (whether married or unmarried) of a minor child die simultaneously.

slightly over twenty million households with children under the age of eighteen but no spouse living with the householder.[7]

All individuals should be concerned about conflicts regarding the selection of a personal representative to administer their estates. Absent testamentary appointment of an executor, a court must appoint a personal representative without express direction from the decedent. The personal representative plays a critical role in the estate administration process because she is typically given authority and discretion to decide whether and how to liquidate property in the estate to satisfy creditor claims and general bequests. Disagreement among beneficiaries regarding selection of the personal representative can lead to expensive and contentious proceedings that dissipate the decedent's estate. The testator can resolve such disagreements in advance by designating an executor in the will.

The high rate of intestacy also raises serious questions of fairness. Demographic analyses reveal that individuals are more likely to have a will if they are white, male, married or formerly married, educated, older, and wealthy; this demographic pattern has endured over time.[8] As a result, the benefits of expanding testamentary freedom (i.e., legal protections for testate estates, dynasty trust legislation, and transfer tax reform) disproportionately flow to those with great wealth, thereby contributing to the growing economic inequality in the United States. For the very wealthy, testamentary freedom and dead-hand control allow for great concentrations of wealth, but for the rest of society, great accumulations of wealth contribute to economic inequality. Studies have shown that individuals who have made a will tend to be white, male, older, and above the median national income.[9]

By contrast, with unintended intestacy, wealth is commonly disbursed among multiple heirs rather than concentrated.[10] This effect compounds the problem of economic inequality because intestate decedents disproportionately belong to the lower and middle economic classes. For decedents with modest estates, the transmission of assets at death permits economic continuity from one generation to the next, but when modest estates are divided among many intestate heirs, economic intergenerational continuity is destroyed. When intended beneficiaries are financially dependent on the succession of property from the decedent, the failure to inherit can be economically devastating. The cost of losing an anticipated inheritance is more economically harmful for those intended beneficiaries than the benefit of a modest windfall inheritance is economically helpful for unintended heirs.

[7] See Profile of General Population and Housing Characteristics, Am. FactFinder, http://factfinder2.census.gov/.

[8] DiRusso, supra note 5, at 44–51; Fellows et al., supra note 4, at 324–25.

[9] See, e.g., *id.* DiRusso, supra note 5.

[10] See B. James Deaton, *Intestate Succession and Heir Property: Implications for Future Research on the Persistence of Poverty in Central Appalachia*, 41 J. Econ. Issues 927, 929 (2007).

Economic disruption is particularly acute in modest estates because the largest asset is almost always the decedent's personal residence. When real property descends to multiple heirs as tenants in common, the fracturing interests make an already modest inheritance even less valuable. If the intended beneficiaries are living in the decedent's primary residence, unintended intestacy can jeopardize their living situation. The problem of fractionation can be prevented by executing a will that identifies a single or small number of beneficiaries rather than allowing property to descend by default to intestate heirs, who can be numerous, remote, and unwilling to cooperate.

THE CURRENT TESTAMENTARY PROCESS DETERS THE CREATION OF WILLS

Given that the law favors will-making, but the majority of people die without a will, why do so many individuals fail to create one? In theory, one answer could be reliance on the statutory default rules, which relieves people of the need to create a will. Empirical studies, however, suggest that individuals lacking a will do not intentionally rely on the default rules.[11] Most individuals do not understand (or claim to understand) even the most basic consequences of dying intestate.

Scholars often explain testamentary procrastination as the product of fear relating to death. According to this view, those who are unwilling to confront the consequences of their own mortality are unlikely to make a will. It is undoubtedly true that humans do not like thinking about or dealing with matters relating to death, but no published empirical finding has established a causal link between such fears and the high rate of intestacy. In fact, opinion surveys suggest that fear of death does not play a major role. For example, in a 1978 Iowa intestacy study, only 4% of respondents said they did not have a will because "they do not like to think about wills" – possibly an implicit reference to contemplating death – and 96% of respondents cited reasons completely unrelated to the psychology of death. Opinion surveys, however, may fail to capture behavioral phenomena accurately, as subjective explanations for one's own behavior tend to be unreliable because humans often do not understand why they engage in certain behavior.

Observation of *actual* behavior points to the conclusion that fear of death, though undoubtedly widespread, is probably not the leading cause of testamentary procrastination. Humans surely harbor fears about their own mortality, but they make plans for the succession of property at death when the process is sufficiently simple, quick, and accessible. In the United States, most transfers of property at death occur outside the probate system through "will substitutes," such as jointly titled property with rights of survivorship, life insurance, and retirement plans that contain a death

11 See Fellows et al., supra note 4, at 339–40; Contemporary Studies Project, supra note 6, at 1077–78.

benefit provision.[12] Will substitutes are popular in part because they avoid the delay and cost of probate, but more importantly, because they are simple to understand, widely available, and quickly executed on standardized forms without the need for legal draftsmanship or witness attestation. For example, most Americans own life insurance, and the majority of contracts in force are individual life insurance policies purchased by the policyholder. Life insurance is so simple to understand and obtain that many individuals purchase their policies directly from insurance carriers over the internet without a broker or agent. The fact that life insurance is so widely purchased, and other forms of non-testamentary transfers are so commonplace, suggests that fear of death is not the primary cause of testamentary procrastination.

Rather than fear of mortality, the more likely cause of testamentary procrastination is the complexity and unique burdens imposed by the testamentary process itself. Most individuals are unfamiliar with the will-making process, and as a result, they hesitate rather than perform the testamentary act. Such behavior is consistent with psychological research on the behavioral phenomenon of procrastination, which suggests that individuals are more likely to procrastinate when confronted by unfamiliar or complex tasks, particularly when the costs of the individual's failure to act are internalized by others. In the will-making context, people perceive the statutorily imposed formalities for executing a will to be complex and unfamiliar, and the costs of failing to act manifest after the person dies and are borne by only the person's intended beneficiaries. Lay testators are likely to perceive two aspects of the will-making process in particular as complex and unfamiliar: (1) the witness attestation requirement, and (2) the need to draft legal language of property conveyance.

The witness attestation requirement distinguishes the will-making process from other acts of legal significance, such as entering into a contract. Although the requirement of obtaining witness signatures may seem simple on its face, the process is unfamiliar to most lay testators and the case law is replete with examples of will contests in which the testator failed to comply with the witness attestation requirement. The need for legal draftsmanship deters the exercise of testamentary freedom because lay individuals are unaccustomed to drafting legal language of conveyance and inadequately trained to do so. Unlike consumer contracts, most of which are unwritten (and those which are in writing are rarely drafted by the consumer), the current will-making process in most states lacks a reliable medium for lay testators to adopt a customizable estate plan without engaging in legal draftsmanship.

Lay individuals are understandably wary of attempting the task on their own and are discouraged from doing so by estate-planning professionals who would prefer to charge a fee for preparing a will or trust.[13] While is it surely advisable to obtain the

[12] John H. Langbein, *The Nonprobate Revolution and the Future of the Law of Succession*, 97 Harv. L. Rev. 1108, 1108 (1984).

[13] Kent D. Schenkel, *Testamentary Fragmentation and the Diminishing Role of the Will: An Argument for Revival*, 41 Creighton L. Rev. 155, 179–80 (2008).

advice of estate-planning counsel, for Americans of modest means, the cost of that advice can serve as a deterrence to the exercise of testamentary freedom – yet another excuse to postpone making a will. The decisions required to formulate a testamentary plan are indeed difficult, so the testamentary process should be designed to alleviate that difficulty rather than exacerbate it. Making a will is difficult, in part, because individuals believe that executing a will involves making final decisions. But wills are freely revocable, so the testamentary process should contain a default advisory that informs the testator that an executed will need not be permanent. The testamentary process should also provide an accessible, transparent medium for revocation. By emphasizing and facilitating the revocability of testamentary documents, the law could reduce the perceived difficulty of decisions involved in planning for the disposition of property at death.

For most individuals with simple estates, drafting an elaborate formal will from scratch is not necessary to memorialize testamentary intent. Most individuals have simple estates and would be satisfied with a basic testamentary instrument that avoids intestacy and could be quickly understood and executed. If the will-making process were more akin to non-testamentary transfers, such as life insurance and pension plan death beneficiary forms, lay individuals would be more likely to handle their own estates and overcome the interference that prevents them from obtaining a will. Better yet, if a testamentary form were an integrated optional component of the compulsory income tax process, individuals who are required to file an income tax return may be less likely to procrastinate in making a will. In short, simplifying the will-making process would likely reduce testamentary procrastination.

A complex will-making process deters self-representation and raises transaction costs, but the result of that deterrence in most cases is intestacy, not increased reliance on attorneys. Professional estate-planning advice may indeed be beneficial, but the will-making process should not be intentionally rendered complex for the purpose of channeling individuals to lawyers. If the goal of inheritance law is to facilitate donative intent rather than to regulate it, then the will-making process should be universally accessible without the need for professional representation.

REFORMING THE TESTAMENTARY PROCESS

Over the last forty years, longstanding adherence to formality and ceremonial tradition have been relaxed in some respects, with a minority of jurisdictions now favoring more informal rules governing the execution and validity of wills. For example, the publication requirement and simultaneous presence rule for witness attestation, which led to many harmless execution errors, were abandoned in the 1969 Uniform Probate Code.[14] In addition to scaling back some of the testamentary formalities, some courts and legislatures now recognize that the purpose of

[14] See Langbein, supra note 12, at 5.

testamentary formalities is to ensure the reliability of wills, not to discourage self-representation or homemade wills.[15] The positive trend toward informalism promotes accessibility and self-representation.

The Trend Toward Informalism

The modern trend of inheritance law also supplies doctrines to cure execution defects when there is sufficient evidence that a will reliably states the testator's intent. In New Jersey, for example, the state Supreme Court has adopted a broad doctrine of substantial compliance, which saves a defective will from automatic invalidity. Rather than denying probate as a matter of course, the court must consider "whether the noncomplying document express[es] the decedent's testamentary intent, and [whether] its form sufficiently approximate[s] the Wills Act formality to enable the court to conclude that it serves the purposes of the Wills Act ..."[16] The New Jersey legislature has further liberalized the law regarding testamentary formalities by adopting the Uniform Probate Code's harmless error rule, which directs courts to treat a defective will as compliant if the proponent adduces clear and convincing evidence that the decedent intended the document to be a will.[17] A minority, but growing number, of states and U.S. territories have adopted both the doctrine of substantial compliance and the harmless error rule.[18] The trend toward informalism increases public access to the will-making process by excusing or forgiving procedural mistakes by lay testators who may be unaware of the technical statutory requirements.

Witness Attestation

The trend toward informalism has not gone far enough to promote universal access to the will-making process because, in all states except for Pennsylvania, witness attestation or notarization (a less onerous form of witness attestation) remains a testamentary requirement for a typewritten will. Under that requirement, the testator must sign or acknowledge her will in the presence of two witnesses who then sign the will within a reasonable period of time. The witness attestation

15 See Mary Louise Fellows & Gregory S. Alexander, *Forty Years of Codification of Estates and Trusts Law: Lessons for the Next Generation*, 40 GA. L. REV. 1049, 1059–64 (2006).

16 In re Will of Ranney, 589 A.2d 1339, 1344 (N.J. 1991) (quoting John H. Langbein, *Substantial Compliance with the Wills Act*, 88 HARV. L. REV. 489 (1975)).

17 N.J. Stat. Ann. § 3B:3–3 (West 2007).

18 A number of jurisdictions have enacted the harmless error rule by statute, using the language from Section 2-502 of the Uniform Probate Code. Haw. Rev. Stat. § 560:2–503 (2010); Mich. Comp. Laws § 700.2503 (2002); Mont. Code Ann. § 72-2-523 (2011); N.J. Stat. Ann. § 3B:3–3; S.D. Codified Laws § 29A-2-503 (2004); Utah Code Ann. § 75-2-503 (LexisNexis 1993 & Supp. 2011); V.I. Code. Ann. tit. 15, § 2-503 (Supp. 2011). Other jurisdictions have enacted variations on the harmless error rule. Cal. Prob. Code § 6110 (West 2009); Colo. Rev. Stat. § 15–11–503 (2011); Ohio Rev. Code Ann. § 2107.24 (West Supp. 2011); Va. Code Ann. § 64.1–49.1 (2007).

requirement is often justified on grounds that the presence of witnesses at the time of execution reduces the likelihood of fraud, duress, or undue influence exerted upon the testator, but in almost all cases of fraud, duress, or undue influence, the document offered for probate complied with the witness attestation requirement. It seems difficult to justify continued application of the witness attestation requirement on those grounds alone.

Although the purpose of witness attestation, like all testamentary formalities, is to increase the reliability of wills, witness attestation imposes unacceptable costs because the requirement is easy to botch and failure to comply is often exploited by disappointed heirs to invalidate wills notwithstanding strong evidence of authenticity. Judicial insistence upon strict compliance with the attestation requirement thus tends to frustrate the decedent's intent rather than facilitate it.

There is also convincing proof that witness attestation is not necessary to prevent the probating of fraudulent wills. Pennsylvania does not require witness attestation, and the state has not become a breeding ground for fraudulent wills. Will substitutes, which are not subject to the attestation requirement, allow property to pass at death outside the probate system, and the success of financial intermediaries that provide will substitutes shows that such transfers are rarely tainted by fraud. Thus, the trend toward informalism has at least one more step before it is complete. Witness attestation should be abolished as a requirement for a valid will.

Holographic and Form Wills

Another positive area of inheritance law reform, the recognition of holographic (handwritten) and statutory form wills, promotes public access to the will-making process by recognizing certain types of homemade wills. Holographic wills are testamentary documents written in the testator's own handwriting and provide a simple way for lay testators to make a homemade will. They are valid in twenty-six states (and under the Uniform Probate Code) without witness attestation because the handwriting sample serves as a proxy for authenticity.[19] Although recognition of holographic wills is a positive step toward liberalizing testamentary formalities, in practice, holographic wills are relatively uncommon. Drafting any will from scratch, whether handwritten or typed, requires legal draftsmanship, and lay testators are understandably wary of attempting that task on their own. As a result, recognition of holographic wills has not meaningfully affected the high rate of intestacy.

Form wills are testamentary documents based on templates that allow testators to fill in the blanks, thereby eliminating the need for legal draftsmanship, but not witness attestation. Commercial form wills have been available for decades, and increased interest in commercial form will services such as Legal Zoom among lay testators demonstrates demand for reform promoting standardization and

[19] Unif. Probate Code § 2-502(b) (2008).

simplification. Some courts, however, have criticized commercial forms as unreliable and potentially confusing to lay testators.

In 1984, the National Conference of Commissioners on Uniform State Laws promulgated the Uniform Statutory Will Act "to simplify and modernize laws dealing with probate" by creating a simple will form for adoption by state legislatures.[20] The statutory form will was intended to serve as an accessible alternative to intestacy without the need for professional counsel. Further, it was supposed to resolve concerns about reliability and usability because it would be designed by state legislatures and, unlike commercial products, would be presumptively valid and enforceable.

The statutory form eliminated the need for legal draftsmanship, one of the primary deterrents to lay testation. But the Uniform Statutory Will Act's model form failed to gain acceptance, with only a small handful of states enacting the model legislation,[21] and in 1996, was no longer recommended by the National Conference of Commissioners on Uniform State Laws.[22] The Uniform Statutory Will Act failed, in large part, because the form relied on the esoteric doctrine of incorporation by reference, thus rendering the boilerplate language too complex for the average lay testator.

The Uniform Statutory Will Act was not successful, but the concept of a statutory form will remains sound. Indeed, some states rejected the model legislation but embraced the underlying concept by enacting a modified statutory form will. Inheritance law should embrace renewed consideration of statutory form wills because they eliminate the need for legal draftsmanship and encourage the exercise of testamentary freedom.

A PROPOSAL FOR STATUTORY REFORM: A "TESTAMENTARY SCHEDULE" ON STATE INDIVIDUAL INCOME TAX RETURN

To promote universal access to the will-making process, this chapter proposes a statutory form will that would be attached to state income tax returns as an optional schedule called a "Testamentary Schedule – Last Will and Testament." This schedule would (1) authorize a simplified statutory form will governed by the same execution formalities as the income tax return, (2) attach the statutory form will to the state individual income tax return as an optional testamentary schedule, (3) assist lay testators in completing the form by providing computerized software similar to the commercial "Turbo Tax" program, and (4) permit electronic filing and storage of completed testamentary schedules. The testamentary schedule would

20 Unif. Statutory Will Act prefatory note (1984).

21 Six states have enacted statutory form wills. Cal. Prob. Code §§ 6220–6227 (West 2009); Me. Rev. Stat. tit. 18, § 2-514 (1998); Mass. Gen. Laws ch. 191B, § 2 (2011); Mich. Comp. Laws § 700.2519 (2002 & Supp. 2011); N.M. Stat. Ann. § 45-2A-3 (2011); Wis. Stat. § 853.55 (2002).

22 Unif. Statutory Will Act, 8B U.L.A. 174 (Supp. 2011).

be governed by the substantive law of wills and could be revoked, amended, or superseded by the execution of another testamentary schedule, revocation form, or formal will or codicil. The testamentary schedule would drastically reduce transaction costs by eliminating the need for legal draftsmanship, by removing the witness attestation requirement, and by simplifying execution procedures.

The testamentary schedule is a novel innovation because it designates the state income tax return as the point of governmental intervention to promote testacy. Integrating the income tax and testamentary processes would promote testacy by efficiently combining complementary tasks that often involve overlapping considerations. In particular, the will-making process requires that the testator be capable of understanding the natural objects of her bounty (i.e., potential beneficiaries) and the nature and extent of her property. In many cases, the income tax process requires similar considerations because taxpayers must identify financial dependents and review income-producing property to report income, deductions, and exemptions properly. Because of the strong factual overlap between taxes and testation, the testamentary schedule's attachment to the income tax return would render the will-making process less onerous than drafting a stand-alone testamentary instrument. The income tax return prompts the testator to consider most of the relevant estate-planning factors, and the testamentary schedule simplifies the will-making process by allowing the testator to record her estate plan in a fill-in-the-blank format.

Integrating the income tax and testamentary processes would yield several advantageous outcomes. First, the testator would confront the testamentary schedule at a time of year when she is already required to contemplate matters of money, income, property, and financial dependents. Second, the testamentary schedule would target individuals most likely to own property at death, such as those who earn income and are therefore required to file an income tax return; if successful, the program could be extended to target other populations not required to complete a state income tax return, perhaps by attaching the schedule to other government forms such as welfare applications or government health benefit registrations. Third, the testamentary schedule would alleviate the problem of "stale wills" because the testamentary schedule's placement on the income tax return would prompt an annual testamentary review. Fourth, the testamentary schedule would alleviate the problem of lost wills because all filed testamentary schedules would be retained by the state until the time of probate. Fifth, the testamentary schedule would harness the care, seriousness, and high rate of compliance with which Americans regard the income tax process. Sixth, individuals who retain skilled professionals to prepare their income tax returns may be encouraged to seek professional estate-planning advice at the same time. Seventh, legal advice for individuals who seek assistance in completing the testamentary schedule will cost less than a formal will drafted from scratch. Eighth, individuals eventually will grow accustomed to dealing with estate planning as an integrated part of the compulsory income tax process, thereby overcoming interference such as procrastination and avoidance.

Other areas of the law already combine widely used administrative processes to promote public awareness of and optional participation in beneficial but obscure government programs. For example, individuals who apply for a state driver's license are asked whether they would like to register as an organ or tissue donor. Although organ donor registration is administratively distinct from the licensing of motor vehicle operators, by combining the driver's licensure process (which is frequently used and universally familiar) with organ donor registration (which is relatively obscure), the law encourages individuals who would otherwise be unaware of the organ donor registration program or registration process to complete the administrative process of becoming an organ donor.

The state income tax return would serve as the point of intervention rather than the federal income tax return because wills are governed by state law, and once executed, the testator would file the will in her state of domicile for safekeeping and ease of probate administration. Seven states, however, do not impose an individual income tax: Alaska, Florida, Nevada, South Dakota, Texas, Washington, and Wyoming. Those states could adopt the testamentary schedule as an independent form and allow testators to file completed testamentary schedules electronically with the state; but of course, those states would lose the benefit of coupling the estate planning and income tax processes. In states that do impose an income tax, the form should also be offered as a standalone instrument for individuals not required to file a tax return.

Proper design of the testamentary schedule would be critical to its success. The testamentary schedule must include all essential elements of a basic will, which, when reduced to its most basic functions, is a donative instrument that: (1) "transfers property at death, amends, supplements, or revokes a prior will, appoints an executor, nominates a guardian, exercises a testamentary power of appointment, or excludes or limits the right of an individual or class to succeed to property of the decedent passing by intestate succession"[23]; (2) complies with testamentary formalities;[24] and (3) is given legal effect when offered for probate.[25] For simple estates, the most important functions of a will include the transfer of property, revocation of prior wills, appointment of an executor, and nomination of a guardian for minor children. The testamentary schedule would serve those basic functions by improving upon existing statutory form wills.

In 1993, Professor Gerry Beyer performed a comprehensive empirical study to assess the design and usability of statutory form wills.[26] Beyer's study remains the only such empirical inquiry. The study results varied according to participants' level of education. Participants with no education above the high school level had the

23 Restatement (Third) of Property: Wills & Other Donative Transfers § 3.1, cmt.a (2003).

24 *Id.* § 3.1.

25 See, e.g., Unif. Probate Code § 3-102 (2008).

26 Gerry W. Beyer, *Statutory Fill-In Will Forms – The First Decade: Theoretical Constructs and Empirical Findings*, 72 Or. L. Rev. 769, 798–99 (1993).

most difficulty, but many of their errors were minor, "such as including gifts of personal property under the section for real property or placing cash gifts to family members in the section for cash gifts to charities."[27] Those errors were minor because the document as a whole contained sufficient expression of the testator's intent to permit probate administration. But other errors, such as misunderstanding the residuary clause, were more serious. Participants with college degrees and students currently enrolled in law school fared much better and were generally able to use and understand the forms. Even though some participants had trouble completing the forms, the vast majority said they welcomed the enactment of statutory form wills. Many participants said the availability of a statutory form would serve as an impetus to obtain a will. Beyer concluded that the advantages of statutory wills strongly outweighed the disadvantages, and that the most common errors could be prevented by improving the forms.

When legislatures amend and draft will forms, they should: (1) provide greater opportunity for individualization; (2) write in plain language; (3) provide detailed instructions, warnings, and explanations which are effectively presented (i.e., in a question and answer format and located on the form where the information is needed); (4) create an effective format; and (5) have straightforward execution procedures.[28]

The proposed testamentary schedule adopts Beyer's recommendations; a sample will and revocation form appear in the Appendix. The proposed form incorporates aspects of the California and Michigan statutory form wills, but provides several innovations, including: (1) relocation of the residuary clause to the beginning of the will under the heading, Primary Beneficiaries; (2) enhanced flexibility for customized estate planning; (3) reliance on information from the testator's most recent state income tax return as a proxy for authenticity; (4) abolishment of witness attestation; (5) inclusion of a simple revocation form; and (6) optional provisions for the testator to record preferences regarding organ donation and disposition of final remains.

Perhaps the most notable feature of the proposed testamentary schedule is the relocation and renaming of the residuary clause. In most wills, specific bequests and cash gifts are recited at the beginning; the residuary clause, which disposes of the balance of the estate, appears at the end. The residuary clause, however, is often the most important provision of the will because it typically distributes the bulk of the estate. In Beyer's study, the residuary clause generated the greatest amount of confusion, which is understandable because first-time testators are unlikely to understand the term "residue" or its critical function in a formal will. To reduce confusion and emphasize its importance, the proposed form relocates the residuary clause to the beginning of the form and describes the provision without using the

[27] *Id.* at 808.
[28] *Id.* at 836.

terms "residue" or "residuary clause." Instead, the provision is simply called "Primary Beneficiaries" and is accompanied by plain English instructions. Thus, the Primary Beneficiaries clause serves all functions of the traditional residuary clause without using terminology that most lay testators find confusing.

Existing statutory form wills severely restrict the number of beneficiaries and specific gifts for the sake of simplicity, and some testators react to those restrictions by altering or abandoning the form. Therefore, the testamentary schedule should provide greater flexibility for estate customization by providing space for at least ten primary beneficiaries, ten personal residence beneficiaries, twenty beneficiaries of specific gifts of tangible personal property, and ten cash gift beneficiaries. Although the proposed form in the Appendix provides space for fewer beneficiaries because of publication formatting constraints, a full-size version of the form would provide space for the recommended number of beneficiaries and, perhaps more importantly, a computerized version of the form would avoid spatial limitations on the number of beneficiaries altogether.

The proposed testamentary schedule includes an optional provision for the testator to record preferences regarding organ donation and the disposition of final remains, intended to supplement existing state programs. Professionally drafted wills often include the testator's preferences regarding the disposition of final remains, but statutory form wills do not.

Additionally, because the testamentary schedule is intended for lay usage, states should strongly consider providing free, computer-guided assistance akin to the TurboTax software popular in the income tax return context. The software should guide the testator through each part of the testamentary schedule using a question-and-answer interview format and generate a draft will based on the testator's responses. The software should also include error-checking features to prevent submission of incomplete forms and errant responses. For example, if the testator opts to assign percentage shares to multiple primary beneficiaries, then the software should ensure that the percentage shares add up to 100%. Introducing this type of technology would be consistent with the current trend promoting public access to the law by helping individuals represent themselves. Courts have long assisted pro se litigants in representing themselves by relaxing the formalities associated with civil litigation. Recently, courts have expanded those efforts by providing technology to help self-represented individuals prepare their own pleadings and litigation forms. States that adopt the proposed testamentary schedule should consider adapting that technology for use by lay testators.

Execution and submission of the testamentary schedule would be governed by many of the same procedural requirements as the state income tax return. The following specific requirements are recommended:

- The testamentary schedule should be completed electronically, but the state should provide a paper version of the form as well.

- For authentication purposes, the testamentary schedule should require information from the testator's most recently filed income tax return (e.g., gross income, total deductions, or adjusted gross income).
- The testamentary schedule should be executed by the testator. For electronic forms, the testator should provide an electronic signature. For handwritten forms, the testator should provide a manual signature.
- The testator should be required to file the executed testamentary schedule with the state for safekeeping. Electronic filing should be encouraged.
- All testamentary schedules on file with the state should be treated with at least the same degree of privacy as personal taxpayer information. Privacy rules should prohibit the state from disclosing filed testamentary schedules to third parties during the testator's life. Upon the testator's death, the state should provide the most recently filed testamentary schedule to parties entitled to file for probate and provide all testamentary schedules filed by the decedent upon request by parties litigating a will contest.
- The testamentary schedule should be attached to the state individual income tax return as an optional schedule and be available as a stand-alone form as well.
- Joint testamentary schedules, wherein two spouses attempt to complete a single testamentary schedule as a reciprocal joint will, should be prohibited to avoid the ambiguities associated with joint wills. Married individuals filing a joint tax return should be required to complete separate testamentary schedules.

Potential criticisms include the possibility of fraud, loss of testamentary privacy, distortion of testamentary intent, failure to appreciate the significance of the testamentary act, and the state's assumption of storage and administrative costs. Incorporating the form wills with income tax filing should help reduce the potential for many of these concerns, and as they arise, changes to the form wills can be made to reduce any of the costs associated with the practice. But it does not seem that the mere potential for these problems, which exist even with attorney-assisted wills, outweigh the benefits of increasing public access to the will-making process.[29]

Historically, the most challenging aspect of estate planning for lay testators involved the sophisticated planning necessary to minimize federal gift and estate tax liability. Until recently, federal gift and estate tax exemption amounts were low enough to impose wealth transfer taxation on relatively small estates. In 1976, for example, the federal estate tax exemption amount was $60,000, so for many (although not most) decedents, tax considerations were a relevant concern. Over the last thirty years, however, Congress has gradually and substantially increased the federal wealth transfer tax exemption amounts. Now, as a result, the federal gift and estate tax only affects a small population of wealthy taxpayers. In 2009, the federal

[29] Reid K. Weisbord, *Wills for Everyone: Helping Individuals Opt out of Intestacy*, 53 B.C. L. Rev. 877, 938–44 (2012).

estate tax exemption amount was $3.5 million, and the Internal Revenue Service received only 14,713 estate tax returns reporting estate tax liability.[30] That year, there were approximately 2.4 million deaths in the United States, so roughly 0.6% of decedents reported an estate tax liability. In 2011, *state* estate tax exemption amounts were also high; among states that impose an estate tax, the average exemption amount was $1.8 million and the median amount, $1 million. Thus, for the vast majority of Americans, death taxes are no longer a relevant estate-planning consideration. The need for professional estate-planning advice has drastically declined, and with it, the potential for lay testators to jeopardize their own interests by handling their own estates.

Self-representation may not be appropriate for wealthy individuals who expect to make transfers exceeding the gift and estate tax exemption amounts. But wealthy individuals are likely to obtain professional estate-planning advice regardless of whether the state provides a statutory form will designed for lay usage. As a precaution, the testamentary schedule should advise users to consult a tax attorney if they expect to leave a large estate. Electronic forms could facilitate effective warnings through the use of appropriate prompts in the testator interview process.

CONCLUSION

Most individuals who want to obtain a will die without one, and rarely do they understand the rules of intestacy or the negative consequences of dying intestate. When unintended, intestacy can wreak economic devastation and social disruption upon the decedent's intended beneficiaries, and in the aggregate, widespread intestacy contributes to the growing problem of economic inequality in the United States.

Many scholars explain the high rate of intestacy as the product of human fears regarding death and mortality, but in the absence of direct empirical evidence supporting that hypothesis, this chapter proposes an alternative explanation for the widespread lapse of testamentary freedom: the obscurity, complexity, and expenses of the will-making process itself.

The proposed testamentary schedule would be governed by the substantive law of wills, but execution formalities would be subject to the procedural rules applicable to the income tax return, including electronic filing procedures. By integrating two complementary tasks – the income tax and estate-planning processes – the testator would encounter the will-making process at an optimal moment, and by creating an annual testamentary routine, reduce the incidence of stale wills. As an empirical matter, adoption of the testamentary schedule would permit a rigorous analysis of

[30] Estate Tax Returns Filed in 2009, IRS (Dec. 2010), available at www.irs.gov/taxstats/indtaxstats/article/0,,id=210646,00.html.

whether the current testamentary process deters the exercise of testamentary freedom. If properly implemented, the number of individuals without a will could be compared before and after introduction of the testamentary schedule. The testamentary schedule would render the will-making process universally accessible, promote the careful exercise of testamentary freedom, and increase the likelihood that the decedent's intent will be expressed and, as a result, implemented.

28

Court Facilitation of Self-Representation

Rachel Ekery

Courts throughout the country are devoting significant resources to develop self-help tools that make court filings and proceedings more accessible to the growing number of pro se litigants. In this chapter, Rachel Ekery presents a comprehensive survey of what courts are doing to leverage technology and attorney assistance through the creation of self-help centers, standardized filing forms, online document assembly, smart forms enabled with electronic filing, and how-to videos on court YouTube channels. These technological advances significantly lower barriers for pro se litigants and are models for other courts to replicate.

This chapter surveys the significant systemic changes that courts are making to increase access to civil justice for pro se litigants. In civil cases, the right to self-representation has been protected by statute in the federal courts since "the beginnings of our Nation,"[1] and is guaranteed by state constitutions, statutes, or procedural rules in the courts of most states.[2] Increasingly, litigants are exercising that right. Most parties, driven by economic necessity, have no other choice.[3]

1 *Faretta v. California*, 433 U.S. 806, 812 (1975); see 28 U.S.C. § 1654 ("In all courts of the United States the parties may plead and conduct their own cases personally or by counsel as, by the rules of such courts, respectively, are permitted to manage and conduct causes therein"). Limited portions of the research for this chapter were also included in Chief Justice Wallace B. Jefferson's speech, *Liberty and Justice for Some: How the Legal System Falls Short in Protecting Basic Rights*, delivered on February 27, 2013, for the Institute of Judicial Administration's Brennan Lecture on State Court and Social Justice at New York University School of Law; see 88 N.Y.U. L. Rev. 1953 (2013).

2 See, e.g., Ala. Const. art. I, § 10 ("That no person shall be barred from prosecuting or defending before any tribunal in this state, by himself or counsel, any civil cause to which he is a party"); N.C. Gen. Stat. § 1–11 (1996) ("A party may appear either in person or by attorney in actions or proceedings in which he is interested"); Tex. R. Civ. P. 7 ("Any party to a suit may appear and prosecute or defend his rights therein, either in person or by an attorney of the court").

3 See, e.g., Ruth Bader Ginsburg, *In Pursuit of the Public Good: Access to Justice in the United States*, 7 Wash. U. J.L. & Pol'y 1 (2001) ("It remains true, however, that the poor, and even the middle class, encounter financial impediments to a day in court. They do not enjoy the secure access available to those with full purses or political muscle"); Susan D. Carle, *Re-Valuing Lawyering for Middle-Income Clients*, 70 Fordham L. Rev. 719, 721 (2001); The Supreme Court of Texas, Misc. Docket No. 11–9046, Order Creating Uniform Forms Task Force, at 1 (Mar. 15, 2011) (observing that increasing numbers of litigants represent themselves because they cannot afford an attorney and are unable to secure representation from legal aid); The Supreme Court of Washington, Order No. 25700-A-1005, at 4 (June 15, 2012), available at www.courts.wa.gov/content/publicUpload/Press%20Releases/25700-A-1005.pdf (noting that 2003 Civil Legal Needs Study showed that the legal system was

But technology has also made self-representation more feasible than before. Court forms, websites, and other resources put a wealth of material at a litigant's fingertips. Information previously available only to trained professionals, and then only for a fee, is now accessible, free of charge, to anyone with access to a computer. The emergence of these resources may lead litigants to believe that a fair outcome can always be achieved without employing a lawyer.[4] It does suggest that attorneys may not be needed in certain cases where courts facilitate self-representation.

The work of courts to enhance the ability of litigants to represent themselves is in part a response to the U.S. Supreme Court's call in *Turner v. Rogers*[5] to look to court-provided safeguards as a substitute for the lack of appointed counsel:

> Those safeguards include (1) notice to the defendant that his "ability to pay" is a critical issue in the contempt proceeding; (2) the use of a form (or the equivalent) to elicit relevant financial information; (3) an opportunity at the hearing for the defendant to respond to statements and questions about his financial status, (*e.g.*, those triggered by his responses on the form); and (4) an express finding by the court that the defendant has the ability to pay.[6]

These measures, in the *Turner* Court's view, could significantly reduce the risk of a failure of due process or erroneous deprivation of liberty.

FORMS AND ONLINE DOCUMENT ASSEMBLY

Forms

One of the safeguards mentioned in *Turner* was court-provided forms to elicit critical information from a self-represented party.[7] Such forms play a central role making the courts more accessible to self-represented litigants.[8] Today, every state provides

unaffordable for moderate-income households – those with incomes between 200% and 400% of the federal poverty level); Texas Access to Justice Commission, *Pro Se Statistics*, at 1, available at www.texasatj.org/files/ExhibitsAQtoReport.pdf (summarizing Legal Services Corporation report showing that 57% of pro se litigants in New York City Family and Housing Courts had incomes under $20,000 per year and that more than 90% of people using court self-help programs in California earned less than $24,000 annually).

4 Several studies have examined why parties represent themselves in court. Two reasons are given more frequently than any others: litigants cannot afford a lawyer, or they believed their case was simple enough to handle on their own. See, e.g., J.M. Greacen, *Self-Represented Litigants and Court and Legal Services Responses to Their Needs: What We Know* (2002); Missouri Supreme Court Joint Commission to Review Pro Se Litigation, *Report to the Supreme Court of Missouri & The Missouri Bar* (2003); New York Office of the Deputy Chief Administrative Judge for Justice Initiatives, *Self-Represented Litigants: Characteristics, Needs, Services* (2005).

5 564 U.S. 431 (2011). 131 S. Ct. 2507, 2520 (2011).

6 *Id.*

7 *Id.* at 2519–20; see also Richard Zorza, Turner v. Rogers: *Improving Due Process for the Self-Represented, Future Trends in State Courts* 2012, National Center for State Courts (2012).

8 See Center on Court Access to Justice for All, *Access Brief: Forms and Document Assembly*, at 1 (2012), available at http://ncsc.contentdm.oclc.org/utils/getfile/collection/accessfair/id/264/filename/265.pdf.

at least some online forms for litigants,[9] and roughly forty states have developed accompanying self-help websites.[10] The five most populous states – California, Texas, New York, Florida, and Illinois – offer a snapshot of the types of online assistance courts give to self-represented litigants, as well as a glimpse into some of the problems encountered in providing such services.

The California courts' website includes an extensive online, self-help center.[11] Published in both English and Spanish,[12] the site helps litigants "find assistance and information, work better with an attorney, and represent [themselves] in some legal matters."[13] The page is divided into sections dealing with different topics, like: getting started, small claims, families and children, divorce or separation, abuse and harassment, eviction and housing, name change, traffic, seniors and conservatorship, and appeals. Within each topic are clear instructions about each proceeding, as well as extensive forms that can be used by litigants. The California courts have provided forms for over thirty years, and there are now more than 1,400 approved forms available.[14] The site also links to the state's self-help centers and family law facilitators, discussed more extensively later.

The Florida courts' homepage includes a "Self Help" section, which provides links to family law self-help centers, family law forms, and assistance in finding a mediator through the Dispute Resolution Center.[15] The forms link includes an explanation of how to use court forms and instructions for completing them. The link has dozens of family law forms covering topics including divorce, paternity, adoption, name change, child support, and domestic violence. The forms also cover most aspects of the litigation process, including filing a petition, conducting discovery, and procuring a judgment.[16] The Florida Supreme Court has also recently approved landlord–tenant forms.[17] Although the Florida courts do not maintain

9 See National Center for State Courts, *Self-Representation State Links*, available at www.ncsc.org/Topics/Access-and-Fairness/Self-Representation/State-Links.aspx?cat=Court%20Forms; see also Texas Access to Justice Commission, *Report to the Supreme Court Advisory Committee, Court's Uniform Forms Task Force* (Apr. 6, 2012).

10 See Center on Court Access to Justice For All, National Center for State Courts, *Forms and Document Assembly*, available at www.ncsc.org/microsites/access-to-justice/home/Topics/Forms-and-Document-Assembly.aspx.

11 California Courts, Online, Self-Help Center, available at www.courts.ca.gov/selfhelp.htm?rdeLocaleAttr=en.

12 California Courts, Centro de Ayuda en Linea, available at www.courts.ca.gov/selfhelp.htm?rdeLocaleAttr=es. Some of the information has also been translated into Chinese, Korean, and Vietnamese. See *id.* at More Languages, available at www.courts.ca.gov/selfhelp-languages.htm.

13 See *id.*

14 Center on Court Access to Justice for All, *Access Brief: Forms and Document Assembly*, at 2 (2012), available at http://ncsc.contentdm.oclc.org/utils/getfile/collection/accessfair/id/264/filename/265.pdf.

15 See Florida State Courts, Self-Help, available at www.flcourts.org/.

16 See Florida State Courts, Family Law Forms, available at www.flcourts.org/gen_public/family/forms_rules/index.shtml#930.

17 See Florida State Courts, Landlord and Tenant Forms, available at www.flcourts.org/gen_public/family/self_help/landlord-tenant.shtml.

those forms, the Florida bar does, and the courts' website provides a link to the forms.[18]

The New York state courts also provide free, do-it-yourself forms that can be completed online and submitted electronically.[19] Their website offers a range of family law forms similar to those offered by states, plus forms covering legal problems in housing, probate and estate administration, and consumer debt.[20] Corresponding YouTube videos guide people through the entire process and provide clear instructions.[21]

The Illinois courts' webpage includes a "Citizen Self-Help" section that links to the Illinois Legal Aid site, the Illinois Child Support site, and the Illinois Lawyer Finder Site.[22] Although the Illinois courts' webpage does not contain forms for litigants, several of the state's intermediate courts provide online forms in a limited set of areas like dissolution of marriage, orders of protection or no contact, and probate affidavits.[23] The Illinois courts have partnered with libraries and Illinois Legal Aid Online to establish interactive, technology-based, self-help legal centers to assist litigants who cannot afford lawyers.[24] In 2012, 77 of Illinois's 102 counties had such centers in public libraries and courthouses.[25]

But like other services designed to help self-represented litigants, court-approved forms can create controversy, as Texas's recent experience shows. In 2010, the Texas Access to Justice Commission, in collaboration with the Office of Court Administration, the Texas Legal Services Center, and the Texas Access to Justice Foundation held a two-day statewide forum on self-represented litigants.[26] Participants discussed the impact pro se litigants have on the justice system and evaluated tools that would enable the courts to steer pro se litigants through the legal system and to operate more efficiently in doing so.[27] It became clear that statewide,

[18] See *id.*

[19] See www.nycourthelp.gov.

[20] See New York CourtHelp, Welcome to the Forms Library!, available at www.nycourthelp.gov./forms.html.

[21] Available at www.youtube.com/watch?v=_34J99kKwDY&feature=youtu.be. In Arizona, the Maricopa County Superior Court offers similar guidance. See www.youtube.com/watch?v=Bq27rkuQ3S8.

[22] See Welcome to Illinois Courts, Citizen Self-Help, available at www.state.il.us/court/default.asp.

[23] See Illinois Second Judicial Circuit Court, Online Forms, available at www.illinoissecondcircuit.info/online_forms.html; Nineteenth Judicial Circuit Court of Lake County, Illinois, Court Forms, available at www.19thcircuitcourt.state.il.us/crt_forms/Pages/default.aspx.

[24] Ill. Legal Aid Online, Our Current Projects, available at www.illinoislegalaidonline.org/index.php?projects (2012); see also James E. Cabral et al., *Using Technology to Increase Access to Justice*, HARV. J. LAW TECHNOL. 241, 247 (2012).

[25] Our Current Projects, supra note 24.

[26] Order Creating Uniform Forms Task Force, Misc. Docket No. 11–9046, at 1 (Tex. 2011), available at www.supreme.courts.state.tx.us/miscdocket/11/11904600.pdf.

[27] *Id.*

standardized forms for pleadings frequently used by self-represented litigants would aid those efforts.[28]

As a result of that discussion, the Supreme Court of Texas appointed a Uniform Forms Task Force to develop standardized forms.[29] Task Force members included judges, private lawyers, legal services attorneys, court clerks, court administrators, and law librarians.[30] Although the Court recognized that the legal system functions most effectively when each litigant is represented by counsel, the Court also noted that parties often appear in courts pro se because they cannot afford an attorney or obtain representation from legal aid organizations.[31] The Court agreed that developing pleading and order forms, approved by the Court for statewide use, would increase access to justice and reduce the strain on courts posed by unrepresented litigants.[32]

The Task Force concluded that family law generally, and divorce in particular, presented the most pressing need.[33] It developed a set of instructions and forms for an uncontested divorce for a couple with no children and no real property. Forty-eight states have court-approved family law forms, and thirty-seven have divorce forms[34] – placing Texas in the distinct minority.[35] Research by the Texas Access to Justice Commission showed that states utilizing such forms reported increased judicial efficiency and economy.[36]

Certain segments of the Texas bar, however, vigorously opposed the forms.[37] The state bar's family law section and other family lawyer groups argued that the court's "foray into uniform forms raise[d] questions about the proper exercise of its power."[38] They complained that the Court did not restrict use of the forms to the

28 *Id.*

29 See *id.*

30 *Id.*

31 *Id.*

32 *Id.*

33 Texas Access to Justice Commission, *A Report to the Supreme Court Advisory Committee from the Texas Access to Justice Commission on the Court's Uniform Forms Task Force*, at 3 (Apr. 6, 2012), available at www.texasatj.org/files/file/041012TAJCReporttoSCACREVISED.pdf.

34 *Id.* at 7; see also Texas Access to Justice Commission, *Exhibits AQ to Report*, at Exhibit G, available at www.texasatj.org/files/ExhibitsAQtoReport.pdf (reporting that only Mississippi and Pennsylvania lacked court-approved family law forms, and reflecting that Texas had court-approved protective order forms).

35 Texas Access to Justice Commission, *A Report to the Supreme Court Advisory Committee from the Texas Access to Justice Commission on the Court's Uniform Forms Task Force*, at 8 (Apr. 6, 2012), available at www.texasatj.org/files/file/041012TAJCReporttoSCACREVISED.pdf; see also Texas Access to Justice Commission, *Exhibits AQ to Report*, at Exhibit G, available at www.texasatj.org/files/ExhibitsAQtoReport.pdf.

36 *Id.*; see also www.texasatj.org/files/file/ExecutiveSummary.pdf.

37 See Family Law Section of the State Bar of Texas, Texas Family Law Foundation, Texas Chapter of the American Academy of Matrimonial Lawyers, and Texas Academy of Family Law Specialists, *Response to the Report of the Uniform Forms Task Force Submitted to the Texas Supreme Court as of January* 11, 2012, available at www.texasatj.org/files/file/FLGResponsetoForms041012.pdf.

38 *Id.* at 5.

indigent (none of the forty-nine states with online forms does),[39] arguing that the Court's goal of increasing access to justice would "not be advanced by assisting those who already have access to justice, i.e., those who *can* afford an attorney."[40] Finally, the associations argued that the development of uniform forms was "beyond the institutional capacity of the Texas Supreme Court and should be abandoned."[41] The state bar president asked the Court to suspend work on the forms.[42] The Court declined to do so, noting that it had a duty to establish "a judicial climate in which people who lack money to hire a lawyer have a reasonable chance to vindicate their rights."[43] Ultimately, the Court approved the forms on November 13, 2012, and recently adopted revised forms incorporating changes made following public comment.[44] The Court cautioned that use of the forms is not required, but "a trial court must not refuse to accept any of the approved forms simply because the applicant used forms or is not represented by counsel."[45] Forms make it easier for self-represented litigants to access the justice system, and courts and litigants generally report positive experiences with forms.[46] Forms may assist not only self-represented litigants, but also lawyers who may be unfamiliar with a particular practice area, making legal services cheaper and more accessible to a wider range of people.[47] In Texas, for example, volunteer attorneys have used the court-approved

[39] See Texas Access to Justice Commission, *Exhibits AQ to Report*, at Exhibit G, available at www.texasatj.org/files/ExhibitsAQtoReport.pdf (reporting that no states limit access to forms to low-income litigants only).

[40] *Id.* at 21.

[41] *Id* at 22.; see also Letter from State Bar of Texas, Family Law Section, to the Supreme Court of Texas (May 2, 2012), available at www.texasatj.org/files/file/FLGSCOTLtrRevised050512.pdf ("If a Supreme Court administrative order endorses forms and instructions that ignore constitutions and statutes, when words in a statute are effectively changed by that court order and when precedent is overshadowed by court ordered forms, the system of law as we have known it will, in fact, have been changed. We have documented the fact that these deviations from our system of law are clearly present in the forms presented to the Court, even after nine months of work by the Task Force").

[42] Letter from Bob Black, President, State Bar of Texas, to Wallace Jefferson, Chief Justice, Tex. Supreme Court (Jan. 5, 2012).

[43] Nathan Koppel, Divorce-by-Form Riles Texas Bar, The Wall Street Journal (Feb. 24, 2012) (quoting letter from Chief Justice Wallace B. Jefferson to State Bar of Texas).

[44] See Order Approving Uniform Forms – Divorce Set One, Supreme Court of Texas (Nov. 13, 2012), available at www.supreme.courts.state.tx.us/miscdocket/12/12919200.pdf. The forms are available at www.supreme.courts.state.tx.us/miscDocket/12/Divorcesetorder.pdf; see also Order Approving Revised Uniform Forms – Divorce Set One, Misc. Docket No. 13–9085 (June 17, 2013), available at www.supreme.courts.state.tx.us/miscdocket/13/13908500.pdf.

[45] Order Approving Revised Uniform Forms – Divorce Set One, Misc. Docket No. 13–9085, at ¶ 2 (June 17, 2013), available at www.supreme.courts.state.tx.us/miscdocket/13/13908500.pdf.

[46] See Texas Access to Justice Commission, State Responses on Standardized Forms, available at www.texasatj.org/files/file/1StateResponsesonStatewideForms.pdf.

[47] Center on Court Access to Justice for All, *Access Brief: Forms and Document Assembly*, at 4 (2012) ("Any program to assist the self-represented litigant must begin with the provision of court forms"), available at http://ncsc.contentdm.oclc.org/utils/getfile/collection/accessfair/id/264/filename/265.pdf.

divorce forms at pro se clinics.[48] Because forms programs are not without controversy, however, court leadership plays a pivotal role in ensuring the success of any form or document assembly program.[49]

Online Document Assembly and Smart Forms

Online document assembly, which is rapidly gaining popularity, is the next frontier for helping the unrepresented navigate the courts. Online document assembly refers to software that asks the user for certain information, often through a step-by-step online "interview," and then populates a form with that information.[50] This method of form completion can be easier than manually filling out forms, especially considering the numerous documents typically required in, say, a family court proceeding.[51] Online document assembly also helps ensure that self-represented litigants accurately complete the requisite forms.[52]

Online document assembly can also be beneficial in cases involving litigants with limited English proficiency. Idaho's document assembly program, for example, provides instructions and requests in English or Spanish, as appropriate, even though the documents that are ultimately generated are in English.[53]

In California, the Orange County Superior Court and the Legal Aid Society of Orange County developed the I-CAN! document assembly system in 2003. I-CAN! stands for Interactive Community Assistance Network, and the network contains thirteen interactive modules addressing legal issues commonly faced by self-represented litigants. The online interviews are accompanied by a video guide in both English and Spanish.[54] By 2012, the system had generated nearly 182,000 pleadings in California, and Orange County judges observed that they could help

48 Angela Morris, *Houston Volunteer Lawyers Use Texas Supreme Court's Pro Se Divorce Forms For Clinic Texas Lawyer*, Tex Parte Blog, available at http://texaslawyer.typepad.com/texas_lawyer_blog/2013/03/houston-volunteer-lawyers-use-texas-supreme-courts-pro-se-divorce-forms-for-clinic.html (2013).

49 Center on Court Access to Justice for All, *Access Brief: Forms and Document Assembly*, at 4 (2012) ("Leadership from the justices of the court of last resort is an important component in beginning a forms development program"), available at http://ncsc.contentdm.oclc.org/utils/getfile/collection/accessfair/id/264/filename/265.pdf.

50 See Katherine Bladow & Claudia Johnson, *Online Document Assembly*, Future Trends in State Courts, at 1 (2008).

51 See *id.* at 3 (observing that document assembly software can greatly reduce "litigant fatigue" associated with the repetitive process of manually filling out forms).

52 See New York's Best Practices Guide: Access to Justice NY State Courts, Document Assembly Programs Best Practice Guide For Court System Development and Implementation Using A2J Author (2013), available at www.nycourts.gov/ip/nya2j/pdfs/BestPractices_courtsystem document_assemblyprograms.pdf.

53 See Bladow & Johnson, supra note 50, at 3.

54 Sample Document Automation Programs for Legal Services, Legal Services Nat'l Tech. Assistance Project, available at http://lsntap.org/?q=node/1407.

six I-CAN!-assisted litigants in the time normally required to assist a single pro se party.[55] I-CAN! is currently used in seven states.[56]

In Minnesota, the courts have taken online document assembly one step further, providing remote review of completed forms. The online Self-Help Center offers document assembly using the I-CAN! program,[57] and once parties have completed the forms online, they can ask the Self-Help Center to review the completed forms before they are filed with the court.[58] The Center's staff can then access the user's computer remotely to review the forms and identify any problems.[59] Thus, "instead of trying to describe which links to click over the telephone or by instant message, a staff person can request permission to take remote control of a visitor's computer and show her how to navigate the website."[60]

Courts are also turning to "smart" forms, which automatically validate the data provided by litigants and check for completeness.[61] Some are e-filing enabled, so that they can be filed with the court once completed.[62] And some tag data, so that it can be integrated with other court systems.[63] In Orange County, California, for example, a self-represented litigant can complete an online template that is then converted into a PDF.[64] For family law cases, the court imports the forms and data generated by this software into the court's family law case management system.[65]

SOCIAL MEDIA

Courts have not yet embraced social media the way the general public has. But these modes of information delivery can increase access to justice, playing a particularly important role in educating the self-represented litigant. According to the National Center for State Courts, posting videos on visual-media-sharing sites is the most popular form of social media that courts use to educate self-represented litigants about the justice system.[66] The Indiana courts were early adopters of this

[55] See James E. Cabral et al., *Using Technology to Enhance Access to Justice*, 26 Harv. J.L. & Tech. 241, 259–60 (2012).

[56] *Id.* at 251; see also I-CAN! Legal, Welcome to I-CAN!, www.icandocs.org/ (offering services in California, Georgia, Massachusetts, Minnesota, North Carolina, Oklahoma, and Virginia).

[57] See Cabral, 26 supra note 55, at 251.

[58] See Minnesota Judicial Branch, Self Help Center, I-CAN! Forms, available at www.mncourts.gov/selfhelp/?page=1011.

[59] Cabral, 26 Harv. J.L. & Tech. at 249.

[60] *Id.*

[61] *Id.* at 252.

[62] *Id.*

[63] *Id.*

[64] *Id.* at 282–83.

[65] *Id.* at 283 (noting that the court uses the *Adobe LiveCycle* software).

[66] See Katherine Bladow & Joyce Raby, *Using Social Media to Support Self-Represented Litigants and Increase Access to Justice*, Future Trends in State Courts 2011, National Center for State Courts (2011), available at http://ncsc.contentdm.oclc.org/cdm/ref/collection/ctmedia/id/29. Examples include Flickr, YouTube, and Vimeo. See *id.* at 35.

technology, establishing a YouTube channel in 2008. The channel now hosts more than 150 videos on wide-ranging topics, many of which are geared toward assisting pro se litigants. There are how-to videos on seeking a protective order, requesting a hearing, preparing pleadings, seeking a summary decree, and preparing for a court date.[67] The California court system – the largest in the nation – created a YouTube channel in 2009.[68] The site hosts over 200 videos covering an array of legal matters. The channel contains a link to the California Courts' Online Self-Help Center.[69] New York's court access program created a YouTube channel in 2010, providing video instruction in several languages, assisting parties with cases in the small claims court, the housing court, and obtaining support modifications in family law matters.[70]

Funded by a grant from the Texas Access to Justice Foundation's Self-Represented Litigants Project, the Lubbock County Bar Association and the Texas Legal Services Center released a nine-minute self-help video geared toward assisting pro se litigants.[71] The video, available on YouTube, emphasizes the difficulty of self-representation and stresses the importance of hiring a lawyer if possible. It also walks litigants through all phases of a civil suit including filing a petition, service, and appearing in court.

Other forms of social media are less prevalent. Courts, like many other institutions, generally do not create new material to post on social networking sites, like Facebook.[72] Rather, they link to existing materials to educate the public about available resources. A notable exception is the Superior Court of Maricopa County, Arizona, which uses the microblogging site, Twitter, to announce pleas in criminal cases, arraignments, and even trial updates.[73]

Social media allow courts to reach a broader audience than they otherwise would, and that audience can be better prepared for court proceedings, increasing efficiency for the courts and parties alike.[74] Social media may be particularly accessible for the middle class, a group with "substantial unmet legal need, but with reliable access to online resources . . . and with sufficient capital (both financial

[67] Indiana Courts, *courts.IN.gov*, YouTube (Sept. 3, 2008), available at www.youtube.com/user/incourts.

[68] California Courts, YouTube (Jan. 30, 2009), available at www.youtube.com/user/CaliforniaCourts/about.

[69] California Courts, *Online Self-Help Center*, available at www.courts.ca.gov/selfhelp.htm.

[70] NYS Courts Access to Justice, YouTube (Jun. 18, 2010), available at www.youtube.com/user/NYCourtsA2J/videos.

[71] See *New Video Helps Low-Income Texans Navigate the Court System*, YouTube (Jul. 8, 2011), available at www.youtube.com/watch?v=NMDOwwRHGX4.

[72] See Bladow & Raby, supra note 66, at 36.

[73] See MC Superior Court @courtpio, available at https://twitter.com/courtpio. A recent post noted: "State v Turley: the first witness of the day has been called. The witness called 911 to report the alleged incident." *Id.* at June 13, 2013.

[74] See Bladow & Raby, supra note 66, at 40 ("Social media . . . allow courts to conduct . . . outreach programs online and to reach the public where they are already congregating, leveraging the limited resources courts have to support the self-represented and increasing access to justice").

and social) to achieve self-represented success with limited assistance from legal service providers."[75]

COURT FACILITATORS AND SELF-HELP CENTERS

As helpful as forms, videos, and websites are, self-represented litigants sometimes need face-to-face assistance.[76] Many states have implemented facilitator programs for self-represented litigants, particularly those involved in family law matters where self-representation is more the rule than the exception. Often, the organized bar presents the most significant opposition to these reforms.

California has one of the most extensive family law facilitator programs in the country. The facilitator program originated in a recommendation from the Governor's Child Support Court Task force.[77] Since 1997, California law has required each county's superior court to maintain a facilitator's office.[78] Each court appoints a licensed attorney with family law experience to manage the office and assist self-represented litigants.[79] The facilitator does not provide legal advice, but helps parties navigate and "demystify" court procedures.[80] Although facilitator services are available to all self-represented litigants, regardless of means,[81] recent data indicate that most users of such services are indigent.[82] Some courts have limited the facilitator program to child support enforcement proceedings, but others include a much broader range of family law matters.[83] Courts benefit from facilitators because they help self-represented parties prepare and submit the correct paperwork and "more fully understand how to present their cases and collect

[75] Cassandra Burke Robertson, *The Facebook Disruption: How Social Media May Transform Civil Litigation and Facilitate Access to Justice*, 65 Ark. L. Rev. 75, 78 (2012) (noting that "[m]iddle-class litigants are likely to experience significant difficulty in paying for legal services – but, at the same time, they have ever-increasing access to information about legal proceedings and support for self-representation").

[76] See, e.g., Reeve Hamilton, Law Community Considers Help for Pro Se Litigants, The Texas Tribune (Apr. 3, 2013) (reporting lawyer Stewart Gagnon's observation that self-represented litigants need more than just forms, "they often they [sic] need someone to actually speak to them").

[77] Administrative Office of the Courts, *Fact Sheet: Child Support Commissioner and Family Law Facilitator Program*, at 1 (2012), available at www.courts.ca.gov/documents/Child_Support.pdf.

[78] Cal. Fam. Code § 10002 (2013); 1996 Cal. Stat. ch. 957.

[79] *Id.* § 10002.

[80] Administrative Office of the [Cal.] Courts, *Fact Sheet: Child Support Commissioner and Family Law Facilitator Program*, at 2 (2012), available at www.courts.ca.gov/documents/Child_Support.pdf.

[81] Cal. Fam. Code § 10003.

[82] See Judicial Council of California, Task Force on Self-Represented Litigants, *Statewide Action Plan for Service Self-Represented Litigants*, at Appendix 2, California Courts' Programs for Self-Represented Litigants, at 52 (2004), available at www.courts.ca.gov/documents/selfreplitsrept.pdf.

[83] Tina L. Rasnow, *Traveling Justice: Providing Court Based Pro Se Assistance to Limited Access Communities*, 29 Fordham Urb. L.J. 1281, 1285 (2002) (noting that Ventura's facilitator office assists with separation, divorce, custody, spousal support, annulment, paternity, grandparent visitation, civil harassment, and domestic violence restraining orders).

support."[84] Judges report significant efficiencies in hearing the pro se calendar because litigants are better prepared, and court clerks reported substantial improvements in the pleadings filed by self-represented litigants.[85] Statewide, the offices register more than 345,000 visits each year.[86]

California has also expanded its facilitator program to other areas of the law, after a task force found that "court-based staffed self-help centers, supervised by attorneys, are the optimum way for courts" to improve access to justice for self-represented litigants.[87] In 2008, the California Judicial Council adopted California Rule of Court 10.960, which states that "[p]roviding access to justice for self-represented litigants is a priority for California courts."[88] The centers must provide neutral, unbiased information and education, and services must be available to "all sides of a case."[89] Self-help centers are now available throughout the state and serve over 450,000 Californians annually in all areas of the law, including what has been described as "the nation's first appellate self-help center."[90] Through a program called Justice Corps, California utilizes Americorps members to guide pro se litigants using the state's self-help centers.[91]

The Fourth Judicial District Court of Minnesota offers two popular self-help centers providing assistance in family law, small claims matters, landlord/tenant disputes, and domestic violence situations.[92] The centers offer forms, lawyer referral services, and free legal clinics staffed by volunteer attorneys.[93] In 2009, the centers handled 43,688 visitors.[94]

Washington has established courthouse facilitator programs in 35 of its 39 counties.[95] The services are heavily utilized: in 2007, facilitators conducted roughly 57,000 customer sessions and made 108,000 customer contacts.[96] A recent study found that most customers were women, had a monthly income of less than $2,000, and had not completed post-secondary education.[97] The study also found that courts

[84] Administrative Office of the Courts, *Fact Sheet*, supra note 77.

[85] Rasnow, supra note 83, at 1285.

[86] Administrative Office of the Courts, *Fact Sheet*, supra note 77.

[87] See Judicial Council of California, Task Force on Self-Represented Litigants, STATEWIDE ACTION PLAN FOR SERVING SELF-REPRESENTED LITIGANTS, at 1 (2004), available at www.courts.ca.gov/documents/selfreplitsrept.pdf.

[88] Cal. R. Ct. 10.960 (a) (2013).

[89] *Id.* 10.960 (d).

[90] Bonnie Hough, Self-Represented Litigants: Family Law: The Response of California's Courts 1 Cal. L. Rev. 15, 120 (Jan. 2010).

[91] Administrative Office of the Courts, Fact Sheet: Justice Corps Program (2010), available at www.courts.ca.gov/documents/JusticeCorps_FactSheet.pdf.

[92] See www.mncourts.gov/district/4/selfhelp.

[93] *Id.*

[94] David Chanen, *The New Legal Aid: Do It Yourself*, MINNEAPOLIS STAR TRIBUNE, Apr. 20, 2010, at 1A.

[95] See Thomas George & Wei Wang, *Washington's Courthouse Facilitator Programs for Self-Represented Litigants in Family Law Cases*, WASHINGTON CENTER FOR COURT RESEARCH, ADMINISTRATIVE OFFICE OF THE COURTS, at 5 (2008), available at www.courts.wa.gov/wsccr/docs/Courthouse%20Facilitator%20Program.pdf.

[96] See *id.*

[97] See *id.*; see also *id.* at 12 (noting that 63% of customers had annual incomes under $12,000).

and litigants alike were pleased with the program. Family law cases involving a facilitator-assisted litigant were more likely to be resolved in a timely manner than were those involving unassisted, self-represented litigants.[98] Facilitator-assisted litigants also reported more positive court experiences and greater trust and confidence in the courts than unassisted pro se parties.[99]

Most of Maryland's circuit courts operate family law self-help centers.[100] The centers are designed to help self-represented litigants in simple, uncontested matters.[101] Center staff evaluate each proceeding, and they advise individuals in contested or complex cases to seek counsel. Florida also provides family law self-help centers in each of its twenty judicial circuits.[102]

Facilitators can provide assistance where geography or a dispersed population makes a physical self-help center unrealistic. The Alaska courts, for example, provide a virtual Family Law Self-Help Center and a toll-free telephone "helpline" for self-represented litigants.[103] Users are advised to seek legal counsel and that the Center does not provide legal services.[104] The site includes dozens of forms organized both by stage of the case and by specific topic.[105] It also includes three sets of educational videos: Divorce and Custody Cases in Alaska, Hearing and Trial Preparation for Family Law Cases, and Domestic Violence Protective Orders.[106]

In Texas, Travis County's self-help center provides facilitators, known as "reference attorneys," to help the approximately 165 self-represented litigants who visit the center each day.[107] The reference attorney program is limited to uncontested family law matters,[108] but the center also provides free legal forms, legal research resources, public-access computers, fax and copy machines, and free help from a law librarian in other matters.[109] Participants are advised that the family law reference attorney can review their paperwork and walk them through the steps of an uncontested family law case, but the reference attorney cannot represent them or provide legal advice.[110] Reference attorneys also participate in the district court's uncontested docket to review the court file, pleadings, and proposed orders of self-represented

98 See *id.*

99 See *id.*

100 See Maryland Courts, Pro Se Assistance, available at http://mdcourts.gov/family/proseassist.html.

101 See, e.g., Montgomery County Circuit Court, Family Law Self Help Center, available at www.montgomerycountymd.gov/circuitcourt/self_Representing/index.html.

102 See Florida State Courts, Family Law Self-Help Centers, available at www.flcourts.org/gen_public/family/self_help/map.shtml.

103 See Alaska Court System Self-Help Center: Family Law, available at www.courts.alaska.gov/shcabout.htm#1b.

104 *Id.*

105 *Id.* at www.courts.alaska.gov/shcforms.htm (including instructions for completing forms as well as necessary forms for each stage of family law proceedings).

106 *Id.* at www.courts.alaska.gov/shcabout.htm#1b.

107 Personal communication with Lisa Rush, manager, Travis County Law Library.

108 *Id.*

109 See Travis County Self-Help Center, available at www.traviscountylawlibrary.org/ProSe_Clinic1.html.

110 See www.traviscountylawlibrary.org/reference_attorney1.html.

family law litigants. The attorney also attaches a checklist to the litigant's paperwork so that the judge can quickly determine whether all procedural requirements have been met.[111] After these steps have been completed, judges can typically complete their review of each case in two or three minutes.[112]

But, as with forms, facilitator programs can generate stiff opposition, often from the bar. After seeing the success of Travis County's efforts to assist pro se filers, Bexar County, Texas, decided to follow suit.[113] County Commissioners approved a plan to create a self-help center in the public law library.[114] The County hired two reference attorneys and a clerk to staff the center.[115]

The commissioners' approval created an uproar. More than 200 attorneys signed a petition protesting the center.[116] Opponents argued that litigants who could afford lawyers would utilize the services and that the County might face liability for providing legal advice.[117] They argued that the center should include an income restriction for its patrons.[118] Supporters disagreed, noting that the center would not cause lawyers to lose business because most pro se filers cannot afford lawyers.[119] The reference attorneys would assist litigants in completing forms but would not provide legal advice.[120] The bar president contended that limiting use to the poor is "similar to saying the public library cannot be available to people who could otherwise go [to a bookstore] to buy their books."[121] In the end, largely due to the opposition, the commissioners scuttled the program.[122]

Courts are also exploring ways in which non-lawyers can increase access to justice. Some states, led by Washington, have begun exploring these alternatives. Over consistent opposition from its bar association, and in an effort to assist the thousands of self-represented litigants appearing in Washington courts, the Washington Supreme Court recently adopted a rule authorizing limited-license

111 Personal communication with Lisa Rush, manager of the Travis County Law Library.

112 *Id.*

113 See Elizabeth Allen, *Lawyers Challenge Legality of Self-Help Bexar Law Center*, San Antonio Express-News, at 3B, Apr. 17, 2008; see also Jonathan Fox, *Opposition Kills Self-Help Center for Pro Se Filers*, Texas Lawyer, Aug. 14, 2008.

114 See Elizabeth Allen, *Commissioners Rethink Law Self-Help Center*, San Antonio Express-News, May 28, 2008, at 10B.

115 Elizabeth Allen, *Lawyers Challenge Legality of Self-Help Bexar Law Center*, San Antonio Express-News, at 3B, Apr. 17, 2008.

116 Jonathan Fox, *Opposition Kills Self-Help Center for Pro Se Filers*, Texas Lawyer, Aug. 14, 2008.

117 *Id.*

118 *Id.*

119 *Id.*

120 *Id.*

121 *Commissioners Rethink Law Self-Help Center*, supra note 124, at 10B.

122 See *id.* (noting that "the argument that resonated most with commissioners – aside from the sheer numbers that opposed the center – was that it would cause lawyers to lose business from even their poorer clients"); see also *id.* (reporting that one speaker told the commissioners that clients "often can scrape up funds from their parents in a custody fight").

legal technicians.[123] Limited-license legal technicians, a close cousin of facilitators, will have greater training and responsibility than paralegals but will not appear in court or negotiate with opposing parties on their clients' behalf.[124] Technicians may assist with court forms, inform clients of applicable procedures and time lines, review and explain pleadings, and identify additional documents that may be needed in a court proceeding. Washington is the first state to adopt such a rule.[125] Noting the objection that the rule posed a threat to the family law bar, the Court explained that the basis of any regulatory scheme, including the court's authority to regulate the practice of law, must be the public interest, and "[p]rotecting the monopoly status of attorneys in any practice area is not a legitimate objective."[126]

California and New York are now following Washington's lead and contemplating their own initiatives on non-lawyer assistance to increase access to justice.[127]

APPELLATE RESOURCES FOR THE SELF-REPRESENTED

Appellate proceedings rely heavily on legal research and written briefs. If court opinions are readily accessible at no cost, it becomes easier for a pro se party to prosecute an appeal. The past two decades have seen the democratization of legal opinions. Previously available only in official reporters or through commercial electronic databases, court opinions are now widely accessible on court websites.[128] Some states have gone a step further, placing their entire library of

[123] See *Supreme Court Adopts Rule Authorizing Non-Lawyers to Assist in Certain Civil Legal Matters*, Washington Courts, June 15, 2012, available at www.courts.wa.gov/newsinfo/?fa=newsinfo.internetdetail&newsid=2136; Washington State Bar Association, *Supreme Court Adopts Limited License Legal Technician Rule*, available at www.wsba.org/News-and-Events/News/Supreme-Court-Adopts-Limited-License-Legal-Technician-Rule; Ethan Bronner, *A Call for Drastic Changes in Educating New Lawyers*, THE NEW YORK TIMES (Feb. 10, 2013).

[124] See *Supreme Court Adopts Rule Authorizing Non-Lawyers to Assist in Certain Civil Legal Matters*, Washington Courts, June 15, 2012, available at www.courts.wa.gov/newsinfo/?fa=newsinfo.internetdetail&newsid=2136 (explaining that technicians may assist with selecting and completing court forms, informing clients of applicable procedures and timelines, reviewing and explaining pleadings, and identifying additional documents that may be needed in a court proceeding).

[125] Washington State Bar Association, *Supreme Court Adopts Limited License Legal Technician Rule*, available at www.wsba.org/News-and-Events/News/Supreme-Court-Adopts-Limited-License-Legal-Technician-Rule.

[126] See In the Matter of the Adoption of New APR 28 – Limited Practice Rule for Limited License Legal Technicians, Supreme Court of Washington, Order No. 25700-A-1005, June 15, 2012, at 7, available at www.courts.wa.gov/content/publicUpload/Press%20Releases/25700-A-1005.pdf.

[127] See Laura Ernde, *State Bar to Look at Limited-Practice Licensing Program*, CALIFORNIA BAR JOURNAL, February 2013, available at www.calbarjournal.com/February2013/TopHeadlines/TH1.aspx; Honorable Jonathan Lippman, The State of the Judiciary 2013: Let Justice Be Done, at 13–14, available at www.nycourts.gov/ctapps/news/SOJ-2013.pdf (describing task force to examine the role that trained and regulated non-lawyer advocates can play in providing out-of-court assistance in areas like housing, consumer credit, and foreclosures).

[128] See, e.g., The Supreme Court of Texas, Orders & Opinions, available at www.supreme.courts.state.tx.us/historical/recent.asp.

case law on their websites and requiring citation to their own public-domain case designator number, as well as internal paragraph numbers, rather than to an official reporter.[129]

Approximately eighteen jurisdictions have adopted some form of public domain citation, making court opinions more accessible to the general public.[130] Although the movement toward public domain citation gained steam in the 1990s, recently it has been stalled. Since the early 1990s, just Arkansas (in 2009) and Illinois (in 2011) have adopted such a system.[131] The Illinois Supreme Court has touted the cost savings of no longer having to purchase official reporters, and it announced that "[t]he official body of Illinois court opinions will now reside on the website of the Illinois Supreme Court, readily available to lawyers, judges and law clerks for official citation and to any member of the public who wishes to read them."[132] As the Chief Justice noted, "[a] lack of printed law reports is no longer a hindrance to legal research."[133] Most self-help assistance at the appellate level comes in the form of online handbooks explaining how to pursue an appeal.[134] Forms, while helpful, are perhaps not as critical as in the trial courts, where there are countless proceedings governed by different pleading rules. Many appellate courts post parties' briefs online, and self-represented litigants can model their briefs on those examples.[135] Some states, like Texas, offer live streaming of oral arguments as well as archived versions of past ones.[136] The California Courts' online self-help center provides an extensive explanation of appealing a judgment, along with numerous forms to assist

[129] See, e.g., Illinois Supreme Court Announces New Public Domain Citation System, Ending Era of Printed Volumes, at 1, available at www.state.il.us/court/media/PressRel/2011/053111.pdf (2011).

[130] See Am. Ass'n of Law Libraries, *Vendor-Neutral Citation Rules Adopted by American Jurisdictions*, available at www.aallnet.org/main-menu/Advocacy/access/citation/neutralrules (last visited May 28, 2013); The Bluebook: A Uniform System of Citation tbl.T1 (Columbia Law Review Ass'n et al. eds. 19th ed. 2010). Those jurisdictions include Arizona, Arkansas, Colorado, Illinois, Louisiana, Maine, Mississippi, Montana, New Mexico, North Dakota, Ohio, Oklahoma, Pennsylvania, South Dakota, Utah, Vermont, Wisconsin, and Wyoming. See *Vendor-Neutral Citation Rules Adopted by American Jurisdictions*, supra; The Bluebook, supra, at tbl.T1.

[131] Am. Ass'n of Law Libraries, *Universal Citation and the American Association of Law Libraries: A White Paper*, 103 Law Libr. J. 335, 335 (2011).

[132] *Id.* at 1.

[133] *Id.* at 2.

[134] See, e.g., State of Idaho Judicial Branch, Supreme Court Appeals, Pro Se Appellate Information, Appellate Handbook, www.isc.idaho.gov/appeals-court/handbook; Massachusetts Appeals Court, Clerk's Guide to Appeals for Lawyers & Self-Represented Litigants, available at www.mass.gov/courts/appealscourt/guide-to-appeals.html; Filing An Appeal In The Supreme Court of Ohio: A Pro Se Guide, Supreme Court of Ohio, available at www.supremecourt.ohio.gov/Publications/proseguide.pdf (2013); Pro Se Guide Appeal Procedures, available at www.utcourts.gov/courts/appell/prose.pdf.

[135] See, e.g., Supreme Court of Texas, Electronic Briefing, available at www.supreme.courts.state.tx.us/ebriefs/ebriefs.asp (posting electronic briefs in many cases, from 1999 through the present); see also *id.*, Guide to Creating Electronic Appellate Briefs, at www.supreme.courts.state.tx.us/pdf/GuideToCreatingElectronicAppellateBriefs2.pdf.

[136] See The Supreme Court of Texas, Welcome to the Supreme Court of Texas, available at www.supreme.courts.state.tx.us/.

litigants with the process.[137] California also asserts that it has established "the first formal state court clinic anywhere for unrepresented appellate litigants."[138] Its website notes that clinic lawyers explain requirements, provide forms, and review paperwork.[139] In appropriate cases, they also attempt to secure pro bono legal representation.[140] Although the clinic is open to anyone, the vast majority of users are indigent.[141] The clinic is staffed by two lawyers from the public-interest law office of the Los Angeles and Beverly Hills Bar Associations.[142]

Several state courts, the Supreme Court of Texas among them,[143] have developed appellate pro bono programs. In Texas, if the Supreme Court decides that a particular case warrants closer study, and one of the parties is pro se, the court refers the case to its pro bono program. The program has been successful, and it is gradually being adopted by other appellate courts throughout the state. Other states use less formal means of assisting indigent pro se parties, either by selecting appellate counsel from a list of volunteer attorneys or by referring the case to a law school clinic. While these programs are laudable, they offer little assistance to those of average means, as participation is typically limited to the indigent.[144]

ACCESS-TO-JUSTICE COMMISSIONS AND A COALITION APPROACH

Access-to-justice commissions provide another means through which courts can assist self-represented litigants, and more than thirty states have developed such commissions.[145] Generally, a state's high court charges a commission with "expand[ing] access to civil justice at all levels for low-income and disadvantaged people in the state ... by assessing their civil legal needs, developing strategies to meet them, and evaluating progress."[146] The commissions typically work in

[137] California Courts, *Online Self-Help Center, Civil Appeals,* available at www.courts.ca.gov/selfhelp-appeals.htm.

[138] *Id.*, Appellate Self-Help Clinic, available at www.courts.ca.gov/2293.htm.

[139] *Id.*

[140] *Id.*

[141] See Court of Appeal, Second Appellate District, Appellate Self-Help Clinic: Drop-In Clinic Helps Litigants Navigate the Maze of Court Procedures, at para. 5, available at www.courts.ca.gov/documents/2dca-man.pdf.

[142] *Id.* at para. 4.

[143] For a general description of the program, see Michael S. Truesdale, *Why I Support Appellate Pro Bono Services (and Why You Should Too)*, 24 App. Advoc., 614, 614–21 (2012).

[144] For example, the Supreme Court of Texas's pro bono program limits eligibility to those with incomes at or below 125% of federal poverty guidelines.

[145] American Bar Association, State Access to Justice Commissions: Lists and Links, available at www.americanbar.org/groups/legal_aid_indigent_defendants/initiatives/resource_center_for_access_to_justice/state_atj_commissions.html (2013).

[146] ABA Resources Center for Access to Justice Initiatives, Definition of Access to Justice Commission, at 1, available at www.americanbar.org/content/dam/aba/administrative/legal_aid_indigent_defendants/ls_sclaid_atj_definition_of_a_commission.authcheckdam.pdf (2011).

partnership with the state's highest court and the highest levels of the organized bar.[147] Access-to-justice commissions are not necessarily limited to assisting the indigent, but "may also include expanding access for moderate income people."[148]

Some states have found that partnerships among various stakeholders, including the courts, access-to-justice commissions, and public libraries effectively marshal resources for self-represented litigants.[149] TexasLawHelp is one such example. Initially funded by the Legal Services Corporation, the website is operated by the Texas Legal Services Center[150] and is now also supported by the Texas Access to Justice Foundation, the Travis County Law Library, and Pro Bono Net.[151] The site provides information on a wide range of legal issues. It also offers free online legal forms, including those recently approved by the Texas Supreme Court,[152] as well as interactive forms that are generated after respondents answer a series of interview questions.[153] This popular resource provides information in English, Spanish, Vietnamese, and Chinese,[154] and more than 400,000 visitors used the website last year.[155] A new "live chat" feature lets visitors correspond with specialists from the Texas Legal Services Center or the Houston Volunteer Lawyers Program, Monday through Friday, from 9:00 a.m. to 5:00 p.m.[156]

CONCLUSION

Courts are providing self-represented litigants with more tools, at a lower cost, than ever before. Technological advances have eliminated many barriers to access faced by pro se parties, and the future holds even greater promise for optimizing their

[147] *Id.* ("Its charge is from and/or recognized by the highest court of the state or equivalent jurisdiction; the highest court and the highest levels of the organized bar are engaged with the commission's efforts and the commission reports regularly to them").

[148] *Id.*

[149] Center on Court Access to Justice for All, a Project of the National Center for State Courts, Access Brief: Self-Help Services, at 7 (2012), available at http://cdm16501.contentdm.oclc.org/utils/getfile/collection/accessfair/id/263/filename/264.pdf ("In practice, some states have found that an effective strategy for developing and implementing self-help services is to build a multi-stakeholder coalition in which, for example, the courts provide the space and staff training, legal aid and the bar provide some of the materials, and libraries provide additional outside service access points").

[150] The Texas Legal Services Center is a nonprofit law office whose mission is "to improve the quality of advocacy and expand availability of legal services for low-income Texans." See TexasLawHelp.org, About Us, http://texaslawhelp.org/about-us.

[151] See TexasLawHelp.org, About Us, http://texaslawhelp.org/about-us.

[152] See *id.*, Texas Supreme Court Approved Divorce Forms, available at http://texaslawhelp.org/issues/family-law-and-domestic-violence/texas-supreme-court-approved-divorce-forms-uncontested-no-minor-children-no-real-property.

[153] See *id.* at Interactive Forms, available at http://texaslawhelp.org/resource/commonly-used-fill-in-forms-online?ref=JSEbP (explaining that users will be redirected to LawHelpInteractive.org to complete the online document assembly process).

[154] *Id.* at http://texaslawhelp.org/.

[155] See *id.*, About Us, http://texaslawhelp.org/about-us.

[156] *Id.*, *About TexasLawHelp.org LiveHelp*, available at http://texaslawhelp.org/resource/about-texaslawhelporg-livehelp?ref=py8mN.

utilization of the courts. It is impossible to predict the precise effects of these developments on society in general, and on the legal system in particular. Perhaps, as some anticipate, the market for lawyers' services will expand as the public's confidence in the efficient administration of justice increases.[157]

One thing is certain: the path to reform will not always be smooth. Innovations are disruptive,[158] and some changes will meet with resistance. Leadership from state courts of last resort is a necessary component in overcoming these obstacles.[159] Only with such backing will reform efforts meet their potential – and will the courts fulfill their mission of making our justice system accessible to all.[160]

[157] See, e.g., Robertson, supra note 75, at 97 (arguing that more individuals will seek judicial resolution of claims and, consequently, lawyer services, if the justice system becomes more affordable); see also Center on Court Access to Justice for All, a Project of the National Center for State Courts, *Access Brief: Self-Help Services*, at 2 (2012), available at http://cdm16501.contentdm.oclc.org/utils/getfile/collection/accessfair/id/263/filename/264.pdf.

("Legal aid attorneys can focus their highly limited resources on those individuals who need more in-depth representation, knowing that the self-represented litigant will find necessary assistance from the court.")

[158] See, e.g., Robertson, supra note 75, at 97 (predicting that "Facebook and other social media are likely to have a disruptive effect on civil litigation"); see also Clayton M. Christensen, The Innovator's Dilemma: When New Technologies Cause Great Firms to Fail 42–9 (1997) (describing how "disruptive innovations" allow consumers at the bottom of a market access to a product or service previously available only to consumers with greater means).

[159] See Barbara Rodriguez Mundell & Wallace B. Jefferson, *Herding Lions: Shared Leadership of State Trial Courts*, Perspectives on State Court Leadership (noting that "a state supreme court must ensure access to, and the availability of, essential court services"), available at http://ncsc.contentdm.oclc.org/cdm/ref/collection/ctadmin/id/1858#img_view_container; Center on Court Access to Justice for All, a Project of the National Center for State Courts, *Access Brief: Self-Help Services*, at 2 (2012), available at http://cdm16501.contentdm.oclc.org/utils/getfile/collection/accessfair/id/263/filename/264.pdf ("[Leadership from the top of the court system . . . is critical").

[160] See Hon. Wallace B. Jefferson, *State of the Judiciary*, at 1, Presented to the 83rd Legislative Session, Austin, Texas, Mar. 6, 2013, available at www.supreme.courts.state.tx.us/pdf/stateofjudiciary.pdf ("Courts exist not to perpetuate the judicial branch for its own sake, but to ensure that the conflicts human beings encounter, whether criminal or civil, are adjudicated in a neutral forum, at an efficient price, producing fair outcomes"); see also Jonathan Fox, *Opposition Kills Self-Help Center for Pro Se Filers*, Texas Lawyer, Aug. 14, 2008 (quoting district judge Karen Pozza, who said that "[w]e are here to make the system work for the public. It is not here to serve us").

29

Limited Representation and Ethical Challenges

Russell Engler

The usual premise of legal representation is that the attorney is to provide a full measure of advice or advocacy appropriate to the needs and resources of the client. The literature on access to justice suggests that a more limited form of representation – sometimes termed "unbundled" legal services – should be encouraged as means of expanding access to legal assistance for Americans of modest means. Unbundling would allow lawyers to offer assistance on discrete tasks, rather than taking on representation over an entire legal matter. Russell Engler in this chapter evaluates the arguments in favor of unbundling in light of research on the effectiveness of limited representation compared to full representation, and the ethical challenges posed in limiting representation to discrete tasks.

The topic of limited representation encompasses ideas captured by a variety of terms, including "unbundled legal services,"[1] "limited scope representation,"[2] "limited assistance representation,"[3] and "limited legal assistance."[4] The concepts emerged as a partial response to the flood of unrepresented litigants and the unaffordability of lawyers for many potential clients. Representation involves a package of discrete tasks, such as gathering facts and advising the client.[5] "Unbundled legal services is a practice

[1] Fern Fisher-Brandveen and Rochelle Klempner, *Unbundled Legal Services: Untying the Bundle in New York State*, 29 FORDHAM URB. L. J. 1107 (2002). This chapter is adapted from my article, *Approaching Ethical Issues Involving Unrepresented Litigants*, 43 CLEARINGHOUSE REV. 377 (Nov.–Dec., 2009), © 2009 Sargent Shriver National Center on Poverty Law.

[2] See, e.g., ABA Section of Litigation, Handbook on Limited Scope Legal Assistance: A Report of the Modest Means Task Force 52–54 (2003)(hereinafter ABA Handbook).

[3] See, e.g., Mass. Sup. Jud. Ct., Order In Re: Limited Assistance Representation (Apr. 10, 2009), available at www.mass.gov/courts/sjc/docs/Rules/Limited_Assistance_Representation_order1 _04–09.pdf.

[4] See *Conference on the Delivery of Legal Services to Low-Income Persons: Professional and Ethical Issues, Report of the Working Group on Limited Legal Assistance*, 67 FORDHAM L. REV. 1819 (1999).

[5] Forrest S. Mosten, *Unbundling of Legal Services and the Family Lawyer*, 28 FAMILY L. Q. 421, 423 (1994). Mosten identifies: "(1) gathering facts, (2) advising the client, (3) discovering facts of the opposing party, (4) researching the law, (5) drafting correspondence and documents, (6) negotiating, and (7) representing the client in court." Because "lawyers generally offer a full service package of discrete tasks that encompass traditional legal representation," *id.* at 422, unbundling also is referred to as "discrete task representation."

in which the lawyer and client agree that the lawyer will provide some, but not all of the work involved in a traditional full service representation."[6]

Long before the emergence of the term "unbundling," legal aid offices, through hotlines and pro se clinics, delivered assistance short of full representation.[7] As assistance programs for the underserved population proliferated, a number of issues emerged for legal aid attorneys, bar associations, and the courts regarding the trend toward unbundling.[8] This chapter briefly explores justifications for the increased use of unbundling as well as emerging questions regarding the effectiveness of unbundling. The chapter then focuses primarily on the ethical issues involved with various forms of unbundling and related issues that arise with the high incidence of self-representation. Given the reality that new forms of assistance will continue to emerge as part of efforts to increase access to justice, the chapter concludes by setting forth a framework for handling ethics questions in these contexts generally.

Proponents articulate four types of arguments in favor of unbundling. First, unbundling is seen as a way to increase access to justice, given the shortage of affordable legal services.[9] Second, some proponents argue that unbundling increases the efficiency of the court system.[10] Third, proponents contend that unbundling empowers clients, providing them with increased choices.[11] Consistent with the trend in which consumers act as their own travel and real estate agents, clients should be in charge of "selecting from lawyers' services only a portion of the full package and contracting with the lawyer accordingly."[12] Finally, some

6 Fisher-Brandveen & Klempner, supra note 1 at 1108. See also, Molly M. Jennings & D. James Greiner, *The Evolution of Unbundling in Litigation Matters: Three Case Studies and a Literature Review*, 89 DENVER U. L. REV. 825, 828 (2012) ("unbundling occurs when a licensed attorney provides a limited set of legal services, in a litigation matter, accompanied by the expectation that the client will proceed pro se on all other aspects of the matter"); ABA Handbook, supra note 3, at 4 ("By 'limited scope legal assistance', we mean a designated service or services, rather than the full package of traditionally offered services. [footnote omitted]. The client and lawyer select the service the lawyer will provide [footnote omitted]").

7 Jennings and Greiner, supra note 6, at 826; Jessica K. Steinberg, *In Pursuit of Justice? Case Outcomes and the Delivery of Unbundled Legal Services*, 18 GEO. J. POV. LAW POL'Y 453, 454 (2011).

8 For a bibliography of articles on unbundling, see Molly M. Jennings & D. James Greiner, *The Evolution of Unbundling in Litigation Matters*, 89 DENVER U. L.REV. 825 (2012), bibliography available online at www.law.du.edu/documents/denver-university-law-review/v89-4/Greiner_ Unbundling_Bibliography.pdf4/Greiner_Unbundling_Bibliography.pdf. For a discussion of arguments in favor of unbundling in the Canadian context, see Samreen Beg & Lorne Sossin, Should Legal Services Be Unbundled?, *in* MIDDLE INCOME ACCESS TO JUSTICE 193 (Michael J. Trebilcock, Anthony J. Duggan & Lorne Mitchell Sossin eds., 2012).

9 Jennings & Greiner, supra note 7, at 831–32; Fisher-Brandveen and Klempner, supra note 2, at 1111–12.

10 Fisher Brandveen & Klempner, supra note 1 at 1112 ("Unbundled legal services benefit the court system because educating and assisting more pro se litigants about civil procedure and evidentiary rules reduce[s] demands on court personnel"; however, "[t]his view is not shared by all members of the judiciary." *Id.*); Jennings & Greiner, supra note 7, at 831–32.

11 Jennings and Greiner, supra note 6, at 832; Fisher Brandveen and Klempner, supra note 7 at 1113.

12 Mosten, supra note 5, at 423. But see Mary Helen McNeal, *Redefining Attorney – Client Roles: Unbundling and Moderate-Income Elderly Clients*, 32 WAKE FOREST L. REV. 295, 335–39 (1997) (cautioning attorneys who may provide unbundled legal services to the elderly).

proponents argue that unbundling increases opportunities for lawyers, attracting clients who can pay some money but cannot afford the price tag for full representation.[13]

Questions about the effectiveness of unbundling have accompanied the calls for increased unbundling at every turn. As early as 1998, a Working Group on Limited Legal Assistance urged that regardless of the details of specific proposals, "limited legal assistance methodologies should be assessed and evaluated."[14] Yet, fifteen years later, "no one knows whether the mainstreaming efforts have in fact realized the goals they were designed to promote."[15] Part of this assessment requires a decision as to the factors that should be evaluated to determine whether an initiative is successful or not.[16] Most clients surveyed as part of the evaluation of the Limited Assistance Representation Pilot Projects in Massachusetts responded that they were "very satisfied" or "satisfied" with being represented on a limited assistance basis.[17] Litigants express satisfaction with self-help programs generally, which often involve unbundling.[18] Yet, a number of studies in the housing area have found that tenants achieve far better results from full representation than from unbundled or limited assistance.[19]

With regard to the justification of affording choice for consumers, Steinberg observes that while the model might offer choice for the middle class, in the low-income context, "the element of choice is effectively nonexistent."[20] Surveys of judges and court personnel show support for assistance programs, although their support for unbundling more generally can vary based on the form of unbundling. [21] Even among the private bar, attitudes are in flux. The bar in Massachusetts resisted a pilot limited representation program in family law; after the program was in operation, attorneys involved overwhelmingly were "satisfied" or "very

13 Jennings & Greiner, supra note 6, at 832; Fisher-Brandveen and Klempner, supra note 1, at 1114; Daniel M. Taubman & John S. Zakhem, *CBA Modest Means Task Force* 2013 *Report*, 42 THE COLORADO LAWYER 103, 110 (2013), available at www.cobar.org/tcl/tcl_articles.cfm?articleid=8327.

14 *Conference on the Delivery of Legal Services to Low-Income Persons*, supra note 4 at 1821.

15 Jennings & Greiner, supra note 6, at 849.

16 For a comparable analysis involving full representation, see, Engler, Chapter in this volume.

17 [Mass.] Supreme Judicial Court Steering Committee on Self-Represented Litigants, Addressing the Needs of Self-Represented Litigants in Our Courts: Final Report and Recommendations 22 (2008) ("SJC Steering Committee Report"), available at www.mass.gov/courts/docs/sjc/docs/self-rep-final-report.pdf. *Id.* at 16–17 (2008).

18 John M. Greacen, *Self-Represented Litigants and Court and Legal Services Responses to Their Needs: What We Know*, at 2 (2002), available at http://bit.ly/cHlF9.

19 Steinberg, supra note 7, at 463; D. James Greiner, Cassandra Wolos Pattanayak, and Jonathan Phillip Hennessey, *The Limits of Unbundled Legal Assistance: A Randomized Study in a Massachusetts District Court and Prospects for the Future*, 126 HARV. L. REV. 901 (2013); *San Francisco Right to Civil Counsel Pilot Program Documentation Report* (May 2014), available at www.sfbos.org/Modules/ShowDocument.aspx?documentid=49157.

20 Steinberg, supra note 7, at 463.

21 See, Greacen, supra note 18, at 2; SJC Steering Committee Report, supra note 17, at 17–22. Judicial attitudes toward ghostwriting, however, are not uniformly positive.

satisfied" with it and recommended its expansion.[22] There is some evidence that unbundling increases pro bono opportunities, yet also concern that unbundling is changing the nature of pro bono work,[23] steering lawyers away from more involved pro bono initiatives in favor of unbundled ones.[24]

ETHICAL ISSUES: UNBUNDLED LEGAL SERVICES GENERALLY

Unbundling raises familiar ethical issues in new contexts and, as with other ethics issues, the rules vary from jurisdiction to jurisdiction. The primary ethical issue beyond ghostwriting, discussed in the next section, involves the scope of representation: to what extent do the ethical rules permit a lawyer–client relationship that delivers services short of full representation? Will clients be forced to accept the model? Will conflict of interest and confidentiality protections be ignored?[25] The growth of court-based assistance programs increased the focus on conflict of interest issues.

American Bar Association (ABA) Model Rule 1.2(c) authorizes lawyers to limit the scope of representation "if the limitation is reasonable under the circumstances and the client gives informed consent."[26] While permission to limit the scope of representation does not alleviate the need to provide competent representation, the standard for competence relates to the extent of the assistance.[27]

Rule 6.5 modifies the conflict of interest rules in the context of nonprofit and court-annexed limited legal services. Under traditional conflict of interest analysis, if a lawyer volunteer at a court-based program assisted a litigant, the lawyer's entire firm or office would be barred from assisting the adverse party.[28] Unlike the traditional analysis under Rules 1.7 and 1.9, only actual knowledge triggers disqualification under Rule 6.5.[29] Unlike Rule 1.10, only the lawyer with knowledge,

[22] *Id.* at 16–17 (2008).

[23] See, e.g., Jennings and Greiner, supra note 7, at 845 ("Some reports suggest that LAR has been used to leverage pro bono assistance . . .").

[24] Esther Lardent, *Are We Shrinking Pro Bono?* The Pro Bono Wire, Pro Bono Institute (May 2014), available at http://archives.informz.net/clients/pbi/archives/archive_4047725.html ("But all too often of late, we seem to equate or conflate pro bono with limited service. This is a most troubling development").

[25] See, e.g., Richard Zorza, *Discrete Task Representation, Ethics and the Big Picture*, 40 FAMILY COURT REVIEW 19 (2002).

[26] See American Bar Association's Model Rules of Professional Conduct (MRPC), Rule 1.2(C), available at www.americanbar.org/groups/professional_responsibility/publications/model_rules_of_professional_conduct/model_rules_of_professional_conduct_table_of_contents.html. The American Bar Association's Ethics 2000 Commission proposed the rule modification discussed in this section.

[27] MRPC 1.2, Comment [7].

[28] *Id.* Rule 1.7–1.10.

[29] *Id.* Rule 6.5(a).

rather than the entire firm, is disqualified.[30] The rule modifications mirror state and local trends[31]

"GHOSTWRITING"

The controversy surrounding one unbundled task – ghostwriting – predates the move toward self-help. Ghostwriting involves a lawyer's preparation of pleadings or other court papers for a litigant who appears without counsel. This fact pattern challenges the unstated assumption in the ethics rules that litigants either are or are not represented by counsel. Decisions characterize ghostwriting as fraud and misrepresentation, arising from the appearance that the litigant is without counsel when a lawyer is pulling the strings.[32] The cases rarely allege specific harm from the alleged deception; that a litigant has received assistance is usually obvious from the court papers.[33]

Bad facts make bad law. The leading ABA opinion, from 1978, involved a lawyer who assisted a litigant at every stage of the proceeding, including trial, without filing an appearance.[34] That opinion relied on cases involving a "habitual litigant who in the past five or six years [had] commenced well over thirty lawsuits against a very large number of defendants."[35] Moreover, "[g]hostwriting complaints are primarily raised by attorneys who wish to maintain their advantage over pro se litigants."[36] The interests of frustrated judges and opposing lawyers drive the case outcomes.

Ethics opinions related to the more typical legal aid scenarios suggest practical solutions. Rather than prohibit ghostwriting, they focus on the extent of the involvement and the nature of disclosure. A pair of New York ethics opinions approved the practice, conditioned on disclosures on the pleadings revealing the assistance.[37]

30 *Id.* Rule 6.5(b).

31 State-by-state activity is available online at the American Bar Association's Access to Justice Resource Center, at www.americanbar.org/groups/delivery_legal_services/resources/pro_se_unbundling_resource_center/court_rules.html (state rules), www.americanbar.org/groups/delivery_legal_services/resources/pro_se_unbundling_resource_center/ethics_opinions.html (State ethics decisions). Maine and Colorado were leaders in adopting rule changes. Jona Goldschmidt, *In Defense of Ghostwriting*, 29 Fordham Urb. L. J. 1145, 1190, nn. 232–33 (2002).

32 See, e.g., ABA Formal Op. 07–446 (2007), available at http://bit.ly/PIR7p, and ABA Comm. on Ethics and Professional Responsibility, Informal Op. 1414 (1978) (discussing Rules 1.2(d), 3.3(b), 4.1(b) and 8.4 (d) and their predecessors); Ellis v. Maine, 448 F.2d 1325 (1st Cir. 1971) (discussing Rule 11 of the Federal Rules of Civil Procedure).

33 Goldschmidt, supra note 31, at 1147–78.

34 ABA Comm. on Ethics and Professional Responsibility, Informal Op. 1414 (1978).

35 Klein v. Spear, Leeds & Kellogg, 309 F. Supp. 341, 342 (S.D.N.Y. 1970); Klein v. H.N. Whitney, Goadby & Co., 341 F. Supp. 699 (S.D.N.Y. 1971).

36 Goldschmidt, supra note 31, at 1158.

37 Compare New York State Bar Ethics Op. 613 (1990), available at http://old.nysba.org/Content/ContentFolders/EthicsOpinions/Opinions601675/EO_613.pdf, with New York City Bar Op. No. 1987–2, http://bit.ly/iwdJm. Each requires disclosure that the litigant received assistance; only the latter requires disclosure of the attorney's identity.

Following New York's adoption of Rule 1.2(c), a different ethics committee held that disclosure no longer was required.[38]

The justifications for ghostwriting prohibitions are under attack.[39] Ghostwriting restrictions ignore the client's interests, the assisting lawyer's interest in not being dragged into the proceeding, and the benefits to the court of coherent papers that articulate claims and arguments, even if ghostwritten. The trend among jurisdictions is to permit ghostwriting through state ethics decisions and court rules.[40] In 2007, the ABA superseded the 1978 opinion on which many ghostwriting decisions relied, replacing it with a formal opinion permitting undisclosed legal assistance.[41]

The trend toward permitting ghostwriting should continue. Lawyers can protect themselves and their clients by disclosing in court papers that assistance was provided. Attorneys will increasingly be comfortable doing so as judges refrain from pressuring them to appear in court and recognize the benefits that flow from coherent filings.

ETHICAL ISSUES: ASSISTANCE PROGRAMS GENERALLY

While unbundling and ghostwriting are the hot-button labels, each component of an assistance program can give rise to ethics issues. The ethics analysis turns on the completeness of issue-spotting.

Lawyer–Client Relationship.

Is a lawyer–client relationship created? Programs that offer information only, without advice, do so in part to make clear that no attorney–client relationship exists.[42] Of course, the line between information and advice is hard to recognize in practice.[43] The use of disclaimers and retainer forms is important, and the briefer the encounter the less likely the relationship is created. Case-law analyzing the relationship starts from the client's perspective, so clarity is crucial.[44]

Scope of Representation

As discussed earlier, lawyers may limit the scope of representation with the client's informed consent under Rule 1.2(c). Attorneys still must represent their clients competently and preserve client confidentiality.

[38] New York County Lawyers' Ass'n Comm. on Professional Ethics, Op. 742 (April 16, 2010), available at www.nycla.org/siteFiles/Publications/Publications1348_0.pdf.

[39] See, e.g., Goldschmidt, supra note 31.

[40] See, e.g., State Bar of Ariz. Comm. On Rules of Prof'l Conduct, Op. 05–06 (2005); Wash. State Rule CR 11(b); Utah Ethics Op. 08–01 (2008).

[41] ABA Formal Op. 07–446 (2007), available at http://bit.ly/PIR7p. For a comparison of decisions that do and do not require disclosure, see *id.*, nn. 3–4.

[42] See, e.g., Zorza, supra note 25, at 22.

[43] See, e.g., John M. Greacen, "No *Legal Advice from Court Personnel*": *What Does That Mean?*, 34 Judges' Journal 10 (Winter 1995).

[44] See, e.g., *Togstad v. Vesely, Otto, Miller & Keefe*, 291 N.W.2d 686, 693 (Minn. 1980) (holding that plaintiff was injured when defendant attorney advised her that she had no medical malpractice claim, despite attorney's claim that no attorney-client relationship was formed).

Competence

A Colorado Ethics Opinion on unbundling illustrates the interrelationship between the scope of representation and unbundling. "[A] lawyer may not so limit the scope of the lawyer's representation as to avoid the obligation to provide meaningful legal advice, nor the responsibility for the consequences of negligent action"; however, "the duty of competence of Rule 1.1 is circumscribed by the scope of the representation agreed to by Rule 1.2."[45] The Model Rules note that the limitation of the representation is "a factor to be considered when determining the legal knowledge, skill, thoroughness and preparation reasonably necessary for the representation."[46] Another factor is whether the lawyer is giving advice or assistance "in an emergency."[47]

Confidentiality

While the measure of competence is affected by the scope of representation, the duty to preserve client confidentiality is not. The prohibitions, and exceptions, set forth in Rule 1.6 apply to both full and partial representation.[48]

Candor

The ghostwriting discussion earlier reveals the relevance of the duty of candor, as embodied in provisions related to fraud, candor, and truthfulness.[49] The duty of candor also explains Rule 1.6(b)'s exceptions to the duty to preserve confidentiality.[50]

Conflicts of Interest

Rule 6.5, discussed earlier, was adopted precisely to avoid the problems caused by applying traditional conflict-of-interest rules to limited assistance programs. The traditional rules, by creating the risk that an entire law office would be "conflicted out" in subsequent encounters with a client, placed an enormous burden on providers of high-volume assistance programs and diminished the pool of those willing to assist. Rule 6.5 responds to these concerns.

Non-Lawyers

Where non-lawyers staff assistance programs, the ethics analysis depends on the tasks performed by the non-lawyers and the supervisory structure. Rules 5.3 and 5.5, regulating Responsibilities of Non-lawyer Assistants and Unauthorized Practice of

45 Colorado Bar Association Ethics Commission, Formal Opinion 101 (1998), available at www.cobar.org/repository/Ethics/FormalEthicsOpion/FormalEthicsOpinion_101_2011.pdf.

46 Rule 1.2, Comment [7].

47 Rule 1.1, Comment [3].

48 Rule 1.6.

49 Rules 1.2(d), 3.3(b), 4.1(b) and 8.4(d).

50 Rule 1.6.

Law, govern.[51] Rule 5.5, Comment [2] illustrates the connection: "This Rule does not prohibit a lawyer from employing the services of paraprofessionals and delegating functions to them, so long as the lawyer supervises the delegated work and retains responsibility for their work."[52] If non-lawyers are not supervised by lawyers, the analysis turns on the tasks involved: by definition, the unauthorized practice of law prohibitions bar acts involving the practice of law. Since providing legal advice is a core component of the practice of law, the distinction often turns on the murky line between information and advice.[53] While unauthorized practice of law statutes, and cases interpreting them, often proscribe specific activities, exceptions to the statutes may include lay representation before certain local courts and state administrative agencies.[54]

Context matters in predicting resistance. Lay assistance might be welcome where no one objects and cases move smoothly, but unwelcome if private lawyers fear losing paying clients to non-lawyers or the goals of opposing counsel are impeded.

Student Practice Rules

Student practice rules frame the analysis where law students are involved. Outside the scope of permissible law student representation, law students are lay advocates. Within the scope of permissible representation, the rules that apply to lawyers apply to law students, establishing obligations for supervisors as well.

Despite the variations in program structure, analysis of the most common ethics labels suggests the governing rules and their application. Given the trend to facilitate self-help and increase access to justice, the relevant interests will generally favor the provision of assistance, with ghostwriting remaining the possible outlier. The systemic analysis mirrors the long-standing Access to Justice dilemma of how to assist more people without delivering second-class justice.

DEALING WITH UNREPRESENTED ADVERSE PARTIES

The prevalence of self-representation raises ethical dilemmas for lawyers in cases pitting lawyers against unrepresented adverse parties. Many lawyers have observed other lawyers "crossing the line" but also have struggled to pursue their own clients' goals in an ethical manner when their own cases implicate this scenario. Cases involving lawyers and unrepresented litigants often settle, under pressure

[51] Rules 5.3, 5.5.

[52] Rule 5.5, Comment [2].

[53] See Derek A. Denckla, *Nonlawyers and the Unauthorized Practice of Law: An Overview of the Legal and Ethical Parameters*, 67 FORDHAM L. REV. 2581, 2588 (1999) (identifying the three categories prohibited by unauthorized practice statutes: (1) representation of another in a court or administrative proceeding, (2) preparing legal instruments or documents that affect legal rights and responsibilities, and (3) advising another of the person's legal rights and responsibilities).

[54] *Id.*

from the court, typically following unmonitored hallway negotiations. Many unrepresented litigants are indigent, silenced by court process and power imbalances, and ill-positioned to distinguish between permissible and impermissible conduct. They appear without counsel not "voluntarily," but due to a shortage of lawyers for the poor. Negotiations between lawyers and lay people are common in administrative proceedings and in transactional contexts as well. With the advent of unbundling, a lawyer may be negotiating with an adverse party who is represented for some portions of the case and unrepresented for others.[55]

The ethical rules do not speak directly to negotiations. Rule 4.1 (Truthfulness in Statements to Others) is the primary source of restrictions where negotiations are between lawyers; Rule 4.3 governs when adverse parties are unrepresented.[56] Rule 4.3 prohibits a lawyer from stating or implying "that the lawyer is disinterested" and from giving "legal advice to a person who is not represented by a lawyer, other than the advice to secure counsel . . ."[57] The analysis applies to interactions with all unrepresented persons, including witnesses, in adverse positions.[58]

Lawyers must refrain from overreaching, misleading, pressuring, and threatening when negotiating with an unrepresented party.[59] The prohibition against advice-giving carries with it prohibitions against persuading an unrepresented litigant to adopt certain terms, making predictions about what will happen in court, and opining on the applicability of the law to the facts of the case beyond the exceptions articulated in the comment.[60] Permissible behavior includes negotiating the terms of a transaction or settling a dispute and informing the unrepresented person of the terms on which the lawyer's client will settle; the lawyer may prepare documents requiring the person's signature and explain the lawyer's own view of the meaning of the document or the underlying legal obligations.[61]

The rules on paper bear little relation to what occurs daily in courts that handle housing, family, and other civil cases in which litigants are often unrepresented. Negotiating tactics that would be standard between lawyers include behavior that is impermissible when the opposing party is unrepresented. Judges and court personnel tacitly condone the behavior when they send unrepresented litigants into the hallway with instructions to discuss settlement, rather than with warnings to protect themselves from attorney misconduct. Ethics decisions rooted in such "settlement discussions" are rare, since unrepresented litigants do not typically file ethics

55 See, e.g., Jennings & Greiner, supra note 6, at 828.

56 Rule 4.3.

57 *Id.*

58 *Id.*

59 See Russell Engler, *Out of Sight and Out of Line: The Need for Regulation of Lawyers' Negotiations with Unrepresented Poor Persons*, 85 California L. Rev. 79 (1997). Rule 4.3 derived from its predecessor in the Code of Professional Responsibility, DR 7–104(A)(2), which succeeded Canon 9 of the Canons of Professional Ethics.

60 *Id.*, at 93–101.

61 Rule 4.3, Comment [2].

complaints against opposing counsel, and disciplinary bodies are unlikely to initiate proceedings.

The absence of meaningful enforcement should not become a license to ignore the rules. Lawyers might negotiate in the presence of court personnel to reduce the incidence of unmonitored negotiations. At a systemic level, weakening the rules to conform to current practice might be tempting. Yet, the ethical rules should demand more where the other party is unrepresented.

The better response is to insure that lawyers understand, and the profession enforces, the existing rules. Demanding adherence to the rules will benefit poor people on balance, since legal aid lawyers face unrepresented adverse parties in only a tiny percentage of the pool of cases pitting a lawyer against an unrepresented litigant. Highlighting the unfairness of scenarios where lawyers routinely face unrepresented litigants might help develop allies in campaigns, including those to expand a civil right to counsel, to correct what is a breakdown of the adversary system.

JUDGES, COURT-CONNECTED MEDIATORS, AND CLERKS

Although beyond the scope of a chapter on limited representation, the high incidence of self-representation implicates the ethical rules governing the conduct of judges, court-connected mediators, clerks, and other court personnel as well. Advocates assist litigants who interact with court players and need to know what to expect. Lawyers undertake representation that requires assessing, supporting, elaborating, and sometimes undoing or challenging what has occurred prior to representation, including amending court filings or vacating defaults or stipulations.[62]

FRAMEWORK, UNDERLYING ASSUMPTIONS, AND ENFORCEMENT REALITIES

The ethical issues applicable to unbundling and self-representation illustrate how traditional ethics training bears little resemblance to our day-to-day challenges. New forms of assistance programs, new labels such as "unbundled" legal services, and a willingness to deal with issues long ignored, such as negotiations with unrepresented

[62] For a discussion of the ethical rules involved for the judges, court-connected mediators and clerks, see, e.g., Russell Engler, *Ethics in Transition: Unrepresented Litigants and the Changing Judicial Role*, 22 NOTRE DAME J. LAW, ETHICS PUBLIC POLICY 367 (2008); Russell Engler, *And Justice for All–Including the Unrepresented Poor: Revisiting the Role of Judges, Mediators, and Clerks*, 67 FORDHAM LAW REV. 1987 (1999); Richard Zorza, *The Disconnect between the Requirements of Judicial Neutrality and Those of the Appearance of Neutrality When Parties Appear Pro Se: Causes, Solutions, Recommendations, and Implications*, 17 GEO. J. LEGAL ETHICS 423, 423 (2004). In 2007, the ABA added a comment to the Model Judicial Code to provide that it is not a violation of the rule requiring impartiality and fairness "to make reasonable accommodations to pro se litigants to have their cases fairly heard." Rule 2.2., comment [4]. For a comparison of the judicial codes of states that have adopted that language or a comparable rule, see www.americanbar.org/content/dam/aba/administrative/professional_responsibility/2_2.authcheckdam.pdf.

parties and the roles of court players, complicate the analysis. New ethical issues will arise as legal aid offices, the private bar, and the courts continue to innovate. The next section therefore offers a framework, drawn from the previous sections, for approaching new ethical issues or variations on existing ethical dilemmas.

FIVE-STEP FRAMEWORK FOR APPROACHING ETHICAL ISSUES

(1) Label the Issue in Ethics Terminology

Is it an issue of client confidentiality? Conflict of interest? The discussion of limited assistance programs reveals the importance of accurate and complete issue-spotting.

(2) Identify the Applicable Rules

Begin with your jurisdiction's analog to the Model Rules (Rules 1.7–1.10 and 6.5, for example, for conflict of interest issues). The applicable law also includes local and national ethics opinions, local court rules, and case law. As with any other area of law, some authority is controlling while ABA Ethics Opinions or decisions from other jurisdictions are instructive.

(3) Apply the Rules

Doing so is easier said than done in some cases, particularly where scenarios that lawyers face are not the ones envisioned by the drafters of the rules. The rules might clarify what steps are prohibited, even if they fail to prescribe the best course of action.

(4) Analyze the Context and Interests of the Players Involved

Compare interpretations of ethical rules facilitating limited assistance programs with cases prohibiting ghostwriting. Context matters.

(5) Assess your Moral Compass on Individual Issues and Your Client's in Systemic Ones

Where ethics rules permit a range of behavior, remember your need to sleep at night and maintain your reputation. Notions of zealous advocacy suggest that we aggressively pursue our client's stated goals at every turn. Yet, ethical rules that emphasize our role as advisor, and that discuss our duties to third parties, the court, and the legal system, imply that a range of behavior is permissible. On systemic issues, the interests of the communities we serve should affect our interpretations of existing ethical rules, or changes we promote.

UNSTATED ASSUMPTIONS IN ETHICS RULES AND ENFORCEMENT REALITIES

Since the ethical rules were not drafted with a focus on settings involving a high incidence of self-representation, articulating unstated assumptions enhances the analysis even where it does not simplify the issues. First, although many people appear without counsel in civil proceedings, few ethical rules acknowledge unrepresented parties. Second, despite the desperate shortage of legal services for the poor, the ethical rules assume that clients have the resources to obtain lawyers.[63] Third, the ethical rules typically assume a full-representation model, a reality challenged by the world of counsel and advice, limited assistance, ghostwriting, and unbundled legal services.[64] Finally, the ethical rules do not envision technological changes, an ongoing challenge for the profession.

Complicating the analysis further, enforcement mechanisms are ill-equipped to respond to many ethical issues involving unrepresented litigants. The legal profession is self-regulated, with rules written by lawyers and judges. Where the interests of lawyers and judges clash with those of non-lawyers and the public, we know whose interests will prevail. In addition, enforcement targets the "bad apple." Lawyer behavior far outside the mainstream is more likely to draw attention than if "everybody does it." Finally, while multiple enforcement mechanisms exist for ethics issues generally, two such mechanisms – the enforcement of ethical rules by disciplinary bodies and legal malpractice cases – typically involve actions between lawyers and their clients. They would be ineffective in regulating the conduct discussed here. A third mechanism, oversight by the court, offers the only viable check on improper conduct.

The unstated assumptions illustrate why unrepresented or partially represented litigants raise such quandaries for lawyers, and also why the discussion connects ethics and politics. The application of rules in our legal system often favors those with power over those without, requiring aggressive and sustained advocacy to counter the pressure. The ethics rules are no different. Our approach to ethics must prevent misconduct and promote good lawyering practices and justice for the poor.

Almost forty years ago, Bellow and Kettleson recognized that our responses to persistent ethical dilemmas in public interest practice were inherently political: "they reflect choices about what is and ought to be the parameters of power between lawyers, clients, and others, and between the public and the profession."[65] Where ethical issues prevent modes of assistance that poor people need, the battle to shape the ethics rules must be part of a law reform agenda, particularly where the battle

63 Rule 4.3(b) permits lawyers to advise an unrepresented person to secure counsel. Rule 1.16(d) envisions that lawyers terminating employment allow "time for employment of other counsel."

64 Rule 6.5, an exception, has not been adopted in all jurisdictions.

65 Gary Bellow & Jeanne Kettleson, *From Ethics to Politics: Confronting Scarcity and Fairness in Public Interest Practice*, 58 Boston Univ. Law Rev. 337, 389 (1978).

might benefit moderate and middle-income clients as well. Our response to the problem of underrepresentation of the poor should include robust and effective assistance programs, revising the roles of the key players, and expanded access to full representation where basic human needs are at stake and lesser forms of assistance cannot protect those basic needs.

At the same time, we must carefully evaluate the impact of new initiatives, including unbundling. For legal aid clients, the paramount issues are less those of ethics than of resource allocation. Beyond the legal aid setting, Access to Justice initiatives should be shaped both by analysis of the application of the ethical rules and the effectiveness of the initiatives in a given setting. Evaluation of case outcomes should guide decisions as to which resources support full representation and which support limited assistance, and which forms of limited assistance are most effective in a given context. With the private bar, a consumer protection analysis should guide any expansion. Clients positioned to make informed choices in retaining legal services for discrete tasks should be permitted to do so, while vulnerable clients, such as the elderly, need protection.

30

Technology Can Solve Much of America's Access to Justice Problem, If We Let It

Benjamin H. Barton

Can the increasing number of online self-help resources created by private companies, the courts, and public agencies help fill the access to justice gap? Benjamin Barton argues that they can. Barton describes the availability of free online forms on state court websites, low-cost document assembly services, like LegalZoom, *and legal advice resources. For routine legal problems, online legal solutions are especially promising.*

This chapter argues that technology is likely to be the best bet for solving these problems. We are at the very beginning of the application of computer power to legal services and we have already seen much that will help increase access to justice: free or low-cost access to the law itself (statutes, regulations, and cases), free or low-cost legal forms, low-cost access to legal advice, etc. Moreover, as computer technology becomes even more sophisticated and we move into more advanced stages of computerization, we may see technology fundamentally reshape the market for legal services.

Two caveats. First, for potential clients who are illiterate or lack access to a computer with internet access, computerization is unlikely to be of much help. Access to the internet is continuing to grow, however. Approximately 70% of Americans have a broadband connection at home, including more than half of households with incomes below $30,000.[1] Almost all public libraries provide free access to the internet and computers as well.[2] Chicago-Kent Law School's A2J project is also beginning to make smartphone versions of their internet access to justice programs,[3] and 61% of Americans own a smartphone.[4] Despite the possibility of access, however, there are significant numbers of Americans incapable of self-help, regardless of technological advances. It is worth noting, however, that if

1 Adi Robertson, *Only 2 Percent of Americans Can't Get Internet Access, but 20% Choose Not To*, THE VERGE, Aug. 26, 013, available at www.theverge.com/2013/8/26/4660008/pew-study-finds-30-percent-americans-have-no-home-broadband.

2 Gretchen Ruethling, Almost All Libraries Offer Free Web Access, N.Y. Times, June 24, 2005, available at www.nytimes.com/2005/06/24/national/24library.html.

3 IIT Chicago–Kent College of Law, A2J, *Access to Justice on a Smartphone*, May 14, 2012, available at www.kentlaw.iit.edu/news/2012/access-to-justice-on-a-smartphone (last visited Nov. 21, 2013).

4 Aaron Smith, *Smartphone Ownership* 2013, PEW INTERNET, June 5, 2013, available at http://pewinternet.org/Reports/2013/Smartphone-Ownership-2013/Findings.aspx.

technology can reach some of the low-hanging fruits of need, legal aid and pro bono efforts could focus more narrowly on the neediest Americans.

Second, technology will not reach all of American legal needs equally. There are at least four different types of legal work the poor and middle class need, and some is more likely to be provided inexpensively by computers than others. The easiest case is access to the raw materials of American law. Thanks to the work of state, local, and federal governments, as well as nonprofits like Cornell Law School's Legal Information Institute (LII),[5] Americans with a computer and an internet connection now have more access to the laws that govern them than ever before. Google and other search engines also make these raw materials easier to find than ever.

Another area of increased access is legal drafting. Wills, forms for powers of attorney, incorporation, and divorce papers can all be obtained online. Commercial providers like *LegalZoom*, and free providers like probono.net and various state court websites provide access to a variety of legal forms. Many of these forms are simple and can be filled out by lay individuals. Interactive forms, which ask users questions and then select and fill out what is appropriate, are the next frontier.

Legal advice is harder to come by, but becoming more available as well. This work tends to be more contextual, and also more protected by rules against the unauthorized practice of law, so this work will be harder to commoditize and sell cheaply. Nevertheless, we have already seen free or reduced-cost legal advice on the internet, and there is reason to believe that the trend will accelerate.

The hardest case is in court litigation work. American judges have always enforced this lawyer prerogative most jealously and it is here that protections against the unauthorized practice of law are at their most powerful. Nevertheless, judges struggling with large pro se dockets are increasingly willing to make it easier to operate in their courts without a lawyer, and online dispute resolution offers a wholly different manner to settle disputes, bypassing courts and lawyers altogether.

The danger to many of these solutions comes from legal restrictions on the "unauthorized practice of law," hostile judges, lawyer recalcitrance, and letting the perfect be the enemy of the good. The greatest danger to the power of technology is the beneficiaries of the status quo. That said, there are early signs that technology is poised to triumph, to the benefit of us all.

ACCESS TO LEGAL MATERIALS

Over the last twenty years or so, free access to law on the internet has become a reality. Federal, state, and local governments have made statutes, regulations, and published cases available for free online and nonprofits like the LII have gathered them in one place.

5 Legal Information Institute, *About*, available at www.law.cornell.edu/lii/about/about_lii (last visited Nov. 21, 2013).

The LII was founded in 1992. Its mission is to provide free online access to law. The website is advanced enough now where it has statutes, court opinions, and regulations from the federal government and all fifty states. It also offers an online legal encyclopedia.[6] Wikipedia also includes a great number of sections devoted to legal cases and concepts.[7]

The availability of these materials is helpful, but the addition of advanced search engines like Google or Yahoo is the real addition. It allows easy access to particular statutes, regulations, or rules if you have the cite (just Google a Federal Rule of Evidence, for example), but it also allows for relatively accurate natural language search. Google has gotten good enough at this to draw the attention of Westlaw and Nexis, who are responding to the competition by creating their own natural language search engines.

None of these resources is perfect, and someone with a legal issue should certainly hesitate before relying on Wikipedia or a Google search if they have a serious legal need. Nevertheless, like the access to medical information on the internet, knowledge is power, and simply having access to the raw materials of American law is a significant change from the past.

DOCUMENT DRAFTING – PROBONO.NET, A2J, AND STATE SUPREME COURTS

Access to the law itself is one thing; access to court filings and other legal documents is another. There has been considerable progress on this front as well. Between free documents provided by state supreme courts, probono.net, and legal aid societies and low-cost document providers like *LegalZoom* and *Rocketlawyer*, ordinary Americans have more access to legal forms than ever before.

The most obvious use of technology is to just post forms and instructions on the internet for download and use. In many cases these forms are posted for free and are available to anyone with internet access and a printer. State supreme courts all over the country have started to offer free, online forms in a multitude of areas. For example, Tennessee has a court-supported self-help website that offers pdfs that can be filled in online and used for uncontested divorces,[8] orders of protection,[9] and various defenses in collection matters.[10] Tennessee is not unusual in this regard; the National Center for State Courts has a page with links to free, online court forms

6 LII, *Wex*, available at www.law.cornell.edu/wex/ (last visited Nov. 21, 2013).

7 See, e.g., Wikipedia, *Due Process*, available at http://en.wikipedia.org/wiki/Due_process (last visited Nov. 21, 2013).

8 Tennessee Administrative Office of the Courts, *Court-Approved Divorce Forms*, available at www.tncourts.gov/help-center/court-approved-divorce-forms (last visited Nov. 21, 2013).

9 Tennessee Administrative Office of the Courts, *Order of Protection Forms*, available at www.tncourts.gov/programs/self-help-center/forms/order-protection-forms (last visited Nov. 21, 2013).

10 Tennessee Administrative Office of the Courts, *Court Approved General Sessions Forms*, available at www.tncourts.gov/node/1436225 (last visited Nov. 21, 2013).

from 49 states and the federal government.[11] Much of the work on these forms has been done by state access to justice commissions. The ABA lists thirty-four different states that have access to justice commissions.[12]

How does it work? The Tennessee site for uncontested divorces is pretty typical. It has five pages of instructions in English or Spanish.[13] The very first set of instructions describes who may use the form: uncontested divorces with no children or property. The instructions walk the applicant through the various forms, explain what to expect in court, and answer some common questions. The applicant then fills out the necessary forms, including the Request for Divorce, the Divorce Agreement, the various filing documents and a draft Final Decree of Divorce. I have served as the faculty supervisor to the student-run University of Tennessee Homeless Legal Advocacy Project since 2001, and while these forms are not for every divorce, we have used them regularly since they came online a few years ago and they have been a lifesaver.

The next level of technical sophistication is interactive forms. Probono.net and Chicago-Kent Law School's A2J project have worked together to create LawHelp Interactive (LHI), an online repository of guided legal form drafting.[14] Since 2009, LHI has created over 145,000 different forms in 28 different states. The forms cover issues like child support and custody, domestic violence, debt collection, foreclosures, evictions, and divorce. The A2J software is especially designed to deal with self-represented litigants who may be uncomfortable filling out a legal form or otherwise confused by legal processes.[15] It takes the user through a guided online "interview," where questions are asked and answered. The program reacts to the questions by guiding the user to the proper form. Once the correct form is selected, the program asks the questions necessary to fill out the form. At the end, the user has a completed legal form.

Consider the A2J and probono.net designed program for an Illinois name change application.[16] The first page asks the user to agree to the terms of use. With that out of

[11] National Center for State Courts, *Self-Representation State Links*, available at www.ncsc.org/Topics/Access-and-Fairness/Self-Representation/State-Links.aspx?cat=Court%20Forms (last visited Nov. 21, 2013).

[12] ABA, *State Access to Justice Commissions: Lists and Links*, available at www.americanbar.org/groups/legal_aid_indigent_defendants/initiatives/resource_center_for_access_to_justice/state_atj_commissions.html (last visited Nov. 21, 2013).

[13] All of the documents described in this paragraph can be found here: Tennessee Administrative Office of the Courts, *Court-Approved Divorce Forms*, available at www.tncourts.gov/help-center/court-approved-divorce-forms (last visited Nov. 21, 2013).

[14] LawHelp Interactive, *About LawHelp Interactive*, available at https://lawhelpinteractive.org/about (last visited Nov. 21, 2013).

[15] IIT Chicago-Kent College of Law, *A2J Author*, available at www.kentlaw.iit.edu/institutes-centers/center-for-access-to-justice-and-technology/a2j-author (last visited Nov. 21, 2013).

[16] LawHelp Interactive, *Illinois Name Change Petition*, available at www.lawhelpinteractive.org/login_form?template_id=template.2009-03-30.3036595798&set_language=en https://www.lawhelpinteractive.org/login_form?template_id=template.2009-03-30.3036595798&set_language=en (last visited Nov. 21, 2013).

the way, an attractive, picture-based road to a courthouse appears, with a series of signposts laying out the steps to completing the form.

For an Illinois name change the first page announces what the program is, Illinois Legal Aid's Online Petition for Change of Name program. The next pages collect personal information (name, date of birth, address, phone number) as well as eligibility information (have you lived in Illinois for longer than six months? Are you a convicted sex offender?). Each of these questions is asked in a simple, straightforward manner. Many include pop-up explanations about why the particular question is necessary.

Once the initial questions are asked and the form is ready to be filled out, the program asks if you would like to access the forms to waive the filing and publication fees and gives instructions about the requirement to publish notice of a name change in a newspaper and how to do it. It then asks about finding a witness for the affidavit section of the form. Once these questions are answered, the form is ready to be printed out and filed. I proceeded through the steps (using made-up Illinois state information) in under 15 minutes and printed out the forms.

Legal Aid Societies are also turning to the internet to try to reach more potential clients. Lawhelp.org has an interactive map of the United States that sends the user to the relevant legal aid website in all 50 states.[17] Twenty-five states use probono.net's LawHelp platform for their websites.[18] Probono.net created the platform to provide a uniform structure for legal aid websites. Each of the sites contains a mix of forms, general information, and specific legal advice. For example, texaslawhelp.org offers advice and forms on a bevy of subjects, including divorce, domestic violence, bankruptcy, eviction, housing discrimination, estate planning, veteran's benefits and many other topics.[19] Legal aid has long provided printed materials and forms to clients they cannot individually help. Just putting all of these publications and forms online alone is a tremendous leap forward.

PRIVATE COMPANIES OFFERING LEGAL FORMS – LEGALZOOM

LegalZoom offers similar services to those listed earlier, for a fee. Like the A2J software, *LegalZoom* takes users through a series of questions and then generates legal documents. For many documents *LegalZoom* provides a review by a nonlawyer scrivener at the end to ensure consistency and to avoid typos.[20] In some cases

[17] Lawhelp.org, *Find Help Near You Now*, available at www.lawhelp.org/find-help/ (last visited Nov. 21, 2013).

[18] Lawhelp.org, *About*, available at www.lawhelp.org/about-us (last visited Nov. 21, 2013).

[19] Texaslawhelp.org, *Homepage*, available at http://texaslawhelp.org/ (last visited Nov. 21, 2013).

[20] LegalZoom.com, *Peace of Mind Review*, available at www.legalzoom.com/assets/modals/modal-legal zoom-peace-of-mind-review.html (last visited Nov. 21, 2013).

LegalZoom also offers review of any document by a lawyer for an additional fee, as little as $39 depending on the document.[21]

The list of *LegalZoom* documents covers almost every type of non-court document you can imagine, including entity formation, trademark searches, contracts, leases, wills, living trusts, powers of attorney, divorce papers, patents, and promissory notes, just to name some.[22] All told, *LegalZoom*'s products available page lists more than seventy documents.[23]

Take, for example, drafting a living will. The basic living will is $39.[24] *LegalZoom* offers a helpful page that differentiates between a Last Will, a Living Trust, and a Living Will, explaining basically what each is for.[25] When you select "living will" you begin to answer a series of relevant questions: name, address, county of residence, etc. Then the site asks a series of questions about life support: would you want it if you are unconscious and have a terminal condition with no hope of recovery? What care would you like if life support is withdrawn? Do you have any additional comments or instructions? Next you decide whether to appoint a healthcare agent and what powers you wish to grant the agent. It closes by asking for your burial wishes. After spending $39, you receive from *LegalZoom* a document created from your answers, which is printed out and mailed to you.[26] The process is simple, inexpensive, quick, and straightforward.

It is harder to find online assistance for contested matters. *LegalZoom* offers documents and support for uncontested divorces only, and includes a description of the difference between an uncontested and contested divorce.[27] Uncontested divorces start at $299.[28] Bankruptcy actually requires a lawyer and a higher fee ($1,599 in Tennessee, for example).[29]

LegalZoom also offers over 160 documents "crafted by top attorneys" for download that the user can fill in herself.[30] The documents come with instructions and are listed from a to z (or from "Academic Letter of Recommendation" to "Workplace

[21] LegalZoom.Com, *Legal Document Review*, available at www.legalzoom.com/legal-document-review/legal-document-review-overview.html (last visited Nov. 21, 2013).

[22] LegalZoom.com, *Our Products and Services*, available at www.legalzoom.com/products-and-services.html (last visited Nov. 21, 2013).

[23] *Id.*

[24] LegalZoom.com, *Living Wills Pricing*, available at www.legalzoom.com/living-wills/living-wills-pricing.html (last visited Nov. 21, 2013).

[25] LegalZoom.com, *Help Me Compare*, available at www.legalzoom.com/wills-estate-planning/summary-compare-wills.html (last visited Nov. 21, 2013).

[26] For a model version provided by *LegalZoom*, see www.legalzoom.com/samples/Living_Will_IL.pdf (last visited Nov. 22, 2013).

[27] LegalZoom, *Divorce Education Center*, available at www.legalzoom.com/divorce-guide/uncontested-contested-divorce.html (last visited Mar. 7, 2013).

[28] LegalZoom, *Divorce*, available at www.legalzoom.com/legal-divorce/divorce-overview.html (last visited Nov. 22, 2013).

[29] LegalZoom, *Pricing for Chapter 7 Bankruptcy Packages*, available at www.legalzoom.com/bankruptcy/bankruptcy-pricing.html (last visited Nov. 22, 2013).

[30] LegalZoom, *All Forms*, available at www.legalzoom.com/legalforms/ (last visited Nov. 22, 2013).

Injury and Illness Report"). The individual forms are mostly priced at $14.95. *LegalZoom* also offers unlimited access to the forms for $7.99 a month or unlimited access plus "attorney support" from the Legal Advantage Plus "attorney plan" for $14.95 a month.[31] A free-standing "attorney plan" runs as little as $9.99 a month.[32]

The user can choose from a panel of lawyers and many of those lawyers have ratings on *LegalZoom*, which puts pressure on the lawyers to provide good service, or to drop off of *LegalZoom*. The plans offer the following services: (1) a user can schedule a time for a half an hour phone consultation with an actual, live lawyer from their State; (2) once a year the user can have a one hour "legal checkup"; (3) the attorney will review documents under 10 pages for no additional charge; longer documents cost more. The lawyer can also choose to write a letter or make a phone call for the user. If more extensive services are needed, the user can hire the lawyer at a *LegalZoom*-negotiated discount. The *Rocketlawyer* program is quite similar in cost and services provided.[33]

Overall, the online reviews in *LegalZoom*'s own "user reviews" section are largely positive, with an overall rating of 4.5 stars as of July 2014.[34] *LegalZoom* has a customer service center and a money-back guarantee for its work. Like other high-profile internet sites, it does appear to take customer satisfaction and online reviews very seriously.

The complaints on *LegalZoom*'s own site are for overbilling for months where the service was not used and for late or inconsiderate lawyers, hardly a *LegalZoom*-only phenomenon. A *Google* search for "LegalZoom scam" or "LegalZoom complaints" provides some more negative reviews, but no showstopping stories of large-scale document failure or consumer harm. Overall there is little to suggest that very many people besides lawyers and bar associations are dissatisfied with *LegalZoom*.

If a more serious dispute breaks out, *LegalZoom*'s Terms and Conditions kick in. Paragraph 13 requires users to arbitrate any disputes along terms similar to other internet service providers.[35] As of right now there are almost no reported cases against *LegalZoom*. The few that do exist are mostly class actions for the unauthorized practice of law. As of July 2014, a Westlaw search of all State and Federal courts finds no lawsuit against *LegalZoom* by an individual, injured customer. This is possibly because of the arbitration clause or the relatively small amounts of damages in any suit or because problems with wills or LLC papers tend to arise years after drafting.

31 LegalZoom, *Legal Forms*, available at www.legalzoom.com/legalforms/bill-of-sale-automobile (last visited Nov. 22, 2013).

32 LegalZoom, *Find an Attorney You Can Trust for Your Family*, available at www.legalzoom.com/attorneys-lawyers/legal-plans/personal (last visited July 28, 2014).

33 Rocketlawyer, *On Call Terms of Service*, available at www.rocketlawyer.com/on-call-terms-of-service.rl (last visited July 28, 2014).

34 *Id.*

35 LegalZoom, *Terms and Conditions*, available at www.legalzoom.com/legal/general-terms/terms-of-service.

At least one law firm has sued *LegalZoom* alleging that the website interferes with the attorney–client relationship and generally treats its lawyers shoddily and unprofessionally. A copy of the complaint is still posted online,[36] but the case was dismissed because of the arbitration clause in 2012 and no more information is available. Overall, *LegalZoom* appears to have a remarkably clean rap sheet for a high-profile company that has been drafting online legal documents for more than a decade.

LegalZoom has drawn some very serious venture capital. According to *Forbes*, *LegalZoom* matches the venture capital checklist: it is a "disruptive model in a huge, decentralized business" and it "targets the high-volume, low-cost business of providing basic consumer and business documents."[37]

In documents filed with the Securities and Exchange Commission, *LegalZoom* claims two million customers over the last 10 years and that its "customers placed approximately 490,000 orders and more than 20% of new California limited liability companies were formed using our online legal platform in 2011."[38]

LegalZoom is hardly alone in the forms market. *Google* owns *Rocket Lawyer*, which is one of *LegalZoom*'s primary competitors. *Rocket Lawyer* actually had more unique visitors than *LegalZoom* in October 2012 (being owned by *Google* has its perks), and has been aggressively pricing its forms, even advertising some as "free."[39]

As noted earlier, legal aid, probono.net, and state courts offer some free forms that essentially compete with *LegalZoom*. In fact, the existence of stiff for-profit forms providers and some free form providers has led to investor skepticism about *LegalZoom*.[40] *LegalZoom* first scheduled its IPO for August, 2011, and then rescheduled due to "market conditions."[41] This is, of course, even better news for access to justice, as the worry about *LegalZoom* is that it is *too expensive*.

It is likely that *LegalZoom* and its competitors will grow in prevalence and as a source of competition for flesh-and-blood lawyers. Lawyers are already worried, but the real concern is that *LegalZoom* and its competitors may soon be more than a cheap and acceptable alternative. *LegalZoom* may eventually be cheaper AND better. Right now lawyers are reaping the benefits of using interactive computer forms themselves, but *LegalZoom* may eventually do a volume of business that will allow them to surpass the quality of any individualized work.

36 Available at www.directlaw.com/Complaint%20&%20Exhibits%20Filed-1.pdf (last visited July 28, 2014).

37 Daniel Fisher, *Silicon Valley Sees Gold in Internet Legal Services*, Forbes, Oct. 5, 2011, available at www.forbes.com/sites/danielfisher/2011/10/05/silicon-valley-sees-gold-in-internet-legal-services/ (last accessed Oct. 18, 2012).

38 *Id.*

39 See Benny Evangelista, *LegalZoom Sues Rocket Lawyer*, S.F. Chronicle, November 28, 2012, available at www.sfgate.com/business/article/LegalZoom-sues-Rocket-Lawyer-4075061.php.

40 See Richard Granat, *LegalZoom's Achilles' Heel: Free Legal Forms*, ELawyering Blog, August 4, 2013, available at www.elawyeringredux.com/2012/08/articles/free-law/legalzooms-achilles-heel-free-legal-forms/.

41 *LegalZoom Delays IPO*, L.A. Biz, Aug. 3, 2012, available at http://newsandinsight.thomsonreuters.com/Securities/News/2012/08_-_August/LegalZoom_IPO_delayed_-_source/.

LAWYERS CAN USE FORMS TOO

Traditional lawyers have tried three responses to the threat of *LegalZoom*. First, they have offered online alternatives that explicitly include lawyer review in the price. These are lawyer/form hybrids, however, where the customer fills in the legal forms and a licensed lawyer "reviews" them. Richard Granat was a pioneer in the field with his fixed-fee divorces in Maryland at *mdfamilylawyer.com*.[42] A simple divorce for a couple with children can be handled by a lawyer for as little as $229, without children $199.[43] *SmartLegalForms* offers legal forms and legal advice by a lawyer in a package deal; with an explicit dig at *LegalZoom*, calling it a more expensive "non-lawyer document preparation service" and "the old way" of internet law.[44]

Second, some lawyers occupy a middle space. Many small firm and solo practitioners' offices are now essentially an intermediary for online forms providers. For example, the National Law Foundation offers "fully editable forms" to lawyers for "as low as $19," covering virtually every type of legal drafting.[45] Similarly, state bar associations are creating online databases of interactive forms for use by their members, with an explicit eye toward "competition from web-based companies like *LegalZoom* and Rocket Lawyer."[46] Between online sites packaging the work of actual lawyers and selling it for peanuts, and regular lawyers feeling the pressure and adopting their own forms-based practices, the price of a real lawyer for some services is in free fall.

Last, if you can't beat 'em, join 'em. As noted earlier, *LegalZoom* and *Rocket Lawyer* and other online providers are starting to sell legal services and advice by flesh-and-blood lawyers through a subscription model or a fixed-price model.[47] The *LegalZoom* subscription model is aggressively priced to try to draw middle-class users. *LegalZoom* promises a lawyer will "review your last will, power of attorney or other legal documents. Get help when you need it from an attorney who knows the laws of your state. Get unlimited number of consultations on new legal matters for one low monthly rate."[48] *Rocket Lawyer* charges "pre-negotiated fees" in its "Rocket Lawyer On Call" program.[49]

42 MDFamilylawyer.com, *Fixed Fee Online Legal Services*, available at www.mdfamilylawyer.com/.

43 *Id.*

44 SmartLegalForms, *SmartLegalForms vs. LegalZoom*, available at www.smartlegalforms.com/smartlegalforms-vs-legalzoom.html.

45 National Law Foundation, *Practical Forms for Attorneys*, available at www.nlfforms.com/.

46 John G. Locallo, *Behind the Technology Curve? The ISBA Can Help*, 100 Ill. B.J. 124 (2012).

47 LegalZoom, *Find an Attorney You Can Trust for Your Family*, available at www.legalzoom.com/attorneys-lawyers/legal-plans/personal.html; Rocket Lawyer, *Get Connected with an On Call Lawyer: Members Save Thousands of Dollars with Pre-Negotiated Rates*, available at www.rocketlawyer.com/find-a-lawyer.rl.

48 LegalZoom, *Find an Attorney You Can Trust for Your Family*, available at www.legalzoom.com/attorneys-lawyers/legal-plans/personal.html?utm_source=pjx&utm_medium=affiliate&utm_campaign=43737&cm_mmc=affiliate-_-pjx-_-43737-_-na.

49 Rocket Lawyer, *Get Connected with an On Call Lawyer*, available at www.rocketlawyer.com/find-a-lawyer.rl.

ONLINE LEGAL ADVICE

Remember that *LegalZoom* and *Rocket Lawyer* and others are already setting a very low online bar for the provision of legal advice by lawyers. That said, even the inexpensive advice they offer may be too expensive in the internet age.

Several different flavors of free online legal advice providers have sprung up. There is the truly free provision of advice in online communities like *MetaTalk*.[50] The acronyms IANAL (I am not a lawyer) and IAALBNYL (I am a lawyer, but not your lawyer)[51] are common intros to question-and-answer sessions on legal matters in these forums. The advice is general and informal, but is available to the public. For example, a *Google* search for "How do I write a will on my own?"[52] leads to ads from *LegalZoom* and *Rocket Lawyer*, but the first result is from wikihow.com and is entitled "How to Write Your Own Last Will and Testament (with Will Template)."[53]

Other websites attempt to leverage free legal advice into business for the answering lawyers. *Avvo* is a website that serves as an attorney evaluation service and offers free legal advice. Users post questions and attorneys answer them publicly. *Avvo* works like "Ask.com" or other crowdsourcing Q&A sites: the answers are stored, browsable, and searchable. *Avvo* also has listings of lawyers, with a controversial multi-factor rating system.[54] *Avvo* makes money through advertising on the site and selling "Avvo pro," a subscription service for lawyers to track their *Avvo* profiles.[55] *Avvo* thus leverages its ratings and traffic to draw lawyers into giving free advice with the hope of gaining paid work. *Avvo* draws traffic/potential clients to the site with free advice or free lawyer ratings.

LawPivot offers more formal and confidential free legal advice. Lawyers answer specific and detailed questions for free, again with an eye toward generating

50 Cassandra Burke Robertson, *The Facebook Disruption: How Social Media May Transform Civil Litigation and Facilitate Access to Justice*, 65 Ark. L. Rev. 75, 84–85 (2012), has a great discussion of this site.

51 MetaTalk, IAALBNYL, available at http://metatalk.metafilter.com/15513/IAALBIANYL.

52 www.google.com/#hl=en&gs_rn=7&gs_ri=psy-ab&qe=aG93IGRvIGkgd3JpdGUgYSB3aWw&qesig=kBqsFOod1_DMnf8JQiP7eQ&pkc=AFgZ2tlfosluMFIskLWyyo6BZ7oZXJJqy8GedMP_7nsAcn8cYAQ5mvGO_pwLKTRuH4mwMOy5rXQzTHcAXOgMWKEh5vetYWOZkg&cp=20&gs_id=26&xhr=t&q=how+do+i+write+a+will+on+my+own&es_nrs=true&pf=p&output=search&sclient=psy-ab&oq=how+do+i+write+a+wil&gs_l=&pbx=1&bav=on.2,or.r_qf.&bvm=bv.44342787,d.eWU&fp=75966c488fe17396&biw=1033&bih=629.

53 www.wikihow.com/Write-Your-Own-Last-Will-and-Testament.

54 Robert J. Ambrogi, *More Reaction to Avvo's Lawyer Ratings*, Law.com Legal Blog Watch, June 6, 2007, available at http://legalblogwatch.typepad.com/legal_blog_watch/2007/06/more_reaction_t.html.

55 Stephen Fairley, *Using Avvo to Market Your Law Firm on the Internet*, The Rainmaker Blog, available at www.therainmakerblog.com/2010/05/articles/law-firm-marketing-1/using-avvo-to-market-your-law-firm-on-the-internet/.

business.[56] *Rocket Lawyer* recently acquired *LawPivot. Rocket Lawyer* has kept *LawPivot* as a free-standing business, but also plans to adopt the Q&A method on its own site.

Internet suppliers are likely to drive the price of legal advice down. Like the provision of forms by *LegalZoom*, much current online provision of legal advice is hardly a threat to lawyers. Much of the advice now given for free online was given for free at cocktail parties in years past, with a similar "this is not legal advice" disclaimer. But, like *LegalZoom*'s forms business, the advice business is a serious matter, and *Avvo, LegalZoom*, and *Rocket Lawyer* are explicitly targeting middle-class consumers who might otherwise hire small firm and solo practitioners. As the technology improves, anyone with access to a computer and the internet may be able to get pretty nuanced legal advice for free or very cheaply.

IN-COURT LITIGATION

LegalZoom, Lawhelp, and other online forms providers do not offer any in-court legal services. The forms are to be used pro se or the users are to hire a lawyer to appear with them in court. In-court litigation looks likely to stay a lawyers-only activity for the foreseeable future. In-court representation of clients is the easiest type of unauthorized practice of law (UPL) for judges to police and it is the area least likely to be attacked by political opponents or lawyer competitors. Since the turn of the nineteenth century American judges have insisted that only lawyers may represent clients in their courts and that will not change anytime soon.

Appearing pro se is always an option and is constitutionally protected in some circumstances.[57] But most American courts have long been relatively unfriendly to pro se representation, expecting pro se litigants to handle their case the way a lawyer would: with timely objections, correct phrasing of questions, limited argument in opening statements, etc.[58]

In some cases lawyers have managed to suppress pro se reforms. For example, the Tennessee Supreme Court has spearheaded a statewide effort to address the hideous problems that poor Tennesseans who cannot afford counsel face when seeking a divorce.[59] Many of the more aggressive reforms, notably form pleading designed for

[56] Leena Rao, *Rocket Lawyer Acquires LawPivot to Add A Quora-Like Q&A Platform to Online Legal Services Site*, TECH CRUNCH, January 14, 2013, available at http://techcrunch.com/2013/01/14/rocket-lawyer-acquires-lawpivot-to-add-a-quora-like-qa-platform-to-online-legal-services-site/.

[57] See Joseph A. Colquitt, *Hybrid Representation: Standing the Two-Sided Coin on Its Edge*, 38 WAKE FOREST L. REV. 55, 57 & n. 10 (2003).

[58] Benjamin H. Barton, *Against Civil Gideon (and for Pro Se Court Reform)*, 62 FLA. L. REV. 1227 (2010).

[59] See Letter from Carl Pierce, Chairman, Tennessee Supreme Court Task Force on the Study of Self-Represented Litigant Issues in Tennessee, to Marcy Easton, President, Tennessee Bar Association (July 30, 2007), available at www.tba.org/tbatoday/news/2007/prosedivorce_letter_090707.pdf.

simple pro se divorces, were dead on arrival – the divorce bar was not going to stand for any changes that threatened their grip on middle- and upper-class divorces.

To a cynical observer the plight of pro se litigants, and the continuing complexity of American court procedures and evidentiary rules, are just advertising for lawyers. In many American courts, all a potential client has to do is watch five minutes of a confused and struggling pro se litigant before deciding to spend the money to hire a lawyer. Change here seems unlikely to come briskly, regardless of technology.

But there are cracks in the armor. Reforms have come in several flavors. From inside the judiciary there has been a conscious effort to push pro se courts to operate in a manner friendlier to their clients – the litigants who appear before them. For example, the American Judicature Society published a guide entitled *Reaching Out or Overreaching: Judicial Ethics and Self-Represented Litigants.*[60] It includes a long list of common-sense things that judges are allowed to do to help pro se litigants, including making procedural accommodations, being courteous, avoiding legal jargon and procedural snafus, explaining the process, avoiding over-familiarity with lawyers in the courtroom, and training court staff so they provide patient, helpful service to self-represented litigants.[61] AJS has also published a set of core materials that gathers the best and most innovative approaches to pro se reform being used nationally.[62] The National Center for State Courts published *The Self-Help Friendly Court: Designed from the Ground Up to Work for People without Lawyers.*[63] While these guides are not perfect or particularly visionary, if pro se courts around the country adopted their suggested reforms, it would make a huge difference in the lives of the indigent, as well as making those courts fairer and more efficient.

There are a number of individual courts that are trying quite innovative approaches. For example, Lois Bloom and Helen Hershkoff describe the creation of a special federal magistrate position in the Eastern District of New York assigned to hear significant categories of pro se matters, the first federal district to assign a single magistrate in this manner.[64] Ronald Staudt and Paula Hannaford have gathered a number of innovative court processes into one National Center for

60 Cynthia Gray, Reaching Out or Overreaching: Judicial Ethics and Self-Represented Litigants 1–2 (2005).

61 Gray, supra note 60, at 1–2.

62 The Self Represented Litigation Network, Core Materials on Self-Represented Litigation Innovation (2006).

63 Richard Zorza, The Self-Help Friendly Court: Designed from the Ground Up to Work for People Without Lawyers (2002), available at www.ncsconline.org/WC/Publications/Res_ProSe_SelfHelpCtPub.pdf. AJS actually has a whole website dedicated to the topic, www.ajs.org/prose/home.asp. See also Richard Zorza, *Self-Represented Litigation and the Access to Justice Revolution in the State Courts: Cross Pollinating Perspectives towards a Dialog for Innovation in the Courts and the Administrative System*, 29 J. Nat'l Assoc. Administrative L. Judiciary 63 (2009).

64 See Lois Bloom and Helen Hershkoff, *Federal Courts, Magistrate Judges, and the Pro Se Plaintiff*, 16 Notre Dame J.L. Ethics Pub. Pol'y 475, 476–77 (2002).

State Courts supported research project.[65] San Antonio and other cities have established specialized pro se courts adopting many of the suggestions for court structure listed earlier.[66]

Court systems, legal aid offices, and other advocates for the poor have also been working hard on offering legal advice and form preparation assistance for pro se litigants. California has a 900-page *Online Self-Help Center* sponsored by their Supreme Court.[67] Utah, Maryland, and other states have followed suit.[68] Lawhelp.org is a probono.net website that is aimed at pro se litigants and forwards the litigants on to each state's legal aid website, many of which are quite helpful.

Some court systems are beginning to experiment with using online dispute resolution (ODR) to fully replace court procedures. Colin Rule directed the *eBay* and *PayPal* ODR systems from 2003 to 2011.[69] EBay and PayPal are natural sites for ODR: they have lots of low-dollar transactions that occur across state and even international lines, making litigation cost prohibitive or simply impossible. The *eBay* ODR process proved exceptionally successful, handling up to 60 million disputes a year, and settling approximately 90% of them with no human input on the company side. Users expressed satisfaction with the program and used *eBay* and *PayPal* more after the ODR experience, regardless of whether they won or lost.[70]

Colin Rule and others licensed the *eBay* software and launched *Modria*, an ODR system for hire.[71] *Modria* sells a "Fairness Engine" that attempts substantive as well as financial settlement of disputes. It starts with a "diagnosis module" that gathers relevant information. A "negotiation module" summarizes areas of agreement and disagreement and makes suggestions for solving the issue. If these do not result in settlement, a "mediation module" with a neutral third party begins and the final step is arbitration.[72] *Modria* claims that the "vast majority" of claims are settled in the first two steps without a human mediator or arbitrator ever becoming involved.[73] Nor

[65] See Ronald W. Staudt and Paula L. Hannaford, *Access to Justice for the Self-Represented Litigant: An Interdisciplinary Investigation by Designers and Lawyers*, 52 SYRACUSE L. REV. 1017 (2002).

[66] See Anita Davis, *A Pro Se Program That Is Also "Pro" Judges, Lawyers, and the Public*, 63 TEX. B.J. 896 (2000).

[67] The Judicial Branch of California, *Online Self-Help Center*, available at www.courtinfo.ca.gov/self help/.

[68] Utah State Courts, *Online Court Assistance Program*, available at www.utcourts.gov/ocap/; Maryland Judiciary, *Family Law Forms*, available at http://mdcourts.gov/family/forms/index.html.

[69] Julia Wilkinson, Colin Rule: From eBay Conflicts to Global Peace Initiatives, ECOMMERCEBYTES.COM, available at www.ecommercebytes.com/cab/abu/y211/m06/abu0289/s05.

[70] Colin Rule, *Quantifying the Economic Benefits of Effective Redress: Large e-Commerce Data Sets and the Cost–Benefit Case for Investing in Dispute Resolution*, 34 U. ARK. L. REV. 1, 1–12 (2012).

[71] See note 71.

[72] Modria, *Our Modular Dispute Resolution System*, available at www.modria.com/resolution-center; see also Thomas Claburn, *Modria's Fairness Engine: Justice on Demand*, INFORMATIONWEEK CLOUD, November 19, 2012, available at www.informationweek.com/cloud-computing/platform/modrias-fair ness-engine-justice-on-deman/240142275.

[73] Modria, *about*, available at www.modria.com/about/.

does *Modria* see itself only as a small-claims alternative for ebusiness: it is targeting bigger-ticket disagreements, as well as complicated issues like patent disputes.[74]

Modria has also built an ODR system for the Canadian State of British Columbia. If British Columbians want to file an appeal of their property assessment, Modria has supplied an online appeal process.[75] This process was successful enough that British Columbia asked *Modria* to design an ODR process for consumer complaints to their consumer protection bureau.[76] Consumers with a complaint about a business are invited to try ODR. If they agree, Consumer Protection BC contacts the business and invites them to participate.[77] From there the *Modria* ODR platform does the rest. One fewer case ends up in small claims court and if the *eBay* experience is typical, both the business and the consumer are satisfied with the process.

We are still in the early stages of the computerized legal services revolution, and there is substantial uncertainty about which approaches will prove successful and lucrative in the long term. The sheer volume of the activity and the type of venture capital involved, however, suggests that technology companies feel confident they can disrupt the current market and replace expensive humans with cheaper information technology. If they are right, and computerized legal services continues to grow, we will see more legal services available for a greater share of Americans than ever before.

BUT UNAUTHORIZED PRACTICE OF LAW?

UPL is prohibited in all fifty states.[78] The definition of the "practice of law" and the levels of enforcement differ from state to state,[79] but at a minimum in no state may a non-lawyer appear in court on behalf of another party.[80] Likewise, non-lawyers may not give "legal advice." State bars have long allowed the publication of "forms books" despite the UPL strictures, but have drawn the line at the provision of advice along with forms.[81]

74 Eric Johnson, *Modria Wants You to Settle Your Workplace Problems (and Even Patent Disputes) Online*, ALL THINGS D, Nov. 24, 2012, available at http://allthingsd.com/20121124/modria-wants-you-to-settle-your-workplace-problems-and-even-patent-disputes-online/.

75 Modria, *Resolution Center: Property Assessment Appeals*, available at www.modria.com/assessment/.

76 Consumer Protection BC, *Resolve Your Dispute*, available at www.consumerprotectionbc.ca/odr.

77 There is a short video describing the process available here: www.odr.info/node/83.

78 Tanina Rostain, *The Emergence of "Law Consultants,"* 75 FORDHAM L. REV. 1397, 1407 & n. 53 (2006).

79 Deborah L. Rhode, *Policing the Professional Monopoly: A Constitutional and Empirical Analysis of Unauthorized Practice Prohibitions*, 34 STAN. L. REV. 1 (1981).

80 Derek A. Denckla, *Nonlawyers and the Unauthorized Practice of Law: An Overview of the Legal and Ethical Parameters*, 67 FORDHAM L. REV. 2581–94 (1999). This rule is relaxed in some administrative settings, see, e.g., Drew A. Swank, *Non-Attorney Social Security Disability Representatives and the Unauthorized Practice of Law*, 36 S. ILL. U. L.J. 223 (2012).

81 See, e.g., *Florida Bar v. Stupica*, 300 So. 2d 683, 686 (Fla. 1974) (providing divorce forms with advice is UPL); *State Ex Rel. Indiana State Bar Association v. Diaz*, 838 N.E.2d 433 (Ind. 2005) (same for immigration forms and advice).

Internet forms providers present a hybrid UPL case. There is not a human offering advice along with the forms, or filling the forms out for someone else, but the websites are packed with instructions and suggestions that look a lot like advice. *LegalZoom*, for example, sells both blank forms for customers to fill in themselves, which courts have found to be virtually identical to a formbook,[82] and interactive forms, where the customers answer questions and *LegalZoom* builds out the forms.[83]

LegalZoom's lawyers have argued that their interactive creation of forms is not UPL because the user provides all of the information and *LegalZoom* merely places the information into the applicable forms.[84] Opponents argue that *LegalZoom*'s interactive forms are not legal products, like a form book, but are actually a legal service: the drafting of documents, and thus clearly UPL.

LegalZoom debuted in 2001 and has thus far has faced only three real UPL challenges. The Washington State Attorney General investigated *LegalZoom* for UPL in 2010. *LegalZoom* settled by paying $20,000 in costs and agreeing not to violate Washington law, while continuing to operate in the state with no changes in their business practices.[85] In 2011, a private lawyer in Missouri filed a class action UPL suit against *LegalZoom*.[86] The case was settled before trial when *LegalZoom* agreed to a small payment and some unspecified changes in its business practices. *LegalZoom* did lose its summary judgment motion and a Missouri Federal District Court did hold that interactive forms are the unauthorized practice of law.[87] The CEO of *LegalZoom* stated that they settled the suit "with little change in [the] business, agreeing mainly to pay lawyers' fees"[88] and *LegalZoom* operates almost exactly the same in Missouri as it does in other states.[89]

LegalZoom has actually brought suit against the state bar in North Carolina, seeking a declaratory judgment that it is not engaging in UPL.[90] So far *LegalZoom*

82 See, e.g., *Janson v. LegalZoom.com, Inc.*, 802 F. Supp. 2d 1053, 1062–63 (W.D. Mo. 2011).

83 *Id.*

84 *Id.* at 1063.

85 NASDAQ OMX GlobeNewswire, *Legalzoom Enters into Agreement with State of Washington*, available at www.globenewswire.com/newsroom/news.html?d=201745 (last accessed Oct. 18, 2012). The settlement itself can be found here: www.atg.wa.gov/uploadedFiles/Home/News/Press_Releases/2010/LegalZoomAOD.pdf.

86 Nathan Kopel, *Seller of Online Legal Forms Settles Unauthorized Practice of Law Suit*, Wall St. J., August 23, 2011, available at http://blogs.wsj.com/law/2011/08/23/seller-of-online-legal-forms-settles-unauthorized-practiced-of-law-suit/ (last accessed Oct. 18, 2012).

87 Janson, 802 F. Supp. at 1064–65.

88 Daniel Fisher, *Silicon Valley Sees Gold in Internet Legal Services*, Forbes, Oct. 5, 2011, available at www.forbes.com/sites/danielfisher/2011/10/05/silicon-valley-sees-gold-in-internet-legal-services/ (last accessed Oct. 18, 2012).

89 *LegalZoom* does not offer the "Peace of Mind Review" of legal documents by non-lawyers in Missouri. See LegalZoom, *Peace of Mind Review*, available at www.legalzoom.com/peace-of-mind-popup.html (last visited Nov. 22, 2013). The Missouri court objected to this aspect of *LegalZoom*'s process, Janson, 802 F. Supp. at 1064.

90 Craig Jarvis, *Online Legal Firm in Bar Fight*, Charlotte News Observer, Oct. 5, 2011, available at www.newsobserver.com/2011/10/05/1540408/online-firm-in-bar-fight.html (last accessed Oct. 18, 2012).

has survived a motion to dismiss, but the District Court has not ruled on the central UPL issue.[91]

WHY SO LITTLE UPL ACTIVITY? AND WHAT WILL BE THE UPSHOT?

There are several reasons for the relative UPL quiet from lawyer regulators. Lawyers have been a little like a frog in a pot of slowly heating water. They did not notice the threat that computerized legal services presented until it was too late. Lawyers were unconcerned when *LegalZoom* started, because it was not really competing with private lawyers. *LegalZoom* fits perfectly with how Clayton Christensen describes disruptive technologies in his book, *The Innovators Dilemma*[92] – it started by servicing the lowest margin part of the market and has gradually inched its way up.

American lawyers currently do very little paid work for the poor and middle class. The staff and lawyers in solo practitioner or small-firm offices spend a great deal of time explaining to potential customers that they cannot afford legal services or explaining why it is so expensive to incorporate a company or to file and prosecute a divorce.

In 2001, when *LegalZoom* started out, anyone willing to incorporate their company or write their will on the internet was very unlikely to be able to afford a lawyer anyway. *LegalZoom* thus was not in direct competition with lawyers; it was merely soaking up a portion of the market lawyers had long since unilaterally abandoned. The first wave of clients *LegalZoom* grabbed were no loss at all. Any potential client who could not afford a "real lawyer" and would settle for a random form that (at first) might not even be particularly suited to their state or jurisdiction was hardly worth losing any sleep over. *LegalZoom* made no attempt, nor could it because of UPL, to snatch any in-court litigation work, which meant that large swaths of small firm practice (like contested divorces and child custody, small commercial lawsuits, criminal defense, etc.) remained unreachable.

As the forms have improved and public acceptance has risen, however, people who could otherwise afford a lawyer have started using online providers. For example, a colleague of mine recently decided to update his will. He called the lawyer who had written the first will ten years ago and was so stunned by the cost that he built a new will on *LegalZoom* for roughly one-tenth the price.

Given *LegalZoom*'s rise, scrutiny will likely increase.[93] Nevertheless, at this point *LegalZoom* is a famous company with a large advertising budget. Any effort to put it out of business in any particular state would bring significant negative attention to

[91] Nate Raymond, *LegalZoom Lawsuit against NC Bar May Proceed*, Thompson Reuters News & Insight, August 29, 2012, available at http://newsandinsight.thomsonreuters.com/Legal/News/2012/08-August/LegalZoom_lawsuit_against_NC_bar_may_proceed__judge/. The order itself is available here: www.ncbusinesscourt.net/opinions/2012_NCBC_47.pdf.

[92] Clayton Christensen, The Innovator's Dilemma: The Revolutionary Book That Will Change the Way You Do Business (2011).

[93] See, e.g., Jonathan G. Blattmachr, *Looking Back and Looking Ahead: Preparing Your Practice for the Future: Do Not Get Behind the Change Curve*, 36 ACTEC J. 1, 19–23 (2010) (arguing that *LegalZoom*

that state's lawyer regulators. For example, in the late 1990s the Texas Bar Association successfully prosecuted an offline program called "Quicken Family Lawyer" for UPL, only to be briskly overruled by the Texas legislature.[94]

In the early 2000s the American Bar Association (ABA) sought to create a model definition of the practice of law,[95] likely as a precursor to increased UPL enforcement. The Department of Justice and the Federal Trade Commission quickly sent the ABA a comment letter objecting to the proposed definition as overbroad and anticompetitive.[96] Given that the ABA settled an antitrust investigation over its accreditation of law schools in 1995,[97] the federal antitrust agencies' letter was a shot across the bow on UPL.

There is also a broader enforcement problem: even if UPL could destroy *LegalZoom*, what about the websites that promise that a lawyer "reviews" the documentation? These sites are priced competitively with *LegalZoom* and are much cheaper than a traditional lawyer, so the problem would persist even with aggressive UPL enforcement.

As for the upshot, it is hard to handicap as a legal matter because UPL and the definition of what constitutes the "practice of law" are notoriously mushy and case specific,[98] so legal analysis is of limited use. As a matter of *realpolitik*, however, I predict the eventual triumph of the online forms providers. Generally speaking UPL enforcement has been at its most robust when aimed against individuals. For example, one of the more notable UPL cases against a computerized form punished the individual who filled an electronic will form for an elderly neighbor, rather than the form provider itself.[99] Similarly, publishers of legal forms have had more success fighting UPL than individual non-lawyer scriveners.[100]

A full-scale attempt to bring computerization to heel via UPL would require a great deal of political will and capital from state supreme courts and other lawyer

service is the unauthorized practice of law and describing his personal, negative experience with *LegalZoom*).

94 *Unauthorized Practice of Law Comm. v. Parsons Tech. Inc.*, 179 F.3d 956, 956 (5th Cir. 1999) (vacating the District Court's injunction banning Quicken Family Lawyer after the Texas Legislature amended its 1939 unauthorized practice of law statute).

95 See Task Force on the Model Definition of the Practice of Law, *Report*, available at www.americanbar.org/content/dam/aba/migrated/cpr/model-def/taskforce_rpt_803.authcheckdam.pdf.

96 Department of Justice and the Federal Trade Commission, *Comments on the American Bar Association's Proposed Model Definition of the Practice of Law*, available at www.justice.gov/atr/public/comments/200604.htm.

97 Department of Justice, *Justice Department and American Bar Association Resolve Charges That the Aba's Process for Accrediting Law Schools Was Misused*, available at www.justice.gov/atr/public/press_releases/1995/0257.htm.

98 See, e.g., Deborah Rhode, *Policing the Professional Monopoly: A Constitutional and Empirical Analysis of Unauthorized Practice Prohibitions*, 34 Stan. L. Rev. 1 (1981).

99 Mathew Rotenberg, Note, *Stifled Justice: The Unauthorized Practice of Law and Internet Legal Resources*, 97 Minn. L. Rev. 709, 709–10 (2012).

100 Catherine J. Lanctot, *Scriveners in Cyberspace: Online Document Preparation and the Unauthorized Practice of Law*, 30 Hofstra L. Rev. 811, 822–36 (2002).

regulators. Truly aggressive moves would be likely to draw federal antitrust and congressional attention. This sort of brinksmanship would hardly be worth it, however, because UPL would be unlikely to bar the hybrid forms providers where lawyers are nominally involved in reviewing the documents.

BUT, QUALITY? QUALITY WILL COME AND JUSTICE WILL FOLLOW

Thus, cheaper access to legal services, advice, and forms through computerization seems likely to become a permanent feature of the landscape, to the great advantage of the many Americans who cannot currently afford such services. But possibly we should decry this change on the basis of consumer safety? For years the objections to unbundled legal services or other self-help aides has been that the poor deserve the same quality of legal work that the wealthy receive, and that *LegalZoom*, self-help aids, and other online aids are clearly deficient. It is true that these first-generation online services may not be as good as a live lawyer, although anyone reading this likely knows a lawyer whose work is already worse than what *LegalZoom* provides. Over time these programs will continue to adjust and improve. Regardless, *LegalZoom*, *Rocketlawyer*, and *LawHelp Interactive* are already clearly superior to nothing, which is what most poor and middle-income Americans can afford.

The quality argument is extremely divisive, because the proponents of free, high-quality individualized legal services by lawyers for the poor and those of moderate income cannot answer who will pay for these services. Moreover, the quality argument has a very hypothetical ring to it. For years lawyers have battled UPL in the alleged public interest. Most UPL complaints come from lawyers and not an aggrieved member of the public.[101] Similarly, any claim that *LegalZoom*, or any other online provider, is dangerous enough to be suppressed should start with actual aggrieved customers of *LegalZoom*, of which there do not appear to be many as of yet. Nor is it true that hiring a lawyer is a guarantee of quality, as the many complaints to bar regulators alone suggests.

More importantly though, technology offers an exit ramp to circular battles over access to justice.

This is the real promise of computerization and pro se court reform. If any thought or effort is put into combining technology with the needs of pro se litigants in courts, something truly revolutionary might emerge. A comparison between the online procedures offered by *Modria* versus what the typical pro se litigant faces in court is staggering. If courts could ever be convinced to let technology loosen the limits court procedures place on pro se litigants, the results would be exceptional: a

[101] See Alan B. Morrison, *Must the Interests of the Client Always Come First?*, 53 Me. L. Rev. 471, 483 n. 19 (2001); Debra Baker, *Is This Woman a Threat to Lawyers?: A Resurgence in Unauthorized Practice Complaints Is Raising Questions about Whether the Court of Public Opinion Will Judge Lawyers as Guardians of the Common Good or Protectors of Their Own Turf*, 85 A.B.A. J., 54, 56 (June 1999).

simple, transparent court system aimed at assisting litigants in a considerate and efficient manner.

Richard Granat, who is an internet entrepreneur, serves on multiple ABA committees and is an old legal aid lawyer himself,[102] immodestly states his life's goal in the mission statement for the LSC Technology Summit: "To use technology to move the United States toward providing service of some form to 100% of persons with a legal need." Let us all hope that we can reach that goal.

[102] Stephanie Francis Ward, *Richard Granat: Internet Obsessive*, ABA, Legal Rebels, available at www.abajournal.com/legalrebels/article/internet_obsessive.

31

Mediation of Employment Disputes at the EEOC

E. Patrick McDermott & Ruth Obar

Mediation is often suggested as an important mechanism for resolving disputes without the costs, financial and psychological, of litigation. The Equal Employment Opportunity Commission (EEOC), a federal agency responsible for the major federal employment discrimination laws, developed a mediation program to help resolve charges that neither the agency nor private lawyers are likely to take on in litigation. The California Department of Fair Employment and Housing (CHFEH) also mediates these cases as a state deferral agency. Patrick McDermott and Ruth Obar report their empirical findings on whether representation by lawyers in mediations affects outcomes at the EEOC and CHFEH.

This chapter provides a quantitative analysis of the experience of claimants pursuing employment discrimination claims at mediation conducted under the auspices of the Equal Employment Opportunity Commission (EEOC). The EEOC mediation program offers pre-investigation mediation for certain cases. The agency's charge-intake process forms the foundation for the selection of these cases for mediation. Cases that appear to have merit at filing are classified as "A" charges; they usually are not eligible for mediation. These charges involve cases where a reasonable cause finding is highly likely or where important "pattern or practice"/systemic issues or other public policy concerns militate against the use of pre-investigation mediation. Where a party requests that an "A" charge be mediated, the District Director and Regional Director have the discretion to permit it.

Charges classified as "B" charges are charges where further investigation is required to make a determination concerning merit. In general, "B" cases are eligible for pre-investigation mediation. However, "B" cases that involve the Equal Pay Act or pattern-or-practice/systemic allegations are not eligible for pre-investigation mediation.

The present program evolved from a February 1991 EEOC pilot mediation program. The program was considered a success; the agency formed a mediation task force to explore the possibility of expanding the program. In 1995, the task force concluded that mediation was a viable process. The EEOC then adopted a policy statement concerning alternative dispute resolution (ADR) that included support for mediation.[1] Using its experience with the pilot program, and the A-B-C classification system as the basis for selection of cases that were deemed appropriate for mediation, the ADR program evolved into its present configuration.

By October 1996, the EEOC mediation program had expanded significantly and, by the end of FY 1997, each district office had a "viable mediation program." For FY 1999, the EEOC budget was increased by $37 million, with $13 million specifically allocated for the mediation program. This increased allocation, a bi-partisan effort, was in part, due to the initial success of the EEOC mediation program.

THE EEOC MEDIATION PROGRAM

The EEOC mediation program uses staff employees as mediators as well as external mediators who are either paid pursuant to an EEOC contract or serve on a pro bono basis. The EEOC provides extensive training to all mediators.

The EEOC contract mediators include, but are not limited to, mediators from the Federal Mediation and Conciliation Service (FMCS). FMCS mediators primarily have been utilized in cases far from offices where internal EEOC mediators and private contractors are unavailable. This guarantees national coverage of charges to be mediated. The external mediators come from a wide variety of backgrounds, including professional neutrals and plaintiff and employer advocates. The EEOC does not train external mediators but rather selects those mediators who are deemed qualified due to training and experience.

Our quantitative analysis of EEOC data contributes to the debate on employment law and ADR by looking at what role representation by counsel plays in a properly designed mediation system.[2] We are not asserting that counsel has no role; rather, our results indicate that (1) mediator self-reporting of mediation events does not support the view that counsel are central to this dispute resolution process; (2) mediation improves procedural fairness whether or not the parties are represented; and (3) employment mediation programs that minimize the role of counsel (California Department of Fair Housing and Employment) appear to be as effective as one of those premised on a more traditional adversarial/representational model (EEOC).

[1] See McDermott et al., available at www.eeoc.gov/eeoc/mediation/report/index.html, An Evaluation of the Equal Employment Opportunity Commission [Sep. 20, 2000]; The EEOC Mediation Program: Mediators' Perspectives on the Parties, Processes, and Outcomes, available at www.eeoc.gov/eeoc/mediation/report/mcdfinal.html [Aug. 1, 2001]; and An Investigation of the Reasons for Lack of Employer Participation in the EEOC Mediation Program, available at www.eeoc.gov/eeoc/mediation/report/study3/index.html [Nov. 2003]. All studies can be found at the EEOC website at www.eeoc.gov/eeoc/mediation/studies.cfm (last accessed Jan. 6, 2015).

[2] We have published results suggesting that the presence of counsel raises the payout at mediation. See E. Patrick McDermott and Ruth Obar, *What's Going On in Mediation: An Empirical Analysis of the Influence of a Mediator's Style on Party Satisfaction and Monetary Benefit*, 9 Harv. Neg. Law Rev. 75 (2004). There may, of course, be a significant selection effect at play: stronger cases on the merits or cases likely to result in larger recoveries will attract counsel, whereas weaker cases and less wealthy claimants will not.

We performed three studies based on EEOC data that provide insight into the role of counsel.[3] While these data were gathered nearly a decade ago, each study remains on the EEOC website.[4] The EEOC continues to use our disputant surveys and report to us that the pattern of data results we reported are recurring today.[5] Thus, they remain instructive. Using our EEOC research as a foundation, we were able to gather data and analyze the pilot mediation program at the California Department of Fair Employment and Housing (CDFEH).

CALIFORNIA DEPARTMENT OF FAIR EMPLOYMENT AND HOUSING SURVEY

We conducted an evaluation of CDFEH pilot mediation program over a three and a half month time frame. We obtained properly completed surveys from 119 mediated cases.[6]

While CDFEH engages in the mediation of statutory employment disputes, this agency's approach differs from the EEOC's in placing more emphasis on the "convening" stage that involves preliminary issue identification, the selection of the mediators, and the role of representatives at the mediation. The EEOC model does provide for any type of formal convening process.

We examined mediator-staffing models, compared internal EEOC data concerning the use of internal staff mediator versus contract mediators, and compared the participant satisfaction and related data for the two programs.

The CDFEH does not use internal personnel or volunteers as mediators. It is generally thought by some CDFEH personnel that using internal mediators would pose the appearance of a credibility problem. CDFEH personnel generally are trained to investigate complaints for merit and not to facilitate a dialogue aimed at achieving a resolution between the complainant and respondent. Instead, the agency uses a pool of external professional mediators. CDFEH employs a detailed 100-point mediator selection process including the hourly rate of the mediator, experience, knowledge, ability, and training.

CDFEH Mediators conduct a "facilitative" form of mediation. Other styles of mediation, such as transformative and evaluative styles, are not supported or

[3] See E. P. McDermott *et al.*, An Evaluation of the Equal Employment Opportunity Commission [Sep. 20, 2000]; McDermott et al., The EEOC Mediation Program: Mediators' Perspectives on the Parties, Processes, and Outcomes August 1, 2001; and McDermott et al., An Investigation of the Reasons for Lack of Employer Participation in the EEOC Mediation Program (undated), all available at www.eeoc.gov/eeoc/mediation/studies.cfm (last accessed Jan. 6, 2015).

[4] *Id.*

[5] Telephone with Stephen Ichniowski, National ADR Coordinator, EEOC, Sep. 9, 2014 (confirming that EEOC continues to use the original surveys with similar data results in the course of on continuing EEOC assessment.)

[6] See McDermott et al., An Evaluation of the California Department of Fair Employment and Housing Pilot Mediation Program, June 24, 2002, available at www.conflict-resolution.org/sitebody/acrobat/California_Research.pdf (last accessed Jan. 6, 2015).

encouraged. The agency provides the external contract mediators with a presentation on the facilitative process, though understanding that in some instances mediators may have a tendency to slip into the evaluative process near the end to close the gap and settle the case. The main reason for promoting the facilitative process is that it allows the complainant and respondent the opportunity to talk about the conditions that started the complaint and their perceptions of what occurred in their own words. The facilitative process also prevents the mediator from becoming an evaluator of the charge or trying to alter the relationship between complainant and respondent.

STUDY RESULTS

EEOC Comprehensive Program Evaluation Study

The EEOC program evaluation study[7] provides data on the experience of represented and pro se parties at mediation. This study surveyed all charging parties, respondents, and mediators in EEOC mediations under the supervision of the 50 EEOC field offices; data were gathered over a five-month rolling time frame from March 1 to July 1, 2000. The sampling technique was to survey all mediations conducted in the EEOC district offices for that time period. This was done to avoid any selection bias issues in identifying a subset of the whole. Analysis showed that the five-month sample was consistent with the overall profile of EEOC mediations.

Our survey instrument included a Charging Party (employee) and Respondent (employer) Satisfaction Survey with 14 five-point Likert-type responses ranging from strongly disagree (1) to strongly agree (5). We also added eight additional questions, five "yes or no" questions, two open-ended questions, and one multiple-choice question. One open-ended question gave participants who did not resolve their claim a chance to explain why they thought their charges were not successfully resolved. The second open-ended question gave participants the opportunity to offer suggestions for improving the mediation process. The multiple-choice question sought to identify the mediation status of the participants. A pretest established that, for most participants, the survey took about five minutes to complete.

The EEOC Mediator Results Survey

The Mediator Results Survey[8] provides more data on the experience of represented versus non-represented parties. Here, we specifically measure the mediators' perceptions of the performance of the legal representatives and "non-legal" representatives.

[7] E. P. McDermott et al., An Evaluation of the Equal Employment Opportunity Commission (Sep. 20, 2000), available at www.eeoc.gov/eeoc/mediation/report/chapter5.html#V.A. (last accessed Jan. 18, 2014).

[8] E. P. McDermott et al., The EEOC Mediation Program: Mediators' Perspectives on the Parties, Processes, and Outcomes (Aug. 1, 2001), available at www.eeoc.gov/eeoc/mediation/report/mcdfinal.html#sdfootnote4sym (last accessed Jan. 18, 2015).

TABLE 31.1 *The five most important barriers to the resolution of the EEOC charge.*

Responses	Ranked #1	Ranked #2	Ranked #3	Ranked #4	Ranked #5	Total*
Positional conduct of the parties						
Charging party's positional conduct	296 (36.50%)	85 (10.48%)	43 (5.30%)	19 (2.34%)	9 (1.11%)	452 (55.73%)
Respondent's positional conduct	158 (19.48%)	121 (14.92%)	60 (7.40%)	25 (3.08%)	11 (1.36%)	375 (46.24%)
Both parties' positional conduct	75 (9.25%)	17 (2.10%)	20 (2.47%)	7 (0.86%)	11 (1.36%)	130 (16.03%
"Table conduct" of the parties						
Charging party's table conduct	50 (6.17%)	75 (9.25%)	40 (4.93%)	19 (2.34%)	7 (0.86%)	191 (23.55%)
Respondent's table conduct	47 (5.8%)	44 (5.43%)	23 (2.84%)	20 (2.47%)	7 (0.86%)	141 (17.39%)
Emotions/attitudes of the parties						
Charging party's emotions	34 (4.19%)	34 (4.19%)	27 (3.33%)	16 (1.97%)	5 (0.62%)	116 (14.3%)
Respondent's emotions	11 (1.36%)	21 (2.59%)	12 (1.48%)	7 (0.86%)	2 (0.25%)	53 (6.54%)
Conduct of the legal and non-legal representatives						
Charging parties' lawyer	36 (4.44%)	42 (5.18%)	20 (2.47%)	5 (0.62%)	5 (0.62%)	108 (13.32%)
Respondent's lawyer	25 (3.08%)	24 (2.96%)	18 (2.22%)	6 (0.74%)	3 (0.37%)	76 (9.37%)
Lawyers of both parties	0 (0.00%)	0 (0.00%)	0 (0.00%)	1 (0.12%)	0 (0.00%)	1 (0.12%)
Charging party's non-legal representatives	7 (0.86%)	6 (0.74%)	3 (0.37%)	1 (0.12%)	2 (0.25%)	19 (2.34%)
Respondent's non-legal representatives	4 (0.49%)	2 (0.25%)	3 (0.37%)	1 (0.12%)	1 (0.12%)	11 (1.36%)
Lack of respondent authority	32 (3.95%)	23 (2.83%)	10 (1.23%)	4 (0.49%)	1 (0.12%)	70 (8.63%)
External factors	20 (2.47%)	11 (1.36%)	9 (1.11%)	4 (0.49%)	1 (0.12%)	45 (5.55%)
Other factors	65 (8.01%)	62 (7.64%)	45 (5.55%)	34 (4.20%)	13 (1.73%)	219 (27.00%)

* *Note:* Total number of unresolved cases is 811. Since some mediators have given multiple reasons, the total number of responses differs from the actual number of unresolved cases. The percentage given is a function of the unresolved cases and not of the responses or participants.

TABLE 31.2 *Specific reasons cited for the non-resolution of the EEOC charge.*

Responses	Frequencies	Percentages*
Charging party's actions	427	52.7
Respondent's actions	373	46.0
Actions of both parties	249	30.7
Actions of the charging party's lawyer	104	12.8
Actions of the respondent's lawyer	54	6.7
Outside factors	67	8.3
Non-legal representatives	24	3.2
Lack of legal representation	6	0.7
Other	6	0.7
Total number of unresolved cases	811	

* *Note:* Total number of unresolved cases is 811. Since some mediators have given multiple reasons, the total number of responses differs from the actual number of unresolved cases. The percentage given is a function of the unresolved cases and not of the responses or participants.

Our data suggest that attorneys may not be as important in mediation as one would posit. We asked mediators in EEOC-mediated cases that did not settle to identify the five most important barriers to resolution. We coded all of the open-ended responses into categories set forth in Table 31.1. Note that in many mediations the role of counsel does not appear to be central to the identified barriers to resolution.

We then looked at the reasons the mediators assigned for the non-resolution of the dispute (Table 31.2). Mediators cited the "lack of legal representation" as a reason for the dispute not being resolved in very few (six) cases. On occasion they identified the conduct of the charging party's lawyer (12.8%) or respondent's lawyer (6.7%) but most often they identified the conduct of the parties as the cause of an unsuccessful mediation. Again, while counsel appears central in a minority of cases, overall the data do not show that the presence or absence of counsel is an important factor identified by the mediators for non-resolution of a dispute.

Based on the mediators' assessments, we then determined the mediation participant identified as "most responsible" for a case not settling and for contributing to mediation barriers. Once again, attorneys do not appear to play a central role, at least in the mediators' perception, in most cases (Table 31.3).

We then measured the "turning points" in a successful mediation. The data show that the performance or presence of counsel was not identified as contributing to a mediation turning point leading to settlement.

Evidence of high participant satisfaction with the mediation process, even for claimants acting without counsel, further suggests a minimal role for representation in EEOC-mediated cases (Table 31.4).

TABLE 31.3 *EEOC mediator perception of responsibility for non-resolution of disputes (inferred from mediators' comments).*

Responses	Frequencies	Percentages*
Both parties equally responsible	266	32.8
Charging party or one of the charging parties	229	28.2
Respondent	180	22.2
Charging party's lawyer	64	7.9
Respondent's lawyer	25	3.1
The lawyers of both parties equally responsible	23	2.8
Charging party's agent	7	0.9
Respondent's agent	4	0.5
Other factor: time (ran out of time)	24	2.9
Total unresolved cases	811	

* *Note:* Total number of unresolved cases is 811. Since some mediators have given multiple reasons, the total number of responses differs from the actual number of unresolved cases. The percentage given is a function of the unresolved cases and not of the responses or respondents.

COMPARISONS: USE OF REPRESENTATIVES

A comparison of our CDFEH data and EEOC data confirm the limited role of counsel in mediated cases (Table 31.5).

In our EEOC survey, only 39% of charging parties and 58% of respondents were represented. A more detailed analysis of disparity in representation is shown in Table 31.6.

In CDFEH mediations, a substantial number of complainants and respondents are coming to the mediation by themselves. A significant majority of complainants (73%) and almost half of the respondents (47%) do not make use of any representatives (Table 31.7). When they bring someone along, it is most likely to be an attorney, not a non-lawyer representative. Respondents are more likely to have legal representation (42% versus 20% for the complainants).

When we place this EEOC and CDFEH representation data side by side, we see what is presented in Table 31.8.

COMPARISONS: PARTY SATISFACTION

For the CDFEH, we found similar high party satisfaction rates. We measured party satisfaction for represented versus non-represented parties. Similar to our EEOC data, we find that mediation can provide party satisfaction on both procedural and distributive dimensions without representation (Table 31.9). These results suggest that the presence of counsel does not significantly affect most satisfaction measures.

TABLE 31.4 *EEOC – participant satisfaction based on representation.**

Statements	Charging party representation		Respondent representation	
	With	Without	With	Without
Procedural elements				
Explanation, scheduling, and voice				
Adequate explanation	4.20	4.28	4.12	4.33
Prompt scheduling	4.26	4.30	4.34	4.46
Understood the process	4.37	4.34	4.50	4.57
Opportunity to present views	4.39	4.38	4.55	4.60
Mediator				
Mediator understood needs	4.26	4.33	4.25	4.39
Mediator helped clarify needs	**4.18**	**4.30**	**4.11**	**4.25**
Mediator neutral in the beginning	4.44	4.43	4.44	4.55
Mediator remained neutral	4.41	4.41	4.40	4.48
Mediator helped develop options	**4.20**	**4.31**	**4.14**	**4.37**
Mediator used fair procedures	4.34	4.32	4.41	4.48
Distributive elements				
Development of realistic options	**3.86**	**4.01**	**3.95**	**4.07**
Satisfaction with the fairness of the session	4.12	4.03	4.27	4.37
Satisfaction with the results	**3.22**	**3.48**	**3.62**	**3.74**

* Satisfaction is measured by the "mean responses" of the participants on a Likert scale (scale of 1 (strongly disagree) to 5 (strongly agree)). Figures in bold refer to statements where a statistically significant difference (evaluated at 95% confidence level) exists between the mean responses of the participants with representation and without representation. The average sample sizes for the respective subgroups are as follows: 680 charging parties with representation and 956 without representation; 900 respondents with representation and 616 without representation.

TABLE 31.5 *Extent of representation by counsel – EEOC mediations.*

	Charging party		Respondent	
	Frequency	Percentage	Frequency	Percentage
With representation	348	39	508	58
Without representation	536	61	370	42
Total	884	100	878	100

TABLE 31.6 *Extent of representation by counsel – EEOC mediations.*

Representation	Frequency	Percentage
Only charging party has representation	89	10.2
Only respondent has representation	250	28.7
Both parties have representation	253	29.0
Neither party has representation	279	32.0
Total number of cases (with complete information on representation)	871	100.0

TABLE 31.7 *Extent of representation by counsel – CDFEH mediations.*

	Complainants		Respondents	
	Frequency	Percentage	Frequency	Percentage
Attorney	23	20	58	42
Other representative	8	7	14	10
No legal/non-legal representative	85	73	65	47
Total	116	100	137	100

Both programs with their different approaches to mediator selection and convening are rated highly by participants. Again, we see that it is the bringing of parties together, regardless of the presence or absence of representation and regardless of the mediation style, that results in an effective program.[9]

9 Here we operationalize "effective" as a program resulting in high participant satisfaction rates on both procedural due process and distributive justice variables.

TABLE 31.8 *Comparison of representation by counsel – CDFEH versus EEOC mediations.*

	CDFEH		EEOC	
	Number of complainants (%)	Number of respondents (%)	Number of charging parties (%)	Number of respondents (%)
With legal/non-legal representative	31 (27%)	72 (53%)	348 (39%)	508 (58%)
No legal/non-legal representative	85 (73%)	65 (47%)	536 (61%)	370 (42%)
Total	116 (100.0%)	137 (100.0%)	884 (100%)	878 (100%)

Note: On an average, representation by counsel in EEOC mediations was about 48% (39% among charging parties and 58% among respondents) and in CDFEH mediations it was about 41% (27% and 53% among complainants and respondents, respectively).

IMPACT OF COUNSEL ON RESOLUTIONS

We also used our EEOC data to engage in a more sophisticated statistical analysis of the relationship between represented and non-represented parties. We examined the role of representation as a variable influencing case settlement at the EEOC.[10] We found, that represented charging parties were less likely to achieve resolutions than unrepresented charging parties. Represented respondents and unrepresented respondents, however, achieved resolutions at about the same rate. We are not sure what caused this difference. One explanation may be that charging parties able to secure counsel have stronger cases and may be less willing to resolve them at the pre-investigation stage. Another possibility is that due to the absence of counsel, unrepresented charging parties are likely to attach a lower value to their claims than they would if they were represented by competent counsel.

Our data[11] showed that if the amount of money obtained in settlement is important, the charging party in employment mediation is at a decided disadvantage without counsel.[12] This disadvantage is even more pronounced in an evaluative

[10] See E. Patrick McDermott and Danny Ervin, *The Influence of Procedural and Distributive Variables on Settlement Rates in Employment Discrimination Mediation*, 2005 J. Disp. Resol. 45 (2005), available at http://scholarship.law.missouri.edu/cgi/viewcontent.cgi?article=1483&context=jdr.

[11] In our EEOC research we had full access to the EEOC's database on case outcomes, including the amounts charging parties received from resolutions. We used these data to measure the relationship of representation to case payout.

[12] See E. Patrick McDermott & Ruth Obar, *"What's Going On" in Mediation: An Empirical Analysis of the Influence of a Mediator's Style on Party Satisfaction and Monetary Benefit*, 9 Harv. Negot. L. Rev. 75 (2004). A comparison of outcomes between cases where claimants are represented and those where proceed pro se does not control for the possibility that cases attracting counsel are likely to be stronger on the merits or more valuable in terms of payout if there is a resolution. There are also methodological challenges to the use of survey research as opposed to direct observation with coding. See E. Patrick McDermott, *Discovering The Importance of Mediator Style – An Interdisciplinary Challenge* 5:4 Negot. Confl. Manag. R. 340–53 (2012).

TABLE 31.9 *Complainant and respondent satisfaction based on representation – CDFEH mediations.**

Statements	Complainants		Respondents	
	With representation	Without representation	With representation	Without representation
Procedural elements				
Explanation, scheduling, and voice				
Prior to my attendance at this mediation session today, I received an adequate explanation about mediation from a CDFEH representative.	4.48	4.40	**4.11**	**4.42**
The mediation was scheduled promptly.	4.60**	4.25**	4.44	4.60
After the mediator's introduction at the mediation session, I felt that I understood the mediation process.	4.55	4.35	4.46	4.61
I (or my representative) had a full opportunity to present my views during the mediation process.	4.61	4.42	4.53	4.61
Mediator				
The mediator understood my needs.	4.52	4.34	4.33	4.50

The mediator helped clarify my needs.	4.52	4.32	4.17	4.34
At the beginning of the mediation, I considered the mediator to be neutral.	4.48	4.43	4.35	4.49
The mediator remained neutral during the session.	4.58	4.39	4.33	4.46
The mediator helped the parties develop options for resolving the charge.	4.48	4.26	4.21	4.29
The procedures used by the mediator in the mediation were fair to me.	4.55	4.25	4.47	4.51
Distributive elements				
Most of the options developed during the mediation session were realistic solutions to resolving the charge.	4.37**	3.96**	4.10	4.27
I was satisfied with the fairness of the mediation session.	**4.42**	**3.96**	4.27	4.38
I was satisfied with the results of the mediation session.	3.40	3.28	3.57	3.61
I obtained what I wanted from this mediation.	3.13	2.73	3.43	3.60
Overall, I was satisfied with today's mediation.	3.74	3.58	4.01	4.14

Mini-win				
If the charge was not resolved/ongoing: I believe that progress was made toward resolution of this claim.	3.30	2.75	3.00	2.58

* Satisfaction is measured by the "mean responses" of the participants on a Likert scale (1 = strongly disagree and 5 = strongly agree). Figures in bold refer to statements where a statistically significant difference (evaluated at 95% confidence level) exists between the mean responses. The average sample sizes for each of the subgroups above are as follows: 30 complainants with representation, 81 complainants without representation, 70 respondents with representation, and 63 respondents without representation.

** There is a significant difference between the means when evaluated at the 90% confidence level.

TABLE 31.10 *Dollar benefit and party representation.*

	Charging party			
	With representation		Without representation	
Actual technique employed	Number of cases	Average dollar benefit	Number of cases	Average dollar benefit
Purely evaluative	34	$31,275.56	61	$5,987.95
Both evaluative and facilitative	16	$16,213.79	47	$4,025.85
Purely facilitative	37	$13,027.54	74	$8,778.52
	Respondent			
	With representation		Without representation	
Actual technique employed	Number of cases	Average dollar benefit	Number of cases	Average dollar benefit
Purely evaluative	59	$16,028.11	37	$13,073.67
Both evaluative and facilitative	34	$8,193.02	27	$6,224.93
Purely facilitative	60	$11,060.96	50	$9,237.39

mediation. Absent legal representation, evaluative mediation appears to result in lower settlement amounts (Table 31.10).

When we compare the variable of representation with the measured mediatory style (facilitative, evaluative, or hybrid), these data indicate that when a purely evaluative mediation is combined with representation, the return to the charging party is far more than if the evaluative mediation was conducted without representation ($31,275.56 versus $5,987.95).

If the evaluative mediation was conducted without representation however, the charging party was worse off than if the mediation was facilitative and without representation ($5,987.95 versus $8,778.52). Thus, the worst possible position for a charging party is evaluative mediation without representation. While our overall results show that the charging party obtains more money in evaluative mediation, this is due to the high payouts when representation is present. This suggests that one of the criticisms of evaluative mediation – that a party may be "strong-armed" by the mediator – is possible. This also suggests that the observed differences in settlement values are driven predominantly by the presence of representation rather than the mediation style.

Unlike the relatively large dollar difference based on representation in an evaluative mediation, a charging party engaged in facilitative mediation with representation does not obtain much more money than if the charging party represented himself or herself ($13,027.54 versus $8,778.52). Facilitative mediation, while establishing a more protective floor for recovery without representation, did not have the same upside potential as does evaluative mediation with representation.

The results of our regression analysis indicate that the presence of a representative on the side of the charging party, the style of the mediator (evaluative), and the type of case (age) are statistically significant variables that contribute to higher dollar settlements. More specifically, the presence of a representative on the side of the charging party raises the average dollar settlement by $12,753 and the use of evaluative tactics results in dollar benefits that are higher by $4,885 on the average. These numbers reinforce the previous findings mentioned earlier: the presence of a representative on the side of the charging party has a significantly higher dollar impact compared to the use of evaluative tactics.[13]

CONCLUSION

We have provided a range of measurements that place the role of counsel in an intriguing light where it is only one part of the mediation process, and counsel arguably does not play a central role in mediation dispute resolution and party satisfaction. There can be high settlement rates and high party satisfaction without counsel. But the presence of counsel suggests higher settlement amounts. While it is a truism that one is better off with counsel than without, the more intriguing inquiry is how well can an unrepresented person do in the mediation process.

13 In a work in progress we address the issue of settlement asymmetry. Here we are attempting to see how similar perceptions of the mediation process or factors (symmetry) contribute to settlement. The EEOC data show that where each side is represented the likelihood of settlement decreases.

32

AAA Consumer Arbitration

Christopher R. Drahozal

Organizations that administer arbitration and other ADR services can by rulemaking, in consultation with industry and claimant groups, improve the fairness of the process for the parties. Consumer disputes present a particular challenge for arbitration systems when the small size of an individual consumer's claim may, as a practical matter, preclude even assertion of the claim. This is a problem also in litigation, but class actions, which can aggregate small clains, may be more readily available in court. Christopher Drahozal examines the initiatives of the American Arbitration Association, the leading ADR provider in the country, to promote fair consumer arbitrations.

Whether arbitration – resolution of a dispute by a private judge rather than in the public court system – increases or reduces access to justice is hotly debated.[1] Samuel Estreicher, for instance, urges that "[a] properly designed arbitration system . . . can do a better job of delivering accessible justice for average claimants than a litigation-based approach."[2] Others, notably Jean Sternlight and David Schwartz, argue that arbitration increases costs and discourages lawyers from taking consumer cases, thereby reducing consumer access to justice but increasing corporate profits.[3]

This chapter does not take sides in that debate. Instead, it seeks to advance the debate by presenting information on arbitrations involving disputes between consumers and businesses that are administered by the American Arbitration

[1] For an empirical debate on the subject, examining data from AAA employment arbitrations, compare Theodore Eisenberg & Elizabeth Hill, *Arbitration and Litigation of Employment Claims: An Empirical Comparison*, Disp. Resol. J. (Nov. 2003–Jan. 2004), at 44, 45, with David S. Schwartz, *Mandatory Arbitration and Fairness*, 84 Notre Dame L. Rev. 1247, 1297–309 (2009). See generally Christopher R. Drahozal, *Arbitration Costs and Forum Accessibility: Empirical Evidence*, 41 U. Mich. J.L. Reform 813, 833–35 (2008).

[2] E.g., Samuel Estreicher, *Saturns for Rickshaws: The Stakes in the Debate over Predispute Employment Arbitration Agreements*, 16 Ohio St. J. on Disp. Resol. 559, 563 (2001); see also *Allied Bruce Terminix Cos. v. Dobson*, 513 U.S. 265, 280 (1995) (stating that "arbitration's advantages often would seem helpful to individuals, say, complaining about a product, who need a less expensive alternative to litigation").

[3] E.g., Jean R. Sternlight, *Creeping Mandatory Arbitration: Is It Just?*, 57 Stan. L. Rev. 1631, 1654–55 (2005).

Association (AAA).[4] During 2010–12, the AAA received over 7,000 consumer arbitration filings,[5] and is commonly named in consumer arbitration clauses as the sole administrator or one of several administrators of consumer arbitrations.[6] The types of businesses involved in AAA consumer arbitrations include credit card issuers and other consumer lenders, cell phone companies, car dealers, mobile home sellers, real estate brokers, home builders, insurance companies and extended warranty providers, and law and accounting firms, among others.[7] AAA consumer arbitration has become a widely used process for resolving disputes between businesses and consumers, and this chapter seeks to provide a better understanding of how that process works.

AAA CONSUMER ARBITRATION PROCEDURES

As noted earlier, businesses commonly name the AAA as the arbitration administrator in their standard form contracts with consumers.[8] The AAA, like other arbitration administrators, does not itself act as the arbitrator – that is, it does not itself issue a binding decision that resolves the parties' dispute. Instead, it administers the arbitration: it promulgates default rules to govern the proceeding[9] and provides services to the parties to facilitate the arbitration, such as maintaining lists of arbitrators, appointing an arbitrator as necessary, handling the logistics of arbitration filings, and so forth. In addition, the AAA has adopted a Consumer Due Process Protocol setting out minimum standards of procedural fairness that govern consumer arbitrations it administers.[10]

[4] For a discussion of the interaction of arbitration clauses and class actions or class arbitration proceedings administered by The American Arbitration Association (AAA), see Rutledge, Chapter 33 in this volume.

[5] Consumer Financial Protection Bureau, Arbitration Study Preliminary Results 60 (Dec. 12, 2013) (hereinafter CFPB Preliminary Report). Roughly one-third of the filings were never perfected (e.g., necessary paperwork not submitted or fees unpaid) so the case did not proceed. *Id.* at 60 n.137.

[6] E.g., *id.* at 34 (stating that as of 2012–13, 55.7% of checking account arbitration clauses, 48.5% of credit card arbitration clauses, and 37.3% of prepaid card arbitration clauses listed the AAA as the sole administrator, and that "over 98% of the relevant account value – whether insured deposits, card loans outstanding, or prepaid load – subject to arbitration clauses in the samples listed the AAA as at least one possible administrator"). Of facilities-based mobile wireless operators (i.e., cell phone companies with their own networks), all but one (11 out of 12) used arbitration clauses as of early 2013, and of the 11 with arbitration clauses, 10 listed the AAA either as the sole arbitration administrator (cell phone companies accounting for 46.2% of customers) or as one of two options (cell phone companies accounting for 37.5% of customers).

[7] See infra text accompanying notes 72–74.

[8] See supra text accompanying note 6. Businesses do not pay a fee to include the AAA as an administrator, nor does the AAA pay a fee to be included (indeed, the AAA may not find out it has been included in an arbitration clause until an arbitration proceeding is filed with it). Instead, as discussed infra notes 21–25, the parties pay fees to the AAA when it administers an arbitration arising out of their contract.

[9] AAA, Consumer-Related Disputes: Supplementary Procedures (Rules effective Sept. 15, 2005; Fees effective March 1, 2013) (hereinafter AAA Consumer Arbitration Rules).

[10] National Consumer Disputes Advisory Committee, Consumer Due Process Protocol (Apr. 17, 1998) (hereinafter Consumer Due Process Protocol).

Supplementary procedures for consumer-related disputes

The AAA has issued consumer arbitration rules to supplement its otherwise applicable commercial arbitration procedures.[11] The consumer rules apply whenever a contract between a business and a consumer specifies the AAA as administrator (or incorporates the AAA rules into the contract) and:

(1) the business has a standardized, systematic application of arbitration clauses with customers;
(2) the terms and conditions of the purchase of standardized, consumable goods or services are non-negotiable or primarily non-negotiable in most of all of its terms, conditions, features, or choices; and
(3) [t]he product or service must be for personal or household use.[12]

When the AAA's consumer rules apply, either party may assert its claim in small claims court, if available, rather than arbitration.[13]

The rules set out how to initiate a claim, under either a pre-dispute or a post-dispute arbitration agreement.[14] Under the AAA consumer rules, the AAA itself appoints the arbitrator. Once it does so, the parties have seven days "to submit any factual objections to that arbitrator's service."[15] The rules provide that a "desk arbitration" – an arbitration decided solely on the basis of documents – is the default approach for a case with no claims over $10,000. But either party can request a hearing, and the arbitrator, likewise, can decide to hold a hearing.[16] If either party seeks over $10,000, "the arbitrator will conduct a hearing unless the parties agree not to have one."[17] The hearing may either be by telephone or in person, and will follow the Expedited Procedures of the AAA's Commercial Arbitration Rules.

After the close of the hearing, the arbitrator has fourteen days in which to decide the case and issue an award.[18] When making the award, "the arbitrator should apply any identified pertinent contract terms, statutes, and legal precedents" and "may

11 AAA Consumer Arbitration Rules, supra note 9; see American Arbitration Association, Commercial Arbitration Rules and Mediation Procedures (Rules effective Oct. 1, 2013) (hereinafter AAA Commercial Arbitration Rules). After this chapter was completed, the AAA issued new, stand-alone consumer arbitration rules. See AAA, Consumer Arbitration Rules (effective Sept. 1, 2014); www.adr.org/cs/idcplg?IdcService=GET_FILE&dDocName=ADRSTAGE2022619&RevisionSelectionMethod=LatestReleased.

12 AAA Consumer Arbitration Rules, supra note 9, Rule C-1(a).

13 *Id.* Rule C-1(d).

14 *Id.* Rules C-2 & C-3. A pre-dispute arbitration agreement is one entered into before a dispute arises; a post-dispute arbitration agreement is one entered into after a dispute has arisen.

15 *Id.* Rule C-4.

16 *Id.* Rule C-5.

17 *Id.* Rule C-6.

18 *Id.* Rule C-7(a).

grant any remedy, relief or outcome that the parties could have received in court."[19] Under the Federal Arbitration Act, the award is subject to review only on limited procedural grounds and, perhaps, for manifest disregard of the law.[20]

Effective March, 1, 2013, the AAA issued a new fee schedule for consumer arbitration cases.[21] For any case, whether brought by the consumer or the business, the consumer pays a filing fee of $200, unless the parties have agreed for the consumer to pay less.[22] The remainder of the filing fees, which range from $1,500 for a case with a sole arbitrator to $2,000 for a case with a three-arbitrator panel, is to be paid by the business. In addition, the business is responsible for all the arbitrators' fees ($750 per case for a documents-only arbitration to $1,500 per day for a telephone or in-person hearing), unless the consumer agrees to pay a share after the dispute has arisen.[23] Although the AAA's commercial arbitration rules permit the arbitrator to reallocate the arbitration fees in the award,[24] the consumer rules provide otherwise: "Arbitrator compensation, expenses ... and administrative fees (which include Filing and Hearing Fees) are not subject to reallocation by the arbitrator(s) except pursuant to applicable law or upon the arbitrator's determination that a claim or counterclaim was filed for purposes of harassment or is patently frivolous."[25]

The AAA's consumer arbitration rules are default rules because, as a general matter, the parties can change the rules by agreement. But the rules contained in the Consumer Due Process Protocol are not default rules, as described in the next section.

Consumer Due Process Protocol

The AAA's Due Process Protocol for Mediation and Arbitration of Consumer Disputes (Consumer Due Process Protocol) sets out a series of principles designed

[19] *Id.* Rule C-7(c).

[20] 9 U.S.C. § 10; see, e.g., *Wachovia Sec., LLC v. Brand*, 671 F.3d 472, 481 & n.7 (4th Cir. 2012) ("manifest disregard of the law" exists when "(1) the applicable legal principle is clearly defined and not subject to reasonable debate; and (2) the arbitrator [ ] refused to heed that legal principle"; and identifying circuit split over its availability as ground for vacating awards).

[21] AAA Consumer Arbitration Rules, supra note 9, "Costs of Arbitration."

[22] Previously, the AAA fees for consumers varied depending on the amount of the case. For claims seeking $10,000 or less, the consumer paid $125 (half of the arbitrator's fee). For claims seeking from $10,000 to $75,000, the consumer paid $375 (again, half of the arbitrator's fee). For claims seeking over $75,000, the AAA applied the standard fee schedule in its Commercial Arbitration Rules. See Christopher R. Drahozal & Samantha Zyontz, *An Empirical Study of AAA Consumer Arbitrations*, 25 Ohio St. J. on Disp. Resol. 843, 863 (2010) (hereinafter Drahozal & Zyontz, *Empirical Study of AAA Consumer Arbitrations*).

[23] AAA Consumer Arbitration Rules, supra note 9, "Costs of Arbitration."

[24] AAA Commercial Arbitration Rules, supra note 11, Rule R-47(c).

[25] AAA Consumer Arbitration Rules, supra note 9, "Costs of Arbitration."

to enhance the fairness of consumer arbitration proceedings.[26] The AAA enforces the Protocol by refusing to administer consumer arbitrations arising out of arbitration clauses that do not comply with the Protocol. This section first sets out the AAA's review process, and then describes the substance of the Protocol.

Protocol Compliance Review

Under the AAA's rules, a party that files a claim in arbitration must submit a copy of the arbitration clause with the filing.[27] For cases seeking under $75,000 in damages, the AAA reviews that clause for compliance with the Consumer Due Process Protocol.[28] If the clause does not comply with the Protocol, the AAA requires the business to waive the offending provision and to commit to change the provision in its contract going forward. If the business does not do so, the AAA will refuse to administer the case and future cases involving the business.[29] Similarly, if the business refuses to pay its share of the fees required by the AAA's Consumer Arbitration Rules, the AAA will refuse to administer the case (unless the consumer pays the business's share of the fees, which is unusual) and future cases involving the business as well.

Most businesses comply with the AAA's efforts to enforce the Protocol.[30] Out of 271 AAA consumer arbitrations seeking under $75,000 and resolved by an award from March through December 2007, 76.8% involved clauses that fully complied with the Protocol; in another 18.8%, the business waived the impermissible provision.[31] The AAA refused to administer an additional 85 cases, and probably an additional 129 cases, that year because of unwaived Protocol violations.[32]

[26] Consumer Due Process Protocol, supra note 10. The Protocol was issued in April 1998 by the National Consumer Disputes Advisory Committee, which included members with backgrounds representing businesses and consumers, as well as members from government and academia. Previously, the AAA had issued an Employment Due Process Protocol. See Task Force on Alternative Dispute Resolution in Employment, Due Process Protocol for Mediation and Arbitration of Statutory Disputes Arising Out of the Employment Relationship (May 9, 1995). Subsequently, it has issued Health Care and Consumer Debt Collection protocols. See Commission on Health Care Dispute Resolution, Health Care Due Process Protocol (July 27, 1998); National Task Force on the Arbitration of Consumer Debt Collection Disputes, Consumer Debt Collection Due Process Protocol (Oct. 2010).

[27] AAA Consumer Arbitration Rules, supra note 9, Rule C-2(a).

[28] For claims seeking over $75,000, the arbitrator is responsible for enforcing the Protocol. Christopher R. Drahozal & Samantha Zyontz, *Private Regulation of Consumer Arbitration*, 79 TENN. L. REV. 289, 308 (2012) (hereinafter Drahozal & Zyontz, *Private Regulation of Consumer Arbitration*).

[29] American Arbitration Association, AAA Review of Consumer Clauses 2 (last visited Nov. 27, 2013), available at www.adr.org.

[30] The empirical findings in this section are from the Searle Study, which is described in more detail infra text accompanying notes 60–105.

[31] Drahozal & Zyontz, *Private Regulation of Consumer Arbitration*, supra note 28, at 327. In 1.1% of the cases, the AAA handled the violation administratively, and in 1.5% of the cases the AAA administered the case as required by a court order. In only 1.8% of cases did the AAA administer a case with an unwaived protocol violation. *Id.*

[32] *Id.* at 330–31.

The most common unwaived Protocol violation, accounting for 42.6% of the cases, was the business's failure to pay its share of the arbitration fees.[33]

The AAA's mechanism for enforcing the Protocol is more effective when the business is the claimant in arbitration than when the business is the respondent. When a business is bringing a claim against a consumer, the business has an incentive to comply with the Protocol because otherwise its case will not proceed in arbitration. But when the consumer is bringing a claim against the business, the incentives are reversed. In such a case, the business may have little incentive to comply because the AAA's refusal to administer the case may preclude the consumer from asserting his or her claim (or at least delay the consumer in doing so). If courts were to hold that a business's failure to comply with the Protocol constitutes a waiver of its right to insist on arbitration, then the business would have an affirmative incentive to comply even when the consumer is bringing the claim. So far, however, courts are split on the issue,[34] and at least some arbitration clauses might be construed as providing that a different arbitration administrator should be substituted for the AAA in that event, which, again, dilutes the business's incentive to comply.[35]

Substance of Protocol compliance review

The Consumer Due Process Protocol consists of fifteen principles that set out basic standards for procedural fairness in consumer arbitration. The following lists each principle of the Protocol and describes the AAA's implementation of that principle in its administration of consumer arbitration cases:[36]

Principle 1. Fundamentally Fair Process. The first Principle of the Due Process Protocol is both a general statement of its goal – to provide fundamental fairness in consumer arbitration – and a catch-all provision. As such, "in reviewing clauses, the AAA is to consider whether the procedures set out in the arbitration clause are unduly one-sided – whether they unduly favor the business in ways not addressed in other principles of the Protocol."[37]

Principle 2. Access to Information. This Principle states that businesses should provide "full and accurate information regarding Consumer ADR Programs."[38] In implementing the Protocol, the AAA only examines the arbitration clause in the parties' contract.[39] As such, "[i]t does not examine the surrounding

[33] *Id.* at 332. The CFPB reported that from 2010 to 2012, the AAA notified 29 businesses that arbitration would not proceed because of their failure to pay their share of the fees. CFPB Preliminary Report, supra note 5, at 117.

[34] Drahozal & Zyontz, supra note 28, at 333–34 & n.216 (citing cases).

[35] *Id.* at 335 n.222.

[36] The rest of this section is adapted from *id.* at 312–15.

[37] *Id.* at 312.

[38] Consumer Due Process Protocol, supra note 10, Principle 2.

[39] See supra text accompanying note 28.

circumstances to evaluate whether the consumer was able to obtain 'full and accurate information' regarding the ADR program."[40]

Principle 3. Independent and Impartial Neutral. The central requirement of a fair arbitration proceeding – indeed, the central requirement of arbitration itself – is an independent and impartial arbitrator.[41] Various contract provisions would violate that requirement: "Certainly a provision permitting the business to select the arbitrator unilaterally or to control the list of prospective arbitrators would violate this Principle. In addition, provisions setting out required qualification for arbitrators likewise might be problematic."[42]

Principle 4. Quality and Competence of Neutrals. This Principle, as construed by the AAA, is directed at the AAA's own processes for screening and training quality arbitrators, although it does manifest itself in the AAA's policy of appointing only lawyers to serve as arbitrators for AAA consumer arbitrations.[43] As such, this Principle adds nothing to the AAA's Protocol compliance review.

Principle 5. Small Claims. As noted earlier, the AAA's consumer rules permit claims to be brought in small claims court even if otherwise within the scope of a consumer arbitration clause.[44] Accordingly, unless an arbitration clause affirmatively forbids the consumer to go to small claims court, this Principle is satisfied.

Principle 6. Reasonable Cost. As a general matter, this Principle is implemented through the fee provisions of the AAA rules. A clause that seeks to override those provisions, such as by requiring the parties to share arbitration costs equally, would violate this Principle.[45]

Principle 7. Reasonably Convenient Location. This Principle seeks to prevent consumers from having to travel substantial distances to attend arbitration hearings. For a national business, "[a] clause that requires arbitration to take place at the business's location would be problematic," while for a business that sells only locally the same provision may well be permissible.[46]

Principle 8. Reasonable Time Limits. This Principle is directed at preventing "undue delay" in arbitration proceedings.[47] The AAA addresses this requirement, in its view, by the time limits in its arbitration rules. "Only if the arbitration clause unduly lengthens those time limits so as to unreasonably delay the arbitration proceeding would there be an issue for the AAA's review."[48]

[40] Drahozal & Zyontz, *Private Regulation of Consumer Arbitration*, supra note 28, at 312.

[41] *Chavarria v. Ralphs Grocery Co.*, 733 F.3d 916, 924–25 (9th Cir. 2013); *Hooters of Am., Inc. v. Phillips*, 173 F.3d 933, 938–39 (4th Cir. 1999).

[42] Drahozal & Zyontz, *Private Regulation of Consumer Arbitration*, supra note 28, at 312.

[43] *Id.*

[44] See supra text accompanying note 13.

[45] Drahozal & Zyontz, *Private Regulation of Consumer Arbitration*, supra note 28, at 313.

[46] *Id.*

[47] Consumer Due Process Protocol, supra note 10, Principle 8.

[48] Drahozal & Zyontz, *Private Regulation of Consumer Arbitration*, supra note 28, at 313–14.

Principle 9. Right to Representation. Parties have the right to the representative of their choice in AAA consumer arbitration.[49] A contract provision that denied that right would violate the Protocol.[50]

Principle 10. Mediation. Because this Principle only encourages the use of mediation, it provides nothing for the AAA to review.[51]

Principle 11. Agreements to Arbitrate. See Principle 2 for further discussion.[52]

Principle 12. Arbitration Hearings. As discussed earlier, the AAA Consumer Arbitration Rules permit the consumer (as well as the business) to request a hearing.[53] A contract provision that required all disputes to be resolved on the basis of documents only would violate this Principle.[54]

Principle 13. Access to Information. This Principle requires the parties to have some degree of access to information in the possession of the other – i.e., some degree of discovery. If an arbitration clause unduly restricted the availability of discovery, it would be inconsistent with this Principle.

Principle 14. Arbitral Remedies. This Principle requires that the arbitrator have the authority "to grant whatever relief would be available in court."[55] It might be interpreted as requiring that remedies available in court, such as punitive damages, always be available in arbitration as well. Alternatively, it might be interpreted as permitting a contract provision to waive the availability of certain remedies, such as punitive damages, as long as such a waiver would be permitted in court under the applicable law. The AAA follows the former interpretation, so that "clauses that preclude the recovery of punitive damages or consequential damages violate this Principle."[56]

Principle 15. Arbitration Awards. Again, the AAA views this Principle as largely addressed by its own rules, although a contract provision that barred written awards likely would be inconsistent with this Principle.[57]

The Consumer Due Process Protocol does not address all issues that may affect the fairness of consumer arbitration proceedings.[58] But the Protocol excludes many of the more egregious provisions in arbitration clauses from AAA consumer arbitrations.

49 AAA Commercial Arbitration Rules, supra note 11, Rule R-26.

50 Drahozal & Zyontz, *Private Regulation of Consumer Arbitration*, supra note 28, at 314.

51 *Id.*

52 See supra text accompanying notes 38–40.

53 See supra text accompanying notes 16–17.

54 Drahozal & Zyontz, *Private Regulation of Consumer Arbitration*, supra note 28, at 314.

55 Consumer Due Process Protocol, supra note 10, Principle 14.

56 Drahozal and Zyontz, *Private Regulation of Consumer Arbitration*, supra note 28, at 314–15.

57 *Id.* at 315.

58 *Cf.* Richard A. Bales, *The Employment Due Process Protocol at Ten: Twenty Unresolved Issues, and a Focus on Conflicts of Interest*, 21 Ohio St. J. on Disp. Resol. 165, 185–96 (2005).

AAA CONSUMER ARBITRATION CASES: EMPIRICAL DATA

Because of the private nature of arbitration proceedings, only limited data are available on what actually happens in AAA consumer arbitrations.[59] One exception is the comprehensive report on AAA consumer arbitration cases issued in 2009 by the Consumer Arbitration Task Force of the Searle Civil Justice Institute (the "Searle Study").[60] The Searle Study examined in depth a sample of 301 AAA consumer arbitrations that were resolved by an award from March through December 2007, as well as a broader dataset (albeit less in depth) of all consumer arbitrations closed by the AAA between 2005 and 2007.[61] Another important addition to the empirical literature is a preliminary report issued in December 2013 by the Consumer Financial Protection Bureau of partial results of its statutorily mandated study of arbitration clauses in consumer financial contracts (the "CFPB Preliminary Report").[62] The CFPB examined 1,241 AAA arbitrations involving credit card, checking account, and payday loan disputes from 2010 through 2012.[63] This part summarizes some of the key empirical findings on AAA consumer arbitrations:

Parties and Claims

Almost all of the AAA consumer arbitrations reviewed in the Searle Study (96.3%) arose out of pre-dispute arbitration clauses – i.e., arbitration clauses in contracts –

59 One source of data are reports filed by the AAA and other arbitration administrators as required by California Civil Procedure Code § 1281.96. For a report describing the information disclosed in the reports, by the AAA and other administrators, see David J. Jung et al., Reporting Consumer Arbitration Data in California: An Analysis of Compliance with California Code of Civil Procedure § 1281.96 (Mar. 15, 2013).

60 The Searle Study is published as: Drahozal & Zyontz, *Empirical Study of AAA Consumer Arbitrations*, supra note 22 (reporting partial results from Searle Preliminary Report (Mar. 2009)); Drahozal and Zyontz, *Private Regulation of Consumer Arbitration*, supra note 28 (reporting remaining results from Searle Preliminary Report); Christopher R. Drahozal and Samantha Zyontz, *Creditor Claims in Arbitration and in Court*, 7 Hastings Bus. L.J. 77 (2011) (hereinafter Drahozal & Zyontz, *Creditor Claims in Arbitration and in Court*) (reporting results from Searle Interim Report (Nov. 2009)).

61 A couple of caveats about the Searle Study are worth noting. First, the arbitrations studied were decided more than eight years ago. Both the legal environment and the AAA rules and practices governing consumer arbitrations have changed in significant ways since then. Second, most, although not all, of the data come from cases in which the arbitrator issued an award. Because cases are not settled randomly, settled cases may differ systematically from awarded cases. As a result, the findings are subject to possible selection biases. See Drahozal & Zyontz, *Empirical Study of AAA Consumer Arbitrations*, supra note 22, at 868–69.

62 12 U.S.C. § 5518(a); see CFPB Preliminary Report, supra note 5.

63 CFPB Preliminary Report, supra note 5, at 58. The results released by the CFPB in its Preliminary Report were limited to "front-end" issues – e.g., the types of claims filed – with nothing reported on "back-end" issues, such as the outcomes of the cases. In March 2015, after this chapter was competed, the CFPB issued its Final Report. See Consumer Financial Protection Bureau, Arbitration Study: Report to Congress, Pursuant to Dodd-Frank Wall Street Reform and Consumer Protection Act § 1028 (a) (March 2015). The CFPB's findings on consumer financial services arbitrations administered by the AAA from 2010 through 2012 appear in Section 5 of the Final Report.

rather than post-dispute arbitration agreements.[64] This finding is consistent with studies of other types of arbitration.[65]

The AAA consumer arbitrations studied predominantly involved claims brought by consumers. Of the awarded cases studied, 79.7% of claims were filed by consumers and only 20.3% by businesses.[66] The Searle Study explained that the types of claims asserted by consumers were diverse, "with consumers asserting claims for non-delivery of goods or services, claims for breach of warranty for defective goods or services, claims under state consumer protection acts, claims under federal consumer protection statutes, and the like."[67]

The amounts claimed in AAA consumer arbitrations are relevant to whether arbitration is an accessible forum for consumers of average means.[68] The amount claimed in the sample of AAA cases resulting in awards averaged $46,131 for consumer claims and $22,037 for business claims (in which the business typically was seeking to recover debts owed by the consumers).[69] Most claims (for both businesses and consumers) sought between $178 and $70,756, although at least twelve consumer claims exceeded $70,756, including one claim seeking $1,200,000.[70] The claim amounts were influenced by the AAA fee schedule, which at the time had graduated fees that varied depending on whether the claim sought less than $10,000, between $10,000 and $75,000, or over $75,000.[71] Not surprisingly, the claims tended to clump at just under the threshold for the higher fee (i.e., at just under $10,000 and just under $75,000). The AAA's new fee schedule with its flat $200 fee regardless of claim size (which, among other things, substantially reduces the fee for consumer claims exceeding $75,000) will no doubt alter this pattern.

The types of businesses involved in the awarded cases varied depending on whether the business was the claimant or the respondent.[72] The most common types of businesses bringing claims against consumers were home builders (21.3% of cases with business claimants), real estate brokers (19.7%), and various other types of service providers like law and accounting firms (32.8%). The most common types of business against which consumers brought claims were car dealers (27.5% of cases with business

64 Drahozal & Zyontz, *Private Regulation of Consumer Arbitration*, supra note 28, at 346 app. 3.

65 *Id.* at 346 & n.243.

66 Drahozal & Zyontz, *Empirical Study of AAA Consumer Arbitrations*, supra note 22, at 871. Counterclaims were filed in 18.9% of the cases (57 of 301), with most counterclaims (46 of 57, or 80.7%) being filed by businesses. *Id.* at 877.

67 *Id.* at 872–73.

68 Determining whether arbitration is more or less accessible than court requires a comparison of comparable cases in the two forums, which the Searle Study did not do.

69 Drahozal & Zyontz, *Empirical Study of AAA Consumer Arbitrations*, supra note 22, at 875.

70 *Id.*

71 For other difficulties in coding the claim amounts, see *id.* at 873–74.

72 The case types in the broader AAA dataset were similar: "Business claimants were mostly service providers: home builders (59 of 455, or 13.0% of cases), real estate brokers (53 of 455, or 11.6% of cases), and other service providers such as law and accounting firms (84 of 455, or 18.5% of cases). Common types of business respondents were motor vehicle dealerships (451 of 2765, or 16.3% of cases) and insurance/warranty companies (207 of 2765, or 7.5% of cases)." *Id.* at 878.

TABLE 32.1 *Types of claims asserted in AAA non-collection consumer arbitrations, as a % of all non-collection AAA consumer arbitrations, 2010–12.*

Types of claims	Credit card arbitrations (%)	Checking account arbitrations (%)	Payday arbitrations (%)
Federal statutory claims	59	23	28
State statutory claims	21	33	90
Fraud claims	5	12	75
Contract claims	28	30	83
Tort claims	7	30	61
General unspecified claims	11	49	7

respondents) and insurance/extended warranty companies (18.3%).[73] Cases involving mass contracting consumer businesses were relatively rare: credit card companies made up just under 10% of both business claimants and respondents and cell phone companies less than 5% of business claimants (and were not respondents in any cases studied).[74]

By comparison, the CFPB Preliminary Report focused exclusively on AAA arbitrations arising out of credit card, checking account, and prepaid loan contracts. For arbitrations not involving a disputed consumer debt, the average amount claimed by consumers against businesses in the arbitrations studied was $38,726, with a median amount claimed of $11,805.[75] Over the three years studied, twenty-three claims (an average of just under eight per year) sought $1,000 or less.[76] The CFPB provided a detailed breakdown of the types of claims asserted by consumers in the consumer financial disputes studied, as shown in Table 32.1.[77]

The CFPB also found evidence that cardholders who brought claims in arbitration tended to have higher incomes than those who did not.[78] The CFPB recognized various qualifications to its data, and was not able to report comparative findings for plaintiffs in court litigation.

Length and Nature of Process

The average length of time from filing to award for the awarded cases in the Searle study was 6.9 months. The median length of time was 5.6 months, with the time ranging from a low of 2.1 months to a high of 2.8 years. Cases brought by businesses

73 *Id.* at 877–78.
74 *Id.* at 878.
75 CFPB Preliminary Report, supra note 5, at 80.
76 *Id.* at 81.
77 *Id.* at 86–87; see also *id.* at 89–91 (identifying common factual bases for consumer claims).
78 *Id.* at 100.

tended to be about ten days shorter on average than cases brought by consumers.[79] Although the data from the Searle Study appear consistent with the view that arbitration is a relatively quick form of dispute resolution, without data from comparable cases in court, it is not possible to evaluate whether arbitration is faster than court, as is often claimed.

While the majority of the AAA consumer arbitrations settled, it appears that a higher proportion of the cases were decided by an award after a hearing than are cases in court. The Searle Study found that 32.1% of cases brought by consumer claimants were resolved by an award, while 49.9% of cases brought by business claimants were resolved by an award.[80] The proportion of cases reaching an arbitral hearing was even greater: over 60% of cases brought by consumer claimants and 65% of cases brought by business claimants.[81] By comparison, the percentage of federal court cases resolved after trial is under 2%.[82] Some of the differences are likely due to selection effects (i.e., differences in cases between arbitration and court), and no doubt the rate of hearings is higher in small claims court than in federal court. That said, it seems likely that at least some of the differences are due to structural differences between arbitration and court.[83]

The higher rate of hearings in AAA arbitrations found by the Searle Study is consistent with a 1983 study by Kritzer and Anderson, in which they examined the total costs incurred by attorneys in cases in state court, federal court, and AAA arbitration.[84] They found that while the costs in AAA arbitration were lower than court litigation for the smallest claims, the costs of AAA arbitration were higher than court litigation for other categories of claims. An important reason that AAA arbitration was more expensive, according to Kritzer and Anderson, was that a "much larger proportion of the cases go through the complete process" – i.e., from filing through the hearing and an award.[85] So viewed, claimants might be more likely to have their "day in court" in arbitration.[86]

79 Drahozal & Zyontz, *Empirical Study of AAA Consumer Arbitrations*, supra note 22, at 892. Again, the data from the broader AAA docket is comparable: the average case took 7.3 months from filing to award, with a median case length of 5.9 months. *Id.* at 895.

80 *Id.* at 879.

81 *Id.* at 881.

82 Marc Galanter, A *World Without Trials?*, 2006 J. Disp. Resol. 7, 12 (2006).

83 A study comparing AAA arbitrations with court cases involving franchise disputes in state and federal courts reached a similar result. See Edward Wood Dunham & David Geronemus, *Lessons from the Resolution of Franchise Disputes*, JAMS Disp. Resol. Alert 1, 3 (Summer 2003) (finding that "8% of franchise disputes in state court were resolved by jury trial or bench trial; 10% of franchise disputes in federal court were resolved by jury trial or bench trial; while 60% of franchise disputes in arbitration were decided by an award").

84 Herbert M. Kritzer & Jill K. Anderson, *The Arbitration Alternative: A Comparative Analysis of Case Processing Time, Disposition Mode, and Cost in the American Arbitration Association and the Courts*, 8 Just. Sys. J. 6, 17 (1983).

85 *Id.*

86 Christopher R. Drahozal, Arbitration Costs and Access to Justice (Mar. 18, 2011), available at www.law.gwu.edu/News/2010–2011Events/Documents/Drahozal%20Submission.pdf.

In just under half the awarded cases studied in the Searle Study (49.8%), the consumer appeared pro se – i.e., was not represented by counsel. Consumer claimants (55.4% of cases with consumer claimants) were more likely to be represented by counsel than consumer respondents (29.5% of cases with consumer respondents).[87] The rates of consumer representation reported in the CFPB Preliminary Report were slightly higher: almost 53% of consumers had attorneys, with 61% of consumer claimants in non-collection cases represented by counsel as compared to 42% of consumer respondents in collection cases.[88] Of those consumers represented by counsel in the debt collection cases studied by the CFPB, "71% were represented by repeat counsel [i.e., counsel who appeared in more than one arbitration in the sample], and 59% were represented by one of only five repeat firms."[89] Of consumers in non-debt collection cases, "77% of represented consumers had a repeat counsel."[90] As noted earlier, without data on comparable cases in court, it is not possible to draw conclusions about whether consumers are more or less likely to be represented by counsel in arbitration than in court.

Outcomes

In the cases examined in the Searle Study, consumers won some relief in 53.3% of the cases they brought, and businesses won some relief in 83.6% of the cases they brought.[91] Prevailing consumers on average were awarded $19,255, which was 52.1% of the amount they claimed. By comparison, prevailing businesses on average were awarded $20,648, which was 93.0% of the amount they claimed.[92] Because consumers and businesses bring different types of claims with different likelihoods of success, comparing consumer win-rates in arbitration to business win-rates in arbitration is not meaningful.[93] Interestingly, though, Marc Galanter has reported that business plaintiffs "won 90% of the cases in which they sued individuals and lost only 50% of the cases in which individuals sued them" in non-personal injury federal court cases[94] – similar percentages to those in AAA consumer arbitrations.

In a more direct comparison between arbitration and court, the Searle Study reviewed the outcomes of debt collection cases in AAA consumer arbitrations as well as the outcomes of debt collection cases in federal court (student loan collection actions) and several state courts. Business claimants won some relief in from 86.2%

87 Drahozal & Zyontz, *Empirical Study of AAA Consumer Arbitrations*, supra note 22, at 903–04.
88 CFPB Preliminary Report, supra note 5, at 73–74.
89 *Id.* at 74.
90 *Id.*
91 Drahozal & Zyontz, *Empirical Study of AAA Consumer Arbitrations*, supra note 22, at 897–98.
92 *Id.* at 899.
93 *Id.* at 901; *cf.* National Center for State Courts, Small Claims & Traffic Courts: Case Management Procedures, Case Characteristics, and Outcomes in 12 Urban Jurisdictions 51–52 (1992).
94 Marc Galanter, *Contract in Court: Or Almost Everything You May or May not Want to Know about Contract Litigation*, 2001 Wis. L. Rev. 577, 600 (based on data on federal court diversity actions from 1986 to 1994, excluding personal injury actions).

to 97.1% of AAA arbitrations and from 98.4% to 100.0% of the court cases.[95] On average, business claimants were awarded from 92.9% to 99.2% of the amount sought in AAA arbitrations and from 96.2% to 99.5% of the amount sought in the court cases.[96] Although consumers fared better in the arbitrations studied than in court, that does not necessarily mean that arbitration is better for consumers than courts. Other factors might account for the differing win and recovery rates. That said, the data do show that the high win-rate and high recovery rate for businesses in the arbitrations studied do not demonstrate that arbitration is biased in favor of businesses. The win-rate and recovery rate are due to the type of case involved – debt collection cases – rather than the forum in which those claims are resolved.[97]

Consumers represented by an attorney tended to win some relief in arbitration more often than consumers without an attorney. Consumer claimants represented by attorneys won some relief in 60.2% of the awarded AAA arbitrations; consumers appearing pro se won some relief in 44.9% of the awarded AAA arbitrations.[98] Consumers represented by attorneys also were awarded higher damages, being awarded on average $27,233 (with a median award of $6,702) while consumers appearing pro se were awarded on average only $5,656 (with a median award of $3,029).[99] These findings are difficult to interpret, however, because of selection effects. Attorneys screen the cases they accept, so that consumers represented by an attorney are likely to have a stronger case than a consumer appearing pro se. As a result, it is difficult to determine whether the greater success of consumers represented by an attorney is due to the attorneys' representation or the strength of the consumer's case.[100]

Consumers sought attorneys' fees in 65 of the 84 cases in which they prevailed and were represented by counsel, and were awarded some amount of attorneys' fees in 63.1% of those cases.[101] The average amount of attorneys' fees awarded (in cases specifying a dollar amount) was $14,574, with a median award of $9,000. Without examining comparable court cases, there is no way to tell whether that is a high rate of recovery or a low rate of recovery. But the data do show that arbitrators are not wholly averse to awarding attorneys' fees to a prevailing consumer.

95 Drahozal & Zyontz, *Creditor Claims in Arbitration and in Court*, supra note 60, at 91.

96 *Id.* at 93.

97 Presumably at least some (if not most) consumer debt disputes are settled before an arbitration or court proceeding is filed. Once a business files a debt collection claim in arbitration or in court, the consumer often does not appear, although the consumer response rate varies widely in the different forums. *Id.* at 96.

98 Drahozal & Zyontz, *Empirical Study of AAA Consumer Arbitration*, supra note 22, at 905.

99 *Id.* at 906.

100 Interestingly, consumers represented by attorneys tended to be awarded a lower percentage of the amount sought (only 44.9%) than consumers appearing pro se, who were awarded on average 64.3% of the amount sought. *Id.* at 907.

101 *Id.* at 902–03.

Finally, while the Searle Study found some evidence of a repeat-player effect in AAA consumer arbitrations (by one definition of repeat business, anyway[102]), it found no evidence of repeat-player bias. Consumer claimants won some relief against repeat businesses in 43.4% of the AAA awarded cases but against non-repeat businesses in 56.1% of the cases.[103] But the likely explanation for this repeat-player effect, according to the Searle Study, is case screening by repeat businesses, not bias by arbitrators: repeat businesses are more likely to settle their weaker cases than non-repeat businesses, leaving only cases in which the repeat business is more likely to prevail to be arbitrated.[104] This case screening explanation for the repeat-player effect is consistent with studies of AAA employment arbitration, which have reached similar conclusions.[105]

CONCLUSION

This chapter has provided an overview of consumer arbitrations administered by the American Arbitration Association, the largest administrator of consumer arbitrations. It does not, of course, purport to resolve the ongoing debate over arbitration and access to justice. A consumer's incentive to bring a claim (and an attorney's incentive to take a case) depends on the costs of the process and the expected outcome in the forum.[106] With the recent amendments to its consumer arbitration rules, the AAA reduced the cost to consumers of bringing claims in arbitration, both by lowering the upfront fees and by largely precluding reallocation of fees to consumers in the award. The expected outcome in arbitration (in particular, relative to the expected outcome in court) presents a much more difficult question because limits to available data preclude comparison of similarly situated claimants. More research remains to be done.[107]

[102] The Searle Study identified a repeat business in two ways: (1) businesses that are involved in more than one arbitration in the sample; and (2) businesses that had additional dealings with the AAA in connection with the AAA's protocol compliance review. *Id.* at 908–09. Businesses identified as repeat businesses under the first definition were not statistically more likely to prevail against consumers in arbitration than other businesses, but businesses identified as repeat businesses under the second definition were. *Id.* at 909–10.

[103] *Id.* at 911. However, prevailing consumers recover roughly the same percentage of the amount sought against repeat and non-repeat businesses. *Id.* at 912–13.

[104] *Id.* at 915.

[105] E.g., Lisa B. Bingham & Shimon Sarraf, *Employment Arbitration before and after the Due Process Protocol for Mediation and Arbitration of Statutory Disputes Arising Out of Employment: Preliminary Evidence that Self-Regulation Makes a Difference, in* ALTERNATE DISPUTE RESOLUTION IN THE EMPLOYMENT ARENA: PROCEEDINGS OF THE NEW YORK UNIVERSITY 53RD ANNUAL CONFERENCE ON LABOR 303, 323 tbl. 2 (Samuel Estreicher & David Sherwyn eds., 2004); see David Sherwyn, Samuel Estreicher & Michael Heise, *Assessing the Case for Employment Arbitration: A New Path for Empirical Research*, 57 STAN. L. REV. 1557, 1571 (2005).

[106] Drahozal, supra note 1, at 833.

[107] Some empirical evidence suggests that arbitration may be a more accessible option than court for employees with small claims, but that evidence has been contested. See supra note 1.

33

Saturns for Rickshaws:

Lessons for Consumer Arbitration and Access to Justice

Dean Peter B. Rutledge

Companies are increasingly requiring consumers to agree to arbitrate disputes they may have over the products or services they purchase. Pre-dispute arbitration agreements are controversial especially for consumer disputes, where, it is feared, consumers will not represent themselves and neither will lawyers come forward because of the small stakes involved in individual claims. Dean Rutledge addresses in this chapter whether consumer arbitration processes can be designed to provide greater access to justice for consumers.

Over a decade ago, Professor Samuel Estreicher laid plain the terms of the policy debate over arbitration of employment disputes.[1] Invoking the provocative and memorable phrase "Saturns for Rickshaws," Estreicher argued that the debate ultimately turned on one's view about the social goals of civil dispute resolution. Prohibiting arbitration clauses in employment disputes might guarantee a "Cadillac" system for the select few who had claims that could attract competent plaintiff's attorneys and plausible damages claims that a jury might buy. Yet for the rest (indeed the majority), civil litigation promised a "rickshaw" system – at best, little or no relief generally because their claims did not have the sticker value to attract competent counsel and, instead, languish on the dockets of understaffed and sometimes incompetent administrative agencies. By contrast, arbitration offered the prospect of "Saturns for all" – making those with "Cadillac" cases slightly worse off but those with "Rickshaw" cases comparatively better off.

While Saturns have disappeared from the new automobile market, Estreicher's metaphor retains its essential relevance to the study of arbitration. Though developed in the context of employment arbitration, it helps to frame the debate over consumer arbitration. One positive question is whether, in the consumer context, arbitration entails the same tradeoff – making a subset of consumers worse off even while making the majority of consumers better off. A related, normative question is whether that particular distribution of benefits is more socially desirable than the distribution of benefits offered by the civil litigation system.

[1] Samuel Estreicher, *Saturns for Rickshaws: The Stakes in the Debate over Predispute Employment Arbitration Agreements*, 18 Ohio St. J. Disp. Res. 559 (2001).

Opinions differ sharply over the answers. To some, arbitration can help solve problems of access to justice by reducing aggregate process costs and expediting the delivery of relief to consumers with meritorious claims.[2] To others, arbitration can exacerbate problems of access to justice by raising costs to the consumer and, when combined with class waivers, removing the incentive of private plaintiffs' attorneys to represent individuals whose small-value claims, due to the class waiver, cannot be aggregated with those of similarly situated individuals.[3]

In my view, Estreicher's thesis holds true for consumer arbitration too: "[a] properly designed arbitration system . . . can do a better job of delivering accessible justice for average claimants than a litigation-based approach." In several respects relevant to this debate, arbitration of consumer-related disputes shares certain features in common with employment arbitration: it can lower process costs, result in favorable results for claimants and lead to prompt resolution of the dispute. Many of these benefits flow from the greater procedural flexibility afforded in arbitration. Critics of consumer arbitration fear that this procedural flexibility could provide a recipe for unfair practices, but in most respects those fears have not come to pass.

While consumer arbitration and employment arbitration are similar, they are certainly not identical. Unlike employment claims, not all consumer claims are of high value, raising the possibility that the low-stakes claim, absent some aggregation mechanism, will deter the consumer from bothering with the suit. This explains why the debate over consumer arbitration has been so extensively tied up with a discussion of class actions, where the class mechanism attempts both to aggregate nominal claims and to supply something akin to group representation. Indeed, class waivers found in consumer arbitration agreements are the one area where the empirical research lends some support to critics' claims that the procedural flexibility afforded by arbitration might actually undercut access to justice.

Yet these differences should not be fatal to arbitration of consumer disputes. It is hardly clear that class litigation vindicates the consumer's interests. Moreover, even when class devices are unavailable in arbitration, alternative mechanisms like aggregate representation by public entities (not bound by the arbitration clause) may provide a better means by which to address residual concerns about consumer access to justice.

[2] See, e.g., Peter B. Rutledge & Christopher R. Drahozal, *Contract and Choice*, 2013 B.Y.U. L. Rev. 1 (2013); Christopher R. Drahozal & Peter B. Rutledge, *Contract and Procedure*, 94 Marquette L. Rev. 1103 (2011). By "process costs," I mean the costs incurred by the parties in resolving a dispute; this includes not only attorneys' fees but also, for example, the costs of complying with discovery. On the concept of process costs, see Stephen J. Ware, *Similarities Between Arbitration and Bankruptcy Litigation*, 11 Nev. L. J. 436 (2011); Christopher R. Drahozal, *Contracting Out of National Law: An Empirical Look at the New Law Merchant*, 80 Notre Dame L. Rev. 523, 531–32 (2005); Stephen J. Ware, *The Effects of Gilmer: Empirical and Other Approaches to the Study of Employment Arbitration*, 16 Ohio St. J. Disp. Res. 735 (2001).

[3] See, e.g., Myriam Gilles, *Killing Them with Kindness: Examining "Consumer-Friendly" Arbitration Clauses after AT&T v. Concepcion*, 88 Notre Dame L. Rev. 825 (2012); Jean Sternlight, *Tsunami: AT&T Mobility LLC v. Concepcion Impedes Access to Justice*, 90 Ore. L. Rev. 703 (2012).

"SATURNS FOR RICKSHAWS": LESSONS FOR CONSUMER ARBITRATION

In "Saturns for Rickshaws," Estreicher identified several features of employment arbitration that made it a superior alternative to civil litigation. It lowered process costs to the employee (that is, the costs of resolving the dispute), offered prompter dispute resolution, and resulted in favorable outcomes for the employee (whether measured by win rates or award amounts). Despite these benefits, Estreicher noted that it was essential for employment arbitration to maintain certain procedural safeguards to avoid unfairness from creeping into the system. These included an experienced bench of employment arbitrators; reasonable opportunity for discovery; written, reasoned opinions; and a cost structure that obligated employers to advance the costs of the arbitration.

In many respects, consumer arbitration displays many of the same redeeming features. To understand how consumer arbitration can reduce process costs, consider a sample case. Assume that a consumer has a complaint against a company about a defective product or a suspicious charge in her bill. The consumer believes she has been wronged and has failed to achieve a mutually agreeable settlement with the company. Suppose that the dispute is weighty enough that the consumer wishes to bring it but not so weighty that she is prepared to miss a day of work to achieve resolution of the matter. Absent arbitration, a small claims court might require the consumer to miss a day's work for a hearing or forgo her claim.[4] By contrast, arbitration can facilitate resolution of that dispute by allowing the parties, either on a pre-dispute or on a post-dispute basis, to agree – indeed to require – that any decision occur entirely on the written submissions of the parties without the need for a live hearing. She can obtain a confirmable award without any need to bear the costs imposed by the non-derogable procedural rules of a litigation forum.

By "unbundling" a dispute from a particular set of procedural rules, arbitration offers the potential to address some of the nettlesome problems of access to justice explored elsewhere in this book. Some of these are well understood. For example, by eliminating a presumptive entitlement to discovery, arbitration can reduce the "process costs" of resolving the dispute.[5] Similarly, by eliminating extensive pleading practice (like motions to dismiss and motions for summary judgment), arbitration can generate results much more quickly.[6] Finally, as noted earlier, by eliminating the requirement of a hearing, arbitration can reduce the costs to a consumer and, in simple cases, the very need for legal representation.[7]

4 For a good summary of the sorts of barriers faced in small claims adjudication, see James C. Turner and Joyce A. McGee, *Small Claims Reform: A Means of Expanding Access to the American Civil Justice System*, 5 U.D.C. L. Rev. 177, 187–88 (2000).

5 See supra note 2.

6 See Robert Summers, *Arbitration Between Attorneys and Clients*, 61 Tex. B. J. 330 (1998).

7 See Nancy A. Welsh, *Mandatory Predispute Arbitration, Structural Bias, and Incentivizing Procedural Safeguards*, 42 Sw. L. Rev. 187 (2012).

TABLE 33.1 *Small claims carve-outs in credit card agreements (2010).*

Type of provision	Number of clauses	% of credit card loans outstanding
Small claims carve-out for cardholder (including ones with damages caps)	42 (68.1%)	98.4
No provision	15 (31.9%)	1.6

While arbitration may be preferable to court in some cases, small claims court might be preferable in others. Arbitration preserves that choice. Arbitration agreements routinely contain "carve outs" reserving to the consumer (or either party) the right to proceed in small claims court. In our study of arbitration agreements in the credit card industry, Chris Drahozal and I found that 68.1% of agreements contained express language carving out small claims proceedings (the remaining agreements did not contain a provision on the matter).[8] When measured as a result of outstanding credit card debt, the results are even starker. Nearly all of the credit card debt subject to an arbitration agreement contains a small claims carve-out; only a fraction does not. Table 33.1 summarizes the results from our database.

Of course, from the consumer's perspective, the above-described saving in process costs afforded by arbitration matters only if the end result is a just one. On this point, the research generally supports the view that it does. As a general matter, most studies of arbitration (whether in the consumer context or otherwise) indicate that it produces favorable results for claimants (whether measured in terms of the "win rate," the recovery, or some comparison between arbitration and litigation baselines).[9] The most recent and methodologically sound study in this area confirms this general trend. A study of approximately 300 AAA consumer arbitrations revealed that "the consumer claimant won some relief against the business defendant more than half of the time."[10] According to the same study, consumers recovered

[8] Rutledge & Drahozal, 2013 B.Y.U. L. Rev. at 21.

[9] See Christopher R. Drahozal & Samantha Zyontz, *An Empirical Study of AAA Consumer Arbitrations*, 25 Ohio St. J. Disp. Res. 843, 852–62 (2010). Of course, a critical research question – with both positive and normative implications – is the proper baseline for measuring favorable or just results. Certain measures – like raw win rates – may be easily measured but do not reveal much about whether the result is a just one (i.e., a $1 award may count as a "win" even when the claimant is seeking thousands of dollars). Other measures – like comparative recovery rates (which compare recoveries between arbitration and litigation in like cases) – may provide more normatively powerful accounts but are extremely difficult to measure. Moreover, any assessment of outcomes confronts a significant risk of selection bias because the universe of the cases studied may not necessarily be representative of the entire range of actual (or potential) disputes. For discussions of the methodological difficulties here, see Drahozal & Zyontz, 25 Ohio St. J. Disp. Res. at 852; Peter B. Rutledge, *Whither Arbitration?*, 6 Geo. J. L. & Pub. Pol'y 549, 556–60 (2008).

[10] Drahozal & Zyontz, 25 Ohio St. J. Disp. Res. at 898.

approximately 50% of the amount sought in their complaint.[11] Perhaps most telling from the perspective of access to justice, the study also considered how consumers fared when they proceeded pro se: "*pro se* consumer claimants won some relief in 44.9% of the cases they brought" (though win rates and recovery rates were higher when the consumer was represented by counsel).[12]

These outcomes, moreover, are usually delivered in an expeditious fashion. Studies of arbitration consistently conclude that median filing times from commencement of the arbitration to issuance of the final award are short – both in absolute terms and relative to comparable data for litigation.[13] The data on consumer arbitration comport with this general trend. AAA consumer arbitrations average approximately six to seven months from median to disposition (documents-only arbitrations that lack an in-person hearing have slightly shorter durations).[14]

These outcomes are undergirded by the "Consumer Due Process Protocol." That protocol was developed in the 1990s by a group of arbitration associations, parties, and counsel who sought to ensure the development of fair procedures in consumer arbitration.[15] The Protocol contains a number of procedural guarantees akin to those recommended by Estreicher in Saturns for Rickshaws. These include a right to resolution of the dispute in a location convenient to the consumer, a right of access to information, a right to reasonable costs, and a right to all available remedies. Since its adoption, the AAA has refused to administer consumer arbitration clauses that are not in compliance with the Protocol.

How widely is the Protocol used? In a 2010 study of arbitration agreements used by credit card companies, Christ Drahozal and I found that nearly all credit card providers offer the option of arbitration administered by the AAA.[16] The AAA is committed to administering arbitrations in accordance with the Due Process Protocol. Table 33.2 summarizes the results.

The AAA aggressively polices arbitration clauses for compliance with the Due Process Protocol. Of 361 consumer arbitrations filed with the American Arbitration Association, Drahozal and Zyontz report only five involved unwaived violations of

[11] *Id.* at 899. Here it should be stressed that the percentages varied with the amount originally sought by the consumer; consumers seeking higher amounts of damages generally recovered a higher percentage of the amount sought. See *id.*

[12] *Id.* at 905. The study does not specify the precise nature of the various consumer arbitration claims under review. Nor did it explicitly compare outcomes in consumer arbitration with outcomes in consumer litigation.

[13] See *id.* at 892.

[14] See Drahozal & Zyontz, 25 Ohio St. J. Disp. Res. at 851–52 and 892–96 (collecting literature and presenting results of consumer arbitration research).

[15] For a discussion of the Protocol's history and development, see Peter B. Rutledge, *Arbitration and the Constitution* 145–56 (Cambridge 2013). A copy of the Protocol may be found on the website of the American Arbitration Association, available at www.adr.org.

[16] Rutledge & Drahozal, 2013 B.Y.U. L. Rev. at 30.

TABLE 33.2 *Choice of provider in arbitration clauses in credit card agreements (2010).*

Provider	Number of clauses	% of credit card loans outstanding
AAA	16 (41.0%)	16.3
AAA or JAMS	13 (33.3%)	81.8
JAMS	2 (5.1%)	.1
AAA, JAMS or NAF	2 (5.1%)	.5
JAMS or NAF	1 (2.6%)	0.0
Other	4 (10.4%)	1.3

the Protocol.[17] Stated otherwise, in 98.2% of the cases, either the arbitration clause complied with the Due Process Protocol or its noncompliance was properly identified and responded to by the AAA. Similarly, in 2007, the AAA refused to administer at least 85 cases, and probably at least 129 cases, because of noncompliance with the Protocol.[18]

Attorney fees represent another type of procedural safeguard that helps to enhance access to justice. For example, the Drahozal and Zyontz study of AAA consumer arbitrations found that arbitrators awarded attorney's fees to prevailing consumer claimants in 63.1% of cases in which the consumer sought such an award.[19] In those cases in which the award of attorneys' fees specified a dollar amount, the average attorney's fee award was $14,574.

Some systems offer much more protection than the Due Process Protocol. Though arbitration is sometimes criticized as imposing costs on consumers (such as arbitrator fees and filing fees) that they do not bear in the civil litigation system, contractual clauses can overcome these risks.[20] The AT&T clause at issue in the recent *Concepcion* decision supplies a good example.[21] As described by the Court, the AT&T Clause

> specifies that AT&T must pay all costs for nonfrivolous claims; that arbitration must take place in the county in which the customer is billed; that, for claims of $10,000 or less, the customer may choose whether the arbitration proceeds in person, by telephone, or based only on submissions; that either party may bring a claim in small claims court in lieu of arbitration; and that the arbitrator may award any form of individual relief, including injunctions and presumably punitive damages. The agreement, moreover, denies AT&T any ability to seek reimbursement of its attorney's fees, and, in the event that a customer receives an arbitration award

17 Christopher R. Drahozal & Samantha Zyontz, *Private Regulation of Consumer Arbitration*, 79 TENN. L. REV. 289, 325 (2012).

18 *Id.* at 330–31.

19 Drahozal & Zyontz, 25 OHIO ST. J. DISP. RES. at 846.

20 See *Green Tree Fin. Corp.-Alabama v. Randolph*, 531 U.S. 79, 93 (2000) (Ginsburg, J., concurring in part and dissenting in part).

21 *AT&T Mobility, LLC v. Concepcion*, 131 S. CT. 1740 (2011).

greater than AT&T's last written settlement offer, requires AT&T to pay a $7,500 minimum recovery and twice the amount of the claimant's attorney's fees.

Here, too, arbitration permits a degree of innovation not possible in the civil litigation system. The civil litigation system fixes its own allocation of court costs, does not allow parties to dictate the forms of hearings, does not enforce one-sided fee-shifting arrangements, and generally does not "reward" a party if its recovery exceeded the company's last settlement offer.[22] (Indeed, in many respects, the civil litigation system imposes more burdens on the consumer – requiring her to pay filing fees, forcing her to attend a hearing, forcing her to cover her own legal fees, and potentially punishing her with costs if her recovery falls below the company's settlement offer.)

To this point, I have considered the procedural flexibility of consumer arbitration in salutary terms. Of course, it might be a double-edged sword, and the theoretical literature has identified a variety of devices such as limits on discovery or limits on remedies that might impede citizens' access to justice. Little empirical work has been done to examine whether those devices are, in fact, employed. For example, in our 2010 study of arbitration clauses in credit card agreements, Drahozal and I found that almost no clauses contained restrictions such as limits on remedies, limits on the time for filing claims, limits on discovery.[23]

The one exception to this trend was class waivers. Our initial 2010 study of forty-seven agreements found that 93.6% of them used such clauses. Subsequent studies told a more complicated story. In a subsequent examination of a more complete set of credit card agreements, we saw that the use was closer to 17% of firms and that for-profit banks were far more likely to use class waivers than member-owned credit unions.[24] However, when the use of arbitration clauses was measured not by firms but by debt load, the usage rate was far higher.[25] The recent preliminary report of the Consumer Financial Protection Bureau confirms our findings that overall utilization rates remain low, when measured by firms, but higher, when measured by debt load.[26]

To summarize this section, consumer arbitration bears many of the hallmarks that Estreicher praised about employment arbitration. It affords consumers greater

22 Admittedly, such reward provisions appear to be rare. In our 2010 study of credit card agreements, we located only one agreement employing such a provision. In that case, the clause stated that the arbitrator should award the consumer "at least $5100 (plus any fees and costs to which you are entitled)" if the consumer requested relief, the company did not provide it, and the arbitrator subsequently awarded at least the amount of relief originally sought by the consumer.

23 Rutledge & Drahozal, 2013 B.Y.U. L. Rev. at 39.

24 See Christopher R. Drahozal & Peter B. Rutledge, *Arbitration Clauses in Credit Card Agreements: An Empirical Study*, 9 J. Empirical Legal Studies 536 (2012).

25 Measuring the usage rate by reference to debt load was difficult. This was due to a settlement in an action against some banks under which they agreed temporarily to remove arbitration clauses from their credit card agreements. See Consumer Financial Protection Bureau, Arbitration Study: Preliminary Results at 22–23 & n. 51.

26 *Id.*

flexibility, decent results, and rapid disposition of their claims. At the same time, various procedural protections, including the Consumer Due Process Protocol and privately developed mechanisms, offer the safeguards that Estreicher deemed essential to ensuring that the promise of improved access to justice not become hollow. Available empirical evidence suggests that the use of these safeguards is widespread and regularly applied. In the next section, I consider how consumer claims differ from employment claims and explore the implications of those differences.

IMPLICATIONS OF HOW CONSUMER DISPUTES DIFFER FROM EMPLOYMENT DISPUTES

Consumer disputes can differ from employment disputes. Centrally, the stakes in some consumer disputes will be smaller than the stakes in some employment disputes. A plaintiff in an employment dispute may have a potentially large damages claim (such as a Title VII claim). By comparison, individual consumers may only suffer relatively small damages due to an alleged violation of consumer law (such as an arguably unlawful charge on a cell phone bill).[27] Absent some mechanism, this feature might discourage individual consumers from bringing claims and, consequently, result in the under-deterrence of some violations of consumer law.[28]

As a result, class actions have taken center stage in the consumer arbitration debate. Class actions potentially might overcome both of these challenges faced in the consumer context. The aggregation of large numbers of small individual claims might provide sufficient financial incentive to proceed with the dispute. Class counsel, moreover, can serve a role akin to an institutional representative on behalf of the individual claimants. Consequently, according to one standard critique of consumer arbitration, class waivers eliminate the core incentive for a consumer to bring a case. If the consumer has only sustained actual injury to the tune of a few dollars, the costs of litigation will almost certainly exceed her expected recovery. Moreover, no attorney will undertake the litigation, even on a contingent fee basis, because the attorney's expected recovery will quickly outstrip the upfront costs she must invest to maintain the litigation.[29] I refer to this problem as the "disaggregation dilemma." Only if the attorney has sufficient financial incentive to undertake the litigation can the disaggregation dilemma be solved.

[27] This is not always the case. Some consumer protection laws contain statutory damages that enhance the consumer's incentive to pursue a claim by raising the potential recovery. See, e.g., *Cicle v. Chase Bank USA*, 583 F.3d 549, 556 (8th Cir. 2009) (discussing statutory damages available under Missouri statute).

[28] In some employment claims, unions can perform this aggregative role. Consumers obviously lack a comparable body.

[29] See *Thorogood v. Sears, Roebuck & Co.*, 547 F.3d 742, 744 (7th Cir. 2008) ("If every small claim had to be litigated separately, the vindication of small claims would be rare. The fixed costs of litigation make it impossible to litigate a $50 claim (our guess – there is no evidence – of what the average claim of a member of the plaintiff's class in this case might be worth) at a cost that would not exceed the value of the claim by many times").

Particularly after *Concepcion*, the disaggregation dilemma has taken on special importance in the field of arbitration. As Drahozal's and my studies of the credit card industry demonstrate, class waivers have grown increasingly common in some industries.[30] Arbitration's critics decry the combination of class waivers and arbitration clauses as the functional equivalent of exculpatory clauses. Because consumers (and their attorneys) lack sufficient financial incentives, cases are never brought; this lack of private enforcement results in under-deterrence.[31] Moreover, to the extent arbitrators feel bound to apply the procedural rules designated by the parties (including the prospective decision not to proceed on an aggregative basis), arbitration's detractors argue there is no likelihood the arbitrator will deem the class waiver unenforceable (a decision, they continue, that could not be reviewed in post-award proceedings). Thus, a great deal of litigation has focused on whether the presence of a class waiver in an arbitration clause renders the clause "unconscionable" (and thus unenforceable) under Section 2 of the Federal Arbitration Act. *Concepcion* struck a blow to this line of argument, although the scope of its holding remains the subject of extensive, ongoing litigation in federal and state courts.

In this legal environment, some might be tempted to declare: "The answer is easy. Amend Section 2 of the FAA to ban class waivers in arbitration agreements. Problem solved!" What I hope to do in this section of the chapter is to sound a note of caution over this approach. The policy debate over the (un)desirability of class waivers in arbitration agreements – particularly as they weigh on issues of access to justice – is far more nuanced, and the prescription proposed by arbitration's critics is not clearly a panacea for consumers.

While the literature on the efficacy of class actions is vast, several recent contributions cast doubt on the utility of class actions as a means of compensating consumers. The effectiveness of the class settlement depends, in part, on the "take rate," that is the frequency with which members of a class actually redeem the benefit offered in the settlement. Several studies of class action settlements find low distribution rates, particularly where consumers must complete a form in order to receive a share of the settlement.[32] As Professor Jaime Dodge has explained, these rates remain low even where the consumer's share is non-trivial.[33] Consequently, Dodge doubts the efficacy of consumer class actions: "many class actions are only

[30] See text in accompanying notes 25–27.

[31] See, e.g., Gilles, 88 Notre Dame L. Rev. at 825, 846.

[32] See Nicholas M. Pace & William B. Rubinstein, *How Transparent Are Class Action Outcomes? Empirical Research on the Availability of Class Action Claims Data* (Rand 2008); Nicholas M. Pace et al., *Insurance Class Actions in the United States* (Rand 2007); Deborah Hensler et al., *Class Action Dilemmas: Pursuing Public Goals for Private Gain* (Rand 2000).

[33] Jaime Dodge, *Disaggregative Mechanisms: The New Frontier of Mass-Claims Resolution Without Class Actions*, 63 Emory L.J. 1253 (2014).

providing compensation to a small fraction of harmed individuals, while preclusion operates to bar these individuals' claims."[34]

Once class actions are cast in a more realistic light, arbitration may do a better job, on the whole, as a means of providing compensation to consumers than class actions. Assuming the consumer chooses to arbitrate, she has a greater likelihood of actually receiving compensation for meritorious claims: the risks entailed with processing of mass claims (that is, non-redemption followed by preclusion against bringing a claim later) drop out. Moreover, most studies have shown (and the Searle report confirms) that actual outcomes in consumer arbitration (whether measured by actual win rates or actual recovery rates) are at least as good as in garden-variety consumer civil litigation.[35]

One mechanism that has increasingly drawn attention in the debates over arbitration and class action has been proceedings brought by public authorities (such as a state attorney general or an administrative agency charged with enforcement, including civil litigation, of a statutory scheme). This argument finds its roots in the Supreme Court's decision in *EEOC v. Waffle House*, which held that arbitration clauses do not bind administrative and other public authorities even when the public authority is suing on behalf of a party whose own claim falls within the scope of the arbitration agreement.[36] In reliance on the *Waffle House* theory, companies employing arbitration agreements with class waivers argue the agreements do not amount to wholesale denials of justice because the public enforcement authority remains available to bring suit in instances where the individual consumers might lack sufficient incentive to do so if they were to proceed on an individualized basis.

This argument, of course, is potentially subject to criticism. One argument, often seen in the post-*Concepcion* litigation, is that public enforcement authorities are overburdened and underfunded. Consequently, reliance on public enforcement mechanisms is, functionally, reliance on at best a limited tool. A second criticism, less widely seen, is that the public enforcement mechanisms might become "captured" by the industries they are asked to regulate through collective litigation. This argument would tap into the rich literature on regulatory capture and postulate that private enforcement mechanisms (as opposed to public ones) are less prone to capture because the incentives of the private class counsel are more closely aligned with those of her client than the incentives of the public regulatory authority.

The invocation of public enforcement mechanisms as a solution to the disaggregation dilemma brings into stark relief the role played by consumer arbitration in questions about access to justice. It is not simply a choice between individualized dispute resolution and aggregate dispute resolution. Rather, it is a choice about individualized dispute resolution backstopped by two very different models of

34 *Id.*
35 See Drahozal & Zyontz, 25 OHIO ST. J. DISP. RES. at 852–62.
36 534 U.S. 279 (2002).

aggregate dispute resolution – one managed by private entrepreneurs, the other administered by the public sector.

The choice may well depend on a mixture of empirical and normative arguments. Empirically, the foregoing discussion has cast some doubt on the efficacy of private class actions as a solution to the disaggregation dilemma. Some recent anecdotal evidence, summarized in the Pepperdine Report of the Consumer Arbitration Discussion Group, suggests public enforcement authorities have provided an effective supplement to situations where consumers might otherwise lack the incentive to pursue their claims on an individualized basis.[37] Of course, whether these anecdotes have broader empirical validity is an extraordinarily difficult question to assess. It would require some conception of the "optimal" level of enforcement, taking into account the possibility of bureaucratic self-aggrandizement and the claim that public bureaucracies could always use more resources. To my knowledge, the empirical resources simply do not exist fully to assess that proposition.

Even accepting the validity of the premise – that public enforcement authorities cannot fully address the disaggregation dilemma created by individualized arbitration – it would not necessarily follow, as a normative matter, that the public enforcement model is inadequate to backstop any "access to justice" impediments created by individualized arbitration of consumer claims. One might reasonably argue public authorities, whether civil or criminal, must regularly set enforcement priorities. These enforcement priorities necessarily mean that some cases will receive the agency's attention while others will not. The deliberation that comes with the setting of those priorities reflects the very nature of our political process and the officials (elected or appointed) who are vested with the authority to enforce the statutes falling under their jurisdiction. If individual voters believe an agency's enforcement priorities do not reflect the popular will, elections (and replacement of those officials) provide a mechanism for resetting those priorities.

To summarize this part: once the unrealistically rosy scenario of class actions is cast aside, individualized arbitration hardly seems to be the monster its skeptics paint it to be. Rather, it simply represents another example of procedural unbundling. To be sure, this form of unbundling gives rise to the disaggregation dilemma. But the solution is not (necessarily) to jettison individualized arbitration altogether. Rather, a variety of mechanisms, including class arbitration and public enforcement mechanisms, exist to resolve the dilemma without the need to invalidate the arbitration clause (or at least the class waiver). The efficacy of these "backstop" mechanisms turns on a host of positive and normative questions that demand further inquiry.

37 See National Roundtable on Consumer and Employment Dispute Resolution, Consumer Arbitration Roundtable Summary Report (Apr. 17, 2012).

CONCLUSION

The available empirical data largely validate the application of Estreicher's "Saturns for Rickshaws" metaphor to consumer arbitration. Arbitration enabled a degree of procedural flexibility while not saddling consumers with the sorts of "unfair" provisions that were feared in the literature but have not materialized in practice. Of course, more could be done. Companies could be more specific in their clauses about cost-sharing rules (a gap that the Consumer Due Process Protocol should address), and companies should consider following the lead of AT&T to ensure that consumers have adequate incentives to proceed with meritorious claims.

To be sure, the limits on these findings must be acknowledged. They concern practices in a single industry and at a single point in time. Particularly as the doctrine in this area changes, it is important to track contracting practices (something Chris Drahozal and I have done in other research).[38] Yet the experience of the credit card industry holds potential lessons for other industries with consumer relationship and counsels caution before accepting the strident but empirically undemonstrated broad-based criticism of arbitration as a tool impeding consumer access to justice.

While arbitration has the potential to improve access to justice, it also carries corresponding risks of defections from the protections afforded by the system of civil litigation. The challenge for scholarship in this area therefore becomes to assess the patterns in various industries. If the sorts of practices exemplified by the AT&T clause are widespread, then arbitration offers great promise as a potential tool for improving access to justice. On the other hand, if such practices prove to be an outlier, then the risks rise that a rule of robust enforceability for arbitration clauses might impede access to justice.

Ultimately, though, whether consumer arbitration is a boon or bane to "justice access" issues depends critically on the baseline by which results are measured. Lawyers (and legal academics) naturally train on disputes actually commenced (or that might be commenced if the barriers could be overcome). But it is worth emphasizing that such actual contested matters only represent the tip of the iceberg regarding consumer affairs. Many differences between consumers and companies, particularly in mass consumer contracting industries like cable television or telecommunications, are resolved or settled without the dispute ever ripening into an actual arbitration. Instead, arbitration merely supplies the end point against which a company can design a whole quilt of dispute resolution models by which customer disputes are resolved. It is precisely the predictability – and enforceability – of this end point that enables companies to estimate their legal costs in cases that go this far. Those predictions enable the company to settle matters expeditiously – and far more cheaply. Companies know that, if the matter is not settled, it will not result in expensive, full-blown litigation but, instead, a less expensive form of arbitration that

[38] See Peter B. Rutledge & Christopher R. Drahozal, *Sticky Arbitration Clauses*, 67 Vanderbilt L. Rev. 955 (2014).

allows for unbundled procedures tailored to the size and stakes of the dispute. This, then, ultimately may be the toughest empirical nut to crack – testing the cases we don't see – and that never ripen – precisely because they are resolved at an early stage – and are so resolved only because they occur against the backdrop of a system of arbitration. While much empirical work remains to be done, this may ultimately be the great legacy of arbitration in improving, rather than harming, the average citizen's access to justice.

34

Employment Arbitration in the Securities Industry

Michael Delikat & Lisa Lupion

The Federal Industry Regulatory Authority (FINRA) maintains a large arbitration system, under federal regulatory auspices, for brokers and dealers in the U.S. securities industry regarding disputes these firms may have with their investors and employees. Michael Delikat and Lisa Lupion examine how the system operates in employment disputes, both where employees are represented by counsel and where they represent themselves.

The Financial Industry Regulatory Authority (FINRA) is the largest non-governmental self-regulatory organization for brokers and dealers doing business in the United States. FINRA was created on July 30, 2007, through a combination of the National Association of Securities Dealers and the New York Stock Exchange.[1] Among its functions, FINRA operates the largest dispute resolution forum in the securities industry, providing arbitration and mediation services for monetary, business, and employment disputes among investors, securities firms, and the employees of securities firms.[2]

Given the number of the organizations and individuals registered[3] with FINRA,[4] FINRA deals with a large volume of arbitrations each year. In each of the last five

1 News Release, NASD and NYSE Member Regulation Combine to Form the Financial Industry Regulatory Authority – FINRA, July 30, 2007 News Release, available at www.finra.org/Newsroom/NewsReleases/2007/P036329.

2 FINRA Arbitration & Mediation website, available at www.finra.org/ArbitrationAndMediation/index.htm.

3 Under the Securities Exchange Act of 1934, most "brokers" or "dealers" must register with FINRA. Broadly speaking, Section 3(a)(4)(A) of Securities Exchange Act, 15 U.S.C. § 78c(a)(4)(A), defines a "broker" as "any person engaged in the business of effecting transactions in securities for the account of others." In other words, any person or entity that executes transactions for others on a securities exchange is a broker. Section 3(a)(5)(A) of the Securities Exchange Act, *id.* § 78c(a)(5)(A), defines a "dealer" as "any person engaged in the business of buying and selling securities for his own account, through a broker or otherwise." A dealer, therefore, includes any person or entity that is buying and selling securities on a continuous basis. Any professional who is actively engaged in an entity's broker-dealer business must be registered through a member entity with FINRA.

4 According to its website, FINRA oversees about 4,245 brokerage firms, about 162,230 branch offices and approximately 630,150 brokers. See *About the Financial Industry Regulatory Authority*, available at www.finra.org/AboutFINRA/.

years (2008–13), there were anywhere from 4,000 to 7,000 arbitration cases filed.[5] These cases can be broadly categorized as some form of a *customer dispute* (e.g., disputes between investors and their individual brokers and broker-dealer firms) or some form of an *employment dispute* (e.g., disputes between individual registered brokers and their employer firms). A wide range of types of controversies fall within these broad categories including margin calls, churning, unauthorized trading, failure to supervise, negligence, omission of facts, breach of contract, breach of fiduciary duty, unsuitability, misrepresentation, discrimination, and compensation disputes.

The majority of the claims filed and the arbitration awards rendered by FINRA would be classified as customer disputes.[6] Nevertheless, because of the professional background of the authors and the important issues raised in employment arbitration, including the arbitration of statutory claims through mandatory arbitration processes, this chapter focuses on the handling of employment disputes in the context of FINRA arbitration. We first consider the rules and procedures that regulate employment arbitrations in FINRA. Next, we look at all of the employment awards issued from January 2009 to December 2012 and offer some conclusions as to how litigants have fared in the forum in a variety of different contexts. Finally, we explore three issues that are critical to determining the impartiality and effectiveness of an arbitral forum: (1) whether parties can effectively litigate their cases as a pro se litigant; (2) whether there is any indication that claimants cannot vindicate their statutory rights; and (3) whether there is any evidence of the "repeat player" effect, which posits that large institutions would benefit from litigating in the same forum on many occasions. Overall, while there are limitations to our analysis based on the often inadequate information provided in FINRA arbitration awards, and FINRA arbitrations are susceptible to "rough justice" or "split the baby" type decisions that might be based more on a sense of fairness than law, we do not see any evidence that would undermine an individual employee's ability to prosecute claims in FINRA arbitration.

OVERVIEW OF FINRA EMPLOYMENT ARBITRATIONS: THE GOVERNING RULES AND PROCEDURES

Employment disputes handled under FINRA auspices are governed by the Code of Arbitration Procedure for Industry Disputes (the "Code").[7] The Code, and any

[5] FINRA Dispute Resolution Statistics, available at www.finra.org/ArbitrationAndMediation/FINRADisputeResolution/AdditionalResources/Statistics/.

[6] See David B. Lipsky, Ronald L. Seeber & J. Ryan Lamare, *The Arbitration of Employment Disputes in the Securities Industry: A Study of FINRA Awards*, 1986–2008, 65 Dis. Res. J., 54 (2010) (noting that employment disputes make up about 23% of all FINRA filings).

[7] FINRA maintains a separate set of rules for customer–broker disputes. The Code of Arbitration Procedure (Customer Code) governs arbitrations between investors and brokers and/or brokerage firms. Both the Customer Code and the Industry Code are available at www.finra.org/ArbitrationAndMediation/Arbitration/Rules/CodeofArbitrationProcedure/index.htm.

changes or amendments to the Code, must be approved by the Securities and Exchange Commission.

As stated in the Code, any dispute that arises out of the business activities of a member or an associated person and is between or among: (i) members; (ii) members and associated persons; or (iii) associated persons, must be arbitrated.[8] Notwithstanding the broad jurisdiction that FINRA enjoys, under the Code, FINRA will not accept all statutory employment claims. FINRA will not accept claims alleging employment discrimination, including sexual harassment, in violation of a statute unless the parties expressly agree to arbitrate such a claim either before or after the dispute arose.[9] Similarly, many claims arising under a "whistleblower" statute are excluded from FINRA arbitration. Specifically, if the statute prohibits the use of pre-dispute arbitration, FINRA will arbitrate the claim under the Code only if the parties agree to arbitrate it after the dispute arose.[10] The Code also excludes class action claims and collective action claims under the Fair Labor Standards Act, the Age Discrimination in Employment Act, or the Equal Pay Act of 1963.[11] Employees looking to assert a claim that is based upon the same facts and law as a court-certified class or collective action, can pursue their claims before FINRA only if the employee can provide some assurance that he or she will not participate in the class or collective action pending in court.[12]

Assuming the claim falls within FINRA's broad jurisdiction, an arbitration is initiated when the complaining party files a statement of claim specifying the relevant facts and remedies requested.[13] Unlike in court, however, failing to assert facts sufficient to state a legally cognizable claim will generally not make the claim susceptible to a motion to dismiss. In fact, the Code specifically provides that a motion to dismiss prior to the conclusion of the party's case in chief is "discouraged."[14] If a motion is filed, the FINRA arbitrators will be permitted to dismiss a party or a claim only if the non-moving party previously released the claims(s) in dispute by signing a settlement agreement or release or if the moving party was not associated with the account, security, or conduct at issue.[15] If the conduct is alleged against the correct party (e.g., the claim is asserted against a registered FINRA entity that did in fact employ the broker/former employee), the Code does not authorize early dismissal of the claim, even if, assuming the facts to be true, the claim would not be viable as a matter of law. The respondent party is expected to file an answer specifying the relevant facts and available defenses to the statement of claim within forty-five days of receipt of the statement of claim.[16]

[8] Code R. 13200.
[9] Code R. 13201(a).
[10] Code R. 13201(b).
[11] Code R. 13204.
[12] *Id.*
[13] Code R. 13302.
[14] Code R. 13504(a)(1).
[15] Code R. 13504(6).
[16] Code R. 13303.

If a party fails to provide a timely answer, or if a party answers a claim that alleges specific facts and contentions with a general denial, or fails to include defenses or relevant facts in its answer that were known to it at the time the answer was filed, the arbitrators can bar the answering party from presenting a defense or the omitted defenses or facts at the hearing.[17]

After the parties have filed claims and answers, FINRA will generate a list of potential arbitrators from the Neutral List Selection System, a computer system that creates a randomly generated list that fit the criteria of the case.[18] The number of arbitrators in a case varies depending on the value of the claims asserted. If the claims are $50,000 or less, one arbitrator will be selected to hear the case.[19] If the claims involve more than $50,000 and less than $100,000, one arbitrator would be selected unless the parties agree in writing to three arbitrators.[20] Finally, three arbitrators would constitute the panel if the claims asserted were more than $100,000 or if the claim was for non-monetary damages.[21]

FINRA arbitrators can be considered "non-public" or "public." An arbitrator is considered to be a non-public arbitrator if, within the past five years, he or she was: (a) associated with, or registered through, a broker or dealer; (b) registered under the Commodity Exchange Act;[22] (c) a member of a commodities exchange or registered futures associate; or (d) associated with a person or firm registered under the Commodity Exchange Act.[23] In addition, the non-public arbitrator category also includes any person who is retired from any of those functions, is an attorney, accountant, or other professional who devoted 20% or more of his or her professional work in the last two years to clients engaged in those activities, or an employee of a bank or financial institution that effects transactions in securities and commodities futures.[24] The concept of the "non-public" arbitrator is akin to an industry insider – a person who seemingly knows and understands the securities industry based upon his or her professional background.

By contrast, an arbitrator is considered a public arbitrator if he or she does not, or has not for a total of twenty years or more, engaged in the conduct or activities described above, and is not the spouse or a family member of someone engaged in such activities.[25] A public arbitrator also includes those individuals who are not investment advisors, or who are not attorneys, accountants, or other professionals

17 Code R. 13308.
18 Code R. 13403.
19 Code R. 13401(a).
20 Code R. 13401(b).
21 Code R. 13401(c).
22 7 U.S.C. § 1 et seq. Individuals can trade commodities and futures without being registered with a FINRA member broker-dealer dealer firm. The FINRA Rules seek to capture all "industry-insiders" in its definition of "non-public" arbitrator by including those financial services employees who are not registered broker-dealers but who trade under the Commodity Exchange Act.
23 Code R. 13100(p).
24 *Id.*
25 Code R. 13100(u).

whose firms derived 10% or more of annual revenue or $50,000 of more in annual revenue in the past two years from professional services rendered to persons or entities performing the activities listed above.[26] Finally, public arbitrators exclude individuals who themselves or their spouses or immediate family members are employed by or officers or directors of an organization that is engaged in the securities business.[27] Unlike the non-public arbitrator, the public arbitrator is intended to be someone with no ties to the security industry who can render a decision.

If the arbitration is between FINRA "members," meaning entities that are registered as brokers or dealers, the dispute would be decided by all non-public arbitrators.[28] If the dispute is between individuals or between an individual and his former employer, the arbitrator would be a public arbitrator if there is to be one neutral, or one non-public arbitrator and two public arbitrators if there is to be a three-person panel.[29]

Notably, whether categorized as a public arbitrator or non-public arbitrator, FINRA arbitrators are generally not required to have any formal legal training as a lawyer or judge.[30] The only exception is for FINRA arbitrations involving claims of statutory discrimination, assuming the parties specifically agreed to resolve such claims through the FINRA arbitration process. Arbitrators hearing statutory employment discrimination cases must have additional qualifications to qualify as the single arbitrator or the chairperson of a panel. Specifically, the arbitrator must have a law degree, membership in a state bar, substantial familiarity with employment law, and ten or more years of legal experience, of which at least five years must be in law practice, law school teaching, government enforcement of equal employment opportunity statutes, experience as a judge, mediator or arbitrator, or experience as an equal employment opportunity officer or in-house counsel.[31]

Once the lists of potential arbitrators are generated through the FINRA Neutral List Selection System, the parties have an opportunity to rank and strike the potential arbitrators. FINRA will appoint the highest-ranked available arbitrator after

[26] *Id.*

[27] *Id.*

[28] Code R. 13402.

[29] *Id.* By contrast, in customer disputes, the investor has the option of having an all-public panel. See Customer Code R. 12403. This change was made with the intention of increasing public confidence in the fairness of the dispute resolution process by allowing the investor to determine whether an industry arbitrator would be appropriate to resolve his or her claims. See News Release, SEC Approves FINRA Proposal to give Investors Permanent Option of All Public Arbitration Panels, Feb. 1, 2011 News Release, available at www.finra.org/Newsroom/NewsReleases/2011/P122877.

[30] The requirements for arbitrators are slightly different in customer disputes. In customer disputes, chairpersons must be public arbitrators. Arbitrators are eligible for the chairperson roster if they have completed chairperson training provided by FINRA and: have a law degree and are a member of a bar of at least one jurisdiction and have served as an arbitrator through award on at least two arbitrations administered by a self-regulatory organization in which hearings were held; or have served as an arbitrator through award on at least three arbitrations administered by a self-regulatory organization in which hearings were held. Customer Code R. 12400 (c).

[31] Code R. 13802(c)(3).

combining the ranked arbitrators from the parties' respective lists and eliminating any arbitrator stricken by a party.[32]

After FINRA appoints an arbitrator or a panel of arbitrators, a party can request that the Director of Dispute Resolution remove an arbitrator if it is reasonable to infer, based on information known at the time of the request, that the arbitrator is biased, lacks impartiality, or has a direct or indirect interest in the outcome of the arbitration.[33] The most common source of information that could form the basis of a request for removal of an arbitrator is information contained in the arbitrator's disclosure reports. All arbitrators are required to disclose: (i) any direct or indirect financial or personal interest in the outcome of the arbitration; (ii) any existing or past financial, business, professional, family, social, or other relationships or circumstances with any party, any party's representative, or anyone that may be a witness; (iii) any of the aforementioned relationships or circumstances involving the arbitrator's family members or current business partners or employers; and (iv) any existing or past service as a mediator for any of the parties.[34] An arbitrator is not specifically required to notify the parties that he or she has served as an arbitrator in another dispute with any one of the parties, although the information provided to parties during the rank-and-strike phase includes any of the arbitrator's publicly available awards and any of the arbitrator's current case assignments.

FINRA provides for discovery, but does not allow for standard interrogatories that would require narrative answers or fact finding and it does not allow for depositions except in very limited circumstances.[35] This more limited discovery is intended to expedite arbitrations to hearing and increase efficiency. As with discovery, FINRA hearings lack some of the formalities of a courtroom. Notably, the Code specifies that the arbitrators are not bound by any state or federal rules of evidence.[36]

The arbitrators have wide latitude in conducting the hearing, including discretion as to the order of the presentation of evidence and arguments and the admissibility of evidence. Once the hearing is concluded, the arbitrators are required to issue an award, signed by the majority of the arbitrators on the panel. Without a joint request from all parties, however, the award need not contain any rationale underlying the award.[37] Indeed, our review of all employment awards issued by FINRA in the last four years, discussed in the following sections, revealed that most of the awards do not state *any* rationale for the award.

32 Code R. 13405 and 13406.
33 Code R. 13410.
34 Code R. 13408.
35 Code R. 13506, 13510.
36 Code R. 13604(a).
37 Code R. 13904.

FINRA EMPLOYMENT AWARDS FROM JANUARY 2009 THROUGH DECEMBER 2012

With few detailed and reasoned decisions, and no clear binding precedents, employment arbitration proceedings before FINRA can be very unpredictable. To help understand how litigants have fared in pursuing or defending employment disputes before FINRA, we collected every employment award issued between January 2009 and December 2012.[38]

The decisions were then classified as claims involving: (1) Form U-5;[39] (2) discrimination; (3) bonus or other compensation claims; (4) wrongful termination; (5) non-compete or raiding; (6) promissory note cases; or (7) general dispute. Cases were considered to be a "general dispute" if there was not sufficient information in the award to ascertain the true nature of the claims asserted. Many cases involve claims falling under more than one category.

There are certain limitations to analyzing FINRA decisions. The most significant impediment is the lack of consistent available information. Notably, FINRA does not utilize any uniform coding system when claims are filed. While one employee might describe his or her claim as a wrongful termination claim, others might generally describe the claim as a contract dispute. Likewise, there are no uniform requirements as to how arbitrators describe the claims asserted in a case in their awards. While the Code mandates that such a description be included, without uniform coding at the filing stage and without much detail in the awards, it is difficult to ascertain the true nature of the claims asserted. The lack of detail in the awards always makes it difficult to appreciate who really "won" the case. The award might indicate several claims at issue, the damages sought, and the damages won. The awards often, however, do not include a breakdown of how the damages were allocated between claims or the basis for that award. As such, the publicly available awards do not necessarily provide a clear picture of the litigation.

Excluding the promissory note and general dispute cases,[40] over 80% of cases that were decided by FINRA arbitrators involved Form U-5 and/or bonus compensation

[38] All arbitration awards reviewed and analyzed in this chapter were obtained via FINRA's electronic database. FINRA's arbitration awards are made available at http://finraawardsonline.finra.org/.

[39] The Form U-5 is the "Uniform Termination Notice for Securities Industry Registration." Broker-dealers, investment advisors, or issuers of securities must use this form to terminate the registration of an individual. In other words, when an employee is terminated, his or her registration with that employer must also be terminated. We used the Form U-5 category to include any cases where there was a claim disputing the employer's completion of the Form U-5. These claims generally arise where the employer indicates some performance defect as an explanation for termination and the employee disputes that characterization.

[40] Because the financial institution is generally the claimant in a promissory note case, we excluded promissory note cases from our evaluation of the outcomes of FINRA awards. In addition, we excluded the category of "general dispute" as we used that category to capture all the awards that provided too little information from which to glean the nature of the case.

claims. There were relatively few claims that could be identified as discrimination claims, comprising only 10% of the considered awards.[41]

Because the study focuses on arbitration *awards*, as opposed to filings, this study is not indicative of the number or type of cases *filed* in FINRA within these categories. If many discrimination cases, for example, are settled prior to hearing, it would not be captured in this analysis, which encompasses only those cases that were actually arbitrated to conclusion and an award was rendered.

ANALYSIS OF OUTCOMES OF FINRA AWARDS

Overall, our study reveals that claimants won more cases than they lost. Excluding the promissory note cases and the general dispute cases, as described above, claimants are awarded some of what was requested in about 63% of the cases that went to hearing from January 2009 through December 2012. An award was deemed a "win" for the claimant if the claimant was awarded any portion of what was requested, including a monetary award of any size or expungement[42] without any financial award.

However, simply describing a case as a "win" for a claimant is insufficient to fully understand the award. Claimants sought damages totaling more than $1 million in 169 cases and were awarded damages in that range in only 31 cases.

When looking at the cases classified as bonus or compensation disputes, for example, claimants were deemed the winner in almost 45% of the cases where awards were rendered. The majority of those awards, however, were monetary awards up to $50,000. Based upon our review, we concluded that a claimant is more likely to recover when the amount sought is less than $50,000. As the requested damages increased, the likelihood of success decreased. In addition, claimants were more successful in compensation cases where the claim arose under a specific compensation or commission plan than when the claim was for an alleged discretionary bonus award. For example, when the award revealed that a complaining party alleged that he or she was entitled to a set sum of money under a specifically named compensation plan, the probability of success increased for the claimant, as compared to the more typical bonus case where the claimant asserts a variety of legal theories in an effort to recover a bonus under a "discretionary bonus" plan.

[41] Discrimination cases represented a larger portion of the employment cases before 1999, when the FINRA rules were changed to make arbitration of employment discrimination claims voluntary. When looking at the employment disputes between 1986 and 2008, 17.1% included a claim of statutory discrimination. *Lipsky* et al., supra note 6, at 55.

[42] The term "expungement" refers to modifying information that has been posted on FINRA's Central Registration Depository system, which tracks information about all broker-dealers and associated persons. See FINRA Rule 2130. Under Rule 2130(b)(1)(A)–(C), arbitrators are permitted to order expungement under the following conditions: (A) the claim, allegation, or information is factually impossible or clearly erroneous; (B) the registered person was not involved in the alleged investment-related sales practice violation, forgery, theft, misappropriation, or conversion of funds; or (C) the claim, allegation, or information is false.

Another category of cases that necessitated further analysis were the U-5 cases. While a pure count of wins suggests that claimants secured favorable outcomes in more than 60% of the U-5 cases in this study, the award in many of these cases was expungement, or expungement with a monetary award of under $50,000.

Like bonus cases, claimants in the wrongful termination and discrimination cases sought extensive sums of money as damages for their claims. In fact, within these categories claimants sought over $1 million in fifty-nine cases, although there were only two awards rendered in that range in the four years covered by our study.

In the raiding and non-compete cases, we noted that while injunctive relief was often sought, it was rarely awarded. Rather, FINRA arbitrators were more inclined to resolve the disputes with monetary awards.

In sum, claimants secured some type of favorable result in more than 50% of cases in which an award was issued from 2009 through 2012, but claimants often recovered a small portion of the damages they had originally sought.

PRO SE LITIGANTS

Having looked at the overall success rates of claimants in FINRA arbitrations, we turned to cases in which a party proceeded in arbitration on a pro se basis. There is no requirement in FINRA cases that an individual be represented by an attorney. In fact, the Code specifies that parties may represent themselves or they can be represented by a person who is not an attorney, so long as it would not run afoul to any state laws prohibiting such representation.[43]

Within the last two years, a party appeared pro se in almost 25% of the employment cases in which an award was rendered. Pro se litigants appeared most frequently in cases that we categorized as having U-5 claims, with approximately 44% of the U-5 cases proceeding with a pro se party.

Notably, pro se litigants secured a favorable result in 54% of the cases in which an employment award was issued in 2011 and 2012. In the bonus and/or compensation dispute cases and in the U-5 cases, the largest two categories of arbitration awards identified in our review, pro se claimants recorded a "win" on 50% of their bonus/compensation claims and 56% of their U-5 claims. In other words, we concluded that pro se parties fared almost as well as all other claimants in FINRA employment arbitrations.

There are several factors that may explain the relatively equivalent results between pro se and represented parties in FINRA arbitrations. First, outside of the statutory employment discrimination setting, employment arbitrators at FINRA need not have a legal degree or background. As such, we suspect that pro se claimants are not "outsiders" to a legal proceeding in which everyone else is well-versed in the law. Second, with a much more restricted use of dispositive motion practice in

[43] Code R. 13208.

FINRA, pro se claimants are not vulnerable to dismissal based on legal technicalities or complicated legal arguments that could cause impediments for pro se litigants in court. Finally, as with the limited motion practice, the fact that pro se parties are not restricted by evidentiary rules in the hearing eliminates technical legal arguments that could restrict a party from presenting his or her case without having representation.

A CLOSER LOOK AT STATUTORY DISCRIMINATION CLAIMS

The appropriateness of arbitrating statutory discrimination claims has often been the subject of commentary and analysis. In particular, the debate over whether such arbitration can or should be mandatorily required has spurred extensive discussion. Responding to that debate, in 1999, the SEC approved a proposed rule, which became effective in 2000, to make arbitration of employment discrimination claims under FINRA auspices voluntary.[44] In connection with the amendment to the Code to remove discrimination claims from the mandatory arbitration requirements, the Code was modified to require arbitrators acting as the chairperson in a case involving statutory discrimination claims to have additional qualifications.[45]

With these changes, FINRA arbitrators have decided fewer statutory discrimination claims.[46] Litigants likely have many varying reasons for not electing to arbitrate their statutory discrimination claims, but we have identified several reasons that, in our opinion are likely motivators: the more structured environment in court provides all parties with a better ability to ascertain their respective case, along with their strengths and weaknesses; broader discovery tools (including depositions), but discovery that is based on rules, provides parties with necessary but not extraneous information; and a meaningful opportunity to limit claims in motion practice.

Given the small sample of discrimination cases for which an award was rendered in 2009 through 2012, it is difficult to reach any definitive conclusions regarding the effectiveness of FINRA as a forum for discrimination cases. Further, because many of the discrimination cases also included other claims, it is impractical, given the limited information provided in FINRA award decisions, to evaluate whether discrimination claims were central to the award or even the extent to which any evidence was presented on the claim even if originally pleaded. Nevertheless, our study indicates that claimants recovered an award in approximately 25% of the cases in which discrimination claims were asserted.[47] Because the discrimination cases

44 See *Lipsky* et al., supra note 6, at 55.

45 See *id.*; see also discussion of Code R. 13802 above.

46 See *Lipsky* et al., supra note 6, at 59 (noting that from 1986 through 1999, there were 288 discrimination awards and 50 discrimination awards from 2000 to 2008).

47 By contrast, when evaluating 186 securities industry arbitration decisions from April 1997 to July 31, 2001, claimants prevailed on their claims in 46.2% of the cases. See Michael Delikat & Morris M. Kleiner, *An Empirical Study of Dispute Resolution Mechanisms: Where Do Plaintiffs Better Vindicate Their Rights?*, 58 Dispute Resolution J. (No. 4, Jan. 2004). The awards in the earlier study were rendered prior to the changes in the Code, which allowed discrimination claimants to proceed outside of FINRA arbitration and also theoretically improved the quality of the decisions in

represent a relatively small number of awards rendered during the time period covered by our study, we cannot conclude that claimants faced any bias in prosecuting their statutory discrimination claims notwithstanding that they recovered damages in roughly 25% of the cases in which the issue arose. To the contrary, with the limited use of motion practice available in FINRA arbitration, we suggest that employees are able to present their evidence at a hearing in relatively more cases than before courts that might dismiss claims prior to trial.

THE "REPEAT PLAYER" EFFECT IN FINRA ARBITRATION

The "repeat player" effect of arbitration is an often cited and much discussed potential flaw in the arbitration process. The concept is that because employers have more arbitration experience in the forum as compared to an individual employee who is likely to be appearing in the forum for the first time, there is an inherent benefit to the employer.

We have not identified any evidence that employers fare better than employees in arbitration due to the relative frequency in which they litigate in FINRA. As described above, claimants actually win more than they lose in FINRA arbitrations. Moreover, as compared in other arbitral fora, we suggest that the claimant's bar is relatively small and well known to FINRA arbitrators. The arbitrators who hear the employment disputes are the same arbitrators that also resolve the customer disputes, and allegations of misconduct by the financial institution could actually undermine any perceived benefit the company might receive as the repeat player. In addition, claimants are often represented by the same attorneys who handle employee-side representation in FINRA. In other words, the claimants, like the institutions, are often represented by attorneys who are also experienced FINRA litigators. Repeat involvement in arbitration may be less significant in this industry because FINRA hears cases in approximately 71 different locations in the United States,[48] generally with arbitrators who live and work near the hearing locations, and FINRA arbitrations are often resolved by three-party panels such that there are varying viewpoints weighing in on every case. In any event, we have not found evidence of the repeat-player effect in FINRA arbitrations.[49]

statutory discrimination cases before FINRA given the enhanced arbitrator qualifications. As such, the decline in the number of cases in which claimants prevailed on their statutory discrimination claim reported in this later study may be a reflection of FINRA rule changes rather than any evidence of bias toward claimants.

48 See FINRA Dispute Resolution Regional Offices and Hearing Locations, available at www.finra.org/ArbitrationAndMediation/Contacts/DRRegionalOfficesHearingLocations/.

49 See *Lipsky* et al., supra note 6, at 58, 60 (concluding that while there was a statistically significant difference between the top five and ten users of the FINRA employment arbitration process when compared to the rest of the firms, other factors, such as the size of the claim and the nature of the charge, are likely more influential to the outcome of the case).

CONCLUSION

Analyzing FINRA decisions remains difficult given the lack of detail often provided by the awards, both in terms of the specific nature of the claims asserted and the rationale for the awards rendered. Nevertheless, our study of four years of FINRA employment arbitration awards reveals that claimants are receiving an award in their favor in the majority of the cases that go to hearing, but that those awards are often smaller than the damages sought. We did not find evidence of structural impediments to litigants effectively vindicating their rights. Rather, we suggest that FINRA creates a framework that encourages the imposition of "rough justice" that could often benefit employees pursuing their claims. Specifically, with a Code that provides for limited motion practice to weed out legally defective claims, the limited legal experience amongst the arbitrators, the lack of legal formalities with respect to evidentiary rulings, and the scarcity of awards that provide reasoning for their decisions, arbitrators are seemingly able to issue awards based on their own sense of fairness rather than having those decisions firmly rooted in law.

35

FINRA Arbitration and Employment Disputes

Ariel B. Wolder

A major concern for employment arbitration is that well-resourced repeat-player employers have an advantage over employees that they would not have in litigation. Ariel Roth analyzes over 400 arbitration cases, administered under the auspices of the Financial Industry Regulatory Authority (FINRA) during a 22-month period, to test whether employers fare better than employees, as claimants, respondents, repeat players, or facing an unrepresented party. The arbitration data show a higher employer win-rate over employees when the employer brings the claim and when the employer is a repeat player, regardless of whether the employee has an attorney. Unrepresented employees had a fifty-fifty chance of winning just like their represented counterparts. This study did not control for selection effects.

Arbitration is an important part of employment law and resolving employment disputes. Many organizations provide employers and employees the opportunity to settle their disputes through arbitration. In fact, increasingly employment contracts state that a claim must be arbitrated as opposed to litigated. This chapter analyzes claims brought to arbitration through the Financial Industry Regulatory Authority (FINRA), the nongovernmental, self-regulatory organization for brokers and dealers in the U.S. securities industry.

First, an employer needs to become a member of FINRA and in order to become a member they need to qualify for that status under the FINRA By Laws.[1] A member as defined by FINRA "is a brokerage firm that has been admitted to membership in FINRA, whether or not the membership has been terminated or cancelled. A brokerage firm may be a partnership, corporation or other legal entity."[2]

[1] FINRA By Laws Article III–IV (found at http://finra.complinet.com/en/display/display_main.html?rbid=2403&element_id=4598) (defining an eligible member as "Any registered broker, dealer, municipal securities broker or dealer, or government securities broker or dealer authorized to transact, and whose regular course of business consists in actually transacting, any branch of the investment banking or securities business in the United States, under the laws of the United States, shall be eligible for membership in the Corporation, except such registered brokers, dealers, or municipal securities brokers or dealers, or government securities brokers or dealers which are excluded under the provisions of Section 3").

[2] Available at www.finra.org/ArbitrationAndMediation/FINRADisputeResolution/AdditionalResources/Glossary/.

The member status extends to employees of the financial employer. According to the official terminology used by FINRA, employees may also be known as associated members.[3]

This study is a supplement to the preexisting literature focusing on FINRA employment arbitration.[4] It looks at arbitration cases over a 22-month period, from March 2010 to December 2012, and includes over 400 cases.[5] One piece of important information added to the study is an analysis of claims brought pro se. Customer cases were excluded.

TYPES OF CASES

Based on the facts of the case and the claims brought, the cases were placed into seven categories. Those categories were retaliation (RD) claims, bonus and compensation (BC) claims, wrongful termination (WT) claims, discrimination (DS) claims, U-5 form (U-5) claims, general dispute (GD) claims, and promissory note (PN) claims. Retaliation claims included stealing and conversion of trade secrets. Bonus and compensation claims involved claims brought by employees for unpaid compensation or bonuses as well as anything else related to a bonus or compensation. Wrongful termination claims were claims brought by former employees who believe they were terminated for improper reasons. Discrimination claims were claims brought by current and former employees for discrimination they faced in the workplace. U-5 claims were brought by former employees alleging that the information placed on their U-5 is improper and should be expunged.[6] These forms are of particular importance for the employee to gain employment in the future because a blemished record can prevent that from happening. Promissory notes are signed by employees when they begin work and are due back to the employer when they leave under certain circumstances. Promissory note claims deal with issues when these notes are not repaid. These types of claims were excluded from the study because they did not have much significance on access to justice.[7] Finally, any employment dispute that did not fit into any of the above-listed

3 Associated Members are defined by FINRA as "any person engaged in the investment banking or securities business who is directly or indirectly controlled by a FINRA member, whether or not they are registered or exempt from registration with FINRA. An associated person includes, but is not limited to, every sole proprietor, partner, officer, director, or branch manager of any FINRA member. This individual may also be referred to as a broker." See *Id.*

4 This is in addition to a study by Michael Delikat & Lisa Lupion, Chapter 34 in this volume.

5 All data were compiled from FINRA database containing records of arbitration actions. All can be found at http://finraawardsonline.finra.org/

6 See generally available at www.finra.org/web/groups/industry/@ip/@comp/@regis/documents/appsupportdocs/p015113.pdf (discussing the ways to fill out the U-5 termination form).

7 Promissory note cases are typically brought by high-level executives and deal with different issues than a typical employment grievance. Promissory note cases tend to turn on the contract terms originally negotiated between the high-level employee and the company. They were excluded mainly because of these reasons. See Delikat-Lupion, Chapter 34.

TABLE 35.1 *Breakdown of cases.*

Case type	Percentage of total cases analyzed
BC	16% (66/414 cases analyzed)
WT	20% (83/414 cases analyzed)
DS	6% (25/414 cases analyzed)
U-5	30% (123/414 cases analyzed)
GD	28% (115/414 cases analyzed)

Note: Discrimination claims do not need to be brought to arbitration under FINRA and therefore there were not many discrimination claims arbitrated as compared to other case types. FINRA Rule 10210.

TABLE 35.2 *Employer outcomes: claimant v. respondent.*

Employer position	Percentage won
Employer as claimant: all cases	70 (46/66 Cases)
Employer as respondent: all cases	44 (119/273 Cases)
Employer as claimant: employer contained more than one case in the dataset	79 (26/33 Cases)
Employer as respondent: employer contained more than one case in the dataset	50 (94/187 Cases)
Employer as respondent: employer contained more than 5 cases in the dataset	50 (61/122)

categories was put into the general dispute category, thereby making the general dispute category the broadest. Table 35.1 provides a breakdown of each case type as compared to the total number of cases analyzed.

The total number is higher than 100% because some cases fit two of the categories. For example, it was very common for a wrongful termination claim to be brought in conjunction with a U-5 claim. As can be seen from the table, the most prominent type of case is a U-5 case, followed by general dispute and wrongful termination cases.

EMPLOYER ARBITRATION ADVANTAGES

One area of interest in the study was whether or not the employer has any systematic advantages over the employee in the arbitration of claims. Employers as a general matter have more resources and experience than employees and for that reason, both in arbitration as well as litigation, will fare better on average than the single-event claimant. The question is whether this "repeat player" advantage has a stronger effect on arbitration because the repeat-player employer has a role in selecting the arbitrator. Table 35.2 looks at how many cases employers win as a claimant and how many they win as a respondent, and to see if the employer outcome changes when the employer has more than one case in the dataset. It should be noted that we are examining only outcomes in the following paragraphs; we are not taking into account the strength of the claim, the arguments made or the quality of the representation for either party.

The first data point analyzed was what percentage of the awards in the dataset where the employer was the claimant was favorable to the employer. The employer won these cases approximately 70% of the time. It makes sense that an employer would have a high win rate on these cases because they would only consider bringing claims that they feel are worthwhile. The employer likely has more information on whether or not they have a good claim either from their own prior experience or access to knowledgeable advisors. It is a different story when the employer is the respondent. In that situation the employer wins about 44% of the time.

Some employers were repeat players and some were not. To analyze the repeat-player effect, all cases that included an employer only once in the dataset were removed. Looking only at repeat-player employers, the employers as claimant won approximately 79% of the time, whereas in the broader dataset the win-rate for employer-claimants was 70%.

On the other hand, when the employer was the respondent, the employer win-rate among awards where employers were repeat players was approximately 50%. This means that repeat players are better off when they are respondents by about 6 percentage points. When the analysis included only employers with five or more cases, the percentage won stayed constant at 50%. Therefore, the data show an employer advantage when the employer brings the case but no strong advantage when the employee is the claimant.

PRO SE CLAIMS

Relevant to the issue of the employee's access to justice, we analyzed the outcomes of cases brought by or defended by employees proceeding pro se. A summary of that data is presented in Table 35.3. Out of the cases analyzed, approximately 23% of the

TABLE 35.3 *Pro se claimants win rate by case type(total pro se cases analyzed: 96).*

Case type	Percentage won: brought by a pro se claimant
All pro se claims	54 (50/93 pro se cases)
BC	50 (7/14 BC pro se cases)
GD	63 (15/24 GD pro se cases)
RD	100 (1/1 RD pro se cases)
WT	40 (4/10 WT pro se cases)
U-5	56 (23/41 U-5 pro se cases)

Note: 2 of the 96 claims were settled and 1 resulted in the claimant failing to appear. These cases were removed from the percentage won analysis.

cases involved a pro se employee. About 84% of the time the pro se employee brought the claim as the claimant. It is important to understand the underlying reason for the employee arbitrating pro se. Of all the different case categories, pro se claimants predominate in U-5 cases. By contrast, in discrimination and retaliation cases each, only one pro se employee was represented in the dataset.

The data do not show that there is an employee disadvantage from proceeding pro se. Approximately half the time the pro se employee won their claim, and half of the time the employee lost. Is this because the rate is 50–50 for all employee claims including represented ones.

REPEAT ARBITRATORS

We also looked at cases where arbitrators appeared more than once in the dataset. We wanted to determine if any arbitrator ruled certain ways in similar cases. The absence of published rationales for cases, the incidence of three-arbitrator panels, and the fact arbitrators decided only a few cases in the dataset confounded analysis here. In any event, we could find no pattern among repeat arbitrators. The dataset would need to be expanded over more years. Since most arbitrators are local, it makes the most sense to analyze this data for each specific location separately.

PROPOSED REFORM

After analyzing hundreds of cases through the FINRA database, a few things became apparent. The site was not easily searchable, the decisions were photocopied PDFs, and the reasoning of the arbitrators and/or the full facts of the case were not in the write-up. In order to increase access to justice for employees, fixing these problems is essential. Step one is to make the database easier to search so that an employee or their agent/representative can review similar cases to determine if the employee should move forward. Allowing employees to review cases could decrease employees' need to spend money on counsel, especially for U-5 claims. Step two is to require arbitrators to complete a checklist as the rationale for their award.

Increasing the information on the write-ups will also be extremely helpful. Analysis of case outcomes and facts will bring arbitration on to a more equal playing field. This recommendation is easier said than done because currently the information is provided free of charge. In order to revamp the database, either the cost of accessing the database or the cost of arbitration would likely need to be increased. These two interests need to be balanced against one another because increasing the cost to the employee is another barrier to accessing the justice they deserve.

36

Arbitration as an Employee-Friendly Forum

Zev J. Eigen & David S. Sherwyn

Zev Eigen and David Sherwyn urge that, at a theoretical level, employment arbitration is superior to litigation because claimants are more likely to obtain a hearing irrespective of their income even if unable to attract counsel; and that empirical studies finding outcomes more favorable to employees in litigation than in arbitration are plagued by serious selection-effect problems.

The only comparison courts and policymakers should be making when assessing whether and to what extent arbitration is superior to litigation as a forum for resolving employment claims is how well does arbitration compare to the reality of employment litigation. Court actions are a problematic forum for addressing most employment disputes. The lower the compensation earned by the employee, the less likely it is that litigation provides a meaningful mode of obtaining redress.[1] Similarly, the more likely an employer is a large, institutional repeat player in litigation, the more likely it is that the employer will be able to exploit the legal system to its advantage in the short run, by avoiding paying damages owed in legitimate claims, and in the long run, by selecting only the best cases to pursue in litigation, maximizing the development of employer-friendly precedent.[2]

The primary objective of an employment dispute system should be to maximize the probability that employees who are actually wronged will recover the damages to which they are entitled – not less, not more. At the same time, the system should minimize the risk of employers having to pay out on baseless claims in order to avoid the costs of defending against such claims. This could be characterized as a distributive justice focus. The system must provide redress for those wronged in violation of the laws irrespective of their income, even if such broader access is obtained at the cost of sacrificing higher-value award for some claimants. This is

[1] See, e.g., David S. Sherwyn, J. Bruce Tracey & Zev J. Eigen, *In Defense of Mandatory Arbitration of Employment Disputes: Saving the Baby, Tossing Out the Bath Water, and Constructing a New Sink in the Process*, 2 U. Pa. J. Lab. & Emp. L. 73, 125–37 (1999).

[2] This is not a new conception. It is part of the set of ideas advanced in 1974 in Marc Galanter's famous piece, *Why the "Haves" Come Out Ahead: Speculations on the Limits of Legal Change*, 9 Law & Soc. Rev. 95 (1974).

perhaps in keeping with Samuel Estreicher's criticism of the litigation system as a "Cadillac" available to a limited percentage of employees, as compared to mandatory arbitration, which is like a "Saturn," and thus available to many more, even if it lacks the fancy bells and whistles of the Cadillac.[3] All else being equal, we prefer a dispute-resolution system that has fewer and lower barriers to its utilization, so that even lower-paid employees have a mode of redress.

A second, related factor is that claimants should not be overcompensated beyond the extent of their legitimate claims. Overcompensation can occur by erroneous decisions of the jury or other trier of fact because the costs of defending claims create settlement value irrespective of the merits. Some have suggested that overcompensation actually furthers compliance objectives because any excess deterrent effect on employers pushes them in the right direction in how they treat protected employees. This is an application of what has been termed the "expressive" function of the law.[4]

It is unclear, however, what effect overcompensation will in fact have. In some cases, the excess damages award may be simply be perceived as "noise" in the system. In other cases, it will change underlying behavior but not necessarily in socially desirable ways. Some employers may avoid hiring individuals from protected classes or reducing hiring levels altogether. Other employers may favor employees from protected classes over more qualified employees outside the protected group.

We distinguish here between Type-I and Type-II errors in adjudicating employment rights disputes. Type-I errors, or "false positive" results, are those in which no violation of the law occurs, but the system of adjudication is nonetheless systematically more likely to reward an employee/plaintiff that alleges employer wrongdoing.[5] Type-I errors are not limited to adjudicated cases only. Non-meritorious cases settled because the costs of defense exceed the costs of settlement are Type-1 errors as well. Type-II errors, or "false negative" results, are those in which a violation of the law occurs, but the system of adjudication is nonetheless systematically less likely to compensate an employee/plaintiff injured by employer wrongdoing.

For high-value claims, in both litigation and arbitration, when an employee suffers a wrong, he is likely to be compensated for it – either through settlement or receipt of a favorable award net of costs paid to obtain the result. In litigation, however, there is a greater likelihood of Type-I errors. This is largely due to the costs of discovery and the unpredictability of jury awards. When claimants are represented by counsel, the costs of the discovery will be much higher than when they

3 Samuel Estreicher, *Saturns for Rickshaws: The Stakes in the Debate over Pre-Dispute Employment Arbitration Agreements*, 16 Ohio St. J. on Disp. Resol. 559, 564 (2001).

4 Richard H. McAdams, *A Focal Point Theory of Expressive Law*, 86 Va. L. Rev. 1649–728 (2000).

5 Joseph L. Gastwirth, *Statistical Issues Arising in Equal Employment Litigation*, 36 Jurimetrics J. 353, 368 (1996).

are unrepresented. Prehearing discovery is more generously available in litigation than in arbitration. In litigation, the risk of above-median jury awards coupled with the costs of discovery creates a non-trivial settlement value for claimants irrespective of the merits.

Arbitration is also a superior forum for lower-value claims likely brought by low-wage earners. In both forums, when a plaintiff/employee brings a baseless claim, he is unlikely to recover. However, because arbitration is a more informal process and dispositive motions are less likely to be entertained by the arbitrator, claimants are more likely to be able to proceed pro se and to obtain a hearing on the merits whether or not they can attract counsel. In addition, many of the arbitration policies that we have reviewed provide that the employer will not bring counsel if the employee does not, thus facilitating self-representation by plaintiffs. These employees get "their day" regardless of the merits. From the plaintiff lawyers' standpoint, a contingency fee in arbitration should be more attractive because a resolution can be more quickly obtained with less motion practice.

A key question is whether employment arbitration works as well in practice as theory would suggest. Over the last twenty years, a good deal of commentary has been written critical of employment arbitration.[6] The basic complaints are that pre-dispute arbitration agreements are unfair to employees because they are deprived of a right to a court action in order to be hired or remain employed,[7] arbitrators are more likely to side with employers who are "repeat players,"[8] and arbitrators award lower damages to employees than do juries.[9] Critics also contend that widespread arbitration will prevent the development of the law because arbitration awards tend not to be published.[10] These arguments have lost some of their force because the arbitration community established arbitration protocols requiring procedural fairness[11] and arbitration organizations are beginning to publish awards in a manner not identifying the parties.

6 See e.g., David Schwartz, *Mandatory Arbitration and Fairness*, 84 Notre Dame L. Rev. 1247–368 (2009); Alexander Colvin, *Employment Arbitration: Empirical Findings and Research Needs*, 64 Disp. Resol. J. 6, 6 (2009); Scott Baker, *A Risk-Based Approach to Mandatory Arbitration*, 83 Or. L. Rev. 861, 891 n.2 (2004).

7 See e.g., Alexander Colvin, *Empirical Research on Employment Arbitration: Clarity Amidst the Sound and Fury?*, 11 Emp. Rts. & Emp. Pol'y J. 405, 406 & n. 3 (2007).

8 See e.g., Lisa B. Bingham, *On Repeat Players, Adhesive Contracts, and the Use of Statistics in Judicial Review of Employment Arbitration Awards*, 29 McGeorge L. Rev. 223, 238–39 (1998).

9 Lisa B. Bingham, *Employment Arbitration: The Repeat Player Effect*, 1 Emp. Rts. & Emp. Pol'y J. 189, 199–200 (1997).

10 See, e.g., Equal Employment Opportunity Comm'n, EEOC Policy Statement on Mandatory Binding Arbitration of Employment Discrimination Disputes as a Condition of Employment (EEOC Notice No. 915.002); see *also* Harry T. Edwards, *Where Are We Heading with Mandatory Arbitration of Statutory Claims in Employment?*, 16 Ga. St. U. L. Rev. 293, 297 (1999).

11 See, e.g., Samuel Estreicher and Zev J. Eigen, *The Forum for Adjudication of Employment Disputes*, in Research Handbook on the Economics of Labor and Employment Law (Michael L. Wachter and Cynthia Estlund eds., 2011); Commission on the Future of Worker-Mgmt. Rel., U.S. Dep't of Lab. and U.S. Dep't of Com., Rep. and Recommendations, GPO-CTLG, L1.2-F 98/2 (1994).

A second wave of anti-arbitration scholarship purports to be supported by empirical data. These studies may be divided into three categories: (1) those that compare plaintiff win or loss rates in arbitration to litigation; (2) those that compare damage awards in arbitration to litigation; and (3) those that compare results in arbitration between repeat-player employers and those who appear for the first time as a party in the arbitration database.[12]

There are two basic selection-effect problems that plague these empirical comparisons of arbitration to litigation. The first is the existence of structural differences between arbitration and litigation such as the greater availability of, and receptivity to, motion practice in court actions. Most arbitration policies do not provide for motions to dismiss or summary judgment motions. Such dispositive motions eliminate a huge percentage of meritless cases from the litigation process.[13] So, the universe of arbitration cases includes more cases that employees should lose because they are not screened out in motions. Second, the cost of bringing a case in arbitration is much lower than the cost of bringing a case in court. So, holding constant the merits of a claim, a plaintiff is more likely to bring his claim to arbitration as compared to litigation. Again, more claims with weaker facts and lower-dollar value claims will be systematically more prevalent in the pool of arbitration cases relative to the pool of litigated cases.

These selection-effect problems could be corrected if the adjudicative forum were randomly assigned. It is our understanding that none of the studies purporting to demonstrate that mandatory arbitration is "worse" than litigation employs such a design.

Another set of studies compare arbitration results of employers who have been in more than one arbitration (termed "repeat player" employers) and those who are first-time parties to an employment arbitration. The double repeat player not only has arbitrated before but has arbitrated before the same arbitrator.[14] The findings of these studies are that repeat players prevail more often than non-repeat players and double repeat players are more successful than mere repeat players.[15]

12 See generally, David Sherwyn et al., *Assessing the Case for Employment Arbitration: A New Path for Empirical Research*, 57 Stan. L. Rev. 1557, 1567–78 (2005) (discussing studies); Bingham, *Repeat Player Effect*, supra note 9. See Sherwyn et al., *New Path*, supra note 12, at 1570–72.

13 Laura Beth Nielsen & Robert L. Nelson, *Rights Realized? An Empirical Analysis of Employment Discrimination Litigation as a Claiming System*, 2005 Wis. L. Rev. 663, 681 (2005); Laura Beth Nielsen & Robert L. Nelson, *Scaling the Pyramid: A Sociolegal Model of Employment Discrimination Litigation*, in Handbook of Employment Discrimination Research: Rights and Realities 3–34 (Laura Beth Nielsen and Robert L. Nelson eds., 2008).

14 Colvin refers to this "double repeat player" effect as the "repeat employer-arbitrator" effect. Colvin, supra note 6, at 430.

15 See Bingham, *Repeat Player Effect* supra note 9, at 213 (finding that "[e]mployees dealing with non-repeat player employers recovered on average 48% of what they demanded, while employees dealing with repeat player employers recovered only 11% of what they demanded"); Colvin, supra note 6, at 430 ("Out of the same sample of 836 awards, employees won only fourteen out of the 124 cases (11.3 percent) involving a repeat employer-arbitrator pair, compared to 151 out of the 712 cases (21.2 percent) that did not involve a repeat employer-arbitrator pair, which was a statistically significant difference . . .").

The conclusion either implicitly or expressly stated is that arbitrators favor the employer who can hire them in the future and, even more so, those who hired them in the past.[16]

These studies do not, however, demonstrate arbitrator bias; nor do they support the claim that arbitration is an unfair forum for employees. There are a number of serious difficulties with this work. First, repeat players are labeled repeat players when their second case is in the dataset.[17] Researchers include the first case in the repeat players' win/loss record.[18] This placement begs the question: how did the arbitrator in the first case know the employer would be a repeat player? A second difficulty is that repeat players are likely to be simply a proxy for large employers with many employees some of whom have employment disputes. These employers are likely to do equally well in both litigation and arbitration simply because of returns to experience. They have more experience with employment claims than their adversary. In addition, because employer-promulgated programs usually provide for mediation or peer review as preliminary steps in the process, strong cases for claimants tend to be settled and do not go to hearing.[19]

Arbitration offers no special advantage for such employers over employees that they do not have in litigation unless they have some informational advantage over employees in arbitrator selection, which these studies do not directly address. In any event, with arbitration organizations increasingly requiring prospective arbitrators to disclose prior cases they have had with the parties and the plaintiff employment bar becoming increasingly organized and sophisticated, any claimed advantage has lost its force.

Professor Colvin's chapter in this volume provides the results of his recent study of 449 arbitration cases. The paper provides the mean and median awards for arbitrations pursuant to employer-promulgated polices versus individual negotiated contracts. The value of such comparisons is limited at best. For example, Colvin reports that the claimant win rate for arbitrations under individual contracts is 64.6% versus 24.7% for those under employer-promulgated policies. These cases are, of course, not comparable because employees working under a negotiated contract are likely to be better paid and have access to competent counsel. Moreover, the issues may be different; employees under a negotiated contract may be arbitrating under the more employee-favorable standard of cause versus the more employer-favorable standards of statutory employment law.

Colvin also finds that arbitration motion practice is on the rise and settlements resolve the majority of cases. Moreover, the average duration of arbitrations is only

16 Colvin, supra note 6, at 427.
17 See *id.* at 427–31.
18 *Id.*
19 *Id.*

one year shorter than the average litigation. He further confirms that claimant win rates are lower than in litigation. He then concludes that his results call into question arbitration's claim of providing access to justice for low-wage workers because, while not as bad as litigation, it's too much like litigation.

What remains undisputed, despite these studies, is that employment arbitration retains the following advantages over comparable litigation: arbitration (1) is significantly faster; (2) is easier to navigate for, and in fact has, more pro se claimants; (3) almost always includes in-house dispute resolution programs that resolve cases even quicker and in a less adversarial fashion, and (4) can be and is used by claimants while still working for the employer. We therefore conclude that arbitration is better than litigation. Is it perfect? No! Can it be better? Yes! That's what employee advocates should be focusing on instead of trying to eliminate the better but flawed alternative to litigation.

37

Access to Justice in Employment Arbitration:

A Critical Look

Alexander J.S. Colvin & Kelly Pike

As one of the editors of this book has argued, arbitration of employment disputes through company-promulgated programs can provide a mode of dispute resolution accessible to, and resulting in a hearing for, employees with incomes and claims that generally do not attract private lawyers. However, reviewing data from the files of a leading arbitration provider, Colvin and Pike suggest in this chapter, though without controlling for possible systematic differences between employees obtaining a hearing in arbitration and employees whose claims survive to trial in court, that employment arbitration results in lower average recoveries than obtainable in private litigation and that arbitrators are showing greater receptivity to entertaining dispositive motions.

Alternative dispute resolution (ADR) procedures, including arbitration, mediation, and other related techniques, are often held out as providing improved conflict resolution compared to litigation along such outcome dimensions as efficiency, equity, and participant voice.[1] From an access to justice perspective, the potential advantage of ADR procedures is that they may reduce the cost and time barriers to access that are created by the inefficiencies of the litigation system. Although ADR procedures do not typically provide the elaborate fact determination and review process of litigation, the argument for them is that they provide both enough equity to disputants and greater opportunity to have disputes voiced that overall access to justice is enhanced.

In the employment area, the most prominent ADR innovation in recent years is the use of arbitration to resolve statutory and other employment law claims. Whereas labor arbitration has long been a central dispute resolution mechanism in unionized workplaces, until the 1990s arbitration was rarely used in the nonunion sector. This changed in the wake of a key 1991 Supreme Court decision, *Gilmer v. Interstate/Johnson Lane*,[2] which held for the first time that a statutory employment claim could be subject to arbitration. Over the course of the 1990s and 2000s a series of court decisions reinforced the basic principle that employment law claims could be subject to arbitration

1 For a fuller discussion, see John W. Budd & Alexander J.S. Colvin, *Improved Metrics for Workplace Dispute Resolution: Efficiency, Equity and Voice*, 47 INDUS. RELS. 460 (July 2008).

2 500 U.S. 20 (1991).

and the courts would enforce these arbitration agreements in most circumstances. A controversial feature of employment arbitration is that many procedures are promulgated by employers as a mandatory term and condition of employment, similar to other non-negotiable human resource policies that employers require employees to follow. The difference here is that these employer-promulgated procedures on which employment is conditioned affect the enforcement of statutory employment rights, leading many critics to refer to them as mandatory arbitration procedures.

Going beyond the question of how employment arbitration agreements are entered into, we can ask to what degree employment arbitration provides access to justice for employees. Certainly analysis of employment litigation indicates that it is often not a particularly accessible or employee-friendly forum for employees to seek justice.[3] Some of the strongest policy arguments in favor of employment arbitration have looked to it as a system that could potentially provide more effective access to justice for employees than does the litigation system.[4] Whether employment arbitration can provide this type of enhanced access to justice for employees will depend on the institutional design of the system and how it functions in practice.

Empirical research on employment arbitration has often been hampered by difficulties in gaining access to data on what is primarily a private procedure for dispute resolution. Some recent research has begun to examine larger-scale datasets that focus on employment arbitration cases that are based on employer-promulgated procedures.[5] A major source of data driving this new research is disclosure mandates placed on arbitration service providers under the California Code of Civil Procedure. However, those disclosure requirements only apply to a limited set of information about each arbitration case, providing only a partial picture of the current state of employment arbitration.

By contrast, in this chapter we examine a new, more detailed dataset of employment arbitration cases administered by the American Arbitration Association (AAA),

3 See, for example, Kevin M. Clermont & Stewart J. Schwab, *How Employment Discrimination Plaintiffs Fare in Federal Court* 1(2) J. EMP. LEG. STUD., 429 (July 2004); Kevin M. Clermont & Stewart J. Schwab, *Employment Discrimination Plaintiffs in Federal Court: From Bad to Worse?*, 3(1) HARV. L. & POL'Y REV. 3 (2009); Laura Beth Nielsen, Robert L. Nelson & Ryon Lancaster, *Individual Justice or Collective Legal Mobilization? Employment Discrimination Litigation in the Post Civil Rights United States* 7(2) J. EMP. LEG. STUD. 175 (2010).

4 For example, in an influential 2001 article, Professor Estreicher analogized employment arbitration to a "Saturn" system of justice, referring to the then prominent economy car line produced by General Motors. He contrasted this to the inequality in the employment litigation system, where a few who were successfully able to access it would receive a Cadillac system of justice with high levels of due process, whereas the larger group of employees who were unable to obtain access to the courts would be left with a Rickshaw system providing no effective access to justice for their claims. See Samuel Estreicher, *Saturns for Rickshaws: The Stakes in the Debate over Pre-Dispute Employment Arbitration Agreements*, 16 OHIO ST. J. ON DISP. RESOL. 559, 563–66 (2001). See also: David Sherwyn, Samuel Estreicher & Michael Heise, *Assessing the Case for Employment Arbitration: A New Path for Empirical Research* 57 STAN. L. REV. 1557 (2005).

5 Alexander J.S. Colvin, *An Empirical Study of Employment Arbitration: Case Outcomes and Processes*, 8(1) J. EMP. LEG. STUD. 1 (Mar. 2011).

which includes information on many important aspects of these cases that are not included in the California Code of Civil Procedure disclosure requirements. With the availability of this new data, we are able to look in more detail at the question of whether employment arbitration has become an effective system for providing access to justice for employees.

THE DATA

In this study, we examine data on all employment arbitration cases that were administered by the AAA nationally and that terminated in an award in 2008. We do not include cases that were withdrawn or settled. Overall there were 449 AAA employment arbitration cases that terminated in an award that year. These AAA files are used by the organization as the basis for its publicly available filings on consumer arbitration cases, which include employment arbitration cases based on employer-promulgated procedures, required under California Civil Code provisions[6] regulating arbitration service providers.[7] In addition, we were able to review in detail the full case files for 217 of the employment arbitration cases, which allowed us to investigate a number of aspects of arbitration proceedings not included in the standard AAA data files.

As with any research that focuses on a particular data source, the nature of the data imposes some limitations that need to be recognized. The AAA is the largest provider of employment arbitration services; however, its practices and cases may not be representative of other service providers or especially what is occurring in ad hoc arbitration cases where there is no arbitration service provider administering the case. Notably, the AAA has written its employment arbitration rules to comply with the terms of the Due Process Protocol developed by a number of leading participants in arbitration in the 1990s.[8] For arbitration cases based on employer-promulgated procedures, the AAA policy is that it will not administer cases under procedures that violate its Protocol.[9] For example, it will only administer the case if the employer pays the arbitrator's fee, apart from a minimal filing fee.[10] As a result,

[6] Cal. Civ. Proc. Code §1281.96 (West 2007).

[7] Colvin, supra note 5, at 1, 407–08.

[8] Some other organizations, notably JAMS in the employment arbitration setting, have also adopted similar due process protections. Current JAMS policy is that it will not administer any employment arbitration that does not meet its minimum fairness standards, which parallel the provisions of the due process protocol, unless the arbitration agreement was individually negotiated by the employee or negotiated with the advice of counsel. JAMS Policy on Employment Arbitration Minimum Standards of Procedural Fairness, effective July 15, 2009, accessed at www.jamsadr.com/minimum-employment-standards on May 31, 2013.

[9] See AAA Employment Arbitration Rules and Mediation Procedures, effective Nov. 1, 2009, available at www.adr.org/aaa/ShowProperty?nodeId=/UCM/ADRSTG_004362&revision=latestreleased (accessed Oct. 24, 2013).

[10] Jacquelyn F. Drucker, *The Protocol in Practice: Reflections, Assessments, Issues for Discussion, and Suggested Actions*, 11 Emp. Rts. & Emp. Pol'y J. 345, 351 (2007).

we may be examining a relatively employee-favorable setting for employment arbitration, particularly in comparison to ad hoc arbitrations where there is no administering organization.

WHAT TYPES OF CLAIMS ARE BROUGHT IN EMPLOYMENT ARBITRATION?

We begin by examining the type of claims brought in employment arbitration and the characteristics of the employees who bring them.

Employer-Promulgated versus Negotiated Arbitration

In employer-promulgated arbitration procedures, the employer adopts arbitration as a standard policy governing dispute resolution with its employees. The employees are then presented with the employment arbitration agreement as a standard form adhesive contract that they must accept or reject on a take-it-or-leave-it basis. The arbitration agreement is a mandatory term and condition of employment in the sense that if the prospective employee does not sign it, then the offer of employment will be rescinded, leading to the moniker of mandatory arbitration. However, other employment arbitration cases arise in the context of individually negotiated agreements. In this setting, the prospective employee is individually negotiating the terms and conditions of employment and not simply adhering to standard employment policies of the organizations. The best-known example of this situation is the negotiation of executive-level employment contracts, which include many non-standard features such as specific termination and severance provisions and individualized compensation and benefit packages. In the course of individually negotiating these contracts, some parties enter into arbitration agreements to resolve any contractual or other disputes that may arise in the course of the relationship. Beyond the differences in their contractual origins, there are good reasons to suspect that the characteristics of the employees and the cases they bring under individually negotiated agreements will differ substantially from their counterparts under employer-promulgated procedures. Individually negotiated agreements are likely to involve wealthier, more sophisticated employees who are more likely to be able to retain better legal counsel. The cases they bring are likely to involve claims based on the individual contracts they have negotiated, which may provide an easier basis for proving claims than employment statutes.

Overall in our dataset we find that employer-promulgated procedure cases are more common, comprising 325 of the 449 total cases (72.4%), whereas individual negotiated agreement cases comprise the remaining 124 cases (27.6%). Our dataset includes all cases administered by the AAA in 2008, so this indicates that the largest portion of employment arbitration by this period involved employer-promulgated procedures.

Claims Initiated by Employers

Another important distinction to make in analyzing arbitration cases is between cases involving claims by employees and those involving claims by employers. Although the typical employment case involves an employee plaintiff making a claim such as being wrongfully terminated or discriminated against in the workplace, there are also some cases involving employer claims. Examples of these types of claims include efforts to recover salary advances paid to employees who quit their employment prior to the end of the pay period or claims seeking to recover severance payments where the employee subsequently breaches the terms of the agreement. In our sample, among cases based on employer-promulgated procedures, 28 of 325 (8.6%) involved claims by employer plaintiffs. By contrast, among cases based on individually negotiated agreements, 20 of 124 (16.1%) involve claims by employers. Although they represent only a small segment of total cases, it is important to account for employer-claimant cases since they may have different characteristics from cases brought by employee plaintiffs. Grouping the two categories of cases together could bias estimates of case characteristics and outcomes.

What Kinds of Employees Bring Claims?

We are able to examine a number of individual characteristics of employees who bring claims in employment arbitration. Of the employee claimants in cases based on employer-promulgated procedures, we find that 54.8% were men and 31.8% were managers. Amongst these employee-claimants, 83.1% had salaries of under $100,000 per year.

By contrast, the characteristics of employee-claimants plaintiffs in individually negotiated agreement cases are very different. Of these employee-claimants, 86.4% are male and 65.8% are managers. Only 20.9% made less than $100,000 per year, whereas 62.7% made between $100,000 and $250,000 per year and 16.4% made over $250,000 per year. This indicates that individually negotiated cases predominantly involved higher-level employees compared to the employees in employer-promulgated procedure cases.

What Damages Are Claimed?

The median claim brought by employee-claimants under employer-promulgated procedures is $167,880. There are some relatively large claims, with the top 10% of claims being $2,000,000 or greater. There are relatively few small claims, with the 25th percentile of the distribution of claims falling at $61,984, meaning that three-quarters of the claims are greater than this amount. This is an important comparison point since some past research has suggested that damages of at least

$60,000 are necessary for it to be feasible to proceed to litigation with an employment case.[11] Our results suggest that the claim amounts in arbitration cases based on employer-promulgated procedures are mostly in the range as those that are seen in litigation.

By comparison, the median or typical claim brought by employee-claimants under individually negotiated agreements is $233,427. There are also relatively few small claims in this category, with the 25th percentile of the claim distribution falling at $88,204. Interestingly, although the size of claims brought under negotiated agreements is higher, the median claim is only 39% larger than that for employer-promulgated procedure claims. This may indicate that despite the generally higher salaries of employees covered by individually negotiated agreements, in either instance it requires a reasonably large potential claim for it to be feasible to bring a claim in arbitration.

How Many Cases Involve Statutory Claims?

The leading cases and much of the debate around mandatory employer-promulgated procedures in employment arbitration has focused on cases involving statutory claims.[12] Major employment statutes such as Title VII of the Civil Rights Act embody important public policies, leading to concerns about the resolution of these statutory rights in the private forum of employment arbitration. Some researchers have suggested that in practice this concern is overblown because cases brought in employment arbitration might not involve many statutory issues.[13] The problem with this argument is that it was based on samples that included mostly cases based on individually negotiated agreements, rather than the cases based on employer-promulgated procedures that have been at the center of debates around employment arbitration. By contrast, in our sample, as noted earlier, most of the cases were based on employer-promulgated procedures. We had access to the complete case files for 217 of the employment arbitration cases that were terminated by an award in 2008, which allowed us to determine the nature of the claims being brought in them. We found that 79 out of 146 cases (54.1%) brought by employees under employer-promulgated procedures involved statutory claims. By contrast only 5 out of 44 cases (11.4%) brought by employees based on individual negotiated agreements involved statutory claims.

11 William M. Howard, *Arbitrating Claims of Employment Discrimination*, 50 Disp. Resol. J. 40, 44 (Oct./Nov. 1995).

12 See, e.g., *Gilmer v. Interstate/Johnson Lane*, 500 U.S. 20 (1991); *Circuit City v. Adams* 532 U.S. 105 (2001).

13 Theodore Eisenberg & Elizabeth Hill, *Arbitration and Litigation of Employment Claims: An Empirical Comparison*, 58 Disp. Resol. J. 44–45 (Nov. 2003/Jan. 2004).

How many Cases Involve Ongoing Employment, i.e., Not Post-Termination Disputes?

Very few cases involve ongoing employment relationships as opposed to disputes that arise following termination of the employment relationship. In only 10 out of 195 cases (5.1%) brought by employees where we could identify the employment status of the plaintiff was there a non-termination situation. If anything this may be an upper estimate of the likelihood of arbitration being used in the context of ongoing employment since we do not know whether the employee continued in employment after the closing of the case. Employment arbitration cases mostly involve employees who have been fired or quit and arbitration does not appear primarily to be a mechanism for resolving conflict in existing employment relationships.

How Many Employees are Self-Represented?

Self-representation is an important phenomenon to consider in evaluating whether employment arbitration in practice provides a more accessible dispute resolution system than litigation. In employment litigation, just under a quarter of employee plaintiffs are self-represented.[14] By comparison, in our sample in 102 out of 325 (31.4%) cases based on employer-promulgated procedures the employee represented himself. This suggests a slightly higher self-representation rate than in litigation, though not a large difference. A large majority of employee plaintiffs in both forums are represented by attorneys. In this area we see a very different pattern for cases based on individually negotiated agreements, where only 10 out of 124 (8.1%) of cases involve self-represented employees. This greater likelihood of attorney representation likely reflects the higher salaries and professional or managerial background of employees involved in individually negotiated agreement cases.

HOW DOES THE PROCESS OF EMPLOYMENT ARBITRATION WORK?

How Many Cases Settle?

Our detailed analysis focuses on the files of cases that were resolved through an award, i.e., a final decision by an arbitrator. However, we are able to examine patterns of type of disposition using a broader dataset of all employment and

[14] Nielsen, Nelson & Lancaster supra note 3, at 175, 200, find in a study of employment discrimination cases filed in federal district courts that 14.8% of plaintiffs were pro se throughout litigation and a further 7.7% initially filed pro se but subsequently obtained representation at some point during the proceedings, making a total of 22.5% of cases that were initially filed by pro se plaintiffs.

consumer cases administered by the AAA. This dataset is provided to the public by the AAA under California Code provisions regulating arbitration service providers. Using this dataset, we calculate that of the employment arbitration cases resolved in 2008, 26.9% were disposed of by an award by an arbitrator. Of the remainder, 13.3% were withdrawn by the plaintiff and 59.5%, were settled. This settlement rate is similar to the 58% settlement rate in federal court employment discrimination litigation reported by Nielsen, Nelson, and Lancaster,[15] indicating that in arbitration as in litigation, the predominant mode of resolution is settlement.

Summary Judgment Motions in Employment Arbitration

One procedural step that is likely to influence the selection process of which cases ultimately go to a hearing is summary judgment. Summary judgment motions are widely used in litigation, with defendant employers frequently obtaining dismissals of employment lawsuits.[16] By contrast, arbitrators traditionally disfavored summary judgment motions. The idea was that arbitration is a process that provides a hearing on the merits of the case without complex procedures or legal formalities. Indeed the absence of motion practice with its potential advantages to employers is one of the strong arguments in favor of employment arbitration being an employee-favorable "Saturn" system of dispute resolution in Estreicher's terms.[17] However, in recent years there have been anecdotal suggestions that motion practice and summary judgments have increased in frequency in employment arbitration as the procedure has become dominated by attorneys accustomed to litigation practice.

We were able to examine this issue in our study by examining the number of employment arbitration cases in which defendants filed summary judgment motions with the arbitrator and the numbers that were granted. We were able to do this for the 217 employment arbitration cases for which we were able to review the full case file, including all motions filed. Overall, we found that motions for summary judgment were made in 52 of 217 cases or 23.9% of the time. Of these motions, 25 were granted in full and 12 in part, indicating some degree of success in 37 cases or 17.1% of the time. We found the highest incidence of successful employer motions in cases brought by employees under employer-promulgated procedures, where there were 43 motions for summary judgment out of 149 cases or 28.9% of the time. These motions were fully granted in 21 cases and partially granted in 12 cases, for a total of 33 cases or 22.1% in which there was some degree of success with a summary judgment motion. Although still occurring in a minority of all cases, these results suggest that summary judgment has become a significant

15 *Id.* at 187.

16 Clermont & Schwab, supra note 3, at 429, 432–36.

17 Estreicher, supra note 4, at 563.

element in employment arbitration and that in a number of cases it results in the plaintiff not being able to obtain a hearing on the merits.

How Long Do Cases Take to be Resolved?

One of the key advantages of arbitration in the area of accessibility is that cases take less time to proceed to a hearing than do cases in litigation. In employment litigation, it is typical for cases to take around two years on average to reach trial, whereas in employment arbitration, time to hearing is more typically around one year.[18] The time to hearing in our sample is consistent with these findings. Among employment arbitration cases in 2008 based on employer-promulgated procedures, we found a mean time from initial filing to resolution following a hearing of 366.9 days and a median of 367 days, almost exactly a year. Among cases that settled in this group, we found a mean time from filing to settlement of 278.9 days and a median of 259 days.

How Much are Arbitrator Fees?

We find that the median or typical arbitrator fee in a case is $9,450, whereas the mean or average arbitrator fee is $15,097, indicating a right-skewed distribution with a few relatively large fee amounts. Arbitrator fees in cases involving employer-promulgated procedures are somewhat lower, with a median fee amount of $8,890 and a mean fee amount of $12,264. Under the AAA rules, which we found were being enforced in the cases we reviewed, the employer is required to pay the full amount of these fees.

WHAT ARE THE OUTCOMES OF EMPLOYMENT ARBITRATION?

What is the Employee Win Rate?

Employee win rates in employment arbitration vary substantially depending on the type of case and whether the employee or the employer is the plaintiff. In the cases based on employer-promulgated procedures where the employee is the claimant, employees won 24.7% of the time. This is using a broad definition of an employee win where there was any finding of liability, even if the amount of damages awarded was relatively small compared to the amount claimed. By contrast, in individually negotiated agreement cases where the employee is the claimant, the employee won 64.6% of the time. This may reflect both the greater sophistication and better counsel available to the generally higher-income group of plaintiffs in these cases. It also may be a product of more of these cases being based on contractual claims that are easier to establish than the statutory discrimination claims more common in

[18] Colvin, supra note 5, at 8.

the employer-promulgated procedure cases. Meanwhile, in cases where the claimant is the employer, there is a relatively high success rate for these employer claimants under either employer-promulgated procedures, 57.1%, or individually negotiated agreements, 66.7%.

What Damage Amounts are Awarded?

Damages exhibit a similar pattern of varying with the type and who is the plaintiff. Focusing initially on the category of cases brought by employee-claimants under employer-promulgated procedures, we find that in the 91 cases where the employee won the case, the median or typical damage award was $39,609. The median claim in these cases was $100,000, indicating that successful employees typically received around 40 cents on each dollar sought. The mean or average damage award received by successful employee-claimants was $81,835, with this larger average reflecting a right-skewed distribution with a few relatively large awards among a greater number of more moderate award amounts. These statistics give us a picture of the outcomes in cases that employees won.

It is also useful to consider the overall nature of outcomes including the cases that employees lost as well as those the employee won.[19] From an economic perspective, this is the expected outcome across all cases, including both the probability of success and the amount won if successful. From a legal system perspective, this is also an important measure because it indicates the average likely outcome for a claimant and his or her attorney, if any. We find that the mean or average damages among the 291 cases brought by employee-claimants under employer-promulgated procedures was $19,967.[20]

The patterns of outcomes look very different when we compare different types of cases and categories of plaintiffs. In cases brought by employee claimants under individually negotiated agreements, the median damage award in the 64 cases won by employees was $75,000 and the average damages were $220,736. For all 99 cases in this category, including employee losses, the average damages were $142,465. As expected, employee plaintiffs recover much more in cases under individually negotiated agreements than under employer-promulgated procedures. This reflects larger amounts claimed in the individually negotiated agreement cases with the median damage claim of a successful plaintiff having been $207,000, so that the typical award of $75,000 represents about 36 cents per dollar claimed, close to the rate for employee-claimants under employer-promulgated procedures. The more noteworthy difference is that the greater chance of success for employee plaintiffs under individually negotiated agreements, combined with the larger

19 Colvin, supra note 5, at 20.

20 For this category of cases, including employee losses as well as wins, the median is not a particularly informative statistic because most employees lost their cases.

amounts being claimed and awarded, means that the overall expected outcome across all cases is $142,465. This is 7.1 times as large as the equivalent expected outcome of $19,967 in the employer-promulgated procedure cases. Damage amounts in cases involving employer-claimants are generally smaller, likely reflecting the different nature of claims in these cases, which are often efforts to recover overpayments or pre-payments of compensation to employees.[21] For employer-promulgated procedure cases with employer-claimants, the median or typical damage award to a successful plaintiff was $10,000 and the mean award was $39,002. For individually negotiated agreement cases with employer plaintiffs, the median award to a successful plaintiff was $36,014 and the mean award was $152,947.

How Common are Punitive Damages?

Punitive damages are a relatively uncommon but increasingly important remedy in that they serve to deter egregious behavior by imposing greater sanctions beyond normal compensatory awards In our dataset we were able to examine the written awards in the 217 cases where we reviewed the full case files and determine whether the damage awards included a punitive damage component. Of these cases, 80 resulted in claimants. Punitive damages were awarded in only three such cases – all involving employer-claimants.

How Common are Attorney Fee Awards and How Large are They?

Another important category of damages in employment law cases are attorney fee awards. This is particularly important as an incentive for plaintiff attorneys to take on cases representing employees who often lack the financial resources to retain counsel out of their personal funds. The prospect of recovering attorney fees provides an incentive for lawyers to take on cases where the provable damages may be relatively modest in nature, such as the lost wages of a lower-paid employee. Attorney fees are recoverable under the key employment statutes, notably in Title VII employment discrimination cases. In the 217 cases where we were able to review the full arbitration case file and written award, we were able to identify when attorney fees had been included as part of the award. We found that overall in cases based on employer-promulgated procedures with employee-claimants, attorney fees were awarded in 17 of the 71 cases (24%) in which there was an award of damages. Among cases that involved a discrimination claim, attorney fees were awarded at a higher rate of 9 out of the 16 (56%) of these cases in which the plaintiff prevailed. The median or typical attorney fee award was $51,710 and the mean attorney fee award was $76,467. In cases based on individually negotiated agreements with employee-claimants attorney fees were awarded in 13 of 64 cases (20%) in

[21] A few employer-plaintiff cases also involved fraud claims.

which there was an award of damages. There were only two cases in this group that involved discrimination claims – in both of these attorney fees were awarded. The median attorney fee award was $48,206 and the mean attorney fee award was $43,618. These figures indicate that while attorney fees are only awarded in a minority of cases in employment arbitration, they can be substantial, which may provide some incentive for plaintiff attorneys to take on these cases.

What Factors Predict Win Rates and Damage Awards?

We have seen that win rates and damage awards vary substantially, depending on whether the case is brought by an employee or an employer plaintiff and whether it is based on an employer-promulgated procedure or an individually negotiated agreement. What other factors influence outcomes in employment arbitration? The strongest predictor of outcomes in the data we examined was whether the employee was self-represented or had representation by an attorney. Looking just at cases with employee-claimants under employer-promulgated procedures, we find that self-represented employees won 17% of cases they brought, whereas employees represented by attorneys won 27.9% of cases they brought. In cases that these claimants won, self-represented employees were awarded an average of $11,071 in damages, whereas employees represented by attorneys won an average of $99,217. Taking into account the chance of winning and the likely damages awarded, the overall mean outcome across all cases, including losses, was $27,722 for employees represented by attorneys, but only $1,781 for self-represented employees. These outcomes are strikingly more meager for self-represented employees. Obviously at least part of what accounts for this difference is that attorneys will only be willing to take cases, particularly under contingency fee arrangements, where there is a reasonable prospect of success and sufficiently high potential damages.

There is also a difference in outcomes depending on whether the case involved claims of discrimination, the key category of statutory claims that has been at the center of much of the debate over employment arbitration. We find that in cases brought by employee-claimants under employer-promulgated procedures, employees won only 17.6% of cases involving claims of discrimination compared to 29.0% of cases involving other types of claims. Where successful in these cases, however, employees who won an award received an average of $116,191 in cases involving discrimination claims, but only an average of $63,940 in cases involving other types of claims. Discrimination claims appear harder to prove, but result in larger damage awards where successful.

IMPLICATIONS

What do our results indicate about the degree to which employer-promulgated arbitration is providing a system for effective employee access to justice?

Some aspects of the current employment arbitration system do accord with an enhancement of access to justice. The time it takes to get a hearing, while arguably still too long at around a year, is shorter than typical in the litigation system. The employees bringing claims under employer-promulgated procedures are mostly of lower- to middle-income levels, earning less than $100,000 a year. Employees do win some cases, just under a quarter of all hearings, and recover some substantial damages, albeit the employee win rates and damage amounts are lower than those found in litigation cases that manage to get to the trial stage. Under the AAA's rules, employers are paying the arbitration fees, which at almost $10,000 per case could otherwise be a substantial barrier to access.

In other respects, however, the picture is less encouraging for the vision of a simple, effective, and accessible system. The typical case in employer-promulgated arbitration is a statutory-claim-based case with a fairly substantial damage claim of well over $100,000, which is the type of case we also typically see in litigation. There are relatively few of the smaller claims that are often seen as excluded from accessibility in the litigation system. Although a third of employees are going to arbitration pro se, not much higher than the one-quarter pro se rate seen in employment litigation, the majority of the two-thirds of employees are proceeding in employment arbitration with representation from attorneys. Furthermore, the self-represented employees have lower success rates and receive much smaller damages. What we are seeing is in some ways a replication of the structure of the litigation system, where employees mostly need attorney representation to successfully proceed with claims.

It is also striking as to the degree to which some of the structural features of the litigation system for how cases proceed are replicated in arbitration. Settlement is the predominant mechanism for resolving cases in litigation, with a smaller number of cases being resolved on preliminary motions and relatively few proceeding to a hearing.[22] Settlement is similarly the resolution mechanism for most cases in arbitration.[23] The perennial problem of how to compare litigation and arbitration outcomes, given that different types of cases may proceed to a hearing, is exacerbated because most cases in both systems are resolved through private settlements where we have limited information on the outcomes. It may be that only the stronger cases in litigation end up going to trial, but it could also be that settlement exerts a similar filtering effect on the cases that

[22] Clermont & Schwab, supra note 3, at 440; Nielsen, Nelson & Lancaster, supra note 3, at 184–88.

[23] Nielsen, Nelson & Lancaster, supra note 3, at 184, find in their study of federal court litigation that 50% of cases are resolved in the early stages of proceedings and a further 8% following summary judgment motions, for a total of 58% of cases resolved through settlement. Similarly, Colvin, supra note 5, at 16, finds in a sample of 3,940 employment arbitration cases that 59% were resolved through settlement. In that latter study there was a difference based on representational status, with a 64.8% settlement rate amongst the 75.1% of cases where the employee was represented by an attorney and a 41.8% settlement rate amongst the 24.9% of cases where the employee was self-represented, which combine to yield the overall settlement rate amongst all employment arbitration cases of 59%.

proceed to a hearing in arbitration. One important structural difference that is often pointed to in litigation is the availability of summary judgment motions, which result in many cases being dismissed before trial, often to the defendant employer's advantage.[24] However, we find that summary judgment motions have increasingly become a feature of the employment arbitration process as well, with such motions being brought in a quarter of the cases we examined and most of these motions being successful.

A key aspect of accessibility is whether the costs of proceeding with a case through the system are low enough to be justifiable given the likely outcomes of the case. The criticism of litigation as a Cadillac system is grounded in the idea that this will only be true in the court system for a strong case with a relatively large damage claim. What do our results tell us about this calculation for employment arbitration under employer-promulgated procedures? The key economic outcome statistic is the average award across all cases, including employee losses, so as to include both the chance of winning and the likely damages that will be awarded if successful. For employee plaintiffs bringing cases under employer-promulgated procedures, this amount is just under $20,000.

How does this compare to the cost of bringing a case? Although we do not have direct evidence on this, our results provide some suggestive parameters to work with. The average arbitrator fee in employer-promulgated cases is just over $12,000. It seems reasonable to assume that an attorney would spend at least as much time working on a case as the arbitrator and likely significantly more given the need to engage in preparation and also to conduct pre-hearing discovery. As a result, this can be viewed as a lower bound estimate on the attorney costs for a represented claimant bringing a case. Another suggestive parameter is the size of attorney fees awarded in cases where such fee requests are granted. We find that the typical attorney fee award in employer-promulgated procedure cases is a little over $50,000. Now it is possible that cases in which attorney fees are awarded tend to be ones involving greater complexity and where the burden of such costs on plaintiff employees is higher than usual. For the sake of illustration, let us suppose that average attorney fees across all cases are only half this amount, or $25,000. This would also be plausible relative to the size of arbitrator fees charged in cases. However, it is also higher, by $5,000, than what we find to be the mean damages outcome across all cases (about $20,000 as noted earlier). Put alternatively, in most cases the cost of obtaining representation to proceed with a case in employment arbitration under employer-promulgated procedures will outweigh the potential damages that can be expected to be recovered in these cases. In cases where attorney fees are awarded, this will offset the costs of bringing a claim; however, as we discussed earlier, successful employee

24 Clermont & Schwab, supra note 3, at 433–35.

claimants only receive attorney fee awards in about a quarter of all cases and just over half of cases in which discrimination is alleged. Most often, bringing cases in employment arbitration will not be economically viable and the system will not be readily accessible to employees. This problem is certainly not unique to employment arbitration. Although we are not analyzing litigation data here, one could certainly argue that there are also related barriers for employees in the litigation system given the well-documented limitations of that system for employee plaintiffs and its high costs for bringing claims.

Now this does not mean that there are no economically viable cases in employment arbitration, and indeed our sample consists of cases that employees chose to proceed with and that employee-side plaintiff attorneys chose to represent. Where the attorney identifies the case as involving a relatively strong likelihood of liability and relatively large provable damages then it may make sense to proceed with the case. We do find that most claims are relatively large, over $100,000, supporting this inference. The possibility of attorney fee awards, which are awarded in a quarter of cases, provides a mechanism for some attorneys to get paid; albeit, given that three-quarters of the cases did not produce such an award, its impact on accessibility is somewhat limited. Furthermore, the one-third of employees who proceed pro se are at least getting a hearing and a small chance of winning some moderate amount of damages with relatively little direct costs in the absence of attorney fees or having to contribute to arbitrator fees. Overall, however, our results indicate that attorney representation is the typical scenario for bringing cases in employment arbitration and that the economic calculus will make it difficult for plaintiff attorneys to accept cases unless they offer relatively high damages and strong prospects of winning. In this respect, employment arbitration may be replicating some of the same barriers to access that exist in employment litigation.

38

Collaborative Technology Improves Access to Justice

Michael J. Wolf

Online dispute resolution (ODR) systems have the potential to resolve cases before they end up in court, reducing costs for litigants and easing the burden of court caseloads. We have limited experience with ODR in the United States, but other countries have found ODR to be helpful even for people without attorneys. In this chapter, Michael Wolf describes international ODR systems and reviews studies that show benefits to unrepresented parties. An ODR mediator can use this technology to conduct intake, gather preliminary documents, and engage parties in a structured online negotiation, making ADR more accessible and affordable to low- and moderate-income Americans.

This chapter describes how international courts use online dispute resolution systems (ODR) to reduce costs and enable litigants to more effectively and efficiently resolve disputes. Courts in the United States can similarly use ODR to overcome hurdles that result from not being represented by a lawyer.

One way to lower barriers to access to justice is to resolve disputes outside the traditional court system. For almost three decades, American courts, from federal circuits to small claims, have been adopting ADR systems and empaneling dispute resolution practitioners to help manage court caseloads.[1] Mediation and other types of court-annexed ADR systems generally are *not* best suited to parties who are looking for vindication, want to establish precedent, or want to maximize short-term recovery. Instead, the most satisfied users of ADR systems tend to be litigants who value quick results, privacy, simplicity, relationship retention, outcome compliance,[2] and who want to minimize cost, risk, time, formality, and conflict.[3]

1 See, e.g., *Alternative Dispute Resolution*, LA. STATE COURTS, available at www.flcourts.org/gen_public/adr/index.shtml (last visited July 20, 2014); *Court-Connected Mediation in Ohio*, SUPREME COURT OF OHIO & OHIO JUDICIAL SYS., available at www.sconet.state.oh.us/JCS/disputeResolution/resources/mediation.asp (last visited July 20, 2014). The views in this article represent those of the author and not the views of the Federal Labor Relations Authority or the U.S. government. An expanded version of this chapter was originally published as Michael J. Wolf, *Collaborative Technology Improves Access to Justice*, 15 N.Y.U. J. Legis. & Pub. Pol'y 759 (2012).

2 Outcome compliance describes agreements that are self-enforcing and which parties are most likely to perform.

3 See, generally, Jennifer E. Shack, *Resolution Sys. Inst., Bibliographic Summary of Cost, Pace, and Satisfaction Studies of Court-Related Mediation Programs* (2nd edn., 2007) (cataloging

Courts can play an important role in the ADR process by using collaborative technology that enables parties to choose methods of dispute resolution other than traditional litigation. This approach can help alleviate the overcrowded dockets of courts around the country, and ODR technologies can provide a less legalistic and more intuitive mechanism for resolving disputes.

Courts might find it cost-effective to also adopt an approved set of online workspaces through which empaneled dispute resolution practitioners can leverage ADR and ODR systems to improve access. Associations of dispute resolution practitioners, local bar associations, and even the Legal Services Corporation might share the tasks of testing and recommending preferred online workspaces and helping with licensing and training.

An ODR model similar to court-annexed ODR was adopted on a trial basis in British Columbia, Canada, by Consumer Protection BC[4] – a not-for-profit corporation – and the Property Assessment Appeal Board[5] – which is a quasi-judicial administrative tribunal. To implement their ODR systems, both organizations partnered with Modria,[6] a U.S.-based global company that specializes in ODR systems. These organizations adopted a version of Modria's "Resolution Center," one example of how ODR tools can be used to help individuals resolve claims without going to court. Parties use Resolution Center to fully explain the nature of their disagreement in writing and to upload any files that support their respective positions.[7] Next, the parties engage in highly structured, text-based negotiations through the Resolution Center website. In the background, Modria's algorithmic tools help parties narrow the differences and work toward agreement.[8] If they resolve the matter at this stage, both sides indicate this on the website.[9] Otherwise, the parties can request assistance from a facilitator or mediator.[10] The mediator helps clarify issues, shares interests and information, brainstorms options, and tries to facilitate resolution. Absent agreement, the moving party can explore other options that might include arbitration or small

evaluations of court-related mediation programs), available at http://courtadr.org/files/MedStudyBiblio2ndEd2.pdf.

4 See www.consumerprotectionbc.ca/about-us and available at www.consumerprotectionbc.ca/odr.

5 See www.assessmentappeal.bc.ca/ and www.assessmentappeal.bc.ca/Resources/ODRHelp.aspx.

6 Modria, which stands for Modular Online Dispute Resolution Implementation Assistance, was founded by Colin Rule, formerly the Director of Online Dispute Resolution at eBay and Pay-Pal. Julia Wilkinson, *Colin Rule: From eBay Conflicts to Global Peace Initiatives*, ECOMMERCEBYTES.COM (June 26, 2011), available at www.ecommercebytes.com/cab/abu/y211/m06/abu0289/s05; see also *Our Team*, MODRIA, available at www.modria.com/team/.

7 See *Frequently Asked Questions*, CONSUMER PROT. B.C., available at www.consumerprotectionbc.ca/faqs-2017.

8 See *Resolution Center*, MODRIA, available at www.modria.com/resolution-center/.

9 If either party fails to perform the agreement, it is up to the other party to enforce it. *Frequently Asked Questions*, CONSUMER PROT. B.C., available at www.consumerprotectionbc.ca/faqs-2017.

10 *Id.* It appears that any assistance from the facilitator or mediator is delivered online.

claims court in Consumer Protection BC cases,[11] or adjudication before the Property Assessment Appeal Board.[12]

Mediators in other countries are already using full-service ODR technologies to reduce the need for costly face-to-face mediation sessions.[13] Soon, as a result of the Directive on ADR and Regulation on ODR passed in 2013 by the European Parliament and the Council of the European Union, consumers will experience the benefits of an EU-wide cross-border ODR system slated for implementation in 2015.[14]

Full-service ODR platforms use online tools to collect preliminary information for an ADR process in which a mediator works with the parties, either online or face-to-face, to resolve the dispute. When applied appropriately, these technologies reduce barriers of time, place, cost, and process in a way that can substantially improve access to justice by people without representation by lawyers. For example, Juripax,[15] a Dutch and German ODR service provider that was recently acquired by U.S.-based Modria,[16] and The Mediation Room,[17] developed in the United Kingdom, offer mediators and parties full-service ODR environments. These are leaders among several online service providers that

[11] See *How Does It Work?*, Consumer Prot. B.C., available at www.consumerprotectionbc.ca/faqs-2017.

[12] See available www.assessmentappeal.bc.ca/InformationSheets/ODRGuide.asp.

[13] See infra text accompanying notes 14 et al.

[14] See *Regulation (EU) No 524/2013 of the European Parliament and of The Council of 21 May 2013, on Online Dispute Resolution for Consumer Disputes and Amending Regulation (EC) No 2006/2004 and Directive 2009/22/EC (Regulation on Consumer ODR)*, Off. J. European Union, L 165/1, available at http://eur-lex.europa.eu/LexUriServ/LexUriServ.do?uri=OJ:L:2013:165:0001:0012:EN:PDF. Also see related EU press release in European Commission – Memo/13/193 12/03/2013, available at http://europa.eu/rapid/press-release_MEMO-13–193_en.htm (last visited July 20, 2014); *New legislation on ADR and ODR for consumer disputes adopted in the European Parliament*, available at http://kluwermediationblog.com/2013/04/09/new-legislation-on-adr-and-odr-for-consumer-disputes-adopted-in-the-european-parliament/; New EU Online Dispute Resolution Regulations, available at www.mediate.com/articles/euodr.cfm. For a constructively critical examination of the new EU legislation, see oped posted by The Mediation Room founder Graham Ross, available at www.modria.com/unintended-consequences-new-eu-law-adrodr/ (last visited July 20, 2014). In addition, the United Nations Commission on International Trade Law (UNCITRAL) established "Working Group III" in 2010 to develop a voluntary, global ODR system primarily for low-value, high-volume, cross-border disputes arising from e-commerce. The Working Group III three-part model, which was still being constructed in 2014, begins with negotiation, followed by facilitated settlement, and, if necessary, final and binding decision by a neutral party. Working Group III intends to develop accreditation criteria and guidelines for providers and neutrals, a framework for case resolution, and enforcement protocols. See *Working Group III 2010 to Present: Online Dispute Resolution*, UNCITRAL, available at www.uncitral.org/uncitral/commission/working_groups/3Online_Dispute_Resolution.html (last visited July 20, 2014). American ODR system designers and implementation leaders should pay careful attention to the work of the European Commission and UNCITRAL.

[15] See description of Juripax, available at www.juripax.com/.

[16] *Id.* Also see Modria, supra at note 7.

[17] See www.themediationroom.com.

enable mediators to create secure workspaces and invite parties to join them in the Cloud.[18]

Before its acquisition by Modria, Juripax mediators could select a template for divorce, employment, e-commerce, personal injury, or construction, and then customize the template and online process to a particular case.[19] To begin, each party established an account on a Juripax server, electronically signed an agreement to engage, and used asynchronous tools[20] to conduct intake and other preliminary processes.[21] The mediator then guided the parties through the remainder of the process, using tools within the online environment, external tools such as telephone, online video, audio communication tools, and when appropriate, face-to-face meetings in order to more effectively resolve disputes.

One use of the Juripax platform in the Netherlands was to submit confidential intake data to the mediator in preparation for face-to-face mediation.[22] Research suggests that parties to employment disputes who use this Juripax function were better prepared for mediation, more likely to engage on a more level playing field, felt more empowered to make decisions on their own, engaged in a more resolution-focused mindset, and achieved time and cost savings of up to 30%.[23] Modria is now introducing its next iteration of technology-assisted case resolution in courts and government agencies in several countries.[24] The study concluded that online divorce mediation is a viable alternative to both offline mediation and other more traditional modes of dispute resolution in divorce.[25]

Given the number of unrepresented litigants in American family law courts,[26] full-service ODR platforms should be considered as an alternative to the courtroom and even face-to-face mediation in appropriate family law cases.

18 Most consumers of internet services experience "the Cloud" as applications running on a collection of remote, publicly accessible hardware and software that, according to the National Institute of Standards and Technology, has five essential characteristics: on-demand self-service, broad network access, resource pooling, rapid elasticity, and measured service. Lee Badger et al., *Nat'l Inst. of Standards & Tech., Cloud Computing Synopsis and Recommendations* 2–1 (2012), available at www.nist.gov/customcf/get_pdf.cfm?pub_id=911075 (last visited July 20, 2014).

19 *Features*, JURIPAX, available at www.youtube.com/watch?v=2WE4R-40CQY (last visited Nov. 9, 2015).

20 In contrast to *synchronous* tools, which permit users to jointly engage in real time, *asynchronous* tools permit users to separately engage in their own time. This can significantly increase the speed and reduce the transaction cost of initiating an ODR case.

21 *Id.*

22 *Id.*

23 *Id.* (mentioning these studies, but not citing the authors).

24 See www.sfexaminer.com/silicon-valley-company-starts-to-take-court-disputes-online/ and note 6 supra.

25 *Id.*

26 Judicial Council of Cal., *Statewide Action Plan for Serving Self-Represented Litigants* 11 (2004) (hereinafter Statewide Action Plan), available at www.courts.ca.gov/documents/selfreplitsrept.pdf.

Full-service ODR platforms also allow dispute resolution practitioners to reduce costs and increase efficiency by using online workspaces to initiate the ADR process, collect and exchange party submissions and responses (and fees), upload and securely share case documents, and use threaded discussion tools to engage in joint sessions and virtual caucuses.[27] Dispute resolution practitioners can create a secure folder in the online workspace to store notes, time and billing records, and confidential materials. An experienced practitioner can manage multiple cases in separate, clearly marked online workspaces and increase efficiency by using a common set of templates, calendars, and task lists across all workspaces. Doing so can help minimize the transaction costs of the dispute resolution process and make better use of the practitioner's limited face-to-face time with parties. This can expedite the resolution of disputes and enable unrepresented parties' participation in aspects of the process without physically being in the same place as the practitioner or other parties. In these ways, the online workspace can break down barriers of time, place, cost, and process associated with litigation and ADR processes.

By reducing the transaction cost of engaging in ADR through the effective leveraging of collaborative technologies like Modria's Resolution Center and Juripax's full-service ODR platform, ADR services can become more accessible to low- and moderate-income disputants. In addition, by using online technology to manage the ADR process more efficiently, practitioners can increase their individual caseloads and thereby lower the average cost-per-case. The combination of reduced costs and greater capacity can allow a larger swath of the population to access ADR systems and resolve disputes outside of the traditional

[27] While working at the Federal Mediation and Conciliation Service and at the National Mediation Board, I created secure, online workspaces for parties to use in many types of dispute resolution processes. For example, I worked with representatives of a major rail carrier and its engineers' union, both of which used separate and joint online workspaces hosted by an internet service provider called iMeet Central (formerly called Central Desktop). iMEET CENTRAL, available at www.imeetcentral.com (last visited Nov. 8, 2015). The parties used the online workspace to prepare for critical negotiations over numerous disputes. During the course of two years, the parties used the online workspace between face-to-face meetings, together with collaborative mind mapping software called FreeMind (http://freemind.sourceforge.net/wiki/index.php/Main_Page, last visited July 20, 2014), to post and maintain an ongoing issues list, a running record of issues discussed, documentation of how various issues were resolved, related resource documents, and voluminous side agreements. Within the secure Central Desktop workspace, they used an online forum for secure threaded discussions, an online calendar and task list to manage action items between synchronous dispute resolution sessions, and a "Team" tab to manage contact information and ensure the security of their information. The online workspace included numerous features that created an excellent user experience, such as an auto-notification to authorized users whenever something changed in the workspace. Another example is a major air carrier and its pilots' association that used an online workspace configured to support joint drafting of several settlement agreements and to securely edit settlement agreements. The workspace provided automatic version tracking, maintained a trail of interpretive comments to minimize future disputes, allowed the parties to easily drag-and-drop to upload and download supporting documents, and permitted the parties to work asynchronously from almost anywhere using computers, tablets, and smartphones.

court system. This increase in the number of cases that are satisfactorily resolved outside of the traditional court system will in turn reduce court system caseloads, allowing quicker resolution of those cases that require court resources. This two-pronged approach can increase the number of Americans with meaningful access to justice, whether outside or inside of the traditional court system.

39

Union Representation in Employment Arbitration

Ann C. Hodges

Employers in recent years have promulgated arbitration programs to resolve disputes with their present and former employees. Arbitration may in many cases provide a lower-cost forum than litigation for resolving such disputes. But the problem of representation of Americans of modest incomes still remains. Ann Hodges explores in this chapter whether labor unions can help address that representation gap.

In the 1980s, the Supreme Court began to enforce agreements to arbitrate statutory claims. The cases involved arbitration agreements between businesses of roughly equal bargaining power. Businesses, however, seized on the judicial approval of arbitration of statutory claims and began to include arbitration agreements in contracts of adhesion with employees and consumers. Arbitration agreements deprive the parties of jury trials. They may limit discovery and other procedures available in court. Perhaps most importantly, they may limit the ability to bring a class action suit, rendering many smaller claims uneconomical.[1] With their long history of representing employees in arbitration, unions have an opportunity to provide representation for employees in these cases, enhancing their ability to enforce their legal rights. Private attorneys who represent employees are rarely attracted to individual arbitration cases because of the often limited potential for damages. In contrast, unions can offer representation as a benefit to recruit new employee members. Additionally, representation in arbitration can become part of a campaign against employer-imposed arbitration systems that limit the legal rights of employees. Accordingly, unions should explore cost-effective methods of providing such benefits to enhance workplace justice.

ARBITRATION OF EMPLOYMENT DISPUTES

For the employer, the arbitral forum offers certain advantages over litigation. It is not public, it is faster and often cheaper than litigation, and the case is not heard

[1] See, e.g., *AT&T Mobility LLC v. Concepcion*, 131 S. Ct. 1740 (2011) (overturning on preemption grounds. California law finding class waiver in arbitration agreement was unconscionable); *American Exp. Co. v. Italian Colors Restaurant*, 133 S. Ct. 2304, 2309 (2013) (ruling that high cost of expert testimony of individual claim relative to class action does not render class waiver unenforceable). An expanded version of this chapter was originally published as Ann C. Hodges, *Trilogy Redux: Using Arbitration to Rebuild the Labor Movement*, 98 Minnesota Law Review 1682 (2014).

by a jury, which may be more sympathetic to an employee than a business. There is some evidence that employers who are sued in arbitration more than once benefit as repeat players in the system.[2] Large employers have this advantage in both arbitration and litigation, although it is plausible that arbitrators may favor such employers if viewed as a source of repeat business. Over time, the employee bar has organized, which can balance the employer's repeat-player advantage for employees who use experienced employment lawyers. And, of course, the class action limitations are extremely valuable, particularly where the employees' claims are of low value individually but large value collectively.[3]

Arbitration is not a panacea for employers, however. In litigation, many employment cases are decided in favor of the employer on summary judgment motions, before a trial is held. Motions for summary judgment are rare in arbitration, although evidence indicates their use is increasing.[4] Further, the arbitrator must be paid directly while judges are paid by the taxpayers. And the ability to appeal arbitration decisions is extremely limited, which is beneficial for the winner, but not the loser.[5] Also, because employee lawyers are likely to challenge arbitral agreements, they may result in costly enforcement litigation.[6] Thus there are some counterincentives for employers considering implementation of an arbitration agreement, but the net advantage is for employers.[7]

While most employer processes allow employees to choose their own representative, if only to ensure enforceability of the agreement,[8] Colvin & Pike's study of employment arbitration found that almost a third of employees in employer-

2 Lisa B. Bingham, *On Repeat Players, Adhesive Contracts, and the Use of Statistics in Judicial Review of Employment Arbitration Awards*, 29 McGeorge L. Rev. 223, 234, 238 (1998); Douglas M. Mahony & Hoyt N. Wheeler, *Adjudication of Workplace Disputes*, *in* Labor and Employment Law and Economics 361, 379–80 (Kenneth G. Dau Schmidt et al. eds., 2009).

3 A prime example would be claims under the Fair Labor Standards Act or state wage law for overtime pay or work off the clock.

4 See Alexander J.S. Colvin & Kelly Pike, Chapter 37 in this volume.

5 Michael Z. Green, *Debunking the Myth of Employer Advantage from Using Mandatory Arbitration for Discrimination Claims*, 31 Rutgers L.J. 399, 426 (2000).

6 *Id.* at 422.

7 See Colvin & Pike, supra note 4.

8 The Due Process Protocol, developed by representatives of the National Academy of Arbitrators, the American Arbitration Association, the American Bar Association, the American Civil Liberties Union, the Federal Mediation and Conciliation Service, the National Employment Lawyers' Association, and the Society of Professionals in Dispute Resolution, set forth the elements for a fair arbitration procedure that included employee choice of representatives. See A Due Process Protocol for Mediation and Arbitration of Statutory Disputes Arising Out of the Employment Relationship, available at http://naarb.org/protocol.asp. The American Arbitration Association will decline to administer arbitration if the process "substantially and materially deviates" from the Due Process Protocol. American Arbitration Association, *Employment Arbitration Rules and Mediation Procedures, AAA's Policy on Employment ADR*, available at www.adr.org/aaa/faces/aoe/lee/lee_search/lee_rule/lee_rule_detail?doc=ADRSTG_004366&_afrLoop=1466211146913426&_afrWindowMode=0&_afrWindowId=360ex3z09_198#%40%3F_afrWindowId%3D360ex3z09_198%26_afrLoop%3D1466211146913426%26doc%3DADRSTG_004366%26_afrWindowMode%3D0%26_adf.ctrl-state%3D360ex3z09_254, last visited Nov. 6, 2015.

promulgated arbitration procedures represented themselves.[9] Further, those employees with representation were far less likely than their employer to have an experienced employment lawyer.[10] Representation was an important predictor of both employee win rates and the amount of damages, which increased substantially with representation.[11] Accordingly, representation of employees could help balance the employer advantage in arbitration.

THE ADVANTAGES OF AN ARBITRATION REPRESENTATION PROGRAM

The Benefits of Union Representation

Unions have existing expertise to assist workers in arbitration of legal claims. Most collective bargaining agreements require arbitration for contractual violations, and unions regularly arbitrate these claims. Thus, union lawyers and union representatives have extensive experience in the arbitral forum. While the employer-created arbitration forum will not be identical to labor arbitration, the experience will still be valuable.[12]

In addition, unions can balance the repeat-player effect that benefits employers in employment arbitration. Data on labor arbitration show relatively high union win rates. Union representation across a range of employment arbitrations should yield a pro-employee repeat-player effect or at least counterbalance the pro-employer effect where claimants are not represented by repeat players in the system. Arbitrators would be less likely to seek to curry favor with the employer knowing that unions will make selection decisions about the arbitrator in the future.

The Benefits for Unions

Even if unions can provide effective representation to employees in employer-promulgated arbitration, there must be an incentive for them to do so. That incentive comes in the form of increased potential for union membership, both initially from employees joining the union to obtain representation and in the long term, through building individual representation into majority representation in

9 Colvin & Pike, supra note 4, at 14.

10 *Id.*

11 *Id.* at. See also Laura J. Cooper et al., *ADR in the Workplace* 652 (2005) (citing study showing that the outcome of disputes is similar when both parties are, or neither party is, represented but where only one party has legal representation, the represented party is more likely to win). *But* see Elizabeth Hill, *Due Process at Low Cost: An Empirical Study of Employment Arbitration under the Auspices of the American Arbitration Association*, 18 Ohio St. J. on Disp. Resol. 777, 800 n. 93, 818 (2003) (finding similar win rates in arbitration for low-income employees with and without counsel).

12 See Ariana Levinson, *What the Awards Tell Us about Labor Arbitration of Employment Discrimination Claims*, 46 U. Mich. J.L. Ref. 789 (2013).

collective bargaining units.[13] Union membership has been declining for many years in the private sector. In the public sector, it has remained relatively steady. There are many explanations for the difference but one way that public-sector unions have retained membership, even in states where collective bargaining is illegal or limited, is by providing legal representation.[14]

Representation in arbitration offers an immediate and tangible value to the employee that is also visible to other employees.[15] Unions can use the opportunity provided by representation to inform the employee(s) of other benefits of membership and representation such as union-sponsored training, collective bargaining agreements, "just cause" protection against discharge, and union representation on the job site. Preparation of employee witnesses for arbitration presents a chance for the client to connect with union members and staff and learn more about the union. Motivated employees who demonstrate leadership potential could be trained to organize and educate workers at the workplace or in the particular industry about the union and the benefits of representation. Indeed, particularly skilled individuals might even be trained to represent employees from their workplace in arbitration of similar claims.[16]

While there is always the potential that an employee who loses in arbitration will blame the union, an effective advocate will educate employees about the risks of loss and demonstrate the value of representation, win or lose. Additionally, representation in arbitration can and should be part of a broader campaign to challenge unfair arbitration provisions imposed by employers.[17]

Another benefit to the union of representing workers in arbitration is ensuring enforcement of the law in all workplaces. Research has demonstrated that

[13] In moving to majority representation, unions must be careful that their legal assistance complies with the restrictions of *Stericycle, Inc.*, 357 N.L.R.B. No. 61 (2011), in order to avoid having a union representation election victory overturned under the National Labor Relations Act. *Stericycle* bars union financing of litigation for employees between the filing of a petition for representation and the election unless the financing is a benefit of membership available to all regardless of the election.

[14] See, e.g., National Education Association, available at www.nea.org/home/34718.htm; American Federation of Teachers, available at www.aft.org/about/member-benefits/aft-legal-and-financial-services; Fraternal Order of Police, available at www.foplegal.com/; Los Angeles Police Protective League, available at http://lapd.com/about/services/.

[15] One difficulty with this strategy is that many cases may involve employees who have been terminated, limiting their continued contact with coworkers. See Colvin and Pike, supra note 4, at 13 (showing only 5% of 217 American Arbitration Association cases in 2008 involved employees who were still employed). It is possible, however, that the availability of union representation in arbitration may encourage more employees to bring claims while still employed.

[16] But pp. 561–63 infra. regarding representation by non-lawyers.

[17] See Ann C. Hodges, *Avoiding Legal Seduction: Reinvigorating the Labor Movement to Balance Corporate Power*, 94 MARQ. L. REV. 889, 899–905 (2011) (discussing risks to unions of excessive reliance on legal action).

employees in unionized workplaces are more likely to enforce their rights.[18] To the extent that greater enforcement by union members is due to the absence of fear of retaliation because of the protection of a union contract, offering representation to workers in a nonunion facility may not necessarily increase enforcement. Another part of the explanation, however, is the union's education of workers about their rights and representational support in enforcing them. Thus, education and representation of workers in unorganized workplaces could result in greater enforcement of laws. Such enforcement will benefit unionized workers also, as their employers will not be threatened by nonunion competitors offering lower prices based on avoidance of legal compliance.

BARRIERS TO UNION REPRESENTATION IN ARBITRATION

While there are benefits to unions and unorganized employees from union representation in employer-imposed arbitration, there are also barriers that must be overcome for such a system to provide employees greater access to justice. The three most significant issues are financing the program, bar requirements, and accountability with corresponding potentiality liability for the union. Additionally, it is possible that once unions initiate such a program, employers could respond by limiting representation in arbitration.

Financing and Bar Requirements

The most immediate challenge is creating a financially viable program. If the union can use lay union representatives rather than attorneys, as it often does in contractual arbitration, the program will be cheaper. But bar requirements may limit the use of lay representatives in some jurisdictions. First, I will discuss other aspects of the program related to financing and then turn to the choice of representative.

Public-sector unions maintain legal assistance programs for members and other bargaining unit employees because the value of the protection convinces many employees to join the organization, though few actually have to utilize the services.[19] In the private sector, unions will need to educate employees about the value of representation, for most are unaware of the difficulty of finding legal representation

[18] See, e.g., David Weil, *Employee Rights, Unions and the Implementation of Labor Policies, in* PROCEEDINGS OF THE FORTY-FIFTH ANNUAL MEETING, INDUS. REL. RES. ASS'N 474, 476 (1993) (analyzing various studies and concluding that unions improve enforcement of laws, including the Fair Labor Standards Act, OSHA, MSHA, certain provisions of ERISA, workers' compensation laws and unemployment compensation laws).

[19] For teachers and police officers, the protection not only applies to legal actions when their own job is threatened but also protection when legal action is taken against them by the public. See, e.g., Virginia Education Ass'n, *VEA Legal Services: Your Safety Net*, available at www.veanea.org/home/legal-services.htm, last visited Nov. 6,, 2015; Fraternal Order of Police, *FOP Legal Defense Plan*, available at www.foplegal.com/, last visited Nov. 6, 2015.

for the arbitration of statutory claims and many will also fail to anticipate the need.[20] If the union can only attract members once the need for representation arises, it will be difficult to construct a financially viable program. Additionally, dues must be set at a reasonable rate for employees to feel that they are worth the benefit offered. They will not be sufficient to cover any individual's costs of representation should it be needed, but should be adequate as a group to help defray the cost to the union.

The design of the program will have a significant impact on costs. Unions will need to determine eligibility requirements, the scope of assistance, and the means of providing assistance. Eligibility requirements will affect costs by establishing when members are eligible to receive assistance and by limiting representation to viable claims. The scope of assistance will dramatically influence costs. Unions must decide whether all legal claims are covered or only particular claims, whether actions in court are covered or only claims in arbitration, and what costs are covered, e.g., only the hearing representational costs or costs of discovery, arbitrator fees, and other associated costs.[21] Unions must also decide whether they will represent employees in challenging biased arbitration programs in court, or only in the actual arbitration. Careful consideration of these options will help the union construct a financially viable program.[22]

There are several ways unions can provide representation in arbitration. Unions could use staff attorneys, outside counsel, or trained union representatives, or they could train employees for self-representation.[23] Alternatively, and perhaps most practical, an arbitration program could be a hybrid of these choices. Some complex cases may require counsel while simpler cases could

[20] Many employees have an inflated view of their rights in the nonunion workplace. See Ian H. Eliasoph, *Know Your (Lack of) Rights: Reexamining the Causes and Effects of Phantom Employment Rights*, 12 EMP. RTS. & EMP. POL'Y J. 197 (2008).

[21] See Judith L. Maute, *Pre-paid and Group Legal Services: Thirty Years after the Storm*, 70 FORDHAM L. REV. 915 (2001) (describing the importance of innovative mechanisms of service delivery, preventive lawyering, and high-quality representation in effective group legal services plans).

[22] See, e.g., Employee Benefits Research Institute, Fundamentals of Employee Benefits Plans 393–96 (6th edn., 2009), available at www.ebri.org/pdf/publications/books/fundamentals/2009/39_Legal-Svcs_OTHER-BENS_Funds-2009_EBRI.pdf (describing the types of plans and limitations often built into legal services plans to contain costs). In addition, consultation with public sector unions, such as the National Education Association and its affiliates, and trade organizations such as Group Legal Services Association could be helpful in structuring viable cost-effective plans. See Group Legal Services Association, *Join GLSA* available at http://glsaonline.org/attorneys/attorneys_-join-glsa/ (last visited Nov. 6, 2015).

[23] It is clear that unions can, without violating bar anti-solicitation and unauthorized practice strictures, offer representation to members using staff attorneys or outside counsel. See *United Mine Workers of America, District 12, v. Illinois State Bar Assoc.*, 389 U.S. 217, 225 (1967) (invalidating on First Amendment grounds Illinois State Bar decision that union's employment of staff attorney to represent members in workers' compensation cases was unauthorized practice of law, concluding the minimal risk of harm did not just the constitutional impairment); *Brotherhood of R.R. Trainmen v. Va. State Bar*, 377 U.S. 1, 7–8 (1964) (reaching similar conclusion with respect to referral of members to specific outside lawyers for representation).

be tried by union representatives or trained employees.[24] In particular, a series of cases that would otherwise be a class action might be tried initially by an attorney who could establish a pattern to be followed by union representatives or employees in later cases.

Financing will be affected in several ways by these choices. Staff attorneys will generally be cheaper than outside counsel, although in today's legal market, the union may be able to negotiate favorable fee arrangements with outside counsel.[25] Attorney fees may be available as a remedy in many cases.[26] Fees may be recovered at market rates, even for attorneys who are paid as staff attorneys, which would enable the union to use them to finance arbitration for other employees.[27] To comply with bar requirements, however, recovered fees should be segregated into a separate fund and used only for legal expenses.[28] Using trained union representatives for some or all cases (subject to bar rules against unauthorized practice of law) would be even less expensive than attorneys and training employees for self-representation could be cheaper yet. Even where attorneys are used, trained union representatives could be used as paralegals in preparing the case, reducing the cost of representation and enabling recovery of fees for their services.[29] Where the choice of representative is based on the case, the decisions must be carefully made by an attorney and the criteria for selection

[24] See Levinson, supra note 12, at 847 (finding union representatives effectively represented employees in many statutory discrimination cases in labor arbitration).

[25] For example, consider the case of a nonprofit group that paid an attorney a $10,000 retainer to represent day laborers in their workers' compensation claims. *D.C. Ethics, Op.* 329 (2005) available at www.dcbar.org/bar-resources/legal-ethics/opinions/opinion329.cfm. The attorney kept 10% of the recovery for each claim and paid back the organization with the first $10,000 collected through this process. The ethics committee of the District of Columbia Bar approved the arrangement because the payment to the nonprofit was not contingent on the amount of the recovery and based on the nonprofit's purpose, there was little likelihood that the nonprofit would interfere with the attorney's professional judgment. Additionally, allowing the practice would further the purpose of making legal services more available to underserved populations.

[26] For example, these employment law statutes authorize the award of attorney fees to prevailing plaintiffs. Fair Labor Standards Act of 1938, 29 U.S.C. § 216(b); Title VII of the Civil Rights Act of 1964, 42 U.S.C. § 2000e-5(k); Americans with Disabilities Act of 1990, 42 U.S.C. § 12205; Family Medical Leave Act, 29 U.S.C. § 2617(a)(3).

[27] See, e.g., *Kean v. Stone*, 966 F.2d 119 (3d Cir.1992); *Am. Fed'n of Gov't Employees v. Fed. Labor Relations Auth.*, 944 F.2d 922 (D.C.Cir. 1991); *Curran v. Dep't of Treasury*, 805 F.2d 1406 (9th Cir. 1986); *Raney v. Fed. Bureau of Prisons*, 222 F.3d 927 (Fed. Cir. 2000). See also *Blum v. Stenson*, 465 U.S. 886 (1984) (allowing full recovery of market rate fees to nonprofit legal services organization although attorney was salaried and had no billing rate). There is no guarantee that an arbitrator will award the same amount of fees or apply the same standards as a court would. Both the American Arbitration Association Rules and the Due Process Protocol, however, require fee awards in accordance with applicable law and the Due Process Protocol goes further to say fees should be awarded in the interests of justice. See Jonathan D. Canter, *The Employment Arbitrator and the Pro Se Party*, 57 Disp. Resol. J. 52, 52–54 (2002).

[28] See *Raney v. Fed. Bureau of Prisons*, 222 F.3d 927, 936–37 (Fed. Cir. 2000).

[29] See, e.g., *Spegon v. Catholic Bishop of Chicago*, 175 F.3d 544, 553 (7th Cir. 1999); *Case v. Unified Sch. Dist. No.* 233, 157 F.3d 1243, 1249 (10th Cir. 1998) (stating fees for paralegal services are recoverable and should be determined in the same manner as lawyers' fees).

must be transparent and available to members at joining to avoid subsequent disappointment and legal claims against the union.

Another approach would be to create a separate legal services program, either exclusive to the union or in combination with other social justice organizations such as worker centers or general legal aid programs.[30] Legal services programs might attract attorneys willing to work at lower rates if they are eligible for loan forgiveness,[31] as well as alleviating any bar concerns about sharing legal fees with nonprofit organizations and insuring independence of attorneys.[32]

The other bar requirement that may impact the program is the prohibition on unauthorized practice of law.[33] This regulation may affect attorneys operating outside of their licensed jurisdiction and non-lawyer union representatives. While historically, unions have been able to use non-lawyer union representatives in contractual arbitration without running afoul of unauthorized practice of law strictures,[34] this may change with the growth of arbitration of statutory and other legal claims.[35] An employer's program of arbitration may permit representation of choice, but this does not prevent the bar from intervening to protect consumers from unauthorized legal practice. The bar may be more concerned if the arbitration

30 Some unions have negotiated legal services programs for employees of particular employers. See, e.g., UAW Legal Services Plan, available at www.uawlsp.com/default.asp (last visited Nov. 6, 2015). Unions have more general plans as well. See Union Plus, *Legal Help for Union Families*, www.unionplus.org/legal-aid-services (last visited Nov. 6, 2015) (offering free consultation and discounted legal assistance to members and retirees of participating unions). Worker centers frequently offer legal assistance as well. See, e.g., Jennifer Gordon, *Suburban Sweatshops* 300–02 (2005); Janice Fine, *Worker Centers: Organizing Communities at the Edge of the Dream* 2 (2006).

31 See U.S. Dep't of Ed., *Public Service Loan Forgiveness Program*, available at http://studentaid.ed.gov/repay-loans/forgiveness-cancellation/charts/public-service#what-kinds-of-employment (last visited Nov. 6, 2015).

32 While some state bar associations have eliminated the ban on fee sharing with nonprofit organizations, as have the ABA Model Rules, other states retain limitations on fee-sharing with non-lawyers. See American Bar Ass'n, Model Rules of Prof'l Conduct R. 5.4(a)(4) (2002); *Ark. Bar Assoc. Op.* RO-95–08 (1995); *Pennsylvania Bar Ass'n. Ethics Op.* 93–162 (1993); *Virginia Legal Ethics Comm. Op.* 1744 (2001) (all permitting fee-sharing with nonprofit organizations). *Cf. Rhode Island Ethics Op.* 2000–5 (2000), available at www.courts.ri.gov/AttorneyResources/ethicsadvisorypanel/Opinions/2000-5.pdf#search=Rhode%2520Island%2520Ethics%2520Opinion%25202000%252D5; *Massachusetts Ethics Op.* 97–6 (1997), available at www.massbar.org/publications/ethics-opinions/1990-1999/1997/opinion-no-97-6; *Texas Ethics Op.* 503 (1994), available at www.legalethicstexas.com/Ethics-Resources/Opinions/Opinion-503.aspx (all finding fee-sharing with nonprofit groups unethical).

33 See Kate Levine, Chapter 41.

34 In 2012, the Rhode Island Supreme Court allowed non-lawyer union representatives in contractual labor arbitration, despite the state's ban on unauthorized practice of law. See In *re Town of Little Compton*, 37 A.3d 85 (R.I. 2012). The court noted that some states explicitly allowed the practice while some had not addressed the issue, but the parties could not find any decisions that had prohibited union representatives from arbitrating contractual claims. 37 A.3d at 90–91. See also CAL.CODE CIV. PRO. §1282.4(h) (authorizing non-lawyers to appear in arbitration under collective bargaining agreements).

35 Kristen M. Blankley et al., *Multijurisdictional ADR Practice: Lessons for Litigators*, 11 CARDOZO J. CONFLICT RESOL. 29, 29–31 (2009); Sande L. Buhai, *Act Like a Lawyer, Be Judged Like A Lawyer: The Standard of Care for the Unlicensed Practice of Law*, 2007 UTAH L. REV. 87, 125–26.

is undertaken for compensation in the form of dues, as the program contemplates, as contrasted with representation by a friend, family member or coworker. Further, an employer who fears that union representation in arbitration may lead to unionization of the workforce may be motivated to report such representation to the bar. Uncertainty about the legal protection available to inadequately represented workers may trigger interest in invoking unauthorized practice of law restrictions.

There is no easy answer to the question of when unauthorized practice of law occurs in arbitration. In contrast to labor arbitration cases,[36] the cases that would be covered by the proposed program will largely involve statutory claims. That they take place in the arbitral forum does not automatically place them outside the unauthorized practice of law prohibition. Such determinations depend on the law of the state. One question will be whether the state has allowed representation by either non-lawyers or out-of-state lawyers in arbitration,[37] which will depend on which state's law applies.[38] In some states, out-of-state attorneys may be able to do a few arbitrations per year without engaging in unauthorized practice or may be able to obtain admission *pro hac vice* for purposes of a particular case.[39]

[36] In finding no unauthorized practice of law by a union representative in *Town of Little Compton*, the court relied in part on the fact that labor arbitration focuses on contractual issues and the law of the shop, with which union representatives were as likely to be as familiar as lawyers, if not more so. 37 A.2d at 93.

[37] See Blankley, supra note 35, at 32–33; Buhai, supra note 35, at 125–26; Virginia State Bar, *Virginia UPL Opinion* 206, Feb. 10, 2004, available at www.vsb.org/site/regulation/virginia-upl-opinion-206 (finding a non-lawyer corporate officer could represent the corporation in arbitration because arbitration was not a tribunal under the rules); Virginia State Bar, *Virginia UPL Opinion* 214, Feb. 27, 2009, available at www.vsb.org/site/regulation/upl-opinion-214 (finding that CPA could not represent for compensation party that was not his employer in an arbitration as it was unauthorized practice of law); Virginia State Bar, *Virginia UPL Opinion* 200, Jan. 21, 2001, available at www.vsb.org/site/regulation/virginia-upl-opinion-200 (finding that an attorney licensed in another jurisdiction could represent existing client in arbitration in Virginia as it was incidental to representation of client in home jurisdiction); Cal. Code Civ. Pro. §1282.4 (authorizing appearance by out-of-state attorneys in arbitrations in California upon approval of the arbitrator after compliance with specified notice requirements). See also Minn. Stat. Ann. 481.02(5) (authorizing any bona fide labor organization to give advice to its members on matters arising out of employment).

[38] Blankley, supra note 35, at 38–43. Some arbitrations may take place in a location other than where the dispute arose, and much of the preparation may take place in yet other jurisdictions, *id.*, although that is probably less likely in workplace arbitrations.

[39] See, e.g., La. Sup. Ct. R., XVII, § 13(B)(6) (allowing participation in and preparation for ADR proceeding without admission to the bar *pro hac vice*); S.C. App. Ct. R. 404(g) (allowing participation in up to three ADR proceedings per year without admission *pro hac vice* if the representation is related to representation of clients in a jurisdiction in which the attorney is licensed to practice); Va. Sup. Ct. R. § 1A:4(10)(c) available at www.courts.state.va.us/courts/scv/rulesofcourt.pdf (allowing an out-of-state lawyer to prepare and participate in an ADR proceeding without admission *pro hac vice*); D.C. App. R. 49(c)(12) (excepting from the bar license requirement attorneys participating in no more than five ADR proceedings per year in DC); *N.J. Unauth. Prac. Op.* 28, 3 N.J.L. 2459, 138 N.J.L.J. 1558, 1994 WL 719208 (N.J. Comm. Unauth. Prac.) (allowing an out-of-state attorney to engage in representation in arbitration without admission to the bar in New Jersey); Md. Rules Gov'g Admission to the Bar R. 14(a), available at www.courts.state.md.us/ble/pdfs/baradmissionrules.pdf (allowing admission *pro hac vice* for arbitration).

In the many jurisdictions that have adopted ABA Model Rule 5.5(c)(3), the questions are easier to answer for attorneys; the rule authorizes licensed attorneys to practice law temporarily in an ADR proceeding if their representation in the case is "reasonably related" to their practice in the jurisdiction where they are licensed.[40] For non-attorneys, however, or attorneys in other jurisdictions, the questions are more complex and require a careful evaluation of state law. Modification of bar rules to allow union representatives to represent their members in claims arising out of their employment would resolve this problem.

Union Liability Issues

An arbitration program will be effective in increasing access to justice only if unions provide the best possible representation, which requires some mechanism for accountability. Additionally, unions must factor the risk of liability into their calculation of whether to institute a program. Some cases will be lost, some workers will be unhappy, and some may bring legal action against the union. While setting realistic expectations regarding the outcome of arbitration will help, it is important to consider what legal claims might be available to dissatisfied workers.

If attorneys are used, ethical standards regarding representation will apply, and malpractice claims will lie against the lawyers who fail in their duty. The union can protect against such claims with malpractice insurance. When representing workers in arbitration under collective bargaining agreements, unions are governed by the duty of fair representation, which imposes liability for representation that is arbitrary, discriminatory or in bad faith.[41] The duty of fair representation, however, is a judicially implied corollary of statutory grants of exclusive representation.[42] Thus, the duty may not apply at all when the union is offering representation to employees who may choose instead to represent themselves because they are not a part of a majority bargaining unit. Employees remain free to choose alternative representation.[43]

Whether or not the statutory duty of fair representation is applicable, negligent representation by a union might give rise to a common law claim of negligence.[44]

40 See ABA Model Rule 5.5(c)(3). Twenty-nine states have adopted this provision although six have modified the rule in ways that may alter its application. Blankley, supra note 35, at 47.

41 See *Vaca v. Sipes*, 386 U.S. 171, 190, 195–96 (1967); *Bowen v. U.S. Postal Serv.*, 459 U.S. 212, 223 (1983).

42 *Steele v. Louisville & Nashville Railroad*, 323 U.S. 192, 204 (1944).

43 See, e.g., *Freeman v. Local Union No. 135, Chauffeurs, Teamsters and Helpers*, 746 F.2d 1316, 1321(7th Cir. 1984) (finding no duty of fair representation requiring appeal of unfavorable grievance arbitration award because the "union does not serve as the exclusive agent for the members of the bargaining unit with respect to . . . [that] particular matter . . ."); *Lacy, et al. v. Local 287, UAW*, 102 L.R.R.M. 2847, 2850 (S.D. Ind., 1979) (finding union owed plaintiffs no duty with respect to filing claim for Trade Readjustment Assistance benefits), *aff'd mem.*, 624 F.2d 1106 (7th Cir. 1980).

44 Some courts have addressed the issue of what standard of care applies to provision of what might be characterized as legal services by non-lawyers. See Buhai, supra note 35, at 97. The issue of the standard is intertwined with the question of what is the practice of law. *Id.* In some cases the courts find

Regardless of the standard, however, there is some risk of liability for unions instituting such a program. Clarification of the accountability standard to be applied would encourage development of representation programs.

Employer Responses

Though current employer programs generally allow employees to choose their own representative and dispute resolution providers actively encourage such choice, employers concerned about union representation of their employees might respond by limiting employee representation choices in these unilaterally promulgated programs. To date limits on representation have not been one of the primary problems with arbitration, perhaps because the cost of representation imposes a natural limit. If employees begin to litigate small claims with union representation, however, representation limits may become a part of employer systems.

One way to challenge such limits would be through service providers such as the American Arbitration Association, which have rules allowing representation of choice and also rely on collectively bargained arbitration for business.[45] Because employment arbitration is unilaterally structured, however, employers could choose providers who would accept such limits. In those cases, legal challenges to representation limits would be necessary. Two possibilities for challenge are the National Labor Relations Act (NLRA)'s protection of employee rights to engage in union and concerted activity and the due process and unconscionability bars to enforcement of unilaterally imposed arbitration agreements.

Any explicit limitation on the use of union representatives or attorneys alone would seem to run afoul of the employee's NLRA Section 7 right to engage in union activity.[46] A general limitation on representation would not implicate Section 7, under current NLRA law. The National Labor Relations Board has held that nonunion employees do not have a Section 7 right to co-employee

non-lawyers should be held to the standard of a lawyer. *Id.* A second approach is to apply a general negligence standard without explicitly defining the standard of care. *Id.* at 97–98. Other cases have declined to apply an attorney standard where a layperson is authorized to engage in representation in a legal forum. *Id.* at 99–100. Generally employees have failed in their efforts to hold lay union representatives to the standard of attorneys in handling cases in the contractual grievance and arbitration procedure. See Ellyn Moscowitz & Victor J. Van Bourg, *Carve-Outs and the Privatization of Workers' Compensation in Collective Bargaining Agreements*, 46 Syr. L. Rev. 1, 52 (1995) (discussing cases).

45 See Sarah Rudolph Cole, *Federalization of Consumer Arbitration*, 2013 U. Chi. Legal Forum 271, 290–91 (advocating implementation of reform by arbitration providers in consumer arbitration).

46 29 U.S.C. §§ 157, 158(a)(1) (protecting employee rights to form, join, and assist unions, as well as to engage in concerted activity for mutual aid or protection and prohibiting interference, restraint, or coercion of employees in the exercise of those rights).

representation in interviews that may lead to discipline, although this position has fluctuated across administrations.[47] The rationale of the most recent decision focused on both the need for confidentiality in investigations and the limited assistance that could be provided by coworkers as compared to union representatives. This decision might support an employer's denial of either union representation in the unorganized workplace or representation by co-employees. Professor Lofaso's suggestion of a statutory change in this ruling to enable union or coworker representation in arbitration would alleviate this problem. Alternatively, the NLRB might reach a different result in the more formal arena of arbitration where union representation is common in other workplaces.

A second alternative would be to challenge limitations on representation as violative of due process requirements since representation choice, at least legal representation, would be available in court. Limits on representation could prevent an employee from vindicating statutory rights. Under an unconscionability analysis, such limits also might be void, particularly if they applied only to the employee and not to the employer.[48] Representation by laypersons, however, whether union representatives or fellow employees, is less susceptible to this argument, since it would not be possible in the judicial forum where most statutory claims covered by arbitration agreements would otherwise be tried.

Finally, any limits on representation would provide fuel to a union-led legislative campaign to challenge unfair arbitration. To deprive employees of their right to litigate, confine them to an arbitration procedure designed by the employer, restrict their right to proceed as a class to reduce their costs, and then bar them from using cost-effective representation seems particularly egregious and might spark legislative action to create a fairer system for employees.

47 See *IBM Corp.*, 341 N.L.R.B. 1288 (2004), *overruling Epilepsy Found.*, 331 N.L.R.B. 676 (2000), and rejecting argument that Section 7 gives employees in the nonunion workplace the right to coworker representation in disciplinary investigations, known as *Weingarten* rights, after the case that established the right in the unionized workplace. In *Materials Research Corp.*, 262 N.L.R.B. 1010 (1982), the Board first found that nonunion employees had a right to coworker representation in disciplinary interviews, but that decision was overruled in *Sears, Roebuck & Co.*, 274 N.L.R.B. 230, 232 (1985), which found that the NLRA compels the conclusion that nonunion employees have no *Weingarten* rights. *E. I. DuPont de Nemours*, 289 N.L.R.B. 627, 630–31 (1988) rejected the *Sears* rationale but decided that the proper balancing of employer and employee rights required limiting *Weingarten* rights to unionized employees. Despite court enforcement, 876 F.2d 11 (3d Cir. 1989), the Board revisited the issue in *Epilepsy Foundation*, concluding that nonunion employees have *Weingarten* rights. Court enforcement followed, 268 F.3d 1095 (D.C. Cir. 2001), but in *IBM*, the Board reversed course once again.

48 *Cf. Armendariz v. California Psychcare Services, Inc.*, 24 Cal. 4th 83, 116–17 (2000)(invalidating arbitration agreement as unconscionable where it required employees to arbitrate their claims against the employer but left the employer free to litigate claims against the employee). It is not uncommon, however, for employers to agree not to use counsel if employees do not. Laura J. Cooper et al., *ADR in the Workplace* 703 (3d ed., 2014). Such a provision might pass muster.

CONCLUSION

The reduction in unionization and the advent of compulsory employment arbitration, combined with the Supreme Court's enforcement of virtually any arbitration agreement, have reduced access to justice for employees despite the existence of many laws designed to protect them from abusive employer practices. Unions, which remain the most powerful employee protective organizations despite their loss of membership, could improve access to justice and increase their membership by developing a program of representation in arbitration for union members in unorganized workplaces. A creative, carefully designed program could meet the needs of both unions and employees, improving enforcement of laws to the benefit of all workers.

40

Legal Representation for New York City's Chinese Immigrant Workers

Aaron Halegua

Any sustainable improvement in access to legal services will require intermediate institutions that provide information about legal rights and assistance in securing those rights. Aaron Halegua in this chapter suggests that the growing phenomenon of "worker centers" may play such a role, especially in immigrant communities.

This chapter explores the challenges that keep Chinese immigrant workers from retaining legal counsel and how various organizations work to overcome those obstacles.

BACKGROUND

The largest population of ethnic Chinese in America today is in New York City. As of 2010, New York City was home to 500,434 Chinese, of whom approximately 73% – over 365,000 individuals – is foreign-born.[1] This population is spread across the numerous "Chinatowns" that now exist not only in Manhattan and Flushing, but also in places like Sunset Park, Bensonhurst and Sheepshead Bay in Brooklyn, and Bayside and Elmhurst in Queens.

The U.S. Census Bureau reports that nearly one in five Chinese in New York City is living below the poverty line.[2] Statistics further show that 31% of the Chinese in New York City never obtained a high school diploma.[3] In addition, many Chinese immigrants come to the United States with very limited, if any, ability to speak and understand English and lack significant opportunities to develop these abilities once they arrive and start working.[4] This lack of education, skills, and language ability

1 Asian American Federation, *Asian Americans in New York City: A Decade of Dynamic Change 2000–2010* 6, 45 (Apr. 2012), available at www.aafny.org/pdf/AAF_nyc2010report.pdf (based on data from the 2010 Census and the American Community Survey conducted by the U.S. Census Bureau).

2 U.S. Census Bureau, *Appendices: Poverty Rates for Selected Detailed Race and Hispanic Groups by State and Place: 2007–2011 (ACSBR/11–17)* 13 (Feb. 2013), available at www.census.gov/hhes/www/poverty/publications/Appendix_Tables1–24.pdf.

3 *Asian Americans in New York City*, supra note 1, at 52.

4 *Id.* at 53 (reporting that 63% of the Chinese population in New York City is of limited English proficiency, compared to the 49% average for all Asians in the city).

sharply narrows the employment opportunities available to these immigrants. As a result, not unlike many other immigrants in New York City, the Chinese are often found working in restaurants, nail salons, laundries or dry cleaners, and the construction industry; driving taxis or livery cabs; performing hospitality or other cleaning jobs; and laboring as home health aides. Further, many workers are limited to jobs in which either the boss or at least certain coworkers speak Chinese – and, perhaps even their specific dialect. Therefore, within these industries that often involve long hours and low wages to begin with, many Chinese immigrants find work at smaller, more informal workplaces in which strict adherence to legal or regulatory requirements is less common. Moreover, survey data show that Chinese-owned businesses, along with Korean and Vietnamese ones, pay among the lowest average wages of Asian-owned businesses.[5]

It is widely known that a large number of these smaller, immigrant-owned and -operated businesses that employ Chinese immigrants fail to comply with at least *some* aspects of the federal and state wage-and-hour laws, even if this noncompliance is not always willful.[6] The more common schemes that employers use to profit at workers' expense include not paying the minimum wage or overtime, "shaving time" or failing to pay workers for all hours worked, stealing tips, making illegal deductions from wages, and forcing employees to pay for the tools, uniforms, or other items needed to perform the job. Some businesses pay employees part of their salary by check and part "off the books" – that is, payment in cash without making deductions, paying taxes, or otherwise reporting these payments to the government. These employers that cheat the government are generally more likely to also cheat their workers.

Chinese immigrants rely on a variety of methods to find work in and around New York City. Employment agencies exist throughout the city's Chinatowns that will, for a fee, provide the phone numbers of business owners across the country seeking to fill low-wage jobs. If the employer is satisfied with the initial phone conversation, the worker can be on a bus to a restaurant in another corner of the country later that day.[7] The classified sections of the Chinese-language newspapers are also filled with job opportunities. However, many immigrants rely primarily on family and friends to help them find work. For instance, when a position opens up in a restaurant, it is common for a current employee to recruit a friend or relative. One

[5] *Id.* at 59.

[6] A 2008 survey of 4,387 low-wage workers in Chicago, Los Angeles, and New York found that 68% of respondents experienced at least one pay-related legal violation in the prior week. Violations were more prevalent among immigrant workers and most prevalent among undocumented workers. Annette Bernhardt et al., *Broken Laws, Unprotected Workers: Violations of Employment and Labor Laws in America's Cities* 1–6 (Center for Urban Economic Development at the University of Illinois-Chicago, Nat'l Employment Law Project and UCLA Institute for Research on Labor and Employment, Sept. 2009), available at www.nelp.org/page/-/brokenlaws/BrokenLawsReport2009.pdf?nocdn=1.

[7] See Sam Dolnick, *Many Immigrants' Job Search Starts in Chinatown*, New York Times, Feb. 22, 2011 (describing how Chinatown's employment agencies operate).

effect of this practice is that workers are very hesitant to oppose the employer, such as by questioning their compensation or filing a lawsuit, as it may reflect badly on the employee who helped them to land that job and could even lead to that person's termination.

A salient feature of the Chinese immigrant population in New York City, which significantly affects the labor market and workers' willingness to seek legal assistance, is the considerable number of undocumented immigrants who lack legal authorization to work in the United States. The U.S. Department of Homeland Security estimates that 280,000 undocumented immigrants from China reside in the country.[8] Many of these individuals are smuggled into the country by "snakeheads" who charge a substantial fee. If someone cannot pay the fee prior to departure, this becomes a debt the immigrant must start repaying once in the U.S. Penalties for nonpayment or late repayment may be severe, including acts of physical violence. This reality creates a huge amount of pressure on these workers to ensure that they are always earning enough money not only to survive in the United States, but also to repay these debts. The employment options available to undocumented workers are even narrower than those of other Chinese immigrants, often being limited to those employers who are willing to ignore – or, in some cases, exploit – their lack of status. Yet, however exploitative this situation may be, many employers expect, and undocumented workers feel, an increased sense of gratitude and obligation due to the employers' willingness to hire someone who lacks legal work authorization.

OBSTACLES TO ACCESSING JUSTICE

Before a lawyer can seek redress for a violation of a worker's employment or labor rights, several things must occur. Most significantly, (1) the worker must be aware that she has rights and that they have been violated, (2) the worker must be willing to seek legal recourse for the violation, and (3) a lawyer must be found and persuaded to take the case. As several chapters in this book demonstrate, different individuals face various obstacles at each of these stages. This chapter focuses on the challenges that are most significant for and particular to low-wage immigrant workers, and where relevant, Chinese workers specifically.

Legal Knowledge

Many workplace violations go unaddressed because Chinese immigrant workers, like many immigrant workers, are unaware of their rights. While most workers understand that some wrong has been committed when an employer simply does not pay them, or pays less than the promised wage, far fewer are aware of the other

8 Michael Hoefer et al., *Estimates of the Unauthorized Immigration Population Residing in the United States: January 2011* 4 (U.S. Department of Homeland Security Office of Immigration Statistics, Mar. 2012), available at www.dhs.gov/xlibrary/assets/statistics/publications/ois_ill_pe_2011.pdf.

legal protections governing their employment. Some Chinese immigrants, even if they have heard of the concepts, do not know the "overtime" rule or the current "minimum wage" applicable to them. Far more Chinese immigrants, who often get paid a daily rate by a nail salon or monthly salary by a restaurant, are unclear on how to actually calculate whether these payment schemes run afoul of minimum wage and overtime rules. Not surprisingly, as we move beyond these most basic concepts, workers know less. For instance, workers hardly ever understand the intricacies of the "tipped minimum wage," 1099 versus a W2 tax treatment, or the "spread of hours" premium.[9] Most workers are similarly unaware of the legal protections concerning discrimination, retaliation, harassment, or the right to organize.

Workers' failure to recognize that their rights have been infringed is particularly poignant among undocumented immigrants. Even those who learn about concepts like minimum wage and overtime still assume that any existing workplace protections do not apply to them or that the avenues for combating violations, such as complaining to government agencies or courts, are unavailable to them.[10] In addition, many immigrants who were paid in cash, or partially in cash, believe that various legal protections are no longer applicable to them. This issue frequently arises among workers who have been fired or laid-off and (mistakenly) believe that they are ineligible to receive unemployment benefits. Employers are often happy to perpetuate workers' lack of knowledge or inaccurate beliefs concerning their legal rights. Many employers fail to comply with the legal requirements to hang posters explaining the minimum wage, overtime, or other employee rights at the workplace, or will tell workers that they are not entitled to some legal protection because they are undocumented or were paid in cash.

Willingness to Sue

Chinese immigrant workers commonly fear that an employer will retaliate against them for taking legal action or even inquiring about the appropriateness of an employment practice – and, based on my experience, this fear is well founded.[11] Workers who have not left their exploitative job are afraid of being harassed at the

9 Both federal and New York State wage-and-hour laws allow employers in certain industries to take a "tip credit" of a defined amount against the minimum wage for workers who routinely receive tips (i.e., pay a "tipped minimum wage"). The "spread of hours" premium refers to the requirement in New York State that employees in certain industries be paid an additional hour of pay when their workday exceeds ten hours.

10 In *Hoffman Plastic Compounds Inc. v. NLRB*, 535 U.S. 137, 152 (2002), the Supreme Court held that the backpay remedy under the National Labor Relations Act for retaliation victims is unavailable to those lacking legal authorization to work in the United States. Lower-court decisions have declined to extend this rule to federal and state wage-and-hour laws that require payment for work that has already been performed. See, e.g., *Colon v. Major Pery St. Corp.*, 987 F. Supp. 2d 451, 453 (S.D.N.Y. 2013).

11 See Bernhardt, supra note 6, at 3 (finding that 43% of surveyed workers who complained to their employer experienced some form of retaliation and the majority of the 20% who did not complain despite experiencing a serious work problem feared some form of retaliation by their employer).

workplace or fired. Even workers who seek to sue a *former* employer may reasonably fear retaliation. Indeed, one Long Island nail salon owner who was sued by his employees, years after the plaintiff had left and the trial had ended, actually appeared at the plaintiff's new place of work in Connecticut and told the manager there that the plaintiff lacked work authorization and should be fired.

Many Chinese immigrant workers also worry that filing a lawsuit will cause them to be seen as a "troublemaker" or otherwise "blacklisted," thus narrowing their employment prospects. Although the number of New York City's Chinese restaurants, retail stores, and massage parlors may seem countless, the job opportunities available for an unskilled Chinese immigrant with poor English are surprisingly limited. Some employers own a large number of businesses – thus, filing a lawsuit against one of those places will likely foreclose working at any of them. The fear of being recognized by a potential future employer also makes workers hesitant to have their name on a court document, testify in court, have their picture in a newspaper, or attend a public protest.

Another common concern for workers is that filing a lawsuit will bring legal troubles upon themselves including, in the case of undocumented workers, a risk of deportation. They worry that either the public nature of a lawsuit or a direct phone call from an angry employer to the immigration authorities will lead to the discovery of their whereabouts and eventual deportation. Aside from deportation, Chinese immigrants also fear that other legal improprieties may become known, such as a failure to report their full income on their tax returns or applications for government benefits. This fear too is well founded. Employers in wage-and-hour cases regularly seek discovery of the workers' immigration status, tax filings, and applications for government benefits in an effort to scare the plaintiffs.[12] Workers weigh these risks in deciding whether or not a lawsuit is worthwhile.

And, of course, nobody likes to be in a lawsuit. For workers who are only paid for the hours or days that they work, the time needed to meet with lawyers, attend a deposition, and participate in a trial carry real economic costs. Moreover, being deposed by a lawyer while your former employer sits across the table or testifying in open court can cause a significant amount of anxiety for anyone, and especially someone not familiar with the legal or court system.

Finding a Willing Lawyer

A good number of attorneys in New York City are now willing to take wage-and-hour cases – namely, claims for unpaid wages, minimum wage and overtime violations,

[12] District courts within the Second Circuit have, for the most part, denied such discovery requests by employers. See *Solis v. Cindy's Total Care, Inc.*, No. 10 Civ. 7242, 2011 WL 5170009, at *1 (S.D.N.Y. Oct. 31, 2011) (holding immigration status irrelevant to wage-and-hour claims); *Melendez v. Primavera Meats, Inc.*, 270 F.R.D. 143, 144 (E.D.N.Y. 2010) (granting plaintiffs' motion for a protective order barring defendants from obtaining their income tax returns).

illegal wage deductions, or the misappropriation of tips – on a contingency basis. These cases are attractive because the violations are relatively straightforward to prove, particularly as the employer bears the burden of maintaining and producing accurate time and pay records, and "double damages," attorneys' fees, and costs are available to prevailing plaintiffs. If a worker's claim, even if for a small amount of damages, will allow for the filing of a collective or class action on behalf of a larger group of workers, many law firms are willing to take such cases. However, there are also attorneys – mostly in small firms or solo practitioners, with varying degrees of experience – willing to represent a single worker or small group of workers. Even if the amount of an individual claim is only in the range of $5,000 or $10,000, several attorneys report that they are willing to attempt to negotiate a resolution of the claim but perhaps not to file a lawsuit if those efforts fail. Some plaintiffs' lawyers complain that the wage-and-hour field has become so "saturated" with attorneys that it is now difficult to sustain a practice focused on low-wage workers, which generally requires a high volume of small cases. Indeed, New York City's Chinese-language newspapers are filled with attorney advertisements encouraging workers who were not paid overtime to call them, even reminding workers that their immigration status is irrelevant and that no payment to the firm is required unless the worker collects.[13]

Despite the seemingly ample number of attorneys interested in wage-and-hour work, the difficulty of actually collecting money from a defendant may still be a powerful deterrent from representing certain low-wage workers. Countless small, family-owned businesses have managed to avoid paying court judgments by engaging in a variety of tactics, including declaring bankruptcy, transferring ownership of the business, or closing the business (and sometimes reopening it under a different name and with different nominal owners). Although employers are personally liable under federal and state labor laws, an employer seeking to evade liability may file for personal bankruptcy or find other ways to shelter his or her assets.[14] Private attorneys are very attuned to this risk and may hesitate to take a case where they suspect that an employer will close the business rather than pay the wages owed. Moreover, it is not uncommon for workers to wait until their employer has shut down the business or fled before contacting a lawyer – strong signals that collection will be extremely difficult.

Outside of the wage-and-hour area, finding competent counsel willing to represent an individual worker is far more difficult. For instance, very few private attorneys will represent a worker appealing the denial of unemployment benefits, for which the attorney is prohibited from collecting a fee unless the client prevails

13 It should be noted that finding a lawyer, particularly one who can accommodate a Chinese-speaking client, can be far more difficult for those working far from New York City or any other Chinatown.

14 See Urban Justice Center et al., *Empty Judgments: The Wage Collection Crisis in New York* 4–25 (Feb. 24, 2015), available at www.sweatny.org/report (identifying $125 million in court judgments and New York State Department of Labor orders that remain unpaid and describing the specific tactics used by employers to evade enforcement).

and the New York State Unemployment Insurance Appeal Board has approved the fee.[15] Attorneys are also less willing to take on discrimination or harassment cases, in which the facts are generally a bit messier, settlement is more difficult, and proving liability is more complex than in wage-and-hour cases. Further, even if discrimination is proved, the "lost wages" for a low-wage worker is likely to be small and the "double damages" that are the norm in wage-and-hour cases are not available.

Finding a lawyer is, of course, not the end of the "access to justice" story. Quality matters, and the quality of the representation provided by law firms varies greatly. For many small firms trying to stay afloat, there are strong incentives to accept a quick settlement for a fraction of what the client is owed rather than continue spending time and money to litigate a case. Indeed, defense attorneys will attest that it is generally far easier to settle a case in which their opposing counsel is a solo practitioner than a nonprofit organization. There are also stories of firms who cross ethical lines in dealing with their immigrant clients. For instance, one immigrant worker has alleged that a law firm that advertises its wage-and-hour services to Chinese and Korean clients allowed him to sign a retainer without explaining the firm's fee structure, failed to provide him with a copy of the retainer agreement, settled his claims without his permission, and then took 50% of the settlement amount – far above the customary one-third retained by most private attorneys.[16]

INTERMEDIATE INSTITUTIONS

Various organizations in New York City, what I call "intermediate institutions," help workers in exploitative situations to find quality attorneys. For instance, labor unions might reach out to underpaid workers in a particular industry that they seek to organize and help those workers litigate wage claims. Religious organizations or the offices of elected officials may refer people to legal-service providers. This section focuses on two other types of institutions that are important to the Chinese immigrant community in New York City: worker centers and social service organizations.

Worker Centers

In recent years, the number of worker centers in New York City has steadily increased, and thirty-seven of the country's 214 such organizations are located here.[17] These institutions are often defined by the ways in which they differ from traditional labor unions. Some worker centers grew out of dissatisfaction with

15 See Yin, Chapter 7 in this volume.

16 Complaint to Disciplinary Committee for the New York State Supreme Court, Appellate Division, First Judicial Department, dated Mar. 14, 2014 (on file with author); Interview of labor rights attorney, MinKwon Center, Flushing, N.Y. (May 21, 2014).

17 Ruth Milkman, *Introduction: Toward a New Labor Movement? Organizing New York City's Precariat*, *in* New Labor in New York: Precarious Workers and the Future of the Labor Movement 2 (Ruth Milkman & Ed Ott eds., 2014). Worker centers have attracted a fair deal of academic attention in

existing unions; however, most were formed to organize in those industries in which unions never had a presence (such as domestic work) or where they ceased to be present (like the restaurant industry). Other worker centers began by advocating for independent contractors to whom many labor and employment law protections do not apply (such as freelancers or taxi and livery cab drivers). Milkman notes that a common feature of these workers is that they belong to the "precariat" – that is, a class of precarious workers in industries with less regulation and labor protections, or where enforcement of those protections is weak.[18]

In terms of structure, Janice Fine describes worker centers as "the inverse of prototypical American unions [,]" as "[t]hey are non-bureaucratic, grass-roots organizations with small budgets, loose membership structures, [and] improvisational cultures and strategies ..."[19] While unions rely almost exclusively on membership dues, worker centers also draw largely on foundation support and other funding sources. These centers generally seek to organize and empower workers through various campaigns, which may be aimed at obtaining concessions from a particular employer, improving standards in an industry, influencing a government agency, or achieving legislative reform. Worker centers employ a variety of tactics, including targeted research and fact-gathering, media outreach, building alliances with politicians or other community groups, public actions such as pickets, protests, and boycotts, as well as litigation.[20] And, in New York alone, worker centers can point to numerous, significant litigation and legislative victories. For example, the Domestic Workers' Bill of Rights and Wage Theft Prevention Act, both passed by the New York Legislature in 2010, began as worker center campaigns.[21]

In New York City, there are two worker centers that specifically seek to provide assistance to Chinese immigrants who have been victims of illegal labor practices: the Chinese Staff & Workers' Association and the MinKwon Center.

Chinese Staff & Workers' Association

Chinese Staff & Workers' Association (CSWA) is one of New York City's oldest and most well-known worker centers, and the most relevant to the Chinese immigrant community. The organization was founded in 1979 by a group of Chinese restaurant workers, largely in response to their frustration with the mainstream union that failed to enforce contracts or address labor code violations in the Chinese restaurants where it represented the employees.[22] However, as noted on its website, CSWA's mission has evolved into "bringing together workers across all trades to fight for our

the past decade. See, e.g., Jennifer Gordon, *Suburban Sweatshops: The Fight for Immigrant Rights* (2007); Janice Fine, *Worker Centers: Organizing Communities at the Edge of the Dream* (2006).

18 Milkman, supra note 17, at 2.

19 Janice Fine, *A Marriage Made in Heaven? Mismatches and Misunderstandings between Worker Centres and Unions*, 45(2) Br, J. Indus. Rels. 335, 341 (2007).

20 Milkman, supra note 17, at 16.

21 *Id.* at 21.

22 See Peter Kwong, *The New Chinatown* 141–42, 148 (1996).

basic legal and human rights in the workplace as well as in the community-at-large."[23] This includes organizing *all* working people, including those in sectors that are excluded from the federal labor laws and those that traditional unions have ignored. Today, CSWA's membership includes nail salon workers, domestic workers, "black car" drivers, garment workers, and many others.

CSWA has engaged in numerous campaigns over the years, both on workplace issues and in other areas. At present, its website lists campaigns addressing working conditions in the service industry, female workers' rights, community displacement, and federal immigration policy. While this chapter focuses primarily on litigation, this is just one of a host of means employed by CSWA to achieve its objectives. For example, the campaign to combat sweatshop conditions includes sponsoring legislation to make it easier for workers to collect judgments, protests outside of exploitative businesses, press conferences, litigation, and providing social services or hosting recreational events to organize more workers.[24]

CSWA sees litigation not simply as a means to remedy the violations suffered by the plaintiffs in a particular case, but as a tool for empowering the plaintiffs and other workers, attracting media attention, and otherwise furthering the goals of a given campaign. Accordingly, CSWA does not assist each and every person who seeks legal advice or wants help finding a lawyer. Instead, it marshals its resources on those cases that will have a broader impact. CSWA also has made a point of not having lawyers on its staff, fearing this would undermine CSWA's mission of empowering workers to see *themselves* as the primary agents of change (through confronting their employer and organizing other workers) who enlist lawyers as allies, rather than viewing lawyers as the silver-bullet solution to the injustices they face. For similar reasons, CSWA maintains a small full-time staff of four to five individuals. The organization relies heavily on members and other volunteers donating their time in order to carry out its work.[25]

By partnering with various legal services providers, as discussed later, CSWA reports to have helped workers obtain over $50 million in back wages. Moreover,

23 The address for CSWA's website is: www.cswa.org. See generally, PeiYao Chen, *Chinese Staff & Workers' Association: A Community-Based Workers' Center Model* 12–21 (2003), available at www.cswa.org/modx/assets/files/cswa%20-%20a%20community-based%20workers%20center%20model.pdf (discussing CSWA's four phases of development.)

24 In addition to its office in Manhattan's Chinatown, CSWA has also been seeking to establish a physical presence in the Chinatowns of Sunset Park, Brooklyn, and Flushing, Queens. The organization's website states that it has over 2,000 members. CSWA's filings with New York State reveal that the organization's total annual revenue has fluctuated in recent years between a high of $650,000 in 2009 and a low of $176,000 in the most recently reported fiscal year, 2012–13. For 2012–13, only a tiny fraction of CSWA's total revenue came from "membership dues" ($1,645) and a small amount from "investment income" ($59,556). The vast majority is from contributions, which CSWA gets through fundraisers, such as an annual Chinese New Year banquet, donations from supporters and members, and contributions from the workers that it helps to recover backpay through litigation.

25 See E. Tammy Kim, *Lawyers as Resource Allies in Workers' Struggles for Social Change*, 13 N.Y. City L. Rev. 213, 225 (2009) (describing the benefits of lawyers partnering with worker centers through a "resource-ally model" as opposed to an "in-house counsel model").

multiple CSWA cases have resulted in landmark rulings: one decision held that a garment manufacturer could be held liable for the employment practices of its subcontractor; another held that common Chinese restaurant practices concerning service and banquet fees constituted an illegal appropriation of workers' tips.[26] More recently, CSWA has litigated numerous cases involving groups of twenty, thirty, or forty plaintiffs against well-known Asian restaurants, such as Saigon Grill, the Ollie's chain, Wu Liang Ye, and Republic, often obtaining large settlements or awards. They also organized a campaign against employment and health conditions in nail salons that included several highly publicized lawsuits. Their "landmark" case against Babi Nails was featured in the *New York Times* investigative report that precipitated New York State Governor Andrew Cuomo to issue a set of emergency measures increasing regulation of that industry.[27] In addition to court litigation, these campaigns have sometimes involved NLRB actions, mostly in response to retaliatory firings by employers, and criminal charges against employers brought by the New York State Attorney General.

CSWA facilitates Chinese immigrants in obtaining legal representation by helping to overcome the obstacles outlined above that keep these workers from ever seeking legal assistance in the first place. First off, CSWA engages in a variety of activities that help to inform Chinese immigrant workers about their legal rights. CSWA encourages its members to discuss these topics with coworkers, friends, and relatives. The organization also raises awareness of labor issues among members' coworkers and community members through its protests outside of restaurants, nail salons, and other places in which its members work. Individuals who are unaware of their rights may also come to CSWA for other reasons but then be educated on these issues. In addition, the organization holds press conferences and works with the media to publicize its protest activities, organizing efforts, and legal victories, which teaches workers about the law, informs them about CSWA and its work, and demonstrates that something can be done to combat the employment practices that these workers likely face in their own jobs.

The most critical function that CSWA plays in the process of obtaining legal representation is giving workers, after having learned their rights, the confidence to then vindicate those rights. As discussed above, Chinese immigrant workers routinely have questions about whether they will be retaliated against, whether they will be blacklisted, or whether they will be deported. CSWA is able to help workers overcome this fear by earning the workers' trust and introducing them to others who have already trodden this course.

26 See *Zheng v. Liberty Apparel Co. Inc.*, 355 F.3d 61 (2d Cir. 2003) (joint employment); *Chan v. Triple* 8 *Palace, Inc.*, No. 03 Civ. 6048 (GEL), 2006 WL 851749, *3–19 (S.D.N.Y. Mar. 30, 2006) (tips, service charges, and banquet fees).

27 See Sarah Maslin Nir, *The Price of Nice Nails*, New York Times, May 7, 2015 (discussing the workers' inability to collect the $474,000 judgment obtained in the case). One of the Governor's reforms requires nail salons to purchase a "wage bond" to ensure money is available to compensate workers who are not paid wages owed.

CSWA builds trust by establishing its expertise and commitment to serving workers' interests. CSWA helps workers to demystify the legal system, litigation process, and other institutions that are largely foreign and often intimidating to Chinese immigrants. CSWA also strives to make workers recognize that the conditions they face are not unique, but simultaneously experienced by a class of workers – and it is this class of workers that CSWA helps. Further, workers involved with CSWA will generally learn of its record of challenging employers' illegal practices and obtaining results, thus reinforcing workers' confidence that CSWA really serves their interests.

Another effective CSWA tactic for instilling confidence in workers is to introduce them to other members who once shared their same fears but have now successfully taken action against their employers. Meeting these individuals is far more encouraging than reading about a lawsuit in the newspaper. Moreover, these interactions give workers a sense that they are part of some larger cause, which can be a powerful motivator. In addition, CSWA's preference for bringing group cases means that most workers will not be "going it alone" in challenging their employer, but will have former or current coworkers alongside them in this action. For an undocumented individual, being part of a group of plaintiffs that also includes several documented workers provides some degree of "cover" that can be particularly comforting.[28]

In the cases that it chooses to litigate, CSWA is generally able to secure high-quality legal representation. CSWA sometimes finds private pro-employee law firms to represent its members either on a contingency or pro bono basis.[29] However, more commonly, CSWA finds a nonprofit or legal aid organization to take the case, which then often finds a law firm to serve as its pro bono co-counsel. In the recent past, CSWA has worked with nonprofits such as the Legal Aid Society, Asian-American Legal Defense and Education Fund, and Urban Justice Center, and through them with major law firms like Davis Polk, Kaye Scholer, Skadden Arps, Shearman & Sterling, and Gibson Dunn. In these relationships, the nonprofit serves as a conduit with the worker center and provides expertise on employment litigation involving low-wage workers; the firms generally contribute their litigation expertise and manpower as well as cover the costs of the litigation.[30] In addition to receiving high-quality representation, the workers also benefit from neither paying any money at the

[28] Although CSWA encourages workers to engage the legal system and use litigation at times, it also educates members about the limits of the existing legal system and the need to improve it. One particular weakness highlighted by CSWA is the ease with which employers can avoid paying judgments. Therefore, CSWA emphasizes that any litigation must be accompanied by organizing in order to be effective. Further, CSWA members, including those taking part in litigation, are often also engaged in organizing for legislative changes.

[29] Some firms that have cooperated with CSWA in this capacity include Gladstein, Reif & Meginniss, Spivak Lipton, Alterman & Boop, and Green Savits.

[30] See Greenberg, Chapter 44, and Dewey et al., Chapter 43 in this volume. The full list of cases brought by CSWA in which such a partnership was used is too long to recite here, but some recent examples include lawsuits against Shanghai Café, Tomo Sushi, Yes Car Service, Wu Liang Ye, Majestic Buffet, Republic, Café Swish, Vine Sushi, Babi Nails, Saigon Grill, Ollie's, Jin Fong, and Kawa Sushi.

outset of their case nor paying the one-third of their recovery that private lawyers customarily charge in contingency cases.

Cases organized by CSWA or other worker centers are attractive to the nonprofit legal service organizations handling labor cases, which seek to leverage their limited resources for a maximum impact. By the time these workers meet the lawyers, they already have some understanding of what litigation entails and are committed to that process. CSWA's preference for group cases also means that the legal aid organization can represent more individuals in a given case while only committing marginally more resources. The staff of CSWA may serve as translators for the often-monolingual clients. Having a group of workers committed to pursuing the litigation together also limits employers' ability to intimidate or buy off a few key plaintiffs. Moreover, as CSWA will often accompany the litigation with protests, media campaigns, and other measures to organize more workers, the case is likely to have an impact beyond just the plaintiffs. Thus, as my former coworker, Hollis Pfitsch, put it, "litigation that supports organizing efforts gets more 'bang' for the legal services budget 'buck.'"[31]

CSWA also facilitates the representation of its members by creating mechanisms for making decisions and communicating information among the plaintiff group. Generally, CSWA will help the group to select "representatives" who are entrusted to approve tactical litigation decisions, not unlike the role played by representatives in a collective or class action.[32] For decisions requiring the input of all plaintiffs, CSWA will assist in conferring with each worker or arranging a convenient meeting time. In addition, and quite significantly, CSWA may help in the decision-making process. For example, if defendants make a lump-sum settlement proposal for the group of plaintiffs, CSWA may offer its experience and expertise to help them decide how to fairly divide this sum among the group. Having represented both groups of workers affiliated with CSWA and groups of unorganized Chinese workers, I can attest that the provision of these services – the logistical help, translation services, assistance with decision-making procedures, etc. – can significantly reduce the burden on the attorney.

That being said, the involvement of a worker center presents certain challenges of its own. Ethical challenges arise from the fact that, while the lawyer generally has a close relationship with the worker center, it is the workers – not the worker center – who are the lawyer's clients. Thus, the attorney must be careful in deciding what information it can and cannot share with the organization and in ensuring that it is carrying out the will of its clients and not simply the organization.[33]

[31] Hollis V. Pfitsch, *Using Fair Labor Standards Act Litigation to Support Immigrant Worker Organizing*, 45(9–10) Clearinghouse Rev. 411, 413 (2012).

[32] CSWA, however, generally disfavors actual class or collective actions both because these mechanisms allow certain workers to free-ride on the efforts of the more committed and active workers and because they create uncertainty as to the class membership and selection of representatives, which threatens CSWA's and its members' control over the case.

[33] See Kim, supra note 25, at 227–30 (discussing ethical issues that arise in working with worker centers).

These cases also face other practical hurdles. Some employers claim that CSWA's tactics are excessive or even extortionist, particularly the staging of protests outside the businesses that it targets, which may prompt the employers to dig in their heels or find ways to attack the organization.[34] For instance, employers have filed counterclaims or initiated lawsuits against worker centers alleging defamation or other torts in response to protest activities.[35] Two workers whom CSWA assisted in recovering back pay also sued the organization, alleging that CSWA illegally compelled (or tried to compel) them to provide it with a portion of their recovery.[36] One management attorney who has represented employers in cases brought by worker centers, including CSWA, believes that these organizations do a "disservice" to the workers by "driving wedges" between the parties, thus both destroying that relationship and impeding settlement. He noted that these cases are very difficult to resolve because they often have an "ideological bent," in which workers view the employer as "evil" or "the enemy" and their ultimate motivation in the case is less clear.[37]

Despite any criticisms of CSWA's methods, the impact of its lawsuits and campaigns is undeniably significant and extends well beyond the individual plaintiffs in those cases. The fear of such lawsuits has increased employer compliance with labor laws, often resulting in higher wages and better working conditions. Further, while employers may complain about the protests or media advocacy that is paired with litigation in many CSWA cases, it is precisely the pressure from these activities that often achieves settlements or results that would not be possible through litigation alone.

MinKwon Center

The MinKwon Center for Community Action, located in Flushing, Queens, is like a social services organization, worker center, and legal aid provider rolled into one. This organization was founded in 1984 as the Young Korean Service and Education Center (YKASEC), which sought "to meet the needs and concerns of the Korean American community through five program areas: Community Organizing & Advocacy, Civic Participation, Social Services, Youth Empowerment, and

34 See Kwong, supra note 22, at 195–96 (noting that CSWA's director has been "accused of extortion and theft and labeled a 'monster,' a 'blood sucker,' and 'public enemy number one'" as well as "received many threats, the seriousness of which cannot be underestimated").

35 See, e.g., *St. Beat Sportswear, Inc. v. Nat'l Mobilization against Sweatshops, et al.*, 698 N.Y.S.2d 820 (N.Y. Sup. Ct. 1999) (alleging that publicity campaign led by CSWA and another worker center constituted tortious interference with employer's business relationships). See also *Sheridan, et al., v. Carter, et al.*, No. 05/18320 (N.Y. Sup. Ct. June 30, 2006) (defamation suit against Domestic Workers United); *B&B Hospitality Group, LLC, et al. v. Restaurant Opportunities Center of NY, et al.*, No. 10/115230 (N.Y. Sup. Ct. Feb. 9, 2011) (defamation suit against Restaurant Opportunities Center of New York).

36 *Xin Wei Lin, et al. v. Chinese Staff & Workers' Ass'n, et al.*, No. 11 Civ. 3944 (RJS), 2012 WL 5457493, *3 (S.D.N.Y. Nov. 8, 2012) *aff'd*, 527 F. App'x 83 (2d Cir. 2013). The district court dismissed all of the plaintiffs' claims.

37 Interview with David Feldman, Moses & Singer, (July 31, 2014).

Culture."[38] However, MinKwon now also offers legal services, including in the field of worker rights, and since roughly 2009, has offered its services beyond Korean immigrants to other marginalized community members, including Flushing's many Chinese immigrants.[39] MinKwon's filings with New York State show that its total revenue in 2008 was just over $500,000, but that number has grown to over $1.5 million for the year 2012 – including $226,849 in government grants and more than $1.3 million from various foundations, corporate donors, and nonprofits.

MinKwon's worker rights advocacy was always sensitive due to the inclusion of business owners in the organization's membership. Nonetheless, as of the summer of 2014, MinKwon had three attorneys on staff, including one who dedicated 90% of her time to labor issues. (The other two lawyers handled immigration and housing matters.) MinKwon's Annual Report for 2013 indicates that it provided social and legal services to over 4,000 community members, and that 9% of them (roughly 360) concerned labor issues. MinKwon's labor attorney estimates that approximately 70% of these individuals are Korean immigrants and the remainder are immigrants from China, of which about two-thirds are ethnic Koreans who lived in the northeastern part of China near the Korean border (*chaoxianzu* in Chinese or *joseonjok* in Korean).

MinKwon's labor work focuses primarily on wage-and-hour violations (40%), unemployment insurance claims (40%), and workers' compensation (10%). A large part of this work is conducting trainings both at MinKwon and in the community as well as educating workers through other means, such as newspaper columns providing legal advice. MinKwon's staff both teaches workers about their legal rights and talks through their fears and concerns of enforcing those rights. For instance, one MinKwon organizer explained how some workers are apologetic when they have not been paid at work, somehow feeling that this is their own fault.[40] In the workers' compensation field, MinKwon established a program with a hospital to assist workers in getting the medical evaluation necessary to file such a claim. Although the organization does not provide representation for these claims, it will provide workers with a list of attorneys who handle such cases.

MinKwon is quite selective in the wage-and-hour cases that it litigates, choosing those that are expected to have a larger impact because the violations are particularly egregious, several workers have come forward, or it involves an important issue. MinKwon tries to avoid cases against small businesses and to focus on cases in which the employer has demonstrated a pattern of abusive practices. Thus, for instance, in one case MinKwon represented a group of restaurant workers who were simply not paid wages for several months; in fact, the Attorney General later brought criminal

[38] MinKwon Center for Community Action 2013 Annual Report 3.

[39] For a thorough description of the organization's history, see generally, Susan McQuade, *Creating "Open Space" to Promote Social Justice: The MinKwon Center for Community Action*, in New Labor in New York 208–26 (2014).

[40] *Id.* at 220.

charges against the individual restaurant owners.[41] In another case, MinKwon represents several workers employed by an ambulette service that did not pay at least one plaintiff any wages for the first two months of his employment.[42] In the past, the organization has assisted workers in employing non-litigation tactics to vindicate their rights, such as forming a picket line outside a Korean restaurant that underpaid its workers.[43] In each of its affirmative wage-and-hour litigations, MinKwon brings in a law firm to serve as co-counsel and provide its services pro bono to the clients. With only a single attorney doing labor cases, MinKwon generally only has two such active wage-and-hour cases at a time. As for discrimination cases, the organization views them as too time-consuming to litigate and therefore refers clients with such issues to the relevant administrative agency.

Social Service Organizations

There are numerous organizations in New York City that provide a wide variety of social services to the Chinese community and Chinese immigrants specifically. Some of the better-known groups include Asian Americans for Equality (AAFE), the Chinese Progressive Association (CPA), and the Chinese-American Planning Council (CPC). There are also several settlement houses in or near Manhattan's Chinatown providing social services to Chinese immigrants, such as the Hamilton-Madison House, University Settlement, and Henry Street Settlement. These organizations provide assistance in areas such as immigration, food stamps, housing and evictions, English language study, and tax advice; they also organize activities for seniors, provide childcare services, and some may organize campaigns around issues affecting the Chinese community.

In around 2010, with my assistance, the Legal Aid Society began a partnership with CPC's Brooklyn office, located in Sunset Park, to establish an employment law clinic. On one Sunday each month, a Chinese-speaking attorney would provide legal consultations to any individual who either made an appointment in advance or walked in on the day of the clinic. Most of the value CPC provided in this partnership stems from its integration into the Chinese community. For instance, many individuals would simply go to CPC with questions about their unemployment insurance, workers' compensation, or other employment-related claim – even though CPC lacked any particular expertise in those areas – because they were familiar with the organization, it was conveniently located, or perhaps they had received CPC's help in the past with another issue. Once CPC launched the clinic, instead of solely translating these people's documents, providing a non-expert

41 *Sung K. Bae, et al. v. Hwan K. Kim, et al.*, No. 11 Civ. 6240 (NG) (E.D.N.Y. 2011) (the civil case).

42 *Nam Sik Pak, et al. v. Vega Transportation Co., Inc., et al.*, No. 13 Civ. 2696 (RML) (E.D.N.Y. 2013).

43 McQuade, supra note 38, at 208–209.

opinion, or directing them to a government office across the river, CPC could instruct them to come back on Sunday to receive a legal consultation.

CPC was also invaluable in publicizing the availability of these legal services and making them attractive to Chinese immigrants. CPC advertised the clinic to those immigrant workers with whom it was already working and through the Chinese-language print and television media, which also ran stories after each clinic educating the Chinese community about an employment law issue. For instance, there were stories emphasizing that undocumented workers were protected by minimum wage and overtime laws, that being paid in cash did not preclude a worker from collecting unemployment insurance, and other topics about which workers often have misconceptions. The newspapers also reported on cases that originated at the clinic and the Legal Aid Society successfully resolved for the client. Moreover, contacting CPC, a reputable organization located in the community, was far more attractive to Chinese immigrants than calling or showing up at the Legal Aid Society – an entity with which they were unfamiliar, that sounds like a government agency, is in a part of downtown Manhattan to which they have never been, and is housed in a building that generally required presentation of an ID upon entering.

The CPC clinic resulted in numerous Chinese workers receiving competent legal representation for their employment issue and many more receiving legal advice. For instance, the Legal Aid Society obtained settlements for a woman with discrimination and retaliation claims against the hotel at which she was the sole Chinese employee, the cook at a small café that did not pay him overtime, a woman who was harassed while employed at a national supermarket chain, and several unpaid construction workers whose employer declared bankruptcy. For most of these workers, due to the nature of their claims, neither a private lawyer nor a worker center such as CSWA would be willing to take their case.

While CPC provided useful logistical support to the attorneys, it was not oriented or structured to help workers cross the line from knowing about their rights to being willing to take legal action. CPC did not have organizers or other workers who could either persuade these individuals of the importance of seeking legal redress or instill in them the confidence that such an effort against their employer could succeed. As a result, I met several workers through the clinic who would come to learn of their legal rights, perhaps even have follow-up meetings in my office, but then decided not to pursue the matter due to any one or combination of the common reasons discussed earlier in this chapter.

It should be noted that finding a willing partner among New York City's social service organizations to establish a labor rights clinic took some searching. Business owners are important members of many of these organizations. Furthermore, these organizations may have programs to train business owners, make loans to small businesses, or place workers into jobs with these employers. Thus, similar to MinKwon's dilemma in this regard, these organizations are often hesitant to partake in activities that may antagonize business owners or be perceived as adverse to their interests. This reality presents a serious limitation on using ethnic-based social service organizations to expand access to legal services for labor disputes.

CONCLUSION

There are large unmet needs for legal representation among Chinese immigrant workers in New York City. Private attorneys are often unwilling to take on potentially meritorious discrimination or retaliation claims for low-wage workers or appear at unemployment insurance hearings that provide limited fees. Legal services attorneys practicing employment law – very few of whom speak Chinese – cannot represent all these individuals by themselves. The private bar has, however, shown far more willingness to take on wage-and-hour matters, even if the quality of the representation is somewhat varied. The obstacles to legal representation in these cases instead lie in workers' lack of knowledge of their rights and, even upon learning this information, their hesitancy to seek legal redress.

This chapter has described how intermediate institutions play an important role in helping Chinese workers to overcome these obstacles and obtain quality representation, as they do in other immigrant communities. Worker centers like CSWA, in addition to the many non-litigation-related things they do to empower workers and address workplace injustices, are able to teach workers about their rights, give them the confidence to take legal action, facilitate their decision-making processes, and connect members with committed and capable lawyers. This model greatly benefits the workers and allows for the efficient use of the legal aid attorneys' resources. Although the impact of CSWA's litigation work certainly expands well beyond the specific plaintiffs involved, particularly in terms of encouraging compliance among more well-established employers, efforts to obtain back pay for past violations still requires direct action on a particular worker's behalf. Yet, the small staffs at worker centers and legal aid organizations limit the number of workers who can receive such help. Moreover, this model is also dependent on large law firms' willingness to fund this litigation both in terms of hard costs and associate hours, which is not limitless. MinKwon is similarly successful in getting information to workers and helping to organize some of them, but faces limitations in bringing litigation due to its small legal staff and inclusion of business owners in its membership. Of course, as these organizations carefully select which cases they will take, there are still many individual workers who are not paired with a lawyer even after seeking out a worker center.

The social-services clinic model is able to deliver legal services to some of those individuals not assisted by worker centers. These groups often are still better able to connect with and disseminate information to immigrant workers in their community than legal aid providers acting on their own; they also provide a more comfortable, approachable, and less threatening environment than a legal aid office.

The logistical support they provide can facilitate a legal aid lawyer's job. However, with no organizing element to their work, this model is less likely to generate group cases where they did not already exist or persuade fearful workers to come forward. Indeed, even operating a labor law clinic in the first place may be difficult for these organizations due to the presence of business owners in their membership base.

Solving the representation puzzle is tricky. Even in the narrow area of trying to meet the legal needs of Chinese immigrant workers, while some models for providing legal services have worked well, no one model is sufficient to provide quality representation to all workers who need it. The lesson learned in studying these multiple models is that we must be flexible and creative in thinking of how to best leverage and combine the limited resources in the community, legal profession, and elsewhere to try to meet this need. In a sense, we in the legal profession need to be like worker centers – continually finding the gaps in existing structures and filling them.

41

Reassessing Unauthorized Practice of Law Rules

Kate Levine

It is a widespread finding of the access-to-legal services literature that representation by a lawyer is unlikely ever to be provided for all Americans who need legal services and are unable to pay for it. This suggests there should a greater receptivity in the legal profession to representation by non-lawyers and enhancement of aids for self-representation. Kate Levine explores in this chapter how state laws prohibiting the "unauthorized practice of law" remain a significant barrier to needed experimentation and reform.

One would think that if poor and middle-income people cannot afford an attorney, they should have an option to obtain representation either from a non-lawyer who, by reason of experience or self-study, has practical expertise in a given area, or from a cost-efficient online form-preparation service. As a formal legal matter, however, those without a license to practice law in a particular jurisdiction are often barred by "unauthorized practice of law" (UPL) statutes or court rules from giving advice or representing individuals in legal matters in a whole host of situations. Notwithstanding evidence that the public desires, and in many cases would benefit from, such informal solutions,[1] successful experience with lay representation before administrative agencies, and the fact that many people, often by necessity, must represent themselves in court proceedings, the organized bar prohibits any incursion into legal practice (as defined by the bar) by laypersons. UPL rules, which exist in every state, are most often enforced not by the executive branch or by private citizens claiming harm, but by state bar committees.[2] The problems inherent in

1 See, e.g., Deborah L. Rhode, *Professionalism in Perspective: Alternative Approaches to Nonlawyer Practice*, 22 N.Y.U. Rev. L. & Soc. Change, 701, 709 (1996) (non-lawyers rank higher than lawyers in 1986 consumer satisfaction survey); and her *Policing the Professional Monopoly: A Constitutional and Empirical Analysis of Unauthorized Practice Prohibitions*, 34 Stan. L. Rev. 1, 3 (1981) (1974 survey found that 82% of respondents felt that many things lawyer handled could be done better by non-lawyers).

2 Deborah L. Rhode & Lucy Buford Ricca, *Protecting the Profession or the Public? Rethinking Unauthorized-Practice Enforcement*, 82 Fordham L. Rev. 2587, 2591 (2014) (2013 survey of UPL committees in forty-two states found that "less than half of [UPL] complaints came from consumers or clients ... Forty-two percent of jurisdictions reported that at least half of complainants were attorneys").

lawyers regulating their own competition are obvious and well documented. [3] Yet these laws remain on the books and are actively enforced in most states.

UPL STATUTES AND ATTEMPTS TO DEFINE THE "PRACTICE OF LAW"

Many of the UPL statutes fail to offer a clear definition of the "practice of law." Some jurisdictions offer no statutory or rule-based definition at all, relying on the courts to define the practice of law on a case-by-case basis, and essentially allow the state bar to control which practices are regulated through selective enforcement. The justification often tendered is that "[i]t would be worse than futile to attempt to formulate a general and universal [definition of the practice of law] which would cover all cases."[4] While the courts in these states define the practice of law as they encounter UPL cases, the decisions are far from a model of clarity. The Indiana Supreme Court, for instance, has repeated in several cases that, "[t]o 'practice law' is to carry on the business of an attorney at law; to do or practice that which an attorney or counselor at law is authorized to do and practice ..." [5] This tautological definition of legal practice does nothing to explain to consumers or providers of services what is allowable and what violates Indiana's UPL rules.

While the states that decline to define the practice of law leave their citizens in an untenable position of having to guess what "the practice of law" means, the situation does not improve all that much in those states that do set out a definition in their statutes and court rules.[6] For instance, the Rules of the Supreme Court of Arizona, characteristic of many states' definitions, state that:

3 See, e.g., *Rhode*, supra note 1; Deborah L. Rhode, *Whatever Happened to Access to Justice?*, 42 *Loy. L.A. L. Rev.* 869 (2009); Gillian K. Hadfield, *Legal Barriers to Innovation: The Growing Economic Cost of Professional Control over Corporate Legal Markets*, 60 STAN. L. REV. 1689, 1717 (2008).

4 *People v. Title Guarantee & Trust Co.*, 227 N.Y. 366, 377–78 (1919); see *Iowa S. Ct. Comm'n on Unauthorized Practice of Law v. Sturgeon*, 635 N.W.2d 679, 681 (Iowa 2001) ("It is neither necessary nor desirable to attempt the formulation of a single, specific definition of what constitutes the practice of law") (quoting Iowa Code of Professional Responsibility for Lawyers); *Mass. Conveyancers Ass'n v. Colonial Title & Escrow, Inc.*, No. Civ.A. 96–2746-C2001, 2001 WL 669280, at *5 (Mass. Super. 2001) (finding that "a comprehensive definition would be impossible to frame" but formulating a general definition); *Cardinal v. Merrill Lynch Realty/Burnet, Inc.*, 433 N.W.2d 864, 867 (Minn. 1988) ("The line between what is and what is not the practice of law cannot be drawn with precision") (quoting *Cowern v. Nelson*, 290 N.W. 795, 797 (Minn. 1940)); *Nebraska ex rel. Johnson v. Childe*, 23 N.W.2d 720, 723 (Neb. 1946) ("An all inclusive definition of what constitutes the practice of law is too difficult for simple statement"); *Gmerek v. State Ethics Comm'n*, 751 A.2d 1241, 1255 (Pa. Commw. Ct. 2000) ("There is no need for present purposes to venture upon a comprehensive survey of the boundaries – necessarily somewhat obscure – which limit the practice of law").

5 *Cincinnati Ins. Co. v. Wills*, 717 N.E.2d 151, 167 (Ind. 1999) (citing *Fink v. Peden*, 214 Ind. 584, 587, 17 N.E.2d 95, 96 (1938)).

6 The following states have court-rule or statutory definitions of the practice of law: Alabama, ALA. CODE § 34-3-6 (2014); Arizona, ARIZ. SUP. CT. R. 31(a); Colorado, COLO. R. CIV. P. 201.3(2); Georgia, GA. CODE ANN. § 15–19–50 (West 2014); Kentucky, KY. SUP. CT. R. 3.020; Louisiana, LA. REV. STAT. ANN. § 37:212 (2014); Maryland, MD. CODE ANN., BUS. OCC. & PROF. § 10–101 (West 2014); Minnesota, MINN. STAT. ANN. § 481.02 (West 2014); Missouri, MO. REV. STAT. § 484.010 (2014); New Mexico, N.M. R. LEGAL ASSIST. 20–102; North Carolina, N.C. GEN. STAT. ANN. § 84–2.1 (West 2014); Rhode Island,

[The] "Practice of law" means providing legal advice or services to or for another by:

(1) preparing any document in any medium intended to affect or secure legal rights for a specific person or entity;
(2) preparing or expressing legal opinions;
(3) representing another in a judicial, quasi-judicial, or administrative proceeding, or other formal dispute resolution process such as arbitration and mediation;
(4) preparing any document through any medium for filing in any court, administrative agency or tribunal for a specific person or entity; or
(5) negotiating legal rights or responsibilities for a specific person or entity.[7]

A layperson (or even a lawyer) might be surprised to learn that the preparation of "any document in any medium" that is intended to affect legal rights comes under the definition of the practice of law in Arizona. Indeed the foregoing list is broad enough to encompass anything from in-court representation, to "expressing" a legal opinion, or to filling out a form that may become the subject of litigation. Not surprisingly, given the breadth of this definition, Arizona has had to list 26 exemptions for activities that would otherwise be considered the practice of law, including representation before a number of agencies, tax-related practice by accountants, and court-approved mediators.[8]

Arizona's over inclusive definition is far from an outlier. To take another example, Wyoming's definition is equally sweeping:

(a) (3) "Practice of law" means providing any legal service for any other person, firm or corporation, with or without compensation, or providing professional legal advice or services where there is a client relationship of trust or reliance, including appearing as an advocate in a representative capacity; drafting pleadings or other documents; or performing any act in such capacity in connection with a prospective or pending proceeding before any court, court commissioner, or referee.
(b) Only active members of the Wyoming State Bar may engage in the practice of law within this state.[9]

In Wyoming, only an attorney may provide "any legal service for any other person ... with or without compensation." This definition, of course, leaves open far more questions than it answers, starting with, what is a "legal service". In its vagueness, this rule potentially covers many things that most of us would not consider "legal," for

R.I. GEN. LAWS ANN. § 11–27-2 (West 2014); Tennessee, TENN. CODE. ANN. § 23-3-101 (West 2014); Texas, TEX. GOV'T CODE ANN. § 81.101 (West 2014); and the District of Columbia, D.C. CT. APP. R. 49.

7 A.Z. ST. SUP. CT. RULES, R. 31(a)(2).

8 *Id.* R. 31(d).

9 WYO. BAR. ASS'N ORG. & GOV'T R 11.

instance, drafting "any document" could refer to assisting with a complex contract, or it could refer to a simple agreement between friends. Similarly, what does "performing any act in connection" with any type of litigation mean? It could mean anything from appearing in court to editing a typo out of a pleading for a relative. These laws and court rules are a trap for the unwary. And, as they are often enforced by bar associations, and through settlements rather than court cases, the "legal service[s]" that have been prohibited are often not available to the public.[10]

The American Bar Association (ABA), despite acknowledging that UPL rules must be revised, has provided little guidance in this area. In 2002, the ABA created a "Task Force," whose stated "challenge" was to:

> [D]etermine the best approach for the Association to address whether to create a model definition of the practice of law that would support the goal to provide the public with better access to legal services, be in concert with governmental concerns about anticompetitive restraints, and provide a basis for effective enforcement of unauthorized practice of law statutes.[11]

Unfortunately, the Task Force's "Proposed Definition" suffers from the same amorphousness as the Arizona and Wyoming rules. It included as prohibited activity any advice about legal rights, drafting any documents that might affect legal rights, and representing anyone before any adjudicative body.[12]

In response, the Department of Justice (DOJ) and Federal Trade Commission (FTC) sent a letter on December 20, 2002, urging the ABA "not to adopt the current proposed Definition," which was "overbroad and could restrain competition between lawyers and nonlawyers to provide similar services to American consumers."[13] The result of adoption would be "to raise costs for consumers and

10 Rhode & Ricca, supra note 2, at 2592 ("[c]lose to half (45 percent) of [state bar association] respondents reported that most, or almost all, of their cases were informally settled, typically through a warning or cease-and-desist letter, and another large percentage reported a high settlement rate without giving specific percentages").

11 ABA Task Force on the Model Definition of the Practice of Law, Challenge Statement, available at www.abanet.org/cpr/model-def/model_def_challenge.html.

12 The proposed Rule included the following activities as the practice of law:

(1) Giving advice or counsel to persons as to their legal rights or responsibilities or to those of others;

(2) Selecting, drafting, or completing legal documents or agreements that affect the legal rights of a person;

(3) Representing a person before an adjudicative body, including, but not limited to, preparing or filing documents or conducting discovery; or

(4) Negotiating legal rights or responsibilities on behalf of a person.

ABA Task Force on the Model Definition of the Practice of Law, Draft (9/18/02), available at www.americanbar.org/groups/professional_responsibility/task_force_model_definition_practice_law/model_definition_definition.html (hereinafter ABA Draft).

13 Letter from the U.S. Dep't of Justice and the Fed. Trade Comm'n to the ABA Task Force on the Model Definition of the Practice of Law (Dec. 20, 2002), available at www.abanet.org/cpr/model-def/ftc.pdf (hereinafter Letter from DOJ and FTC).

limit their competitive choices."[14] The letter concluded that "there is no evidence before the ABA of which we are aware that consumers are hurt by this competition and there is substantial evidence that they benefit from it."[15]

The government agencies' letter did not suggest an alternate definition of the practice of law, but it encouraged further study by the Task Force and a default position that "until demonstrated otherwise, accountants, bankers, real estate brokers and others skilled in business should remain able to provide advice and legal information related to their particular practices without harming the public."[16] Ultimately, the ABA sent the issue back to the states. The Task Force's recommendation, adopted by the ABA in 2003, counseled each state to adopt its own definition of the practice of law.[17]

As we have seen, this "solution" is largely empty because state definitions are invariably vague and over-inclusive. Because of the ABA's and state courts' inability or refusal to define the practice of law clearly, and the power granted to bar associations to enforce UPL rules or common law, lay assistance is prohibited not only in formal court proceedings, but also in many quasi-litigation settings that have been designed specifically to avoid the formalism and costs inherent in court proceedings, even in simple transactions.

UPL LAWS RESTRICT ACCESS TO JUSTICE

UPL laws, whether statutory or common law, continue to be actively enforced by the state bars. In fact, recent years have seen an "uptick" in UPL enforcement activity.[18] These laws reduce access to justice in a number of ways. In the transactional context, they drive up prices for routine transactions such as home-buying, and limit the natural competition that would occur between lawyers and non-lawyers in such areas. Recently, UPL laws have also been used to stymie the internet's potential for enhancing the ability of individuals to represent themselves by restricting online form generators, such as LegalZoom.[19] UPL rules have also been invoked, in the majority of cases by attorneys,[20] to insist on lawyer participation in proceedings that

14 *Id.* Among the benefits, consumers would be allowed to determine what was in their interest, including factors "such as cost, convenience, and the degree of assurance that the necessary documents and commitments are sufficient."

15 *Id.* (emphasis added).

16 *Id.*

17 ABA Task Force on the Model Definition of the Practice of Law, Report to the House of Delegates, Recommendation (2003), available at www.americanbar.org/content/dam/aba/migrated/cpr/model-def/recomm.authcheckdam.pdf.

18 Susan D. Hoppock, *Enforcing Unauthorized Practice of Law Prohibitions: The Emergence of the Private Cause of Action and Its Impact on Effective Enforcement*, 20 Geo. J. Legal Ethics 719, 731 (2007).

19 See generally Catherine J. Lanctot, *Does Legalzoom Have First Amendment Rights?: Some Thoughts about Freedom of Speech and the Unauthorized Practice of Law*, 20 Temp. Pol. & Civ. Rts. L. Rev. 255 (2011).

20 See *Rhode*, supra note 1.

were designed to be less formal and less expensive modes of dispute resolution, such as administrative agencies and arbitration.[21] And in civil litigation, these laws compel a harsh binary choice for litigants. They can either draft the pleadings themselves and appear in court pro se, or pay often prohibitive costs for an attorney to represent them.

Routine Real Estate Transactions

UPL laws are often enforced through bar association correspondence litigation against laypersons doing routine business transactions, whether for compensation or not.[22] Despite the courts' and the bars' claims that these prohibitions are enforced for the public interest, their rulings are based largely on speculative harm to consumers and often, at base, designed to protect the economic livelihood of members of the bar.

While selling or buying real estate involves legal rights, the forms involved in the sale or purchase of a home are often standard documents approved by local boards of realtors.[23] It is not clear why a licensed realtor cannot complete these forms without lawyer assistance. In some states, such as New Jersey[24] and Arizona, [25] no attorney is needed to complete the buying or selling of a home. In Georgia, Florida, Illinois, Massachusetts, and South Carolina, on the other hand, you cannot purchase or sell your home without hiring an attorney to supervise the filing of deeds, mortgage agreements, and closing contracts.[26]

21 See, e.g., In re Estate of Rowley, 444 C.D. 2013, 2013 WL 6795208 (Pa. Commw. Ct. Dec. 23, 2013) ("It is well settled that with a few exceptions, non-attorneys may not represent parties before ... most administrative agencies"); *Nisha, LLC v. TriBuilt Const. Grp., LLC*, 388 S.W.3d 444, 445 (Ark. 2012) (non-lawyer not allowed to represent party to arbitration in Arkansas).

22 See, e.g., *The Florida Bar v. Smania*, 701 So. 2d 835, 836 (Fla. 1997) (in case where two non-lawyers tried to appear in court for a party without compensation, the Florida Supreme Court permanently enjoined the non-lawyers and ruled that "compensation is not a necessary element of proving that an individual has engaged in the unlicensed practice of law").

23 See, e.g., New Jersey Association OF Realators Standard Form OF Real Estate Contract, available at http://bhnj.com/pdf/contract.pdf; see also *New Jersey State Bar Ass'n v. New Jersey Ass'n of Realtor Boards*, 461 A.2*d* 1112, 1113 (1983) (approving consent decree, which allowed "real estate brokers and salespersons ... to prepare certain types of residential sales and lease agreements if these agreements contain specified provisions" including a provision for attorney review of contract.)

24 *In re Opinion No. 26 of Comm. on Unauthorized Practice of Law*, 654 A.2d 1344, 1351 (N.J. 1995) (Hereinafter "*Opinion No. 26*"). (included in the rules set out by the opinion is a three-day review period during which a buyer or seller may contact an attorney. If the attorney finds a problem with the forms, he or she may cancel the closing contract).

25 In 1962, Arizona amended its Constitution to allow real estate brokers to draft all forms relating to a sale after the State's Supreme Court prohibited such conduct as illegal under the unauthorized practice of law rules. See ARIZ. CONST. art. XXVI, § 1.

26 *In re UPL Advisory Op.* 2003–2, 588 S.E.2d 741, 742 (Ga. 2003); *Mass. Conveyancers Ass'n v. Colonial Title & Escrow, Inc.*, CIV. A. 96–2746-C, 2001 WL 669280 (Mass. Super. Ct. June 5, 2001); *State v. Buyers Serv. Co.*, 357 S.E.2d 15, 19 (S.C. 1987); *Keyes Co. v. Dade Cnty. Bar Ass'n*, 46 So. 2d 605, 606 (Fla. 1950); *People ex rel. Ill. State Bar Ass'n v. Schafer*, 404 Ill. 45, 53, 87 N.E.2d 773, 777 (1949).

In 1995, after years of dispute between the state bar and state realtors associations, the New Jersey Supreme Court decided that consumers could buy or sell homes without the assistance of an attorney. In New Jersey, at the time, the practice in the northern part of the state was to require an attorney to supervise the transaction whereas, in the southern part of the state, the practice was "that from the beginning of the transaction to the end, neither seller nor buyer [wa]s represented by counsel. Every aspect of the transaction is handled by others, every document drafted by others, including the contract of sale, affidavit of title, bond and mortgage."[27] In response to this split in practice, the state's bar Committee on Unauthorized Practice of Law had issued an opinion stating that the following actions involved the UPL:[28]

> (1) the ordering of a title search and abstract by a real estate broker;[29] (2) the preparation of conveyance documents either by a title company or by an attorney retained by the broker;[30] (3) the removal of exceptions to the title by a title company; involving rendering legal opinions and lawyer activity;[31] and (4) the practice by title companies of conducting closings or settlements without the presence of attorneys.[32]

The committee summed up the consumer's "simpl[e]" choice: "either retain competent legal counsel, or select your own title insurer, and review the title commitment yourself, accepting the consequences of your choice to proceed to closing without legal advice or assistance with respect to the exceptions appearing therein."[33] It explained that:

> If a buyer or seller [chooses] to appear at closing without an attorney, the title clerk cannot provide legal advice, draft legal instruments, interpret legal documents or otherwise purport to protect the legal interests of the unrepresented

27 *Opinion* No. 26, 654 A.2d at 1346.

28 *NJ Unauth.Prac.Op.* 26, 130 N.J. L.J. 882 (1992).

29 *Id.* The bar committee had "answered" this question in an opinion from 1972. See *NJ Unauth.Prac.Op.* 11, 95 *N.J. L.J.* 1345 (1972).

30 For this prohibition, the bar cited to *Cape May County Bar Association v. Ludlam*, 45 *N.J.* 121, 125 (1965), where the New Jersey Supreme Court had held that "practice of law embraces the art of conveying, which has been defined as 'a term including both the science and art of transferring titles to real estate from one man to another." *Id.*

31 The bar opinion stated that "In *New Jersey State Bar Ass'n. v. Northern N.J. Mtge. Associates*, 32 *N.J.* 430 (1960), the[state] Supreme Court held that a title company's participating in clearing objections to the title which necessarily involved some legal opinion and activity constituted the unauthorized practice of law." *Id.*

32 The bar opinion noted that "in *New Jersey State Bar Ass'n v. New Jersey Ass'n of Realtor Boards*, 93 *N.J.* 470 (1983), the [state] Supreme Court ... approved a consent judgment. The settlement, as approved by the Court, allows the realtor to consummate the contract phase of the transaction (provided that contract contains the court approved language allowing a three day attorney review period), with attorneys handling the actual transfer of title.

33 *Supplement to NJ Unauth.Prac.Op.* 26, 131 *N.J. L.J.* 910 (1992).

buyer or seller at the closing without engaging in the unauthorized practice of law.[34]

In other words, if a consumer chose not to retain an attorney, the other agents to the transaction had the choice either to engage in the UPL or refuse to aid the unrepresented consumer in any way.

The New Jersey Supreme Court, rejected the bar's determination. It held that "the public interest does not require that the parties be deprived of the right to choose to proceed without a lawyer [in buying or selling a home]."[35] Specifically, the court ruled, so long as notice of the potential dangers of proceeding without an attorney[36] was provided by a real estate broker to a buyer and seller along with the contract of sale neither party needed to be represented by counsel. Moreover the ruling allowed real estate brokers to "order abstracts, title binders and title policies" and allowed title companies to "participate in clearing up ... minor objections ... such as marital status and money liens customarily paid at closing, but not ... easements, covenants or other serious legal objections to title." [37]

Despite possible complications to a real estate transaction, as a general matter, the court reasoned, "it takes a very short sentence to describe what apparently occurs [at the closing of a real estate transaction]: the deal closes, satisfactory to buyer and seller in practically all cases."[38] It also pointed out the "absence of proof [of damage to consumers]," which, "[wa]s particularly impressive" in this context because "the dispute between the realtors and the bar is of long duration, with the parties and their counsel singularly able and highly motivated to supply such proof as may exist."[39] On the other hand, years of evidence from these opposing practices made clear that the cost savings to individual consumers in southern New Jersey were real and substantial.[40]

By contrast, in 2003, the Georgia Supreme Court affirmed its state UPL committee's decision that "the preparation and execution of a deed of conveyance on behalf of another and facilitation of its execution by anyone other than a duly licensed

[34] *Id.*

[35] *Opinion No.* 26, 654 A.2d at 1345.

[36] The court drafted the notice and appended it to its Opinion as "Appendix A." The notice informs the unrepresented party that the real estate broker is not an attorney; that they represent the (other party); that the agent may not give legal advice; that the contract of sale is the most important part of the transaction, determines the party's rights and responsibilities, and may be cancelled by an attorney up to three days after signing; that without an attorney, the buyer in particular may not receive help if legal issues arise with the contract, and that retention of an attorney is up to the consumer. See *Id.* at 1363–64.

[37] *Id.* at 1361.

[38] *Id.* at 1351.

[39] *Id.* at 1346.

[40] *Id.* The Court found that in northern New Jersey, where the practice was to require legal representation, the seller spent an average of $750 and the buyer $1,000 on attorney's fees. In the southern part of the state where transactions proceeded without attorneys, the buyer spent nothing and the seller might spend $90 on engaging a lawyer to prepare a deed and affidavit of title.

Georgia attorney constitutes the unauthorized practice of law."[41] The high court, like the bar committee before it, cited no allegation or proof of harm to consumers from allowing a non-lawyer to prepare a deed of conveyance.[42] The basic position was the belief "that the public interest is best protected when a licensed Georgia attorney, trained to recognize the rights at issue during a property conveyance, oversees the entire transaction."[43]

Implicit in Georgia's decision and similar decisions from other states that insist on attorney participation in all real estate transactions is that the public is not capable of making an informed decision about whether or not to retain an attorney when buying or selling a home.[44] This decision for consumers has real consequences – depending on the value of a home and resources of the consumer, the cost of a lawyer's services could be material to the transaction. Of course, a competent lawyer is usually preferable to self-representation, particularly in a situation where the transaction is not routine – as for instance when a search turns up a cloud on the property title. It is doubtful, however, that an attorney is necessary in every case and, more importantly, that the consumer and the realtor will be unable to identify situations requiring a lawyer's assistance on their own. The only group that clearly benefits from decisions like that in Georgia is the real estate bar.

Online Form Preparation

The emerging enforcement of UPL laws against online form generators is an even stronger case against the bars' enforcement of such laws. These actions are stifling a large-scale access to justice tool without any showing that such services harm the public. Companies like LegalZoom provide consumers with low-cost standardized form creation. By all accounts, LegalZoom has been incredibly popular; in 2011, 20% of all new businesses in California were formed using LegalZoom.[45]

Many state bar associations have enforced UPL laws against LegalZoom almost since its inception. Beginning in 2008, the bars of North Carolina, Connecticut, and Pennsylvania have issued advisory opinions, cease-and-desist letters, or brought

41 *In re UPL Advisory Opinion* 2003–2, 588 S.E.2d 741, 742 (Ga. 2003)

42 See *id.*; Ga. Bar Ass'n Standing Comm. on UPL, Advisory Op. 2 (2003).

43 *In re UPL Advisory Opinion* 2003–2, 588 S.E.2d at 742.

44 See e.g., *Mass. Conveyancers Ass'n, Inc.*, CIV. A. 96–2746-C, 2001 WL 669280 (ruling that lawyers must be involved in real estate conveyances because "lawyers are better qualified to handle settlements because they are more knowledgeable about the legal issues and more likely to identify a problem than are non-attorney closing agents"); *State v. Buyers Serv. Co., Inc.*, 357 S.E.2d at 19 ("We are convinced that real estate and mortgage loan closings should be conducted only under the supervision of attorneys, who have the ability to furnish their clients legal advice should the need arise and fall under the regulatory rules of this court. Again, protection of the public is of paramount concern").

45 Anthony Ha, LegalZoom Files for $120M IPO, Saw $156M in Revenue Last Year, available at http://techcrunch.com/2012/05/11/legalzoom-ipo/. The company did not end up going public. See LegalZoom Delays IPO, L.A. Biz (Aug. 3, 2012, 12:32 PM), available at www.bizjournals.com/losangeles/news/2012/08/03/legalzoom-delays-ipo.html.

successful suits declaring LegalZoom's operations to constitute UPL.[46] In other states, including Ohio, Arkansas, Texas, and Missouri, private lawsuits have been filed and are in various stages of resolution.[47]

In a 2010 opinion, the Pennsylvania bar ruled that not only LegalZoom but all "Legal Document Preparation Services" (LDPS) violated the state's UPL prohibition.[48] According to the opinion, LDPS are companies that:

> [O]ffer legal forms and advice online or in person to laypersons in Pennsylvania who are contemplating litigation, filings with administrative bodies, and the creation of business entities in Pennsylvania as well as personal estate planning and the like. In the vernacular of their marketing approach, the documents offered are typically "inexpensive" or "cheap" Wills, Trusts, Incorporations or LLC's, and Divorce pleadings.[49]

Despite the breadth of the opinion, the bar group did not mention a single instance of harm to a consumer from the use of an LDPS. [50] Instead, the state bar relied on language from a 1937 state Supreme Court opinion warning in the abstract against "the intrusion of inexpert and unlicensed persons in the practice of law . . ."[51] Absent was any acknowledgement that consumers will not always have the option to hire an attorney when performing routine legal transactions.

In *Janson v. LegalZoom*,[52] a Missouri federal district court ruled similarly to the Pennsylvania bar opinion when it allowed a class action UPL claim by consumers against LegalZoom to proceed past the summary judgment stage. The court reasoned that, while the provision of legal forms was allowed under Missouri state law, LegalZoom still may have violated the state's UPL rule because it went beyond providing forms by offering assistance to consumers once they inputted their information. Drawing on earlier Missouri decisions allowing the provision of "do-it-yourself kits," where a consumer was provided a blank form but given no further

[46] Letter from N.C. Bar Ass'n. Auth. Prac. Comm. to LegalZoom.com, Inc. (May 5, 2008), available at www.directlaw.com/LegalZoom%2020080326%20LOC.pdf; Conn. Comm. on UPL, Informal Op. 01 (2008); Ohio Sup. Ct. Bd. on UPL, Advisory Op. 03 (2008) (addressing legal document preparation services generally); Pa. Bar Ass'n UPL Comm., Formal Op. 10 (2010).

[47] See *LegalZoom.com. v. McIllwain*, 2013 Ark. 370 (2013); *Solotko v. LegalZoom.com*, No. 03–10–0075 (CV), 2013 WL 3724770 (July 11, 2013); *Lowry v. LegalZoom.Com, Inc.*, No. 4:11CV02259, 2012 WL 2953109 (N.D. Ohio July 19, 2012); *Janson v. LegalZoom.com, Inc.*, 802 F. Supp. 2d 1053, 1060 (W.D. Mo. 2011).

[48] 42 Pa. CONS. STAT. ANN. § 2524(a) (West 2014). Subsection (c) states that an injunction may be used as a penalty for violation of subsection (a). "[A]ny person, including, but not limited to, a paralegal or legal assistant, who within this Commonwealth shall practice law, or who shall hold himself out to the public as being entitled to practice law, or use or advertise the title of lawyer, attorney at law, attorney and counselor at law, counselor, or the equivalent in any language, in such a manner as to convey the impression that he is a practitioner of the law of any jurisdiction, without being an attorney at law . . . Commits a misdemeanor . . ."

[49] Pa. Bar Ass'n UPL Comm. Formal Op. 01 (2010).

[50] *Id.*

[51] *Id.*

[52] *Janson v. LegalZoom.com, Inc.*, 802 F. Supp. 2d 1053 (W.D. Mo. 2011).

help in filling it out, or where the forms required only "clerical" services to complete,[53] the court ruled that:

> LegalZoom's sale of blank forms over the internet does not constitute the unauthorized practice of law. Nor would LegalZoom be engaging in the unauthorized practice of law if it sold general instructions to accompany those blank forms over the internet (as may already be the case).[54]

What placed LegalZoom into the realm of unauthorized "form preparer" was its offer to help consumers with completing forms – the site promised that, after the consumer answered a few questions, "we'll do it for you."[55] In other words, LegalZoom's offer of assistance to consumers presented the danger to the public interest that Missouri's UPL rules were allegedly designed to protect. This ruling was made despite the plaintiffs' acknowledgement that they did not believe they were receiving legal advice when they opted to use LegalZoom's services.[56]

Even where LegalZoom has come to agreements with states or been successful in court, it is only to sell blank forms, not to aid consumers. Very recently, the South Carolina Supreme Court approved an order by a special master approving a settlement through which LegalZoom could operate in that state.[57] In order to operate, however, LegalZoom had to promise to offer residents only forms that were already available to them through other state agencies; ensure that residents answers were entered "verbatim"; that, in any "review" of the documents by LegalZoom, no change was made to the form without contacting the consumer and rerecording her answers verbatim; and that LegalZoom made clear on its website that it was not offering legal services. By making these promises in the order, LegalZoom confirmed that its function was akin to a "scrivener" or "someone who does nothing more than record verbatim what the [customer] says."[58]

In short, tailored services potentially harm the public, while merely providing a form with no assistance does no such harm. Yet these tailored services are exactly what ordinary citizens are unable to obtain for their routine transactions, due to the cost of retaining a traditional attorney. These rulings allow a consumer to fill out

53 *Id.* (citing *In re. Thompson*, 574 S.W.2d 365 (1978) (allowing sale of do-it-yourself divorce kit); *Holes v. Crier*, 363 Mo. 26, 247 S.W.2d 855 (1952) (allowing real estate agents to fill out routine forms as long as they were ancillary to routine business and brokers did not charge extra fee for service).

54 *Janson*, 802 F. Supp. 2d at 1064.

55 *Id.* at 1060.

56 *Id.*

57 See South Carolina Approves LegalZoom Business Model, available at www.reuters.com/article/2014/04/22/idUSnGNX1hzWlp+1c4+GNW20140422.

58 Report and Recommendation, *Medlock v. LegalZoom.com, Inc.*, Case No. 2012–208067 (S.C. Sup. Ct. Oct. 25, 2013), available at www.scbar.org/LinkClick.aspx?fileticket=GbQPsiTIoL4%3D&tabid=144. The North Carolina Supreme Court, meanwhile, recently denied LegalZoom's motion to dismiss an action brought against it by the state bar association because it was not convinced that LegalZoom gave no legal advice. See *LegalZoom.com, Inc. v. N. Carolina State Bar*, No. 11 CVS 15111, 2014 WL 1213242 (N.C. Super. Ct. Mar. 24, 2014).

legal forms without assistance but deny her the ability to make an informed choice about whether or not to engage the services of an online document preparer.

Lay Representation Before Non-judicial Bodies

Bar associations also pursue UPL claims against laypersons participating as representatives in non-judicial bodies, such as administrative agencies and in arbitration. Despite many years of successful lay appearances before federal administrative agencies,[59] some states continue to prohibit lay assistance with state administrative agency hearings. Similarly, in the world of arbitration, a forum designed specifically as an alternative to formal litigation, bar associations and courts in several states maintain that lay representation is prohibited by their UPL rules.

Representation Before Federal Agencies

Federal law authorizes administrative agencies to issue regulations to determine whether lay representatives may appear before them;[60] most agencies have done so.[61] Several states have taken a similar approach.[62] Experience at the federal level has shown that laypersons are able to represent clients at an agency hearing.[63] Particularly notable for its longevity and success is non-lawyer practice at the United States Patent Office (USPO) and before the Internal Revenue Service (IRS) and United States Tax Court.

Patent practice is known for its particularly complicated legal rules. Yet the USPO has long allowed lay representation,[64] provided non-lawyer "agents" fulfill the

[59] See e.g., *Sperry v. Florida ex rel. Fla. Bar*, 373 U.S. 379, 382 (1963) (noting the success of non-lawyer representation before Patent Office); Herbert M. Rosenthal, *Report of the Commission on Nonlawyer Practice*, 7 Prof. Law. 12, 12–13 (1995). (Recommending that "the states . . . Consider nonlawyer representation of individuals in state administrative agency proceedings, as long as the nonlawyer representatives are subject to the agencies' standards of practice and discipline").

[60] 5 U.S.C. § 500.

[61] See, e.g., 31 C.F.R. § 10.3(b), (c) (authorizing non-lawyer representation before United States Tax Court); 20 C.F.R. § 404.1705(b) (authorizing non-lawyer representation before the Social Security Administration); 37 C.F.R. § 11.6 (b) (authorizing non-lawyer representation before the United States Patent Office).

[62] See, e.g., ABA Standing Comm. on Client Prot., 2012 Survey of Unlicensed Practice of Law Committees 1–8 chart 2 (2012), available at www.americanbar.org/content/dam/aba/administrative/professional_responsibility/2012_upl_report_charts.authcheckdam.pdf (Of states that responded to survey, the following allowed non-lawyer participation at agency proceedings: Arizona, Arkansas, Colorado, Connecticut (if permitted by agency regulations), Delaware, Washington, DC, Florida, Indiana, Iowa (if permitted by agency regulations), Kentucky, Maine, Missouri, Montana, Nebraska, New Mexico, North Dakota, Oregon, Pennsylvania, South Dakota, Tennessee, Texas, Utah, Virginia, Washington (if permitted by agency regulations), Wisconsin).

[63] *Sperry*, supra *note* 59.

[64] See 37 C.F.R. § 11.6 (b) ("Any citizen of the United States who is not an attorney, and who fulfills the requirements of this part may be registered as a patent agent to practice before the Office").

USPO's requirements for practicing before it.[65] In *Sperry v. Florida*,[66] the Supreme Court overturned a Florida Supreme Court ruling enjoining a non-lawyer from aiding Florida citizens with federal patent applications. Although the Court acknowledged that the activities in question violated Florida's UPL laws, it ruled Florida's laws were preempted by the federal law allowing non-lawyers to represent clients in federal patent matters.

The USPO's experience with lay patent representation had proven extremely successful.[67] Indeed, the USPO had found "no significant difference between lawyers and non-lawyers either with respect to their ability to handle the work or with respect to their ethical conduct."[68] The Office, it should be noted, has created its own system for registering and disciplining those who practiced before it, minimizing any impact that the bar's disciplinary system might have on the ethics of its practitioners.[69]

In a similar vein, certified public accountants (CPAs) and other non-lawyer "enrolled agents" are permitted to prepare taxation materials and appear at hearings before the IRS[70] and the United States Tax Court,[71] so long as they pass a written examination. The Tax Court, which has allowed non-lawyers to represent claimants since 1966, requires adherence to both the Federal Rules of Evidence[72] and the ABA's Model Rules of Professional Conduct for Attorneys.[73]

65 See 37 C.F.R. § 11.7 (establishing requirements for patent agents, including passing a registration exam, showing moral fitness, and scientific and technical expertise, and competence to represent clients before the Board).

66 *Sperry*, 404. supra note 59 at ("[T]he order enjoining petitioner must be vacated since it prohibits him from performing tasks which are incident to the preparation and prosecution of patent applications before the Patent Office.")

67 *Id.* at 383, 402.

68 *Id.* at 402.

69 *Id.*

70 31 C.F.R. § 10.3(b) (CPAs), (c) (Enrolled Agents); 31 C.F.R. § 10.4(a) ("Enrollment as an enrolled agent upon examination. The Commissioner, or delegate, will grant enrollment as an enrolled agent to an applicant eighteen years of age or older who demonstrates special competence in tax matters by written examination administered by, or administered under the oversight of, the Internal Revenue Service, who possesses a current or otherwise valid preparer tax identification number or other prescribed identifying number, and who has not engaged in any conduct that would justify the suspension or disbarment of any practitioner under the provisions of this part").

71 Tax Ct. R. 200(3) ("Nonattorney Applicants. An applicant who is not an attorney at law must, as a condition of being admitted to practice, file with the Admissions Clerk at the address listed in paragraph (b) of this Rule, a completed application accompanied by a fee to be established by the Court. See Appendix II. In addition, such an applicant must, as a condition of being admitted to practice, satisfy the Court, by means of a written examination given by the Court, that the applicant possesses the requisite qualifications to provide competent representation before the Court").

72 26 U.S.C. § 7453 (2012) ("[T]he proceedings of the Tax Court and its divisions shall be conducted in accordance with such rules of practice and procedure (other than rules of evidence) as the Tax Court may prescribe and in accordance with the rules of evidence applicable in trials without a jury in the United States District Court of the District of Columbia")

73 Tax Ct. R. 201(a) ("Practitioners before the Court shall carry on their practice in accordance with the letter and spirit of the Model Rules of Professional Conduct of the American Bar Association").

Representation before state agencies

Unlike those areas preempted by federal laws, non-lawyers are an integral part of many state agencies' practices, despite state and local bars' attempts to stymie this longstanding practice. As the Supreme Court of Ohio noted in *Cleveland Bar Assn. v. Comp Management, Inc.*, non-lawyer agents represented at least one party in 95% of hearings before the state's Industrial Commission.[74] In that decision, the Court refused to affirm a report by the bar association that practice before the Industrial Commission violated the state's UPL rules. The Court pointed out that:

> It is no secret that a full confirmation of the [bar's] report in this case would substantially alter the administrative landscape. [It] would immediately vitiate Industrial Commission procedures that have been in place for more than 30 years, ban virtually all nonlawyer involvement in the hearing process, significantly, if not drastically, curtail the business of actuarial firms, and, to a lesser extent, impair the ability of unions to represent their members, and increase the premium costs and attorney fees for workers' compensation claims in Ohio.[75]

Refusing to approve the regime change suggested by the Cleveland Bar Association, the Ohio high court ruled that "nonlawyers who appear and practice in a representative capacity before the Industrial Commission and the Bureau of Workers' Compensation are not engaged in the unauthorized practice of law."[76]

In other jurisdictions, like Pennsylvania[77], Idaho,[78] and Colorado, the default rule is that lay representation in agency proceedings is presumptively the UPL and the courts must decide the propriety of lay representation at state agency hearings on a case-by-case basis. This insistence on a case-by-case determination effectively cancels any efficiency or cost-saving benefits of a rule allowing lay representation in principle because each litigant wishing to be represented by a layperson must litigate whether or not she may proceed. Moreover, the decisions confuse, rather than clarify, the state of the law.

In some jurisdictions, the UPL jurisprudence is confusing and contradictory. For example, in *Denver Bar Ass'n v. Pub. Utilities Comm'n*, the Supreme Court of Colorado invalidated a bright-line rule allowing non-lawyers to appear before the

[74] 818 N.E.2d 1181, 1188. (2004).

[75] *Id.*

[76] *Id.* at 1189.

[77] See, e.g., In re Estate of Rowley, 444 C.D. 2013, 2013 WL 6795208 (Pa. Commw. Ct. Dec. 23, 2013) ("It is well settled that with a few exceptions, non-attorneys may not represent parties before the Pennsylvania courts and most administrative agencies").

[78] See *Idaho State Bar Ass'n v. Idaho Pub. Utilities Comm'n*, 102 Idaho 672, 676, 637 P.2d 1168, 1172 (1981) ("Inasmuch [the agency's rules] profess to empower third persons unconnected with the entity and acting in a representative capacity in proceedings before the Commission to engage in activities constituting the practice of law, the Commission in adopting these subsections has infringed upon the inherent and singularly judicial power granted by the constitution to this court to define and regulate the practice of law").

Public Utilities Commission in all circumstances.[79] In so holding, the Court maintained that it was "[t]he character of the act done, rather than that it is performed before the Commission, is the factor which is decisive of whether it constitutes the practice of law."[80] In a later case, however, a Colorado appellate court held that "proceedings at an Industrial Commission hearing are sufficiently informal so as to permit the employer's representative to question witnesses and introduce evidence when invited to do so by a hearing officer."[81] Yet if one were to look at the "character of the act done," as mandated by *Denver Bar Ass'n*, questioning witnesses and introducing evidence is surely on the "practice of law" side of the equation. Thus, if a Colorado citizen cannot afford or does not wish to have a lawyer represent her at an agency hearing, she has very little guidance from the courts about whether or when she may engage a lay representative.

There is, moreover, despite a broad range of experience with lay representation before administrative agencies, no evidence that properly regulated lay advocates cannot represent clients at least as satisfactorily as lawyers.[82] In any event, the competence of lay representatives should be policed by the agencies themselves or the state Attorneys General, who are not burdened by the conflict of interest inherent in the bar's scrutiny of such practices.

Arbitration

Arbitration should be a congenial forum for lay representation. It was developed to avoid the cost, formality, and delay that attach to court proceedings. It would seem clear that arbitration, particularly when it is private, should not fall within the ambit of state UPL rules about litigation. Not surprisingly, the American Arbitration Association, the leading arbitration services organization, allows parties to be represented by non-lawyers.[83]

Moreover, non-lawyer representation at arbitration hearings has a long and successful history in the context of labor disputes. As the Supreme Court of Rhode Island recently noted in *In re Town of Little Compton*,[84] "private arbitration [has since 1960] been the central and distinctive feature of our collective

[79] 391 P.2d 467, 471 (Co. 1964).
[80] *Id.* at 471.
[81] *Ross v. Industrial Comm'n*, 566 P.2d 367, 369 (Co. App. 1977).
[82] See *Sperry*, supra note 59 at 382.
[83] See, e.g., American Arbitration Association, Employment Arbitration Rules and Procedures, Rule 19 "Representation," available at www.adr.org/aaa/faces/rules/searchrules/rulesdetail?doc=ADRSTG_004366&_afrLoop=2327416919884672&_afrWindowMode=0&_afrWindowId=14uvbktiva_435#%40%3F_afrWindowId%3D14uvbktiva_435%26_afrLoop%3D2327416919884672%26doc%3DADRSTG_004366%26_afrWindowMode%3D0%26_adf.ctrl-state%3D14uvbktiva_491; see also, *Nisha, LLC v. TriBuilt Const. Grp., LLC*, 388 S.W.3d 444, 446 (Ark. 2012) (noting that "under the American Arbitration Association (AAA) rules, which governed the arbitration proceeding at issue, any party could be represented by counsel, pro se, or 'by any other representative of that party's choosing'").
[84] 37 A.3d 85, 90 (R.I. 2012).

bargaining system" and that while "most ... states ... have not considered whether nonlawyer representation in labor arbitration is [UPL] ... those states that have addressed this issue have generally permitted the practice."[85] The court pointed to rules in California, Connecticut, Utah, and Washington that expressly allow the practice, and a 2008 case where the Supreme Court of Ohio ruled that, because arbitration did not rely on the same strict and formal rules of traditional litigation, non-lawyers were allowed to represent parties at labor arbitrations.[86] Moreover, the Rhode Island high court was unable to find any state that disallowed the common practice. Yet equally clear was that allowing non-lawyer representation violated in terms the state's UPL rules prohibiting, "without limitation, an activity that constitutes the practice of law as "the doing of any act for another person usually done by attorneys at law in the course of their profession."[87]

The court held that "because of the long-standing involvement of non-lawyer union employees at public grievance arbitrations," the practice would be allowed to continue for the immediate future. But it made no change to the state's over-inclusive UPL law, stating it would reserve the "deci[sion] [about] the generic issue of nonlawyers participating in public grievance arbitrations" for "the future."[88]

Where non-lawyer representation in arbitration is barred or restricted, the decisions focus on the acts performed by a representative at an arbitration that are similar to formal litigation rather than on the purpose of arbitration or the harm caused to the parties represented.[89] For instance, in 2012, the Supreme Court of Arkansas held, in *Nisha, LLC v. TriBuilt Const. Grp., LLC*, that a corporation could not be represented by a non-lawyer in an arbitration proceeding, even if the representative was an employee under Arkansas' UPL statute, a non-lawyer could not "tender or furnish legal services or advice," or "render legal services of any kind in actions or proceedings of any nature."[90] The UPL prohibition applied in this case because, as in formal litigation, the parties in an arbitration have "the right to be heard, present

[85] *Id.*

[86] *Id.* at 90–91. See also CONN. R. SUPER. CT. § 2–44A(b) ("Whether or not it constitutes the practice of law, the following activities by any person are permitted: * * *(4) Participating in labor negotiations, arbitrations, or conciliations arising under collective bargaining rights or agreements"); UTAH SUP. CT. R. PROF'L PRAC. 14–802(c) ("Whether or not it constitutes the practice of law, the following activity by a nonlawyer, who is not otherwise claiming to be a lawyer or to be able to practice law, is permitted: * * * (10) Participating in labor negotiations, arbitrations or conciliations arising under collective bargaining rights or agreements or as otherwise allowed by law"); WASH. GEN. R. 24(b) ("Whether or not they constitute the practice of law, the following are permitted: * * * (5) Participation in labor negotiations, arbitrations or conciliations arising under collective bargaining rights or agreements"); CAL. CIV. PROC. CODE § 1282.4(a) and 1282.4(h) (West 2014).

[87] *In re Town of Little Compton*, 37 A.3d 85 (R.I.2012) at 94–95.

[88] *Id.* at 95.

[89] See, e.g., *Nisha, LLC v. TriBuilt Const. Grp., LLC*, 388 S.W.3d 444, 445 (2012); County, No. CV737595; *Disciplinary Counsel v. Alexicole, Inc.*, 822 N.E.2d 348 (Oh. 2004); *The Florida Bar v. Rapoport*, 845 So. 2d 874 (Fla. 2003); *In re Creasy*, 198 Ariz. 539, 12 P.3d 214 (2000).

[90] *Id.* (*citing* 16 A.C.A. § 16–22–211 (West 2011)).

evidence material to the controversy, and cross-examine witnesses appearing at the hearing ..." [91] The Arkansas high court made no suggestion that the corporation or its employees were damaged by their decision to forgo counsel. In fact, it was the other party to the arbitration who had objected after the corporation decided to appoint one of its employees to represent it at the private arbitration.[92] Nor, in this instance, could the Court suggest that the business was not making an informed decision, as it had retained and then released attorneys once the proceeding was moved to arbitration.[93]

The Supreme Court of Ohio made a similar decision in *Disciplinary Counsel v. Alexicole, Inc.*[94] when it fined a non-lawyer corporation for, and enjoined it from, representing parties in a securities arbitration proceeding.[95] Although the representative in question had never "held himself out" as an attorney, he represented parties in securities arbitrations, and, during that process, "regularly prepares statements of claims, conducts discovery, participates in prehearing conferences, negotiates settlements, and participates in mediation and arbitration hearings."[96]

Decisions like *Nisha, LLC.* and *Alexicole* undermine the advantages of arbitration for litigants who cannot afford counsel or who may simply prefer lay representation. Indeed, they detract from the central purpose of arbitration – allowing the parties to design their own dispute resolution procedure free of the formalities and costs of court litigation.

Non-Lawyer Assistance in Formal litigation

In the realm of lay representation in formal court proceedings, the UPL world is much clearer, although arguably even more hostile to non-lawyer representation. Almost every state explicitly forbids a party to be represented by a non-lawyer in court, or to receive aid from a non-lawyer in preparing court documents.[97] This requirement is perhaps the most defensible from the perspective of the bar associations: court rules are complicated, and deciding whether a layperson could adequately prepare pleadings or represent another in court would be administratively

91 *Id.* at 449.
92 *Id.* at 446.
93 *Id.* at 447.
94 822 N.E.2d 348 (Oh. 2004).
95 *Id. at* 349.
96 *Id.*
97 Denckla, supra note 1, at 2589 (1999) ("Almost every American court has prohibited nonlawyers from appearing before them"). See, e.g., GA. CODE. ANN. § 5–19–50 ("The practice of law in this state is defined as: (1) Representing litigants in court and preparing pleadings and other papers incident to any action or special proceedings in any court or other judicial body") (West 2014); MINN. STAT. ANN. § 481.02(1) ("Prohibitions. It shall be unlawful for any person or association of persons, except members of the bar of Minnesota admitted and licensed to practice as attorneys at law, to appear as attorney or counselor at law in any action or proceeding in any court in this state to maintain, conduct, or defend the same, except personally as a party thereto ... or to prepare legal documents") (West 2014).

difficult. These objections, however, say nothing about whether or not individual litigants benefit from the rule. Indeed, any public-interest justification comes up against a formidable theoretical obstacle: the allowance of self-representation.

But why should lay representation be barred when self-representation is a constitutional right in the criminal context and is permitted in the civil context by constitution or statute in every state?[98] Moreover, the refusal to allow lay assistance is based on a misleading premise that the choice for a litigant is between lay assistance or a lawyer when, in many cases, the real alternative is between lay assistance and appearing pro se. The fallacy of this "choice" is illustrated by the fact that three out of five civil litigants appear pro se not because they choose to but because no lawyer is available to them.[99] Thus, if the right question is asked – whether or not the public is better off with *no* assistance or lay assistance – the prohibition of lay assistance in formal litigation becomes much less defensible as in the interest of the public

Written Submissions

In *Johnson v. Avery*,[100] the U.S. Supreme Court ruled that Tennessee could not prohibit non-lawyer assistance by so-called "jailhouse lawyers" to inmates drafting *habeas corpus* and other civil petitions because the state did "not provide an available alternative to the assistance provided by other inmates."[101] The Court found that, because many prisoners were illiterate or poorly educated, "if such prisoners cannot have the assistance of a 'jailhouse lawyer,' their possibly valid constitutional claims will never be heard in any court." It reasoned that Tennessee's refusal to provide reasonable alternatives was akin to "adopt[ing] and enforce[ing] a rule forbidding illiterate or poorly educated prisoners to file habeas corpus petitions." Thus, Tennessee's refusal to provide assistance to prisoners or to allow inmate assistance "denied [prisoners] access to the courts."[102]

Justice Douglas' concurrence made clear that at least one member of the Court saw this ruling as a referendum on UPL laws rather than a decision focused only on the rights of incarcerated persons:

98 Federal law permits parties to appear pro se in all cases. See 28 U.S.C. § 1654, ("In all courts of the United States the parties may plead and conduct their own cases personally"); Nina Ingwer VanWormer, *Help at Your Fingertips: A Twenty-First Century Response to the Pro Se Phenomenon*, 60 VAND. L. REV. 983, 988 (2007) (although they use "various mechanisms ... states widely recognize civil litigants' right to proceed pro se").

99 See Alicia M. Farley, *An Important Piece of the Bundle: How Limited Appearances Can Provide an Ethically Sound Way to Increase Access to Justice for Pro Se Litigants*, 20 GEO. J. LEGAL ETHICS 563, 564–65.

100 393 U.S. 483, 488 (1969).

101 *Id.* at 490 ("[U]nless and until the State provides some reasonable alternative to assist inmates in the preparation of petitions for post-conviction relief, it may not validly enforce a regulation ... barring inmates from furnishing such assistance to other prisoners"). But see *Turner v. Am. Bar Ass'n*, 407 F. Supp. 451, 478 (N.D. Tex. 1975) (multidistrict litigation holding that there is no constitutional right for a criminal defendant to have an "unlicensed layperson represent them in [c]ourt proceedings").

102 *Johnson, supra note* 100, *at* 487–88.

> [N]ot enough lawyers to manage or supervise [civil claims]; and much of the basic work done requires no special legal talent. Yet there is a closed-shop philosophy in the legal profession that cuts down drastically active roles for laymen . . .
>
> Laymen in and out of prison should be allowed to act as "next friend" to any person in the preparation of any paper or document or claim, so long as he does not hold himself out as practicing law or as being a member of the Bar. [103]

While the majority confined its holding to the *habeas* petitions of inmates, Justice Douglas wrote that the eradication of the "closed-shop philosophy" of lawyers, and the acceptance of lay assistance, should be equally applied to the situation of poor and even middle-income litigants in any civil claim for which no free or low-cost legal assistance was provided.

The Supreme Court took a small step toward Douglas' view when it held, in *Wolff v. McDonnell*,[104] that inmate assistance was to be allowed for all civil claims by indigent prisoners, not just for *habeas* petitions. There, Nebraska was required to allow lay assistance to a prisoner for a "civil rights" petition when it did not provide reasonable alternatives. The Court noted that the State had "read [*Johnson*] too narrowly" to apply only to "habeas actions." The right of access to the courts, upon which *Johnson* was premised, "applied equally to any allegation "concerning violations of fundamental constitutional rights."[105]

Despite the potential of the Court's rulings in *Johnson* and *Wolff* to create pressure to allow lay assistance in other contexts where, although fundamental rights are implicated, no meaningful access to an attorney is provided, lower courts have restricted that case to its facts.[106]

A 2013 case from the Ohio Supreme Court is illustrative. In *Cleveland Metro. Bar Assn. v. McGinnis*,[107] the Court approved a bar opinion that sanctioned McGinnis and fined her $6,000 for "accepting $40" to prepare a pleading in an eviction proceeding, and for holding herself out as a lawyer by posting a flyer that stated, "Forrestine's Law, Inc. Avoid expensive attorney fees."[108] Although the claimant submitted an affidavit, no mention was made about whether he had been confused by the flyer, whether his pleadings were prepared improperly or whether he had

[103] *Id.* at 491–92 (Douglas, J., concurring).
[104] 418 U.S. 539, 579 (1974).
[105] *Id.* at 578.
[106] See, e.g., *Dunn v. The Florida Bar*, 726 F. Supp. 1261, 1275 (M.D. Fla. 1988) (*Johnson* does not extend to lay assistance with divorce); *Nowicki v. Voss*, 103 F.3d 133 (7th Cir. 1996) (*Johnson* applies only to "extremely limited circumstances that entitle an indigent prisoner to receive the assistance of a layperson"); but see *Matter of Bright*, 171 B.R. 799, 806 (Bankr. E.D. Mich. 1994) (holding that lay assistance in bankruptcy pleadings is not the UPL because "[t]he organized bar, which has not made available the minimal counseling which would enable a person to exercise his right of self-representation, cannot be heard to say that the service which it does not provide is the practice of law").
[107] 998 N.E.2d 474, 476 (Oh. 2013)
[108] This advertisement might well be considered misleading and might be the subject of regulation regardless of whether the services performed in this case should be disallowed in all instances.

been successful in fighting the eviction. The Court flatly ruled that the flyer was misleading, and that the claimants "legal rights were undoubtedly affected" by the preparation of pleadings.[109] This case demonstrates ideally the way that our civil and criminal laws are able to deal with egregious non-attorney actions, such as masquerading as a lawyer – no UPL law is necessary for an action against McGinnis for fraud.[110] More significantly, however, this case reflects the ease with which bar associations can challenge lay practice, regardless of whether a blanket denial of such assistance is in the public's interest or whether there are any meaningful alternatives for individuals who prefer lay assistance with pleadings to no representation at all.

One alleged obstacle to lay assistance with pleadings is that it dissolves the traditional attorney–client relationship, which imagines the attorney representing her client from before the first pleading to the resolution of a case. In this regard, however, the practice of "unbundling" or "ghostwriting" by attorneys is instructive. A number of states now allow attorneys to draft court documents for a person who intends to represent herself pro se in a court proceeding. In such circumstances, the attorney does not sign the documents or appear in court, but merely drafts the documents for a fee. The ABA declared "ghostwriting" to be permissible in a 2007 ethics opinion,[111] and at least 18 state bar associations have concurred. Most of those states do not even require the attorney or litigant to disclose the fact that any assistance was given.[112] When Colorado approved unbundling, it reasoned that consumers were able to evaluate the "risks and benefits" of limited representation.[113] The same trust in consumers should apply to lay representation in the form of assistance with court pleadings, motions, and appeals. A consumer able to weigh the

[109] *Cleveland Metro. Bar Assn.*, 998 N.E.2d at 476.

[110] For instance, in Ohio, impersonating an attorney is a first-degree misdemeanor. See Oh. Rev. Code Ann. §§ 4705.07, 4705.99.

[111] ABA, Standing Comm. On Ethics and Prof. Resp., Formal Op. 07–446. See Engler, Chapter 29, in this volume.

[112] Alabama, Alaska, Arizona, California, Colorado, Maine, Michigan, Minnesota, New Mexico, North Carolina, Utah, Vermont, Washington, and the District of Columbia allow anonymous ghostwriting by attorneys. See Ala. Bar Ass'n, Ethics Op. 10–01 (2010); Colo. Bar Ass'n, Op. 101 (Amended 2006); Me. State Bar Ass'n, Ethics Op. 89 (1988); Mich. State Bar Ass'n, Ethics Op. RI-347 (2010); Minn. State Bar Ass'n Pro Se Implementation Comm., Final Report; N.M. R. Prof'l Conduct 16–303 cmt. 15 (2008); N.C. State Bar Ass'n Ethics Comm., Formal Op. 2005–10 (2005); Or. Bar Ass'n, Op. 11–183 (2011); Utah State Bar, Ethics Advisory Op. 08–01 (2008); Vt. R. Prof'l Conduct 1.2 cmt. 3 (2008); Wash. Super. Ct. R. 11(b); D.C. Bar Ass'n, Ethics Op. 330 (2005). Florida, New Hampshire, Tennessee, and Virginia allow ghostwriting but insist that the assistance is disclosed. See Fla. R. Prof'l Conduct 4–1.2 (2008); N.H. Super. Ct. R. 15(f); Tenn. Sup. Ct. Bd. of Prof'l Responsibility, Formal Op. 2007-F-153 (2007); Va. State Bar Ass'n, Legal Ethics Op. 1127 (1988).

[113] See Marcus J. Lock, *Increasing Access to Justice: Expanding the Role of Nonlawyers in the Delivery of Legal Services to Low-Income Coloradans*, 72 U. Colo. L. Rev. 459, 489 (2001) (quoting the comments section to the Colorado rule allowing unbundling and arguing that the same logic should be applied to lay representation in Colorado).

risks and benefits of unbundled attorney services should be equally able to evaluate whether to use lay representation. As in nearly all areas discussed in this chapter, most people who can afford an attorney will, of course, hire one to draft pleadings as well as represent them in the courtroom, but a person without the means to do so should not be left with no choice but to prepare court documents on his or her own.

Lay Assistance In Court

Although it is taken as gospel that only an attorney can make court appearances on behalf of a litigant, we should be skeptical of even this prohibition of lay assistance. Although courts insist on a bright-line rule against lay assistance, all states permit self-representation, either by constitution or statute. The reasons for allowing self-representation also support allowing lay assistance.

In the criminal context, although the right to self-representation is guaranteed in the Sixth Amendment, courts have refused to extend that right to lay assistance.[114] The reasoning behind the right to self-representation, however, extends to recognizing a litigant's right to choose her representative. The Supreme Court's decision in *Faretta v. California* was rooted in the notion that the Sixth Amendment "grants to the accused personally the right to make his defense."[115] Because it was the defendant who was affected by the outcome of a criminal trial, the Court reasoned that it was "the defendant . . . who must be free . . . to decide whether . . . counsel is to his advantage . . ."[116] And while a defendant might not be as capable as an attorney to try a case, "a layperson . . . is as capable as any lawyer of making an intelligent choice" about whether he or she wants an attorney. Ignoring this, said the Court, "would impair the worth of [the constitutional right to an attorney] by treating [it as an] empty verbalism[]."[117]

If a defendant is as capable as any lawyer of making an intelligent choice to represent herself, a defendant should be allowed to make the same choice about whether to engage a lay assistant. Moreover, in the civil context, where no right to a state-provided attorney exists, the "right" to self-representation granted by every state, becomes an "empty verbalism." When litigants have no access to an attorney, there is no choice; self-representation is the only option. Yet courts prohibiting lay assistance routinely proceed without acknowledging this issue. For instance, in *Ippolito v. Florida*, a federal district court dismissed a number of claims made by a group of laypersons "associated with several non-profit organizations, such as Pro Se Litigants of America, Inc., and the Defenders of Life and Property, Inc." who wished to represent clients in court.[118] In doing so, the court focused on the level of knowledge necessary to practice law, stating that:

[114] See, e.g., *United States v. Hoffman*, 733 F.2d 596, 599–600 (9th Cir. 1984); *Turner v. ABA*, 407 F.Supp. 451 (N.D. Tx. 1975).

[115] *Faretta v. Ca.*, 422 U.S. 806, 819 (1975).

[116] *Id.* at 833.

[117] *Id.* at 815 (quotations omitted).

[118] *Ippolito v. State of Fla.*, 824 F. Supp. 1562, 1564–65 (M.D. Fla. 1993).

> it is unlikely that an average person could effectively prepare a case for trial, appear in court, and make an effective argument before a judge or a jury. Unskilled laymen attempting to argue their own case, or on behalf of another, would be inordinately disadvantaged. For these reasons, the Bar has become an indispensable component of the modern legal system.[119]

While it is hard to dispute that an "unskilled" layperson is generally less capable of performing in court than an attorney, this statement assumes that the choice facing litigants is whether to hire an attorney or to proceed without one, which it simply is not. The court listed a number of high-stakes cases in which representation by a non-lawyer might be disastrous for her client.[120] Of course, in certain cases, or perhaps certain categories of cases, a state or court might decide that only attorneys are competent to deal with the complex legal issues involved. And, in such high-stakes cases, there are likely many lawyers willing to become involved. But in lower-level cases, where legal issues are routine and returns to the representative small, such a high-minded view of the law and those who may practice it does not protect individual litigants.

In contrast, lay assistance is broadly accepted in other countries, including Canada and England. In Canada "nonlawyer agents" are allowed to represent litigants in small claims, family law, traffic, and minor criminal cases, so long as a court is satisfied that the agent is qualified.[121] Similarly, English courts routinely allow non-lawyers, called "*McKenzie* friends," including spouses, siblings, and accountants, to assist pro se litigants.[122] *McKenzie* friends are "not allowed to address the court but may sit at the counsel table, make suggestions quietly, refer the *pro se* party to documents, take notes, suggest questions for examination or cross-examination, and so forth."[123] In both jurisdictions, non-lawyer representation or pro se assistance is allowed only at the discretion of the courts.[124] But, unlike in America, the default position is that a party may be assisted in court by a person of her choice. The standard in British courts is that the "justices must when considering an application that a friend assists an unrepresented defendant strive to ensure by

[119] *Id.* at 1568.

[120] *Id.* ("When a 15-year-old girl is murdered by a parolee five months after he is released from prison despite a history as a sex offender, when a driver is severely injured when her vehicle is struck by a fleeing suspect being pursued by a police officer, when a citizen's liberty is jeopardized by an unlawful prosecution, and when a landowner is deprived of all economically viable use of her property without just compensation, the victims seek legal counsel – competent, skilled attorneys – to remedy the alleged injustice and obtain remuneration for their injuries. In each instance, the legal profession is called upon to assist in the resolution of these matters.")

[121] Jack Goldschmidt, Autonomy and "Gray-Area" Pro Se Defendants: Ensuring Competence to Guarantee Freedom, 6 Nw. J. L. & Soc. Pol'y 130, 173–74 (2011).

[122] *Id.*

[123] *Id.*

[124] See, e.g., *R. v. Dick* [2002] B.C.L.R. 27 (noting that it is the court's discretion whether to allow a non-lawyer representative in a British Columbia court); *R. v. Leicester City Justices, et al.*, (1991) W.L.R. 974 (A.C.) (Same, in British Judicial system).

their decision that no injustice will be done if they refuse the application and that the proceedings bear the appearance of fairness."[125] This is a far cry from the essentially absolute prohibition on non-lawyer assistants in American courtrooms.

If American jurisdictions are unable or unwilling to provide a right to counsel in civil cases, they should consider relaxing their UPL laws and setting up systems by which they can ensure that a non-lawyer representative is capable of representing a litigant in an individual case. It is true that allowing lay representatives to appear in court may impose additional administrative costs, but those costs are outweighed by the benefits to the justice system overall of allowing litigants to receive some representation when the alternative is fending for themselves in court.

CONCRETE STEPS FORWARD FOR BAR ASSOCIATIONS AND COURTS

There are a number of steps that bar associations can take to reduce the protectionist implications of their UPL enforcement, ranging from abolishing their UPL Committees altogether to instituting training and disciplinary systems for non-lawyer assistance. Courts, with the power to change their states' UPL laws and the standards by which cases are judged, are also in a particularly good position to ensure that only UPL practices that actually harm consumers are proscribed.

A dramatic but realistic step that bar associations can take is to abolish their UPL Committees. In 2010, Montana did just that. The Montana Supreme Court adopted the bar association's recommendation that both entities should remove themselves from enforcing UPL laws. Noting that the "array of persons and institutions that provide legal or legally-related services to members of the public are, literally, too numerous to list," and the fact that "what constitutes the practice of law . . . is by no means clearly defined," the high court dissolved the state's committee on unauthorized practice.[126]

As Montana's decision suggests, the bars and courts should focus on regulating the actions of those who are admitted to practice law.[127] Unfortunately, there is no shortage of work to be done in this area.[128] Short of abolishing UPL committees, state bar associations can work to ensure that lay representatives have the knowledge

[125] *R. v. Leicester City Justices, et al.*, (1991) W.L.R. 974 (A.C.).

[126] *Id.*

[127] Another area where UPL committees might be useful is regulating those who hold themselves out as lawyers. This issue is particularly live in the immigration context where non-lawyers bill themselves as "notarios," which translates to notary, but in certain Latin countries also means a legal professional. See Leslie C. Levin, *The Monopoly Myth and Other Tales About the Superiority of Lawyers*, 82 Ford, L. Rev. 2611, 2616 (2014) ("Notarios are not trained in immigration law – which is substantively complex – and their inaccurate advice can have devastating consequences, including removal of their clients from the country in cases where removal would not have otherwise occurred"); Travis B. Olsen, *Combating "Notario Fraud" Locally*, 22 Berkeley La Raza L.J. 383, 385–86 (2012).

[128] See, e.g., Anita Bernstein, *Pitfalls Ahead: A Manifesto for the Training of Lawyers*, 94 Cornell L. Rev. 479, 487 (2009).

necessary to perform limited legal functions, and to ensure that there is a system of discipline in place to enforce appropriate standards. In Washington State, the bar's "Practice of Law Board" proposed, and its Supreme Court approved, a new rule entitling "Limited License Technicians" to perform discrete legal services in areas of law approved by a "Limited License Technician Board"[129] and the Washington Supreme Court.[130] LLTs are allowed to "select and complete court forms," "review and explain pleadings," and identify other necessary court documents, among other services. The rule, similar to many attorney admission rules, establishes age, moral fitness, and education requirements,[131] an application process, and "Continuing Licensing Requirements." The Rule also tasks the Board with instituting disciplinary proceedings and provides that an LLT owes her client the same "duty of care" applied to Washington Attorneys.[132] New York and California are currently considering similar proposals.[133] These requirements go a long way to answering concerns about the lack of admission requirements and disciplinary systems available to ensure competent non-lawyer assistants.

On the other hand, states should be wary of creating an expensive apparatus of licensing and discipline that prices low-income consumers out of the market for LLTs. Moreover, instituting an LLT system should not replace other possible market solutions for those who cannot afford access to an attorney. While an LLT may be a very good alternative for a consumer who wants a representative with some legal training, we should not simply replace the current binary choice of an attorney or self-representation with another economically prohibitive system of hiring an attorney, an LLT, or representing oneself. Even states that have taken this step should look closely at reforming or abolishing their UPL laws and practices and

[129] Wash. A.P.R. 28(C) (the board consists of nine lawyers and four non-lawyers).

[130] See *In the Matter of the Adoption of New APR 28 – Limited Practice Rule for Limited License Legal Technicians*, Order no. 25700-A-1005 (Wa. Sup. Ct., June 15, 2012), available at www.courts.wa.gov/content/publicUpload/Press%20Releases/25700-A-1005.pdf.

[131] *Id.* The educational requirements are:

(a) (i) An associate degree or equivalent program, or a bachelor degree, in paralegal/legal assistant studies approved by the ABA or the Board, together with a minimum of two years experience as a paralegal/legal assistant doing substantive law-related work under the supervision of a lawyer, provided that at least one year is under a Washington lawyer; or

(ii) A post-baccalaureate certificate program in paralegal/legal assistant studies approved by the Board, together with a minimum of three years experience as a paralegal/legal assistant doing substantive law-related work under the supervision of a lawyer, provided that at least one year is under a Washington lawyer; and

(b) Complete at least 20 hours of pro bono legal services in Washington as approved by the Board, within two years prior to taking the LLT examination.

[132] Wash. A.P.R. 28(A)-(F).

[133] See Jonathan Lippman, C.J., "The State of The Judiciary" at 12, available at www.nycourts.gov/ctapps/news/SOJ-2013.pdf; Working Group Recommendation: Support of Limited License Program and Possible Governance Structures (June 17, 2013), available at http://board.calbar.ca.gov/docs/agendaItem/Public/agendaitem1000010722.pdf.

trusting that consumers will be able to make their own cost–benefit analysis when deciding what kind of assistance they want with their personal legal issues.

Short of voluntary dissolution of UPL enforcement committees by the bars, courts and legislatures should carefully consider revising their UPL rules. States could reform their UPL statutes and rules to allow many services currently considered UPL. They could restrict their definitions of the practice of law to in-court litigation, or they could reduce their role in the regulation of non-lawyers by redefining who falls under the auspices of court regulation. This would require a potentially radical but also realistic shift in the courts' and bars' vision of their regulatory power – currently the default is that courts define what the "practice of law" is, and any layperson found to be performing such services is engaged in the UPL. It would be better to confine the definition of the "practice of law" to those who are admitted to the bar or hold themselves out as attorneys, and craft a separate set of rules to allow lay assistance outside of court and ensure competent lay representation in court.

UPLs are touted by bar associations as a means of protecting the public from unscrupulous, negligent lay practitioners. But those laws are an overbroad means of providing such protection, because they bar lay representation altogether. Tort law protections are preferable to prohibitory regulation. As Washington did with its LLT program, a number of states have already required a "standard of care" for those who perform quasi-legal services that is equal to the duty of care standard applied to attorneys.[134] This approach could be extended to all non-lawyer representations. In fact, while rarely discussed in the UPL context, a number of courts have recognized a private action, whether in contract or tort, against anyone who performs legal services, barred or not, and have held them to the same standard of care that is required of an attorney.[135]

Access to quality attorneys is, of course, the goal of almost anyone writing about access to justice. Yet, as numerous studies have shown, where less complex matters are concerned, most attorneys are not competing to provide services to low-income or even middle-income Americans.[136] Instead, these consumers and litigants are

[134] See Sande L. Buhai, Act Like A Lawyer, Be Judged Like A Lawyer: The Standard of Care for the Unlicensed Practice of Law, 2007 UTAH L. REV. 87, 94 (2007) (discussing duty of care standard for lay representatives).

[135] *Id.* at 88 ("A majority of courts have held that one who provides legal services, regardless of whether licensed or authorized, should be held to the standard of care applicable to attorneys providing those same services"); see, e.g., *Jones v. Allstate Ins. Co.*, 45 P.3d 1068, 1081 (Wa. 2002) (Court finds that insurance claims adjuster violated UPL rules and negligently advised consumers. Because the "claims adjuster was engaged in the practice of law . . . [she] shall be held to the standard of care of a practicing attorney"); *Buscemi v. Intachai*, 730 So. 2d 329, 330 (Fla. Dist. Ct. App. 1999) (negligence action against non-lawyer who was found to have given negligent advice on marriage dissolution. The court found that "whether a lawyer or not, if [a person] undertakes to give legal advice, he is subject to a standard of due care").

[136] See, e.g., Legal Services Corporation, Documenting the Justice Gap in America: The Current Unmet Civil Needs of Low Income Americans 1–13 (2009), available at www.lsc.gov/pdfs/documenting_the_justice_gap_in_america_2009.pdf; Farley, supra n. 99.

forced to forgo legal transactions, or to represent themselves. Allowing a choice of non-lawyer assistance will fill a gap in services, not encroach upon the business of the bar. In the small segment of practice where non-attorneys actually do compete with attorneys, lawyers may be forced to lower their fees or to show clients that their services are worth the cost. While this may affect attorneys on the margin, the benefit to the public certainly outweighs the cost to the bar. If the bar is serious about increasing access to justice and unwilling or unable to provide legal services to those without means, it cannot continue to uphold and enforce outdated and rigid UPL rules.

42

The *Pyett* Protocol:

Collectively-Bargained Grievance Arbitration as a Forum for Individual Statutory Employment Claims

Terry Meginniss & Paul Salvatore

Unions and employers have historically been able to resolve labor disputes through a negotiated grievance and arbitration process. Until a 2009 decision of the Supreme Court, it was not clear if this process could be used for statutory employment claims of individual employees represented by unions. That decision suggested an affirmative answer to the question but raised issues of fairness to represented employees when unions declined to go to arbitration. Terry Meginniss and Paul Salvatore report on the "Protocol" they have negotiated and on their clients' behalf administer in the commercial building industry of New York City for precisely such cases.

In 2009, the U.S. Supreme Court in 14 *Penn Plaza LLC v. Pyett*[1] decided that a provision in a collective bargaining agreement (CBA) entered into between an employer and a union that waives the right of covered employees to pursue statutory claims of discrimination in a judicial forum is enforceable, provided that the waiver is both specific and clear and provided that the bargaining agreement creates a sufficient alternative forum for the pursuit of those claims. The Court's holding has been cheered by some and denigrated by others. Those who have welcomed the decision emphasize that (1) the decision authorizes the use of arbitration, a cost-effective and speedy forum, for employers and employees to resolve employment discrimination disputes by a neutral party; (2) the decision will have the salutary effect of easing the burden on an already crowded judicial system; and (3) the Court honored the abilities of arbitrators to hear and rule on these matters.

The Supreme Court's ruling left open a vexing question, however. In *Pyett*, the employees argued that the bargaining agreement's arbitration provision provided the union with the exclusive right to determine whether to bring their discrimination claim to arbitration. They asserted that, because the union had declined to bring the claim to arbitration, they had to be afforded the opportunity to pursue the claim in

Parts of this chapter were originally published as Terry Meginniss and Paul Salvatore, Response to an Unresolved Issue from Pyett: The NYC Real Estate Industry Protocol, in The Challenge for Collective Bargaining | Proceedings of the New York University 65th Annual Conference on Labor, (eds. Michael Z. Green and Sam Estreicher, Matthew Bender & Co. Inc, 2013).

1 556 U.S. 247 (2009).

court; otherwise the mandatory arbitration provision would have effectively extinguished altogether their right to vindicate the protections guaranteed by the statute. The Court did not decide this issue. After the decision, New York courts heard cases applying the same arbitration provision as the one at issue in *Pyett*, and addressed the issue of individual access with differing results – in some cases, courts have held that the union's refusal to pursue the grievance to arbitration acted as a waiver of the plaintiff's statutory rights, thereby relieving the plaintiff of the contract's waiver of access to a judicial forum, and in others, courts have compelled arbitration, regardless of initial union support.

Against this legal backdrop, the Realty Advisory Board on Labor Relations, Inc. (RAB), and SEIU Local 32BJ (the Union) have adopted a Protocol and Agreement for handling discrimination claims. The Protocol does not attempt to dispose of the legal question of whether an individual employee has effectively waived his/her right to a judicial forum when he/she seeks to pursue a discrimination claim that the Union has declined to pursue in the contractual arbitration forum; the Protocol does, however, afford the individual and his/her employer a cost-effective framework for resolving those claims.

THE PYETT DECISION

In 14 *Penn Plaza v. Pyett*, the Court held that arbitration was a suitable vehicle for the vindication of the substantive rights protected in anti-discrimination laws. The Court explained that parties' decision in the CBA "to resolve [Age Discrimination in Employment Act (ADEA)] claims by way of arbitration instead of litigation does not waive [the] statutory right to be free from workplace discrimination; it waives only the right to seek relief from a court in the first instance." [2]

The individual plaintiffs at issue in *Pyett* were long-standing employees in a commercial office building who were reassigned from positions as night watchmen to less desirable positions as night porters and light duty cleaners, allegedly due to their age. They brought suit against the employer and building owners under the ADEA, New York State Human Rights Law (NYSHRL), and the New York City Human Rights Law (NYCHRL). Defendants, commercial building owners/managers, filed a motion to compel arbitration, asserting that the CBA required plaintiffs to arbitrate such claims. The plaintiffs argued that, if the CBA were construed to require arbitration, it would effect a substantive waiver of their statutory rights because the union had declined to take their statutory discrimination claims to arbitration. The Supreme Court did not decide that issue. While holding that a CBA provision that "clearly and unmistakably" required union members to arbitrate ADEA claims was enforceable as a matter of federal law, it remanded the case to allow the lower court to resolve whether the CBA allowed the union, acting as a gatekeeper of the arbitration process,

[2] *Id.* at 265.

to prevent the individual employees from "effectively vindicating" their rights in the arbitral forum.

The dissenters in *Pyett* criticized the majority's reasoning, but noted that the Court's holding may have little practical effect. Because, the dissenters urged, unions typically control access to the arbitration forum created in a CBA, and, at least with respect to those claims the union chooses not to arbitrate, the employee would have to be granted access to a judicial forum to avoid having the employee's substantive claim altogether extinguished.

LOWER COURTS' INTERPRETATIONS OF PYETT

Following *Pyett*, the lower courts have devolved several principles concerning whether an individual whose terms of employment were covered by a CBA that expressly waives the right to proceed on statutory discrimination claims in a judicial forum may, nevertheless, do so.

The lower courts have looked first to whether the language in the collective bargaining agreement was sufficient to waive the right to proceed on the statutory claim in a judicial forum. It is common ground that the waiver must be both "explicitly stated" and "clear and unmistakable." A number of lower courts have declined to find a waiver where the bargaining agreement's definition of what is arbitrable was broadly stated and the contract included a general no-discrimination clause but did not specifically reference statutory discrimination provisions. [3] On the other hand, a few courts have held that a CBA that generally prohibits discrimination and provides for the arbitration of such claims *does* provide a "sufficiently clear and unmistakable waiver." [4] In other instances, courts have found a waiver where the contract language did not name specific statutes, but did include references that were sufficiently descriptive of statutory claims that it was clear the parties intended statutory discrimination claims to be included.[5]

3 See, e.g., *Evans v. Wayne County*, No. 2:10-CV-11275, 2011 WL 5546230, at *4–5 (E.D. Mich. Nov. 10, 2011); *Pulkkinen v. Fairpoint Commcn's, Inc.*, No. 09-cv-99-P-H, 2010 U.S. Dist. LEXIS 23917, at *15 (D. Me. Feb. 23, 2010 *Manuele v. City of Springfield, Ill.*, 718 F.Supp.2d 939 (C.D. Ill. 2010); *Barnes v. Harsthorn*, No. 09–2299, 2010 WL 3540919 (C.D. Ill. July 15, 2010); *Alderman v. 21 Club, Inc.*, 733 F. Supp.2d 461 (S.D.N.Y. 2010).

4 See *Cardine v. Holten Meat, Inc.*, No. 10-cv-309-MJR-DGW, 2010 WL 5014327, at *1 (S.D. Ill. Dec. 3, 2010) (holding that a CBA that included a no-discrimination provision passed the "clear and unmistakable" waiver standard; the provision stated only that the "Employer and the Union agree not to discriminate against any employee for reasons of sex, race, religion, age, national origin, handicap [or] union activity. This Section is subject to the grievance and arbitration provision"); *Jensen v. Calumet Carton Co.*, No. 11 C 2785, 2011 WL 5078875, at *3 (N.D. Ill. Oct. 25, 2010).

5 See, e.g., *Thomspon v. Air Transp. Int't LLC*, 664 F.3d 723, 726–27 (8th Cir. 2011) (holding that arbitration clause, which required "claims of discrimination arising within the employment relationship between the Company and the Crewmembers, whether such claims are made under the collective bargaining agreement or in state or federal court and alleged to be violations of state or federal law . . . are to be addressed, resolved and finalized" under the grievance procedure can serve to "waive the judicial forum as an avenue for bringing federal statutory claims and state anti-discrimination claims as part of a mandatory arbitration agreement").

Where the courts have determined that the contract explicitly provides for arbitration of statutory discrimination claims, and provides that those claims may only be litigated in the parties' grievance and arbitration procedure, courts have made two further inquiries before barring litigation in the judicial forum: (1) whether the plaintiff sought to have his or her claim arbitrated; and (2) whether the union declined to take the matter to arbitration.

With respect to the first inquiry, lower courts have dismissed claims where the bargaining agreement provided for a waiver of the right to litigate discrimination claims in a judicial forum and the plaintiff never sought to have the union bring the claim to the contractual arbitration forum. Dismissal in these circumstances represents the imposition of a kind of exhaustion requirement.[6]

The second inquiry has a more complicated history. Where the employee has sought to have the union bring the discrimination claim to arbitration and the union has declined to do so, employees have argued that barring litigation in a judicial forum can have the effect of altogether extinguishing the claim without any hearing at all. Some courts – interpreting the same CBA language as in *Pyett* – have allowed plaintiffs to pursue their claims in court if the union declined to pursue them in arbitration. In *Kravar v. Triangle Servs., Inc.*,[7] the district court held that the plaintiff could proceed with litigation of her claim in federal court simply because the union had declined to advance the claim to arbitration. The court noted that "there is little question that if Ms. Kravar's union prevented her from arbitrating her disability discrimination claims, the CBA's arbitration provision may not be enforced as to her . . ." Similarly, in *Borrero v. Ruppert Hous. Co.*,[8] the court dismissed without prejudice, permitting the plaintiff to seek to have the union invoke arbitration on the claim, but providing that the plaintiff could bring the matter back to court if the union prevented him from litigating the claim in that forum. Also in *Morris v. Temco Serv. Indus.*,[9] the court held that "[a]lthough an agreement to arbitrate is enforceable against an employee who withdrew or otherwise decided not to pursue his grievance, the record shows that it was not Morris but the Union which chose to abandon her discrimination claims"; thus the arbitration provision of the employee's CBA could not be enforced against the plaintiff.

LABOR AND MANAGEMENT'S ADOPTION OF "NO-DISCRIMINATION PROTOCOL"

Neither the RAB nor the Union (the bargaining parties in *Pyett*) was a party to *Kravar, Borrero,* or *Morris*. A central question in those cases – whether the CBA

6 See, e.g., *Johnson v. Tishman Speyer Props., L.P.*, No. 09 Civ. 1959 (WHP), 2009 WL 3364038, at *4 (S.D.N.Y. Oct. 16, 2009; see also *Borrero v. Ruppert Hous. Co.*, No. 08-CV-5869 (HB), 2009 WL 1748060, at *2 (S.D.N.Y. June 19, 2009).

7 No. 1:06-CV-07858-RJH, 2009 WL 1392595 (S.D.N.Y. May 19, 2009).

8 No. 08-CV-5869 (HB), 2009 WL 1748060, at *2 (S.D.N.Y. June 19, 2009).

9 No. 09 Civ. 6194 (WHP), 2010 WL 3291810, at *5 (S.D.N.Y. Aug. 12, 2010).

provided that an individual employee must submit his or her claim to arbitration when the union has declined to pursue it to the regular contractual arbitration forum – is an issue that remains in dispute between the RAB and 32BJ. In each of these cases, the RAB and 32BJ were left in the very uncomfortable position of watching the courts interpret their bargaining agreement without the benefit of the evidence on bargaining history and context that only the union and the employer could provide.

Knowing that the courts might decide the central question in a way that at least one of the parties would find incorrect, the RAB and 32BJ agreed to *directly* arbitrate the issue. The case was brought to arbitration in February 2010, but, shortly before the hearing, the parties reached an agreement to take a different, beneficial, course. The parties adopted the "No-Discrimination Protocol" (the "Protocol") (attached as an "Appendix") that would govern all statutory discrimination claims, including claims brought by individual employees if the union declined to pursue those claims.

In the Protocol, the RAB and the Union parties agreed to leave the central legal issue undecided, at least for the time being – whether the CBA's no-discrimination and arbitration clauses require an individual employee to submit his or her statutory discrimination claim to some arbitration forum even when the union has declined to advance the claim to the regular contractual arbitration forum. The dispute between the RAB and 32BJ on that subject remains, and either party is permitted to invoke arbitration of the issue at any time with thirty days' written notice to the other.

The Protocol establishes a mediation process and also provides for assistance to individual employees and employers seeking to arbitrate claims where mediation has failed in instances in which the Union declined to seek arbitration of the claim. The first step, the mediation process, is a mandatory step for all such claims. The Protocol establishes a panel of mediators selected by the RAB and 32BJ from which the parties may choose, and all costs of the mediation are borne equally by the RAB and 32BJ. The mediators are given robust plenary power to require production of evidence and position statements, as well as confer separately with each party in order to vigorously pursue settlement. A pre-mediation conference must be scheduled within thirty days of the mediator's appointment. At the conclusion of the mediation, the mediator may make a settlement proposal to the parties. The mediator also has authority to order sanctions if he or she believes one or both of the parties failed to comply with his or her directives in good faith. The parties' experience with the Protocol over the last two years is such that a great number of claims are resolved in mediation.

If mediation does not resolve the matter, the individual employee or employees, regardless of whether they are represented by counsel, may pursue their claims as they see fit in arbitration. The RAB and 32BJ prepared a list of employment discrimination trained and qualified arbitrators from the American Arbitration

Association (AAA) to hear the claims, but the union will not otherwise participate in or pay for the arbitration. All terms of the arbitration, including financial compensation, are to be worked out between the litigating parties, with the RAB usually representing the employer.

After the initial period where the parties implemented the Protocol as a "pilot program," the parties recognized its success and incorporated its terms into their master agreements at the end of 2011.

JUDICIAL RESPONSE TO THE PROTOCOL

A number of courts and government agencies have deferred to the process outlined by the parties in the Protocol. A few months after the parties agreed to the Protocol, the U.S. District Court in the Southern District of New York, in *Duraku v. Tishman Speyer Properties*,[10] stayed an individual's claim pending arbitration, noting that arbitration should ensue even if the union declined to bring the claim. In other post-Protocol cases, courts in the Southern District of New York have similarly held that the parties' arbitration provision did *not* constitute a prospective waiver of plaintiffs' statutory rights since plaintiffs were entitled to bring the grievances to arbitration with or without union support.[11]

EXAMPLES OF THE "PROTOCOL" IN ACTION

Overall, since the Protocol's enactment, twenty-nine individuals have brought discrimination claims. Of those twenty-nine, all but one have proceeded to mediation and seven have settled (with an additional case that may be settled shortly). Approximately sixteen cases have proceeded to arbitration during this time period with others to follow. The following anecdotes illustrate how productive the Protocol is as a mechanism for dispute resolution.

An example of the Protocol in action occurred in a matter involving Zija Cukovic, who was terminated on February 25, 2008.[12] Mr. Cukovic filed a grievance with 32BJ alleging his termination was without just cause due to the employer's alleged discrimination on the basis of national origin, age, and disability. 32BJ declined to take the matter to arbitration. Mr. Cukovic filed a complaint in the U.S. District

[10] 714 F.Supp.2d 470 (S.D.N.Y. 2010).

[11] See, e.g., *Gildea v. Bldg. Mgmt.*, No. 10 CIV. 3347 (DAB), 2011 WL 4343464 (S.D.N.Y. Aug. 16, 2011); *Garcia v. Newmark Knight Frank & 641 Owner, LLC*, No. 09 Cv. 4599 (BSJ), 2010 U.S. Dist. LEXIS 142619 (S.D.N.Y. July 28, 2010); and *Veliz v. Collins Bldg. Servs., Inc.*, 10 Civ. 00615 (RJH), 2011 U.S. Dist. LEXIS 109351, at *13–14 (S.D.N.Y. Sept. 26, 2011) ("The court held that 'Veliz's claims against [the employer] are dismissed without prejudice because if the CBA operates to preclude Veliz's attempt, if any, to resolve his statutory claims through the procedures set forth therein, the CBA will be unenforceable and Veliz will have the right to re-file his claim in federal cour'").

[12] *Cukovic v. Tecmo Serv. Indus., Inc.*, No. 09 Civ. 6233 (AKH), 2010 U.S. Dist. LEXIS 77717, at *1–2 (S.D.N.Y. July 30, 2010).

Court for the Southern District of New York, alleging discrimination due to national origin and age. The court stayed the discrimination claim pending the outcome of the procedures under the Protocol.[13] Unable to resolve the claim in mediation, Mr. Cukovic brought the matter before Arbitrator Mona Glazer, and the claims were dismissed as lacking merit.[14]

While the RAB and 32BJ do not agree on the central legal issue that gave rise to the establishment of the Protocol, they agree that implementation of the Protocol has been successful because it frequently leads to resolutions without costly litigation. In particular, the Protocol's mediation is a forum where individual plaintiffs have a chance to tell their stories to an interested neutral party – often, the opportunity to be heard is something the individual plaintiff greatly values. Also, the very fact that the RAB and 32BJ have declined to finally decide the reserved question is useful to the mediation effort – neither party knows for certain whether the case will be litigated in a judicial forum or in arbitration, and to the extent that this is an issue of significance to the parties, the very uncertainty about the outcome should provide a further incentive to settle the merits in mediation. However, the RAB and 32BJ expect that as great number of these claims will be resolved in mediation and in fact, the parties' experience has been consistent with that expectation.

While the Protocol, by its terms, does not settle the issue of whether an employee desiring to pursue a discrimination claim that the Union has declined to take to arbitration may proceed in court, the RAB and the Union recognized that some of these claims will be litigated in some forum (and not settled in mediation), and that the litigation may raise legal and/or procedural issues that are of concern to the RAB and the Union. For example, neither collective bargaining party will look favorably on the prospect that overlapping claims might be litigated simultaneously in each tribunal (e.g., the union's claim that an employee was discharged "without just cause" would be litigated in the union–employer arbitration forum while the individual employee's claim that he was discharged for discriminatory reasons – a claim that the union had declined to pursue – would be litigated in another).[15]

[13] *Id.* at *4.

[14] *In re Cukovic and Tecmo Servs. Indus., Inc.* (2012) (Arb. Glazer).

[15] Similar problems are also presented when the Union asserts in the contractual arbitration forum both the claim that the employee was discharged without just cause, and the claim that the employee was discharged for discriminatory reasons. The first of these is a claim that is commonly advanced in union–employer arbitration under a collective bargaining agreement, and arbitrators have traditionally held that, in those cases, the employer carries the burden of proof of just cause for discharge and would be called upon to present its case first. See Elkouri & Elkouri, *How Arbitration Works* 949 (BNA 6th ed. 2003). On the other hand, the employee bringing a claim that he/she has been discriminated against in violation of a state or federal statute would generally carry the burden of proof (and generally the burden of production) on that claim and would be called upon to present his/her claim first. The parties to arbitrations in which both claims are litigated frequently fence over these competing obligations: Who goes first? How does the arbitrator sort out the varying burdens? If the arbitrator reaches the decision that the employee was disciplined without just cause, must he/she decide the discrimination claim? In addition, the RAB and the Union have agreed that the procedural devices available to a discrimination plaintiff in a judicial forum, including discovery, will be available to the

Additional problems are presented if the individual member demands relief that is inconsistent with the bargaining agreement, or if the member advances a construction of the bargaining agreement that either the Union or the RAB believes is wrong. Of course, if the individual is litigating these issues in a judicial forum and the Union or the RAB believe that their own interests may be affected in the litigation, each will have no way to protect those interests other than to seek intervention. With respect to litigation in an arbitral forum, the RAB and the Union included in the Protocol certain provisions intended to protect, to the extent feasible, against the harm of decisions that impact adversely on their interests. The Protocol includes language to the effect (1) that an arbitrator's decision on an individual claim will have no precedential effect with respect to the construction of the underlying contract; and (2) that the arbitrator hearing claims under the Protocol shall not be empowered to require alteration of any existing agreement between the RAB and the Union.

To date, however, these vexing issues have surfaced only rarely and have not posed insurmountable problems for the various parties. Indeed, the bulk of claims brought under the Protocol are "garden-variety," where the underlying facts and circumstances of the alleged adverse employment action overlap as the basis for both the breach of the CBA and the discrimination claims. In light of the nature of the building service industry employment relationship, the parties anticipate that "garden-variety" claims – quite suitable for resolution under the Protocol – will continue to dominate.

CONCLUSION

The Supreme Court's ruling in 14 *Penn Plaza v. Pyett* affirmed that the parties in a collective bargaining relationship may agree to pre-dispute mandatory arbitration for statutory discrimination claims. The legal issue of whether courts, under these circumstances, would bar employees from bringing suit if the union declined to pursue the claim in arbitration has been set aside by the RAB and 32BJ. Instead, the parties adopted a two-step process providing for mandatory mediation and a potential arbitration forum in the event mediation fails. The Protocol is an effective dispute resolution mechanism for the more than 60,000 commercial real estate workers in New York City subject to the parties' collective bargaining agreements. The parties' experience with the Protocol has been resoundingly positive.

Union advancing the claim that an employee was discharged without cause. Certainly, resort to discovery often results in the final disposition of the claim being delayed. While the time it takes to reach a final resolution of the discrimination claim in arbitration is likely to be shorter than the time it would take to reach a final disposition of the claim in court, it is likely to be considerably longer than the time it takes to dispose of the traditional just cause claim. Unions face the prospect that an aggrieved member with a valid claim is out of work a longer period of time when the discrimination claim is added to the arbitration mix; employers face the prospect of a much larger backpay award in that event.

The Protocol has worked well for New York's commercial real estate industry, and it may work for other sophisticated employer–union relationships with similarly strong grievance arbitration infrastructures and dedication to employees' civil rights.

APPENDIX

No-Discrimination Protocol[16]

The parties to this Agreement, the Union and RAB, believe that it is in the best interests of all involved – – employees/members, employers, the Union, the RAB and the public interest – – to promptly, fairly and efficiently resolve claims of workplace discrimination, as covered above (collectively "claims"). Such claims are very often intertwined with contractual disputes under this Agreement. The RAB, on behalf of its members, maintains that it is committed to refrain from unlawful discrimination. The Union maintains it will pursue its policy of evaluating such claims and bringing those claims to arbitration where appropriate. To this end, the parties, notwithstanding the continuing disagreement between them described below, establish the following system of mediation and arbitration applicable to all such claims, whenever they arise. The Union and RAB want those covered by this Agreement and any individual attorneys representing them to be aware of this protocol.

As background, following the decision of the Supreme Court in 14 *Penn Plaza*, 556 U.S. 247 (2009), the RAB and the Union have had a dispute about the meaning of the "no discrimination clause" and the grievance and arbitration clauses in the collective bargaining agreements ("CBAs") entered into between these parties. The Union contends that the CBAs do not make provision for arbitration of any claims that the Union does not choose to take to arbitration, including statutory discrimination claims, and therefore, individual employees are not barred from pursuing their discrimination claims in court where the Union has declined to pursue them in arbitration. The RAB contends that the CBAs provide for arbitration of all individual claims, even where the Union has declined to bring such claims to arbitration.

The parties agree that, should either the Union or the RAB deem it appropriate or necessary to do so, that party may bring to arbitration the question so reserved. The parties intend that the reserved question may only be resolved in an arbitration between them and not in any form of judicial proceeding. The outcome of the reserved question hinges on collective bargaining language and bargaining history, which are subjects properly suited for arbitration. Such arbitration may be

[16] The parties intend this provision to apply to all collective bargaining agreements between them superseding the "Agreement & Protocol" entered into [on] February 17, 2010.

commenced on 30 days' written notice to the other party. The arbitrator for such arbitration shall be Roberta Golick, unless she is unable to serve, in which case the parties shall agree upon an arbitrator, and failing agreement shall submit the case to arbitration before the American Arbitration Association, in New York City.

Notwithstanding the above disagreement, in 2010, the parties initiated the pilot program provided for in this section (Agreement and Protocol, February 17, 2010, the "No-Discrimination Protocol") as an alternative to arbitrating their disagreement. The parties have now agreed to include the No-Discrimination Protocol as part of this Agreement, as set forth below. The Union and the RAB agree that the provisions of this Protocol do not resolve the reserved question. Neither the inclusion of this Protocol in the CBAs nor the terms of the Protocol shall be understood to advance either party's contention as to the meaning of the CBAs with regard to the reserved question, and neither party will make any representation to the contrary.

Mediation

A. Whenever it is claimed that an employer has violated the no discrimination clause (including claims based in statute), whether such claim is made by the Union or by an individual employee, notice shall be provided of such claim to the Union, the RAB and the affected employee(s), and the matter shall be submitted to mediation, absent prior resolution through informal means. A notice of claim shall be filed within the applicable statutory statute of limitations, provided that if an employee has timely filed such claim in a forum provided for by statute, the claim will not be considered time-barred.

B. Promptly following receipt of the notice, the administrator of the Office of Contract Arbitrator (OCA), 370 Seventh Avenue, New York, NY, shall appoint a Mediator from the Mediation Panel described below. All mediators on the panel shall be attorneys with appropriate training and experience in the conduct of mediations and significant knowledge of employment discrimination statutes. The Mediation Panel shall be a distinct panel from the Contract Arbitrator Panel. A person listed on the Mediation Panel will be removed when either the Union or the RAB gives notice to the other party that such person's name shall be removed. A person may be added to the Mediation Panel list upon mutual agreement of the Union and the RAB. The Union and RAB mutually commit to appointing mediators with appropriate skill and experience, as they view mediation as the important step in which many claims will be resolved.

C. OCA shall appoint a Mediator from the Mediation Panel. Such appointments shall be made by a random selection (*e.g.* "spinning the wheel") of available panel members.

D. Within 30 days of being appointed, the Mediator shall notify the parties of his/her appointment and schedule a pre-mediation conference. (For this purpose, "Parties" refers to the person or entity asserting the claim and the respondent/defendant.) At the conference, the Parties shall discuss such matters as they deem relevant to the mediation process, including discovery. The Mediator shall have the authority, after consulting with the Parties, to (1) schedule dates for the exchange of information and position statements, and (2) schedule a date for mediation. Any disputes shall be decided by the Mediator. In the event the Mediator concludes that there has not been good faith compliance with his/her directive, including directives as to the holding of conferences and the conduct of discovery, the Mediator may, after notice and an opportunity to be heard, order appropriate sanctions.
E. The entire mediation process is a compromise negotiation for the purposes of the Federal Rules of Evidence and the New York rules of evidence.
F. At the mediation, each party shall be entitled to present witnesses and/or documentary evidence. The Mediator shall be entitled to meet separately with each Party for the purpose of exploring settlement.
G. At the conclusion of the mediation, the Mediator shall be entitled to make a proposal to the Parties of a settlement agreement. Neither Party shall be required to adopt the proposal.
H. Mediation shall be completed before the claim is litigated on the merits. However, if the Union alleges the claim of a violation of the no discrimination clause, the Union may proceed directly to arbitration and bypass this Mediation procedure if it so chooses.
I. The fees of the Mediator shall be split equally between the Union and the RAB. The Union and RAB shall provide language interpreters at their jointly shared cost.

Arbitration

A. The undertakings described here with respect to arbitration apply to those circumstances in which the Union has declined to take an individual employee's employment discrimination claim under the no discrimination clause of the CBA (including statutory claims) to arbitration and the employee is desirous of litigating the claim. The forum described here will be available to employers and employees who are represented by counsel and to those who are unrepresented by counsel.
B. The Union and the RAB have elicited from the American Arbitration Association a list of arbitrators who (1) are attorneys, and (2) are qualified to decide employment discrimination cases. In the event that an employee and RAB member employer seek arbitration of a discrimination claim in the

circumstances described in paragraph A, the list of arbitrators provided by the AAA shall be made available to the individual employee and the RAB member employer by the administrator of OCA. The manner by which selection is made by the RAB member employer and the individual employee and the extent to which each shall bear responsibility for the costs of the arbitrator shall be decided between them. A person may be added to or removed from the Statutory Arbitration Panel list upon mutual agreement of the Union and the RAB. Any such arbitrations shall be conducted pursuant to the AAA National Rules for Employment Disputes, except those rules pertaining to administration by the AAA and the payment of fees, and any disputes about the manner of proceeding shall be decided by the arbitrator selected.

C. The hearings in any arbitration provided for in the preceding paragraph may be held at the OCA, however, it is understood that this forum is not a forum provided for in the collective bargaining agreement.

D. The Union will not be a party to the arbitration described above and the arbitrator shall not have authority to award relief that would require amendment of the CBA or other agreement(s) between the Union and the RAB or conflict with any provision of any CBAs or such other agreement(s). Any mediation and/or arbitration outcome shall have no precedential value with respect to the interpretation of the CBAs or other agreement(s) between the Union and the RAB.

PART IV

Creating a Culture of Service

43

Integrating Pro Bono with the Law Firm's Business

Lisa Dewey, Anne Geraghty Helms, Sara Andrews, Roberta Ritvo & Richard Gruenberger

Both to further training and career-enhancing opportunities for young lawyers and provide counsel for Americans unable to afford a lawyer, law firms should seek to integrate pro bono commitments with their business objectives. Lisa Dewey and her colleagues describe the innovative efforts of their firm.

This chapter offers strategies for successfully weaving a strong pro bono culture into the ethos and business strategy of every law firm. It also considers the role that the law firm community should play in responding to this country's access to justice crisis.

DEVELOPING AND MAINTAINING A STRONG PRO BONO PROGRAM

It is easy enough to say that every law firm should have a strong pro bono program, that pro bono should be a part of every law firm's culture, and that pro bono must be treated as part of the firm's core business, not as a sideshow or afterthought. But what are the core building blocks of a strong pro bono program? Using DLA Piper's U.S. program as one example (and we recognize that there are hundreds of other great programs and there is not a one-size-fits-all approach), we discuss how to create a pro bono culture, how it becomes a part of the firm's business plan, and what infrastructure is needed to maintain a pro bono program at a large law firm.

DLA Piper's Pro Bono Program

DLA Piper's pro bono program is situated in a large, global firm.[1] The firm is the product of multiple mergers, dating back to the creation of Piper Rudnick in 1999. As the firm grew, lawyers brought their own tradition of pro bono – and this common culture of service was part of what ultimately made the firm's growth successful. Piper & Marbury, for instance, was a Baltimore-based firm that had created a "branch office" storefront legal clinic in East Baltimore in 1969, staffed by two full-

[1] See www.dlapiper.com/global/about/ourhistory/.

time lawyers from the firm and junior lawyers, many who then became partners, rotated through the clinic.[2] The experience of providing frontline pro bono assistance helped instill an enduring service ethic there.

The pro bono practice expanded to reflect the firm's international scope, and in 1999 DLA Piper created a full-time pro bono position. As the firm grew, so did the U.S. pro bono team,[3] which expanded to include a researcher and four full-time counsels.

In 2005, DLA Piper's pro bono program took on a new, global dimension with the creation of New Perimeter,[4] a unique nonprofit affiliate whose mission is to provide long-term pro bono legal assistance in under served regions around the world to support access to justice, social and economic development, and sound legal institutions. New Perimeter does this primarily in developing and post-conflict countries. Through New Perimeter, teams of lawyers from the firm's global offices work on pro bono projects (many averaging between 3 and 5 years) that frequently involve travel to a developing country.

DLA Piper also created[5] the Krantz Fellowship Program in June 2012, hosting two fellows who dedicate their first year at the firm to pro bono work while earning the same salary as other first-year lawyers. During their Fellowship, they work with a wide variety of lawyers, often from multiple offices; have extensive client interaction; and take on a wide array of projects.

Pro Bono and Firm Culture

The first and most essential ingredient for establishing a robust pro bono program is support and drive from the firm's top leadership. At DLA Piper, for instance, firm leadership includes pro bono in its firm-wide communications, and is seen as actively involved in strategic planning for our pro bono program. And pro bono team leadership participates in management meetings.

Pro bono work should also be emphasized and rewarded. Like many firms, DLA Piper also backs up its commitment to pro bono through lawyer incentives, for instance by providing firm credit hours and evaluating lawyers' pro bono work in the same way as billable work. Recognizing pro bono achievements not only builds morale internally but also nurtures a culture of doing and expecting pro bono.[6]

A vibrant pro bono program also strengthens the law firm's culture as a whole. It can unite people across offices, practice groups, and the world – offering opportunities to work with colleagues outside of one's usual network, and sometimes

[2] One of the junior lawyers who volunteered in the Baltimore clinic eventually became global co-chair of the firm.

[3] DLA Piper also has an international pro bono team led by a full-time pro bono partner.

[4] See www.newperimeter.org.

[5] See Sara Randazzo, *DLA Piper Associates Will Be Paid to Do Good*, AM LAW DAILY, Aug. 29, 2011.

[6] See Reena N. Glazer, *Revisiting the Business Case for Law Firm Pro Bono*, S. TEX. L. REV., 563, 585 (2010).

opening the door to new billable work.[7] It provides other intangible benefits, like fostering motivation and cultivating loyalty, making for a tighter-knit and happier firm, which can play a critical role for the growing number of merging firms.[8]

Pro Bono: It's Good for Business

In 2000, Esther Lardent laid out in an article, *The Business Case for Pro Bono*, several compelling arguments for firms to incorporate pro bono in their business plans – beyond it simply being the right thing to do.[9] Lardent also points out that pro bono work tends to make lawyers happy, that happy lawyers are less likely to leave, and that firms save costs by not having to replace lawyers after substantially investing to recruit and train them.

Aligning pro bono with the firm's other goals – from recruiting to professional development to diversity and inclusion – also furthers the firm's business platform. Pro bono is a great way for firms to attract, support, train, and retain top talent. With recruiting, for instance, law students increasingly seek out law firms with respected, established pro bono programs that match their personal commitments to doing good. And in marketing, a prominent pro bono program and vocal support for doing good unquestionably distinguishes a firm in a competitive market and improves its brand.

Pro bono also promotes professional development by affording lawyers an efficient and inexpensive way to develop their skills and careers. Pro bono and professional development go hand in hand, especially given current market pressures, which include corporate clients who are reluctant to pay to train new associates. In fact, pro bono is considered a critical professional development tool for young lawyers. Pro bono often is a necessary outlet for junior associates to undertake more advanced tasks, such as interviewing clients, negotiating leases or contracts, and appearing in court.[10] And it also offers experience in less tangible (and therefore less teachable) skills like exercising good judgment and demonstrating leadership. Of course, pro bono also grants perspective to our lawyers and nurtures a connection to the communities where we live and work.

In one example at DLA Piper, a corporate-and-securities associate who assisted on a merger of three nonprofit organizations told us:

7 See http://thepbeye.probonoinst.org/2012/02/13/video-wdpb-lisa-dewey-dla-piper/ (Lisa Dewey describes several reasons why pro bono is important).

8 See Yoann Kassi-Vivier, Jennifer Pawlowski & Carol Guttery, *Demonstrating the Business Value of Pro Bono Service*, Taproot Foundation (2012).

9 Esther Lardent, *Making the Business Case for Pro Bono*, Pro Bono Institute Law Firm Pro Bono Project (2000), available at www2.nycbar.org/mp3/DoingWellByDoingGood/pbi_businesscase.pdf.

10 See Scott L. Cummings & Rebecca L. Sandefur, *Beyond the Numbers: What We Know – and Should Know – About American Pro Bono*, Harvard L. & Pol'y Rev., 83, 98 (2013). ("A recent study of early-career associates in large firms suggests that pro bono work may be part of broader career development strategy . . .").

> I had the chance to attend the client's meeting of the Board of Directors where the proposed transaction was presented to the members. While I have worked on many corporate transactions . . . this was the first time that I was invited to attend a board meeting . . . It was fascinating to see the Board's process as they considered the merits of the proposed transaction.

In another instance, one of the firm's partners remembers her opportunity to argue a pro bono case before the Federal Court of Appeals for the District of Columbia Circuit.

> I argued on appeal before three judges, including our current Supreme Court Justice John Roberts. Arguing the appeal was a thrilling experience for me as a seventh-year lawyer. I remember being asked a question by then Judge Roberts during the argument . . . My pro bono case allowed me a fantastic opportunity to argue before the person who now holds the highest judicial office in our country. It is a memory I cherish.

For senior lawyers, too, pro bono offers a chance to do something they always wanted to do but never had the time, as well as an opportunity to mentor younger attorneys and try something new.

Beyond all these benefits, there is one other critical reason for law firms to integrate pro bono with their business plans: our clients demand it. Our clients increasingly not only wish to know that we have strong pro bono programs (and requests for proposals for legal work increasingly include questions about our pro bono commitment), but also look at their law firms to help provide infrastructure and support so that their own lawyers can participate in pro bono as well.

The Nuts and Bolts of a Pro Bono Program

THE IMPORTANCE OF STAFFING AND INFRASTRUCTURE[11] So, what are the elements of a strong pro bono program? As a law firm grows, so does the importance of building a robust infrastructure around pro bono which ensures that the program operates smoothly for volunteers and within the firm's broader structures.

To begin with, firms must consider how they wish to treat pro bono from a policy standpoint, determining what types of work count as pro bono; how to manage the program; how pro bono matters are approved; how to handle costs in pro bono matters; how to recognize pro bono internally and organize events promoting pro bono; how to support legal services organizations; and how to treat pro bono work within the firm for compensation, review, and bonus purposes.[12] And they must consider whether associates and partners will be required to do a certain number of hours of pro bono work and whether they will receive billable credit for that work.

[11] The Pro Bono Institute provides technical assistance to its member firms on these issues and is a wealth of information and help.

[12] See Scott L. Cummings & Deborah L. Rhode, *Managing Pro Bono: Doing Well by Doing Better*, FORDHAM L. REV. 2357, 2386 (2010).

Firms also must decide who should manage their pro bono programs. This can be (and at many firms is) done by a vigorous and involved pro bono committee[13] responsible for staffing matters, setting priorities, and sometimes acting as an approving body for new matters. As the size and sophistication of pro bono programs grow, and because of the added expertise that a full-time professional can bring, many large law firms now rely on a dedicated lawyer or team of lawyers to build and sustain these programs.[14]

Whether a full-time professional or a committee, those who manage pro bono programs at law firms must focus on making pro bono accessible to volunteers while operating in harmony with the firm's other business priorities and concerns. Of course, this begins with developing and offering matters about which their lawyers feel passionate and through which they can make a difference – including in areas that complement the skill sets of both litigators and transactional attorneys, such as complicated nonprofit mergers, microfinance work, real estate and employment work, and service as outside counsel to qualifying nonprofit organizations. It therefore is essential to develop and maintain good working relationships with outside legal service providers and nonprofits, as well as other lawyers within the firm.

Those who manage pro bono programs also ensure that training, mentoring, and support are available for lawyers who may be unfamiliar with the practice area relevant to the pro bono client's matter.[15] Attorney mentors, either within the law firm or from an outside legal service provider can answer questions, provide guidance, and help fill in the gaps.

In addition to these responsibilities, pro bono counsel must monitor the pro bono program from a risk-management perspective, ensuring that pro bono matters do not generate conflicts,[16] that these matters are properly supervised, and that participating lawyers take appropriate steps, such as preparing engagement letters or properly transitioning cases when leaving the firm. Pro bono counsel are responsible for reporting on pro bono activities, both externally and internally; overseeing any pro

[13] Committees tend to work best when they are diverse in terms of practice area, geography, and perspective – in addition to being committed to pro bono and its benefits. The Pro Bono Institute's Law Firm Pro Bono Project has useful information concerning pro bono committees, including best practices for committee structure, membership, size, mandate, and resources. See Pro Bono Institute, *Best Practices for Creating and Maintaining an Efficient and Effective Law Firm Pro Bono Committee* (2011).

[14] See Scott L. Cummings, *The Politics of Pro Bono*, 52 UCLA L. Rev. 1, 4 (2004).

[15] Technology is playing an increasingly important role in the support of pro bono volunteers as well. Through webinar technology, attorneys can be trained either live or at their convenience at their own desks. Shared online platforms, such as eRooms, provide volunteer attorneys access to trainings, model documents, sample briefs, and work product needed to represent his or her client. And websites like Probono.net, which is dedicated to increasing access to justice through innovative uses of technology and increased volunteer lawyer participation, provide a one-stop shop for anyone looking to engage in pro bono.

[16] See Cummings & Sandefur, supra note 9, at 96 (discussing pro bono and types of conflicts that can emerge at law firms).

bono-related marketing; and developing the firm's pro bono policy, sample retainer letters, and processes for tracking cases, hours, and costs. They also must develop relationships with other internal firm functions – like recruitment and professional development – and report to management on the overall goals and outcomes of the pro bono practice.

To provide an example, DLA Piper helped create a pro bono program with the National Veterans Legal Services Program (NVLSP) to help veterans apply for Combat-Related Special Compensation (CRSC), a Department of Defense benefit. No one was helping veterans access these funds and, indeed, many veterans were not even aware of the program. Under the leadership of a firm lawyer in Texas who is a veteran and active member of the Texas Air National Guard, the management of a paralegal in California, and a team of paralegals who obtain medical and military records needed to prepare the applications, lawyers from nearly every U.S. office at the firm have helped over 150 veterans and have partnered with corporate clients to help dozens more.[17] More important still is the big-picture impact – NVLSP now refers CRSC cases to over 35 law firms and corporations.

COLLABORATION IS KEY Corporate clients, other law firms, legal-service providers, and community organizations contribute their own set of skills, resources, and expertise to pro bono projects.

Teaming with corporate clients An increasing number of in-house legal departments are embracing pro bono. Many are signing the Corporate Pro Bono Challenge, a pledge taken by in-house legal departments to contribute pro bono legal services.[18] And law firms are teaming ever more often with their corporate clients to help them fulfill that pledge.[19] Law firms with established pro bono programs can help our in-house clients by providing technical assistance, helping legal departments who do not have the benefit of full-time pro bono counsel create infrastructure for their programs; developing and managing projects; and coordinating training for their lawyers. We can also either co-counsel on pro bono matters – which helps relieve some of the pressure when taking on larger, time-consuming projects – or help in-house lawyers find manageable opportunities on their own.

Performing pro bono alongside clients also offers firm attorneys the opportunity to build closer relationships with their clients. When it comes to pro bono teaming, equity is the key to the relationships between law firms and in-house counsel. And as with law firms, it is also important that in-house legal departments have top-down support for their pro bono programs.

[17] DLA Piper has partnered with Verizon (as well as a couple of other in-house departments) on this project.
[18] See www.corporateprobono.org.
[19] See Glazer, supra note 5, at 573.

DLA Piper has collaborated with well over a dozen of its corporate clients on pro bono.[20] We have worked with clients to jointly represent nonprofit organizations, to staff local legal services clinics, and to provide direct assistance to low-income clients.

Partnering with legal services providers Legal services providers (LSPs) are in the trenches every day serving those without access to justice. Law firms, on the other hand, lack the infrastructure to directly reach potential clients. LSPs are essential for direct services pro bono programs. They can conduct initial interviews with clients, determine their eligibility for free legal assistance, train volunteers, offer expertise on substantive law, and provide mentoring to firm lawyers. LSPs are experts in their areas of the law and can help law firm attorneys find and handle matters in a wide variety of areas. Indeed, our relationships with LSPs form the very foundation of our pro bono program – so much so that having a pro bono program without them would be exceedingly difficult.

REFLECTION, FEEDBACK, AND FLEXIBILITY The ultimate goal is to develop a pro bono program that is user-friendly, strategic, and impactful. But how can you evaluate the success of a pro bono program? To answer this question, we must reflect on what we are doing, whether we are fulfilling our goals, and whether we are meeting the expectations of our program's many stakeholders, including the firm, our lawyers, our clients, and the community at large.

For the past several years, the DLA Piper pro bono team has engaged in periodic reflection and strategic planning. One goal was to survey our lawyers and find out how our pro bono program is viewed internally, including its perceived weaknesses and strengths, and what motivates our lawyers to do pro bono. Lawyers viewed pro bono opportunities as readily available and accessible to them. They also found that pro bono was an excellent integration tool. Associates articulated a moral imperative for doing pro bono and also found it important as a professional development tool. We used this feedback to improve the program.

PRO BONO CAN BE FUN: BE CREATIVE IN DEVELOPING YOUR PRO BONO PROGRAM

Lawyers who agree to provide free legal services to those who cannot afford a lawyer are donating their time and talent – their most valuable resources – in the process. Pro bono should be as accessible, easy, and rewarding as possible for lawyers. One of the ways we do that is by developing creative and engaging pro bono projects, a few of which are described in more detail in the following.

[20] See http://dlapiperprobono.com/collaboration/corporate-clients/.

New Perimeter and Global Pro Bono

As law firms have gone global, so has pro bono. DLA Piper's New Perimeter program, created in 2005, is an example of this phenomenon. New Perimeter is a nonprofit affiliate of the firm dedicated to delivering long-term pro bono legal assistance in under served regions around the world. It has worked on over fifty major projects involving hundreds of DLA Piper lawyers worldwide focusing on access to justice, social and economic development, and sound legal institutions in Africa, Asia, Latin America, and the Balkans. For example, lawyers worked with the National Center for State Courts over a period of ten years to help draft legislation creating the court system and system of public prosecution in Kosovo, to train lawyers in the newly created Kosovo Ministry of Justice, to work with the Kosovo Chamber of Advocates to review and revise the laws and regulations affecting the legal profession, and to help develop strategies for increasing the number of women lawyers in Kosovo. In the area of women's rights, lawyers assisted a human rights organization in taking testimony from Zimbabwean women who were tortured because of their political affiliations. And in the area of economic development, we have worked for the government of East Timor to help it consider creating special economic zones to encourage economic development.[21]

Some key features of New Perimeter are:

- its Advisory Board composed of leading public-interest and private-sector lawyers who provide invaluable feedback on existing projects and guidance on the program's direction,
- long-term partnerships with local nonprofit organizations, academic institutions, and governmental entities,
- opportunities for our lawyers to work alongside partner organizations in country for one to two weeks at a time,
- frequent engagement with clients for feedback on the program,
- a competitive application process to match lawyers with projects,
- a comprehensive orientation process for project staff, and
- an evaluation process at the completion of a project to assess and measure the impact of the program.

Instituting and running a program like New Perimeter requires a significant investment in time and resources. But the firm benefits from the high satisfaction ratings of participating attorneys, external recognition of the program,[22] and the program's role in supporting employee recruitment, retention, professional development, and cross-border collaboration.

[21] See www.newperimeter.org.

[22] For instance, *The American Lawyer* recently recognized New Perimeter with its Global Citizenship Award. See www.newperimeter.org/about/news/2013/global-citizenship-award-lifetime-achievement.html.

Clinics

The reality for lawyers in private practice is that they must fit their pro bono commitments into the larger demands of practice. Legal clinics are an excellent way to deliver a service, while making pro bono accessible through limited representation and therefore predictable workload commitments.[23] This feature makes clinics a vehicle for firm partnerships with corporate counsel.

DLA Piper has created over a dozen clinics around the country that deliver legal services to the underserved,[24] and the firm has participated in several others. Typically, the firm – sometimes with a client's legal department – teams with a legal service provider to assist with screening pro bono-eligible clients and on site-support. And either the firm or the legal service provider must organize issues like staffing, intake, follow-up, and volunteer support.

Legal clinics can take many forms and cover myriad substantive areas. For example:

- **General advice clinics:** Many clinics are designed to provide general advice, intake, and referral services to clients on various legal issues. DLA Piper's legal clinic in the Woodlawn Community of Chicago partners once a month with LAF (formerly the Legal Assistance Foundation of Metropolitan Chicago) to offer advice on a range of legal issues. A full-time fellow at LAF, partially funded by DLA Piper, administers the clinic and runs volunteer training. LAF also sends to each clinic a lawyer who is an expert in poverty law who can advise DLA Piper lawyer volunteers. Many cases are handled at the clinic while others are discussed later with volunteers who type their notes after their interviews and meet after the clinic to discuss how the cases will be referred (often to other LAF or DLA Piper attorneys)..
- **Brief services clinics**: Other clinics offer discrete and immediate legal services to clients. DLA Piper and in-house counsel from Cigna work with the Senior Law Center, a nonprofit that assists elderly people in Philadelphia and throughout the state. Together they run an advance-directives clinic which helps to address the Center's long waiting list for free "life planning" services. Before the clinic, Senior Law Center enrolls seniors, screens them for eligibility and capacity, and counsels them on the decisions they will be making at the clinic, including seeking input from their doctors on end-of-life health decisions. On the day of the clinic, volunteers from DLA Piper and Cigna pair up to meet with the clients and draw up advance directives such as basic wills, healthcare proxies, living wills, and powers of attorney. Senior Law Center staff are present to welcome and organize clients, answer questions, address

[23] Legal hotlines are another variation of a legal clinic where pro bono volunteers can provide limited assistance over the phone from the comfort of their own desks.

[24] See http://viewer.zmags.com/publication/0f5f8b29#/0f5f8b29/24. In addition to creating three legal clinics at VA hospitals, we help manage clinics in Baltimore, Chicago, Palo Alto, Philadelphia, Sacramento, San Francisco, and Washington, DC.

problems, review documents, and support the volunteers. All paperwork is completed at the clinic, and volunteers do not advise on any issues other than advance directives. DLA Piper, like many large law firms, has also participated in several Clinic in a Box® programs, a project created by Corporate Pro Bono®, a partnership project of Pro Bono Institute and the Association of Corporate Counsel, to advise nonprofit organizations or small businesses about their legal needs. At these clinics, lawyers receive brief training and then conduct a one-time legal audit of the client organizations in areas such as real estate, employment, IP, and corporate governance.

- **Training and initial client meeting clinics:** One increasingly popular model features clinics where lawyers receive training and then attend an initial client meeting where they gather documents, conduct an interview, and initiate the work sought by the client. For example, as part of the firm's partnership with Verizon to represent survivors of intimate-partner violence, DLA Piper has created U Visa clinics across the country. Volunteers attend training a week or two before the clinic and receive their client's file at the training or soon thereafter. At the clinic, the volunteers meet with their clients for the first time. Lawyers typically make substantial progress on their clients' applications while receiving onsite mentoring by a legal services provider. After the clinic, the volunteers work individually to complete and submit the application. This type of clinic is most appropriate for fairly routine matters requiring small time commitments of generally under 20 hours.
- **Virtual clinics**: A result of advancing technology, the "virtual clinic" permits volunteers to provide the same type of assistance they would deliver at a live clinic. But instead of attending a clinic outside the office, volunteers assist clients from their computers. DLA Piper has worked with other organizations to staff "virtual clinics" where volunteer lawyers join the clinic remotely by computer, using video- and document-sharing technology to interview potential clients, review documents, and provide advice. Clients are community members seeking general legal advice on subjects such as family law, contracts, labor and employment, and consumer law.

Signature Projects

In 2000, DLA Piper helped pioneer the signature project model. These large-scale, multi-year projects were developed in partnership with nonprofit organizations, academic institutions, philanthropic foundations, and corporate clients with the hope that, by working together, we could develop innovative solutions to vexing social problems and help society's most vulnerable members. Offices looking to create signature projects started with committees that led inclusive needs-assessment processes in their communities and ensured that there was sufficient internal support and enthusiasm for the chosen subject matters. We then selected project leaders who committed to devoting substantial time to managing these projects.

The firm's first signature projects addressed the backlog of adoption cases in Washington, DC, with the Children's Law Center, and took on juvenile justice cases in Chicago, partnering with Northwestern University School of Law's Blum Legal Clinic. Our real estate practice launched the first national project, helping victims of Hurricane Katrina secure over $1.7 million to rebuild and clear title to their land so they could access federal and state rebuilding grants and after resolving heirs property issues.

DLA Piper has five national signature project areas:

1. Advancing Education's Promise
2. Serving Those Who Serve Our Country
3. Advocates Against Intimate Partner Violence
4. Feeding the Hungry In Our Global Neighborhood
5. Second Chances for Juveniles[25]

The implementation of these signature project areas differs from office to office; every office participates in at least one of the signature areas, and most participate in multiple projects. Signature projects thus provide a sense of community for lawyers and staff to come together in support of a common goal.[26]

Signature projects additionally allow our lawyers to gain and leverage experience in particular subject areas over time. This, in turn, relieves some of the pressure from our LSP partners to continually train and mentor our lawyers. The firm also can set and track goals for the work over time, enabling us to report on impact. For instance, we know that after Hurricane Katrina our lawyers were able to help clients secure over $1.7 million to rebuild after resolving heirs property issues. And, ultimately, we can address systemic issues we encounter first-hand through signature projects. For example, after representing dozens of juveniles in Chicago, our lawyers identified and worked to remedy systemic problems impeding our young clients from re-enrolling in school after spending time in custodial detention.

THE LAW FIRM AS AN IMPORTANT VOICE FOR ACCESS TO JUSTICE

Well-resourced law firms have a unique responsibility to address the crisis in access to the courts for people of average means.

How Can Law Firms Help?

First, large firm lawyers can use their leverage as leaders in the profession to shine a spotlight on this need and to call for greater funding for legal aid. Firm leaders also

[25] See www.dlapiperprobono.com.

[26] Several of our signature projects provide non-legal opportunities for our lawyers and staff to work side by side on the focus areas of our projects. For instance, we regularly volunteer at area food banks, tutor children at risk, and volunteer at Stand Down events to help veterans.

can educate lawyers within their own firms about why representing individuals of limited means is important.

Often, just exposing a lawyer to the problems people face trying to access our justice system can improve a lawyer's understanding of a civil legal system impacting people of limited means. It leaves an impression when a new lawyer – or even a seasoned partner – sits down at the table for the first time across from a person who breaks down in tears because she has done everything right – kept meticulous documents, followed up as required, made payments on time – but is still at risk of losing her home because of a bureaucratic mix-up. These eye opening experiences can convert lawyers into lifelong champions of legal aid.

Those who run pro bono programs also can work to ensure that they are responding to the most pressing needs in their communities by maximizing the value of their attorneys' resources and talents. As pro bono leaders, we must continually adapt to the changing environment while also calling for changes that we see are needed. More and more, pro bono counsel are asking themselves tough questions and measuring outcomes so that we can act on the data we collect.

The Pro Bono Institute has convened a Task Force on Pro Bono Measurement and Metrics, employing the pro bono services of Deloitte to provide a roadmap for measuring the impact of pro bono efforts on the community.[27] Ideally, these and other efforts will help law firm leaders tailor pro bono programs to best serve those who cannot afford a lawyer.

Finally, law firms can (and most do) help by prioritizing legal aid in their charitable giving programs. Without adequately funded legal services organizations, even the best and most well-intentioned law firm lawyers will have a hard time providing effective pro bono representation.

Promising Developments in Pro Bono

Citing the desperate need and law firms' obligation to do more would be unfair without also recognizing the work being done by many across the country to engage law firms. Although this list is by no means exhaustive, these are examples of how firms are responding to the crisis in legal assistance.

Legal Services Corporation Pro Bono Task Force

The Legal Services Corporation convened a Pro Bono Task Force to consider how to better engage pro bono lawyers. The Task Force recommended amending certain internal LSC regulations to better encourage the use of pro bono and non-lawyer volunteers in grantee programs; revising certain state-law practice rules to

[27] See Glazer, supra note 5, at 589; Cummings & Sandefur, supra note 9, at 105–109 (suggesting ways "toward better pro bono intelligence"); Cummings & Rhode, supra note 11 at 2401–408.

incentivize pro bono; and modifying how LSC provides technical support to its grantees.

The Association of Pro Bono Counsel (APBCo) IMPACT Project

Recognizing the potential for a full-time lawyer to develop much more sophisticated and strategic pro bono programs, law firm management teams began creating pro bono counsel positions at their firms. Once the number of lawyers in these pro bono counsel positions reached critical mass, they created the Association of Pro Bono Counsel (APBCo), a membership organization dedicated to the support and professional development of full-time pro bono counsel and coordinators at commercial law firms. Today, APBCo has grown to have over 150 members from law firms across the country.[28] APBCo is also now engaged in access to justice work, having launched IMPACT (Involving More Pro Bono Attorneys in our Community Together) to work collaboratively in several cities across the country on a range of issues.

In Chicago, for instance, local law firm counsel met with one another and with leadership in the legal aid community to discuss existing programs and the gaps in those programs where the private bar could add value. After discussing the significant obstacles the more than 3.9 million men and women with criminal records in Illinois face in obtaining employment, licenses, and housing, several of the legal aid agencies working on these issues identified a new one area where no legal aid organizations were providing assistance. The Illinois legislature recently had adopted laws that opened the door for many individuals who were ineligible for expungement to apply for either a Certificate of Good Conduct (certification by a local court that the person has been rehabilitated, thereby removing statutory employment bars and shielding employers from liability based on criminal records) or a waiver to work in the healthcare industry. The processes for obtaining both are relatively straightforward for a lawyer, and the APBCo firms agreed to launch a series of clinics to assist individuals applying for either form of relief.[29]

Other Innovative Efforts

Other firms and companies are innovating similarly unique models for closing the justice gap.[30] For instance, Thomson Reuters, which owns the Westlaw

28 Association of Pro Bono Counsel, *Pro Bono FAQ*, available at www.google.com/url?sa=t&rct=j&q=&esrc=s&frm=1&source=web&cd=1&ved=0CCkQFjAA&url=http%3A%2F%2Fwww.americanbarfoundation.org%2Fuploads%2Fcms%2Fdocuments%2Faccess_across_america_first_report_of_the_civil_justice_infrastructure_mapping_project.pdf&ei=aw7DUvKWFKPmyQGg8IHYCw&usg=AFQjCNHOZywfn6Ya4UmcU4PWJsu2fkutOQ.

29 See Steven Schulman, Latonia Haney Keith & Kevin Curnin, *The Year Ahead in Pro Bono*, Law 360, Jan. 2014, at 2, available at www.law360.com/articles/497965/the-year-ahead-in-pro-bono.

30 Sheldon Krantz's recent book, which highlights problems with and suggested reforms to the legal profession, cited the example of Bickel & Brewer for their innovative Storefront program. The firm's lawyers and staff volunteer at the Storefront, and clients are charged based on their ability to pay. Proceeds from the Storefront go to the Bickel & Brewer Foundation, which, in turn, supports

legal research service used by most law firms, recently launched the Do Justice program to offer free legal research for law firm lawyers doing pro bono work.[31] Nonprofits, like Appleseed Centers, throughout the country are leveraging the resources of corporate counsel and firms to work on systemic change to increase access to civil justice.[32] Many firms also are becoming more creative in delivering pro bono services by exploring the inventive use of technology to create virtual legal clinics.

Law Firms Working with Law Schools to Promote Access to Justice

As pressures increase for law schools to better prepare their students by providing more practical and experiential opportunities, those schools are turning to law firms for partnership and assistance.

For example, our Woodlawn Legal Clinic in Chicago is just blocks away from the University of Chicago Law School.[33] Students involved in the school's Pro Bono Service Initiative had been looking for volunteer opportunities and learned that our legal clinic was the only place where they could provide direct legal services in their own community (besides the school's own clinical program), so they approached the firm about participating. We now have at least two law students at every clinic helping our lawyers to interview clients and preparing interview notes for our lawyers' review.

More firms Should Make Pro Bono Part of Their Business Plans and Everyday Life

Over the past few decades, the world of pro bono has had much good news to report. The number of hours dedicated by law firms has exploded, and pro bono has become part of the culture and fabric of most large law firms.

But we need more. Pro bono service has been declining since 2009 – by about 400,000 hours per year (PBI report). And the total number of pro bono hours reported to *Am Law* amounts to only about three pro bono hours per lawyer each year.[34] And in most firms, associates do the heavy lifting with too few partners

community organizations. *The Legal Profession: What Is Wrong and How to Fix It* (LexisNexis 2013) at 120.

31 http://info.legalsolutions.thomsonreuters.com/westlaw/do-justice/default.aspx.

32 Appleseed is a terrific example of a nonprofit working on social justice issues by promoting systemic change and leveraging the resources of pro bono lawyers and firms.

33 DLA Piper has teamed with several law schools on pro bono projects over the years, including Northwestern's Bluhm Legal Clinic, Georgetown's International Women's Clinic, Hastings Law School, University of Maryland Carey School of Law, and most recently, University of Michigan's International Transactions Clinic.

34 Krantz, supra note 30, at 80. Although these numbers only reflect the time reported by the 134 signatories to the PBI Pro Bono Challenge program, they likely reflect a large percentage of all pro bono activity. See also Glazer supra note 5, at 570.

involved in pro bono cases. Associates report twice as much pro bono as partners. At a time when some firms have more partners than associates this is a troubling statistic.[35]

Even with strong, well-staffed programs, the need is – and will continue to be – crushing. And as long as it is so, law firms must continue to look for ways to build robust, creative, and collaborative programs that enable their lawyers to help meet that need.

[35] Krantz, supra note 30, at 79.

44

Facilitating Law Firm Pro Bono in Transactional Cases

Daniel L. Greenberg

In creating a culture of service, can law firms engage transactional lawyers in pro bono work too? In this chapter, Daniel Greenberg argues that firms can, if their pro bono programs move beyond litigation and incorporate transactional projects that build on the skills and knowledge of what their transactional lawyers do. At Greenberg's firm, their pro bono program successfully recruits volunteer transactional lawyers to represent nonprofits just like they represent their corporate clients advising on real estate issues, drafting contract language, or addressing intellectual property concerns. –Eds.

Any analysis of access to justice for Americans of average means must take note of the pro bono programs of major law firms. They are a huge potential source of advocacy for individual Americans of average means, and for the organizations that advocate for them. To maximize that potential, these firms will need to expand their services not by doing more of the same, but by rethinking the structure of their pro bono programs. This chapter argues that when a firm adopts a transactional pro bono model, thus transforming the scope of its services, not only will Americans of average means benefit, but the firm, its partners and associates will end up benefitting as well.

Historically, as is still the case in most law firms today, pro bono work has been tied to the firm's litigation practice. In the 1950s, the NAACP Legal Defense Fund, Inc. used courts to jump-start the civil rights movement. In 1963, President John F. Kennedy enlisted fifty of the country's largest law firms to work for equal justice through litigation with the creation of The Lawyers Committee for Civil Rights under Law. Framing large issues in law reform terms, and using class action litigation as its tool, private lawyers attacked segregation, discriminatory education and election laws, and other civil rights violations in federal courts that were largely sympathetic to their cause. Simultaneously, new legal services arose with a focus on the rights of poor people. These programs collaborated with big law firms in their quest for housing rights, access to government benefits, and consumer protections. Later, advocates in the women's, anti-war, and environmental movements emulated this model. To this day, big test-case litigation – often in partnership with public interest organizations such as the American Civil Liberties Union, the Lambda

Legal Defense Fund, and the NAACP – is the primary mode by which large law firms deliver pro bono services.

If the issue at hand is important enough, advocacy for an individual of whatever means frequently springs from these large test cases. Large firms with litigation-centered pro bono programs have spent thousands of hours of lawyer time on capital appeals and habeas corpus applications from southern states, or on asylum applications from those fleeing political repression. In these cases, there is little doubt that the litigation model has helped individuals while affecting significant changes in the law. Major challenges to existing policies in education, housing, government benefits, civil rights, death penalty, and many other areas could never have been brought but for the resources of large law firms. Some of these cases, particularly those involving civil rights, civil liberties, and due process rights when benefits such as unemployment insurance are wrongfully withheld, directly impact Americans of average means.

The structure of law firms makes them particularly well-suited to collaboration with the public interest organizations bringing such suits, because the firms possess the resources the NGOs lack. Partners can strategize as to the best ways to structure the litigation. Associates can devote thousands of hours to research, brief writing, and depositions. Paralegals can scan voluminous documents, file papers, and monitor deadlines. The firm as a whole can use these matters as training tools, permitting less experienced associates to take on responsibilities not yet permitted them with regard to billable clients. These associates develop the very skills they will need to advocate effectively for their corporate clients who may be faced with a securities class action lawsuit or other large-scale litigation. Of additional benefit to the firm is the fact that these cases allow the firm to be publicly identified with popular causes, often generating the kind of enormous favorable publicity that will help grow their client base.

The litigation pro bono model does have serious limitations, however. Most practice areas of big law firms focus on transactional work, not litigation. Lawyers attracted to finance, intellectual property, employment, tax, and real estate may be ill-suited to write a brief, depose a witness, or appear in court. The focus on big test-case lawsuits has created the anomaly that 80% of the firm's pro bono work is done by the 20% of the lawyers who are litigators, and non-litigators are left out. This imbalance serves neither law firm nor pro bono client. By placing transactional work at the center of big law firm pro bono practices, Americans of average means are lifted directly into the pro bono net without any connection to large, test-case legal challenges.

The modern large corporate law firm is global, with hundreds, even thousands of attorneys. Alert to the interactions between merger and acquisition, financing, real estate, intellectual property, and employment issues, they maximize profits for themselves, while providing continuity of care to their clients, by acting as a full-service law firm, even adding personal services such as trusts and estates to their arsenal. Traditionally, most firms saw no way to apply this structure to their pro bono work. As one corporate partner remarked to me: "somehow poverty organizations just don't seem to be interested in merging together two multinational institutions." Instead, firms have relied on clearinghouse not-for-profits that send weekly emails describing the rare transactional opportunities aimed at non-litigators, which are immediately snapped up.

When I ran The Legal Aid Society in New York, I, too, tended to reach out to firms predominantly for our mission-driven work. I was seeking assistance that directly affected our clients in distress. This was, after all, the reason I became its leader: a commitment to clients and their legal needs. Occasionally a real estate issue would arise, or a problem in our HR department needed outside legal help, at which point I would ask for one-off assistance from a Board member, who would ask her firm for help. But mostly I looked to large law firms for their litigation resources.

What I learned first-hand at Legal Aid is that all not-for-profits are also in essence small businesses. Consequently, their leaders need to act as CEOs. Ideally they should have a strong business background, and yet most executive directors, no matter how capably they serve their missions, have spent their careers avoiding business decisions of any sort. They could make up for this deficit by hiring savvy business people to help them build an infrastructure that will keep their organizations running smoothly. Yet they are loathe to do so, for every dollar spent on a CFO or assistant comes at the expense of client services. What they do instead is muddle through until a problem gets out of hand, when they may turn to an attorney on their board to bail them out. Too often the delay has made matters worse: small matters have mushroomed into major problems.

At Schulte Roth & Zabel, we embarked on an expanded, nontraditional pro bono program that asked transactional lawyers to do for nonprofits what they do for their paying clients: act as the nonprofit's general counsel. Simultaneously, we asked the executive directors of dozens of not-for-profits to use us as corporate organizational lawyers serving the organization's needs beyond the mission-driven needs of its clients. This resulted in an influx of non-litigation matters that could be spread throughout the firm. To understand the breadth of these issues, here is a sampling of how the various practice areas responded to our change in direction:

Real estate: Space is an issue for all not-for-profits. Partners help them decide whether to buy or rent. For most nonprofits, who lease property, associates review initial agreements, renewals, and modifications. They insure air conditioning or heat if the office is used on weekends. They interpret letters from landlords and the regulations they cite. If a city or state are the landlords – not uncommon with not-for-profits – they bring their expertise to advocacy. They avert court proceedings by arranging payouts for organizations in financial distress.

Employment: Myriad HR and board-related issues vex organizations. It often seems that our clients' HR directors have us on speed-dial. Now no employee is terminated without consulting us. ERISA and pension issues are handled. Employee handbooks, contracts for job offers, and policies on everything from whistle-blowers to conflicts of interest, are reviewed. Board decisions are analyzed so that its decisions comport with state and local statutes; we also make sure there is enough D and O insurance to protect them if they go wrong. Alerts about changes in the law are proactively sent. And when complaints are sent to administrative agencies we handle those as well. The skills our employment attorneys garner are entirely relevant to the billable work they do for the large not-for-profit organizations and educational institutions they primarily represent.

Intellectual property: These attorneys review the dozens of contracts that our clients have with other entities. They create Memos of Understanding that serve as the structure for collaboration. They trademark names and copyright programs, software, and training material organizations develop. They have prevented others from infringing on the branded name on which our clients fund-raise. In some instances, by scrutinizing their clients' websites, they have prevented clients from inadvertently infringing on the rights of others. For example, a client that was reprinting large parts of newspaper articles about its work was advised to create links to the newspaper's website. The result was a better-looking page, as well as a lawful one. And in a striking example of a swift response to a client's needs, an organization giving medical aid to Haiti in the aftermath of its devastating earthquake had a plane filled with equipment and volunteers set to go in Boston, when the pilot refused to take off. His position was that the aircraft, which was generally used by its owner and his family, was inadequately insured. Within two hours a partner who specialized in airplane insurance secured a one-shot $10 million policy and the plane took off.

Trust and estates: Under a program designed by an organization committed to the needs of elders, lawyers have done dozens of simple wills, and often settled their estates. They have created trust agreements allowing wealthy individuals during their lifetimes to leave their assets to a client organization. In collaboration with a local law school, they have trained graduating law students on how to serve Americans of average means and not-for-profit clients in their communities. Our lawyers have also assisted charitable organizations in registering with state attorneys general, using knowledge gained from their work with foundations created by their billable clients. Importantly, the pro bono groups we represent have sometimes received grants from these foundations when, not uncommonly, the foundations have sought advice from counsel on identifying worthy recipients.

Bankruptcy: When a local hospital in a working-class section of Queens was closing, a neighborhood health center sought to keep its primary care facility open. Our bankruptcy practice represented the center and, with the assistance of the finance group, successfully intervened in the proceeding. Lawyers in this group regularly assist Americans of average means with debt issues, counseling, training, and filing bankruptcy petitions.

Tax: Tax lawyers have helped dozens of not-for-profits obtain 501(c)(3) status, find sponsors that obviate the need for a separate identity, or amend their certificates of incorporation. They review state laws and analyze how and when not-for-profits need to register with state authorities. They help with compliance on filing 990 forms and answer questions about the deductibility of certain contributions. They help organizations go out of business, merge, or take over similar entities. Particularly at election time, they help clients navigate political activity that might jeopardize not-for-profit status. And they have given many of our clients advice on the tax consequences of hiring U.S. citizens working at their overseas sites.

Corporate/finance: The business practice areas are a rich source of assistance to our clients, especially those whose mission involves economic development. We have helped structure the financial arrangements for an NGO that builds housing in the South Bronx, and for an enterprise that seeks to bring an ice hockey rink to abandoned property there. We give legal advice and mentoring to dozens of newly created micro-businesses in this country and overseas. Business transactions attorneys routinely review organizational contracts and those for individuals. For example, we represent working-class artists with contract issues. Finance attorneys help structure organizations so that a loss of revenue for one project does not necessarily impact other parts of its work. Insurance attorneys are available for the numerous issues that arise: they once had to recommend securing kidnap insurance for an organization involved in a rural area of a third-world country. our attorneys even researched the possibility of creating a hedge fund whose profits would be directed solely toward the financing of a not-for-profit.

Ethics: At some point many of our client organizations, especially those with a mission relating to law, face ethical issues. Our experts here are swift to respond. A few of the issues we have helped to resolve are: the limits of the attorney–client relationship; the responsibilities of board members who are attorneys; conflicts issues; attorneys as organizers; the right to practice in a foreign jurisdiction; and the collection of referral fees.

All attorneys: Virtually all not-for-profit clients need legal research at some point, frequently on issues directly related to Americans of average means. Through an agreement with Lexis and Westlaw, our firm can comfortably allow associates across its practice areas to meet those needs. Attorneys in our hedge fund practice area, for example, created a detailed handbook for use by employers who hire low-income workers. In preparing this handbook, which integrates government programs with private company benefits, the attorneys discovered that a breadwinner with a large family may be eligible for food stamps, and that many employees can apply for the Earned Income Tax Credit. Our associates researched the existence of all such programs, and made them accessible to the human resources departments of small businesses. Non-litigators have engaged in hundreds of similar research projects over the years.

Other firm-wide, non-litigation activities abound. Dozens of our lawyers have done election protection work, insuring, in a non-partisan manner, access to the voting booth. Chinese Americans of all incomes have received translation services from public agencies through our advocacy work. Attorneys with a background in criminal law are called upon to counsel organizations during investigations. Spanish-speaking attorneys helped a group of Guatemalan Indians seek justice. Working groups across practices have advocated for a UN Convention on the Elderly, for prosecutorial rigor on behalf of rape victims in Africa, for internet security in China, and for environmental justice in Israel. Our attorneys have gathered judicial rulings on equal opportunity, religious freedom, innocence, and exonerations in criminal matters; and human rights at home and abroad for use in reports by our client organizations. Firm-wide pro bono activities are not restricted to the legal staff: our HR people helped a not-for-profit reorganize its HR department, and our IT staff routinely lend their technical expertise to our clients.

To understand the depth of our pro bono practice beyond the sampling of practice areas mentioned earlier, it may be useful to concretize these services in one specific organization. Sanctuary for Families is a domestic violence organization that helps battered women through court advocacy, counseling, and securing physical protection from their abusers. There is no means test for its services, since even women of more than moderate means who flee their spouses may have no access to their former resources. In 2005 Sanctuary for Families seemed an ideal vehicle to test the general counsel model. With the benefit of eight years of assistance behind us, it is instructive to see how this has functioned, as well as its impact on Americans of average means.

Sanctuary has a number of shelter sites throughout New York City. A real estate partner has been intimately involved in overseeing associates who have helped the organization decide whether it is prudent to rent or to buy space. Associates have reviewed a number of leases, and have insured that clauses concerning adequate protection for anonymity are included. When the police came to question a client, a former assistant district attorney, now specializing in foreign corrupt practices, resurrected her former career and accompanied the client to the interview. Trust and estates attorneys created a system for multi-year contributions, and tax associates answered sales tax questions about the sale of goods. A partner who specializes in evaluating ethical issues has responded to a variety of questions, including whether judges can be trainers at its seminars, and whether a subpoena could be quashed on attorney–client grounds. And yes, litigation associates continued to secure Orders of Protection in family court, and helped the organization secure attorney's fees for a law reform case. The sum of these interactions is that Sanctuary runs smoothly, as legal problems that could undermine its mission are either avoided altogether or are dealt with before they cause serious damage. More, as an unforeseen bonus, a partner with numerous positive interactions with the organization joined its Board of Directors.

Immigrant groups and those working overseas also benefit from our corporate and transactional work. Organizations that run hospitals in Haiti, Lesotho, Malawi, and those serving the Uyghur people of China, are clients. Others build schools in Rwanda, educate girls in Kenya, minister to Ethiopian refugees, and bring Israeli solar energy technology to Africa. Asylees from all over the world are represented at hearings, and we obtain administrative regularization of status for foreign-born youngsters.

The benefits of this transactional pro bono model for multiple constituencies should by now be clear. It results in direct services to individuals of average means, or ongoing assistance to groups whose missions enhance their quality of life. Seniors, immigrants, artists, victims of domestic violence, micro-entrepreneurs, and those seeking bankruptcy relief will find exceptionally talented lawyers willing to represent them. For the organizations that advocate for them, it means that the executive director has a dedicated law firm that is, in effect, on retainer, with a cadre of attorneys to whom they can turn. With this resource at hand, at no cost, organizations are quick to consult before problems veer out of control.

In extolling the benefits of this model for clients, we should not lose sight of the value it has for firms and their partners and associates. The *American Lawyer* magazine, whose AmLaw 100 listing of the most profitable law firms is frequently credited with turning the legal industry from a collegial profession into a cut-throat business industry, also tracks pro bono work in a special issue called "The A List." The publication of the average number of hours a firm devotes to pro bono has become a significant public relations opportunity. It has created a huge incentive for firms to support pro bono work, with concrete consequences for their profitability.

Law firms also recognize that their largest private, billable clients care about pro bono work. Corporations that care about their own diversity, charitable giving and the volunteer work of their employees are likely to query their attorneys about these same issues. Potential as well as current clients become aware of the positive publicity these cases engender, either from news reports or from the firm's newsletter. Pro bono activity is monitored and measured and, by implication, becomes part of the calculus of which firms to engage. With increased competition among law firms to attract and keep clients, firms that remain insensitive or inflexible to potential clients' pro bono needs do so at some risk.

Legal recruiting at the top law schools is also helped by a vibrant pro bono program. Students often ask about the types of non-billable matters the firm undertakes, and whether the hours devoted to them are credited toward their target hours for the year. Partners are eager to discuss pro bono initiatives because not only do the hours count, but the students can be assured that they will be called upon to engage in important pro bono activity regardless of the practice area to which they have been assigned. One partner noted that the transactional pro bono model has emerged as a significant talking point during interviews because it is so different from that of other firms. At a time when law schools increasingly teach students "to think like a lawyer" devoid of practical application, and given that many law firms can ill afford to take up the slack, pro bono work provides an invaluable education to young associates and a necessary measuring stick for partners. If partners are able to evaluate this work, those evaluations become a part of the end-of-the year review, and eventually a factor in major decisions, including whether an associate becomes a partner.

Associates, too, gain an enormous amount from this model. It involves them in matters directly related to the skill-base they seek to develop. These matters tend to be discrete, which means they can do important work within a manageable schedule. They are likely to have greater responsibility for every phase of the representation than is typical with billable clients. Indeed, it may be their only chance to meet a real client. That they are involved with public interest organizations whose missions are laudable, and that these clients are far more likely to say "thank you," also can be great morale boosters. Little wonder that associates who are otherwise uninterested in going to court flock to these matters and develop long-term relationships with the clients they serve. Even when they leave the firm, as most do, associates often find work in smaller venues where what they have learned in their transactional pro bono work will become invaluable in servicing paying clients.

The transactional pro bono model works. Between April 2005, when our program began, and year-end, the percentage of pro bono done by the 16% of the firm in the litigation practice dropped from 45% to 36%. This level remained constant in 2006, despite our undertaking of a class action lawsuit in Louisiana challenging FEMA's handling of Hurricane Katrina. The level did rise slightly over the next few years, but never reached the 2004 level until 2012, when a massive lawsuit challenging the indigent defense system in upstate New York required tens of thousands of hours. Yet even here, the firm seeks to engage associates who are non-litigators, using dozens of associates across the practice areas for research and writing.

As leaders in the legal profession – in the academy, in firms and in public service – struggle to invent newer and better ways to insure access to justice for people at all income levels, pro bono will continue to be an important resource. Novel ideas on expanding its use are essential, and broadening the involvement of associates and partners who cannot, or do not want to, engage in litigation is just one way to bring new resources to bear. The transactional pro bono model benefits clients and the firm, helping to resolve problems while it teaches new skills. It may not in and of itself fix the access to justice problem for Americans of average means, but with creativity and tenacity it is certainly part of the solution.

45

What Bar Associations Can Do to Improve Access to Civil Justice

Lynn M. Kelly

Bar associations continue to be a critical resource for engaging lawyers in pro bono work to help people who cannot afford to hire a lawyer. Lynn Kelly, the executive director of the New York City Bar's Justice Center, describes in this chapter how the Center has expanded its pro bono initiatives to help moderate-income Americans.

With 24,000 members, the Association of the Bar of the City of New York ("City Bar") is a large and prestigious voluntary local bar whose members include lawyers at many of the country's leading law firms as well as in-house counsel and the full range of the legal profession. Members may apply to serve on 160 committees, organized by subject area, that make legislative and policy recommendations. The City Bar Justice Center has a staff of 30 employees and a handful of full-time volunteers and matches 1,000 cases a year with pro bono attorneys it recruits, trains, and mentors as needed. The City Bar Justice Center leverages more than $20 million worth of donated legal time annually and helps 20,000 New Yorkers through staff and pro bono efforts. One of the distinctive features of the City Bar Justice Center is its rapid response to emerging areas of legal needs because it can recruit and quickly train hundreds of pro bono attorney volunteers and host the trainings and legal clinics in the large main meeting hall at the City Bar Association located in midtown Manhattan.

FROM THE POOR TO PEOPLE OF AVERAGE MEANS: AN EVOLVING ROLE FOR PRO BONO WORK

Starting in the 1960s, the City Bar was a forum for major discussions about the obligation of lawyers to assist the poor and was an early supporter of government-funded neighborhood legal services. This thrust was part of the growing attention to poverty within the legal field and society as a whole. It would take some twenty-five years after the City Bar began creating pro bono programs for the poor, for the bar to begin a program targeted to moderate-income clients who could not afford lawyers – now known as "Monday Night Law."

Volunteer spinoffs from the bar

In the 1960s and 1970s, the City Bar underwent a shift away from its historical position as an elite professional association and toward the view that the profession should respond to unmet legal needs. Younger City Bar members fomented serious debate with the suggestion that the City Bar sponsor a public interest law firm to be staffed with salaried attorneys and funded by levies drawn on the large firms. The proposal was addressed, in part, by the founding, in 1976, of a new organization called the New York Lawyers for the Public Interest (NYLPI) with three City Bar presidents among its founders. NYLPI's goal was increasing legal services to the poor through screening and channeling public law opportunities to participating large law firms.

In 1984, the City Bar created a second pro bono organization from the work of the Access to Legal Services Committee called the Volunteers of Legal Service (VOLS) in the face of cuts made in federal funding of legal services for the poor. The VOLS model distinguished itself in three ways: it required a collective, formal agreement of twenty-nine participating large law firms to meet or exceed an annual goal of thirty hours of pro bono work per attorney limited to low-income clients; it addressed civil legal issues; and it matched law firms with the local law offices of the Legal Services Corporation. Within a year's time VOLS became a separate nonprofit organization. By 1985, VOLS had recruited more than 60 law firms and 20 corporations into its program. The incubation of two entirely new pro bono institutions out of the City Bar – NYLPI and VOLS – reflected the growing capacity of New York's legal community to address the legal needs of low-income New Yorkers in the face of limited government funding for civil representation and the bar's role in fostering those discussions.

City Bar presidents over the last fifty years have regarded access to legal services for the poor as one of their highest priorities. Along with the leadership and permanent staff of the Bar, the City Bar's committee structure helped to provide direct service ideas, trainings, and guidance on substantive law and structuring of pro bono projects. Frequently, the committees were also a source of volunteers.

Focusing on Specific Legal Needs: Immigration and Homelessness

In the 1980s, the City Bar responded to the increase in documented and undocumented immigrants. The City Bar's Committee on Immigration and Nationality Law started a project to train and mobilize pro bono lawyers to assist on Haitian asylum claims. Then, following the 1986 amnesty law, which provided for a one-year window during which potentially 800,000 undocumented immigrants in New York City could apply to legalize their status, the City Bar Fund hired an attorney to train scores of pro bono volunteers to process amnesty applications for over 600 people. The City Bar has continued to mobilize pro bono efforts to respond to the city's major immigration needs. These projects are popular with immigration specialists and young associates at large law firms interested in international human rights. The first global pro bono center at the City Bar was created as the Cyrus R. Vance Center for International Justice in 1991.

In 1987, the City Bar created the Community Outreach Law Program (COLP).[1] COLP won awards and became a model for bar association legal clinics nationally seeking to provide direct legal services to urban communities. COLP initiated many legal services projects including projects in the Housing Court to prevent evictions and in Family Court to assist battered women, using summer associates as volunteers. In 1991, with the creation of the Project on the Homeless, COLP provided a coordinator and helped to create a weekly clinic to provide free onsite legal counseling to the homeless population. Nearly 2,000 cases were assigned to City Bar volunteers in a 15 month period of which three-quarters involved counseling and one quarter involved direct representation at fair hearings challenging welfare errors.

As COLP was expanded, targeted projects provided training by experts on specific legal areas so that the volunteers could be recruited from any practice background or corporate legal department therefore expanding the pool of potential pro bono attorneys. Between 1991 and 1992, COLP trained over 1,000 lawyers who were expected to take at least one pro bono case in return. COLP also developed projects including: Guardian Ad Litem, AIDS Counseling, Domestic Violence, Hostos Center for Women's and Immigrants' Rights, and a legal clinic with Bellevue Hospital which trained hospital social workers to identify legal issues and provided a telephone helpline if needed for consultation with an attorney with expertise in family, immigration, or elder law. Programs were also created in the areas of matrimonial law, bankruptcy, counseling for the homeless, cancer patient rights, elder law, public benefits, law-related education, adoption, and children's rights.

"Monday Night Law": Volunteers for Moderate-Income Clients

In the 1990s the City Bar became increasingly concerned with the lack of legal services affordable to moderate-income New Yorkers. The Young Lawyers Committee started "Monday Night Law" (MNL) in 1991 with teams of trained volunteer attorneys counseling low- and moderate-income clients. Monday Night Law, now sponsored by the City Bar's Committee on Legal Services for Persons of Moderate Means, requires that volunteer lawyers have at least two years of practice experience, and there is a training every fall for new recruits. MNL runs a free evening clinic at the City Bar with 130 volunteers organized into four teams for the year offering free in-person consultations to over 1,000

[1] COLP was subsequently named for a former president, Robert B. McKay (City Bar president, 1984–86).

clients a year. The free consultations cover bankruptcy, consumer, employment, family, landlord–tenant, and small business law. The City Bar Justice Center certifies pro bono Continung Legal Education (CLE) credits for MNL volunteers and provides administrative and translation support. More than two decades after it started, MNL remains a successful, almost entirely volunteer-driven clinic. Appointments are made for the MNL clinic through the City Bar's Legal Referral Service (see Chapter 16 of this volume for a description of the referral service), and the program makes 45–60 appointments for each MNL clinic, which run four Monday nights a month (excluding August and September when new volunteers are recruited and trained). There is a one-third no-show rate on appointments, so 30–40 clients on average are seen at MNL. MNL is popular with volunteer attorneys and with clients.

Mobilizing Volunteer Responses to a Mass Crisis

Prior to 2001, no portion of the low-income civil justice sector in New York City, including the City Bar Fund, was experienced in mobilizing volunteer resources on a massive scale. However, the attacks on the World Trade Center on September 11, 2001, presented an unprecedented and urgent civic challenge to the organized bar. The families of those killed were in shock and needed immediate legal help to obtain expedited death certificates, file health and life insurance claims, obtain Social Security and other survivors' benefits, workers' compensation, and navigate Surrogate's Court. The families of survivors included low-income, middle-income, and high-income families. All who asked would receive pro bono legal services whether they could afford to pay or not. No subsequent response to the various natural disasters has lowered the economic screening barrier for free legal help in the way that the 9/11 attacks did. From a pro bono viewpoint, the 9/11 tragedy unleashed the strongest pro bono response in New York City's history from lawyers and is a useful model for increasing pro bono representation to all income levels after a disaster.

In the week after September 11, 2001, the legal profession in New York came together, coordinated by the City Bar and the Chief Judge of the New York State courts, and forged a new coordinated mass disaster legal response model. More than 4,000 individuals of all income levels affected by the 9/11 disaster were represented on a pro bono basis by volunteer lawyers. Approximately 3,000 attorneys received training through the City Bar and in-house law firm programs using City Bar resources. A "facilitator model" was developed so that the clients could have all their legal needs identified and managed by one attorney designated as the facilitator for a particular client. This departed from the dominant model of pro bono in which volunteers specialize in one area and the client must self-identify what help they need or get referred from one lawyer to the next. The 9/11 pro bono model sought to spare the client the stress of hunting down the additional help needed and instead that need would be identified by the facilitator who would then match the need with various resources.

The various bar association groups with members in New York City agreed to specialize in different areas at the outset of the 9/11 clinics, which made it easier to sort volunteers and cases. The Legal Aid Society and Legal Services NYC served as facilitators identifying the legal needs, they provided direct representation to clients and they trained and advised volunteer lawyers from the private sector. Other legal services providers addressed particular issues or populations. Law firms were the largest source of volunteer attorneys and the preexisting pro bono structures at the largest law firms made it easier to organize volunteers and match cases. By 2001, many large firms had hired pro bono coordinators, so they became the liaison to match cases with the firm's volunteer lawyers. Probono.net provided online information, communication, and resources to all enrolled volunteers. Large law firms were able to dedicate staff to the effort and several sent multiple attorneys on secondment to the City Bar for a number of months to help organize the response while continuing to be paid by their law firms. The City Bar was able to rapidly mobilize its existing Legal Referral Service (LRS)[2] for telephone intake of victims needing legal assistance and lawyers seeking to volunteer.

Since 9/11, the City Bar's pro bono services model has grown into the City Bar Justice Center. The City Bar Justice Center has a staff of 30 full-time employees who recruit, train, mentor, screen, and match pro bono matters. This model leverages more than $20 million worth of donated legal time annually and helps 20,000 New Yorkers. Since 9/11, the pro bono disaster response model at the City Bar has been tested by disasters including Hurricane Katrina in New Orleans, which sent displaced people to New York City and elsewhere, and Superstorm Sandy in 2012.

INCREASING LEGAL NEEDS OF PEOPLE OF AVERAGE MEANS

The Great Recession started in 2008 and added huge numbers of the formerly middle class into the pool of New Yorkers who could not afford counsel. This included litigants – the homeowners and others with crushing credit card and student loan debt who were falling out of the middle class and being sued by financial institutions. The corporations bringing suit were required to be represented by counsel leaving the uneven playing field spectacle of thousands of pro se New Yorkers attempting to defend lawsuits commenced by debt collection law firms. Commencing in 2010, in the face of New York State's 2.3 million litigants without counsel, New York's Chief Judge Jonathan Lippman[3] spearheaded an unprecedented multi-year effort to expand state funding for legal services and pro

[2] See Charne, Chapter 16 in this volume.
[3] See Chief Judge Lippman's Overview in this volume.

bono programs and to encourage more lawyers to donate pro bono services to low-income New Yorkers in need of help with the basic necessities of life. First, the Chief Judge added significant funding for low-income legal services to the Judiciary budget. Then, the Chief Judge broadened the pool of volunteers with a series of targeted court rules. First, a new law student admission requirement of 50 pro bono hours, followed by pro bono time and donation reporting requirements, broadening the eligibility for out-of-state licensed in-house counsel who want to volunteer, a revitalized lawyer emeritus program starting at age 50 (the "baby boomer" retirees) and a Pro Bono Scholars Program to be implemented in 2015 to give law students a chance to take the New York bar exam after two and a half years and then do pro bono work for their last semester of law school.

The new legal needs for working families revealed by the Great Recession – consumer debt, bankruptcy, mortgage foreclosure, student loan debt – tended to be in areas of law not traditionally covered by legal aid and legal services programs in New York City. At the City Bar Justice Center, a new project, the Lawyers Foreclosure Intervention Network, was started with the support of the Federal Reserve Bank of New York. The City Bar Justice Center's Consumer Bankruptcy Project developed a waiting list longer than six months for pro bono help on a simple bankruptcy. The waiting list continued to grow as many formerly employed people remained out of work beyond the expanded unemployment assistance program as the recession wore on. The longer they were out of work, the more legal needs they had.

The City Bar Justice Center's Legal Hotline became a tremendous resource for moderate- and low-income people in New York City during the recession. Because it has flexible income guidelines and is able to provide basic information and advice without screening for income, the Legal Hotline is able to help a broader range of New Yorkers. Out of the pool of 20,000 New Yorkers helped each year by the Justice Center, half of the cases are assisted through the Legal Hotline. For bar associations hoping to provide a great service to the community, a Legal Hotline is a great start, and it is particularly convenient for the elderly and mobility impaired. Surveys of client satisfaction with the Legal Hotline have shown that callers are very pleased to reach an attorney who will speak with them over the phone about their matters. Expectations are made clear from the beginning of the call that only advice can be given, and the Legal Hotline will not be able to match most callers with a free lawyer through one of our projects. In addition, the types of calls are limited to questions that can be answered over the telephone or with a limited amount of legal research and follow-up.

The Legal Hotline is also used to screen clients for the Consumer Bankruptcy Project and sends out a detailed screening questionnaire, which saves the project from having to spend time to screen out inappropriate cases. The Legal Hotline in 2013 piloted a new Planning and Estates Law Project (PELP) where more advanced trust and estates questions are referred to a pro bono panel of experts. They review the questions and give advice to the hotline attorneys on how to respond. Funds were raised to hire a project coordinator to manage the administration of the PELP project and assist the Legal Hotline. PELP then was able to add a new monthly clinic with over 150 households helped in the first year. At the clinic, the pro bono T & E attorneys aided by local law student volunteers go over the paperwork, help the client to fill out any forms, and give the client legal advice on his or her case. In addition the PELP volunteer lawyers are working on drafting simple forms that can be used by pro se people in the Surrogate's Court.

During the recession, the City Bar Justice Center experienced a great increase in hotline requests for help from individuals who were being sued on their credit card, medical, and student loan debts. As these cases ballooned in the courts as well, new funding in 2010 from the Office of Court Administration allowed the City Bar Justice Center to add several part-time lawyers to expand the Legal Hotline. The hotline increased its capacity serving 20% more calls, assisting 1,000 callers each month.

Those calling the Legal Hotline include people who may be working but are seeking free help because they cannot afford legal counsel. They are frequently referred by both the federal and state courts, which have reduced their staff size due to budget cuts. The City Bar Justice Center doesn't screen for income and assets for cases where it is only giving advice on the hotline and not referring to one of the projects for extended representation. The usual income cutoff for free legal services is that a person's income must fall below 250% of the poverty line; some of the City Bar Justice Center's projects serve workers whose income is up to 400% of poverty. During the foreclosure crisis, the City Bar Justice Center and other low-income legal service programs in NYC starting helping large numbers of people with a home, but no money to pay for a lawyer to defend a foreclosure case.

Ms. P, for example, is a single mother of two children, with high monthly expenses for child care and commuting to work. When her gas expenses rose to $400 a month and her rent increased, she was $300 short every month and she went into debt. She worked all available overtime, which further increased her childcare costs, but she still couldn't make ends meet. She came home to the stress of daily creditor phone calls and letters, threats of garnishment, and the possibility of losing her rented home. She called the City Bar Justice Center's Legal Hotline, which referred her to the Consumer Bankruptcy Project at the City Bar Justice Center. The Consumer Bankruptcy Project matched her with a pro bono attorney who helped her complete the form to file pro se for a discharge of her debts in bankruptcy. With a discharge in bankruptcy, this family got a fresh start out from under the accumulated debt.

Another example of working families assisted by the City Bar Justice Center is a husband and wife who were the parents of two adult children, one a disabled son the mother looked after at home and one in college. The family went into debt when the disabled son was hospitalized and his bills were astronomical. As a landscaping contractor, the father earned close to $70,000 a year, and the family lived in a two-family home with rental income to help cover the mortgage. But all his income was focused on the medical debt, and they fell behind on their consumer and mortgage debt. A shoddy debt management company consolidated the debt, took payments from the family and failed to send payments to the creditors. In a panic, the family sought help from the City Bar Justice Center, which successfully matched them with a pro bono attorney to discharge the debt in bankruptcy.

MODELS FOR LEVERAGING ATTORNEY VOLUNTEERS

In using attorney volunteers to help close the justice gap, the City Bar Justice Center has learned several lessons that would be helpful for other bar associations seeking to help low- and moderate-income people:

- Develop mass clinics to serve individuals in specific subject areas. Whenever the Justice Center can, we turn an unmet legal need into a clinic because it allows the Justice Center to reach more people. Our large clinics cover areas like veteran's disability benefits, immigration relief, and the 9/11 reopened victim's compensation fund. We run smaller clinics in the paper-intensive consumer bankruptcy area and with our Neighborhood Entrepreneur Law Project (NELP). Clinics are popular with clients and pro bono attorneys. New York has an ethics rule waiving conflicts screening for brief services at pro bono clinics, which has helped to increase interest in this form of pro bono.
- Schedule clinic appointments. For mass clinics, individuals schedule prearranged appointments and are usually given a reminder call through a third-party screener or a staff member of the City Bar Justice Center. For example, the Legal Referral Service makes the appointments for Monday Night Law, or staff of elected officials book appointments for the City Bar Justice Center's Deferred Action for Childhood Arrivals Clinic. There is generally a no-show rate of up to 20% for clinics. To reduce the chance of pro bono attorneys sitting around with no client, the Justice Center staggers the appointments at one-hour intervals over the first two hours of a three-hour clinic and does telephone, email, or text client reminders. If a bar association wants to do pro bono clinics but is short on resources, it is possible to partner with community groups and train them to screen clients who might benefit from a legal consultation and use a shared online scheduling calendar for the appointments.
- Unbundle legal services so that pro bono attorneys can be trained to tackle one issue. Each lawyer must disclose that only one portion of a case will be handled and advise the client of alternatives if he or she would prefer to get full representation. For many legal needs, there is no full representation available for free or at an affordable rate. Anyone designing programs for clients with court or administrative agency cases must familiarize themselves with the local

rules on unbundling because for some issues, some courts do not permit unbundling.

- Leverage experts who volunteer by "bookending" them, placing them at the beginning or end of client intake. For example, the City Bar Justice Center collaborates with experts and specialty bar associations like the American Immigration Lawyers Association to screen and do a final review on cases in complex areas like immigration before the client checks out of a pro bono clinic. Attorney volunteers who are not experts conduct the more time-consuming functions, like interviewing a client or filling out of forms.
- Use technology to make trainings easily accessible to pro bono attorney volunteers. The City Bar Justice Center tapes most trainings and makes them available to law firms and individual lawyers who cannot attend the live training. We collaborate with ProBonoNet to post trainings online.
- Invest in a full- or part-time staff support for the pro bono projects. Even one staff attorney or non-attorney project coordinator working with volunteers and coordinating legal work can make a huge difference on bar association projects. A firm may be willing to send an associate to help start a pro bono program for 6 months or a year. A retired lawyer might commit to a year helping to build a pro bono project. There needs to be a point person, even a non-lawyer, at the bar association to help coordinate the allocation of pro bono resources and to screen cases and make appointments. Equal Justice Works Fellowships and Americorps are other possible sources for staffing for bar association pro bono programs.
- Make programs self-sustaining. Finding funding to serve the needs of people who cannot afford attorneys is challenging for bar association-run pro bono projects. There are foundations willing to fund projects serving low-income people as an anti-poverty strategy. However, households over 250% of poverty are screened out of most free legal services programs and pro bono programs. In fact, cases of moderate-income people cannot be counted toward their pro bono hour requirements in New York and under the American Lawyer Magazine Am Law 100 standards. One solution is to host an annual gala or luncheon with participating firms, corporate legal departments, and lawyers purchasing tables to support the pro bono programming. The advantage to special event funding is that it doesn't saddle the pro bono program with ongoing reporting requirements or onerous financial screening for eligibility as do some government and private foundation grants. The City Bar Justice Center gala raises about one-quarter of our operating budget in unrestricted funding for the City Bar Justice Center. Some groups successfully use a sliding-scale low bono fee to represent working families, particularly in the immigration context, but the Justice Center does not charge clients.

- Establish a capacity for full representation. Some clients need full representation, and some lawyers want a more in-depth pro bono experience through impact cases or cases requiring complex problem-solving issues.
- Be transparent about what the program offers. If the program is an unbundled one, make sure whoever is scheduling the appointments notifies each and every potential client that this program doesn't promise to give them an attorney; it just gets them a free one-on-one half-an-hour consultation. Managing client expectations is important. Our experience with the MNL is that clients are grateful for lawyers who are willing to interview them, sort through their legal problems and advise without further representation.
- Recognize that pro bono does not work for every subject matter area. In order for a bar association to operate a successful pro bono program, the volunteers have to want to do work in that area of the law, and there has to be an unmet need.
- Use client satisfaction surveys to evaluate programs. These surveys are helpful to determine whether an unbundled service actually helps clients resolve their legal problems. On some projects, we have learned that clients could not actually complete filing certain applications on their own despite being advised about how to do it. We learned on an immigrant detention project that when immigrants were bonded out of detention, many were able to raise the money to hire their own lawyers and no longer needed the City Bar Justice Center, freeing up that resource for the next client.
- Obtain malpractice insurance. Bar association-sponsored pro bono programs must make sure that their malpractice insurance covers the activities of pro bono volunteers or limit the program to attorneys who provide proof of malpractice insurance. As new players such as in-house counsel, law students, law graduates, and retired lawyers are encouraged to do more pro bono, the issue of malpractice coverage must be resolved so that the work is covered, and the clients are protected.

The findings of the American Bar Association (ABA)'s Supporting Justice III Report in March 2013 are useful for bar associations that are creating programs for people of moderate means. First, the findings show that it helps to have the cases screened by a trusted bar association or other trusted institutional source. The ABA report found that one-third of lawyers were willing to accept an unfamiliar pro bono client if they knew the referral source.[4] Second, 79% of pro bono lawyers did not report any areas in which they could have used more support. The support they received from bar association pro bono programs includes: form document samples (21%), CLE (16%), sample pleadings (15%), and regular check-ins (15%).

[4] ABA Standing Committee on Pro Bono and Public Service, Supporting Justice III: A Report on the Pro Bono Work of America's Lawyers (2013), available at www.americanbar.org/content/dam/aba/administrative/probono_public_service/ls_pb_Supporting_Justice_III_final.authcheckdam.pdf.

As the work of New York City's Bar Association shows, thousands of individuals who cannot afford a lawyer can be served through pro bono programs. The pro bono programs developed by the City Bar Justice Center, including the free legal hotline, could be helpful in many other parts of the country. The next frontier is to use technology such as online applications to increase intake efficiencies so that pro bono programs can help more people. There is a role for bar associations to continue providing access to justice for individuals of average means through trainings on low bono pricing of legal services and helping the implementation of initiatives to create areas where non-lawyers can help individuals with legal needs. Newly minted attorneys without job offers may create more affordable approaches for legal needs of moderate-income people.

46

The Teaching Law Office:

Service and Learning in the Law School Years

Jeanne Charn

Jeanne Charn describes in this chapter the evolution of Harvard's pioneering teaching law office and the benefits of this model for both the law students and their clients. Present-day clinical programs can look to the teaching law office as a realistic, replicable model for serving the legal needs of people of modest means.

What role should law school clinics play in education for practice, particularly, though not exclusively, in the law school years? Is law student immersion in a high-quality, high-volume law practice an educational necessity that generates substantial client service? Decades of experience in a teaching law office at Harvard Law School suggests that clinics can make a substantial contribution to access to legal services both as direct providers and as developers of cost- and outcome-effective legal services.

THE "HARVARD MODEL"

The notion of a so-called "Harvard Model" of clinical education is rooted in the concept of a teaching law office analogous to the teaching hospital in graduate and post graduate medical education. The teaching law office idea involves an insistence that service and learning are not in tension but inextricably intertwined; a commitment to clinical practice in a fully functioning law office; an emphasis on the distinctive educational role of expert advocates mentoring novice students;[1] a deliberate decision to prioritize the everyday legal needs of low- and moderate-income clients of the clinic; and a focus on what it takes to assure high-quality legal services.

The teaching law office at Harvard has accommodated many students and served hundreds of clients annually.[2] It evolved in four distinct phases.

[1] Oral History Interview with Gary Bellow, Gary Bellow Oral History, Zona Hostetler, conducted by Zona Hostetler (1999–02–17), available at https://repository.library.georgetown.edu/handle/10822/709332.

[2] The Center opened over 1,000 cases annually in 1983 and 1984. Legal Services Center: 10 Year Report of Cases Opened (on file with the author).

1964–1971: CLAO

Before the Johnson administration created the federally funded legal services program and the Council on Legal Education for Professional Responsibility (CLEPR) launched modern clinics, an informal faculty committee at Harvard conceived of and sponsored the Community Legal Assistance Office (CLAO). In the 1964–65 academic year, Committee members placed 34 students in the offices of the Boston Legal Aid Society but were not satisfied with the arrangement. Federal funding from the Office of Economic Opportunity (OEO) enabled the CLAO to test the efficacy of law student volunteers working with experienced, full-time legal aid lawyers. CLAO director John Ferren hired staff, sited the office in a low-income neighborhood a half hour from campus, and solicited student volunteers. The original plan was for forty students but over 200 showed up at an informational meeting. Seventy-five were admitted. In subsequent years CLAO accepted 100 student volunteers each year.

CLAO made a substantial contribution to the legal needs of low-income people in the area. From 1967 to 1969, staff and students saw over 4,000 clients and closed 2,860 matters that went beyond brief advice. The office typically had about 800 active cases.[3]

The CLAO experiment ended in 1971.[4] Its legacy was faculty who understood the value of a law school-affiliated practice center involving many students, serving thousands of clients, critically examining innovative approaches to delivering legal services, and offering students educational opportunities not available in the law school classroom. In all these respects, CLAO anticipated the academic clinical program (i.e., courses with classroom and clinical components for credit).

1971–1978: *the Lawyering Process Years*

Coincidentally with the end of CLAO, the law school had a new dean, Albert Sacks, who prioritized developing a clinical program. Dean Sacks wanted opportunities for students to take direct responsibility for lawyer work on the CLAO model and he wanted intellectual content that warranted academic credit. Gary Bellow was the Dean's choice to lead Harvard's program and his appointment with full tenure signified the School's commitment to clinical education on the CLAO/Bellow model. Gary's accomplishments as a public defender and legal aid lawyer were legendary. As a 1972 report commissioned by CLEPR pointed out, Bellow's

[3] CLAO information from a March 1970 report by John M. Ferren and A. Van C. Lanckton, CLAO *Harvard's Community Legal Assistance Office: A History, Analysis and Proposal* (on file with the author).

[4] OEO transferred funds to Cambridge and Somerville Legal Services.

Lawyering Process course had "… an intellectual originality and strength not matched in the other clinical programs we observed."[5] He had a remarkable capacity to critically examine his experience and make explicit what he called "the lawyering process."[6] Early in 1973, I was hired as assistant dean and director of administration of the School's clinical programs.

In the first iteration of Harvard's academic clinical program, students enrolled for three credits in "The Lawyering Process" course. They practiced in legal aid and public defender offices for four credits and many added a writing credit. Clinical fellows, funded by a CLEPR grant that began in the CLAO years, supervised students and were simultaneously admitted to a two-year LLM program. The quality of supervision was good, but we weren't satisfied with outsourcing the crucial practice component. While we had hoped for close collaboration with local offices, staff attorneys saw the clinical supervisors and students in their midst as marginal to their core service mission and were, for the most part, disinterested in service innovations. We had too little influence on the practice systems and routines that affected the quality of lawyer work. We needed a law office that was a school *and* a laboratory for innovation *and* a high-volume, high-quality service provider.

1978–1982: *Third-Year Bridge to Practice*

By 1978 the Carter Administration had put in place a strong board of directors for the Legal Services Corporation (LSC) with Thomas Ehrlich as president and Hillary Rodham as chair. Increased funding for legal services was creating thousands of new jobs, and we saw an opportunity to address problems we had observed in legal aid offices. We developed a proposal for a Legal Services Institute that would offer 3Ls an eleven-month program of courses, supervised practice, clinical seminars, research, and writing. The third year of law school would become a bridge to legal services practice. We approached LSC with the idea of regional Institutes that would be laboratories for service innovations and offer internships for 3Ls entering legal services practice after law school. LSC executives were willing to provide financial and programmatic support for a pilot project at Harvard Law. In October 1978 the LSC Board approved participation in the Institute experiment. A month later the faculty voted unanimously to support the project. The backbone of the Institute was the partnership between Harvard Law School and Greater Boston Legal Services (GBLS), the largest

5 Lance Liebman & Felice Levin to Robert Goldmann, "Memorandum," July 19, 1972 (on file with the author) at 0, 19.

6 Gary Bellow & Beatrice Moulton, *The Lawyering Process: Clinical Instruction in Advocacy* (1978); Jeanne Charn, *Service and Learning: Reflections on Three Decades of the* Lawyering Process *at Harvard Law School*, 10 Clin. L. Rev. 75, 79 (2003–04).

legal services provider in the region and an LSC grantee. GBLS was fiscal agent and managed funds for the Institute from LSC and Harvard Law.[7]

The pilot program accommodated twenty-five students. Eight seats were reserved for Harvard 3Ls, eight for Northeastern 3Ls, and the remaining seats were available to applicants from any law school willing to award academic credit for the Institute program. We spent eighteen months building the law practice and developing the curriculum for students due in July 1980. In January 1979, Gary and I left the Cambridge campus to teach and practice full-time at the Institute.

We set out to innovate in many areas: we made wide use of paralegals, were early adopters of technology in teaching and to support practice. We gathered detailed knowledge about the characteristics of the neighborhoods where our clients lived to better understand the context of their legal problems, and met with organizers and other service providers to learn about their goals and begin conversations about how we could work together.

Service Innovations

An example of the laboratory potential of the Institute was a claim we developed and then exported to the private bar. We had a docket of cases involving lead paint hazards prevalent in old, poorly maintained housing. We could not find lawyers to pursue damage claims for children with elevated lead levels but no obvious impairments. We found a researcher at Children's Hospital who had identified subtle learning and behavioral problems in children with low lead levels. Relying on these research results, we filed two cases that settled for about $50,000.

With these results, we recruited solo and small-firm lawyers to take similar cases. The potential recovery per case had been too low to attract major personal injury firms but cost of developing the claim was too great for solo and small firm lawyers to incur. By making a one-time investment to test the viability of the claim, we enabled a market that might never have emerged and expanded access to contingent fee legal assistance for children harmed by lead paint.

At the same time that we developed lawyer-led strategies, we developed a pro se divorce clinic and later a pro se eviction defense clinic. We trained staff at our community partners to provide basic legal help and make appropriate referrals to the Institute. Thirty-five years ago these now widely accepted ideas were new and controversial.

Quality Assurance

A core goal of the Institute was to develop and institutionalize internal systems to increase both the quality and quantity of service to clients. We established

[7] Annual LSC funding was: $350,000 in 1979 and $500,000 in 1980, 1981, and 1982 for a total of $1,850,000. In 2014 dollars, LSC and HLS support combined would total just under $7.6 million over four calendar years. Available at www.bls.gov/data/inflation_calculator.html.

a committee that set standards for all aspects of practice. Staff working in every substantive area set guidelines for case handling and documentation of requests for brief advice and assistance. We produced desk references and practice memos for quick access to practice information.

We set benchmarks for outcomes based on the success of experienced attorneys, and set protocols that captured evolving best practices. We reviewed every closed case and random samples of cases in process for compliance with file keeping requirements and recent activity. And finally, we collected data, standardized by case type, on every representation in the office.

Courses and Study at the Institute

Institute students were in residence July through May so that we could frontload introductory material before students began practice and coursework. Courses included poverty law, lawyering skills, and the legal profession. We did not grade students but built evaluation into every aspect of the program so that students could internalize habits of self and peer assessment. Students completed two analytic papers, one of which grew out of small group work with faculty on a project related to some aspect of lawyering or service delivery. We had political science, urban planning, and law school scholars-in-residence doing research, teaching units of courses, and collaborating with students on their projects.

The Institute experiment ended in June 1982 after the first Reagan administration cut funding. I know of no effort that has departed so radically from the conventional law school paradigm and restructured the third year as a career-specific capstone experience. In a high-volume law office serving hundreds of needy clients, not only did JDs master basic skills and internalize important professional values, the program also generated intellectual excitement, attracted prominent researchers, and inspired impressive scholarship.

1984–2006: *the Legal Services Center*

Since 1984, what is now the WilmerHale Legal Services Center has been the law school's largest civil practice site with as many as eighty students per semester in peak years. The Legal Services Center evolved into a full-fledged teaching law office focused on service delivery innovations and practice-based learning. With a much larger staff and many more students, the Center had more areas of practice and served many more clients than the Institute. Of particular relevance to this volume, the Center expanded to serve moderate-income clients, charged fees and co-payments for many services, provided phone advice, and supported self-help. The following are a few of the practice management and service innovations that Center staff developed:

AIDS Law Project

In cooperation with Boston AIDS Action Committee, we were one of the first, if not the very first, providers of legal assistance for people who were HIV+ or suffered from Aids. Center staff offered assistance on issues such as access to medical care, privacy issues, settlement of insurance policies, and estate planning. Teams made emergency visits to hospice and hospital bedsides to complete testamentary documents.

Medical and Legal Services Project

In collaboration with Brigham and Women's Hospital, we provided legal check-ups for low-income patients in a large primary care practice. Medical and law students partnered to provide services, and for several years we offered participating students a course on legal needs and healthcare taught with our Partner, Dr. JudyAnn Bigby, at Harvard Medical School. We also carried out a research project on the impact of legal advice on patients' health status. The Center's collaboration with Brigham Women's became a prototype for medical and legal service projects now supported by Boston Medical Center.

Foreclosure Prevention and Debt Problems

In response to a housing bubble and repair scams that victimized homeowners in our service area in the late 1990s, we began helping clients threatened with foreclosure or burdened with unsustainable debt. Outcomes in our first twenty-seven cases included two foreclosures and two short sales, six workouts that prevented foreclosure, and seventeen market sales that preserved equity ranging from a few thousand dollars to a high in one case of $155,000.

Income from Service

Since the Institute years, we had sought statutory attorney fees from opponents. In the mid-1990s we expanded assistance to moderate-income people and began charging co-payments for many services. The income increased resources for the Center and gave students opportunities to discuss fees and costs with clients. In time, income from client service generated $200,000 annually. Sources of income included: reimbursement of costs and fees advanced from the Center's litigation budget (reimbursement was not sought from very-low-income clients), statutory fees from opponents, co-payments from moderate-income and business clients, and fees permitted in successful social security disability cases.[8] By the 1990s, HLS was fiscal agent for the Center and received, administered, and accounted for income from GBLS and from client service. We left proceeds

8 SSA allows a percentage of the client's back benefits for counsel fees. The Center took about half the permitted amount.

from a few large fee awards in a Center account and with that security, the law school allowed us to budget annually based on projected service income.

Quality Assurance
We continued to develop service protocols and to track and analyze outcomes on every case. We instituted a comprehensive system of annual performance evaluations of all staff that included written comments and scored aspects of performance. Practice units set quantity as well as quality standards. We found that staff members who set quality benchmarks often completed the most cases. High performers accomplished this with strong supervision skills and excellent case and practice management.

Pro bono Assistance
In the 1990s, HLS alumni at WilmerHale funded a permanent home for the Center and began to donate hundreds of pro bono hours every year. Through my tenure as director, the firm had a partner in residence who represented clients and supervised students at the Center.

SUPERVISION BY TEACHERS WHO PRACTICE

The Center became a practice site for clinical work connected to Harvard Law courses with required clinical components and other courses with clinic options. With many courses connected to the Center, students could enroll for a second semester and some were with us throughout their 2L and 3L years.

More students required more supervisors, so we returned to the model in which experienced advocates supervised students enrolled in large classes taught by professors and lecturers. The crucial difference was that we had our own law office. We set the quality and productivity standards and hired experienced lawyers and paralegals that we titled "Clinical Instructors" or "CIs." Over time, we added post-JD fellows and invited some to continue for three more years as Senior Fellows.

By the 1990–91 academic year, the Center had 20 attorney and paralegal CI staff to supervise up to eighty students per semester. Supervisor-to-student ratios were low – three to five students per supervisor – so that student caseloads could be high. CI interaction with students was frequent and less bounded than in the classroom, the practice instructor demonstrated as well as instructed, and assessment was pervasive, never "blind," and multi-dimensional. The core task for CIs was mentoring students but we expanded their role to include the following:

Assessing Student Performance

CIs assessed student performance through frequent, informal feedback and formal assessments at mid-term and the end of the semester. A standardized instrument (similar to the form used for annual staff reviews) included a report on advocacy tasks accomplished, qualitative assessments supported by specific examples from student work, and a scale for assessing progress. Students self-assessed on the same instrument.

Leading a Workshop

In the Center's second decade, CIs developed and led a one-credit workshop for their students. Workshops began with an intensive introduction to law, procedure, and practice protocols, but the heart of the workshop was "Rounds," similar to grand rounds in medicine. Following a structured format, students presented challenging issues in their cases and commented on peer presentations.

Protecting Clients

Students took on as much of the representation as their capacities warranted, but CIs took the lead when needed. This arrangement emphasized learning by observing and an important dimension of self-assessment: recognizing tasks that are beyond one's present skill level.

The CI model was and remains controversial among clinicians because it embraces differential roles and status in clinical teaching.[9] We chose *not* to follow the national norm of seeking tenure or tenure-like status for all long-term clinical faculty. Gary joined HLS with conventional tenure and others followed him but we built the clinical program around a large, direct client service law practice staffed by 20 or more instructor-practitioners. We sought CIs who loved practice, were very good at it, could articulate the complex perceptions and understandings they had learned in practice, and found it challenging and satisfying to contribute to shaping the next generation of practitioners. Practice knowledge is, after all, cumulative and collegial. It evolves among peers within their work and professional organizations and is passed on from experts to novices – thus the persistence and universality of apprenticeship and mentoring in professional life.

We found practical as well as educational advantages. CIs are on a professional not academic calendar so clients are served and new clients accepted year-round. CIs "cover" for colleagues on leave just as in every busy law practice. CIs and full-time interns continue service in the summer, so clients are never transferred to temporary staff. By adding CI staff we could easily scale up to meet student demand or begin new areas of practice linked to HLS courses.

9 See Steve Wizner & Jane Aiken, *Teaching and Doing: The Role of Law School Clinics in Enhancing Access to Justice*, 73 FORDHAM L. REV. 997, 1000–1002 (2004).

EDUCATIONAL PREMISES OF HARVARD'S TEACHING LAW OFFICE

The evolution of the teaching law office reflected our best efforts to operationalize our understandings of how novices learn their craft, internalize the profession's norms, and master the performance demands of direct client service. As our experience grew and we explored the literature on professional expertise and management of "learning organizations," we were better able to articulate the premises underlying the teaching law office. Foremost among these were the following.

Ethics, Choice, and Responsibility

The ethical and value dimensions of practice cannot be learned through study alone. Ethics and values are internalized in roles where choices must be made and responsibility for outcomes shouldered:

> There is a deeper part of us which must be reached if the ethical lesson is to stay with us for future use, and which cannot be reached by the same teaching methods that are so valuable in teaching the doctrinal part of the law school curriculum ... No one can learn to be controlled by ethical principles by standing outside a problem and commenting on it ... Only in a clinic, where the teacher and the student are personally involved; where they have to take action and face the consequences; where they undergo tensions which upset their emotions and take away their peace of mind, is there opportunity to develop the moral fiber and the proper instincts for dealing with ethical problems in a professionally responsible way.[10]

Immersion in Specialized Practice

We never veered from our conviction that deep experience in a high-quality professional environment is the most effective, efficient, and certain path from novice to expert and ethical practitioner. Immersion in a specialized area of practice is the starting point for professional development. Students need enough task repetition and observations to internalize practice scripts and strategies. We sought broad task not broad substantive exposure and required students to begin in a specific field and gain as much experience as possible in one or several semesters. We made no effort to screen for "teachable" cases. If a case became too complex, the CI took over. If a client withdrew the student took on another case. Our goal was to incorporate novices into the flow of office work offering them as much direct responsibility as they could handle.

[10] Counsel on Legal Educ. for Prof'l Responsibility, Third Biennial Report 9 (1973–74) (William Pincus, the President's Report).

Tacit Learning and the Practice Environment

Novices learn tacitly, picking up cues about how to act and what is accepted in practice from the routines and systems they experience and observe. The structure and personal interactions of practice – the law office, courts and court personnel, opposing parties – are powerful teachers. We could control only the law office and our own actions, so we paid careful attention to the messages implicit in our behavior, case protocols, and office systems. We sought congruence between what we said and what we did, how we structured work and how we interacted in our practice community.

Learning What We Know

Models of what competent lawyers do help make explicit what has been learned tacitly and often experienced as intuitive. "Learning what we know" is a reflective effort to make explicit the complex understandings and behavior of high-performing practitioners. Explicit descriptions provide conventions for communication that facilitate exploration of complex or elusive experience and ideas. Models of good lawyering suggest criteria for assessing one's own and others' work, for generating strategic possibilities, and anticipating ethical, tactical, and strategic difficulties. The protocol project of the Center is an example of capturing knowledge distributed among practitioners and making explicit and reviewable the scripts, micro-strategies, short–cuts, and risk assessments that may have been learned tacitly.

The hallmark of expert problem-solving is *forward* reasoning from the client's circumstances to one or a few of the more plausible paths to resolution. Through experience in hundreds of cases of a particular type, experts see client problems in a context that is broader than law. Experts understand that the problems clients bring are ill-defined with legal, economic, interpersonal, and other aspects that cannot be teased apart. Experts also understand that their clients' problems are inherently indeterminate, meaning there is irresolvable uncertainty about the exact outcome even though experts usually have a good idea of the range of possible outcomes.

Research on professional expertise further suggests the following:

(1) When experts encounter problems outside their field, they revert to novice-like reasoning.

(2) It is likely that becoming expert in a second area of practice is easier than the first and achieving expertise in a third field is easier still because we learn "how to learn" in and through action.

(3) Observing the experience of others, both peers and more experienced practitioners, is additive. Practice experience can be "borrowed" from colleagues. "Rounds" exercises are a structured approach to expanding the volume of student case experience in a semester of clinical work.

(4) Although learning from and through experience is unavoidable and occurs tacitly, consciousness of the process enhances learning.
(5) It is likely that more complex typologies, better pattern-recognition and matching skills, and understanding the nature of in-practice expertise correlate with higher levels of expert performance.

These are the complexities and dynamics of reasoning, prediction, judgment, and action under conditions of uncertainty.

TEACHING LAW OFFICES AND THE ACCESS PROBLEM

I conclude with a few thoughts about the teaching law office as a site for service and learning.

Harvard's multi-decade experience in a large teaching law office demonstrates that meeting students' needs for mentoring in practice produces a substantial service by-product. We need not and should not subordinate learning to high-volume service because a well-managed practice center will achieve both. In a large office like the Center, students have many choices. They can elect litigation, administrative, transaction, or planning practices and represent individuals or entities.

The teaching law office concept is gaining currency. The ABA reports a remarkable increase in post graduate lawyer incubators, similar to teaching law offices, that offer a year or more of mentored practice and learning the business side of law practice. In 2012 there were three programs. As of early 2015 the ABA documents thirty-six.[11] Many are law school affiliated, others are collaborations among law schools and a few partner with not-for-profits. All see their operations as expanding access for populations who, at present, are managing in a law-thick world without benefit of legal advice. The Center's experience points to opportunities for linking clinical work in the law school years to post-grad incubators to produce a modern apprenticeship.[12]

[11] ABA Standing Committee on Delivery of Legal Services, "Incubator/Residency Program," available at www.americanbar.org/groups/delivery_legal_services/initiatives_awards/program_main.html.

[12] The United States is the only country in the world whose legal profession does not require some period of mentored practice prior to full licensure.

47

The Emergency-Room Law School Clinic

Joy Radice & Randy Hertz

What would a legal clinic look like that responded immediately and directly to the most pressing legal needs of working Americans? Modeled after an emergency-room medical rotation, Radice & Hertz envision an emergency-room clinic where law students are assigned to conduct intake, triage, and diagnose potential clients' legal problems, and ultimately counsel or represent them in matters ranging from creating wills to fighting housing evictions.

Assessments of the nature and efficacy of legal education often compare the field unfavorably to medical education. It is typically said that our society wouldn't allow a new physician to treat patients without having gone through adequate clinical fieldwork instruction in addition to classroom learning, and yet we allow new lawyers to represent clients in profoundly consequential matters without having previously engaged in actual practice under expert supervision. With the very recent changes in the accreditation standards for law schools that come into effect next year, all law students will now have to take six credits of "skills instruction," but even this new rule will not require student practice during law school since it can be entirely satisfied with simulation courses.[1]

Looking to medical education for guidance, we will explore whether the emergency room of a teaching hospital can serve as a model for a "full immersion" law school clinic that would teach law students the complete array of cognitive and practical skills that are essential for effective lawyering. This chapter proposes an emergency-room clinic that would parallel emergency-room rotations for third-year medical students.[2] As in medical school, law students would take classroom courses to ground them in substantive knowledge and professional values before they enter the emergency room. Once in the emergency-room clinic, law

1 2014–2015 ABA Standards and Rules of Procedure for Approval of Law School (2014). In Chapter 3, Rule 303 now requires every law student to complete "one or more experiential course(s) totaling at least six credit hours. An experiential course must be a simulation course, a law clinic, or a field placement."

2 We assume that the model we present here would be adapted to fit the specific orientation of a law school: adjusted to fit, for example, the typical career patterns of a law school's student body, the particular goals of the law school, and the other types of courses the school offers.

students would conduct intake, employ diagnostic skills, and pursue remedies under expert supervision and training, just as medical students do. In addition to serving educational goals, this clinic is a model for how law schools can respond directly to the civil access to justice crisis documented elsewhere in this book by representing low- and moderate-income individuals.[3]

A CLIENT-DRIVEN MODEL

In the clinic, as in a hospital emergency room, students would conduct intake, triage client issues, and offer consultation and representation. The chapters in this book paint a clear picture of the far-ranging unmet civil legal needs that an emergency-room clinic can address. Many of these needs relate to core areas of a law school curriculum and the subjects tested on the bar exam: property, civil procedure, contracts, bankruptcy, family law, housing, employment, and trusts and estates. The clinic would expose students to transactional work, litigation, negotiation, and mediation. Students could, for example, draft wills, petition for divorces, represent clients at unemployment hearings or in housing trials, rewrite leases, negotiate basic contract disputes, incorporate a nonprofit, file bankruptcies, prepare asylum petitions, and resolve issues in small claims court.[4]

In the clinic's client-centered intake system, as in a hospital's intake procedure, a student would interview a potential client to gather information about the immediate legal problem, while determining whether any peripheral, non-urgent legal needs exist. A client who comes to the clinic with a housing eviction case, for example, may also need advice about consumer debt, and may not even realize this need. Or a client who comes in with a minor contract dispute may also need a lawyer to draft a will or power of attorney.

Presumably a clinic of this sort would need to set financial eligibility requirements but any such criteria should take into account the problem, discussed elsewhere in this book, that moderate-income people are being priced out of legal representation. Legal markets vary dramatically by geographic location, but all have significant portions of the population who cannot afford a lawyer. Family income eligibility requirements for a clinic of this sort should not be as restrictive as the rule for eligibility for legal services, which is that an individual must fall within 200% of the poverty line. For clients in higher moderate-income ranges who still cannot afford average attorney rates, law schools could develop sliding-scale fee

[3] Each law school could define income eligibility requirements, but student practice orders may have to be rewritten to reflect this. Some clinical programs are currently limited to serving very-low-income people because their state student practice order defines eligibility by using legal aid's income eligibility guidelines.

[4] Part I of this volume documents the range of areas from immigration to bankruptcy where a dramatic percentage of litigants are not represented by lawyers. Many of these cases would lend themselves to student attorney representation in an emergency-room clinic.

schedules that require minimal payments based on income, family size, and ability to pay.[5]

Each emergency room legal clinic would respond to the unmet needs specific to a law school's geographic area. For example, depending upon the region, there might be a more or less pressing need for helping clients gain access to healthcare, or deal with immigration issues, or cope with housing-related problems. Legal services organizations similarly vary their services and allocation of legal resources based on the communities they serve.

Conducting a local-needs assessment with the help of the local bar and legal services organizations would allow law schools to predict the types of cases the clinic would undertake and the legal expertise needed to staff the clinic. The assessment should consider the types of legal services offered by local lawyers and their cost so that the clinic does not inadvertently take affordable work away from the private bar. Pro bono clinics, which are surfacing throughout the country, can also serve as good indicators of the types of civil problems people face without a lawyer.

The idea of a legal clinic that serves a range of civil legal needs is not new, of course. During the early years of clinical education, law school clinics offered the first models for civil legal services organizations.[6] A central aim of clinical education was to open the doors of the courthouse to the poor. Jeanne Charn's chapter on the evolution of Harvard's clinical program is one such example. Many programs, like the clinical program at the University of Tennessee, were the primary legal services providers in their communities, and students in those programs handled high caseloads.[7] The emergency-room model would build on this rich history by expanding eligibility well beyond the 125%-of-the-poverty-line criteria of federally funded legal services organizations that many clinics apply.[8]

THE LEGAL ROTATION

After the completion of their second year, participants in the emergency-room legal clinic would be sworn in under a state student practice order by a senior local judge to mark symbolically the transition from student to student-practitioner.

[5] St. Andrew Legal Clinic in Oregon is an example of a public interest law firm that represents moderate-income people and charges fees based on a sliding scale in predominantly family law cases. Approximately 65% of the clinic's $1.8 million in revenue comes from client fees with the remainder from grants and private sources. See www.salcgroup.org/about-us (last accessed Jan. 21, 2015).

[6] J.P. "Sandy" Ogilvy, *The Early Development of Clinical Legal Education and Legal Ethics Instruction in U.S. Law Schools*, 16 CLINICAL L. REV. 1, 7 (2009).

[7] Douglas A. Blaze, *Deja Vu All Over Again: Reflections on Fifty Years of Clinical Education*, 64 TENN. L. REV. 939, 952–53 (1997).

[8] Section 1007(a)(2) of the Legal Services Corporation Act, 42 U.S.C. § 2996f(a)(2). Legal services organizations can accept clients up to 200% of the poverty line under certain circumstances. LSC 2015 Income Guidelines, 45 C.F.R. § 1611.5(a). See also Chapter 15 for further details on federal-funded civil legal services income eligibility.

This ritual would parallel the white coat ceremony in medical school in which medical students don their first doctor's coat to signify their entrance into the profession.[9]

Triaging Matters

Students would begin the clinic at different times so that the number of students is proportionate to the number of supervisors, and also to ensure staffing of the clinic throughout the year. At intake, students would interview potential clients and begin to diagnose the legal issues they raise. They would consult with supervising attorneys to figure out how to prioritize the cases and counsel clients at the outset. The operating premise of the clinic would be that clinic students will help the client and take the matter. Many clients may ask questions that have relatively simple answers but some questions may be too complicated or raise legal issues too difficult for a law school-based clinic to handle. At intake, the client could be offered assistance along a spectrum: the student-attorney counsels the client, but no legal action is needed; the student-attorney is able to offer legal advice or assistance that day, and the case is closed; the student-attorney accepts the case and is assigned to work with the client and schedules a follow-up meeting; or the clinic is unable to assist the client because the case is too complicated for the students' skill level, but the student makes a serious effort to refer the client to other existing resources (e.g., legal aid, pro bono clinics, or "low bono" attorneys).

Rotation Models

Schools can design legal rotations in different ways based on pedagogical considerations. The simplest model would assign students to matters randomly as they come in during intake, regardless of the legal issue(s) they present. Under this model, the clinic would be like an emergency-room rotation. Like medical students staffing an emergency room, the students would experience an unpredictable set of legal issues based on the needs of the clients who arrive during that rotation.

There are a number of benefits of such a model. First, the students would be exposed to several areas of law, and the focus of the rotation would be on how to be creative problem-solvers. Each matter, regardless of its substantive legal focus, will require students to identify and research the applicable legal principles, and the students will immediately have to understand the difficulty of

[9] Jennifer S. Bard, *What We Can Learn from Our Colleagues in Medicine about Teaching Students How to Practice Their Chosen Profession*, 36 J.L. MED. & ETHICS 841, 843 (2008) (explaining that Texas Tech and other schools currently have similar ceremonies for their students).

ascertaining the facts, and appreciate the need to listen carefully to and evaluate the client's account and needs, and to devise potential options for solving the problem.

Second, as in the hospital emergency room, this model furthers a goal of meeting the urgent legal needs of clients. Third, this model would be the least administratively burdensome because matters would not have to be organized by any particular characteristic and the assignment of cases would not have to be coordinated for certain students or supervising attorneys. Finally, students can take one client from intake to completion of their case, and that could include serving one client on a variety of types of matters.

A downside to this model is that students would not have input in the types of matters that they are assigned. Students who want to learn bankruptcy or contracts, for example, would have no guarantee that they would have matters in these areas. Depending on the variety of cases in a given intake, some students may feel overwhelmed by too many new areas of law at one time, while others may not encounter much variety at all. The focus of this rotation would not be "learning" how to do a specific type of case, but the process a lawyer goes through in answering legal questions in areas of the law that are new to them.

In medical school, students also rotate through mandatory specialties (the emergency room is only one of them) and choose one elective rotation.[10] The emergency-room clinic could mimic this approach in two different ways. One model would emphasize rotating students through specific practice areas over their nine months in the clinic. Some legal rotations could be mandatory while others are elective. For example, in one emergency-room clinic, each student could study in three rotations for three months apiece. A law school could determine that one or two rotations are mandatory for every clinic student, while other areas are elective, based on student preferences expressed prior to the beginning of clinic. (For example, a law school might decide to make family law and estate planning mandatory for all clinic students while allowing students to elect additional areas like housing, business law, immigration, and/or bankruptcy.) Placement in the elective rotations could be through student rankings and a lottery or bidding.

Another model could divide each law student's emergency-room clinic experience into two, five-month rotations – one that focuses on transactional work and the other on litigation. Mimicking law firms that have litigation and transactional practice areas, students could be required to experience both practice areas, and

[10] Stephen Ellmann at New York Law School has developed a clinical third year, building on a different type of medical rotation in which students spend their entire third year in three 9-week, full-time, clinical rotations for 24 credits. The experiences include drafting legislation and brief writing at the Division of Legal Counsel at the New York City Law Department; assisting in civil litigation matters at the Legal Aid Society; and working on administrative law matters at the New York City Department of Health and Mental Hygiene. Stephen Ellmann, *The Clinical Year Begins*, 21 CLIN. L. REV. 337 (2015).

evaluate how the decision-making, pace, negotiations, and problem-solving can be similar or different.

Under either approach, the administration of the clinic would be more complicated when matters have to be categorized and supervised under specific practice areas. Intake procedures would have to identify the type of matter and rotation area, the students who are in that rotation, and the supervisors assigned to that rotation. In hospitals, the different specialties that lead to medical school rotations – cardiac, obstetrics, pediatrics – are designed as the way the hospitals treat patients. The medical students are placed with doctors in their predetermined rotations. If the emergency room clinic were to take a similar approach, the administrative burden and added costs of organizing the matters would not be on an outside organization but on the legal clinic itself.

Although the emergency-room clinic could follow different models, the least costly and administratively intensive would be the one that functions like an actual emergency room. Students would serve clients primarily on a first-come-first-served basis, and decide whether they can offer advice at intake, take the matter, or refer the client to other community resources.

A TEACHING LAW FIRM

There have been numerous calls, over the years, for reforming legal education to expand skills instruction and clinical legal education. In 1921, in the *Reed Report*, the Carnegie Foundation for the Advancement of Teaching criticized law schools for not offering skills training.[11] In the ensuing two decades, John Bradway and Jerome Frank articulated a vision of an in-house legal clinic as a fundamental part of legal education.[12] In the 1960s and 70s, the Council on Legal Education for Professional Responsibility (CLEPR) stimulated the incorporation of clinical methodology in law schools throughout the country.[13] Yet, in 1992, when the ABA Section of Legal Education and Admissions to the Bar looked carefully at the state of legal education, the resulting "MacCrate Report" found that law schools were not doing nearly enough to teach law students the skills and values essential for competent legal practice.[14] That was the finding as well when the Carnegie Foundation examined the quality of legal education in

[11] Alfred Z. Reed, Training for the Public Profession of the Law: Historical Development and Principal Contemporary Problems of Legal Education in the United States, With Some Account of Conditions in England and Canada, Bulletin No. 15 (1921).

[12] Jerome Frank, *Why Not a Clinical-Lawyer School?*, 81 U. Pa. L. Rev. 907 (1933). John S. Bradway, *The Objectives of Legal Aid Clinic Work*, 24 Wash. U. L.Q. 173, 176 (1939).

[13] See Ogilvy, supra note 6.

[14] Section of Legal Educ. and Admissions to the Bar, Am. Bar Ass'n, Legal Education and Professional Development – An Educational Continuum (Report of the Task Force on Law Schools and the Profession: Narrowing the Gap, 1992).

2007 and documented the need for integration of "theoretical and practical legal knowledge and professional identity."[15]

The clinic we are proposing here would remedy the foregoing criticisms of traditional legal education, teaching the knowledge, skills, and values, that are essential for effective lawyering by:

1. carefully scaffolding supervision that encourages students to take ownership of their cases;
2. a live-client case method that teaches problem-solving;
3. skills training that focuses on the core competencies of lawyering; and
4. a classroom component of case rounds that engages students in self-reflection and peer critique.

Scaffolding Supervision: the Legal Resident and Teaching Lawyer

Supervision in the legal rotation would mirror supervision in medical rotations.[16] In teaching hospitals, medical students learn from a model of "plan–do–reflect," working in small teams alongside residents and attending doctors. A resident physician is a recent medical school graduate who is considered both a student and health provider. As a student, the resident is supervised by senior attending physicians and receives more independence over time. The resident works on a team of health providers including third-year medical students, who will shadow residents. The resident is responsible for diagnosing medical problems for new patients and setting up treatment plans. An attending doctor is a senior, experienced doctor who completed a residency (and sometimes a fellowship) and is ultimately responsible for the direct supervision of medical students and residents.

Similarly in the emergency-room legal clinic, students will be assigned to small teams supervised by "legal residents," and larger teams supervised by experienced "attendings," or Teaching Lawyers.

a. Legal Residents – recent law graduates – would supervise the third-year student attorneys and be present in the clinic daily to guide students heavily at the beginning of their clinic experience and less so over time.[17] Like medical residents, law students who have finished a rotation in the

[15] William M. Sullivan et al., *Educating Lawyers* (2007) at 13.

[16] Jayne W. Barnard & Mark Greenspan, *Incremental Bar Admission: Lessons from the Medical Profession*, 53 J. LEGAL EDUC. 340, 343 (2003).

[17] Many schools have developed post graduate programs to encourage students to open solo practices (such as the incubators described in Gomez-Velez, Chapter 48 in this volume, CUNY Law School's Community-Based and Community Empowering Clinics); while others, have created fellowships like Georgetown's Prettyman Fellowship, for graduates. Each year, three post graduate fellows at Georgetown begin a two-year fellowship that can lead to an LLM. During their first year, they manage their own criminal caseload. In their second year, they supervise students in Georgetown's clinical

emergency-room clinic could apply for a clinical fellowship in which they would supervise 3Ls and work with senior Teaching Lawyers for one year.

In the emergency-room clinic, Legal Residents would supervise 3Ls and would also represent clients in more complicated cases. As cases come in through intake, Legal Residents would consult with the full-time instructors (termed "Teaching Lawyers") to determine case assignment. The Legal Residents would have teams of six to eight students and would be responsible for preparing their students to lead case rounds, attending routine court appearances, and working with the students on their cases. A Legal Resident could help students edit documents, offer advice on client counseling, or strategize with students about negotiation.

b. The Teaching Lawyer would supervise the Legal Residents and student attorneys in the emergency-room clinic, and work under the supervision of the director of the clinic. The Teaching Lawyer would supervise two or three teams of Legal Residents and meet weekly with students, attend case rounds, supervise critical court appearances like hearings and trials, and grade the students.

Some Teaching Lawyers would be full- or part-time supervisors, while others might be adjuncts who consult on certain types of cases. Many clinical programs currently leverage the resources of expert practicing lawyers by appointing them as part-time professors who work several hours a week in the clinic or house their team of supervisees at their law office.

Some of the Teaching Lawyers should be full-time clinical professors who can train the part-time Teaching Lawyers in clinical instruction techniques, co-teach seminar classes, and provide guidance and support in supervising student attorneys.

Teaching Lawyers could also identify lawyers in the community who are willing to consult on cases. For example, a practicing business attorney could help students working with a client who has a business plan and is seeking financing, or a family law attorney could help students with a complicated asset issue in a contested divorce. Some of these lawyers could be adjuncts, but others might want to help as part of their pro bono service to the bar. By developing a list of these expert resources, the Teaching Lawyers could leverage their own teaching expertise with the type of expertise needed for a case. Not all supervising attorneys need to be full time or paid. Pro bono attorneys may also be interested in staffing intake days to help students answer questions and make determinations about whether the clinic can take a matter.

program who represent clients in misdemeanor and juvenile cases. The fellows are supervised by four faculty members. See CDPAC Graduate Teaching Fellowships at www.law.georgetown.edu/academics/academic-programs/clinical-programs/our-clinics/criminal-defense-prisoner-advocacy/graduate-teaching-fellowships.cfm (last visited Jan. 12, 2015).

As in teaching hospitals, supervision in the legal rotation would be critical to its success. Students would learn through their work on cases, strategizing with their supervisor and peers, and then reflecting on their decisions, making supervision a key part of that learning experience.[18] The model for supervision should draw heavily on the best practices for effective clinical teaching and supervision that clinical legal education has spent more than five decades developing.[19]

A clinic director would need to oversee the emergency-room clinic, supervise the Legal Resident and Teaching Lawyers, and administer the allocation of students to clinical rotations.

The Live-Client Case Method

Practicing attorneys have to be problem-solvers. The teaching in live-client clinics would focus on aspects of practice that are transferable to any legal practice: researching and applying law, investigating and developing facts, and decision-making in situations with real consequences. The clinic would also be a formative place for students to begin developing a professional identity. Students can take time in clinic to think about and discuss how to form their professional reputation. They can begin the process of intentional formation of a professional identity by focusing in the right ways on the types of relationships they develop with clients, the communications they have with opposing counsel, their court appearances, and networking at and volunteering for local bar associations.

Developing Core Competencies

Student participants in the emergency-room clinic would begin by attending a one-day orientation and a skills boot camp to introduce them to the basic competencies of lawyering.[20] These competencies would form the foundation for supervisor feedback and evaluation throughout the semester.

The lawyering competencies taught in this clinic would extend to any type of law practice. Competencies evaluated as part of clinic could include professional judgment, communication, management of effort, legal reasoning, working with colleagues and opposing counsel, conflict resolution, emotional intelligence, and professional responsibility. The cases will be vehicles for more than learning how to diagnose, research, and analyze legal issues.

[18] Peter Joy, *The Cost of Clinical Legal Education*, 32 B.C.J.L. & Soc. Just. 309, 320 (2012). See Donald A. Schön, *Educating the Reflective Practitioner*, 2 Clinical L. Rev. 231 (1995).

[19] See David R. Barnhizer, *The Clinical Method of Legal Instruction: Its Theory and Implementation*, 30 J. Legal Educ. 67 (1979); Peter T. Hoffman, *The Stages of the Clinical Supervisory Relationship*, 3 Antioch L. Rev. 301 (1985); Ann Shalleck, *Clinical Contexts: Theory and Practice in Law and Supervision*, 21 N.Y.U. Rev. L. & Soc. Ch. 109 (1993–94).

[20] Rubrics in clinical courses currently identify these competencies for students and are used for weekly supervision meetings, mid-semester evaluations, and final grading assessments.

Students will learn how to investigate facts, adhere to the client's goals, develop and evaluate alternative strategies, and reflect on decisions. They will begin developing professional relationships with clients, judges, and opposing counsel, and be challenged to manage their time effectively, especially as a part of a team. The cases will also raise ethical issues affecting their client's choices.

The clinic orientation would acclimate the students to the new practice setting by giving them instruction in office procedures, staff support, and case management systems. The boot camp, which could occur during their 2L year, would introduce students to theories of interviewing, counseling, legal writing, negotiation, and drafting prior to their clinic rotation. The case rounds seminar described later would use students' emergency-room cases as a "textbook" to build on decisional and statutory law learned in first- and second-year courses and to provide (and, often, reinforce) skills training. This type of intentional sequencing of legal analysis, skills, and competencies will improve student performance in the clinic and after law school.[21]

The legal rotation would prepare law students with core lawyering competencies and teach students professional responsibility, values, and professionalism.

Legal Case Rounds

The students would have a weekly 3-credit, case rounds seminar, of a sort that is familiar to clinical teachers.[22] The benefits of case rounds are described in Jeanne Charn's chapter in this volume. In medicine, Grand Rounds for doctors are commonplace and are most effective when they are used to "disseminate knowledge, change physician behavior, and improve patient outcomes."[23] Similarly, the legal rounds session would teach students how to learn from their cases by sharing student experiences, exploring applications of legal principles, and evaluating lawyering strategies being used in the cases. The Teaching Lawyer and Legal Residents would participate in case rounds, and the students would be trained in how to lead them. The rounds would raise challenging questions about the lawyer's decision-making, legal values and ethics, and professionalism.

POTENTIAL OBJECTIONS TO THE EMERGENCY-ROOM CLINIC PROPOSAL

Will two years of law school classroom courses be enough to prepare the students for handling cases in a context like this?

To integrate the emergency-room clinic, law schools will have to reconfigure course offerings so that all mandatory doctrinal courses are available to first- and second-year

[21] See Margaret Barry, *Practice Ready: Are We There Yet?*, 32 B.C. J.L. & Soc. Just. 247 (2012).

[22] Susan Bryant & Elliott Milstein, *Rounds: A "Signature Pedagogy" for Clinical Education?*, 14 Clinical L. Rev. 195 (2007).

[23] Shaifali Sandal et al., *Can We Make Grand Rounds "Grand" Again*, 5 J. Grad. Med. Educ. 560 (2013).

students. Many students already try to cover their mandatory courses prior to their third year. A legal clinic on the emergency-room model may also encourage consideration of whether there should be a mandatory two-year curriculum offering students only a few electives.[24] This would allow law students to take classroom courses that faculty feel are essential to graduation but are not currently mandatory.

Are Medical Schools So Different from Law Schools that the Analogy is Not Useful?

An obvious, critical difference between medical and law schools is that there is no already-existing institution in the legal context like a hospital emergency room. This is, of course, a comment not only about the transferability of the medical model to legal education, but more broadly about the reasons for the current gap in legal services for low- and moderate-income individuals. Whereas all indigent and moderate-income individuals and families can turn to an emergency room for medical care, and may qualify for federal funding like Medicaid, there are no comparable resources for legal services. Accordingly, law schools would have to think creatively about the potential sources for free or low-cost spaces or conducting intake on a large scale. Natural partners for the clinic that could offer free or affordable space include law firms, churches, legal aid officers, the law school itself, affiliated-university buildings, bar associations, the courts, public housing units, and local nonprofits like large soup kitchens or homeless shelters. By collaborating with interdisciplinary organizations, law schools may attract different sources of funding from private foundations, bar associations, and government grants. The early clinical programs that helped launch some of the first legal aid organizations used a range of outside financial resources to jump-start their programs.

The emergency-room clinic could coordinate with legal services organizations, pro bono projects and bar referral services during the triage phase of intake, directing some clients to other available local resources. The clinic rotation should not duplicate the services that legal services organizations already provide or serve the client base they already represent. This model is intended to expand legal services to legal areas not already addressed by legal services and to clients who are above legal services' income eligibility guideline of 125% of the poverty line.[25]

Would an Emergency-Room Clinic be More Expensive than Current Clinics?

Not necessarily. This clinic would be a different way of using existing resources. Many in-house clinics under the supervision of faculty focus on one or a few

[24] Washington & Lee Law School has a third-year curriculum that is entirely experiential, combining skills simulation courses with either a clinic or an externship. As a result, the law school restructured its first- and second-year curriculum to guarantee that students would have a foundation for their new third-year structure.

[25] Financial eligibility policies, 45 C.F.R. § 1611.3 (Sept. 7, 2005).

specialty areas of law and assign 8–12 students to a professor for five, six, or seven credits a semester. The emergency room clinic would not use more resources and actually might save money when compared to clinics taught exclusively by full-time clinical faculty.

The cost of setting up an emergency-room clinic would be similar to the cost of a high-volume hybrid of in-house clinic and externships, which many schools have. In these programs, full-time clinical faculty work together with practicing attorneys and fellows in supervising students, thereby reducing the overall cost of the clinic and expanding the number of students who can participate in the clinic.

The supervisory structure proposed earlier is designed to reduce costs and to do so by employing a model that has proven effective in medical rotations. The emergency-room model would provide adjunct salaries to part-time Teaching Lawyers, and modest post graduate fellowships to Legal Residents, which is a common approach to help supplement the supervision of full-time clinical faculty.

The emergency-room model might also draw support from previously untapped external funding sources. Just as the Ford Foundation was willing to provide seed money for clinics in the 1960s and 1970s through the auspices of CLEPR, federal agencies and private foundation grants may be willing to invest in emergency-room clinics across the country. Some of the agencies or foundations may be drawn to the proposal as a means of enhancing the quality of legal education; others might favor it as a means to ameliorate the shortcomings of our system of civil legal services; and some might by attracted by both goals.

Law schools would no doubt need to be creative about finding resources to run a clinical legal rotation on a long-term basis. But there may be unexplored partnerships that could generate the necessary permanent financial commitment. A state's civil access to justice initiative may be interested (especially if endorsed by a State Supreme Court Chief Justice) to work with law schools to raise an endowment that supports a pro bono/law school emergency-room partnership. State bars might help fund the clinic through bar fees, or state governments might increase lawyer professional taxes to support an access to justice clinic.

Will Students be Overwhelmed and Ill-Equipped to Counsel Clients About a Wide Range of Issues?

If it is indeed the case that students will feel overwhelmed by having to confront a wide range of types of legal problems, the clinic could regulate student assignments so that students begin with a limited number of subject matter areas and add more over time. Although no student caseload would look the same, supervising attorneys could carefully structure clinic intake and assignments so that students are exposed to new areas of the law incrementally. In intake, students can identify and interview clients with similar legal issues (e.g., family law cases, debtor-creditor cases, housing cases), and then be assigned to cases in one of those areas. After a student has logged in a certain amount of time working on cases in one field, Teaching Supervisors could add other areas. This process of organically folding in new legal issues can address the overload concern without disadvantaging the client base by unduly restricting the clinic to specified areas of the law. This approach would have the fringe benefit of modeling for students how they can expand their practice to new areas when they are practicing on their own after graduation.

CREATING A CULTURE OF SERVICE

The earlier chapters on pro bono service highlight the important commitments that have been made by law firms, law schools, legal aid, and bar associations to increase the quantity and quality of pro bono resources for low- and moderate-income Americans. The calls to action described in the introduction by former Chief Justice Jefferson and Chief Judge Lippman reflect the dire need for the legal profession to inculcate a culture of service for unmet legal needs.

To respond to this need, law schools have increasingly engaged students in pro bono projects with local legal aid organizations, on alternative spring-break trips, or in partnerships with local nonprofits like homeless shelters and hospitals. Law schools even offer incentives to students – awards at graduation or recognition by local bar leaders – for participating in such programs. An emergency-room rotation of the sort we are proposing here is another way for law schools to instill a culture of pro bono service before a student graduates. The hope is that its promise of rigorous training in skills and competencies will attract students not previously inclined to participate in pro bono programs. And in doing so, it will train future lawyers in the trenches of the access to justice crisis and encourage them to raise questions about how the legal profession should respond.

48

CUNY Law School's Community-Based and Community-Empowering Clinics

Natalie Gomez-Velez

Law school clinics can seek to integrate their pedagogical objectives with the needs of the community in which they are based. Natalie Gomez-Velez discusses the innovative clinics of this type at CUNY School of Law.

Social justice law practice requires meaningful engagement with clients and communities. For low-income and marginalized clients, the need for individual legal representation often is accompanied by multi-faceted, systemic, socio-legal issues that require attention and response if the representation is to be effective. Law schools have an important role to play in training students for holistic representation and providing tools that support not only excellent legal representation but also a range of strategies to improve access to justice to individuals and communities as part of effective practice and professional obligation.

From its inception, the City University of New York (CUNY) School of Law's mission-driven commitment to clinical legal education and social justice lawyering has included deep and broad work preparing students for community-based practice designed to address both individual and systemic social justice concerns. Contrary to recent narratives about too many lawyers and not enough legal work, CUNY Law's program has long focused on an awareness of the scarcity of available lawyers to address legal issues related to basic human needs and the impact of this gap on access to justice for all but the wealthiest individuals and communities.

CUNY Law's curriculum requires every student to engage in supervised practice in a clinic or concentration before s/he graduates. The clinics and concentrations[1] are the culmination of the law school's integrated curriculum. The curriculum includes doctrinal courses alongside simulated practice or "lawyering" courses that are offered in the first and second years. The lawyering sequence is designed to complement and strengthen student understanding of doctrinal materials while engaging students in legal writing, research, client interviewing, counseling, negotiation, and oral advocacy.

[1] CUNY Law's concentrations are externship practicums involving student placements in public interest law offices combined with intensive classroom instruction and simulation.

This chapter will focus on four of the clinics: Economic Justice Project (EJP), Community Economic Development (CED), Immigrant and Non-Citizen Rights (INCR), and Elder Law, to provide examples of how the clinical model operates in various civil practice contexts.

ECONOMIC JUSTICE PROJECT

The Challenge

CUNY Law launched the EJP in 1997 in the wake of the crisis created for many students as a result of regressive welfare reform legislation. The 1996 welfare reform law[2] imposed workfare requirements[3] that made it difficult if not impossible for students pursuing higher education as a gateway out of poverty. Welfare reform abolished the Aid to Families with Dependent Children (AFDC) program, which had provided a federal safety net for indigent families and their children, and replaced it with Temporary Assistance to Needy Families (TANF), a benefits program that was explicitly temporary and accompanied by workfare requirements. New York City's then-mayor Rudolph Giuliani aggressively embraced the workfare concept, imposing one of the most stringent welfare-to-work schemes in the nation. New York City required more hours of "work activity" than required under either state or federal law.[4]

The City's approach to workfare in terms of required hours, location of work sites, and reporting requirements made it extremely difficult for TANF recipients to attend college. This had a huge impact on students attending the CUNY – a large public university whose mission is to provide an opportunity ladder and help lift New Yorkers out of poverty through access to higher education. Thousands of individuals who had been pursuing CUNY degrees were forced to leave school to fulfill workfare requirements. Most of the affected students were single mothers seeking the education and credentials necessary to obtain jobs that would lift them and their families out of poverty.

The Model

The EJP responded by training and enlisting CUNY Law students to provide direct representation to hundreds of CUNY undergraduates, collaborating closely with

2 Personal Responsibility and Work Opportunity Reconciliation Act, Pub.L.No. 104–193, 110 Stat. 2105 (codified at 42 U.S.C. §§ 601–1788) (eliminating the federal statutory entitlement to welfare benefits created under the Aid to Families of Dependent Children program and imposing work requirements for the receipt of public assistance for people in poverty).

3 "Workfare" refers to the work requirements associated with the receipt of public assistance under welfare reform.

4 For example, under state and federal law, single parents of children under six were required to work twenty hours per week, see N.Y. Soc. Serv. L. § 335-b(3) (McKinney 2001), but New York City required the same individuals to work for thirty-five hours per week.

and supporting the organizing and political efforts of CUNY's Welfare Rights Initiative (WRI) and other grass-roots organizations. WRI of CUNY's Hunter College has as its immediate goal helping welfare recipients enrolled in CUNY colleges to "stay in school and to agitate for reforms that expand welfare recipients' access to higher education."[5]

EJP student interns provide legal assistance to eligible CUNY students by representing them in administrative benefits hearings and appeals, and resolving related issues. For example, WRI referred a case to EJP in which the City of New York sought to terminate welfare benefits of a Bronx woman with two children for failure to complete a workfare assignment. The assignment was inconsistent with the woman's medical limitations and conflicted with her academic schedule at CUNY's Bronx Community College where she was working toward a business degree. The EJP legal intern filed an appeal contesting the proposed termination of benefits and argued successfully at the administrative hearing to reverse the City's action and restore the client's benefits.

In the course of handling the welfare issue, the EJP intern learned about an eviction action filed against the client's family in Bronx Housing Court. The intern accompanied the client to Housing Court where the landlord agreed to discontinue the eviction action. The legal intern then worked with the client to locate appropriate medical services and advised the client about how to remain in college without risking another termination of welfare benefits. The client graduated with an Associate's Degree the following June.

In representing the client, the EJP intern experienced the multiple ways that the socio-legal context can derail motivated students from pursuing a college degree.

EJP interns complement direct representation with legislative action to amend the public benefits law and regulations. EJP interns recently worked with advocates to secure reauthorization of New York State's Workstudy/Internship law, which prohibits workfare assignments that unreasonably interfere with a college student's academic schedule and allows work study and internship hours to count toward a student's workfare requirement.[6]

The Pedagogy

EJP is a hybrid lawyering seminar and clinic.[7] It exemplifies the law school's broader curricular goals of bridging theory, doctrine, practice, and skills and moving students from simulated practice to client representation in individual administrative hearings and in more systemic legal and social change efforts.

5 See Welfare Rights Initiative web page at http://wri-ny.org/.

6 See WRI advocacy efforts related to the Work Study/Internship bill at http://wri-ny.org/2013/06/wri-alert-s1419-key-senators-need-to-know-about-s1419/.

7 For a description of CUNY Law's fourth-semester lawyering model, see www.law.cuny.edu/academics/courses/lawyering-seminars.html.

The Public Benefits lawyering seminar is offered as a co-requisite with a course on Social Welfare Law and Policy. These courses teach students the complex substantive and procedural law related to the provision of public benefits and place that law in a broader social context. The lawyering seminar engages students in the range of skills students will need to represent CUNY undergraduates in benefits hearings.

COMMUNITY ECONOMIC DEVELOPMENT CLINIC

The Challenge

At a time of economic crisis, government and private disinvestment, growing inequality, and a reduction in public services, community-based organizations have emerged as important local lifelines. However, these organizations face a range of challenges. Uncertain financial support, lean infrastructure, top-down agenda-setting through layers of regulatory and programmatic reporting, and fiscal oversight requirements require a difficult balancing act – how to focus on program delivery while also keeping close track of all financial, reporting, and regulatory requirements.[8]

The Model

CUNY's CED clinic is primarily a transactional clinic that responds to the legal needs of community-based organizations to ensure that they remain in compliance with legal, regulatory, and funding requirements.[9] The clinic deliberately offers necessary legal expertise through a process that avoids the traditional authoritarian role played by lawyers, replacing it with a collaborative counseling approach.

An example of the collaborative, participatory transactional model is the establishment of Colors, a worker-owned restaurant with the goals of providing worker-owners a living wage, better working conditions, and pay equity while beginning to transform the restaurant industry using a worker-ownership structure. The initial organizing entity, ROC-NY, together with a nonprofit law firm and the CED clinic, engaged in a collaborative process with the workers in choosing the legal team, engaging in counseling, establishing the organization's governing structure, and making other key decisions. Much thought and planning were given to equalizing roles and opening spaces for all members to communicate and for the lawyers to listen.[10]

8 See, e.g., Nicole Dandridge, *Choking Out Local Community Service Organizations: Rising Federal Tax Regulation and Its Impact on Small Non-Profit Entities*, 99 Ky. L.J. 695 (2010–11); Daniel S. Shah, *Lawyering for Empowerment: Community Development and Social Change*, 6 Clin. L. Rev. 217 (1999).

9 See, e.g., Alicia Alvarez, *Community Economic Development Clinics: What's Poverty Got to Do with It?* 34 Fordham Urb. L.J. 1269 (2007).

10 See Carmen Huertas-Noble, *Promoting Worker-Owned Cooperatives as a CED Empowerment Strategy: A Case Study of Colors and Lawyering in Support of Participatory Decision-making and Meaningful Social Change*, 17 Clin. L. Rev. 255, 277 (2010). Colors is an ongoing nonprofit restaurant owned by ROC United. See www.colorsrestaurantnyc.com; www.rocunited.org. Professor

Among the key, client-centered decisions was the determination of who among the members would be selected to sit on the Board of Directors and how to correct for the salary and job assignment disparities. Through the collaborative process, the group settled on director positions connected to work teams representing different jobs along the traditional hierarchy. To achieve the overarching goals of the participants, the legal team, based on input from the group, created a two-tier LLC structure for the restaurant that balanced the interests of the stakeholders and enabled the worker-owners gradually and seamlessly to gain majority control of the entity.[11]

The transaction involved students in multiple legal issues including corporate structure and governance, real estate, employment, and tax questions. Students researched and identified key legal issues, and engaged in interviewing, fact investigation, and document preparation.

Professor Carmen Huertas-Noble continues this approach to community economic development and has expanded it to address a range of local community needs. Student work includes assisting start-up organizations with incorporation and/or obtaining tax-exempt status, as well as more complex CED projects such as creating a unionized worker-owned cooperative, negotiating and drafting contracts, and counseling organizational clients on employment and governance issues. The clinic also provides legal support to tenant associations seeking repairs and safe, affordable housing. Clinic clients range from large, established nonprofits to small community groups seeking to incorporate, reorganize, or solve problems. This range provides clinic students a variety of models and strategies of community organizing, development, and empowerment. It also places the model in a broader social, legal, and political context.[12]

The Pedagogy

The CED clinic is a one-semester, twelve-credit clinic. Classroom work focuses on CED theory and practice, community lawyering in furtherance of social justice, legal ethics, and various substantive areas of law related to not-for-profits and their legal needs. To enroll in the CED clinic, students are encouraged to take either the lawyering seminar in Community Economic Development or Non-Profit Law to receive a preference in the enrollment process. Other students must demonstrate experience with community organizing and community development.

The pedagogical component of the clinic is further enhanced through "rounds" discussions during which clinic students regularly review, reflect on, and critique

Huertas-Noble continues the CED clinic's worker-ownership focus through its Worker Cooperative Law Project and its Non-Profit Legal Support Project.

11 *Id.* at 280–82.

12 See, generally, Sheila R. Foster, Brian Glick, *Integrative Lawyering: Navigating the Political Economy of Urban Redevelopment*, 95 Cal. L. Rev. 1999 (2007).

their work and engage in problem-solving to increase the effectiveness of their interactions and representation.[13] Students therefore come away from the CED clinic with concrete skills and knowledge of transactional work, while engaging deeply in complex areas of client–lawyer relations, ethics, and professional identity.

IMMIGRATION AND NON-CITIZENS RIGHTS CLINIC

The Challenge

CUNY's INRC[14] represents, supports, and assets the rights of vulnerable immigrants and noncitizens – either through individual legal representation or as groups. By supporting and representing vulnerable immigrants and noncitizens, the INRC aims to train law students to become thoughtful, principled, skilled, and committed public interest lawyers.

The Model

The INRC was one of the first immigration law clinics in the nation and has a long, distinguished record of litigation and advocacy in this area. INRC's docket has evolved to meet changing community needs. Cases generally are selected strategically to test or develop an area of law within existing areas of faculty expertise. For example, the clinic recently has focused on matters involving legal permanent residents who have criminal convictions, domestic-violence survivors facing immigration issues, and asylum-seekers in deportation proceedings. In connection with concerns about the post-9/11 treatment of noncitizens, INRC students also have provided supervised representation of prisoners of various nationalities who are or have been held at United States military facilities at Guantánamo Bay, Cuba; Bagram Air Base, Afghanistan; and other detention sites worldwide in federal trial and appellate courts and before military commissions. INRC students also provide support to immigrant community organizations and labor groups in non-litigation advocacy, organizing, and consciousness-raising, including "know-your-rights" trainings.[15]

Representing Immigrant Workers and Families

Much of INRC's work on behalf of immigrant workers and families involves supervised representation of individuals in federal and immigration court proceedings at the administrative, trial, and appellate levels. These cases generally are referred by community organizations and are selected with a social and economic justice strategy in mind to respond to patterns of injustice.

[13] See Susan Bryant, Elliot S. Millstein, *Rounds: A "Signature Pedagogy" for Clinical Education?* 14 Clinical L. Rev. 195 (2007).

[14] The INRC is in the process of a name change from "Immigrant & Refugee Rights Clinic."

[15] See description of CLEAR at www.law.cuny.edu/academics/clinics/immigration/clear.html.

For example, INRC students have litigated in federal district court on behalf of immigrant kitchen workers deprived of regular and overtime pay against a high-end chain of Manhattan restaurants and on behalf of a domestic worker subject to exploitative work conditions, including an hourly wage below $2 per hour. Students also have litigated before immigration judges on behalf of a woman in deportation proceedings who sought immigration status independent of the physically and emotionally abusive husband from whom she has escaped, and on behalf of a 23-year-old man seeking refugee status because his home was bulldozed and his father was killed by the government in his home country due to his involvement in opposition politics.[16]

In addition to individual representation, INRC students engage in community education, policy and advocacy work targeting law, regulations, and policies that inhibit the fair and just treatment of immigrants and noncitizens. Much of this work is designed not only to educate and provide assistance to communities, but also to strengthen existing community assistance and problem-solving resources through a collaborative model that better equips communities to handle ongoing needs in circumstances where full-scope individual representation cannot be provided.

For example, the INRC uses a "collaborative individual law model" to serve immigrant women facing domestic abuse. This model combines individual, limited-scope representation with client education and community organizing to address systemic issues as well as individual client needs.[17]

Another INRC approach envisions community organizing and empowerment as critical components in effective legal representation of the poor as among its goals.[18] This model includes engagement of the clinic with community needs and the development of the clinic as a "center of activity" in the community. For example, to address wage and hour violations targeting immigrant workers, INRC faculty and students moved beyond addressing a docket of individual cases and used "the clinic's scarce legal resources to support organizing and collective action for broader reform in an industry."[19]

The synergistic combination of short-term, individualized representation and broader community work helps prepare clinic students, litigants, and community members to work as partners and problem-solvers with respect to both immediate legal needs and longer-term issues.

Representing Detainees and CLEAR

Starting in 2009, in collaboration with law firms and advocacy organizations, INRC began representing detainees of various nationalities currently or previously held at

[16] See description of INRC at www.law.cuny.edu/academics/clinics/immigration.html.

[17] See Alizabeth Newman, *Bridging the Justice Gap: Building Community by Responding to Individual Need*, 17 Clinical L. Rev. 615, 639 (2011).

[18] Sameer M. Ashar, *Law Clinics and Collective Mobilization*, 14 Clinical L. Rev. 355 (2008).

[19] *Id.* at 391–92.

American facilities at Guantánamo Bay, Cuba, at Bagram Air Base, Afghanistan, at so-called "Black Sites,"[20] and at other detention sites established by the United States worldwide. INRC students have drafted, filed, and argued motions in federal district court; drafted appellate and Supreme Court merits briefs; and engaged in negotiations with U.S. government agencies. Students also have conducted privileged meetings with clients at the U.S. military prison facilities at Guantánamo Bay, Cuba.[21]

In addition, INRC has recognized the growing local need for legal assistance for individuals and communities under surveillance and/or investigation based on ethnic or religious background or association who have not been charged with any crime. In response, INRC in partnership with CUNY Law's Criminal Defense Clinic (CDC) initiated the Creating Law Enforcement Accountability & Responsibility (CLEAR) project. Working with advocacy and community-based organizations, CLEAR provides legal assistance and engages in lawful and constructive responses to aggressive post-9/11 law enforcement practices implemented in the name of national security and counterterrorism. CLEAR addresses the underserved legal needs of Muslim, Arab, South Asian, and other communities in New York City through representation, legal consultation, public education for rights awareness, and community organizing.[22] For example, with the American Civil Liberties Union (ACLU) and the New York Civil Liberties Union (NYCLU), CLEAR filed a federal lawsuit challenging the New York City Police Department's unconstitutional policy and practice of targeting entire Muslim communities for discriminatory and suspicionless surveillance.[23] In addition, CLEAR represents community members and leaders as they respond to "voluntary interview" requests from the FBI and NYPD as well as individuals served with grand jury and trial subpoenas and during law enforcement searches. CLEAR provides legal advice related to safe charitable giving options; and offers counsel and legal representation to clients who face difficulties and delays in international and domestic travel because of heightened and targeted U.S. government searches and scrutiny.

CLEAR teams also engage in community education, facilitating "know-your-rights" workshops at mosques, Muslim student associations, and other community centers. CLEAR workshops typically center on individual rights related to law enforcement interactions; dealing with informants and infiltration; charitable giving; and domestic and international travel.

CLEAR teams also support local community organizing campaigns focused on responding to overzealous law enforcement policies and practices related to

20 For information about "Black Sites" for Extraordinary Rendition of suspected enemy combatants, see www.pbs.org/wgbh/pages/frontline/iraq-war-on-terror/mapping-the-cias-secret-prisons/.

21 See INRC description at www.law.cuny.edu/academics/clinics/immigration.html.

22 See, generally, Ramzi Kassem and Amna Akbar, Are Muslims Allowed Rights, Al Jazeera Online (Nov. 28, 2011) www.aljazeera.com/indepth/opinion/2011/11/2011112415501938290.html.

23 The case is *Raza v. City of New York*, 13-CV-3448 (E.D.N.Y.). It is currently proceeding before the district court. The City recently filed an answer to the Complaint and preliminary discovery issues are being addressed as of this writing.

counterterrorism. CLEAR has worked closely with key community organizations and coalitions, including the Muslim American Civil Liberties Coalition (MACLC) and the Majlis ash-Shura in New York City. Recently, CLEAR helped organize community responses to confirmed reports of extensive, systemic NYPD surveillance of local Muslim communities.[24] CLEAR students and supervising attorneys assisted more than twenty local organizations with campaigns to record and document the volume, nature, and impacts of Muslim community encounters with law enforcement.

The Pedagogy

The INRC is a two-semester, sixteen-credit clinic. Clinic students participate in about five hours of seminar per week (in addition to fieldwork, research and written work, and supervisor meetings with faculty). Because INRC runs along the two tracks described earlier, the coursework consists of a mix of substantive law and policy review in immigration and its intersection with criminal law, labor law, family law, and gender issues, as well as law and policy involving the treatment of noncitizen detainees imprisoned without charge and/or on suspicion of being enemy combatants or a "national security threat." The coursework includes intensive practice work addressing professional responsibility, negotiating client collaboration, immigration practice and procedure, federal court practice, fact development, cultural competence (including working with interpreters and with diverse communities), and trial skills. The coursework is designed to provide students with a practical and theoretical foundation for legal and policy work affecting immigrants and noncitizens.

ELDER LAW CLINIC

The Challenge

The population of elderly Americans is significant and is projected to increase dramatically in the near future. Poor and vulnerable elderly persons, particularly those with diminished capacity, experience increased risks of neglect, exploitation, and abuse. The same is true for people facing physical and mental incapacity.[25] There is a crucial need for legal assistance, oversight, and continued systemic approaches to improve the safety, autonomy, and quality of life for vulnerable elderly and incapacitated persons. This is the mission of CUNY's Elder Law Clinic (ELC).

[24] See CLEAR description at www.law.cuny.edu/academics/clinics/immigration/clear.html.

[25] See, generally, Nina A. Kohn, Jeremy A. Blumenthal & Amy T. Campbell, *Supported Decision-Making: A Viable Alternative to Guardianship?* 117 PENN St. L. REV. 1111, 1137–38 (2013).

The Model

In the ELC, students engage in supervised representation of clients and often their families, grappling with a variety of legal issues and problems related to aging and incapacity.[26] The ELC works primarily in the areas of adult guardianships, estate and incapacity planning, and government benefits. Clinic students examine the theory, doctrine, and practice of elder law, and develop the skills necessary to provide high-quality representation focused on understanding and responding to the client's goals and wishes. That representation is focused on understanding and responding to the client's goals and wishes.

For example, student-attorneys in the ELC serve as court evaluators and represent parties in adult guardianship proceedings under Article 81 of the New York Mental Hygiene Law;[27] draft wills, trusts, and advance directives; counsel clients about government benefits, including Medicaid, Medicare, and Social Security; and represent clients in Surrogate's Court proceedings involving probate of wills and administration of estates. In addition, ELC student-attorneys participate in projects that complement individual casework and foster necessary systemic change.

Some recent accomplishments of ELC student-attorneys include (1) successfully recommending that an elderly woman evacuated from a nursing home during Hurricane Sandy be permitted to return home to her apartment with home care; (2) preventing a relative who neglected an elderly woman from being appointed her guardian and facilitating her discharge back to her home community; and (3) reconstructing the identity and history of an elderly man who had checked into a hospital with no memory, thus enabling the court to create a guardianship and plan of care responsive to his unique needs.[28]

ELC also works with clients on estate planning, an example of preventive law practice. For example, an elderly couple sought to provide for an adult child who was receiving government disability benefits. The ELC legal intern held numerous counseling sessions with the clients, explaining the complex maze of laws governing estate planning, Medicaid eligibility and estate recovery, and supplemental needs trusts. Together, the intern and clients created an estate plan with wills, advance directives, supplemental needs trusts, and arrangements for future contingencies, which was so responsive to the family's needs that they told the intern that she had "saved their lives."[29]

Interns also work on a variety of projects designed to address systemic issues beyond the capabilities of individual representation. For example, ELC legal interns

26 See www.law.cuny.edu/academics/clinics/elder.html.

27 See *Id.* at 331, see also Poverty, Guardianship, and the Vulnerable Elderly: Human Narrative and Statistical Patterns in a Snapshot of Adult Guardianship Cases in New York City, Georgetown Journal of Poverty Law and Policy, Vol. 16, No. 2 (Spring 2009).

28 See Elder Law Clinic description at CUNY Law web page at www.law.cuny.edu/academics/clinics/elder.html.

29 *Id.*

established an Article 81 Guardianship Pro Se project, in which interns prepare pro se materials[30] and help people who need to be appointed guardians complete and file the pleadings in Supreme Court. ELC interns are currently developing an "A2J" Guided Interview software program as part of the Access to Justice Clinical Course Project[31] for Article 81 pro se litigants in collaboration with the Article 81 Pro Se Project of the New York Legal Assistance Group. ELC interns also have engaged in community education "know your rights" presentations on various elder law issues, including adult guardianships, Medicare, and healthcare directives.

The Pedagogy

ELC is a one-semester, twelve-credit clinic that integrates theory, doctrine, and practice through issues arising from aging and incapacity, adult guardianships, wills, trusts, advance directives, estate planning, government benefits, and the interplay among these different areas. While working in the elder-law practice context, ELC students gain skills and knowledge transferable to other legal practice contexts. These include intensive attention to interviewing, counseling, and human interaction in difficult circumstances, close attention to interrelated legal, regulatory, and factual issues, careful drafting and revision, and complex problem-solving. Students also examine how ethnicity, race, and culture impact their practice. Finally, their individualized representation informs areas for reform in adult guardianships under Article 81 of the New York State Mental Hygiene Law.

POST-GRADUATE MODELS THAT SUPPORT COMMUNITY LAWYERING AND BUILDING COMMUNITY-BASED PRACTICES

CUNY law school also has been at the forefront in designing structured, innovative approaches to serving individuals and communities in need not only during law school but also after graduation.

The Challenge

The Community Legal Resource Network (CLRN) was initially designed to support solo and small firm community-based practice for high-need and average-need clients. Established in 1998, CLRN is a collaborative that supports CUNY Law School graduates as they work to set up and run solo or small-group practices devoted to serving pressing needs of the poor and disadvantaged in communities that are underserved by lawyers. With a focus on serving individuals and communities often

30 See "Guide to Becoming a Guardian without a Lawyer," www.law.cuny.edu/academics/clinics/elder/Becoming-A-Guardian-Without-A-Lawyer.pdf.

31 See http://a2jclinic.classcaster.net; www.kentlaw.iit.edu/institutes-centers/center-for-access-to-justice-and-technology/a2j-author.

priced out of legal services, CLRN was designed to support the development of "low bono" and community-based practices to help address this huge legal services gap.

The Model: Professional Development Pedagogy and Support

CLRN supports "successful community law practice by providing the networking, infrastructure assistance, business planning, sharing of legal and law practice expertise, and continuing legal education options that are taken for granted in large law firms serving wealthy clients."[32] CLRN's founding goal was to support excellent representation of low- and moderate-income clients through a network of solo and small firm practices committed to improving access to justice. Through mentoring support, training, and peer resources, and networking support, CLRN helps new attorneys avoid floundering in isolated, economically precarious, situations. With CLRN's support, CUNY alumni have launched and established solo and small firm practices serving local communities in New York City and surrounding areas. As community law practice and professional development needs evolved and expanded, CLRN adopted new models to help serve those needs.

In late 2007, CLRN established a project, the Incubator for Justice, in Manhattan.[33] Based in part on feedback from CLRN alumni about the challenges of establishing a solo or small firm practice and on an interest in supporting forms of practice that would more effectively address the justice gap for low- and moderate-income individuals and communities, the Incubator provides more robust support to CUNY Law alumni in establishing community practices that are viable, innovative, and consistent with social justice goals.

The Incubator trains CLRN members, over an eighteen-month period, in basic business issues such as forms of organization, billing, record-keeping, technology, bookkeeping, and taxes. At the same time, the Incubator facilitates participants' involvement in larger justice initiatives and in subject-based training in immigration law, housing and employment law, and other topics that will arise continually as participating attorneys build their practices. The Incubator also provides concrete start-up support such as low-cost office space and supplies in a CUNY Law alumnus's law office suite.[34] Since its inception, the Incubator has supported the establishment of solo and small firm practices, including new forms of community

[32] Natalie Gomez-Velez, *Structured Discrete Task Representation to Bridge the Justice Gap: CUNY Law School's LaunchPad for Justice in Partnership with Courts and Communities*, 16 CUNY Law Review 21, 35 (2012).

[33] See Delece Smith-Barrow, *Consider Law Schools with In-House Firms, Incubators* U.S. News & World Report (June 17, 2013) at www.usnews.com/education/best-graduate-schools/top-law-schools/articles/2013/06/17/consider-law-schools-with-in-house-firms-incubators_print.html (describing CUNY Law's Incubator as first of its kind).

[34] See Jonathan D. Glater, *Lawyers Can Learn How to Be Businesslike*, N.Y. Times, Jan. 9, 2008, at B6.

practice designed to provide legal support to address the difficulties brought on by the recession and ongoing economic crisis and systemic issues requiring creative legal responses.[35] The Incubator model has been so successful that several other law schools have adopted it and currently run similar Incubator programs.[36]

A DYNAMIC VISION OF LIFELONG LEARNING

CLRN and its Incubator project provide initial and ongoing support through a sophisticated networking, modeling, and mentoring program to help members become financially, professionally, and personally successful as community lawyers. The model is dynamic. CLRN has evolved over the years to respond to existing and ongoing challenges arising out of changes in law practice and the legal market as well as evolving community legal needs. CLRN's vision is to use professional development to support each lawyer's success while also supporting collective work to establish effective and innovative legal services delivery models to improve access to justice for underserved low- and moderate-income people. Part of CLRN's work today is to institutionalize the lessons learned thus far. Through the use of technology to systematize practices, structures, and procedures, current and future participants will have the benefit of CLRN's institutional knowledge of a range of social justice community practice methods. CLRN also is enhancing its "longitudinal law school" vision, integrating its work with CUNY Law students throughout law school, rather than only upon graduation. Maintaining the commitment to serving CUNY alumni as lifelong learners eager to address systemic issues of injustice, while proactively evaluating an evolving legal market operating within dynamic social and political climates, CLRN's goal

[35] For example, the Incubator helped CUNY Law alumni establish the Health Care Rights Initiative (HCRI). HCRI is a not-for-profit education and advocacy organization that provides free and low-cost advocacy to individuals and families through the often confusing process of medical care insurance claims. See Health Care Rights Initiative web page at http://hcri.org/?page_id-40. Another Incubator-supported project, Common Law, is a novel form of community-based practice serving both individual legal needs and related systemic community concerns. Through a combination of discrete task representation, community education, and organizing, Common Law's foreclosure legal clinic works in active participation with clients and community members to help tackle individual cases and address systemic issues related to the massive foreclosure crisis facing its Queens, New York, community. See http://commonlawnyc.org/?page_id-344.

[36] See, e.g., Fern Fisher, *Launch Pads and Incubators: Providing Access to Justice Using Law Graduates and New Lawyers*, 53 No. 1 JUDGES' J. 4 (2014). CLRN also established the first Launch Pad for Justice, a structured pro bono apprenticeship project in partnership with local courts. Launch Pad is designed to train and support law students and law graduates in providing urgently needed legal assistance to otherwise unrepresented litigants in housing, family, and consumer matters. See Gomez-Velez, supra note 33.

is to broaden its reach in serving CUNY law's mission-driven, social justice law students and graduates.

CONCLUSION

Consistent with its social justice mission, CUNY Law School has, since its inception, established and developed holistic and empowering models of law teaching and practice designed to serve individuals and communities in need. The clinics and programs described here provide some examples of this work.

49

A New Law School in Texas to Address Unmet Legal Needs

Dean Royal Furgeson, Ellen Pryor, Cheryl Wattley, Valerie James & Eric Porterfield

Creating a culture of service in the legal profession should begin in law school. This chapter, authored by Judge Furgeson and several founding members of the University of North Texas Dallas College of Law (UNT) faculty, offers an example of how law schools can prepare law students for careers representing low- and moderate-income Americans.

The University of North Texas Dallas College of Law has set ambitious goals. We are a new law school. Classes have just started, and the work is only just beginning. Even so, our approach to every facet of the College of Law experience is designed to help expand access to legal services for all, including un- or underserved working Americans, such as the middle class and small businesses.

Our overall objective is to expand access to an excellent legal education while keeping costs – and student debt – low, and constructing a curriculum with an emphasis on practice skills and community service. Students will be sensitized to the needs of the underserved, while equipping them with the skills to deliver those services, unencumbered by the debt that makes delivering lower-cost legal services difficult.

ADMISSIONS: EXPANDING ACCESS

The College of Law admits and seeks to admit students who have the demonstrated potential to be excellent lawyers but may not otherwise have a realistic opportunity to access legal education, due to cost, geography, and the current dominance of the LSAT in both admissions decisions and awarding scholarships. We have low tuition and intend to keep it low.

For our inaugural class, the College of Law charged just $14,040 per year for full-time tuition. The inaugural 2014 class also received a partial tuition waiver, bringing tuition to just $12,540. We just welcomed our second entering class and modestly raised tuition for full-time students to $15,267. The College of Law also offers a part-time evening program, allowing students to keep their day jobs, offsetting some of the total expense of attending law school. And the geographic location of the College of Law in downtown Dallas opens opportunities for those who do not want or could not afford to move a long distance to attend law school.

Texas Supreme Court Chief Justice Nathan Hecht spoke at our law school's Inaugural Convocation and emphasized these points when he said, "Many of you already have jobs and commitments, and in UNT Dallas College of Law, you now have a shot at a dream you thought was gone. For others, a legal education was never within financial reach, and now it is."[1]

Our status as a new institution provides unanticipated benefits because we do not have the burden of legacy costs such as expensive physical plants and other long-term, preexisting financial commitments. Maintaining our affordable tuition is a primary goal. We plan to meet this goal by spending funds on those things that improve outcomes rather than spending money to improve rankings in national surveys.

Our approach to admissions and our commitment to affordable tuition expands access to students from a diverse range of socioeconomic backgrounds. And, by providing a legal education to working, diverse persons who are themselves motivated to pursue a legal education because of their appreciation of individuals' need for legal services, we hope to contribute to closing the gap in access to legal services between the elites and everyone else, including the middle class.

Nearly as important as controlling costs and debt is avoiding overemphasis on LSAT scores in admissions decisions. But what do LSAT scores have to do with assisting underserved populations like the middle class? And how does expanding access to legal education help with broadening the provision of legal services? By opening legal education to students who come from underserved populations, including the middle class, we believe there will be increased access to legal services for those populations. Those students, having observed or even experienced the burdens of inadequate access to legal representation, will be uniquely motivated to provide assistance to those under-represented populations.

As a currently unaccredited institution, the College of Law does not qualify to participate in the ranking assessment, a circumstance that we have chosen to use to our advantage. We emphasize to prospective students that we will take a holistic approach to admissions. Thus, we examine GPAs, we look at work history, and we review LSAT scores. But we also encourage applicants to come to the College of Law for a personal interview, to share with us their reasons and motivations for wanting to attend law school. During those meetings, students have the opportunity to demonstrate their qualifications and fitness for admission. And our admissions personnel have a chance to develop a personalized evaluation of the student.

For our inaugural class, this approach has had a most positive result. The class is varied, with a one-to-one ratio of men to women, a wide range of ages with the

[1] Hon. Nathan L. Hecht, Chief Justice, The Supreme Court of Texas, Keynote Address at the University of North Texas Dallas College of Law Inaugural Convocation, 3 (Aug. 10, 2014), http://pdfserver.amlaw.com/tx/JusticeHechtConvocationSpeech_08102014.pdf

average age of 33.5 years, almost all Texas residents, and ethnic diversity of 48%. Our students have wide professional experiences – from traditional students straight from undergraduate education to seasoned professionals – doctors, bankers, entrepreneurs, paralegals, retired military service members, police officers, educators, and a variety of public servants. And our second entering class has very similar demographics.

COMPETENCY-BASED CURRICULUM AND COURSE DESIGN, COMMUNITY ENGAGEMENT AND MENTORSHIP

The College of Law has the uncommon opportunity to design its curriculum from the ground up, drawing on the extensive body of research addressing methods of improving legal education.

The College of Law intends to be a positive model for change consistent with this research. Our goal is to prepare students with respect to the full range of practice-related competencies, and to instill in them the confidence that they have attained such preparedness. To that end, we have followed several principles in designing our curriculum. First, having identified the practice-related competencies that guide our program, we will design and map our curriculum in accordance with those competencies.[2] Second, we have designed our courses around the achievement of learning outcomes, identifying goal-level outcomes, general learning outcomes, and more specific learning outcomes for each course. For example, a goal-level outcome may be to pass the bar exam or have the skills a competent entry-level lawyer should have. Working backward from such goals allows us to identify skills such as writing, critical thinking, and knowledge and application of legal doctrines. For a doctrinal course like Civil Procedure, a general learning outcome may be to understand subject matter jurisdiction in federal court. A more specific learning outcome might be to know the elements of subject matter jurisdiction tests and how to apply them. An even more specific learning outcome may be to critically assess different arguments in complex or unclear subject matter jurisdiction scenarios. Again, this backward design allows us to create our multiple assessments so we can evaluate whether our students are achieving these outcomes. Third, in every course, we will engage in multiple formative and summative student assessments tied to these learning outcomes. We have entered our program-level and course-level learning outcomes into our learning management system and testing-assessment

[2] For our program-level competencies, we gained much insight from the following: National Board of Law Examiners, NCBE Job Analysis: A Study of the Newly Licensed Lawyer (2012), available at www.ncbex.org/assets/media_files/Research/AMP-Final-2012-NCBE-Newly-Licensed-Lawyer-JAR.pdf; Neil W. Hamilton, Verna Monson & Jerome M. Organ, *Encouraging Each Student's Personal Responsibility for Core Competencies Including Professionalism*, 21 PROFESSIONAL LAWYER No. 3, at 1 (2012); William D. Henderson, A *Blueprint for Change*, 40 PEPPERDINE L. REV. 461 (2013); Marjorie M. Schultz & Sheldon Zedeck, *Predicting Lawyer Effectiveness Broadening the Basis for Law School Admissions Decisions*, 36 LAW & SOC. INQUIRY 620 (2011).

software. Thus, our assessments can be tagged to all associated learning outcomes, and we can accumulate significant information about overall and individual student progress on all learning outcomes.

Fourth, because competencies require incremental and iterative development, we will "thread" skills and abilities throughout the upper-level curriculum. For instance, three-hour doctrinal classes will follow a "2 + 1" model, in which one hour reflects application of the material in the form of writing, research, problem solving, and other skills. To implement this approach, we require eight writing "segments," eight research segments, and ten segments in other skills (such as negotiation). A writing segment is defined as a "writing assignment that (1) correlates in scope and complexity with significant written work product that lawyers prepare; and (2) on which the student receives formative and summative assessment." (The research segments and skills segments are defined similarly.) Fifth, students will be required to take at least two courses that fall within the following categories: practicum, externship, or clinic.

We also have taken advantage of the unique opportunity to use many of the exercises and programs that are being used individually by other law schools or recommended directly to students.[3] For example, even before classes began, all of our incoming class took the Myers Briggs Type Indicator assessment and attended a two-hour feedback session to explore how personality type can influence interactions with clients, judges, and other attorneys. They took the VARK learning style assessment to identify their strengths and challenges in learning. They took the Core Grammar for Lawyers diagnostic test and completed grammar learning modules. They wrote reflective pieces designed to encourage the development of a "plan, do, reflect" approach to learning that will transfer to the representation of clients. But above all, the students are challenged to be active in their legal education, just as they will be active in handling cases on behalf of their clients.

Because a significant number of our students may elect to practice in solo or small firms, we are developing courses and programs that will optimize their ability to be successful. Every student is required to take Principles of Accounting and Finance for Lawyers (or place out of the class by demonstrating proficiency in the learning outcomes for the class). Our required third-year Practice Foundation III course will examine the business components of running a law practice, including marketing, client development, and strategic planning. While we are using some of the same technology that is used by other law schools such as Canvas (similar to Blackboard) and Exam Soft, we are also piloting a Student Course Management Program with Clio, a cloud-based case management software. Clio, responding positively to our idea, adapted its program for use by our students throughout their academic course of study. Instead of case files, our students will create "course" files. They will use the

[3] See Michael Hunter Schwartz, *Expert Learning for Law Students* (2008).

software to track their study time, group work, and other activities similar to the time record keeping of practicing attorneys. Calendaring, document creation, and collaboration will be managed through Clio, again much in the same way that the software is used by lawyers. By the time they graduate, our students will be comfortable with many of the organizational and procedural aspects of a law practice through the use of this software. They will be as prepared as possible to open their own solo practices or join small firms as active associates. And as described earlier, solo and small firm practices seem to offer the best possibility to assist those who need but cannot afford legal services.

In addition to our credit courses, we are implementing two programs, the Community Engagement Program and the Louis A. Bedford Jr. Mentorship Program, that will introduce our students to the Dallas legal community and social issues that impact our area. These programs are designed to instill in our students a connection to various segments of our community that are in need of legal assistance. The Community Engagement Program has been established to provide our students with opportunities to make those connections and have those experiences. Our Community Engagement Program places students with nonprofit organizations and governmental agencies for five hours of volunteer service a month. We have intentionally not scheduled classes for Monday through Wednesday mornings for our day students. Those mornings have been kept available so that our students can utilize two of those mornings monthly for their community placement. For our evening students, placements have been developed that can be done either on Saturday morning or through independent work that students self-schedule.

The community placements include organizations such as Catholic Charities, City Square, Human Rights Initiative, Dallas Child Advocacy Center, Doors (a prison re-entry program), Dallas County Dispute Resolution Center, Dallas County Public Defender's Office, Dallas City Attorney's Office, Legal Hospice of Texas, and the Dallas Independent School District – a wide array of nonprofit, governmental, and public interest organizations. Students have ranked their interests in listed community issues and, as far as possible, will be matched with a placement relating to one of their areas of interest.

Through the selection of the community partners, our students will interact with persons who are in need of services, often times legal. They will come face to face with persons who have had to turn to the nonprofit organizations and agencies for help. They will encounter the deficiencies in our current system of delivery of legal services that fail so many working Americans. These personal experiences, we believe, will give our students an appreciation of the importance of and need for access to legal services. With such an appreciation, our students, even if not directly involved in the delivery of legal services to working Americans, are more likely to seek avenues by which they can use their skills and talents to address this under-representation. Staying connected to interest areas that brought the student to law school in the first place and to those who are in need of, but cannot afford, legal help can help sensitize our students to the needs of underserved populations like the middle class.

Our other program, the Judge Louis A. Bedford Jr. Mentorship Program, blends book club, Inn of Court, and traditional mentorship formats into a collective study of community concerns. By working with mentor attorneys, our students will research social issues with the perspective of being problem solvers. The chance to confront, early in their law school career, current human and societal issues (such as the flow of unaccompanied minors now coming to Texas) will enhance our students' awareness of the wide range of legal needs.

These two programs, along with our curriculum development, reflect the culture that we are striving to create at the College of Law. We emphasize that lawyers are problem solvers and that, as lawyers, we have an obligation to use our skills and talents to address community concerns. We intentionally connect students to the needs of the community in which they live, which also keeps them connected to the desire to serve. We teach that our skills, talents, and values as lawyers are carefully formed and groomed to be worthy of the trust and confidence that our clients and others place in us. And as we progress to externships and live client clinics in the second and third years, we will give priority to identifying placements and creating clinics that serve un- or under represented persons and entrepreneurs.

HOW WILL WE KNOW IF WE ARE SUCCEEDING?

As we embark on this journey of building an educational institution, we are ever mindful that we have to assess what we are doing, that we have to measure the impact of our work. We use surveys to get our students' feedback with respect to our programming. We are using formative as well as summative assessments in our classes. We have worked with consultants with significant expertise in pedagogy and assessment, both in law schools and otherwise, to identify and map out key competencies and determine how to create and maintain analytics to measure those competencies. For example, we have implemented an assessment tool called Exam Soft. Students' quizzes, essays, and written work product can be created, delivered, and evaluated using this software. Perhaps one of the most important features of this technology is that we can "tag" each question or issue on which we assess our students with our learning outcomes and goals. When we assess students, we will be able to determine not just how they performed on a particular question, but whether they are mastering learning outcomes and developing the key competencies necessary to be a member of the bar.

Our greatest measure of effectiveness, however, will be our students and what they choose to do with the values and priorities we have tried to instill in them. We believe that, if our students are convinced we are honest with them, then they will take to heart what we say. They will pay attention to us when we emphasize that they can be a part of the solution to providing legal access to our vast un- or under served population. And it starts from the beginning.

In April 2013, we welcomed the inaugural class of the UNT Dallas College of Law in a full-day admitted students' session. Our take-away message for them was short and blunt: "There are no jobs for law graduates in today's market. To repeat, there are no jobs. So, if you are coming to our law school with the expectation that, in three years, you will have a job waiting for you, think again." We told them that, after graduation, they must "make their own way" in the legal profession. At the same time, we pledged to these new students that we would do everything we could to prepare them for that road ahead. We would provide them with an instructional model designed to enhance learning and retention. With a faculty committed to collaboration, so that learning outcomes in all courses are clear and uniform. With a mentorship program that will introduce them to lots of lawyers, offer excellent opportunities for interaction, and make it possible for them to observe practitioners at work. And, finally, with a continuous and wide selection of externships and experiential programming that will enable them to learn what the practice of law is all about.

AND SO WE BEGIN

As this chapter went to publication, we welcomed our second academic class. There has been valuable collaboration between faculty, important consultation with librarians, and significant work with our IT personnel. We have spent hours talking about the culture of our school and how to convey our emphasis on professionalism. We have admitted two classes that are already inclined to provide legal service to un- or under served people, because they come from working backgrounds. We will make sure we nurture and encourage students interested in being a part of the solution to providing legal access to our vast un- or under served population, now and in the future. We will do this and more because we are committed, individually and as an institution, to our stated mission: "to improve access to justice for underserved legal needs."

50

Public Service Residency in Lieu of the Third Year of Law School

Samuel Estreicher & Randal S. Milch

The proposal by Samuel Estreicher and Randal Milch, which can be implemented by a change in state supreme court rules, would allow students to become licensed to practice after completing two years of a prescribed law school curriculum and one year of a paid internship working principally on public service matters, broadly defined to include representation of poor and middle-class individuals and families. Law schools will not have to change their degree requirements but many will be under pressure to provide offerings that will be worth the year of tuition and foregone income; they will have to "earn" the third year, rather than have it imposed by law.

President Obama's remarks on the utility of the third year of law school[1] have rekindled public debate over the value of requiring students to finish three years of law school before they can take the bar examination and practice law. We are proposing a Public Service Residency Program as a practical alternative to the third year of law school. We believe that this Program, which can be flexibly implemented in accordance with local legal and political requirements, will produce new lawyers with greater experience and less debt, and thus with more to offer to prospective employers and greater freedom to take legal jobs of their choice and further the needs of the community.

The Public Service Residency Program would be an option that students might select. It would not require law schools or the ABA to change their current requirements for a JD degree.

The parameters of the proposal (which would require action by the State Supreme Court) are set out later, but the nuts and bolts are simple. After completing a core curriculum in the first two years of law school, participating students would, beginning in the summer after the second year, undertake a year's Public Service Residency with a participating law firm, corporate legal office, government agency, or nongovernmental organization. These sponsoring organizations would be responsible for providing the Residents with three things: supervised legal work on behalf of one or more clients involved in public service

[1] http://dealbook.nytimes.com/2013/08/23/obama-says-law-school-should-be-two-years-not-three/.

matters, compensation, and certification at the year's end of the Resident's satisfactory performance. There is no requirement that the sponsoring organization offer the Resident a permanent position at the end of the Residency. After completion of the Residency, the Resident would receive a waiver from the State Supreme Court to permit the student to sit for the State Bar Examination without completion of the third year of law school or a JD degree. Assuming success on the bar examination and satisfaction of the applicable character and fitness requirements, the student may either be licensed like any other lawyer permitted to practice law in the State (the applicable character and fitness requirements).

The State may wish to adopt the Program on an experimental or pilot basis and review the Program after three to five years of experience.

THE PROPOSAL

General Description

The [name of State] Public Service Residency Program ("Residency" or "Program") will allow students who successfully have completed a prescribed course of study for the first two years of law ("Prescribed Course of Study"), if selected, to work on Public Service Matters (defined later) under the supervision of a legal employer at a rate in pay in excess of the State minimum wage ("Prescribed Rate of Pay"). Upon the successful completion of a year of service in the Program, the student will receive a waiver from the [State Supreme Court] permitting the student to sit for the State bar without completion of the third year of law school. If the student passes the bar examination and satisfies the applicable character and fitness requirements, the student will be licensed to practice law in the State.

Selection Process

Students would apply for selection to the Program in February of their second year in law school by submitting to the program administrator their resume, law school transcript and proof of probable completion of the Prescribed Course of Study by no later than May 31 of that year. These applications will then be forwarded to law firms or other legal organizations, private or public, nonprofit or for-profit, located in the State that have indicated interest in participating in the Program ("Participating Practice Organization" or "Organization").

Certification of Participating Organizations

A Participating Organization will have previously registered with the Program administrator to certify that they will have Public Service Matters for the student

Residents to work on during the Residency and they will be able to provide ongoing supervision of the Resident's work.

Size of the Residency Program

The size of the Program shall be set no later than January 15 of each year in a process determined by [the State Supreme Court].

Prescribed Course of Study

Students wishing to participate in the Program will be required to receive a passing grade in a prescribed two-year course of study. The following courses, either taught in the traditional manner or integrated into courses emphasizing practical skills upon approval of the State Supreme Court, should be required: Civil Procedure, Contracts, Corporations, Creditors' Remedies (or Bankruptcy), Constitutional Law, Criminal Law, Evidence, Legal Research and Writing, Legislation, Property, Moot Court, Professional Responsibility, Real Estate Transactions, Taxation, Torts, and Trial Practice. The particular order in which these courses are taken will be determined by the students' law school.

Obligations of Participating Practice Organizations

A Participating Practice Organization must (a) provide at least 1,500 hours of work on Public Service Matters (as defined later); (b) supervise and train the Resident in the same manner as it would any of its junior associate lawyers; (c) compensate the Resident at no less than the Prescribed Rate of Pay; and (d) after the completion of the public service year, certify that the Resident has satisfactorily performed his/her work assignments and conducted him- or herself in a professionally responsible and competent manner. The Organization may, but would have no obligation to, offer employment to the Resident at the end of the Residency. Compensation for any post-Program employment will be determined by the employer and employee in the normal course.

Public Service Matters

This term is defined inclusively to include law reform, work for the government and nonprofit organizations, and direct legal services to poor and average-income individuals or families.

Resident Feedback

Residents would be required three times during the Residency to provide the Program Administrator with a written description of their experience and of the degree and quality of supervision they are receiving. If in the opinion of the Program Administrator, a Participating Organization has not provided the Resident with 1,500 hours of Public Service Matters or adequate supervision of the Resident's work during the Residency, that Organization will not be certified for future years.

Index